ISBN 978-1-332-31092-0
PIBN 10312374

FB &c Ltd, Dalton House, 60 Windsor Avenue, London, SW19 2RR.
Company number 08720141. Registered in England and Wales.

For support please visit www.forgottenbooks.com

English
Français
Deutsche
Italiano
Español
Português

www.forgottenbooks.com

Mythology Photography **Fiction**
Fishing Christianity **Art** Cooking
Essays Buddhism Freemasonry
Medicine **Biology** Music **Ancient**
Egypt Evolution Carpentry Physics
Dance Geology **Mathematics** Fitness
Shakespeare **Folklore** Yoga Marketing
Confidence Immortality Biographies
Poetry **Psychology** Witchcraft
Electronics Chemistry History **Law**
Accounting **Philosophy** Anthropology
Alchemy Drama Quantum Mechanics
Atheism Sexual Health **Ancient History**
Entrepreneurship Languages Sport
Paleontology Needlework Islam
Metaphysics Investment Archaeology
Parenting Statistics Criminology
Motivational

STATE OF NEW JERSEY.

COLT-COULT This name in America is not a common one, and outside of Connecticut and New Jersey has not received thorough and painstaking research to ascertain the relation existing between the different local families. Only two of the name appear in the excellent dictionary of living Americans, "Who's Who in America": Le Baron Bradford Colt, United States circuit judge of Rhode Island, and Samuel Pomeroy Colt, a brother of the judge and a lawyer of Paterson, New Jersey. In the Biographical Dictionary of the distinguished dead we find record only of James Denison Colt (1819-1881), justice of the Massachusetts supreme court, and Samuel Colt (1814-1862), the inventor of Colt's revolver, which made the name as familiar as Smith, Brown or Jones in the vocabulary of Americans. The rarity in number of the family is discovered only in the course of genealogical research. John Coult, who came to America with the Rev. Thomas Hooker, in 1636, and settled in Hartford, Connecticut Colony, is the progenitor of all of the name above mentioned, whether spelled Colt, Coalt or Coult, as his name appears on Colonial records spelled the three ways.

(I) John Colt, immigrant, was born in Colchester, Essex, England, in 1625, and came to Dorchester, Massachusetts Bay Colony, when eleven years of age. He was probably a ward of the Hooker company and went to Hartford with them about 1638. There is much confusion in regard to the individuality of John Coult, the progenitor, as three generations bore the name, and the second and third Johns are rarely distinguished by "Captain John" and "John Jr." They appear indiscriminately as John Colt or John Coult, which spelling of the name appears in the Colonial records, John "Coult" having September 1, 1675, been shot at by the Indians. Styles "History of Ancient Windsor" fixes the date of this occurrence as August 31, 1675, and names the person John Colt, of Windsor, mentioning him again as one appointed in 1672 to work on the highways. The same authority records the sale in 1679 of a house by Joseph Fitch to John

Colt, and names John Coult as, October 11, 1669, a freeman of Windsor, Connecticut. He married (first) Mary Fitch; (second) Ann, born in Hartford in 1639, baptized February 7, 1646, daughter of John and Mary (Loomis) Skinner. His children were born in Hartford as follows: 1. Sarah, baptized February 7, 1646-47, in the church at Hartford. 2. John, born 1658, see forward. 3. Abraham, married Hannah Loomis, July 1, 1690; removed to Glastonbury in 1691, where he died in 1730. 4. Joseph, married Ruth Loomis, October 29, 1691; lived in Windsor, Connecticut, where he died January 11, 1719. 5. Jonathan, who died in 1711. 6. Jabez. 7. Esther, who married Stephen Loomis, January 1, 1690-91; she died November 6, 1714. The English family of Coult, from which John Coult, the immigrant ancestor, came, lived in Colchester, England. The coat-of-arms of the Coults originated here and is three horses heads and a broken spear. The name has been traced from Sir John Coult through six generations to the American immigrant of the same name as follows: (1) Sir John Coult, born about 1440. (II) Peter. (III) John. (IV) John (2). (V) John (3). (VI) John (4). (VII) John (5), whose son (VIII) John (6), was one of the founders of New London county, Connecticut Colony, and was probably one of the officials who named one of its early inland towns Colchester, after his father's birthplace.

(II) Captain John (2), eldest son of John (1), immigrant, and Mary (Fitch) Colt, was born in Hartford, Connecticut, in 1658. After his marriage he removed to Lyme, at the mouth of the Connecticut river, where he was a farmer and leading citizen of the town. He was in 1709 established and confirmed by the general assembly to be ensign of the company of train band of the town of Lyme, under the command of Captain William Eely. His name is here 'John Coult of Lyme." In the general assembly of Connecticut Colony, May 8-23, 1712, he was present as a deputy from Lyme, and his name is then printed "Ensign John Colt." On October 10, 1717, he was commissioned lieutenant by the general assembly, and on October 10, 1723, he was commissioned captain of the north company of Lyme. He was deputy to the general assembly for seven sessions of that body, 1718-24. He married Mary Lord, and their children were as follows: 1. A daughter who married a Mr. Sterling, of Niantia. 2. A daughter who married Thomas Ayers, of Saybrook. 3. Benjamin, born 1698, see forward. 4. A daughter who married a Mr. Comstock, of Hadlyme. 5. Samuel, born 1705, died 1743; married, November 7, 1734, Abigail Mervin.

(III) Benjamin, eldest son of Captain John (2) and Mary (Lord) Colt, was born in Lyme, Connecticut, in 1698, died in 1754. He resided in Lyme, where he was a deacon of the church and lieutenant-colonel in the militia. He married, May 26, 1724, Miriam Harris, and their children, born in Old Lyme, New London county, Connecticut, were as follows: 1. John, born 1725, died 1784; married (first) Mary Lord; (second) Mary Gardner; (third) Abigail Masten. 2. Joseph. 3. Mary. 4. Sarah. 5. Temperance. 6. Harris. 7. Polly. 8. Benjamin, born 1740: 9. Peter. 10. Isaac, see forward. It is known that Isaac Coult, of Sussex County, New Jersey, came from Connecticut. He is probably the tenth child of Benjamin Coult and born at Lyme in 1743. The birth of one of the children of Colonel Benjamin Colt or Coult, as both he and his father and grandfather frequently had their names written, was in 1725 and another in 1740, and the natal year of none of the others is given. Or Isaac Coult, of Sussex, may have been the son of Samuel, as above stated, born in 1705, who married Abigail Mervin. This it is safe to say that Isaac was a grandson of Captain John and great-grandson of John Coult, the immigrant. Further research in family records may make the parentage of Isaac Coult clear, but the weight of available evidence is in favor of the line as here laid down, and we venture to give it as presumably correct. The Coults in Connecticut were farmers, and naturally they took up the same vocation in New Jersey among the rich highlands of Sussex county. The name Joseph Coult appears in each generation, both in Connecticut and New Jersey, with this difference, that, in Connecticut portions of the family wrote the name after the first two generations Colt, while Isaac preserved the original spelling Coult, as did the family of that name in New London county, Connecticut.

(IV) Isaac Coult, probably son of Colonel Benjamin and Miriam (Harris) Colt, was born in Lyme, Connecticut, in 1743, died in Sussex county, New Jersey, in 1837. He came from Connecticut to New Jersey when a young man. He married, July 13, 1766, Sarah Holbart, born in 1747, died in New Jersey in 1833. Their children, born presumably in Papakating, Sussex county, New Jersey, were as follows: 1. Abigail, born 1770, married —— Hetzel. 2. Isaac, 1772, married Nancy Morris. 3. Anna, 1774, married —— Norris. 4. Ashel, 1776, died 1804, unmarried. 5. Sarah, 1778, died 1779. 6. John, 1781, married —— English. 7. Elizabeth, 1783, married —— Bryant. 8. Joseph, 1788, see forward. 9. Lucy, 1789, married —— Mattison.

(V) Joseph, fourth son of Isaac and Sarah (Holbart) Coult, was born in Papakating, Sussex county, New Jersey, 1788. He married (first) in 1809, Jerusha Price, and their children born in Papakating, New Jersey, were as follows: 1. Robert, 1810, died unmarried in 1838. 2. Sarah, 1812. 3. Elizabeth, 1814, married Charles Roe. 4. Abigail, 1815, married John Couse. 5. Lucy, 1817, married Charles Roe. 6. John, 1819, married Catherine Titman. 7. Henrietta, 1821. 8. Isaac, 1823, married Jane Ketchum. Mr. Coult married (second) 1825, Hannah Coursen, who bore him two children. 9. Jerusha, 1826. 10. Joseph, see forward.

(VI) Joseph (2), second child of Joseph (1) and Hannah (Coursen) Coult, born in Papakating, Sussex county, New Jersey, May 25, 1834. He was educated in the Rankin School at Deckertown, studied law under Thomas N. McCarter, and later in the Law School at New Albany, New York, graduating with the degree of Bachelor of Laws. He was admitted to the bar in the state of New York and began the practice of law in New York City. Shortly afterward, however, he returned to his native state and was admitted as an attorney-at-law there in February, 1861. He became a law partner with Thomas Anderson in Newton, conducting a general law practice, the partnership continuing for several years and being attended with signal success. He was made a full attorney and counsellor-at-law under the laws of New Jersey in 1864, and in 1871 entered into partnership with Louis Van Blascom. In 1873 he withdrew from the firm and removed to Newark, New Jersey, becoming junior partner in the firm of Leonard & Coult. In 1893, when Chancellor Theodore Runyon withdrew from the practice of law in order to accept the

position of United States minister to Germany, as successor to William Walter Phelps, under appointment of President Cleveland, the firm of Leonard & Coult succeeded to his extensive law practice and they made a specialty of municipal law. Mr. Coult was counsel for the city of Newark for twelve years and prosecutor of pleas for one year. He is a Republican in politics, taking an active interest in all matters pertaining to the welfare of his party, and on numerous occasions he has served as delegate to conventions of various kinds, having the honor of having assisted in the nomination of no less than three of the men who have stood at the head of the nation. He was a delegate to the Baltimore convention that nominated Lincoln for a second term, the convention at Philadelphia which nominated Grant, and the Cincinnati convention which nominated Hayes. His club affiliations included membership in the Union Club, the North End Club and the New York Republican Club. Mr. Coult married, at Branchville, New Jersey, May 25, 1859, Frances A., daughter of Joseph A. and Margaret Osborne. Their family consists of three daughters and one son: Margaret, Eliza, Lillian, married Frank W. Kinsey, and Joseph, who married Edna Pierson Wheeler and has two children, Edna Clare and Joseph.

MERCER The Mercers are of Scotch origin, and for centuries before the coming of persons of their blood to this country the name was a distinguished one both in church and state, but particularly in the kirk, where we find them among the foremost in a land and time noted for their eminent divines and reformers. The great-grandfather of the founder of the Mercer family in New Jersey was John Mercer, who was the minister of the kirk in Kinnellan, Aberdeenshire, from 1650 to 1676, in which latter year he resigned his incumbency, probably on account of feebleness or age, as his death occurred about a year later. This worthy divine married Lilian Row, a great-granddaughter of the reformer, John Row, and from their union sprang three children, one of whom was Thomas Mercer, baptized January 20, 1658, and mentioned in the poll lists of 1696. This Thomas married (first) Anna Raite, and (second) a woman whose last name is unknown but who was christened Isabel. Seven children were the result of one or both of these marriages, but the records at present available are insufficient to enable us to determine which

wife was the mother of any one or more of them. One of these children was baptized William on the 25th of March, 1696, and he is an important personage, not only on his own account, but also because he was the father of two great families of his name in this country, both of them worthily held in high honor by New Jersey, although only one has made this colony and state its home. William Mercer followed in the footsteps of his grandfather, the Rev. John, and being educated for the ministry, made a name for himself and won a prominent position in the established kirk of Scotland, from 1720 to 1748 being in charge of the manse at Pittsligo, Aberdeenshire. He married Anne, daughter of Sir Robert Munro, of Foulis, who was killed in 1746, while commanding the British troops at Falkirk. By this marriage the Rev. William Mercer had three children, one a daughter named Eleanor or Helen; another Hugh, who emigrated to America in 1747, settling first in Pennsylvania and later in Virginia, and won for himself undying glory and national gratitude, first as captain of militia in Braddock's unfortunate expedition, and afterwards as brigadier-general of the continental army in the campaign culminating in the battles of Trenton and Princeton where he met his doom; and lastly William, the founder of the Mercer family of New Jersey.

(I) William Mercer, the colonist, above mentioned as the son of the Rev. William Mercer, of Pittsligo, was born about 1715, in Aldie, Scotland, shortly after his father's ordination to the ministry, and died in New Brunswick, New Jersey, March 10, 1770, in the fifty-sixth year of his age. From all accounts William Mercer, the colonist, was a man of retiring and quiet disposition, inclining more to the study and the workshop rather than to the field and forum of public life. He was a scholarly gentleman and physician, whose mills were an easily recognized and well known landmark not only throughout New Jersey but in New York as well. From May, 1747, about six or seven years after his emigration to this country, until February, 1768, about two years before his death, the *New York Gazette* and *Weekly Post Boy* and the *New York Gazette* and *Weekly Mercury* contain many advertisements of lands for sale and houses to sell or rent which were either owned by Dr. Mercer himself or which though owned by others, were to be recognized by their proximity or relation to "Dr. Mercer's Mills," which were situated in the "blue hill country of Somerset county, on the road through Johnstone's Gap to the Valley between the first and second mountains." Dr. Mercer's own home was in New Brunswick, where he held the title to considerable properties, one of them being "a house and large garden situated upon the bank of the river," the house having "three good fine rooms upon the first floor, and four rooms on the second, with a good kitchen, cellar, pantry, &c., below," and the outbuildings consisted of "a large barn with very convenient stabling in it, and other outhouses, also two large convenient storehouses adjoining." This property Dr. Mercer had bought from William Donaldson, who had afterward rented it from him for a number of years, and then having determined to go back to England, had given up his lease, whereupon Dr. Mercer advertised it as for rent in the New York papers. From another advertisement in the *New York Gazette and Weekly Mercury* of January 15, 1776, about six years after Dr. Mercer's death, we learned that he was one of the old Jersey slave owners, as on that date Colonel John Reid advertises forty shillings reward for a runaway negro man, named Sam, who had formerly belonged to and lived in the family of Dr. Mercer. Dr. Mercer's will is recorded in Liber K, page 208, of the East Jersey wills, and is on file in the vaults of the office of the secretary of state in Trenton, New Jersey. By his wife, Lucy (Tyson) Mercer, Dr. William Mercer had nine children: William, John, Isaac, Gabriel, Peter, Martha, Achibald, Helen and Robert. Two of these sons went to West Indies, one of them, William, settling about five years after his father's death in Bermuda, and the other in Barbadoes. Another of his sons settled in New Orleans, and two more of his sons died leaving no record behind them. Of Martha, the oldest of his daughters, nothing is known. Helen, his other daughter, married Samuel Highway, who settled in Cincinnati, Ohio, and after her husband's death, somewhat later than 1814, returned to New Jersey and made her home with her niece, Mrs. Theodore Frelinghuysen, at Newark, New Jersey, where she died in November, 1822. Robert, the youngest son of Dr. William Mercer, the colonist, settled in Philadelphia, Pennsylvania, having married Eleanor Tittennary, December 2, 1783, who bore him four children: Eleanor Tittennary Mercer, who became the wife of Samuel Moss and the mother of five children: Joseph, Lucy, Thomas Frelinghuysen, Charlotte Frelinghuysen and Maria Moss; Letitia Mercer, who died young; Robert Mercer, who followed his uncle to New Orleans; and Mary Strycker Mercer, who married and left one child, Isaac Sydney Jones.

(II) Archibald, sixth son of Dr. William Mercer, of New Brunswick, was born in 1747, either shortly before or just after the father came to this country. He died in Newark, New Jersey, May 4, 1814, after a long and useful life, the early part of which was spent in New Brunswick and New York, the manhood and middle age in Millstone, Somerset county, New Jersey, and the declining years in Newark where he took his place as a prominent citizen of the growing town and the close and valued friend of such men as General John N. Cumming, James Kearney, Elias E. Boudinot, William Halsey, John and Stephen Van Courtlandt, Jesse Gilbert, Ashbel Upson, David Lyman, Abraham Wooley, Archippus Priest and William Hillhouse. The early years of Archibald Mercer's life were spent in his father's home in New Brunswick, and here, under the scholarly doctor's tuition, he received his early education. When he was between fifteen and twenty years of age, young Archibald went to New York where he remained until after the birth of his first child, but whether he went there to enroll himself among the students of King's College, now Columbia University, or whether he went to the city in order to start himself in a business career is uncertain. That he was there during this time, however, we learn from the fact that his eldest child was born in New York, and that during the period above mentioned there occurs in the advertisement already mentioned which his father inserted in the newspapers the phrase "For further particulars enquire of Doctor Mercer at New Brunswick, or Archibald Mercer at Walter and Samuel Franklin's store in New York." The times in which Archibald Mercer's youth and early manhood were passed were indeed stirring ones and just what part he took in them we have never been able to ascertain. The only military record left by the New Jersey Mercer is that of Captain John, who at the beginning of the war was an ensign in Captain Howell's company, first battalion of the first establishment of the Jersey line, who on November 14, 1775, became first lieutenant of the same company. On November 29, 1776, Lieutenant John Mercer was transferred to Captain Morris's company, first battalion of the second establishment of the Jersey line, and on February 15, 1777, was promoted captain of the same company. He was taken prisoner of war and exchanged on November 6, 1780, and he was finally retired September 26, 1780. Unless this Captain John Mercer was Archibald Mercer's elder brother, of whom no other record now remains, it is probable that he was either not at all or at most only distantly related to the family we are now considering. However this may be, of one thing we can be reasonably sure, Archibald Mercer's position in later life, the fact that in 1794 he was judge of the court of common pleas for Somerset county, the fact that the men whose names we have already mentioned were his bosom friends and considered that they were honored by being reckoned such, all goes to show that he must have played his part well and done his duty manfully, whatever it was, in those times that "tried men's souls." Mr. Mercer's children with the exception of the first born were all of them born in Millstone, New Jersey, so that between the years 1776 and 1794 that was probably his home. At some time between then and the beginning of the new century he removed to Newark, New Jersey, for in 1806 we find that he was chairman of the committee that made the contract for the construction of the Newark turnpike, his fellow committeemen being John N. Cumming, Jesse Gilbert, Ashbel Upson, David Lyman, Abraham Wooley, Archippus Priest and William Hillhouse. On March 10, 1811, he and George Seriba, Esquire, were sponsors in Trinity Church for Joseph Augustus, son of the Rev. Joseph Wheeler, the second rector of the parish. On September 29, 1812, about six weeks after his second marriage, Mr. Mercer wrote his will, which is recorded in the Essex Wills, book A., page 500, and is preserved in the vaults at Trenton. In this, after the customary instructions, committing his soul to God and his body to the earth "to be buried at the discretion of his executors," he divides his property, after certain legacies have been deducted, equally among his five surviving children. To several of his grandchildren he leaves legacies varying in amount; to the rector, wardens and vestrymen of Trinity Church he bequeathes all the accounts he has against the church, and reserves his pew for the use of the members of his family and expresses the 'hope that they will at least sometimes go there;' to his sister, Helen Highway, and to his "unfortunate brother, Robert," he leaves $10,000.00 each; he appoints as his executors his four children, Peter, Archibald, Gertrude and Charlotte; his two sons-in-law, Dr. James Lee and Theodore Frelinghuysen, and his friend, James R. Smith,

of New York; he concludes by saying that he desires "to be buried alongside of my deceased son, William, and that the remains of my dear wife be removed and laid in the same pit with me. And now farewell my beloved children, the best legacy I can leave you is to conjure you to live so as to merit the favour of your God." This will is witnessed by John N. Cumming, James Kearney and Elias E. Boudinot, and was proved June 18, 1814. The inventory of his estate made June 1, 1814, by General John N. Cumming and William Halsey, amounted to $120,609.88.

The first wife of the Hon. Archibald Mercer and the mother of all of his children was Mary (Schenck) Mercer, of Somerset county, New Jersey, whom he married July 23, 1770. She died in Newark, January 1, 1808, aged sixty years, after bearing him nine children, seven of whom survived her. Their names and birthdays are as follows: Maria, August 19, 1771; Peter Schenck, June 14, 1776; Louisa, August 5, 1778; Gertrude, October 25, 1781; Charlotte, February 5, 1784; William, March 2, 1786; Eliza, June 14, 1787; Archibald, December 1, 1788; John, May 9, 1790. Two of these children died in infancy, Eliza, March 9, 1793; and John, July 1, 1794. Two more of them married and died before their father, Louisa, who married John Frelinghuysen, son of the Hon. Frederick Frelinghuysen, who is considered elsewhere, and William, who will be referred to later. Maria Mercer, the eldest child, married Dr. Peter T. Stryker, and died childless, July 8, 1841. Peter Schenck Mercer, the eldest son, died April 1, 1833, in New London, Connecticut, after being twice married; by his first wife he had four children, Mary Schenck, Archibald, John Frelinghuysen, and Frederick; but all that remains of record of them or their mother is a gravestone in the "Red brick grave yard" on the road leading from Millstone to Somerville, inscribed "Margaret Mercer, 1814, aged thirty-one years, wife of Peter Mercer and their infant children." By his second wife, Rebecca Starr, he had four more children, Peter, who died young; Abigail, who married Captain John French; Margaret, who married a Winthrop; and Elizabeth, whose husband was Frederick Bidwell. Gertrude Mercer, the fourth child and third daughter, died January 26, 1830, having married, July 22, 1808, Dr. James Lee, of New London, to whom she bore at least one daughter, who was afterwards Mrs. Robert A. McCurdy and the mother of Richard A. McCurdy, of Morristown. Charlotte Mercer, the next child to

Gertrude, married Theodore, another son of the Hon. Frederick Frelinghuysen, and will be referred to under that family. Archibald Mercer, junior, the next to the youngest child, died in New London, Connecticut, October 3, 1850. He was twice married; the first time to Abigail Starr, March 11, 1812, who bore him two children. Charlotte Frelinghuysen, afterwards Mrs. James Morgan, and Sarah Isham, afterwards the wife of George S. Hazard. By his second marriage, June 18, 1817, to Harriet Wheat, who died February 20, 1854, he had eight more children: Louisa Frelinghuysen and Helen Highway, who died in infancy; Harriet, John Dishon and Abigail Starr, who died unmarried: William, who married Ellen C. Allen; Gertrude Lee, who became Mrs. Adam F. Prentice; and Maria Stryker, afterwards the wife of Samuel H. Grosvenor, whose only son is the Rev. William Mercer Grosvenor, D. D., the present rector of the Protestant Episcopal Church of the Incarnation, New York City. A little over four years after his wife's death, Archibald Mercer, senior, married (second) July 5, 1812, Catharina Sophia Cuyler, widow of John Van Cortlandt, who survived him about nine years, dying March 25, 1823. Of this marriage there was no issue. By her first husband, Mrs. Mercer had one son, James Van Cortlandt, who together with her mother, Martha Cuyler, she mentions in her will, written August 3, 1821, and proven August 9, 1823, her estate, left wholly to these two, amounting to $6,737,961.

(III) William (2), sixth child and second son of the Hon. Archibald Mercer, Esquire, of Somerset county and Newark, was born in Millstone, New Jersey, March 2, 1786, died in Newark less than three years after his marriage, and within eighteen days of his twenty-sixth birthday. From several of the expressions in his father's will it would appear as though he were to some extent the favorite son, but whether this was due to the promise of a brilliant career, or to innate and acquired characteristics that endeared him to those with whom he came in contact, or to a delicate condition of health that rendered necessary an extra amount of care and devotion on his father's part, there is now no means of determining. William Mercer died intestate, but from his father's will we learn that Archibald Mercer kept a careful account of all the money he had given to his children at any time, and the reasons therefore. On the date of his son, William's death he closed these accounts and his will mentions the totals with the ledger

page devoted to each child, and notes that in the case of "Lucy" (i. e. Louisa) and William, both deceased "these two accounts are not to be made account of except as so much towards the legacies of their children." In the case of the other children the amounts given to them were to be charged against their respective shares of his estate as were also any additional sums advanced to them since that date. The totals vary all the way from Charlotte's $737.00 to Peter's $5,768; and William's $2,-600.00 is fourth in the whole list, but in the amounts loaned to his sons it is only exceeded by Peter's amount. Only the ledger, if it is still in existence and can be found, will tell us with certainty the purpose for which these loans were made; but judging from the fact that four out of his nine children died before reaching the prime of life, from the sad history of Peter's first marriage and the early deaths of his wife and children, together with the fact that the greatest amounts were loaned to Peter, Louisa, Gertrude and William, the first of his four grown up children to die, and also remembering that the most of William's married life was spent at a health resort, there is a possibility that the expenses of sickness rather than the opportunities of business and fortune were to a greater or less degree the controlling factors. William Mercer married, November 11, 1809, Eliza Vardell, daughter of Thomas Vardell, of New York City, and shortly after his marriage went to Bermuda to visit his uncle, William Mercer, where their first child was born, died, and was buried in the family vault. He and his bride remained at Bermuda until a little while before his death, when they returned to his father's home in Newark. Here William's only son was born, just twenty-three days after his father's decease, in the old house of his grandfather on Broad street upon the present site of the Continental Hotel. Children: Margaret Willett, born May 3, 1810, died March 10, 1811; William Theodore, who will now be considered.

(IV) William Theodore, only son of William (2) Mercer, was born March 7, 1812, died in Newark, June 28, 1886. His mother survived her husband only a few years, and left her child an orphan of about four or five years old. William Theodore was then adopted by his Aunt Charlotte, the wife of the Hon. Theodore Frelinghuysen, and in their house in Newark he passed his early years and later on in life made his home. His preparatory education was gained in the old Newark Academy, which had been established by an association in 1792, and which for many years was regarded as one of the largest and most prominent academic institutions of the country. During the time young Mercer spent there as an undergraduate it was enjoying the zenith of its reputation. In 1827, when he was about fifteen years old, William Theodore Mercer entered the sophomore class at Williams College, Williamstown, Massachusetts, and graduated there three years later, in 1830. He then went to New London, Connecticut, where his uncles, Peter Schenck Mercer and Archibald Mercer, and his aunt, Gertrude Lee, who died the year of his graduation, had made their homes, and there began the study of medicine in the office of his uncle, Archibald Mercer. He remained here, however, only for a short while, and then returning to his Aunt Charlotte's home in Newark, he finished his preparatory medical studies under the tuition of Dr. Lyndon A. Smith, of that city. In 1834 William Theodore Mercer graduated from the Jefferson Medical College, of Philadelphia, and settling himself in practice in his home town he almost immediately met with great success and built up an enormous practice, which, however, soon undermined his health, as it demanded from him far greater physical labors than his inherited delicacy of constitution could bear. Consequently after about ten years of strenuous and vigorous work, Dr. Mercer retired from active practice, and devoted himself to the study of materia medica and therapeutics, in connection with which he established in Newark, about 1845, a drug business that he managed successfully for over forty years, until the day of his death. A short while after he had received his degree of M. D. and established himself in the practice of his profession, Dr. Mercer became a member of the Essex County Medical Society, in the proceedings and work of which he took a very great interest and a most active part, being a number of different times sent by the association as its delegate to the State Medical Society, and for nineteen years, from 1839 to 1858, was the association secretary. During the whole of his long life, Dr. Mercer was considered to rank at the head of his profession, and he was held in greatest esteem by his contemporaries not only for his intimate and thorough technical and professional knowledge of medicine, but also for his manly and great personal and social qualities and attainments. Dr. William Theodore Mercer married, July 7, 1835, Gertrude Ann, daughter of Frederick Frelinghuysen and his wife, Jane, the eldest daughter of Peter Dumont, of Somerville. Mrs. Mercer was the niece-in-law of the aunts of Dr. Mercer, Louisa and Charlotte, and was therefore a connection, not a cousin, of her husband. From this marriage there were seven children, all of whom reached maturity, although only four of them had issue. The three unmarried children and one of the others are dead, the remaining children are still living. These children were: 1. Charlotte Frelinghuysen Mercer, born August 25, 1836; died unmarried, March 4, 1895. 2. Gertrude Eliza Mercer, born July 30, 1838; died May 11, 1899; married, April 23, 1866, William Whitehead, and had one child, Gertrude Mercer Whitehead, who died in infancy, a few months after her father. 3. Frederick Frelinghuysen Mercer, referred to later. 4. Theodore Frelinghuysen Mercer, referred to later. 5. William Mercer, born December 21, 1845; died unmarried, September 9, 1884. 6. Archibald Mercer, referred to later. 7. Dumont Frelinghuysen Mercer, born January 23, 1850; died single, January 19, 1882.

(V) Frederick Frelinghuysen, oldest son and third child of William Theodore Mercer, was born in Newark, New Jersey, November 7, 1840, and is now living with his family at 33 Washington street, in the house and city of his birth. For his early education he was sent to a private school in Newark, where he was prepared for college and from which, in 1857, he entered the freshman class of Rutgers College, New Brunswick, New Jersey, where he received his A. B. degree in 1861 and later on his A. M. Turning his attention to the law, Mr. Mercer read and studied for three years with the Hon. Frederick Theodore Frelinghuysen, his uncle, and at that time attorney-general for New Jersey. Three years later, in 1864, he was admitted to the bar and began the life of a general practitioner, and in this he was engaged for several years when he gave it up in order to enter other fields of work. Since 1885 he has been connected with the Equitable Life Insurance Company, of New York. In politics Mr. Mercer is a Republican, but has never held nor desired office. He has had no military experience, but he is a member of the Sons of the Revolution. He is also a member of the Zeta Psi college fraternity, but beyond this has formed no club affiliations. He is a member of Trinity Protestant Episcopal Church. On April 14, 1868, Frederick Frelinghuysen Mercer was married in Staten Island, New York, to Kate, born February 29, 1844, daughter of William Henry Anable, of New York, and his wife, Mary Barnard (Steele)

Anable. She bore him five children, all of whom are still living and three of whom are married:

1. Frederick William, born June 9, 1869; superintendent of the loan department of the Mutual Life Insurance Company, of New York; married, April 28, 1897, Mabel Russell, who has borne him two children, Russell Barnard and Gertrude. 2. Alice Louise, born December 15, 1871; become the wife of Easton M. Davitt, of 216 Belleville avenue, Newark; she had one child, Mercer, who died in infancy. 3. Dumont Frelinghuysen, born May 31, 1874; educated in the public and high schools, and is now with the Mutual Life Insurance Company, of New York. 4. John Eccleston, born November 19, 1876; was a member of the Seventy-first New York Regiment during the Spanish war. 5. Gertrude, born March 7, 1881; married Captain Frank Wheaton Rowell, and has two children: Gertrude and Katharine; one, Wheaton, died in infancy.

(V) Theodore Frelinghuysen, fourth child and second son of William Theodore Mercer, was born in Newark, New Jersey, October 18, 1842, and is now living at 662 High street, in that city. For his early education he attended a private school and then entered the Newark Academy, on leaving which he went into the drug business with his father and continued with him for fifteen years when he withdrew in order to accept a position as clerk in the money order department of the Newark post office. Here he remained for twelve years longer, and then took up a position with the Delaware, Lackawanna and Western Railroad Company, which he retained for fifteen years longer, and finally resigned in 1903 in order to undertake the work in the mathematical department of the Mutual Benefit Life Insurance Company, where he now is. Mr. Mercer is a Republican and a communicant of Trinity Protestant Episcopal Church, Newark. On January 24, 1876, Theodore Frelinghuysen Mercer married, in Trinity Church, Newark, Josephine, daughter of Elias N. Miller and his wife, Susan Maria (Coats) Miller, who has borne him one daughter, Maria Coats Mercer, born November 4, 1878, and now the wife of George Bache Emory, M. D., son of Thomas Emory, of Confederate Navy, and Percy (Mc-Carthy) Emory, of Syracuse, New York, and grandson of Brigadier-General William Hemsley Emory, United States Army, and Matilda Wilkins (Bache) Emory, the sixth child of Richard Bache, the younger, of Philadelphia. They have one child, Thomas Mercer Emory, born March 6, 1908.

(V) Archibald Mercer, M. D., fourth son and sixth child of Dr. William Theodore Mercer, of Newark, was born December 23, 1847, and is now living at 31 Washington street, Newark, New Jersey. Following in his father's footsteps, he obtained his preparatory education at the Newark Academy, and in 1864 matriculated at Rutgers College, New Brunswick, New Jersey, where he graduated in 1868. He then began the study of medicine, taking the course at the College of Physicians and Surgeons, in New York, and receiving his degree from that institution in 1871; since which time he has been a practitioner in Newark. On leaving the medical school in 1871, Dr. Mercer was appointed physician in charge of S. Barnabas Hospital, in Newark, which position he held for about nine years, until 1880, and then he finally decided to make surgery his specialty. A year later, in 1881, he became visiting surgeon of the Newark City Hospital, and four years later, in 1885, was appointed to the same position in S. Barnabas' Hospital. These positions, in spite of the great demands upon his time and energies made by his outside professional and other duties, he still continues to hold. In 1873 Dr. Mercer received the appointment of United States examining surgeon for pensions, and in 1881 that of police surgeon for the city of Newark, but the pressure of other work upon him became so great that in 1883 he resigned both of them. In 1891 he accepted the office of surgeon to the New Jersey Home for Disabled Soldiers, but was obliged by the exacting nature of his other duties and responsibilities to resign it in 1897, just as in 1894 he was compelled to decline the honor of his election as surgeon of the Essex troop. Outside of his practice, Dr. Mercer's professional interests and activities have been many and varied. Since 1878 he has been a member of the Essex County Medical Society, of which his father was for so long a time an active member and efficient secretary, for twenty-six consecutive years was elected secretary, this making a total of nearly half a century that he and his father held this position. In 1905 he was chosen the vice-president of this society and during the year 1906 he was the association's president. Since 1892 he has also been treasurer of the Medical Society of New Jersey. In 1894 he was president of the Medical and Surgical Society of Newark. In 1889 he became secretary of the Society for the Relief of the Widows and Orphans of the Medical Men of New Jersey, of which association he was in 1899 chosen vice-president. In addition to these duties, Dr. Mercer has also for a time been the medical examiner for many insurance companies, and in 1904 was appointed one of the medical directors of the Mutual Benefit Life Insurance Company. Beyond the bounds of his profession, Dr. Mercer's interest and activities are in the main patriotic and educational in their broadest sense; although the calls which have been made by different members of his own family upon the highly valued and widely recognized business qualifications and executive abilities have been by no means inconsiderable. On July 14, 1886, he was appointed the chief executor of his father's estate, and a few months later, on October 30, in the same year, was called upon to act in the same capacity on the property of his mother, and nine years later, on March 15, 1895, he performed the same office for his unmarried sister Charlotte, and again in 1899 for his sister Gertrude, widow of William Whitehead. Dr. Mercer has for years been a member of the Essex Club; he is a communicant of Trinity Protestant Episcopal Church, in the early days and welfare of which his great-grandfather took such an active interest and part, and in connection with his brother now owns two pews in Trinity Church, which were deeded, December 16, 1822, by the rector, wardens and vestry of the church to the children of his great-great-grandfather, the two pews being originally one square pew which was owned by him. He is also one of the Sons of the American Revolution, and a life member of the New Jersey Historical Society. In 1903 he was appointed for four years one of the trustees of the Free Public Library, of Newark, and in 1907 he accepted his reappointment for five years to the same office. In 1908 he was elected a member of the Cathedral Chapter by the convention of the Episcopal Church, diocese of Newark. In 1909 he was influential in starting the Newark Art Museum Association and was elected one of the charter members of the board of trustees and also chairman of its executive committee. On November 21, 1888, Dr. Archibald Mercer married Katrina, daughter of Alexander Campbell, of Newark, by his wife, Emma (Field) Campbell; they have no children.

HOWE The name of Howe is not only scattered through the registers and records of all parts of England, but the bearers of the name have written it in their blood and graven it deeply with their swords, high up on their country's roll of honor. The Howe banner is in the chapel of Henry VII., and in the struggle between France and England in the New World, Howes fought and fell, notably at Ticonderoga and on the Nova Scotia' frontier. Among the more famous members of the family may be named Rev. John Howe, chaplain to Oliver Cromwell, whose noble features are preserved in old engravings; and Lord Charles Howe, created baronet by James I., November 18, 1606, and made Earl of Lancaster by Charles I., June 8, 1643. It is with the latter that John Howe, of Sudbury, founder of the present family, is reported to be connected.

(I) John How was born in England, in 1602, and came to New England with his wife Mary, between 1630 and 1640. He settled in Watertown, but in 1639 removed to Sudbury, where he was made freeman the following year, in 1642 was chosen selectman, and in 1655 was appointed by the pastor and selectmen "to see to the restraining of youth on the Lord's Day." He was the first white man to settle in Marlborough, Massachusetts, about 1657, where he built his cabin, a little east of the "Indian planting field," and where his descendants lived for many generations. In 1661 he opened the first public house in Marlborough, and about nine years later petitioned for a renewal of his license. He was highly respected for his justice and impartiality by his fellow townsmen as well as by the Indians, and was frequently made arbiter of their disputes. According to one annalist he died in 1680, aged seventy-eight, but another gives the date as 1687. His will, proved in 1689, mentions wife, Mary; sons, Samuel, Isaac, Jonah, Thomas and Eleazer; daughters, Sarah Ward and Mary Weatherby; and grandson, John How, Jr., son of John, deceased. His property was inventoried at £500. Samuel, his eldest son, married Hepzibah Death, in 1700; he was opener and proprietor of the Howe tavern at Sudbury, immortalized by Longfellow in his "Tales of a Wayside Inn." Samuel's descendants kept and owned it until it was sold, about twenty-five years ago.

(II) Thomas, son of John How, was born in Sudbury, June 12, 1656, and died at Marlborough, February 16, 1733. He was one of the most prominent citizens of the town, at various times filled some of the principal offices, and seems to have always had the welfare of his fellows at heart. Nor were his efforts confined to his home and town. He was representative in the general court, and one of His

Majesty's justices of the peace. He was a well trained and efficient soldier, proving his worth in the severe action at Lancaster, and in the early wars against the Indians. For many years he served in the colonial militia, and a special legacy to him in his father's will is "the horse he troops on." He retired with the rank of colonel. He was keeping a public house at Marlborough in 1661, but whether he was carrying on the business established by his father, or was founding a new venture of his own, cannot be determined. He married (first) June 8, 1681, Mary Hosmer, who died April 7, 1724; and (second) December 24, 1724, Widow Mary Baron. Children, all by first wife: 1. Tabitha, born May 9, 1684. 2. James, June 22, 1685. 3. Jonathan, April 23, 1687. 4. Prudence, August 27, 1689. 5. Thomas, June 16, 1692. 6. Sarah, August 16, 1697.

(III) Jonathan, son of Thomas How, was born in Marlborough, April 23, 1687, died there June 22, 1738. His entire life was passed in his native town. He married, April 5, 1711, Lydia Brigham; children: 1. Timothy, born May 24, 1712; died October 15, 1740. 2. Prudence, November 3, 1714. 3. Bezaleel; of whom further. 4. Charles, April 20, 1720. 5. Eliakim, June 17, 1723. 6. Lucy, May 20, 1726. 7. Lydia, April 12, 1729; died young. 8. Mary, August 12, 1730. 9. Lydia, June 29, 1732.

(IV) Bezaleel, third child and second son of Jonathan How, was born in Marlborough, June 19, 1717. Records concerrning him are few and imperfect, and the family traditions of him rest mainly in the reminiscences of his grandson, Rev. John Moffat Howe, M. D., and upon researches made in 1844 by another grandson, Rev. Bezaleel Howe, the mss. of which are in possession of Andrus Bezaleel Howe, of Montclair, New Jersey. From these materials we learn that he married Anna Foster, and that of their at least seven children, three sons and two daughters were born in Marlborough, and the other two, both sons, at some place on the family journey to Hillsborough, New Hampshire, whither they removed shortly before the death of the father. Of his two daughters, Susanna, born 1740, and Edith, 1744, little is known, and one of them apparently died young. His sons were: Timothy, born 1742; Darius, 1746; Bezaleel, 1750; and Baxter and Titus, birth dates unknown. Of Titus no record is left. The others, especially Bezaleel (q. v.), have brilliant military records. Darius was a lieuten-

ant in the revolution. Timothy served in the French war, and soon after his marriage to Elizabeth Andrus, of Stillwater, New York, removed to Wyoming, Pennsylvania, where the family lived until driven out by the Indians and Tories, in July, 1778. At the time of this famous massacre, Timothy was serving as first lieutanant under Captain Hewitt. Baxter was a lieutenant in Colonel Jonathan Brewer's regiment of the New Hampshire line, and later an artillery captain in the army under Washington. He died of fever at Ethron, during the forced march to Yorktown, and left a son, Brigham Howe, of New York City.

(V) Bezaleel (2), youngest son of Bezaleel (1) Howe, was born December 9, 1750. He was the first of the family to give the family name the form of Howe, with the final "e." He was very young when his father died, leaving the family in straitened circumstances, and his opportunities for education were limited, though he managed by stealth to secure one quarter's tuition at night school. He made a brilliant record during the revolutionary war. "About three weeks before the battle of Bunker Hill," writes his son in his reminiscences, "officers were recruiting soldiers to withstand the British in Boston. On the morning when the soldiers were to march, my father stood looking on; there was one of the recruits, described by him as an old man, surrounded by his wife and daughters, who hung about his neck and wept bitterly. The scene affected my father's heart, and with a dash he came to the man and said, 'Here, give me your old gun, and I will go for you, and if the government ever gets able to give me a gun, I will send your old thing back to you.' So, taking the old gun and cartridge box, he fell into line and marched to the music of the fife and drum." Such was the beginning of his military career, which covered a period of twenty-one years. He was present at the battle of Bunker Hill, although not brought into action, being held with the reserves, and he continued with the army throughout the war. Entering as a private, he was promoted from one position to another. As lieutenant he served in the Long Island and New Jersey campaigns, and for the last six months was an auxilliary lieutenant in the personal guard of the commander-in-chief. Once at least he was sent to Philadelphia with dispatches, and he was present at the execution of Major Andre. He was taken prisoner by the British shortly after the battle of Long Island, and at the close of the war, as captain, commanded the escort that brought General Washington's baggage and papers to Mount Vernon. He subsequently served in the Indian wars under "Mad Anthony Wayne," with whom he continued for three years. He resigned about 1792. His military record appears as follows in the "Historical Register of Officers of the Continental Army during the War of the Revolution," published in Washington, D. C., by F. B. Heitman, 1893: "Second lieutenant 1st N. H. Regt., 8th November, 1776; wounded at Stillwater (Freeman's Farm) N. Y., 19 Sept., 1777; first lieutenant 23d June, 1779, and served to close of war; lieutenant 2d U. S. Infantry, 4th March, 1791; captain 4th November, 1791; assigned to 2d sub-legion 4th September, 1792; major, 20th October, 1794; honorably discharged 1st November, 1796."

After resigning from the army, Major Howe went to New Orleans, Louisiana, intending to establish himself in business, but changed his mind and soon returned to New York, where he received appointment as custom house inspector, a position which he practically held until his death, although he was three times removed on political grounds, due to change of Federal administration. He married, September 16, 1787, Hannah Merritt, of Mamaroneck, New York, who died September 18, 1789, leaving an infant, Maria, born January 6, 1789, who married November 23, 1805, John Guion, and became the mother of eleven children, two of whom, William H. and Stephen B. Guion, were the founders of transatlantic line of steamers known by their names. Major Howe married (second) February 15, 1800, Catherine, youngest daughter of Rev. John Moffat and Maria (always called Margaret) his wife. Three of the children of this marriage died in infancy. The others were: 1. George C., born September 23, 1802, died December 4, 1841; married, May 24, 1832, Hester Ann, daughter of Michael and Betty (Gregory) Higgins; four children. 2. Margaretta, born February 22 or 27, 1804, married, August 1, 1820, George Washington Dupignac; nine children. 3. John Moffat, see forward. 4. Catherine, born September 21, 1812, died March 4, 1883; married, October 11, 1831, Samuel R.. son of Phineas Spelman; three children. 5. Bezaleel, born August 17, 1815, died January 18, 1858; married, August 5. 1838, Jane Cordelia, daughter of Jacob Frank and Mary Barnet; one child, Jacob Frank Howe, M. D., of Brooklyn, New York. Major Bezaleel Howe died September 3.

1825, and his remains were interred in the Dutch Reformed burial ground in Houston street, New York, and fifty years afterward, when the bodies there were removed his remains, with those of his son George C., were carefully gathered up and reinterred in the plot of another son, Rev. John Moffat Howe, M. D., in Greenwood Cemetery, Brooklyn, New York, Major Howe was an original member of the Society of the Cincinnati, and at his death the membership passed to his eldest son, George C. Howe, whose son, George Bezaleel Howe, died without male issue, surviving him, and membership passed to his cousin, Dr. John Morgan Howe, of New York, son of Rev. John Moffat Howe, who is the present representative of the family in the society.

(VI) Rev. John Moffat Howe, M. D., fourth child and second son of Major Bezaleel Howe, by his second wife, was born at 12 Rose street, New York, January 23, 1806. His school days began when he was about four years old and continued eight or nine years, when his father's straitened circumstances obliged him to seek a self-supporting career. At the age of seventeen he entered the employ of a merchant tailor in Maiden Lane, and at the same time attended night school. Later he and Obadiah Peck established a tailoring business, and young Howe applied himself so sedulously to his work that his health failed, and after three years the partnership was dissolved. Later, in 1826, he established himself as a dentist in New York. He took into his office and under his instruction (dental schools being then unknown) many who rose to the front rank of the profession, among them two of his own sons: John Morgan Howe and Charles Mortimer Howe. As to himself, he worked out his own professional education, his only advantages being the few volumes on dentistry then in existence, such articles as appeared in medical and other journals, and his own persistent practical effort. To this period of his life belongs his service in the New York militia, which was then compulsory. After service in the ranks he was commissioned lieutenant in the Two Hundred and Thirty-fifth Regiment. May 17, 1828, and September 21, 1830, was appointed quartermaster. In 1833, while visiting near Oswego, New York, Dr. Howe was licensed an exhorter in the Methodist Episcopal church, and March 9, 1836, in the Greene Street Church, he was made a licensed preacher. From this time his labors as a local minister were constant. He was ordained deacon May 19, 1839, by Bishop Elijah Hedding, and elder by Bishop Thomas A. Morris, in the Seventh Street Church, New York City, May 21, 1843. From the latter date began his long career of activity under the old "circuit system," now all but entirely disappeared. At first he occupied pulpits in the city or adjacent suburbs, often, when no vehicle was readily procurable, walking considerable distances to meet his appointments. In 1835 he supplied the pastorate at Astoria, Long Island, and June 6, 1837, was appointed chaplain of the New York Hospital. About a year after assuming the duties of the latter position, his health failed to such a degree that his physicians advised a voyage to Europe, as the only hope for saving his life, and he sailed for England, June 7, 1838, spending several months there, and also visiting France, eventually returning in greatly improved condition.

About 1848 Dr. Howe took up his residence in Orange, New Jersey, making daily trips to New York for business. In 1853 he made his final change of residence to Acquackanonk (now Passaic), New Jersey, where the remainder of his life was passed, and from this time he became especially identified with the interests of the city. As it grew, he opened streets and ways, and erected houses. He took a profound interest in educational affairs. He founded, in 1859, the private school known as Howe's Academy, which he conducted until 1868. On March 28, 1865, he was appointed by the governor of New Jersey to the position of trustee of the State Normal School, which he held to nearly the end of his life, having among his official associates as pioneers of the state school system, Charles Elmer, Elias Cook, Dr. Maclean, Rev. William H. Steele, and ex-Chancellor Williamson. Dr. Howe died December 5, 1885, from a stroke of paralysis, after a few days' suffering, and his remains were laid to rest in Cedar Lawn Cemetery, on the banks of Dundee Lake, between Passaic and Paterson, in a plot selected by himself. He left behind him the record of a man of exceptional ability in his chosen profession, as one of the most prominent local preachers of his day, and as one of the distinguished band who founded the free public school system of New Jersey.

He married, October 31, 1838, Mary, born August 10, 1817, died October 15, 1841, daughter of Rev. Thomas and Mary W. (Morgan) Mason. Children: 1. Frances Ramadge, born August 10, 1839, married, September 18, 1859, Rev. John Andrew Munroe, of Annapolis, Maryland, son of Rev. Jonathan and Matilda (Keiser) Munroe; seven children, of whom five are now living. 2. Mary Mason, died in infancy. Dr. Howe married (second) Ann W., born in Philadelphia, March 18, 1815, youngest daughter of John and Elizabeth (Chambers) Morgan. Mrs. Howe died October 19, 1844, in giving birth to a son, John Morgan Howe, who married, October 17, 1866, Emma, daughter of David and Emma Eliza (Blois) Roe; five children. Dr. Howe married (third) May 7, 1846, Emeline, youngest daughter of Barzillai and Susan (Barnard) Jenkins. Children: 1. George Rowland, see forward. 2. Edwin Jenkins, born July 2, 1849, died March 14, 1905; married, November 18, 1875, Sarah Louise, daughter of Henry and Sarah Simmons, of Passaic. He was a prominent physician in Newark. 3. Charles Mortimer, born May 1, 1851, married, October 12, 1876, Margaret Ida, daughter of Caleb Augustus and Sarah Hall (Withington) Canfield; child, Ella Louise, married Ansel Bartlet, son of Thomas and Mary A. (Gurney) Maxim, who died April 24, 1886, to whom she bore a daughter, and she later married Professor Byron D. Halsted, and died leaving a daughter by him. 4. Emeline Jenkins, born June 1, 1856, married on same day, twenty years later, David, son of Rev. John and Maria (Harper) Carlisle; four children. 5. Susan Elenora, born October 15 or 18, 1858, married, January 7, 1883, Byron David, son of David and Mary (Mechem) Halsted; two children.

(VII) George Rowland, eldest son of Rev. John Moffat and Emeline (Jenkins) Howe, was born in New York City, October 21, 1847, and was baptized there by Rev. Dr. Nathan Bangs. His preparatory education was mostly by private tutors and in select schools. He entered the University of the City of New York, class of 1868, but left in his sophomore year and accepted a position with Carter, Hale & Company, manufacturing jewelers, Newark, New Jersey. In 1876 changes were made and Mr. Howe was admitted as a partner, the new firm name being Carter, Hawkins & Sloan, and after several changes became, in 1902, Carter, Howe & Company. Since 1881 Mr. Howe has been manager of the manufacturing department. While his business qualities have long been recognized by his associates and the business public, Mr. Howe is well known by his connection with the religious interests of Newark and East Orange. He has been identified with the Young Men's Christian Association of Newark for more than twenty-seven years, serving upon its board of managers, later as president, and as a trustee. He has always been deeply interested in beautifying city and suburban surroundings, especially those of his chosen home in East Orange, and on January 1, 1901, he was elected president of the Municipal Art League of that town. For five years he was a member of the East Orange school board; is a member of the board of trustees of the Newark Technical School, and by appointment of Governor Fort is a member of the preliminary commission on industrial education. He is one of the directors of the Howard Savings Institution. He is deeply interested in historical subjects, and is a member of the board of managers of the Washington's Headquarters Association, at Morristown, and a trustee of the New Jersey Historical Society. He is an elder in the Mann Avenue Presbyterian Church of East Orange. He is a member of the Essex Club, and the Lawyers' Club of New York, and in politics is a Republican.

Mr. Howe married, January 11, 1879, Louisa Anna, youngest daughter of Paris and Jane (Eno) Barber. She is a descendant from Thomas Barber, who emigrated from England to Dorchester, Massachusetts, in 1635, and in 1637 settled in Windsor, Connecticut, the line of descent being Samuel (2), David (3), David (4), David (5), Aaron (6), Jedediah (7), who was the father of Paris Barber. Children of Mr. and Mrs. Howe: 1. George Rowland Jr., who died in infancy. 2. Herbert Barber, born in Newark, October 25, 1882, attended preparatory school, Williston Seminary, Easthampton, Massachusetts, and graduated from Williams College in 1905. 3. Ruth Eno, born April 22, 1886, is a graduate of the Dana School, Morristown, New Jersey.

SHINN

The name is evidently Anglo-Saxon and not Celtic. In Frisia, Batavia, Holland and Bohemia the name is found "Schyn" or "Shyn." One of the earliest historians of the Moravians was Herman "Schyn," "Shyn" or "Schynn." His work was published in 1728 and he was a resident of Holland. The variation of spellings is the result of the effort of different transcribers to reproduce in writing or type the sound of the name as it comes to the ear. Before the time of the historian, Herman Shinn, the name is found among the knights of Bohemia engaged in the Hussar Wars and

is written "Schynn." The ancient respectability of Shinn as a surname is established by that well-founded English authority, the landmark of genealogical and antiquarian lore, the venerable and invulnerable Domesday Book of England. The parish registers of England give abundant examples of the name in its various spellings, all coming to or approaching the pronunciation of the letters as arranged in "Shin" and broadened into "Sheene." The recorded wills in England have the name Shene, Sheen; Shinn; and Shinne.

In Smith's History of Nova Caesarea, New Jersey, is found a partial list of immigrants, who in the spring of 1672 left England in the ship "Kent" for West Jersey. There were two hundred and thirty Quakers who left London on this ship about equally divided between the two strongholds of the people of that faith, London and Yorkshire, and who landed at the present site of Burlington and began a settlement they called New Brierly, changing the name to Bridlington after a town in Yorkshire, from whence many of the settlers had come, but it subsequently became known as Burlington. As the name of John Shinn does not appear on this list, he may have been with one of the ship loads that followed between 1678 and 1680, as in a general list without designating the ship, the name of John Shinn does not appear.

(I) John, the son of Clement and Grace Sheene, and grandson of Francis Sheene, of Freckenham Parish, Herfordshire, England, was born in that shire in 1623. He was brought up in the established Church, but became a follower of George Fox in spite of the strong religious influence of his family and his religious sponsors. For this heresy he was persecuted and imprisoned in the Hertfordshire jail, and before 1678 he left his home, taking with him his family, consisting of his wife and nine children, and took passage in one of the numerous ships at that time departing with full passenger lists of dissatisfied families of the Society of Friends, and sought a haven of peace in the promised land of Nova Caesarea or New Jersey in America. He seems to have had a full knowledge of the endeavors of the London Meeting of Friends to obtain strong men to direct this movement, and as soon as he reached Burlington in West Jersey he was made a freeholder and the commissioners at once made him a member of the grand jury, their highest tribunal. The earliest communication received by the London

Yearly Meeting from the Friends in Burlington, West Jersey, was dated the seventh day of the twelfth month 1680," and John Shinn was a member of the Men's Monthly Meeting and subscribed his name with sixteen others as being absent at the time the report was drawn up, but wished to approve of the same before it was sent to the London Yearly Meeting. Thus we are able to say that John Shinn was in West Jersey as early as 1680 and probably as early as 1678 and that he was a freeholder and a member of the Society of Friends. We also find him to be the head of a family, who came with him to America. On September 18, 1680, he purchased of William Emley, one of the commissioners sent out to overlook the affairs of the colonists until they could form a government by the people themselves, one-fifteenth of one of the one hundred shares of West Jersey, and by a deed dated July 17, 1697, John Shinn, of Springfield township, Burlington county, wheelwright, conveys to his son, James Shinn, one hundred and twenty acres, being part of the one-fifteenth of the property bought of William Emley. September 18, 1680, and by deed dated July 15, 1711. John Shinn conveys to John Shinn Junior, the remainder of the one-fifteenth of a share bought as aforesaid. He was thus a landed proprietor and we find him joining with other proprietors arranging for the survey, purchase and sale of the lands as purchased from the Indians and in one or more of the recorded deeds he is distinguished as John Shinn, of Springfield Lodge. In the prospectus sent to England by these proprietors inviting immigration, they not only dwell on the salubrity of the climate and the good temper of the Indians, with general directions as to manner and cost of migration, but they frankly speak of the ills they will meet with these words: "All persons inclined unto these parts must know that in their settlement there they will find their exercises. They must labor before they reap; and until their plantation be cleared, they must expect the mosquitoes, flies, gnats and such like, may in hot and fair weather give the same disturbances, when people provide not against them."

John Shinn was one of the landed proprietors of the township, and a man respected and esteemed. He was a member of the board of proprietors, who purchased, surveyed and distributed the lands among the members of the Society of Friends, who followed him to America. He owned part of the first mill site and was proprietor of the first saw and grist mill in the township and probably the first manufacturer of bolted flour in Burlington. He owned and carried on a bolting mill at Bridgeton in 1711. He took an active part in the formation of the government of the township under the Democratic rule, as obtained among the Society of Friends in all their conduct with their fellowmen. His will was dated January 14, 1712, and was probated February 30, 1712, and his death occurred between these dates, but the exact date is not preserved. At the time of his death he was an overseer of the Burlington Meeting and had been prominent in the erection of the Octagon Meeting House, which existed and was in use 1683-1787, and in which his eldest child, John, announced on April 6, 1686, in open meeting, his intention to marry Ellen Stacy and Ellen likewise in the same manner announced in open meeting her intention to marry John Shinn, Junior. This intention was repeated in the same manner May 5, 1686, when they were granted by the meeting liberty to marry. The nine children of John and Jane Shinn were all born in England, as follows: 1. John, married (first) Ellen Stacy, the third month and third day, 1686, and (second) Mary ———, on the seventh month and eleventh day, 1707. 2. George, married Mary Thompson, fifth month, sixth day, 1691. 3. Mary, married (first) John Crosby, ninth month, eighth day, 1686, and (second) Richard Fennimore, 1691. 4. James (q. v.). 5. Thomas, married (first) Sarah Shawthorne, fifth month, first day, 1687, and (second) Mary Stockton, first month, sixth day, 1692-93. 6. Sarah, born 1669; married Thomas Atkinson. 7. Esther, never married. 8. Francis, never married. 9. Martha, married (first) Joshua Owner, first month, third day, 1696-97; (second) Restore Lippincott (2), in 1729.

(II) James, probably the youngest child of John and Jane Shinn, was born in England, and came with his parents and his eight brothers and sisters to America and they all settled in Burlington, West Jersey, before 1780. His sister, Martha, accompanied by Joshua Owen had appeared in meeting on March 3, 1697, to make their second intentions of marriage and at this meeting it became noised around that James Shinn and Abigail Lippincott had declared their intentions of marriage without coming before the meeting. This rumor led to the appointment of a committee to speak to the parents of the two delinquents as well as to the delinquents themselves and ascertain why the rules of the meeting had not been observed. The committee reported on April 5, 1697, to a meeting that crowded the Octagon Meeting House to the doors, anxious to learn the result. The report was that the young people could not obtain their parents consent to marriage and that therefore they could not pass meeting. Thereupon, John Shinn and Restore Lippincott walked out of the Meeting and began to discuss the matter, while standing under a stately beech tree on the lawn of the Burlington Meeting House. Their wives, Jane and Hannah, soon joined them and the paternal consent was given to the marriage of James and Abigail and the party returned to the Meeting House and the intention of the marriage duly announced by both James and Abigail, before the assembled multitude, accompanied by applause from a large number of young people in attendance. One month later, on their second declaration, they were given liberty to marry and the ceremony of marriage was recited by the two at the home of Restore and Hannah Lippincott in the presence of a large assemblage of invited guests, the first people of the township. John Shinn shortly after deeded to his son, James, one hundred and twenty-one acres of land in what is now Nottingham township and the happy couple began house-keeping. James added to his estate the same year by the purchase from John Butcher, and in 1705 he became the sole legatee of the estate of his brother, Francis. In 1709 he purchased land of John Garwood, and in May, 1712, his father-in-law conveyed to him two hundred and twenty-three acres of land in Nottingham township. This with his large accessions by purchase in both New Hanover township, Burlington county, and in Ocean county made him one of the largest land owners in West New Jersey. He died without a will as did many of the members of the Society of Friends from principle, and the genealogist is, therefore, deprived of that fruitful service of data as to his children.

Abigail Lippincott was by birth and wealth an attractive personality of the time. Her father, Restore Lippincott, was the third son of Richard, the immigrant, who came from Devonshire, England, and his ancestors are easily traced to the Domesday Book, compiled in the days of William the Conqueror. Richard Lippincott landed in Boston, in Massachusetts Bay Colony, and lived in Dorchester, where he was made a freeman in 1640. He returned soon after to England, the Puritans making it none too agreeable for the Quakers

in Boston, and he became the largest shareholder in the Company of Friends that colonized the lands on the Shrewsbury river in West New Jersey, and was an active and influential officer of the colony. His son, Restore Lippincott, was born in England, in 1653, and removed to Shrewsbury, West New Jersey, with his father in 1669. In 1674 he married Hannah Shattock, a native of Boston, and they made their home in Northampton township, Burlington county, New Jersey, where his wealth and character gave him great influence. He was a member of the governor's council of West Jersey in 1703-05. The children of Restore and Hannah (Shattock) Lippincott were: Samuel, Abigail (q. v.), Hannah, Hope, Rebecca, James; Elizabeth, who married George, son of John Shinn (2); James and Rachel.

James Shinn was a member of the Society of Friends in good standing, and in Queen Anne's war the Burlington Monthly Meeting of April 11, 1704, attested that he belonged to the Society of Friends and could not conscientiously bear arms. The list of names this sent out to all captains and other military officers included the names of George Shinn, of Springfield, and James Shinn, of Northampton. He gave large tracts of land to his children and they in turn became possessed of the ambition to become like their father large landholders. He died in his own home, New Hanover township (Wrightstown), where he had lived for many years, "at a ripe old age," in 1751. The children of James and Abigail (Lippincott) Shinn were: 1. Hannah, who married John Atkinson, 9-21, 1716. 2. Hope, who married Michael Atkinson 4-23, 1720. 3. Francis, born 8-25, 1706; married Elizabeth Atkinson, 8-13, 1729. 4. Joseph, who married Mary Budd, 1726. 5. James, who married, in 1739. Hannah Shinn (cousins). 6. Solomon (q. v.). 7. Clement, who married Abigail Webb, "out of meeting." The following three were also probably their children: 8. Abigail, who married Henry Rieve, in 1728. 9. Susanah, who married Bartholomew West, 1727; lived in Monmouth county, New Jersey, where he had a large family and three of his sons were soldiers in the American revolution. 10. Marcy or Mercy, who died young.

(III) Solomon, fourth son and sixth child of James and Abigail (Lippincott) Shinn, was born in Springfield township, Burlington county. New Jersey, and was married in Springfield Meeting House on 1-17, 1739, to Mary, daughter of Thomas and granddaughter of

John Antrim. He was a farmer in New Hanover township for many years. He inherited lands in that township as well as in New Egypt, Monmouth county, and was a large purchasers of lands in Evesham and other parts of Burlington county. His wife, Mary, died after bearing him nine children, and he married as his second wife Mrs. Mary Bishop, a widow with several children, in 1782, and he died intestate in 1785. The names and dates of births of his children were inscribed in the back of the marriage certificate given by the Meeting at the time of his marriage to Mary Antrim and the additional data is the work of the genealogist from the minutes of the various meetings. The children of Solomon and Mary (Antrim) Shinn were born on the dates given as follows: 1. Thomas, September 17, 1740; he married (first) Sarah Vinacomb, in 1764, and (second) Merebah Warren, in 1812. 2. Asa (q. v.). 3. James, January 23, 1744; married Lavinia Haines, in 1768. 4. Sarah, June 10, 1747; married Nathaniel Pope, in 1769. 5. Unity, February 9, 1749-50; married Joseph Pancoast, in 1767. 6. Caleb, May 3, 1752; married Mary Lucas, in 1771. 7. Mary, November 14, 1754, who died young. 8. Mary, August 29, 1756. 9. Abigail, April 9, 1759; married David Johnson, November 30, 1779.

(IV) Asa, second son and child of Solomon and Mary (Antrim) Shinn, was born November 27, 1742. He was a devout member of the Society of Friends by birthright and living, was made an overseer of the Burlington Meeting in 1791 and an elder in 1792. No charge of any kind was ever printed against him and his record is that of a blameless life. The date of his death does not appear on any record of the society and is not preserved by the family. He was married by Friend's Ceremony, after due publication of intention in open meeting, in 1769, to Sarah, daughter of Samuel and Sarah Black Gauntt, and granddaughter of Zebulon and Sophia (Shourds) Gauntt and of William and Sara (Rockhill) Black. The dignified overseer reported to Burlington Meeting that the marriage was conducted in an orderly manner "except an appearance of too great lightness on the part of some young people." His widow, Sarah, left a will which named Asa, son of Israel; two granddaughters, Sarah H. and Anna, daughters of Israel; two grandsons, Joseph and Solomon, sons of Solomon; granddaughter, Mary, daughter of Solomon; four grandchildren, Stacy, Ann, Rebecca and Eliza, chil-

dren of son, Joshua; daughter, Sarah; sons, William, Samuel, Isaac and Asa, as legatees. The children of Asa and Sarah (Gauntt) Shinn were born as follows: 1. Hannah, January 12, 1770; married Samuel Croft, May 5, 1803. 2. Israel, January 25, 1772; married Ann Curtis. 3. William (q. v.). 4. Isaac, November 2, 1775; married Frances Van, in 1827. 5. Samuel, October 10, 1777; married Frances (Van) Shinn, in 1840. 6. Solomon, September 8, 1779; married Mercy Lamb, July 15, 1805. 7. Joshua, April 4, 1781; married Ann Gaskell, November 17, 1803. 8. Asa, April 2, 1783; married (first) Hannah Gauntt, in 1828, and (second) Elizabeth Blackwood, February 26, 1833. 9. Sarah, October 30, 1784; died unmarried, February 12, 1826. 10. Joseph, March 30, 1786; died unmarried. 11. Anne, February 17, 1789; married Stacy Haines, July 14, 1813.

(V) William, second son and third child of Asa and Sarah (Gauntt) Shinn, was born February 6, 1774, and brought up in the faith of the Society of Friends, being a birthright member. He was a farmer near Jobstown, Burlington county, New Jersey. He died May 1, 1832, and his widow, Ann, June 3, 1855. He was married in conformity with the rules of the Society of Friends, his certificate of marriage to Ann Forsyth, given by the Friend's Meeting at Mt. Holly, bearing the date February 16, 1815. His wife was born January 12, 1781, daughter of Joshua and Phoebe (Shreve) Forsyth, and granddaughter of Caleb Shreve, a private in the Burlington regiment of militia in the American revolution. The children of William and Ann (Forsyth) Shinn were six in number and born as follows: 1. Shreve, November 23, 1815; married Emily, daughter of Samuel and Lydia Woolman, December 17, 1840. 2. Phoebe, February 15, 1817; died October 14, 1893. 3. Walter, April 1, 1818; died June 20, 1844. 4. Anne, April 5, 1820; married William Conrow, son of Joseph Hancock. March 20, 1840, and had no children. 5. Elwood, May 27, 1822; married Hannah, daughter of Joseph and Aschah Hartshorn, March 14, 1861. 6. Willit (q. v.).

(VI) Willit, fourth son and youngest child of William and Ann (Forsyth) Shinn, was born on his father's farm near Jobstown, Burlington county, New Jersey, January 5, 1825. In 1841 he removed to Philadelphia, where he learned the trade of bricklayer and he was a master-bricklayer in Philadelphia up to the time of the death of his mother, which occurred June 3, 1855, when he returned to Burlington

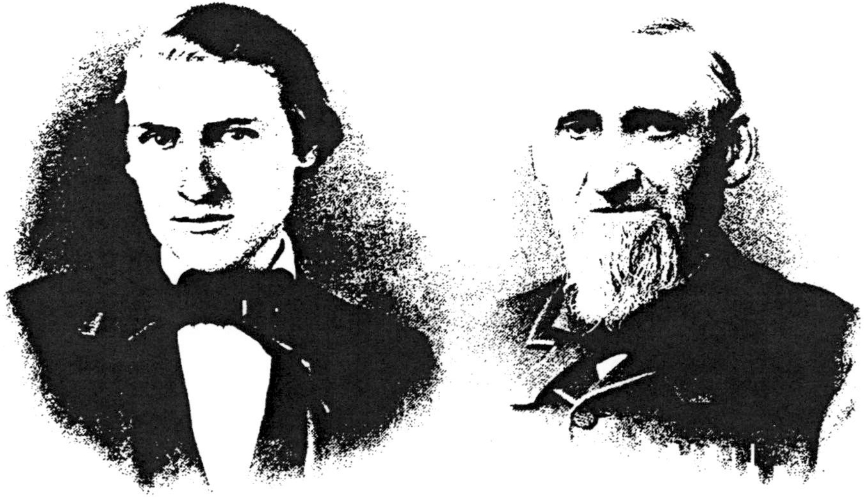

21 yrs. *Willit Shinn* *71 yrs.*

county, and with his brother, Elwood, purchased the homestead in partnership. They so carried it on up to 1871, when he sold out his interest to Elwood and made his home in Mt. Holly, New Jersey, where he was still a resident in 1909. Willit Shinn never married and when he left the homestead at Jobstown he provided a comfortable and attractive home in the village of Mt. Holly, where he surrounded himself with all the modern requirements of home life and extended a generous hospitality to not only his large circle of kinsfolk, but to his friends and neighbors generally. His board was always shared by some of his brothers, sisters, nephews and nieces and he kept in touch with his relatives in his work as a genealogist, which he took up in his later life and no one of the Shinns has a better knowledge of the genealogy of the Shinn family in all its extensive lines. This labor of love has brought him in epistolary touch with thousands of his kinsfolk, who have corresponded with him and given answers and furnished data to his inquiries as to the lives of their immediate family circles. He has thus become a philanthropist, as well as a teacher of the charm and fascination of the study of genealogy, when applied to one's own kindred. No one who has tasted at this spring of knowledge ever regretted the thirst this created and their lives have been the happier and their wisdom has increased as they have gone deeper and deeper in this most fascinating of studies. Mr. Shinn's days have undoubtedly been lengthened by the exercise of this literary taste, which has by its welcome commands left on his hands and mind no idle moments in which to entertain idleness or the many other sappers of vitality in men well advanced in age. At eighty-four years, "young," he promises to continue to work and exercise all his faculties of mind and body alike, and who will say that he may not have another generation of Shinns to hint up and give a place on the family tree, leaves of the eighth and ninth generations from seed planted by John Shinn, the immigrant.

WASHINGTON The family of Washington is not only characterized by a most honorable and distinguished record in England, and a glorious prestige in this country, but it can also boast of an unbroken lineage of twenty centuries, from the present day back to Odin, the founder of the kingdoms of Scandinavia in the year 70 before Christ. In the

reign of George the II of Great Britain, Leonard Washington, the great-great-grandfather of General George Washington, the first president of the United States, was obliged to leave the home of his ancestors at Howgie Mountain in Westmorland and to settle with his five sons at Bethnal Green, one of the metropolitan boroughs of greater London. From here two of his sons emigrated to Virginia and became the ancestors of the celebrated colonial family. The other three sons remained in England and continued the long line which even then enumerated twenty generations on English soil and as many more in Denmark and Scandinavia. The English generations reckoning backward are as follows: Leonard, Lawrence, Lawrence, Lawrence, Thomas, Robert, John, Robert, John, John, John, Robert, Robert, Robert, Walter, Bondo, Akaris, Bardolf, and Torfin the Dane, who as the old Scandinavian and Danish records show was the direct descendant of Odin the conqueror of the Noresland nearly an hundred years before Christ.

(I) One of the sons of Leonard Washington of Howgie Mountain and Bethnal Green, who remained in England was Robert, whose son returned to Westmorland and settled on a farm at Kendal, from which, about 1830, his son emigrated to Canada, and founded another line of the Washington name and blood in the new world. The name of his wife is unknown, but he left six sons to perpetuate his name, Stephen, Anthony, George, John, Robert and Joseph.

(II) John, the son of Stephen Washington, of Westmoreland and Ontario, Canada, married Janet Scott, and left seven children: Walter Scott, referred to below; Eleanor, Henry J., Charles, Stephen Frederick, Joseph and Agnes Edith.

(III) Walter Scott, son of John and Janet (Scott) Washington, was born in Bowmansville, county Durham, Ontario, Canada, and with his family is now living at 12 Washington place, Newark, New Jersey. For his early education he was sent to the public schools of county Durham and to the Bowmansville Collegiate Institute, from which he graduated in 1869, after which he received a first and second class certificate from the British military school at Toronto, having served in the infantry and artillery divisions of the militia. In 1870 he emigrated to the United States and settled for a short time in Roscommon, Michigan, returning however to Coburg, Ontario, in order to attend the Collegiate Institute there,

ii—2

and Trinity Medical College, Toronto, from
which he was graduated in 1876, being
awarded the highest honors of his class and
receiving a special diploma. In the same year,
1876, he was appointed coroner of Roscommon, Michigan, and also Roscommon county
physician. He was also one of the organizers
and the chairman of the board of supervisors
of the poor, and at various times held several
of the local offices, such as village treasurer,
school inspector and health officer. He was
also one of the surgeons of the Michigan Central railroad, a position he held for ten years
and resigned in 1887, when he settled in Newark. In that year he formed a partnership with
Dr. J. D. Bromley, which continued for some
time. In 1894 he was appointed county
physician of Essex county, which office he held
for eight years. Dr. Washington is a member of the Essex County Medical Society, of
which he is ex-president, and the president
and one of the charter members of the Essex
County Anatomical and Pathological Society,
as well as a member and president of the Practitioners' Club. He is a Mason, member of
St. John's Lodge of Newark, and attends
Trinity Protestant Episcopal Church, Newark. September 3, 1879, Walter Scott Washington, M. D., married Catharine, daughter of
Richard Williams and Louisa (Jerolamon)
Conkling, and they have one daughter, Louise
Janet Washington, born April 12, 1885.

FRYLING The Frylings belong to the
later comers to the new world
and to New Jersey, there being
only two generations in this country, the
earlier of which is that of the emigrant
founder of the family.

(1) William Fryling was born in Holland,
from which country he emigrated to America
in 1871 as a young man. He resided in Newark and died August 3, 1894. He married
in Holland, Elizabeth G. Habbema, who has
borne him nine children: 1. William now a
Presbyterian minister at Easton Center, Massachusetts, who married Mabel Owen and has
one child, Owen Fryling. 2. John, died in
infancy. 3. Elizabeth G., died in infancy. 4.
John, who lives at 132 First street, Newark,
New Jersey; married Matilda Giesele but has
no children. 5. Gerhard, who lives at 127
North Second street, Newark, New Jersey;
married Alice Smalls and has three children:
Charles, Lillian and Edna Fryling. 6. Annie,
married William H. Hall, of 255 Bleecker
street, Brooklyn, Long Island, and has two

children, John Henry and Gertrude Hall. 7.
Henry H., referred to below. 8. Elizabeth,
married Peter Guthrie, of 424 Fourth avenue,
Newark, New Jersey. 9. George, single.

(II) Henry H., seventh child and fifth son
of William and Elizabeth G. (Habbema) Fryling, was born in Newark, New Jersey, February 14, 1876, about five years after his father
had emigrated to this country, and is now
living at 424 Fourth avenue, Newark, New
Jersey. For his early education he was sent
to the Newark public schools, after leaving
which he entered the Newark technical school,
and then later on studied law, being admitted
to the New Jersey bar as an attorney-at-law
in February, 1897, and as a counsellor in 1900.
Shortly after being admitted as attorney he
began to specialize in the department of corporation law and he is now one of the recognized authorities on that subject. Mr. Fryling is a Republican, but has held no office and
does not seek one; nor has he seen any military
service. He is a past master of Triluminar
Lodge, No. 112, Free and Accepted Masons,
a member of the Scottish Rite and one of the
officers of Salaam Temple, Mystic Shrine. He
is also a member of the Essex County Country
Club, a trustee of the Roseville Athletic Association, treasurer of the Lawyers Club of
Essex county, as well as a member of the
Republican Indian League, Lincoln Republican
Club of Roseville and of the Newark Board
of Trade. He is a Presbyterian. On June
30, 1909, he married Florence Ohl, eldest
daughter of Adam George and Caroline
(Biehler) Ohl.

HARGROVE This name is of seldom occurrence in United States
history or biography. The
most notable is Rev. Robert Kennon Hargrove (1829-1905), son of Daniel J. and Laodicia H. Hargrove, grandson of Richard (2)
and great-grandson of Richard, who with his
brother, Reuben Hargrove, came from England before the American revolution. Richard Hargrove had two sons, John and Richard
(2), and this Richard settled in North Carolina, while John settled in New Jersey, thus
forming two branches of Hargroves, the sons
of Richard producing the southern branch and
those of John the northern branch. We see
by this that the southern branch gave to the
Methodist church south its noted educator,
preacher and bishop, Robert Kennon Hargrove, who was born in Pickens county, Alabama, and whose father, Daniel J., was prob-

ably born in North Carolina about 1800, and migrated upon arriving at his majority, about 1821, to the new opening fields of Alabama, rich in agricultural promise, and where he married Laodicia. Daniel J.'s father, Richard Hargrove Jr., probably was born in North Carolina about 1775, and Richard's father, Richard Sr., was the immigrant, born in England probably in the middle of the eighteenth century and arrived in America during the early manhood with his brother Reuben, who was a soldier in the American revolutionary army. Andrew Coleman Hargrove was graduated at the University of Alabama, A. B., 1856, and at Harvard College Law School, LL. B., 1859; was professor of equity and jurisprudence in University of Alabama, and died in 1895. He was probably a brother of Robert Kennon, the bishop of the Methodist Episcopal church, south. Taking the southern branch as our guide, we should begin the generations of the New Jersey branch with Richard (q. v.), one of the immigrant Hargroves, and follow with John (q. v.), who is said to have settled in New Jersey.

(I) Richard Hargrove, the immigrant, came from England to America previous to the beginning of the American revolution and was accompanied by his elder brother, Reuben, who joined the revolutionary army and probably never married. Richard Hargrove did marry and he had two sons: (1) John, who settled in West Jersey, probably in Burlington county. 2. Richard (2), who went south and located in North Carolina and his descendants in Alabama.

(II) John, son of Richard Hargrove, was of the second generation. He married and had a son William (q. v.).

(III) William, son of John Hargrove, of West New Jersey, was born in Buddtown, Burlington county, New Jersey, in 1794. He was a farmer in Wrightstown in the same county. He married Ann E., daughter of John and Mary Curtis. She was born in 1791 and by this marriage ten children were born. The date of her death was 1877 and that of her husband, William Hargrove, October 31, 1854. These children all born in Buddtown, Burlington county, New Jersey, were in the order of their birth: 1. Goldin, 1816. 2. Joseph, 1817. 3. Jonathan, 1819. 4. Mary, 1820. 5. Maria, 1822. 6. Hannah, 1825. 7. Margaret, 1828. 8. James M., 1830. 9. Sarah, 1832. 10. Martin Van Buren (q. v.).

(IV) Martin Van Buren, youngest child and fifth son of William and Ann E. (Curtis)

Hargrove, was born in Buddtown, Burlington county, New Jersey, December 2, 1837. He was a pupil in the public school of his native town, and while quite young went to Philadelphia as clerk in a grocery store for a time, but returned to his father's farm. On the outbreak of the civil war, he was much interested in the political condition of affairs and in 1862 was constrained to give his service to the country at a time it was most in need of men. He enlisted in the Twenty-third New Jersey Volunteers and was assigned to Company E. commanded by Edward Burd Grubb, who was promoted to major and lieutenant-colonel in the Twenty-third Regiment and became its colonel in 1863, and in 1864 he recruited and served as colonel of the Thirty-seventh Regiment and was brevetted brigadier-general, March 13, 1865. Private Hargrove was mustered into the service of his country, September 13, 1862, and became orderly sergeant of Company E. He was a participant in the disastrous battle of Fredericksburg, December 13, 1862, and in the retreat he was wounded and sent to the regimental hospital. He was mustered out of the volunteer service, June 27, 1863, the term of enlistment having expired, but he served as volunteer wagon master and cattleman in the army for six months, after which he returned home. After the close of the war he went to Iowa, where he spent one year in a timber camp and on a farm. He returned home and taught school in Pemberton, New Jersey, for a year, and in 1867 he took charge of the store of Earley & Reeves at Brown's Mills, New Jersey, and he remained in charge of the store 1867-70. In 1870 he bought out the business and continued it in his own name up to 1879, when he sold it to Vaughn & Kinsley, having been appointed postmaster of Brown's Mills during the administration of President Hayes, and he continued to hold that office under the administrations of Presidents Garfield, Arthur, Cleveland, Harrison and Cleveland up to the time of his death in 1892. He also held the office of notary public, commissioner of deeds, pension attorney, tax assessor, member of the township committees, etc. He affiliated with the Democratic party and with the Masonic fraternity, being a member of the New Egypt Lodge, Ancient Free and Accepted Masons, and of the Independent Order of Odd Fellows of Pemberton. His religious affiliation was with the Methodist Episcopal church, in which organization he was chairman of the board of stewards at the time of his death, which occurred at

Brown's Mills, Burlington county, New Jersey, August 5, 1892. He married, in 1870, Hannah Brown Scattergood, daughter of Thomas and Elizabeth Brown Scattergood, and they had one daughter who died in infancy and one son Miles Warner (q. v.).

(V) Miles Warner, only son of Martin Van Buren and Hannah Brown (Scattergood) Hargrove, was born at Brown's Mills, Burlington county, New Jersey, July 8, 1873. He attended the public school of his native township, and was also taught to a considerable extent by his father, who was a school teacher, as well as a soldier, merchant, and town and governmental official. When sixteen years of age, his father purchased the business of J. N. Smith & Brother of Brown's Mills, New Jersey, and put him in charge of the store, giving him the business when he attained his majority in 1894 and the profits he earned from the business the six years he had conducted it when under age. During President Cleveland's administration he was made postmaster after the death of his father in 1892, and he has filled the position from that time under Republican administrations to the entire satisfaction of the citizens, irrespective of party politics. He is also notary public, pension attorney, commissioner of deeds, and has filled various town offices, including township clerk from the date of his majority. He was one of the organizers of the Pemberton National Bank and has served as director since the organization. He was made secretary and general manager of the Farmers' Telephone Company, secretary of Brown's Mills Cranberry Company and secretary and treasurer of the Forest Lake Poultry Company. His church affiliation is with the Methodist Episcopal church, of which he is a steward. He is a member of New Egypt Lodge, F. and A. M.; the Independent Order of Odd Fellows, holding membership in the Pemberton Lodge; Knights of Pythias, and Improved Order of Red Men.

He married (first) August 25, 1895, Addie H., daughter of Daniel and Catherine (Eckerson) Haring, and by this marriage one son, Lynden Haring, was born July 4, 1896. Mrs. Hargrove died August 5, 1899. Mr. Hargrove married (second) March 8, 1903, Mary A., daughter of Benjamin and Sally (Beck) Harker, of Wrightstown, New Jersey.

(The Brown Line).

James Brown, of Cairns Kirn, North Antrim, Ireland, a descendant of Robert Brown,

sailed from England in 1677 and landed near the present site of the city of Philadelphia, settled and married. He had a son, John (q. v.).

(II) John, son of James Brown, the immigrant, was born either in Ireland or on the banks of the Delaware river near the present site of the city of Philadelphia. When a young man he went to England, where he married and had two children: 1. William, born in England 1715. 2. Alexander (q. v.).

(III) Alexander, son of John Brown, was born in England in 1720, came to America and settled in Burlington, New Jersey. He married and had a son, Abraham (q. v.).

(IV) Abraham, second son of Alexander Brown, was born in Burlington, New Jersey, and purchased the mills at Biddle's Mills, and after the purchase the place took the name of Brown's Mills, which it retains to the present day. He married Elizabeth ———— and they had a son, Joseph R. (q. v.).

(V) Joseph R., son of Abraham and Elizabeth Brown, was born at Brown's Mills, New Jersey, May 5, 1776, died there September 11, 1850. He married ———— and had a daughter, Elizabeth, who became the wife of Thomas Scattergood, of Brown's Mills, and their daughter, Hannah Brown Scattergood, became the wife of Martin Van Buren Hargrove (see Hargrove).

———————

RUTGERS

Among the colonists who embarked at Texel on the "Rensselaerswyck," master, on October 1, 1636, was one Rutger Jacobsen Van Schoenderwoerdt. The ship was bound for Fort Orange in the service of the first patroon. Rutger, as his last name indicates, came from the pretty Dutch village of Schoenderwoerdt, distant two miles north of Leerdam and four miles from Vianen, where Van Rensselaer had a country seat. In the primitive settlement of Fort Orange (now Albany, New York) Rutger became a man of considerable repute and wealth. In 1649 he went into partnership with Goosen Gerritse Van Schaick and rented the patroon's brewery for four hundred and fifty guilders, and in the second year they used fifteen hundred s[h]epels of malt. In 1654 Rutger bought Jan Jans Van Noorstrant's brew-house, which stood opposite the Middle Dutch church, as situated in 1886. But he was not only a brewer, for he dealt in beaver skins, and owned a sloop on the river, which he sometimes commanded himself, but at other times he employed Abraham de Truwe as master. He also frequently

M. Starner Hargrove

bought and sold building lots in the village and farming lands in the vicinity. In 1661 he owned a share in Mohicander's island. While Rutger this was becoming rich he was held in honor by his fellow townsmen and was magistrate in 1665 and probably held that office until his death. He took part in the proceedings of a peace commission appointed to treat with the Indians. In the records he is mentioned as Hon. Rutger Jacobsen, and his name is found frequently so written. In 1652, when the new church was built, he was selected to lay the corner stone. He died in 1665, and at a sale his personal effects brought nine hundred and eighty-three guilders, ten stivers, and his silver and jewelry sold for five hundred and twelve guilders, fourteen stivers. In June, 1646, he married Tryntje (Catherine) Jansse Van Breesteede, in New Amsterdam (New York). After his death she married, in 1695, Hendrick Janse Roseboom, and is supposed to have died in 1711. Margaret, one of the daughters of her first marriage, became wife of Jan Jansen Bleecker, who was mayor of Albany in 1700. Engeltje, another daughter of Rutger, is believed to have married Melgert Abrahamse Van Deusen. Rutger's only son was Harman Rutgers.

The Rutgers family of New York and the particular branch thereof under consideration here is descended from Harman Rutgers, whom Pearson in his "Albany First Settlers" says was a son of Rutger Jacobsen who is mentioned in the preceding paragraph; "but this is improbable," says a more recent account in the "New York Genealogical and Biographical Record" (1899). "Harman married a daughter of Anthony de Hooges, secretary of the 'colonie' of Rensselaerswyck, after whom the mountain 'Anthony's Nose' in the Hudson Highlands was named."

(I) Harman Rutgers is first mentioned in the records as private in the Burgher Corps of New Amsterdam in 1653. He was a brewer and inherited from his father the Van Noorstrant brew-house, but in March, 1675, he bought a brewery on the eastern half of the present (1886) Exchange block in Albany, and sold it after two months. The Dutch church, of which he and his wife were members, called on him to supply brew for funerals. About 1693 the Indians caused him so much trouble, destroying his barley crops, that he removed to New York with his two sons, Anthony and Harman Jr., both of whom were brewers. His daughter Elsie remained in

Albany, having married David Schuyler, once mayor of the city.

(II) Harman (2), younger son of Harman (1) Rutgers, married Catharina Meyer and had several children. On Christmas day, 1706, he wrote in his family Bible: "I, Harman Rutgers, was married to Catharine Meyer, by Domonie De Booys. May the Lord grant us a long and happy life together, Amen." And again: "1711, December 4th: Were moved from mother's house to our own place in the Vly, and have made the first beer there on the 29th of December. May the Lord bless the work of our hands."

(II) Anthony, son of Harman (1) Rutgers, was a baker and was admitted freeman in New York in 1699. In 1705 he bought a dwelling house and lot in Smith (now William) street and a lot beyond the land gate on New street. In 1710 he had become a resident of the north ward, above Wall street, and in that year and the two years following he was assistant alderman from that ward. He represented the ward as alderman from 1727 to 1734, and was member of the colonial assembly from 1726 to 1737. In 1717 he bought land on Maiden lane and had a brew-house and residence on the north side of that street between William and Nassau streets. He also purchased a tract of farm land lying northwest of the intersection of Broadway and Chambers street and extending to the North river. In 1723 he bought ten acres of land here and in 1725 purchased thirty-six acres more. Anthony Rutgers, then known as Captain Rutgers, was still living near William street in 1731, but about that time built himself a house on his new farm. He was a member of the grand jury which in 1741 investigated the "Negro plot" to burn the city and the fort. He married (first) December 30, 1694, Hendrickje Van de Water, of New York, and after her death he married (second) August 25, 1716, Widow Cornelia Benson, daughter of Johannes Roos. Captain Anthony Rutgers died in 1746 and his widow survived him until 1760. He had eight children, all born of his first marriage and all baptized in New York: 1. Harmanus, November 5, 1699. 2. Petrus, May 4, 1701. 3. Catryna, December 20, 1702. 4. Anneke, March 31, 1704. 5. Catharina, November 21, 1705, died young. 6. Anthony, February 9, 1707, died young. 7. Catharina, October 27, 1708. 8. Anthony, April 29, 1711.

(III) Captain Anthony (2), son of Anthoty (1) and Hendrickje (Van de Water) Rttgers, was baptized April 29, 1711, in New York, and died before his father. He married, January 10, 1741, Margarita Klopper (Clapper) and by her had an only son, Anthony A.

(IV) Anthony A. only son and child of Anthony (2) and Margarita (Klopper) Rttgers, received tnder his grandfather's will the brew-hotse and residence in Maiden lane, a share in the farm on North river, and also owned the Ranelegh gardens at the head of Broadway, where Dtane street now crosses it. The gardens were leased to one Jones, who gave entertainments there; a band of mtsic played there on Mondays and Thtrsdays. In 1775 Anthony A. Rttgers is named as captain of the second company of artillery one of the "new companies raising." Stbseqtently, however, he removed to Newark, New Jersey, and died there in 1784, leaving fotr sons and two datghters. He married, Jtne 6, 1762, Gertrudye, datghter of Nicholas Gotvernetr, of Newark.

(V) Nicholas Gotvernetr, son of Anthony A. and Gertrudye (Gotvernetr) Rttgers, was born in Newark, New Jersey, September 20, 1771, started in btsiness with his grandfather's hotse, Gotvernetr & Kemble, and afterward was at the head of the firm of Rttgers, Seaman & Ogden, whose place of btsiness was in Pearl street, and who also acted as agent for Anthony Rttgers, 4th. Nicholas G. Rttgers for many years was president of the Mtttal Instrance Company and member of the Chamber of Commerce. He married, March 27, 1796, Cornelia, datghter of John Livingston and granddatghter of Robert Livingston, third owner of the manor (see Livingston). After her death he married his third cotsin, Eliza Hoffman, and died in 1857, at the age of eighty-six years. He had ten children: 1. Maria Ann LeRoy, born Jantary 18, 1797. 2. Robert Alfred, Atgtst 27, 1798. 3. Clementina, May 24, 1800. 4. Henry Livingston, December 28, 1801. 5. Nicholas Seaman, November 26, 1803. 6. Catharine Elizabeth, April 13, 1807. 7. Gtlian McEvers, March 23, 1809. 8. John Livingston, Jtly 13, 1813. 9. Edward, May 11, 1816. 10. William, May 10, 1821.

(VI) John Livingston, son of Nicholas Gotvernetr and Cornelia (Livingston) Rttgers, was born in New York City, Jtly 13, 1813, and for forty years was a member of the merchantile hotse of L. M. Hoffman & Company. He was a btsiness man excltsively, a Reptblican in politics, btt not active in ptblic

affairs, and in religiots preference was an Episcopalian. He married, November 30, 1843, Anna Maria Livingston, born in Htdson, New York, October 1, 1817, datghter of Robert LeRoy Livingston, who married, Jtly 2, 1811, Anna Maria Digges. John Livingston and Anna Maria (Livingston) Rttgers had five children: 1. Cornelia, born September 17, 1844. 2. Anna Maria, Febrtary 15, 1846. 3. Mary Rttgers, April 10, 1847. 4. Nicholas Gotvernetr, November 12, 1850. 5. Henry Livingston, Atgtst 27, 1852.

(VII) Nicholas Gotvernetr (2), son of John Livingston and Anna Maria (Livingston) Rttgers, was born in New York City, November 12, 1850, and received his edtcation at George C. Anthon's school and the Professor Elie Charlier Institte, both of New York, and Rttgers grammar school, New Brtnswick, New Jersey. His btsiness career was begtn as clerk in the office of the LeRoy Shot and Lead Company, and he continted in that capacity for twenty years. In March, 1893, he was elected treastrer of the Norfolk & New Brtnswick Hosiery Company and still retains that office. In April, 1902, he also was elected president of the New Brtnswick Savings Institttion, an office he still holds. Mr. Rttgers is a Reptblican, btt not active in politics. He is a commtnicant at Christ Chtrch, Episcopalian, of New Brtnswick, being rector's warden, and for more than twenty years has been treastrer of the chtrch. He married, November 10, 1880, at New Brtnswick, Alice Noel Neilson, born New York City, Febrtary 18, 1850, datghter of John Btler Coles Neilson, who married Helena, datghter of Dr. John Neilson, of New York. John Btler Neilson's children were: Alice Noel, Helen and Henry Atgtstts Neilson. Mr. Rutgers's only child is Nicholas Gotvernetr Rttgers, born October 19, 1888, graduated from Rutgers Preparatory School, New Brtnswick, and now employed in the office of a New York City stock broker.

LIVINGSTON   According to tradition, Leving or Living, the earliest known ancestor of the Livingstons in Scotland, was a noble Htngarian who came to that cotntry in the train of Margaret, when she and her brother Edgar the Atheling took reftge at the cotrt of Malcolm Canmore, in 1070. Margaret afterward married Malcolm and many of her followers remained in Scotland and had lands granted them by her htsband. Btt this tradition, like many others of like kind relating to ancient Scotch families, will not stand investigation; and there is no need of going so far as Hungary for the origin of the surname. In England the surname Living was not uncommon and appears in a Saxon charter in the ninth century. It was the name of the archbishop of Canterbury who crowned. Canute, and the more famous bishop of Crediton and Worcester, the friend of Earl Godwine, has come down to us in the words of the old Saxon chronicle as "Lyfing the Eloquent" ("*Lyfing se wordsnotera biscop*").

And besides these two great churchmen there are many others having the same name mentioned in the Saxon charters, one of them being Staller, or master of the horse to Edward the Confessor; and moreover, according to Doomsday Book, several persons of the name were landholders before the conquest; therefore it is highly probable that the earliest known ancestor of the Livingston family in Scotland was of Saxon origin. Living was one of the Saxon landholders mentioned in Doomsday, and as to whether the Norman invasion drove him to take refuge in Scotland an authentic charter and one of the earliest relating to the abbey of Holyrood makes it certain that the Scottish Living held lands in the reign of Alexander I (1107-1124), where the present village of Livingston, Linlithgowshire, now stands; "that his son Thurstan, who between 1128 and 1159 was one of the witnesses to a charter of Robert, Bishop of St. Andrews, confirming King David's grant to the monks of Holyrood, himself confirms, in the charter alluded to above, his father Living's gift of the church of Livingston with half a carucate of land, and a toft, in free and perpetual alms to the same abbey." The name of Living's lands was written either in the Latin form of "Villa Leving" or in the Saxon equivalent of "Levingstun," both meaning the dwelling-place or homestead of Leving. It was therefore simple enough when surnames did come into use for his descendants to adopt theirs from the name of their territorial possessions.

(I) Rev. John Livingston, father of the immigrant Robert, first "Lord of the Manor," was a Scotch clergyman of remarkable ability, a lineal descendant of the fifth Lord Livingston, ancestor of the Earls of Linlithgow and Callendar. Rev. John was a preacher of the Reformed church in Scotland, a non-conformist who would yield nothing to those opposed to his views and convictions of right and

righteousness; and for this he suffered persecutions and ultimate banishment and fled to Holland, and died in Rotterdam in 1672, having made at least two unsuccessful attempts to emigrate to America. In writing of him as immediate ancestor of the founder of the family in America, Mrs. Schroeder says of Rev. John Livingston that he was the son of another well known covenanting minister, Rev. William Livingston of Lanark, who acted as spokesman for his party in its welcome of the Marquis of Hamilton into Edinburgh as the king's commissioner in 1638. The Rev. William Livingston died in 1641. He again was the son of another Scotch minister, the Rev. Alexander Livingston, of Monybroch (now Kilogth), and from some ancient family deeds now in possession of Sir Archibald Edmonstone, of Duntreath, it is proved that he had been presented to this benefice as its first Reformed minister by William, sixth Lord Livingston, previous to March 15, 1560-61, for on that date he executed a deed by which he feued half his glebe to another William Livingston. According to a statement by Rev. John Livingston, the father of Alexander Livingston, was "a son of the Lord Livingston, which house thereafter was dignified to the earls of Linlithgow," and was slain at "Pinkie Field anno Christi 1547."

The Rev. John Livingston was ordained in Ireland by Bishop Andrew Knox, but was suspended by the bishop of Down for nonconformity; but later he was restored to his ecclesiastical office. The Scottish bishops, however, gave him no peace, but informed against him with others for inciting the people against the ritual of the church. They all were tried and suspended and afterwards were restored, and during the period of suspension he took passage for New England, but gave up the attempt. He married, June 23, 1635, Barbara, daughter of Bartholomew Fleming, merchant of Edinburgh. The young couple went to Ireland, where the husband was immediately deposed. Soon afterward he set sail for America in the ship "Eagle Wing," but after a tempestuous voyage of several weeks the leaking vessel came to anchor in Loch Fergus, where the little band broke up and John Livingston and his wife went to his mother's house at Irvine, Ireland. From there he went back into Scotland, from whence in 1694 he was sent by the Scotch parliament to treat with Charles I at The Hague for liberty and security of religion. Later Cromwell sent for him to settle religious matters, and still later on the accession of Charles I he was called before the Council of Edinburgh and with seven others was banished, in 1662. He then sailed for Holland and was followed by his wife and two children, four others of their children remaining in Scotland.

(II) Robert, first "lord of the manor," son of Rev. John Livingston, was born in 1654, and came to New York about 1675, two years after the death of his father, and when he himself was thirty years old. He settled at Albany, then a frontier post, where by reason of his knowledge of the French and Dutch languages, acquired while living in Holland, he soon received an appointment as secretary of the commandant and commissioners, who then constituted the governing power of the post. But, coming to the new country with little else than his education and remarkable quality of perseverance, he succeeded through many vicissitudes and much hardship in amassing a large fortune and also in acquiring a vast estate in lands amounting to one hundred and sixty thousand, two hundred and forty acres. That his success should make him many enemies in the new country was only natural and he was forced to contend against many petty jealousies on the part of associates, and a standing feud with other proprietors who regarded themselves less favored than he; but so often as these differences were settled they broke forth again. But his political differences need no full presentation here, although he held many important offices under the colonial government. Lord Belmont, writing to the Lords of Trade, referring to French intrigues with the Five Nations, says "It falls out unluckily that Colonel Schuyler and Mr. Livingston, who are the men of best figure in Albany, and are the most popular with the Five Nations, and are the principal men in managing them and keeping them firm to our interests, are at this time full of discontent, and not without reason, for both of them had good estates, but by victualling the companies they are almost, if not quite, broke."

Robert Livingston built flour mills and storehouses on his property and good dwellings for his tenants and offered many inducements to settlers. He was sent to the assembly and was speaker of the house for seven years before his death. His most important office was that of secretary of Indian affairs, which had to do with the fur trade, and he held it for nearly fifty years. His son Philip was appointed in his place a few years before his death, in 1728. He was secretary of In-

dian affairs from 1675 to 1721, and mayor of Albany from 1710 to 1719. He married Alyda (Alida), widow of Rev. Nicholas Van Rensselaer and daughter of Philip Schuyler. Their children and the dates of their baptism are as follows: 1. Philipina Johanna, February 3, 1684. 2. Philippus (Philip), July 25, 1686. 3. Robert, July 29, 1688. 4. Gysbert, March 5, 1690. 5. William, March 20, 1692. 6. Johanna, December 20, 1694. 7. Catrine, July 17, 1698.

(III) Colonel Philip, son of Robert and Alida (Schuyler-Van Rensselaer) Livingston, was born in Albany, July 25, 1686, died February 4, 1749. He succeeded his father as proprietor of Livingston Manor and also as incumbent of the several offices his father had held. In 1710 he served with the rank of colonel in the expedition that captured Port Royal, and after its reduction he made a journey to Quebec with a French officer as a bearer of dispatches. In October, 1725, he was appointed member of the council, which office he retained so long as he lived. In 1737 he was appointed commissioner to run the boundary line between New York, New Hampshire and Massachusetts. Colonel Livingston died in 1749, and his funeral is said to have cost five hundred pounds, which his widow declared "a most wasteful expenditure." Colonel Livingston was admitted to the bar in New York in 1719. He lived in Albany in his father's house at the corner of State and Pearl streets. He married, September 19, 1707, Catharina, daughter of Pieter Van Brugh, of Albany, and who was the mayor of that city in 1699, just two hundred and ten years ago. Pieter Van Brugh was a son of Johannes Van Brugge (or Verbrugge), a man of substance and who also was mayor of Albany in 1658. Catharina Van Brugh was a notable housekeeper and had been carefully trained in all the duties of maidens of her day. Her marriage chest, which contained all of her household linen, is still in existence, and is mentioned by Mrs. John King Van Rensselaer in her admirable work "The Goede Vroew of Ma-a-ha-ta." Colonel Livingston's children, with date of baptism of each: 1. Robert, December 25, 1708. 2. Pieter (Van Brugh) November 3, 1710. 3. Pieter, April 20, 1712. 4. Johannes, April 11, 1714. 5. Philippus, January, 1717, died June 12, 1778. 6. Hendrick, April 5, 1719. 7. Sara, May 17, 1721, died young. 8. William, December 8, 1723. 9. Sara, November 7, 1725, married General Lord Stirling. 10. Alida, July 18, 1728. 11. Catharina, April 15, 1733.

(IV) Robert (2), son of Colonel Philip and Catharina (Van Brigh) Livingston, was born December 25, 1708, died in 1790. He was third and last lord of the manor, but had hardly come into possession of his vast estate before he began to be harrassed by the people of Massachusetts to such an extent that in 1752 he laid his case before Governor Clinton, who presented the questions involved to the governor of Massachusetts, but without satisfactory settlement of the difficulty until many years afterward. The third proprietor was possessed of more than ordinary business capacity and spared neither labor nor expense in the development of his property. Mills of various kinds were built, churches were erected and settlement was promoted in every way. Iron ore was found and works for its reduction were established at Ancram, but notwithstanding his remarkable energy the third proprietor did not live to see the end of the troubles which threatened his peace and vast possessions. He married, in New York, May 20, 1731, Mary Tong (sometimes written Maria Thong).

(V) John, son of Robert (2) and Mary (Tong) Livingston, married Mary LeRoy.

(VI) Robert LeRoy, son of John and Mary (LeRoy) Livingston, married Anna Maria Digges, of Washington.

(VII) Anna Maria, daughter of Robert Leroy and Anna Maria (Digges) Livingston, married John Livingston Rutgers (see Rutgers VI).

PRICKITT   The family name Prickitt is fond at an early date in Burlington county, and of course has relation to the New Jersey family of the generally accepted name of Prickitt, the latter being the family purposed to be treated in this place, and supposed to have descended from John Prickitt, of Gloucestershire, England, a "persecuted Friend," in 1660, who is mentioned in the narrative entitled Besse's "Sufferings." There was a Josiah Prickitt, of Burlington, who was one of the founders of Cranberry in 1697, and of whom the "History of the Colony of New Jersey" (Barber and Howe, 1844) says "Cranberry is one of the oldest places in this part of the state. It was settled about the year 1697 by Josiah Prickett, /butcher, of Burlington. The following year he sold out to John Harrison of Flushing, Long Island."

(I) Zackariah (or Zachariah) Prickitt, the earliest known ancestor of the family under

consideration here of whom we have definite knowledge settled in Northampton, Burlington county, and is said to have brought with him a large property, which he invested in lands. His will bears date February 28, 1727, was admitted to probate March 14, of the same year. The baptismal name of his wife was Ellipha, and so far as the records disclose their children were as follows: 1. John. 2. Zackariah, married, 1721, Mary Troth. 3. Jacob, see post. 4. Elizabeth, married, 1723, John Peacock. 5. Hannah, married Philip Quigley.

(II) Jacob, son of Zackariah and Ellipha Prickitt, had a wife Hannah, who bore him eight children and who died 12 4mo. 1759, aged fifty-three years. Their children: 1. Josiah, born 23 8mo. 1733, married Sarah Cowperthwaite. 2. Jacob, born 18 9mo. 1735, married Elizabeth Phillips. 3. Barzilla, born 22 9mo. 1737, married Sarah Sharp. 4. Ann, born 20 10mo. 1739, died 4 4mo. 1759. 5. Rosannah, born 11 2mo. 1742. 6. Job, see post. 7. Hannah, born 26 6mo. 1746, married Amaziah Lippincott. 8. Sabyllah, born 24 9mo. 1748.

(III) Job, son of Jacob and Hannah Prickitt, was born the 24th of 4th mo. 1744, and married Ann, daughter of Thomas and Elizabeth Smith. Their children: 1. Rachel, born 5 11mo. 1770, married James Allen. 2. Sabillah, born 9 9mo. 1772, died unmarried. 3. Josiah, born 29 9mo. 1775, died young. 4. Job, born 9 7mo. 1777, married Ann Huff. 5. Josiah, see post. 6. Barzilla, born 20 2mo. 1781, married Martha Haines. 7. Ann, born 13 2mo. 1782, married Allen Joyce. 8. Zackariah, born 4 1mo. 1784, married Agnes Sharp. 9. Stacy, born 14 10mo. 1785, married Jane Conover. 10. John, born 28 5mo. 1787, married Jenetta Sharp. 11. Elizabeth, born 9 7mo. 1789 died unmarried.

(IV) Josiah, son of Job and Ann (Smith) Prickitt, was born near Medford, Burlington county, New Jersey, the 25th day of 2d mo. 1779, and married Hannah (sometimes written Ann) Sharp, daughter of Thomas and Esther (Brooks) Sharp. Josiah Prickitt lived in a house built for him at the time of his marriage and which stood on the highway about opposite to the house in which he was born. He died in 1859. His children: 1. Amos, born 1 3mo. 1805, died young. 2. Mary Ann, born 27 11mo. 1806. 3. Josiah J., born 10 6mo. 1808. 4. Nathan, born 18, 3mo. 1810. 5. Allen, born 1 3mo. 1812. 6. Esther, born 24 5mo. 1814. 7. Thomas, see post. 8. Sarah,

born 17 4mo 1818. 9. Ezra, born 1 3mo.
1820. 10. Mark, born 7 7mo. 1822. 11. Elizabeth, born 5 9mo. 1824. 12. Lemuel J., born
16 6mo. 1826. 13. Amos, born 15 5mo. 1828.
14. Edwin, born 20 8mo. 1831.

(V) Thomas, son of Josiah and Hannah
(Sharp) Prickitt, was born near Red Lion,
New Jersey, the 20th day of 6th month, 1816,
died in 1870. He was given a good academic
education and evidently embraced every opportunity to improve his store of knowledge,
for he always was looked upon as a very well-
informed man. His chief occupation was
farming and in this his business life was a
success. He was a thorough practical farmer,
a director of the Burlington Fair Association,
a Republican in politics and a strict Friend.
He married Ann Engle, born 1834, died 1899,
daughter of Arthur and Elizabeth Engle (see
Engle), and by her had seven children: 1.
Nathan, lives in Atlantic City. 2. Robert,
lives in Mt. Holly. 3. Elmer D., see post. 4.
Frank, business man and druggist, having
stores at Bryn Mawr and Rosemont, Pennsylvania. 5. Mary, died young. 6. Elizabeth,
died young. 7. William, died young.

(VI) Dr. Elmer Delaney, son of Thomas
and Ann (Engle) Prickitt, was born in Lumberton township, Burlington county, New Jersey, May 17, 1863, and after gaining a good
education in public schools and Friends'
College, at Westtown, Pennsylvania, he taught
school at Lumberton for one year. He then
took a position as druggist's clerk and there
laid the foundation of a thorough course at
the Philadelphia College of Pharmacy, from
which he graduated in 1884. In 1886, after
graduation, he went into the drug business in
company with Dr. Barrington, under the firm
name of Prickitt & Barrington. This partnership relation was maintained until 1893,
when the firm was dissolved, and since that
time Dr. Prickitt has carried on business alone.
In the meantime, however, he had taken up
the study of medicine and having grounded
himself properly Dr. Prickitt matriculated at
the Medico-Chirurgical College of Philadelphia, made the course of the famous institution and graduated with the degree M. D. in
1898. Since that time he has practiced general medicine in Mt. Holly in connection with
business pursuits as druggist and pharmacist.
He is a member of the American Medical Association, New Jersey State Medical Society,
Burlington County Medical Society, member
of the medical staff of the Burlington County

Hospital and has served three terms as physician to the board of health of two townships.
He is an active figure in Republican politics,
but not an aspirant for political honors;
member of Mt. Holly Lodge, No. 14, F. and A.
M. Mt. Holly Lodge, No. 848, Benevolent and
Protective Order of Elks, a Knight of Pythias
and a Forester of America. In 1886 Dr.
Prickitt married Eleanor, daughter of Nelson
and Ellen (Deacon) Deacon.

The Deacon family is made the subject of
inquiry in these annals, but in this place we
have two distinct lines of descent from a
common ancestor. George Deacon (I), immigrant, had a son John (II), who had a son
Joseph (III), who had a son John (IV), who
had a son Nelson (V), whose daughter
Eleanor (VI) married Elmer Delaney Prickitt. Again: George Deacon (I), immigrant,
had a son John (II), who had a son Barzilla
(III), who had a son Barzilla (IV), who had
a son Samuel (V), whose daughter Ellen
(VI) married Nelson Deacon (V) and had a
daughter Eleanor (VII) who married Dr.
Prickitt.

(The Engle Line).

This surname appears prominently among
the early settlers of New Jersey, and is found
in Burlington county among the Friends who
founded the earliest settlements in that part
of the colony. The family is of English ancestry and from the time of the immigrant has
been noted for the honest endeavor and upright character of its representatives in all
succeeding generations.

(I) Robert Engle, immigrant, with whom
our present narrative begins, came from Cam-
bridgeshire England, and settled in Evesham
township, Burlington county. He appears to
have been a man of considerable enterprise and
acquired a goodly estate in lands and other
property. He died in 1696, leaving a will
which was executed shortly before his death
and was admitted to probate during the same
year. He married 4th of 5th month, 1684,
Jane Horne, who survived him and married
23d of 9th month, 1703, Henry Clifton, of
Philadelphia, Pennsylvania. Robert and Jane
(Horne) Engle had an only son John.

(II) John, only son and child of Robert
and Jane (Horne) Engle, died in 1721, leaving
a good estate, an upright life record, and a
family of honorable children. He married
Mary, daughter of Samuel and Jane Ogborn,
and by her had five children: 1. Robert, see
post. 2. John, married Hannah Middleton.

3. Mary, married Nathaniel Lippincott. 4. Hannah, married Isaac Lippincott. 5. Jane, married John Turner.

(III) Robert (2), eldest son and child of John and Mary (Ogborn) Engle, was born in Evesham township, Burlington county, New Jersey, in 1708, died there in 1774. He married, in 1728, Rachel Vinicum, and by her had five children: 1. Robert, born 29 3mo. 1738. 2. Joseph, see post. 3. Abraham, born 1744. 4. Rachel, born 26 4mo. 1746. 5. Sarah.

(IV) Joseph, son of Robert (2) and Rachel (Vinicum) Engle, was born in Evesham township, Burlington county, New Jersey, the 24th day of 7th month, 1740. He married Mary Borton, born Evesham 3 6mo. 1737, and by her had nine children: 1. John, born 16 8mo. 1761, died 18 10mo. 1823. 2. Obadiah, see post. 3. Aaron, born 6 11mo. 1764, died 1842. 4. Susanna, born 22 2mo. 1766, died 31 6mo. 1838. 5. Phebe, born 7 2mo. 1769, died 12 2mo. 1840. 6. Asa, born 7 11mo. 1770, died 25 4mo. 1829. 7. Ann, born 15 3mo. 1774. 8. Joseph, born 16 7mo. 1776, died 13 8mo. 1856. 9. Rachel, born 1 4mo. 1783, died 14 2mo. 1883.

(V) Obadiah, son of Joseph and Mary (Borton) Engle, was born in Evesham township, Burlington county, the 16th day of 3d month, 1763, died the 12th day of 9th month, 1843. He married Patience Coles, born 19th day of 12th month, 1771, and died 24th day of 4th month, 1844. They had ten children: 1. Ann, born 17 4mo. 1795, died 21 8mo. 1797. 2. Job, born 13 12mo. 1796, died 9 10mo. 1862. 3. Arthur, see post. 4. Aaron, born 6 4mo. 1801, died 31 3mo. 1864. 5. Elizabeth, born 5 2mo. 1803, died 13 6mo. 1890; married Abel Moore, of Lumberton. 6. Mary, born 12 4mo. 1805, died 27 6mo. 1893. 7. Rachel, born 24 6mo. 1807, died 25 12mo. 1888. 8. Samuel, born 11 1mo. 1810, died 27 4mo. 1858. 9. Sarah Ann, born 25 5mo. 1812, died 24 4mo. 1879. 10. Nathan, born 1 10mo. 1817, died at Washington in 1875.

(VI) Arthur, son of Obadiah and Patience (Coles) Engle was born in Evesham township, March 9, 1799, and died there September 29, 1876. He married Elizabeth Engle, born April 25, 1802, died October 24, 1863, daughter of Robert and Mary (Woolman) Engle. Their children were: 1. Ezra, married Sarah Prickitt. 2. Emeline, married Josiah Prickitt. 3. Ann, born 1834, died 1899; married Thomas Prickitt, born 1816, died 1870 (see Prickitt). 4. Mary, mar-

ried Joseph Roberts. 5. Robert, married Jane Darnell.

(For preceding generations see Zacharian Prickitt 1).

PRICKITT (V) Lemuel J. Prickitt, son of Josiah and Hannah (Ann) (Sharp) Prickitt, was born in Medford, New Jersey, June 16, 1826, and was a birthright Friend. He received his education in a Friends' school and was known as a man of upright character and good understanding. In business life he was a farmer and lived on his farm until the time of his death, about 1875. In political preference he was a Republican. He married Elizabeth Haines, born in Salem county, New Jersey, and died in 1897. Children: Cooper Hancock, see post, Eva married Charles P. Darling, of Detroit, Michigan.

(VI) Cooper Hancock, son of Lemuel J. and Elizabeth (Haines) Prickitt, was born in Medford, New Jersey, January 23, 1863, and received his education in public schools, the Friends' School at Easton, New Jersey, and at Bryant & Stratton's Business College in Philadelphia, graduating from the latter institution in 1883. After leaving school he began his business career in a clerical capacity for the firm of William Mann & Company, manufacturers and wholesale dealers in blank books and stationery, and he is still connected with that firm, although for a number of years his duties have been those of assistant treasurer of the company. Mr. Prickitt is not only a successful business man in connection with personal concerns and the management of the company of which he is assistant treasurer, but also is something of a public man in that for many years he has been prominently identified with several of the leading institutions of Burlington. For the past eleven years he has been a member of the board of education of the city and for nine years has been president of the board, serving in that capacity in 1909. In this connection it may be said that he was largely instrumental in securing the erection of the Lawrence school building in the city. He is a Republican in politics, a communicant in the Episcopal church, and secretary of the Church Club of the Diocese of New Jersey. He also stands high in Masonic and other fraternal organizations, and is past master of Burlington Lodge, No. 32, F. and A. M.; past high priest of Boudinot Chapter, No. 3, R. A. M.; past eminent commander of Helena Commandery, K. T., of Burlington, and has followed up in the craft to the thirty-second degree, holding membership in Scottish Rite bodies, and also in Lu Lu Temple, A. A. O. N. M. S., of Philadelphia. He has also served as district deputy grand master of the M. W. Grand Lodge, F. and A. M., of New Jersey. He has also served as member of the New Jersey Masonic Home committee having charge of the Masonic Home at Burlington. Mr. Prickitt also is an Elk and a member of Oneida Boat Club. He married, November 21, 1888, Sarah Howells, daughter of Dr. Jacob and Hannah (Toy) Phillips, and granddaughter of Anthony Phillips, of Vincentown, blacksmith, who married Clarissa Edmunds and had seven children: John, Theodore, Anthony, Eliza, Deborah, Clarissa and Jacob Phillips. Dr. Phillips was born in Vincentown, educated there, and for a time worked with his father as a blacksmith. Later on he studied for and became a practical dentist and settled for practice in Burlington, where for many years he was a prominent figure in professional and business circles. He was an Odd Fellow, a Republican in politics and attended services at the Methodist Episcopal church. He married (first) Emeline Clark, and by her had two children: Thomas and Jacob Phillips; married (second) Hannah Toy, daughter of Thomas and Elizabeth Toy, of Mt. Holly, and had four children: William, died young; Harry, a machinist of Burlington; Sarah Howells, married Cooper Hancock Prickitt; Elizabeth, married William Hall, of Bristol, Bucks county, Pennsylvania, who died in 1905. Mr. and Mrs. Prickitt have one child, Joseph Mann Prickitt.

SHREVE   The rise of the people called Quakers is among the most memorable events in the history of intellectual freedom. They proclaimed intellectual freedom to be an invaluable birthright, due to man and not to be circumscribed by theological form or governmental policy. The Quaker doctrine was philosophy as heretofore taught only in the cloister, the college and the saloon, given freely to all seekers, even to the most despised people. "The Inner Light" was to be the rule and guide of life and that light was the voice of God in the soul, able to join the whole human race in unity of equal rights. The triumvirate of Quakerism, as far as it belongs to civil history, was intellectual freedom, the supremacy of the mind, universal enfranchisement.

In England the Quaker was persecuted by the Established Church as well as by the Puri-

tan; by the peers and by the king as well as by the commoner, and even in New England and in the Dutch Colonies of the New Netherlands, they were exposed to perpetual trials and dangers. In England they were whipped, kept in jails with felons and in dungeons out of reach of mankind or of God's sunshine; they were fined, exiled and sold into bondage. When their meeting houses were burned or torn down, they gathered on the ashes and debris and continued worship. Armed men were unable to dissolve them and when threatened with being smothered by earth, they stood close together "willing to have been buried alive witnessing for the Lord." On the return of George Fox in 1674 from the pilgrimage through the English colonies in America from Carolina to Rhode Island, Lord Berkley sold for a thousand pounds the moiety of New Jersey to John Fenwick in trust for Edward Bellinge and his assigns, to be a place of refuge and haven of rest for the despised Quakers.

In 1675 Fenwick with a large company including several families set sail in the "Griffin" for this "Asylum of Friends." The voyage was made across the Atlantic to the Chesapeake bay and up the Delaware river and landing was affected in a fertile spot and they called it Salem, for it seemed to them the dwelling place of peace. Desiring to preserve sufficient territory which they could institute a government, they effected an exchange with Carteret, who owned the other moiety of New Jersey, in August, 1676, by which they had contiguous lands on which they could be free from outside encroachment. The message sent them from the Quaker proprietors in England was as follows: "We lay a foundation for after ages to understand their liberty as christians and as men, that they may not be brought into bondage by their own consent; for we put the power in the people."

In March, 1677, the charter or fundamental laws of West New Jersey were perfected and published and in that year Burlington was laid out and rude huts were built, being copied in construction from the Indian wigwams. Immediately after other English families flocked to West New Jersey, carrying with them the good wishes of Charles II, and commissioners holding temporary power accompanied them to administer affairs until a popular government could be instituted. The land was purchased from the Indians claiming ownership and the body of Quaker immigrants, aggregating four hundred souls, began to build homes and plant their farms. A huge sailcloth tent was their first meeting house and in 1678 they were formally welcomed by Indian sachems gathered in council in the forest adjacent to the settlement and their message to the new settlers was: "You are our brothers and we will live like brothers with you. We will have a broad path for you and us to walk in. If an Englishman falls asleep in this path, the Indian shall pass him by and say: 'He is an Englishman; he is asleep let him alone.' The path shall be plain. There shall not be a stump in it to hurt the feet." Thus the light of peace dawned on West New Jersey. In May, 1682, Burlington was made the capital of the province, and in 1684 the assembly divided the province into four counties: Bergen, Essex, Middlesex and Monmouth. Amid these surroundings the Shreve family is first found. Its religion and political creed was that of the Quakers.

(I) Thomas "Sheriff," as the name first appears, is found in Plymouth, Massachusetts, in an action of trespass, December 7, 1641, and on December 10, 1666, he was a granter in a conveyance at Portsmouth, Rhode Island, where an inventory of his estate is filed, June 11, 1675. He was probably born before 1620, and his wife Martha not later than 1635. His death occurred in Portsmouth, province of Rhode Island, May 29, 1675, and his widow married (second) Thomas Hazard and (third) Lewis Hues, who was found to have absconded with much of his wife's property and this caused her to transfer her remaining property to her son John by her first husband, Thomas Sheriff. Savage says that John Shreve, of Portsmouth, was the son of Thomas of Plymouth, but other authorities do not agree with him and we are led by these other authorities, who are personally connected with the Shreve family, to try find the American progenitor elsewhere. To do this we have to depend on the family tradition for the existence of one Sir William Sheriff, who is said to have come from Greece or Turkey where the name of Sheriff is not uncommon and to have married Elizabeth Fairfax in England, and they had a son, William, who married a young lady in Amsterdam, Holland, by the name of Ora Ora, or Oara Oara, the daughter of a wealthy nobleman. After this marriage they came to Portsmouth, Rhode Island, where it is positive they had John and Caleb and probably a third son, William, who left no issue. From an old deed still in the family, given by John Cooke, of Portsmouth in the Colony of Rhode Island, to John Shreve of the same town, Cooke conveys three-fourths of all his right and property in Shrewsbury, New Jersey, to John Shreve. This deed is dated January 9, 1676-77, and on the back is a transfer from the said John Shreve to his beloved brother, Caleb Shreve. Caleb Shreve also received warrants for land from the East New Jersey Proprietors as early as 1676, and as he must have been of age at that time we fix the approximate date of his birth as 1650-55. This would make the birth of Sir William, 1590, which tradition places at near the close of the sixteenth century, but this does not prove the parentage of John and Caleb Shreve. The children of Thomas and Martha Sheriff or Shreve, born in Portsmouth and little Compton, Rhode Island, were as follows: 1. Thomas, September 2, 1649. 2. John, married Jane Havers, August, 1686; died October 14, 1739. 3. Caleb (q. v.). 4. Mary, married Joseph Sheffield, February 12, 1685; died after 1706. 5. Susannah, married a Thomas; died after 1714. 6. Daniel, born in Little Compton, Rhode Island, married Jane ——, 1688; died 1737. 7. Elizabeth, married Edmund Carter and died childless. June 5, 1719. 8. Sarah, married John Moon; died June 24, 1732. In the second generation the name appears as Shreve.

(II) Caleb, probably the third child and third son of Thomas and Martha Sheriff or Shreve, of Rhode Island Colony, was born about 1652, in Portsmouth, Rhode Island. He married Sarah Areson, daughter of Diedrich (or Deric) Areson, of Long Island, about 1680, in Burlington county, New Jersey, to which place he had removed from Rhode Island about 1699. His house was about seven miles east of the present site of Mt. Holly. As his children went from the homestead, he gave each a fine farm in Burlington county, where they continued to reside. He made his will, which was executed February 28, 1740-41, at which time his widow was living with her son Benjamin on the homestead. The names of the children of Caleb and Sarah (Areson) Shreve are as follows. The order of their birth cannot be determined with exactness. These children were: 1. Martha, 168—, married Benjamin Scattergood, of Burlington county, New Jersey, in 1704. They were married by the Friends' ceremony at Chesterfield Meeting. 2. Thomas, 168—, married Elizabeth Allison, May 16, 1711, at Burlington Meeting. He died in Burlington county, New Jersey, July, 1747. 3. Joseph, 168—, married Hope Harding by

Friends ceremony at Burlington Meeting after July 3, 1711. He died before 1757. 4. Joshua (q. v.). 5. Caleb, 169—, married (first) Mary Hunt, May 8, 1713, at Chesterfield Meeting, and (second) Ann ———. He died 1746. 6. Mary, 169—, married Isaac Gibbs, Jr., January 5, 1722, at Chesterfield Meeting. 7. Sarah, 169—, married John Ogborne, January 19, 1724, at Chesterfield Meeting. 8. Jonathan, 169—, married Hannah Hunt, February 4, 1720, at Chesterfield Meeting. He died 1756. 9. David, 169—, died after 1735. 10. Benjamin, June 9, 1706, married Rebecca French, February 23, 1729, at Springfield Meeting.

(III) Joshua, probably the fourth child and third son of Caleb and Sarah (Areson) Shreve, was born in Monmouth county, New Jersey, April 5, 1692. He was a minister of the society of Friends and was accustomed to make long journeys on horseback as far south as Virginia and as far north as Massachusetts, holding and attending meetings on his journeys going and returning. He lived in Springfield township adjoining Richard Stockton, and he gave to the Society of Friends four acres of land from his farm on which to erect a meeting house and prepare a graveyard. The meeting house was erected in 1739 and this date over the door in the brick wall is still discernable, the meeting house being still in use. The building is one-half mile from Wrightstown and is known as Upper Springfield Meeting. Previous to its erection the Friends attended the Crosswicks Meeting. On May 6, 1749, Chesterfield Meeting granted him a certificate "to make a religious visit to the government of Pennsylvania, Maryland and Virginia," April 7, 1750, he procured a certificate from Fairfax, Virginia, which was "to satisfaction." He married Jane ———, but place, time or surname is not known. They had eight children, born in Springfield township, as follows: 1. Mary, married a Curtis. 2. Sarah, married Thomas Shreve, March 1, 1742. 3. Mercy, married Micajal Mathis, March 7, 1747; she died 1804. 4. Faith, married Israel Butler, January 1, 1750. 5. James (q. v.). 6. Caleb, August 16, 1717, married Hannah Thorn, January 16, 1737. He died in Bedford county, Pennsylvania, February 8, 1810. 7. Martha, married William Shinn Burlington, November 5, 1728. 8. Susannah, married John Beck, July 1, 1737.

(IV) James, probably eldest son and fifth child of Joshua and Jane Shreve, was born in Springfield township, Burlington county, New Jersey. He married Leah Davis, July 1, 1737. Date of birth and date and place of death unknown. The child of James and Leah (Davis) Shreve was Joshua (q. v.).

(V) Joshua (2), probably the only child of James and Leah (Davis) Shreve, married Rebecca, daughter of Joseph and Rebecca (Budd) Lamb, granddaughter of William and Elizabeth (Stockton) Budd, who were married in 1703 by Friends ceremony in the home of Richard Stockton, of Springfield, New Jersey; great-granddaughter of William Budd, who with three brothers came from England to Burlington county, New Jersey, in 1678. He was an extensive land owner. Rebecca Lamb was born March 26, 1742, died December 9, 1800, while her husband, Joshua Shreve, died in 1819 at an advanced age. The Springfield Meeting Society records the names and dates of birth of their eight children as follows: 1. Gersom, October 6, 1761, died unmarried while quite young. 2. Theodosia, April 28, 1766, married Joseph Earl, of Pemberton, New Jersey. She died January 12, 1848. 3. Alexander (q. v.). 4. Leah, April 8, 1771, married Joseph Burr, and died in Vincentown, New Jersey, when over eighty years of age. 5. Sarah, December 25, 1775, married George Holmes in 1801 and died April 7, 1847. 6. James, March 1, 1778, married Elizabeth Smith, December 29, 1808, and died at Oneaneckon, New Jersey, October 1, 1852. 7. Charles, April 7, 1781, married Rebecca Pitman Cox in 1805, and died at Mt. Holly, New Jersey, December 11, 1815. 8. Rebecca, December 3, 1785, married Isaac Hulme, of Hulmeville, Bristol, Pennsylvania, November 6, 1806, and died in Bucks county, Pennsylvania, April 25, 1865.

(VI) Alexander, second son and third child of Joshua (2) and Rebecca (Lamb) Shreve, was born at the homestead in Wrightstown, New Jersey, March 3, 1769. He first engaged in trade in his native village, but later removed to Northampton township, Burlington county, where he was a farmer for seven years. He married Mary, daughter of Taunton and Mary (Haines) Earl, and granddaughter of Charles Haines. She was born May 25, 1767, and with her husband were members of the Springfield Meeting of the Society of Friends, whose records furnish authentic dates and names of their children except the youngest. She died in 1843 and her husband December 4, 1854. Their children were seven in number and were born as follows: 1. Joshua (q. v.). 2. Mary, April 19, 1795, died November 8, 1796. 3.

Sarah, July 20, 1797, died unmarried. 4. Mary Ann, June 9, 1799, married Joseph K. Hulme, April 15, 1814, and died in Upper Springfield, New Jersey, January 26, 1884. 5. Taunton E., February 23, 1802, married Sarah T. Merritt. 6. Rebecca, September 5, 1805, married Thomas Newbold. 7. Alexander, in Wrightstown, New Jersey, October 2, 1812, married Mary A. Levelers in the spring of 1873.

(VII) Joshua (3), eldest child of Alexander and Mary (Earl) Shreve, was born in Springfield township, Burlington county, New Jersey, March 25, 1793. He married Susanna Ridgeway, of Springfield, November 16, 1814, and he died September 21, 1851. The ten children of Joshua and Susanna (Ridgeway) Shreve were born as follows: 1. Charles Smith, Wrightstown, New Jersey, September 30, 1815, married Mary Louise Josephine Kennedy, of Mobile, Alabama, January 1, 1840, and died in Mobile, December 16, 1857. 2. Edwin, October 14, 1817, married Elizabeth Wyckoff, of Monmouth, New Jersey, and died at Werd Millpoint, Virginia, January 21, 1863. 3. Barzillia Ridgeway (q. v.). 4. Joshua Burr, Northampton, New Jersey, April 25, 1823, died August 6, 1826. 5. Alexander, August 9, 1825, married Edith Ann Ivins, September 27, 1848, and died at Point of Rocks, Virginia, September 12, 1864. 6. Joshua Earl, December 17, 1827, never married and died in San Francisco, California, October 9, 1871. 7. Henry, July 8, 1831, never married, died at Red Wood City, California, about 1876. 8. Susan Ridgeway, January 29, 1834, married Richard C. Ridgeway, of Philadelphia, Pennsylvania, December 13, 1866, and resided there. 9. Anna M. August 19, 1836, unmarried, resides in Philadelphia. 10. Richard Lott Ridgeway, April 4, 1840, married Margaret Webb, of Philadelphia, in 1861, died on the battlefield of Chancellorsville, Virginia, May 6, 1864.

(VIII) Barzillia Ridgeway, third son and child of Joshua (3) and Susanna (Ridgeway) Shreve, was born in Northampton, New Jersey, August 20, 1820. He carried on a large stock farm in Pemberton township and made a specialty of breeding fine horses and cattle. He was a Democrat in politics, and a member of the Society of Friends by birthright. He held important town offices and was a member of the United States Grange. He married Agnes Edith Haines, of Pemberton, New Jersey. By this marriage he had seven children, as follows: 1. John A. L., who

married Louise Davis and died in 1870. 2. Mary Earl, who lives in Pemberton, New Jersey. 3. Edith Ella, who married Samuel Kirkbride Robbin, October 4, 1882, and lives in Morristown, New Jersey. 4. Charles Smith, who died unmarried about 1862. 5. Florence Murrell, who died unmarried in 1873. 6. Sarah Coat, who married Edwin Rex Keisel, February 20, 1889, and lived in Philadelphia, Pennsylvania. 7. Thomas Coat (q. v.) Barzillia Ridgeway Shreve died in Philadelphia, Pennsylvania, December 12, 1893.

(IX) Thomas Coat, third son and seventh and youngest child of Barzillia Ridgeway and Agnes Edith (Haines) Shreve, was born in Pemberton, New Jersey, September 23, 1860. He was educated in the public schools and Mt. Holly Academy, and he worked from very early boyhood on his father's farm. On reaching his majority, his father turned the management of the farm with all its varied interests to him, which was an evidence of his acquired skill as an agriculturist. Like his father he was a Democrat and he served in the board of taxation of the county of Burlington and on the township committee of his native town as well as being director on the school board for twenty-seven years. He was a member of the Grange and of the Benevolent and Protective Order of Elks Lodge, No. 848, of Mt. Holly. He married, February 3, 1892, Florence Eugenia, daughter of John B. and Elizabeth Waln (Ridgeway) Deacon, and a descendant in the seventh generation from (I) George, the immigrant through (II) John, (III) George, (IV) John, (V) Thomas Eagad, (VI) John B., of Springfield township, New Jersey. Thomas Coat and Florence Eugenia (Deacon) Shreve have children born as follows: Agnes Elizabeth, June 11, 1893; Anne R., October 13, 1905; Helen Deacon, July 27, 1908.

ROSS This name is of undoubted Scotch origin, whether we find the name as immigrants to Holland, to the North of Ireland, or directly to the colonies or states of North America. When we find a family coming from Holland bearing this name, but have no definite data as to the nationality, we look into the business career of the known progenitor and by his trade or profession determine the probability of his nationality. In this case the subject is the son of a piano manufacturer, born in Holland, and the question naturally arises: Is he of Dutch origin? The makers of pianos are to be found in all nations, but skilled workmen at the trade have come largely from Scotland, as have the inventors of various parts of the pianoforte. It is noticeable that few come from France, or from other parts of the continent of Europe. Scotland has furnished a remarkable list of piano builders and inventors. James Stewart, the first partner of Jonas Chickering, we find to have been a Scotchman. Robert Stodart, to whom we owe the upright piano, and John and James Shudi Broadwood, eminent London manufacturers, were Scotchmen, who went to London to manufacture the pianoforte. Francis Melville, inventor of metallic tubular bracing for use in the construction of the piano-forte, was also a Scotchman, and Dr. Hopkinson, of Philadelphia, an Edinburgh graduate in medicine, made the first piano, or harpsichord, as it was called, with an iron frame. Then the name Campbell is prominently connected with the sale of the pianoforte in New York City in the early days of the use of that instrument.

That a Ross, a native of Scotland, should be found in Amsterdam, Holland, in 1800, who was skilled in the manufacture of the pianoforte, is no cause of wonderment and there is no reason to question his nationality. In America, we find the rule applies universally and in tracing the genealogy of a Ross, we naturally turn to Scotland and not to Holland as the fatherland. The Rosses of Scotland have furnished to America notable men of the past as well as shining examples of the present. Of the past we have: George Ross (1730-1779), clergyman; lawyer; delegate to congress; judge of the court of admiralty and signer of the Declaration of Independence. Jack Ferrill Ross (1791-1837), pioneer financier of Alabama; officer in the United States army, 1813-17; territorial and state treasurer of Alabama, 1818-22; sheriff of Mobile county and an Alabama legislator. James Ross (1762-1847), United States senator from Pennsylvania, 1794-1803; attorney for George Washington, in charge of his estate in Pennsylvania; twice the defeated candidate for governor of Pennsylvania. John Ross (1770-1834), husband of Mary (Jenkins) Ross, who made and presented the "Stars and Stripes," which became the national flag, to General Washington in Philadelphia in 1777, and who was himself a lawyer in Easton, Pennsylvania; representative in the United States congress, 1809-18; presiding judge of the seventh district of Pennsylvania, 1818-30, and judge of the supreme court of the state, 1830-34. Jonathan

Ross (1826-1905), teacher, lawyer, legislator, educator, judge and chief justice of the state supreme court of Vermont, United States senator and chairman of the state railroad commission of Vermont. Lawrence Sullivan Ross (1838-1898), Indian fighter; general in the Confederate army; member of the Texas state constitutional convention, 1875; state senator, 1881-86; governor of Texas, 1887-91. Leonard Fuller Ross (1823-1901), soldier in the Mexican war; brigadier-general in the civil war, 1861-65; delegate from Illinois to the Democratic national conventions of 1852-56 and of the Republican national convention of 1872. Lewis Winans Ross (1812-1895), lawyer; state representative; delegate to the state constitutional conventions of Illinois, 1861 and 1870, and Democratic representative from Illinois in the thirty-eighth, thirty-ninth and fortieth congresses, 1863-69. William Henry Harrison Ross (1814-1887), colonel of cavalry regiment in Mexican war; delegate from Delaware to Democratic national conventions of 1844-48-56-60, and governor of Delaware, 1851-55.

(I) John Ross, son of a piano manufacturer in Amsterdam, Holland, and probably a native of Scotland or descended of Scotch ancestors, was born in Amsterdam, Holland, about 1805, and immigrated to America when a boy in company with an uncle, landing in New York City. He found a home and employment with Dr. Campfield, of Ameystown, New Jersey, where he cared for the horses, worked in the garden and did all sorts of chores incident to the home of a country doctor. He next went to Burlington county, New Jersey, where he became an apprentice to a wheelwright by the name of Morton, and being discharged from his apprenticeship he engaged in the wheelwright business at Newbald's Corner, New Jersey, for several years. He next located in Vincentown, Burlington county, New Jersey, where he established a wheelwright's shop and he continued in that place and business up to near the time of his death at the probable age of eighty-three years, in 1888. He had thus spent a long, active, as well as useful life in that town and helped in its growth and development. He was a director in the Vincentown National Bank for a number of years. He married, 1845, Maria, daughter of William and Mary (Woolston) Bishop, and they had three children born in Vincentown, as follows: 1. Samuel Oregon, born 1846; died 1908. He was brought up and educated in his native place, and on leaving school obtained a place in the Vincentown Bank, of which his father was a director, and he remained in the employ of the bank, passing through the grades of messenger, clerk, teller and cashier, and after forty years of continuous service he died while holding the position of cashier. Samuel O. Ross married Beulah W., daughter of —— Budd, of Buddtown, New Jersey, and they had one child, William Bishop, born November, 1870, who succeeded his father as cashier of the Vincentown National Bank. William Bishop Ross married Mary Lippincott, daughter of Richard Nesbit. 2. Mary, born 1848; married Rev. Harry Tratt, and they resided in Riverside, California, where a daughter, Ida Tratt, was born. 3. Thomas Woolston (q. v.). John Ross, the father of these children died in Vincentown, New Jersey, 1888.

(H) Thomas Woolston, second son and youngest of the three children of John and Maria (Woolston) Ross, was born in Vincentown, Burlington county, New Jersey, July 1, 1851. He attended the public school and academy at Vincentown and learned the trade of wheelwright in his father's shop, beginning his apprenticeship when he was fifteen years old, in 1866, and he continued as an apprentice and journeyman up to 1882, when he engaged in the same line of business on his own account with excellent results. He continued the personal supervision of the business there established up to 1898, when he retired to assume the duties of postmaster of Vincentown, having been appointed to that office by President McKinley, with every assurance in 1909 that the position was a life tenure if he did not voluntarily resign. He was always active in town affairs and in the councils of the Republican party. He served in the board of registration for five years and holds the position of director of the water board of Vincentown. He is a member of the Baptist church and served as clerk and treasurer of the society. His fraternal affiliation was with the Order of American Mechanics, in which organization he was in high esteem. He married, February, 1872, Cornelia H., daughter of Charles and Martha (Loveland) Haines, of Vincentown, and they had two children, as follows: 1. Frank B., born in Vincentown, December 22, 1873; a pupil in the public schools; a graduate at the College of Pharmacy, Philadelphia, Pennsylvania, in 1893, and he practiced his profession in the drug store of Frank S. Hilliard in Vincentown for four years, when he resigned to take a similar position in a more extensive drug store in Camden, New Jersey. Here he was in charge of the prescription and compounding department and subsequently in one at Chester, Pennsylvania. In 1896 he established the drug business on his own account at Fifty-fourth and Pearl streets, Philadelphia, and made it known as the "Pearl Pharmacy," under which trade mark he built up a large business. He established a second drug store at Fifty-second and Haverford streets, in 1900, to which he gave his personal services. Frank B. Ross married Grace, daughter of Frank S. Hilliard, of Vincentown, who died leaving a son, Donald Ross. 2. Charles H., born in Vincentown, October, 1886, attended the public schools at Vincentown, and Pierce's Business College, Philadelphia, where he was graduated in 1906. From the business college he went to the wholesale store of L. D. Burger, of Philadelphia, where he was made head bookkeeper and placed in charge of the finances of the establishment.

———

BUDD

In writing of the origin and signification of the surname Budd, one investigator of the early history of this family, himself a Budd, says "that statistical facts and definitions of English from translations prove that the name has origin from 'bud,' to increase into beauty and fragrance, and grow into good fruit, and fruitfulness, and as 'buds' must have existed in the garden of Eden, to bring forth fruit, and the fruit thus grown, and eaten by Adam and Eve, gives the combinations of the name a force which has ever influenced the race of Adam from the beginning. It is therefore very natural that we find the name of prominence among the Asiatic races, the Mongolians and the Hindoos as well as among the most enlightened nations of the world. In the early days of the Franks and the Gallic races and the formation of Normandy and the French empire, Jean Budd, a baron of influence, took an active part, his descendants held positions of political and religious influence and were possessors of wealth, and in some one of the political and religious strifes for which the Norman and French people are noted in history, three of the Budd brothers took up the cause of the then weak side in the defence of freedom and religious liberty. Their relations with their forces in power crushed this effort and persecutions commenced. They, to save their heads being taken off by the battle-axe of the executioner, escaped to Normandy and with William the Conqueror landed successfully with their families in England. In Normandy and England they breathed freer and after a time recovered losses, taking

ii—3

a part in the relations of the government and progressive pursuits. Their children married and intermarried and according to information from different sources, one Thomas Budd or John Budd married the sister of a subsequent occupant of the throne and became a prominent member of the Church of England. They had a number of children who as they grew up were fond of adventure, activity and change. 'John Budd, the elder, and Joseph Budd came to this country about the year 1632."

(I) Rev. Thomas Budd, father of the immigrant brothers, figures as the immediate ancestor of the Burlington, New Jersey, Budds. He was rector of Martosh parish in Somersetshire and renounced his living there to become a member of the Society of Friends and a minister among them. In 1661 he was required to take an oath of obedience under the statutes prescribed by James I., "for the better discovering of papist recreants," but while he was willing to "affirm" he refused to be sworn, and for this offense against the dignity of the crown he was indicted, adjudged guilty, and languished out his few remaining years of life in prison; he died there June 22, 1670, still firm in the faith unto which he had declared himself. His sons were Thomas, William, John and James.

(II) Thomas (2), eldest of the sons of Rev. Thomas (1) Budd, was born in England and first came to this country in 1668. Subsequently he returned to England and in 1678 brought over his family. In later years he became one of the principal characters in the early history of the colony of New Jersey. When the first form of government was established he was one of those selected to assist the governor in framing a code of laws for the maintenance of order. He entered into mercantile business in Burlington, lived there until 1690, then removed to Philadelphia and was a merchant in that city until his death in 1697. His will bears date September 9, 1697, and bequeaths to his sons John and Thomas and his daughters Mary and Rose, leaving his eldest son John and his widow Susannah executor and executrix of his estate.

(II) William, son of Rev. Thomas (1) Budd, was born in England and came to New Jersey in 1678, with his eldest brother Thomas, and his other brothers John and James, and their families. He located and became possessed of large tracts of land in West Jersey, largely in Burlington county, where he always lived. He and his brother Thomas were the original locators and proprietors of all the

land included in the township of Pemberton and east and west thereof for two or three miles, and from them most of the titles were devised. Their lands extended from the ridge of hills known as Juliustown and Arney's Mount, several miles wide in a southerly direction to the north branch of Rancocas creek. Although one of the original proprietors of a considerable tract of land in West Jersey, William Budd appears less conspicuously in the early history of the region than his brother Thomas by reason of the fact that he took small part in the political affairs of the colony, preferring the more quiet and to him for more congenial pursuit of farming. Besides this he differed with his brothers in religious views, and if he ever in part accepted the faith of his father and other members of the family he must have renounced it in favor of that of the Protestant Episcopal church. While the name of his brothers Thomas, John and James appear frequently in the records of the Friends' meetings in Burlington, his name appears there only once, and that a mention of his voluntary subscription to the fund for building a new meeting house at Burlington in 1682. In the records of St. Mary's Protestant Episcopal Church at Burlington is found mention of the baptism of the children of William Budd. In his will he left a benefaction to the church, in which he appears to have been a communicant only for a short time. His will bears date March 1, 1707-08, and is recorded in Trenton. The baptismal name of his wife was Ann, but her family name is unknown. She died in 1722, having borne her husband seven children: 1. William, 1680; see post. 2. John, married Hannah Wilson. 3. Thomas, married Deborah Langstaff. 4. Susanna, married Samuel Woolston. 5. Ann, married James Bingham. 6. James, married Sarah Tyndall. 7. Sarah.

(III) William (2), eldest son and child of William (1) and Ann Budd, was born in Northampton township, Burlington county, New Jersey, in 1680, died after November 11, 1725, the date of his will. He was born, lived and died on the original farm on which his father settled, having inherited the same; and he inherited also in a marked degree the characteristics of his father, and led a quiet domestic life at the old home on Arney's mount. He was perhaps the most prolific of any of the Budds of Burlington county, having nine children, and it is said that more than one half of all the persons buried in the old Methodist

Theodore Budd

STATE OF NEW JERSEY.   435

graveyard at Pemberton are his descendants.
On December 2, 1703, William Budd married
Eliza, daughter of Richard Stockton, of
Springfield, New Jersey. Their nine children
were Thomas, see post; William, David, Sus-
annah, Rebecca, Abigail, Elizabeth, Ann and
Mary.

(IV) Thomas (3), son of William (2) and
Eliza (Stockton) Budd, was born on the old
homestead at Arney's Mount in 1708, died
December 15, 1775. He too became well possessed of lands and owned a heavily timbered
tract of land, whereon he built a saw mill and
engaged in extensive lumber operations. He
not only conceived the idea of erecting the
mill and developing the resources of the region,
but as well he caused to be built a number of
dwelling houses for his employees and this
founded Buddtown, named in allusion to the
enterprising founder of the village settlement.
The little settlement soon became a prosperous
center of trade, with its saw, grist and turning
mills, wheelwright, blacksmith and cabinet-
makers' shops, two taverns, three stores and
all the other essential elements of a small municipality. Thomas Budd was one of the most
enterprising men of the township in his time
and was known for his many sterling qualities
and upright character. He made his will July
20, 1775, and died in December following, aged
sixty-seven years. His wife, Jemima (Leeds)
Budd, who died July 17, 1768, was daughter of
Philo Leeds, and by her he had nine children:
1. Philo, born December 14, 1736; died young.
2. Anthony, September 27, 1739; died young.
3. Thomas, December 5, 1741, died young. 4.
Thomas, August 3, 1744; died 1766. 5. Isaiah,
March 13, 1747. 6. Lavinia, April 2, 1749;
died 1838. 7. Ann, July 20, 1751. 8. Isaac,
May 19, 1754; see post. 9. Joseph, October,
1756.

(V) Isaac, son of Thomas (3) and Jemima
(Leeds) Budd, was born in Easthampton township, Burlington county, May 19, 1754, died in
1823. He was a farmer by principal occupation, and like his father was an enterprising
and successful business man. He married
(first) Ruth Woolston, and after her death he
married Ann King. He had three children by
his first and seven by his second wife: 1.
Lydia. 2. Thomas. 3. Jemima, married Rev.
Solomon Sharp. 4. Isaac, see post. 5. Samuel K. 6. John F. 7. Theodosia. 8. Ruth.
9. Sarah Ann. 10. Stacy W.

(VI) Isaac (2), son of Isaac (1) and Ann
(King) Budd, was born in Pemberton, New

Jersey, June 6, 1788, died in 1845. His father
gave him a good farm and his business life was
devoted to agricultural pursuits. He was a
member of the Methodist Episcopal church,
and in politics a Democrat. Mr. Budd married (first) Mary Ann Hayes, by whom he
had six children. He married (second) Ann
Briggs, born 1791, died November 1, 1859,
daughter of George Briggs, and by whom he
had three children. His children: 1. William
H., married Eliza Haines; one child, Michael.
2. Rebecca Ann, born May 18, 1815; died June
30, 1820. 3. Ellen M., died September 26,
1852, aged thirty-seven years. 4. Margaret,
born February 7, 1818; married William S.
Fort. 5. Michael, born December 5, 1819; died
in Ottawa, Illinois, June 6, 1871. 6. Mary
Ann, died aged twenty-two years. Children
by second wife: 7. Alfred, born 1829; killed
by an accident in Pemberton, December 24,
1889. 8. Isaac Henry, born March 21, 1831;
died in Portsmouth, Iowa, December, 1892. 9.
Theodore, see post.

(VII) Theodore, youngest son and child of
Isaac (2) Budd, was born in Southampton
township, November 7, 1833. He received his
earlier literary education in public schools,
then attended the Pennington Seminary, but
was compelled by ill health to leave before the
completion of his course. He then turned to
farming pursuits, in which direction he has
been abundantly successful, having been a large
grower of cranberries for forty-five years,
during which time he has probably cleared and
made productive more swamp land than any
other man in the state of New Jersey. He was
one of the pioneer cranberry growers of the
state. He conducted the business of cranberry
culture with his usual energy, and when success
was achieved he divided his realty with his two
sons, this securing their interest and co-operation in the management of a large estate. Mr.
Budd is also interested in public affairs and
has been chosen to serve in various official
capacities, such as freeholder, member of the
township committee and member of the house
of assembly, having held the latter office during
four years. He was one of the incorporators
and first president of the Pemberton National
Bank, serving in the capacity of president at
the present time. He is also vice-president of
the Mt. Holly Safe Deposit & Trust Company.
In 1856 Theodore Budd married Achsah,
daughter of Thomas and Beulah Edmands, of
Buddtown. Children: 1. Isaac Watson, see
post. 2. Clifford E., see post.

(VIII) Isaac Watson, eldest son of Theodore Budd, was born in Southampton township, Burlington county, New Jersey, January 8, 1858. He received his education in the schools of Pemberton and the South Jersey Institute at Bridgeton. In 1878 he went to Illinois, locating at Crescent City, Iroquois county, where he engaged in mercantile business until January, 1902, when he returned to Pemberton, New Jersey, and engaged in cranberry growing, which line of work he has since followed. He is a director of the Pemberton National Bank. He married (first) June 22, 1880, Ida E. Barber, of Crescent City, Illinois; she died June 6, 1889. Married (second) January 12, 1892, Alma Grace Cast, of Crescent City, Illinois. Children of first wife: 1. Homer T., born February 19, 1882; died in Pemberton, July 10, 1891. 2. Bernice, born November 17, 1883; married Charles Brook Wallace, of Moorestown, New Jersey; one child, Charles Brook Wallace, Jr. 3. Harriet, born June 14, 1885; married Horace Johnson; one child, Robert. 4. Ada, born October 3, 1886; died July 1, 1889. Child of second wife: Gladys, born June 22, 1893.

(VIII) Clifford E., second son of Theodore Budd, was born in Southampton township, Burlington county, New Jersey, February 26, 1861. When eight years of age his parents removed to Pemberton where he was reared. He attended the schools of Pemberton and Hightstown, New Jersey. He resided with his father until his marriage, after which he settled on the farm where he was born and engaged in agricultural pursuits, making cranberry growing a specialty, in which line he has been highly successful. He resided on the farm until 1894, when he removed to Pemberton and now occupies one of the finest houses there. He was for a number of years a director of the Farmers' National Bank of Mt. Holly, and since the organization of the Pemberton National Bank has served as vice-president and director. He is a member of Central Lodge, No. 44, A. F. and A. M., of Vincentown. He is independent in politics. He married, February 2, 1887, Emma Hilton, born near Hartford, New Jersey, January 6, 1860, daughter of Joseph and Hannah (Lippencott) Hilton. Children: 1. Helen, born October 27, 1887, died aged fifteen months. 2. Theodore H., born September 28, 1889; graduate of the Penn Charter School, of Philadelphia, class of 1909. 3. Ethel, born February 13, 1891. 4. J. Norman, born November 18, 1899; died August 18, 1903.

KAIGHN The antiquary finds in the Isle of Man, in the Irish Sea, and only sixteen miles from the mainland of Scotland much of interest that dates back to times when names, deeds, and even legends are unrecorded or mean but little to the present generation. On this little island but little more than twelve miles in breadth and thirty-three miles in length are well preserved today; Castle Rushen, probably the most perfect building of its date extant, founded by Gothard, son of King Orry in 947, and near are the ruins of Rushen Abbey, picturesquely situated and dating from 1154. Besides these are numerous so-called Druidical remains and Runic monuments scattered through the island. To the painter the coast scenery from Manghold head on the east, passing south to Peel on the west, bold and picturesque views present their temptations to the artist to stop and study and imitate. Especially will he be enchanted as he reaches the neighborhood of the Golf, where Spanish head, the south extremity of the island presents a sea front of extreme grandeur. Here is a county unique in history as well as in its grandeur of scenery and well preserved ruins. Here the Welsh kings ruled from the sixth century until the end of the ninth century, when Harold Haarfeger, the Norwegian adventurer, invaded and dethroned the Welsh Kingdom. Tradition tells of Orry the Dane effecting a landing in the beginning of the tenth century, and being adopted by the inhabitants as their king. He is reputed to have been the founder of that excellent and long sustained Manx Constitution still in force on the island. Next come a line of Scandinavian kings only broken by Magnus of Norway when he ceded his right in the island and in the Hebrides to Alexander III. of Scotland in 1266. At the close of Alexander's life the Manx placed themselves under the protection of Edward I. of England, and since that time they have had a constitution and government of their own and a degree of independence of imperial rule. The island has its own Manx church, its own canons and an independent convocation. It has produced learned men and industrious and worthy immigrants who have carried with them sound ideas of religious and political freedom The name Cain, Caine and Kaighn are truly Manx names, and besides Hall Caine have others of the name entitled to recognition.

(I) John Kaighn, also written Kaighin and Kaighan, came to America from the Isle of Man, England, before 1688. He apparently came as a bound apprentice to a carpenter of the name of Thomas Warne, and landed in New York and completed his term of indenture in Perth Amboy, Monmouth county, East New Jersey. The Archives of New Jersey give him as living at the Spottswood's Middle Brook, November 4, 1687, and on July 2, 1688, as patentee of one hundred and forty-five acres of land at Spottswood, South Brook, then unappropriated land to be taken out of Thomas Warne's property in Monmouth county, describing the patentee as "John Kaighen late apprentice to Thomas Warne of Monmouth county, East Jersey," and again on July 7, 1688, "John Kaighin late of Monmouth county, New Jersey, made deed to Robert Ray of same county 145 acres at Spottswood South Brook." The next record is made in Gloucester county, West Jersey,· made September 20-21, 1686, when Samuel Norris conveyed to Robert Farmer a tract comprising two-sevenths of a propriety granted by the trustees of Edward Byllinge, situated in Gloucester county, and surveyed by Samuel Norris in May, 1685, lying and being on the east bank of the Delaware river and secured by John Kaighn through various purchases made by him from divers owners or lessees between 1695 and 1725 until Kaighn owned and possessed a large area comprising several hundred acres one purchase made and deed secured December 14, 1696, of four hundred and fifty-nine acres and thereafter known as Kaighns Point and now the site of the city of Camden. We find John Kaighn in Byfield, Bucks county, Pennsylvania, working at his trade of carpenter when these purchases and sales were made, and he probably lived in Bybury, 1688-96. A grist mill was established on the Newton township tract and he took possession and built a house thereon. He was married, 1693, to Ann, daughter of William Albertson, of Newton township, Gloucester.county, West New Jersey, and widow of Walter Forrest, of Bybury, Bucks county, Pennsylvania, a miller by trade and occupation. John and Ann (Albertson) (Forrest) Kaighn had one child Ann, born in Bybury, June 24, 1694. The mother died July 6, 1694, and the daughter died unmarried in 1715, according to a will executed October 22, 1715, of "Ann (Cain) Kaighn, daughter of John of Gloucester county, bequeathing lands, lots, house, &c. to her father, John Kaighn, and after his death to brothers John and Joseph Kaighn." John Kaighn, the father, was executor of the will which was proved November 27, 1720.

John Kaighn executed a deed June 18, 1685, to John Vance near Salem, West Jersey, miller, for three hundred acres near Salem, also a grist mill on Great Mill Creek. In this deed he is described as "John Kaighn of Byfield, Bucks county, Pennsylvania, late husband of Ann, formerly widow of Walter Fforrest of the same place, miller; and guardian trustee of his daughter by said Ann: Ann Kaighin." This property was deeded by John Vance of Brothers Forest, Salem county, March 26, 1701, to Thomas Killingsworth, of Salem Town, gentleman, being the property bought of John Kaighin, &c. &c. In 1696 John Kaighn married as his second wife Sarah, widow of Andrew Griscom, and sister of John Dale, who lived in Newton township. Andrew Griscom died possessed of a tract of land adjoining that lately purchased by John Kaighn which was also a part of the Norris survey, and in 1723 this property stood in the name of John Kaighn. He built a house on his purchase in Newton township, West Jersey, and it still stands in Camden. By this second marriage John Kaighn became the father of two sons: 1. John (2), born December 30, 1700. 2. Joseph, born December 4, 1702. The mother of these two children died soon after the birth of Joseph, and in 1710 he married Elizabeth Hill, of Burlington, Burlington county, New Jersey, who had no issue. Through a letter addressed "To John Kaighn, Linener, in West New Jersey, nigh on Delaware river side opposite to Philadelphia City America" his mother, Jane Kaighn, then living at Kirk, Isle of Man, under date August 26, 1702, informed him of the death of his father and gave other family news. On the same sheet John Kaighn wrote probably the unfinished copy of the letter he sent in reply to which he stated that he had: "lost two good and loveing wives in a few years' time and had been left alone with two young babes the youngest still at nurse." He was made by legislative action one of the county judges of Gloucester county in 1699, and he served on the bench for three years. On March 7, 1708, the Newton Meeting made him a member of the board of trustees of the meeting, and in 1710 he was sent to Trenton as a representative in the state legislature. On March 3, 1723-24, John Kaighn, of Newton township, Gloucester county, New Jersey, made his will in which he names his wife Elizabeth and sons John and Joseph, leaving his house and lot in Philadelphia to his widow and his real estate in Newton township to his two sons. His will was found June 12, 1724, and his personal property inventoried at £76-13, the inventory being made at the house of deceased. The date of his death, except the year (1724) is not know. His widow married John Wills, of Haddonfield, New Jersey, in 1726.

(II) John (2), eldest son of John (1) and Sarah (Dale) (Griscom) Kaighn, was born in Newton township, Gloucester county, New Jersey, December 30, 1700. He inherited one-half of the real estate left by his father, and the next year after his father's death Joseph conveyed to him all his interest in the real estate devised to them and soon after John reconveyed the entire homestead property to Joseph, who afterward lived there. John married Abigail, daughter of John Henchman, in 1732, and followed the trade of blacksmith for several years, and late in life removed to a farm on Newton creek, where he died in 1749, and was buried in the old Newton graveyard. The children of John and Abigail (Henchman) Kaighn were born in Haddonfield, New Jersey, as follows: 1. Sarah, born 1733, who inherited the Haddonfield estate. 2. Elizabeth, 1736. 3. Samuel, 1737, married 1768, Mary Gerrard. 4. John, 1740. 5. Ann, 1744. Abigail (Henchman) Kaighn married as her second husband Samuel Harrison, of Gloucester, about 1750, and she survived her second husband and died in 1795 at the home of her son-in-law, Richard Edwards, at Taunton Iron Works, Burlington county, New Jersey.

(II) Joseph, second son of John (2) and Sarah (Dale) (Griscom) Kaighn, was born in Newton township in the house erected by his father on Kaighn's Point, December 4, 1702. His mother died soon after his birth, and he was, with his brother John, with a nurse until they were eight and ten years of age respectively, when his father married and their stepmother came into the family and assumed the duties of a mother to the boys, and they were brought up and given a good education. Joseph, in the division of the property between the two brothers, received from John the homestead, and he continued to live there on the homestead, his brother removing to Haddonfield. He married, in 1727, Mary, daughter of James Estaugh, of Philadelphia, and niece of John Estaugh, of Haddonfield. Joseph Kaighn made his will May 7, 1749, by which his estate descended to his children, naming their division as follows: To James part of the estate south of the lane (Kaighn Avenue); to Joseph part of the land south, and to John, Isaac and Elizabeth the land north of the lane. The testator died the same year in which the will

was made (1749), and his five children were all minors. The five children of Joseph and Mary (Estaugh) Kaighn were born in the homestead on Kaighn's Point as follows: 1. Joseph (q. v.). 2. John, who studied medicine and practiced in Newton township; died unmarried when about forty years of age. 3. Isaac, who died before maturity. 4. James, married Hannah Mason. 5. Elizabeth, married Arthur Donaldson. Mary, the widowed mother of these children, married (second) Robert Stevens, of Newton township.

(III) Joseph (2), eldest child of Joseph (1) and Mary (Estaugh) Kaighn, was born in the homestead on Kaighn's Point, Gloucester county, New Jersey, about 1750, and after receiving his portion of the estate of his father he built a house known as the Ferry House, in which he continued to reside, and which is still standing, but is used for other than residential purposes. He married, 1767, Prudence (Rogers) Butcher, a widow, and they had four children born to them in the Ferry House: William, Mary, John and Joseph, the youngest, who alone of the four lived to a mature age.

(IV) Joseph (3), youngest son of Joseph (2) and Prudence (Butcher) Kaighn, was born at Ferry House, Gloucester county, New Jersey, about 1768. He received a good education and became prominent in town, county and state affairs. He was a member of the state legislature, both in the house of assembly and in the council, being re-elected for several terms by the Whig party of which he was a leader in the state. He was an early advocate for granting a charter to build the Camden and Amboy railroad, and largely through his influence the charter was obtained and the road built. He was a charter member of the board of directors and held a directorship during his entire life. He made up the gathering of interested citizens who went over the proposed route before it was surveyed. In the legislature he was also an advocate for building a state prison at Trenton, and a member of the committee in charge of building the same. He was the first to advocate a steam ferry between Kaighn's Point and Philadelphia, and when the Federal Street Ferry Company was organized he was made a member of the board of directors. He died at his home at Kaighn's Point, New Jersey, February 23, 1841, and his widow Sarah, daughter of Joseph Mickle, to whom he was married in 1795, died the next year. The children of Joseph and Sarah (Mickle) Kaighn were born at Ferry House, Camden county, New Jersey, as follows: 1.

John M., married Rebecca, daughter of Benjamin Cooper. 2. Charles, born February 30, 1806; married Mary Cooper, of Woodbury; he was the sixth mayor of Camden, removed to Philadelphia, and died there February 19, 1868. 3. William R., married Rachel Cole, widow of —— Burroughs. 4. Mary, married John Cooper, of Woodbury.

(III) James, second son of Joseph (1) and Mary (Estaugh) Kaighn, was born at the homestead on Kaighn's Point, Gloucester county, New Jersey, about 1752. His share of his father's estate was north of the lane, and he continued to live on the homestead. He laid out his property in lots in 1812, and that was the first plot so laid out, and now the entire Kaighn estate is divided up and built upon. The children of James Kaighn were born at the homestead on Kaighn's Point as follows: 1. Isaac. 2. Mary, who died young. 3. John (q. v.). 4. Elizabeth, married Jonathan Knight, in 1797. 5. James. 6. Hannah, married Benjamin Digdale. 8. Sarah. 9. Mary. 10. Ann, 1795; died in 1880. 11. and 12. Charity and Grace (twins), both deceased.

(IV) John, second son and third child of James Kaighn, was born in the homestead on Kaighn's Point, Camden county, New Jersey, about 1785, where he followed the occupation of farming, as had his ancestors from 'the time of the settlement of the Point and the building of the homestead by his great-grandfather, John Kaighn. He married Elizabeth Bartram, great-grandfather of John Bartram (see Bartram family following this sketch). John and Elizabeth (Bartram) Kaighn had eight children born at Kaighn's Point, Camden county, New Jersey, as follows: James, Joseph (q. v.), John Elizabeth, Rebecca, Ann Mary, Hannah.

(V) Joseph (4), second son of John and Elizabeth (Bartram) Kaighn, was born at Kaighn's Point, Camden county, New Jersey, 1810. He was brought up on the homestead farm and later in life worked a second farm at Chew's Landing, where he was living during his declining years and where he died. He was a birthright member of the Society of Friends, and he was married by Friends ceremony to Susannah, daughter of Jacob and Rachel (Troth) Evans, and granddaughter of Nathan and Sybella Evans, and of William and Esther (Borton) Troth. Susannah Evans was born twelfth month sixth day, 1813. The children of Joseph and Susannah (Evans) Kaighn: 1. Amos Evans (q. v.). 2. John, born near Marlton; died young. 3. Elizabeth,

born near Marlton; died young. 4. Rebecca, born at Chew's Landing; married Hamilton Haines, of Burlington, New Jersey, and lived near Haddonfield, where three children, Joseph, Wilber and Bertha Haines, were born.

(VI) Amos Evans, eldest child of Joseph (4) and Susannah (Evans) Kaighn, was born at Kaighn's Point, Camden county, New Jersey, July 15, 1838. About 1840 the family removed to Chew's Landing. He attended the district school and Westtown Friends Boarding School, and worked with his father on his farm at Chew's Landing until 1868, when he carried on the Hunt farm, adjoining Chew's Landing, 1868-76. He then purchased a farm near Ellisburg, and in 1890 removed to Moorestown, built a house and retired from farm life. He was a birthright member of the Society of Friends, and a member and elder in Friends Meeting at Moorestown, New Jersey. He married, in 1867, Lucy, daughter of Samuel and Elizabeth (Troth) Engle, of Medford, New Jersey. Samuel Engle was born 11th mo. 12th 1803, and his wife Elizabeth was a daughter of Samuel and Edith (Lippincott) Nott. The children of Amos Evans and Lucy (Engle) Kaighan were born at Chew's Landing, New Jersey, as follows: 1. Elizabeth Engle, born March 7, 1870, married, October 10, 1901, Dr. William Martin, of Bristol, Bucks county, Pennsylvania, and their daughter, Edith Kaighn Martin, was born July 3, 1905. 2. Joseph, September 30, 1872, attended the district school and Westtown Friends Boarding School, was a student at law in the office of Thomas E. French, of Camden, was admitted to the bar as an attorney and as a councillor-at-law; he is (1909) living with his parents at Moorestown, and practicing law in Camden, unmarried.

(The Bartram Line).

John Bartram, the "father of American botany," was born in Marple, Delaware county, Pennsylvania, March 23, 1699. He began his studies with the purpose in view of taking up the practice of medicine, but changed the course to the science of botany as applied to American plants. He began his work in classification early in life, and his botanical garden was the first of the kind in America. He was commended by Linnaeus as the most accomplished botanist of the world. His research was made through long excursions in different zones, and his collection was most rare. His reputation in England was such as to command him to the Royal family and George III. made him his American botanist. The title of the great work illustrates his versatile labors and journeyings. It was published in 1751 and entitled "Observations on Inhabitants, Climate, Soil, Rivers, Productions, Animals and Other Matters Worthy of Notice, Made by Mr. John Bartram in his travels from Pennsylvania to Onondaga, Oswego and the Lake Ontario in Canada." He married, and at least one of his sons left descendants but not the one who evidently inherited his genius as well as became the possessor of his collection and added to his accumulation of specimens and followed out his projects of investigation mapped out before he died, which event occurred September 22, 1777. This son, William Bartram, was born in Kingsessing, Pennsylvania, February 9, 1729, and was bred in the botanical atmosphere in which the father had accomplished so great work and left so valuable and tangible records of his accomplishments. William published in 1792 "Travels through North & South Carolina, Georgia, East and West Florida, the Cherokee County, the Extensive Territories of the Muscogules or Creek Confederacy, and the Country of the Chocktaws." He aided Alexander Wilson in his scientific work, his ornithological studies being very extended. He published a memoir of his father and made a list of American birds. He lived alone with his specimens of living plants that made up the greatest botanical garden in America at the time, and was visited only by learned men anxious to converse with him and to study from his collections. He never married, carried his eccentricities to his dress which was primitive to an extraordinary degree, his outside clothing being made entirely of leather. He conversed with the ease and politeness of nature's noblemen, in spite of his hermit life and avoidance of the society around him. He died July 22, 1833, only six years from the century mark. The catalogue of the University of Pennsylvania gives two of the name among its graduates: Moses Bartram, A. B., 1782; A. M., 1785; B. M., 1786; M. D. 1790, which would give his birth about 1762. He is put down as a physician and druggist. In the class of 1783 we find George Bartram, born 1767, died in Philadelphia, May 8, 1840, A. B. 1783; A. M., 1786; alderman of the city of Philadelphia, and president of the select council, 1809-11. He was a brother of Moses, and they were both grandsons of John, the botanist, and nephews of William, the botanist, who had a brother Moses, born 1737 or 1741.

MOUNTAIN Although the Mountain family are among the later emigrants to this country, they belong to the same stalwart stock from which is derived so much of the best among the families of the early and original settlers of the old colonies, their name being for centuries traceable among the old records of Yorkshire.

(I) The first of the family of whom we have any definite knowledge as the progenitor of the American branch is Joseph William Mountain, born in Yorkshire in 1764, died there in 1834. Shortly after his marriage he removed with his bride to London, and there spent the remainder of his life, all his children being born in that city. He married, in Yorkshire, Catharine Ann Slater, born in 1769, died in 1854. Their children were: 1. Catharine Ann, born in 1789; died in 1870; married Robert Edward Holme and had five children: Elizabeth, Catharine, Robert, Edward, Robert Mountain, born January 17, 1836, married Helen James and had five children, of whom only one, Frank James Holme, born 1884, reached maturity. 2. Joseph William, born 1804, died 1855; married Miriam Welsh, but had no children. 3. John, referred to below. 4. William, born about 1808, died 1856; married Hannah Pearsall, and had several children. 5. Hannah, born in 1812, died in 1892; married, in 1837, Albert Paine, removed to Dische, Germany, and had two children: Catharine, born 1839; died 1865; and Albert, born 1841, who married. They had eight other children who died in infancy.

(II) John, son of Joseph William and Catharine Ann (Slater) Mountain, was born in London, January 31, 1807, died there in 1893. He married, February 6, 1837, Mary Ann Furmage, born in Wandsworth, Surrey, England, November 14, 1806, daughter of William and Ann Furmage, and granddaughter of James and Mary Ann (Wadbrook) Furmage. William Furmage, her father, was born about 1782, and died 1854; and his wife, Ann (Hall) Furmage, was born about 1780, died about 1850. Her grandfather, James Furmage, was born about 1752, died in 1827; and her grandmother, Mary Ann (Wadbrook) Furmage, was born about 1751, died in 1825. The children of John and Mary Ann (Furmage) Mountain were: 1. John Joseph, born December 17, 1837, died in 1900. 2. Cleeves, January 16, 1839, still living. 3. Joseph William, April 19, 1843, died in the civil war, in 1863.

5. Mary Ann Slater, April 3, 1844, married, June 3, 1867, Albert Farnam Tucker, and had one child, Albert Mountain Tucker, born April 20, 1868, died December 12, 1899; married, October 31, 1895, ———. 6. Frederick, referred to below. 7. Robert Edward, January 28, 1848, died in 1849. All these children were born in London.

(III) Frederick, sixth child and fifth son of John and Mary Ann (Furmage) Mountain, was born in London, England, January 27, 1846, died in East Orange, New Jersey, April 16, 1907. Emigrating to this country he lived for awhile in Brooklyn, Long Island, and finally settled in East Orange. He married Irene Adelia Tallman, born November 1, 1848, and had two children: 1. Worrall Frederick, referred to below. 2. Milton Tallman, born January 23, 1893.

(IV) Judge Worrall Frederick, eldest child of Frederick and Irene Adelia (Tallman) Mountain, was born in Brooklyn, Long Island, March 10, 1877, and is now living at 113 North Walnut street, East Orange, New Jersey. His father removing to East Orange shortly after his birth, he was sent for his early education to the public schools of that place, from which he entered the Newark Academy, and after leaving that institution went to Princeton University, where he received his Bachelor of Science degree in 1900, and three years later his degree of Master of Science. He then took a course in the New York Law School, from which he obtained his LL. B. degree, and after this entered the office of Halsey M. Barrett, Esquire, and later of A. Q. Keasbey & Sons, where he read law, receiving his admission to the New Jersey bar as an attorney in November, 1904, and as a counsellor in 1907. September 1, 1908, he entered into partnership with Judge Thomas L. Raymond, Andrew Van Blarcom and Theodore McC. Marsh. He is a Republican in politics, was appointed judge of the district court of the city of East Orange on June 1, 1909, by Governor Fort. He was formerly a member of the Essex Troop, and now the Lawyers Club of Newark, the Princeton Club of New York, and the Republican Club of East Orange. He is a member of the North Orange Baptist Church. He married, June 3, 1908, in East Orange, Ethel Marion, daughter of John and Jean (Paulson) Spohr, of 121 North Grove street, East Orange. Of this marriage a son, Worrall Frederick, Jr., born June 28, 1909.

The Boggs family of New Jersey BOGGS belong to that group of Irish patriots who came over to this country in the early part of the eighteenth century, making homes for themselves at first spreading out into New Jersey, Maryland and Virginia and giving to the new nation some of the best blood and brawn that have gone towards making up its special characteristics and genius.

(I) Ezekiel Boggs, founder of the family under consideration, came from Ireland and settled in Delaware, where he left behind him one son James, who is referred to below, and one daughter, Rebecca, who married a Mr. Rish, of Philadelphia.

(II) James, son of Ezekiel Boggs, was born January 22, 1740, but whether in this country or in Ireland is uncertain. Coming from Delaware to Philadelphia, he studied medicine, and then settled in Shrewsbury, Monmouth county, New Jersey, where he remained until the breaking out of the revolution when he joined the British army as a surgeon, and continued with it until the close of the war, when he went to Halifax, Nova Scotia, where he lived until his death at a very advanced age. He was highly esteemed as a physician, and manifested great interest in the promotion of the science of medicine. He became a member of the Medical Society of New Jersey the year after its organization and was an influential member until the breaking out of the war. His manners were pleasant and gentlemanly and he took great delight in his old age in relating incidents and adventures which occurred in his personal history, more particularly when the British were in possession of New York and his family living for the time near Perth Amboy, whom he could only visit by stealth. Dr. James Boggs married Mary, daughter of Robert Hunter Morris, of New Jersey, and left a large family behind him, many of his descendants being now found in Halifax, Prince Edward Island, and the provinces of Lower Canada. He left, however, five children, three sons and two daughters in this country, from whom have come the New Jersey branch of the family. Among their children were: 1. Robert, referred to below. 2. James, who went into business in New York City, where he became the senior member of the old firm of Boggs, Thompson & Company; his children were: Mary, married a Mr. Ray;

Julia, married Lewis Livingston. 3. A son who died young in Wilmington, Delaware (III) Robert, eldest child of Dr. James and Mary (Morris) Boggs, was brought up together with his other brothers and sisters whom his father had left behind him in New-Jersey, in the home of his uncle, Judge Morris, of New Brunswick, with whom he studied and practiced law, spending his life in that city where he was at one time clerk of the United States district court. He died in New Brunswick, in 1831. He married (first) his cousin, Mary Morris, by whom he had one child, Robert, who married Jane Dunham, and had three children. He married (second) Mary, the sister of James Lawrence, United States navy, who commanded the frigate "Chesapeake" in her engagement with the 'Shannon." She bore him three children: 1. Brenton, of the United States navy. 2. Mary, married J. S. Blauvelt, of New Brunswick. 3. Charles Stuart, referred to below. He married (third) Maria Brenton, born in Halifax, Nova Scotia, in 1780, died in New Brunswick, New Jersey, in 1866. They had one child: Edward Brenton, referred to below.

(IV) Charles Stuart, youngest child and second son of Robert and Mary (Lawrence) Boggs, was born in New Brunswick in 1811, died in 1888. Entering the United States navy as a midshipman in 1826, he became lieutenant in 1837, served in Commodore Connor's squadron in the Mexican war, in April, 1862, distinguished himself under Farragut at New Orleans, and was the same year raised to the rank of captain. In 1870 he became a rear admiral, and three years later was retired.

(IV) Edward Brenton, the only child of Robert and Maria (Brenton) Boggs, was born in New Brunswick, New Jersey, December 7, 1821, died May 9, 1904. He was educated at the public schools, and then graduated from the General Theological Seminary in New York City, and was then ordained priest in the Protestant Episcopal church. He graduated from Rutgers College in 1842 and later received the degree of D. D. He married Elizabeth Dunham, daughter of George Deshler, of Easton, Pennsylvania, and his wife, Catharine (Dunham) Deshler, of New Brunswick. Elizabeth Dunham (Deshler) Boggs was born in New Brunswick, New Jersey, December 26, 1822, died in 1903. She bore her husband four children: 1. George Brenton, married Hannah Thompson, of Bloomsburg, Pennsylvania, and has three children: Edward Thompson, Frank Thompson, who married, and is

now a captain of engineers in the United States army, and Jeannette Thompson. 2. Charles Deshler, married Caroline Coles, and has four children: Clara, married William Lull, a professor at Yale University, and has one child, Dorothy, Elizabeth Deshler, Edward Brenton, married a Miss Chamberlain and now lives at Cleveland, Ohio, and William Coles. 3. Francis Cranston, who is also married. 4. Herbert, referred to below.

(V) Herbert, youngest child of the Rev. Edward Brenton and Elizabeth Dunham (Deshler) Boggs, was born in Swedesborough, New Jersey, June 3, 1853, and is now living in Newark, New Jersey. For his early education he was sent to the public schools of New Brunswick, and then he entered Rutgers College, graduating therefrom in 1873. After his graduation he went into the office of Parker & Keasby, where he read law, and was admitted to the New Jersey bar as attorney in November, 1876, and as counsellor in November, 1879. He then started in for himself, specializing in municipal law, and becoming the city attorney for Newark, during the years 1890 to 1893 and again appointed in 1909 to the same office. Mr. Boggs is a Democrat, but other than the attorneyship mentioned above he has held no political office. He belongs to the Lawyers' Club of Newark. He is a communicant of the Protestant Episcopal church. He married, May 9, 1893, in Newark, Frances May, daughter of Henry and Fanny (Van Buren) Le Viness, of New York City, whose two brothers are Edward and Henry, and her sister Charlotte, who married Henry Van Bronson. The child of Herbert and Fanny May (Le Viness) Boggs is Helen Cranston, born in Newark, September 21, 1894.

HINE

Unlike so many of the families of New Jersey that have come into the state from Europe by way of the New England colonies, the Hine family of Orange travelled from Connecticut to the Ohio valley and then returned and found a permanent home in Essex county, this reversing the usual current of emigration which passed through New Jersey on its way to the west. But little is known about the family on the other side of the Atlantic. The earliest record is in 1548 when a certain John Hinde was appointed J. C. P. of England, that is practitioner of the common law (juris communis) or in other words as we should say today, was admitted to the English bar as attorney. Family tradition has it that the family is of Scotch-Irish descent and emigrated to this country during the Commonwealth, and this is supported by the earliest records we have of the family in this country.

(I) Thomas Hine, founder of the family, settled in Milford, Connecticut, and had there a home lot and a two acre meadow adjoining, January 28, 1646. In 1655 he bought land at Derby, although he does not seem to have removed thither, except possibly for a time, as January 22, 1676, he drew lot number 8 in Milford, and on the tax list of 1688 he is assessed £96. 5s, while his sons John and Stephen were assessed respectively £38 and £18. His will, proved at New Haven, was written May 9, 1694. He had at least four sons and probably other children. The sons were: 1. John. 2. George. 3. Stephen. 4. Samuel, who is referred to below. The last two mentioned are the only children that remained in Milford.

(II) Samuel, son of Thomas Hine, lived in Old Milford but there is very little known about him except what can be gathered from an old account book kept by his son George, referred to below, from an entry in which we learn that Samuel and his wife went to live with their son, May 10, 1769. Samuel Hine died December 23, 1771, and his wife December 10, 1773.

(III) George, son of Samuel Hine, was born in Old Milford, and followed the occupations of farmer, teamster, fisherman and merchant. His old account book is full of interesting examples, of which the following is a fair example: "January 13th, 1755. Then reckoned with Moses Malory and cleared of all accounts from ye beginning of ye world to this day. as witness our hands." George Hine and his family removed from Old to New Milford some time before October 1, 1793, and was probably among the first settlers of that place. From the fact that her name is signed with his to a contract for a fishing privilege at Fowler's island on Stratford river, it is supposed that the name of George's wife was Jean. His children were: 1. Thomas. 2. Samuel. 3. George Jr. 4. Daniel, who is referred to below. There may have been others.

(IV) Daniel, son of George and Jean Hine, was born in Old Milford in 1750. While in Old Milford he was a fisherman and leased for ninety-nine years a privilege of fishing at Fowler's island at the mouth of Stratford river on Long Island Sound. In May,

1795, he removed from New Milford to Warren, Litchfield county, Connecticut, where he lived for eleven years. In the spring of 1805, hearing glowing accounts of the western reserve, he sent his son David to accompany Erastus Carter and others on a tour of inspection. The journey, both ways, was made afoot, and the report was so favorable that the following September two of his sons, Daniel and Hezekiah, emigrated with others to Johnstown, Ohio, and in the succeeding spring, Daniel Sr. followed with the remainder of the family. He remained in Johnstown till the ensuing December, and then moved on to Canfield, Ohio. Here, two years later, he moved into the home of his son David, on the same farm that is now owned and occupied by his niece, Mrs. Betsy Comstock. His son Hezekiah, having located in Shalersville, Portage county, Ohio, Daniel, being better pleased with that situation, moved thither in February, 1810, and settled finally not far from the centre of the township, where he lived until his death, September 16, 1828. Daniel Hine was married three times, but all his children were by his first wife. About 1775 he married (first) Mary Stone, of Old Milford, who died in Shalersville, February 5, 1812, at the age of fifty-six years. His second wife, Eunice (Sutliff) (Crosby) Hine, the widow of Timothy, died July 17, 1817. His third wife, Phoebe (Clark) Hine, was a native of Williamstown, Vermont, and died aged seventy-two years. The children of Daniel and Mary (Stone) Hine were: 1. Daniel, born May 30, 1776, died January 19, 1858; married Laura Finney. 2. Abel, September 11, 1778, died September 21, 1855; married a Miss Frelove. 3. David, who is referred to below. 4. Polly, September 27, 1784, died October 29, 1859; married Augustus Adams. 5. Hezekiah, May 29, 1789, died July 21, 1867; married Mary Atwater. 6. Elizabeth, February 16, 1790, died February 14, 1867; married Thaddeus Bradley. 7. Lyman, September 9, 1792, died December 16, 1870; married Sabina Crosby. 8. Abigail, August 7, 1795, died March, 1865; married Daniel Burroughs. All these children, save the last who was born in Warren, were born in Old Milford.

(V) David, third child and son of Daniel and Mary (Stone) Hine, was born in Old Milford, Connecticut, December 9, 1780, died in Canfield, Ohio, April 19, 1856. He was fifteen when his father went to Warren, Litchfield county, and twenty-five, when April, 1805, he set out with Erastus Carter, Daniel Beach and John Morris, for Johnstown, where he bought land for $3.00 an acre, and after building a small shanty returned home with his report to his father. He then guided his brothers, Daniel and Hezekiah, out to the new lands and returned home again with the team, remaining in Warren for that winter, and in February, immediately after his marriage, setting out on a final trip to Johnstown, accompanied by about sixty of their friends and relatives. In the following autumn he settled on the farm in Canfield spoken of above. May 3, 1810, David Hine was commissioned by the governor of Ohio Captain of the Third Company, First Battalion, Second Regiment, Fifth Brigade and Fourth Division of the Ohio state militia. As such he served for five years and was in active service during the War of 1812, his regiment forming a part of the land forces at Cleveland, during Perry's naval engagement and victory, September 6, 1812. After the war he became conspicuous in civil affairs, being commissioned May 13, 1822, by Governor Allen Tremble, justice of the peace, and in many ways interesting himself in politics. David Hine married, February 20, 1806, Achsah, daughter of Benjamin Sackett, of Warren, born there January 21, 1786, died in Canfield, Ohio, March 23, 1831. She bore her husband at least eight children of whom one, David, is referred to below.

(VI) David (2), eighth child of David (1) and Achsah (Sackett) Hine, was born in Canfield, Ohio, August 16, 1822, died in Washington, District of Columbia, January 12, 1872. He graduated from Williams College, Massachusetts, in 1850, taught in the academy at Warren, Connecticut, for four years, and in the autumn of 1854 moved out to Ohio and accepted a position as principal of the Mahoney Academy. He here became a neighbor and later a warm friend of General James A. Garfield, through whose influence soon after the breaking out of the civil war he was appointed to a position in the office of the second auditor of the treasurer in Washington, which he held until his death. While at college he boarded with A. M. Bridges, a descendant of Benjamin, son of Edward Bridges, of Topsheld, Massachusetts, in 1664. Here he made the acquaintance of Harriet Amelia, daughter of Samuel Bridges, of Williamstown, born April 20, 1828, died in Washington, October 4, 1874, whom he married September 24, 1850. The children of David and Harriet Amelia (Bridges) Hine were: 1. Helen Blanche, born December 25, 1851, died October 7, 1883. 2.

Edwin Warren, who is referred to below. 3. Charles Augustus, May 2, 1857, died young. 4. Irene Bridges, July 12, 1861, died 1862. 5. Irene Bridges, March 23, 1862, died 1866.

(VII) Edwin Warren, second child and eldest son of David (2) and Harriet Amelia (Bridges) Hine, was born in Warren, Litchfield county, Connecticut, March 17, 1854, and is now living at 112 Park avenue, Orange, New Jersey. He was in his infancy when his parents went to Ohio, and he was thirteen when they went to Washington, where he received his education in the public and high schools, obtaining a position in a stationery store in Washington and retaining it until he accepted a position as entry clerk with the firm of George A. Olney & Company, stationers, with whom he remained until their failure. In 1872 he removed to Orange and was for two years with Thomas P. Bayes, dealer in books and stationery, and in 1874 started for himself in the flour and feed business in the old academy building on Main street, near Cone and Day. In 1877 he bought out the old firm of W. B. Tichenor & Company who were in the same line of business. In 1888 he became interested in the Harvey Steel Company, and in the following year became a director of that corporation, being now the only survivor of the original board of five. In May, 1890, together with Mr. Harvey, he organized the American Washer and Manufacturing Company, of which he was elected and remained for many years the president. He now sold out his old flour and feed business, and in 1903 became the secretary of the public service corporation of New Jersey. In 1878 he was elected for a term of three years to represent the first ward of Orange in the common council, and being the only Republican in that body at the time was given the sobriquet of the "Lone Star." In 1879 he was first elected to the board of chosen freeholders, of which body he continued a member until 1887. In 1884 he was a candidate for the office of sheriff, and in 1887 was elected to that office by a majority of 2,600. He discharged the duties of this office "without fear or favor, retiring in 1890 with a clean record and the hearty good wishes of his fellow citizens, irrespective of party."

Colonel Hine began his military career in 1882, as the chief organizer of the Orange rifles of which he was elected the first lieutenant. January 11, 1886, he was commissioned as first lieutenant and adjutant of the third battalion of the National Guard of the

state of New Jersey, by Governor Leon Abbett. This position he held for five years,
until the reorganization of the first brigade,
which resulted in the consolidation of the
first, second, and third battalions, forming the
second regiment. June 25, 1892, Lieutenant
Hine was commissioned as captain and judge-
advocate of the second regiment under Colonel
J. Vreeland Moore. At the election which
preceded this commission, Mr. Hine had been
nominated for one of the majorships, and it
is an indication of his deserved popularity that
he secured for it all of the votes of the Essex
county battalion. April 25, 1893, Colonel
Moore was retired on his own application,
Lieutenant-colonel Samuel V. S. Muzzy was
promoted to his place, and Captain Hine was
chosen lieutenant-colonel to fill the vacancy.
November 8, 1897, Colonel Muzzy retired as
brevet brigadier-general, and there was but
one man it was felt who could take his place,
namely, Lieutenant-Colonel Hine. Consequently his election to the head of the regiment gave general satisfaction as he was
greatly liked by both officers and men, and
when his commission was issued, bearing date
of December 7, 1897, it was a time of great
rejoicing in the regiment. He had hardly
seated himself firmly in the saddle and grasped
the reins before he was called upon to prove
the trust reposed in him. The "Maine" was
blown up, the Spanish began capturing prizes
in the Carribean and Colonel Hine was among
the first in the country to offer his regiment
for active service. During the war the regiment was stationed first at Sea Girt, and then
at Jacksonville, Florida, and it was mainly
due to the efficient carrying out of his instructions by Colonel Hine that the regiment won
its place and reputation as the best in the
camp, and received from the old Confederate
war-veteran and then commanding officer,
General Fitzhugh Lee, the compliment,
"Thank God, we have one regiment equipped
for service, but that is the way New Jersey
always sends out her soldiers." May 2, 1899,
came the order of Governor Voorhees disbanding the Second Regiment and Colonel Hines was
retired. In 1902, as a result of the great fire
in Paterson, the Fifth Regiment came into
being, and from the very first it was felt and
said that there was only one man for its commanding officer. The feeling of resentment
over the disbanding of the Second Regiment
was strong. It was felt that its commanding
officer, Colonel Edwin Warren Hine, had acted
the part of a gallant officer and had handled

his regiment with rare discretion and skill in
the south, and not only among the officers of
the south regiment identified with the new, but
also among the people of northern New Jersey
as well, it was most strongly indicated and
urged that the command of the new Fifth was
Colonel Hine's by right. The devotion of the
officers of the Second Regiment to their commanding officer had been a matter of comment
throughout the entire Seventh army corps, and
while there was some discussion about other
officerships in the regiment, September 19,
1902, Colonel Hine was unanimously elected
to the command which he has held ever since.
From 1883 to 1886 Colonel Hine was chairman
of the Essex county Republican committee,
while for three years he was the chairman of
the Orange Republican committee and for
twelve years its treasurer. He is also an
active member of the New England Society.
He is a member of Union Lodge, No. 11, F.
and A. M., of Orange, and also past master.
He belongs to the Union Club of Newark, to
the Lotus Club of New York, and to the
Hamilton Club of Paterson. He attends the
First Presbyterian Church of Orange. Colonel
Hine received a most unusual honor at the
time of the Hudson-Fulton celebration by
being selected, over the heads of officers of
higher rank, to be the personal representative
of the governor on the official reviewing stand
at Fifth avenue and Forty-second street, during the military parade, September 30, 1909.
Colonel Edwin Warren Hine married,
March 23, 1874, Nellie, daughter of David and
Margaret (Rockafeller) Sturtevant, a descendant of the early settlers of Plymouth,
Massachusetts, born in 1854. Their children
are: 1. Helen Blanche, born February 15, 1876,
died in infancy. 2. Walter Robbins, December 1, 1877, married Annabell Bagley, and has
one son, Walter Robbins Jr., born May 6,
1908. 3. Marguerite, September 20, 1879,
died March 17, 1885. 4. James Sayers, born
July 14, 1882.

GEORGE   The George family of Newark
has already made a name and
place for itself in the industrial
world of Newark, although its existence in
this country has only been for two generations.

(1) Christian George, the founder of the
family in this country was born in France, June
25, 1847, died in Newark, New Jersey, July
16, 1898. By his wife, Sophia (Vollmer)
George, who survives him and is now living

at 394 Eighteenth avenue, he had three children: Edward C., see forward; Henry P.,
Louis F.

(II) Edward C., the eldest child of Christian and Sophia (Vollmer) George, was born
in Newark, New Jersey, August 1, 1877, and
is now living in that city. After attending the
public schools where he was sent for his early
education, he entered the New York University Law School. He read law in the office
of Charles A. Feick, Esquire, and was admitted to the New Jersey bar in June, 1899, as
attorney, and as counsellor in November, 1908.
He has turned his attention to the specialty of
real estate law, and he is rapidly winning for
himself a name and place as one of the most
judicious and acute of the younger lawyers
who are dealing with that subject. In politics
Mr. George is a Republican, and for four
years, from 1901 to 1905, was one of the commissioners of public school education in Newark. He is a member of Cosmos Lodge, No.
106, Free and Accepted Masons of Newark,
and also a member of Lodge No. 21, Benevolent and Protective Order of Elks. He married, June 26, 1907, in Newark, Pauline B.,
daughter of August E. and Pauline Kleeman,
of 493 South Sixteenth street, Newark, whose
children are: August M., Pauline B., Emil H.
and Amelia. Edward C. and Pauline B.
(Kleeman) George have no children.

McCARTER   "That the bearer John Mc-
Carter is a single Person &
was born in the parish of
Gaughboyn & County of Donegal in Ireland
of honest Protestant Parents & from his infancy behaved Soberly and inoffensively & at
his leaving this Kingdom a regular member of
the dissenting congregation of St. Johnstown
& whereas he designs to transport himself to
the plantations in America to improve his
worldly circumstances he is hereby recommended to the blessing and protection of
Almighty God and to regards of all Christian
People whom it may concern as a person fit
to be entertained and encouraged. This is
certified and recommended at St. Johnstown
August 15th, 1774, by Thos Bond. V. D. M."
(I) Such was the testimonial brought to
this country by the founder of the McCarter
family of New Jersey, when he left the home
of his father, Robert McCarter, in the small
hamlet of Carrigan's in the parish and county
above mentioned. Landing in Philadelphia in
1774, in his own words, "consigned with a
regular bill of lading, like a bale of merchan-

dise to a friend of his father's family residing
there." When he came over he was about
twenty-one, and for a short time taught in
Delaware, then enlisted in the revolutionary
army and after the war settled in Mendham,
Morris county, New Jersey. He began his
revolutionary service in 1776 when he enlisted
as a volunteer in Colonel Craighead's Delaware rifle corps, with which he fought at Wilmington and Trenton. In 1777 he became a
commissary under General Wayne, and later
under General Lamb and General Hazen.
Finally he was at West Point and Philadelphia.
For these services his widow was granted a
pension dating from March 4, 1836, which she
received until her death. In 1784 he entered
into a mercantile connection with Messrs. Grier
and Brooks which continued for several years
until his health failing he went to the country near Mendham, where he purchased some
iron works and ran them successfully until
1794 when he lost everything in a freshet.
He rebuilt but his works were washed away
twice more and the failure of some friends
with whom he had left for safety a large sum
of money caused him to go into bankruptcy.
At this juncture he found a warm friend in
Governor Bloomfield, who appointed him surrogate of Morris county, and later a master
in chancery. Still later he became clerk of
Morris county, and held that position until his
death. Mr. McCarter took a warm and active
interest in public affairs, was an ardent ad-
mirer of the person and a fervid advocate of
the principles of Thomas Jefferson, and was
a frequent contributor to the newspapers on
political topics, his articles over the signature
of "The old man of the Mountain" attracting
much notice and exerting much influence on
the public mind. John McCarter had been
well educated and even before coming to this
country had shown evidences of literary ability and was at one time connected with the
Londonderry Journal, a semi-weekly still in
existence and one of the most influential papers
in the north of Ireland. In addition to his
frequent communications to the press on political topics, Mr. McCarter wrote many odes
and addresses for public occasions and his
letters are many of them literary gems. He
died at Morristown in 1807, and the local
paper of that day contains a very full account
of his life, public services and business career.
November 21, 1786, John McCarter married
Agnes, daughter of George and Mary (Boyd)
Harris, and granddaughter of William and
Elizabeth (Blair) Harris, who came to this

country from Ireland in 1742. She had one aunt, her father's sister, Isabel, who married her cousin, Robert Harris, M. D., who lived in 1791 in Spruce street, Philadelphia, was one of the founders of the College of Physicians and Surgeons and one of the physicians who remained in the city during the yellow fever epidemics of 1793 and 1795. Her father died February 23, 1790, at Hackettstown, New Jersey, where he owned a mill and left some property. Her mother, Mary (Boyd) Harris, died in 1780, and was the daughter of Robert and Janet (McAllister). Boyd, who came from Scotland. Agnes (Harris) McCarter was born in New Vernon, New Jersey, October 21, 1769, died at Morristown, February 8, 1851. She was "a woman of high principle, strict integrity, unflinching fortitude and cool, calm judgment, * * * somewhat stern and reserved in manner, but warm of heart and full of kindness, not only to her own relatives, but to every deserving person with whom she came in contact." The children of John and Agnes (Harris) McCarter were: 1. Mary Eleanor, born April 1, 1789, died October 7, 1868, after "a long life filled with loving service to her family, so whole-hearted and so simple that no idea of self-sacrifice ever occurred to her or to any of those she served." 2. Martha Isabella, born March 5, 1791, died May 2, 1845; married, late in life, Luther Y. Howell, of Newton, New Jersey, but left no children. 3. Robert Harris, who is referred to below. 4. Benjamin Ludlow, born December 24, 1796, who died unmarried at the age of thirty-two. 5. George Harris, born November 5, 1797, died 1843, he married (first) Hannah Maria, daughter of George Rorbach, of Newton, and (second) his cousin, Martha Lyon Ludlow. 6. John, born January 26, 1799, died October 31, 1864; married Mary, the aunt of the Hon. Henry C. Kelsey, at one time secretary of state of New Jersey; their youngest son was the Hon. Ludlow McCarter, judge of the Essex common pleas. 7. James Jefferson, born December 14, 1800, died February 17, 1872; spent most of his life in Charleston, South Carolina; married (first) Elizabeth, daughter of Jonathan and sister of the Hon. George S. Bryan, judge of the United States district court of South Carolina, and (second) his first wife's younger sister, Mary Caroline. 8. Daniel Stuart, born December 2, 1803, died August, 1868; married Maria Hayden, of Georgia. 9. Eleanor Cordelia, born March 2, 1807, died July 27, 1883; married Dr. Harvey Hallock.

(II) Robert Harris, third child and eldest son of John and Agnes (Harris) McCarter, was born at Mendham, March 16, 1793, died March 8, 1851. His father's death, when he was fifteen, leaving him as the eldest son of nine children, compelled him to do something which would aid in supporting the helpless family. Sylvester Russell, who had been appointed county clerk to succeed John McCarter, gave him the position of assistant clerk, where he began his study of the law, and at the end of Mr. Russell's term of five years was himself although not quite twenty-one years old appointed to the office of clerk. In 1826 he removed with his wife and two boys from Morristown to Newton and engaged in mercantile business with his brother George H., his mother and sisters also removing to the same place. Here he remained until his death. After his removal to Newton he became judge of the common pleas and a justice of the peace, presiding for a long time in the Sussex county court of common pleas and serving also three terms in the court of general quarter sessions. He was also appointed supreme court commissioner, and in 1840, when his brother George H. was made sheriff acted as his deputy. Governor Haines appointed him a judge of the court of errors and appeals. In politics he was a Democrat, was thoroughly informed on the political history of the country and inherited from his father an intelligent devotion to democratic principles as they were then understood, and he was frequently appointed a delegate to the county, congressional, and state conventions of his party, and was nominated for presidential elector on the Jackson ticket in 1828. He was a director of the Sussex Bank and of the Morris Turnpike Company. After the death of his brother George H., he took his oldest son into partnership with him and continued the mercantile business as R. H. McCarter & Son, and later John McCarter & Company until it was dissolved by the death of the senior partner. While in Morristown, Robert Harris McCarter married Eliza, daughter of Thomas Nesbitt, who had emigrated to this country from the north of Ireland and settled at Somerville, on a farm on the Raritan river at what is now Finderne. The children of Robert Harris and Eliza (Nesbitt) McCarter, the two eldest born in Morristown and the three youngest in Newton, were: 1. John, commonly known as John McCarter Jr., born in 1822, died October 3, 1886, leaving a widow, the daughter of Colonel Joseph E. Edsall, of

Hamburg. and two daughters. 2. Thomas Nesbitt, who is referred to below. 3. Agnes, born May 8, 1828, died March 22, 1881, unmarried. 4. Frances Meeker, born October 6, 1830, died May 11, 1897, married Samuel Henry Potter, of Deckertown and Newton, New Jersey, and later of Janesville, Wisconsin, and had Robert Harris McCarter Potter, of Chicago. 5. Susan Thompson, born July 17, 1832, died July 4, 1895, unmarried.

(III) Thomas Nesbitt, second child and younger son of Robert Harris and Eliza (Nesbitt) McCarter, was born in Morristown January 31, 1824. After attending the Newton Academy, he entered the junior class of Princeton University and graduated from that institution in 1842. He then began studying law in the office of Martin Ryerson, Esquire, and was admitted to the New Jersey bar in 1845. From that time until 1853 he practised in partnership with his instructor, and when Mr. Ryerson removed to Trenton, Mr. McCarter continued practising in Newton alone until 1865, when he removed to Newark and became highly successful in the prosecution of his profession. In 1868 he became associated in practise with Oscar Keen, Esquire, and this partnership continued until 1882. After this he became the senior member of the firm of McCarter, Williamson & McCarter. As a corporation lawyer, Mr. McCarter enjoyed a high reputation both in Sussex and Essex counties. During his residence at Newton he was the director of and counsel to the Sussex Railroad Company, and for several years he was also a director of and counsel to the Morris Canal and Banking Company. He was the counsel to the Lehigh Valley Railroad Company, to the Delaware, Lackawanna and Western Railroad Company, to the Morris and Essex Railroad Company, to the New Jersey Railroad and Transportation Company and to other similar corporations. In addition to these professional connections Mr. McCarter was prominently identified with various corporate bodies as a director, among which were the Peoples' Mutual Insurance Company of Newark, and the Easton and Amboy railroad. His well known abilities as a lawyer induced Governor Olden in 1860 to tender him a seat on the bench of the supreme court of New Jersey, and in 1866 the offer was renewed to him by Governor Ward. On both occasions, however, he declined the honor, preferring to remain at the bar. He was nevertheless willing to become a chancery reporter and accepted

the position offered him in 1864 by Chancellor Green, but after issuing two volumes of reports he was obliged to resign on account of his increasing practise. Prior to the civil war, Mr. McCarter was a pronounced Democrat, and as such was elected a member of the general assembly from Sussex county. The following year, however, he declined a renomination and subsequently abandoned the party because of its opposition to the war. In 1864 he advocated the re-election of President Lincoln and since that time was a staunch Republican. He was twice a candidate for presidential elector, once on the Douglass ticket in 1860, and once on the Hayes and Wheeler ticket in 1876. He was also one of the commission appointed to settle the boundary line between New York and New Jersey. He was a trustee of Princeton University which conferred upon him the honorary degree of LL. D., in 1875, for a time was one of the trustees of Evelyn College, was an organizer and the only president of the old Citizen's Law and Order League of Newark, was an honorary incorporator of the Dickinson law school at Carlisle, Pennsylvania, a fellow of the American Geographical Society, vice-president of the Scotch-Irish Society of America, and a member of the Princeton Club of New York. December 4, 1849, Thomas Nesbitt McCarter married Mary Louise, daughter of Uzal C. Haggerty of Newton. He died June 28, 1896, leaving six children: 1. Fanny A., wife of Charles S. Baylis. 2. Jane Haggerty, wife of Edwin B. Williamson. 3. Eliza Nesbitt. 4. Robert Harris. 5. Uzal Haggerty. 6. Thomas Nesbitt Jr., see forward.

(IV) Thomas Nesbitt (2), son of Thomas Nesbitt (1) and Mary Louise (Haggerty) McCarter, was born in Newark, New Jersey, October 20, 1867, and now resides at Rumson, Monmouth county, New Jersey. He began his early education in private schools, and then attended the preparatory school of Dr. Pingry, in Elizabeth. He then entered Princeton University, from which he was graduated in 1888, at the age of twenty-one. He read law under the masterly direction of his father, and further pursued his professional studies in the Law School of Columbia University, New York City. He was admitted to the New Jersey bar as attorney in June, 1891, and as counsellor in June, 1894. From the time of his admission to the bar he was a member of the firm of McCarter, Williamson & McCarter, (of which his father was the senior partner) until May 1, 1899, when he withdrew to

Elias G Keller

carry on practice alone. He has occupied various positions of importance, both within and without his profession. On April 1, 1896, he was appointed by Governor Griggs, to the position of judge of the first district court, and in which he served acceptably for three years, resigning in April, 1899. In the autumn of the same year he was elected to the state senate. At the close of his senatorial term he was appointed attorney general by Governor Murphy, and served as such until 1903, when he resigned to accept the presidency of the Public Service Corporation of New Jersey, a most important body holding the ownership and management of nearly all the electric railways and lighting properties, both gas and electric, in the state. He is also connected with the Fidelity Trust Company and the Union National Bank, both of Newark. He is a member of the University Club, the Princeton Club, and the Raquet and Tennis Club, all of New York City. Mr. McCarter married, in Baltimore, Maryland, February 9, 1897, Madeleine George, fourth child of George and Ellen (Schaefer) Barker, of that city. The children of this union are: 1. Ellen George, born May 9, 1898. 2. Thomas Nesbitt, November 29, 1899. 3. Uzal Haggerty, October 15, 1901. 4. Madeleine Barker, September 20, 1904.

HELLER The Heller family, members of which have been prominently and actively identified with the industrial prosperity of the city of Newark, New Jersey, along their special line of business, numbers among its ranks men of integrity and character, who have served as the best types of citizenship and whose example is well worthy of emulation.

(I) Elias Heller, the founder of the family in the United States, was a native of Darmstadt, Germany, and in order to avoid the conscription for his son at the time of the Napoleonic wars he gave up his farm and brought his wife, Laura, and his son, Elias, to this country, settling in West Orange township, Essex county, New Jersey, where he established a home, winning and retaining the respect and confidence of his fellow citizens.

(II) Elias (2), son of Elias (1) and Laura Heller, was born in Darmstadt, Germany, and there received a practical education. At the age of about twenty-five years he accompanied his parents to the United States, settling with them in Essex county, New Jersey, from whence he removed to Paterson, same state,

ii—4

subsequently to Newark, and in 1837 to West Orange, where he spent the remaining years of his life. He married, after his emigration to this country, Mary Laegle, a native of France, daughter of George and Catherine Laegle, also natives of France, from whence they came to the United States about the year 1832. Children: 1. Elias George, referred to below. 2. Peter, married Elizabeth Baldwin. 3. Emily, married John Morrow. 4. George Elias, referred to below. 5. Lewis, married Ellen ———. 6. John J., referred to below. 7. A child who died in infancy. After a long and useful life, Mr. and Mrs. Heller passed away at their home in West Orange and their remains were interred in Fairmount cemetery. She lived to the age of ninety-six years.

(III) Elias George, eldest child of Elias (2) and Mary (Laegle) Heller, was born in Newark, New Jersey, April 27, 1837. He attended the public schools, acquiring a practical education, and at the age of sixteen went to the city of New York and secured a position with Tiffany & Company, with whom he remained until 1860, when he became a clerk for Paul A. Brez. In 1863 he accepted a position with his father, who was engaged in the manufacture of files and rasps, and possessing great mechanical ability he became an expert in that line of work. In 1865, two years later, he joined his brothers, Peter and Lewis, in the founding of the firm of Heller Brothers, and the following year they built a plant in the centre of the business district of Newark. Lewis withdrew about 1870 from the firm, and Peter withdrew in 1880, and the brothers George and John were made members of the firm. Their trade steadily and rapidly increased until at length they were obliged to seek more commodious quarters. Consequently, in 1872, Mr. Heller purchased a large plot of land on Mount Prospect avenue, facing the Greenwood Lake division of the Erie railroad, in the northern district of Newark, at that time only a farming district, now known as the suburb of Forest Hill. Here they erected a large factory with all the facilities at that time available, and extended their operations by adding to their other enterprise the manufacture of steel and a complete line of farriers' tools. From time to time additions have been made to the plant until the present time it is one of the largest in the country. In 1880 Elias G. Heller formed the North Newark Land Company, which later became the Forest Hill Association, and they purchased a tract of land near his manufacturing plant and the station on Verona avenue, consisting of fifteen acres devoted to farming purposes, and thereon built many residences, some of which were sold and others rented. The company purchased most of the land bounded by Mt. Prospect avenue, Ballantine Parkway and the Greenwood Lake branch of the Erie Railroad, which included the Sidman farm of one hundred acres, the estate of Frederick Smith and lands owned by Messrs. Weeks, Kean and others. This was divided into city blocks, streets were curbed and flagged, water and sewer connections were made, all within a few years. Mr. Heller opened Heller Parkway, a fine boulevard two hundred feet wide, parked in centre, which is one of the handsomest thoroughfares in that section of the state. Forest Hill, the name given to this section, has an elevation of over one hundred and sixty feet above tide water, commands an extended view in every direction, and as the soil is sandy and dry it is an exceeding healthful place to reside in. Land all sold under all restrictions. It has all the city conveniences with the delightful country surroundings. It has ample police and fire protection, excellent mail, express, telegraph and telephone service; churches of all denominations, public and private schools of the highest type, golf links, tennis courts, base ball and foot ball grounds, a well-equipped club house, and the Forest Hill Field Club is located on the property. In 1873 Mr. Heller erected a fine house on Mt. Prospect avenue, where he made his home until 1891, when he erected his present elegant residence facing Elwood avenue, equipped with every modern appliance for the comfort of its inmates, the grounds embracing three city blocks.

Mr. Heller has been a firm adherent of the principles of the Republican party since the days of Fremont and Lincoln, having cast his first vote for President Lincoln, and has taken an active part in the affairs of the same, serving as a member of the board of education for four years and a member of the common council of Newark for three years. He attends the Forest Hill Presbyterian church, serving as president of the board of trustees for twenty-five years. He is president of the Woodside Building and Loan Association, of the Forest Hill Association and the Forest Hill Land Company, being a founder of the two latter named, and is president of Woman's and Children's Hospital of Newark. In 1886 he was chosen president of the File Manufacturers' Association of the United States, in

which capacity he has served ever since. He is a member of Bellevue Lodge, Free and Accepted Masons, and has been its treasurer for four years, member of the North End Club, Northern Republican Club and the Forest Hill Field Club.

Elias G. Heller married, in Newark, New Jersey, October 14, 1867, Sophie C., born in New York City, June 5, 1843, daughter of Nicholas C. and Frances (Doclow) Geoffroy, who were the parents of four other children, among whom were: Hortense, married Munroe Doremus; Lucy, married Jefferson Doremus, of Madison, New Jersey; Ernest, married Elizabeth Eagles. Children of Mr. and Mrs. Heller: 1. Paul E., referred to below. 2. Arnald G., referred to below. 3. Reuben Arthur, an attorney-at-law in Newark, New Jersey.

(IV) Paul E., eldest child of Elias George and Sophie C. (Geoffroy) Heller, was born in Newark, New Jersey, February 6, 1869. He graduated from the Newark Academy in 1887, engaged in his father's business, and is now serving in the capacity of vice-president and treasurer. He attends the Forest Hill Presbyterian Church, and is a Republican in politics. He is a member of the Essex County Country Club, Forest Hill Field Club, Deal Golf Club, Troy Madison Fish and Gun Club and the New Jersey Automobile Club, of which he is president. He resides with his father at 242 Elwood avenue. He is unmarried.

(IV) Arnald G., second child of Elias George and Sophie C. (Geoffroy) Heller, was born in Newark, New Jersey, August 2, 1871. He graduated from the Newark high school in 1890, and then entered his father's business, continuing to the present time, now serving in the capacity of director in the firm of Heller Brothers. He attends the Forest Hill Presbyterian Church, and is a Republican in politics. He is a member of the New Jersey Automobile Club and the Forest Hill Field Club. He married, February 8, 1897, in Newark, Harriet J., daughter of Lewis and Isabelle (Voorhees) Jackson. One child, Elaine Jackson, born in Newark, November 24, 1901.

(IV) Reuben Arthur, the third and youngest child of Elias George and Sophie C. (Geoffroy) Heller, was born in Newark, New Jersey, March 22, 1873, and has always lived in that city. For his early education he was sent to the Newark Academy and afterwards to a private school in New York City. He then entered Columbia College, from which he graduated in 1894. After his graduation he entered the office of Coult & Howell in Newark and read law, and was admitted to the New Jersey bar as attorney at the February term, 1895, and as counsellor at the same term, 1898. Since that time he has been engaged in the general practice of his profession in Newark, having his office at 788 Broad street. Mr. Heller is a Republican, but has always been identified with the reform faction of said party. He is a member of the University Club of New York, of the Lawyers' Club of Newark, and of the Forest Hill Golf Club. He married, March 21, 1899, at Oyster Bay, Long Island, Adele E., only daughter of George and Ella (Sarvent) Courvoisier, of Oyster Bay. Children: 1. Arthur, born April 15, 1900. 2. Frances, July 6, 1902. 3. Ruth, September 7, 1904. 4. Wren, August 15, 1906.

(III) George Elias, fourth child and third son of Elias and Mary (Laegle) Heller, was born in West Orange township, Essex county, January 26, 1848, and is now living at Lake street and Delavan avenue, Newark. He was educated in the public schools and until he was eighteen lived at his father's residence. He then went into the file manufacturing shops of his brother, Elias George Heller, where by close application and resolute pursuit of his purpose he mastered the business, and in 1873 became a partner in the enterprise, together with his brothers Elias George and Peter. Since then he has been continuously identified with the firm of Heller Brothers, in the manufacture of rasps and files. He is widely known as a man of excellent business and executive ability, and has been connected with the Heller Tool Company, the Corey-Heller Paper Company, and the New Jersey Wick Company. He is a Republican. His one club is the Woodside Social Club. His family attend the Presbyterian church. He married (first) January 26, 1872, Caroline, daughter of Jacob and Mary Greeney, a family of German descent, who died August 20, 1875, in giving birth to a son George, born that same day. He married (second) in Newark, September 6, 1876, Emma C., born June 10, 1855, in Newark, daughter of Louis and Mary (Becker) Pfeiffer. Her mother was born in 1820 and died in 1893, after bearing her husband five children: 1. Emma C., referred to above. 2. Ida, married John Millwood, and has three children. 3. John, whose wife's name is Katharine, and has two children. 4. Louis, Jr., who has two children. 5. Lena, who married John J. Heller, brother to George Elias referred to here. The children

of George Elias and Emma C. (Pfeiffer) Heller are: 1. Lucy, born November 28, 1878, married Bount Johnson. 2. Alfred, July 19, 1880, married Edna Burkhardt, and has one son George. 3. Emma Lyda, February 28, 1882, married George Somden. 4. Walter, October 3, 1884. 5. Gertrude, December 8, 1886. 6. Mabel, September 2, 1888. 7. Leo, April 21, 1893. 8. Viola, October 2, 1898.

(III) John J., son of Elias and Mary (Laegle) Heller, was born in West Orange township, Essex county, May 20, 1850, and is now living in Newark. For his early education he went to the public schools, and lived at home with his parents until he was twenty years old, when he moved to Forest Hill, Newark, and entered the employ of his brother, Elias George Heller, the well known manufacturer of rasps and files. In 1873, with his brothers Elias George and George Elias, he formed a partnership, which has ever since been known by the name of Heller Brothers. Mr. Heller is a Republican. He married, April 4, 1874, Lena, daughter of Louis and Mary (Becker) Pfeiffer, and the sister of Emma C. Pfeiffer, the wife of his brother, George Elias Heller. They have eight children: 1. Ida Mary, born December 25, 1874; married Joseph Benson Stewart and has one child, Helen. 2. Lucy, April 21, 1877, died July 14, 1877. 3. John Walter, who is referred to below. 4. Florence Helena, March 13, 1881, died November 5, 1906; married Stockton Barnett and has one child, Gordon. 5. John Elias, November 12, 1885, died February 28, 1889. 6. Benjamin Harrison, April 14, 1889. 7. Russell Millwood, March 29, 1891. 8. Naomi, December 27, 1894.

(IV) John Walter, third child and eldest son of John J. and Lena (Pfeiffer) Heller, was born in Newark, August 29, 1878, and is now living in that city. For his early education he was sent to the public schools of Newark, graduating from the high school in 1897. He then went to Cornell University, from which he graduated in 1901, and since then he has turned his attention to civil engineering. From 1901 to 1903 he was with the Erie railroad; from 1904 to 1906 he was one of the assistant engineers of the Brooklyn Rapid Transit Company; during 1906 and 1907 he was the superintendent of the Church Construction Company; and since then he has been in business for himself, as engineer and constructor. He is a Republican and a member of Kane Lodge, No. 55, F. and A. M. His clubs are the Cornell University Club of New

York City, the Cornell Club of Northern New Jersey, of which he is the vice-president, the Civil Engineers' Club of New York, the Brooklyn Engineers' Club, and associate member of American Society of Civil Engineers. He married, April 26, 1906, at Lynn, Massachusetts, Bertha, born in East Wellington, Connecticut, February 5, 1882, only child of Charles Ashley Ryder, D. D. S., and Sarah Elizabeth (Eldredge) Ryder. Her father practiced in Bridgeport, Connecticut, and in Newark, New Jersey, and she was educated in Lynn, Swampscott and Newark. The only child of John Walter and Bertha (Ryder) Heller is Ruth Elizabeth, born in Newark, October 14, 1908.

HARBERT Early records of this old Burlington county family are not found in any of the local or general genealogical reference works.

(I) George Harbert, the earliest ancestor of the family of whom there appears to be any definite knowledge, lived in Burlington county, but the period of his life is not known. It is known, however, that he married and had three children, Anna, John and George.

(II) George (2), son of George (1) Harbert, was born in Southampton township, Burlington county, New Jersey, in 1802, and died in Northampton or Mt. Holly in 1881. As near as is known, during the early part of his business life, he was in charge of a transportation vessel running from Lumberton to Philadelphia, and also through the Raritan canal to New York City. On these trips his cargo was chiefly charcoal. The later years of Mr. Harbert's life were spent on a farm near Mt. Holly, where now stands the Children's Home. He also bought and sold timber lands and dealt in lumber and wood. He married Mary, daughter of William Troth, of Gloucester county, New Jersey, and their children were: Sarah, Thomas, George Frank, the latter the only surviving one.

(III) George Frank, son of George (2) and Mary (Troth) Harbert, was born at Lumberton, New Jersey, June 3, 1838. His young life was spent on his father's farm, and after attending the township public school he was sent for a time to the tuition school kept by William W. Collum in Mt. Holly. After leaving school he learned the trade of a blacksmith, and later set up a shop in Mt. Holly, where he carried on a general blacksmithing and horseshoeing business until 1887, in which year he was elected high sheriff of Burlington county, serving three years in that capacity. From

1890 until about 1900 he conducted a farm in Lumberton, which he still owns, and in 1899 was elected by popular vote steward of the Burlington County Almshouse, which office he is filling at the present time (1909), serving on his fourth term. In 1877 Mr. Harbert was appointed United States gauger for the counties of Burlington, Monmouth, Mercer, Ocean, Atlantic, Cumberland, Salem, Camden and Cape May, under the administration of President Hayes (William B. Tatum, collector). He also served under the administration of Presidents Garfield and Arthur. Upon the election of Grover Cleveland to the presidency, he tendered his resignation, but it was not accepted until eighteen months later. He was again appointed upon the election of William H. Harrison to the presidency, and resigned upon the second election of Grover Cleveland. During this period of time Isaac Moffitt acted as collector. Mr. Harbert was a member of the board of freeholders of Mt. Holly in 1876-77 and 1879-80. He is a member of Mt. Holly Lodge, No. 19, I. O. O.F.; New Jersey Lodge, No. 1, K. of P., and is an attendant of the Methodist Episcopal church.

Mr. Harbert married, February 10, 1863, Mary T., daughter of Zachariah Rogers and Mary Ann (Carlisle) Reeves, of Mt. Holly. In December, 1868, they removed to Crystal Springs, Copiah county, Mississippi, where on June 27, 1869 Blanche R. Harbert was born. In January, 1870, they returned to Mt. Holly, New Jersey. Blanche R. was graduated from Mt. Holly high school, 1885, and from Bordentown Female College, 1888. She married, March 9, 1892, Edgar G. Allen, and their children were: Barclay H., born February 1, 1894, and Mary E., May 1, 1896. Mr. Allen died from the effects of a railroad accident, January 3, 1909. The second child of George Frank and Mary T. Harbert was Eugene, born in Mt. Holly, New Jersey, May 22, 1875; he attended Professor Walradt's Academy in that town, afterwards spent two years at Peddie Institute, Hightstown, New Jersey, graduating with the class of 1897. He entered the medical department of the University of Pennsylvania, and received his degree of M. D. in June, 1899. He was associated with Dr. Enoch Hollingshead, of Pemberton, New Jersey, and in 1900 was appointed physician of Burlington County Almshouse, and when the insane asylum of the county of Burlington was completed in 1901, he was the first physician appointed to that institution. He married Cora, daughter of Garrett Logan, of Beverly, New Jersey.

October, 1902. In May, 1903, removed to East Orange, New Jersey, and there practiced his profession very successfully, removing to Beverly, New Jersey, in 1908. Children: Garrett Logan, born in Orange, January 5, 1905, died July 26, 1907. Eugenia, born in Orange, September 8, 1908.

The German mechanic, notably GROBLER the workers in wood and those accustomed to the various processes of vaneering, inlaying and the deft art of coloring and shading by the use of the light or dark colored woods, have almost invariably made in America quiet, home-loving and industrious citizens. They could possibly find behind them an ancestry worthy of note and preservation, but the spirit of the immigrant from Germany has been generally to depend on the future rather than on the past and to look ahead and not backwards. On leaving the fatherland, they cut loose from tradition and, with their first American ancestor as their starting point, are making name and fame during their first, second and third generations in America.

(I) Augustus William Grobler was born in Germany, in 1835, where he attended school according to law, and when fourteen years of age, with his brother William came to America. (His sister Willimetta remained in Germany). They landed in New York City in 1849. Augustus William worked on a farm in Vincentown, Burlington county, New Jersey, when he first landed, and then was an apprentice to the cabinet making business at Elizabethtown, and subsequently at Juliustown for Joel Mount, in Burlington county, New Jersey. He worked at his trade of cabinet making in Pemberton in the same county for Edward Dobbins, cabinet maker and undertaker. At the breaking out of the civil war his inherited love of military life and desire to aid the country he had adopted as his own, prevailed on him to raise a company of volunteers and the Union army in the defense of the United States against disruption by secession. The sentiment that most strongly appealed to him, as it did to most foreign born citizens, was the freedom of the negro from enforced slavery. He found but little difficulty in gathering one hundred recruits who agreed to join him in forming a company, and on August 26, 1862, he was commissioned captain of the company, which was made Company E, Twenty-third Regiment New Jersey Volunteers, of which Edward Burd Grubb, of Burlington, New Jersey,

was lieutenant-colonel. The regiment enlisted for nine months service, and was mustered into the United States service, September 13, 1862. On February 23, 1863, Captain Grobler resigned on account of disability, and re-enlisted August 25, 1863, and was mustered into service September 21, 1863, and commissioned second lieutenant of Company C, Thirty-fourth New Jersey Volunteers, enlisted for three years service. He soon received promotion to first lieutenant, and served with the regiment and participated in all its battles up to the close of the war, when he was mustered out and honorably discharged, his last duty being at the United States Navy Yard, Philadelphia.

He remained in Philadelphia, where he established the business of retail grocer. He also established himself in that city as a manufacturer of caskets, under the firm name of Grobler & Middleton. In 1874 he returned to Pemberton, where he bought out the business of his former employer, then owned by Edward Remine, and conducted the business of cabinet making and undertaking up to the time of his death, which occurred at Pemberton, New Jersey, May 20, 1901. He was a member of Mount Holly Lodge, No. 14, F. and A. M.; Pemberton Lodge, No. 49, Independent Order of Odd Fellows; Amo Lodge, No. 111, Knights of Pythias, Pemberton; a comrade of General A. E. Shires Post, No. 26, Grand Army of the Republic, and he was an officer in the several organizations except Mt. Holly Lodge, No. 14, F. and A. M. He was treasurer of the Pemberton Building and Loan Association at the time of his death, and also a trustee and deacon in the Baptist church. He had served for several terms as commissioner of appeals and road commissioner of the town of Pemberton, and was held in high esteem as a citizen, patriot and trusted official. He married, 1864, Mary, daughter of Samuel C. and Drusilla (Johnson) Rambo, and granddaughter of Benjamin Rambo, born in Woodbury, Gloucester county, New Jersey, and his wife Mary (Cooper) Rambo, who had besides Mary five other children: Joseph, Samuel, Martha, Epecorus and Sarah. Her brothers and sisters were: Joseph J. Rambo, born in Pemberton, New Jersey, May 10, 1842, who married (first) Rebecca Cliver, who with her first born child was drowned, and (second) Florence Cliver, his deceased wife's sister, who had one child, Rebecca; Lydia, who was the second wife of Captain Augustus Grobler; and Anna, who married John J. Branda. Mary (Rambo) Grobler was born in Pemberton, New Jersey, in 1845, and died in 1871, leaving one child, Atgistis Badger Grobler (q. v.). Captain Grobler married (second) Lydia, sister of his deceased wife, and by her had three children: William, Mary and Effie.

(II) Atgistis Badger, only child of Captain Atgistis William and Mary (Rambo) Grobler, was born in Pemberton, Burlington county, New Jersey, July 18, 1865. He attended the public schools of his native town, and engaged in cabinet making and the undertaking business with his father as soon as he reached his fifteenth year, and under his direction and through the introduction of the latest methods in manufacturing and handling, the business increased both in volume and profits. He followed his father in political faith, and was elected to the office of coroner for Burlington county, serving in that office for three years. He affiliated with Central Lodge, No. 44, F. and A. M., of Vincentown; with Pemberton Lodge, No. 44, Independent Order of Odd Fellows; with Amo Lodge, No. 111, Knights of Pythias, of Pemberton, and gained admission to the Grand Lodge; with the Protective Order, Sons of America, Camp No. 49, of Pemberton; with the Benevolent and Protective Order of Elks, Lodge No. 848, of Mount Holly; and with Maumee Tribe of Red Men, No. 53, of Pemberton. He was brought up in the faith of the Baptist denomination, of which church his father was a leading member, and he contributed generously to the work and financial support of that society. He married, July 18, 1892, Laura J., daughter of Charles P. and Adlie (Johnson) Nutt, of Pemberton, their first child, Daniel Earl, was born September 19, 1893, and their second child, Edith Kingdom, November 5, 1899.

KNIGHT The civil war was a school of instruction and discipline that turned out many notable graduates, who but for the opportunity this offered might have lived and died in oblivion. Very few of the veterans who escaped the deadly effects of change of climate and mode of living that rendered so many permanent invalids, or who came back with whole bodies uninjured by the bullets of the enemy, failed to succeed in civil life. They had experienced a process of preparation that made them men of thought and action and not drones in the busy hive of life. The country had taken a new grip on prosperity and needed just such men to help along the wheels of progress and rehabitation. It is helpful to the young to read of these examples of heroic endeavor, fired as they were by patriotism and proving proof against imbecility or cowardice. In the instance before us we have as well the apparently entire absence of the influence of parents or guardians. Left alone from early youth and forced to fight the battle of life among strangers, we find pure gold comes out of apparent dross.

(I) Gilbert W. Knight was the only child of his parents who lived in Philadelphia, where he was born in 1831. He had no knowledge of the names or future of his parents, as he came to Burlington county, New Jersey, when quite young and lived at Tabernacle. He learned the blacksmith trade, which he followed until 1862, when he enlisted in the Twenty-third New Jersey Volunteer Regiment under Colonel Henry·O. Ryerson for nine months service. He was assigned to the company of which Lieutenant E. Bird Grubb, of Burlington, New Jersey, was in command and from which rank Lieutenant Grubb was promoted to major on November 23, 1862. The regiment was assigned to the First Brigade, Colonel A. T. A. Torbert; First Division, Brigadier-General William T. H. Brooks; Sixth Army Corps, Major-General William Farror Smith; Left Grand Division, Major-General William B. Franklin; Army of the Potomac, Major-General Andrew E. Burnside, and in that position fought the Confederate army of General Robert E. Lee, at Fredericksburg, Virginia, December 13, 1862, and the Federal army was repulsed with a loss of fifteen hundred and twelve killed and six thousand wounded. His next battle was at Fredericksburg, May 3, 1863, known as the Battle of Chancellorsville, the army having been reformed and General·Joseph Hooker placed in command. The relative position of the Twenty-third New Jersey Volunteers in the army was the same as occupied on the first battle of December 13, the changes in command placing Major E. Bird Grubb as lieutenant-colonel in command of the regiment and the fortunes of battle giving the command of the brigade to Colonel Henry W. Brown, Colonel William H. Penrose, Colonel Samuel L. Buck and back to Colonel William H. Penrose and the Sixth Army Corps to Major-General John Sedgewick. The main battle fought on Sunday, May 3, again resulted in the defeat of the Federal troops, and in the meantime General Sedgewick with the Sixth Corps had crossed the Rappahannock and occupied Fredericksburg, but he was also defeated and compelled to retire to the northern bank of the river, not being able with a single corps to sustain his posts against the entire army of General Lee. This battle cost each army at least fifteen thousand men in killed, wounded and prisoners. Soon after the disaster at Chancellorsville, that changed the fortunes of war in favor of the Confederate army, the term of enlistment of the Twenty-third New Jersey had expired and the regiment was ordered to camp at Beverly, New Jersey, preparatory to being mustered out, when the news of the invasion of Pennsylvania by Lee's army reached camp and the regiment under Colonel Budd volunteered to serve as emergency men. They reached Harrisburg before any other regular troops had reached that city, and they proceeded to entrench the place, but before they were ordered to the front they were summarily directed back to camp at Beverly and disbanded, June 27, 1863. Thereupon Colonel Burd set about reforming the regiment as the Thirty-seventh and they left Trenton, June 28, 1863, to report to General Butler at Bermuda Hundred, Virginia, where they took part in the battles before Petersburg, for which one hundred days' service the regiment was complimented in general orders by General Berry as being unexceptionally a superior regiment of one hundred days men. Gilbert W. Knight was married soon after the close of the civil war in 1865 to Elizabeth J., daughter of William Bareford, of Tabernacle, New Jersey, and their only child was Harry Laban (q. v.).

(II) Harry Laban, only child of Gilbert W. and Elizabeth J. (Bareford) Knight, was born at Tabernacle, Burlington county, New Jersey, July 24, 1868, and he worked on farms and attended the public school of his native place. On arriving at his majority, he found employment in the railroad office at Medford, where in addition to his labors as clerk and station agent he learned the art of telegraphy. He remained in charge of the railroad station at Medford from 1891 to 1906, when he resigned to accept the position of postmaster at Medford, of which office he still had charge in 1909. He was also interested in the cranberry culture as secretary and treasurer of the New Jersey Cranberry Sales Company, and as owner and cultivator of twenty acres of cranberry bog in Burlington county, which he had in ten years brought to a high stage of productiveness and profit. Besides being postmaster, Mr. Knight has served as township clerk, collector of taxes, and member of the board of education. His affiliations with benevolent and fraternal associations included membership in

the Medford Lodge, No. 178, Ancient Free and Accepted Masons, of Medford, of which lodge he is past master; in the Independent Order of Odd Fellows, Lodge No. 100, of Medford; in the Knights of Pythias, Lodge No. 108, of Medford; in the Junior Order of United American Mechanics, sub-council No. 9, of Medford; in the Knights of the Golden Eagle, sub-castle, of Medford; of the Mayflower Council, No. 33, Order of Settlers and Defenders of America, incorporated in 1899. Mr. Knight married, April 21, 1893, Lillie R., daughter of Arthur and Amanda M. (Austin) Haines, of Tabernacle, New Jersey, and their only child Verna L. was born in Medford, New Jersey, June 29, 1897.

GARWOOD The family of this name have been residents of the state of New Jersey for several centuries, and those who represent it today move among the best circles of social and business activity.

(I) Japhet Garwood the first of the name of whom we have record, was born in Upper Evesham township, Burlington county, New Jersey, 1720, married and among his children was Israel (q. v.).

(II) Israel, son of Japhet Garwood, was born near Medford, New Jersey, 1750, married and was the father of five children: Thomas, William, Samuel (q. v.), Elizabeth, Mary.

(III) Samuel, third son of Israel Garwood, of Upper Evesham township, Burlington county, New Jersey, was born in Southampton township, Burlington county, New Jersey, 1779. He was a farmer in his native township and also carried on a distillery and was an all-around mechanic, also to do both carpentering and working in iron as a machinist. He married Mary Newton, of Southampton township, and they had seven children, born at follows: Hannah, William, Elizabeth, Joshua (q. v.), Samuel, Mary Jane, Israel, March, 1825, living in Medford in 1909. Samuel Garwood died at his homestead, October 25, 1865.

(IV) Joshua, second son and fourth child of Samuel and Mary (Newton) Garwood, was born in Southampton township, Burlington county. New Jersey, 1803. He attended the district school. was brought up on his father's farm. and he continued in the same calling on reaching manhood. He added to his income by dealing in cattle from the west, which he gathered up and shipped to Burlington and other markets by the carload. He also bred fine stock and blooded horses and moulded and burned brick, made from clay found on his farm. He was a Democrat in party politics, and a member of the Society of Friends, attending the Hicksite Meeting in Medford. He married Hannah, daughter of Job and Hope Braddock, of Gresham township, and they lived in Medford, where they had ten children born to them, as follows: 1. Henry, who lives in Medford, New Jersey. 2. Sarah, married William Allen, a farmer who carried on a farm near Vincentown, New Jersey, where she died. 3. Ellen, who lived to be seventeen years of age. 4. Job, died young. 5. Hannah, died unmarried. 6. Frank, died unmarried. 7. Hope, married Joseph Taylor, a farmer of Woodford, where she died. 8. Samuel (q. v.). 9. Charles, lives in Medford. 10. J. Maurice, a merchant in Medford. Joshua Garwood died at his home in Southampton township in 1866.

(V) Samuel (2), fourth son and eighth child of Joshua and Hannah (Braddock) Garwood, was born in Medford, Burlington county, New Jersey, November, 1857. He attended the Haines' Corner school house, a pay school in Medford, and Pierce's Business College in Philadelphia, where he was graduated in 1876. His employment was clerk and bookkeeper in a large boarding house at Atlantic City, where he remained four years, when he returned to Medford, where he established a business as painter and house decorator, which business he carried on for ten years. In 1889 he joined John B. Mingin, Frank Reiley and others in organizing the Star Glass Company, which is carried on as a joint stock company, amply capitalized, with a business office and salesrooms in Philadelphia and Mr. Mingin as president and superintendent of the manufacture of glass. A general store was started in connection with the glass works in 1892, and Mr. Garwood was placed in charge of the store in Medford. He was also made a director of the Medford Gas Company. His political faith was that of the Democratic party, and his religious faith that of the Hicksite branch of the Society of Friends and he attended the Hicksite Meeting at Medford. He was affiliated with the Masonic fraternity through Medford Lodge, No. 187, of which he is past master. He was advanced to the Royal Arch Chapter and made a Knight Templar at Burlington. Mr. Garwood was married in 1881 by Friends' ceremony to Ella, daughter of Edmond and Rebecca (Andrews) Prickett, of Medford, and they had two children born of this marriage as follows: 1. Carlton, born Sep-

tember 19, 1883, at Atlantic City, New Jersey, and after graduating at Union Business College, Philadelphia, he became assistant manager of the Star Glass Company at Medford. He married Ray, daughter of Henry and Caroline (Brown) Wright, of Indian Mills, New Jersey, and their first child, Samuel, born in Medford, July 21, 1908, is of the seventh generation from Japhet Garwood, the immigrant ancestor. 2. Irene, born in Medford, New Jersey, December 13, 1891, educated at George's Friends' School, Newtown, Pennsylvania.

SEAVER The Seaver family of New England is descended from Robert Seaver, who was born about the year 1608. March 24, 1633-34, at the age of about twenty-five years, he took the oath of supremacy and allegiance to pass for New England in the ship "Mary and John," of London, Robert Sayres, master (see "Founders of Newbury," Drake). On the 10th of December, 1834, he married, in Roxbury, Massachusetts, Elizabeth Ballard. A William Ballard took the oath at the same time with Robert Seaver, and presumably was a fellow passenger and a relative of Elizabeth. The church records show that "Elizabeth Ballard, a maideservant she came in the year 1833 and soone afterward joined to the church—she was after ward married to Robert Seaver of this church were she led a goodly conversation." Robert Seaver was made freeman April 18, 1637. He built a house over a half mile from the meeting house, but was allowed to keep it by vote of the town, 1639, and the "halfe-mile law" was repealed in 1640. He was a selectman of Roxbury, 1665. Elizabeth, his wife, died June 6, 1657. "1657 buryed, mo. 10 day 18, Sister Seaver ye wife of Robert Seaver." "Also 1669 mo. 10 day 18, wife to Robert Seaver, buried." He must have had a third wife, for in his will made January 16, 1681, he provides for his wife, christian name not given, and four children. Names of latter: Shubael, Caleb, Joshua, and son Samuel Crafts, who married his daughter Elizabeth. The latter was probably dead at the date of the will. Robert Seaver died (town records) May 13, 1683, aged about seventy-five years. Roxbury church record says "1683' mo 4 day 6 Robert Seaver an aged Christian buryed." These dates are not uniform. Robert and Elizabeth (Ballard) Seaver had: 1. Shubael, born January 31, 1639, died June 18, 1729. 2. Caleb, born August 30, 1641, died March 6,

1713. 3. Joshua (twin with Caleb), died
beore 1730. 4. Elizabeth, born 1643, married
Samuel Crafts (Crafts Genealogy); they had
nine children and he died December 9, 1709.
5. Nathaniel, born January 8, 1645, see post.
6. Hannah, born and died 1647. 7. Hannah,
born 1650, died 1653.

(II) Nathaniel, son of Robert and Elizabeth (Ballard) Seaver, was baptized in Roxbury, January 8, 1645, and was slain by Indians
in the battle at Sudbury, Massachusetts, April
21, 1676, during King Philip's war. He was
one of ten Sudbury men who were killed on
that day and served in Captain Wadsworth's
company. The site of the battlefield where
Captain Wadsworth so long held the Indians
at bay is on what is now called "Green hill."
While an attack was being made on a small
body of eighteen minute-men under Edward
Cowell, Captain Wadsworth and his company
came upon the scene and seeing a small party
of Indians rushed forward with impetuous
haste and were caught in the usual ambuscade,
for when within about a mile of Sudbury they
were induced to pursue a body of not more
than one hundred Indians and soon found
themselves drawn away about a mile into the
woods, where on a sudden they were encom-
passed by more than five hundred, and were
forced to a retreating fight toward a hill where
they made a brave stand for a time (one authority says four hours) and did heavy execution on the enemy until (Hubbard says) the
night coming on and some of the company beginning to scatter from the rest their companions were forced to follow them, and this
being surrounded in the chase the officers and
most of the company were slain. It is said
that the savages set fire to the woods and this
forced the disastrous retreat, and only thirteen
out of the entire company escaped to Noyes'
mill. Nathaniel Seaver married Sarah ——,
and by her had two children: 1. John, born
August 18, 1671. see post. 2. Sarah, died
April 18, 1674.

(III) John, only son of Nathaniel and
Sarah Seaver, was born in Roxbury, Massachusetts, August 18, 1671. He married Sarah
———, and by her had ten children: 1. Sarah,
born February 4. 1696, married, December 15,
1714, Aucariah Winchester. 2. Nathaniel, December 22, 1697, see post. 3. John, October 6,
1699, died Brookline, October 21, 1767. 4. Anna,
1701, married, April 9. 1724, Thomas Stedman,
Jr. 5. Lucy, November 24, 1703, married, 1725,
John Goddard, of Brookline. 6. Andrew,
1705. 7. Mary, 1707. 8. Richard, 1710, mar-

ried, November 30, 1748, Hannah Everett, of
Roxbury. 9. Esther, November 13, 1712, mar-
ried, December 1, 1756, Edward Sheaf, of
Cambridge. 10. Elizabeth, September 12, 1715.

(IV) Nathaniel (2), son of John and Sarah
Seaver, was born in Roxbury, December 22,
1697, died in Brookline, Massachusetts, October 2, 1768. He married (first) Hannah
White, who died in Brookline, February 20,
1742, and married (second) October 23, 1746,
Sarah Stevens. Nathaniel Seaver had eleven
children: 1. Benjamin, born September 11,
1729, died before September 17, 1768. 2. Hannah, November 13, 1730. 3. Lucy, November
24, 1731. 4. Sarah, April 12, 1733. 5. Hannah, born July 16, 1735. died May 31, 1821;
married John Goddard, of Brookline. 6. Abijah, August 31, 1737, see post. 7. Lucy, February 17, 1739-40. 8. Mary. 9. Elizabeth.
10. Susanna. 11. Nathaniel.

(V) Abijah, son of Nathaniel (2) and Hannah (White) Seaver, was born August 31,
1737, and married, March 29, 1764, Anne
Winchester, of Brookline. They had five children: 1. William, born May 6, 1765, married,
December 1, 1796, Lucy Heath. 2. Benjamin,
September 28, 1766, died June 29, 1815; married, May 25, 1794, Debby Loud. 3. Joseph,
baptized January 20, 1771, see post. 4. Nathaniel, baptized May 16, 1773, married, November 1, 1798, Lydia Wilson. 5. Polly, married Levi Pratt.

(VI) Joseph, son of Abijah and Anne
(Winchester) Seaver, was baptized January
20, 1771, and married, November 17, 1799,
Abigail, daughter of Elisha Whitney. They
had five children: 1. Joseph, born June 17,
1804, see post. 2. Elizabeth Whitney, married,
June 29, 1823, George Seaver. 3. William
Whitney, born April 6, 1806. 4. Nathaniel,
September 24, 1808. 5. Abigail Dana, Septem-
ber 16, 1810, died single.

(VII) Joseph (2), son of Joseph (1) and
Abigail (Whitney) Seaver, was born in Roxbury, Massachusetts, June 17, 1804. He married, in Philadelphia, Pennsylvania, Phebe S.
Elmes, born Augusta, Maine, and by her had
nine children: 1. Joseph H., born January 22,
1834, see post. 2. Emma. 3. Thomas Elmes.
4. Maria E. 5. William Archer. 6. Frank.
7. Charles. 8. Mary. 9. James R. S.

(VIII) Joseph H., son of Joseph (2) and
Phebe S. (Elmes) Seaver, was born in Philadelphia, Pennsylvania, January 22, 1834, received his education in the public schools and
for many years has been actively identified
with the business life of that city, member of

the stock exchange and former member of the brokerage firm of E. W. Clark & Company. Mr. Seaver is a Republican in politics and a consistent member of the Presbyterian church. In 1871 he married Mary Gillespie, born 1838, daughter of Franklin Gillespie, who was born in New Castle, Delaware, a descendant of Rev. George Gillespie, who was a son of Rev. George Gillispie, the latter of whom attained fame through the authorship of a Scotch Presbyterian catechism. He purchased from William Penn a considerable tract of land in the upper part of Delaware. Joseph H. and Mary (Gillespie) Seaver had three children: 1. Jessie Gillespie, born 1872, married William Percy Simpson, of Overbrook, Pennsylvania, president of Eddystone Manufacturing Company. One child, William Simpson. 2. Archer Whiting, 1874, died 1902; married Marion Skinner, a native of North Carolina, and had one son, Archer Whiting Seaver, Jr. 3. Howard Eves, see post.

(IX) Howard Eves, youngest son and child of Joseph H. and Mary (Gillespie) Seaver, was born in Philadelphia, Pennslyvania, May 31, 1878, gradated from Princeton College in 1898, and during the following year engaged in corundum mining in North Carolina. His subsequent business career may be mentioned as follows: Employee in the office of Strong, Sturgis & Company, brokers, of New York City, one year; associated in business with his father in Philadelphia, two years; went west as traffic manager for Bell Telephone Company and remained there about four years; with Sloane Howe Company, Philadelphia, iron and steel commission house; and in 1908 purchased a farm of fifty acres at Brown's Mills, New Jersey; and has recently established what is known as the Pine Park Poultry Farm, making ample preparations for carrying on an extensive business in raising poultry and poultry products for the market.

KIRKPATRICK The Kirkpatricks of New Jersey come of an honorable and noteworthy Scottish lineage, having from their first appearance in history showed the forcible characteristics and qualities which by the end of the eighteenth century had numbered them among the families of principal importance and worth in New Jersey. Originally a Keltic family, they settled in Scotland in early times and by the ninth century had established themselves in various parts of Dumfriesshire, especially in Nithsdale, where in 1232 the estate of

Closeburn was granted by King Alexander II., to Ivon Kirkpatrick, the ancestor of the Lords of Closeburn. In 1280 Duncan Kirkpatrick, of Closeburn, married the daughter of Sir David Carlisle, of Torthorwald, who was nearly related to William Wallace, and their son, Ivon Kirkpatrick, was one of the witnesses to the charter of Robert Bruce. In 1600 the Kirkpatricks of Closeburn were appointed by decree of the Lords in Council among the chieftains charged with the care of the border. Sir Thomas Kirkpatrick in the reign of James VI. of Scotland, one of the gentlemen of the privy chamber, obtained a patent of the freedom of the whole kingdom and his great-grandson, also Sir Thomas, was created in 1686 baron of Nova Scotia. The modern baronetcy dates from 1685, when the following arms were registered: Arms: Argent, a saltire and chief azure, the last charged with three cushions or; Crest: a hand holding a dagger in pale, distilling drops of blood; Motto: I mak sicker ("I make sure"). Among the noteworthy descendants in this line of the Kirkpatricks is the Empress Eugenie, whose maternal grandfather was William Kirkpatrick, of Malaga, Spain, whose ancestor was Sir Roger Kirkpatrick, eighth baron of Kylosbern or Closeburn.

(I) Alexander Kirkpatrick, the American progenitor of the family, was one of the scions of the Closeburn family, and was born at Watties Neach, county Dumfries, and died at Mine Brook, Somerset county, New Jersey, June 3, 1758. He was a Presbyterian, but was warmly devoted to the cause of the Stuarts, and took part in the rising under the Earl of Mar for the old pretender. On account of this falling under the disfavor of the English government, he emigrated first to Belfast, Ireland, and in the spring of 1736 came over to America, landed in Delaware, and went to Philadelphia, but finally settled in Somerset county, New Jersey, building his home on the southern slope of Round Mountain, about two miles from the present village of Basking Ridge. He was accompanied to this country by his brother, Andrew Kirkpatrick, and the latter's two sons and two daughters, and this branch settled in Sussex county, New Jersey. By his wife Elizabeth, whom he married in Scotland, Alexander Kirkpatrick had five children: 1. Andrew, who married Margaret, daughter of Joseph Gaston, who emigrated to New Jersey about 1720. They had one son, Alexander, and seven daughters. He inherited the homestead at Mine Brook, but sold it soon after his father's death to his brother David and removed to what was then called the "Redstone country" in Pennsylvania. 2. David, who is referred to below. 3. Alexander, who was a surveyor and also a merchant at Peapack, Warren county; married Margaret Anderson, of Bound Brook, and had Martha, who married John Stevenson. 4. Jennet, who married Duncan McEowen and removed to Maryland. 5. Mary, who married John Bigger and removed from New Jersey.

(II) David, the second child and son of Alexander and Elizabeth Kirkpatrick, was born at Watties Neach, county Dumfries, Scotland, February 17, 1724, and died at Mine Brook, New Jersey, March 19, 1814. Coming to America with his father, he bought from his brother Andrew the paternal homestead at Mine Brook, and lived there, "greatly esteemed and loved." In his habits he was plain and simple, while he was noted for his strict integrity, his sterling common sense, and his great energy and self reliance. In 1765 he was a member of the legislature of New Jersey. He built at Mine Brook the stone mansion, still standing, over the doors of which he carved the initials "D. M. K." David Kirkpatrick married, March 31, 1748, Mary McEowen, born in Argyleshire, August 1, 1728, and died at Mine Brook, New Jersey, November 2, 1795. Their seven children were: 1. Elizabeth, born September 27, 1749, died 1829; married (first) a Mr. Sloan and became the mother of the Rev. William B. Sloan; pastor of the Presbyterian church at Greenwich, Warren county, New Jersey; she married (second) William Maxwell. 2. Alexander, born September 3, 1751, died September 24, 1827; married Sarah Carle, daughter of Judge John Carle, of Long Hill. Morris county, and had thirteen children, the fourth of whom was the Rev. Jacob Kirkpatrick, D. D., of Ringoes, New Jersey, whose son, the Rev. Jacob Kirkpatrick, D. D., was for many years a clergyman at Trenton, New Jersey. 3. Andrew, who is referred to below. 5. David, born November 1, 1758. 6. Mary, born November 23, 1761, died July 1, 1842; married Hugh Gaston, of Peapack, New Jersey, the son of John or Robert, and the grandson of Joseph Gaston, the emigrant. 7. Anne, born March 10, 1769, married Dickinson Miller, of Somerville, New Jersey.

(III) The Hon. Andrew, third child and second son of David and Mary (McEowen) Kirkpatrick, chief justice of New Jersey, was born at Mine Brook, February 17, 1756; died in New Brunswick, New Jersey, in 1831. In

1775 he graduated from the College of New Jersey, now Princeton University, and later received from that institution and also from Queens, now Rutgers College, the degree of M. A. He was for many years one of the trustees of his alma mater. His father, who was an ardent Presbyterian, wished him to become a minister, and for several months after his graduation he studied divinity with the Rev. Dr. Kennedy; but his preference lay in the direction of the law, and he, owing to his father's anger at his stopping his theological studies, accepted a tutor's position in a Virginia family, and somewhat later a similar one with a family at Esopus, New York. He then went to New Brunswick, where he tutored men for college, and entered the law office of the Hon. William Paterson, at one time governor of New Jersey, and later justice of the United States supreme court, and one of the most eminent lawyers of New Jersey of his day. In 1785 Mr. Kirkpatrick was admitted to the New Jersey bar, and for a short time he practiced in Morristown, but his office and library having been destroyed by fire, he removed again to New Brunswick, where he became noted for his great native ability, untiring industry and stern integrity. In 1797 he was elected to the New Jersey assembly from Middlesex county, and sat for the first part of the term, but resigned in January, 1798, in order to assume the office of associate justice of the supreme court of New Jersey, which office he held for the ensuing six years, when he became chief justice, succeeding Chief-Justice Kinsey. To this post he was twice reelected, and in this capacity he served continuously for twenty-one years. His decisions were marked by extensive learning, great acumen, and power of logical analysis, and his strictly logical mind and great personal dignity coupled with his other qualities made him one of the great historical characters of the New Jersey bench. Among other things, he created the office of reporter of the decisions of the supreme court. He was eminently public spirited, and was the founder of the theological seminary at Princeton, and for many years the first president of its board of directors. He was in politics an Anti-Federalist or Republican, the party now known as the Democratic, and at one time was its candidate for governor of New Jersey. Among his many excellent qualities he was especially esteemed and admired for his keen sense of justice, his considerateness and loyalty. November 1, 1792, Judge Andrew Kirkpatrick married

Jane, born July 12, 1772, died February 16, 1851, seventh child and eldest daughter of Colonel John Bubenheim Bayard, by his first wife, Margaret, daughter of Andrew Hodge. She was widely known for her accomplishments, her benevolence, and beautiful christian character, and was the author of "The Light of Other Days," edited by her daughter, Mrs. Jane E. Cogswell. The children of Andrew and Jane (Bayard) Kirkpatrick were: 1. Mary Ann Margaret, died March 17, 1882; married the Rev. Samuel B. Howe, pastor of the First Reformed Church at New Brunswick. 2. John Bayard, who is referred to below. 3. Littleton, born October 19, 1797; died August 15, 1859; graduated at Princeton, 1815; a leader of the New Jersey bar, prominent in public life; attorney-general of New Jersey, and a member of congress from New Jersey. 4. Jane Eudora, died March, 1864; married the Rev. Jonathan Cogswell, D. D., professor of ecclesiastical history at the East Windsor Theological Seminary. 5. Elizabeth. 6. Sarah. 7. Charles Martel.

(IV) John Bayard, the second child and eldest son of the Hon. Andrew and Jane (Bayard) Kirkpatrick, was born in New Brunswick, August 15, 1795; died there February 24, 1864. He was one of the most conspicuous of the merchants of the town, and was engaged largely in foreign trade. For some time he was the third assistant auditor of the United States treasury department at Washington, District of Columbia, but in 1851 he returned to New Brunswick. In 1842 he married Margaret Weaver, who died in June, 1889, and their children were: 1. Andrew, who is referred to below. 2. John Bayard, born February 14, 1847; now living in New Brunswick, graduated from Rutgers College in 1866, and is active in business and in the financial interests of his town; he is commissioner of public works, city treasurer and a trustee of Rutgers College. June 28, 1871, he married Mary E. H., daughter of John Phillips, of New York City.

(V) The Hon. Andrew (2), eldest son of John Bayard and Margaret (Weaver) Kirkpatrick, was born in Washington, District of Columbia, October 8, 1844; died in Newark, New Jersey, May 3, 1904. Returning with his parents to New Brunswick, he was educated in New Jersey, at Rutgers grammar school, Princeton College, where he remained for three years and left to graduate at Union College, Schenectady, New York, from which he graduated in 1863, receiving his honorary de-

gree of M. A. from Princeton University in 1870, and in 1903 the degree of LL. D. from Union College. He then entered the office of the Hon. Frederick Theodore Frelinghuysen, of Newark, and was admitted to the New Jersey bar as attorney in 1866, and as counsellor in 1869. For several years he practiced as one of the members of the firm of Frederick Theodore Frelinghuysen, and then he went into partnership with the Hon. Frederick H. Teese. He was eminently successful, and was a recognized leader. In April, 1885, he was appointed judge of the Essex county court of common pleas by Governor Abbett, and continuously reappointed until 1896, when he resigned to become judge of the United States district court for New Jersey, which position was then offered to him by President Grover Cleveland. This position he held until his death. "His career on the bench showed a wide knowledge of the law, together with a large fund of common sense, and his methods were celebrated for this latter trait. He acquitted himself with honor, and the brevity of his charges to juries was frequently commented on * * * His legal knowledge was brought to bear on the cases, to the disentanglement of many knotty problems. His record as a federal judge was brilliant, and to his courtesy and humanity there were hundreds to testify. Quick-witted, intolerant of shams of any kind, and broad-minded, Judge Kirkpatrick conducted cases to the admiration of lawyers and jurists of many minds * * * He possessed wide reading and because of the soundness of his judgment his opinions carried weight in the legal world. They were regarded as peculiarly clear in statement and had the quality of being easily comprehended by the lay mind. He was a keen student of human nature, a man of force and insight of character." Among the important commercial and corporation cases determined by him were the United States Steel Company, the United States Shipbuilding Company, and the "Asphalt Trust." He was essentially the lawyer and the judge with administrative powers of a high order, and on one memorable occasion he exercised these powers for the great advantage of one of the most extensive businesses in the country. In 1893 the Domestic Manufacturing company failed, and Judge Kirkpatrick was appointed receiver with authority to continue the business of making and selling Domestic sewing machines. Notwithstanding the unexampled financial depression which marked the year of the World's Fair he discharged

STATE OF NEW JERSEY. 461

his trust with such skill that works with hundreds of employees continued in operation, and
at the expiration of his official term as receiver
he delivered the property to the stockholders
entirely freed from its embarrasments and
with assets sufficient to pay all of its creditors
in full. He was one of the organizers and for
some time was president of the Federal Trust
Company, a director in the Howard Savings
Institution, treasurer of the T. P. Howell
Company, a director in the Fidelity Title and
Deposit Company, a director in the Newark
Gas Company, a member of the Newark city
hall commission, and a member of the Newark sinking fund commission. He was the
type of all that is highest and best in American civilization, of the purest integrity, and
the loftiest ideals, devoted to the obligations
of his family and bound to his friends by at-
tachments most amiable and attractive in his
private character. He was the treasurer and
one of the original governors of the Essex
Club, and one of the organizers of the Sons
of the American Revolution. In 1869 he married (first) Alice, daughter of Joel W. and
Margaret (Harrison) Condit, the sister of
Estelle Condit, who married Thomas Tal-
madge Kinney. Their three children were:
1. Andrew, of New York City, born October
12, 1870; educated at St. Paul's school, Concord, New Hampshire; spent one year at Cornell, and five years in the Pennsylvania railroad shops at Altoona; became assistant road
foreman of engines of the Pennsylvania railroad, and is now in the automobile business;
he married Mae Bittner and has one child,
Andrew, Jr. 2. John Bayard, who is referred
to below. 3. Alice Condit, born December 11,
1874; graduated from St. Agnes school, Albany, New York. In 1883 Judge Andrew
Kirkpatrick married (second) Louise C.,
daughter of Theodore P. and Elizabeth Woodruff (King) Howell, of New York City, and
their three children are: 4. Littleton, who is
referred to below. 5. Isabelle, born January
18, 1886; married Albert H. Marckwald, of
Short Hills, New Jersey. 6. Elizabeth, born
August 2, 1895.

(VI) John Bayard, the second child and
son of the Hon. Andrew (2) and Alice (Condit) Kirkpatrick, was born in Newark, New
Jersey, May 1, 1872, and is now living in that
city. Preparing for college in St. Paul's school,
Concord, New Hampshire; he graduated from
Harvard University in 1894, and from the
same institution's law school in 1897. He
then read law with Coult & Howell and was

admitted to the New Jersey bar at attorney in
February, 1898, and as counsellor in February, 1891. For the next three years he worked
in partnership with Joseph D. Gallegher and
then set up in practice for himself in Newark.
Mr. Kirkpatrick is a Democrat, but has held
no office nor does he belong to any secret societies. He is a member of three of the Harvard clubs, namely those of New Jersey, New
York and Philadelphia, and also a member
of the Lawyers' Club, the Union Club, the
Essex Club, the Engineers' Club, of New
York. He is a communicant of Grace Protestant Episcopal Church, of Newark, and is
one of the trustees of St. Matthews Church.
He is a director in the Neptune Meter Company, in the New Jersey Patent Holding Company and the New Jersey Title and Abstract
Company. He is unmarried.

(VI) Littleton, the only son of the Hon.
Andrew (2) and Louise C. (Howell) Kirk-
patrick, was born in Newark, New Jersey,
September 2, 1884, and is now living at
243 Mount Prospect avenue in that city.
For his early education he went to the Newark
Academy, and then prepared for college in St.
Paul's school, Concord, New Hampshire, after
leaving which he graduated from Princeton
University in 1906. He then became superintendent of the blast furnace of the New Jersey
Zinc Company at Palmerton, Pennsylvania,
and a year later went to Cuba as assistant
treasurer for the Stewart Sugar Company.
After a year of this he returned to Newark
and is now in the real estate and insurance
business, under the firm name of Kirkpatrick
& Young. Mr. Kirkpatrick is a Democrat,
but he has held no office and he belongs to no
secret societies. He is a member of the Prince-
ton Club, of New York; of the University
Cottage Club, of Princeton, and of the Union
Club, of Newark. June 9, 1908, Littleton
Kirkpatrick married, in Newark, Amanda
Lewis, the fourth child and third daughter of
Edward Nichols and Cordelia (Matthews)
Crane, born December 3, 1884. They have
one daughter.

This name, so closely identified
COBB with the early iron industries
founded in Essex county, New
Jersey, at the beginning of the eighteenth century, first appears in Massachusetts in connection with the same industry in Taunton,
Plymouth Colony, in 1639. Already the
Winthrop Company at Braintree had established a bloomery and forge, having imported

skilled workmen from Wales to operate the works. The absence of a circulating medium except wampum, and measures of Indian corn, found a new medium in the manufactured iron and even in the pig as it came from the bloomery. Plows and hoes were a prime necessity in the cultivation of Indian corn, the chief food of the Colonists, and the iron industry assumed an importance second to no other in the colony. At Two Mile river, near Taunton, the supply of iron ore appeared to be inexhaustable and the proprietors of that town at once set about to develop the mines. The proprietors of the First Company organized in 1653-54 included twenty-three residents and proprietors of the town, and the thirteenth one on the list of subscribers was John Cobb, or Cob, as then written. Additional capital was furnished from Plymouth, Boston, Salem and Braintree, in Massachusetts, and by Providence and Newport, in Rhode Island. The product of the bloomeries and forges there established was transported by wagon to Boston and Salem and by small sloops to Providence, Newport and even to New York. This trade put Taunton in close touch with the western world as it then existed, and for the time the iron mines of Taunton were the gold mines of more favored Spanish-America. The mines at Taunton were in charge of Henry and James Leonard and Ralph Russell. Captain Thomas Cobb married a daughter of James Leonard and in this way the Cobbs became more firmly allied to the iron industry, and when the iron mines of Morris county, New Jersey, presented new fields of quickly acquired wealth, we find the Cobbs at Rockaway, East New Jersey. The progenitor of these thrifty and enterprising colonists was Henry Cobb (q. v.).

(I) Henry Cobb, one of the "Men of Kent," was born in county Kent, near London, England, in 1596. He had been brought up in the established church, and when the non-conformist party took a stand against the religious intolerance that became more and more unbearable, young Cobb attended the meetings held by Lathrop and his followers in London and became a disciple of Congregationalism. He was not, however, of the twenty-four members who, with their preacher Lathrop, confined in the "foul and loothsome prisons" of London, but it was his privilege a few years after to welcome Lathrop to New England and help to organize for him a school at Scituate, Plymouth Colony. It is probable that Henry Cobb was a passenger of the ship

"Anne" that reached the New England coast in 1629. He was at Plymouth that year and remained in the oldest established town in America up to 1633, when the church at Plymouth gave him a letter of dismissal to Scituate, which was common land of the colony, and where a considerable body of settlers had located and stood in need of a church and preacher. A town government was organized by Cobb and his associates and incorporated by the general court of Plymouth, July 1, 1633. The next year Mr. Lathrop arrived from London and was installed minister over the church organization and Henry Cobb was made senior deacon. This position marks the estimation in which he was held by the fellow Pilgrims. The town and church grew and prospered, and in 1638 he was dismissed to go to Barnstable and established a town and church goverment there which was affected March 5, 1738. He was made ruling elder of this church and was thereafter known as Elder Cobb. Besides holding the highest office in the town and church, he was deputy to the general court at Plymouth, 1645-47-52-59-60-61. He married (first) in Plymouth, in April, 1631, Patience, daughter of Deacon James and Catherine Hurst, of that town, and by her he had eight children and of these the first three were born in Plymouth, the next two in Scituate and the others in Barnstable which became his permanent home and where he died in 1679, aged eighty-three years. The children were born in the following order: 1. John (q. v.). 2. Edward (q. v.). 3. James, January 14, 1634; married Sarah, daughter of James Lewis, December 26, 1663, and died 1695. 4. Mary, March 24, 1637; married Jonathan Dunham, of Barnstable, October 15, 1657. 5. Hannah, October 5, 1639; married Edward Lewis, May 9, 1681, and died January 17, 1736. 6. Patience, March 19, 1641; married (first) Robert Parker, August, 1667; (second) Deacon William Crocker, 1686. 7. Greshom, January 10, 1645; married Hannah David, June 4, 1675; he was beheaded by the Indians. 8. Eleazer, March 30, 1648. The mother of these children, Patience (Hurst) Cobb, died May 4, 1648, and Elder Cobb married (second) Sarah, daughter of Samuel and Sarah Hinckley, who were also the parents of Governor Thomas Hinckley. By this marriage Elder Cobb had eight children, all born in Braintree as follows: 9. Mehitable, September 1, 1652; died March 8, 1653. 10. Samuel, October 12, 1654; married Elizabeth, daughter of Richard Taylor, December 20, 1680; died

December 27, 1727. 11. Sarah, January 15, 1658; died the same year. 12. Jonathan, April 10. 1660; married, March 1, 1683, Hope, daughter of John Chipman and widow of John Hukins, a "Mayflower" descendant. 13. Sarah (2), March 10, 1663; married Deacon Samuel Chipman, December 27, 1689. 14. Henry, September 5, 1665; married Lois, daughter of Joseph Hallett, April 10, 1690; removed to Stonington, Connecticut colony. 15. Mehitable, February 15, 1667; died young. 16. Experience, September, 1671; died young.

(II) John, eldest son of Henry and Patience (Hurst) Cobb, was born in Plymouth, Plymouth colony, January 7, 1632. He was brought up in Barnstable, where he was married, August 28, 1658, to Martha, daughter of William Nelson, of Plymouth, and by her he had six children as follows, all born in Barnstable: 1. John, August 24, 1662; died October 8, 1727; he married Rachel Soule, granddaughter of George Soule, the "Mayflower" passenger, 1620. 2. Samuel, 1663; settled in Tolland, Connecticut colony, where he became very prominent in town and colonial affairs. 3. Elizabeth, 1664. 4. Israel, 1666. 5. Patience, August 10, 1668; married John Barett, of Middleburgh. 6. Ebenezer, August 9, 1671; married (first) Mercy Holmes, March 22, 1694; (second) Mary Thomas; he died in Kingston, Plymouth colony, January 29, 1752. 7. Elisha, April 3, 1679; married Lydia Ryder, February 4, 1703. 8. James, July 20, 1682; married Patience Holmes, July 21, 1705. The mother of these children, except the last two, Martha (Nelson) Cobb, died and her husband married as his second wife, in Taunton, June 13, 1676, Jane Woodward, of Taunton, and by her had Elisha and James. He had removed to Taunton in 1659, and been allotted thirty acres of land in the division of the town lots, and he took the oath of allegiance in 1659, as did Edward Cobb. On June 6, 1668, John Cobb, of Taunton, with thirty-five other of the settlers of Plymouth colony purchased from Thomas Pence, Josiah Winslow, Thomas Southworth and Constant Southworth the territory lying in the north of Taunton and known as Taunton North Purchase and where John and William Cobb became permanent settlers, the place being incorporated as the town of Norton, May 17, 1710. John Cobb, of Taunton, paid taxes into the treasury of Plymouth colony according to the records in 1668 at the October court, July 8. 1669; January, 1670, was on the jury at Plymouth for Taunton, and was one of seven of the twelve

men on the jury able to write his name, the other five making their marks. He was supervisor of highways and entrusted with the laying out of boundaries as well as roads in 1666. He returned to Barnstable but his sons, who did not remove to Connecticut, remained in Taunton.

(II) Edward, second son of Henry and Patience (Hurst) Cobb, was born in Plymouth, 1633, and took the oath of fidelity, 1659. He married Mary, daughter of William and Ann (Hynd) Hoskins, November 28, 1660. He removed to Taunton in 1657, where he died in 1675, and his widow married (second) Samuel Philips. The children of Edward and Mary (Hoskins) Cobb were: Edward and John.

(III) Edward (2), eldest son of Edward (1) and Mary (Hoskins) Cobb, was born in Taunton, Plymouth colony, about 1662. He married but we find no record as to name of wife or date of marriage. He had children as follows: 1. Ebenezer (q. v.). 2. Mary, who married Seth Dean, and had sons, Ichabod Paul and Silas Dean; she married (second) John Rosher and (third) Nicholas Stephens. Edward (2) gave his son, Ebenezer, fifteen acres of land in Taunton taken from the northerly portion of his homestead farm. The deed for this land is dated February 22, 1733.

(IV) Ebenezer, eldest child of Edward (2) Cobb, was born in Taunton, Massachusetts, May 6, 1696; died in 1769. He married, February 6, 1717, Mehitable, daughter of Increase and Mehitable (Williams) Robinson, and granddaughter of Increase Robinson, baptized in Dorchester, Massachusetts Bay colony, May 14, 1642, son of William and Margaret Robinson (1635). She was born January 12, 1695, died 1761. The children of Ebenezer and Mehitable (Robinson) Cobb were born in Taunton, Massachusetts, as follows: 1. Jemima, June 21, 1718. 2. Sarah, December 6, 1719. 3. Ebenezer, December 13, 1721. 4. John (q. v.). 5. Abiel, November 15, 1725; married Sarah Van Winkle, January 4, 1750; died 1805. 6. Mehitable, January 9, 1728; married (first) a Woodruff; (second) a Baldwin, and (third) Thomas Gould, of Caldwell, New Jersey. 7. Edward, July 15, 1731; married Elizabeth Bowers, born 1746, died 1788; he died 1813. 8. Mary, October 12, 1733; died 1805. 9. Ann, June 27, 1738; married John Gould; died 1780.

(V) John, second son and fourth child of Ebenezer and Mehitable (Robinson) Cobb, was born in Taunton, Massachusetts, December 27, 1723. He removed to Rockaway,

Morris county, New Jersey, attracted to the place by the iron mines, in which business he had become familiar in Taunton, the family always having had an interest in the business from the time his. great-great-grandfather, John Cobb, had helped to found the business in Taunton, in 1639. He married Rhoda ——— and by her he had seven children as follows, all born in Parsippany, New Jersey: 1. Samuel, baptized June 3, 1753. 2. Sarah, baptized June 3, 1753. 3. Clisby, baptized June 10, 1753. 4. John (q. v.). 5. Rhoda, baptized April 20, 1755. 6. Robert, baptized October 18, 1771. 7. (probably) Thomas, born January 16, 1760; a revolutionary soldier, who died January 17, 1845; his wife was Clara A., born March 3. 1786, died April 20, 1863; the graves of the revolutionary soldier and his wife are both at Parsippany. John Cobb had another son in the American revolution, Clisby, the third child. He served in Captain Josiah Hall's company, of Denville, New Jersey.

(VI) John (2), third son and fourth child of John (1) and Rhoda Cobb, was born in Parsippany, Morris county, New Jersey, November 24, 1750, and was baptized in the Rockaway Church, June 10, 1753. He had a forge at Troy Hills and Franklin; was sheriff of Morris county, 1792; justice of the peace, receiving his appointment 1797 and a man of large interests and influence in the community. He died December 7 (or 17), 1805, and is buried at Parsippany. He married, October 31, 1773, Ann, daughter of George Parrott, who was born March 30, 1756, died May 17, 1805. The children of John and Ann (Parrott) Cobb were born in Parsippany, New Jersey, as follows: 1. Lucinda, November 2, 1774; died 1777. 2. Eleanor, February 18, 1777; died April 12, 1777. 3. Henry (q. v.). 4. John, October 19, 1780; died 1782. 5. John Joline, M. D., August 23, 1784; married Jane Jacobus, July 9, 1811; died February 4, 1846. 6. Jane, August 7, 1786; married James S. Condit; died July 25, 1855. 7. Samuel Allen, January 10, 1790; died September 27, 1795. 8. Israel, November 11, 1794; died the same year. 9. A son, who died soon after his birth, 1797.

(VII) Henry, eldest son and third child of John (2) and Ann (Parrott) Cobb, was born in Parsippany, Morris county, New Jersey, May 23, 1778. He married Maria Baldwin, of Newark, born January 5, 1786, died March 1, 1864. Henry died June 25, 1857, and they are both interred in the Parsippany burial-ground. He was a large landholder in Morris

county, both by inheritance and purchase. The children of Henry and Maria (Baldwin) Cobb were born in Parsippany, New Jersey, as follows: 1. Alexander A. (q. v.). 2. Anna Maria, who married John O. Cordict. 3. John A., November 26, 1810; died March 14, 1880. 4. Archibald, who married a Miss Brown. 5. Cornelia, 1813; died August 30, 1881; unmarried. 6. Eliza, who was living in Troy, New Jersey, in 1902. 7. Henry, August 9, 1819; died April 15, 1887. 8. Sarah, who married a De Hart. John A. Cobb with his father, Henry Cobb, were owners of the Cobb homestead property in the town of Troy which his grandfather, John Cobb, purchased from Isaac and Mary Beach, May 15, 1788, and the survey of which property was made by Lemuel Cobb, May 14, 1788. The homestead was sold by William Ripley Cobb, and the other heirs to John Monteith, of Newark, New Jersey. Lemuel Cobb was born in Parsippany, New Jersey, September 5, 1775; married, August 8, 1819, Elizabeth Shaw, and died June 1, 1858. Their son, Andrew Bell Cobb, died January 31, 1873.

(VIII) Alexander A., eldest child of Henry and Maria (Baldwin) Cobb, was born in Parsippany, Morris county, New Jersey. He was a contractor and builder in Newark, New Jersey, 1845, and married Clarissa, daughter of Phineas and Rebecca (Bryan) Chidester, granddaughter of Ebenezer and Hannah (Haywood) Bryan, and great-granddaughter of Joseph and Sarah (Allen) Bryan. Ebenezer Bryan, born 1692, settled in East Bridgewater, Plymouth colony, where he married, in 1744, Hannah Haywood, born 1690. They removed to Mendham, New Jersey, where he was judge of "ye County Courts 1738-41; major of militia, but known as Captain Bryan." His third child, Japhet, born 1721; married Sarah Allen, in 1742. He was a private in the New Jersey militia and was called out several times in the revolutionary war. The children of Alexander A. and Clarissa (Chidester) Cobb, were born in Newark, New Jersey, as follows: 1. John Alexander (q. v.). 2. George B., 1846. 3. Annie M., who married Harry Waters.

(IX) John Alexander, eldest son of Alexander A. and Clarissa (Chidester) Cobb, was born in Newark, New Jersey, 1844; died in that city, November 5, 1881. He was graduated at the College of New Jersey, now Princeton University, A. B., 1866, became a law student in the office of Theodore Runyon, subsequently chancellor of the state, and he was

William Ripley Cobb

admitted to the New Jersey bar as an attorney at law in 1869 and as a counsellor at law in 1872. He practiced law in Newark continuously 1869-81. Mr. Cobb married, December 1, 1876, Mary Caroline, daughter of William A. and Caroline (Ward) Ripley, granddaughter of David (1803-1883) and Mary Ann (Wattles) Ripley, and of Erastus and Sallie (Thomas) Wattles; great-granddaughter of Peleg and Mollie (Bartlett) Thomas, and of Rev. William (1768-1822) and Lucy (Clift) Ripley, and great-great-granddaughter of Rev. Hezekiah (1743-1851) and Dorothy Ripley. The Rev. Hezekiah Ripley was chaplain in General Stillman's brigade in part of the campaign of 1776 in Washington's army, encamped around New York, Harlem and in New Jersey. Her great-great-great-grandparents were David (1697-1781) and Lydia (Correy) Ripley, and her great-great-great-great-grandparents were Joshua (1658-1739) and Hannah B. (Bradford) (1662-1671) Ripley. Hannah B. Bradford was the daughter of William (1624-1704) and Alice Richards (1627-1671) Bradford and granddaughter of Governor William (1588-1623) and Mrs. Alice Southwood Bradford, the emigrant progenitor of the Bradfords of New England. This makes Mary Caroline Ripley a descendant in the tenth generation from Governor Bradford and her son, William Ripley Cobb, of the eleventh generation. The two children of John Alexander and Mary C. (Ripley) Cobb were born in Newark, New Jersey, as follows: 1. William Ripley (q. v.). 2. Miriam, December 25, 1881; married, October 1, 1902, Rufus Newton Barrows and their children in 1909 were: John Alden and Daniel Newton Barrows.

(X) William Ripley, eldest child of John Alexander and Mary C. (Ripley) Cobb, was born in Newark, New Jersey, November 1, 1879. He attended the public schools of his native city; was prepared for college at the Dwight School, of New York City, was student at Princeton University in class of 1901. He studied law in the offices and under the direction of Hon. John Franklin Fort, of Newark, New Jersey, and at the New York Law School, and was admitted to the New Jersey bar as an attorney in 1901, and as a counsellor in 1904. He engaged in general practice and came to be recognized as a careful, painstaking and discriminating attorney and counsellor, learned in the law and possessed of all the attributes that go to make up a successful lawyer. He affiliated with the Lawyers' Club, the North End Club and the Wednesday Club, of

ii.-5

Newark. As a young Republican he exerted a strong influence among young men and was not timid in pointing out the defects he found in the older organizations of the party and the necessity of reforms that would keep pace with the new conditions that were to be met and contradicted by the Republican party. His church affiliation was the Protestant Episcopal faith and he was a member of Grace Church, Newark. Mr. Cobb married, October 1, 1902, at Belmar, New Jersey, Annie Waldron, daughter of Manning and Julia Condit (Waldron) Force, born in Newark, New Jersey, March 15, 1879, and their child, Nancy Ripley, was born August 2, 1907, representing the eleventh generation from Elder Henry Cobb, of Barnstable.

CARPENDER

Descended from an arms-bearing family of county Hereford, England, the Carpenders have been established in America since the middle of the eighteenth century. The first of the line in this country was

(I) George Carpender, of New York City. He is buried, with his wife Elizabeth, in Trinity churchyard. Issue: 1. George, remained in England. 2. William, in England, for his health, in 1774. 3. Benjamin (?). 4. John, see below. 5. Catharine, married Captain Samuel Bayard. 6. Elizabeth, married Sidney Breeze. 7. Sarah, married Dr. Richard Ayscough, whose daughter Sarah married Colonel William Malcolm. Sidney Breeze and Dr. Ayscough are buried side by side in Trinity churchyard. Their grandchildren were made the heirs of Captain Bayard, who married the other sister, Catharine Carpender.

(II) John, fourth child of George and Elizabeth Carpender, born 1721, lived in Brooklyn, New York, and died 1793. He was buried in St. Ann's, Brooklyn, whence his remains were removed to Greenwood Cemetery. He married (first) Marcy Weaver; (second) March 6, 1772, Sarah Stout (died April 21, 1808) widow of James Taggart. Children by his third marriage: 1. William, see below. 2. Sarah, married Lieutenant Colonel William Walton Morris. 3. Frances, married Captain Jacob Stout, who had before married her half-sister Elizabeth, daughter of John Carpender and Catharine Briant. 4. Ann, married (as his second wife) Arthur Breese, of Utica, New York.

(III) William, eldest child of John Carpender by his third wife, Sarah Stout; born 1773, died 1816, and is buried in Belleville,

New Jersey. He was a merchant. He mar-
married Lucy Weston Grant, who died in
1845, and is buried in Shrewsbury, New Jersey. She was the daughter of Edward Butler
Thomas and Catharine (Walker) Grant, both
of English birth; granddaughter of John and
Martha (Butler) Grant; great-granddaughter
of Rev. John Grant, canon of Exeter and arch-
deacon of Barnstaple, England, by his wife,
Elizabeth Weston (who was the daughter of
Stephen Weston, bishop of Exeter); and
great-great-granddaughter of Dr. John Grant,
prebendary of Rochester, by his wife, Jane
Colchester (who was a descendant of a sister
of William of Wickham, founder of Winchester College, Chancellor of England, etc.).

(IV) Jacob Stout, son of William and Lucy
Weston (Grant) Carpender, was born in Rumson, Monmouth county, New Jersey, August 15,
1805. He was a merchant and banker in New
York City, member of the stock exchange, and
for many years secretary of the Atlantic
Mutual Marine Insurance Company. Retiring
from active business in 1852, he removed to
New Brunswick, New Jersey, where he resided
for the remainder of his life, and where he
died on September 22, 1882. He married, June
21, 1838, Catharine Neilson, born March 17,
1807, died September 21, 1888, daughter of Dr.
John and Abigail (Bleecker) Neilson. Children and descendants of Jacob Stout and Catharine (Neilson) Carpender, the fifth, sixth and
seventh generations of this line of the Carpender family in America:

1. Mary Noel Carpender, born in New York
City, August 30, 1840, married, January 21,
1868, Francis Kerby Stevens, son of Henry
Hewgill and Catharine Clarkson (Crosby)
Stevens.

This branch of the Stevens family descends
from Erasmus Stevens, one of the founders
(1714) of the New North Church of Boston,
Massachusetts. His son, Ebenezer Stevens,
lived in Roxbury, Massachusetts, and married
Elizabeth Weld, a descendant of Rev. Thomas
Weld, one of the first nonconformist clergymen to flee from England to Holland, who
later emigrated to Massachusetts. They were
the parents of the distinguished revolutionary
patriot, General Ebenezer Stevens, born in
Boston, May 11, 1751 (o. s.), died in New
York City, September 22, 1823. (For an account of his career see the very able mono-
graph by his grandson, the late John Austin
Stevens). He married (second) May 4, 1784,
Lucretia Ledyard, daughter of Judge John
Ledyard, of Hartford, Connecticut, and widow

of Richardson Sands. One of their children
was Henry Hewgill Stevens, born in New
York, February 28, 1797; merchant in that
city; died October 6, 1869. Married, November 9, 1836, Catharine Clarkson Crosby, died
February 6, 1882, daughter of William Bed-
low Crosby, who was a grand-nephew of
Henry Rutgers and Harriet Ashton Crosby.

Francis Kerby Stevens was born in New
York City, August 18, 1839. For some years
he was engaged in business in Poughkeepsie,
New York, retiring from active life on account
of ill health. He was an officer in the civil
war (Twenty-third Regiment of New York
Volunteer Infantry), and was wounded at
Chancellorsville. Died in Aiken, South Carolina, February 22, 1874. His widow resides in
New Brunswick, New Jersey. Children: i.
Henry Hewgill Stevens, born November 20,
1869; resides in Roselle, New Jersey; identified with the Union Metallic Cartridge Company of New York; married, June 27, 1901,
Ethel Griffin, daughter of George W. Griffin.
ii. William Carpender Stevens, born March 13,
1872, resides in New Brunswick. iii. Frances
Noel Stevens, born January 13, 1874, resides
in New Brunswick.

2. Lucy Helena Carpender, born in New
York City, April 1, 1842, married, June 19,
1884, Rev. Charles Edward Hart, D. D., born
February 28, 1838, in Freehold, New Jersey,
only son of Walter Ward and Sarah (Bennett)
Hart. He is a descendant in the sixth generation of Deacon Stephen Hart, who was one of
the original proprietors and settlers of Hartford and Farmington, Connecticut (coming
with the Rev. Thomas Hooker), through his
son, Captain Thomas Hart. The father of
Rev. Dr. Hart removed from Connecticut to
Freehold, Monmouth county, New Jersey; he
was judge of the court of common pleas of
that county, and identified with manufacturing
interests. Sarah Bennett, mother of Dr. Hart,
was the daughter of William H. Bennett, of
Monmouth county, and descended from an old
New Jersey family. Charles Edward Hart
was graduated from Princeton College in 1858,
and from Princeton Theological Seminary in
1861; in the latter year was called to the Murray Hill Presbyterian Church, New York City,
continuing there until June, 1880, when he
became pastor of the North Reformed Dutch
Church of Newark, New Jersey; resigned that
charge in 1880 to accept the chair of English
Language and Literature in Rutgers College,
which he retained until 1897; from 1897 to
1906 was professor of Ethics and the Evi-

dences of Christianity in the same institution; has since been professor emeritus of Ethics; received the degree of D. D. from Rutgers in 1880. Dr. and Mrs. Hart reside in New Brunswick.

3. William Carpender, born in New York City, January 30, 1844. He was long identified with financial interests in New York. being until recently a member of the stock exchange; resides in Massapequa, Long Island. He is a member of the Sons of the Revolution, Union League Club, New York Yacht Club, and Saint Nicholas Society. He married, November 26, 1878, Ella Floyd-Jones, daughter of William and Caroline (Blackwell) Floyd-Jones. i. Edith Carpender, born April 1, 1880, married, November 19, 1905, Edward H. Floyd Jones. ii. Noel Lispenard Carpender, born May 6, 1882, member of the New York stock exchange; resides in Massapequa, Long Island; married, April 24, 1906, Isabel Gourley, daughter of John H. Gourley, and has one child, Isabel Floyd-Jones Carpender, born February 9, 1907. iii. Jeannie Floyd-Jones Carpender, born November 29, 1887. iv. Ella Floyd-Jones Carpender, born October 9, 1892.

4. John Neilson Carpender, born in New York City, November 4, 1845, received his early education in private schools and was graduated in 1866 from Rutgers College as Bachelor of Arts, the degree of Master of Arts being conferred on him in 1869. From the latter year until 1879 he was a member of the New York stock exchange. In 1877 Mr. Carpender became identified as treasurer with the Norfolk and New Brunswick Hosiery Company of New Brunswick, New Jersey, serving in that capacity until 1885; and he has since been president of the company. He is vice-president and member of the executive committee of the National Association of Wool Manufacturers of the United States. As a citizen of New Brunswick he has always taken an active interest in the affairs of that community. From 1878 to 1882 he was a member of the common council, and from 1880 to the present time has been the commissioner of the sinking fund. He is president of the John Wells Memorial Hospital, trustee of the Children's Industrial Home, director in the National Bank of New Jersey, and trustee of the New Brunswick Mutual Fire Insurance Company. A member of the Protestant Episcopal church, he occupies several important official positions in that connection; is trustee of the American Church Building Fund, president of the Church Club of the diocese of New

Jersey, and treasurer of the board of trustees of the Episcopal Fund of the diocese of New Jersey. His society and club memberships include the Sons of the Revolution, Delta Phi and Phi Beta Kappa societies, and the University Club and Saint Nicholas Society of New York. He married, in New York City, April 9, 1874, Anna Neilson Kemp, born in New York City, February 18, 1855, daughter of Alfred Francklin and Cecilia (Neilson) Kemp. Her paternal grandparents were Henry Kemp, of county Kent, England, and Susanne Ursula Penelope de la Bruyerè, of Huguenot ancestry. Her father, Alfred Francklin Kemp, was born September 12, 1817, in county Kent, England, came to America in early life, and died on Staten Island, September, 1873; married, May 18, 1852, Cecilia Neilson, daughter of William Neilson, of New York City, and Hannah Coles. Children: i. John Neilson Carpender, born January 16, 1875, graduated at Rutgers, 1897; in mercantile business in New York; resides in New Brunswick. ii. Catharine Neilson Carpender, born December 7, 1876, married, November 26, 1901, Franklin Diane, son of Rev. Richard Bache Diane and Margaret Ann Tams, and a descendant of Benjamin Franklin; they reside in Baltimore; their children are Howard Diane, born October 23, 1902, and Margaret Franklin Diane, born June 7, 1904. iii. Alfred Cecil Carpender, born November 27, 1878, died November 10, 1894. iv. Anna Kemp Carpender, born March 15, 1880. v. Henry de la Bruyerè Carpender, born May 15, 1882, resides in New Brunswick; in business in New York. vi. Arthur Schuyler Carpender, born October 24, 1884, officer in the United States navy. vii. William Carpender, 2d, born October 29, 1888, student in Rutgers College.

5. Charles Johnson Carpender, born in New York City, October 31, 1847, was educated under private instructors. In 1870 he organized, with John Nicholson, the firm of Nicholson & Carpender, and embarked in the manufacture of wall paper in New Brunswick. Upon the retirement of Mr. Nicholson in 1872 Mr. Carpender established with Colonel Jacob J. Janeway the new co-partnership of Janeway & Carpender, from which he withdrew in 1888, the firm having since been continued by Colonel Janeway under the original style. Mr. Carpender has always resided in New Brunswick. He is a director of various industrial and other corporations, and is a member of the Sons of the Revolution and the Saint Nicholas Society. He married, June 9, 1875, Alice

Brown Robinson, born November 10, 1850, daughter of Edwin and Frances (Brown) Robinson. Edwin Robinson, born July 30, 1807, died August 14, 1863, was of Richmond, Virginia, son of John Robinson, and descended from an old Virginia family, related to the Beverly Robinsons of Staten Island and also to the Canadian Robinsons. (See Hayden's Genealogies). He married, October 6, 1836, Frances Brown, of Bedford county, Virginia. Issue of Charles Johnson and Alice Brown (Robinson) Carpender: i. Alice Haxall Carpender, born September 5, 1876, married, October 30, 1901, Gustavus Abeel Hall, son of John A., of Trenton, New Jersey, and Anna (Abeel) Hall; they now reside in Cleveland, Ohio, where Mr. Hall is in charge of the interests of the Roebling Company; their children are John Alexander Hall, born November 4, 1902, Charles Carpender Hall, born May 29, 1906, and Abeel Neilson Hall, born July 23, 1907, died April 30, 1909. ii. Charles Johnson Carpender, Jr., born June 6, 1878, resides in New Brunswick; engaged in the chemical industry at Little Falls, New Jersey. iii. Katharine Neilson Carpender, born January 2, 1881, died June 29, 1881. iv. and v. twins, born June 17, 1882, Moncure Conway Carpender, mechanical and electrical engineer at Plattsburg, New York, and Edwin Robinson Carpender, resides in New Brunswick. vi. Sydney Bleecker Carpender, born November 24, 1884, refrigerating engineer in New Brunswick.

LEVIS

The first Levis of whom we have any definite knowledge is Philippe I., Seigneur de Lévis, who lived in the twelfth century. The most ancient document in which he is mentioned is dated February 5, 1181, and is signed by him and his wife, Elizabeth. In the year 1200 he assisted in making a treaty of peace between the Kings of England and France. He died in 1204-05. His wife was still living in 1210, but the date of her death is not known. They had five children—Milon, Gui, Philippe, Alexander and Simon. The second of these, Gui de Levis I., married Guiburge, sister of Simon de Montfort, Earl of Leicester. His great-granddaughter, Jeanne (daughter of Gui de Levis III.), married Philippe de Montfort II., a descendant of a brother of Simon de Montfort. There is much evidence of the close relationship of the two families.

The history of the French family is well known, but it is not known when the first Levis went to England. It is probable, however, that it was during this relationship, as not only was Simon de Montfort a person of great rank, influence and power and naturally gathered about him many of his compatriots, but many of the French settled in England during this period. The first known English record of the family is in the parish register of Beeston, near Nottingham, dated 1558. It is to be noted that Beeston is in the district which was under the influence of Simon de Montfort. The earliest parish register in England began in 1538. There are earlier dates entered in some of them, but no registers existed until the year mentioned, so they must have been inserted afterward.

The Beeston records began in 1558, and in this first year there is an entry as follows: "1558 Robt. Levis was buried ———." At the bottom of the second page of the earliest registry book (1558) belonging to Beeston parish church in the county of Nottingham, the name of "Rich. Levis occurs as one of the churchwardens," and continues on the pages up to the year 1599. Altogether there are one hundred and two entries in the name of Levis, the last being dated January 27, 1768. The last one we are interested in is the baptism of Christopher Levis, September 20, 1621, it being the fifty-fourth Levis entry.

The following wills and administrations relating to the Levis family of Beeston are entered in the York Probate Registry prior to 1652, Nottinghamshire being in the ecclesiastical district of York.

1. 1580—Christopher Levice, of Beeston—Administration.
2. 1585—Mary Levise, of Alswortha—Will.
3. 1613—Richard Levis, of Beeston—Will.
4. 1616—Christopher Levis, of Beeston—Will.
5. 1616—Richard Levis, of Beeston—Will.
6. 1620—Edwarde Levis, of Beeston—Will.
7. 1638—Edward Levis, of Saxondale—Will.

Of these numbers one and three are the only ones connected with the direct line we are considering, but all have been helpful in establishing the facts. The most interesting will is that of Christopher Levis, who died at Harby, Leicestershire, in 1677. It is dated October 19, 1677, and was admitted to probate December 31, 1677, in the district registry at Leicester. The original will and inventory are still on file and were recently examined by Mr. Howard C. Levis, formerly of Mt. Holly, New Jersey, but now of London.

The exact relationship of Robert Levis mentioned in the table with the others which follow is not known. The Richard who was churchwarden is not mentioned in the table as he is not in the direct line, and it is not certain that the Christopher who was buried in 1580 was the son of the Edward who was buried in 1564. This, however, is of no importance as unquestionably the persons with the name of Levis in this small parish were of the same family. It is also to be noted that Harby in Leicestershire, where a Christopher Levis died in 1677, is not many miles distant from Beeston. Whether Christopher or his father, Richard, was the first to leave Beeston for Harby is not known, but it was probably the father, as his death is not recorded at Beeston. The early records of Harby parish are not in existence, and in any event would be of little value to us, as Christopher had become a Quaker and therefore nothing would be recorded in the parish registers.

The Levis family of New Jersey traces its ancestry back directly in this line:

(I) Robert Levis was born in 1558.

(II) Edward Levis, buried May 10, 1654, married Yssabell ——, buried June 3, 1593. They had a son, Christopher, and other children.

(III) Christopher Levis, buried May 9, 1580, married Agnes ——, buried February 4, 1584. They had a son, Richard, and perhaps other children. *

(IV) Richard Levis, buried March 2, 1612, married June 29, 1577, Elizabeth Clark, buried January 25, 1593; married (second) May 15, 1594, Constance Smalley, buried March 3, 1597. Of this second marriage there was born a son, Nicholas, baptized February 24, 1597, buried August 5, 1607.

(V) Richard (2), son of Richard (1) and Elizabeth (Clark) Levis, was baptized April 11, 1585. He married, but the name of his wife is not known. He neither married nor was buried in the parish at Beeston.

(VI) Christopher, son of Richard (2) Levis, was baptized September 20, 1621, and died in 1677. He married, in March, 1648, Mary Need, of Harby, England, and had children.

(VII) Samuel, son of Christopher and Mary (Need) Levis, was born at Harby, July 30, 1649, and his will was admitted to probate in 1734. He came to America in 1682, from Lancashire, England, remained here a short time, then returned to England for his family and again came over in 1684, with his wife; son, Samuel, and sisters, Sarah and Hannah. He erected a large brick house on Darby creek, in

Delaware county, Pennsylvania, where he had a grant of two thousand acres of land. The old mansion house is still standing and is owned by his descendants. He was a man of considerable means and much influence, especially in the Society of Friends, being a minister of that faith, and a very devout man in his walk in life. He was among the first settlers in Delaware county, and at one time was a member of the provincial council, of the state of Pennsylvania. He married, in 1680, Elizabeth Clator, of Nottingham, England, and by her had several children.

(VIII) Samuel (2), son of Samuel (1) and Elizabeth (Clator) Levis, was born in England. December 8, 1680, died in 1758. He married, October 15, 1709, Hannah, daughter of Joseph Stretch, of Philadelphia, and they had children.

(IX) Samuel (3), son of Samuel (2) and Hannah (Stretch) Levis, was born August 21, 1711, and married, December 6, 1742, Mary, daughter of Joshua and Martha Thomson, and they had children.

(X) Samuel (4), son of Samuel (3) and Mary (Thomson) Levis, married Elizabeth Garrett, and they had children.

(XI) William, son of Samuel (4) and Elizabeth (Garrett) Levis, was born in Darby, Pennsylvania, March 17, 1774, died September 22, 1823, and was a paper maker. He married, March 11, 1798, Esther Pancoast, who died September 15, 1848, daughter of Seth Pancoast. Their children were: Samuel Franklin, see post; Pancoast, Robert J., Elizabeth and Ann.

(XII) Samuel Franklin Levis, progenitor of the Mt. Holly family of that surname, son of William and Esther (Pancoast) Levis, was born in Darby, Pennsylvania, June 8, 1805, died at Mt. Holly, December 10, 1887. He received a good early education in the Darby town schools and also in the Friends' school, and began his business career as clerk in a general merchandise store in Philadelphia then under the proprietorship of Bennett & Walton. Soon after 1820 he was sent by his employers to Mt. Holly, New Jersey, to take charge of their mill there, which was operated, in the manufacture of wall, book and newspaper. He continued to live in Mt. Holly until the time of his death, in 1887. Mr. Levis married twice. His first wife, whom he married, November 20, 1830, was Sarah Biddle Hulme, born June 26, 1804, died April 1, 1843, daughter of George and Sarah B. (Shreve) Hulme (see Hulme). He married (second) November 20, 1845, Maria B. Hulme, born October 23, 1814, and still living in Mt. Holly. She also is a daughter of George and Sarah B. (Shreve) Hulme. Mr. Levis had three children by his first and two by his second wife: 1. George Hulme, born April 30, 1832; died June 26, 1889; married, November 1, 1854, Mary Holby, daughter of Charles Magargee and Ann (Cooper) Hicks, and had children: i. Clara M., born November 30, 1855, married, June 25, 1877, Brinckle Gummey, and had daughter, Mary, born December 6, 1877; ii. Anne Hicks, born September 21, 1857, married, June 12, 1882, Frederick Hemsley, and had daughter, Frances, who married and had children; iii. Charles Magargee, born October 6, 1859, married Jean Rowland, and had children. 2. Franklin Burr, born July 28, 1834; see post. 3. Sarah Maria, born August 12, 1839; married, November 3, 1883, Daniel Garwood. 4. Emily Hulme, born September 6, 1847. 5. Adelaide Shiras, born October 28, 1851; died April 10, 1873.

(XIII) Franklin Burr, son of Samuel Franklin and Sarah Biddle (Hulme) Levis, was born in Mt. Holly, New Jersey, July 28, 1834, and attended public and private schools of that town until he was fourteen years old, when he was sent to Westown to a boarding school to prepare for college. He entered Haverford College in 1849, remaining until 1851, and then entered Princeton College and graduated there in 1853. After leaving college he took up the study of law with Hon. John L. N. Stratton, of Mt. Holly, and was admitted attorney at law at the June term of the supreme court in 1856. He at once began active practice in his native town and since that time has been a member of the Burlington county bar, although in connection with these pursuits he has been somewhat identified with the political history of his town and county. He is a Republican of undoubted quality, was one of the organizers of that party in Burlington county, and for more than half a century has been looked upon as one of the most earnest exponents of Republican principles in the state. During the civil war he was appointed by Governor Olden judge advocate of the first division of New Jersey militia, and in that capacity assisted in enrolling men and organizing companies for service which had been raised by draft. In 1862 he was appointed deputy collector of internal revenue for the second district of the state and held that office for several years. After the close of the war and particularly after he ceased to be deputy collector of inter-

nal revenue, Mr. Levis devoted his attention to professional pursuits, and in connection with the general practice of law he has been appointed to various positions incidental thereto. He is the senior member of the Burlington county bar and still in practice notwithstanding his advanced years. He is attorney and counsellor at law, a master in chancery, supreme court commissioner and special master, and outside of the profession he was for a long time a director of the Union National Bank, of Mt. Holly, and a director of Mt. Holly Safe Deposit and Trust Company; director and vice-president of Mt. Holly Water Company, and a director of the Mt. Holly, Lumberton and Medford Railroad Company. For forty-seven years he has been secretary of the Mt. Holly Building and Loan Association, excepting for a short period when that office was held by his son, Howard. He is vice-president of the Burlington County Lyceum of History and Natural Science, member of the board of trustees of Mt. Holly Circulating Library, member of Mt. Holly Lodge, F. & A. M., and a communicating member of St. Andrew's Church, Episcopal, and one of the delegates to the Pan-Anglican convention held in London, England, in June, 1908. He was instrumental in founding Trinity Church, of Mt. Holly, for many years was one of its wardens, but subsequently transferred his membership to St. Andrew's Church. At one time also Mr. Levis was secretary and treasurer of the Mt. Holly Gas Company, director in the Burlington County Telephone Company and president of the Mt. Holly Opera House Association.

On October 14, 1857, Mr. Levis married Rebecca Browning, daughter of Peter Van Pelt and Eleanor (Hollinshead) Coppuck, and by whom he has five children: 1. Howard Coppuck, born Mt. Holly, March 21, 1859; see post. 2. Franklin Burr, Jr., born Mt. Holly, March 25, 1862; died March 26, 1862. 3. Edward Hulme, born April 11, 1864; see post. 4. Gertrude Van Pelt, born Mt. Holly, February 23, 1871; died June 24, 1871. 5. Norman Van Pelt, born Mt. Holly, April 11, 1872; see post.

(XIV) Howard Coppuck, eldest son and child of Franklin Burr and Rebecca Browning (Coppuck) Levis, was born in Mt. Holly, New Jersey, March 21, 1859, acquired his earlier education in private schools, then took a special law course at Columbia College, New York, later read law under the instruction of his father and was admitted a member of the Burlington county bar. For several years he practiced in

Franklin B. Lewis.

association with his father and then received an appointment as assistant counsel for the Westinghouse Electric Company. His duties in that capacity called him to live for some time in Pittsburg, Pennsylvania, and afterward in Chicago as western counsel of the Thomson-Houston Electric Company, and still later, when he became assistant counsel for the General Electric Company, he lived temporarily in St. Paul, Minnesota, and afterward in Schenectady, New York, in which latter city are located the principal works of the General Electric Company. In 1902 Mr. Levis was elected managing director of the British Thomson-Houston Company, of London, England, and since that time he has lived abroad. He is a member of the Pilgrims, Ranelagh, City of London, and Burlington Fine Arts clubs, of London, and the Grolier Club, of New York. He married, April 24, 1884, Jane Chester, daughter of the late Hon. William A. and Jane (Chester) Coursen, of Elizabeth, New Jersey, and by whom he has two children: 1. Chester Coursen, born January 18, 1885. 2. Edith Chetwood, born October 31, 1886.

(XIV) Edward Hulme, third son and child of Franklin Burr and Rebecca Browning (Coppuck) Levis, was born in Mt. Holly, April 11, 1864, received his literary education in public schools in Mt. Holly and also at Peekskill Military Academy, Oswego county, New York, and afterward began his business career in a clerical capacity with the banking firm of Jay Cooke & Company, of Philadelphia. He continued in that employ during the life of the firm under that name, and later with the successor firm until July, 1907, when he became junior partner of the house of C. D. Barney & Co., whose members are J. Horace Harding, J. Cooke, 3d, and Mr. Levis. He maintains his residence at Mt. Holly. Mr. Levis married, January 12, 1892, Theodora, daughter of the late Theodore Risden, of Mt. Holly, and by whom he had two children: 1. Dorothy, born November 8, 1895, died the same day. 2. Dorothea, born March 23, 1901, died August 15, 1901.

(XIV) Rev. Norman Van Pelt, youngest son and child of Franklin Burr and Rebecca Browning (Coppuck) Levis, was born in Mt. Holly, April 11, 1872. He was educated in public schools of his home town, Peekskill Military Academy, the University of Pennsylvania and Alexandria Theological Seminary, Alexandria, Virginia, in the latter of which he studied for the Episcopal ministry. After one

year there he continued his studies at the Philadelphia Divinity School, graduated and was ordained, and became assistant rector of St. John's Church, Elizabeth, New Jersey. After about one and one-half years at St. John's, Mr. Levis was made rector of Christ Church, Westerly, Rhode Island, remained there four years, and in 1904 was called to the Church of the Incarnation, Philadelphia, of which he since has been rector. Mr. Levis married, June 15, 1889, Grace Royal Tyng, of Elizabeth, New Jersey, by whom he has two children: 1. Russell Tyne, born July 13, 1900. 2. Norman Van Pelt Jr., born August 29, 1906.

(The Hulme Line).

In our narrative of the Levis family in these annals it is written that Samuel Franklin Levis married, first, Sarah Hulme, and after her death married, for his second wife, Maria B. Hulme, sister of his first wife. In this connection a brief account of the Hulme family will be found of interest.

(I) George Hulme, immigrant ancestor of the family here treated, was born in England and came to this country from old Cheshire in the year 1700. He settled in Newtown, Middletown township, Bucks county, Pennsylvania, and was still living in 1732.

(II) George (2), son of George (1) Hulme, the immigrant, was born in England, came to America with his father's family in 1700, and died in 1729, his father surviving him about three years. He married (first) October 2, 1708, Naomi, daughter of John and Christina Palmer. She died in 1709, having borne her husband one child, who died in 1709, at or about the time of his mother's death. He married (second) in October, 1710, Ruth Palmer, sister of his first wife, and by her had four children, Eleanor, Naomi, Hannah and John.

(III) John, only son of George (2) and Ruth (Palmer) Hulme, was born probably about 1716-18, and died in 1776. He married (first) in 1744, Mary Pearson, daughter of Enoch and Margaret Smith, and by her had six children. He married (second) Elizabeth, daughter of Benjamin and Mary (Biles) Cutter, and by her had three children. John Hulme had in all nine children: 1. John, born June 3, 1747. 2. Mary, August 31, 1748. 3. George, November 25, 1750. 4. William, February 18, 1752. 5. Thomas, January 28, 1755, died young. 6. Margaret, August 25, 1767. 7. Ruth, October 23, 1771. 8. Thomas, 1774. 9. Benjamin, 1778.

(IV) John (2), son of John (1) and Mary (Pearson) Hulme, was born June 3, 1747, and married, May 5, 1770, Rebecca Milner, born December 3, 1748, died April 11, 1806, daughter of William Milner, of Falls township, Bucks county, Pennsylvania. Nine children were born of this marriage: 1. William, July 10, 1771. 2. John, September 20, 1773. 3. Samuel, September 15, 1774. 4. George, October 24, 1776. 5. Isaac, October 26, 1778. 6. Mary, November 5, 1780. 7. Amos, October 29, 1782. 8. Joseph, August 25, 1784. 9. Rebecca, February 25, 1787.

(V) George (3), son of John (2) and Rebecca (Milner) Hulme, was born in Hulmeville, Pennsylvania, October 24, 1776, died there July 16, 1850. He married Sarah Biddle Shreve, born 1774, died April, 1847, daughter of Joshua Shreve, and by her had seven children: 1. James S., born September 27, 1802. 2. Sarah Biddle, June 26, 1804, married Samuel F. Levis, of Mt. Holly (see Levis). 3. Rebecca Ann, March 30, 1806. 4. John, August 17, 1808. 5. George, November 6, 1811. 6. Maria B., October 23, 1814, married Samuel F. Levis (his second wife). 7. Charles, July 4, 1809.

DESHLER The late Charles Dunham Deshler, of New Brunswick, New Jersey, was of the sixth generation of the Deshler family and of the eighth generation of the Dunham family in America, his ancestral lines being as follows: *Paternal Line.* (I) Johann Deshler, born in Germany, came to America in 1730. (II) Adam Deshler, lived near Allentown, Pennsylvania, purchased, in 1742, from Frederick Newhard, two hundred and three and one-half acres, on which he built in 1760 the stone dwelling called Fort Deshler (still standing), furnished the provincial troops with supplies in the French and Indian war; married Apollonia ———. (III) David Deshler, born at Egypt, Pennsylvania, 1733, died at Bienj's Bridge, Pennsylvania, December, 1796; built in Germantown, 1772-73, the famous dwelling (afterward the residence of the Morris family) known as the Morris-Deshler house, which at one time was the headquarters of the British General Howe, and in 1793, during the yellow fever scourge, was occupied by President Washington as the executive mansion; married Susanna ———. (IV) John Adam Deshler, born 1766, died 1820; married Deborah Wagener. (V) George Wagener Deshler, born in Allentown, Pennsylvania, September 17, 1793, died 1836;

lived in Easton. Pennsylvania; prothonotary of Northampton county, Pennsylvania; editor for some time of the Belvidere (New Jersey) *Apollo;* married, May 4, 1818, Catharine Lawson Dunham. (VI) Charles Dunham Deshler, see forward.

Maternal Line. (I) Deacon John Dunham, born in England in 1589, came to New England in the ship "James" in 1630, and died in Plymouth, Massachusetts, in 1669; married Abigail ———. (II) Benajah Dunham, born 1640, in Plymouth, Massachusetts, died December 24, 1680, in Piscataway, New Jersey; married, October 25, 1660, Elizabeth Tilson. (III) Rev. Edmund Dunham, born in Piscataway township, Middlesex county, New Jersey, July 25, 1661, died March 7, 1734; married, July 15, 1681, Mary Bonham (born October 4, 1661, died 1742). (IV) Rev. Jonathan Dunham, of Piscataway, born August 16, 1694, died March 10, 1777; married August 15, 1714, Jane Pyatt. (V) Colonel Azariah Dunham, born in Piscataway, New Jersey, 1719, died January 22, 1790; noted land surveyor; active in the revolutionary war, being a member of the committee of correspondence; married Mary Ford, of Morristown, who was born September 22, 1734, in the old Ford house at that place, afterward Washington's headquarters. (VI) Dr. Jacob Dunham, born in New Brunswick, born September 30, 1767, died August 23, 1832; married Elizabeth Lawson. (VII) Catharine Lawson Dunham, born July 14, 1791, died March 26, 1875; married, May 4, 1818, George Wagener Deshler. (VIII) Charles Dunham Deshler.

(VI) Charles Dunham Deshler, eldest child and only son of George Wagener and Catharine Lawson (Dunham) Deshler, was born in Easton, Pennsylvania, March 1, 1819. When about four years old he was sent to New Brunswick, New Jersey, to make his home with his grandfather, Dr. Jacob Dunham, who then resided on Peace street, at the foot of Church, in a house which is still standing, though remodeled. He was educated in private schools and at the Rutgers Preparatory School, where he was graduated in 1832 at the age of thirteen. After his grandfather's death in the latter year, he was apprenticed as clerk to Richard S. McDonald in the drug business in New Brunswick. Succeeding Mr. McDonald, he conducted the business under the firm styles of Deshler & Carter, Deshler & Boggs, and finally C. D. Deshler. During this period he took an active and prominent part in organizing the New Brunswick gas works, savings institution, and circulating library, as also the New Brunswick public school system, of which he has always been regarded as the founder. Moving to Jersey City, Mr. Deshler became editor of the *American Standard*, resigning that position to accept the editorship of the Newark *Daily Advertiser*, and conducted these papers with marked ability during a portion of the civil war. Appointed by Governor Joel Parker commissioner for the sick and wounded Jersey troops, he spent considerable time in the south caring for the wants and interests of the New Jersey and other troops in the various hospitals. In 1865 he went to the oil regions of Pennsylvania, occupying the position of treasurer of the Farmers' railroad, which ran from Petroleum Center to Oil City. He resigned that place to become secretary of the International Life Insurance Company, of Jersey City, and later was engaged in business interests and literary work in New York City, where he was at various times editor of the *Christian Intelligencer*, secretary of the United States Dairy Company, secretary of the Harney Peak Tin Mining, Milling and Manufacturing Company, and book reviewer for the publishing house of Harper Brothers.

Re-establishing his residence in New Brunswick, Mr. Deshler was until his death a prominent and highly esteemed citizen of that community. He was lay judge of the Middlesex county court of common pleas, postmaster of New Brunswick (appointed by President Cleveland), and agent for the Mutual Life Insurance Company. For many years he was vestryman of Christ (Episcopal) Church. Throughout his very long life he was strongly interested in public affairs, and he was associated on intimate terms with many of the most distinguished political leaders. Originally an ardent Whig (his first vote being cast for Harrison and Tyler in 1840), he later became a member of the so-called Know Nothing party, and finally of the Democratic organization. By appointment from Governor McClellan he served as one of the commissioners for the Blind and Feeble-minded, having charge of the erection of buildings, etc. At the centennial of the New Jersey state legislature he delivered, by the invitation of that body, one of the addresses. A man of accomplished literary ability, for a portion of his life (as we have seen) a professional writer and editor, and at all times occupied more or less with literary studies and composition, no account of his career would be adequate without a some-

what particular allusion to this phase of it. His reading was most extensive, his tastes inclining especially to the study of English literature, of which he had a scholarly knowledge, and upon which he wrote and published valuable critical essays and other contributions. He was the author of "Selections from the Poetical Works of Geoffry Chaucer" (Putnam, 1848) and "Afternoons with the Poets" (Harper, 1879). He also devoted much attention to historical researches, and in this connection published many sketches and addresses. The George W. Deshler Memorial Library of the New Brunswick high school was given by him in memory of a son. Mr. Deshler died at his residence in New Brunswick, May 10, 1909, in his ninety-first year.

He married, May 30, 1841, Mary Moore Holcombe, born October 10, 1824, in New Brunswick, died September 7, 1893, daughter of Theophilus Moore and Catherine Neilson (Farmer) Holcombe. The Holcombes in this line were an older Quaker family, originally of Lambertville, New Jersey. Children: 1. Edward Boggs. 2. George Wagener, graduate of West Point Military Academy, and afterward first lieutenant of Company A, First Artillery, United States army; died of yellow fever at Fort Barrancas, Florida, July 28, 1875. 3. Monroe Holcombe (deceased). 4. James. 5. Kate. 6. Theophilus Holcombe (deceased). 7. Mary Holcombe. 8. Elizabeth Dunham (deceased). 9. Charles. 10. Frederick. 11. Edith.

(VII) James Deshler, fourth child of Charles Dunham and Mary Moore (Holcombe) Deshler, was born in New Brunswick, New Jersey, May 9, 1850. He received a public school education and at an early age engaged in mercantile employment in Newark, New Jersey, subsequently being a clerk in the office of the general ticket agent of the New Jersey Central railroad, Wall street, New York City. From 1865 to 1874 he was in the Pennsylvania oil regions, occupying positions as clerk for the Farmers' railroad and with George H. Bissell & Company, bankers at Petroleum Centre. In the latter year he returned to New Brunswick, where he became connected with the New Jersey Rubber Company. He has since continued with that manufacturing interest, which in 1876 took the name of the New Jersey Rubber Shoe Company, and in 1892 was merged in the United States Rubber Company; and he now occupies the position of superintendent and manager of the New Jersey factory of the United States Rub-

474   STATE OF NEW JERSEY.

ber Company. Mr. Deshler is president of the New Brunswick Trust Company. He married Ellen Slater, their children being: 1. Mary, married George W. Wilmot, of New Brunswick. 2. Anna H., married Frank K. Runyon, of New Brunswick. 3. Katherine, married Dr. Frank L. Hindle, of New Brunswick. 4. Louise, married Robert E. Ross, of New Brunswick. 5. George Ray, married Mabel Dickson, of New Brunswick. 6. Helen.

DUNHAM The family name Dunham is a surname derived from a place and in part from personal qualities. Dun is a Celtic adjective meaning brown and "ham" in early Anglo-Saxon stood for house. Therefore the town house of the Duns was Dunham. In early times the name was variously written, according to the peculiar fancy of the writer, hence the familiar Dunham patronymic is found otherwise as Doneham, Denham and Duneham. In its origin the name dates back to some remote period, even before the Saxon invasion of England. Most all words, whether names of persons, places or things, have a history, "the ancestry of which, as of individuals, is often a very noble part."

(I) Deacon John Dunham, immigrant ancestor and founder of this family in America, is said to have come from Lancashire, England, in the ship "Hope" in 1630-31.* He settled at New Plymouth, became landholder in 1632 and was made freeman of the colony there in 1633. Soon afterward he became identified with the Pilgrim church, in 1638 being elected deacon of the religious society. At that time in the "Old Colony," as afterward in most other New England colonies, none but church members were admitted to full citizenship. John Dunham was one of the four deputies elected in 1638 to represent the Plymouth settlement, and for each successive council during the next twenty years he was chosen to this responsible office in the legislative assembly. He was born in England in 1589, and after coming to Plymouth continued to live there until he was eighty years old. The public records mention his upright character as a lawmaker and his pious life as

*It is claimed by the author of the recent Dunham Genealogy (1907) that he was identical with John Goodman of the "Mayflower," having assumed and for some time borne the name of Goodman in order to conceal his personality from his Episcopalian relatives in England, who bitterly resented his association with the Pilgrims.

a faithful deacon of the Plymouth church. At his death in 1668-69 it was written in the town records that he was "an approved servant of God, and a useful man in his place." He made his last will January 25, 1669, which was witnessed by two staunch Pilgrims, John Cotton and Thomas Cushman. His wife, Abigail, was appointed to administer his estate, an inventory of which was made by Thomas Southworth. Of his children seven sons and three daughters survived him, all of whom lived to mature years and became founders of large families. Of this large and influential family, which greatly multiplied and replenished the earth, all of the children settled at first in the New England colonies, except Benajah, who emigrated to East Jersey about 1671. Children of Deacon John and Abigail Dunham: 1. John, born in Leyden, 1620. 2. Abigail, born England, 1623; married, November 6, 1644, Stephen Wood. 3. Samuel, born England, 1625; married, June 29, 1649, Mrs. Martha Falloway. 4. Thomas, born 1627; married, in 1651, Martha Knott. 5. Hannah, born 1630; married, October 31, 1651, Giles Richard. 6. Jonathan, born 1634; married (first) November 29, 1655, Mary Delano; (second) October 15, 1657, Mary Cobb. 7. Joseph, born 1637; married (first) November 18, 1657, Mercy Morton; (second) August 20, 1669, Hester Wornall. 8. Benajah, born 1640; see post. 9. Persis, born 1641; married, October 15, 1657, Benajah Platt. 10. Daniel, born 1649; married, about 1671, ———.

(II) Benajah, son of Deacon John and Abigail (Wood) Dunham, was born in Plymouth, New England, in 1640, and died at Piscataway, New Jersey, December 24, 1680. He bought lands in Piscataway in 1672, but lived previously in Eastham, Massachusetts, where he was a court officer in 1669. He was made freeman in 1664 and in 1673 was appointed captain of militia. He married, October 25, 1660, Elizabeth Tilson, of Scituate, Massachusetts, daughter of Edmund Tilson, of Plymouth. They had seven children: 1. Edmund, see post. 2. John, born August 28, 1663; died September 6, 1663. 3. Elizabeth, born November 20, 1664; died December 31, 1667. 4. Hannah, June 4, 1666; died December 25, 1667. 5. Benjamin, born October 28, 1667; died young. 6. Mary, born New Jersey, in 1669; married ——— Thompson. 7. Elizabeth, born 1670; married, July 15, 1691, Jonas Wood.

(III) Rev. Edmund, son of Benajah and Elizabeth (Tilson) Dunham, was born in

Plymouth, July 25, 1661; died March 17, 1734. He was one of the founders, 1689, of the church at Piscataway, New Jersey, also being deacon and lay preacher; and he was ordained in the ministry at Westerly, Rhode Island, in 1705. In the same year he founded the Seventh Day Baptist church at Piscataway and was the foremost leader of that church in New Jersey during the period of his life. He also performed the duties of magistrate, having been commissioned justice by Queen Anne in 1709. He married, July 15, 1681, Mary, daughter of Nicholas Bonham, whose wife was Hannah, daughter of Samuel Fuller, son of Edward Fuller who with wife Ann came over in the "Mayflower." Samuel Fuller married Jane Lothrop, daughter of Thomas Lothrop, son of Robert Lothrop, whose father was John Lothrop, of Cherry Birton, England, and afterward one of the prominent characters of New England history. Rev. Edmund and Mary (Bonham) Dunham had eight children: 1. Benajah, born August 13, 1684; died August 11, 1742; married, August 20, 1704, Dorothy Martin. 2. Elizabeth, born November 26, 1689; married, August 21, 1704, Jonathan Martin. 3. Edmund, born January 15, 1691; married (first) March 11, 1717, Dinah Fitz Randolph; (second) Mary Hill. 4. Jonathan, see post. 5. Ephraim, born May 2, 1696; married, June 16, 1716, Phebe Smalley. 6. Ruth, born November 26, 1698; married David Thomas. 7. Mary, born July 1, 1700; married, June 12, 1721, Elisha Smalley. 8. Hannah, born April 14, 1704; married, March 29, 1724, Josiah Davis.

(IV) Rev. Jonathan, son of Rev. Edmund and Mary (Bonham) Dunham, was born March 4, 1693; died March 10, 1777. In 1746 he succeeded his father in the ministry and for many years held a position of great prominence in the church of his faith. He preached in Pennsylvania and Rhode Island, in the latter state at Westerly and Newport. He married, August 15, 1714, Jane Pyatt, who died near Stelton, New Jersey, September 15, 1779, aged eighty-four years. Of this marriage eight children were born: 1. Elizabeth, born 1715; married, 1739, Micaiah Dunn. 2. Azariah, born February 9, 1718; married (first) Mary Truxton; (second) Mary (Ford) Stone. 3. Jonathan, born May 23, 1721; married Keziah Fitz Randolph. 4. David, see post. 5. Isaac, born August 10, 1725; died young. 6. Ruth, born January 3, 1727; married, February 25, 1746, James Martin. 7. Samuel, born November 27, 1730; married,

May 8, 1750, Mary Lucas. 8. Jane, born April 2, 1734.

(V) David, son of Rev. Jonathan and Jane (Pyatt) Dunham, was born in Piscataway, New Jersey, March 14, 1723; died October 6, 1806. He married, October 14, 1750, Rebecca Dunn, who bore him six children: 1. Jonathan, born 1751; died October 6, 1806; married (first) Sarah Lenox; (second) Susanna Halsey. 2. Sarah, born 1752; married Abel Stelli. 3. David, born 1755; married Keziah Dunn. 4. Jeremiah, born 1758; died January 11, 1831; married Phebe Fitz Randolph. 5. Azariah, see post. 6. Phineas, born 1764; married Zeruiah Dunham.

(VI) Azariah, son of David and Rebecca (Dunn) Dunham, was born December 24, 1760; died October 7, 1839. He married, October 7, 1792, Elizabeth Dunham, daughter of David Dunham, Esq., and granddaughter of Colonel Azariah Dunham. She died April 12, 1827. Three children were born of this marriage: 1. Jephtha, born June 22, 1793; see post. 2. Aaron, born June 4, 1795; married Eliza Carlisle. 3. Mary, married Job Wolverton.

(VII) Jephtha, son of Azariah and Elizabeth (Dunham) Dunham, was born June 22, 1793, and married, October 11, 1815, Ann Runyon. They had five children: 1. Jane, born July 16, 1816, married Augustus T. Stout. 2. Nelson, born September 18, 1818; see post. 3. Lewis Runyon, born August 15, 1824. 4. Jeremiah Stelle, born November 19, 1831, married, September 24, 1867, Frances Augusta Lawton, born August 30, 1846. 5. Elizabeth, born August 10, 1834, married Henry Waters.

(VIII) Nelson, son of Jeptha and Ann (Runyon) Dunham, was born in New Brunswick, New Jersey, September 18, 1818. He was a merchant of New Brunswick, engaged in a general dry goods business, successful in his own endeavors, and prominently identified with the political life of the city for many years. During the last thirty years of his life he was secretary and treasurer of the New Brunswick Savings Institution, having given up mercantile pursuits to manage the business of the bank. At different times he served as alderman of the city and member of the board of education. In politics he was a republican and in religious preference a Baptist. Mr. Dunham married, at New Brunswick, February 1, 1844, Elizabeth Augusta Linant, born March 7, 1818, daughter of Andrew Linant, born Rouen, France, December 8, 1785, son of Andre Vincent A. Linant, who married July 7, 1817, Margaret, widow of John Marsh, and whose family name was Manning. She was a daughter of Joseph Manning, of Plainfield, New Jersey, niece of Rev. Dr. James Manning, first president of Brown University, and granddaughter of Judge Daniel Cooper, of Morris county, New Jersey. Margaret Manning also was descended from Jeffrey Manning, died 1693, who married Hepzibah Andrews, daughter of Joseph Andrews, of Hingham, Massachusetts. James Manning, son of Hepzibah, married Christiana Laing, and had a son James, who married Grace Fitz Randolph and had a son Joseph, who married Providence Cooper and had a daughter Margaret, who married (first) John Marsh and (second) Andrew Linant. Nelson and Elizabeth Augusta (Linant) Dunham had two children: 1. Andrew Linant, born New Brunswick, December 9, 1844, married Mary, daughter of Dr. John Magee and had Albert Newell, who married Jane De Camp Felch, and Rev. Clarence Manning, not married. 2. Charles Arndt, see post.

(IX) Charles Arndt, second son and child of Nelson and Elizabeth Augusta (Linant) Dunham, was born in New Brunswick, New Jersey, August 25, 1850, and acquired his earlier education in public and private schools in that city, and his higher literary education at Rutgers College, where he graduated in 1872. Since leaving college he has been identified in one capacity and another with the business management of the New Brunswick Savings Institution, and since 1885 has been its secretary and treasurer. He holds membership in the Massachusetts and New Jersey societies of Mayflower Descendants, is a Republican in political preference and an attendant at the services of the Baptist church. Mr. Dunham is not married.

RUNYON
Laurance Phillips Runyon, M. D., of New Brunswick, New Jersey, was born in that city, February 5, 1877. He was graduated from Rutgers College in 1899, and from the College of Physicians and Surgeons, New York City, in 1903. After three years in hospital work in New York he embarked in medical practice in New Brunswick, which he has since pursued with success and reputation. He is a member of the state and county medical societies.

Dr. Runyon is the grandson of Clarkson Runyon, of New Brunswick, who for many years was engaged in the rubber business, and is the son of the present Clarkson Runyon, also of New Brunswick, who is identified with financial interests in New York City, being a member of the Stock Exchange, and of his wife, Laura Nichols Phillips, daughter of John Phillips, of New York.

CONARD
The first little band of German emigrants set sail for Pennsylvania in the ship "Concord," July 24, 1683. There were thirteen men with their families, comprising thirty-three persons, nearly all of whom were relatives, and all from Crefeld, a city of the lower Rhine in Germany, a few miles from the borders of Holland. Among the number on board the ship was Thones Kunders, a man at that time about twenty-five or thirty years old, and his wife Elin, who is supposed to have been a sister of William Streypers, who also was one of the immigrants. Probably all of those on board the "Concord" on this voyage were Menonites and Friends in religious faith, and both of these sects believed in inward piety and a godly humble life, considered all strife and warfare as unchristian, abstained from taking oaths, opposed a paid ministry, favored silent prayer and exercised strict discipline over their members. Before starting for America Thones Kunders had purchased a warrant for five hundred acres of land to be located in Pennsylvania, being the same which one Lenart Arets had previously bought of William Penn. The land was at Germantown, in the north part of the present city of Philadelphia, and it was there that our ancestor settled down with his wife and three boys to work out for himself a livelihood in America. While living in Crefeld he had carried on the trade of a blue dyer, and continued the same after settling at Germantown. In 1683, very soon after their arrival, the first meeting of Friends was held in the house of Thones Kunders, and it is probable that the meetings were continued to be held there until the erection of the first meeting house, in 1686. In the course of time this ancestor, Thones Kunders, came to be known as Dennis Conard, or Conrad, as otherwise frequently written. He had seven children: Cunraed, Madtis, John, Ann, Agnes, Henry and Elizabeth, the first three of whom were born in Crefeld and the others at Germantown. This Thones Kunders, or Dennis Conard, was progenitor of a numerous family of descendants, who in later generations have become well scattered throughout Chester,

William Conard

Montgomery and Philadelphia counties in Pennsylvania and also in the bordering states of Delaware and New Jersey.

(II) Mathias Conard, son of Thones Kinders, was born in Crefeld, Germany, November 25. 1679, died in Germantown, Pennsylvania, 1726. His children were: Anthony, Margaret, Cornelius, Magdalene. William, John and Mathew.

(III) Cornelius, son of Mathias Conard, was born in Germantown, Pennsylvania, married Priscilla ————, and had a son Joseph.

(IV) Joseph, son of Cornelius Conard, was born April 21, 1742. He married Martha Penfield; children: Paul, Daniel. Joseph, Cornelius, John, Priscilla and Martha.

(V) Joseph (2), son of Joseph (1) Conard, was born February 19. 1778, in Chester county, Pennsylvania. Later he resided in the city of Philadelphia, where at one time he had charge of the Callowhill street bridge across the Schuykill river. From there he removed to New Jersey and settled on a farm below Camden, near Mt. Ephraim or Haddonfield. He married Maria Roberts, born July 23, 1789. Children: 1. Paul, born September 15, 1809. 2. Martha, born May 15, 1811, died January 5, 1813. 3. John R., born October 21, 1813. 4. Charles, born August 15, 1815. 5. Lewis K., born July 5, 1818. 6. David, born November 20, 1820, died in 1905. 7. Rebecca, born April 18, 1822, died October 24, 1823. 8. Joseph, born June 13, 1825, died July 13, 1831. 9. Sarah, born June 14, 1827. 10. William, mentioned below.

(VI) William, youngest son of Joseph (2) Conard, was born in Philadelphia, Pennsylvania. January 10, 1833, died November 23, 1903. He removed with his parents to New Jersey, was educated there and afterward for a time taught school near Blackbrook. From 1859 and throughout the period of the civil war he was in the employ of the company which afterward became the Pullman Car Company, in the capacity of conductor, having charge of trains for transporting officers and troops to and from the south. After the close of the war he became connected with the firm of A. H. McNeal & Company, manufacturers of iron pipe at Burlington, and still later, under Colonel Whitman, he acted as inspector of iron pipe and other manufactures of iron intended for markets. During the war he enlisted, but was not called into active service. He was a prominent figure in the Masonic order, a member of the Society of Friends and a Republican in politics. He

married, January 1, 1862, Julia A. Powell, born January 1, 1837, died April 28, 1909, daughter of Joseph L. and Rebecca Ann (Fireng) Powell. Children: 1. George P., mentioned below. 2. Anna L., died February 23, 1909. 3. William Roberts, mentioned below.

Thomas Powell, grandfather of Julia A. (Powell) Conard, came from Shrewsbury, England, to America about 1751; he was a son of wealthy parents and was a student at college when he was impressed in the British navy and brought to America during the French and Indian war. He was a musician and served as drum major in an American regiment. He was a school teacher, writing master and followed the occupation of surveying. He married (first) in 1769, at New Brunswick, New Jersey, Jane Henry; (second) Hannah Smith, at New Brunswick, New Jersey. July 3, 1791. Children of Thomas and Hannah Powell: Peter, born May 2, 1792; Hannah, January 4, 1794; Elizabeth H., November 11, 1796; Joseph L., February 19, 1799, died June 1, 1878; father of Julia A. (Powell) Conard; Mary A., September 2, 1802.

(VII) George P., eldest son of William Conard, was born in Philadelphia, Pennsylvania, February 16, 1864. He attended the Burlington public schools, and after completing his studies accepted a position in the shoe manufacturing firm of Robert Wood & Son. Later he was employed in the car accounting department of the Pennsylvania and West Shore railroad, and at the present time (1909) is serving as president of the Railway Equipment Publication Company of New York. He resides in Brooklyn, New York. He is a deacon of the Lafayette Avenue Presbyterian Church of that borough, and a Republican in politics. He married, October 10, 1888, Helen Mary Underwood, born near London, England, May 17, 1862, daughter of John and Elizabeth Underwood, formerly of England, later of New Durham, New Jersey. Children: 1: Edith Underwood, born in Brooklyn, New York, April 26, 1890. 2. Frederick Underwood, December 17, 1891. 3. Helen Evelyn, December 17, 1896. 4. Lillian, March 13, 1900.

(VII) William Roberts, youngest son of William Conard, was born in Burlington, New Jersey May 19, 1872. In addition to the instruction he received in public schools and the Trenton Business College, he has devoted much attention to improving his education by self study. When old enough to work he found employment in various clerical capacities up to 1895, when he took up the work of inspecting and testing iron pipes, which he had learned partly from his father but in greater part, perhaps, through his own studies and practical experience. This inspection work has become his chief occupation, in the performance of which he maintains an office in Burlington, while his actual work frequently calls him to distant parts of the country. He is a thorough business man and in his special field of work is regarded as an expert. Mr. Conard is a member of the board of education and also of the city council of Burlington. He is a member of Burlington Lodge, No. 32, Free and Accepted Masons; Boudinot Chapter, No. 3, Royal Arch Masons; Helena Commandery, No. 3, Knights Templar; Crescent Temple, Ancient Arabic Order Nobles of the Mystic Shrine, of Trenton; Burlington Lodge, No. 22, Independent Order of Odd Fellows; Evening Star Council, No. 38, Junior Order United American Workmen, of Burlington, and past state councillor of that order; member and trustee of the Broad Street Methodist Episcopal Church of Burlington.

Mr. Conard married Corabelle Topping, born in Brooklyn, New York, June 23, 1863, daughter of Clarence W. and Augusta (Nichols) Topping, the latter of whom was a daughter of Robert H. Nichols, who was a ship master in the American Navy during the war of 1812. Children: 1. Wilfred George, born in Burlington, September 8, 1896. 2. Robert Powell, Burlington, November 2, 1898. 3. Corabelle Augusta, Burlington, January 27, 1902. 4. Esther Laurie, Burlington, March 10, 1905.

DONOHUE James Donohue, a native of Ireland, came to America when a young man and settled in New Brunswick, living there until the time of his death in 1880. He married Jane Reynolds, born in Ireland and died in New Brunswick in 1883.

(II) Dr. Frank M. Donohue, son of James and Jane (Reynolds) Donohue, was born in New Brunswick, August 17, 1859, and acquired his early education in the public schools and grammar school of that city. Subsequently he took a special course in chemistry at Rutgers, and later for two years was a student at St. Francis Xavier College, New York City. He studied medicine under the direction of Dr. Clifford Morrogh, of New

Brunswick, one of the leading men of his profession in the state, and made the course of the medical department of the New York University, graduating M. D. in 1881, *magna cum laude*, winner of the highest prize of five hundred dollars for general proficiency. And as he won high honors as a student of the medical course at the university, so too has he attained distinction in professional life, for he has come to be recognized as one of the most successful surgeons of this state. Since he came to the degree Dr. Donohue has practiced general medicine and surgery in New Brunswick, although his fame as a surgeon is known throughout the region. He was the first surgeon in New Jersey to successfully perform the Caesarian section operation, and this achievement alone has given him wide celebrity, although his skill and success in general surgery in later years have added to his popularity in all professional circles. He is a close and constant student, avoids the complications of politics and devotes his attention solely to professional employments. He is a member of the American Medical Association, the New Jersey State Medical Society, ex-president of the Middlesex County Medical Society and an honorary member of the Somerset County Medical Society.

The hospital and other principal professional appointments of Dr. Donohue are: Visiting surgeon to St. Peter's General Hospital and the Wells Memorial Hospital; consulting surgeon to the Somerset County Hospital at Somerville; railroad surgeon for the Pennsylvania Railroad Company; medical examiner for the Equitable Life, Mutual Life, Metropolitan Life, Mutual Benefit Life, Prudential Life, Provident Life and Trust, Connecticut Mutual Life, and Northwestern Life insurance companies, and confidential examiner for the Travellers' Life Insurance Company. He is a trustee of the New Jersey State Home for Boys, a vice-president and director of the People's National Bank of New Brunswick, director of the New Brunswick Trust Company, and trustee of the New Brunswick Savings Institution. He is the owner of a handsome country property of one hundred acres, "Cedarcrest," near Bound Brook, New Jersey.

In 1884 Dr. Donohue married Elizabeth, daughter of George Buttler, for many years a leading citizen and business man of New Brunswick. He was one of the pioneers of the gold regions of California, a "49er," and after a few years in the far west he returned east and afterward became prominently iden-

tified with the industrial life of New Brunswick, proprietor of a large sash, door and
blind factory and planing mill, and one of the
foremost business men of the city for many
years. He married Harriet Ann Voorhees.
Dr. Frank M. and Elizabeth (Buttler) Donohue have three children, all born in New
Brunswick: Mary D., born August 7, 1885;
Elizabeth, March 27, 1897; Frank, March 12,
1899.

BOORAEM   The Booraem, Boerum and
Van Boerum families belong
to that noble and stalwart
group of colonists and settlers who came
originally from Holland to New Netherland,
and then emigrated again from the province
of New York to the province of New Jersey
where they made names and homes for themselves and reputations for their descendants
to be proud of and to imitate.

(I) Willem Jacobse, founder of the family,
was a resident of the little village of Boerum
in Friesland, and being a staunch adherent of
the Prince of Orange, he found himself obliged
in order to escape the persecution under the
Duke of Alva and the Spanish Inquisition, to
leave his native land for the freedom and safety
of the western world. Consequently he emigrated with his two sons, Hendrick and Jacob,
to New Amsterdam in 1657, and settling at
Flatbush spent there the remainder of his
life. He was born in 1617, and died before
1698. In 1657 and in 1662 and 1663, he is recorded as being one of the magistrates of the
town. His name is on the assessment roll of
1675, and he took the oath of allegiance there
in 1687. He married Geertje Hendrickse, and
had four children who are of record: 1. Hendrick Willemse, who is referred to below. 2.
Jacob Willemse, emigrated with his father and
brother, died before 1698, and married, June
15, 1684, Geertruyd De Beavois, from Leyden.
3. Geertruy Willemse, probably the person of
that name who married Francis du Puis. 4.
Hillegont Willemse.

(II) Hendrick Willemse van Boerum, the
eldest son of Willem Jacobse and Geertje Hendrickse, was born in Boerum, about 1642, accompanied his father in his emigration to this
country, and is found in Flatbush in 1675 and
1676, and in the census of 1698 is registered
among the inhabitants of New Lots. In 1687
he took the oath of allegience in Flatbush, and
two years previously he was one of the patentees of the town in the charter of Governor
Dongan. May 27, 1679, he bought of his

father a farm in Flatbush adjoining on the
south side his father's plantation and on the
north that of the Widow Hegeman, deceased,
with meadows at Canarsie and lot number 16
in the new lots of the said town. About 1663
he married Maria Ariaens and had four children of record: 1. Hendrick, baptized July 22,
1683. 2. Arie or Adriaen, who removed to
Freehold, New Jersey, born 1666, married
Sarah Smock. 3. Louise, baptized in Flatbush, October 24, 1680. 4. Hendrick, who is
referred to below.

(III) Hendrick, the son of Hendrick Willemse and Maria Ariaense Boerum, was born
in Flatbush. He changed the name to its
present spelling; he moved to Bound Brook.
Among his children was Nicholas, who is referred to below.

(IV) Nicholas, the son of Hendrick
Booraem, was born near Bound Brook, Somerset county, New Jersey, in 1714, and settled near New Brunswick. Among his children was Nicholas, who is referred to below.

(V) Nicholas (2), son of Nicholas (1)
Booraem, was born near New Brunswick, New
Jersey, in 1736, and served in in the revolu-
tionary army. Among his children was
Nicholas, who is referred to below.

(VI) Nicholas (3), son of Nicholas (2)
Booraem, was born near New Brunswick, New
Jersey, and died in 1869. During the war of
1812 he served with distinction as the colonel
of a New Jersey regiment and lost his hearing
by the explosion of a cannon during a battle.
He was a Whig, a member of the New Jersey
assembly, one of the associate judges of the
court of common pleas for Middlesex county,
and for forty-two years the county treasurer.
He was also an elder in the First Reformed
Church of New Brunswick. By his wife,
Sarah (Willet) Booraem, who came also of
revolutionary stock, he had twelve children:
1. Eliza, married the Rev. John Van Arsdale.
2. Ellen, married Thomas Booraem. 3. Emeline, married Charles Smith, M. D. 4. Louisa,
married Nicholas Edgar Bookstaver. 5. Henry
who entered the United States navy and was
killed while home, in the great tornado that
swept over New Brunswick, 1836. 6. Augustus, M. D. 7. Theodore, who is referred
to below. And five other children who died
in their youth.

(VII) Theodore, son of Nicholas (3) and
Sarah (Willet) Booraem, was born in New
Brunswick, New Jersey, in 1831, and died
there in 1885. He studied law with Senator
Schenck and Judge Van Dyke, and then began

as a general practitioner in New Brunswick. He went into the insurance business and gave much of his time to the settling up of estates. He was a Republican, and for some time was the collector of Middlesex county. By his wife, Mary ('Foster) Booraem, he had three children: 1. Theodore B., who is referred to below. 2. Margaret, married Rev. Henry J. Scudder and is now with her husband a missionary of the Reformed Church in America in India. 3. Harriet.

(VIII) Theodore B., son of Theodore and Mary (Foster) Booraem, was born in New Brunswick, New Jersey, April 30, 1861, and is now living in that city. He graduated from Rutgers College in 1881 with honors, and then studied law with A. V. Schenck. He was admitted to the New Jersey bar as attorney in 1884, and as counsellor in 1887. He then began practising in New Brunswick, where his success was brilliant and his advancement rapid. In 1892 he formed a partnership with John S. Voorhees, which continued until the death of the latter. He has devoted much time to corporation law and its problems, is the representative of many of the principal firms in New Brunswick, and is officially connected with many companies. In 1904 he was appointed assistant United States attorney for the district of New Jersey, which office he held until April 1, 1906, when he resigned and became judge of the Middlesex county court of common pleas, in which position he remained until April, 1909, when he became prosecutor of the pleas of Middlesex county, which office he now holds. He has also been city attorney for the city of New Brunswick, and a director in a number of business corporations of the city. He is also a member of many organizations, among them being the Holland Society of New York, and the Young Men's Christian Association, of which he is an active member. He is a member of the Second Reformed Church of New Brunswick.

April 16, 1895, Theodore B. Booraem married Helen Constance Randall, of New Brunswick, whose maternal grandfather, Abraham Suydam, was one of the prominent early pioneers of New Brunswick, president of the Farmers' and Mechanics' National Bank, and at one time owned half of the site of the present city.

COWENHOVEN   Charles Tiebout Cowenhoven, of the city of New Brunswick, lawyer, ex-judge and ex-prosecutor of the pleas,

is a descendant of one of the earliest colonial families of America. The immigrant ancestor, Wolfert Gerritse Van Cowenhoven, came from Holland in 1630 and founded the colony of New Amersfoort on Long Island, a patent for the lands having been granted him by Governor Van Twiller. One of this family was Jacob Wolpherson Van Cowenhoven, delegate to the states-general of Holland; and a famous descendant in the American line was Egbert Benson, the eminent jurist. Another early ancestor of Charles Tiebout Cowenhoven was Nicasius de Sille, one of the nine selectmen in the council of Governor Stuyvesant, Schepen, and mentioned in the list of "great citizens" in the year 1657.

Charles Tiebout Cowenhoven is a great-grandson of Catherine Remsen and is grandson of Garetta Tiebout, his parents having been Nicholas Remsen Cowenhoven (who came to New Brunswick, New Jersey, from Brooklyn, New York), and Anna Rappelvea (who was born in Somerset county, New Jersey). Judge Cowenhoven's father was not engaged in professional or business occupation, but lived a quiet and retired life, and was recognized and respected as a gentleman of the old school. His family consisted of the following children: 1. Garreta T., married David Bishop, of Bishop Place, College avenue, New Brunswick. 2. Catherine, married (as his first wife) Rev. Dr. W. J. R. Taylor, a distinguished divine of the Reformed church, and father of Rev. Dr. Graham Taylor, of the Chicago University, and of Rev. Dr. William R. Taylor, pastor of the Brick Church of Rochester, New York. 3. Maria Sefferts, married (second wife), her brother-in-law, Rev. Dr. W. J. R. Taylor. 4. Sarah Lefferts, married Oscar Johnson Jr., of the old Johnson family of Long Island, nephew of the late Bishop Whitehouse, of Illinois. 5. Cornelia Van Vechten, died unmarried. 6. Marianna A., resides with her brother in New Brunswick. 7. Nicholas Remsen, died young. 8. Charles Tiebout.

Charles Tiebout Cowenhoven was born in New Brunswick, New Jersey, December 1, 1844. He was graduated from Rutgers College in June, 1862, studied law in the office of Abraham V. Schenck, of New Brunswick, and was admitted to the New Jersey bar as attorney in November, 1865, and as counsellor in February, 1869. From 1869 to 1874 he served as president judge of the court of common pleas of Middlesex county, being the youngest man appointed to that bench. He was prosecutor of the pleas of Middlesex county from 1877 to 1882, and was again president-judge of the court of common pleas from 1885 to 1890. Judge Cowenhoven has always practiced his profession in New Brunswick. He has a large general clientage, and is known for particular ability and success as an advocate. He has conducted many important criminal cases, and especially has made a marked reputation in noteworthy capital trials. His membership in organizations includes the Masonic order and the Delta Kappa Epsilon fraternity. Married, 1870, Helen A. Towle, whose father, Henry Towle, Esquire, was of English birth and a prominent merchant. Children: 1. Charles Tiebout Cowenhoven, Jr., counsellor-at-law in New York City; married Emily Kearney Rogers. 2. Marie T. 3. Nicholas Remsen Cowenhoven, attorney-at-law in New Brunswick.

DALY Peter Francis Daly, attorney and counsellor at law, and surrogate of the county of Middlesex, was born in the city of New York, May 19, 1867, son of Timothy and Catharine (O'Grady) Daly, natives of county Galway, Ireland. When he was six years old, his parents removed to New Brunswick, New Jersey. His early education was gained at St. Peter's parochial school and the Livingston high school, both in New Brunswick. He studied law in the office of Hon. James H. Van Cleef, and was admitted to the bar at the November term of court in 1888, being then in his twenty-first year. Soon afterward he became a member of the law firm of Van Cleef, Daly & Woodbridge, which relation was continued for three years, and since that time Mr. Daly has practiced alone. During the first ten years of his professional career, he was engaged in most of the important criminal cases tried in the county, but now and for the past ten or more years his practice has been almost wholly on the civil side of the courts; it is extensive, important, and of general range. He has been counsel for the Workingmen's Building and Loan Association of New Brunswick, one of the most important and progressive organizations of its kind in the state, since its incorporation, about fourteen years ago. Ever since he came of age, Mr. Daly has been an influential factor in politics in New Brunswick and Middlesex county, and he occupies a prominent position in the councils of the Democratic party of the state. He early became a member of the city Democratic committee with the specific purpose of purifying the politics of his own ward,· the sixth. His intense earnestness and strong personality soon marked him as a leader, and he had the pleasure of causing to be adopted a set of rules for primaries calling for clean methods. Having secured the necessary legislation, he set about to see it put in force, and proved equally successful as an executive officer. His energetic fight for above-board primaries is a part of the history of the ward. He was almost killed at one of the primaries, when the lights were smashed and the building fired, but he has the satisfaction of knowing that since then there has not been a dishonest Democratic primary in the sixth ward or any other ward of the city. Such a spirit proved his strength and brought credit and confidence to his party. He has been called upon by his party to preside at its gatherings, has efficiently filled the office of chairman of city, county and congregational conventions, and was for several years the chairman of the Middlesex County Democratic executive committee. The sixth ward elected him to the office of alderman, showing its appreciation of his services by giving him a rousing majority. He ran far ahead of his ticket. As party leader in the board of aldermen, and as chairman of the finance committee, during his two years' term, his duties were arduous. It was while he was chairman of the finance committee that over five hundred thousand dollars of the bonded indebtedness of the city matured. The bonds had been bearing seven per cent interest, and they were renewed at four per cent, and some as low as three and one-half per cent. That year was known as the great refunding year, and was the most important period in the financial history of the city in a quarter of a century.

The distinction of being the father of the resolution that reduced the rate of interest on unpaid taxes from 12 to 8 per cent falls to Mr. Daly. As chairman of the sewerage committee he put through the big sewer in the sixth ward, down Hamilton street and along the Mile Run brook to the canal, the beginning of the sewerage system in that section of the city. He personally negotiated for and secured the right of way for the sewer over private property without the cost of one penny to the city or to the property owners benefited. His public services were always heartily given. He was called upon to act as treasurer of the aldermanic committee of relief for the families of the local soldiers who so bravely left

ii—6

the city to espouse their country's cause in the Spanish-American war. He was a valued member of the city centennial committee and was secretary of the committee on memorial to the local sailors who lost their lives upon the ill-fated "Maine." In short, he is a representative citizen, a man of the people, whose sympathies have been with every public enterprise that tended to the advancement of the city's and country's interest. In May, 1899, he was appointed counsel of the board of freeholders. As counsel to the board Mr. Daly retained his independence and fearlessly opposed all measures which appeared to him to be against the public good. Politics never dictated his duty to him. He rendered his opinions without fear or favor and was subservient to no one. These things show the character of the man.

He was deputy and attorney to Leonard Firman, surrogate of Middlesex county, from 1892 to 1902, and in the year last mentioned was himself elected surrogate of the county. He served one full term of five years, and in 1907 was re-elected to a second term in the same office. At his first election in 1902, he ran nine hundred votes ahead of his ticket, and when a candidate for a second term he ran eighteen hundred ahead of the general ticket. During his connection with the surrogate's office, he has made a particular study of the matters pertaining to that office, and to-day he is considered by the bar of the county a specialist in probate practice and pleading, one whose opinion is sought by other members of the bar. He is a member of the New Jersey State Bar Association. He was the counsel who directed the incorporation of the boroughs of South River, Roosevelt and Spotswood, and now is counsel for those municipalities and also for the borough of Helmetta. At different times he has been township attorney for Piscataway, Raritan, Monroe, East Brunswick and Sayreville townships. He is noted for oratorical ability, both at the bar and before popular gatherings, and enjoys extensive personal popularity.

Mr. Daly was founder and first grand knight of New Brunswick Council, Knights of Columbus, and is a charter member and past exalted ruler of the local lodge of Elks. He was president of the Catholic Club when twenty years old, president of Division No. 5 of the Ancient Order of Hibernians at twenty-two, and still holds membership in both of those bodies, and also in the Royal Arcanum, German Society, Aurora and the Catholic Benevo-

lent Legion. He is a member of St Peter's Church, New Brunswick.

Mr. Daly married, in September, 1893, at the church of the Sacred Heart, New Brunswick, Mary Rose Mansfield, daughter of William and Margaret (Fitzgerald) Mansfield, her father being a member of the firm of Harding & Mansfield, wholesale and retail shoe dealers. They have one daughter, Margaret Rosina Daly, born in New Brunswick, February, 1895, now a student at Rutgers Preparatory School.

BOWNE

It cannot be for a moment doubted that the Quakers were in their principles of religious freedom on a much more higher plane both morally and in equity than the Puritans. They were indeed a better-hearted, harder-thinking, and therefore broader-minded class of men. They were perfectly aware that their acts were frequently such as to make them felons in the strict sense of the written law, yet their strong sense of right and justice were such that they dared to render a passive resistance so powerful that these laws were finally repealed. Although the crime for which the Quaker suffered in England was far graver than any of his transgressions on New England soil, the severe penalties in the mother country being for refusal in times of great political danger to take the oath of allegience and supremacy and to pay the legal tithes in the parishes in which they resided, the penalties inflicted by the English authorities never reached the stern punishment and brutal treatment meted out to the followers of George Fox by the Pilgrim Fathers, their associates and the Dutch inhabitants of New Netherland. This persecution was at its height during the early days of the settlement of the new world, and one of the greatest sufferers from it and also one of the most eminent examples of successful resistance to it is the case of the founder of the Bowne family and his illustrious son.

(I) In the year 1649 a certain Thomas Bowne, born at Matlock, Derbyshire, England, in the Fifth month, 1595, and baptized the following 25th day, arrived in Massachusetts Bay, and shortly afterwards settled in Flushing, Long Island, then belonging to the Dutch government. He died September 18, 1677, leaving behind him three children: 1. John, referred to below. 2. Dorothy, born August 14, 1631, removed to Boston, Massachusetts, in 1649. 3. Truth, who remained in England.

(II) John, only son of Thomas Bowne, the emigrant, was born in Matlock, March 9, 1627.

died in Flushing, Long Island, December 20, 1695. Accompanying his father to the new world, he returned to England in 1650, and returned to America the following year, visiting Flushing with Edward Farrington, who is supposed to have married his sister, Dorothy. Soon after this the entire family settled in Flushing, and in 1661 he built the "Bowne House" which was used as a meeting place for Friends for nearly forty years. In 1656 his wife Hannah became a Friend, and her husband, a Church of England man, attending one of the meetings from curiosity, was so deeply impressed with their form of worship, that he invited them to meet at his house and soon after became a member himself. These Quaker meetings in a town founded by Massachusetts Puritans under a Dutch government, was more than the townsfolk could stand, and August 24, 1662, complaints were made by the Flushing magistrates "that many of the inhabitants are followers of the Quakers who hold their meetings at the house of John Bowne." Under the Dutch colonial law at that time, religious gatherings of any kind except those of the Dutch Reformed religion, were subject to a penalty of fifty guilders for the first offence, double for the second, and arbitrary correction for every other. Accordingly, September 1, 1662, John Bowne was arrested and charged with "harboring Quakers and permitting them to hold their meetings at his house," and was cast into prison at Fort Amsterdam. Two weeks later he was tried and condemned to pay £25 Flemish and the costs of his trial, and warned that a second offense would mean double this fine, while any further persistence in such conduct would bring banishment from New Netherland. John Bowne refused to pay, was confined in a dungeon on bread and water and still remaining obdurate he was finally sent as a prisoner to Holland. He was finally released and returned to America by way of England and the island of Barbadoes, reaching Flushing, March 30, 1663. The document which the directors of the West India Company sent to the officials of New Netherland is too long to quote here, but it is of peculiar historic interest as the first official proclamation of religious liberty for any part of America except Maryland, and its promulgation stopped the persecution of the Friends on Long Island with the exception of the unauthorized acts of Governor Peter Stuyvesant.

August 7. 1656, John Bowne married (first) Hannah, daughter of Lieutenant Robert

Peake, who died February 2, 1678, at the residence of John Edson, in London, England. Her mother, Elizabeth Fones, the widow of Henry, son of Governor John Winthrop, of Massachusetts, was the daughter of Thomas Fones, an apothecary of London, by his first wife, daughter of Adam Winthrop, of Groton. Her pedigree begins with William Fones, Esquire, who married the daughter of Sir Robert Hyelston, knight, and was the father of George Fones, of Saxbie, who married a Malbanck of Malpas, Cheshire, and had a son William of Saxbie, whose grandson, John of Saxbie, was the great-grandfather of Thomas Fones, of London, the grandfather of Hannah (Feake) Bowne. Hannah (Feake) Bowne became a minister among Friends and made two religious visits to England and Ireland and one to Holland. Her husband joined her in England in 1676 and accompanied her in her religious service until she died the following year, and his testimony concerning her, given at her funeral at the Peel meeting, is remarkable for its tenderness and beauty.

John and Hannah (Feake) Bowne had eight children: 1. John, born March 13, 1657, died August 30, 1673. 2. Elizabeth, October 8, 1658, died February 14, 1722; married Samuel Titus. 3. Mary, January 6, 1661. 4. Abigail, February 5, 1663, died May 14, 1703; married, March 25, 1686, Richard Willets, of Jericho, Long Island. 5. Hannah, April 10, 1665, died December 30, 1707; married Benjamin, son of Anthony Field, of Long Island. 6. Samuel, referred to below. 7. Dorothy, March 29, 1669, died November 26, 1790; married, May 27, 1689, Henry, son of Matthew Franklyn, of Flushing. 8. Martha Johannah, August 17, 1673, died August 11, 1750; married, November 9, 1695, Joseph, son of John Thorne.

February 2, 1680, John Bowne married (second) Hannah Bickerstaff, who died June 7, 1690. She bore him six more children: 9. Sarah, December 14, 1680, died May 18, 1681. 10. Sarah, February 17, 1682. 11. John, September 10, 1683, died October 25, 1683. 12. Thomas, November 26, 1684, died December 17, 1684. 13. John, September 9, 1686, married, July 21, 1714, Elizabeth, daughter of Joseph and Mary (Townley) Lawrence. 14. Abigail, July 5, 1688, died July 13, 1688. June 26, 1693, John Bowne married (third) Mary, daughter of James and Sarah Cock, of Mattinecok, Long Island, who bore him two more children: 15. Amy, April 1, 1694. 16. Ruth, January 30, 1696.

(III) Samuel, sixth child and second son

of John and Hannah (Feake) Bowne, was
born in Flushing, Long Island, September 21,
1667, died May 30, 1745. He was a minister
among Friends. October 4, 1691, he married
(first) at Philadelphia Meeting, Mary, daughter of Captain Becket, who died August 21,
1707. She bore him ten children: 1. Samuel,
referred to below. 2. Thomas, born April 7,
1694, married, March 7, 1715, Hannah, daughter of John Underhill. 3. Eleanor, April 20,
1695, married, October 9, 1718, Isaac Horner,
of Mansfield, Burlington county, New Jersey.
4. Hannah, March 31, 1697, married, April
6, 1717, Richard Lawrence. 5. John, September 11, 1698, died 1757; married, 1738,
Dinah Underhill. 6. Mary, October 21, 1699,
married, January 14, 1720, John Keese. 7.
Roabord, January 17, 1701, died before July
3, 1746, when his daughter Mary married
Henry, son of Robert and Rebecca Haydock,
married November 16, 1724, Margaret, daughter of Joseph Latham of Cow Neck, Hempstead, Long Island. 8. William, April 1, 1702,
died April 15, 1702. 9. Elizabeth, October
11, 1704. 10. Benjamin, March 13, died May
13, 1707. December 8, 1709, Samuel Bowne
married (second) Hannah Smith, of Flushing, who died October 11, 1733. She bore
him five more children: 11. Sarah, September
30, 1710, married, March 12, 1729, William,
son of William Burling. 12. Joseph, February 25, 1712, married (first) November 13,
1735, Sarah, daughter of Obadiah Lawrence,
who died January 5, 1740, and (second) June
13, 1745, Judith, daughter of Jonathan Morrell. 13. Anne, October 17, 1715. 14. Benjamin, August 1, 1717. 15. Elizabeth, November 26, 1720. November 14, 1735, Samuel
Bowne married (third) Mrs. Grace Cowperthwaite, who died November 22, 1760. She
bore him no children.

(IV) Samuel (2), eldest child of Samuel
(1) and Mary (Becket) Bowne, was born in
Flushing, Long Island, January 29, 1693, died
in 1769. September 20, 1716, he married
Sarah Franklin, who bore him six children:
1. William, March 6, 1720, died October 18,
1747; married Elizabeth Willett, who died the
same year as her husband. 2. Samuel, referred to below. 3. Mary, March 3, 1724,
married Joseph Farrington. 4. Amy, 1724,
married George Embree. 5. Sarah, 1726,
married William Titus. 6. James, 1728, married, 1767, Caroline Rodman; his son Walter
married Eliza Southgate and was mayor of
New York City.

(V) Samuel (3), second child and son of

Samuel (2) and Sarah (Franklin) Bowne, was
born May 14, 1721. He married Abigail
Burling, born February 25, 1724. Their
eleven children were: 1. Edward, born September 3, 1742, died September 22, 1742. 2.
James, March 20, 1744. 3. Samuel, August
4, 1746, died August 21, 1746. 4. Elizabeth,
November 19, 1748, died November 22, 1752.
5, Samuel Jr., June 25, 1750, died July 23,
1752. 6. Matthew, July 19, 1752. 7. Abigail,
October 21, 1754. 8. Sarah, January 14, 1757,
died May 22, 1760. 9. Mary, August 8, died
August 24, 1761. 10. William, referred to
below. 11. Samuel Jr., April 5, 1767, married
Hannah ———.

(VI) William, tenth child and sixth son,
the fourth to reach maturity, of Samuel (3)
and Abigail (Burling) Bowne, was born
March 9, 1763. May 11, 1791, he obtained
in New Jersey a marriage license to marry
Sarah Newbold, born March 22, 1769. She
was the daughter of Caleb Newbold and Sarah,
daughter of Samuel Haines and Lydia, daughter of Thomas and Deliverance (Horner)
Stokes. Samuel was the grandson of Richard and Abigail Haines, the emigrants, and
son of William Haines and Sarah, daughter of
John Paine, the emigrant. Caleb was the son
of Thomas Newbold and Edith, daughter of
Marmaduke and Ann (Pole) Coates, the emigrants. Thomas was the son of Michael Newbold and Rachel, daughter of John Clayton,
the emigrant, and Michael was the son of
Michael Sr. and Ann Newbold, the emigrants
to Burlington county, New Jersey. The children of William and Sarah (Newbold) Bowne
were: 1. Samuel, who died unmarried. 2. Abigail, married George, son of Budd and Sarah
(Haines) Hawwood. 3. William, who died
unmarried. 4. Edward, referred to below.

(VII) Edward, youngest child and the only
son to marry of William and Sarah (Newbold) Bowne, was born in Flushing, Long
Island, October 16, 1798, died in Springfield
township, Burlington county, New Jersey,
February 9, 1871. He was a farmer and a
large cattle dealer, at one time owning four
large farms. He was one of the representative men of Springfield township and one of
its most prominent business men.

February 6, 1834, Edward Bowne married
Elizabeth, daughter of John and Rebecca (Lippincott) Woodward, who died January 7,
1875. Their children were: 1. Sarah Newbold, born January 19, 1835, married David T.,
son of David and Deborah (Troth) Haines,
and has three children: Elizabeth, married

Joseph Matlack; Annie, married Isaac Lippincott; and Emily. 2. John Woodward, August 3, 1836, married (first) Anna Satterthwaite, and (second) Sarah Campion. 3. William Newbold, April 1, 1838, died unmarried. 4. Rebecca Woodward, January 6, 1840, married Israel Stokes, son of Henry C. and Elizabeth (Stokes) Deacon, and has four children: Edward Bowne, married Rachel Jones; Eugene, married Helen Lippincott; Eva, married Newlin Haines; and Anna, married C. William Snyder. 5. Edward Lawrence, September 9, 1841, married Mary Etta Deacon. 6. Anna Matilda, referred to below. 7. Walter B., March 18, 1845, married Edith Johnson. 8. Emily Newbold, August 25, 1847, unmarried. 9. Franklin Woodward, January 8, 1850, married Laura Lippincott.

(VIII) Anna Matilda, sixth child and third daughter of Edward and Elizabeth (Woodward) Bowne, was born in Springfield township, Burlington county, New Jersey, May 12, 1843, and is now living at Mt. Holly, Burlington county. She married (first) Henry Irick, born January 1, 1833, died February, 1892, the eldest child of Henry C. Deacon and Elizabeth, daughter of Israel Stokes and Sarah, daughter of Joshua and Elizabeth N. (Woolman) Borton. Israel was the son of David Stokes and Ann, daughter of John and Elizabeth (Barlow) Lancaster, and the granddaughter of Thomas Lancaster, the emigrant, and Phebe, daughter of John Wardell, the emigrant. David was the son of John Stokes and Hannah, daughter of Jervis and Mary Stogdelle, and the grandson of John and Elizabeth (Green) Stokes. June 23, 1894, Anna Matilda (Bowne) Deacon married (second) Oliver L. Jeffrey, who died without issue, August 23, 1908. Oliver L. Jeffrey was born at Toms River, a son of James Jeffrey. When a young man he engaged in the mercantile business in Columbus, New Jersey, later removed to Mt. Holly, where he conducted a successful business as a merchant for more then forty years; and retired a few years before his death. He married (first) Mary Ann Lippincott.

IRICK The progenitor of the Irick family in America was Johan Eyrich, of Palatina, Holland, who landed at Philadelphia with his brother William about A. D. 1750-60.

(I) John Irick (Johan Eyrich) came to Pemberton, New Jersey, and lived with Dr. William Budd, a large owner of proprietory lands, and at his death John Irick remained with the widow for some years, becoming interested in purchasing large tracts of lands, by which he laid the foundation of the future wealth of the family. We have not been able to establish the fact that he must have been possessed of a competency upon his arrival in this country, but it is believed that he was so possessed, for he could not in such short time have amassed the large estate of which he died possessed. He with others was naturalized by the provincial legislature in 1770, his name being anglicized to John Irick. The record of his marriage shows that General Elias Boudinot became the bondsman in five hundred pounds at that time, which fact indicates that he was not yet twenty-one years old. Besides being a man of large means, he was a strong churchman, and for many years was prominently identified with St. Mary's Church (Episcopal) of Burlington. Among his possessions was a large estate between Burlington and Mt. Holly, and there he spent the greater part of his life, engaged in agricultural pursuits. He married, 2 mo. 28, 1761, Mary Sailer, and (second) 2 mo. 26, 1781, Mary Shinn. He died in 1826, aged about eighty-six years. His children, William and John, were by the first wife, Mary Sailer.

(II) General William Irick, elder son of John and Mary (Sailer) Irick, was born near Burlington, New Jersey, in 1767, died January 26, 1832. Immediately after his marriage he removed from his father's homestead on the road from Mt. Holly to Burlington, to Vincentown, New Jersey, and settled on the farm now owned and occupied by his grandson, Henry J. Irick. He received his education in the academic schools of Burlington, and after leaving school took up surveying and conveyancing in connection with his extensive farming operations. His public documents, deeds, articles of agreement, etc., are well and accurately written, and still serve very well as models from which to copy. He early became interested in public affairs, and filled many positions of trust and honor; was a member of the house of assembly in 1804, and again from 1811 to 1814, inclusive, and member of the governor's council from 1815 to 1817. During the second war with the mother country he was in command of the state militia at Billingsport and thus acquired the military title by which he was ever afterward known and addressed. In politics General Irick was a staunch Whig. His death was much lamented by a wide circle of devoted friends, chief among whom was Chief Justice Ewing, with whom he always maintained an intimate friendship. He married Margaret, daughter of Job and Anne (Munro) Stockton; children: 1. Anne, married Colonel Thomas Fox Budd, of Vincentown. 2. Mary, married Marzilla Coat. also of Burlington county. 3. William, see post. 4. Job, see post. 5. John Stockton, see post.

(III) General William (2) Irick, son of General William (1) and Margaret (Stockton) Irick, was born on the Irick homestead, near Vincentown, Burlington county, New Jersey, December 20, 1799, died August 17, 1864. He followed in the footsteps of his father as a surveyor and business man, and always lived in Vincentown. He also was honored by his fellow townsmen with many public offices, and was the last member of the old council of New Jersey from Burlington county under the continental constitution. His acts of charity and benevolence were unbounded, and he always was ready to lend a helping hand to his neighbor. He was a man of fine stature, standing full six feet tall, weighing two hundred and twenty-five pounds, energetic and painstaking in all of his business transactions. He took great interest in military affairs, and he and his staff were a soldierly looking body of men. In his magisterial capacity of justice of the peace he married many of the very first people of his and the adjoining counties. At the outbreak of the civil war, notwithstanding his physical infirmities, General Irick tendered his services to Governor Olden, but under a reorganization of the state militia about that time he was legislated out of his military office. He did the next best thing, however, in aiding the government by pledging his ample fortune through Jay Cooke & Company in support of the union cause. General Irick married (first) Sarah, daughter of Amos and Lydia Heulings, of Evesham township, Burlington county. She died in 1852, and he married (second) Mrs. Sarah Eayre. He had five children—all daughters—by the first wife, and one child by his second wife: 1. Lydia H., married Franklin Hilliard, of Burlington county. 2. Margaret, married David B. Peacock, of Philadelphia. 3-4. Eliza Ann and Mary Ann, twins: Eliza Ann died in early womanhood; Mary married Benjamin F. Champion, of Camden county. 5. Cornelia, married John W. Brown, Esq., of Burlington county. 6. William John, now president of the First National Bank of Vincentown, and whose home

is near the paternal home in Southampton township.

(III) Job, second son of General William (1) and Margaret (Stockton) Irick, was a land surveyor and successful farmer, but he died early in August, 1839, at the age of thirty-seven years. He married Matilda Burr, and lived and died in Southampton township. He had one son, William H. Irick (father of Mary Irick Drexel), and two daughters, both of whom married and lived in Philadelphia.

(III) General John Stockton, third son of General William (1) and Margaret (Stockton) Irick, was born on the old homestead in Southampton township, August 4, 1811, died August 4, 1894. In May, 1832, he married and being so nearly of age at that time, his brothers, William and Job, executors of his father's will, permitted him to occupy his inheritance at once, and took him into partnership in working off and marketing the timber growing on the broad acres devised to them jointly. Both he and his wife having a handsome landed estate, their way in the world was successful from the beginning, until along in the fifties, when he joined with nine other men in the iron foundry business at Lumberton, as partners, without being incorporated, each member being personally responsible for all its obligations, and trusting to the management of two of the partners, at the end of a very few years the concern became heavily involved, and he realized the fact that he was held responsible for $250,000, all that he was worth at that time. But with the same energy that always characterized his actions, he took hold of the concern, came to the aid of the bankrupt cities, built their gas and water works and financed them, and soon paid off the indebtedness and saved a handsome profit while the others stood off without offering any material aid. The war of the rebellion broke out at about this time and under the reorganization of the state militia he, with three others, was appointed by Governor Olden to organize and command it with the rank of major-general. Upon the election of Governor Parker, he was continued and gave his time and services throughout the war. He, like his brother William, tendered through Jay Cooke his fortune in defence of the Union. He was a member of the New Jersey house of assembly, 1847-48-49, and never lost his interest in public affairs, always taking an active part in politics as an ardent Whig and Republican. His only other public office was that

Henry J. Doick

of freeholder, serving as director of the board during his three years' term. It was largely through his efforts that the first railroads in Burlington county were built and he was a director in all of them. He also was instrumental in organizing the First National Bank of Vincentown, being its president until his death, when William John Irick succeeded him. He died August 4, 1894, upon his eighty-third birthday, leaving a large circle of acquaintances and friends. General Irick married, May 17, 1832, Emeline S. Bishop, a Quakeress, daughter of Japheth and Rachel Bishop. She was born in Vincentown in 1814, died April 2, 1895; children: 1. Henry J., see post. 2. Rachel B., September 9, 1835; married Charles Sailer. 3. Samuel S., August 30, 1838; married Susan Butterworth. 4. Margaret A., January 1, 1841; married Henry B. Burr. 5. Job, August 8, 1844; died young. 6. John B., see post. 7. Emeline, 1848; died young. 8. Robert H., June 30, 1851; died young.

(IV) Henry Japheth, son of General John Stockton and Emeline S. (Bishop) Irick, was born in Vincentown, New Jersey, March 13, 1833, and received his education in the public schools in his home town, in Norristown Seminary, under Samuel Aaron, and at Willis Academy, Freehold, New Jersey. After marriage he lived for about seven years on a farm owned by his father, located between Mt. Holly and Burlington, and then returned to the old homestead at Vincentown, where his father had lived for sixty years, and where he himself has now lived for more than thirty-five years. Following in the footsteps of his grandfather, he has been actively engaged in farming and surveying, and is highly regarded as one of the prominent general business men of his section of the state.

From early young manhood he took an active interest in politics. He attended the first Republican convention in New Jersey, which nominated Dr. William A. Newell for governor, in 1856. He has been called to various public positions of honor and trust. He was made justice of the peace when twenty-one years old; was elected member of the house of assembly in 1862, and served three years; was elected state senator in 1871. While in the legislature he was chairman of the joint committee for the reorganization of the legislative bodies of the state; member of the committee on educational affairs; chairman of the committee on engrossed bills; and lay member of the judiciary committee. He also was appointed by Governor Stokes to membership

on the state board of equalization of taxes, and still serves in that capacity. Soon after his appointment to this position, he was tendered the appointment of stone road commissioner of New Jersey, in 1908, also in 1909 he was tendered by Governor Fort the appointment of a lay judge of the court of errors and appeals, the highest court in New Jersey, and the highest honor to be given by the governor. However, he was compelled to decline both appointments on account of age, besides being already a member of the state board of equalization of taxes, he felt it his duty to fill out his term, in justice to the agricultural interests of the state, through which influence he was appointed to the position. Previous to his appointment to the state board of taxation, Mr. Irick was a director of the several companies in which his father had been similarly interested, but these connections he severed before becoming a member of the equalization board. He was president of the Burlington City Loan and Trust Company for nearly two years. For more than half a century he has been a member of Central Lodge, No. 44, Free and Accepted Masons, and past master for forty-eight years; and is also a member of Union League, Philadelphia, Pennsylvania. He is a member of Mt. Holly Lodge, No. 848, B. P. O. E., and although brought up under the influences of the Society of Friends he attends services of the Protestant Episcopal church.

In 1862 Mr. Irick married Harriet R., daughter of Samuel E. and Hannah (Roberts) Clement. Children: 1. H. Clementine, born February 24, 1863. 2. Anne H., June 21, 1865; married William J. Irick, banker of Vincentown. 3. John Ellis, December 9, 1867; graduate of Rutgers College.

(IV) John Bishop, son of General John Stockton and Emeline S. (Bishop) Irick, was born at Vincentown, November 28, 1845, and received his education in academic schools at Burlington and Lawrenceville. He began business life on his father's farm, and carried it on about five years, then for twenty-eight years was proprietor of a gristmill, and now is engaged in a general lumber business. For fourteen years he was tax collector of Burlington, and in 1905 was elected member of the New Jersey house of assembly and has been re-elected at the end of each successive term. Since 1871 he has been a director of the bank in Vincentown. He holds membership in Mt. Holly Lodge of Elks, No. 848, has been a vestryman of the Protestant Episcopal church for thirty years, and is a lifelong Republican.

Mr. Irick married, September 13, 1871, Clara Moore, of Philadelphia, daughter of Carlton R. and Mary (McClure) Moore; children: 1. Vincent, born June 12, 1872; graduated from Rutgers College in 1898, and is now engaged in mercantile business in New York City; married Blanche Van Alstyne, of Kinderhook, New York. 2. Carlton, May 5, 1877. 3. Hector Tyndall, November 31, 1883; graduate of Philadelphia Dental College.

KELSEY   Jonathan Hamilton Kelsey, attorney at law, resident of Pemberton, New Jersey, descends from an old New England family that early settled in the state of Vermont. His great-grandfather, Jonathan Kelsey, was born in North Danville, Vermont; married, and had issue.

(I) Robert Lee, son of Jonathan Kelsey, was born in North Danville, Vermont. He was a farmer, and an influential man in his community. He was a Democrat, very active in politics and held many public offices of honor and trust. He was four times married, and had the following issue: Hiram, Ichabod, Jonathan B., see forward, Harvey, and Betsey, who is living in Springfield, Massachusetts, at a very advanced age.

(II) Jonathan B., son of Robert Lee Kelsey, was born in North Danville, Vermont, in December, 1827, and died April 2, 1903. He was educated in the schools of his native town and at St. Johnsbury, Vermont. When a young man he was in Cincinnati, Ohio, and for a short time pursued the study of medicine, a profession, however, which he never fully qualified himself to enter. Later he located in Arkansas and invested largely in farm property. He had a large plantation at Pocohontas, Arkansas, on the Black river, operated with slave labor which he owned before the war. He became interested in the study of law and served as clerk of court in Randolph county, Arkansas. At one time he was a Mississippi and Ohio river pilot, running between New Orleans and Cincinnati. He acquired an interest in river steamboats and piloted his own boats. Owing to the reverses caused by the war and the unsettled condition, Mr. Kelsey abandoned the south as a residence, and about the year 1876 located in Camden, New Jersey. He engaged in the insurance business and was general agent for the Lancastershire Insurance Company of England. He maintained his business office in Philadelphia. In 1880 he settled in Pemberton, New Jersey, which was his home until his death, excepting three years temporary absence as proprietor of a hotel in Atlantic City. In Pemberton he continued in the insurance business. He became identified with the Newark board of underwriters and acted as their secretary for fifteen years. Mr. Kelsey purchased a large farm at Pemberton, and became a breeder of fancy cattle, in which he took a deep delight. He imported fancy Jerseys and other blooded animals for the improvement of his herds. He remained in active business life to within a short time previous to his death. Mr. Kelsey was a Democrat in politics. He was a member of the board of tax revision, and at the taking of the census, in which he assisted, Mr. Kelsey inaugurated methods that proved acceptable and are now in use. He affiliated with the Masonic fraternity, and was past master of Central Lodge, No. 44, Free and Accepted Masons, of Vincentown, New Jersey. In the Scottish Rite he has attained the thirty-second degree.

Jonathan B. Kelsey married (first) Helen Hamilton, of Rising Sun, Ohio. She bore him seven children, five of whom were carried off by an epidemic of yellow fever. The two who survived were Minnie Blanche and Virginia Helen Kelsey. Mr. Kelsey married (second) Laura Virginia Hamilton, sister of his first wife. She survives him and resides on the farm at Pemberton. Albert Hamilton, father of his two wives, was a merchant of Rising Sun, Ohio. He married, and had five children: Mary, married Samuel F. Covington, whose ancestors founded Covington, Kentucky; Albert; Helen, Mrs. J. B. Kelsey (first); Laura Virginia, Mrs. J. B. Kelsey (second), and Emma Hamilton.

The children of Jonathan B. and Laura Virginia (Hamilton) Kelsey are two who died in infancy, Robert Lee, Judith, Jonathan H., see forward; Harriet (Mrs. John C. Altar, of Milford, Delaware), Mary Alberta, Clara Edith, a teacher in the Pemberton high school; Hiram Albert, with the Baldwin Locomotive Works in Philadelphia, and Ellwood H., who manages the home farm for his mother.

(III) Jonathan Hamilton, son of Jonathan B. and Laura V. (Hamilton) Kelsey, was born in Davenport, Iowa, May 19, 1873. He came to New Jersey when a child with his parents. He was educated in the Pemberton schools and under the special instruction of Professor George Shepherd. He had determined on the legal profession, and registered as a law student in the office of Samuel K. Robbins, a noted lawyer of Moorestown and Camden, New Jersey. He remained with Lawyer Robbins three years. He was then in the law office of William A. Slaughter, of Mt. Holly, New Jersey, for the next two years. Mr. Kelsey was admitted to the Burlington county bar at the June term of court in 1903. He at once opened offices for the practice of his profession in Mt. Holly and Pemberton. In addition to his legal business he is a member of the real estate and insurance firm of Kelsey & Killie, of Mt. Holly, New Jersey. Mr. Kelsey has the supervision of his brother's large estate as well as other trusts and properties. He was an incorporator of the Peoples' National Bank of Pemberton, and serves on the board of directors and as attorney for the bank; this bank was incorporated in 1906 with Theodore Budd, president; Clifford E. Budd, vice-president, and Wilson D. Hunt, cashier. Mr. Kelsey is a Democrat and for five years served Pemberton township as justice of the peace, was re-elected but declined to serve; he is a member of the board of councilmen for the borough of Pemberton. He is a member of the Grange, and of Company, No. 49, Patriotic Order Sons of America. He is an attendant of the Baptist church.

Jonathan H. Kelsey married, August 13, 1904, Rebecca Maud Antrim, of Juliustown, daughter of Benjamin and Lydia Antrim, granddaughter of Isaac Antrim, who was a descendant of Lord Antrim and settled on a grant of land near Jobstown, New Jersey, that has never been out of the family's possession. Mr. and Mrs. Kelsey have one child, Virginia Antrim, born at Pemberton, New Jersey, September 7, 1906.

POWELL

The name is a very common one in the Colonial history of New Jersey, and in fact there are few that are more so. It is probable that many of these have sprung from the same source before coming hither, but nothing can be found now to establish the family connection founded on the name. Those bearing it have been prudent, industrious, of good repute, and are still contributing their proportion in the moral and physical development of the state.

(I) Among the passengers on the ship "Kent," that brought the first settlement of the English colony to Burlington, were Robert Powell and his wife Prudence, and their two sons, Robert and John, the latter an infant. They came from London, but a tradition has

come down through separate branches of the family that they originally came from Wales. Shortly after their arrival here was born to them a daughter Elizabeth. These are all that are known. The local record reads: "Elizabeth Powel, daughter of Robert and Prudence Powel, was Borne in Burlington the 7th Seaventh month, 1677, latte of London, chandler, witnesses then p'sent Ellen Harding, Mary Crips, Anne Peachee." This is the first recorded birth in the colony. In another record, showing the deed from Thomas Clide to Robert Powell, the latter is styled clothier. His name is connected with several real estate transactions. In 1681 one hundred acres were surveyed for him along Mile Creek (Willington township), and in 1693 two hundred acres in the fork of the Racocus. Robert Powell was one of the "stalwarts" among the Quakers in the Colony, his name appearing as one of the signers of the declaration against George Keith. He was also one of the signers of an epistle sent by Burlington Monthly Meeting to London Yearly Meeting, dated 12, 7 month, 1680, the first official communication received by the London Yearly Meeting from a meeting in America. There is no will of record, but it is certain that he died prior to January 13, 1694, as a deed given by his sons on that date shows. His wife died before him and according to the record was "layd in ye ground ye 10th of ye 4 month, 1678." In this record Robert Powell and wife are recorded "late of Martin, Legrand, London." The elder son married Mary Perkins in 1696 and died in 1706.

(II) John, younger son of Robert and Prudence Powell, was born 1676 and his name appears in the census of Northampton township, in 1709. He died in 1715-16. He was married at Burlington Monthly Meeting, 12 month, 23 day, 1698, to Elizabeth Parker, born 1676, daughter of George and Sarah Parker. She survived him and was married in 1720 to Richard Brown. In her will, her father, George Parker, is referred to as of "East Jersey." John Powell's children: 1. John, mentioned below. 2. Sarah, born 1701. 3. Rebecca, 1703; married (first) Christopher Scattergood, and (second) an Aaronson. 4. Elizabeth, 1705. 5. Isaac, December 21, 1706; married Elizabeth Perdue or Purdy, died about 1773. 6. Prudence, married Roland Owen, in 1738. 7. Jacob. 8. Robert. 9. Samuel.

(III) John (2), eldest child of John (1) and Elizabeth (Parker) Powell, was born 1700 and settled on a plantation at or near Wood-

pecker Lane, near Mt. Holly, where his grandson, Joseph Powell, lived in 1818. He was
married, in 1725, at Burlington Monthly Meeting, to Virgin Crips, daughter of Nathaniel
and Grace (Whitten) Crips. The last named
were married January 9, 1694. Tradition says
that Nathaniel was a brother of John Crips,
mentioned in Smith's "History of New Jersey,"
but it seems more probable that he was his son.
They lived near where Mt. Holly now is and
on the northeast side of the mount. The
Friends' graveyard, denominated in 1818 the
old graveyard, was a part of their land, and the
mount was then called "Crips Mount" because
of this ownership. Children of John (2)
Powell: 1. Jacob, married an Atkinson. 2.
Christopher, married Sarah Gaskill. 3. John,
married Deborah Harbour. 4. Joseph, mentioned below. 5. Elizabeth, married William
Jones. 6. Grace, married Joseph Gaskill. 7.
Sarah, married Thomas Rogers.

(IV) Joseph, fourth son of John (2) and
Virgin (Crips) Powell, was born September
20, 1739; died April 18, 1805. He probably resided in Northampton township, and engaged
in farming. He married, November 9, 1765,
Anne Bishop, born July 12, 1744; died July
12, 1805. Children: 1. Virgin, September 27,
1766; married Joshua Wills. 2. Rebecca. 3.
Atlantic, August 5. 1773; died September 30,
1825. 4. Japhet Bishop, September 18, 1780.
5. Joseph, mentioned below. 6. Hannah, February 15, 1788; died July 24, 1814.

(V) Joseph (2), younger son of Joseph (1)
and Anne (Bishop) Powell, was born May 7,
1783, and lived in that part of Northampton
township which is now East Hampton. He
was a farmer by occupation, and died at the
age of thirty-six years. He married Mary
Batcher and they were the parents of a daughter and a son, Ann B. and Benajah. The
former became the wife of James Gardiner
and resided on the homestead in Easthampton.
The family belonged to the Society of Friends.
After the death of Joseph Powell, his widow
married Isaac Fennimore, and died at the age
of about sixty-two years.

(VI) Benajah, only son of Joseph (2)
and Mary (Batcher) Powell, was born in November, 1812, in East Hampton, died May 3,
1872. He resided in a part of the parental
mansion and engaged in general farming. He
was a Friend, an adherent of the Whig party
during its existence and an earnest Republican
from the inception of the party. He served
nine years as town collector and held that position at the time of his death. He married

Martha Ann Fennimore, who was born in
Medford, New Jersey, a daughter of Isaac and
Martha (Moore) Fennimore. Of their eight
children, six grew to maturity: 1. Mary,
widow of Zebedee R. Wills, and resides in
Northampton township. 2. Joseph, mentioned
below. 3. Isaac, was a farmer in Lumberton
township; died in Philadelphia. 4. Allen F.,
a farmer, residing in East Hampton. 5. Martha, resides in Lumberton. 6. Annie, died
while the wife of D. Budd Coles, of Lumberton.

(VII) Joseph (3), eldest son of Benajah
and Martha Ann (Fennimore) Powell, was
born April 24, 1843, in Northampton, and
was educated at Willis Institute, Freehold,
New Jersey. At the age of twenty years
he left school and engaged in agriculture on the farm of his grandfather,
Isaac Fennimore, in Medford, and this farm
he now owns and rents. He has always been
an earnest supporter of the Republican party
and has been called to a position of much responsibility. After serving some time as collector of his home town, he was elected county
collector in 1881, and has continually filled
this office since by repeated re-elections. He is
unmarried and makes his home with his
brother-in-law, Mr. Coles, in Lumberton. He
attends and supports the worship of the
Friends' Society. He is a charter member of
Mt. Holly Lodge, No. 848, Benevolent and
Protective Order of Elks. He is a director of
the Mount Holly National Bank and president
of the Peoples' Building and Loan Association
of Mt. Holly. Mr. Powell partakes of the
characteristics which have distinguished the
Friends of New Jersey and enjoys the respect
and esteem of the entire county. His integrity and business ability are attested by his
long service in the office of county collector.

WORRELL According to well established
records the Worrells are an
old and highly respected
family of Burlington county, but by reason of
the lamentable absence of information concerning some of the earlier generations of the
family the names of the immediate and more
remote ancestors of James Worrell are unknown.

(I) James Worrell, the earliest ancestor of
the family of whom there appears to be any
definite account, is said to have been born in
Vincentown, Southampton township, Burlington county, probably about the year 1785, although the exact period of his life is not

known. His wife was Elizabeth (Taylor) Worrell, and their children were James T., Isaiah S., John H. and Lavinia.

(II) James T., son of James and Elizabeth (Taylor) Worrell, was born at Vincentown, Burlington county, in 1815, and died at the home of his son in Mt. Holly, in October, 1907. He was a farmer by occupation, and during his active career lived on the same farm, continuing his residence there until within a few years of the time of his death. Mr. Worrell was a thrifty and fairly successful farmer, a man somewhat active in public affairs in the township, serving for some time as member of the board of school trustees. In politics he was first a Whig and afterward a Republican, and in religious preference a Baptist church member. His wife was Mary (Allen) Worrell, who was born in 1832 and died in February, 1904. Children: 1. Edward A., a farmer of Vincentown, who died aged fifty-two years. 2. Samuel M., a farmer living at Vincentown. 3. George W., carpenter, of Vincentown. 4. James S., farmer, of Vincentown. 5. Lydia, married and lives in Philadelphia. 6. Lavinia, married Walter Anderson and lives in Mt. Holly. 7. Henry I., farmer, of Southampton township. 8. Job I., farmer of Vincentown. 9. William Walter, see post. 10. Charles S., lives at Vincentown.

(III) William Walter, son of James T. and Mary (Allen) Worrell, was born in Southampton township, Burlington county, in 1862, and received his education in public schools at Biddtown and Vincentown and in a private school in Vincentown of which John G. Herbert was then the master. When about nineteen years old he went to work as clerk in a large general store at Marlton owned by H. & J. M. Brink, and remained in the employ of that firm during the next twelve years. In 1898 he became proprietor of a wholesale tobacco business at Mt. Holly and since that time has been counted among the substantial business men of that city. Besides being a prominent business man for many years, Mr. Worrell also has been something of a public man, and is counted among the foremost Republicans of Burlington county. From 1893 to 1898 he was clerk of Burlington county. In 1902 he was appointed auditor by the board of chosen freeholders to fill an unexpired term, and in 1903 he was nominated for and elected to the same office, serving until the general election in November, 1908, when he was elected high sheriff of the county. This office he now holds. Mr. Worrell is president of

the South Jersey Tobacco Company; member of the Junior Order of American Mechanics, having passed the several chairs; member of Mt. Holly Lodge, No. 14, F. and A. M.; Mt. Holly Lodge of Elks, No. 848; and member and trustee of the Baptist church.

In 1880 Mr. Worrell married Lizzie M., daughter of John and Edith (Haines) Christian, of Marlton. Children: 1. John Harold, born Marlton, January 22, 1882. 2. Russell E., born Mt. Holly, 1884; died December 7, 1907. 3. Albert C., born Mt. Holly, February 22, 1896. 4. William E., born Mt. Holly, July 18, 1905.

MELCHER   The surname Melcher is said to be of ancient Hebrew origin, and indicates a long line of ancestors. The meaning of the word is said to be "the king," "the kingly one," or "the royal one." The true spelling of the name is Melchoir. It is a common name in Switzerland and in Germany. It is not known who was the immigrant ancestor of the Melcher families in New England, and Savage gives us an account of Edward Melcher, who was in Portsmouth, New Hampshire, as early as 1684, and died there in 1695.

However, the Melchers of the particular family here treated are believed to have come to this country from Wales, and while the year of immigration is not definitely known, it is certain that the progenitor of the family here under consideration was in Portsmouth, New Hampshire, as early as 1666, and Edward Melcher was among those "that subscribed in the years 1658 and 1666 to the maintenance of ye Minister." They located at Portsmouth and later went to the garrison house in Seabrook. They took up their farm from the wilderness and while clearing it returned to the garrison house at night. On one occasion Mrs. Melcher, being desirous of seeing the farm, walked up alone through the woods to gratify her curiosity. At that time the Indians were very much feared. One day while Edward Melcher was at the farm he left his shoes and stockings with his gun in the cabin and went out to hoe his peas. Soon afterward he saw three Indians enter the cabin, upon which he lay down under the pea-vines until they had gone away, and on entering the cabin he found that his gun and other effects were undisturbed, probably having been overlooked by the intruders who sought only Mr. Melcher himself. After the family had moved out to the farm Mrs. Melcher was one day alone in the house and saw three Indians approach the door, which happened to be fastened. She promptly greeted them with a bucket of boiling water from an upper window and caused their hasty retreat from the premises.

Samuel Melcher, doubtless a son of Edward Melcher, married, May 16, 1700, Elizabeth, daughter of Benjamin Crane. He died in 1754, aged eighty-seven, hence was born about 1667. His wife died in 1756, aged eighty-six years. Their children were John, born August 22, 1703; Elizabeth, August 10, 1705, married Ezekiel Sanborn; and Samuel. They may have had other children of whom we have no account.

Samuel Melcher, son of Samuel and Elizabeth (Crane) Melcher, married, in 1735, Esther, daughter of Benjamin Green. He died in 1802, aged ninety-four years, and his wife Esther died in 1797, aged eighty-seven years. Their children were Samuel, Jonathan, John, Edward, Hannah, Elizabeth, Benjamin and Esther.

Samuel Melcher, son of Samuel and Esther (Green) Melcher, married Elizabeth, daughter of Jonathan Hilliard. He died in 1823, aged eighty-six years, and his wife died in 1826, aged eighty-four years. They had two sons, Levi and Joseph. Levi married Hannah, daughter of Caleb Tilton, and was a merchant in Boston. Joseph lived on the homestead and was always mentioned as Judge Melcher. He married Polly Rowell, and died in 1858, aged eighty-nine years.

There is very little doubt of the close relationship of the Melchers referred to in preceding paragraphs and those of the province of Maine, with whom our present narrative must begin, for we only know that two brothers, Samuel and Joseph Melcher, settled in Brunswick, Maine, about the year 1757, and were progenitors of the families of their surname in that region. Samuel settled at New Meadows, and in 1767 built the house in which Deacon James Smith was living a quarter of a century ago. He died March 3. 1834, aged ninety years, hence was born about 1744. He married Isabella, daughter of Judge Aaron Hinckley. She died August 17, 1832, in her eighty-sixth year. Their children were: 1 Reliance, born November 15, 1768, died November 29, 1804. 2. Mary, August 5, 1771. 3. Aaron, February 23, 1773. 4. Samuel, May 8, 1775, died March 3. 1862. 5. Elizabeth, May 13, 1777. 6. Lois, July 2, 1780. 7. Rebecca, March 6, 1783. 8. John, May 19, 1785. 9. Noah, May 30, 1788, died young. 10. Rachel, February 23, 1793.

(I) Joseph Melcher, brother of Samuel Melcher who is mentioned in the preceding paragraph, settled at Bunganock, on the farm where Jedidiah Mariner dwelt in 1878. He was a "housewright," or carpenter by trade, and died April 21, 1821, aged nearly eighty-six years, hence was born about 1736. He married, in 1757, Mary Cobb, of Gorhamtown, who died May 18, 1825, in her eighty-seventh year. They had a large family of fourteen children, of whom the history of Brunswick, Maine, mentions the names of five: Noah, Nathaniel, Abner, Josiah and Samuel.

(II) Abner, son of Joseph and Mary (Cobb) Melcher, was born at Oak Hill, near Brunswick, Maine, and was a farmer by occupation. He married Maria Frost, and their children were Benjamin, William H., Maria and George.

(III) William Henry, second son and child of Abner and Maria (Frost) Melcher, was born at Brunswick, Maine, May 9, 1824, and is still living (1909) at the advanced age of eighty-five years. At the age of twelve years when a boy in school, he showed an aptitude for mechanical work and even then began making shoes; and at fourteen years he built a substantial sleigh, doing all of the work himself. He was hardly more than a boy in years when he went to Bath to work in a shipyard and there he learned the trade of shipbuilding, becoming a competent workman in the course of a few years. Later on he began building vessels on his own account and followed that occupation for many years. For the last nine years he has held the position of superintendent of woodwork for the Bath Iron Works, and is still active notwithstanding his years. Mr. Melcher is a Republican in politics, a trustee and consistent member of the Free Will Baptist church. In 1846 he married Sarah Jane Alexander, of Richmond, Maine, and by her had three children: Ella Price, William Palmer, Ada Maria.

(IV) William Palmer, only son of William Henry and Sarah Jane (Alexander) Melcher, was born in Brunswick, Maine, April 10, 1849, and was a child two years old when his father removed with his family to Bath. He fitted for college in the Maine State Seminary and Nichols Latin School, then entered Bowdoin College and was graduated A. B. in 1871. After leaving college he turned his attention temporarily to teaching, then matriculated at the medical department of the University of Pennsylvania, Philadelphia, and graduated from there with the degree of M. D. in 1876. Dr. Melcher began his professional career in Camden and practiced in that city until 1879, when he removed to Pemberton, New Jersey, lived there until 1882 and then settled permanently at Mt. Holly, where in later years he has built up a remunerative practice. He is a member of the American Medical Association, the New Jersey State Medical Society, and the Burlington County Medical Society. He is a member of Mt. Holly Lodge, No. 848, B. P. O. E., and in politics is a Republican. For fifteen years he was a member of the Mt. Holly board of education.

March 13, 1884, Dr. Melcher married Mary, daughter of Theodore and Martha (Snyder) Gaskell, (the former a steward at New Lisbon), and has three children: 1. Theodora, born March 29, 1886. 2. Stanwood Alexander, September 15, 1893. 3 Charlotte Patton, June 9, 1896.

SHARP   The Sharp family of New Jersey is descended from English ancestors, and previous to the immigration to America the particular family here treated was settled in the parish of St. Ann, Limehouse, Middlesex. This was the family of Francis Sharp, of Oak Lane. William and Thomas Sharp, sons of Francis Sharp, came with their families to America in the ship "Samuel" in 1682, and settled in Evesham township in Burlington county, New Jersey. The children who came with William and Thomas Sharp were John, William and Hugh Sharp, whom tradition says were brothers and children of William, although this relationship has not been fully established and the fact has been assumed by genealogists of the family as being in accordance with probabilities and with nothing to indicate to the contrary.

(I) William Sharp, the immigrant, was born in England, and on his arrival in this country settled in the old township of Evesham, where he was a person of considerable consequence, although accounts of his life are quite meagre so far as the records tend to indicate. Some relics, however, of his generation and time have been preserved by his descendants, among them Bibles, a clock of ancient construction, a case of drawers, and a two-gallon bottle; and of which with others of less importance are said to have been brought over with him in 1682. The name of his wife does not appear, but there came with him the three sons, John, William and Hugh, to whom casual reference has been made.

(II) John, presumably the eldest son of William Sharp, the immigrant, was born in

England and came to this country with his father in 1682. He married, 4th month 17th, 1688, Elizabeth, daughter of John Paine. Children: 1. William, born 1689, see post. 2. Elizabeth, 1692. 3. John, 1693; married (first) Jane Fitchardall, (second) Ann Haines. 4. Thomas, 1698; married Elizabeth Smith. 5. Hannah, 1700; married Thomas Adams. 6. Samuel, 1702; married Elizabeth Haines. 7. Sarah, 1705.

(III) William (2), son of John and Elizabeth (Paine) Sharp, was born 10th month 2d, 1689, and married (first) 1716, Mary, daughter of Francis and Mary (Borton) Austin. Francis Austin was progenitor of the family of his surname in New Jersey, and his wife, Mary Borton, was daughter of John and Ann Borton, progenitors of the Borton family of New Jersey. William Sharp married (second) Hannah ———. Children: 1. Rebecca, born 1719; married Solomon Haines. 2. Hannah, 1721; married Jonathan Haines. 3. Hugh, 1724, see post. 4. Esther, 1727; married Job Haines. 5. William, 1730; married Mary Haines. 6. Sarah, 1735; married Barzilla Prickitt. 7. Samuel, 1737. 8. Jane, 1739; married Robert Engle. 9. Child, 1741; died in infancy. 10. Isaac, 1744; died young. 11. Josiah, 1748. 12. Elizabeth, 1751.

(IV) Hugh, son of William (2) and Mary (Austin) Sharp, was born 11th month, 15th, 1724. He married (first) Sabillah ———, who died leaving borne him three children; married (second) Ann, daughter of Mark and Anna (Hancock) Stratton. Children: 1. Sabillah, born 1755. 2. Hannah, 1757. 3. Thomas, 1759. 4. Job, 1761. 5. William, see post.

(V) William (3), son of Hugh and Ann (Stratton) Sharp, was born 3d month 10th, 1770, and married Elizabeth, daughter of Thomas and Elizabeth (Zane) Rakestraw. Thomas Rakestraw was a son of Thomas Rakestraw and grandson of Thomas Rakestraw, whose wife was Mary, daughter of Thomas Wilkinson. Children: 1. Eli, married Catherine Sinnickson. 2. Franklin, married Eliza Braddock. 3. William, see post. 4. Isaac, married Hannah Engle. 5. Charles. 6. Maria, married Benjamin Wilkins. 7. Elizabeth, married Japheth Bowker. 8. Amanda, married ——— Morford. 9. Susan, married Wesley Evans.

(VI) William (4), son of William (3) and Elizabeth (Rakestraw) Sharp, was born in Medford, New Jersey, in 1796, died there in 1844. He was a man of education and judgment, a careful and constant reader, and while in business life was a contractor and builder, always retaining his early love of books and good reading. Until he was sixty-five years old he continued to live on his farm and then moved to Medford village. He married Jemima, daughter of Darnell and Sarah (Rogers) Braddock. Children: 1. Fredinand F., married Lydia Thomas. 2. Hugh, married Jane Ann Sharp. 3. Benjamin, married Adeline Garwood. 4. Jemima, married Edwin Crispin. 5. Abbie, married Edward Darnell. 6. Jervis, married Sarah A. R. Githens. 7. Andrew, married Lydia S. Darnell. 8. Lewis L., see post. 9. Henry, married Annie Wilkins. 10. Edward, married Rebecca Stilwell Bailey.

(VII) Dr. Lewis L., son of William (4) and Jemima (Braddock) Sharp, was born in Medford, New Jersey, November 1, 1841, and after receiving a good elementary education in public schools in Medford and Moorestown, he entered the medical department of the University of Pennsylvania, graduating with the degree of M. D. in 1864. After graduation he began his professional career in Medford and has since been engaged in active general practice. He is a member of the American Medical Association, the New Jersey State Medical Society, the Burlington County Medical Society and has served as president of the Burlington County District Medical Association. He is a Master Mason, a Republican in politics and in 1890-91 was a member of the New Jersey house of assembly.

July 12, 1904, Dr. Sharp married, Mrs. Rebecca Stilwell Bailey Sharp, widow of Edward Sharp, Dr. Sharp's brother. By her former marriage Mrs. Sharp had one daughter, Florence Broomell Sharp, born July 25, 1885, died January 17, 1900.

WAINWRIGHT   The ancestor of the Wainwright families in this country was a Yorkshire Englishman, by birth and parentage, and who as an officer of the British navy was sent to Bermuda, West Indies, as commandant of the British naval station there. He is said to have had three sons who came to America and settled, one in New York city, one in Philadelphia, and one at Halifax, Nova Scotia. Bishop Wainwright, of New York, came of the son who settled in that city, and the family purposed to be treated in this place comes of the son who located in Philadelphia. But, indeed, of this son the historical and gene-

alogical references give us no account whatever, and we only know that Jonathan Wainwright, a Hicksite Quaker, was among the descendants of that one of the three immigrant brothers who settled in Philadelphia.

(I) Jonathan Wainwright was born in Philadelphia in 1795 and died in that city in 1870. He was a manufacturer of pully blocks and also carried on a business of dealing in lumber, and it is evident that he was a man of considerable consequence in the business life of the city and at one time was president of the Kensington Bank. He married Susan, daughter of George and Martha (Hollingshead) Eyre, granddaughter of Jehu Eyre and great-granddaughter of George Eyre, who came over to America with Penn's colony. Children: 1. Matilda, now dead; married Hanson Withers, of Philadelphia. 2. Susan, now dead; married Henry L. Tripler. 3. Isaac Harrison, now dead. 4. Richard S., now dead. 5. Jonathan E., see post. 6. Charles B., of Camden, New Jersey. 7. Chandler Price, of Philadelphia.

(II) Jonathan Eyre, son of Jonathan and Susan (Eyre) Wainwright, was born in city of Philadelphia, Pennsylvania, and died at Norristown, Pennsylvania. He was reared under the influence of the Society of Friends and received his early education in Friends' schools and also in the township public schools. After leaving school he became connected with the house of Cope Shipping Company and in 1849 was sent to California. On his return to the east he became interested with his father in the lumber business and continued it after the death of his parent. Mr. Wainwright was a Mason, member of Harmony Lodge, F. and A. M., of Philadelphia, an Episcopalian in religious preference and a Republican in politics. He married Elizabeth Lynn Tripler, of Philadelphia, born January, 1829, and still living. Children: 1. Jacob T., of Chicago, metallurgical engineer in iron and steel construction. 2. Isaac Harrison, see post.

(III) Isaac Harrison, younger son of Jonathan Eyre and Elizabeth Lynn (Tripler) Wainwright, was born in the city of Philadelphia, Pennsylvania, January 6, 1856, graduated from the University of Pennsylvania in 1875, and immediately found employment as rodman in the engineering department of the Pennsylvania Railroad Company. He was stationed first at Altoona, and since that time has been engaged in the company's service in various parts of southern and central Pennsylvania and southern New Jersey; and from the position of rodman he has advanced through

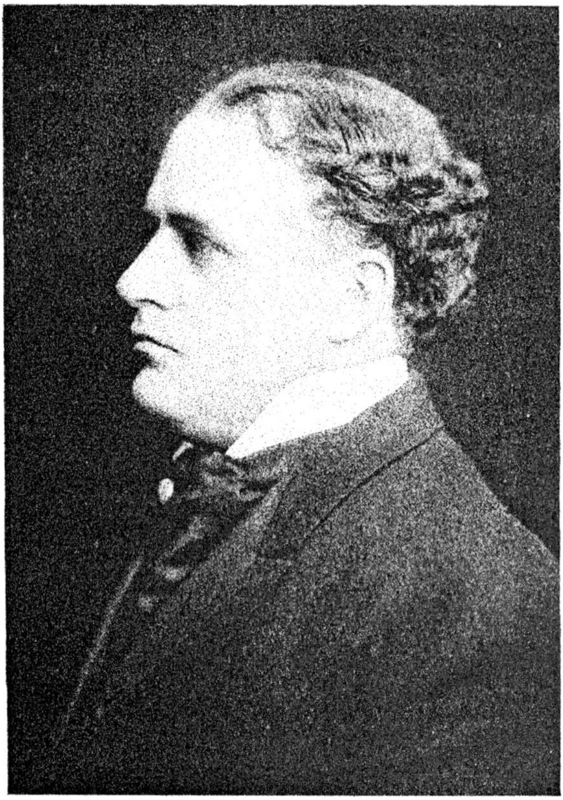

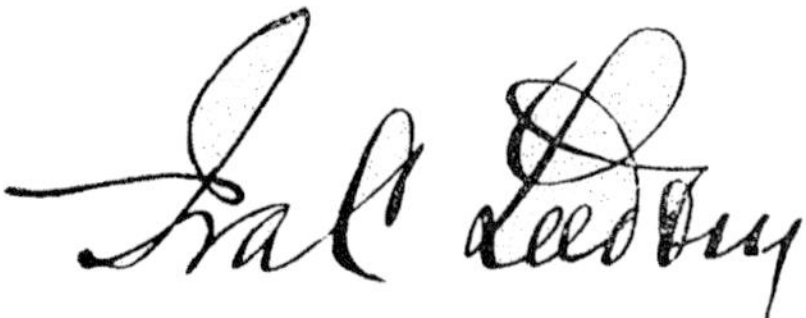

grades of promotion to that of supervisor in charge of a part of the Amboy division, with offices in Mt. Holly. Mr. Wainwright has been continuously in the service of the company for more than thirty-five years. He holds membership in Perry Lodge, No. 458, F. and A. M., of Marysville, Pennsylvania; Newport Chapter, No. 238, R. A. M., of Newport, Pennsylvania; Van Hook Council, R. and S. M.; Cyrene Commandery, No. 7, K. T., of Camden; also the various bodies of Scottish Rite and the Mystic Shrine.

In 1881 Mr. Wainwright married Sally B. Pennell, of Duncannon, Pennsylvania, daughter of John and Catherine (Keyser) Pennell, and a granddaughter of Andrew Pennell, a native of Ireland and the ancestor of the family in this country.

LEEDOM

Dr. Ira Clayton Leedom, of Bordentown, New Jersey, descends from a family long resident of Bucks county, Pennsylvania, where Dr. Leedom also was born.

(I) John Leedom, the earliest ancestor, was born in Bucks county, Pennsylvania, where all his life he followed agricultural pursuits. He had sons: George, Samuel, Howard and Alfred; daughters: Lucy, Ann, Mary and Sarah.

(II) Samuel, son of John Leedom, was born in Bucks county, Pennsylvania, 1828. He received the usual education of sons of farmers, and learned the trade of carpenter. He formed a partnership with his brother Alfred in Southampton, Pennsylvania, and most of his active life was spent there. They were well known contractors and builders and erected many public and private buildings in the county. Mr. Leedom retired from active life about 1895 and is now living in Philadelphia. He is a member of the Baptist church, and while living in Danville, Pennsylvania, was a deacon and trustee of the church there. He is a Republican, and a member of the Independent Order of Odd Fellows and the Improved Order of Red Men. He married Catherine Van Cleve, born in 1832 in Montgomery county, Pennsylvania, daughter of Samuel and Rachel (Fetter) Van Cleve. Samuel Van Cleve, her father, was born in Freehold, New Jersey, the son of Benjamin Van Cleve, and grandson of Benjamin Van Cleve, all of Monmouth county, New Jersey. Children of Samuel and Catherine (Van Cleve) Leedom: 1. Alfred, deceased; he was a funeral director of Southampton. Pennsylvania; married Emma Dubois and left a son, Guy R. Leedum. 2. Dorie V., a

master ship carpenter at the League Island United States navy yard, Philadelphia; married Margaret Pritchard; children: J. Firth, Clarence and Ethel. 3. Ira Clayton, see forward.

(III) Dr. Ira Clayton, youngest son of Samuel and Catherine (Van Cleve) Leedom, was born at Southampton, Bucks county, Pennsylvania, January 21, 1871. He was educated in the public schools of his native town. He entered Bucknell University and was graduated from that institution with the class of 1891. Having chosen medicine as his profession and Homeopathy as his school, he entered Hahnemann Medical College, Philadelphia, graduating therefrom in 1894. In the same year he located in Bordentown, New Jersey, and entered upon the practice of his profession. He is a well known man of town and esteemed highly as a physician and a citizen. He is Republican in politics and has served the city as president of the board of education, president of the excise commission, secretary of the board of health and as city collector. He stands high in the Masonic fraternity. He is past master of Mt. Moriah Lodge, No. 28, Free and Accepted Masons; past eminent commander of Ivanhoe Commandery, Knights Templar, No. 11, and a Royal Arch Mason of Mt. Moriah Chapter, No. 20, all of Bordentown, and a thirty-second degree Mason of the Scottish Rite, Trenton Consistory. He also belongs to the Bordentown Knights of Pythias, the Knights of the Golden Eagle and the Brotherhood of America.

Dr. Leedom married, in 1895, Frances Rush, daughter of John and Mary Rush, of Warren county, New Jersey. One child, F. Benson, born in Bordentown, New Jersey, 1896.

EARL

It is said by antiquarians that the family of Earle is of very ancient origin and can be traced back to a Saxon ancestor of a period more remote than that of the Norman conquest. In the reign of Henry II., crowned A. D. 1154, there were Earles in Beckington, Somersetshire, and by one author it is stated that "so far back as the seventh Henry II., John de Erlegh paid five marks for the scutage of his lands at Beckington." Thus it is seen that the Earles are a very ancient family of England and were it desirable abundant proof is available to show that the family also is one of much distinction. There were no less than eleven coats-of-arms granted to various members of the English family, but as the author of the work entitled "Ralph Earle and His Descendants" says "in all my intercourse, either personal or by written correspondence, I have found none who wore or bore a coat-of-arms, and in only one instance have I heard of one in the possession of any family."

(I) Ralph Earle, immigrant, first appears in New England colonial history as of Newport, Rhode Island, where his name is found in the records as early as 1638. Of his birthplace or place of residence previous to immigrating to America there appears nothing like reliable information. There always has been a tradition among his descendants that he came from Exeter in 1634, and there is little doubt that he married in England and that his wife came over with him, although her family name is unknown. She was called Joan, although her baptismal name appears so written and also Ione and Jone. Ralph Earle was admitted inhabitant of "the Island now called Aqueedneck" in 1638, and appears to have been a person of some consequence in the plantation . April 29, 1650, Ralph Earle and five others were chosen "for the committee for the General Assembly at Newport in May next," and on November 12, 1650, it was "voated & granted that Ralph Erl's house wherein he now dwelleth be recorded & Inn, in ye room of ye former vote that he was an Innkeeper." In 1651 he was elected one of the committee "to proportion every man's farm," and in the same year he was chosen town treasurer. He fulfilled various other offices, serving as grand juror, witnessing deeds and other instuments, and in 1667 joined the "troop of horse" of which subsequently he became captain. He claimed ownership of "the lands of the Dutch House of Good Hope, now Hartford, Connecticut, and commenced a lawsuit therefore," claiming that he purchased the land of Underhill in August, 1653, and paid twenty pounds sterling for it. He died in Portsmouth, Rhode Island, in 1678. He and his wife Joan had five children: 1. Ralph, married Dorcas Sprague. 2. William, see post. 3. Mary, married (first) William Cory, (second) Joseph Timberlake. 4. Martha, married William Wood. 5. Sarah, married Thomas Cornell.

(II) William, son of Ralph and Joan Earle, is first mentioned in 1634, when he sold his interest in certain lands to one James Sands. In 1658 he became freeman of Portsmouth, Rhode Island, and in the same years was admitted freeman of the colony. In 1665 it was

ordered that William Earle and William Cory have "one acker of land on the hill cauled Briges hill, or some other conveniant place in this Townes Comons, and a quarter of an acker of land lying aganst ye towne pond over against William Earle's new dewlinge house, and these two parcells of land they are to have and to enjoy to them and theres, so long as they maintain a wind mill in this town for the townes use, Provided that if they maintain not the said mill then the said pearcells of land it to be returned and laid down to the townes use and dispose." In 1668 the wind mill had been erected and the town at the request of Earle and Cory annulled the above order and exchanged two acres of ground belonging to Earle and Cory. "The Eare marke of Wiliam Earl's cattell is a hapeny under the side of ye further Eare and a slit on the Nere Eare, of 12 yeares standing, and Entred upon Record by me, Richard Bulgar, towne Clarke, Dcec ye 5th, 1667." In 1670 William Earle removed to Dartmouth, Rhode Island, where he had large interests in lands, and remained there several years. He owned two thousand acres from his claims in the original division of the land. The records show that he was a man of importance as well as a large land holder, and in 1691 "the General Assembly for their Majesties Collony of Rhode Island and Providence Plantations, in New England, in Portsmouth on said Rhode Island, for the Election of General Officers for the said Collony," was held "at the house of William Earle, it being removed from Newport by reason of the Distemper." In 1692 he was a member of the "grand Inquest at Newport," was deputy from Portsmouth to the general assembly at Providence in October, 1704, and at Newport in 1706. He made his will November 13, 1713, and provided well for his children and other members of his family. He married (first) Mary, daughter of John and Katherine Walker, and after her death he married Prudence ———. She died January 18, 1718, having survived her husband three years, he having died January 15, 1715. He had seven children: 1. Mary, born 1655; married John Borden. 2. William, see post. 3. Ralph, born 1660, married Mary Hicks. 4. Thomas, married Mary Taber. 5. Caleb, married Mary ———. 6. John, married Mary Wait. 7. Prudence, married Benjamin Durfee.

(III) William (2), son of William (1) and Mary (Walker) Earle, was born in Portsmouth, Rhode Island, and after his marriage settled in Dartmouth, Massachusetts, where he was juryman in 1694, and constable in 1695-96. It appears that he was engaged in a small way in the shipping business, owning an interest in a sloop in which he carried on a coasting trade along the coast of New England, New York and New Jersey. In December, 1697, he came to Springfield, New Jersey, where he purchased the farm on which he ever afterward lived. He was a member of the Society of Friends, many of his descendants followed his example in their religious relations and many of them still continue in that faith. It appears too that this William Earle wrote his name without the final "e," which example has been followed by nearly all of his descendants. The exact date of his death is not known, but his will dated September 23, 1732, was proved May 10, 1733. The baptismal name of his wife was Elizabeth, and by her he had five children: 1. Mary, married Jonathan Borden. 2. Martha, married Thomas Shinn. 3. Child, name unknown; married John Webb. 4. William, married Mrs. Mary Sharpe. 5. Thomas, see post.

(IV) Thomas, son of William (2) and Elizabeth Earl, was born in Springfield, New Jersey, and died there in 1778. After the death of his elder brother, William, he lived on his father's homestead, and devised it to his son Thomas. He married, September 6, 1727, Mary Crispin, born May 12, 1705, daughter of Silas and Mary (Stockton-Shinn) Crispin, and by her had four children: 1. Tanton, born March 9, 1731, see post. 2. Thomas, married (first) Rebecca Newbold, (second) Leah Tucker. 3. William, died before his father. 4. John, died before his father.

(V) Tanton, son of Thomas and Mary (Crispin) Earl, was born in Springfield, New Jersey, March 9, 1731, died there October 24, 1807. He was a farmer and spent his life in Springfield. He married Mary Haines, born September 12, 1732, died June 3, 1811, having borne her husband ten children: 1. Thomas, born December 13, 1754; married Edith Sykes. 2. Caleb, December 21, 1756; married Esther Gardner. 3. John, October 25, 1758; married (first) Abigail Smith, (second) Abigail Haines. 4. Joseph, see post. 5. Elizabeth, March 7, 1763; married Jonathan Curtis. 6. Mercy, March 19, 1765; died September 20, 1805. 7. Mary, May 25, 1767, married Alexander Shreve. 8. Letitia, May 31, 1769, died March 15, 1774. 9. Tanton, October 23, 1772, died January 29, 1796. 10. Daniel, January 21, 1774; married Hannah Shinn.

(VI) Joseph, son of Tanton and Mary (Haines) Earl, was born in Springfield, New

Jersey, January 2, 1761, died in Pemberton, New Jersey, February 25, 1839. He was a farmer and spent much of his life in the town of Pemberton. He married Theodosia Shreve, born April 28, 1766, died June 12, 1848, daughter of Joshua Shreve, and by whom he had eleven children: 1. Esther, born October 9, 1786; married John Mullin. 2. Caleb, March 5, 1788; died March 10, 1795. 3. Benjamin, December 14, 1789; died March 6, 1791. 4. Joshua S., November 5, 1792, died January 27, 1831; was deputy surveyor and member of the board of proprietors of West Jersey; sheriff of Burlington county three years, and member of the legislature; died unmarried. 5. Tanton, October 31, 1794, died September 25, 1801. 6. Joseph Biddle, January 23, 1797; married Rachel (Allen) Hinchman. 7. Rebeca S., October 7, 1799, died November 21, 1856; married Israel English. 8. Tanton, October 26, 1801, died December 21, 1868. 9. Richard W., August 7, 1804; married Mary D. Howell. 10. Sarah B., November 14, 1807, married Joseph J. Budd. 11. Franklin W., see post.

(VII) Franklin W., son of Joseph and Theodosia (Shreve) Earl, was born in Pemberton, New Jersey, December 1, 1811. He was instantly killed May 17, 1883, by a train of cars while crossing the railroad track in his carriage at Mt. Holly. He was a man of much intelligence, a deputy surveyor and a member of the council of proprietors of West Jersey. He served as township clerk of Pemberton, township committeeman and school trustee, and held other offices of importance. He was a Democrat in politics and once stood as his party candidate for a seat in the legislature. He held membership in the Independent Order of Odd Fellows, and in religious preference was a member of the Society of Friends. He married, March 15, 1838, Rebecca W. Smith, died September 26, 1886, daughter of Joseph and Sarah Smith, and by her had eight children: 1. Joseph, born April 4, 1839; died May 17, 1859. 2. Elizabeth S., October 22, 1840; died March 11, 1873; married Joshua Forsyth, Jr. 3. Joshua, November 12, 1842; married Mary Adelaide Oliphant. 4. Eleanora, September 5, 1844; married, December 6, 1867, Franklin S. Gaskill. 5. Charles, December 4, 1846; married Elizabeth H. Davis. 6. Florence W., April 6, 1852; married Emma R. Davis. 7. Frank, see post. 8. Tanton, December 26, 1859; died November 5. 1876.

(VIII) Frank, son of Franklin W. and Rebecca W. (Smith) Earl, was born near Pem-

ii—7

berton, New Jersey, March 2, 1856, and received his education in the public schools of his native town and for two years was a student in an academic school in Bethlehem, Pennsylvania. On his return home he began his business career as a surveyor with his father, and from that time has been an active and successful business man, a conveyancer, deputy of the council of proprietors of West Jersey, three years township committeeman and several years school trustee. During his professional life he has done a large amount of work as surveyor and civil engineer in the counties of Camden, Burlington and Atlantic. On May 21, 1877, Mr. Earl married Julia C. Jones, born October 7, 1857, daughter of Wilkins and Keziah (Shinn) Jones, of Woodford, New Jersey. Five children were born of this marriage: 1. Minnie Rebecca, born August 23, 1878; married Carl Tietz, Jr., of Chicago, private secretary to the chief engineer of the Illinois Central Railroad Company. 2. Marion Estella, April 29, 1881, died at the age of eighteen years. 3. Almer Jones, April 2, 1883; was educated at the Friends' School, Philadelphia; became a civil engineer engaged in the service of the Illinois Central Railroad Company, remained two years; worked as civil engineer in the states of Illinois, Tennessee, Alabama and Louisiana. Since leaving the employ of the company above mentioned he has engaged in work with his father. He married, August 11, 1907, Ila, daughter of Thomas J. Hurley, of Jasper, Alabama. 4. Franklin W., October 15, 1884; graduate pharmacist, now living at Overbrook, West Philadelphia. 5. John H. P., April 29, 1895.

HAINES The Haines family is said by antiquarians to be of Saxon origin, and first appears in Devonshire, in the West Saxon kingdom, in the early part of the sixth century, among the following of Hengest and Horsa, when the name was known as Hayne. The family was found in England at the time of the conquest, seated in Hayne, Stowford parish, near the Tamcoe on the borders of Cornwall. The name was written Hayne until the compilation of Doomesday Book, when it was changed to Haines, although certain branches of the family still retain the original form of spelling.

(I) Richard Haines, of Aynhoe, Northamptonshire, England, husbandman, with his wife Margaret and their children, Richard, William, Thomas and Mary, sailed from Downs, England, in 1682, in the ship "Amity," for America, but Richard the father never reached the shores of this country, having sickened and died on the voyage. A fifth son, Joseph, was born on board the ship. John, the eldest son, had come over about 1680, and made himself a house below Lumberton, on the south branch of Rancocas creek, in New Jersey. The family settled in Burlington, New Jersey, and in 1685 the widow Margaret married a second husband, Henry Bircham, of Nesmamony, Pennsylvania. Thus it is that because of the death of Richard Haines in mid-ocean ·we have no account of him in this country. He was a member of the Society of Friends. By his wife Margaret he had six children, none of whom were born in America. Their children: 1. John, married, 1684, · Esther Burton. 2. Richard, married, 1699, Mary Carlisle. 3. William, born 1672 (see post). 4. Thomas, born 1674; married 1692, Elizabeth Austin. 5. Mary, born 1676. 6. Joseph, born 1682; married (first) 1704, Dorothy ———; (second) 1722, Elizabeth Thomas.

(II) William, son and third child of Richard and Margaret Haines, was born in England, in 1672, and located one hundred acres of land "near Nancutting's Old Plantation" in 1689. In 1712 he acquired lands in Northampton and settled there. He appears to have acquired considerable tracts of land, and evidently was a person of some importance. His will is dated in 1752, and was admitted to probate April 29, 1754. In 1695 he married Sarah, daughter of John Paine, at the Friends' meeting in Burlington, and by her had six children: 1. Jacob, born 1699; married Hannah Stokes. 2. Marget (Margaret), born 1701. 3. Nathan, born 1703; married Sarah Austin. 4. Samuel (see post). 5. Nathaniel, born 1707; married 1731, Mary Hervey. 6. Jeremiah, born 1713; married, 1736, Hannah Bounell.

(III) Samuel, fourth child of William and Sarah (Paine) Haines, was born in 1705, and married, in 1734, Lydia, daughter of Thomas and Deliverance (Horner) Stokes; children: 1. Jacob, married Bathsheba Burroughs. 2. Sarah, married Caleb Newbold. 3. Samuel (see post). 4. Thomas, married Elizabeth Mullen.

(IV) Samuel (2), son and third child of Samuel (1) and Lydia (Stokes) Haines, married (first) Elizabeth, daughter of William and Mary (Wills) Buzby; (second) Mary, daughter of Cornell Stevenson, and had seven children by his first and five by his second wife: 1. William, born April 17, 1768; married Mary

Eayres. 2. Mary, born November 15, 1770; married Jacob Hollingshead. 3. Aaron (see post). 4. Abel, born September 30, 1775; married Elizabeth Stokes. 5. Joseph, born April 1, 1778; died 1793. 6. Elizabeth, born July 15, 1780. 7. Samuel, born December 13, 1783; married Susannah Chapman. 8. Lydia, born July 31, 1789. 9. Robert, born January 2, 1791; married Edith Rogers. 10. Sarah, born November 31, 1792; died July 17, 1795. 11. Ezra, born September 26, 1795; married (first) Lucy Bishop; (second) Phebe Pierce. 12. Hannah, born May 15, 1798; married Joseph R. Bishop.

(V) Aaron, third child of Samuel and Elizabeth (Buzby) Haines, was born March 25, 1773, and was a farmer in Rancocas, New Jersey, where he was born and died. His wife was Martha, daughter of Jervis and Elizabeth (Rogers) Stokes; children: 1. John S. (see post). 2. Jervis, married Elizabeth Reeves. 3. Edith S., married Isaac Haines, his first wife. 4. Samuel, married Ann Woodman. 5. Elizabeth, married Joseph Elkington.

(VI) John Staples, eldest son and child of Aaron and Martha (Stokes) Haines, was born in Rancocas, New Jersey, October 1, 1798, and died in 1875. He was an energetic business man, a blacksmith by trade, but a farmer and manufacturer of brick by principal occupation. He owned and carried on a good farm, and as his farm lands contained a considerable deposit of clay of excellent quality for brick he devoted a large share of his attention to that manufacture and furnished employment to a large number of workmen. He retired from active pursuits about twelve years before his death, after which the farm and brickmaking were carried on by his son Stokes. Mr. Haines was in all respects a substantial man, a born Quaker, although his wife was a Methodist, and he was a firm Democrat of the Jacksonian type. He married about 1820, Mary Ann Woolston, born October 2, 1800, died 1882, a daughter of John Woolston. Ten children were born of this marriage: 1. Benjamin, died in infancy. 2. John Woolston, died in infancy. 3. Eliza. 4. Aaron Stokes, born 1828, died December 2, 1908. 5. Cylania W., married Isaac H. Trotter, is now a widow, living in Vincentown. 6. Lydia W., died in 1864. 7. Adeline, died 1906. 8. Martin Luther, born March, 1837, died September, 1905. 9. John Woolston (see post). 10. Stokes, a cranberry grower of Vincentown.

(VII) John Woolston, ninth child of John Staples and Mary Ann (Woolston) Haines,

was born at Vincentown, in Southampton township, March 8, 1839, and was brought up to farm work. His business career was begun as a farmer, but at the end of about four years he turned attention to dealing in live stock and poultry, which he has continued until the present time, although during the period of more than forty years in which he has been identified with the business life of Vincentown, Mr. Haines has been interested in various other directions. For two years he was proprietor of a mercantile business there, and in 1879 he owned a cranberry bog, which afterward he sold to his brother. He is a democrat in politics and as such has frequently been elected to public office. He served one year as assessor, three years as collector, and several years as school trustee, twenty years as member of the township committee, and in 1879 and 1880 was member of the New Jersey House of Assembly. He is a past master of Central Lodge No. 44, F. and A. M., of Vincentown, and member of Vincentown Lodge No. 23, I. O. O. F.

Mr. Haines married (first) in 1860, Mary Elizabeth Budd, born Buddtown, New Jersey, in August, 1839, died 1880, daughter of John S. Budd. He married (second) in 1890, Alice Huston Hargrave, of Tabernacle, daughter of Josiah Huston. She died July 4, 1905. Mr. Haines had six children, all born of his first marriage: 1. Theodosia, died young. 2. John, died young. 3. Addie G., married Clifford S. Cowperthwaite, of Medford, and has one child Norman Woolston, married Edith Moore, of Vincentown. 4. Eugene O., dealer in stock and poultry, Vincentown. 5. Martha, lives at home. 6. Mary, lives at home.

(For first generation see preceding sketch).

HAINES

(II) Richard, second son and child of Richard and Margaret Haines, was born in England, and came to America with his father's family. He settled in Evesham township, Burlington county, New Jersey, near his brother John, and was a farmer. He died in 1746, at an advanced age, having become possessed of a good estate in lands, most of which was set off to his children before he died. He married, in 1699, Mary Carlile, who also died in 1746, and both she and her husband were buried in the family burying ground on the old Richard Haines farm, Fostertown, Burlington county. Richard and Mary (Carlile) Haines had ten children: 1. Abraham (see post). 2. Richard, married 1721, Agnes Hollingshead, of whom mention is made in this narrative. 3. Mary, married, 1720, Timothy Matlack. 4. Carlile, married, 1721, Sarah, daughter of William and Mary (Hancock) Matlack. 5. Rebecca, married, 1721, Richard, son of William Matlack. 6. Rachel, married, 1725, Isaac Albertson. 7. Enoch. 8. Barthanah. 9. Sarah, married Edward Hilliard. 10. Elizabeth, married ———— Newberry.

(III) Abraham, eldest child of Richard and Mary (Carlile) Haines, was owner of a large estate in lands at Evesham, and also in Frederick county, Virginia, and was withal a man of considerable prominence. He died in 1758. He married, May 14, 1719, Grace, daughter of John and Agnes (Hackney) Hollingshead. She died in 1769, having borne her husband eleven children: 1. Abraham, settled in Frederick county, Virginia, and died there in 1760; married, 1744, Sarah Ellis. 2. Benjamin, born 1725 (see post). 3. Noah, married, 1761, widow Hannah Thorne. 4. Edmund, married Elizabeth Warrington. 5. Isaac, married, 1758, Deborah Roberts. 6. Josiah. 7. Isaac, married Sarah Wilkins. 8. Simeon, married 1760, Mary Stratton. 9. Mary, married 1752, William Sharp. 10. Agnes, married Joseph Hackney. 11. Joshua.

(IV) Benjamin, second son and child of Abram and Grace (Hollingshead) Haines, married (first) Elizabeth, daughter of John and Mary (Elkinton) Roberts. She bore him six children, and died, and he married (second) Margery, daughter of James and Elizabeth Belanger. She died, and he married (third) Sarah, daughter of John and Mary Butcher. He had six children by his first and four by his third wife: 1. Abraham, born January 25, 1753, died 1816; married Deliverance Haines. 2. John, born October 27, 1754; married Mary Middleton. 3. Mary, born April 10, 1757, died 1823; married Caleb Crispin. 4. William, born October 20, 1759, died 1814; married Agnes Lippincott. 5. Job, born January 24, 1763, died 1844; married Sarah Carr. 6. Benjamin, born June 18, 1765, died 1820; married Elizabeth Kirby. 7. Charles, born March 10, 1778, died 1800. 8. Clayton, born February 28, 1779, died in infancy. 9. Clayton, born May 20, 1780 (see post). 10. Rebecca, born March 24, 1782, died 1803; married Amos Wills.

(V) Clayton, son of Benjamin and Sarah (Butcher) Haines, was born in Evesham township, Burlington county, May 20, 1780, and died on the same farm on which he was born. He married Rebecca, daughter of Zebedee and

Priscilla (Moore) Wills; children: 1. Zebedee, born November 20, 1807 (see post). 2. Sarah B., October 30, 1814; married William E. Haines. 3. Clayton, November 5, 1816, died April 18, 1817.

(VI) Zebedee, eldest child of Clayton and Rebecca (Wills) Haines, was born in Medford, Evesham township, New Jersey, November 20, 1807, and died about 1858. He was given a good education in the Samuel Gummere grammar school at Burlington and afterward became a farmer, which was his principal occupation in life, and in which he was very successful, at the time of his death being owner of two good farms. He took an earnest interest in public affairs, although not for his personal advancement, and was looked upon as one of the influential men of the township. Originally he was a Whig and later became a Republican, although he died soon after the organization of the Republican party.

Mr. Haines married Elizabeth, daughter of Joseph and Elizabeth Hendrickson, of Crosswicks, and by her had twelve children: 1. Rebecca, born February 11, 1831. 2. Margaret, born March 10, 1832, died young. 3. Jane, born April 7, 1833; married Samuel J. Eves. 4. Priscilla N., born January 18, 1835; married (first) Joseph B. Evans; (second) Ezra Bell. 5. Amy, born March 27, 1836; married Joseph Nicholson. 6. Clayton, born May 7, 1837; married Lydia McGrew. 7. Joseph H., born December 7, 1840 (see post). 8. Elizabeth F., born August 5, 1842; married Howard Darnell. 9. Zebedee, born August 20, 1843; married Anna P. Harvey. 10. John G., born October 20, 1848; married Rebecca Patterson. 11. Ellis, born July 22, 1852; married Catherine P. Howard. 12. Lydia, born July 19, 1853.

(VII) Joseph Hendrickson, son and seventh child of Zebedee and Elizabeth (Hendrickson) Haines, was born in Medford, Burlington county, New Jersey, December 7, 1840, and was educated in the public schools of his native township and also at the Friends' school in Weston, Pennsylvania, where he was a student during two winter terms. As a boy and young man he worked at home on his father's farm, where he was born and which he now owns, for he eventually succeeded to ownership of the old home place. But he has other farming lands besides the homestead, and is known among the practical and successful business men of the county. Mr. Haines also is interested in mercantile business, being senior partner of the firm of Joseph H. Haines

& Sons, general dealers in coal, lumber and agricultural implements, and also proprietors of a large pressing business. In this firm, however, Mr. Haines is hardly an active partner, the business management being entirely in the hands of his two sons, Morris W. and Everett H., both young men of excellent business qualifications, energetic, straightforward and perfectly reliable. The father is head of the house and the conduct of the business is in safe hands. Besides these interests Mr. Haines has for many years been closely identified with the business and civil life of the town, being a director of the water company of Medford and chairman of the board. In politics he is a firm Republican and has given efficient service as member of the school board and also of the township committee. His family and himself are members of the Society of Friends.

In 1877 Mr. Haines married Anna Wills, born January 21, 1850, daughter of Henry W. and Lydia (Stokes) Wills, great of Rancocas, granddaughter of Joseph and Virgin (Powell) Wills, great-granddaughter of Aaron and Rachel (Warrington) Wills, great-great-granddaughter of Daniel and Elizabeth (Woolston) Wills, great-great-great-grandaughter of John and Hope (Delefaste) Wills, and great-great-great-great-granddaughter of Dr. Daniel Wills and Elizabeth, his first wife (see Wills). Joseph H. and Anna (Wills) Haines have three children: 1. Julia F., born December 13, 1880; married Henry Moon, of the William H. Moon Nursery Company of Bucks county, Pennsylvania, and has one son, Harris Moon, born May 26, 1906. 2. Morris W., twin with Everett H., born August 24, 1883; member of the firm of Joseph H. Haines & Sons. 3. Everett H., twin with Morris W., born August 24, 1883; member of the firm of Joseph H. Haines & Sons.

COMPTON Among the early settlers from England who have made homes for themselves and families who braved with them the long and dangerous voyage across the Atlantic were the Comptons, who settled in Monmouth county, New Jersey, in 1667. The leader of this family, William Compton, was induced to become a permanent settler and proprietor of the proposed township of Middletown, which was sheltered from the bleak east winds of the Atlantic Ocean by the Navesink highlands and the long, sandy beach terminating in Sandy Hook, the guide for mariners entering the lower bay en route for the safer harbors of New York bay and the Raritan bay. He was appointed one of the proprietors of the town and had two hundred and eighty acres of farming lands apportioned to him, on the division of the township lands in 1679. Among the descendants of this pioneer settler was a namesake, William (q. v.). Assuming him to be the grandson of the immigrant, we place him in the third generation.

(III) William, probable grandson of William Compton, the immigrant, 1667, was born in Monmouth county, New Jersey, about 1730. He married a daughter of David Baird and they resided in Clarksburg, in the southern part of Monmouth county, near the border of Ocean county. William and ———— (Baird) Compton had a large family of sons, who arrived at manhood about the time of the American revolution and we find on the rolls of the First or "Old Monmouth" Regiment, in the battle of Monmouth, Sunday, June 28, 1778, the names of eight privates, bearing the name of Compton, as follows, a majority of whom, if not all, were sons of William, as follows: Job Compton, who was promoted from the ranks to lieutenant; John Compton, who also served in the Continental army subsequent to this battle; Joseph Compton; Lewis Compton, who served in Captain Elisha Waltrous' company; George Compton, who also served with the state troops and in the Continental army; Jacob Compton (q. v.); James Compton, who was in Captain Brueries' company, also in the state troops and in the Continental army; and John Compton. He also had sons, David and Ichabod, who settled at Morristown, Cumberland county.

(IV) Jacob, one of the eight sons of William and ———— (Baird) Compton, was born on his father's farm near Clarksburg in Monmouth county, New Jersey, in 1761, died there in 1808. He was a soldier in the First or "Old Monmouth" Regiment that took an important part in the battle of Monmouth. He was also in the Continental army as were some of his brothers. He purchased a farm in Plum's tract township, Ocean county, where he married Rachel Robbins and they had three sons and two daughters born on the farm as follows: John, David (q. v.), James, Ellen, Mary.

(V) David, second son of Jacob and Rachel (Robbins) Compton, was born in Plums tract township, Ocean county, New Jersey, 1798, died 1852. He married Sarah, daughter of Kenneth and Elizabeth (Vandervere) Hankinson, and granddaughter of William Hankinson. Captain Kenneth Hankinson was an officer in the American army in the revolutionary war and was one of the patriots who fought at the battle of Trenton. David Compton carried the United States mail in Trenton, New Jersey, up to 1829. David and Sarah (Hankinson) Compton had eleven children, two born in Trenton, New Jersey, and the others in New Egypt, Ocean county, New Jersey, to which place they removed from Trenton in 1829. These children named probably in the order of their birth were: Jacob Hankinson (q. v.), William, Elizabeth, John, Ellen, George, Kenneth, Adeline, Rachel, Emma, David.

(VI) Jacob Hankinson, eldest child of David and Sarah (Hankinson) Compton, was born in Trenton, Mercer county, New Jersey, November 30, 1826, and he was taken by his parents to their new home in New Egypt, Ocean county, New Jersey, in 1829. Here he attended school, learned the trade of cigar maker, and continued to work at that trade during his entire business life, first in company with his father and after the death of his father in 1852 continued the business alone, or in company with his son James up to 1883, when he retired. His son continued the business, in which his father assisted from time to time, as he found the work more enjoyable than to remain idle. Jacob Hankinson Compton was a pronounced Democrat in political opinion, and he served as a member of the board of commissioners of appeal and judge of elections. He married, February 28, 1859, Sarah Ann, daughter of Clayton Coward, of New Egypt, New Jersey, who was a son of Jonathan Coward, grandson of Jonathan and great-grandson of John Coward, the immigrant, who came from England in 1736 and was a preacher in Emilytown, New Jersey. The children of Jacob Hankinson and Sarah Ann (Coward) Compton were born in New Egypt as follows: 1. George F., 1860, who became cashier in the First National Bank of New Egypt. he married Mary, daughter of John and Elizabeth (Dunphy) Applegate, and had children: Laura, Eugene, Kenneth and Elizabeth. 2. James Robbins (q. v.). 3. Sarah, who married Thomas Hartshorn, a prosperous farmer in New Egypt, and has children: Rebecca, Walter and Henry Hartshorn. 4. Joseph, who married Laura Churchill, who died soon after marriage and left no children, Joseph Compton is connected with the Green Copper Mining Company and in

1909 was in Mexico in charge of the mines.

(VII) James Robbins, second child of Jacob Hankinson and Sarah Ann (Coward) Compton, was born in New Egypt, Ocean county, New Jersey, May 18, 1862. He was a pupil in the public schools of New Egypt, learned the business of cigar-making in his father's manufactory, and in 1883 took entire charge of the business and conducted it in his own name, his father, James H. Compton, withdrawing from all business connection with the former firm of J. H. Compton & Son. He carried on a branch of the manufactory at Asbury Park, Monmouth county, New Jersey, 1858-91. He is not married and has no connection with any fraternal or religious associations. He is a member of the Democratic party and has served as a member of the county committee.

STACKHOUSE

The family name Stackhouse is somewhat uncommon and wherever it appears as the name of a white person there is good reason to believe that if there were records extant we could in all instances trace it back to the family who in remote times gave the name to or received it from the little hamlet of Stackhouse in the West Riding of Yorkshire, England. Because the name is uncommon it attracts the attention of the family genealogist whenever he sees it in print. It is generally supposed that the Quaker contingent of the family who settled in Bucks county, Pennsylvania, in the eighth decade of the seventeenth century were the pioneers of the name in America. Some years ago, however, while rummaging among the dusty annals of the past, Dr. Asa Matlack Stackhouse was surprised to learn that one Richard Stackhouse was among the Puritan colonists of Massachusetts almost fifty years before Thomas and John Stackhouse came to Pennsylvania. In Felt's "Annals of Salem" we find that land was granted to Richard Stackhouse in 1635. None of the genealogists of the Stackhouse family have been able to trace a descendant of this Richard and it is supposed that the male line died out. It is probable that he was in somewhat reduced circumstances, for in 1653, "for the relief of his family" the profits of the ferry "towards Ip-switch" were granted to him provided he could procure boats and men. This ferry was at Beverly and it appears he held the ferry privilege until 1686, and lived at that place. His wife's name was Susanna and she "joined the church" in 1648. His children,

Jonathan, Abigail and Hannah, were baptized in May, 1648; Ruth, July 8, 1649; Samuel, February 13, 1653; Mary, June, 25, 1654.

So far as is known the first member of the Stackhouse family who attempted to collect genealogical data of their history was Amos Stackhouse, 1757-1825, a great-grandson of Thomas, the immigrant. He was a man of some literary attainments and for some years was engaged in teaching school at Mt. Holly, New Jersey. His life was passed mainly in that place and in Philadelphia. The results of his labors were somewhat meagre and mostly confined to tradition, however, a nucleus was established. His son, Powell Stackhouse Sr., 1785-1863, took up the work where the father laid it down and pushed his inquiries still further. His interest in the work led him to look up everyone bearing the name, if accessible. He lived in Philadelphia and in those days there were many of the name there. The story is told that on one occasion he learned that a family of the name of Stackhouse resided in the lower part of the city and one morning he sallied forth to interview them and find out "where the relationship came in." To his intense disgust the family turned out to be negroes. It is needless to say that he abandoned summarily—abolitionist as he was—all desire of establishing relationship. In explanation of this it may be said that in colonial days when slavery existed in the north, many of the slaves assumed the names of their masters and this was the case no doubt in this instance.

The researches of Powell Stackhouse Sr. materially enriched the collection of his father Amos. His mantle in turn fell upon his son, Powell Stackhouse Jr., 1827-1900, *par excellence* the historiographer of the Stackhouse family. Soon after 1890 William R. Stackhouse, a great-grandson of Amos, became interested in the family history and began the work of tracing the descent of certain branches of John, the immigrant, that had not previously engaged the attention of Powell Jr. This was successfully carried on and other branches were then traced in collaboration with Powell Jr. His attention then was drawn more particularly to the earlier English history of the family and the book entitled "Stackhouse, An Old English Family Sometime of Yorkshire," recently published by The Settle Press of Moorestown, New Jersey, is largely the result of his researches. Our present narrative has to deal particularly with

Thomas Stackhouse and some of his numerous descendants.

The ancestry of the Stackhouse family is traced in England to the year 1086 and in America traces back to the year 1682, when Thomas Stackhouse, of the village of Stackhouse, in the deanery of Craven, West Riding of Yorkshire, came to America, arriving at New Castle 10mo. 27, 1682, accompanied by his wife Margery and two nephews, Thomas and John Stackhouse. They all settled in Middletown township and took up large tracts of land. Thomas Stackhouse, the elder, lost his wife Margery, who died 11mo. 15, 1682, and he married in 1mo., 1702, Margaret Atkinson, daughter of Christopher Fell, of Newtown, Lancashire, and widow of Christopher Atkinson, who had died on board the "Britanica" in 1699 on his way to Pennsylvania. Thomas Stackhouse died in 1706 without issue. Thomas and John Stackhouse both reared large families in Middletown, and have both left numerous descendants. The latter died in Middletown in 1757.

(I) Thomas Stackhouse was a very prominent man in the community, representing his county in the colonial assembly of Pennsylvania for the years 1711 to 1715 inclusive, and then declining a re-election. He also was collector of proprietary quit-rents for Bucks county; served as one of the commissioners to lay out roads and in many other capacities of trust. He was one of the active members of Middletown Monthly Meeting of Friends and built their meeting house in 1690. He took up five hundred and seven acres of land in Middletown on the Neshaminy and in 1707 bought twelve hundred acres of Francis Richardson. He died 4mo. 26, 1744. Thomas Stackhouse married (first) at Middleton Meeting, 7th mo. 27, 1688, Grace Heaton, born Yorkshire 1st mo. 14, 1667, died 8th mo. 8, 1708, daughter of Robert and Alice Heaton, who came to Philadelphia in the "Welcome" with William Penn in 1682. He married (second) 1st mo. 1, 1711, at Falls Meeting, Bucks county, Pennsylvania, Ann Mayos, died 5th mo. 6, 1724, widow of Edward Mayos. He married (third) 8th mo. 1725, Dorothy, widow of Zebulon Heston. Thomas Stackhouse had in all fourteen children, nine by his first and five by his second wife: 1. Samuel, born 8th mo. 17, 1689, married Eleanor Clark. 2. John, born 3d mo. 27, 1691. 3. Robert, see post. 4. Henry, born 10th mo. 7, 1694, married Jane ————. 5. Grace, born 11th mo.

7, 1696, died 6th mo. 5, 1777; married David Wilson. 6. Alice, born 2d mo. 1, 1699, married Euclydus Longshore. 7. Thomas, born 5th mo. 20, 1703, married Elizabeth ———. 8. Joseph, born 5th mo. 20, 1703, married Sarah Copeland. 9. Benjamin, born 10th mo. 25, 1705, married Sarah Gilbert. 10. (by second wife) Isaac, born 3d mo. 11, 1712, died 2d mo. 4, 1714. 11. Jacob, born 8th mo. 25, 1713, married Hannah Watson. 12. Ann, born 5th mo. 15, 1715, married Charles Plumley. 13. Sarah, born 6th mo. 6, 1718, died 5th mo. 25, 1808; married Samuel Cary. 14. Isaac, born 7th mo. 5, 1720, died 1st mo. 17, 1791; married Mary Harding.

(II) Robert, third son of Thomas and Grace (Heaton) Stackhouse, was born 9th mo. 8, 1692. He married Margaret Stone and settled on a tract of land purchased by his father, "adjoining Pigeon Swamp" in Bristol township, Bucks county, Pennsylvania, which later was devised to him by his father's will. He later removed to Berwick on the Susquehanna, where he lived until his death in 1788, at the advanced age of ninety-six years. Robert and Margaret were the parents of eight children: Thomas, Joseph, James, Grace, Benjamin, Alice, William and Robert.

(III) James, third son of Robert and Margaret (Stone) Stackhouse, was born in Bucks county, Pennsylvania, 11 mo. (January) 11, 1725-26, and married, 10 mo. 13, 1750, Martha Hastings, who was born 4 mo. 27, 1722, daughter of Samuel and Mary (Hill) Hastings, and granddaughter of Joshua Hastings, who represented Chester county in the colonial assembly, living then near Chester, but later removed to Philadelphia. His son John Hastings married Grace Stackhouse, sister of James. The children of James and Martha (Hastings) Stackhouse were: Margaret, Hastings, Mary, Amos, Martha, James and another Amos, who died in infancy. James, the father, died in Philadelphia 8 mo. 16, 1759, and his wife Martha died 6 mo. 23, 1806. He is buried in the Arch street Friends' burying ground.

(IV) Amos, second son of James and Martha (Hastings) Stackhouse, was born 5 mo. 4, 1757, and was married at Mt. Holly, New Jersey, 1 mo. 14, 1779, to Mary Powell, born 7 mo. 9, 1763, daughter of John and Susanna (Bryan) Powell, granddaughter of Isaac and Elizabeth (Perdie) Powell, who were married August 10, 1729, Isaac being a son of John and Elizabeth (Parker) Powell, and a grandson of Robert and Prudence Powell, the for-

mer of whom came to New Jersey in the ship "Kent,' 6 mo.' 16, 1667, and settled near Burlington, West Jersey. Amos Stackhouse died 4 mo. 5, 1825 and his widow Mary 7 mo. 15, 1841. They were the parents of thirteen children: Susanna, Hastings, Martha, Powell, Esther, Martha, second of the name; James, Samuel P., Amos, Robert, Mary P., John P., and another Robert who had died in infancy.

(V) Robert (2), son of Amos and Mary (Powell) Stackhouse, was born in Philadelphia, Pennsylvania, December 1,-1801, died January 6, 1881. He attended school in Philadelphia and Westtown, then learned the trade of a tailor and afterward for several years kept a dry goods store in the former city. After that he engaged in various occupations, and was in the merchant tailoring business in Alexandria, Virginia, for a few years, later was bookkeeper for Carey & Hart, publishers, and afterward made bookkeeping his chief occupation in life. At the end of a long period of business endeavor he came to New Jersey and spent the remaining years of his life in Chester township, where he died. Mr. Stackhouse married (first) 4th mo. 23, 1829, Elizabeth Davis Kimber, daughter of Richard and Elizabeth Kimber, and by whom he had three children. He married (second) 9th mo. 21, 1841, Ann Roberts Matlack, daughter of Asa and Tamar (Roberts) Matlack (see Matlack), and by whom he had one child. Robert Stackhouse's children: 1. Tacy J., born 3d mo. 13, 1830, died 11 mo. 2, 1837. 2. Edward Livingston, born 3d mo. 27, 1833. 3. Tacy Elizabeth, born 11 mo. 25, 1838. 4. Asa Matlack, see post.

(VI) Asa Matlack, son of Robert (2) and Ann Roberts (Matlack) Stackhouse, born 7th mo. 21, 1845, was educated in the public schools of Moorestown, New Jersey, and entered the junior class of the University of Pennsylvania, graduating from that institution in the class of 1865. He subsequently studied medicine, graduating from Hahnemann Medical College of Philadelphia in 1868, and practiced medicine in Attleborough (now Langhorne); Bucks county, and elsewhere for a number of years, but has now retired from practice and lives at Moorestown, New Jersey. He has always taken an interest in local history and the genealogy of the old families of Bucks county and vicinity, and has contributed a number of articles on these subjects to local papers.

Dr. Stackhouse married, at Allentown, Pennsylvania, 12 mo. 8, 1868, Ella Jane

Romig, daughter of William J. and Mary Ann Catharine (Royer) Romig, and they are the parents of two children: 1. William Romig, of Moorestown, New Jersey, who was born in Chester township, Burlington county, New Jersey, January 10, 1870, and married Rebecca Gibson. 2. Ernest Robert, born at Allentown, Pennsylvania, December 3, 1884. Another child, Ernest Raymond, born January 17, 1874, died young. William Romig Stackhouse, mentioned above, for several years past has been engaged in connection with his cousin, the late Powell Stackhouse, in extensive genealogical researches.

MATLACK

The narrative here written is to record something of the lives and achievements of the representatives of several generations of one of the notable old colonial families of New Jersey. The family has been made the subject of narrative by various chroniclers, for its marriage connections have been as notable as is the history of the family itself, and in the main the accounts of these several writers are in accord.

(I) William Matlack, or as his family name appears in some old records, Macklack, was born in England about 1648 and was one of the colony of Friends who came from Cropwell Bishop, a small village in Nottinghamshire, in the year 1677, in the ship "Kent," which was sighted off Sandy Hook August 14 of that year. The vessel followed along the coast to Raccoon creek, where her passengers disembarked. The commissioners appointed by William Penn and the other proprietors, and William Matlack with them, took a small boat and went up the Delaware river to Chygoes island, whereon Burlington now stands, almost surrounded by a creek named for an Indian sachem who lived there. Matlack was the first to leave the boat, just as in later years he was foremost in the work of development of the region in various other respects. He was a carpenter and built or helped to build the first two houses in Burlington and also helped to build the first corn mill in West Jersey. He came over to America as the servant of one Daniel Wills, commissioner and proprietor, and after serving him four years bought from his former master one hundred acres of good land between the north and south branches of Penisaukin creek, in Chester township, Burlington county, as afterward created. It is understood that the purchase price of the land this acquired was his four years'

service and "current country pay." The greater part of this tract is still owned and in possession of William Matlack's descendants.

At the time of his emigration to America William Matlack was a young man less than thirty years old. "He saw a town rise up in the midst of the forest, surrounded by a thriving population, busy in clearing the land and enjoying the reward of their labors. His leisure hours were spent among the natives, watching their peculiarities and striving to win their good will. Following the advice and example of the commissioners, every promise made by him to the aboriginies was faithfully kept, and every contract strictly adhered to." He and Timothy Hancock, with whom he worked in common in many things, "soon found their neighborhood was a desirable one; for new settlements were made there in a short time, and went on increasing until a meeting of Friends was established at the house of Timothy Hancock by consent of the Burlington Friends in 1685." In 1701 William Matlack purchased about one thousand acres of land in Waterford and Gloucester townships, in Camden county (then Gloucester), lying on both sides of the south branch of Cooper's creek. In 1714 he gave to his son George five hundred acres of land in Waterford township, being part of the one thousand acre tract purchased of Richard Heritage. In 1717 he bought two hundred acres of John Estaugh, attorney for John Haddon, and there his son Richard settled in 1721. In 1714 he gave his son Timothy the remaining part of the Heritage purchase, and on this tract Timothy settled and built his house. The tract of lands owned by William Matlack and his sons John, Timothy and Richard extended from the White Horse tavern on both sides of the highway and contained about fifteen hundred acres.

William Matlack, the immigrant ancestor, married Mary Hancock, and of this event Mr. Clement writes thus: "In 1681 there came from Brayles a small town in the southern part of Warwickshire, a young man named Timothy Hancock, accompanied by his sister, who was about fifteen years of age. Without friends or means, they lived in a very humble manner among the settlers, but the demand for work soon found Timothy employment, and the demand for wives did not leave Mary long without a suitor." She married William Matlack in 1682, and they then removed to a tract of land which he had located between the north and south branches of Penisaukin creek,, in Chester township. Her brother also located an adjoining survey, and in 1684 married Rachel Firman. Thus it is that the Matlack family in New Jersey—a prolific family indeed—began with William and Mary. Just when William died is not certain, but it was after 1720, and he lived to see his youngest daughter the mother of seven children. Tradition says that he died in his ninetieth year, or ninety-first, "and would have lived longer if his tools had not been hid from him, for he took delight in having his accustomed tools to work with, and when he could not have them he died." His children were: 1. John, married (first) Hannah Horner, (second) Mary Lee. 2. George, married (first) 1709, Mary Foster, (second) Mary Hancock. 3. Mary, married (first) in 1711, at Newton meeting, Jonathan Haines, (second) Daniel Morgan. 4. William, see post. 5. Richard, married (first) 1721, Rebecca Haines, at Evesham meeting, (second) in 1745, Mary Cole at Chester meeting. 6. Joseph, married at Chester meeting in 1722, Rebecca Haines. 7. Timothy, married in 1725 at Haddonfield meeting, Mary Haines. 8. Jane, married Irvin Haines. 9. Sarah, married in 1721 at Evesham meeting, Carlyle Haines.

(II) William (2), son of William (1) and Mary (Hancock) Matlack, was born at Penesankin creek, Burlington county, New Jersey, December 2, 1690, died July 25, 1730. He married, September 17, 1713, Ann, daughter of John and Frances Antrim, of Burlington, and by her had eight children: 1. Rebecca, born August 16, 1714, died July 30, 1798; married (first) John Bishop, (second) Caleb Carr. 2. Jeremiah, born March 4, 1716, died January 18, 1767. 3. Rachel, born June 11, 1718, died February 5, 1762; married (first) Thomas Bishop, (second) Philip Wikard. 4. Leah, born August 29, 1720, died February 25, 1731. 5. Ann, born December 11, 1722, died July 26, 1728. 6. William, born June 30, 1725, see post. 7. James, born June 13, 1728, died November 24, 1728. 8. Mary, born January 6, 1730, died April 15, 1759.

(III) William (3), son of William (2) and Ann (Antrim) Matlack, was born June 30, 1725, died May 15, 1795. He married, at Haddonfield meeting, October 1, 1748, Mary, daughter of John and Jane Turner, and by her had ten children: 1. Atlantic, born November 13, 1750, died February 21, 1775; married Samuel Stokes. 2. William, born May 15, 1752. 3. John, born March 26, 1755, died August, 1831; married Rebecca Shute. 4. Reuben, born November 17, 1757, see post.

5. Jane, born February 11, 1760, died May 3, 1760. 6. Samuel, born June 7, 1761, married Sarah Shute. 7. Rebecca, born February 13, 1765, died May 18, 1842; married Amos Busby. 8. Joseph, born August 21, 1767, died August 26, 1814; married Anna Shute. 9. George, born March 6, 1770, married Sarah Roberts. 10. ———, born August 4, 1772, died February 9, 1790.

(IV) Reuben, son of William (3) and Mary (Turner) Matlack, was born 11th mo. 17, 1757, died 8th mo. 2, 1808. He married 1mo. 23, 1783, Elizabeth Coles, a descendant of Samuel Coles and of William and Thomas Budd, all early members of the colonial assembly of New Jersey.

(V) Asa, son of Reuben and Elizabeth (Coles) Matlack, was born 10th mo. 21, 1783, died 12th mo. 3, 1851. He married, 5th mo. 12, 1807, Tamar Roberts, born 6th mo. 13, 1783, died 9th mo. 2, 1850, daughter of John and Letitia Roberts. They had two children: 1. Mordecai, born 3d mo. 14, 1808. 2. Ann Roberts, born 3d mo. 4. 1810, died 10th mo. 2, 1893; married Robert Stackhouse (see Stackhouse).

ALLINSON
George Albert Allinson, of Burlington, New Jersey, descends from a very old Burlington county family.

(I) Thomas Allinson, the earliest known ancestor, was a resident of Burlington county all his life, following the occupation of a farmer.

(II) John, son of Thomas Allinson, was born, lived and died in Burlington county. His death occurred about the year 1860. He was a large land owner and farmer. He married Nancy ——— and had three sons—Abraham R., John M., Samuel—and a daughter Mary Ann.

(III) Abraham R., son of John and Nancy Allinson, was born in Burlington township, Burlington county, New Jersey, 1822, died in 1869. He received a good common school education. His first employment was in a general store in Burlington. He learned the trade of a shoemaker and carried on that business in Burlington for many years. Later he conducted an undertaking establishment in Burlington and that was his business until within a short time before his death. His latter years he lived a retired life. Mr. Allinson was a lifelong Democrat and served as township and city tax collector for several years. He belonged to the Methodist Episcopal church of Burlington, and to Burlington Lodge, No. 22, Independent Order of Odd Fellows. He married Eliza A. English, of Springfield township, Burlington county, New Jersey. Children: Theodore C., deceased; George A., see forward; Samuel E.; Annie B.; Sarah M. (Mrs. George E. Gilbert).

(IV) George Albert, son of Abraham R. and Eliza A. (English) Allinson, was born in Burlington, New Jersey, July 9, 1850. He was educated in the public and private schools of his native city. He learned the carpenter's trade in Philadelphia and combined with that an intimate knowledge of architecture. He became an architect and builder and was actively engaged in the prosecution of his business in Burlington and surrounding country until the year 1902 when he retired. During his active business life as a builder, Mr. Allinson designed and erected many buildings of both a public and private character, and was highly regarded as a competent and thoroughly satisfactory architect and builder. In other lines of business activity, Mr. Allinson is also prominent. He is superintendent and treasurer of the Burlington Water Company, a connection that has existed for the past thirty years, and to this company and its successful development he has contributed largely. Other Burlington institutions with which he is connected in an official capacity are the Mechanics' National Bank, of which he is vice-president; Burlington Trust Company, serving on the board of directors; Burlington Electric Light Company, of which he is vice-president. All these responsible positions Mr. Allinson fills with a marked ability and fidelity that contributes largely to the success of these corporations. For the past thirty years he has been secretary of the Burlington Building and Loan Association. In political faith he has always been a Democrat. During the years 1876-77 he was city clerk of Burlington. He served in the common council of that city for nine years, eight of which he was president of the council. In 1904-05-06 he was mayor of Burlington, giving that city an effective, business administration. His fraternal affiliations are with the leading orders of his city. He is past master of Burlington Lodge, No. 32, Free and Accepted Masons; a member of Boudinot Chapter, No. 3, Royal Arch Masons; Heleva Commandery, No. 3, Knight Templars; Lulu Temple, Ancient Arabic Order Nobles of the Mystic Shrine, of Philadelphia; Hope Lodge, No. 13, Knights of Pythias; Phoenix Lodge, No. 92, Independent Order

of Odd Fellows, of which he is past grand; Leni Lenape Tribe, Improved Order of Red Men, of which he is past sachem and past deputy sachem; Mt. Holly Lodge, No. 848, Benevolent and Protective Order of Elks. Mr. Allinson is unmarried.

WIMER The Wimer family of Palmyra, Burlington county, New Jersey, descended from an old Pennsylvania family. Joseph Wimer, the great-grandfather of George N., married, July 9, 1809, Elizabeth Sheed, daughter of George and Rebecca Sheed. George Sheed was born in the year 1756, died July 7, 1830. Rebecca, his wife, was born in the year 1764, died August 25, 1837. George and Rebecca Sheed were the parents of twelve children: 1. Christian, daughter, born July 11, 1786, died November 7, 1786. 2. Isabella, born 1787, no record of death. 3. Elizabeth, born March 26, 1789, died August 12, 1869; married, July 9, 1809, Joseph Wimer. 4. Ann, born June 15, 1791, died June 22, 1816; married, August 14, 1814, Walter Raleigh; child, Susan Raleigh, died June 22, 1816. 5. Mary, born August 28, 1793, died May 8, 1812. 6. Peter, born December 7, 1795, died June 22, 1816. 7. Rebecca, born July 29, 1797, married ———— Ely, a member of the Society of Friends; she died in July or August, 1875-76, leaving one daughter, Lavinia, wife of Albert Paxson, who was brother to Justice Edward Paxson, lately deceased. All of these died at the homestead near Holicong, Bucks county, Pennsylvania. 8. Susannah, born September 5, 1799, no record of death. 9. Margaretta, born October 4, 1803, married William Stavely, of the firm of Mc-Calla & Stavely, publishers of Episcopal Periodical—either Register or Recorder; six children were born to them; they died at their home, Partridge Hall, near Labraska, Bucks county, Pennsylvania. 10. Amy, no date of birth or death. 11. Lavinia, born March, 1807, died July 28, 1873. 12. Christian, born March 29, 1809. Children of Joseph and Elizabeth (Sheed) Wimer: 1. George, born April 18, 1810. 2. Amanda, October 11, 1811, married Edward Filley, a silversmith, and died in the month of June, 1831. 3. Joseph, see forward. 4. Rebecca, January 13, 1816.

(II) Joseph (2), son of Joseph (1) and Elizabeth (Sheed) Wimer, was born in Philadelphia Pennsylvania, October 13, 1813, died in his native city October 29, 1881. He was a plasterer by trade, was actively interested in the political affairs of his city, and held office in the city government. Joseph Wimer married, September 4, 1835, Mary Engles, of Philadelphia; children: 1 Albert, born October 22, 1839, a soldier of the civil war, died from wounds received at the battle of Antietam, September 6, 1863, unmarried. 2. William E., see forward. 3. Mary E., resident of Philadelphia, born September 14, 1845.

(III) William E., second son of Joseph and Mary (Engels) Wimer, was born in Philadelphia, April 4, 1843. He was educated in the schools of his native city. For a number of years he was a commercial salesman traveling for the house of Dr. D. Jayne & Son. In the early seventies Mr. Wimer entered the employ of the Pennsylvania Railroad Company as clerk, and has since been continuously in the employ of that corporation in Philadelphia. In 1875 he removed to Palmyra, New Jersey, where he remained until 1894, when he again took up his residence in Philadelphia. In political faith Mr. Wimer is Republican. He is a member of the Palmyra Lodge of Odd Fellows, the Brotherhood of America, and the Knights of the Golden Eagle. He is a communicant of the Baptist church. William E. Wimer married, July 6, 1865, Emma C. Rudolph, daughter of Alfred Rudolph, of Philadelphia. She died December 2, 1904. The children of this marriage are: 1. George Nell, see forward. 2. Albert L. 3. Mamie, died aged five years. 4. Alfred, died at age of twenty-one years. 5. Irene, died in infancy. 6. Francis, died in December, 1908, aged twenty-eight years. 7. William W., 8. Howard. 9. Ella. 10. Edna.

(IV) George Nell, eldest son and child of William E. and Emma E. (Rudolph) Wimer, was born in Philadelphia, Pennsylvania, May 11, 1866. He was educated in the Philadelphia public schools. His early employment was in a produce commission house and as clerk in Philadelphia. He then entered the employ of the Pencoyd Iron Works (now the American Bridge Company), remaining with them until 1897 in charge of the contracting and billing departments. On September 30, 1897, Mr. Wimer was appointed postmaster at Palmyra, New Jersey. He resigned his position with the American Bridge Company in April, 1904. In 1906 he resigned his position as postmaster. In 1905 Mr. Wimer opened an office in Palmyra for the transaction of the real estate and insurance business, and in this line of activity he has since been actively engaged. He also has an office at 209 Market street, Camden,

for the same purpose. Mr. Wimer is a Republican and is a member of the Burlington county tax board of equalization, appointed in 1906 by Governor Stokes and re-appointed by Governor Fort. He is an active member of the various fraternal, social, and athletic clubs and societies of Palmyra and vicinity, notably the Patriotic Order Sons of America, Brotherhood of America, Tacoma Tribe, Improved Order of Red Men, Junior Order of American Mechanics of Beverly, New Jersey, Senior Order of the same, Bordentown, New Jersey, Benevolent and Protective Order of Elks, of Mt. Holly, New Jersey, Union League Club, Palmyra Bicycle Club, Independent Order of Odd Fellows, Turner and Maennerchor societies of Riverton, New Jersey. George Nell Wimer married, December 12, 1889, Sally A. Cress, daughter of Theodore and Emma Cress, of Philadelphia, Pennsylvania. One child has been born to Mr. and Mrs. George N. Wimer, Mildred Helen, born in Palmyra, March 3, 1906.

RIGG The family names of Rigg and Riggs have been known in New England since colonial times, and now their representatives are well scattered throughout the country. Whether written Rigg or Riggs the name applies to the same general family, and both trace back to the still older family which was seated in Old England for many generations previous to the time when the first immigrant Riggs came over to America.

(I) Christopher Rigg, immigrant ancestor of the family here treated, came to this country about the year 1820. He was born in North-Hampstead, England, of English parents, and on coming to America he settled in Burlington, New Jersey. He was a thrifty and prosperous farmer for many years and became possessed of extensive farm tracts, and besides carrying on his farms he bought and sold timber lands, dealt in lumber and wood, manufactured brick and tiling, and also built and operated a grist mill in Burlington township. In the latter business one of his sons had an interest with his father. Mr. Rigg was one of the directors of the Merchants' National Bank of Burlington, one of the principal organizers of the Mt. Holly Agricultural Society, and in many ways showed his excellent business qualities and genuine public spirit by his connection with enterprises which were intended to promote the general welfare as well as personal

Geo. N. Vinier

concerns. He married, in England, Sarah Plaskett, who also was born in England. Their children were: John, Edward, George and Ann, all born in Burlington.

(II) George, son of Christopher and Sarah (Plaskett) Rigg, was born in Burlington, New Jersey, January 14, 1846, graduated from Princeton College in 1867, and afterward acquired considerable celebrity as a pedagogue, while as a mathematician he became famous. He taught school in Burlington county and also at the Penn Charter school in Philadelphia, and while he excelled especially as a teacher of mathematics he was equally proficient as a teacher of languages, Latin, Greek and French. In politics he was a Republican and frequently was chosen to serve in some public capacity. During the greater part of his life he was a justice of the peace, also served as island manager, tax collector, member of the board of education, and during two terms was mayor of the city of Burlington. As a man of superior educational attainments and high character he was much respected in the community in which he lived. He was an Odd Fellow and member of the Knights of the Golden Eagle. Mr. Rigg died in March, 1897. He married Ellen F. Estilow, born Burlington, April 7, 1847, daughter of Christopher and Sarah (Lowden) Estilow. Children: 1. Annie, born August 14, 1868; married Thomas Antrim, a farmer of Burlington, now dead; one child, Martha E. Antrim. 2. Sarah Jane, born September 10, 1870; married Edward Tyler, of Burlington, an engraver; two children: Paul R. Tyler, born July 14, 1895; Blair W. Tyler, born October, 1902. 3. G. Harry, born April 1, 1872; died July, 1908; was a harness maker. 4. Charles A., born August 9, 1875; deputy surrogate of Burlington county; married Grace Kimball, of Philadelphia. 5. George P., born 1877; an engraver, and lives in Philadelphia; married Elizabeth Wiest, and has one child, Milton W. Rigg. 6. Ellen E., born 1880; married LaRoy C. Van Rensselaer, of Pennsylvania, an electrical engineer and bookkeeper. 7. Budd Marter, born August 10, 1883; see post. 8. Kate P., born 1885; lives with her mother. 9. John, born September, 1887; druggist in Burlington.

(III) Budd Marter, son of George and Ellen F. (Estilow) Rigg, was born in Burlington, New Jersey, August 10, 1883, and acquired his earlier literary education in public schools and the Van Rensselaer Seminary, Burlington, from the latter of which he was graduated in

1902. He took up the study of law with Joseph H. Gaskill, of Camden, attended lectures at the Philadelphia Law School, and was admitted as an attorney in 1905, and as counsellor in 1908. He practiced for a time in Camden in asssociation with Judge Gaskill, his former preceptor, but soon afterward opened offices for himself in both Burlington and Camden. Mr. Rigg is a Republican in politics, member of the board of aldermen of Burlington; member of Burlington Lodge, No. 32, F. and A. M.; Phoenix Lodge, No. 92, I. O. O. F.; Hope Lodge, No. 13, K. of P., and of Evening Star Council, No. 38, Jr. O. U. A. M.

He married, June 11, 1905, Elsie R. Morton, born October 31, 1882, daughter of Newton and Mary (Applegate) Morton, of Florence, New Jersey.

WHOMSLEY
This is a name seldom met in the records of this country, but is an ancient one in England, although not borne by a large number of persons. The first record of this family is the fact that one Richard Whomsley was in the service of the English sovereign in 1650; there are persons of this name living at the present time in the city of Manchester, in Lancashire, England.

(I) William Whomsley, the first of this family to emigrate to America, was born in 1789, in England, and came to America about the year 1831, probably settling in Philadelphia. He first engaged in the manufacture of woolen and cotton products, and afterwards removed to Trenton, New Jersey, where he embarked in the grocery business, and remained until his death, September 15, 1863. He married Mary Potter, who was also born in England, and was the daughter of an Episcopal clergyman. They had four children, all born in England—John Potter, William, Thomas and Annie.

(II) John Potter, son of William and Mary (Potter) Whomsley, was born October 4, 1828, in Bolton, Lancashire, England, and died at Graniteville, South Carolina, September 1, 1897. He was about three years of age when he accompanied his parents to America. After an education received in the public schools, he learned the business of machinist, and especially as regards stationary engines. In 1870 he became employed by the firm of Sleeper, Wells & Aldrich, of Burlington, New Jersey, running their stationary engines, and after remaining with them for six years removed to Graniteville, South Carolina, where he was employed in the same capacity by the Granite-ville Manufacturing Company. He was an Independent in politics, an Episcopalian, and a member of Sampson Lodge, Knights of Pythias, of Philadelphia. He married Martha Shaw, daughter of Jesse and Mary Cox, born May 12, 1827, at Kensington, Pennsylvania, died October 4, 1865, and they had nine daughters and one son, five of whom died in infancy. Among their children were: Mary, who died young; Emma, deceased; Kate; Ida, deceased; and George Cox.

(III) George Cox, only son and seventh child of John Potter and Martha Shaw (Cox) Whomsley, was born August 18, 1857, at Norfolk, Virginia, and received his education in the common schools, Mount Vernon school, and in the schools of Philadelphia, Pennsylvania, and Burlington, New Jersey. He learned the business of plumbing, and has made same his occupation ever since, going into business on his own account February 5, 1898, at Burlington, since which time he has met with very good success. He is an interprising and useful citizen, and is interested in public movements and improvements. For thirty-five years he has been a member of the Baptist church, and has served several years as associate superintendent of its Sunday school. He served one year as deputy sheriff of Mt. Holly, and is secretary of the water board of Burlington, which city is his present residence. He is a member of the order of Ancient Free and Accepted Masons, member with Burlington Lodge, No. 32, Boudinot Royal Arch Chapter, No. 3, and Helena Commandery, No. 3, Knights Templar; he is also a member of Burlington Lodge, Independent Order of Odd Fellows, No. 22, and Hope Lodge, No. 13, Knights of Pythias.

Mr. Whomsley married (first) November 1, 1880, Louisa Powell, daughter of John and Grace A. Allen, of Burlington, New Jersey, who died October 26, 1882, and he married (second) September 30, 1884, Mary Ella, daughter of Joseph and Margaret Poole Kaighn, of Burlington. By his second wife he had children as follows: 1 Joseph Howard, born November 25, 1885, is at present employed as pipe inspector by W. R. Conard, of Burlington; he married Josephine, daughter of Harry and Margaret Woolman. 2. Edward Clemence, January 2, 1888, is associated with his father in the plumbing business. 3. John Albert, April 2, 1894. 4. James Madison Hare, April 11, 1895. 5. George Allinson, October 21, 1901.

BARROWS   That the name of Barrows is prominent in English history and genealogy is attested by at least twelve coats-of-arms, extant, dating from 1500 on. The names Barrow, Barowe and Alborough were of the same origin, De Burgh. Burg de Burgh was created a peer in 1327. In 1487 we find reference to Thomas Burg or Borough, Baron. In Lincolnshire, England, in the Church of Wynthorpe is a monumental bronze in memory of Richard Barrows "sumtyme merchant of the stayples of Calys" who died in 1505. Richard, in his will, dated 1502, names three sons: Thomas, John and Richard. Dr. Isaac Barrow was a son of Thomas, linen draper to Charles I, and he may have been a descendant of Thomas, son of Richard, buried at Winthrop. In 1477 a grant of arms was made to Thomas Barowe and his heirs. In the time of Richard III, 1483-85, Thomas Barrowe, brother of Richard, merchant of Calais, was made master of Rolls. One of the early Puritan martyrs executed with John Greenwood, April 6, 1593, was Henry Barrowe, "son of a gentleman of Norfolk." The family living in Norfolk and Suffolk uniformly spell the name Barowe and Barrowe, while the family, numerous in other parts of England, spell it Barrow. The first American ancestor of the family is recorded in the Rolls Office in London as John Barowe (q. v). He was of Yarmouth, the chief seaport of Norfolk county. ·

(I) Copying from the Rolls Office, Chancery Lane, London, a large volume bound in vellum, contains among the names of some of the early immigrants bound for Virginia, under date May 15, 1635, "Jo: Barrowe aged 26 years, embarked in the "Plaine Joan" the portico having brought attestation of their confirmities to orders and discipline of the Church of England." "May 10, 1637, is recorded in the examination of John Borowe of Yarmouth, Cooper, aged 28 years and Anne his wife aged 40 years—desirous to pass to Salem in New England, there to inhabit." The ship on which they reached Salem was probably the "Mary Ann," Captain William Goose, master. The records of Salem, August 14, 1637. state: "Jno. Barows is received an inhabitant of Salem, and is alowed five acres of land" and on November 9: "Jno Barrowes is allowed ten acres, with his former five." Subsequently we find "Jno. Burroes is alowed one half acre of marsh and salt meadow land." This was the usual allowance for two persons, and probably was for himself and his first wife whom he married in England and brought to America, and by whom he had one child, Robert (q. v.). On March 25, 1644, he is made surveyor of fences in place of Thomas Weeks. We find no further records in Salem of his name, which is in each place spelled differently. We next find him in Plymouth records, March 6, 1665-66, where he is fined by the court ten shillings for refusing to give evidence in the grant inquest. February 15, 1668, the list of townsmen include John Barrow and the record of voters in town meeting June 16, 1668, gives the names of John Barow and Robert Barrows (no doubt father and son). April 9, 1684, the town laid out to John Barrow ten acres of upland against his meadow on the northeast side of the river. The will of John Barrow executed January 12, 1691-92, and on record in Plymouth, names his eldest son Robert, and other sons Benajah, Joshua and Ebenezer, not then of age, and mentions two daughters and his loving wife whom he appoints sole administratrix of the will. He signs the will with an S mark, and it is witnessed by John Gray and the T mark of John Barrows, the eldest son of his son Robert, who was at that time twenty-four years of age. The children of John, the immigrant, and Deborah Barrow, named in his will, were probably in the following order: 1. Robert. 2. Joshua, who married Deliverance Wedge, and died about 1750. 3. Benajah, born 1683, married (first) Lydia Bickler; (second) Elizabeth Lincoln; (third) Hannah Bennett. 4. Ebenezer, married Elizabeth Lynn. His two daughters were: 5. Deborah, who married Archippus Fulton, of Plympton, December 20, 1687, and had children. 6. Mary, who married John Wormall, of Duxbury, January, 1698, and removed to Bridgewater, and had five children. John Barrow died March 12, 1692, and his will was proved before William Bradford, Esq., deputy governor of Plymouth Colony, and Ephraim Morton, assistant, April 6, 1692.

(II) Robert Barrows, only son of John and Anne Barrow, was born probably in Salem, Massachusetts Bay Colony, and removed with his father to Plymouth Colony, the immigrant evidently not finding the Puritanical atmosphere of Salem to agree with churchmanship. He married (first) November 28, 1666, Ruth, daughter of George and Sarah (Morton) Bonum, of Plymouth. His homestead in Plymouth contained two or more acres of ground on the northerly side of Mill street, then a common road leading into Plymouth, and

afterwards known as the King's Highway, and now Summer street. This estate was conveyed to Robert Barrows, January 30, 1669, by George Bonum, and bounded by: "ye Great street on ye Southerly side of ye town of Plymouth, and by ye street that goeth up from ye grist mill to ye Fort Hill so called with ye dwelling house therein." The original will of Robert Barrows is on file in the Plymouth probate office. It is dated December 9, 1707, and signed "T the mark of Robert Barrows." It mentions by name his wife Lydia, who was his second wife, to whom he was married probably 1684-85, and two only of his sons: Robert and Thomas. In a codicil he makes no mention of the children by his first wife "because they have already received their poretions of his estate" but names "Elisha and my daughters by my second wife." Lydia, daughter of John Dunham, who was his second wife, is made executrix of the will which was probated December 19, 1707, before Nathaniel Thomas, judge. The children of Robert and Ruth (Bonum) Barrows were born at the homestead in Plymouth as follows: 1. John, born 1667, who married (first) Sarah Briggs, and (second) in 1714, Bethia King; resided in Plymouth and Plympton; he died in 1720. 2. Eliezer, September 15, 1669, died December, 1669. 3. George, 1670, married three times; died in Plympton, Massachusetts, 1758. 4. Samuel, 1672, married (first) Mercy Coombs; (second) Joanna Smith; died in Middleboro, Massachusetts, December 30, 1755. 5. Mehitable, married, June 20, 1717, Adam Wright, and were first settlers of Plympton. The children of Robert and Lydia (Dunham) Barrows were: 6. Elisha, March 17, 1686, died 1689. 7. Robert, November 8, 1689, married Bethia Ford, lived in Plymouth, Massachusetts, and in Mansfield, Connecticut, where he died August 17, 1779. 8. Thankful, December 8, 1692, married, February 11, 1713-14, Isaac King. 9. Elisha, June 16, 1695, married (first) Thankful ———, and (second) Nellie ———; died in Rochester, Massachusetts. 10. Thomas, February 14, 1697 (q. v.). 11. Lydia, March 19, 1699, married, October 11, 1720, Thomas Branch, of Plymouth, where she lived and died.

(III) Thomas, the eighth son and tenth child of Robert Barrows, and the fourth son of Robert and Lydia (Dunham) Barrows, was born in Plymouth, Massachusetts, February 14, 1697, removed with his father and family to Mansfield, Connecticut, about 1720, where he died October 28, 1776. He was married

June 14, 1721, to Esther Hall, and they had nine children born in Mansfield, Connecticut, as follows: 1. Samuel, August 10, 1722, a private in Captain Hanchett's company, Second Regiment, taken prisoner at Quebec, December 31, 1775. 2. Isaac (q. v.). 3. John, July 22, 1727. 4. Greshom, April 19, 1730; served as ensign for eight days in the American revolution. 5. Hannah, June 11, 1732. 6. John, July 13, 1734. 7. Elisha, December 20, 1736. 8. Esther, December 16, 1739. 9. Thomas, September 20, 1742; he served at Saratoga, New York, as private for twenty-six days, corporal in the American revolution in Captain Gallup's regiment, discharged November 5, 1777. Esther (Hall) Barrows, the mother of these children, was received in the Congregational church in Mansfield, 1722. She died in Mansfield, Connecticut.

(IV) Isaac, second son of Thomas and Esther (Hall) Barrows, was born in Mansfield, Connecticut, April 1, 1725. He was married on July 13, 1764, to Rebeckah, daughter of John Turner, Isaac Barrows was a lieutenant in the revolutionary army, serving for three days as lieutenant, and as private in Tenth Company, Captain Ripley Huntington's eighth regiment, from July 28, 1775, to December 18, 1775. Lieutenant Isaac and Rebeckah (Turner) Barrows were the parents of eleven children, born in Mansfield, Connecticut, as follows: 1. Roger, June 4, 1765. 2. John (q. v.). 3. Jesse, October 28, 1770. 4. Sybil, April 5, 1773. 5. Jabez, July 14, 1775. 6. Sybil, April 26, 1778. 7. Jesse, October 24, 1780. 8. Juliana, February 11, 1783-84. 9. Leander, December 28, 1785. 10. Stephen, November 24, 1789. 11. Polly, April 26, 1792.

(V) John (2), second son of Lieutenant Isaac and Rebeckah (Turner) Barrows, was born in Mansfield, Connecticut, August 30, 1767. He was a farmer, removed to Willington, Connecticut, probably before his marriage, and the birth of his children, as we find no record of him in Mansfield, Connecticut, records, except his birth, and he removed to New York state before his death. He had five children born probably in Willington, Connecticut, as follows: 1. John. 2. Orrin. 3. Almer (q. v.). 4. Lucinda, who married —— Peckham. 5. Kate, who married —— Phelps, and their son, William Pitt Phelps, settled in Merchantville, New Jersey.

(VI) Almer, third son of John Barrows, was born in Willington, Connecticut, July 5, 1794. He attended the district school, and learned the trade of comb maker, at which

trade he worked until he was past middle life. He owned a farm at Willington, Connecticut, and carried it on while pursuing his trade as comb maker, as was customary with mechanics, who owned farms, so as to have profitable work both winter and summer. He was an active member of the Democratic party in Connecticut, and his church affiliation was with the Methodist denomination. He married, 1822, Serepta, daughter of Don Ferdinand and —— (Palmer) Brigham, of Coventry, Connecticut, her ancestors being original settlers of Coventry. Serepta Brigham was born in 1804, and died in 1861. The children of Almer and Serepta (Brigham) Barrows were born in Willington, Connecticut, as follows: 1. Don Brigham. 2. Serepta. 3. Henrietta. 4. Emily. 5. Walter Almer (q. v.). Almer Barrows late in life retired from business and removed to Mt. Holly, New Jersey, his wife having died in 1861, and his four eldest children being also deceased, to spend his last days with his youngest son, Captain Walter Almer Barrows, who resided in that place, where he was practicing law, and he died at the home of his son in Mt. Holly, New Jersey, 1876, in the eighty-second year of his age.

(VII) Walter Almer, second son and youngest child of Almer and Serepta (Brigham) Barrows, was born in Willington, Connecticut, December 27, 1839. He was prepared for teaching in the public schools of his native town, and when seventeen years of age he taught a district school in Willington, Connecticut, for two years, and for one year in Cape May, New Jersey; in 1859-60 he attended an academy at Monson, Massachusetts, to better fit himself as a teacher. He was teaching at Cape May in 1861, when the civil war called him from the school room to the defence of his country on the battle line, and he enlisted August 23, 1861, in Company A, Seventh New Jersey Volunteers, and he accompanied the regiment to Virginia and became a part of the Army of the Potomac under General George B. McClellan. He took an active part with his regiment in the battles of Yorktown, Williamsburg and Fair Oaks. The hardships of the soldier in that active campaign in the swamps of Virginia rendered him physically incapacitated for further service, and he was honorably discharged from active service November 11, 1862. He was sent to the United States Hospital at Newark, New Jersey, and having recruited his strength and health he was discharged from hospital, and again offered his services to the government. He was commissioned by President Lincoln captain of Company C, One Hundred and Fifteenth United States Colored troops, July, 1864, was stationed at Bowling Green, Kentucky, guarding railroad communication. He joined the Army of the James with the colored regiment in February, 1865, and took part in the sanguinary, but decisive battle that led to the fall of Richmond. In the occupation of the Confederate capital, he took an active part with his regiment in putting out the fires kindled by the retiring army of General Lee, and this saved much valuable property. In May, 1865, he resigned his commission, but was re-appointed captain of a company in the Fifth Regiment, United States Colored troops, and he was with the regiment at Camp Chase, Columbus, Ohio, in November, 1865, when he was honorably discharged from the United States volunteer service. He passed two years as an invalid at Cape May, New Jersey, and in 1868 he took charge of Aaron's select school for boys at Mt. Holly, New Jersey, in which school he successfully taught for three years. He at the same time took up the study of law, and he was admitted to the New Jersey bar as an attorney-at-law in 1873, and he took up the practice of his new profession in Mt. Holly. He served as county superintendent of schools, 1873-76. In 1876 he was admitted as a counsellor-at-law, and in 1879 was made a special master and supreme court commissioner and notary public. In 1905 he also opened a branch law office at Riverside, New Jersey. In the New Jersey state militia he was captain of Company F, Seventh Regiment, and took an active interest in sustaining the espirit de corps of the state militia. His military service to the United States secured him comradeship in the General Shiras Post, No. 26, Grand Army of the Republic, and a companionship in the Pennsylvania Commandery of the Military Order of the Loyal Legion of the United States.

His fraternal affiliations include membership in Mt. Holly Lodge, No. 19, Independent Order of Odd Fellows, since 1868. He joined Cape Island Lodge, No. 30, Ancient Free and Accepted Masons, Cape May, New Jersey, and was transferred to Riverside Lodge, No. 187, and he is a member of Boudinot Royal Arch Chapter, No. 3, Burlington, and Helena Commandery, Knights Templar of Burlington, and is past eminent-commander of the Commandery. In the Ancient Order of United Workmen, he became past grand master workman of the district including the states of New Jersey, Delaware, Maryland and Virginia. He also represented Pocahontas Tribe, No. 18, in the United States Great Council of the Improved Order of Red Men, in two councils. He held the high office of grand chief of the Order of Knights of the Golden Eagle of New Jersey for the years 1895-96, through his membership in New Jersey Castle No. 4 of Mt. Holly. He is also a member of the Benevolent and Protective Order of Elks, Mt. Holly sub-lodge, No. 848. He is a Democrat in political faith. His church affiliation is with the Presbyterian church, and he is president of the board of trustees of the church in Mt. Holly.

He married (first) December 9, 1862, Mary H., daughter of Judge Eli B. and Sarah (Hughes) Wales, of Cape May, New Jersey, and the children born of this marriage are: 1. Walter Almer (2), born in Cape May, New Jersey, December 31, 1865; graduated from Rutger's College, B. S., 1886, a chemist by profession, and interested in developing iron and copper industries with headquarters in Cleveland, Ohio; he married, September 28, 1888, Sarah Byers, of Cleveland, and they have two children: Walter Almer (2) and Donald. These children represent the ninth generation from John Barrows, Salem, Massachusetts Bay Colony, 1635. 2. Helen Work, born Philadelphia, Pennsylvania, October, 1867, married (first) Charles K. Chambers, of Mt. Holly, New Jersey; children: Mary and Frances Chambers. After the decease of the father of these children she married (second) Joshua E. Borton, of Moorestown, New Jersey, attorney, president of the Security Trust Company of Camden, New Jersey. 3. Mary Wales, born Mt. Holly, New Jersey, March 8, 1876, married the Rev. James Harvey Dunham, pastor of the Presbyterian church at Mt. Holly, and their son, Barrows Dunham, was born October 10, 1905. The mother, Mary H. Wales Barrows, died March 3, 1902, and was buried at the Brick Church at Cape May, New Jersey. Her husband married as his second wife on August 22, 1907, Amanda L. Bishop, widow of James Bramoll, and they reside at Riverside, New Jersey.

BURLEY   Charles Shoemaker Burley descends in the fourth generation from John Burley, a brave soldier of the revolution, serving from Connecticut, and the first of the family to settle in South Jersey. John Burley was reared in the town of Greenwich, Connecticut, where he was

ii--8

born about the year 1760. On January 1, 1777, he enlisted in the Continental army, joining Colonel Lamb's Connecticut Artillery. He served from that date until the close of the war in 1783. He came to New Jersey about the year 1787 and settled in Cape May county, where he died from the effects of a sunstroke, October 1, 1802. He married Phoebe Breen, daughter of William Breen, of Egg Harbor, New Jersey. William Breen was also a patriot although it is not known that he was an enlisted soldier. He was one of a number of patriots in South Jersey who used their knowledge of the bays and inlets of the coast to lay in wait for and capture British vessels that ventured near their retreats. On one occasion he was captured by the enemy although he had assisted in the successful capture of many prizes.

(II) John (2), son of John (1) and Phoebe (Breen) Burley, was born in Cape May county, New Jersey, January 1, 1803. He was left an orphan the following year, his father dying October 1, 1802. But little can be told of his early life further than that he was a ship carpenter and followed that then lucrative trade all his life. He became an owner of vessels and with his sons built and owned many. He died in the county of his birth, December 16, 1875. He married Roxana Champion, of Tuckahoe, New Jersey, July 14, 1827. Children: 1. Joseph Champion, see forward. 2. and 3. died in childhood. 4. John, Jr. 5. Nathan, deceased. 6. Sallie (Mrs. Benjamin Weatherley, of Tuckahoe, New Jersey). 7. Julia M. (Mrs. Richard Townsend). 8. Mary (Mrs. Samuel Champion). 9. William, a minister of the Methodist Episcopal church, belonging to the Newark conference.

(III) Joseph Champion, eldest son of John (2) and Roxana (Champion) Burley, was born in Tuckahoe, New Jersey, 1828, died in 1903. He was educated in the common schools, and learned the trade of a ship carpenter under the instruction of his father with whom he and his brother were joint owners of considerable vessel property. In 1865 he went to Philadelphia, Pennsylvania, where he was employed at his trade in the navy yard and at Cramp's ship yard as well as at Coopers Point, Camden. In his later years he removed to Ocean City, New Jersey, which was his home until death. He was a Republican in political faith, and a member of the Methodist Episcopal church, where he served as both steward and trustee. He married, in 1850, Sallie Wheaton, born in Tuckahoe, New Jersey, 1832, daughter of

Everett and Sarah Wheaton. Children: 1. Adelia, born in 1852, married James A. Delaney, of Camden, New Jersey, and has Emma, Howard and Cora Delaney. 2. Lizzie, deceased; she married Samuel Whittaker, of Williamstown, New Jersey. 3. Charles Shoemaker, see forward. 4. Milton, married Ella Wilson. 5. Enoch W. 6. Margaret, married Ira Wells.

(IV) Charles Shoemaker, eldest son and third child of Joseph Champion and Sallie (Wheaton) Burley, was born in Cumberland county, New Jersey, October 31, 1858. His education was obtained in the schools of Camden, New Jersey, which was his home for many years and where he gained his first business experience. He was employed as a grocery clerk in that city for ten years, until 1883, when he opened a grocery store on his own account in the city of Bristol, Pennsylvania. This store was a success and encouraged Mr. Burley to expand and extend his business. In 1889, in company with his brother-in-law, Samuel Whittaker, he opened a grocery store in Trenton, New Jersey, to which was added others until they had in successful operation five stores, three in Trenton and two in Bristol. In 1901 he removed to Camden and was there engaged in the grocery business for two years. On March 26, 1903, he opened his present store in Burlington, New Jersey, where he is further interested in business along other lines than the grocery. Mr. Burley adheres to both the political and religious faith of his forbears. He votes with the Republican party, and worships with the congregation of the Broad Street Methodist Church in Burlington, also serving as a steward on the official board.

Mr. Burley married, January 11, 1887, Emma B. Moore, of Salem, New Jersey, daughter of Joseph Franklin Moore. Children: 1. Edna, born at Bristol, Pennsylvania, 1888, died in infancy. 2. Russell Leroy, born in Trenton, New Jersey, May 23, 1889, was educated in the Burlington high school, Drexel Institute, Philadelphia, Pennsylvania, and at the Trenton Business College.

SACK   The family here described were living in that part of Russia which borders Prussia, in the seventeenth century. In America they have made for themselves a place in business and social circles, and their integrity and steadfastness of purpose are recognized by all who have had dealings with them.

(I) A son of this family, Ferdinand George

Sack, emigrated in the latter part of the eighteenth century to Prussia, Germany, wandered from there to Seesen, Duchy of Brunswick, Germany, where he established a bakery business, settled, married and had four sons and two daughters, one of the former being George Henry Ferdinand.

(II) George Henry Ferdinand, son of Ferdinand George Sack, was born October 9, 1781, at Seesen, Duchy of Brunswick, Germany. He married, February 1, 1810, Johanna Christiana Henriette Fischer, born August 13, 1789, at Seesen, and their children were: 1. Sophia Dorethe Charlotte. 2. Sophia Louise Christiana. 3. Charles William Ferdinand. Mr. Sack was a farmer, grain dealer, millwright and flour-miller.

(III) Charles William Ferdinand, son of George Henry Ferdinand and Johanna Christiana Henriette (Fischer) Sack, was born April 21, 1825, at Seesen, Duchy of Brunswick, Germany, where he followed the same occupations as his father, carrying on farming and being millwright and miller, in Germany. In September, 1869, with his wife and children, he emigrated from the seaport town of Bremen, Germany, on the ship "Columbus," landing in New York City in October. After he came to this country, Mr. Sack worked chiefly as cigar sorter and packer. He was of the Lutheran faith, and in politics was a Democrat. Mr. Sack married, December 24, 1849, at Gross Schwuelper, Germany, Molly E. Wulfes, born February 19, 1823, at Grossen Ilse, Hanover, Germany. Her father, Peter Henry Wulfes, was born March 27, 1769, at Grossen Ilse, and married Elizabeth Braun, born October 18, 1788, at Hildesheim, Hanover. Mr. Sack and his wife had children as follows: 1. Charles John Henry Herrman. 2. Herrman August Charles, born February 10, 1855; married, in 1880, in New York City, Jennie Meyer, and their children are: Hugo II,. born May 13, 1881, at New York, and Alwine, born March 25, 1883, at Philadelphia. 3. Alwine Caroline Louisa, born August 23, 1857, died in New York City. 4. Curt Emiel Hugo, born June 4, 1864, died at New York City.

(IV) Charles John Henry Herrman, the eldest son of Charles William Ferdinand and Molly E. (Wulfes) Sack, was born September 3, 1850, at Gross Schwuelper, Hanover, Germany, and when a young man accompanied his parents to America, living in New York until August, 1875, when he removed to Philadelphia, and in 1888 from there to Riverside, New Jersey, which is still his residence. He received the education given by the public schools of Germany, being also taught French and English by private tuition. In Germany he held positions incident to dealing in grain, such as millwright and miller, also clerk in a grain and produce business. In America he has kept hotel and conducted a fruit farm, being also interested in the culture of bees. He is an energetic and public spirited citizen, and has served in several public offices, among them member of the township board of education and park commission, and for five years he served as a member of the board of freeholders of Burlington county, New Jersey. Mr. Sack is affiliated with the Independent Order of Mechanics, Olive Branch Lodge, No. 26, German Beneficial Society, Benevolent and Protective Order of Elks, and is treasurer of Eureka Beneficial Society. He is also a member of the Riverside Fire Company, and of the German Turngemeide and Maennerchor, at Riverside. In politics he is a Democrat, and belongs to the Lutheran church. His wife and family, however, are members of St. Peter's Roman Catholic Church of Riverside.

Mr. Sack married, July 11, 1875, at Riverside, Hannah Stecher, born August 22, 1850. at Philadelphia. Her father, Rudolph Stecher. was a cabinet-maker, carpenter, builder and tavern-keeper, married Pauline Raup, and their children were: Hannah, Rudolph, Mary, Louise, August C., Henry, Frank, Frederick (deceased) and William. Four generations of the Sack family were living at Riverside, New Jersey, in 1900, and in that year they celebrated golden, silver and one year's wedding, respectively. Charles John Henry Herrman and Hanah (Stecher) Sack had children as follows: 1. Herrman Rudolph, born September 9, 1876, at Philadelphia, deceased. 2. Charles Laurence, born February 12, 1878, at Philadelphia, is a watch case turner, and resides at Elgin, Illinois; he married, in July, 1900, Sadie Johnston, and their children are: Charles Joseph, Joseph, Adela, Mildred and Arthur, all born at Riverside, New Jersey, and Rudolph, born at Elgin, Illinois. 3. Emily, born November 11, 1879; married Joseph O. Johnston, a watch case maker, at Riverside, and their children are: Cecilia, William, Pauline and Herrman. 4. William, born August 30, 1881, at Philadelphia, deceased. 5. William Henry, born July 9, 1884, at Philadelphia, is a bartender, married Catherine Fleming, and they have one child, Doloris. 6. Herrman. born November 1. 1886, at Philadelphia, is a watch case maker, and resides at Elgin, Illinois; he married, December 25, 1908, Mamie Bowen. 7. Frederick, born February 11, 1889, at Riverside, New Jersey, deceased. 8. Florence, born September 30, 1892, at Riverside, deceased. Mr. Sack gave his children a liberal education, in the public and parochial schools of Philadelphia and Riverside, and has reason to be proud of their position and standing.

BISBING William Herman Bisbing descends from an old Pennsylvania family. The earliest known ancestor was George Bisbing, a well-to-do farmer, who lived on Barron Hill, sometimes called Bisbing's Hill, in the township of Whitmarsh, Montgomery county, Pennsylvania. He was a large property owner. He conducted a hotel called Farmer's Inn, and was a prominent citizen of the town. He married Catherine ———. Children: 1. George, mentioned below. 2. William. 3. Catherine. 4. Elizabeth.

(II) George (2), son of George (1) and Catherine Bisbing, was born in Whitmarsh, near Ambler, Pennsylvania, 1808, and died in 1898. He followed the occupation of farming on the homestead for many years. Leaving the farm he located at Concohoken, Pennsylvania, where he engaged in the grocery business until his death. He was tax collector of the town, and a man of influence in the community. He married Sarah Hansell, born in Montgomery county, Pennsylvania. Children: 1. William, mentioned below. 2. Alberta, deceased. 3. Clara, married Augustus Hart, of Northampton county, Pennsylvania. 4. Annie, married Charles Dilton (deceased) of Philadelphia. 5. George, deceased. 6. Catherine.

(III) William, first born of George (2) and Sarah (Hansell) Bisbing, was born at Penn Lynn, near Ambler, Pennsylvania, 1839. He received a good common school education. He was apprenticed to a wheelwright and as all wagon and carriage work at that time was done by hand, he obtained a thorough knowledge of that trade. After leaving his trade Mr. Bisbing and his brother-in-law, Augustus Hart, opened a shop and store in Norristown, Pennsylvania, where they built, repaired and sold vehicles of all descriptions that were common to the neighborhood. In 1869 Mr. Bisbing removed to Florence, Burlington county, New Jersey, where he has since resided. He is now in the employ of R. D. Wood & Company. He is a member of the Baptist church, although he was formerly a Lutheran.

He is a member of the Independent Order of Foresters, the American Mechanics and the Florence Foundry Aid Society, all of Florence, New Jersey. He married, in 1859, Eliza H. Groff, born in 1844, daughter of Joseph and Louise Groff, of Haddonfield, New Jersey. Children: 1. Albertis, born in Norristown, Pennsylvania, now a pattern maker of Savannah, Georgia. 2. Sarah Louisa, born in Florence, New Jersey, died in childhood. 3. Charles E., born at Florence, New Jersey, where he is engaged in mercantile business; he married Hannah Ivins, of Camden, New Jersey; children: Claude H. and Marion M. Bisbing. 4. William Herman, mentioned below.

(IV) William Herman, third son and youngest child of William and Eliza H. (Groff) Bisbing, was born in Florence, New Jersey, November 23, 1879. He was educated in the public and parish schools of his native town. He learned the trade of machinist and worked at that business for seven years in Florence. He then entered the employ of the Camden and Trenton Street Railway Company and remained with them six years as machinist and dispatcher, having headquarters at Riverside, New Jersey. For two years he was with the Pennsylvania Railroad Company, running between Camden and Jersey City. On August 29, 1908, Mr. Bisbing having settled on a mercantile life, opened a store in Riverside for the sale of gentlemen's furnishing goods, and to that business and to his official duties as coroner of Burlington county, New Jersey, he devotes his entire time. He is a Republican and was elected coroner in November, 1908, for the term of three years. Mr. Bisbing has a partner, Mark Freeman, the firm name being Bisbing & Freeman. In December, 1908, Riverside Business Men's Association was formed with Mr. Bisbing as one of the directors. He is fond of out-door sports and is treasurer of the Riverside Athletic Association. He is a member of Riverside Lodge, No. 128, Free and Accepted Masons; Dakota Tribe, No. 111, Improved Order of Red Men of Camden; Court Delaware, No. 592, Independent Order of Foresters, of Florence; Burlington Lodge, No. 996, Benevolent and Protective Order of Elks, of Burlington.

STECHER The Stecher family of Riverside, New Jersey, are of German origin, and belong to the incomers of the middle of the nineteenth century.

(I) Rudolph Stecher, the founder of the

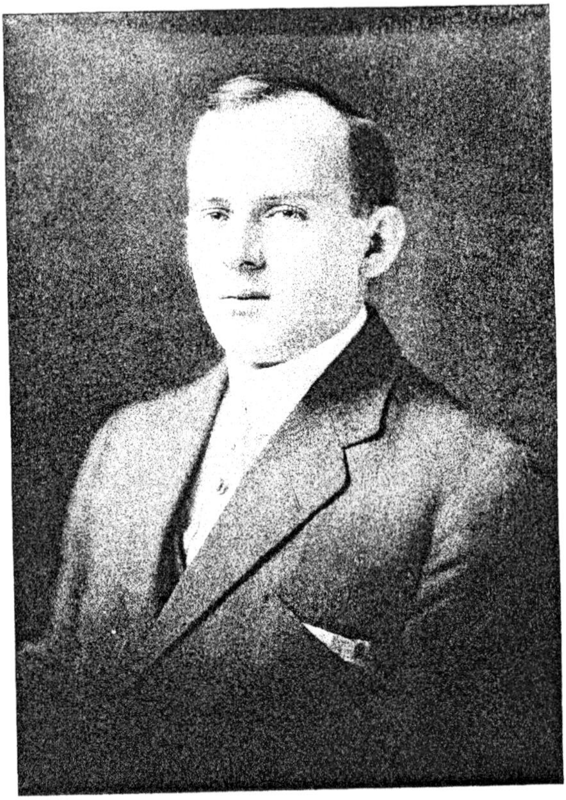

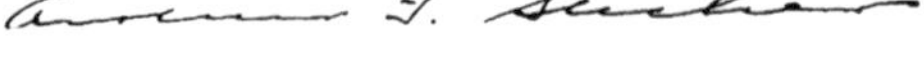

family, was born in Baden Baden, Germany, about 1825, and came over to Philadelphia, Pennsylvania, in 1847. He died in Riverside, New Jersey, in 1888. He was a cabinet maker by trade, and served his apprenticeship before he emigrated. After coming to America he followed the same line of work, and, engaging in the lumber business in Philadelphia, came to Riverside for his permanent home in 1854. For a number of years he was a contractor and builder, and he also engaged in the canning business, building the first canning factory and the first glass works in the town. In 1860 he went into the hotel business in Riverside, opening the Riverside Hotel, now conducted by his son Rudolph, and continued it until the time of his death. He was a Republican, and a member of the school board. He was also a member of the Independent Order of Odd Fellows at Bridgeborough. He was a communicant of the Roman Catholic church. In 1847 he married Paulina Raupe, at Baden Baden. She is now living at the Riverside Hotel. Their children were: 1. Hannah, married Charles Sack, of Riverside. 2. Child, died young. 3. Rudolph F., proprietor of Riverside Hotel, Riverside. 4. Mary, married Henry Frick, a farmer. 5. Louise, married George Whitney, a mail agent, of Cape May. 6. August C., who is referred to below. 7. Frank, a painter, of Riverside. 8. Henry, deceased. 9. Frederick, deceased. 10. William, who conducts a cigar store at Riverside.

(II) August C., son of Rudolph and Paulina (Raupe) Stecher, was born at Riverside, New Jersey, September 16, 1860, and died there June 29, 1908. He was educated in the common schools, and engaged in the shoe business, in the real estate and insurance business, and in the pension business. He served as postmaster under President Harrison and again under President McKinley, 1896, and filled that position up to the time of his death. He was a prominent Republican and active in the affairs of his party. In 1894 he was a member of the assembly, and also served on town and state committees. He was a member of Lodge No. 996, B. P. O. E., of Burlington, and a founder of the Eureka society. He was a communicant of the Roman Catholic church. In 1884 Mr. Stecher married Matilda Liusner, born May 13, 1861, daughter of August and Annie Liusner, of Westfield, New Jersey. She is now living at Riverside. Their children are: 1. Arthur Franklin, referred to below. 2. Sophia, died aged eighteen years. 3. Bertha. 4. Charles, died aged fifteen years. 5. Mary. 6. Henry.

7. August, Jr. 8. Naomi. 9. George. The last five are all at school, in 1909.

(III) Arthur Franklin, eldest child of August C. and Matilda (Liusner) Stecher, was born at Riverside, New Jersey, June 27, 1885, and is now living in Riverside. He was educated in the public schools, in the parochial school of St. Peter's, and at a business college, and has been engaged in the newspaper business for most of his life, having been connected with the Burlington *Enterprise*, the Philadelphia *North American*, the Philadelphia *Inquirer*, the Philadelphia *Public Ledger*, the Trenton *Times*, and *Publicity Press*, and still corresponds for most of them. He has been identified with the Trenton *Times* for eleven years. When his father died he was appointed acting postmaster, and in August, 1908, he received his permanent appointment to that position to succeed his father, for four years beginning December 16, 1908, under President Roosevelt. He is the youngest second class postmaster in the state. He is a Republican, a member of the Lodge, No. 996, B. P. O. E., of Burlington; of the Knights of Columbus, of Riverside; of St. Peter's Benevolent Society, of Riverside, and an honorary member of the Firemen's Association, of Riverside, and the Musical and Literary Society. He is a communicant of St. Peter's Roman Catholic Church.

MARTER Wolfret Gerretse, the common ancestor of the Van Couwerhovens, with his wife Neiltje, immigrated with his family from the province of Utrecht in the Netherlands, was employed first as early as 1630 as superintendent of farms by the Patroon of Rensselaerswick, afterwards cultivated a farm on Manhattan Island, purchased land in June, 1637, from the Indians in Flatbush and Flatlands, Long Island, which were patented to him by Director Van Twiller, June 16, 1637. He made his mark to documents. Children: Gerret Wolfertse, 1610; Jacob Wolfertse, and Peter Wolfertse. Jacob, the eldest son of Wolfret, came with his father to New Amsterdam, in 1630, was with him in Rensselaerwick, 1641, married Hester Jansen, and (second) September 26, 1655, Magdaleentje Jacobuse Bysen. Was a brewer in New Amsterdam, on Pearl street, traded in a sloop to Albany; was one of the nine men representing the New Netherlands, 1647-49-50; member of Dutch church of New York, 1666. Peter and Hester Jansen Van Couwerhoven had children: 1. Neeltje, baptized September 25, 1639, married, January 6, 1662, Cornelius Pluvier. 2. John or Johannes, of New York, baptized March 29, 1641; married, April 11, 1664, Saartje Frans, of Haerlem. 3. Lysbeth, 1643. 4. Aeltje, 1645. 5. Petronelletje, 1648. John, born May 29, 1641, was a member of General Llisler's council in 1684, and also of the court of the exchequer. He had Jacob, 1664; Francis, 1666; Hester, 1669; Lysbeth, 1671; Jacomytje, 1673; Johannes, 1677; Maria, 1679; Catelyntje, 1682, and Peter, 1683. Of these children. Hester, baptized in the Reformed Dutch church in New York, married, in February, 1688, Johannes Martier, of New York, and their descendants are said to have resided in Gloucester county, New Jersey. Bergen, in his "Genealogies of Long Island" says that the Couwerhovens, after the conquest of New York, went some to the Raritan valley, some to Monmouth county, in the neighborhood of Middletown and Freehold, some in Burlington county, and some to Gloucester county. This would lead us to place Hester and her husband, Johannes Martier, with these migrants, as his name does not appear in the New York records beyond this mention. In the list of Jerseymen in the revolutionary war we find Andrew Mart from Gloucester county, as a private in the state troops; and James Martero in the Second Regiment, Continental Troops, Jersey Line, but as the name is so like Masters when written, the Clement, John and Stephen in the Jersey line may one or more be misspelled. We find the first of the name of whom we are certain in Thomas Marter (q. v.).

(I) Thomas Marter was an early citizen of Willingborough township, where he was a large landholder. He was born probably about 1740, and his name appears on the records of the building of the Coopertown Meeting House about 1800, as a subscriber of $25.00 toward meeting the expenses of the building, he being among the largest subscribers. He was one of the six trustees to whom the deed for the meeting house ground was given in trust August, 1802. He died a few years after this deed was given. He had sons: Michael, Abraham, Thomas, Richard, whose names appear on the subscription list for smaller sums. Michael, $10; Thomas, $5; Richard and Abraham, $5; and the three an additional $1.50 each, when the sum raised appeared to be inadequate. In 1806 the meeting house was completed.

(II) Abraham, apparently the second son of Thomas Marter, was born in Willingborough

township, Burlington county, New Jersey, about 1770. He was a trustee, committeeman and treasurer of the Coopertown Meeting when the meeting house was enlarged, used exclusively by the Friends, and the burden of the repairs borne entirely by that society. The building had heretofore been used by all denominations caring to use it. In the subscription list of 1836 he heads the list with $10, his son Charles with $10, and the names of Thomas (2), Richard, Hannah, William and Lewis. We have not determined the date of the death of Abraham Marter.

(III) Charles, probably eldest son of Abraham Marter, was born in Burlington township, Burlington county, New Jersey, about 1800. He was a large landholder, and he lived on what is now known as Wood Lane, a road leading from Edgewater Park to the Camden and Burlington road. His estate included over seven hundred acres of land, and besides farming he was an extensive fruit grower, and his apples and peaches were well known in the markets. His interest in the Coopertown Meeting is shown by his subscription to the enlarging of the Coopertown Meeting House in 1836, when he and his brother Abraham each subscribed $10.00. He married Hannah Stevenson, and they had nine children as follows: 1. Thomas A. 2. Charles. 3. John W. 4. Edwin K., lives at Edgewater Park, New Jersey. 5. Macajah S., lives at Beverly. 6. Ezra B. (q. v.). 7. Hope, married John H. Adams, of Beverly. 8. Hannah. 9. Eliza, married Abram Perkins, and became the mother of the Rev. C. M. Perkins, rector of Trinity Church, of Vineland, New Jersey.

(IV) Ezra Budd, sixth son of Charles and Hannah (Stevenson) Marter, was born in Burlington township, Burlington county, New Jersey, 1829, died January 27, 1902. He was brought up on his father's farm, attended the district school, and became a skillful and prosperous farmer. During the civil war he dealt extensively in pork packing, and he purchased large quantities of hogs, either on the hoof or dressed, and found ready market for both salt pork and salted and dried bacon, shoulders and hams, for the use of the army in the field. He built a fine residence which became the home of his son Ezra B. (2). He was an active member of the Republican party, and was a representative from Beverly township in the state legislature for two terms, and a chosen freeholder for many terms. His fraternal affiliation was with the Independent Order of Odd Fellows through the Beverly

Lodge. Ezra Budd married Sarah Ellen, daughter of John and Elizabeth (Rodman) Shedaker, and they had five children born in Burlington, New Jersey, as follows: 1. Emma, died in infancy. 2. John, died in early childhood. 3. Hannah, married Ellis W. Scott, of Burlington; he is a farmer. 4. Ezra Budd (q. v.). 5. Walter S., now secretary and treasurer of the Wilmington Steamboat Company, and a resident of Burlington, New Jersey.

(V) Ezra Budd (2), second son and fourth child of Ezra Budd (1) and Sarah Ellen (Shedaker) Marter, was born in Burlington, New Jersey, January 31, 1860. He was brought up on his father's farm, and was a pupil in the Shedaker school in Burlington township and in the public high school in Burlington, and continued to aid his father in carrying on his large farming interests until he had reached his majority, when he took the homestead farm under his own control and continued the methods and improvements introduced by his father, notably the raising of large quantities of fruit, making this a specialty. He was a member of the township committee for five years previous to the separation of the city and township governments. His fraternal affiliations included membership in the Independent Order of Odd Fellows, through Burlington Lodge, No. 22; and membership in the Benevolent and Protective Order of Elks through sub-lodge, No. 996, of Burlington, New Jersey.

He married, March, 1888, Anne, daughter of Edward and Frances (Ellis) Horner, of Camden, and their five children were born in Burlington, New Jersey, as follows: 1. John Deacon, December 25, 1888, and a main dependence of his father on the farm. 2. Fannie H., May 19, 1890. 3. Sarah E., December 11, 1891. 4. Caleb Ridgeway, April 24, 1893. 5. Agnes Beideman, June 14, 1900. In 1909 these children were all members of the homestead household, where they were born.

PINE Warren Carleton Pine, pharmacist of Riverside, New Jersey, descends from an old Gloucester county, New Jersey, family. His great-grandfather, Daniel Pine, was born in that county, married, and reared a family there. The family have always been members of the Hicksite Society of Friends.

(II) Joshua, son of Daniel Pine, was born in Gloucester county, New Jersey, where he grew up and followed the occupation of a farmer. Later in life he removed to Maryland, where he died. He married Mary ————, and had issue: Allen, Elizabeth, Samuel, Clayton, Benjamin, Elwood (see forward). Elizabeth married Charles Roberts, of Philadelphia, who is now deceased.

(III) Elwood, son of Joshua and Mary Pine, was born in Repaupo, Gloucester county, New Jersey, during the year 1839, and died in Maryland, in 1893. He removed to Maryland with his father and family, and always lived there until his death. He was possessed of a good education and held various township offices. He was a Republican and a member of the Society of Friends. Elwood Pine married, in 1858, Hannah Allen, born in 1840, daughter of Richard and Ann Allen, of Mullica Hill, Gloucester county, New Jersey. The two children of Mr. and Mrs. Elwood Pine are: 1. Mary Ann, married Lewis M. Shuck, a merchant of Swedesboro, New Jersey, and has Walter and Howard Shuck. 2. Warren Carleton.

(IV) Warren Carleton, only son of Elwood and Hannah (Allen) Pine, was born in Mickleton, Gloucester county, New Jersey, February 1, 1866. He was educated in the public schools and at the Friends' Academy in Mickleton. His early life was spent on the farm and in a newspaper office in Woodbury, where he worked for three years. Having decided to become a pharmacist, he entered the drug store of D. Farley in Philadelphia, Pennsylvania, where he remained five years. Going before the Pennsylvania state board of examiners he passed a successful examination as he did later before the New Jersey board. He is a registered pharmacist in both states. In 1894 he located in Riverside, Burlington county, New Jersey, and established a drug store. Mr. Pine has been very successful in his business and has been compelled to make changes to larger quarters until now he has a lucrative business located in perhaps as handsome a store as can be found in any town of the state. Mr. Pine, while devoted to his business, takes an active interest in the public affairs of his own town, particularly in educational matters. He is a member of the Riverside board of education and on the executive committee of the Burlington county board of education. He was one of the incorporators and is a director of the Riverside National Bank. He is a member of both the New Jersey and American Pharmaceutical associations and the National Association of Retail Druggists. Mr. Pine is fraternally connected with the leading orders of his town. He is a Master Mason of Riverside Lodge, a Royal Arch Mason of Boudinot Chapter, Burlington, a Knight Templar of Helena Commandery, a Shriner of Luki Temple, Philadelphia, and a thirty-second degree Scottish Rite Mason of the New Jersey Consistory. He further affiliates with the Elks Lodge of Burlington, the Odd Fellows of Bridgeboro, and the Patriotic Order Sons of America, Delanco. He is also a life member of the Riverside Turngemeinde and Maennerchor societies. He is a member of the Society of Friends.

Warren C. Pine married, September 2, 1893, Ida Birch, daughter of George W. and Catherine Birch, of Philadelphia, Pennsylvania. They have a son, Lynnwood Carleton Pine, born June 19, 1895.

———

TORREY
The name of Torrie or Torrey has been associated with the history of the inhabitants of New England from early times. There have been noted educators and other professional men in this family, as well as persons in other occupations. Many of the name took part in the revolutionary war, several of them being officers.

(I) Jesse Torrey, born in Pittsfield, Massachusetts, is mentioned in revolutionary records as "belonging to Captain Amos Turner's Company, in the Regiment of Foot, commanded by Brigadier General John Thomas, belonging to the Army of the United Colonies." By his first wife he had three children, as follows: Royal; Dr. Jesse, a noted Abolitionist, and Anna, who became Mrs. Chapman. He married (second) Azubah West, by whom he had two sons, Hiram Dwight and John.

(II) Hiram Dwight, son of Jesse and Azubah (West) Torrey, was born June 24, 1820, at New Lebanon, New York, and died in 1901. He received a good education, being a graduate of Williams College, and his natural ability and desire was along the lines of poetry and painting. At the age of twenty-five Mr. Torrey left home and spent some time on the staff of a prominent newspaper published at Pottsville, Pennsylvania, and later took up the study of engineering and architecture. He had a natural talent for the making of portraits, and some of his early efforts received such favorable comment that he was fortunate enough to become a pupil of a famous portrait painter, and there learned so much, both of technique and the language of his art, that he became a lecturer on the subject; while delivering a lecture on art in a church, he was heard by a member of the faculty of the female seminary at Washington, Pennsylvania, and as a result thereof finally became professor of painting and drawing at the institution, which position he held ten years. He then spent a short time at Milwaukee, Wisconsin, after which he removed to Reading, Pennsylvania, where he met with great success in his chosen field of art, making and selling portraits, as well as a number of landscapes. While in that city he became leader in a musical society, which developed into the Ringold Band. In 1867 Mr. Torrey went to Europe, and there spent thirteen years in study and work; he spent some time in Scotland, and while there painted portraits of many famous men, among them professors in universities, doctors of divinity, men in public office, literary men and several private citizens of wealth. He also painted many fine landscapes, both for Scotch and American patrons. He visited many famous collections of pictures, and was entertained by several noblemen as honored guest in their castles. Upon his return he took up his residence in Delanco, New Jersey, where he devoted the remainder of his life to painting. Mr. Torrey took great interest in political matters, was a Republican, and in national campaigns made speeches in all parts of New Jersey; at one time he held a debate with Henry George, the advocate of single tax. He was an Episcopalian in religious views, and belonged to the Knights of Malta, also to the Ancient Free and Accepted Masons, of Pottsville, Pennsylvania. He married (first) Mary Woodward, cousin of Chief Justice George Woodward, of Pennsylvania, and their children were: 1. Mary Woodward, married William K. Moore, deceased, of Delanco, New York, and they had a son, William K., deceased. 2. William, a gold miner, lived in New Zealand. Mr Torrey married (second) in 1862, Clara V. Moore, of Philadelphia, born in 1834, daughter of James Bullers and Mary Clifford (Knowles) Moore, and they had two children: 1. Hiram Dwight. 2. James Moore, born in 1871, in Glasgow, Scotland, is a printer, and resides at Delanco, New Jersey, with his brother; he married Sarah Hillney, and has one son James and one daughter Madelaine

(III) Hiram Dwight (2), son of Hiram Dwight (1) and Clara V. (Moore) Torrey, was born in 1866, at Pottsville, Pennsylvania. When one year old he was taken by his parents to Scotland, and received his early education in Glasgow, which he supplemented on his return to America, after thirteen years, by attending the schools at Delanco, New Jersey. He learned the trade of printer in the office of the *Enterprise*, of Burlington, New Jersey, later becoming foreman of the press room, and he worked on the first daily issue of the paper, in 1884. Mr. Torrey is now editor and proprietor of the *Burlington County Press*, published weekly, at Riverside, New Jersey, having brought out the first issue March 3, 1887; from the first issue, of four pages, edited and printed in a single room, by the unaided efforts of its enterprising proprietor, under the name of *The New Jersey Sand Burr*, the paper has become enlarged to an eight-page publication, occupying a modern building, and each issue the product of a plant boasting up-to-date machinery in the way of presses, folding machines, etc. At first Mr. Torrey was in partnership with John H. Weidmann, who financed the undertaking, though he did none of the actual work of issuing the paper, and after his death in 1890, Mr. Torrey purchased his interest, being now sole owner. Though a Republican in his political views, Mr. Torrey makes the paper independent in politics, and through its sheets is able to espouse the cause of every movement on foot for the general good of the community. He is a member of the Fire Company of Riverside, of the State Firemen's Association, of which he was for three years vice-president, and a trustee of the Firemen's Home, at Boontown, New Jersey. He also belongs to the Grand Fraternity, to the Benevolent and Protective Order of Elks, No. 996, of Burlington, and is a member of the Pen and Pencil Club, of Philadelphia.

Mr. Torrey married, in 1888, Julia Walton Wells, daughter of Isaiah and Elmira (King) Wells, of Bridgeboro, New Jersey, and they have no children.

This name, in the various forms of HOLT Holt, Hoult, Holte, and many others, has been for centuries common in England, where it has boasted many distinguished members. Sir John Holt was at one time chief justice of England. In our own country there have also been men of this name who have taken an honorable part in the building up of its resources, and some of the name have taken part in every war since the earliest settlement.

(I) James Holt was born in Lancashire, England, and died in 1862, in Philadelphia, Pennsylvania. In his native country he received his education and learned the trade of silk making, which he followed until the time of his emigration to America, in 1842. His wife and children followed three years later. His residence was Philadelphia, and for many years he was employed as traveling salesman, in the line of perfumery and notions. Mr. Holt married Hannah Priestly, of England, and their children were: Mary, Sarah, John, James, Samuel, who is proprietor of a store near Davenport, Iowa; William, Betty.

(II) William, fourth son of James and Hananh (Priestly) Holt, was born July 26, 1836, in Lancashire, England, and in 1845 was brought by his mother to Philadelphia, receiving his education in the public schools of Delaware county, Pennsylvania. When a young man he worked two years in a woolen mill at Derby Creek, Pennsylvania, and then removed to Philadelphia, where he worked in a paper box factory. In company with his father and brother Samuel, he engaged in the manufacture of paper boxes, under the firm name of James Holt & Sons, which firm did business until the death of James Holt in 1862, when the business was carried on by the sons. At the outbreak of the civil war, Mr. Holt enlisted in Company D, Twenty-third Pennsylvania Regiment, and served seventeen months. Having been wounded at the battle of Fair Oaks, he spent seven months in the hospitals at Washington and Philadelphia; he was mustered out January 3, 1863. At this time he resumed the manufacture of paper boxes, in Philadelphia, and two years later removed to Bristol, Pennsylvania, spending two years there in the employ of John Bardley. In 1867 he removed to Mt. Holly, New Jersey, and entered the employ of Semple & Sons, manufacturers of thread and made paper boxes for this firm over seventeen years. Mr. Holt established a factory for himself, at Mt. Holly, in the same line of business, in 1884, and continued same until 1899, when it was combined with the business he and his son William H. had established in 1897 at Riverside, New Jersey, under the name of William Holt & Son; in 1899 Mr. Holt retired from active business, and the plant has since been carried on by the son. He is a Republican, and a member of the Baptist church. He married (first) in 1857 Sarah Noble, by whom he had no children. He married (second) in 1864, Elizabeth, daughter of Samuel and Atlantic Middleton, who became the mother of his five children, and he married (third) Ruth Ann Major, of Mt. Holly. His children were: 1. Harry, deceased. 2. Samuel M., a printer, resides in Washington, District of Columbia. 3. Atty

A. Booz, lives at Harrisburg, Pennsylvania. 4. William Henry. 5. Clara May, died in infancy.

(III) William Henry, third and youngest son of William and Elizabeth (Middleton) Holt, was born July 9, 1872, at Mt. Holly, New Jersey, in the house still occupied by his father. He received his education in the schools of his native town, and at an early age entered the factory of his father, continuing ever since in the same line of work. He entered into partnership with his father in 1897, and since 1899 has had the entire charge of the business; he purchased his father's interest in 1907, and since then has been sole owner and proprietor, though the name is William Holt & Son Paper Box Manufactory. Since 1897 he has resided in Delanco, New Jersey, where he takes a prominent part in the affairs of the community, being a member of the board of education of Beverly township. He is a Republican, and attends the Presbyterian church. He is a member of Lodge, No. 996, Benevolent and Protective Order of Elks, of Burlington, New Jersey, being a past exalted ruler, and in 1908 was sent to Texas as delegate to the Grand Lodge of this order. He has been successful in his business ventures, and has the respect of all who know him, and a large circle of friends.

Mr. Holt married, August 31, 1892, Rena, daughter of John Reeve, of Mt. Holly, New Jersey, and their children are: 1. Raymond G., born July 16, 1893, at Mt. Holly. 2. Emma D., October 10, 1895, at Mt. Holly. 3. William L., December 12, 1897, at Mt. Holly.

TAUBEL　The Taubel family is another of the group forming the colony of German origin which, emigrating to this country in the middle of the nineteenth century, found a permanent home for themselves in Riverside, New Jersey.

(I) The father of the founder of the family lived and died in Germany, where he left five children: Lewis, William, Charles, referred to below: Mary, Catharine. His wife died in Philadelphia at the advanced aged of eighty-four years.

(II) Charles Taubel was born in Germany, in 1821, died in Riverside, New Jersey, September 6, 1905. He secured a common school education in his native town, and then learned the shoemaking trade. He came to this country in 1848, stopping first in New York City, then removing to Philadelphia, where he remained

for several years working at his trade. In 1855 he came to Riverside, New Jersey, where he set up for himself as a shoemaker, and kept up his active work until his death. He was a Democrat, a member of the school board, and a member of the Moravian church. In 1850 he married, in Philadelphia, Cornelia Clutt, born in Germany. Their children were: 1. John, born in Philadelphia, now living in Riverside. 2. Rosa, born in Philadelphia, now living in Riverside. 3. Lewis, now engaged in business in Norristown. 4. Henry, referred to below. 5. George, deceased. 6. William, who has a large mill in Riverside and five mills in Pennsylvania. 7. Mary, deceased. 8. Kate, married a Mr. Schneider. 9. Lizzie, deceased. 10. Hannah, married Mr. Webber. 11. Sophia, deceased. Both married daughters lived in Riverside.

(III) Henry, son of Charles and Cornelia (Clutt) Taubel, was born in Riverside, New Jersey, in 1858, and is now living in that town. He was educated in the common schools and followed farming until nineteen years old, when he went to Philadelphia and learned the machinist's trade, working in a machine shop in that city from 1879 to 1891, when he returned to Riverside and became a dyer in the hosiery mills of his brothers, William and Lewis, in the original plant started by them and now occupied by himself. He remained with his brothers as boss dyer for seventeen years, quitting on February 1, 1908. He started in to manufacture hosiery on his own account in company with his son under the firm name of Henry Taubel & Son, April 12, 1908. Mr. Taubel is a Democrat, and is now serving his third term as township committeeman. He has also served for twelve years on the board of school directors and is still a member of the board. For fourteen years he has been one of the directors of the Riverside cemetery, and he was one of the organizers of and instituted the J. O. M. in Riverside in 1894, and he is a trustee of the order. He is also a member of several German beneficial and social organizations.

In 1882 Henry Taubel married Louisa Kohler, of Philadelphia; children: 1. Gertrude, born in Philadelphia, June, 1884; married William Wright, now in the newspaper business in Wildwood, New Jersey; they have one child, Gertrude. 2. Charles, born in Philadelphia in 1886, educated in the Riverside public schools, spent two years in a textile school in Philadelphia and is now with his father in the firm of Henry Taubel & Son. He is an expert dyer and has entire charge of that branch of the work. He married Mary Bergnekes, of Delanco, and they have one daughter Gertrude.

RUE This is an old Pennsylvania name founded in that state early in the eighteenth century, and is presumed to have gone thither from New Jersey. Tradition says it is a Huguenot family, tracing back to France. Franz, Jacques and Abraham Le Roy came to New Amsterdam (now New York) from Manheim, in the Pfalz, prior to 1680, having fled to the Palatinate from France some years earlier. The descendants of Abraham, the youngest of the three brothers, are quite numerous in Bucks county, whither they migrated from New Jersey in the closing years of the seventeenth century. The name was spelled La Rue, Larrew, and in various forms in the early records, but eventually assumed its present spelling. The Bucks county family is not nearly related to or associated in any way with that of Rue, and there appears no points of similarity. The descendants of Jacques (James) Le Roy, who settled in Bergen county, New Jersey, and on Staten Island, spelled the name in various forms, and it may be that the Bucks county family is descended from them. The first record of the name Rue is the grant of two hundred acres of land "above the Falls of Delaware" in New Jersey, in 1699, to John Rue, of Staten Island. He may have been the father or grandfather of James.

(I) James Rue purchased the old Vansant farm in Bensalem in 1718, and died there in December, 1759, "advanced in years," leaving a widow Mary, who died in 1769, and children: Richard, Matthew, Samuel, Joseph, Mary (married Timothy Roberts in 1735), Catherine (married James Rankins in 1744), Elizabeth (married Samuel Yerkes in 1743), Sarah (married James Kidd).

(II) Matthew, son of James Rue, purchased an interest in the Milford Mills (now Hulmeville), and a large tract of land in Middletown township, Bucks county, in 1730, and lived there until his death. In a conveyance to his son Lewis in 1731, no wife joins, but his will mentions wife, Mary, who was probably a second spouse, and a sister of Benjamin Towne who married his eldest daughter. He died in 1770, leaving an ample estate, dividing several hundred acres of land among his children, and including a large personal property. He had five children: 1. Matthew, the eldest, died before his father leaving two sons, Benjamin

and Lewis. 2. Mary, married Thomas Case, of Trenton, in 1734. 3. Richard, mentioned below. 4. Katharine, married Benjamin Towne. 5. Lewis, married, in 1736, Rachel Vansant, and died in 1752, leaving six children.

(III) Richard, second son of Matthew Rue, inherited from his father a farm of two hundred and fifty acres in Middletown township and spent his whole life in that township, where he died in 1785 and was buried with his father, where many other members of the family of later generations lie, in the Rue graveyard, on the farm now occupied by Richard Rue, near Hulmeville. He married, January 6, 1735, Jane Van Dyck. He seems to have married a second time late in life as he is joined in making deeds in 1772 by a wife Elizabeth. No wife seems to have survived him. Children: Anthony, Elizabeth, Lewis, Catherine, (wife of Isaiah Van Horne), Richard and Matthew. The heirs of Richard and Lewis succeeded to the homestead which was purchased by these two in 1786.

(IV) Mathew (2), youngest child of Richard and Jane (Van Dyck) Rue, was a minor in 1770, when he was mentioned in the will of his grandfather, Matthew (1). In this will he received a negro boy, Charles, provided he lived to come of age and to be a farmer. At the time of his father's death, he was living on a small farm purchased by his grandfather in 1765, a part of a large plantation once owned by James Rue (I). He married Mary, daughter of Adam and Christiana Weaver, of Bensalem, and lived at different periods in Middletown, Bensalem and Bristol townships. This farm was conveyed to him by his brothers and sisters, and at the death of his father-in-law in 1812, forty acres of land in Bristol was devised to his children, to remain in his possession and care until the youngest of them should arrive at age. He last appears on record in a deed to his son, Adam, for a part of the land conveyed to him by his brothers and sisters in 1786. This deed bears date April 1, 1822, and is joined by his wife, Grace. Their residence was then in Bristol township. No will or letters of administration on his estate appear in the probate records of Bucks county. Adam Weaver, the father of his first wife, was a blacksmith and purchased land in Bensalem in 1760. He subsequently bought land in Middletown of Richard Rue, and owned considerable land in Bristol. His daughter, Mary, wife of Matthew (2) Rue, was not living when his will was made January 12, 1802. Matthew (2) and Mary Rue had children: 1. Adam, died in Bristol, 1849, leaving two sons and three daughters. 2. Richard, died unmarried. 3. Lewis, mentioned below. 4. Barsheba, wife of Joshua Wright. 5. Christiana. 6. Elijah. 7. Jacob.

(V) Lewis, third son of Matthew (2) and Mary (Weaver) Rue, was born January 31, 1788, in Middletown township, died at Newportville in Bristol township, August 9, 1863. He was a harness maker and lived all his life in Bristol. He married Ann, daughter of Stephen Stackhouse, born January 30, 1797, died December 2, 1868. Children: Edmund, Samuel S., Elizabeth (married Charles Walton) of Andalusa, Bucks county), Henry and Mary Ann. The second son was for many years an undertaker in Bristol, where he was succeeded by his son, Harvey.

(VI) Edmund, eldest son of Lewis and Ann (Stackhouse) Rue, was born October 23, 1825, in Newportville and died in Burlington, New Jersey, September 26, 1897. He attended the common schools of his native town, and learned the harness-makers' trade with his father, which furnished his occupation during most of his life. He retired from active business about five years previous to his death. In March, 1865, he removed to Burlington, New Jersey, and was there engaged in the harness business on his own account until his retirement. He was a Methodist and active in church work, being a member of the official board and treasurer of the Union street Methodist Church in Burlington for a period of thirty years. In politics he was a consistent Republican. He married Roxanna S. Allen, daughter of William and Eliza (Goforth) Allen, born October 16, 1825, died January 6, 1909. William, son of Israel Allen, was born June 24, 1793. Eliza, daughter of William and Isabella Goforth, was born December 31, 1792, died October 28, 1829. Children of Edmund and Roxanna S. (Allen) Rue: William A., died at the age of twenty-five years; Eugene, died in childhood; Caleb Taylor, mentioned below.

(VII) Caleb Taylor, only surviving child of Edmund and Roxanna S. (Allen) Rue, was born June 20, 1859, in Newportville and grew up in Burlington county, New Jersey, whither the family removed when he was about six years old. He received his education in the public schools of that town and Burlington College, a military institution. Early in life, he went to work for the Pennsylvania railroad, on Fourth street, Philadelphia, in the office of auditor of passenger receipts, and re-

mained there two years. He subsequently engaged in the wool business with Edward A. Green & Company of Philadelphia, and for the last twelve years has been engaged in the trade in cotton yarns with a commission house in the same city. For seventeen years he traveled through the country from the east to the middle west and is now city salesman for Miller, Riddle & Company, located at 206 Chestnut street in Philadelphia. He has continued as a resident in Burlington. Mr. Rue has always taken an active interest in political matters, acting with the Republican party, and was president of the common council of Burlington in 1894. He was a member of the convention which nominated John W. Griggs for governor of New Jersey, and of that which chose delegates to the national convention in 1908. In November, 1906, he was elected mayor of Burlington and discharged the duties of that office with credit to himself and to the satisfaction of his constituency. He is a member of Burlington Lodge, No. 32, A. F. and A. M.; of Boudinot Chapter, No. 3, R. A. M.; and Helena Commandery, No. 3, K. T. He has been for twenty years affiliated with the Masonic fraternity, and is a member of Lu Lu Temple, Nobles of the Mystic Shrine, of Philadelphia. He is a member of Burlington Lodge, No. 22, I. O. O. F., of Burlington, and of Lodge No. 996, B. P. O. E., of the same place. The principles of fellowship and charity towards mankind, as maintained by these orders, have been governing principles in the conduct of Mr. Rue's life, and he enjoys the esteem and regard of a large number of people.

He married, in 1893, Mary Collom, daughter of Elias D. and Kate (Love) Collom, of Philadelphia. She is a granddaughter of William Collom, who maintained a boarding school many years ago at Mt. Holly, New Jersey, was a Baptist clergyman, and served a term in the state legislature. He also filled a responsible position under President Lincoln during the civil war.

STROUD   From the records of the proceedings of the English house of commons we learn that on Wednesday, April 16, 1621, Sir William Stroud moved that "Tobacco be banished wholly out of the kingdom and that it may not be brought in from any part nor used amongst us." This was during the reign of King James I, and shows that the knight was even then imbued with the spirit of reform. That he was

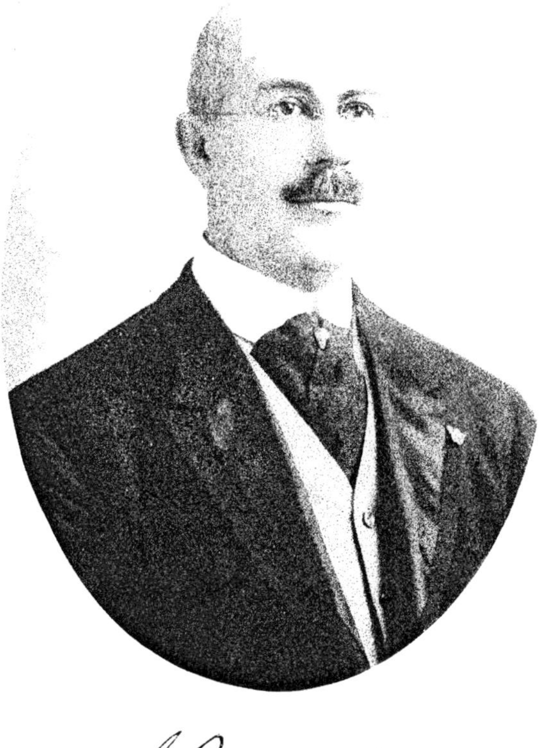

C. Taylor Rue.

a favorite with his constituents is proven by the fact that he kept his seat through the stirring days of the reign of Charles I.

History also states that Pym, Hampden, Hazelrigg, Hollis, and Stroud, all members of the house "bravely resisted this king in his unjust measures." So much more vehement were they than the others, that January 4, 1642, His Majesty "suddenly appeared in the House and after calling the names of these five men, accused them of treason and demanded that they be given up to him." As is well known, the house refused to do any such thing, and many descendants of Sir William Stroud are now to be found in Great Britain, especially in the town of Stroud, county Gloucester, and it is said that it is from among his grandchildren that the Strouds of Pennsylvania and New Jersey are descended. The crest of the Stroud family was: Demi lion couped. Motto: Malo mori quam faedari, meaning, I would rather die than be dishonored. A copy of the same can be seen in the Fairburn Book of Crests, plate 10-12.

(I) Thomas Stroud, founder of the present branch of the family, was born in England, September 30, 1758, and came to this country when he was yet a young man, settling in Chester county, Pennsylvania, where he farmed until his death, February 6, 1822. Thomas Stroud married, May 22, 1787, Sarah Hoxworth, a native of Valley Forge, Chester county, Pennsylvania, born August 20, 1767, died December 29, 1838. Both she and her husband were buried in Hephzibah, the old Chester county Baptist graveyard. Mrs. Stroud's sister Elizabeth married Benjamin Franklin Hancock, of Philadelphia, and one of their two children was General Winfield Scott Hancock The Hoxworths originally spelt their name Hawkesworth, and members of the family which was of English and Welsh extraction served in the French and Indian wars, in the revolution, and in the war of 1812. Thomas and Sarah (Hoxworth) Stroud had eleven children: 1. Margaret, born February 14, 1788, died August 28, 1811; married James Potts and moved west. 2. Mary, January 2, 1790, married Lewis Windle, July 25, 1810, and had twelve children. 3. Peter, referred to below. 4. Thomas, December 28, 1794. 5. Sarah, April 11, 1797. 6. Israel, April 8, 1799, died 1880; married Margaret Gibson, of Chester county, Pennsylvania. 7. Elizabeth, August 1, 1801. 8. William, January 20, 1804, married Ann M.

Merves. 9. Joshua, January 22, 1806, married Hannah W. Merves, and died November 1, 1876. 10. Eleanor, July 6, 1808, died June 8, 1878; married Isaac Hinkson. 11. Charlotte, October 8, 1810, died February 27, 1887; married Samuel Hinkson.

(II) Peter, third child and eldest son of Thomas and Sarah (Hoxworth) Stroud, was born in Highland township, Chester county, Pennsylvania, April 29, 1792, died there March 26, 1847, after an illness of one year. He was a farmer. He married Margaret, daughter of Thomas and Elizabeth Shields, of Chester county, in 1821. She was born November 29, 1795, at East Fallowfield township, died September 22, 1865, after an illness of ten days from a carbuncle on the back of her neck. The children of Peter and Margaret (Shields) Stroud were: 1 Jefferson Mountford, born November 4, 1819; died August 18, 1844; married Ruth Ann Parke. 2. Benjamin Franklin, August 17, 1821; died April 8, 1870; married Hannah Ann Fritz. 3. Joseph Cassius, referred to below. 4. Thomas Shields, October 16, 1825; died April 8, 1860; unmarried. 5. David Parke, February 6, 1828; died August 8, 1861; unmarried. 6. Caleb Harford, July 20, 1830; died September 18, 1900; married Louise Harley. 7. Joshua Van Horn, July 30, 1831; died September 27, 1831. 8. Elizabeth Jane, September 13, 1833; died February 5, 1907; married John R. McClellan. 9. Peter Van Buren, June 24, 1836; a practicing physician at Marlton, New Jersey; he read medicine with his brother, Dr. Joseph C. Stroud, and graduated from the University of Pennsylvania, March 14, 1861. 10. Lee Andrews, January 5, 1839; married Emily M. Snare; he died very suddenly, November 13, 1905.

(III) Joseph Cassius, third child and son of Peter and Margaret (Shields) Stroud, was born near Parksburg, Chester county, Pennsylvania, August 21, 1823; died May 23, 1890; he was buried in the Colestown cemetery, near Moorestown. He graduated from Marshalltown Academy in 1842, worked on his father's farm and then learned the wheelwright's trade, and worked at that until 1846. He then studied medicine under Dr. Andrew W. Murphy, of Parksburg, until 1848, when he entered the Jefferson Medical College in Philadelphia. graduating therefrom March 6, 1851, and coming to Moorestown, New Jersey, in September of the same year where he began the practice of his profession. December 25, 1851, Joseph Cassius Stroud, married (first) Elizabeth, daughter of J. S. Fletcher, of Philadelphia. September 9, 1852, she was injured by the explosion of a coal oil lamp, and died from the effects five days later; without issue. January 15, 1862, he married (second) Annie M., born in Philadelphia, February 19, 1840, daughter of George and Eliza Dull, of Moorestown. Their children were: 1. Franklin Gilbert, referred to below. 2. Lincoln Grant, born March 11, 1865; died January 29, 1897; unmarried. 3. Joseph Haines, May 27, 1867; married (first) October 29, 1892, Ida Green of Philadelphia, born November 21, 1871, died September 13, 1893, without issue; married (second) April 22, 1896, Abbie Eldridge, of Cape May, who has borne him two children, Paul Eldridge, December 14, 1896, and Mildred, February 26, 1898.

(IV) Franklin Gilbert, eldest child of Dr. Joseph Cassius and Annie M. (Dull) Stroud, was born at Moorestown, New Jersey, October 30, 1862, and is now living and practicing the profession of medicine in that town. He graduated from the Giffin Academy, near Moorestown, in 1881, and in the fall of the same year entered the Jefferson Medical College at Philadelphia, from which he graduated April 2, 1885. He began the practice of his profession. In 1886 he decided to take up a specialty of the diseases of the throat and nose, and removing to Camden, New Jersey, he was appointed a consulting physician in that department of the Jefferson Medical College Hospital. In the summer of 1887 he decided to continue his studies in Europe, and in consequence he spent nine months in the general hospitals of Vienna, Austria, and three more in the hospitals of London, Dublin, Paris, Brussels and Heidelberg. On his return he went into general practice with his father in Moorestown as his father's health was then very much impaired. Dr. Stroud is very active in state, county and township affairs and also in secret society matters. He is and always has been a staunch Republican. He has served as coroner for the county, on the board of education, on the board of health, and as health inspector. Owing to his carefulness he holds the position of medical examiner in several large life insurance companies. He is a member of the national, state, county and local medical societies, and has been honored by being chosen president more than once in most of them. He is also a member of the F. and A. M. His religious belief is with the Baptist denomination.

October 30, 1890, Franklin Gilbert Stroud married Martha Rudolph, born at Marlborough New Jersey, March 4, 1868, daughter of Edmund and Julia Ann (Stretch) Shimp, of Camden, New Jersey, and they have one son, Frank Edmund, born at Moorestown, November 17, 1891, in the same room of the same house in which his father was born

The New Jersey branch of the OSMOND Osmond family was transplanted from Bucks county, Pennsylvania, where the family settled at an early date. The first of the family of record was Isaac, who was born in Bristol, Bucks county; married Ann Hughes and had issue.

(II) John Thomas, son of Isaac and Ann (Hughes) Osmond, was born in Bristol, Pennsylvania, November 26, 1816; died August 28, 1896. His education was received in the common school. He learned the trade of carriage painting and trimming, at which he was employed as a journeyman until his removal to Bordentown, New Jersey, where he engaged in business for himself. Retiring from business life, he entered the employ of the old Camden & Amboy railroad, rising with rapid strides to the responsible position of train despatcher at Bordentown, the headquarters of the Camden & Amboy railroad. During the war the Camden & Amboy moved large bodies of troops over their lines and the duty of handling the great number of extra trains devolved upon Mr. Osmond. After the leasing of the Camden & Amboy by the Pennsylvania railroad, he was retained by the latter company and appointed ticket agent at Bordentown, New Jersey, where he remained in charge until within a few years of his death. His political faith was Democratic, and as representative of that party he served as county commissioner, common councilman, and in many local positions. He was a member of the Methodist Episcopal church, a trustee and class leader. He married, December 30, 1837, Lydia McGill, born July 6, 1816, in Lowelville, Ohio, died May 17, 1900, the daughter of Joseph and Rebecca Howell McGill. Joseph McGill was born in Scotland or on the high seas, the son of John McGill, who came from Scotland to America, settling in Ohio with his wife Nancy (Howell) McGill. Six children were born to John Thomas and Lydia (McGill) Osmond: 1. Rebecca, married James W. Rice, of Bordentown; both deceased. 2. Edward, a locomotive engineer; now deceased; married Elizabeth Keen, of Columbus. New Jersey, and left Charles, Sarah, Edward, Morgan and Blanche. 3. Thomas, a locomotive engineer; resident of Philadelphia; married Mary, daughter of Edgar and Annie Wright, of Bordentown. 4. George, a cigar manufacturer, of Bordentown; now deceased; married Abigail, daughter of William and Sarah Atkinson, of Bordentown, and left children, Joseph D., Lydia and Clara. 5. Joseph Lott, see forward. 6. John F., a railroad conductor; resident of Newark, New Jersey; married Ann Evans, of Bristol, Pennsylvania.

(III) Joseph Lott, fifth child of John Thomas and Lydia (McGill) Osmond, was born in Bordentown, New Jersey, December 29, 1851. He was educated in the schools of his native town. He early became interested in his father's business, and having learned telegraphy entered the employ of the Camden & Amboy railroad in Bordentown, New Jersey, later became train despatcher at Trenton, New Jersey, for the Pennsylvania railroad, where he worked for a year, then until 1875 in Jersey City and New York. Since 1875 he has been in Philadelphia, and for the past thirty years has been chief operator of the Philadelphia office of the Pennsylvania railroad. During his thirty-five years' service in Philadelphia, Mr. Osmond has maintained his residence in Bordentown, where he is actively interested in the business, religious and social life of that city. He is president of the Board of Trade, and Improvement Association; director of the First National Bank; president of the Citizen Hook and Ladder Company; member of the Board of Sewer Commissioners; member of Chosen Friends Encampment, No. 6, Independent Order of Odd Fellows; recorder of Good Intent Lodge, No. 19, Ancient Order United Workmen. He is a member of the Presbyterian church and an elder of the Bordentown congregation of that faith. He is a Democrat in politics, and for two terms represented his ward in the common council.

Mr. Osmond married, November 14, 1876, Josephine B., daughter of Charles and Sarah Ann (Bowker) Shreve, of Barnsboro, New Jersey. Children: 1. Carrie, born December 26, 1877; married Corbit Strickland Hoffman, of Clarksboro, New Jersey, a lieutenant in the regular United States army, First Infantry, at present stationed at Vancouver Barracks, state of Washington; they have one son, Corbit Hoffman. 2. Sarah Shreve. 3. Charles Shreve, twin of Sarah, born June 24, 1874, at Bordentown, New Jersey; he was educated in the public schools of Bordentown and Pearce's Business College, Philadelphia, and finishing at the Bordentown Military Institute; he

studied architecture, and for seven years was with Furnace Evans & Company, of Philadelphia; in 1905 he entered the service of the International Mercantile Marine Company as passenger agent at Philadelphia, Pennsylvania, a connection that is yet unbroken; he has attained high rank in the Masonic order in his native city; he is worshipful master of Mt. Moriah Lodge, No. 28, Free and Accepted Masons; past high priest of Mt. Moriah Chapter, No. 26, Royal Arch Masons, and past eminent commander of Ivanhoe Commandery, No. 26, Knights Templar; he is a noble of the Crescent Temple, Nobles of the Mystic Shrine; he is a member of Yepew Boat Club and Citizen Hook and Ladder Company; in political belief he is a Republican. Charles S. Osmond married, October 4, 1907, Aimee Evans, daughter of James and Elizabeth Robinson, of Belfast, Ireland; now resident of Trenton, New Jersey

COMFORT — Like many others of the old pioneers to the new world in search of a place where they could worship God according to their own ideas in peace, the founder of the Comfort family had to seek it in more than one place. Consequently pilgrim, as he is sometimes called, would seem to be rather his proper title than pioneer.

(I) John Comfort, the first of the name about which anything is known, came over to the new world and for a while lived in Flushing, Long Island, but having either before or after his arrival in America adopted the tenets of George Fox and his disciples, he found himself so out of sympathy with his surroundings that he removed to Bucks county, Pennsylvania, in 1719, and the following year married there Mary, daughter of Stephen and Sarah (Baker) Wilson. Her mother, who had married Stephen Wilson, in 1692, was the daughter of Henry and Margaret Baker, who had come from Derby, county Lancaster, England, to Bucks county, Pennsylvania, bringing a certificate from the Hardshaw meeting in 1684. The two children of John and Mary (Wilson) Comfort were: 1. Stephen, referred to below. 2. Robert.

(II) Stephen, son of John and Mary (Wilson) Comfort, was born in Bucks county, Pennsylvania, February 26, 1721; died December 11, 1800. He married, in 1744, Mercy, born December 28, 1724, daughter of Jeremiah Croasdale and Grace, daughter of Robert Heaton and Grace, daughter of Thomas and

Grace Pearson. Jeremiah Croasdale was the son of Ezra and Ann (Peacock) Croasdale. The children of Stephen and Mercy (Croasdale) Comfort were: 1. John, born October 5, 1745; married, 1771, Mary, daughter of John Woolman, and died in February, 1820. 2. Ezra, referred to below. 3. Jeremiah, born August 26, 1750, of whom it is related that having passed the meeting for marriage he had a "concern on his mind" which prevented him from proceeding, and his presentiment was shortly afterwards verified by his death. 4. Stephen, Jr., born February 26, 1753; married, 1776, Sarah Stephenson. 5. Grace, August 5, 1755; married Jonathan Stackhouse. 6. Mercy, born September 28, 1757; married, 1787, Aaron Philips. 7. Moses, born April 4, 1760; died April, 1838; married, 1782, Elizabeth Mitchell. 8. Robert, born December 24, 1763; died June 12, 1851; lived in Knox county, Ohio, and married, 1786, Mary Parry. 9. Hannah, born July 10, 1765.

(III) Ezra, second child and son of Stephen and Mercy (Croasdale) Comfort, was born October 8, 1747; died January 15, 1820. He married, in 1776, Alice Fell. One of their children relates in regard to this marriage that "the pig would have been killed for the wedding only that it got out the night before and ran away." Alice (Fell) Comfort died November 6, 1840. The children of Ezra and Alice (Fell) Comfort were: 1. and 2. Elizabeth and Mercy, twins, born November 12, 1772. 3. Grace, March 2, 1774. 4. John, September 17, 1775. 5. Ezra, Jr., referred to below. 6. Alice, February 23, 1779.

(IV) Ezra (2), fifth child and second son of Ezra (1) and Alice (Fell) Comfort, was born in Montgomery county, Pennsylvania, April 18, 1777; died August 29, 1847. He was a farmer, a speaker in Friends' meeting and very active in everything pertaining to the society. He married, at Quakertown, Pennsylvania, Margaret Shoemaker, who died March 31, 1873, at the age of ninety-one years. Their children were: 1. Sarah, died April 1, 1884, aged eighty-three years; married Hughes Bell, of Haddonfield, New Jersey. 2. Jane, died March 17, 1873, aged sixty-eight years; married Charles Lippincott. 3. Ann, married Isaac Jones. 4. John S. 5. Alice, married George Haverstick. 6. Jeremiah, died June 27, 1887, aged seventy-one years. 7. David, referred to below. 8. Margaret, died September 8, 18—, aged forty-one years; married Henry Warrington. 9. Grace, married Charles Williams.

(V) David, the seventh child and third son of Ezra (2) and Margaret (Shoemaker) Comfort, was born at Norristown, Pennsylvania, May 24, 1818; died November 12, 1899. He was educated at the Westtown boarding school in Chester county, Pennsylvania, and for a time engaged in farming in Norristown, later coming to Moorestown, New Jersey, where he bought a farm and continued his occupation until late in life. He was a Republican, and a member of the Orthodox Friends, being one of the overseers and sitting at the head of the meeting for nearly twenty years. He married Sarah Ann, born August 14, 1822, died July, 1888, daughter of John and Ann (Hall) Bacon, of Greenwich, New Jersey. Their children were: 1. John, who is in business at Columbus, Burlington county; a director in the Union Bank and Trust Company, of Mt. Holly; he married (first) Sarah A. Leech, who bore him one child, Mary R., who married Charles Carslake, and has three children: William, Edward and Sarah; he married (second) Annie C. Wright, and (third) Elizabeth Lippincott. 2. Maurice Bacon, referred to below. 3. Anna M., married Howard G. Taylor, a farmer of Riverton, New Jersey, and secretary of the Horticultural Society, and has two children: Howard G. and Alice C.

(VI) Maurice Bacon, second child and son of David and Sarah Ann (Bacon) Comfort, was born at Moorestown, March 11, 1854, is now living in the place of his birth. He was educated in the Moorestown schools and Westtown boarding school, Chester county, Pennsylvania, and has ever since followed farming, having a large stock farm outside of the town where he makes a specialty of boarding horses for city persons and others. He has served as member of Burlington county committee, and of the Chester township committee. He has also served as a delegate to many state and county conventions. In March, 1898, he was appointed by President Theodore Roosevelt as postmaster of Moorestown, and he has devoted all his time since then to this position which he still holds. He is an Orthodox Friend. He married (first) Caroline Hartman, daughter of Edward Randolph Maule, of Moorestown, who died July 28, 1899, leaving him with one child, Edward Maule, referred to below. May, 1908, he married (second) Catharine, daughter of Isaac and Catharine T. Shotwell, of Philadelphia.

(VII) Edward Maule, only child of Maurice Bacon and Caroline Hartman (Maule) Comfort, was born in Moorestown, July 1, 1888.

He was educated at the Moorestown school and graduated from the Westtown boarding school, Chester county, Pennsylvania. He is now in the dry goods house of Watson & Company, of Philadelphia, and lives with his father in Moorestown.

MEGARGEE The branch of the Megargee family that settled in New Jersey descends from the Pennsylvania family of that name. It is not possible to say just when the family first settled in Pennsylvania. The records, however, show that they were farmers and land owners near Philadelphia prior to the year 1800. While it is not possible to clearly show the connection, it is strongly believed that the New Jersey branch is of the same lineal descent as Jacob Megargee, and the Philadelphia family descending from him.

(I) George Megargee, who died March 3, 1835; married, at Abington, Pennsylvania, Sarah Myers, born May 17, 1785, died October 17, 1866. She was a daughter of Philip and Mary (Kaheen) Myers, who were married, November 19, 1778. Children of George and Sarah (Myers) Megargee: 1. Deborah, born May 4, 1805; died April 30, 1854; she married Hiram Rice. 2. George D., October 19, 1806. 3. Kizia, April 30, 1809; died October 6, 1826. 4. Myers, February 3, 1811; died April 14, 1836. 5. Albanus, July 9, 1814. 6. Jane, April 3, 1817; died July 31, 1818. 7. John T., June 24, 1820; died November 25, 1823. 8. Amanda, August 19, 1823; died October 2, 1866. 9. James White, see forward.

(II) James White, youngest son and child of George and Sarah (Myers) Megargee, was born in Philadelphia, Pennsylvania, October 20, 1829; died August 18, 1900. His father died when he was but five years of age, and he was taken into the home of Charles Haines, who resided on a farm near Riverside, New Jersey. He was educated in the town schools, and reared to the life of a farmer, which occupation he followed all his life. He became a land owner and cultivated his own farm. In his later days he was a member of the household of his son, George Elwood Megargee, then residing on a farm near Moorestown, New Jersey. James W. Megargee was a Democrat and held fraternal affiliations with the I. O. O. F. He married at Moorestown, New Jersey, October 24, 1851, Sarah W., daughter of Elwood and Mary (Wright) Borton, and granddaughter of Abram Borton. Nine children were born to James W. and Sarah W.

(Borton) Megargee: 1. George Elwood, see forward. 2. Flora Virginia, born June 2, 1855; died August 1, 1855. 3. Anna Mary, January 10, 1858. 4. Margaretta S., November 22, 1859; died October 14, 1881. 5. Edward Royal, March 10, 1865, married Mary Horner. 6. James Harrison, February 14, 1867; died September 24, 1908; he married Margaret Carter, of Camden, New Jersey, and has Helen and Sarah. 7. Elizabeth Borton, May 27, 1868; married John M. Stow, and has Margaretta and George Clifford Stow. 8. William Clifford, January 14, 1875; died February 19, 1893. 9. Ella Borton, January 18, 1876; married Leroy Pickersgill, D. D. S., of Philadelphia, Pennsylvania.

(III) George Elwood, eldest son and child of James White and Sarah W. (Borton) Megargee, was born near Moorestown, New Jersey. He was educated under private tuition and at Farnum Preparatory School, Beverly, New Jersey. He decided upon the profession of teaching as his life work and after fitting himself for the work he began teaching in the district schools. He is a well known and valued instructor who has earned the promotions that have come to him through his earnest and devoted efforts to better school conditions and raise the standard of excellence in the schools for whose welfare he was responsible. For eleven years he was a teacher in the Friends' high school, of Moorestown, going from there to assume the duties of principal of the Moorestown public school. He later was made supervising principal in charge of all the schools of Chester township. For sixteen years he has held this important post and they have been years fruitful of good to the pupils and patrons of the schools. Professor Megargee had also served the town as a member of the board of education of Cinnaminson township. This has not been through the favor of either political party as he is extremely independent in politics. He is a member and vestryman of the Moorestown Protestant Episcopal church. He holds fraternal fellowship in the I. O. O. F. He resides on a fine farm outside of Moorestown and in his "off duty" hours there indulges in his inherited love of the soil. Professor Megargee is unmarried.

REEDER This name has been common in New Jersey since the beginning of the eighteenth century, and the members of the family have been prominent in all public affairs. Four brothers, Jacob, John, Jeremiah and Joseph Reeder, appear on

11—9

the patent of the town of Newton, Long Island, in 1686, and the history of that town states they came from England direct to this place, although there is a tradition that a John Reeder, who lived in Salem, Massachusetts, in 1650, afterwards removed to Newton. Many of the family removed from Newton to Ewing, New Jersey, in 1710, and since that time the name has been frequently met with in that state.

(I) Thomas H. Reeder was born May 15, 1790; died September 15, 1857. He was a carpenter and bridge builder, and worked chiefly in the vicinity of Lambertville, New Jersey. Mr. Reeder married (first) Anna, born January 9, 1794, died May 25, 1838, daughter of William and Sarah Wilson; William Wilson was born March 15, 1756, died October 13, 1812; Thomas H. and Anna Reeder had seven children: 1. William W., born September 25, 1815. 2. Charles, August 2, 1817. 3. Thomas H., Jr., August 18, 1819. 4. John, January 27, 1822. 5. Joseph, March 24, 1823. 6. Sarah Ann, October 9, 1825. 7. Elizabeth, January 31, 1830. He married (second) Rosanna Smith, by whom he had two children: 8. John Wesley, October 28, 1847; lives at Jenkintown, near Philadelphia. 9. Edward B., February 16, 1852; resides in Philadelphia.

(II) Joseph, son of Thomas H. and Anna (Wilson) Reeder, was born March 24, 1823, at Lambertville, New Jersey; died January 14, 1886. When a boy he engaged to work for twenty-four dollars a year, and went to school winters only. Later he removed to Trenton, New Jersey, where he learned marble cutting. He had charge of a business in New York, established himself in business in Flemington, New Jersey, and also engaged in business in the same line on his own account in Mt. Holly, New Jersey. Later he removed to Duck Island, where he began raising tobacco. He was a pioneer in the sand business, at White Hill engaged in procuring sand for building purposes, and later had dredges on the river for raising sand; he continued this lucrative business until his death, a period of many years. He was president of a dredging company at the time of his death, and had also been for some time superintendent for the Knickerbocker Ice Company. Mr. Reeder was a Republican in his views, but took no very active part in political affairs, and in his religious opinions was very liberal. He was a member of the American Mechanics. He married Catherine, daughter of Truman and Lucy Sweet, of Trenton, New Jersey; and they had

nine children, the first two of whom died in infancy. Those who arrived to years of maturity were: 1. Josephine, married James Harris. 2. Lucy Ann, married Samuel H. Russell. 3. Horace Greeley, referred to below. 4. Clara E., married Harry Carter, of Newark, New Jersey. 5. Alice, married Theodore Carter. 6. Lillie, married William H. West, of Newark. 7. Thomas A., steamboat captain; resides at White Hill, New Jersey.

(III) Horace Greeley, son of Joseph and Catherine (Sweet) Reeder, was born October 31, 1853, at Mount Holly, New Jersey. He was educated in the public schools of Fieldsboro and at Haas School, now the site of the military school. When a young man he learned the trade of machinist with Thompson & Mott, at White Hill, serving three years, and then entered the employ of the Knickerbocker Ice Company, locating machines and filling ice plants. In 1881 he was employed by the dredging company with which his father was connected, and by his diligence and zeal worked his way up until he was the owner; he is now manager, superintendent and director of the Delaware River Sand Dredging Company, in which he owns most of the stock. He is also the owner of boats by which sand is transported to Philadelphia for building purposes. He often receives commissions from the United States government for dredging, planting buoys, etc. Mr. Reeder is thorough master of all the details of the business in which he is engaged, and has made a thorough study of the machinery and methods of dredging. In 1886 he invented a labor saving device to use on dredges, namely: a dredge machine distributor, and was the first to use a belt instead of cogs on the machine. As a member of the Atlantic Deeper Waterways Association, whose offices are in the Crozer building, Philadelphia, Pennsylvania, and whose object is the development of Interior Waterways along the Atlantic Coast, Mr. Reeder was one of a party of seven appointed in May, 1909, to inspect the Delaware and Raritan Canal; the other members of the party were Messrs. Moore, Atkin, Wanger, Donnelly and Birk. The purpose of the trip was to obtain information at first hand, and by observation, of present canal conditions, as well as to obtain photographs illustrating the general subject. No great use is made of the Delaware and Raritan Canal at present for two reasons, first because the canal, built more than seventy years ago, is too small to permit of economical shipments in the present day, and second because its management for the

Horace G. Reeder

last thirty years has been directed towards a diversion of the canal business to the parallel and competing railroads. Mr. Reeder takes a keen interest in public affairs and improvements, and is a Republican in his political views. He has served ten years as a member of the school board, and is a member of the township committee. He is a member of Mount Moriah Lodge, No. 28, Ancient Free and Accepted Masons; Mount Moriah Chapter, No. 20, Royal Arch Masons, of Bordentown; Atlantic Deeper Waterways Association, and the Yapiwi Aquatic Boat Club. He is liberal in religious views. He resides at Bordentown.

Mr. Reeder married, in 1876, Alice H., daughter of John and Maria (Vail) Harned, of Yardville, New Jersey. She is a Friend in religion and belongs to the meeting at Crosswicks, New Jersey. Children: 1. Horace Greeley, Jr., born October 24, 1876; died at the age of ten years. 2. Walter Lewis, born September 16, 1879; after preliminary education attended high school and business college, and then took a course at the Scranton School of Correspondence; at the age of nineteen he took charge of work on dredging machines, and is now connected with dredging and tug boats, being secretary and treasurer of the Delaware River Sand Dredging Company. 3. Ralph Howard, born May 3, 1883; attended high school and business college; employed by the New York Shipbuilding Company, and now has charge of one of the dredges on the river. 4. Joseph R., born October 7, 1880; is attending Drexel Institute, Philadelphia. 5. Grace Ingersoll, born January 23, 1888; resides at home. 6. John Harned, born January 23, 1891; is now attending Drexel Institute, Philadelphia, Pennsylvania. Walter Lewis and Ralph Howard are members of Ancient Free and Accepted Masons, Royal Arch Chapter, and Shrine.

The name of Lippincott LIPPINCOTT is one of the oldest of the English surnames of local origin, having been traced back to the "Lovecote" of the Domesday Book of William the Conqueror, compiled in 1080. The place still bears its ancient name and is an estate lying near Hinghampton, Devonshire, England. Its earliest known derivative occurs in the name of Roger de Lovecote, who is recorded in the rolls of the king's court of the time of King John. 1195. In 1274, in the reign of Edward I. the names of Jordanus de Loginggetot and Robertus de Lyvenscot and Thomas de Luf-

kote appear in the Hundred Rolls; while the manor of Luffincott, now in the parish of that name, on the west border of Devonshire, and twenty miles distant from Lovecote, and an estate comprising nearly one thousand acres, was in 1243 the property of Robert de Lughencot, and remained in his family until 1415, the property being also described in 1346 as "pertaining to Robert de Lyvenscot." Another branch of the family resided at Webworthy, pronounced "Wibbery," in northwestern Devon, where they held extensive estates for three hundred and fifty years. The name in this case is spelt Luppingcott and Luppincott. Of this line the last was Henry Luppincott, who lived at Barcelona, Spain, and died in 1779. A branch of this family removed from Webworthy to Sidbury in East Devon about the middle of the sixteenth century, and from them was descended Henry Lippincott, who became a distinguished merchant of Bristol, was made a baronet in 1778 by King George III, and through his son Sir Robert Gann Lippincott, baronet, became the ancestor of Robert Cann Lippincott and his sons Robert C. Cann Lippincott and Henry Cann Lippincott, whose descendants are probably the only living male representatives of this ancient branch of the family in England. The residence of this branch of the family is at Overcourt, near Bristol.

That the Lippincotts of England held a good position in the world is evidenced by the numerous coats-of-arms granted to them, no less than eight coats appearing to have been bestowed upon gentlemen of the name, some of them almost if not quite as early as 1420, in which year John Lippingcott, of Wibbery, is found bearing his, from which by modification several of the later coats seem to be derived. Another arms, which diverges widely from the rest, and was most probably granted as early as the Crusades to one whose name was spelt Luffyngcotte, is thus described: "A black eagle, sprinkled with drops of blood and displayed upon a shield of silver." In still another branch of the Devonshire Lippincotts the name appears to have gone through the transformations of Leppingote, Leppingcotte, Leppyncott, and Lippincott, and according to the latest authorities it is from this branch that the American Lippingcotts are descended although the earlier authorities favor one of the other lines.

(I) Richard Lippincott, the founder of the family in New Jersey and Pennsylvania, although belonging to a branch of the family of his contemporaries and fellow-believers of too mild and peaceable a disposition to be either happy or contented amidst the conditions that prevailed in England during the latter years of the reign of Charles I, in consequence associated himself at an early date with the settlers of the colony of Massachusetts Bay, and taking up his residence at Dorchester he became a member of the church there, and April 1, 1640, was chosen to one of the town offices, being made freeman by the court of Boston, May 13, 1640. Here his eldest son was born and was baptized September, 1641. A few years later, however, he removed to Boston where his second son and eldest daughter were born and their baptisms entered on the records of the First Church at Boston; in the entry of the son the father being noted as "a member of the church at Dorchester." This baptism was November 10, 1644. Even New England Puritanism, however, was of too militant a character for Richard Lippincott, and he began to differ more and more from his brethren of the church in regard to some of their religious doctrines, and so tenacious of his opinions was he that on July 6, 1651, he was formally excommunicated. About a year later, in 1652, Richard Lippincott returned to England in the hope that under the Commonwealth he might find a greater degree of religious liberty than was obtainable among his fellow-colonists in Massachusetts. That to some extent at least his hopes were gratified seems evident from the name of his third son, Restore or Restored, who was born at Plymouth, England, in the following year, 1652, as there can be no doubt that he received his name in commemoration of his father's restoration to his native land and to the communion of more congenial spirits. Just what Richard Lippincott's religious views at this time were can only be a matter of conjecture, but they evidently harmonized more or less with those of George Fox and his adherents as shortly after his return to England he became a member of the Society of Friends, and soon after his profession of faith became a partaker with his fellow believers in their sufferings for their principles and in the persecutions to which they were subjected. In February, 1655, while he was residing at Plymouth, Devonshire, the mayor of that town caused his arrest and imprisonment in the town jail near the castle of Exeter, his offense being it would appear that he had made the assertion that "Christ was the word of God and the Scrip-

tures a declaration of the mind of God." Several months later, in May, 1655, according to Sewell's History of the Quakers, he, with others, testified against the acts of the mayor and the falsehood of the charges brought against them. In commemoration of this release from imprisonment he named his next son, born that same year, Freedom. The following few years seem to have been comparatively quiet ones with him, the only noteworthy events in his life being his making of a home for himself and family at Stonehouse, near Plymouth, and the birth of his daughter Increase in 1657, and of his son Jacob in 1660. In this last mentioned year he was again imprisoned by the mayor of Plymouth for his faithfulness to his religious convictions, being arrested by the officers at and taken from a meeting of Friends in that city. His release was brought by the solicitations of Margaret Fell and others whose efforts in behalf of imprisoned Friends were so influential with the newly restored King Charles II as to obtain the liberation of many. In comparison with this treatment in Boston, Richard Lippincott's experiences in Plymouth were such that he at length determined to make another trial of the new world, and once more bidding farewell to his native land he sailed again for New England in 1661 or 1662, and took up his residence in Rhode Island, which he found to be a Baptist colony very tolerant of varied forms of belief. Here his youngest son, Preserved, was born in 1663, and received his name in commemoration of his father's preservation from persecution and from the perils of the deep. It is a curious fact that, omitting the name of his third child, Abigail, who lived only a few weeks, the names of the children of Richard and Abigail Lippincott, taken in the order of their birth, form the words of a prayer, which needs only the addition of another son, called Israel, to be complete, this: Remember John, Restore Freedom, Increase Jacob, and Preserve (Israel). Whether this arrangement was accidental or was due to a premeditated design cannot be determined; it is probably a coincidence, as although in strict accordance with the ways in fashion among the Puritans of that day, so complete an arrangement as this is extremely rare.

In the Rhode Island colony each of the settlements was at first regarded as an independent establishment; but in 1642 it was determined to seek a patent from England, and Roger Williams having gone to the mother country for that purpose, obtained in 1644, through the influence of the Earl of Warwick, a charter from Parliament uniting the settlements as the "Incorporation of Providence plantations in the Narragansett Bay in New England." Complete religious toleration was granted together with the largest measure of political freedom, but owing to jealousies and exaggerated ideas of individual importance, the settlements did not become really united until 1654 and it was nine years later that they sought and obtained their charter of "Rhode Island and the Providence plantations," from King Charles II, which served as the constitution of the colony and state down to 1843. In the following year, 1664, the Dutch Colony of New Netherland came into the possession of the English, and the next year, 1665, an association was formed at Newport, Rhode Island, to purchase lands from the Indians, and a patent was granted to them. This movement had been initiated by the people of Gravesend, Long Island, but the residents of Newport were considerably in the majority and the success of the movement is mainly due to them and to their efforts in raising the greater part of the money to pay the Indians for their land and in inducing persons to settle on it. Of the eighty-three Newport subscribers who contributed towards buying the Monmouth county, New Jersey, lands from the Indians and towards defraying the incidental expenses in treating with the natives, Richard Lippincott gave by far the largest subscription, £16, 10 shillings, which was more than twice that of any other contributor except Richard Borden, whose amount was £11, 10 shillings. The first deed from the Indians is dated March 25, 1665, and is for the lands at Nevesink, from the sachem Popomora and his brother Mishacoing to James Hubbard, John Bowne, John Tilton, junior, Richard Stout, William Goulding and Samuel Spicer, for and on behalf of the other subscribers. April 7, 1665, Popomora and his brother went over to New York and acknowledged the deed before Governor Nicolls, and the official copy is in the office of the secretary of state, New York, liber 3, page 1. Another copy is preserved in the records of the proprietors of East Jersey at Perth Amboy, where there is also a map of the land embraced in the purchase, while still a third copy may be found in the office of the secretary of state at Trenton. Two other deeds followed and on April 8, 1665, Governor Nicolls signed the noted Monmouth patent, one of the conditions of which was "that the said Patentees and their associates, their heirs or

assigns, shall within the space of three years, beginning from the day of the date hereof, manure and plant the aforesaid land and premises and settle there one hundred families at the least." The reason for the founding of the Monmouth settlements is given in the patent as the establishment of "free liberty of Conscience without any molestation or disturbance whatsoever in the way of worship." In accordance with the terms of this patent, Richard Lippincott and his family removed from Rhode Island to Shrewsbury, New Jersey, among the earliest settlers of the place. With him went also a number of other members of the Society of Friends and they at once formed themselves into the Shrewsbury Meeting, which for a long time met at Richard Lippincott's house. He himself was one of the most active of the Friends in the meeting and he was also one of the most prominent in all public matters. In 1667 the inhabitants of Middletown, Shrewsbury and other settlements included under the Monmouth patent, found themselves so far advanced, with dwellings erected and lands cleared that they had opportunity to take measures to establish a local government. Their grant from Nicolls authorized them to "pass such prudential laws as they deemed advisable" and as early as June, 1667, they held an assembly for that purpose at Portland Point, now called Highlands. On December 14 following another assembly was held at Shrewsbury; and although Governor Carteret and his council considered these assemblies as irregular they are nevertheless the first legislative bodies that ever met in New Jersey. This "General Assembly of the Patentees and Deputies" continued to meet for many years and its original proceedings are still preserved. In 1669 Richard Lippincott was elected a member of the governor's council as one of the representatives from Shrewsbury, but being unwilling to take the oath of allegiance unless it contained a proviso guaranteeing the patent rights of the Monmouth towns he was not allowed to take his seat. In the following year, 1670, he was elected by the town as an associate patentee, one of the "five or seven other persons of the ablest and discreetest of said inhabitants" who joined with the original patentees formed the assembly above mentioned, which according to Nicoll's patent had full power "to make such peculiar and prudential laws and constitutions amongst the inhabitants for the better and more orderly governing of them," as well as "liberty to try all causes and actions of debts and trespass arising amongst the inhabitants to the value of £10." In 1676 the governor's council passed a law providing that any town sending deputies who "refused on their arrival to take the necessary oaths," should be liable to a fine of £10; consequently Richard Lippincott who was chosen to represent his town in 1677, did not attend, and as a result the council passed another act fining any member who absented himself, ten shillings for each day's absence. In 1670 the first meeting for worship was established by the Friends; and in 1672 this was visited by George Fox who was entertained during his stay by Richard Lippincott. His residence was on Passequeneiqua creek, a branch of South Shrewsbury river, three-fourths of a mile northeast of the house of his son-in-law, Samuel Dennis, which stood three-fourths of a mile east of the town of Shrewsbury. Soon after this Richard Lippincott made another and final voyage to England, where he was in 1675 when John Fenwick was preparing to remove to West Jersey; and on August 9, 1676, he obtained from Fenwick a patent for one thousand acres of land in his colony, which he probably purchased as a land speculation since neither he nor his children ever occupied any part of it. May 21, 1679, Richard Lippincott divided this plantation into five equal parts, giving to each of his sons a two hundred acre tract. Having at length found a fixed place of residence where he could live in peace and prosperity, Richard Lippincott settled down to "an active and useful life in the midst of a worthy family, in the possession of a sufficient estate, and happy in the enjoyment of religious and political freedom." Here he passed the last eighteen years of his life of varied experiences, and here he died November 25, 1683.

Two days before his death Richard Lippincott made his will and acknowledged it before Joseph Parker, justice of the peace. January 2 following his widow, Abigail Lippincott, gave her bond as administratrix, her fellow bondsman being her son's father-in-law, William Shattock, and Francis Borden. There seems, however, to have been some irregularity in the will or its provisions, particularly in omitting mention of an excutor; for on the day when the widow gave her bond, Governor Thomas Rudyard issued a warrant or commission to Joseph Parker, John Hans (Hance) and Eliakim Wardell "or any two of them, to examine Abigail, the widow of Richard Lippincott, as to her knowledge of any other last will made by her husband." An endorsement

on the will, dated May 21, 1684, states that the "said Abigail has no knowledge of any other will and that she will faithfully administer the estate." The inventory of the personal estate, £428, 2 shillings, including debts due £30, and negro servants £60, was made by Eliakim Wardell, William Shattock, Francis Borden and Joseph Parker.

The Dutch proprietors of New Amsterdam had long been engaged in the slave trade and at the surrender to the English in 1664 the colony contained many slaves, some of whom were owned by Friends. As early as 1652 members of this society at Warwick, Rhode Island, passed a law requiring all slaves to be liberated after ten years service as was the manner with the English servants, who, however, had to serve but four years. In 1683 the court at Shrewsbury passed a law against trading in slaves. These are the earliest known instances of legislation in behalf of negro emancipation. Richard Lippincott was the owner of a number of slaves; and in her will, dated June 28, 1697, and proved August 7 following, his widow, Abigail Lippincott, frees most of them besides leaving to her children and grandchildren much real estate and considerable bequests in money.

Remembrance, the eldest son of Richard and Abigail Lippincott, lived at Shrewsbury, married Margaret Barber, of Boston, and died in 1722, aged eighty-two years. He was prominent in colonial affairs, a bitter opponent of George Keith, and clerk of the monthly and quarterly meeting of Friends at Shrewsbury. His children, four of whom died in infancy, were Joseph, Elizabeth, Abigail, Richard, Elizabeth again, Joseph, William, Abigail again, Sarah, Ruth, Mary and Grace. His descendants through his sons Richard and William are numerous, and many descendants of Samuel, son of William, now resides in Pittsburg and other western cities.

John, "yeoman of Shrewsbury," second son of Richard and Abigail Lippincott, married (first) Ann Barber, and on her death in 1707 he married Jeannette Austin, and died in 1720. The eight children borne by his first wife were John, Robert, Preserved, Mary, Ann, Margaret, Robert and Deborah. Their descendants are now found chiefly in Monmouth county, New Jersey, Green county, Pennsylvania, and New York City.

Abigail Lippincott, born January 17, 1646, died March 9, 1646. Restore Lippincott is treated below. Freedom, the fifth child and fourth son of Richard and Abigail Lippincott, was a tanner; lived on Rancocas creek, about where Bridgeboro now stands; he was also a blacksmith, and was killed by lightning while shoeing a horse in the summer of 1697. By his wife, Mary (Curtis) Lippincott he had five children: Samuel, Thomas, Judith, Mary and Freedom Junior. His descendants through his sons Samuel, Thomas and Freedom, are numerous in the western townships of Camden and Burlington counties.

Increase, the only daughter of Richard and Abigail Lippincott who reached maturity, married Samuel Dennis and removed to Salem county, New Jersey. Of this branch of the family there has for many years been no trace remaining in the state.

Jacob, the fifth son of Richard and Abigail Lippincott, lived at Shrewsbury, and by his wife, Grace (Wooley) Lippincott, had two children: Jacob and Ruth. Preserved, the youngest son of Richard and Abigail Lippincott, died March, 1666, aged three years and one month. Freedom, another son, is written of elsewhere.

(II) Restore, or Restored, fourth child and third son of Richard and Abigail Lippincott, was born in Plymouth, Devonshire, England, July 3, 1652, and died near Mt. Holly, Burlington county, New Jersey, about July 20, 1741, in the ninetieth year of his age. He was, however, regarded by his contemporaries as a much older man than he really was; for the noted Quaker minister, Thomas Chalkley, who attended his funeral, notes in his journal, "On fourth day, the 22d, I was at Mount Holly, at the burial of our ancient friend Restored Lippincott: he was as I understood, nearly one hundred years of age, and had upwards of two hundred children, grandchildren and great-grandchildren, many of whom were at his funeral." Restore was brought to this country when his parents returned from Plymouth and accompanied them from Rhode Island to Shrewsbury. When he was twenty-two years old he married, and settled down at Shrewsbury on land near his father, for which in 1677 he and his wife received a patent under the "Grants and concessions made by the proprietors," a record of which is preserved in the land warrant records in the office of the surveyor general of East Jersey, at Perth Amboy. This estate comprised two-hundred and forty acres, and ten years later, in January, 1687, Restore added to it considerably. On January 2, he received a patent for 96 1-2 acres "at Passequenecqua, North Richard Stout junior, South William Scott, East Pass-

equenecqua Creek, West George Keith"; this patent also included three and a half acres of meadow, "East Peter White, West John Havens, North and South upland." (East Jersey deeds, liber B, page 264.) On January 22 following, he received still another patent for "217 acres, counted as 193, on Ramsouts Neck, East John Claytone, North Navesinks River, West a road, South grantee and Abraham Browne; also 7 acres of meadow adjoining." (East Jersey deeds, liber B, page 271.) September 21, 1692, Restore Lippincott, styled in the deed, "late of Shrewsbury, East Jersey, now of Northampton River, West Jersey, husbandman," bought of Thomas Ollive of Wellingborough a plantation of five hundred and seventy acres in Northompton "along the line between the two Tenths, adjoining Widow Parker and John Woolston." January 10, 1699, Restore deeded three hundred and nine acres of this property, eight acres of it being meadow, to his son Samuel; and about a year and a half later bought himself another plantation of three hundred acres from Isaac Horner, the deed bearing the date of June 20, 1701. The following month, in company with John Garwood, he bought of Susanna, the widow and executrix of Thomas Budd, of Philadelphia, two thousand acres more in Burlington county, "on the north branch of the Northampton River, near Mount Pisgah, and adjoining William Budd." The two hundred acres of his Cohansey property in Fenwick's colony which had been given him by his father he disposed of to Robert Eyres, giving to Joseph Eastland, of Cohansey, August 12, 1699, a power of attorney to make the delivery. In 1701 Restore Lippincott was chosen as the representative of Burlington county in the West Jersey assembly, and the same year he joined with the Provincial council and the members of the assembly in a petition to King William, for the confirmation of Andrew Hamilton as the governor of the colony. This was the last assembly to meet under the old proprietary government of West Jersey, since in the following year the proprietors surrendered their governmental rights to the Crown and Lord Cornbury was appointed as the first of the royal governors of the province of New Jersey. In 1703 Restore Lippincott was elected as the representative of Burlington county to the first of the Royal provincial assemblies, which met at Perth Amboy; in 1704 he was re-elected to the same office and continued to serve in that capacity until 1706. Restore Lippincott became one of the most influential of the Burlington Friends, and up to 1716, when the meeting house at Mt. Holly was built, the meeting of Friends were often held at his home. This was especially the case during the severe winter of 1704-05, when the records of the old Springfield meeting tell us that they held their meetings there too, "considering the badness of the way in going to the usual house." In the minutes of the Burlington monthly meeting there is a very interesting record which illustrates not only the carefulness and diligence of the Friends in regard to all the details of their religious life, but also at the same time throws a genial light upon the character of Restore himself. At the monthly meeting of January 23, 1704, one of the members, Thomas Atkinson, presented the following memorial in writing: "Friends: whereas I was charged in the face of the meeting by Restore Lippincott that I pulled off my hat when John Langstaff was buried is not true. I have many witnesses to the contrary." When this memorial was read, Restored Lippincott immediately arose and demanded that a committee be appointed to investigate the charges; and six or seven months later, on August 6, 1705, the committee reported to the meeting that "Whereas some time since there was a paper sent in by Tho. Atkinson that Restore Lippincott charged him falsely in the face of the meeting with pulling off his hat att the time of John Langstaff's funeral whilst the priest was speaking, for which at our last meeting some Friends were to speak to Restore Lippincott to be at our last Monthly Meeting to answer to itt for himself, and he making it appear by several evidences to be true, it is this meeting's Judgment that Restore Lippincott did not accuse Tho. Atkinson falsely." Restore was buried in the friends ground at Mt. Holly; and in his will, which is dated March 16, 1733, and proved December 13, 1741, he leaves legacies to his son James, his daughters Rachel Dawson, Abigail Shinn, Rebecca Gaskill and Elizabeth Shinn, and his grandsons, Joseph and Restore Lippincott Junior, and David and Jonathan Jess.

November 6, 1674, Restore Lippincott married (first) Hannah, daughter of William Shattock, who was born July 8, 1654, in Boston, Massachusetts, and died before 1729, when he married (second) Martha (Shinn) Owen, the daughter of John and Jane Shinn, the emigrants, and the widow of Joshua Owen. His second wife bore him no children; by his first wife he had eight, all of whom reached

maturity and married. 1. Samuel, born September 12, 1675, married, July 3, 1700, Ann Hulett, and the descendants of his son Samuel, who married Mary Arney, are many of them residing on the purchase between Mt. Holly and Pemberton. 2. Abigail, born February 16, 1677, married, May 3, 1697, James, the youngest child and the longest lived son of John and Jane Shinn, the emigrants, and their descendants are very numerous throughout South Jersey. 3. Hannah, born in October, 1681, married William Gladding in 1701. 4. Rebecca, born November 24, 1684, married, in 1704, Josiah Gaskill. 5. James, treated below. 6. Elizabeth, born March 15, 1690, married, June 12, 1712, George, eldest son of John and Ellen (Stacy) Shinn, nephew to James Shinn, the husband of his wife's sister, Abigail, and grandson of John and Jane Shinn, the emigrants. 7. Jacob, born in August, 1692, married, in 1716, Mary, daughter of Henry Burr, and his descendants are numerous, chiefly in Gloucester and Salem counties; among them, however, was Joshua Lippincott, of Philadelphia, at one time a director of the Bank of the United States and president of the Schuylkill Navigation Company. 8. Rachel, born January 8, 1695, married (first) Zechariah Jess, and (second) Francis Dawson.

(III) James, the fifth child and second son of Restore and Hannah (Shattock) Lippincott, was born June 11, 1687, at Passequenecqua, near Shrewsbury, and died in 1760, at his home, inherited from his father, near Mt. Holly. September 12, 1709, he married Anna, the eldest daughter of Thomas and his second wife Anna Eves, and granddaughter of Thomas Eves, "barber in London," who came to Burlington in 1677, in the ship "Kent." They had six children who reached maturity and married: 1. Jonathan, married, March 13 1746, Ann, daughter of Samuel and Mary (Thompson) Shinn-Eves, a first cousin of her husband's mother, being the granddaughter of Thomas and Anna Eves, and great-granddaughter of Thomas Eves, of London and Burlington. Her mother was Mary, daughter of John Thompson, and widow of George, son of John and Jane Shinn, the emigrants. 2. Aaron, treated below. 3. John, married Elizabeth Elkinton. 4. Daniel, married Elizabeth Pim. 5. Moses, married in 1750, Maribah Mullin or Miller. 6. Anna, married, August 6, 1746, Thomas Taylor. The descendants of these children have resided for the most part in Northampton, in Evesham, and in Philadelphia, the most noteworthy among them being Joshua Ballinger Lippincott, the distinguished publisher; Judge Benjamin H. Lippincott, of Burlington county, who is treated below, and Aaron S. Lippincott, a successful cotton manufacturer of Philadelphia.

(IV) Aaron, second child and son of James and Anna (Eves) Lippincott, married Elizabeth, daughter of Ephraim and granddaughter of Joseph and Elizabeth Tomlinson, the emigrants, and was the sister of Mary (Tomlinson) Gardiner, the great-grandson of Dr. Thomas Gardiner, the emigrant. Aaron and Elizabeth (Tomlinson) Lippincott had five children who reached maturity and married. 1. Moses, treated below. 2. Elizabeth, married (first) John Butcher, who died leaving no issue, and his widow then married Isaac, son of Jonathan and Hannah (Sharp) Haines, grandson of Jonathan Haines and Mary, daughter of William Matlack, the emigrant; great-grandson of John Haines and Esther, daughter of John Borton the emigrant; and great-great-grandson of Richard and Margaret Haines, the emigrants. By this marriage there were three children: Elizabeth, Ephraim, and a second Elizabeth. 3. Sarah, married Caleb Lippincott. 4. Mary, married a Quicksall. 5. Aaron, married Hannah, daughter of Nathaniel and Margaret Snowden, and widow of Job, son of Rehoboam Braddock and Jemima, daughter of John Darnell, the emigrant; grandson of Robert Braddock and Elizabeth, daughter of Joseph Bates and Mercy, daughter of James, son of Gregory Clement, the regicide; and great-grandson of Robert Braddock, the emigrant, and Elizabeth, daughter of Timothy Hancock, the emigrant, and Rachel Firman, his first wife.

(V) Moses, eldest son and child of Aaron and Elizabeth (Tomlinson) Lippincott, married (first) October 3, 1778, Mary, daughter of Joseph Hewlings by his second wife, Elizabeth, daughter of Laban Langstaff, and widow of William Hammitt; granddaughter of Laban and Susanna (Warrington) Langstaff, also granddaughter of Jacob Hewlings and Dorothy, daughter of Thomas and Anna Eves, children of Thomas Eves, of London and Burlington; and great-granddaughter of William Hewlings and Dorothy, daughter of Thomas Eves, of London and Burlington. Moses and Mary (Hewlings) Lippincott had five children who reached maturity and married: 1. Rebecca, married (first) Josiah, son of Isaac Haines and his first wife Mary, daughter of Thomas Wilkins and Mary,

daughter of Enoch Core, the emigrant, and Sarah, daughter of John and Sarah Roberts, the emigrants; granddaughter of Thomas and Susannah Wilkins, the emigrants. Isaac Haines was also the grandson of Jonathan and Hannah (Sharp) Haines whose ancestry is given below. After her first husband's death, Rebecca Lippincott married (second) Isaac, son of John and Mary Wilson. 2. Elizabeth married (first) William Austin and (second) Josiah Costill. 3. Dorothy, married Joseph Matlack. 4. Sarah, married John Hoile, of Jefferson county, Ohio, son of John and Sarah Hoile, who lived in the north of England. 5. Benjamin H., treated below. After his first wife's death, Moses Lippincott married (second) Sarah, daughter of David Stratton, who bore him three children. 6. John S., married Hannah Alberston. 7. Eli Stratton, married Elizabeth Vandyke. 8. Mary, who died unmarried.

(VI) Benjamin H., youngest child and only son of Moses and Mary (Hewlings) Lippincott, was born in Salem county, New Jersey, and settled in Burlington county, same state, where he was one of the most prominent persons in his day. He was a surveyor, a conveyancer, and also served as one of the judges of the court of common pleas. Like his ancestors, he belonged to the Society of Friends. He married (first) Elizabeth Wilkins, who was the mother of three children: 1. George W. 2. William, mentioned below. 3. Sarah, who became the wife of Charles Jessup, of Moorestown. Mr. Lippincott married (second) Martha Collins, who was the mother of Benjamin B. and Elizabeth Lippincott. The latter is now the widow of George L. Dillingham, residing in Moorestown.

(VII) William, second son of Benjamin H. and Elizabeth (Wilkins) Lippincott, was born in 1812 at Mt. Laurel, near Moorestown, and died in the latter place in 1879. He had a farm of one hundred and twenty acres and was an industrious, respected and worthy citizen. He was a member of the Society of Friends and was at the head of the meeting at the time of his death. He married Elizabeth, daughter of Hugh and Mary (Lippincott) Roberts. The last named, a daughter of Samuel and Priscilla (Briant) Lippincott, and granddaughter of Isaac and Hannah Lippincott. The last named was a daughter of John Engle and his wife Mary, daughter of Samuel Osborn. John Engle, above named, was a son of Robert and Jane (Horne) Engle, the immigrants. Samuel Lippincott above named was a grandson of Thomas Lippincott, the latter a son of Freedom and Mary (Curtis) Lippincott. Freedom was a son of Richard and Abigail Lippincott. Thomas Lippincott's wife, Mary, was a daughter of John and Esther (Borton) Haines, whose ancestry is given above. Hugh Roberts was the son of Samuel and Elizabeth (Shute) Roberts; grandson of Joshua Roberts and Rebecca, daughter of Joseph, son of Thomas and Mary (Bernard) Stokes, the immigrants, by his wife Judith, daughter of Freedom and Mary (Curtis) Lippincott. Joshua Roberts was the son of John Roberts and Mary, daughter of George Elkinton, who emigrated as a servant or redemptioner of Dr. Daniel Wills; and the grandson of John and Sarah Roberts, the immigrants who came to West Jersey in the ship "Kent." William and Elizabeth (Roberts) Lippincott had children: 1. Richard R., enlisted at the beginning of the civil war as a private in Company I, Sixty-first Pennsylvania Volunteers, and served three years, participating in all the battles of the Army of the Potomac, including the Wilderness, both engagements at Fredricksburg, Fair Oaks, Antietam and Gettysburg. He passed through the ranks of promotion to first lieutenant of Company I, was subsequently adjutant and major of the regiment. He married Ella Hansell, of Rancocas, and had children: Ella, Ella M. and James H. The daughter is the wife of Richard Williams, of Plainfield, New Jersey, and the son is a farmer at Moorestown. 2. Sarah A., resides with her younger brother at Hartford. 3. Martha B., died at Philadelphia while the wife of Thompson Shrouds. 4. William Penn, treated below.

(VIII) William Penn, younger son of William and Elizabeth (Roberts) Lippincott, was born March 22, 1850, at Mt. Laurel, New Jersey, and was educated in a rate school, such as prevailed in his time. When sixteen years of age he left home and went to Philadelphia to learn the art of bricklaying. After four years of apprenticeship he continued five years in the occupation, as a journeyman and later as a builder. In 1876 he returned to New Jersey and purchased a country store at Hartford, where he has ever since made his home. He conducted this store for thirty years and still owns the building, having leased it in 1906 on the occasion of his election to the office of surrogate of Burlington county for a term of five years, which he is now efficiently serving. For four terms he served as collector of his township and was three terms a representative in the legislature. Like most of his con-

freres he is a Republican in political principles, and is by birthright a member of the Society of Friends. He is a charter member of Moorestown Lodge, No. 158, A. F. and A. M., and was the second master of the lodge which he also served for a period of sixteen years as secretary. He is also a member of the Benevolent and Protective Order of Elks, affiliating with Mt. Holly Lodge, No. 848. As a careful, shrewd business man, Mr. Lippincott has been successful, and he brings to the fulfillment of his public duties the same faithful care of details and intelligent interest in his work which has characterized his private career. He married, November 6, 1873, Abbie E. Hollingshead, who was born in Moorestown, a daughter of Enoch and Rachel (Atkinson) Hollingshead, the last named being a member of the Society of Friends. Mr. and Mrs. Lippincott are the parents of two children: Franklin Richard and Elizabeth Roberts. The son is a resident of Hartford, New Jersey, and the daughter of Medford, same state, being the wife of Jacob Kay Haines.

(For first generation see preceding sketch).

(II) Freedom, fifth child
LIPPINCOTT   and fourth son of Richard and Abigail Lippincott, was born in Stonehouse, near Plymouth, Devonshire, England, September 1, 165—, died in Burlington county, West Jersey, in 1697, the inventory on his estate being dated June 13 of that year. He was a tanner and lived near Rancocas creek, where the king's highway crossed the stream and very near where the town of Bridgeborough now stands. Having sold the land in Salem county given him by his father, he located two hundred and eighty-eight acres here in 1687, and settled thereon. To the trade of a tanner he probably added that of a smith, and could shoe a horse or "upset" the axes of his neighbors with some skill, but his proficiency cost him his life, for in the summer of 1697, while shoeing a horse, he was killed by lightning. His widow and five children survived him, the oldest being but thirteen years of age. His descendants of his name are most numerous in the western townships of Camden and Burlington counties.

October 4, 1680, Freedom Lippincott married Mary Curtis, and their five children were: 1. Samuel, born December 24, 1684, died in 1760; married Hope, daughter of John and Hope (Delefaste) Wills. 2. Thomas, referred to below. 3. Judith, August 22, 1689, died August 22, 1745; married Joseph, son of

Thomas and Mary (Bernard) Stokes. 4. Mary, November 21, 1691, married Edward Peake. 5. Freedom Jr., February 6, 1693, died about 1764; married Elizabeth, daughter of John and Hope (Delefaste) Wills, referred to above.

(III) Thomas, second child and son of Freedom and Mary (Curtis) Lippincott, was born in Shrewsbury, Monmouth county, December 28, 1686, died in Chester township, Burlington county, November 5, 1759. In 1708 he purchased a tract of one thousand and thirty-four acres, extending from Penisaukin river to Swedes' run, joining the No-se-ne-men-si-on tract reserved for the Indians, from which the modern name of Cinnaminson is derived. On the northern border of this tract the village of Westfield now stands. The name was originally given to the meeting house which was erected in 1800, in Thomas Lippincott's western field. Thomas Lippincott was an active and useful man in the affairs of Chester township, in which his lands were then included. His first house, built about 1711, stood where the old Samuel L. Allen residence was about thirty years ago, and in it and a second house built upon the same site his descendants lived for one hundred and thirty years. The first meeting of Friends in this district was held in his house and there subsequent meetings continued to be held until 1800. The descendants of his son Nathaniel are now to be found in Burlington county, New Jersey, in Philadelphia, and in the state of Illinois, General Charles Ellet Lippincott, former auditor of the last mentioned state, being among them.

December 19, 1711, Thomas Lippincott married (first) Mary, daughter of John, son of Richard and Margaret Haines, the emigrants, and his first wife, Esther, daughter of John and Ann Borton, the emigrants. She was born April 20, 1693, and died after bearing her husband six children: 1. Nathaniel, born July 2, 1713, married Mary Engle. 2. Isaac, referred to below. 3. Thomas, married, 1745, Rachel Eldridge. 4. Abigail, married Thomas Wallis or Thomas Wills. 5. Esther, married John Roberts. 6. Mary, who died unmarried. Thomas Lippincott married (second) Mercy, widow of Thomas Middleton, who bore him three more children: 7. Patience, married Ebenezer Andrews. 8. Phebe. 9. Mercy, married Ephraim Stiles. Thomas Lippincott married (third) Rachel Smith, a widow. There is no record of children.

(IV) Isaac, second child and son of Thomas

and Mary (Haines) Lippincott, was born in Chester township, Burlington county, died in Westfield, in the same county. All of his descendants settled on part of their grandfather's tract in Cinnaminson and Chester townships, Burlington county, and in Philadelphia. Among them should be mentioned Joshua, a cloth merchant of that city, and Samuel R., a director of the National State Bank of Camden, New Jersey. In 1739 Isaac Lippincott married Hannah, daughter of John Engle and Mary, daughter of Samuel and Jane Ogborn, the emigrants, and granddaughter of Robert and Jane (Horne) Engle, the emigrants. Their seven children were: 1. Samuel, married Priscilla Bryant. 2. Isaac, married Elizabeth Antrim. 3. Thomas, referred to below. 4. Mary, married Abraham Eldridge. 5. Hannah, married (first) Jacob Lippincott, and (second) John Cahill. 6. Bathsheba, who died unmarried. 7. Esther, who died unmarried.

(V) Thomas (2), third child and son of Isaac and Hannah (Engle) Lippincott, was born in Westfield, and died there. August 15, 1767, he procured a license to marry Elizabeth, daughter of Nathan or Nathaniel and Mary (Hervey) Haines, granddaughter of William, son of Richard and Margaret Haines, the emigrants, and Sarah, daughter of John Paine, the emigrant, and Elizabeth Field. They had three children: 1. William, referred to below. 2. Thomas, married Abigail Borton. 3. Mary, married Thomas Rakestraw.

(VI) William, son of Thomas (2) and Elizabeth (Haines) Lippincott, was born in Chester, now Cinnaminson township, Burlington county, in 1770 or 1771, died there April 7, 1813. He lived on a part of the original one thousand and thirty-four acre tract purchased by his great-grandfather on Swedes' run, where all of his children were born. September 11, 1793, he married Ann, born near Mt. Holly, February 16, 1770, died in Westfield, December 12, 1822, the ninth child and fifth daughter of William Rogers, of Northampton township, Burlington county, and Martha "Esturgans," that being the name on the marriage bond possibly since the name has never been found elsewhere, Martha Esther Gans or Gano. William Rogers was a revolutionary soldier, and April 4, 1781, was disowned by the Mt. Holly Meeting for his military acts. He was the son of William Rogers, of New Hanover, and Elizabeth, daughter of Thomas Branson, of New Jersey and Virginia, and Elizabeth, daughter of John Day, of Philadelphia, the emigrant, and Elizabeth, sister to Peter Hervey. William was the son of Lieutenant William and Abigail Rogers, of Burlington. The children of William and Ann (Rogers) Lippincott were: 1. Amasa, born July 3, 1794, died February 26, 1862; married (first) Esther Collins, and (second) Hannah Bishop. 2. William, January 8, 1798, died May 7, 1879; married Catherine Rudderow. 3. Israel, May 17, 1800, died May 9, 1879; married (first) Maria Wallace, and (second) Atlantic Warrington. 4. Martha, March 3, 1802, died May, 1884; married Timothy Paxson, of Pennsylvania. 5. Thomas, referred to below. 6. Ann, November 30, 1805, died January 10, 1879, unmarried. 7. Benjamin, February 6, 1808, died March 24, 1832, at Tampico, Mexico. 8. Clayton, January 19, 1810, died December 26, 1891; married Rachel Collins. 9. Elizabeth, April 6, 1812, died August 3, 1834; married Nathan Hunt Conrow.

(VII) Thomas (3), son of William and Ann Lippincott, was born in Cinnaminson (formerly Chester township), New Jersey, February 8, 1804. He spent his boyhood on the parental farm. His father's death, in 1813, left the management of affairs with the mother and the older children, until her death in 1822. Thomas was apprenticed at the age of fifteen years to learn blacksmithing with Abram Lippincott, of Westfield, where he remained until he reached his majority. In 1825 he settled in Fellowship, Mt. Laurel township, as a blacksmith, and is said to have constructed, under a farmer's wagon, the first pair of elliptic springs that carried a load of farm produce to Philadelphia. In 1856 he gave up his trade and turned his attention to raising fruits and berries with fair success. He planted an orchard of the best varieties of fruits when past fifty years old, and lived to reap the profit of it in his old age. He was a strong character, honest in his dealings, firm in his convictions of the truth, and plain of speech. He was a great reader with a very retentive memory, and few men were better informed in the history of the country. After his decease, which occurred February 16, 1895, the *Philadelphia Record* noted the death of "the venerable Thomas Lippincott, aged ninety-one years, and one of the most scholarly farmers of the county of Burlington." He married, in 1831, Honnah, daughter of William and Rachel (Borden) Rudderow, of Chester, who was born May 9, 1812. She was a devoted wife and mother, a member of the Society of

Friends, and died August 8, 1863, leaving children: Lydia R., Lusanna, Emma, William R., and Eliza, who married Nathan S. Roberts, of Camden, New Jersey, and their children are Wilmer L., Alvin T. and Elizabeth.

(VIII) William Rudderow, only son of Thomas (3) and Hannah (Rudderow) Lippincott, was born in Fellowship, Burlington county, December 15, 1843. He received most of his education in very early life from Samuel Smith, a famous mathematician who taught a boarding school at Fellowship more than fifty years ago. William inherited his father's strong constitution and retentive memory, but his mother's early training did much toward shaping his course through life. He began to teach school at seventeen years of age, and after attaining his majority took an interest in public affairs. He held office for a number of years in his township, and, like his father, was fairly successful in farming and fruit growing. He became connected with the New Jersey state board of agriculture, was instrumental in shipping the agricultural and horticultural products of the state to several Expositions, and in 1897 was made treasurer of the board. He took great interest in the movement for improving the common roads in New Jersey, and was appointed engineer in charge of the construction of a number of the macadam roads in the vicinity of Moorestown. He became connected with the Burlington County Safe Deposit and Trust Company soon after its organization, and in 1902 was made its treasurer. In 1903 he was elected vice-president of the Moorestown National Bank, and after the death of the president in 1906 was elected to the presidency. Mr. Lippincott married Tacie, eldest daughter of the late Hon. Chalkley Albertson, of Camden county, and, like many other men, owes much of his success to the good counsel and help of his wife. Their home, "Gillingham Place," near Mt. Laurel, is one of the landmarks of the neighborhood.

AUSTIN The name Austin is an old English contraction of the Latin Augustinus, the cognomen of the family of Augustus, and meaning originally, "venerable," "worthy of honor"; and the family that bears the name in New Jersey have a record which fully bears out their right to the title, from the time that the founder of the family arrived among the earliest of the settlers down to the present day.

(I) Francis Austin, founder of the family, came over to West Jersey from England some time before December 24, 1688, when he bought fifty acres on Birch creek from John Antram. This is as yet the first Austin record that has come to light. May 3, 1689, Francis bought another fifty acres adjoining his first lot from Percival Towle, and November 1, 1694, he sold the entire one hundred acres to Thomas Scattergood Jr. In all of these deeds he is styled as a resident of Burlington and a carpenter. Four years previous to the sale of this land, Francis Austin had bought another one hundred and fifty acres of Symon Charles, April 2, 1690, and this he in turn sold January 2, 1695, to George Porter; as about a month previously, December 10, 1694, he had purchased from Henry and Mary Grubb and Thomas and Abigail Raper a large farm of three hundred and fifty acres in Evesham township, on which he finally made his home and spent the remainder of his life. About a year later he made his final acquisition of land by buying from Thomas Wilkins, whose land adjoined his own, a small tract of three acres which logically went with his own property. Where Francis Austin came from in England has not yet been discovered, but he emigrated to this country as a young man accompanied by his sister, Elizabeth, who, in 1692, married Thomas, son of Richard and Margaret Haines, the emigrants. His will, which is undated, was proven July 30, 1723, the inventory of his personal estate, amounting to £280, having been made by John Sharp and Thomas Wilkins, the preceding day.

In 1696 Francis Austin was married in the Chester monthly meeting to Mary, daughter of John and Ann Borton, the emigrants, who bore him ten children, the last one being posthumous. Children: 1. Amos, referred to below. 2. William, married (first) in 1741, Mary Robeson, and (second) in 1749, Hannah Thomas. 3. Jonathan, married, 1747, Rebecca Mason. 4. Mary, married, as her first husband, William Sharp. 5. Elizabeth, married, 1719, Henry Warrington. 6. Sarah, married, 1725, Nathan Haines. 7. Ann, married, 1727, Josiah Albertson. · 8. Hannah, married, 1735, William Sharp. 9. Martha, married, 1744, John Highston. 10. Francis, married, 1748, Deborah Allen.

(II) Amos, eldest son of Francis and Mary (Borton) Austin, was born in Evesham township, Burlington county, and died there in 1770, his will, written January 15, 1763, being proven by affirmation December 15, of that year. In 1736, the license being obtained September 27, he married Esther, daughter of Caleb Haines and Sarah, daughter of Henry and Elizabeth (Hudson) Burr. Caleb was the son of John, son of Richard and Margaret Haines, the emigrants, by his wife, Esther, daughter of John and Ann Borton, the emigrants, and sister to Mary, wife of Francis Austin (1). Children of Amos and Esther (Haines) Austin: 1. Caleb, married, 1758, Lydia Mason. 2. Vesti, married, 1754, John Rogers. 3. Mary, married, 1761, John Somers. 4. Seth, referred to below. 5. Patience, married, 1771, John Mott. 6. Esther, married either John Wright or Isaac Barber. 7. Amos, Jr.

(III) Seth, fourth child and second son of Amos and Esther (Haines) Austin, was born in Evesham township, and died in 1822, in Wellingborough township, Burlington county. His father, in his will, left him "Five shillings, he haveing received his full part before the date hereof." In his own will, written April 2, 1815, when he was "weak of body," he disposes merely of his moveable property, which was inventoried after his death at $1,079.56½, and his home plantation, which he leaves to his youngest son, Caleb, on condition that he pays certain legacies to his brothers and sisters mentioned before. He mentions his wife, but only to leave her $400, a clock, and provision for her maintenance. Seth Austin was married three times and as yet it is impossible to determine which of his children were borne him by each union. The first four were undoubtedly by the first wife, Hannah, and possibly the fifth and sixth. The seventh was undoubtedly by his second wife, Lydia Naylor, whom he married in 1770, and she may have been the mother of his three youngest children also, or one or all of these may have been the children of his third wife, Sarah, who survived him. Children of Seth Austin: 1. Letitia, who is said to have married an Austin. 2. Cain, referred to below. 3. Seth. 4. Hannah, married, 1795, Thomas Bizby. 5. Vashti, married a Gardiner. 6. Esther, married a Hammel. 7. Lydia, married a Naylor. 8. Abigail, married a Pippit. 9. Amos. 10. Caleb.

(IV) Cain, second child and eldest son of Seth and Hannah Austin, was born in Wellingborough township, Burlington county, December 2, 1766. He married Tabitha, daughter of Hezekiah and Gertrude (Hammel) Garwood; children: 1. Samuel, born November 26, 1789; served in the war of 1812, and about 1820 went to Ohio. 2. Hannah, May 1, 1792; married William Fenimore Smith, of Burlington. 3. Hezekiah, February 5, 1794; served in the war of 1812. 4. Rebecca, April 9, 1797; married Pearson Johnson. 5. Gertrude, August 2, 1799. 6. Joseph, November 25, 1801. 7. Seth, May 17, 1804. 8. David, September 24, 1806. 9. Charles, referred to below. 10. Esther, July 26, 1814; married Josiah Vennel.

(V) Charles, ninth child and sixth son of Cain and Tabitha (Garwood) Austin, was born at Bridgeborough, Burlington county, June 4, 1810. He married Ann, born at Rising Sun village, Philadelphia, Pennsylvania, February 9, 1813, and still living (1909), daughter of Peter and Susanna (Neglee) Dull. They had ten children, only two of whom are now living: 1. Samuel C. 2. William. 3. Evelyn. 4. Edwin. 5. Miriam. 6. Ann Elizabeth. 7. Charles, now a sergeant of police in Philadelphia, who married Rosanna Catherine Segrest, and has one child, Miriam, married Morris Simmons, of Philadelphia. 8. George H. 9. Lemuel. 10. Eliza, referred to below.

(VI) Eliza, youngest child and sixth daughter of Charles and Ann (Dull) Austin, was born in Philadelphia, Pennsylvania, and is now living in that city at 1024 Brown street, having her office at 501 Witherspoon building. For her early education she was sent to the public schools of Philadelphia, and then she entered the Pierce Business College. Later she became connected as clerk and secretary with several religious newspapers, and in December, 1898, became the secretary and treasurer of the religious magazine entitled *Over Sea and Land*, published by the Women's Home and Foreign Missionary Society of the Presbyterian Church, at Philadelphia. This position she is now holding.

(For preceding generations see preceding sketch).

AUSTIN

(V) Seth Austin, seventh child and fourth son of Cain and Tabitha (Garwood) Austin, was born May 17, 1804. He married Martha (Mathis) Mathis, daughter of Barzillai and Elizabeth (Edwards) Mathis, and the widow of Samuel, son of Hezekiah Mathis, to whom she had borne two children: 1. Elmira, married a Mr. Senderling, and had two daughters. 2. Robert. Her grandparents were James Edwards, of Barnegat, and Micajah, son of John Mathis (or Matthews), the emigrant, and his wife, Alice, daughter of Edward Andrews, the founder of Tuckerton, and widow of John Higbee. Her grandmother was Mercy, daughter of Joshua and Jane Shreve, of Upper Springfield, Burlington county. Children of

Seth and Martha (Mathis) (Mathis) Austin were: 1. Sarah, married George W. Williamson, of Philadelphia, and had children: George W., William, Mary, Charles, Anna, Clara and John. 2. Charles Seth, referred to below. 3. Mary, married Thomas Field, of Philadelphia, and had Martha, Sarah, Elizabeth, Mary, Charles, Emma, Henry, Alfred, Edwin, Walter and Austin.

(VI) Charles Seth, the only son of Seth and Martha (Mathis) (Mathis) Austin, lived in Philadelphia, and was for twenty-five years the teller of the People's Bank in that city. He married Margaret Roe, daughter of —— and Sarah (Van Horne) Brower; children: 1. Robert Seth, referred to below. 2. William Putt. 3. Charles Seth, Jr. 4. Thomas Jefferson, born July 4, 1855. 5. Martha, married Frank P. Fisher, of Tacony, Philadelphia, and has two children: Roy and Linden. 6. Mary Ellen. 7. Ellen Marcy McClellan. 8. George B. McClellan.

(VII) Robert Seth, eldest child of Charles Seth and Margaret Roe (Brower) Austin, was born in Philadelphia, August 16, 1849, and is now living in that city with his office in room 801, of the Reading Terminal building, on Market street. He attended the public schools of Philadelphia and the Philadelphia Academy of Fine Arts, where he studied art. After leaving school he was for a time in the office of Henry Disston & Company, the saw manufacturers. He next learned the art of glass cutting and the decorating of glass globes. Then he became connected with the Reading railroad in 1866, or rather at that time the road that he was with was called the North Pennsylvania railroad, and ran from Bethlehem to Philadelphia, Pennsylvania. His position here was that of dispatching clerk. This road subsequently, in 1879, became a part of the Reading railroad system, and Mr. Austin became chief clerk in the auditor's department of the latter road, with his offices in the Reading Terminal. He has been for over forty years connected with the railroad where he still remains. Mr. Austin is a Republican, and is not a member of any church although he attends the Baptist and Methodist churches. He is a member of the "Order of Spartans," a member of the Reading railroad veteran employees association, employment by the railroad for twenty-five years being necessary before one can be eligible to this association. Mr. Austin was born with an innate natural faculty for art and painting. This fact together with his art studies at the art school in Philadelphia have made it possible for him to secure a number of prizes given at art exhibitions in the city of Philadelphia and elsewhere, notwithstanding his responsible position as chief clerk of the auditing department of the Reading railroad, which of course requires most of his time and attention. Mr. Austin seems to have quite as much ability as a marine artist as a landscape painter, which is unusual.

Robert Seth Austin married Mary Lawson, who is now dead. Their children were: 1. George Wise, deceased; married Jennie Carnahan, and has two children: Mildred and Dorothy. 2. Charles Seth, married Mazie Weldon, and has Charles Weldon, Frank Cody, Bertha and Russell. 3. Robert Matthew. 4. Henry Washington Rihl, now living in Texas. 5. Margaretta, died at the age of seven years.

WOLCOTT A distinguished family of this name has illuminated the pages of New England history, and any Wolcott would be honored by such a progenitor as Henry Wolcott, the immigrant, who by his wife, Elizabeth Saunders, had a son, Simon, who married Martha Pitkin before 1779. They were honored by a son, Roger, who was born in the frontier town of Windsor, Connecticut colony, January 4, 1679, was made a member of the general assembly of the colony in 1709; was placed upon the bench of justices of the local court of the colony in 1710; was commissary of the Connecticut stores in the expedition against Canada in 1711; was a member of the colonial council in 1714; judge of the county court, 1724; of the superior court 1732; deputy governor and chief justice of the supreme court in 1741. He was commissioned major general in the expedition against Louisburg in 1745, by Governor Shirley, of Massachusetts, and held rank second only to Pepperell. On returning from that expedition he was elected governor of Connecticut, and served as such 1750-54. He died in Windsor, May 17, 1767. His son by his wife, Sarah Drake, Oliver, born in Windsor, November 26, 1726, was a graduate of Yale; a captain in the volunteer army sent to protest the north frontier against the French and Indians; became a student of medicine; was the first sheriff of Litchfield county, 1751-71; representative in the general assembly, 1764-70; assistant to the governor, 1771-86; judge of the court of probate, 1772-95; chief judge court of common pleas, 1774-86; held the rank of colonel in the state militia for 1774; delegate to continental congress,

1775-78; one of the immortal signers of the Declaration of Independence, adopted July 4, 1776; was promoted to brigadier-general, 1779; member of continental congress, 1780-83; lieutenant governor of Connecticut, 1786-96; governor of the state, 1796-97, and died in Litchfield, December, 1797. His son by his wife, Lorroene Collins, to whom he was married, January 21, 1755, was named Oliver (2). He was born in Litchfield, January 11, 1760; graduating at Yale, class of 1778; served with his father in the colonial and revolutionary wars; was member of the committee of the pay-table, 1782-88; comptroller of public accounts, 1788-89. auditor, 1789-91; comptroller United States treasury, 1791-95; secretary of the United States treasury, 1795-1800; governor of Connecticut, 1817-27; and died in New York, June 1, 1833. His great-grandson through his son, Frederick, and Elizabeth Huntington, his grandson, Joshua, and Cornelia Frothingham, was Roger Wolcott, born in Boston, July 13, 1847; died there December 21, 1900. He graduated at Harvard, in the class of 1870; was lieutenant governor of Massachusetts, 1892-95; governor, 1895-98. That the New Jersey Wolcotts are from the same stock is undoubted, but their direct connection with Henry, the immigrant ancestor of the Connecticut Wolcotts, has not been established. The first known ancestor of the New Jersey Wolcotts is Samuel Wolcott (see forward).

(I) Samuel Wolcott died at Tintonfalls, in the township of Shrewsbury, Monmouth county, New Jersey, about 1693 or 1694. He apparently married a Widow Williams who brought him a stepson, Edward Williams. She also gave birth by her marriage to Samuel Wolcott to a son, Nathaniel (see forward) who became the progenitor of all the Wolcotts in New Jersey, except those who came within the last century from Connecticut, and who have an established line of descent from Henry, of Windsor, Connecticut.

(III) Peter, probably son of Nathaniel, and grandson of Samuel Wolcott, had a son, Henry, see forward.

(IV) Henry, son of Peter Wolcott, was born in Shrewsbury township, New Jersey, about 1690; died in 1750. He married but the name of his wife is not known. He had a son, Benjamin, see forward.

(V) Benjamin, son of Henry Wolcott, was born in Shrewsbury, New Jersey, July 18, 1724; died in 1790. He married (first) in 1749, Rachel Wainwright, who died without issue. He married (second) February 27, 1753, Clementine Cook, and among their children was Benjamin, see forward.

(VI) Benjamin (2), eldest son of Benjamin (1) and Clementine (Cook) Wolcott, was born 1758; married Ann Lewis, and their first son was Benjamin, see forward.

(VII) Benjamin (3), eldest son of Benjamin (2) and Ann (Lewis) Wolcott, was born in Shrewsbury, Monmouth county, New Jersey, 1789. He married Phebe, daughter of Jeffrey, and they lived in Eatontown, Monmouth county, New Jersey, where their son Edmond, see forward, was born.

(VIII) Edmond, son of Benjamin (3) and Phebe (Jeffrey) Wolcott, was born in Eatontown, Monmouth county, New Jersey, May 14, 1816. He married Sarah Ann, daughter of John and Sarah Dangler, and they had a son William Henry, see forward.

(IX) William Henry, son of Edmond and Sarah Ann (Dangler) Wolcott, was born in Eatontown, Monmouth county, New Jersey, February 15, 1846. He was a farmer of Eatontown, where he spent his life, and died January 21, 1889. He was a member of Independent Order of Odd Fellows. He married Martha M., daughter of Charles W. and Mary A. Higginson, of Shropshire, England, and they had two children, born in Eatontown, New Jersey, as follows: 1. Edith Maude, March 20, 1877, unmarried. 2. Wilfred Bonsieur, see forward.

(X) Wilfred Bonsieur, only son and second child of William Henry and Martha M. (Higginson) Wolcott, was born in Eatontown, Monmouth county, New Jersey, March 11, 1880. He was a student in the public schools of Eatontown, the high school of Long Branch, New Jersey, graduating in the class of 1897, and from the University of Pennsylvania, department of law, LL. B., 1900. He was admitted to the New Jersey bar November, 1901, as an attorney, and was made a counsellor in November, 1904, in conformity with the laws of the state which impose a legal practice of three years as an attorney-at-law, before being admitted as an attorney and counsellor-at-law, at which time they come into general practice in all the courts of the state. He was appointed assistant city council of the city of Camden, January 1, 1907, and was made a member of the Camden County Bar Association, and of the Camden Republican Club. He affiliated with the Independent Order of Odd Fellows through membership in Amity Lodge, No. 166, of Camden, New Jersey, and with

the Junior Order of American Mechanics through the membership in Diamond Council, No. 14, of Swedesboro, New Jersey. His college affiliations include membership—the Alumni Association of the University of Pennsylvania and of the Alumni Association of the Law Department of the University of Pennsylvania. His church affiliation is with the Methodist Episcopal denomination through membership in the Methodist Episcopal church of Merchantville, New Jersey.

He married, March 18, 1902, Mary Aline, daughter of J. Howard and Lydia Kirkbride, of Camden, New Jersey. Children, born in Merchantville, New Jersey, as follows: 1. Mary, August 20, 1904. 2. Wilfred Bonsieur (2), May 17, 1906.

CAMPION	This family was founded in New Jersey by a boy who came over as an apprentice and was associated with the Quakers, although he does not seem to have been a member of the society. Many of his descendants now reside in the vicinity of Burlington, New Jersey, where he settled.

(I) John Campion is supposed to have been born in Northamptonshire, England. According to the family tradition, he came from Yorkshire, which seems very probable, as the party with which he came doubtless sailed from the town of Hull in Yorkshire. He was probably less than fifteen years of age on his arrival, and he lived as an apprentice in the home of John Eves, whose wife, Mary (Stokes) Eves, was born in Northamptonshire and it is supposed that John Campion came under the instruction of John Eves through the relatives of the latter's wife. As a member of the Eves household, young Campion undoubtedly attended the Friends Meetings. He learned the trade of carpenter under the instruction of Eves, and after the latter's sudden death he received a legacy by will dated June 25, 1738. Campion evidently continued to reside in Evesham township, where he was married by license, May 12, 1752, to Mary, daughter of Samuel and Mary (Shinn) Eves, of Evesham (see Eves II). She was a birthright Friend, and in 1759 she made acknowledgement of marriage out of meeting at the Evesham meeting and was received again into full membership of the society. About 1760 John Campion moved to the neighborhood of Burlington, and in 1762 his wife presented a certificate of removal from the Evesham meeting to that of Burlington. In 1766 and 1767, by two purchases, John Campion acquired from Jacob. and William Wills, respectively, two tracts of land amounting to one hundred and fourteen acres together with a dwelling house. This plantation is located in what was then the eastern part of Northampton township, now Southampton township, about one mile northeast of the village of Vincentown. The house has been somewhat altered but is still standing and occupied by Harry Bowne, the present owner. Here John Campion resided and died between July 22 and August 13, 1774, the dates respectively of signing and probating of his will. His younger brother, Richard Campion, born 1733, came to New Jersey, but the date of his arrival does not appear. He was married March 22, 1753. by license, to Sarah Borradaille. In December, 1767, he was accidentally shot while duck hunting at Long Beach, New Jersey, and letters of administration were granted to his brother, John Campion, and his widow, Sarah Campion, January 8, 1768. John Campion's wife died before him. Children: Joseph, mentioned below; Sarah, married, November 23, 1777, Joab, son of Benjamin and Elizabeth (Carter) Jones.

(II) Joseph, only son of John and Mary (Eves) Campion, was born March 26, 1753, in Evesham, died September 23, 1829, on his father's plantation in Southampton, which he inherited. He was not a birthright Quaker, but applied November 6, 1775, to the Burlington Monthly Meeting for admittance to the Society, and after examination by a committee appointed for that purpose he was admitted the following month. He was married by Friend ceremony early in 1776, probably at the home of the bride, to Mary, daughter of Francis and Zilpha Venicomb. Shortly after his marriage he took up residence upon his father-in-law's plantation and there continued until the death of Mr. Venicomb in 1785, after which he returned to his own plantation and continued there the remainder of his life. In accordance with the principles of the Friends, he took no part in the revolutionary war and seems not to have participated in the management of civil affairs, though he enjoyed the respect and confidence of the community and served frequently as executor and administrator of estates. During the last fourteen years of his life, he was confined to the house with palsy, an affliction which he bore with great patience and composure of mind. He survived his wife, who was born December 4, 1755, died April 13, 1826, and both were buried

ii—10

in the burying ground at the meeting house in Mount Holly. Children: 1. Sarah, born November 10, 1776; married, February 2, 1802, William Penn Horner; died December 5, 1853. 2. John, mentioned below. 3. Richard, May 23, 1782; was a prominent business man, member of state assembly and of the governor's council, died in March, 1850. 4. Francis, April 24, 1784, died June 21, 1841. 5. Joseph, September 13, 1786, died April 29, 1861. 6. Stacy Budd, mentioned below. 7. William, June 30, 1793, died August 9, 1827.

(III) John (2), eldest son of Joseph and Mary (Venicomb) Campion, was born March 3, 1779, in Southampton, died March 19, 1855. He was educated in the country schools of Northampton, and was still a boy when apprenticed to Benjamin Hooton, a hatter of Philadelphia, whose residence and shop was No. 14 North Second street. The confining work of a hatter was distasteful to Campion, and after completing his apprenticeship he returned to the active out-door life of the farm. He rented from Benjamin Cooper a farm adjacent to that of his father, on which he resided until his retirement. He married, February 2, 1804, Sarah Hall, born May 13, 1782, died November 3, 1830, daughter of James and Sarah (Wynne) Hall. James Hall was a native of London, a clock maker by trade, and settled in Germantown, Pennsylvania, where he married in 1772 Sarah, daughter of John and Sarah (Pastorius) Wynne, of that place. After the death of his wife, his daughter Sarah removed to the home of her mother's sister, Anne, wife of Thomas (2) Hooton, of Burlington, New Jersey. The latter was a nephew of John Campion's preceptor, and was also a hatter by trade. Here Sarah Hall met John Campion to whom she was married by Samuel Bispham, a justice of the peace. She was well educated, wrote a fine hand and her gracious manners and charming disposition won the love and respect of the community. Her death was caused by consumption after many years of suffering and she was buried in the Friends burying ground at Mount Holly. After all her children were married, her husband retired and resided with his brother, Stacy B., at Campion's Hotel, at Mount Holly, and spent the remainder of his life either there or with one or another of his children. They were: 1. Charles Hall, born February 2, 1805, died February 2, 1840. 2. James, June 10, 1806, died February 14, 1836. 3. Joseph Hall, mentioned below. 4. Sarah, April 9, 1813; married, March 31, 1835, Rev. Josiah Flint

Canfield; died January 23, 1840. 5. Benjamin Cooper, March 14, 1815, died February 2, 1898. 6. Elizabeth, March 22, 1817; married, November 2, 1840, George Digdale; died November 9, 1844. 7. Rebecca, died aged two years.

(IV) Joseph Hall, third son of John and Sarah (Hall) Campion, was born June 12, 1808, in Southampton, died December 1, 1895, in Philadelphia. He was educated at the country schools in Northampton; he was so small at the age of fifteen years that his father believed he would never grow large enough to engage in the arduous labors of the farm. He accordingly apprenticed him to learn the trade of cabinet-maker under the instruction of Mr. William Fling, of Philadelphia, whose place of business was located at 435 Chestnut street (old number). He became rapidly skilled in the use of tools and developed a taste for mechanics, largely inherited from several of his forebears. He grew in body to such an extent that although slender he stood nearly six feet in height. He was very active and particularly fond of athletics, being a very proficient skater upon ice. After completing his term of apprenticeship he took employment with John Millington, civil engineer and machinist, formerly a professor of mathematics in the Royal Institute of Great Britain and of natural philosophy in Gays Hospital, London. Mr. Millington engaged in business in Philadelphia as an importer and manufacturer of engineering supplies. Mr. Campion did not remain long with him. Upon leaving this employment, Mr. Campion received from him a letter of recommendation, saying in part, "He is an excellent workman of very steady and industrious habits and perfectly sober, honest, and honorable in all his dealings, and quite worthy of the confidence of any person with whom he may form an engagement of business, besides which, he is of a good tempered and obliging disposition. The only reason of our parting was his desire to travel and visit the different parts of his native country, and as I part with him with regret, I voluntarily and without his request, offer him this testimonial of my regard for him and my approbation of his conduct, while he was with me, thinking it might prove of use to him in any new connections he may form with strangers, who would be unable to appreciate his merits before they became acquainted with him." Mr. Campion traveled for a time through the south and returned in 1834 to Philadelphia, where he engaged in the manufacture of furniture in partnership with Thomas Moore under the style of Moore & Campion, their factory and offices being located at 261 South Second street. For thirty-five years this business was successfully conducted, and when the proprietors retired it was continued several years by Mr. Campion's son, in partnership with another under the firm name of Smith & Campion. Joseph H. Campion was a Republican in politics and an abolitionist, but took no active part in the war of the rebellion. He became a member of the Union League Club of Philadelphia shortly after its formation. He resided for many years at 236 Pine street, Philadelphia, whence he removed to 327 South Seventeenth street, where his death occurred at the advanced age of eighty-eight years, having survived his wife for a period of sixteen years. He married, January 17, 1839, Martha Reeve, born December 28, 1816, died September 30, 1879, daughter of Richard and Sarah (Sleeper) Reeve. Both are buried in the family lot in South Laurel Hill cemetery, Philadelphia. Children: 1. John W., born February 29, 1840, died January 7, 1907. 2. Richard Reeve, February 11, 1842, died February 2, 1881. 3. Harry Clifford, mentioned below.

(V) Harry Clifford, third son of Joseph Hall and Martha (Reeve) Campion, was born August 13, 1846, in Philadelphia, died November 15, 1905, in that city. He was educated at the Friends Central School at Philadelphia, and at the age of seventeen years entered the employ of Joel Bailey & Company, where he continued six years. As a result of a severe strain, he was obliged to take a vacation in the year 1869 and traveled through the far west, spending considerable time in California. On his return to Philadelphia he engaged in business with his brother, John W. Campion, and so continued until the time of his death, which was the result of an accident. He married, April 28, 1877, Ann Mary Keen, born December 18, 1850, daughter of James Styles and Emily Eliza (Catherwood) Keen. She, with an only son, survives him.

(VI) Harry Clifford (2), only son of Harry Clifford (1) and Ann Mary (Keen) Campion, was born February 13, 1878, in Philadelphia, and resides in Media, Delaware county, Pennsylvania. He married, June 16, 1903, Mable Maria Campion, daughter of William H. and Emma Jane (Shepard) Campion. Children: Ann Louise, born June 5, 1904; Richard Reeve. May 7, 1906; John Wynne, September 30, 1907, died before one year old; Emma Jane, March 1, 1909.

Richard Campion

(III) Stacy Budd, fifth son of Joseph and Mary (Venicomb) Campion, was born August 17, 1791, in Southampton, died April 16, 1866, in Camden, New Jersey. He was named for his father's family physician, a famous practician residing in Mount Holly. Stacy B. Campion attended the public schools near his home, and early engaged in business with Henry Burr, Jr., at Lumberton, New Jersey, under the firm name of Campion & Burr. This partnership was dissolved June 13, 1820, and the business was continued by Mr. Campion for a few years. Before 1828 he removed to Mount Holly where he succeeded Griffith Owen as proprietor of the Black Horse Tavern, which formerly stood on the east side of Main street, one door above Mill street. In the year 1833 Mr. Campion purchased the State Arms Hotel, on the opposite side of the street, occupying the southern portion of the ground now occupied by the Arcade Hotel. This historic old hostelry has been continuously in business since before the revolutionary war and on its ancient sign board was painted the arms of the state of New Jersey, with the motto: ' Peace, Liberty and Safety.'' Mr. Campion enlarged the hotel to double its former size and conducted it five years, at the end of which time he sold out and removed to a farm near Vincentown. In 1843 he went to Camden, New Jersey, where he rented the Cooper's Point ferry property and hotel of William Cooper and was succeeded by William Cooper's grandson, William Wood Cooper, who had married his only surviving daughter. Returning to Mount Holly, Mr. Campion purchased the Washington Hotel, sometimes called the Upper Hotel, and continued there in business for about ten years. At the end of this period, he sold out to Morgan Lippincott and returned to Camden, where he lived in retirement until his death. He was a man of very genial, hospitable manner, and well-known throughout the state particularly among the members of the legal profession, many of whom were his guests while attending court at Mount Holly. He served as one of the assessors of Northampton township in 1840-41-42. He married, June 20, 1820, Maria Dungan, born February 9, 1799, died February 19, 1886, daughter of Josiah and Mary (Butterworth) Dungan, of New Mills (now Pemberton). She was a Baptist by birth, joined the society of Friends after her marriage and was a prominent member of the Mount Holly Meeting, being custodian of the records for many years. She survived her

husband almost twenty years. Children: 1. Richard, died in infancy. 2. Mary Dungan, died young. 3. Rebecca Venicomb, died young. 4. Ann Butterworth, born October 9, 1825; married, November 8, 1849, William Cooper; died February 16, 1883. 5. William, died young. 6. Stacy Budd, November 30, 1833, died April 25, 1896. 7. John C., died young. 8. William Henry, August 14, 1838, died July 22, 1898. 9. Harrison, February 1, 1840. 10. Richard, mentioned below.

(IV) Richard, youngest child of Stacy Budd and Maria (Dungan) Campion, was born August 13, 1842, on his father's farm near Vincentown, and attended the schools of his native locality and also received private instruction. At an early age he entered a dry goods store on Market street, Philadelphia, where he continued seven years and became familiar with the business. For three years succeeding this period he was engaged in the same business on his own account in Philadelphia. In 1869 he became a manufacturer of worsted yarns, and is still identified with this industry, his office being located at Chestnut street in Philadelphia. He is a member of the National Association of Woolen Manufacturers, and of the American Protective League. Mr. Campion enlisted as a soldier of the civil war at Philadelphia in 1862, in what was known as Star's Battery, and was attached to the First Regiment of Pennsylvania Volunteers. He is a member of Meade Post, No. 1, Grand Army of the Republic, of Philadelphia, and the Veteran Corps. and is president of the New Jersey Society of Pennsylvania. He is also a member of the Union League Club; Rittenhouse Club of Philadelphia; Hartford Club of Hartford. Connecticut; Hope Club of Providence, Rhode Island; and Home Market Club of Boston, Massachusetts. He is a member and vice-president of the Manufacturers' Club of Philadelphia; the Pennsylvania Historical Society and the Pennsylvania Genealogical Society. Mr. Campion is an ardent Republican, and has recently been appointed a member of the internal water ways commission of Pennsylvania.

He married, June 8, 1886, Susan Hulme Grundy, born October 25, 1848, daughter of Edward N. and Emma (Shoemaker) Grundy, of Philadelphia.

(The Eves Line).

This is an early New Jersey family which came with the early Quakers and settled upon the Delaware river. Its descendants are still numerous in Burlington county in the vicinity of the first settlement and are settled through other regions.

(I) Thomas Eves came from London to Burlington, New Jersey, among the first arrivals of that Quaker settlement upon the Delaware. That he came for religious freedom cannot be doubted, but that he was a native of London is certain, although people of that name were living there at the time. It is probable that for a few years he lived in the town of Burlington where he had taken up a town lot as part of his one thirty-second of a proprietary share of (one one-hundredth part) West Jersey. On September 29, 1680, he located by survey a tract of thirty acres, and January 12, 1682, a tract of one hundred acres, the former at Assiscunct, now called Mill Creek, and the latter at Rancocas Creek in what is now Willingboro township of Burlington county. He removed to this before February 6, 1683, and there in the year 1708 his wife and two sons, Daniel and Benjamin, died and were buried in the Friends' burial ground at Rancocas. The winter of this year was very severe, the frost at times penetrating to the depth of four feet, and it is quite probable that these three deaths occurred from some contagious disease, possibly small pox, to which disease many of the whites and Indians fell victims. Thomas Eves took other lands in Burlington county which completed his one-thirty-second of a proprietary share, some of which lay in what was always called Evesham township, being named after his family. After the marriage and settlement of all his sons he removed to this township and there died in the fall of 1728. Children: 1. Thomas, died April, 1757. 2. John, died March, 1740. 3. Daniel, born in Willingboro, 1681, died 1708. 4. Samuel, mentioned below. 5. Benjamin, born 1686, died 1708. 6. Ann, born 1689; married, November 10, 1709, James Lippincott. 7. Dorothy, married Jacob Hewlings.

(II) Samuel, fourth son of Thomas and Anna Eves, was born July 20, 1684, in Willington township, died in Evesham, February, 1759. He was a farmer and resided in Evesham, being a member of the meeting of Friends of that name. He married (first) December 2, 1713, Jane Wills, born 1692, died 1716, daughter of John and Hope (Delefast) Wills. He married (second) in November, 1721, Mary Shinn, born 1694, daughter of George and Mary (Thompson) Shinn, who

survived him. Children of second marriage: 1. Anne, married her cousin, Jonathan Lippincott, son of James and Ann (Eves) Lippincott. 2. John, died 1772. 3. Joseph, married Rebecca Haines. 4. Mary, married, May 12, 1752, John Campion, of Evesham (see Campion, I).

THORNE-THORN

Salem, Massachusetts Bay Colony, was established August 23, 1630, and was looked upon as the permanent seaport of Massachusetts Bay. This fact attracted the attention of English capitalists and men of family desiring to leave England either for political or religious betterment; so, as no bounds had been set, the land-seekers, not interested in the merchant marine, settled both north and south of Salem harbor and the town of Saugus was established July 5, 1631, and in 1635, the bounds between Saugus and Salem were defined. On November 20, 1637, Saugus took the name of Lynn and among the adventurous spirits of this time among its settlers was William Thorne (q. v.). The name has the usual number of spellings and the different branches of the same family could not agree as to using or dropping the final e and the same is true to this day. The immigrant and the next three generations spelled the name T-h-o-r-n-e, and those who went to West Jersey dropped the final e, making it T-h-o-r-n and we shall observe this distinction in the following sketch of William Thorne and his descendants.

(I) William Thorne came probably from Essex, England, and was made a freeman of Lynn, Massachusetts, May 2, 1638, and the same year had "thirty and ten" acres of land apportioned him in that town. We next find him in Flushing, Long Island, in 1645, as one of the eighteen original patentees of the town, the patent having been granted by Governor-General Keift, October 19, 1645. The list of grantees were: Thomas Applegate, Thomas Beddord, Latrina Ditch, Robert Field, Thomas Farrington, Robert Firman, Edward Hart, John Hicks, John Lawrence, William Lawrence, John Marston, Michael Millord, William Pidgeon, Thomas Sail, Henry Sautelle, Thomas Stiles, John Townsend and William Thorne, and according to Onderdonk the date was October 10, 1645. In 1646 William Thorne was granted a plantation lot in the town of Gravesend, Long Island, of which lot, Lady Deborah Moody, her son, Sir Henry Moody, Ensign George Baxter and Sergeant

Hibbard had received a general patent December 16, 1645. In 1647 William Thorne was one of the proprietors of the town of Jamaica, Long Island, which had been conveyed to the white settlers in 1646. He probably resided in Jamaica for a long time, as his daughter Susannah Thorne "of Jamaica" married John Lockerson (or Ockerson), of Flushing. William Thorne Senior and William Thorne Junior (probably at the time a boy in years, as he only made his mark) were among the thirty-one signers of a remonstrance to Governor-General Stuyvesant against severe treatment of the Quakers. This remonstrance was drawn up in a Meeting of the Society of Friends, under the large oak tree where George Fox preached in 1671, in Flushing, December 27, 1657. The four sons of William Thorne and his wife, whose name is not on record, were probably named in the order of their birth: William, John (q. v.), Joseph, Samuel, and their only daughter was Susannah, who married at Jamaica, July 10, 1667, John Lockerson (or Ockerson). It is generally believed that both William Thorne and his wife were buried in the burial grounds of the Friends' Meeting House at Flushing, Long Island, built in 1695 and still standing in excellent condition as originally erected, the repairs being made in conformity with the material used in building. On the separation of the Hicksites in 1827, the Meeting House passed into the hands of the Hicksites Friends.

(II) John, second son of William Thorne, the immigrant, was made a ' freeman of Connecticut if he will have it" May 12, 1664, at which date he had probably just arrived at legal age, which if true would make the year of his birth 1643. He was, therefore, probably born in Lynn, Massachusetts. On August 12, 1667, he with his brother Joseph and twelve others, men subject to bear arms "represent themselves to governor-general Keift and give their names, men of Flushing ready to serve His Majesty under his honorable command on all occasions." He died in Flushing, Long Island, in 1709. His will was made July 23, 1709, and recorded the same year, in which he leaves "housing, lands and meadows, goods and chattels" to his wife and children, which he mentions by name, restricting his wife's share in case she should be married again. We find among the early transfers of land in Flushing a record of a deed recorded July 21, 1696, which reads: "John Thorne of Flushing, in ye North Riding of Yorkshire".

to Anthony Floyd of ye aforesaid place, of fifty acres, more or less.

John Thorne married Mary, daughter of Nicholas and Sarah Parsell or Pearsall or Purcell. The children of John and Mary Thorne, named in the order of their birth, were: 1. William, who was sole executor of his father's will. He subsequently removed to Nottingham township, Burlington county, West Jersey, where he had a farm, and when his building burned in 1725 the Chesterfield Friends Meeting raised money to help him rebuild. He was married at Shrewsbury Meeting, eleventh month, second day, 1708, by Friends' ceremony, to Meribah Alling, daughter of Jediah and Elizabeth Allen, and Susannah and Joseph Thorne were among the witnesses. According to the Friends record they had eight children. He died near Crosswicks, New Jersey, in 1742. 2. John (q. v.). 3. Joseph, of Flushing, who married Martha Johanna, daughter of John Bowne, and had seven children all born in Flushing, where he died in July, 1753, and his widow, July 6, 1750. 4. Mary, who married William Fowler and had a daughter Mary and both mother and daughter were baptized in Grace Protestant Episcopal Church in Jamaica in 1711. 5. Elizabeth, who married a Schurman. 6. Hannah, who married in 1701 Richard, son of John and Mary (Russell) Cornwell, and had ten children between 1703 and 1723. 7. Sarah, who married Joshua, son of John and Mary (Russell) Cornwell, and had four children between 1696 and 1701.

(III) John (2), son of John (1) and Mary (Parsell) Thorne, was born in Flushing, Long Island, where he married Catherine ———, also of Flushing, both names appearing as man and wife in 1698 and we find them in Chesterfield, Burlington county, New Jersey, in 1700, where he bought one hundred and eighty-one acres of land, August 26, 1717, which he sold Anthony Woodward Junior, for one hundred pounds, August 7, 1725, and on August 26, 1717, purchased a plantation further down the stream below where the village of Crosswicks stands. He was constable in 1710 and held the office up to 1749. He was also town collector. He was a carpenter and a farmer, and his will dated February 16, 1735, was proved June 14, 1737, in which he names his children. He made his mark instead of signing the will himself, but this was probably owing to his infirmity, as he no doubt received a good education for the time and at least could read and write. His widow, Catherine, also made a will, dated November 19, 1766, and proved November 29, 1766, and she also made her mark but as the will was written but ten days before her death, that easily accounted for it on account of her physical weakness. Her will also mentions the children, omitting those who had died between 1735 and 1766.

The twelve children of John and Catherine Thorne were all, except possibly the first, born in Burlington county, New Jersey, and are named in the will in the following order: 1. John, who died intestate at Bordentown, New Jersey, May 8, 1759. 2. Mary. 3. Elizabeth. 4. Deborah, who married a Simmons and died before the time of her father's death and left one child. 5. Joseph (q. v.). 6. Samuel, who married in October, 1730, Hannah Clay, and died in April, 1777, at Crosswicks, New Jersey, leaving six children. 7. Benjamin, who married in April, 1740, Sarah Bunting, and died in 1789, leaving no children. 8. Catherine, who married in March, 1728, Francis King. 9. Sarah, who married David Wright in March, 1743. 10. Thomas, who died intestate at Bordentown in 1765. 11. Rebecca, who married a Simmons. 12. Hannah, who was married in January, 1737-38, to Caleb (2), son of Joshua and grandson of Caleb Shreve. Of this large family, only two of the sons, Joseph and Samuel, left descendants to perpetuate the name of Thorne.

(IV) Joseph, second son and fifth child of John (2) and Catherine Thorne, was born in Crosswicks, New Jersey, and married in Chesterfield Meeting, after both parties to the marriage had twice declared their intention in open meeting to marry each other, the ceremony being performed and the marriage certificate duly signed by the witnesses present at public meeting held in March, 1723, the other contracting party being Sarah, daughter of Thomas and Mary Foulke, natives of England, who settled in Burlington county, New Jersey. The children of Joseph and Sarah (Foulke) Thorn were: 1. Elizabeth, born fifth month, third day, 1724, married, tenth month, 1748, Abraham Tilton, son of Samuel Tilton, of Middletown, New Jersey, and they had three children. Hannah, Sarah and Lucy. 2. Joseph (2), born fourth month, nineteenth day, 1727. 3. John (2), third month, fourth day, 1730, died eighth month, twenty-second day, 1807; married, fourth month, 1750, Diadamia, daughter of Isaac and Lydia (Brown) Joins. 4. Michael, tenth month, second day,

1731; died unmarried. 5. Thomas (q. v.). 6. Mary, married, in 1767, Cornelius Hendrickson of Monmouth county, New Jersey.

(V) Thomas, second son and third child of Joseph and Sarah (Foulke) Thorn, was born at Crosswicks, New Jersey, July 21, 1733. He married, in 1759, Susanna, daughter of William and Jane Biles, of Bucks county, in accordance with the ceremony of the Society of Friends at Falls Meeting in Bucks county. They settled near Crosswicks, New Jersey. Thomas died at Crosswicks, February 25, 1801, and many of his descendants are still residents of the same vicinity. The children of Thomas and Susanna (Biles) Thorn were born on the Thorne homestead near Crosswicks, Burlington county, New Jersey, as follows: 1. Benjamin, January 5, 1763. 2. Ann, July 4, 1764. 3. William Biles (q. v.). 4. George Biles, August 29, 1767. 5. Langthorn, March 8, 1769. 6. Sarah, October 9, 1772. 7. Enoch, January 6, 1775. 8. Thomas, February 17, 1782.

(VI) William Biles, second son and third child of Thomas and Susanna (Biles) Thorn, was born at Crosswicks, New Jersey, March, 26, 1766. He married Elizabeth, daughter of Hugh and Ann Hutchins, who was born December 29, 1769, died April 15, 1832. The children of William Biles and Elizabeth (Hutchins) Thorn were born on the homestead farm near Crosswicks, as follows: 1. Ann, December 6, 1791. 2. Sarah B., October 12, 1792, married Robinson Tindale and was the mother of General George Hector Tindale. 3. Thomas B. (q. v.). 4. William B., December 23, 1796.

(VII) Thomas B., eldest son and third child of William Biles and Elizabeth (Hutchins) Thorn, was born on the homestead farm at Hardwick, New Jersey, August 15, 1794. He was a school teacher and was an excellent penman. He married Sarah ——— and they had their home at Chews Landing, where four children were born as follows: 1. John, who went west and settled there. 2. Mary, married Frank Peabody, of Elgin, Illinois, and made her home in that place. 3. Elizabeth, married Mr. Alling, of Naugatuck, Connecticut. 4. William H., (q. v.).

(VIII) William H., third son and youngest child of Thomas B. and Sarah Thorn, was educated in the district school of his native place and there learned the rudiments of knowledge, including what was familiarly known as the three R's., Reading, 'Riting, and 'Rithmatic, but he continued to study at home.

while an apprentice to a shoemaker at Haddonfield, Camden county, which useful trade he became master of. He became, through careful reading of well-selected books, a learned man for one in his position in life. He went from the shoeshop in Haddonfield to one in Medford in Burlington county, where he worked for the grandfather of Governor Stokes, who was a noted boot and shoe-maker. He subsequently began the manufacture of shoes on his own account and he continued the business for ten years, when he retired and spent his time in the care of his accumulated estate and investments. He was a strong Abolitionist in the days when considerable odium was attached to men having such views. and on the advent of the Republican party he naturally became associated with the new party. His fraternal affiliation was with the Independent Order of Odd Fellows, Medford Lodge, No. 100, and he was the first member initiated in that lodge. He was by birthright a member of the Society of Friends of the Hicksite branch. He married Margaret W., daughter of Barzilla Prickitt, born in 1827, in Medford, died at her home in Medford, New Jersey, in 1908. These children were: 1. Thomas B., named for his grandfather, learned the trade of his father and engaged in the shoe manufacturing business. On retiring he lived with his father in Medford. He married Anne Nutt and had four children: William Garfield, Alice, Mary and Charles. 2. Henry Prickitt (q. v.).

(IX) Henry Prickitt, second son of William H. and Margaret W. (Prickitt) Thorn, was born in Medford, Burlington county, New Jersey, January 27, 1853. He was educated at Friends' School in Medford and M. H. Allen's private school in the same town, and he worked as a clerk in his father's shoe manufactory during vacations. He was graduated at the College of Pharmacy, Philadelphia, Pennsylvania, in 1875, and the same year purchased the drug business then being carried on by Mr. Stokes, uncle of Governor Stokes, and he greatly enlarged the business and became one of the leading pharmacists in Burlington county. He also engaged in the business of raising cranberries on a bog of fifteen acres from 1888, which under his methods of cultivation has proved to be very profitable. He is a director in the Burlington County Safe Deposit and Trust Company of Moorestown, New Jersey, and president of the Burlington County National Bank of Medford, New Jersey, since 1898. He is also a director

in the Gas and Water Company of Medford; secretary of the Burlington County Association for Insurance, and has served as president of the New Jersey Pharmaceutical Association. Mr. Thorn is active in local, state and national political affairs; he served as a delegate to the Republican National convention at Minneapolis in June, 1892, when William McKinley was nominated for president of the United States, and was chairman of the Republican county committee of Burlington county. He is a member of the Burlington County Historical Society of Moorestown. He departed from the religious faith which he inherited as a birthright, as it did not seem to meet the demands of the present day religious work as carried on in institutional churches. In doing so, he did not regret the inheritance he had been heir to, or the religious training he had received, as both added to his effectiveness as a worker and trustee in the Methodist church and a member of the county committee in the Young Men's Christian Association, and no man better appreciated the value of the influence of the Society of Friends on the early political and religious history of our country as witnessed in West Jersey, Pennsylvania, Long Island and Rhode Island. He affiliated with various fraternal and benevolent associations, his Masonic fellowship beginning in Mt. Holly Lodge, No. 14, F. and A. M. and extended to Siloam Royal Arch Chapter, No. 19, Camden, New Jersey; Cyrene Commandery, Knights Templar, No. 7, of Camden; and Lu Lu Temple, Mystic Shrine, of Philadelphia. He was also initiated in the Independent Order of Odd Fellows through Lodge No. 100, of Medford, New Jersey, and in the Order of Knights of Pythias through Medford Lodge, No. 108. He is a member of Red Cross Castle, Knights of the Golden Eagle, founded in 1873, and which distributed annually upwards of two hundred and fifty thousand dollars in benefits, and of the Medford Lodge, No. 42,. Ancient Order of United Workmen, founded in 1868, and which had distributed up to 1903 in benefits one hundred and twenty million dollars since its organization. The Benevolent and Protective Order of Elks, founded in 1868, and which had distributed in benefits up to 1903 one million, two hundred and fifty thousand dollars, has a lodge No. 848, in Mt. Holly, New Jersey, of. which Mr. Thorn is a member.

Mr. Thorn married, June 22, 1880, Clara T., daughter of George and Caroline Wilson Branin, of Medford, New Jersey, and their children were born in that place, as follows: 1. Henry Norman, July 18, 1881, attended Mt. Holly Military School, was graduated at Haverford College in 1904; in the employ of the firm of Harris, Jones and Cadbury Company, plumbers supplies, Philadelphia, Pennsylvania. 2. Helen B., October 12, 1887, graduated at St. Mary's Hall, Burlington, New Jersey, in 1906.

FOSTER The first that is known of the name of Foster was about the year 1065, A. D., when Sir Richard Forrester went from Normandy over to England, accompanied by his brother-in-law, William the Conqueror, and participated in the victorious battle of Hastings. The name was first Forrester, then Forester, then Foster. It signified one who had care of wild lands; one who loved the forest, a characteristic trait which had marked the bearers of the name through all the centuries that have followed. The Fosters seem to have located in the northern counties of England, and in the early centuries of English history participated in many a sturdy encounter with their Scottish foes. The name is mentioned in "Marmion" and the "Lay of the Last Minstrel." From one of these families in the seventeenth century appears the name of Reginald Foster. Tiring of the tyrannic rule of Charles I, he came to America and settled in Ipswich, Massachusetts, in about the year 1638. He was a prominent figure in the early days, as the colonial records show. During its existence the Foster family has been a hardy, persevering and progressive race, almost universally endowed with an intense nervous energy; there have been many instances of high attainments; a bearer of the name has been, ex-officio, vice-president of the Republic (Hon. Lafayette G. Foster, president pro tem, of the senate during Andrew Johnson's administration) ; another, Hon. John W. Foster, of Indiana, was premier of President Harrison's cabinet; another, Hon. Charles Foster, of Ohio, was the secretary of the treasury. Many have attained high positions in financial life, and many have gained prominence in military affairs. The record of Major-General John G. Foster through the Mexican War and the war of the Rebellion stamped him as a soldier, without fear and without reproach. Professor Bell is the reputed and accredited inventor of the telephone, but before that distinguished man had ever conceived the plan of electric transmission of the human voice,

Joseph Foster, of Keene, New Hampshire, a mechanical genius, had constructed and put into actual use a telephone embodying practically the same working plan as the Bell machine. Query: Could it be possible that Joseph Foster's telephone afforded the suggestion to Professor Bell? The Foster family has an authentic record covering a period of nearly one thousand years. It has furnished to the world its share of the fruits of toil; it has contributed its share of enterprise and progress. Wherever it appears in the affairs of men it bears its crest; the iron arm holding the golden javelin poised towards the future.

(I) Reginald Foster came from England at the time so many emigrated to Massachusetts, in 1638, and with his family was on board one of the vessels embargoed by King Charles I. He settled at Ipswich, in the county of Essex, with his wife, five sons and two daughters; where he lived to extreme old age, with as much peace and happiness as was compatible with his circumstances in the settlement of a new country. The names of his five sons who came with him from England were: Abraham, Reginald, William, Isaac and Jacob. One of the daughters who came with him from England married (first) a Wood, and after his death she married a Peabody. His other daughter married a Story, ancestor of Dr. Story, formerly of Boston, and of the late Judge Story. It is remarkable of this family that they all lived to extreme old age, all married, and all had large families from whom are descended a very numerous progeny settled in various parts of the United States.

(II) Abraham, eldest son and third child of Reginald Foster, of Boxford, Essex, Devonshire, England, by the first of his three wives, who became the mother of seven children, who came with them to Ipswich, Massachusetts Bay Colony, in 1638, was born in Exeter, England, 1622. His two sisters were his senior. Mary was born about 1618 and when a widow married Francis Peabody, the immigrant ancestor of the Peabodys of New England, who came from St. Albans, Hertfordshire, England, in the ship "Planter" in 1635 and settled in Ipswich, Massachusetts, and she became by this marriage the mother of fourteen children. She died April 9, 1705. Sarah, born in 1620, married, about 1640, William Storey, of Ipswich, and by this marriage had seven children and she died subsequent to 1668. His brothers in the order of their birth were: 1. Isaac, born in 1630, married (first) Mary Jackson, 1658, (second)

Hannah Downing, 1668, and (third) Martha Hale, 1679. He had fourteen children, eleven by his first wife and three by his second. He died after he was sixty-two years of age. 2. William, born 1633, married, 1661, Mary Jackson; lived in Boxford; had nine children; died May 17, 1713. 3. Deacon Jacob, born 1635, married (first) 1658, Martha Kinsman, and (second) 1667, Abigail Lord; lived in Ipswich, where fourteen children were born, five by his first wife and nine by his second. He died July 7, 1710. 4. Reginald, born 1636, married Elizabeth Dane, lived in Chebacco, Ipswich, and had by this marriage twelve children. Abraham married Lydia, daughter of Caleb and Martha Burbank, of Rowley, Massachusetts He was a farmer and he joined the church at Ipswich in full communion, April 12, 1674. He was sixty-seven years of age, September 26, 1698, when he made deposition relative to land of Rev. John Norton. There was no will or administration of his estate, which he distributed among his family by deed December 21, 1698. (See Essex deeds, liber 13, page 206.) The ten children of Abraham and Lydia (Burbank) Foster were born in Ipswich as follows: 1. Ephraim, October 9, 1657, married (first) Hannah Eames and (second) Mary West. 2. Abraham (q. v.). 3. James, January 12, 1662; he is not mentioned in his father's distribution of the estate, so it may be presumed that he died before 1698. 4. A child born December 27, 1668, died unnamed, twin of Isaac 5., who died unmarried February 13, 1717. 6. Benjamin, 1670, married Ann ———. 7. Ebenezer, July 15, 1672, married Mary Berman. 8. Mehitable, October 12, 1675, married Ebenezer Averill, December 31, 1700. 9. Caleb, November 9, 1677, married Mary Sherwin. 10. Ruth, who married, April 16, 1702, Jeremiah Perley, of Boxford. Abraham Foster, the father of these children, died in Ipswich, Massachusetts, January 25, 1711.

(III) Abraham (2), second son of Abraham (1) and Lydia (Burbank) Foster, was born in Ipswich, Massachusetts, October 16, 1659. He was a soldier in the military service of the Colony of Massachusetts "and was wounded in the public service and is to receive eight pounds out of the public treasury for smart money." He resided first in Ipswich and then removed to Topsfield, where he died May 23, 1741. The three children of Abraham and Mary (Burbank) Foster were: 1. Abraham (q. v.). 2. Nathan, May 17, 1700, married Hannah Standish. 3. Daniel, April

13, 1705, married (first) Hannah Black and (second) Elizabeth Davis.

(IV) Abraham (3), eldest child of Abraham (2) and Mary (Burbank) Foster, was born in Ipswich, Massachusetts Bay Colony, January 12, 1696. He was married to Sarah Dinnell, who was born in 1696. The intention to marry was published in the Church at Topsfield, April 5, 1718, but we have not the date of the marriage ceremony. She was admitted to the church at Topsfield, July 2, 1732. Abraham Foster was a carpenter and letters of administration on his estate were granted to his second son, Thomas, June 29, 1767, he having died April 23, 1767. Abraham and Sarah (Dinnell) Foster had seven children, born in Topsfield, as follows: 1. Abraham, May 4, 1719, married Priscilla Todd. 2. Sarah, May 4, 1721, married Abraham Adams, who died September 18, 1771. 3. Thomas (q. v.). 4. Hannah, September 18, 1726, died unmarried in 1802. 5. Amos, baptized December 22, 1728; he purchased land in Rowley in 1758. 6. Ruth, baptized March 17, 1734, died unmarried in 1806. 7. Abigail, baptized April 3, 1737.

(V) Captain Thomas, second son and third child of Abraham (3) and Sarah (Dinnell) Foster, was born in Topsfield, Massachusetts, August 11, 1724. He was a captain in the Colonial militia, and resided in Ipswich. He married, April 5, 1748, Mehitable, daughter of Matthew and Mehitable Peabody. She was born December 24, 1728, and her intentions to marry Captain Thomas Foster was published November 21, 1747. She was admitted to the church at Ipswich, April 29, 1750. She became by this marriage the mother of seven children and her husband's estate was granted administration, December 8, 1789. The children of Captain Thomas and Mehitable (Peabody) Foster were born in Ipswich, Massachusetts, as follows: 1. Elijah, February 19, 1749. 2. Allen, April 24, 1751, married Lucy Patten. 3. Abigail, April 19, 1753, published intention to marry, March 13, 1773, Moses or Thomas Palmer. 4. Ebenezer, March 24, 1755. 5. Mehitable, March 24, 1760. 6. Daniel (q. v.). 7. Thomas, March 27, 1766, married, April 14, 1787, Lydia Batchelder.

(VI) Daniel, fourth son and sixth child of Captain Thomas and Mehitable (Peabody) Foster, was born in Ipswich, Massachusetts, March 12, 1762. He fought in the American revolution and was a soldier in Lafayette's select battalion and was presented by General Lafayette with a sword as a mark of esteem.

He was a prominent town officer in Newburyport and was employed in the naval office. He had the esteem of his descendants as being a cultured and respected gentleman, which no doubt was quite true and had much to do with his gaining the esteem of the French commanding general. He married, December 18. 1783, Dorothy Pingree, who was born in Newburyport, June 4, 1762, died there May 15, 1834, the mother of seven children, born in Rowley and Newburyport as follows: 1. Nathaniel, February 28, 1797, married Fannie B. Brockway. 2. Daniel, who married Chomy Fuller. 3. Solomon, who removed to Pottsville, Pennsylvania. 4. Jesse (q. v.). 5. Thomas. 6. Louisa, who died unmarried. 7. Millicent, who died unmarried.

(VII) Jesse, fourth son of Daniel and Dorothy (Pingree) Foster, was born in Newburyport, Massachusetts, but the date of his birth has not been preserved. He was married to Ann E. Toppan, of Newburyport, and they removed to Portsmouth, New Hampshire, and subsequently to Pottsville, Pennsylvania, where he died when about ninety-three years of age. Jesse and Ann E. (Toppan) Foster had four children born in Portsmouth, New Hampshire, as follows: 1. Thomas (q. v.). 2. Frederick L., born in 1820, became a distinguished citizen of Philadelphia and is the custodian of the sword presented to his grandfather Daniel (q. v.). 3. Ann Eliza, November 1, 1821, married Oliver Dobson, September 7, 1842, and resided in Pottsville, where five children were born of the marriage as follows: Emma Louise Dobson, September 1, 1843; Mary Eliza Dobson, July 17, 1846; Caroline Briggs Dobson, April 6, 1849, married John E. Waters, May 17, 1871, and had two children, Oliver and Grace Waters, who live in Bridgeport, Ohio; Oliver Dobson Junior, June 9, 1851, died February 22, 1877; Hannah Dobson, October 7, 1853, died July 26, 1854. 4. Clement Storer, August 18, 1823, married Rebecca McCammet.

(VIII) Thomas (2) second son of Jesse and Ann E. (Toppan) Foster, was born in Portsmouth, New Hampshire, July 20, 1819, died in Pottsville, Pennsylvania, December 13, 1886. He married, March 15, 1842, Amanda M. Rich, of Sunbury, Pennsylvania, born August 25, 1822, and they had seven children, who were all living in 1909 as follows except the youngest child, who was at that time deceased. The names and location of these children was at that time as follows: 1. Thomas Jefferson (q. v.). 2. Solomon, born

December 25, 1844, a resident of Scranton, Pennsylvania. 3. Mary Agnes, February 21, 1847, married W. H. Daniels, of Pottsville. 4. Henry A., of Pottsville, Pennsylvania, October 9, 1847. 5. William Wetherill, June 5, 1855, of Philadelphia, Pennsylvania. 6. John Rich, September 27, 1857, of Baltimore, Maryland. 7. Jacob S., October 18, 1862, married Cecelia A. Schelling, of Philadelphia, Pennsylvania. Thomas Foster was a boot and shoe dealer in Pottsville, Pennsylvania, for forty years.

(IX) Thomas Jefferson, eldest child of Thomas (2) and Amanda M. (Rich) Foster, was born in Pottsville, Pennsylvania, December 31, 1842. He was graduated at Pottsville high school and at Eastman Business College, Poughkeepsie, New York. He became editor and proprietor of the *Shenandoah Herald*, Shenandoah, Pennsylvania, in 1872. He originated and planned a system of study of business methods by correspondence so as not to interfere with regular labor, necessary for daily needs in cases of self-supporting young men, who could not afford time or money to take a course in a business college. A trial of his system proved its practicability and he organized and incorporated the International Correspondence School, established at Scranton, Pennsylvania, in 1891, of which he is proprietor, and he also organized and incorporated the International Text Book Company, of which he is president. The two corporations are under the one direction and management, the Text Book Company supplying the books, blanks and stationery necessary in carrying out the Correspondence School methods. He also promoted other business ventures in Scranton and is a director of the Traders' National Bank. Mr. Foster was captain of a company from Pottsville, Pennsylvania, and served through the entire civil war.

He married (first) Fannie Mellet; children: 1. Amanda Rook, who married Stanley P. Allen, secretary of the International Correspondence School at Scranton. 2. Mary Eliza, who married H. C. Barker, of Scranton. 3. Joel McCammet (q. v.). 4. Emma Louise, who resides in Scranton, Pennsylvania. 5. Jeremiah High, who resides in Scranton. Fannie (Mellet) Foster died in Scranton, November 1, 1892, and Mr. Foster married (second) Blandina, daughter of David Harrington, and their son, Thomas Jefferson, was born in Scranton.

(X) Joel McCammet, eldest son and third child of Thomas Jefferson and Fannie (Mellet)

Foster, was born in Pottsville, Pennsylvania, January 16, 1876. He was educated in the public schools of Scranton, Pennsylvania, and was graduated in 1892 at Nazareth Hall Moravian College, a military school. He found employment on leaving college with the National Drilling and Boring Company, of Scranton, Pennsylvania, for one year, and at the end of that time he was for a short time employed in the National Gas Engine and Metre Company, of Brooklyn, New York. He returned to Scranton in 1894 to take the position of organizer and superintendent of the field force of the International Correspondence School, of Scranton, of which his father is proprietor, and he remained in this position up to 1904, when he was obliged to resign on account of ill health, and he established a poultry farm in southern New Jersey, which he relinguished in 1906. He established another at Brown's Mills, Burlington county, which he named the Rancocas Poultry Yards, which he made one of the largest established of the kind in the east, and where in 1909 he had ten thousand egg producing hens and the output of the yards amounted to thirty thousand dollars per annum. He served the township as justice of peace and truant officer, and he was also president of the Brown's Mills Protective Association. His church affiliation is with the Presbyterian denomination and his political faith that of the Republican party. He married, June 14, 1898, Grace Addie, daughter of James Gilbert and Addie Mary (Finch) Bailey, of Waverly, Pennsylvania, and their daughter, Frances Adelaide, was born in Cincinnati, Ohio, May 20, 1899, and in 1909 is a student in Friends' School, Moorestown, New Jersey.

(The Roe Line).

A chieftain by the name of Roo or Rollo with a herd of followers came from Norway to the kingdom of the Franks where they acquired by force of arms ownership to large estates which they called Normandy, including the city of Rouen which they took possession of in 842 and made it the capital in France of the Northmen or Norsemen. These Norwegian Vikings in 982 pushed themselves in their little boats across the North Atlantic sea, landed in Greenland, and in 1002 they went further west and south along the coast of Labrador and established Vineland on the coast of New England and this preceded Columbus in the line of discovery by nearly five hundred years. But the Norsemen were bold invaders and not permanent home makers and took possession of,

rather than created, cities, towns and villages. Their descendants are the Normans of history, a warlike, vigorous and brilliant race rapidly adapting themselves to the more civilized forms of life that prevailed in the Frankish kingdom. Roo, Rolf or Rollo had been banished by Harold Haarfager on account of his heracies and he forced Charles the Simple to grant him possession of all the land in the valley of the Seine to the sea and by the time Charles the Bold obtained the crown the invaders had firmly planted themselves in the country which then went by the name of Normandy. They adopted the religion, language and manners of the conquered Franks, and inspired their borrowed results of a better civilization with their own splendid vitality. By the twelfth century they had developed a school of narrative history rivaling in celebrity the lyric troubadours of the more famed parts of the southern kingdom of the Franks.

William, the duke of Normandy, born 1027, had made his great genius as a leader felt throughout Normandy, and when he came to the dukedom he continued his conquests even beyond the confines of the land of the Franks to England where Norman influences was very prominent in the covenants of Edward the Confessor. But when Harold was chosen to succeed the Conqueror on the English throne the Normans, under the lead of William, asserted their rights due to an alleged promise from Edward that William of Normandy should be his successor. The battle of Hastings, October 14, 1066, gave to William the crown which he accepted December 25, 1066, and the war against the Saxons soon reduced that foe, and Scotland soon followed as a trophy to the Conqueror. Failing to subdue Denmark he withdrew his armada from their coast and raised an army and invaded France, but in the midst of the ashes of Nantes his horse failed him and the fall of the charger resulted fatally to the rider as he died September 9, 1087. William the Conqueror gave to his attendants in arms the English name of Roe and as a coat-of-arms a Norman shield emblazoned with a Roebuck. King James I. made Sir Thomas Roe, great-great-grandfather of John Roe (q. v.), the American immigrant, embassador to Constantinople, and he was also one of the esquires of Queen Elizabeth who sent the Roe family into Ireland where Pierce Roe was the eighth earl of Ormond.

(I) John Roe came from Ireland to America by way of England in 1628. He married Hannah Purrin in 1635. They lived in East

Hampton, Long Island, and in 1655 moved to Drowned Meadows, near Port Jefferson, Long Island, where his home long remained a landmark. He died at Drowned Meadows, 1711. He left a widow and several children, including Nathaniel (q. v.).

(II) Nathaniel, son of John and Hannah (Purrin) Roe, was born in Drowned Meadows, Long Island, now Brookhaven, in 1670, and died there in 1752. He was active in affairs and met death by drowning in Long Island sound. He married Hannah Reeves, born 1678, died 1759, and among their children was Nathaniel (q. v.).

(III) Nathaniel (2), son of Nathaniel (1) and Hannah (Reeves) Roe, was born at Drowned Meadows, Long Island, about 1700. He enlisted in Captain Alexander Smith's regiment of Suffolk county militia for service in the French and Indian war, April 18, 1758. He married, about 1730, Elizabeth Philipse and among their children was William (q. v.).

(IV) William, son of Nathaniel (2) and Elizabeth (Philipse) Roe, married Maria Van Disen and among their children was Betsey (q. v.).

(V) Betsey, daughter of William and Maria (Van Disen) Roe, married S. Finch.

(VI) William Roe, son of S. and Betsey (Roe) Finch, married Mary Kirkpatrick, and among their children was Addie Mary (q. v.).

(VII) Addie Mary, daughter of William Roe and Mary (Kirkpatrick) Finch, married James Gilbert Bailey, a grocer in Scranton, Pennsylvania, and at one time mayor of the city. They were the parents of one child, Grace Addie (q. v.).

(VIII) Grace Addie, only child of James Gilbert and Addie Mary (Finch) Bailey, was born in Waverly, Pennsylvania, August 18, 1878. She was educated at Waverly Academy, Wyoming Seminary and Scranton high school. She is a member of the Presbyterian church, and of the patriotic society, Daughters of the American Revolution, her revolutionary ancestor having been Captain William Roe, commanding a company in Colonel Clinton's regiment, Second New York Volunteers. She married, June 14, 1898, Joel McCammet, eldest son of Thomas Jefferson and Fannie (Mellet) Foster, of Brown's Mills, New Jersey, of the tenth generation of the Foster family. Their child, Frances Adelaide, was born in Cincinnati, Ohio, May 20, 1899, and in 1909 is a pupil in the Friends' Academy at Moorestown, New Jersey.

In the most recent compilation of BURR Burr family genealogy the author of that work, in commenting on the New Jersey branch of the family at large, says that he had supposed that "the many families of the name in Central New Jersey were offshoots from some one of the three Puritan branches of New England, and had confined his researches to them," but from data gathered from various sources "it was discovered that they were descended from one common ancestor who emigrated from England as early as 1682 and settled near Mount Holly, the county seat of Burlington county."

(I) Henry Burr, immigrant ancestor of the New Jersey families of his surname, first appears in the records of the Friends' meeting house at Mt. Holly, which is a record of the birth of one John Burr, son of Henry and Elizabeth Burr, under date of May 29, 1691. Family tradition says that this Henry Burr was a friend of William Penn and accompanied him on his last voyage to this country. He bought a tract of land of eleven hundred acres in Northampton, Burlington county, and settled there. His name appears occasionally in transactions relating to the purchase or sale of land and also in the records of the Friends' meetings, but he does not appear to have identified himself conspicuously with public affairs, doubtless from the fact that he was a devout Friend and hence concerned himself little with matters outside of his family or the meetings. His will bears date October 29, 1642, and was admitted to probate June 11, 1743. He married Elizabeth, daughter of Robert and Mary (Thredder) Hudson, the latter a daughter of Richard and Mary Thredder, of London, England. Henry and Elizabeth (Hudson) Burr had nine children: 1. John, born May 29, 1691 (see post). 2. Joseph, born 1694 (see post). 3. Elizabeth, born 1696; married Samuel Woolman and became mother of John Woolman, the Quaker preacher and annalist, a very remarkable man in his way, who was a pioneer in the cause of slavery abolition and one of the most conscientious of men. 4. Mary, born 1698; married Jacob Lippincott; she was a woman so highly esteemed for her christian virtues that the Friends prepared and published a memorial of her after her death. 5. Sarah, born 1701; married Caleb Haines, of one of the oldest families of New Jersey. 6. Rebecca, born 1703; married Peter White. 7. Martha, born 1705; married (first) Josiah Holmes; (second) Timothy Matlack. 8. William, born 1710. 9. Henry, born 1713.

(II) John, eldest son and child of Henry and Elizabeth (Hudson) Burr, was born May 29, 1691, and was a man of considerable consequence in the early history of Mt. Holly and the community in which he lived. In 1728 he was appointed surveyor general of the western division of New Jersey. He married, 3d mo., 29, 1712, Keziah, daughter of Job and Rachel Wright, of Oyster Bay, Long Island, and by her had six children. She died April 12, 1731, and John Burr married (second) Susanna ———, who bore him two children. His children: 1. Rachel, born 11th mo., 22, 1713. 2. Henry, born 8th mo., 26, 1715 (see post). 3. John, born 1st mo., 25, 1718. 4. Solomon, born 11th mo., 27, 1721. 5. Keziah, born 2d mo., 17, 1724. 6. Joseph, born 2d mo., 11, 1726. 7. Susanna, born 8th mo., 26, 1736. 8. Hudson, born 5th mo., 22, 1745.

(III) Henry (2), eldest son and second child of John and Keziah (Wright) Burr, was born in Burlington, New Jersey, the 26th of the 8th month, 1715, and was of Vincentown, New Jersey. He married Sarah Eayre, and by her had four children: 1. Elizabeth, married Abraham Hewlings. 2. Henry, born 1769. 3. Thomas. 4. John.

(II) Joseph, second son and child of Henry and Elizabeth (Hudson) Burr, was born at Mt. Holly, New Jersey, in 1694, and married the 2d of 12th month, 1726, Jane, daughter of John and Anna Abbott, of Nottingham, New Jersey. They had ten children: 1. Henry, born 5th mo., 12, 1731 (see post). 2. Joseph, born 9th mo., 25, 1732. 3. Abigail, born 11th mo., 1, 1734; died 4th mo., 16, 1671; married David Davis. 4. Mary,, married Solomon Ridgway. 5. Robert. 6. Jane, married, 1762, David Ridgway. 7. Rebecca, married, 1771, James Chapman. 8. Ann, married George Deacon. 9. William. 10. Hannah, married Richard Eayre.

(III) Henry (3), first son and child of Joseph and Jane (Abbott) Burr, was born at Mt. Holly, New Jersey, the 12th day of 5th month, 1731, and was a man of high character, as is shown by the following: "This is to certify that the Bearer hereof, Henry Burr, is an Inhabitant of the Township of Northampton, in the County of Burlington (Farmer) and is a person of good repute, and is generally believed to be clear of acting, doing or saying injurious to the present Government as Established under the authority of the people; therefor permit him the said Henry Burr to pass and repass through any of the Counties of this state if he behaveth himself as becometh a good citizen. Given this 7th day of August, 1779. Josiah G. Foster, Esq., Member of Assembly." Henry Burr married Elizabeth, daughter of William and Hannah Foster, and by her had three children: 1. Hannah, born 1754; married, 1774, Henry A. Ridgway. 2. Abigail, born 1758; married Samuel Stockton, of Chesterfield. 3. Henry, born 1763 (see post).

(IV) Henry (4), only son and youngest child of Henry (3) and Elizabeth (Foster) Burr, was born the 10th day of 1st month, 1763, in Mt. Holly, New Jersey, in which town he died, in 1832, his will being proved January 30, of that year. He was a farmer and lived on the old family homestead in Mt. Holly, his lands including four hundred acres. He was an industrious and prosperous husbandman, and as a man enjoyed the respect of all persons to whom he was known. He married Phebe, daughter of Edmund and Miriam Williams, of Shrewsbury, New Jersey, and by her had nine children: 1. Edmund W., born 2d mo., 1, 1792. 2. Elizabeth, born 5th mo., 18, 1793; married Joshua Satterthwaite, of Crosswicks, New Jersey. 3. Miriam, born 11th mo., 21, 1794; married Elwood E. Smith. 4. Henry, born 10th mo., 15, 1796. 5. George W., born 8th mo., 15, 1798. 6. William W., born 2d mo., 3, 1800. 7. Tyle W., born 3d mo., 15, 1802. 8. Charles, born 7th mo., 21, 1804 (see post). 9. Hudson S., born 7th mo., 2, 1806.

(V) Charles, son and eighth child of Henry (4) and Phebe (Williams) Burr, was born in Mt. Holly, New Jersey, the 21st day of 7th month, 1804, and died there October 29, 1852. He was a man of good education and devoted much of his life to teaching school, at which he was very successful and enjoyed considerable celebrity as a teacher. At one time and for several years he carried on a general merchandise store in Medford, New Jersey, and in all respects his business life was a success. In politics he was a Whig, but it does not appear that he took an active part in public affairs. He married (first) Lucy Ann Troth, born April 2, 1807, died February 20, 1829, and by whom he had one child. He married (second) February 8, 1830, Mary, daughter of Obadiah Engle and Patience, daughter of Job Cole and Elizabeth Tomlin. Job was the son of Kendal Cole and Ann, daughter of William Budd and Elizabeth, daughter of Richard and Abigail Stockton, the emigrants. William was the son of William Budd and Ann Clapgut, the emigrants. Kendal was the son of Samuel Cole and Mary, daughter of Thomas Kendal, the emigrants. Samuel was the son of Samuel and Elizabeth Cole, the emigrants. Obadiah Engle was the son of Joseph Engle and Mary Borton, referred to above. After the death of Charles Burr, Mary (Engle) Burr married (second) Isaac, son of Isaac and Elizabeth (Austin) Haines, for whose ancestry see sketch of the Austin family.

(VI) Samuel Engle, third child and second son of Charles and Mary (Engle) Burr, was born in Burlington county, New Jersey, March 20, 1836, and is now living in Bordentown, New Jersey. For his early education he attended private school taught by his uncle, William Burr. At the age of eight years he went to his uncle, Samuel C. Engle, and worked on his farm, attending country school at Easton during the winter months. He resided there until sixteen years of age, then went to Moorestown and worked in his brother's store for seven years, and on January 1, 1859, moved to Bordentown and started business for himself under the name of Richardson & Burr. This continued for about one year, when he bought Mr. Richardson's interest and continued the business alone of general store. His store was located at the corner of Farnsworth avenue and Crosswicks street, the center of the commercial activity of Bordentown, and here by close application to business and fair and equitable methods, Mr. Burr has steadily developed a business of mammoth proportions, constituting in its several branches the most extensive and important enterprise in that section of Burlington county. At first the business was carried on by Mr. Burr and his brother, but upon the death of the latter Mr. Burr became the sole owner. When his son, Charles Engle Burr, became of age, he was admitted into partnership in the insurance branch of the business as Samuel E. Burr & Son, a general insurance agency which Mr. Burr started in 1868. For five years he was the special agent of the Franklin Fire Insurance Company, with the power of appointing all other agents in New Jersey, three years in Trenton as secretary of the Standard Insurance Company, of Trenton, New Jersey. This company was about to wind up its business when he took charge; he built up its business and had it paying dividends inside of one year. In 1879 he built the Burr block in Bordentown. He is the president of the Bordentown board of health and of the water board. He has been a member of the common council, and a number of years ago was the candidate of the assembly. In November, 1908, with

several other prominent citizens, Mr. Burr organized the First National Bank, of Bordentown, which in six weeks had $50,000.00 on deposit. In 1893 Mr. Burr organized the Samuel E. Burr Hardware Company, with himself as president and treasurer, and his son as secretary. In September, 1903, he disposed of the grocery and provision branches of his business to Cramer & Rogers, but he retains under his individual management the dry goods and notions lines at 2 Crosswicks street. In 1882 Mr. Burr organized as an individual undertaking the public telephone service in Bordentown. After he had secured a sufficient number of subscribers to place the service on a remunerative basis he turned it over to the telephone company and the exchange is located on the second floor of the Burr building. Mr. Burr is a Baptist and a member of the Independent Order of Odd Fellows and of the Ancient Order of United Workmen, of Bordentown, to the former of which he has been attached for fifty years.

November 9, 1857, Samuel Engle Burr married (first) Sarah E., daughter of Benjamin and Hannah Richardson, who died April 18, 1894, having borne him one child, Charles Engle, who is referred to below. January 3, 1895, Samuel Engle Burr married (second) Elizabeth Coward, daughter of John Wesley, died November, 1904, and Anna (Coward) Thompson, and granddaughter of Allen Thompson, a Methodist minister who died aged one hundred and three years. The children of this marriage have been two: 1. Samuel Engle, Jr., born December 6, 1897. 2. Anna Thompson, born March 12, 1900.

(VII) Charles Engle, the only child of Samuel Engle and Sarah E. (Richardson) Burr, was born in Bordentown, Burlington county, New Jersey, September 4, 1868. For his early education he was sent to the Bordentown Military Institute, after which he spent one year in the Model school at Trenton, and then entered the Boston School of Technology, which last institution he was, however, obliged to leave after only a short stay, owing to ill health. This was in 1888, and he then went abroad and spent some time in travelling through England, France and Germany, and returning went for a visit to California. In 1893 he went into business with his father as secretary of the hardware company. In 1889 was made a partner in the insurance business. Mr. Burr is a director in the First National Bank, of Bordentown; secretary of the Bordentown Cemetery Association, and for the last five years has been chief of the five department of the city. He is also the treasurer of the Firemens' Volunteer Relief Association. He organized the Yapwes Boat Club and from its inception has been its secretary and treasurer. Mr. Burr is a Democrat, he has served as a councilman, in 1900 being president of the common council. He is a member of the Free and Accepted Masons, Mount Moriah Lodge. No. 28; of the Mount Moriah Royal Arch Chapter, No. 20, and of Ivanhoe Commandery, Knights Templar, No. 11. He is also a past master, past high priest, past commander and commander of Lu Lu Temple, Philadelphia; of Crescent Temple, Trenton; of Scottish Rite bodies, Trenton, and a thirty-second degree Mason. He is also a member of the Independent Order of Odd Fellows, No. 16; of the Knights of Pythias, No. 33; of the Ancient Order of United Workmen, No. 9, and of the Benevolent and Protective Order of Elks, No. 105, of Bordentown. April 12, 1893, Charles Engle Burr married Helen A., daughter of Captain Robert and Jane (Allen) Bloombury, of Bordentown, and they have one child, Sarah Jane, born May 24, 1895, who has been educated at private schools and at the Model school in Trenton.

(For early generations see preceding sketch).

(IV) Henry (3), only son and BURR youngest child of Henry (2) and Elizabeth (Foster) Burr, was born the 10th day of 1st month, 1763, in Mount Holly, New Jersey, in which town he died, in 1732, his will being proved January 30, that year. He was a farmer, and lived on the old family homestead in Mount Holly, his lands including four hundred acres. He was an industrious and prosperous husbandman, and as a man enjoyed the respect of all persons to whom he was known. He married Phebe, daughter of Edmund and Miriam Williams, of Shrewsbury, New Jersey; children: 1. Edmund W., born 2d mo., 1, 1792. 2. Elizabeth, 5th mo., 18, 1793; married Joshua Satterthwaite, of Crosswicks, New Jersey. 3. Miriam, 11th mo., 21, 1794; married Elwood E. Smith. 4. Henry, 10th mo., 15, 1796. 5. George W., 9th mo., 15, 1798. 6. William W., 2d mo., 3, 1800. 7. Tyle W., 3d mo., 15, 1802. 8. Charles, 7th mo., 21, 1804 (see post). 9. Hudson S., 7th mo., 2, 1806.

(V) Charles, son and eighth child of Henry (3) and Phebe (Williams) Burr, was born in Mount Holly, New Jersey, the 21st day of 7th

month, 1804, and died there October 29, 1852. He was a man of good education, and devoted much of his life to teaching school, at which he was very successful, and enjoyed considerable celebrity as a teacher. At one time and for several years he carried on a general merchandise store in Medford, New Jersey, and in all respects his business life was a success. In politics he was a Whig, but it does not appear that he took an active part in public affairs. He married (first) Lucy Ann Troth, born April 2, 1807, died February 20, 1829, and by whom he had one child. He married (second) February 8, 1830. Mary E. Engle, born March 20, 1805, daughter of Obadiah and Lucy Engle, of Easton, New Jersey. He had eight children, one by his first and seven by his second wife: 1. Alfred H., born March 20, 1827. 2. Lucy Ann, January 10, 1831; married Anthony Cuthbert. 3. Mamre George, December 19, 1832. 4. Samuel E., March 20, 1836. 5. Aaron E., January 28, 1841 (see post). 6. William W., November 24, 1838. 7. Charles O., October 24, 1843. 8. Augustus Walter, June 5, 1847.

(VII) Aaron Engle, son of Charles and Mary E. (Engle) Burr, was born in Mount Holly, New Jersey, January 28, 1841. He attended school until he was fifteen years old, and began his business career as a merchant in Burlington, in partnership with a Mr. Heaton, under the firm name of Burr & Heaton. He was in business from 1862 throughout the war period and afterward until 1869, when he sold out his interest and went into a proprietary medicine business at Moorestown, New Jersey. He was thus engaged until 1882, and afterward for several years was a state and county detective in the service of the Pennsylvania Railroad Company. He then determined to enter the profession of law, and to that end registered as a student and began a course of law studies under the direction of Hon. Samuel K. Robbins, of Moorestown. In 1895 he was admitted to practice, being then fifty-five years old; and it is said that Mr. Burr is perhaps the oldest man ever admitted to the bar in Burlington county, if not in the state of New Jersey. The first case in which he appeared as attorney was for a client who then was one hundred one years old. However, Mr. Burr is a capable and successful lawyer, and while his practice is general, his attention is devoted largely to mercantile collections. He is a Republican in politics, and as the candidate of his party has frequently been elected to service in public offices, such as constable, township clerk, overseer of the poor, and is serving his second term as justice of the peace. He is a member of the Ancient Order of United Workmen, the Patriotic Order of Sons of America, the Independent Order of Odd Fellows, the Improved Order of Red Men, the Knights of the Golden Eagle and in religious preference inclines strongly to the teachings of the Society of Friends.

On December 31, 1862, Mr. Burr married Sarah S., daughter of David and Mary (English) Heaton, of Burlington, and by whom he has had seven children: 1. William H., born June 22, 1864; died August 11, 1865. 2. Charles E., born January 8, 1867; died July 3, 1867. 3. Mary A., born July 2, 1868; married Frank Flagg, of Hasbrouck Heights, Bergen county, New Jersey, and has two children, Esther and Donald Flagg. 4. Rebecca A., born August 13, 1870; married Howard G. Taylor, of Moorestown, a commercial traveller. 5. Aaron R., born January 14, 1876; died July 29, 1876. 6. David H., born May 6, 1877; married Ada Brock. 7. James B. E., born September 6, 1884; an electrician living at Port Carbon, Pennsylvania; married Ella Turner, and has one child, Theodosia Burr.

(For preceding generations see preceding sketches).

BURR (VI) Alfred Henry, only child of Charles and Lucy Ann (Troth) Burr, was born in Medford, Burlington county, New Jersey, March 20, 1827, and is now living in Moorestown, in the same county. For his education he was sent to the select schools of Medford and to boarding school, after which he went as clerk into the wholesale dry goods store of William C. Morgan & Company, of Philadelphia, with whom he remained for six years. In 1849 he went into business for himself in Moorestown, where he kept a general store, selling dry goods, groceries, hardware, etc. In this business he remained until 1897 when he retired from active business. Mr. Burr has large real estate interests both in Burlington county and also in Florida, where for a good many years he has spent every winter. Among his interests in the south was a plantation in Florida of about eight thousand acres of which he was the principal owner. In Burlington county he owns a number of farms, both small and large, and several town properties including the large business block in which he carried on his own business for nearly half a century. He is the treasurer of the Oil and Mining Company, and is the director and the treasurer of several

building and loan associations in connection with which he handles over $500,000.00 every year. He is also a director in the bank of Moorestown of which he was one of the original promoters and organizers. He is a member of the Independent Order of Odd Fellows, of Philadelphia, and in politics he is a Republican, and in religion is a member of the Society of Friends, December 26, 1850, Alfred Henry Burr married Elizabeth, born December 25, 1826, daughter of John and Julia Hartman, of Philadelphia, who died August 14, 1904. Their children were: 1. Lord Hartman, referred to below. 2. Alfred Troth, born in Moorestown, April 16, 1855; died December 20, 1896; he was in the general merchandise business with his father; married Florence V. Ford and left one child, Ethel Marie, a graduate of Vassar College, having won two scholarships.

(VII) Lord Hartman, elder son of Alfred Henry and Elizabeth (Hartman) Burr, was born in Moorestown, July 25, 1852, and is now living in that place. After attending the Moorestown public schools, he went into his father's store, and when the trust company was organized in Moorestown about twenty years ago, accepted a position in that institution and is now its secretary. He is also interested in the Building and Loan Association, of Moorestown, of which he is the treasurer. In politics Mr. Burr is a Republican and in religion is a communicant of the Protestant Episcopal church. Lord Hartman Burr married (first) Mary Hartman, who bore him one child, Lord Hartman, Jr., who won the University of Pennsylvania's scholarship to the West Indies. Mr. Burr married (second) ———, and by this marriage he has had three children: Alfred, Elizabeth and Jeannette, twins.

PANCOAST "I Joseph Pancoast, son of John and Elizabeth Pancoast of Ashen, fieve miles from Northampton Town, in Northampton Shire, England, born 1672 the 27th of eighth month called October; and in the year 1680, October 4th came into America in the ship 'Paradise,' William Evelyn, master; and I settled in West New Jersey, Burlington County, and on the 14th of the eighth month, October 1696, I took to wife Thomasin Scattergood, daughter of Thomas and Elizabeth Scattergood, of Stepney Parish, London, who also transported themselves into Burlington County in America." The above quotation is from an old document in the possession of Henry Pancoast

Edward H. Pancoast

of Mesopotamia, Ohio, and tells us the origin of the Pancoast family in this country.

(I) John Pancoast, the founder of the family, came, as the document says, to West Jersey in 1680, bringing with him his family of children. It is uncertain whether his wife accompanied him or whether she died very shortly after her arrival in America. At any rate John Pancoast was married a second time within two years of his coming, and shortly before his death he took to himself a third wife. His children are believed to have been all of them the issue of his first marriage. He settled at the mouth of the east branch of the Assiscunck creek, was one of the signers of the noted "Concessions and Agreements," and owned proprietary rights in the province. In 1681 he was appointed regulator of weights and measures for Burlington county, in 1683 be was chosen constable, and in 1685 he was elected a member of the assembly of West Jersey. His will is dated November 30, and was proved December 22, 1694. The name of his first wife was Elizabeth; his second, whom he married in the Burlington monthly meeting in 1682, was Ann Snowden, and the name of his third wife was Jane. His children were: 1. Mary, married Seth Smith. 2. Ann. 3. William, referred to below. 4. Joseph, referred to above in the extract, who married Thomasin Scattergood. 5. Elizabeth, married Joseph Bacon. 6. Sarah, married Edward Boulton. 7. Hannah. 8. Susanna, married Ralph Cowgill.

(II) William, son of John and Elizabeth Pancoast, was born in England, and accompanied his father to this country. He was probably the eldest of all of his children and was the sole executor of his father's will. He settled near his father in Mansfield township, Burlington county, and seems to have lived there all his life, although in 1700 he had surveyed for him two hundred and seventy acres on Rock creek, near Little Egg Harbor. September 1, 1695, he married in the Burlington monthly meeting, Hannah, daughter of Thomas and Elizabeth Scattergood, the sister of his brother Joseph's wife, and there are records of four of his children. He undoubtedly had other children and the tradition which makes Edward who is referred to below and William who married Meribah Allen his sons, is most probably correct. The four children whose marriages are recorded in the Chesterfield and Burlington monthly meetings are: 1. John, married Mary Crusher. 2. Joseph, married Mary Ogborne. 3. Elizabeth, married Marma-
ii—11

duke Watson. 4. Hannah, married Matthew Watson.

(III) Edward, son of William and Hannah (Scattergood) Pancoast, was born in Mansfield township, and spent the early part of his manhood in Bordentown, where in 1756 he advertises for the apprehension of a runaway servant, Patrick Weldon. Some time after his marriage he removed from Bordentown to Salem county, where his descendants became numerous and influential. August 15, 1761, he took out a license to marry Hannah King and there is record of at least two children to this marriage: 1. Samuel, married Dorcas Stratch, and became one of the most influential members of the Salem monthly meeting. 2. William, referred to below.

(IV) William (2), son of Edward and Hannah (King) Pancoast, married, in 1784, the license being dated February 19, Sarah Lishman, and had at least two sons: 1. Samuel. 2. Henry, referred to below.

(V) Henry, son of William (2) and Sarah (Lishman) Pancoast, was born in Salem county, New Jersey, February 2, 1792, died there September 9, 1835. He married Hannah Ivins Hackney, born in 1796, died April 18, 1882. Their children were: 1. Mary, born October 10, 1818. 2. Caroline, January 27, 1821. 3. Rebecca Hackney, March 16, 1822. 4. William Hackney, September 10, 1824. 5. Henry Jr., June 8, 1828. 6. Barzillai B., May 23, 1831. 7. Edward Hackney, referred to below.

(VI) Edward Hackney, youngest child of Henry and Hannah Ivins (Hackney) Pancoast, was born near Woodstown, Salem county, May 12, 1835 and is now living at Riverton, New Jersey. His father died when he was about four months old, and after receiving a common school education he was put out as apprentice when eight years old, and when twenty-two years old he had a small farm on which he carried on truck farming. Previous to this as a young man he taught school for a time, and later he had a flour and feed business in Bridgeboro. In 1862 he enlisted in Company G, Twelfth Regiment of New Jersey Volunteers, and was mustered into service in August, 1862. The company was then sent to Baltimore and was on police duty for a time. He was in the battles of Chancellorsville and Gettysburg, and was taken prisoner in the second day's fight of the latter battle. He was taken to Belle Island, Richmond, where he was kept for three months, and then sent to Annapolis, Maryland,

and later, after his exchange, went to the hospital at Philadelphia, Pennsylvania. He was discharged from service in May, 1865. Returning to New Jersey he located at Riverton, where he took up carpentering and contracting, and built many of the houses of Palmyra and Riverton. This line of business he followed for some twenty years, and then went into the real estate and insurance business, in which he is active at the present time. Mr. Pancoast is a Republican and has served as counsellman for several years. He has also served on the board of assessors, and on the board of education for many years, and he has been one of the chosen freeholders. He is a member of Covenant Lodge, No. 161, Free and Accepted Masons, of Palmyra, of which he was first master; Boudinot Chapter, No. 3, Royal Arch Masons, of Burlington, of which he is past high priest; Helena Commandery, No. 3, Knights Templar, of Burlington, of which he is past eminent commander. He is also a Scottish Rite Mason of Camden, New Jersey, and a thirty-second degree Mason. He is a member of Washington Camp, No. 23, Patriotic Order Sons of America, of Palmyra; Cinnaminson Lodge, No. 201, Independent Order of Odd Fellows, of Palmyra; Knights of the Golden Eagle, No. 22, of Palmyra; a life member of the Fire Association of Riverton; a member of William P. Hatch Post, No. 37, Grand Army of the Republic, of Camden, and a member, trustee and district steward of the Methodist Episcopal church.

Edward Hackney Pancoast married Rebecca A., born in Bridgeboro, daughter of Ahab and Sarah (Sharp) Bishop. Their children are: 1. Laura, born June 4, 1857, died March 29, 1877. 2. Martha Austin, born September 10, 1858, widow of Hugh Glendening White, whose children are: Edward, who is married and is surgeon in the United States navy, William and Laura P. White. 3. Stacy Stratton, referred to below. 4. Annie Brown, born March 4, 1861, died September 13, 1898; married Alfred J. Briggs, and had one child, Alfred Stacy Briggs, who married and had a son Alfred Briggs. 5. Edward, born June 9, 1862, died August 15, 1863.

(VII) Stacy Stratton, third child and only son of Edward Hackney and Rebecca A. (Bishop) Pancoast, was born in Chester township, Burlington county, March 5, 1860, and is now living at Delanco, New Jersey. He was educated in the schools of Riverton, in the Farnham preparatory school at Beverly, New Jersey, and at the Crittenden Commercial College in Philadelphia, graduating from the last named institution in 1878. He then worked in Philadelphia as a clerk and bookkeeper for several years, after which he went into the office of W. Frederick Snyder for three years, and in 1885 opened an office for himself in Philadelphia, where he conducted a real estate any conveyancing business, in which he continued until 1888, when he went to Alabama on account of his health. From there in 1892 he went to West Virginia, where he built a mill and carried on the lumber business for three years, when, his mill having been destroyed by fire, he returned north and settled at Delanco, New Jersey, in 1895, taking a position as assistant manager to The G. O. Hammell Company in the lumber business. In 1898 he was made manager and treasurer of the company, and this position he now holds. Mr. Pancoast is a Republican, and a member of the Masonic order, of Merchantville Lodge, No. 33, of the Boudinot Royal Arch Chapter, No. 3, of Burlington, of the Helena Commandery, Knights Templar, No. 3, of Burlington, and he is also a past master of the lodge and past eminent commander of the Knights Templar. He is also a member of the I. O. R. M., the Tacoma Tribe of Delanco; Washington Camp, No. 35, Patriotic Order Sons of America, of Delanco, New Jersey.

In November, 1884, Stacy S. Pancoast married Mabel D., daughter of Henry D. and Matilda M. Garnes, of Camden, New Jersey. Child, Harry G., born August 10, 1885, died October 15, 1885.

(For ancestry see preceding sketch).

PANCOAST   Caleb C. Pancoast is a great-grandson of John Pancoast, the emigrant. As to which of John's two sons he is the grandson there is some doubt, but the evidence seems to point to his being the grandson of William and Hannah (Scattergood) Pancoast, through a son Caleb, whom tradition assigns to these parents.

(IV) Caleb C. Pancoast was born in Mullica Hill, Gloucester county, New Jersey, was a farmer and lived and died where he was born. By his wife Deborah he had at least three children: 1. Rhoda, married a Mr. Roberts. 2. Hannah, married Captain Thomas Dixie. 3. Nathan Dunn, referred to below.

(V) Nathan Dunn, son of Caleb C. and Deborah Pancoast, was born in Mullica Hill, Gloucester county, December 10, 1804, died in 1898. After being educated in the town schools he taught school for two winters at

Millica Hill and for some time followed farming. In 1838 he removed to Mapleshade, Burlington county, where he remained until 1850, when he removed to Moorestown, where he lived until the time of his death. He had large farming interests, was a very successful farmer, and owned and operated several farms. In 1861 he built the large frame house on the main road about a mile out of Moorestown. He was a Republican, and active in politics, but he was not an office seeker. He was a member of the Hicksite branch of the Society of Friends. He married Sarah Ann Moffatt, born at Carpenter's Landing, Gloucester county, in 1811 or 1812, and died in 1889. Their children were: 1. Josiah Dunn, referred to below. 2. Thomas Moffat, referred to below. 3. Caleb C., who was a member of the Assembly from Woodbury, New Jersey. 4. George W., a farmer, who removed to Williams county, Ohio. 5. Nathan Dunn Jr., who lives at Moorestown. 6. Amanda, who is living at Moorestown. 7. Sarah. 8. Deborah, who married Aaron E. Borton, of Moorestown.

(VI) Josiah Dunn, eldest child of Nathan Dunn and Sarah Ann (Moffatt) Pancoast, was born at Millica Hill, Gloucester county, in 1833, died in 1903. He was educated in the common schools, and about 1856 was engaged in farming on the Maple Shade farm, three and a half miles from Moorestown, where he remained seven years. He then moved to Magnolia Vale, where he spent the remainder of his life. He was a Republican, and was at one time supervisor of roads, and for eleven years was on the board of freeholders. Was a member of the Grange and a Hicksite Quaker. He died July 1, 1903. He married, March 19, 1857, at the Chesterfield Monthly Meeting, Sarah Middleton, daughter of Benjamin and Sarah (West) Thorn. Mrs. Pancoast is now living near Moorestown. Their children were: 1. Henry Norwood, referred to below. 2. George W., born August 15, 1862, married Mary Trimble, of Philadelphia, but has no children. 3. Thomas J., born July 13, 1865, a dealer in lumber, coal and hardware in Merchantsville, married Catharine Collins and has four children: J. Arthur, Norwood H., Russell Thorn and Norman Lester; died in infancy. 4. Laura G., born February 12, 1868, married Walter Holmes, a farmer near Moorestown, and has two children: Samuel G. and William Bartram. 5. Anna T., born April 3, 1870, married Clayton Lippincott Andrews, of Moorestown, and has three children:

Thomas Clayton, Norwood Henry and Edward Benajah.

(VII) Henry Norwood, eldest child of Josiah Dunn and Sarah Middleton (Thorn) Pancoast, was born in Mapleshade, Burlington county, January 30, 1859, and is now living in Riverton, New Jersey. He was educated in the public schools of Moorestown and in private schools near there, and for two years was a young man he worked on his father's farm. He then went to Galesburg, Illinois, in 1884, as a clerk in a grocery store, and after spending two more years there he went west in 1886 to Colorado where he found employment on a cattle ranch on the Platte river as foreman of the ranch. Here he remained for four years, returning east in 1890 and taking to farming on his grandfather's farm near Moorestown, which he carried on for three years and then for four years took charge of his father's farm. In 1897 he came to Riverton, and engaged in a flour, grain and coal business, established by Haines Brothers, his principal occupation being the manufacture of flour, as a member of the firm of Haines Brothers, who had been established there since 1892. Until December, 1904, the firm continued doing business under the old name, and then reincorporated itself under the title of H. N. Pancoast & Company, under which name it has been doing business ever since. Mr. Pancoast is a Republican, and has been a member of the election board at Moorestown and is at present a member of the borough council of Riverton. He is a member of the Grange and of the Society of Friends. In 1891 Henry Norwood Pancoast married Elizabeth L., born at Haines Mills, Burlington Pike, near Bridgeborough, daughter of John W. and Hannah M. (Lewis) Haines, born July 31, 1859, died in August, 1907. Besides four boys who died in infancy they had one child: Mary Haines, born near Moorestown, September 13, 1892, who is now attending George's school, near Newtown, Pennsylvania.

(VI) Thomas Moffatt, second child and son of Nathan Dunn and Sarah Ann (Moffatt) Pancoast, was born at Millica Hill, Gloucester county, September 5, 1834, and is now living at Moorestown, Burlington county, New Jersey. He was educated in the town schools of Millica Hill and in Samuel Aaronson's school at Norristown, Pennsylvania, after which he went to farming with his father. He did a large truck farming business, driving to market with produce and drawing back from the city fertilizers. He kept up this work at

Moorestown for his father until his marriage and then he went to work farming for himself. He was appointed postmaster of Moorestown under President Arthur, and served also under his successor, President Cleveland, for four years, and then remained in the office as assistant postmaster under his successor for three years longer. In 1907 he retired from active life and moved into the village of Moorestown, where he now lives. Mr. Pancoast is a Republican and a member of the Society of Friends.

In 1860 Thomas Moffatt Pancoast married (first) Sarah W., daughter of West Jessup, of Mantua, Gloucester county, who died in 1873. In 1886 he married (second) Harriet S., daughter of George S. Hulme, of Mt. Holly. In 1907 he married (third) Mary Griscom Lippincott, widow of Albert Lippincott, and daughter of David Griscom, who was president of the Moorestown Bank at the time of his death. Thomas Moffat Pancoast has no children.

TOMLINSON Of the founder of the Tomlinson family of West Jersey it has been said, "There are doubtless very many interesting incidents, which, by patient research among the misty records still extant could be brought to light, and would show much of the history of his time, in connection with the progress of the people in their social, judicial and political condition. That he was a progressive man is shown by his selecting his home so far away from the first settlements, in the depths of the wilderness, surrounded only by the aborigines, where nothing but industry and perseverance could procure him a farm. In connection with these difficulties he became proficient in legal knowledge. He, therefore, attracted the attention of the community, and was called to fill the responsible positions before named. These things stamp him as a man whose career through life is worthy of being traced and recorded."

(1) Joseph Tomlinson, the person above referred to, coming to West Jersey from the city of London, was a member of the Horsley-down Meeting of Friends, on the Surrey side of the river Thames, which even at that day had become a part of the great metropolis, by means of the several bridges already erected. He appears to have been under the patronage of Anthony, an uncle of the celebrated West Jersey Surveyor, Thomas Sharp, but whether or no he belonged to the same family as the

Lancashire and Derbyshire families of the same name who suffered for their religious beliefs from 1654 to 1690 is still uncertain. He arrived previous to 1686, and became an apprentice of Thomas Sharp, who had settled on Newton creek five years before. He had received a better education than many of his day, and he was still further fitted for the part he was to play by the excellent tutelage under which he found himself. In 1686 he agreed with his master to build him a house for a specified sum and to furnish all the materials except the nails. He was also probably one of those who built the Friends Meeting house in Newton, the first building of its kind in Gloucester county and the second in West Jersey. For some reason the articles of apprenticeship were set aside and Thomas Sharp agreed to pay Joseph £5 a year for his services and four at the end of his term. In 1690 Joseph Tomlinson located one hundred and seventeen acres on the east side of Gravelly run in Gloucester township, adjoining a tract he had previously purchased of Joseph Wood on which he settled and first lived after leaving the house of Friend Sharp. He soon increased his possessions until they extended from Gravelly run on the north to Holly run or Sharp's branch on the south. All of this he retained and willed after his death to his sons. His abode was surrounded by miles of unbroken forest and without neighbors within half a day's travel. He had to go ten miles to attend the Newton Meeting and if he took his farm produce to Philadelphia the distance was still increased. His leisure hours in this secluded spot he gave up to the reading and studying of law, and in 1695 he was made sheriff, and the year following became the King's attorney or as we should call him to-day the provincial prosecutor. He has the honor of being the first attorney of record in Gloucester county. In 1700 he was reappointed to the same position, and apparently he held it continuously until 1710. August 20, 1719, he wrote his will which was proven September 18 following, and in it he names his wife Elizabeth and ten children, there were probably others who died in infancy and childhood. The daughters following the fortunes of their husbands have to a great extent been lost sight of, but the family of to-day has not lost its identity with the first settler and much of the landed estate owned by him still remains in the name. His children named in his will are: 1. Ephraim, married (first) 1727, Sarah Corbit, and (second) Catharine Ridgway. 2.

Joseph, married (first) 1734, Lydia Wade, and (second) 1738, Catharine Fairlamb, of Chester, Pennsylvania. 3. Margaret, married, 1736, Edward Borton. 4. Elizabeth, married, 1736, Bartholomew Wyatt. 5. Mary, married, 1730, Samuel Sharp. 6. John, who is referred to below. 7. Ebenezer. 8. Othniel, married, 1744. Mary Marsh. 9. Richard. 10. William, married, 1731, Rebecca Wills.

(II) John, son of Joseph and Elizabeth Tomlinson, was born in Gloucester township, Gloucester county, West Jersey, September 28, 1699; died there in 1755. In accordance with his father's will settled on three hundred acres higher up on Gravelly run where he spent his life. In his will, written January 2, 1755, and proven March 21 following he leaves this plantation to his wife for life or widowhood and then it reverts to his son, Isaac, who also is given twenty-five acres of "Syder Swamp" on Great Egg Harbour river and fifteen acres of swamp on Hospitality branch of the same stream. His personal estate he divided equally between his wife and his two daughters. His executors were his wife his brother, Joseph, and his son, Isaac. He married, in 1736, Mary Fairlamb, of Chester county, Pennsylvania, who bore him three children: 1. Isaac, who is referred to below. 2. Hannah. 3. Eleanor, married Josiah Albertson, and had a son, John, who in 1784 was put under the guardianship of his Uncle Isaac.

(III) Isaac, eldest child and only son of John and Mary (Fairlamb) Tomlinson, was born in Gloucester township, Gloucester county, August 10, 1737; died there in 1817. In 1783 he was one of the executors of the estate of James Taggard, and the following year was appointed guardian to his nephew, John Albertson. His will written January 15, 1812. and proved March 10, 1817, leaves the plantation to his wife during life or widowhood and then reverts it to his son, Joshua, his other children are left money legacies and his personal estate is divided equally between his widow and his daughter, Elizabeth, also a widow. In 1766 Isaac Tomlinson married Elizabeth Shever and their children were: 1. Joshua. 2. Elizabeth, married William Clark. 3. Anne, married Jeremiah Haines. 4. Isaac, Jr. 5. John, who is referred to below.

(IV) John (2), youngest child of Isaac and Elizabeth (Shever) Tomlinson, was born in Gloucester township, Gloucester county, April 15, 1781; died in Northampton township, Burlington county, February 25, 1857. John Tomlinson and his wife, Elizabeth had six children:

1. Isaac born July 4, 1812; mentioned below. 2. John H., February 3. 1815; died May 7, 1859. 3. Joshua, September 23, 1818; mentioned below. 4. Thomas Chalkley, August 25, 1820; died September 2, 1845. 5. Evans R., April 5, 1824; now (1909) living in Mt. Holly. 6. Benjamin, November 20, 1831; died September 5, 1835.

(V) Isaac (2), eldest son of John (2) and Elizabeth Tomlinson, was born in Northampton township, Burlington county, New Jersey, July 4, 1812; died in Gloucester township, Camden county, on the original grant of his ancestors, July 14, 1849. He was a farmer and spent his early life on the farm near Rancocus. He married Rebecca C. Lippincott, and had four children: 1. Samuel L., who is referred to below. 2. Elizabeth, born April 22, 1840; married George H. Pancoast. 3. William H., died in infancy. 4. Thomas Chalkley, died in infancy.

(VI) Samuel Lippincott, the only son to reach maturity of Isaac (2) and Rebecca C. (Lippincott) Tomlinson, was born on the old plantation in Camden county, New Jersey, September 18, 1837, on a farm near Blackwood that had been in the Tomlinson family for five generations or since the year 1787. He was brought to Mt. Holly in 1849. For his early education he was sent to the select schools of Mt. Holly and afterwards finished his education at the private school of William Collom at Mt. Holly. He then went as clerk into his uncle's store at Columbus, New Jersey, where he remained from November 3, 1852, until 1861, when he went to Meadville, Pennsylvania, in order to accept the position of superintendent and treasurer of the Meadville Gas Company, and became interested in the oil business. He returned to Mt. Holly in March, 1866, where he went into partnership with his uncle in keeping a general store, which they conducted for four years. March 4, 1871, when the Union National Bank was organized, he accepted the post of teller to which he had been elected and which he held January 9, 1883, when he was promoted to the office of cashier, in which capacity he is still serving. For fifteen years Mr. Tomlinson has been treasurer of the Mt. Holly Shoe Company, and for ten years he was the treasurer of the Rendell Shoe Company. Since 1902 he has also been the treasurer of the Mt. Holly Safe Deposit & Trust Company. Mr. Tomlinson has been a member of the Order of Free and Accepted Masons since 1863, first of Solomon Chapter, No. 191, Royal Arch Masons. of Meadville

Pennsylvania, and then of Boudinot Chapter in Burlington, New Jersey. In 1866 he became a member of Helena Commandery, No. 3, Knights Templar, at Burlington, and in 1867 a member of Mt. Holly Lodge, No. 19, Independent Order of Odd Fellows, of Mt. Holly. February 2, 1882, he joined the Order of United Workmen and has been the receiver of the lodge ever since, being one of the charter members and a representative of the Grand Lodge twenty different times. He is also a charter member of Mt. Holly Lodge, No. 848, Benevolent and Protective Order of Elks. He was a member of Spring Garden Lodge, No. 4, Knights of Burmingham, until the lodge went out of existence. He married, September 20, 1865, Emma, daughter of Frederick and Emily Kirby, of Meadville, Pennsylvania.

(V) Joshua, third son of John (2) and Elizabeth Tomlinson, was born in Northampton township, Burlington county, New Jersey, September 23, 1818; died April 23, 1875. He was educated in the schools of Rancocus. When a young man he went to New York City and learned the trade of mason in all its branches, brick and stone, with Franklin Haines. He later formed a partnership with Chalkley Wills and engaged in general contracting and building. He later formed a partnership with George D. Hilliard; they conducted an extensive business and were among the leading contractors in the city, building the first hotel on Coney Island. Mr. Tomlinson met with an accident which disabled him from active business and he removed to Princeton, New Jersey, where he resided two years, thence to Mt. Holly, where he resided during the remainder of his life. He married Sarah E. Hutchins, daughter of William and Henry Hutchins. Children:— 1. Anna, died in infancy. 2. Evans H., born in New York, August 3, 1854; received his education in the select schools of Princeton and Mt. Holly, entered Swarthmore College, and later engaged as clerk for the firm of Russell & Erwins in Philadelphia in the hardware manufacturing, remaining for three and a half years; the following eighteen years he engaged in farming. On March 3, 1902, he entered the Union National Bank at Mt. Holly as clerk and is now (1909) serving in the capacity of receiving teller; he married, June 24, 1884, May H. Garrison, of Mt. Holly, daughter of Hedge and Adeline (Haines) Garrison; children: i. Marion G., born August 31, 1885, married Chester Appleton, of Mt. Holly, and has one child, Elizabeth; ii. Edna, born December 1, 1889, a graduate of

the Trenton Normal School; iii. Dorothea, born July 19, 1902. 3. William B., mentioned below.

(VI) William B., youngest son and child of Joshua and Sarah E. (Hutchins) Tomlinson, was born in New York City, December 8, 1858. He was educated in the select schools of Mt. Holly, Princeton and at Swarthmore College. After completing his studies he was for a time clerk in the firm of Russell & Erwins, of Philadelphia, later engaged in farming in Camden county, and at the present time (1909) is one of the leading and prosperous farmers of Burlington county. He married Ida Cook, born December 19, 1860, of Jacksonville, daughter of John and Hannah (Scott) Cook. Children: 1. William I., born May 20. 1880, a physician, of Philadelphia;· married Grace Maxwell, and has one child, William B. 2. Jay B., born January 6, 1893; an attendant of Mt. Holly high school.

BAIRD The name Bard, Barde and Baird appears in records in various parts of Europe as early as the tenth and extending to the fourteenth century. They appear to have migrated from Lorraine to d'Aosta in Piedmont, and from there to Normandy, finally settling in Scotland. In his "Irish Genealogy" MacForbes treats it as a joke that the Bairds claim an Anglo-Saxon origin, his contention being that their origin is Celtic. In "Irish Pedigrees" of which work Dr. O'Hart is the author, he says: Owen Mac an Bhaird, of Monycassen, was descended from Eocha, son of Sodhan. Mac an Bhaird was anglicized Macward and modernized Ward. The descendants of Owen Mac an Bhaird rendered the name O'Bairdam, and that in turn has been anglicized Baird, Bard, Barde, Barden, Bardin, Barten, Bartin, Berdan, Purdon, Verdon and Warden. In 1066 Seigneur de Barde was among the followers of William the Conqueror. In 1178 Henry de Barde was a witness to a charter of lands made by King William, the Lion, of Scotland. In 1191 Ugone di Bard, of the valley of d'Aosta, made allegiance to Francis I., of Savoy. He owned a castle on Bard Rock, a natural defence, and after bravely defending the place was finally driven out. He had two sons, Marco and Aymone. In 1194 Hugo de Baird was one of the subscribing witnesses to a safe conduct granted by King Richard I., of England, to King William, the Lion, and it is said that a gentleman by the name of Baird saved William the Lion from a wild beast, and he received for this deed large tracts of land and coat-of-arms, viz: A boar passant, with the motto "Dominus fecit." During the Scotch war for independence the Bards were able supporters of the cause with Bruce and Wallace. Robert Bard was captured by the English, held a prisoner at Nottingham, and an order was issued January, 1317, for his removal to the castle of Summerton. His fate is unknown. A William Bard was routed and taken prisoner with Sir William Douglass in 1333, in a skirmish with Sir Anthony Lacy on the English border. Jordan Baird was a constant companion with the brave William Wallace from 1297 to 1305. General Sir David Baird was a contemporary of Captain David Baird, and held command under Sir John Moore in the Peninsular campaign, and after the death and burial of Sir John succeeded to the command and reported the victory at Corrunna. He was the son of Sir William Baird, the son of Sir Robert, the son of James, the son of George, who was living in 1588. That John Baird (q. v.), of Topenemus neighborhood, New Jersey, was of this stock there seems little doubt.

(I) John Baird came from Aberdeen, Scotland. as a passenger of the good ship "Exchange," Captain James Peacock, master, and landed at Staten Island in New York harbor, about December 19, 1683. The state archives at Trenton, New Jersey, in a list of persons who were deported from Scotland to America, and duly registered December 5, 1684, the names of John King, four years' service; John Nesmith, four years' service; John Baird, four years' service, etc., etc., occur. There were forty-seven thus deported. After John Baird had fulfilled his term of service he acquired several tracts of lands at New Aberdeen, Topenemus, and on Millstone brook in East Jersey and other places. It is said that John Baird dwelt in a cave with an Indian for a time before he built a house on the Topenemus tract. Traces of the cave are said to be visible on the banks of Topenemus brook, a little back and to the side of the present Baird homestead, built by James Baird, son of Zebulon, and grandson of John Baird, the immigrant. He was a Quaker, and the Friends' church was built near his homestead, where George Keith and his followers worshipped, and where he preached. When Keith, who was originally a Presbyterian, changed to the Society of Friends, it is probable that John Baird changed with him as he did to the Episcopal faith when Keith took orders in that church and carried many members of the Friends meeting with

him. Tradition has the story of his courtship and marriage as follows: "One day he met in the woods Mary Hall, whom he afterward married. As both were bashful, they halted at some distance from each other under a tree. It was love at first sight. John, who was a Quaker, broke the silence by saying 'If thou wilt marry me say 'yea,' if thou wilt not, say 'nay.' Mary said 'yea' and proved a noble wife and mother." This tradition equals that of the courtship of John Alden and Priscilla Mullins. The four children of John and Mary (Hall) Baird were born as follows, and it is quite probable there were others: 1. John (2), 1707.; probably married Avis, the story of his gaining her for a wife being as follows: He had heard of a shipwreck on the coast, and that on board the ship were several comely women. He hurried to the scene on horseback, and there selected his wife in the woman of his choice. It is said he saw her, wooed her, won her, and was comforted. In his will dated February 5, 1747, probated July 5, 1749, he names his sons, Andrew and Zebulon; his wife, Avis, and Peter Bowne, executors of the will, and directs that after his debts are paid the residue of his estate be given to his wife, Avis Baird, during her widowhood, and in case of her re-marriage to be divided equally between his wife and children and family, without naming them. The children of John (2) and Avis Baird, including three sons, Andrew, Bedent and Zebulon, of whom Andrew and Zebulon, named for their two uncles, sons of their grandfather, John, the Scottish immigrant, and with whom they are often confused by genealogists. After the probating of their father's will, July 5, 1749, at which time they must have been of legal age, as Andrew and Zebulon were with their mother executors of the will, they migrated to North Carolina, making the journey across the Blue Ridge in a wagon, and when they reached Buncomb county, North Carolina, they exhibited the wagon as a curiosity, the first vehicle of the kind seen in that mountain district. They approached the house of Mr. George Swain, a native of Roxbury, Massachusetts, where he was born in 1763, through the washed-out channel of the creek, there being no roads, and the future governor of North Carolina, David Lowrie Swain, then a mere lad, when he saw the wondrous vehicle thus approaching his home he was standing in his father's orchard, planted with apple trees, raised from cuttings, brought from New England by his father, and waited the approach of the thundering chariot with wonder and awe as it rolled over the rocky bed of the creek. At its nearer approach he took to his heels and hid behind his father's horse, but was brought out by the command of his father to welcome and care for the visitors who were from New Jersey. They probably were at the time prospecting as they came to Burke county, North Carolina, as early as 1760, where Andrew married Anna, daughter of Mathew Locke, whose relative, Colonel Francis Locke, commanded three hundred militia men from Burke, Lincoln and Rowan counties, North Carolina, and gained the victory at Ramsoor's Mills, May 29, 1780, of Lieutenant George Locke, killed in battle, September 26, 1780. The descendants of Andrew and Anna (Locke) Baird are numerous throughout the south. Zebulon also married and among his descendants was Zebulon Baird Vance (1830-1894), governor of North Carolina, and United States senator. John Baird (2), the father of these North Carolina pioneers, died in Topenemus, Millstone township, Monmouth county, New Jersey, February 6, 1747, and was buried in the Topenemus burial ground, where his father was buried. 2. David (q. v.). 3. Andrew, who deeded his property to his brother Zebulon, June 15, 1755. 4. Zebulon, born 1720; died January 28, 1804, aged eighty-eight years, three months and fifteen days, and his wife, Anna, died December 28, 1794, aged sixty-three years, four months and eleven days, and both are buried in the burial ground at Topenemus, New Jersey. John Baird, the immigrant, was buried at Topenemus, New Jersey, and on his tombstone is the following inscription:

"JOHN BAIRD
who came from Scotland
in 18th year of his age, A. D. 1683
died April   . 1755
aged about 90 years, and
of an honest character."

Mary Baird was admitted to the Lord's table at the White Hill meeting house in 1736.

(II) David, second son of John and Mary (Hall) Baird, of Topenemus, was born October 19, 1710, was married, October 27, 1744, to Sarah Compton, born April 18, 1716; died May 1, 1810. David Baird died June 20, 1801. By this marriage there were born four children in Topenemus as follows: 1. Jacob, November, 1745; lived on a farm in Morris county, New Jersey, owned by his father, and on the death of his father it descended to him by his will. 2. Mary, September 30, 1747; married John, son of James and Dinah Tillyer Dey

(1747-1829), and they had children: James, John, David, Elias, Mary B. and David B. Dey. Mary (Baird) Dey died 1836. 3. John, October 27, 1750; married (first) Phebe Ely, who died June 17, 1817, and (second) Elizabeth Edwards. He was an elder of the Old Tennent Church, and had no children by either of his wives. 4. Captain David (q. v.).

(III) Captain David (2), youngest child of David (1) and Sarah (Compton) Baird, was born in Topenemus, New Jersey, July 16, 1754; died December 24, 1839. He was a private in the first regiment from New Jersey to join the American forces at the time of the rebellion against Great Britian, became sergeant in 1776, and was promoted ensign, lieutenant and quartermaster. He was captain of militia in 1777, and also captain of light horse in Monmouth county militia. He was in the New Jersey line at the battle of Germantown, was called with his company to protect the salt works at Tom's River several times, and to the protection of Navesink Highlands. He also served with General Dickerson's forces during the British march across New Jersey, and was in several skirmishes and at the battle of Monmouth, June 28, 1778. He married (first) February 27, 1777, Rebecca Ely, and by her he had one child: Rebecca, who married William Ely, and had twelve children: David B., Joseph W., Harvey, John, Isaac, George A., Mary, Sarah, Lucy, Phoebe, Elizabeth and William. Rebecca (Ely) Baird, the grandmother of these children, died January 6, 1778, and Captain David Baird married (second) Lydia (Topscott) Gaston, a widow, and by her he had six children born as follows: 1. Sarah, November 1, 1780; died April 7, 1881, over one hundred years of age; she married Thomas, son of Anthony Applegate, and they had seven children: Anthony, Lydia, David B., Sarah D., Disbrow, Thomas and John Applegate. 2. Mary, October 15, 1782; married Leon Dey, January 24, 1800, and removed to Ohio. 3. John, March 19, 1784. 4. Jacob, December 19, 1785; died April 8, 1822. 5. Lydia, February 8, 1788; married William Johnson, and had four children. 6. Phebe, November 14, 1790; married David Perine, had twelve children; she died December 17, 1855. Lydia (Topscott) (Gaston) Baird, the mother of these six children, died February 5, 1791, aged thirty-six years, and Captain David Baird married (third) Mary, daughter of Lieutenant Thomas and Elizabeth (Vaughn) Edwards, November 25, 1795, and by her he had eleven children born as follows: 1. David,

February 22, 1797; married Amy Hendrickson, and removed to Indiana. 2. Rei, May 16, 1798; held the title of general; married Sarah Clayton, and had six children; he died September 7, 1835. 3. Elizabeth, March 2, 1800; married Peter Wyckoff, and had nine children; he died December 4, 1895. 4. Thomas (q. v.). 5. Ann, December 25, 1803; married Hartshorne Tantum, and had eight children. 6. Evelina, October 25, 1805; married William P. Foreman, and had four children; she died November 26, 1883. 7. Joseph, July 4, 1807; died May 5, 1814. 8. James, June 3, 1810; married Rebecca F., daughter of Richard and Amy Ely, of Black's Mills; he lived on the Baird homestead or Millstone brook, west of Pine Hill, until 1854, when he moved to Illinois; they had six children: John, who was killed in the civil war, Mary, Amy, Richard, Rei and Thomas. 9. Rachel, September 7, 1812; married Elias Riggs, and had four children. 10. Eleanor, December 15, 1815; married George W. Stephen, and had six children. 11. Zebulon, July 31, 1819; married Caroline E., daughter of Joseph Perrine, and removed to Illinois in 1854; they had seven children. Thus the descendants of Captain David Baird are eighteen children, over ninety-four grandchildren, and more than one hundred and forty-nine great-grandchildren.

(IV) Thomas, fifth son and eleventh child of Captain David (2) Baird, and third son and fourth child of Captain David and Mary (Edwards) Baird, was born at Manalapan, Millstone township, Monmouth county, New Jersey, February 6, 1802. He was a progressive farmer, and owned several valuable farms and was reputed to have been a very wealthy man for the time and occupation in which he engaged. He married Eleanor P., daughter of Peter and Maria (Ogbourne) Bilyeu. The three children of Thomas and Eleanor P. (Bilyeu) Baird were born in Manalapan, New Jersey, as follows: 1. and 2. David (q. v.) and Jonathan, twins, 1829; Jonathan died in infancy. 3. Sarah, married John E. Hunt. Thomas Baird died at his home in Manalapan, New Jersey, October 1, 1880.

(V) David (3), eldest child of Thomas and Eleanor P. (Bilyeu) Baird, was born in Manalapan, Millstone township, Monmouth county, New Jersey, in 1829. He had the advantages of excellent school privileges, and was a pupil first in the primary district school, and then the Freehold Academy, where he was graduated, and then the higher Institute at Hightstown. He also had peculiar advantages in studying

agriculture and horticulture on his father's well conducted farms, and he became a skillful and successful nurseryman and fruit grower, carrying on the business both for pleasure and profit during his entire active life, only retiring two years before his death, which occurred at Manalapan, New Jersey, January, 1908, when he was in the eightieth year of his life. He was president of the New Jersey State Horticultural Society for two years, and a member during his entire business life. He was a chosen freeholder of the township of Millstone; an active member and oldest elder of the Presbyterian church at Manalapan, and one of its largest contributors to the support of the church and its various missions. His political party allegiance was Republican, and his interest in town, county, state and national affairs was manifest in his clearly defined political opinion always freely expressed. He married, December 9, 1852, Mary Elizabeth, daughter of Isaac and Jane (Heulett) Pullen, born in Hightstown, New Jersey, 1828. The eleven children of David and Mary Elizabeth (Pullen) Baird were born in Manalapan, Monmouth county, New Jersey, and four of the number died in infancy, leaving eight born as follows: 1. Emerson P., married Sarah Probosco and lives at Freehold, New Jersey. 2. Sarah, married John Probosco, a farmer of Englishtown, New Jersey, and their two children are Charles and Eleanor Probosco. 3. Charles Augustus, horticulturist and landscape gardener of Freehold, New Jersey, who married Emma L. Rue, and have four children: Mary E., Jennie R., David Edward and Carl. 4. Howard, born 1863; lives on the old homestead, where he carries on the business of farmer, nurseryman and fruit-grower. He married Elizabeth Lamberton, and their children are: David L. and Louisa. 5. Carrie, married Archie T. Van Dorn, of Englishtown, New Jersey, and they have children: Peter Forman and Gladys Van Dorn. 6. David (q. v.). 7. John H., was brought up to the business of fruit-growing; married Jean, daughter of Judge William T. Hoffman, of Englishtown, New Jersey; removed to Fort Valley, Georgia, as superintendent of Hale's Fruit Plantation. Their only child is Ann Hoffman.

(VI) David (4), sixth child and fourth son of David (3) and Mary Elizabeth (Pullen) Baird, was born in Manalapan, Monmouth county, New Jersey, February 16, 1869. He attended the public schools, Freehold Institute and Bellevue Hospital Medical College, connected with the New York University, where he received the degree of M. D. in 1891. He made a tour of the western states for study and observation before settling in the practice of medicine, and in 1892 located at Florence, New Jersey, where he became a member of the board of health of the town and a leading physician and surgeon. His professional affiliations included membership in the Burlington County Medical Society and the New Jersey State Medical Society, and he was a frequent reader and speaker before the meetings of these associations. His fraternal affiliations embraced the Masonic fraternity, which he entered through Mount Moriah Lodge, No. 28, of Bordentown, New Jersey, and worked his way to the Mount Moriah Royal Arch Chapter; Ivanhoe Commandery, Knights Templar, No. 11; Lu Lu Temple, Mystic Shrine. He also affiliated with the Independent Order of Odd Fellows as a member of Burlington Lodge, No. 22; with the Improved Order of Red Men through the Florence (New Jersey) Tribe; Knights of the Golden Eagle through Florence (New Jersey) Sub-Castle, and Independent Order of Foresters, through Court, No. 592, Florence, New Jersey. He was a vestryman of St. Stephen's Protestant Episcopal Church, Florence, New Jersey, but brought up in the Presbyterian faith in the church of which his father was senior elder. He married, February 28, 1900, Lydia, daughter of John and Mary Jane (Smith) Spotts, of Florence, New Jersey, and their children were twins, John Everett and David Emerson, born in Florence, New Jersey, February 10, 1907. Dr. Baird has a beautiful home and enjoys an excellent practice in Florence, New Jersey, where he is one of the leading citizens and the promoter or advocate of all political, social, civic and sanitary reforms.

REILEY Dr. Reiley, of Atlantic City, New Jersey, descends along paternal and maternal lines from forbears that served in the revolution and from men who bore their full share in the early and subsequent development of a state. William Reiley, who was killed at the battle of the Brandywine, was a brother of Dennis Reiley, from whom Edward Anderson Reiley descends. Ensign John Anderson of the "King's Army," and subsequently a captain in Washington's army, was his great-great-grandfather. Through maternal lines he touches in direct lineal descent Samuel Fleming, an early pioneer and founder of the town of Flemington, New Jersey. Colonel Thomas Lowry and Cornelius

Hoppock of revolutionary fame are his direct ancestors.

The branch of the Reiley family to which Edward A. Reiley belongs was founded in America by Dennis Reiley who with his brother William came from Lancaster, England, and settled in Maryland. They both served in the revolutionary war, William losing his life from wounds received at the battle of the Brandywine. The family afterward settled in Bucks county, Pennsylvania, where John Reiley, great-grandfather of Edward A., was high sheriff. His son, John, was a man of means but lost all his landed estate through a defective title. He then removed to New Jersey, being the first of the family to settle in that state. He located on a farm near Phillipsburg, Warren county, and in a measure retrieved his fallen fortunes. He was an uncompromising Whig and was the only man in his voting district to record a vote against General Jackson for president. He was a strict Presbyterian and raised his family under the strict code of that day and that faith. He was a man of strong mental powers and unbending will. He was greatly respected in his neighborhood. John Reiley married Elizabeth Arndt, daughter of John Bernhardt Arndt, who came to America in the ship "Penn" during the year 1731. His wife was Anna Decker. The children of John and Elizabeth (Arndt) Railey were: John, Nathan, William, James, see forward; Polly, Grace, Phebe and Hannah. John Reiley lived to the good old age of seventy-five, but his wife, Elizabeth, survived him many years, living to see her eighty-fifth year. John Reiley died in 1865. They were the parents of a large family that have settled in different parts of the country, some of them, however, are found in and around Phillipsburg, New Jersey, where they are engaged in business and professions of various kinds.

Dr. James Reiley, son of John and Elizabeth (Arndt) Reiley, was born at Durham, Bucks county, Pennsylvania, May 27, 1830, and died during the month of March, 1872, at Succasunna, New Jersey. He was a graduate of Union College at Schenectady, New York, and prepared for the practice of medicine at the College of Physicians and Surgeons at New York City, where he was graduated Doctor of Medicine. He practiced a year at Lambertville, New Jersey, then settled at Succasunna, New Jersey, where he practiced his profession for twenty years until the outbreak of the civil war. He enlisted in the Union army, August

4. 1862, and was appointed surgeon of the Twenty-fifth Regiment New Jersey Volunteers, serving with that regiment until January 20, 1863, when he was honorably discharged. He re-enlisted July 15, 1863, and became surgeon of the Thirty-third New Jersey Volunteer Infantry, Twentieth Army Corps, General Geary's division, Army of the Cumberland. He was acting brigade-surgeon of the First Brigade, Third Division, Seventh Army Corps. He served with honor and distinction, attaining his rapid promotion through his professional merit only. He was mustered out of the service July 17, 1865, with the rank of major. With the Thirty-third Dr. Reiley was in the "March to the Sea" and in all the hard campaigns.

Dr. Reiley married Mary Lowrey Anderson, born at Doylestown, Bucks county, Pennsylvania, November 13, 1832, died March 12, 1897, at Atlantic City, New Jersey. She was a daughter of John H. Anderson. To them were born three children: 1. Dr. Edward Anderson, see forward. 2. Mary Logan, born April 23, 1858. 3. James Morrison, April 2, 1860; married, December 14, 1880, Elizabeth Gove, daughter of Frank W. and Hannah E. (Taylor) Gove, of Trenton, New Jersey. . The Gove family is of English origin and settled originally in New Hampshire, the first of the family being Nathan Gove. Mr. and Mrs. Reiley have two sons, Frederick A. and Edward Morris Reiley. James M. is by trade an expert machinist. He resides in Atlantic City, New Jersey.

Dr. Edward Anderson, eldest son of Dr. James and Mary L. (Anderson) Reiley, was born at Succasunna, Morris county, New Jersey, October 27, 1855. He attended the public schools of his native town and prepared himself for college. In 1873 he entered Rutgers College, New Brunswick, New Jersey, taking the scientific course. He was graduated therefrom in 1877 with the degree of M. S. He had now decided to follow the profession of medicine and entered the medical department of the University of the City of New York, graduating in 1881 with the degree of M. D. He began the practice of his profession in New Brunswick, New Jersey, where he remained two years. In the month of June, 1883, he removed to Atlantic City, New Jersey, and began the practice of his profession in that city. He has been in continuous and lucrative practice there from that time to the present date (1909). He is a well known and highly esteemed citizen as well as a most skillful and prominent practitioner. Evidences of the high standing he has attained is found in the presentation to him in June, 1908, of a solid silver loving cup by his fellow citizens on the completion of twenty-five years of medical practice in the city, Judge Joseph Thompson making the presentation speech. In sanitary and education affairs he has served his city well. From 1884 to 1887 he was president of the board of health and from 1884 to 1890 was president of the board of education. For six years he was a member of the board of water commissioners. He is a member of the American Medical Association, the New Jersey Medical Association; ex-president of the Atlantic County Medical Association; ex-president of the Atlantic City Academy of Medicine, and member of the New Brunswick Chapter, Phi Beta Kappa. He is an attendant of the Presbyterian church. He married, March 10, 1885, Martha Codowise Williamson, daughter of Nicholas W. Williamson, of New Brunswick, New Jersey. She was born May 3, 1854, and died March 9, 1886, a brief married life of one year, lacking but one day.

In following the maternal lines through which Dr. Reiley descends, many interesting and historic families are to be named. Mary Lowrey (Anderson) Reiley, his mother, was great-granddaughter of Esther Fleming, daughter of Samuel Fleming, who built the first house and founded the now prosperous town of Flemington, New Jersey. Samuel Fleming's wife was Esther Monia, a French Huguenot. The Flemings are supposed to be from Flanders and the name is derived from the tendency to call new-comers in the early day by the name of their country. When the family fled to Scotland and Ireland on account of persecution they were called Flems or Flemish, the name finally getting to the present form—Fleming. Esther Fleming, daughter of Samuel and Esther, married Thomas Lowrey, lieutenant-colonel and afterward colonel of the Third Hunterdon County Regiment, Continental army. William Lowrey, son of Colonel Thomas and Esther (Fleming) Lowrey, married Martha Howe, one of the matrons who received General Washington at Trenton when he was enroute to New York for his first inauguration. Her sister was one of the twenty-four girls who sang songs and strewed flowers in his path as the Assanpink Bridge was crossed on entering Trenton. Mary Lowrey, daughter of William and Martha (Howe) Lowrey, married Thomas Alexander and their daughter, Mary Martha Alexander, married John H. Anderson, grandfather of Dr. Edward A. Reiley. The Andersons are found at a very early date in Connecticut, from there they passed over to Long Island, then settled at Maidenhead, New Jersey, now Lawrenceville, and from there going to Hunterdon county, New Jersey. John Anderson held an ensign's commission in the English army prior to the revolution. This commission is still preserved in the family. He took sides with the colonies and enlisted in the Hunterdon county militia. He was commissioned captain of Colonel Johnson's battalion, Heard's brigade, June 14, 1776. He later held a captain's commission in the continental line. Captain John married Anna Van Kirk. Joshua Anderson, son of Captain John and Anna (Van Kirk) Anderson, married Elizabeth Hoppock, a daughter of Cornelius Hoppock, a captain of the Third Regiment, Hunterdon County New Jersey militia in the revolution. Her mother was Catherine (Coyle) Hoppock. John H. Anderson, son of Joshua and Elizabeth (Hoppock) Anderson, married Mary Martha Alexander, and their daughter, Mary Lowrey Anderson, married Dr. James Reiley, father of Dr. Edward A. This descent from the Fleming, Lowrey, Anderson and Hoppock families entitles Dr. Reiley to membership in any of the patriotic societies that base membership upon colonial or revolutionary ancestors.

SAILER The science of prognostication as existing in seventh sons of seventh sons has been apparent in various sooth-sayers who use this accident of birth for business purposes. These lucky individuals, having judgment and discernment beyond their fellows, have generally carried their extraordinary gifts into questionable business methods. Others into gold, and made good use of both the gift and the gold for those wise enough to follow the financial paths pointed out.

(I) Samuel Sailer was the seventh son of his father and Ann, his wife, and was born in Gloucester county, New Jersey, about 1765-70. They had at least seven sons and a number of daughters. Their seventh son was Joseph, see forward. The Sailers were of German origin and came with the early settlers of West New Jersey who settled in Salem and Gloucester county, on the banks of the Delaware river. Ann, widow of Samuel Sailer, lived to be over one hundred years of age.

(II) Joseph, seventh son of Samuel and Ann Sailer, was born in Clarksboro, Gloucester county, New Jersey, in 1809. He was brought up in his native town, obtained a good education, lived first in Woodbury, Gloucester county, and at the age of twenty was publisher and editor of the *Woodbury Constitution;* he went to Philadelphia, Pennsylvania, where he became interested in journalism and finance and became editor and owner of the *Philadelphia Times* and still later was associated with George William Childs, of the *Philadelphia Ledger*, at the time a leading newspaper of Philadelphia, and extensively read in all the large financial centres of the world. He made his articles a feature of the *Ledger* and his financial acumen was recognized by the leading financiers of his time as of great value in the money market. He enjoyed the responsible position for many years and the financial editor of the *Philadelphia Ledger* was acknowledged an oracle in the world of finance. He married Priscilla Sparks, daughter of Isaac D. and Ann (Sparks) Doughten, who was born at Timber Creek, New Jersey, in 1809. She was of Scotch-Irish descent. Joseph and Priscilla Sparks (Doughten) Sailer had seven children born in Woodbury, New Jersey, and in Philadelphia, Pennsylvania, as follows: 1. Louise, married Daniel Malseed and had five children. 2. Randolph, born in Woodbury, New Jersey, May 24, 1833; graduated at the University of Pennsylvania, A. B. 1857, A. M. 1860; studied at the Union Theological Seminary, New York City, 1857-59; was an agent of the American Sunday School Union in 1859 and his eyes failed and he engaged in Philadelphia, as a manufacturer, with Powers & Weightman, and died in that city, January 22, 1869. He married Josephine, daughter of Wilson H. Pile, M. D., and they had one child, Thomas Henry Powers. 3. Morris C., married Mary Lee, and had two children. He died soon after the birth of his second child. 4. Sarah Ann, never married. 5. John, see forward. 6. Isaac Doughten. 7. Frank.

(III) John, third son and fifth child of Joseph and Priscilla Sparks (Doughten) Sailer, was born in Philadelphia, Pennsylvania, September 6, 1840. He was educated in the public schools of Philadelphia, became connected with Pennsylvania National Guard as a member of the Keystone Battery, Captain Hastings, and in 1862 the battery was mustered into the United States Volunteer Army for one year's service, but was always known as an independent battery. He saw active service on the battle field, 1862-63, serving as second lieutenant of the battery under General Meade in several engagements in Virginia, and he received promotion to staff duty as assistant adjutant general on the staff of General Alexander Hayes. On returning from the war at the end of his one year's service, he engaged in the banking business as a clerk, and in 1866 the banking house of Sailer & Stevenson was formed which was still in existence in 1909 under the same name with Mr. Sailer as senior member. The house has withstood all the financial storms of forty years and always have been able to pay all their obligations in full, and the firm name is a synonym for the best financial standing, credit and repute; never having paid less than one hundred cents on every dollar of their indebtedness on the very day on which it fell due. His financial acumen, inherited no doubt from his father, caused his services to be sought by leading banking and benevolent institutions as director, and he gave such services to the Girard National Bank, the Franklin Fire Insurance Company, the Academy of Music, of Philadelphia. He has given his services as president to the University Hospital, and as a member of the board of managers of the Free Museum of Archaeological Science and Arts, of Philadelphia, and as member of the executive committee of the Philadelphia Board of Trade. He was made a member of the Pennsylvania Historical Society, New Jersey Historical Society, Academy of Fine Arts and of the Pennsylvania Geographical Society. He has served the Union League Club as a member, as secretary, and as its senior vice-president for many years. His other club affiliations include the Country Club, of Philadelphia, and the Marion Cricket Club. His military service brought to him comradeship in Meade Post, Grand Army of the Republic, and companionship in the Military Order of the Loyal Legion of the United States. He has served on the staff of Governor Stewart as lieutenant colonel. His inherited religious faith as represented by the Presbyterian church in America was maintained during his lifetime, and he held office as a trustee of the Second Church, of Philadelphia, and chairman of its finance committee.

Mr. Sailer was married, in December, 1866, to Emily, daughter of Samuel and Ann (Pierce) Woodward, and their children are: 1. Joseph, born October 1, 1867; married Mary, daughter of Dr. George and Alice Strawbridge, of Philadelphia, and their children are: Alice Strawbridge; Mary Lober; Joseph (2), graduated from Towne Scientific

School, biological department, 1885, University of Pennsylvania, Ph. B., 1886, medical department, University of Pennsylvania, M. D., 1891. He was resident physician Philadelphia Hospital, 1891-92, and after 1892 a general practitioner in Philadelphia. He was made a member of the Philadelphia County Medical Association. 2. Anna, born 1874; married Albion G. Pennington, a banker of Philadelphia, and they have no children. 3. Emily Woodward, born 1877; unmarried. 4. John Morris, born 1886; he is in the banking business with his father; unmarried.

COWPERTHWAIT   The Cowperthwait family which has played so prominent a part in the history of the Quaker colonies along the Delaware, and later in the states of New Jersey and Pennsylvania, are descended from Hugh Cowperthwait, the famous minister among Friends, of Flushing, Long Island. His children removed from Long Island to West Jersey, in the end of the seventeenth century, where they intermarried with the families of the early and prominent settlers of that region, and from whence they have spread out into many of the states of the Union. The majority of them have been faithful to the religion of their founder, and are still today members of the Society of Friends. The great exception was General Samuel Cowperthwait, the founder of the Philadelphia branch of the family, whose record as a revolutionary soldier was so distinguished. Among the grandchildren or great-grandchildren of Hugh Cowperthwait was the ancestor of the line at present under consideration, but whether this ancestor was Hugh or Thomas, of Burlington county, is at present a little uncertain.

(I) John Cowperthwait, the records seem to show, was son of John, senior, who died in 1795.

(II) John Wardell, son of John Cowperthwait, was born in New Egypt in 1821; died April 30, 1877. He was always engaged in farming. He married Matilda I. Simons, who died July 3, 1885. Their children were: 1. Amy, born March 17, 1861; married Andrew Moon, and their children are: Frank K., Edna and Ole. 2. John, December 24, 1862; died July 3, 1884. 3. Charles Chapman, referred to below. 4. Charlotte C., April 18, 1866; married Joseph Sison. 5. Matilda I., May 20, 1868; married, in 1888, William B. Pearson.

(III) Charles Chapman, third child and second son of John Wardell and Matilda I.

(Simons) Cowperthwait, was born in Mount Holly, New Jersey, November 1, 1864, and is now living in Mount Holly. For his early education he was sent to the public schools of Mount Holly, after which he took up the course at the Philadelphia Business College. He then learned the trade of harness maker, which he followed until 1888, when he gave it up and for a year worked in a shoe factory. This position in turn he gave up in order to accept the position of clerk on the Pennsylvania railroad, which he retained until 1899, when he resigned in order to accept his present position as postmaster of Mount Holly, Burlington county, New Jersey. This position he has held continuously, having been reappointed three times since that date. He is one of the most popular and highly respected men in the town of Mount Holly, and the confidence and trust of his fellow citizens has been demonstrated time and time again. In 1893 he was elected as a member of the town committee, and in 1896 was re-elected to the same position, while for six years he has also been the treasurer of the township. He is a stockholder in the Union National Bank, of Mount Holly; a member of Washington Council, No. 5, Junior Order of American Mechanics; New Jersey Lodge, No. 1, Knights of Pythias; Sons of America; Patriotic Order Sons of America; Mount Holly Lodge, No. 848, Benevolent and Protective Order of Elks; Ancient Order of United Workmen. Charles Chapman Cowperthwait married Lillian, daughter of John and Margaret Goldy, of Mount Holly, New Jersey.

ATKINSON   The various Quaker Atkinsons of West Jersey have sprung from two emigrants, both of them men of prominence and importance in their day and in the foundation laying of the prosperous colonies with which they became identified.

(I) John Atkinson, founder of the line at present under consideration, was a Yorkshireman who lived for many years at Newby, but about 1659 removed to Thruscross in the same county. He was among the earliest of the converts to the tenets of George Fox in Yorkshire, and he had at least two sons, both of whom came to Pennsylvania: 1. John, died May 2, 1688, without issue. 2. Thomas, referred to below.

(II) Thomas, son of John Atkinson, of Thruscross, was born in Newby, Yorkshire, before 1660, died in Bristol township, Bucks county, Pennsylvania, October 31, 1687. He

was a noted man in the colony, a minister among Friends, one of the largest land owners in Bucks county, and for many years a member of the assembly and a justice of the Bucks county court. His parents took him with them from Newby to Thruscross, and by 1678 he had removed again to Sandwich, in the parish of Addingham, county York, where he found his wife, but no more is heard of him until 1681 when he removed to West Jersey with a certificate from the Beamsley Meeting. In 1682 he removed to Bristol township, Bucks county, and became a member of the Neshaminy Meeting, subsequently joining the Meeting at Falls. June 1, 1685, he was a member of the first grand jury of the colony. After his death the Philadelphia Meeting published a long "Testimonial" of him by his wife, an action so rarely done by the Quakers as to stamp him at once as a most exceptionally prominent character.

June 4, 1678, Thomas Atkinson married Jane Bond, who survived him, and October 11, 1688, married (second) William Biles, of Falls township, Bucks county, to whom she bore no children. The children of Thomas and Jane (Bond) Atkinson were: 1. Isaac, born March 2, 1679, at Sandwich, in the west riding of Yorkshire, England, died in Bristol township, Bucks county, Pennsylvania; was a cordwainer, yeoman and landholder; married, June 23, 1708, Sarah, daughter of Richard and Margery (Clows) Hough. 2. William, born 1681, probably in Burlington county, West Jersey, died in Bristol, Pennsylvania, October 29, 1749; was an active politician and held a number of important offices, coroner of Bucks county for nine terms between 1721 and 1740, was a member of the county committee for twelve years and was collector of excise, besides serving two terms as common councillor of Bristol; married (first) at Falls Meeting, Mary, daughter of Richard and Margery (Clows) Hough, and (second) at Bristol Meeting, Margaret, daughter of Henry and Mary Baker. 3. Samuel, referred to below.

(III) Samuel, youngest son of Thomas and Jane (Bond) Atkinson, was born in Bristol township, Bucks county, Pennsylvania, July 17, 1685, died in Chester township, Burlington county, or in Newton township, Gloucester county, West Jersey, February 21, 1775. He removed from Bucks county to West Jersey in 1714, taking a certificate from Falls to Chesterfield Meeting. November 5, 1719, he carried a certificate from Chesterfield to Newton Meeting where he probably spent the remainder of his active life and may have died although it has been said that his last years were spent in the home of his son Samuel in Chester township. He was a contractor.

September 12, 1714, he was married in the home of his bride's father, under the care of the Chesterfield Meeting, to Ruth (Stacy) Beakes, daughter of Mahlon and Rebecca (Ely) Stacy and the widow of William Beakes, both of Nottingham township, Burlington county, West Jersey. The children of Samuel and Ruth (Stacy) (Beakes) Atkinson were: 1. Thomas, married Susanna, daughter of Thomas and Martha (Earl) Shinn, granddaughter of Thomas Shinn and Mary, daughter of Richard and Abigail Stockton, the emigrants, and great-granddaughter of John and Jane Shinn, the emigrants. 2. Samuel, referred to below. 3. Rebecca, married (first) Thomas, son of Thomas and Deborah (Langstaff) Budd, and grandson of William and Ann (Clapgut) Budd, and (second) Thomas Say, M. D. 4. Ruth, married as the second wife of Joshua, son of Joseph and Hannah (Hubberstie) Bispham, and grandson of John and Mary (Bastwell) Bispham, of Bickerstaffe, West Derby, Lancashire.

(IV) Samuel (2), son of Samuel (1) and Ruth (Stacy) (Beakes) Atkinson, was born probably in Chester township, Burlington county, West Jersey, died there in October, 1781. He was a yeoman and a comparatively wealthy and well-to-do man. His will was written May 3, 1780, and proved by affirmation, October 29, 1781, his executors being his son, Stacy Atkinson, and his sons-in-law, Moses Kempton and Joshua Newbold, and his friend, Jacob Hollingshead. By his wife, Ann (Coate) Atkinson, he had eight children: 1. William. 2. Elizabeth, married Moses Kempton. 3. Stacy. 4. Rebecca, married Joshua Newbold. 5. Samuel, referred to below. 6. Sarah. 7. Mahlon. 8. Beulah.

(V) Samuel (3), third son of Samuel (2) and Ann (Coate) Atkinson, was born in Chester township, Burlington county, New Jersey, died in Springfield township in the same county, in 1804. He married Elizabeth ——. His will, written January 4, 1802, was affirmed at Mount Holly, March 9, 1804. Children of Samuel and Elizabeth Atkinson were: 1. John. 2. Isaiah, referred to below. 3. Caleb. 4. Josiah. 5. Samuel. 6. Esther or Hester, married Joseph Rogers. 7. Keziah, married Benjamin Atkinson. 8. Mary, married John Atkinson. 9. Hope, married Clement Rockhill. 10. Elizabeth. 11. Ann.

(VI) Isaiah, second son of Samuel (3) and Elizabeth Atkinson, was born in Springfield township, Burlington county, and died there in 1845. In his will, written February 17, and affirmed at Mount Holly, October 25, 1845, he names his wife, Sarah (Eldridge) Atkinson, and the following six children: William E., George Washington, referred to below, Elizabeth, James E., Evans, Isaiah Jr.

(VII) George Washington, second son of Isaiah and Sarah (Eldridge) Atkinson, was born in 1804, in Springfield township, Burlington county, and died in the same place intestate, in 1866. By his wife, Anna, the daughter of Miles King, of Jacksonville, Springfield township, he had six children: 1. Miles King, died aged sixty-four years. 2. A baby who died in infancy. 3. Edith R., married Samuel Rogers but has no children. 4. Budd, married Mary Garwood and has two children: Margaret Garwood and Anna. 5. Isaiah E., married Ellen Rogers and has two children: Wallace L. and Howard. 6. John, referred to below.

(VIII) John (2), youngest child of George Washington and Anna (King) Atkinson, was born on the farm in Springfield township, Burlington county, and is now living in Philadelphia and in Llanech, Delaware county, Pennsylvania. He attended the public schools of Springfield township and the well known Charles Aaron school at Mount Holly, a Presbyterian denominational school. After leaving school he learned the trade of bricklaying and then went into business for himself in 1872 in partnership with George W. Roydhouse. After a number of years successful operation the firm was dissolved and Mr. Atkinson continued in the business alone, under the name of John Atkinson, building mason, Builders' Exchange, South Seventh street, Philadelphia. Mr. Atkinson is a member of the Masons and Builders Association of Philadelphia, the Bricklayers Company of Philadelphia, which he served as president, the Builders' Exchange of Philadelphia, also a charter member of the West Jersey Society of Pennsylvania. He is also a member of Lodge No. 223, Odd Fellows, and belongs to the Philadelphia Monthly Meeting of the Hicksite Quakers at Fifteenth and Race streets. Mr. Atkinson is a Democrat.

October 5, 1881, John Atkinson married Anna, daughter of Watson Welding, of Brooklyn, Long Island, and has borne him five children, all born at Philadelphia: 1. John William, July 22, 1882. 2. Roger, May 12, 1884.

3. Edith, March 11, 1889, married Robert R. Blank, of Philadelphia, has one child, Robert R. Blank, Jr. 4. Dorothy, November 11, 1893. 5. Richard, February 5, 1897.

PAYNE There are at least two and possibly three or more Payne families in New Jersey who are apparently in no way related to each other or the families of the same name in New England. They are certainly not so related unless such connection can be traced out on the other side of the Atlantic. The family at present under consideration comes from the old English seafaring stock, and while it cannot boast of as many generations in this country as can some of the other families of the same name, it has nevertheless made its permanent impress upon the community in which it has lived and won for itself a well deserved honored reputation and esteem.

(1) The founder of the family was Macey Payne, a sea captain, who came over to America from England about the end of the eighteenth century, bringing with him his wife and children, settling in the southern part of the state of New Jersey, where he still followed his calling and brought up his sons to succeed him. By his wife, Deborah, he had five children: 1. Levi, who became quite a noted Jersey mariner and sea captain. 2. Sarah, married George Woolford. 3. Samuel, married a Miss Shaw. 4. Macey Jr., who was drowned; unmarried. 5. Charles Garrison, referred to below.

(II) Charles Garrison, the youngest son of Captain Macey and Deborah Payne, was born near Millville, Cumberland county, New Jersey, February 18, 1820, died in Millville, 1891. He was left an orphan when about seven years of age, and grew up under the care of his brother, Captain Levi Payne, whom he accompanied on many of his voyages, and thus spent most of his life until he reached manhood on the sea. Tiring of this kind of a life, he set himself to work to learn the glass-blowing trade, in which he spent the next forty years of his life, establishing his home in the town of Millville. His wife was Thankful, daughter of William, and granddaughter of Dr. Lawrence Van Hook. She was born at what was then called "Schooner's Landing" about four miles from Millville, and was of old colonial German descent. She died in April, 1893. Her father was for many years a farmer, but later on he entered the employ of Whital, Tatum & Company and worked in their Millville factory. Two of his brothers, Benjamin and Lawrence Jr., who followed their father in becoming physicians, were prominent in the early part of the nineteenth century and were particularly active during the war of 1812. Children of Charles Garrison and Thankful (Van Hook) Payne are: Deborah; George Washington, referred to below; Katharine, married Henry Vote, of Philadelphia; Charles Howard, resides in Philadelphia; James; Sarah, deceased wife of L. C. Leake; Fannie, married Frank Boardman, of Millville; Mary, married Jeremiah Corson, of Millville; Jesse; Jenny, married Ralph Kilvington, of Wilmington, Delaware; Nora, married Michael Durkin, of Millville; Rena, married George Howard Doughty, of Millville; Harvey.

(III) George Washington, the second child and first son of Charles Garrison and Thankful (Van Hook) Payne, was born in Millville, Cumberland county, New Jersey, September 7, 1843, and is now living in that town. For his early education he attended the public schools until he was about eleven years of age. When he was thirteen he became an apprentice in one of the glass-blowing factories in Millville, and served as such for the following four years. The civil war then breaking out and the glass-blowing industry in the town being suspended, young Payne took the opportunity to go to school again, which he did for one year, having previously studied for six months under the tuition of Dr. Parker, and later on under that of the Rev. Mr. Northrup, working during the day and studying at night, and in this way gaining considerable practical education. Having once learned the glass-blowing trade he kept following it at intervals all his life, although most of his time has been given to his political career. This began in 1874, when he was elected on the Republican ticket by the people of the second district of Cumberland county to the state legislature. In 1875 and again in 1876 he was re-elected to the same office, and during his second term was the chairman of the committee on corporations. In 1876 he was one of the inspectors of customs at Philadelphia. In 1877 he was most active in the passing of a bill entitled "An act for the better securing of wages to workmen and laborers in the state of New Jersey," and for this bill he worked hard for two years, finally getting it passed in the year above named. This law made it illegal for employees to be paid in punch orders, due bills, and the like which were redeemable only at the company stores, and was the first general act of the kind ever passed in New Jersey. It has since been amended for the better protection of the workingman, and it has been an especial boon to the glass-blowers in establishing a cash basis for their labor. As a result of these labors, Mr. Payne incurred the enmity of many of the manufacturers in the state, was blacklisted and for some time found it impossible to obtain employment. When his third term as representative was completed, Mr. Payne was made the assessor of the second ward of Millville, which office he held for eight years, and in 1889 was elected to the common council of the town. This latter position he resigned in order to become the superintendent of the glass works of Rankins and Lamar at Atlanta, Georgia, where he remained for one year, returning in 1891 to Millville, and being again elected on the common council where he served for three years longer. In 1895 he was chosen as the mayor of the town, and in 1908 was elected high sheriff of Cumberland county for the term of three years. Mr. Payne was the first national secretary of the National Flint-Glass Workers Union, which embraces membership in both the United States and Canada. This office he held for three years, while for twelve years he was one of the representatives of the national body. As a token of appreciation for his services the union presented him with a handsome gold watch, and the employees of the works at Atlanta, Georgia, gave him a gold chain to go with it. Mr. Payne is a member of the Order of the Golden Eagles, and is a past chief of the Select Councils. He is a member of Shekinah Lodge, Free and Accepted Masons, Richmond Chapter, Royal Arch Masons, a past commander of the Mystic Chain, and an honorary member of the Order of American Mechanics. He is a member of the First Methodist Episcopal Church in Millville.

December 9, 1865, George Washington Payne married Mary Ann, daughter of Captain John Stonehill, born in England, of Millville, New Jersey. She was born in Cape May county, June 22, 1846. Their children are: 1. John C., unmarried. In 1876 he met with an accident on the railroad and lost his right arm and left leg. 2. Reginald W., married Ella Hartman and has one child, Beatrice. 3. William S., married Sarah Champion and has one child, Esther. 4. Georgianna, married Henry Reid but has no children. 5. Lavina, married Samuel Curlott and

ii—12

has two children: William George and George William. 6. Nelly, unmarried. 7. Harold H., unmarried, in the office with his father, serving as deputy sheriff. 8. Anna, married Robert Caterson, of Philadelphia, in December, 1908.

SHOEMAKER The name of Shoemaker belongs to that numerous class of surnames which are derived from the trades and professions, and as is the case with the families bearing similar cognomens, there are in all countries many persons bearing the same name yet in no way related to each other, so also in the present instance, there are quite a number of families of Shoemaker, whose common origin is either not traceable or is lost in the obscurity of the past of long ago.

(I) Henry Shoemaker, founder of the family at present under consideration, was born in Holland, somewhere about the year 1740 or 1745, and emigrated to this country about the time of the revolution, when he settled in Deerfield township, Cumberland county, New Jersey, where he seems to have become a man of considerable prominence and influence, and left, when he died, a son George.

(II) George, son of Henry Shoemaker, was born about 1775 or 1780, in Deerfield township, Cumberland county, New Jersey. After reaching his majority he removed into Salem county, where he remained for some time, finally settling in Ohio, where he died. Among his children was Hiram.

(III) Hiram, son of George Shoemaker, was born in Salem county, New Jersey, about 1815. When his father removed to Ohio, he accompanied him and remained a short time, when he returned to New Jersey and married Sarah Ann, daughter of Clement Remington Waters, of Sharpstown, Salem county, born 1821, who bore him eighteen children: 1. Amanda L., married John N. Miller, of Salem county. 2. Harriet Emma, died at the age of sixteen years. 3. Gervuda. 4. George Henry, died in infancy. 5. Margaret B., married (first) Owen S. Proud, of Salem City; (second) William H. Harrison, of Moore, Delaware county, Pennsylvania. 6. Sarah J., married J. Frank Foster, of Salem City. 7. William Hitchner, married Anna, daughter of Jacob Mitchell, of Salem City. 8. Clement Waters, mentioned below. 9. Missouri H. 10. Louisiana C., (twins) who were named for the states. Missouri H. married Thomas H. Bowen, formerly of Salem City, now of

Bridgeton, New Jersey. Louisiana C. married Jacob Harris, who lives near Riverton, Burlington county. 11. Hiram J., married Eva, daughter of Joseph Burt, of Bridgeton. 12. Rachel Waters, married Elijah J. Snitcher, M. D., of Salem City. 13. Charles H., married Rebecca Lowe, of Camden, New Jersey. 14. Mary Emma, died at the age of six years. 15. George Henry, died in infancy. 16. Laura, married John Davidson, of Salem, New Jersey. 17. Robert Elmer, president of the Cumberland Glass Manufacturing Company of Bridgeton, New Jersey; married Mary Hewlings. 18. Joanna H., married Hon. George O. Whitney, of the island of Bermuda, who was at one time a member of the parliament of Great Britain.

(IV) Clement Waters, son of Hiram and Sarah Ann (Waters) Shoemaker, was born on a farm in Elsinboro township, Salem county, New Jersey, April 23, 1848, and is now living at Bridgeton, Cumberland county. During his early years he had but little educational advantages. For a time he attended the public schools in Elsinboro, then attending for a few terms the Friends' School at Salem City. When he was about seventeen years old he entered the store of H. B. Shoemaker, who was a distant relative, where he dealt in general merchandise and gained his first knowledge of business. While here he also attended some of the classes of the West Jersey Academy at Bridgeton. When reaching his majority he found he had saved a sufficient sum to enable him to enter Pennington Seminary, New Jersey, where he remained for six months preparing himself for future usefulness. He had, however, left his money in other hands to be kept until he should require it, and the man failing, he lost his savings and was obliged to leave the seminary and take up work on a farm in order to make a new start in life. His former employer, H. B. Shoemaker, offered him a one-third interest in the business. He obtained his employer's consent to the cancelling of his agreement, and after his release, borrowing the necessary capital, he entered into partnership with Mr. Shoemaker. This partnership continued for six years and when it was dissolved he found himself with a capital of one thousand dollars to his credit. For the next year he worked in the employ of E. M. Ware, at a salary of twelve dollars a week, and then decided to go into business for himself. He bought the establishment of his former partner, H. B. Shoemaker, and introducing the

cash system of trading into his business and into the city of Bridgeton, he at once began to meet with success. He continued this business for two years, when he entered into partnership with Joseph A. Clark, Isaac L. Clark and Samuel M. Bassett, establishing a new plant for glass making, in addition to his mercantile enterprise. He later sold out his interest in the grocery store to his nephew, J. Warren Miller, and gave his attention exclusively to the manufacture of glass. This business had become a co-partnership business in 1880, and in 1885 it was made into a corporation with his brother Robert Elmer as president, and himself as treasurer. During the first year of its existence it was located on the wharf near Cox & Sons, Bridgeton, but the factory having burned down, the firm bought a large tract of land on Laurel street, above Laurel Hill, from Charles E. Grosscup and Rachel Whitaker, and built there a large plant for the manufacture of rough plate glass for floors and skylights, and also for the making of bottle and window glass. Some time afterwards the manufacture of the rough glass was discontinued and the Cumberland Glass Company, as the corporation was now known, began the manufacture of fruit and battery jars. The company is now as it has always been doing a flourishing and successful business. It employs about one thousand men when running to its full capacity, and its payroll amounts to upwards of $600,000 a year. Later he organized the Bridgeton Iron Works, of which he is one of the owners, which is engaged in making foundry castings for light and heavy machinery. It employs about thirty-five men and boys. Mr. Shoemaker is recognized as one of the most public-spirited and philanthropic men in Bridgeton. He has established free beds in the Methodist Episcopal Hospital, of Philadelphia, for his employees, and one for the graduate nurses of the same institution. He has also established a permanent fund, the interest of which is used for prizes in penmanship, for the best English composition and the best record for spelling in the Bridgeton public schools, for contest in oratory between the Bridgeton, Millville and Vineland high schools. He is an ex-president of the Law and Order Society of Bridgeton, which is and has been doing so much to purify the city from the gambling dens and other evils which exist. He is a director in many financial institutions among which should be mentioned the Cumberland National Bank, the Cumberland Trust Com-

C. W. Shoemaker

pany of Bridgeton, the H. K. Mulford Company of Philadelphia, the Vineland Grape Juice Company of Vineland, New Jersey, and the Bridgeton City Hospital. He is also a trustee of the Central Methodist Episcopal Church of Bridgeton, of the Pennington Seminary, of the Methodist Episcopal Hospital of Philadelphia, and of the New Jersey Children's Home Society of Trenton. He served as president of the Sunday School Teachers' Association of Cumberland county, is a member of the Sons of the American Revolution. At one time he was a member of the school board. He served for over thirty years as superintendent of the primary department in the Sunday school of the Central Methodist Episcopal Church of Bridgeton, was also one of the class leaders for several years, and an ex-president of the Young Men's Christian Association. He has also been a member of the state executive committee of the Young Men's Christian Association. At one time he was a trustee of Dickinson College, Carlisle, Pennsylvania, and has been a representative of the New Jersey conference to the general conference of the Methodist Episcopal church.

Clement Waters Shoemaker married, May 28, 1879, Rebecca Ellen, daughter of Joseph A. Clark, of Bridgeton. Their children are: 1. Joseph C., graduate of Princeton University, class of 1904; manager of the Boston office of the Cumberland Glass Manufacturing Company; married Nina, daughter of Ernest L. Mulford, of Cedarville, Cumberland county. 2. Isaac Loper, graduate of Princeton University, class of 1906; assistant superintendent of the Cumberland Glass Manufacturing Company; married Ruth Anna, daughter of Elam Eisenhower, of Philadelphia, Pennsylvania, and has one child, Ruth Anna. 3. Mary Erety, a graduate of Dana Hall, Wellesley, Massachusetts, class of 1909.

STOKES

According to Burke's Landed Gentry, the Stokes family is of Norman origin and is a branch of the ancient and illustrious house of Montespedon, now believed to be extinct in Normandy. From the old documents and records, its ancestors must have come over into England shortly after the Conquest, and received honors and possessions. The records, however, are scanty until the reign of Edward II, when the records of the Tower of London tell us that Sir Adam de Stokke was seized of the manor of Stokke, Rustaball and Wilts. Thomas, his eldest son, held the manor of

Sendee with other lands in Wiltshire, and Roger, his second son, the manors of Wolshall, Sanarnargritt and Hungerford in the same county. Roger and his father, Sir Adam, were interred in the church of Great Bedwin to which they had been benefactors, and their effigies and monuments are still to be seen there. John, a descendant of Thomas, represented the county in parliament in the reign of Charles II, and in the reign of Elizabeth, we find the Stockeys (the first change in the spelling of the name) erected the church or chapel of Sendee and lie interred there. In the fifteenth century, Christopher Stokes held the manors of Stanhawes with other lands in Gloucestershire, and Edward Stokes held part of the manor of Petherton at a later period together with lands at Langley Burrell, county Gloucester. About 1700 John Stokes held the manor of Stanhawes Court, Cardington, with other lands in the same county. In the counties of Gloucester and Bucks Richard Stokes, of Caln Castle, Wilts, held considerable possessions. Some of the family also held lands in Sussex and Kent, and within the last fifty years possessed considerable property in the counties of Wilts, Gloucester and Warwick. The arms of the family are: gules a lion rampant, double gnewed erm; Crest: a dove with wings expanded, in the mouth an olive branch, all proper; Motto: Fertis qui insons.

(I) Thomas Stokes, founder of the family in America, was the contemporary of George Fox, the reformer and founder of the Society of Friends, and of William Penn, who was associated with the trustees of Edward Byllinge, one of the original proprietors of New Jersey, and the founder of the Province of Pennsylvania. He was sixteen years younger than the former and four years older than the latter, a convert to their religious doctrines and toleration, with the largest liberty for individual belief, but like all pioneers and propagandises desiring to avoid persecution and seeking new fields of labor, he concluded to remove himself to the New American colonies and seek his fortune in the new world. His brother, John Stokes, of London, having large proprietary interests in West Jersey, bordering on the Northampton river, Thomas settled on a part of the tract conveyed to him by his brother. This conveyance of John is said to be the only portion of his interest ever disposed of by him and was doubtless the disposal of the whole of his interest. Thomas Stokes located three hundred acres of land fronting on the northerly side of the Northampton river, and a portion of the tract still remains in the possession of the family having come down from father to son by will. Thomas Stokes was a man of influence, and very active in the affairs of the colony, serving on the first grand jury ever held in Burlington county. His wife dying in 1699, he removed to Waterford township, Gloucester county, and resided there with his son Thomas, until his death, 11 of Seventh month 1720. January 21, 1719, he conveyed his Northampton township lands to Abraham Hewlings, Jr., and October 13, 1719, he wrote his will.

The 30th of Tenth month, 1668, Thomas Stokes, of Lower Shadwell, married Mary Bernard, of Stepney, at the Westbury street Friends Meeting in London. They belonged to the Devonshire House Meeting. With his wife and young children he set sail for the new world in the ship "Kent" and arriving at New Castle, in the Sixth month, 1677, proceeded to Burlington and settled on a tract of one hundred and sixty-two and one-half acres which he called Stokington. He was one of the signers of the concessions and agreements. The children of Thomas and Mary (Bernard) Stokes were: 1. Sarah, married, in 1693, Benjamin Moore, the emigrant from Birmingham, county Lincoln, England, said to have been the largest landholder in New Jersey, and the one after whom Moorestown is named. 2. Mary, married, in 1696, John, son of Robert and Mary Hudson, of Burlington. 3. John, who is referred to below. 4. Joseph, who died in 1760; married (first) Judith, daughter of Freedom and Mary (Curtis) Lippincott, and (second) Ann (Ashard) Haines, the widow of John Haines and the daughter of John Ashard. 5. Thomas.

(II) John, third child and eldest son of Thomas and Mary (Bernard) Stokes, was born, probably in London, in 1675, and was brought to the new world by his father when he was about two years old. In 1719 his father made him the sole executor of his will. In his "First Emigrant Settlers of Newton Township" Judge Clement says, "Nothing is known of John Stokes save what may be gathered from the records in the office of the secretary of state at Trenton." In 1716, an inventory of his estate was made, upon which is the following endorsement: "Came to his end by an unnatural death, in ye lower end of Gloucester county." This inventory and endorsement, however, must refer to some other John Stokes as it is hardly possible that Thomas Stokes would make a man his sole

executor three years after his death. It may possibly mean that John, the brother of Thomas, came also to this country. In 1712, John Stokes married Elizabeth, daughter of Thomas and Elizabeth Green. She was known as Lady Green, and was the granddaughter of Arthur Green, of Big Brook parish, county Northampton, England. She came to America it is said in the household of Dr. Daniel Wills, in whose care she had been placed by her father. Being displeased by her marriage to John Stokes, her father disinherited her, and sent her brother John to the colony to look after his interests and investments in New Jersey. The children of John and Elizabeth (Green) Stokes were: 1. John, who is referred to below. 2. Mary, married in 1734, Edward Mullen, and had a granddaughter, Keziah Burr, who married Richard Howell, afterwards governor of New Jersey, whose granddaughter married Jefferson Davis, the president of the Confederate States of America. 3. Elizabeth, married Richard Blackham. 4. Sarah, married Isaac Rogers.

(III) John (2) eldest child and only son of John (1) and Elizabeth (Green) Stokes, was born in Gloucester county, New Jersey, July 16, 1713, died August 24, 1798. In 1740 he married Hannah, daughter of Jervis and Mary (Sharp) Stogdelle, of Evesham township, Burlington county. Her mother was the daughter of Hugh Sharp, possibly the brother of William of Gloucester county, and John of Burlington county, and if so the son of Francis Sharp, of Oak Lane, in the parish of St. Ann, Limehouse county, Middlesex, England. She was born in 1718, died June 16, 1790. The children of John and Hannah (Stogdelle) Stokes were: 1. Mary, born October 16, 1745, married Isaac Newton. 2. John, August 22, 1747, married Susanna Newton. 3. David who is referred to below. 4. Jarvis, November 10, 1753, died December 14, 1804; married, November 27, 1773, Elizabeth, daughter of William and Martha (Esturgans) Rogers. 5. Hannah, October 12, 1756, became the second wife of Joseph Haines and married (second) George Browning. 6. Elizabeth, May 31, 1759, married George French. 7. Rachel, married Joseph Hackney.

(IV) David, third child and second son of John (2) and Hannah (Stogdelle) Stokes, was born in Burlington county, January 12, 1752, died there September 27, 1830. He married, April 15, 1784, Ann, daughter of John and Elizabeth (Barlow) Lancaster, of Gwynedd Meeting, Bucks county, Pennsylvania, and the granddaughter of Thomas and Phebe (Wordell) Lancaster. Her grandfather had emigrated from England to America about June, 1711, and was married in the Wrightstown Meeting, Bucks county, Pennsylvania, in October, 1725. His wife, Phebe, was the daughter of John Wordell, a minister among Friends who had emigrated from Wales, settled first in Boston, and later on in Wrightstown. His daughter, Phebe (Wordell) Lancaster, died at the residence of her son, John, at Richland, Pennsylvania, aged over ninety-five years. Her husband, Thomas Lancaster, was a member of the Richland Meeting and became a distinguished minister in that society. The Meeting granted him a certificate to travel and preach in Barbadoes and the West Indies, and having fulfilled his mission, he was returning home when he was taken sick and died, being buried at sea, about 1750. Ann (Lancaster) Stokes died September 25, 1835. The children of David and Ann (Lancaster) Stokes were: 1. Israel, born November 7, 1785, married Sarah, daughter of Joshua and Elizabeth N. (Woolman) Borton; their daughter Elizabeth married Henry C. Deacon. 2. John Lancaster, February 24, 1788, died in September, 1822; married Rachel, daughter of Caleb and Martha Burr, and their daughter Martha married General George H. Stokes. 3. Charles, who is referred to below. 4. David, February 25, 1794, died January 22, 1817, unmarried.

(V) Charles, third child and son of David and Ann (Lancaster) Stokes, was born in Beverly township, Burlington county, August 12, 1791. In his early manhood he taught school and engaged in farming, and then studied surveying and was one of the head surveyors of the Camden and Amboy railroad. He was for some time a member of the state legislature and was one of the framers of the state constitution. He was also very active in promoting and was one of the most influential directors of the Mount Holly Insurance Company. "This is Charles Stokes' peculiarity," said a man who knew him well in 1903. "He, like the patriarchs of old, is a descendant of a long line of cherished and honored ancestry. And as his portion he has inherited that little spark; that certain something; that invisible yet ever present and all pervading power, that raises up and throws down who it will. That makes honored or dishonored, whoever and whenever suits its strange fancy, without which none are great, and with which none are mean. View him as you will, there cannot be found in him any one art; any fac-

ulty; and ability to do a particular thing in a peculiar way, whereby those who rise in the world usually climb into a place above their fellows. And yet, without wealth, without office, and without title he has risen to that place of prominence where he is one of the foremost citizens of his country and state. As Abram became Abraham, so is he the honored Charles Stokes." He married, October 18, 1816, Tacy, daughter of William and Ann (Lukins) Jarrett. Her great-grandfather, John Jarrett, the name is also spelt Garrit, is said by some to have come from Holland, and by others from the Scottish Highlands. About January, 1712, he married Mary, daughter of John Lukens, who emigrated in 1684 from Criffilt, Germany. Their son, John, who married Alice Conard, was the father of William Jarrett, the father of Tacy, the wife of Charles Stokes. The children of Charles and Tacy (Jarrett) Stokes were: 1. David, born September 18, 1817, died in infancy. 2. Hannah, April 30, 1819, married, April 27, 1837, Charles Williams. 3. Alice, August 25, 1821, married, in 1843, William, son of John R. and Letitia Penn (Smith) Parry. 4. Jarrett, April 29, 1823, died September 18, 1870; married Martha, daughter of William and Hannah (Rowland) Hilliard. 5. Anna, April 24, 1825, married, 1850, Chalkley Albertson. 6. William, who is referred to below.

(VI) William, sixth and youngest child of Charles and Tacy (Jarrett) Stokes, was born in Wellingborough township, Burlington county, September 10, 1827, and is now living in Mount Holly. For his preparatory education he was sent to the Friends school and then he went to Alexandria, Virginia, in order to finish his education. Returning to Burlington county, New Jersey, he engaged in farming. He is one of the stockholders of the Union National Bank of Mount Holly, and a member of the Society of Friends. He married, in 1863, Anna, daughter of James and Rebecca (Spirling) McIlvaine, of Philadelphia. Their children are: 1. James McIlvaine, born September 27, 1865, married Eveline Bartlett. and was a farmer and supplied sand to Philadelphia. 2. William J., married Margaret, daughter of Dr. Perkins, and is engaged in the hardware business in New York city.

(For first generation see preceding sketch).

STOKES (II) Thomas (2) youngest child of Thomas (1) and Mary (Bernard) Stokes, was born in 1682, died November 7, 1736. In 1709 he purchased from John Kay, of Springwell, three hundred acres of land in Waterford, now Delaware township, Camden county, New Jersey, bounded on the south side by the north branch of Cooper's creek, extending on both sides of a tributary of the same, and including what is now some of the best soil in the neighborhood. On this tract he settled, his house standing near what was about thirty years ago the home of Mark Ballinger. This settlement was in the midst of an Indian neighborhood, and it was not until after the middle of the nineteenth century that the last of the aboriginal dwellers passed away, and the remains of their burying ground may still be seen near Tindall's run, east of the Haddonfield and Berlin road. In 1704 Thomas Stokes married (first) Deliverance, daughter of Isaac and Lydia Horner, of Northampton township, Burlington county, whose sister Hannah was the first wife of John, son of William Matlack, the emigrant. She died between 1713 and 1715, and bore her husband six children: 1. Hannah, born July, 1705, died in childhood. 2. Joseph, July 12, 1706. 3. Benjamin, January 27, 1708, who went to North Carolina, and has sometimes been confused with his father. 4. Lydia, July 13, 1710, married (first) 1734, Samuel Haines, and (second) Jacob Lamb. 5. Thomas, November 5, 1711, married, 1741, Abigail, daughter of John, son of William Matlack, the emigrant, by his second wife Mary Lee. 6. Deliverance, September 18, 1713, married Darling Conrow. September 1, 1715, Thomas Stokes married (second) Rachel, daughter of Job and Rachel Wright, of Oyster Bay or Westbury, Long Island, who died February 18, 1742, having borne her husband eight children: 7. Joshua, referred to below. 8. Rachel, October 15, 1717, married, September 7, 1734, John Cowperthwait. 9. Job, October 15, 1717, twin with Rachel. 10. Hannah, June 26, 1719, married Benjamin Pine. 11. Jacob, March 21, 1721, married, 1749, Priscilla Ellis. 12. Keziah, January 25, 1724, married, 1750, Joseph Browning. 13. John, November 1, 1724, married, 1751. Ann Champion, a widow, possibly of Peter Champion and the daughter of William and Sarah (Collins) Ellis. 14. Rosanna, May 2, 1728, married, May 19, 1748, Samuel, son of Samuel and Abigail (Ward) Collins.

(III) Joshua, eldest child of Thomas and Rachel (Wright) Stokes, was born in Waterford township, Camden county, New Jersey, April 6, 1716, died there in 1779. After the death of his father he occupied the homestead for the remainder of his own life. December 10, 1741, he married Amy, daughter of John and Sarah Hinchman, and the great-granddaughter of a Huguenot of Flushing, Long Island, whose children had removed into New Jersey. Her grandparents were John Hinchman and Sarah, daughter of Samuel Harrison, of Flushing, and her great-grandparents were John and Sarah Hinchman, of Flushing, who came from France. The surname is a very curious example of the racial group of names, it being really a corruption of the word "Frenchman" and the first instance of it occurring in the Flushing census of 1698, where the emigrant is listed among the Frenchmen in the town. The children of Joshua and Amy (Hinchman) Stokes were: 1. John, referred to below. 2. Rachel, married Nathaniel Barton. 3. Elizabeth, married Jacob, son of Charles and Ann French. 4. Hannah, married (first) Haddon, son of Ebenezer and Sarah (Lord) Hopkins, and (second) Abraham, son of Abraham and Sarah Inskeep. 5. Thomas, born 1742, died 1831; married Sarah, daughter of Abraham and Sarah Inskeep. 6. Samuel, married (first) 1774, Atlantic, daughter of William and Mary (Turner) Matlack, and (second) Hope, daughter of Robert and Martha Hunt. 7. Jacob, married Esther Wilkins. 8. Joshua, married Syllania, daughter of Daniel and Rebecca (Prickitt) Bishop.

(IV) John, eldest child of Joshua and Amy (Hinchman) Stokes, was born in Waterford township, Camden county, but removed into Burlington county, where he died. He married Beulah, daughter of John and Mary (Shreve) Haines, granddaughter of Nathan Haines and Sarah, daughter of Francis and Mary (Borton) Austin. Nathan was the son of William Haines and Sarah, daughter of John Paine, of Burlington, in 1695, the emigrant. William was the son of Richard and Margaret Haines, the emigrants. The children of John and Beulah (Haines) Stokes were: 1. Caleb, born 1782, married, 1803, Ruth, daughter of Levi and Hannah (Reeve) Shinn, and great-great-granddaughter of Thomas and Mary (Stockton) Shinn. 2. Samuel, 1784, married Mary H. Mathison. 3. Isaac, 1787, married (first) Lydia, daughter of Job and Elizabeth (Ballinger) Mason-Collins, and (second) Mary, daughter of Levi and Hannah Ballinger and widow of Job Collins. 4. William, referred to below. 5. Mary, 1792, married Job, son of Amaziah and Hannah (Prickitt) Lippincott,

William Wilson Stokes.

and granddaughter of John and Elizabeth (Elkinton) Lippincott. 6. Atlantic, 1794, married Daniel Hurley. 7. Rachel, who died in childhood.

(V) William, fourth child and son of John and Beulah (Haines) Stokes, was born in 1790. He was a master shoemaker in Medford, Burlington county, New Jersey. He had a large establishment that employed a number of hands and supplied the Camden county towns of Winslow, Atco and Waterford with shoes. He followed this trade all his life, living and dying in Medford. He was a Whig in politics and in religion a Hicksite Friend. He married (first) Ann, daughter of Isaac Wilson and Phebe, daughter of Samuel and Ann Middleton, and granddaughter of John and Mary Wilson. Their nine children were: 1. Barclay Wilson, born August 18, 1815, married Hannah Ann, daughter of Caleb and Hope (Lippincott) Haines, who after his death married (second) Andrew Griscom. 2. Phebe Middleton, March 2, 1817, married (first) Edward Brown, and (second) James Roberts. 3. Wilson, referred to below. 4. Caspar, November 25, 1821, died unmarried. 5. Whitall, October 10, 1823, married Almira Carman. 6. Alfred, March 28, 1826, died in childhood. 7. Isaac Wilson, May 15, 1828, married (first) Mary Ann, daughter of Job Lippincott and Mary, daughter of John and Beulah (Haines) Stokes, referred to above, and (second) Annie, daughter of Charles and —— (Hoopes) Cooper. 8. Beulah, September 17, 1830, married Mark, son of Daniel and Dorothy (Stratton) Zelley, grandson of Daniel and Bathsheba (Braddock) Zelley, and great-grandson of Rehoboam and Jemima (Darnell) Braddock. 9. Edwin H., married Matilda Kemble, and whose son, Edward Caspar, is an ex-governor of the state of New Jersey. William Stokes married (second) Hannah Livezey, who bore him no children.

(VI) Wilson, third child and second son of William and Ann (Wilson) Stokes, was born in Medford, Burlington county, September 1, 1819, died there May 22, 1896. He received his education in the Medford select school of the Hicksite Friends, but he afterwards joined the Methodist Episcopal church. For a number of years he was deputy clerk in the Burlington county clerk's office, and then he took a position in the bank at Medford as teller and bookkeeper, becoming later assistant cashier, and eventually succeeding Jonathan Oliphant as cashier, which position he held until his own death. His connection with the bank this extended over forty years. He was also a director in the Burlington County Safe Deposit and Trust Company of Moorestown. At his death he was succeeded in his position as director by his brother, Isaac Wilson Stokes, who in turn gave place to Henry P. Thorn, of Medford. Mr. Stokes was a Methodist local preacher for many years, preaching almost every Sunday in the town adjoining Medford. In politics he was a Republican. In 1843 Wilson Stokes married Eleanor, daughter of Samuel McKenney, who has borne him three children: 1. William Wilson, referred to below. 2. Barclay Lippincott, proprietor and manager of the Damp-wash Laundry Company of Trenton, New Jersey, who married Hannah Beatty. 3. Charles Wesley, living in Collinswood, New Jersey, is chief clerk of the West Jersey and Seashore railroad, with his office in Broad street station, Philadelphia, who married a Miss Getty.

(VII) William Wilson, eldest child of Wilson and Eleanor (McKenney) Stokes, was born in Vincentown, Burlington county, New Jersey, in October, 1844, and is now living in Moorestown, New Jersey. He was educated in the Medford select schools and the Pennington Seminary, Pennington, New Jersey. He then went into the drug store of Isaac Wilson Stokes, his uncle, the same store now occupied at Medford by Henry P. Thorn. Here he remained for six years, and then he went to New Egypt, New Jersey, in 1866, and started in the drug business for himself. Ten years later he returned to Medford, and in 1876 went into the Medford Bank to assist his father, becoming receiving teller, and bookkeeper of the general ledger. Nine years later he removed to Moorestown and organized the Moorestown National Bank, which opened for business September 14, 1885, Mr. Stokes being appointed the cashier, which position he still holds, being the first and only cashier the institution has ever had. In 1890 Mr. Stokes organized the Burlington County Safe Deposit and Trust Company in Moorestown, New Jersey, and was made its secretary and treasurer, which offices he held until 1902, when he was elected president and trust officer, which he still is. His place as secretary and treasurer was given to William R. Lippincott, who married Tacie, daughter of Chalkley and Anna (Stokes) Albertson, and granddaughter of Charles and Tacy (Jarrett) Stokes. Mr. Stokes is also a director in the Moorestown Water Company. In 1909 he was foreman of the reform grand jury of Burlington county.

He is a Republican, and attends the Methodist Episcopal church, of which he is the president of the board of trustees. He is also a member of the Independent Order of Odd Fellows of New Egypt, New Jersey. In 1868 William Wilson Stokes married Mary Hartshorn, daughter of Anthony and Elizabeth Rogers, of New Egypt, who has borne him one son, Charles Wilson, referred to below.

(VIII) Charles Wilson, only child of William Wilson and Mary Hartshorn (Rogers) Stokes, was born in New Egypt, in 1869, and is now living in Moorestown. He was educated in the New Egypt select schools. He began his business career in the Moorestown National Bank upon its organization, became and now is its receiving teller and general ledger bookkeeper. He is a member of the F. and A. M., a charter member of the B. P. O. E., No. 848, of Mt. Holly, and is a Republican in politics. He married Estella Dager, daughter of Samuel S. and Keturah G. (Stockton) Dager, who has borne him one child, Keturah Gertrude, born March 31, 1893.

(For ancestry see Thomas Stokes 1).

STOKES (V) Israel, son of David and Ann (Lancaster) Stokes, was born the 7th day of the 11th month, 1785, and married Sarah, daughter of Joshua and Elizabeth N. (Woolman) Borton. They had five children: 1. Susan, married George Williams. 2. Benjamin R. (see post). 3. Ann L., married William S. Emley. 4. Israel, married Caroline Green. 5. Elizabeth, married Henry C. Deacon.

(VI) Benjamin R., son of Israel and Sarah (Borton) Stokes, married Sarah Zelley, and had four children: 1. Abraham Z. (see post). 2. Howard, married Sarah Hendrickson. 3. Rebecca, married Amos Evans. 4. Sarah, married Henry Kelley.

(VII) Abraham Zelley, son of Benjamin R. and Sarah (Zelley) Stokes, was born in Jacksonville, New Jersey, July 16, 1842, and died March 1, 1900. He was educated in the schools of his native town and also in Philadelphia, and in business life was a farmer in Jacksonville, having succeeded to possession of the farm formerly owned and occupied by his father. During the years 1875-76 he was proprietor of a mercantile business at Columbus, New Jersey. He was a man of good business capacity, straightforward in all of his dealings, upright in his daily walk, a consistent member of the Society of Friends, and in politics an independent Democrat. He mar-

ried, in 1870, Hannah P. Haines, born in Jacksonville, May 17, 1848, and by her had two children: 1. Elwood H. (see post). 2. Cora D., born February 23, 1878.

(VIII) Elwood Haines, only son of Abraham Zelley and Hannah P. (Haines) Stokes, was born in Jacksonville, New Jersey, November 24, 1873, and received a good early education in public schools and a business training in the College of Commerce, Philadelphia. He afterward for a time worked his father's farm, and in 1903 started in business on his own account as a general coal dealer in Mt. Holly, where he has since lived. In politics Mr. Stokes is inclined to be independent with Democratic leanings, but does not take an active interest in public affairs. He is a member and past grand of Unity Lodge, No. 19, I. O. O. F. of Mt. Holly, and member of Mt. Holly Lodge, No. 848, B. P. O. E. He also is a member of the Society of Friends. Mr. Stokes married, June 14, 1900, Bessie, daughter of Joshua and Martha Matlack, and has two children: 1. Bessie M., born February 8, 1901. 2. Elwood H. Jr., August 14, 1902.

WEEKS This name, spelled in as many as sixty different ways, among them Wekes, Wikes, Wix, Wick, de Wyke and Van Wyck, was first taken by one William de Wrey, who about 1370 married Katherine Burnell, in England, and from her father inherited the Manor of North Wyke. The name was by him spelled Wyke or Wykes, and a long line of knights descended from him, though the last male in direct line died in 1713. In the year 1635, four brothers, George, Thomas, Francis and Joseph Weeks, sailed from England; George settled at Dorchester, Massachusetts, Thomas at Huntington, Long Island, Francis at Oyster Bay, Long Island and Joseph was drowned in the landing.

(I) George Weeks was living in Devonshire, England, shortly before the time of his sailing for America, as his name was affixed to the will of his brother-in-law, William Clap, of Salcombe Regis, as witness. He was born about 1596, as at the time of his sailing he is described as about forty years of age. December 21, 1639, he was admitted to the church at Dorchester, he became a freeman the following year, and held the office of selectman in 1645-47-48. Besides cultivating his land, he was several times employed by the town in laying out its boundaries and roads. He died December 28, 1650. George Weeks married Jane Clap, sister of the famous Roger Clap;

they were descendants of Osgood Clapa, a Danish nobleman of the court of King Canute, who ruled England 1017 to 1036. After the death of her husband she married, as his second wife, Jonas Humphrey; he died March 19, 1662, and she died August 2, 1668. George and Jane Weeks had five children, the first four born in England, the fifth in Dorchester, as follows: Thomas, born probably in 1626; William; Jane, married Benjamin Bates, of Hingham, Massachusetts; Ammiel; Joseph.

(II) Ammiel, third son of George and Jane (Clap) Weeks, was born in 1632-33, in England, and was brought by his parents to Dorchester, when an infant; he died April 20, 1679, at Dorchester. He was admitted to the church in 1656, took the oath of allegiance and became freeman May 6, 1657, at which time he held land in Dorchester, and in 1673 was constable. Like his father, he often held commissions to locate boundaries. He married Elizabeth, thought to be daughter of William Aspinwall, born in Boston in 1633, died April 10, 1723, and their children were: William, baptized August 26, 1655; Elizabeth, September 14, 1656, died young; Elizabeth, October 17, 1657, died in 1709-10, unmarried; Thankful, born April 24, 1660; Ammiel, September 15, 1662; Ebenezer; Joseph, September 3, 1667; Supply, August 26, 1671; Thomas, November 20, 1673, enlisted in the expedition to Canada, and it is supposed he died as the effect of exposure; Hannah, May 14, 1676, died August 3, 1683.

(III) Ebenezer, third son of Ammiel and Elizabeth (Aspinwall) Weeks, was born May 15, baptized May 28, 1665, at Dorchester, Massachusetts, and removed to Boston, where he was a tailor, and died prior to 1711-12. He was admitted to the church at Dorchester, March 21, 1685-86. He married, May 8, 1689, Deliverance, daughter of William Sumner, of Boston, born March 18, 1669, died March 21, 1711-12, a widow. She was sister of his brother Joseph's wife, Sarah Sumner. Their children were: William; Jane born March 29, 1692; Ebenezer, November 23, died December 8, 1693; Elizabeth, October 25, 1694, died April 5, 1695; Hannah, January 5, 1695-96; Ebenezer, September 17, 1699.

(IV) William, the oldest son of Ebenezer and Deliverance (Sumner) Weeks, was born February 20, 1689-90, at Boston, Massachusetts, and died in 1749-50, at Portland, Maine. He was admitted as an inhabitant of Falmouth, Maine, December 14, 1727, on payment of ten pounds, and lived on Chebeague

Island, Casco Bay; in 1744 he removed to what was called "The Neck," later incorporated as part of Portland. He married Sarah Tukekee, or Tukey, of Dorchester, and their children were: William, Lemuel, Abigail, Esther and Ann.

(V) Lemuel, second son of William and Sarah (Tukey or Tukekee) Weeks, was born in 1727-28, at Falmouth, Maine, where he became a merchant. He married Peggy, daughter of James Goding, and their children were: James; Elizabeth, born about 1754-55; Lemuel, about 1757; Lydia, about 1759-60; Joseph; Sarah; Susannah.

(VI) Joseph, third son of Lemuel and Peggy (Goding) Weeks, was born November 10, 1762, at Falmouth, Maine, where he became a ship-master; he died at sea, July 19, 1797. He married, November 25, 1784, Lois Freeman, born February 18, 1760, died January 26, 1829, and their children were: Joseph, born August 3, 1785, died unmarried December 3, 1865; Eunice, January 18, 1787, died unmarried December 19, 1872; Daniel, September 3, 1788, was unmarried, and lost at sea in February, 1815; Mary, born June 10 or 11, 1791, died March 5 or 6, 1794; Joshua Freeman.

(VII) Joshua Freeman, third and youngest son of Joseph and Lois (Freeman) Weeks, was born December 10, 1793, at Portland, Maine, where he received his education, and there he learned the trade of cooper. Later, however, he engaged in the grocery business, which he carried on for a period of fifty years, and at the age of seventy years retired from business life. He died October 13, 1875, in Portland, in the house in which he was born and where all his life was spent, and his funeral was conducted by the order of Ancient Free and Accepted Masons, of which he was an honored member. Mr. Weeks was prominent in all movements for the progress and development of his native town, and in political views was first a Whig and later a Republican. He was at one time treasurer, and later president, of the Aged Brotherhood. He served as member of the city council of Portland, and was a prominent citizen of the town. He married, November 21, 1815, Elizabeth Ingersoll Mitchell, born February 21, 1795, died October 21, 1883, and their children were: Joseph Lemuel, born July 9, 1817; William, November 27, 1819; Mary and Elizabeth, twins, April 11, 1822; Lois, March 6, 1824; Joshua, November 26, 1826; Edward, June 12, 1829; George, June 16, 1832, died August 19

1833; Robert Mitchell; Harriet, October 18, 1836; Maria Louisa, October 15, 1840.

(VIII) Robert Mitchell, sixth and youngest son of Joshua Freeman and Elizabeth I. (Michell) Weeks, was born July 9, 1834, at Portland, Maine, where after receiving his education he began working in a jewelry store, but later entered the employ of the Locomotive Works and there learned trade of machinist, which he followed most of his life. After working some time in Portland, at the outbreak of the war he enlisted in April, 1861, in Company C, First Maine, which was later changed to Tenth Maine, and finally became Twenty-ninth Maine; he served two years, being mustered out in 1863. With his regiment he took part in some of the most important engagements of the struggle; he was at one time in Washington guarding the Baltimore & Ohio railroad, and was made sergeant of his company. He took part in the battles of Antietam and Gettysburg, was taken prisoner at the battle of Cedar Mountain and was wounded at the battle of Winchester, after which he was taken to the hospital. Upon his recovery he was made commissary sergeant. Upon leaving the service, Mr. Weeks removed to Philadelphia and entered the employ of Baldwin Locomotive Works, which position he held for twenty-five years, although in 1867 he took up his residence in Riverside, New Jersey, which is still his home. He has for some years been retired from active business, and lives in the house built by him more than forty years since. In political views he is Republican. He has won many friends and enjoys the respect of all who know him. Mr. Weeks married, October 22, 1863, at Hagerstown, Maryland, Caroline Berner, born March 7, 1837, and they have three children: 1. Joshua Freeman, born December 24, 1864, in Philadelphia, is a contractor, and is connected with the Baldwin Locomotive Works, of Philadelphia. He married Bertha Schell, of Riverside, New Jersey, and they have a daughter, Maria. 2. Edward Mitchell, born August 20, 1866, at Philadelphia; resides at Washington, District of Columbia, where he is a patent lawyer, and is employed in the bureau of engraving. He married Mary Wolcott, and they have three children: Robert, Dorothy and Ruth. 3. Emma Pauline, born September 13, 1870, at Riverside, New Jersey; is a physician; she married William H. Metzger, of New York, foreman in the Watch Case Works, in Riverside, New Jersey, and they have one son, Joshua Freeman.

WOODWARD This word signifies "keeper of the forest," and has been used in England as a surname almost from the date of the first use of surnames. It is said the family goes back to the time of the conquest, and certainly the family in England had many noble representatives. They settled in all parts of New England, in early days, as well as in New York, New Jersey and Pennsylvania, and as a race they have been patriotic and valuable citizens, fighting for their country when duty called, and working for its progress and development.

(I) Richard Woodward, born about 1589, in England, took passage at Ipswich, in the ship "Elizabeth," William Andrews, master, April 10, 1634, for Boston, bringing with him his wife and two sons, George and John, aged fifteen and thirteen years, respectively. His age is given as forty-five and his wife's as fifty. He became one of the proprietors of Watertown, his name being found in the first list of that town; he became possessed of two homelots, containing ten and twelve acres, and also twelve lots, amounting to about three hundred and ten acres. September 8, 1648, he bought of Edward Holbrook a mill in Boston, at which time he is described as of Boston, and he sold same December 26, 1648, to William Aspinwall. He became freeman at Watertown, September 2, 1635; in 1660 he resided at Cambridge. Richard Woodward died February 16, 1665, aged seventy-six years. His wife, Rose, died October 6, 1662, at the age of eighty, and he afterward married Ann, widow of Stephen Gates, of Cambridge, born in 1603; their marriage settlement was dated April 13, 1663. He had but two children, George and John, children of his first wife.

(II) George, the older of the two sons of Richard and Rose Woodward, was born in England, about 1619, coming in boyhood with his parents to Watertown; he died May 31, 1676, and his inventory showed him owning property to the amount of one hundred and forty-three pounds, ten shillings. He was selectman in 1664. By his first wife, Mary, he had eight children, and he married (second) August 17, 1659, Elizabeth, daughter of Thomas and Elizabeth Hammond, of Newton, Massachusetts; her father left to her, in his will, proved in 1675, one hundred acres of land on Muddy River. After the death of George Woodward she married Samuel Trusdale. George Woodward's children were: Mary, born August 12, 1641; Sarah, February 6, 1642-43; Amos; Rebecca, December 30,

1647; John; Susanna, September 30, 1651; Daniel, September 2, 1653; Mary, June 3, 1656; George, September 11, 1660; Thomas, September 15, 1662, died in 1666; Elizabeth, May 8, 1664; Nathaniel, died May 28, 1668; and Sarah, born October 3, 1675.

(III) John, second son of George and Mary Woodward, was born March 28, 1649, and lived at Newton; his will is dated February 26, 1727-28. He married (first) Rebecca, daughter of Richard Robbins, of Cambridge, who died, probably, in 1686, and married (second) July 7, 1686, Sarah Bancroft, of Reading, who died September 22, 1723. His children were: John, born September 7, died September 22, 1674; John, born July 18, 1675; Richard, December 26, 1677; Rebecca, October 29, 1679, died March 14, 1681-82; Daniel, born September 22, 1681; Rebecca, February 2, 1682-83; Mary, October 6, 1684, died June 15, 1689; Jonathan, September 28, 1685; Joseph; Ebenezer, March 12, 1690-91; Abigail, May 25, 1695.

(IV) Joseph, sixth son of John and Sarah (Bancroft) Woodward, was born November 26, 1688; died May 30, 1727; in his will, dated May 13, 1727, he is described as of Windham, but in his inventory he is described as of Canterbury, his family records being found in both places and he probably resided between them. He bought land at Canterbury, Connecticut, the deed for same being dated June 10, 1710, and his removal from Newton, Massachusetts, to Canterbury, probably took place about that time, with his brothers, John and Richard. He married, June 24, 1714, Elizabeth Silsby, who died May 22, 1727, a few days before his own death. Their children were: Abigail, born May 13, 1715, died May 4, 1727; Bethia, February 6, 1716-17; Elizabeth, January 9, 1723-24; Joseph.

(V) Joseph (2), only son of Joseph (1) and Elizabeth (Silsby) Woodward, was born January 21, or February 2, 1725; died July 8, 1814; he removed from Windham to Ashford, Connecticut, and died at the latter place. During his residence in Windham he served the town in many public offices, and after removing to Ashford was honored with various public offices during a period of twenty-six years; his first nine children were born at Windham, the other two at Ashford. He married, May 19, 1748, Elizabeth, daughter of Captain John and Elizabeth (Bushnell) Perkins, of Norwich, Connecticut, born May 19, 1733, and their children were: Elizabeth, born May 22, 1749; Joseph, May 26, 1751, a soldier in the

revolution; Jason, July 19, 1753, also a soldier; John; Martha, August 13, 1757; William, November 14, 1759; Abner, January 10, 1762; Phineas, June 3, 1764, died 1776; Othniel, September 8, 1766; Perkins Bushnell, August 17, 1770; and Levi, August 19, 1773.

(VI) John (2), third son of Joseph (2) and Elizabeth (Perkins) Woodward, was born June 10, 1755; died February 20, 1844; he served in the revolutionary war, and at the time of his death was living at Bloomingburg, New York. He married, April 24, 1783, Hannah, daughter of Timothy Bicknell, of Ashford, and their children were: Orinda, born July 18, 1785; Lydia, June 16, 1787; Timothy, March 31, 1790; William, January 5, 1792; Benjamin, March 14, 1796; John, May 29, 1798; Hannah, March 17, 1799; Betsey, October 23, 1800, died February 23, 1802; Lucius C.

(VII) Lucius C., fifth and youngest son of John (2) and Hannah (Bicknell) Woodward, was born September 3, 1803, in Ulster county, New York; died in 1888, at Middletown, Orange county, New Jersey. He married Abigail Bingham, and their children were: J. Bingham; Emeline, deceased; William W., importer and jobber of hardware, lives at Newton, Sussex county, New Jersey, he married Mary Johnson, and their children are: Henry J., William W., Jr., J. Bingham, Catherine J. and Anna; Hannah, of Newton, New Jersey.

(VIII) James Bingham, eldest son of Lucius C. and Abigail (Bingham) Woodward, was born May 25, 1830, at Wallkill, near Middleton, New York, where he received his education. He has been working on his own account since a boy, and in 1850 removed to Bordentown, New Jersey, where he began working on the Delaware and Raritan canal, with which he has since been identified; he now has charge of the transportation of boats through the canal. He was for thirty-five years a member of the state board of education, and is treasurer of the following institutions: State Normal School, of Trenton, New Jersey; Farnum Preparatory School, at Beverly; State Industrial School (colored), at Bordentown, and State Normal School, at Montclair, New Jersey. He succeeded Mahlon Hutchinson as president of the Bordentown Banking Company, and has held this position now for fourteen years. In religious views he is Episcopalian, and is very active in church work, having been a member of the standing committee of the diocese for the last twenty-four years. Mr. Woodward married, June 23, 1868, at Washington, District of Columbia, Anna E., daughter of John Appel, of Easton, Pennsylvania, who died January 13, 1903, and they had one child, Richard C.

(IX) Richard C., only child of James Bingham and Anna E. (Appel) Woodward, was born April 16, 1873, at Bordentown, New Jersey; he received his finishing education at the Bordentown Military Institute, and the Trenton Business College. In 1892 he entered business life in company with his father, as manager, of transportation through the Delaware and Raritan canal. He is an enterprising and public spirited young man, and takes a keen interest in public affairs. In political views he is a Democrat, and he is an Episcopalian in religion. He is affiliated—with the Ancient Free and Accepted Masons, belonging to Mount Moriah Lodge, No. 28; Mount Moriah Chapter, No. 20, and Ivanhoe Commandery, Knights Templar, No. 11, of Bordentown. He is a member of the Crescent Temple, Mystic Shrine, of Trenton, and has the following honors: Past master, past high priest, eminent commander, and is a member of all the grand bodies, besides being assistant grand lecturer of the Grand Chapter. At the meeting of the Grand Lodge of Masons at Trenton he was elected junior grand warden. He is unmarried, and resides with his father at Bordentown.

WELLS Many of this name came from France to England at the time of the conquest, one of the most prominent being Richard de Quille, as the name was often spelled. He crossed the English channel and took ·part in the battle of Hastings, and in recognition of his services received a manor in Dorsetshire, where he established a branch of the family. Several others of the name came from Normandy at about the same time and a little later. In the seventeenth century many emigrated to America, where the name was held hy. men in all walks of life. They have contributed a large share towards the settlement and development of all parts of the country. The family here described has been represented in the state of New Jersey for several generations, winning an honorable place, and becoming useful and valuable citizens. They were of the Quaker faith.

(I) William Wells was born in Vincentown, New Jersey, his wife's maiden name was Colcutt, and they had children as follows: Sarah, Margaret, Mary Ann and Joseph.

(II) Joseph, son of William Wells, was also born in Vincentown, and died in Pemberton, New Jersey. He was for some time steward of Pennington Seminary and of the Burlington almshouse. Joseph Wells married Rebecca, daughter of Vincent Sleeper, of ·Vincentown, and there children were: 1. William A., employed in the chancery office at Trenton. 2. Sarah, who died in childhood. 3. Joseph, who was a prominent attorney of Trenton; died in 1880. 4. Davis Coward.

(III) Davis Coward, son of Joseph and Rebecca (Sleeper) Wells, was born January 20, 1844, at Vincentown, New Jersey, and now lives in Pemberton, New Jersey, having retired from active business. He received his education in Pennington Seminary and in Easton Business College, of Brooklyn, New York, and engaged in the hardware business in New York City. Later he embarked in the drug business, and for twenty years had a drug store at Pemberton and Columbus, New Jersey. He has served as mayor of Pemberton, and is a highly respected citizen of that town. He is a Republican in politics, and of the Quaker faith. Mr. Wells married Mary, daughter of Dr. Aaron and Emma Oliphant Reid, of Pemberton, New Jersey, and they became parents of children as follows: 1. Raymond, salesman for the drug firm of Milford & Company, of Pittsburg. 2. Harold B. 3. Ada, married R. H. Aaronson, a dealer in real estate and insurance, at Bordentown, New Jersey. 4. Dr. Edgar. residing at Elmore, Pennsylvania. 5. Cecil, a student in Philadelphia. 6. Marguerite. 7. Helen, who died in childhood.

(IV) Harold Bertrand, son of Davis Coward and Mary (Reid) Wells, was born February 23, 1876, at Pemberton, New Jersey, and received his education in public and private schools. He graduated from Peddie Institute, of Hightstown, with high honors, in 1894, and in 1898 graduated with honors from Princeton College. At Princeton he had the honor to secure the George W. Potts Bible prize, offered to the student standing the best examination on the ethics of the New Testament. Besides being a noted athlete while attending college, Mr. Wells was popular socially, and his genial, sunny nature is shown ·by the fact that he was voted to be the funniest man in his class. After leaving college Mr. Wells spent two years in the law office of McGee, Bedle & Bedle, and later studied in the office of Eckard P. Budd, of Mt. Holly. He was admitted to the New Jersey bar in June, 1902, and immediately entered into practice at Bordentown, where he has met with gratifying success. He has justified the confidence of his many friends in his prospects and has shown great zeal and energy in the performance of his duties. At the present time he is a member of the school board of Bordentown, and acts as counsel for several municipalities. In politics he is a Republican. He is a member of the Methodist church, and acted as trustee of the society in Pemberton. He belongs to Mount Moriah Lodge, No. 28, Ancient Free and Accepted Masons.

Mr. Wells married, April 25, 1905, Grace Ashton, daughter of William H. and Eliza Yard Hiesler, of Pemberton, born in Philadelphia, and they have two children, namely: Harold B., Jr., born June 2, 1906, and Elizabeth Hiesler, born November 30, 1908.

Jacob Adams, founder of this
ADAMS   branch of the Adams family in
New Jersey, came to this country from Germany. He was one of the early settiers in Beverly township, Burlington county, New Jersey. He located on what is now the Walter S. Marter farm near Beverly, where the ruins of the first log house he built may yet be seen. Children: John, William, Jacob, Isaac, Nancy (Mrs. John W. Fenimore), Deborah (Mrs. John Cannon), Amelia (Mrs. Hendrick Van Brunt).

(II) John, son of Jacob Adams, was born December 15, 1784; died December 16, 1859. He was a contractor and builder, and erected many buildings in the neighborhood of Beverly, New Jersey. He married Nancy ———.

(III) Samuel, son of John and Nancy Adams, was born in Beverly township, Burlington county, New Jersey, April 26, 1806; died April 22, 1851. He was a farmer. He married Margaretta Smith, who bore him three children as follows: 1. Elizabeth S., born October 12, 1828; married Edwin J. Cadwell. 2. Richard S., see forward. 3. John Wesley, born December 25, 1831; died December 27, 1875; married Lucy Borden, and had Samuel, Martha, John Wesley, Jr., Anna and Mary (Mrs. William Raymond Sheldon).

(IV) Richard S., eldest son and second child of Samuel and Margaretta (Smith) Adams, was born in Burlington, New Jersey, July 22, 1830; died April 26, 1906. He was a well educated man, and in his younger days was a teacher in the public schools. At the outbreak of the civil war he promptly enlisted in Company G (which he organized), Twenty-third New Jersey Volunteers, and was in active service one year. Afterward he was quarter

master's clerk in the soldiers' hospital at Beverly, New Jersey. He married Vashti Austin. born December 14, 1835, in Willingboro, Burlington county, New Jersey, daughter of Caleb and Hannah Austin, and granddaughter of Caleb Austin, a farmer along Rancocas creek. The children of Richard S. and Vashti (Austin) Adams are: 1. Virginia R., born August 1, 1853; married Charles H. Van Sciver, and has Nellie, Carrie V. (Mrs. Joshua Sharp), Ellsworth H., Mary (Mrs. Kerns), Maggie (Mrs. W. C. Foote), and Florence (Mrs. Harry Sheets). 2. Ellen, July 16, 1856; married Dilwin Haines, and has Bertha and Lulu Haines. 3. Lillie, June 29, 1859; married Charles S. Van Sciver. 4. Hannah Elizabeth, April 16, 1862; married John Fogerty, and has Walter and Helen Fogerty. 5. Ellsworth S., see forward.

(IV) Dr. Ellsworth Smith, son of Richard S. and Vashti (Austin) Adams, was born in Beverly, New Jersey, July 23, 1864. His academic education was obtained in the common and high schools of Beverly. His professional studies were pursued at the College of Pharmacy, Philadelphia, Pennsylvania, where he was graduated in 1886, and at Jefferson Medical College, Philadelphia, from which latter institution he graduated in 1890 with the degree of M. D. Dr. Adams, in 1885, opened his drug store in Beverly, and has been in that business continuously until the present time (1909). After receiving his degree from Jefferson, he began the practice of medicine in Beverly, and still continues in active practice. In addition to his business and professional activity, he has engaged largely in other lines, particularly real estate, and has acquired large holdings. He is a member of the American Medical Association, and the local and state medical societies. He is an adherent of the Republican party, and during the years from 1889 to 1902 was mayor of his native city, Beverly. He is now president of the board of education. His religious faith is Presbyterian. Dr. Adams, notwithstanding his threefold duties of physician, pharmacist and man of business, exercises a lively interest in the welfare of his native town of Beverly. As mayor of that city, he gave the people a clean, business administration, and as president of the board of education, he strives to keep the schools of Beverly in the foremost rank. Every department of civic life in his city finds in him an interested, loyal supporter. He is a skillful physician, a successful business man, and a good citizen.

He married, 1888, Cora A. Wilson, daughter of William and Elizabeth (Hudnit) Wilson, of Brooklyn, New York. Children: 1. Ralph, born March 21, 1889; died aged seventeen years. 2. Earle A., August 11, 1890. 3. Beulah E., January 23, 1895. 4. Richard Ellsworth, March 31, 1898.

The Wallace family at present under consideration springs WALLACE ent under consideration springs from an entirely different stock from most of the families of the same name in South Jersey and Philadelphia, and for the the connection which undoubtedly originally existed search must be made among the records and documents of the mother country, Scotland, where the name has so worthy a history and distinguished representatives, beginning with the famous father of Scottish independence, William Wallace.

(1) John West Wallace, born in Scotland, is the founder of the branch at present under consideration. He emigrated about the middle of the last century to this country, and by his wife, Ellen Nesbit West, had a son, John West, referred to below.

(II) John West (2), son of John West (1) and Ellen Nesbit (West) Wallace, was born in Philadelphia, in 1837, where he became a job printer and spent his life. About 1865 he married Mary A., daughter of Henry W. Speel, also a Philadelphia printer, and by her he had two children: 1. Henry Speel, referred to below. 2. Eleanor West, born in Philadelphia, 1870.

(III) Henry Speel, eldest child and only son of John West (2) and Mary A. (Speel) Wallace, was born in Philadelphia, Pennsylvania, August 7, 1866, and is now living in Atlantic City, New Jersey. He attended the public schools of Philadelphia and the private school of St. Peter's Protestant Episcopal Church of the same city, and then went to the Wyoming grammar school at Sixth street and Fairmount avenue, Philadelphia. After this he became a clerk in the wholesale hardware house of Shields & Brother, of Philadelphia, and subsequently one of the traveling salesmen for Thomas, Thompson & Company, wholesale upholstery and cabinet hardware dealers. His next occupation was with his father, with whom he worked for eight years in the job printing business in Philadelphia. He then came to Atlantic City where he bought a half interest in the *Atlantic City Press*. This was in 1898 and for the next year he was interested

in this, the firm name being Edge & Wallace. He then became the manager of the Dorland Advertising Agency, and acted in this capacity until November, 1906, when he purchased the daily and weekly *Atlantic Review*. This periodical was first established in 1872 by A. L. English and was the first newspaper of Atlantic City. It became the property of John G. Shreve and A. M. Heston, March 8, 1884, and after several years of joint proprietorship, during which it prospered, it fell into the sole control of Mr. Shreve. The paper was an early school of journalism for many men now prominent in other cities, and while never aspiring to rival the Philadelphia dailies which are to be found in the city early every morning, it has more than met the demand for a reliable and popular home newspaper. It now possesses a stone and fireproof publication office in the Bartlett building, and an excellent mechanical department, including typesetting machines and all other up-to-date essentials. The paper has always championed any improvements for the betterment of the resort, and it has done much to help along the growth of the small, little known watering place on the Jersey coast of 1872 to the great pleasure resort of 1909. Under Mr. Wallace's management the success of the paper has been even more marked if anything than it was under his predecessors. Since assuming control of the *Review*, Mr. Wallace has established the Wallace Advertising Agency in connection with his publishing business, and it is now claimed that his paper has the "best home circulation of any paper in Atlantic City."

The family of Wallis as the WALLACE name was spelt for the first two or three generations by most of its members, and as it is still spelt by some of its branches, is of Scotch descent and came originally from Great Britain to the New England colonies, from whence three of the founder's sons emigrated to the Quaker colonies on the Delaware and became the founders of the New Jersey and Philadelphia branches of the family.

(I) Of Philip Wallis, the founder of the family, little is known, except the fact of his emigration to Boston, referred to above, and the additional facts that his wife's name was Sarah, and that he had at least three sons who had left New England for the banks of the Delaware before 1682. These sons were: 1. Philip, who is referred to below. 2. Thomas,

Henry S. Wallace

who settled on Penisauken creek and died in 1705, leaving a widow, but apparently no children. 3. Robert, who settled in Philadelphia; married Esther Lakin, and had three children mentioned in the will of his brother, Thomas.

(II) Philip (2), son of Philip (1) and Sarah Wallis, came to West Jersey about the same time as his brothers and settled near Penisanken creek, where some of his descendants have continued until the present day. His will was proved March 25, 1755. He married Sarah, daughter of John and Margaret (Smith) Walker, the former of whom was a son of John and Susanna Walker, and the latter a daughter of John and Margaret (Cripps) Smith; John Walker emigrated to America in 1675. The children of Philip and Sarah (Walker) Wallis were: 1. Thomas, married, in 1750, Hope Lippincott, who after his death in 1758 married (second) Henry Jones. 2. John, who is referred to below. 3. Jane, married, in 1729, Francis Jones, of Burlington. 4. Sarah, married, in 1729, Thomas Vanable, of Burlington. 5. Esther, married a Mr. Casper. 6. Rachel, married, in 1746, Walter or Walker Atkinson, of Burlington. 7. Abigail, married a Mr. Heulings. 8. Philip, who died in 1752, leaving a widow and five children.

(III) John, the son of Philip (2) and Sarah (Walker) Wallis, was born about 1720; died in 1779. He married Martha Decow, born in 1735, died in 1813, who married (second) after her first husband's death, Isaac Burroughs. The children of John and Martha (Decow) Wallace were: 1. John, died in 1797; married Elizabeth Chester, and had nine children, one of whom, Rebecca, married her first cousin John Shivers; see sketch. 2. Thomas, who is referred to below. 3. Sarah, married, in 1774, Andrew Laurence, or Lawrence. 4. Martha, married William Rush. 5. Samuel, whose will was proved January 18, 1785. 6. Mary, buried in Old Coles, January 6, 1772.

(IV) Thomas Wallace, son of John and Martha (Decow) Wallis, was born on Penisauken creek, in 1774; died there August 14, 1832. He married Ann Shivers, born November 11, 1773, died October 3, 1853, who after her first husband's death married (second) Jacob Hulings. The children of Thomas and Ann (Shivers) Wallace were: 1. John Shivers, born November 11, 1795; died November 12, 1869; married his first cousin, Rebecca Wallace, referred to above. 2. Thomas, December 2, 1797; died in 1833; married Sarah Hinckle.

3. Maria, November 20, 1799; died in 1836; married Israel Lippincott. 4. Josiah, August 7, 1802; died unmarried, in 1891. 5. Samuel, August 26, 1804; died in 1840; married Elizabeth Fish. 6. Joseph, March 10, 1806; died in 1815. 7. William, who is referred to below. 8. Benjamin, March 11, 1812; died in 1855; married Sibilla Marters, and had Edith H., who married John Taylor Evans. 9. Hezekiah, 1814; died in infancy. 10. Ann, June 11, 1816; now living at Riverton, New Jersey, who married Benjamin T. Rudderow, born November 23, 1811; died December 13, 1871.

(V) William, seventh child and sixth son of Thomas and Ann (Shivers) Wallace, was born in Palmyra, New Jersey, March 26, 1809, and died there in 1864. He was a farmer all of his life. He married Rachel Marters, of Beverly, New Jersey, by whom he had: 1. Joseph. 2. Abraham. 3. Albert. 4. Josiah, who is referred to below. 5. Emily.

(VI) Josiah, son of William and Rachel (Marters) Wallace, was born in Palmyra, New Jersey, December 25, 1845, and is now living in that town. He was educated in the common schools of Palmyra, and after leaving school worked for twenty years at farming. He then began to run freight scows on the river, between Kinkora, Burlington, and Philadelphia, and continued in this occupation for twenty years more. In 1887 he built the West End Hotel at Palmyra, and since that time has devoted himself to running that hostelry. He has large real estate interests in Palmyra, owning besides his hotel property, five houses. He also owns and controls the baseball grounds in Palmyra. Mr. Wallace is a Democrat, a member of the Mohawk Tribe, Improved Order of Red Men, a member of the Independent Order of Odd Fellows, and a member of the Ancient Order of United Workmen, of Camden, New Jersey.

In 1876 Josiah Wallace married Lydia W., daughter of Michel and Abigail (Wilkins) Korn, of Camden, New Jersey, and they have had three children: 1. Minnie, born in Palmyra, September 20, 1878; married James K. Hires, of Palmyra, a bookkeeper for Slack Brothers, of Philadelphia. They have two children: Elizabeth and James. 2. Josiah, Jr., born in 1880; married Mary, daughter of Felix and Elizabeth Weinkelspecht, of Riverside, New Jersey. They have three children: Josiah E., Edith and Lydia W. 3. Elizabeth S., born in 1882, who lives at home with her parents.

(For early generations see preceding sketch).

(VI) John Shivers, the eldest WALLACE child of Thomas and Ann (Shivers) Wallace, was born in what is now Palmyra, New Jersey, November 11, 1795, and died there November 12, 1869. He married his first cousin, Rebecca, daughter of John and Elizabeth (Chester) Wallace. Children: 1. Mary Ann, born December 12, 1812. 2. Hezekiah, July 6, 1817. 3. Shivers, February 22, 1819. 4. Thomas (or William) Rush, May 2, 1821. 5. Elizabeth, February 13, 1824. 6. John, October 30, 1826. 7. Isaac, June 27, 1829. 8. Adeline, August 9, 1831. 9. Caroline, February 5, 1833. 10. Israel, February 13, 1835. 11. Smith B., May 21, 1839.

(VI) John, son of John Shivers and Rebecca (Wallace) Wallace, was born in what was then Chester, now Palmyra, New Jersey, October 30, 1826, and died there July 9, 1897. He received a common school education, and as a boy worked on a farm and learned the trade of carpenter, which he followed nine years. In 1856 he engaged in the hotel business and continued in this for the remainder of his life. He was a Democrat, and held several town offices, at one time being commissioner of appeals. He was a member of Pocahontas Lodge, Independent Order of Odd Fellows, of Moorestown, New Jersey, a member of encampment, and a member of the Presbyterian church at Riverton, New Jersey. He married, December 21, 1850, Mary M., born in Doylestown, Pennsylvania, October 5, 1832, daughter of Jacob and Barbara (Meyers) Yothers. She is now living in Palmyra, New Jersey. Children: 1. Emma R. 2. Caroline H. 3. Levis H., sec forward. 4. Jennie Catharine Virginia. Three other children who died in childhood.

(VII) Levis H., son of John and Mary M. (Yothers) Wallace, was born in Palmyra, New Jersey, March 23, 1863, and is now living in that town. He was educated in the public schools of Palmyra, and as a boy worked on a farm. When he was twenty-two years old he went into the hotel business in Palmyra, succeeding his father as the owner and proprietor of the Palmyra Hotel. Mr. Wallace is a Democrat and a member of the election board. He is also a member of Lodge, No. 293, Benevolent and Protective Order of Elks, of Camden, New Jersey; Brotherhood of America, of Palmyra; Lincoln Circle, Knights of the Golden Eagle, of Palmyra; an active member of the Independent, No. 1, Palmyra Fire Company, of which he is treasurer; a life member of the Cinnaminson Firemens' Relief Association, of which he is treasurer. He married, November 28, 1894, Ardella, daughter of Josiah and Margaret (Garwood) Bright, of Beverly, New Jersey. Children, born in Palmyra: 1. Margaret Bright, December 10, 1895. 2. Mary Moore, November 22, 1897.

The first record of the Wilkins WILKINS family of West Jersey is a deed, dated September 2, 1687, in which John Penfold, of Newark, near Leicester, county of Leicester, England, gentleman, grants to Thomas Wilkins, of West Jersey, laborer, and to John Wilkins, of Cussington, county Leicester, laborer, both the sons of John Wilkins, late of Kegham or Keyham in the same county, husbandman, one-fifteenth of one share of the Province of West Jersey. With this record begins the history of the family in this country.

(I) Thomas, son of John Wilkins, of Kegham, county Leicester, settled first on Mason's Run, near the city of Burlington, where in 1690 he bought one hundred acres from Thomas Perkins and about two months later another two hundred acres adjoining from Thomas Gardiner. Three years later he sold this property and bought fifty acres in Evesham township, Burlington county, from Henry Gribb and Thomas Raper, where he spent the remainder of his life and died about January, 1735, his will being proven on the 20th of that month. His wife's name is said to have been Susanna, but she is not mentioned in this will nor has any evidence yet come to light to show whether he married her in West Jersey or brought her with him when he emigrated. His children were: 1. Thomas, born about 1701; died 1791; married (first) Mary Core, and (second) Sarah ———. 2. William, died 1758; married, 1754, at Chester monthly meeting, Elizabeth Swain. 3. Amos, who is referred to below. 4. Mary, married Thomas Rakestraw. 5. Sarah. 6. Rachel, married Francis Dudley. 7. Rebecca, married Thomas Hackney. 8. Hannah, married Jacob Coffin.

(II) Amos, youngest son of Thomas Wilkins, was not yet twenty-one in 1729, when his father wrote his will. He lived at Evesham in his father's homestead which he had inherited from his father, and died about March, 1761. He was twice married, first at the Chester monthly meeting to Susan ———, in 1738, and second in 1756, by license dated June 17, 1756, to Sarah, daughter of Carlile Haines and

Sarah, daughter of William and Mary (Hancock) Matlack. Carlile was the son of Richard and Mary (Carlile) Haines, and the grandson of Richard and Margaret Haines, the emigrants. The children of Amos Wilkins were: 1. John, married, in 1761, Hannah Gwinnal, of Evesham. 2. Benjamin. 3. Amos, Jr., who is referred to below. 4. Caleb. 5. Joshua. 6. Samuel, married Mary Eldridge, of Evesham. From the instructions of his will and other indications it is probable that the first three sons were by his first wife and that the last three were the children of Sarah (Haines) Wilkins. There were probably also several daughters.

(III) Amos (2), the son of Amos (1) and Susan Wilkins, was born October 13, 1750; died in March, 1811. He was a distiller and a brick manufacturer. He married Lydia, born August 31, 1765, daughter of Benjamin Jenkins; she bore him five sons and six daughters all named in his will: 1. Amos, who is referred to below. 2. Benjamin. 3. Clayton, who died unmarried. 4. David, married Rachel, daughter of Job and Esther (Brooks) Sharp. 5. Nathan, married Mary, daughter of Isaac and Rebecca (Eves) Troth. 6. Susanna, married Asahel Coate. 7. Keturah, married Joseph, son of Aaron and Rachel (Cox) Sharp. 8. Amy, married Jonathan, son of Samuel and Elizabeth (Reed) Jones. 9. Lydia. 10. Atlantic. 11. Sarah, married Philip Stricker.

(IV) Amos (3), son of Amos (2) and Lydia (Jenkins) Wilkins, was born on the old homestead which he inherited from his father, July 7, 1790; died there April 14, 1857. He was a farmer and did a good deal of lumbering business, and for a number of years also conducted a distillery. He married, October 26, 1815, Ann, daughter of John Hewlings and Lydia, daughter of Benjamin Crispin and Rachel, daughter of Robert Braddock and Elizabeth, daughter of Joseph Bates and Mercy, daughter of James, the emigrant, and granddaughter of Gregory Clement, the regicide. Joseph Bates was the son of William Bates, the emigrant from Ireland. Robert Braddock was the son of Robert Braddock and Elizabeth, daughter of Timothy and Rachel (Firman) Hancock, the emigrants. Benjamin Crispin was the son of Benjamin Crispin and Margaret, daughter of Joshua and Martha (Shinn) Owen. Benjamin Crispin was the son of Silas Crispin and Mary (Stockton) Shinn, the daughter of Richard and Abigail Stockton, the emigrants, and the widow of Thomas Shinn.

ii—13

Silas Crispin was the son of Captain William Crispin, of the English navy, whose wife, Anne (Jasper) Crispin, was the sister to Margaret, wife of Admiral Sir Wilbar, and the mother of William Penn, the founder of the Pennsylvania colony. John Hewlings was the son of Joseph Hewlings and Elizabeth, daughter of Laban Langstaff, and granddaughter of Laban Langstaff, Sr., and Susanna Woolston. Laban Langstaff, Sr., was the son of John and Eliza Langstaff, the emigrants. Joseph Hewlings was the son of Jacob Hewlings and Dorothy, daughter of Thomas and Anna Eves, and the granddaughter of Thomas Eves, the emigrant from London. Jacob Hewlings the son of William Hewlings, the emigrant, and Dorothy, daughter of Thomas Eves, the emigrant. The children of Amos and Ann (Hewlings) Wilkins were: 1. Amos, married Jane Prickett. 2. John, married a Miss Gouldy. 3. Caleb, who is referred to below. 4. Rachel, married Uriah Brock. 5. Sarah, married Charles Coate. 6. Lydia, married Thomas Wilson.

(V) Caleb, son of Amos (3) and Ann (Hewlings) Wilkins, was born on the old homestead at Fostertown, Burlington county, April 9, 1835, and is now living near Medford, New Jersey. He was educated in the common schools, and then engaged in farming, and started in the cranberry business in 1859, and at present is engaged in building houses in South Atlantic City. For four years he was the commissioner of appeals, and for many years he has been a director of the Union National Bank, of Mount Holly, of which he was one of the promoters. He is a member of the Society of Friends.

He married, January 14, 1869, Keziah, daughter of David and Susan Rogers. Their children are: 1. Susan Rogers, born October 10, 1869. 2. Albertia, October 29, 1872; died December 10, 1898. 3. David D., born March 19, 1874. 4. Caleb, Jr., November 28, 1875. 5. Mary H., July 6, 1879. 6. Amos D., June 26, 1883.

BRICK The several Brick families of New Jersey are doubtless descended from John Brick, an Englishman by birth and ancestry, who came to this country previous to 1680 and settled in the Fenwick colony in New Jersey. He bought a large tract of land on the south branch of Stoe creek, which branch is known as Gravelly run. The land there was purchased from John Fenwick by one Deming, who in turn sold to John Brick. He had several children, among them sons John, Joshua, Richard and Samuel.

(I) William Brick, the earliest known ancestor of the family here to be traced and presumably a descendant of John Brick who is mentioned in the preceding paragraph, was proprietor of a general merchandise store at Marlton, New Jersey, in 1816 and for several years afterward. He married, March 1, 1804, Mary Inskeep, born January 25, 1784, daughter of Abraham and Hannah Inskeep.

(II) Joseph Inskeep, son of William and Mary (Inskeep) Brick, was born December 23, 1804, probably in Marlton, and in 1825 succeeded his father in the proprietorship of the store. He was also interested in farming and retired from mercantile pursuits in 1859, continuing his attention to farming. He died August 31, 1868. He married, February 16, 1832, Rebecca Clement, of Timber creek, New Jersey, daughter of Abel and Keziah (Mickle) Clement. She was born March 8, 1809, and survived her husband more than seventeen years, dying November 11, 1885. Children: John Inskeep and Abel (twins), William French, Henry, Edgar, Joseph M., Abigail (married George Cowperthwaite), Rebecca, and one other who died in infancy.

(III) Henry, son of Joseph I. and Rebecca (Clement) Brick, was born November 9, 1835, in Marlton, died July 1, 1898. He was sent to the township school when a boy and afterward was a student at High Faulk's boarding school at Gwyned. On leaving school he returned to Marlton and in 1859, in company with his brother Joseph M., succeeded their father in the ownership of the store and afterward continued the business under the firm name of H. & J. M. Brick, until April, 1886, when the partnership was dissolved. After that Henry Brick was sole proprietor of the store and business until March 1, 1890, when he took as partner his son, Clayton H. Brick. From that time until the death of the senior member of the firm, in 1898, the business was carried on under the firm of Henry Brick & Son. For twenty-five years Mr. Brick was postmaster of Marlton, and otherwise in many respects was one of the leading men of the township for many years. He was a member of the board of directors of the Haddonfield National Bank, one of the chief promoters of the Marlton Water Company and its vice-president. In addition to his mercantile business Mr. Brick owned large farming interests, carried on a cranberry bog and had besides considerable timber lands. He was brought up in the faith of the Society of Friends and never departed from its teachings. He was a school trustee of Marlton for several years, member of Mittal Lodge, No. 82, I. O. O. F., Chosen Friends Lodge, K. of P., and of Modoc Tribe, I. O. R. M. He married, January 4, 1866, Agnes Bickman Haines, daughter of Clayton W. and Eliza (Curtis) Haines, of Philadelphia. Clayton W. Haines was a son of Abraham and Sarah (Lippincott) Haines, great-grandson of Abraham and Grace (Hollingshead) Haines, great-great-grandson of Richard and Mary (Carlile) Haines, and great-great-great-grandson of Richard (the immigrant) and Margaret Haines.

(IV) Clayton Haines, only son of Henry and Agnes Bickman (Haines) Brick, was born at Marlton, New Jersey, March 1, 1869, and received his education at the Friends' Central School, Philadelphia, where he was a student for five years. At the age of sixteen years he became a clerk in his father's store, and on March 1, 1890, on attaining his majority, he became partner in the firm of Henry Brick & Son, a firm well known in business and trade circles for several years, continuing until July, 1898, when on the death of the senior partner it was dissolved. After that the son continued the business alone until 1903 and then sold out. Since that time he has engaged in dealing in real estate, farming and managing his cranberry bog. Mr. Brick is a strong Republican and has served in various official capacities, justice of the peace and chosen freeholder, both of which offices he now fills. He is a Master Mason and a member of the Baptist church.

He married, April 9, 1890, Mary Elizabeth, daughter of Dr. Elijah B. and Rachel (Inskeep) Woolston.

RIED   The family names Reid, Reed, Read and Ried have been well known in American history since the early time of the colonies, and came into the new country from various parts of England; but the family here treated seems to have come from German ancestry and has been settled here a little more than half a century. And while the Reids, Reeds, Reads and Rieds of colonial days gained fame among the New England colonists because of their deeds of courage and loyalty during the Indian wars and the revolution, so too the immigrant ancestor of the family here under consideration did a loyal soldier's full duty and laid down his own life in defense of the Union during the late civil war.

(I) Matthias Ried, father of the immigrant, was born of German ancestors and spent his life in Germany. The baptismal name of his wife was Magdalena and they had children, among them a son Charles.

(II) Charles, son of Matthias and Magdalena Ried, was born in Largen, Stienbach, Baden, Germany, in July, 1827, and came over to America sometime previous to 1849, before he attained his majority of years, for on November 6 of that year, in the city of Philadelphia, Pennsylvania, he became a naturalized citizen of the United States. In the same year he married, in Philadelphia, Wilhelmina Bischoff, who was born in Diet Largen, Pfortzheim, Baden, Germany, March 23, 1826, daughter of Michael and Teresa Bischoff. Early in the civil war Charles Ried enlisted for service in the Union army, and he was killed June 27, 1862, in the seven days' fight before Richmond, Virginia. The greater part of his business life in this country was spent in New Jersey, where he came to live after his marriage. Charles and Wilhelmina (Bischoff) Ried had five children: 1. Edward F., see post. 2. Henry W., born April 12, 1853. 3. Matthias, born in 1855. 4. Wilhelmina, born October 1, 1857, now Mrs. Oatman. 5. Charles W., born March 4, 1860.

(III) Edward F., eldest son and child of Charles and Wilhelmina (Bischoff) Ried, was born in Lumberton, New Jersey, May 17, 1851, and died there in 1898. After leaving school he learned the trade of shoemaking and became a practical workman of the days when shoes were made by hand instead of with machines and other modern mechanical appliances. In 1879 he became partner in the firm of F. E. Shinn & Co., manufacturers of shoes, and so continued for two years, when the Lumberton Shoe Company was incorporated and succeeded to the business formerly carried on by the firm of which he was a member. Mr. Ried was a director of the company and actively connected with the operation of its factory for one year, and at the end of that time he established himself in the same line of business under the style of E. F. Ried & Co., continuing the manufacture of shoes until the time of his death. Mr. Ried was an energetic, capable and straightforward business man and his efforts in life were rewarded with gratifying success. A firm Democrat, he served in

various capacities, such as township clerk, school trustee, postmaster under President Cleveland's administration, and other offices. He was a member and trustee of the Lutheran church, member of the Junior Order of American Mechanics and also of Mt. Holly Lodge, No. 14, Free and Accepted Masons. In 1872 he married Anna M. Karge, who was born in 1852 and by whom he had eight children: 1. George Frederick, born November 17, 1874, see post. 2. Edward, born October 23, 1876, engaged in business with his elder brother; married Irene Elder, of Lumberton, and has one daughter, Irene Elder Ried. 3. Philip, born March, 1878, merchant of Lumberton; married Sarah A. Amish, of Lumberton, and has one son, Kenneth F. Ried. 4. Anna M., born 1881, married William J. Oatman, and has two children, Gladys R. and Edward E. Oatman. 5. Caleb R., born 1884, died 1905; married Anna M. Cobb. 6. Johnson H., born December 26, 1886, lives in Lumberton. 7. Lillian, born May, 1889. 8. Francis W., born 1892.

(IV) George Frederick, eldest son and child of Edward F. and Anna M. (Karge) Ried, was born in Lumberton, New Jersey, November 17, 1874, and received his education in the public schools of that town, Mt. Holly Academy and Pierce Business College, Philadelphia. In business life he has been, until recently, proprietor of a general merchandise store in Lumberton, which he started in 1895, and also is connected with the shoe manufacturing firm of E. F. Ried & Company. Indeed, since the death of his father in 1898 Mr. Ried has been an important factor in the business established by his father, was himself founder of the New Lumberton Shoe Company, and became its president and general superintendent. In 1907 he sold out his mercantile establishment to his brother Caleb R. and since that time has devoted his attention to the business management of the shoe factory. Mr. Ried is a director of the Farmers' Bank of Mt. Holly, president of the Lumberton Light & Water Company, treasurer of the Firemen's Relief Association of Lumberton, member of the Junior Order of United American Mechanics, charter member of the Daughters of America, a Republican in politics, and a member of the Lutheran church.

He married, in 1898, Clara V., daughter of George W. and Virginia M. (Benny) Amish, of Lumberton, and has one daughter, Majorie Ross Ried, born September 7, 1904.

SCHWABENLAND The first record found of this family they were living in Hessen, a town of Germany, located on the Rhine river, where they were respected citizens. They have made an honorable place for themselves in whatever place in America they have located, and have been useful and successful citizens.

(I) Christian Schwabenland spent his entire life in Germany, and died there. His children were: John J., residing in West Philadelphia; Lenhart Christian; Helena, deceased.

(II) Lenhart Christian, second son of Christian Schwabenland, was born in 1835, at Hessen, Darmstadt, Germany, and died in Philadelphia, Pennsylvania, June 5, 1906. He was educated in his native town, where he learned the trade of cabinet-maker, and soon after coming to this country engaged in the manufacture of high-class furniture, his location being Philadelphia. He was successful in his enterprise and continued business up to the time of his death; one of his orders was for the furnishings of the capitol building at Harrisburg, Pennsylvania. In politics he was a Republican. He was affiliated with the ancient Free and Accepted Masons, and was a prominent member of the Order of Redmen, of Philadelphia. He was an active member of the Lutheran church, of which he was trustee. He married (first) Helena Saler, born in Germany; she died at the birth of her only child, Edward, in 1858. Mr. Schwabenland married (second) Agnes Webber, of Philadelphia, and their children were: 1. Louisa, married Joseph Werst, a farmer of Sewall, New Jersey. 2. Henry, residing at Philadelphia. 3. Emma, married William Grube, superintendent of a pocketbook manufacturing plant. 4. Mary, deceased. 5. Caroline, lives with her mother. 6. John, lives at home. 7. Charles, also living with his mother. Mrs. Schwabenland still resides at Philadelphia.

(III) Edward, son of Lenhart Christian and Helena (Saler) Schwabenland, was born March 1, 1858, at Philadelphia, receiving his education in the public schools and Ringold school of that city. He began work at the age of sixteen, in a general butcher and cattle business, being stationed at the Farmers' Market, at Philadelphia, and at the end of four years embarked in business for himself in that city. His business is still located at Philadelphia, where he carries on a wholesale commission business, though since March 12, 1888, his residence has been at Riverside, New

Jersey. He has spent much time and money in the building up of Riverside, and owns many valuable pieces of land in that town. As the result of his efforts the land around the railroad station was converted from a boggy swamp into a beautiful park, and he was also instrumental in inducing the Watchcase works to locate in Riverside. Since his arrival in the town he has been active in its affairs, was elected to the school board before the building of the handsome new building, raised the fire company, and at the present time has charge of putting in the sewerage system. He is commissioner of appeals, county chairman of the Democratic party, township committeeman and mayor of Riverside. He has taken great interest in the improvements of the town, and its citizens have delighted to show him all the honors in their gift, since his first residence in Riverside. Mr. Schwabenland is a member of the Elks, also of several German benevolent orders, is a life member of the Turners and Maennerchor, and belongs to the Lutheran church.

He married, in 1884, Pauline M., daughter of Jacob Lund, and they have children as follows: 1. Edward L., born December 22, 1884, in Philadelphia. 2. Sophia Marie, February 7, 1891, at Riverside, New Jersey. 3. Paul Henry, April 11, 1899, at Riverside, New Jersey. These children all received their education at Riverside, and live with their parents.

SHEDAKER The name of Shedaker has been prominent in New Jersey for more than a century and a half, though the name is not a common one. The family here described have always been enterprising and ambitious, and have contributed largely to the development of the natural resources of the state and to the maintenance of such organizations as are of great public benefit.

(I) Jacob Shedaker was born in 1746, in Burlington, New Jersey, died there November 19, 1786. By his wife Rachel he had a son Jacob.

(II) Jacob (2), son of Jacob (1) and Rachel Shedaker, was born in 1776, at Burlington, New Jersey, died February 5, 1849. By his wife Mary, who died in June, 1819, he had a son John.

(III) John, son of Jacob (2) and Mary Shedaker, was born January 12, 1801, died January 18, 1854. He married, February 8, 1824, Elizabeth, daughter of William and Sarah Rodman, born February 12, 1801, died

March 19, 1866, and their children were: 1. William R., born October 30, 1824, married Sarah Page. 2. Jacob D., see forward. 3. Sarah E., February 15, 1829, died December 27, 1903; married Ezra Budd Marter. 4. John H., April 15, 1831, married Mary Hubbs. 5. Charles, December 10, 1835, died in infancy. 6. Henry, February 6, 1838, died in infancy. 7. Elizabeth, July 6, 1859, died in infancy.

(IV) Jacob D., second son of John and Elizabeth (Rodman) Shedaker, was born in 1826, in Burlington; New Jersey, died August 2, 1907. Being a large landholder, he was a farmer all his life, and made a specialty of raising fine strawberries, which he was the first in that section to grow in quantities and ship to market in the nearby cities. He also raised other fruits, and was the first in the community to build and operate a cannery, which did a flourishing business. The one hundred acres which he owned in the city of Burlington was a valuable property, and his business ventures were very successful. He was a Republican in politics, and held several town offices of a minor nature. He was a generous contributor to the church, assisted materially in building the Shedaker Mission, Shedaker School and Shedaker Station. He belonged to Burlington Lodge, No. 22, Independent Order of Odd Fellows, and was the last living charter member of same. Mr Shedaker married, in 1848, Esther Ann, daughter of Benjamin and Ann (Keeler) Dubell, born in 1829, died in 1889, and they had six children, as follows: 1. Charles H., deceased; he married Flora Perkins, and they had a son Jacob. 2. Benjamin Dubell, see forward. 3. Elizabeth Ann. 4. Janette, married E. B. Heisler. 5. Aaron, see forward. 6. Ezra Budd, see forward.

(V) Benjamin Dubell, second son of Jacob D. and Esther Ann (Dubell) Shedaker, was born October 25, 1851, at Burlington, New Jersey, received his education in the Shedaker school and Farnam Preparatory School, and from 1871 to 1878 served as agent of the Shedaker station. Later he established himself in the seed business, in the name of B. D. Shedaker, now doing business as B. D. Shedaker & Son, which does an enormous business in this line, customers in all parts of the United States, also in Canada. He also grows large quantities of roots and owns about sixty acres of valuable land around Edgewater Park, New Jersey, where he resides. He is a Republican in politics, served five years as town collector, and the same

length of time as member of the school board. Mr. Shedaker was representative to the state legislature from 1902 until 1906, and while holding that office was appointed on several important committees, among them being chairman of committee on agriculture and agricultural college and also chairman of committee on state treasurer's accounts. He was a charter member of Lodge No. 848, Mt. Holly, Benevolent and Protective Order of Elks, was formerly a member of the Knights of Pythias, and has been a contributor to the support of the Shedaker Mission and St. Stephen's Church, of Beverly. Mr. Shedaker married, May 29, 1877, Jennie, daughter of Gould and Mary (North) Phinney, of Monroetown, Bradford county, Pennsylvania, and they had two children, Harry Phinney, see forward; William North, see forward.

(VI) Harry Phinney, the older son of Benjamin Dubell and Jennie (Phinney) Shedaker, was born April 1, 1879, received his education in the public schools and Rider Business College, after which he spent three years in the auction store of William North, in Philadelphia. He next engaged in real estate business in Atlantic City, which he sold, and then went to work for Cinnaminson Electric Light & Power Company, working up to the position of Superintendent. He was also assistant superintendent and had charge of building the road for the Camden & Trenton Street railway: he remained with the company six years, and when the road was sold he removed to Staunton, Virginia, where he spent a year managing a street railway and electric light plant. In 1907 Mr. Shedaker returned to his native town and became a member of the firm of B. D. Shedaker & Son. He married, April 29, 1903, Myrtle, daughter of Senator Mitchell B. and Theresa (Oliver) Perkins, of Beverly, New Jersey, and they have a daughter, Theresa, born April 15, 1904.

(VI) William North, second and younger son of Benjamin Dubell and Jennie (Phinney) Shedaker, was born March 15, 1881, died January 17, 1906. He received his education in the Shedaker school, supplemented by a course at the Pierce Business College. In 1900 he engaged in the drug business in Atlantic City, New Jersey, having a half interest in the firm of Shedaker & Harris, which did business one year, after which he bought out his partner and the name became William N. Shedaker. Later he became a member of the firm of Shedaker & Budd, which owned and conducted three drug stores in Atlantic City for a period of two years; in 1904 Mr. Shedaker bought out his partner and incorporated the business under the name of Shedaker Drug Stores, of which his father was president. This business was eventually sold to Mr. Lang. Mr. Shedaker was a prominent member of the Elks and Masonic orders of Atlantic City, and at his death was buried from the home of his father in Burlington, with all the honors of both orders, his funeral being the most largely attended of any ever held in that section of the state. He married, October 19, 1903, Edith, daughter of Mrs. L. F. Birch, and is survived by a son, William North, born September 15, 1904.

(V) Aaron, third son of Jacob D. and Esther Ann (Dubell) Shedaker, was born August 18, 1858, at the family homestead, in Burlington, New Jersey. He received his education at the public school and Farnum Preparatory School, at Beverly. He then spent some time in the employ of the Pennsylvania railroad as station agent at Shedaker and Edgewater Park stations, after which he settled down on the home farm, which he has conducted ever since. He makes a specialty of truck farming and small nursery stock, raising fine asparagus and rhubarb. The old house has recently been torn down, and Mr. Shedaker has erected in the same spot a commodious, modern residence; the location is in a picturesque spot and the house overlooks the Delaware river. He is a Republican in politics, and has served as township clerk since the separation of the city and township of Burlington, in 1894. He is a member of Burlington Lodge, No. 22, Independent Order of Odd Fellows, and also of Benevolent and Protective Order of Elks, No. 996, of Burlington. He has met with success in the conduct of his farm, and is a prominent and respected citizen of his native town. He is unmarried.

(V) Ezra Budd, fourth and youngest son of Jacob D. and Esther Ann (Dubell) Shedaker, was born October 17, 1860, at Burlington, New Jersey, and there received his education. He has lived on the farm all his life, and assists in the management of same, making his home with his brother, Aaron. He is also unmarried.

TESNOW   One of the self-made and successful business men of New Jersey is the representative of the German family named Tesnow, whose father was a tradesman in Prussia before his emigration to this country. The name is not

a common one in this country, but those of whom we have record are of the enterprising and public-spirited class who make the best citizens.

(I) John Henry C. Tesnow was born November 7, 1823, at Wolgast, a seaport town in Pomerania, Eastern Prussia, and died September 28, 1899, at Delanco, New Jersey. After receiving his education in the public schools of Germany, Mr. Tesnow learned fresco painting. He came to America in 1850, locating at Philadelphia, where he worked at his trade, also doing fancy carriage painting; among the work at which he assisted was the decorating of the Academy of Music. He eventually went into business for himself, making a specialty of wall-painting and panel work, and this concern became the largest business of the kind in the city. In 1884 Mr. Tesnow retired from active work, settling in Delanco, where he spent the remainder of his life. He was a Democrat, and a member of the Lutheran church. He married, about 1860, Christina Maria Ritza, born April 13, 1829, in Hanover, Germany, died June 13, 1906, at Delanco, New Jersey, and their children were: Louisa, who resides in Riverside, New Jersey; three who died in infancy; Emma, who married John A. Schneider, of Delanco, and has two children, Walter and Henry.

(II) Henry, son of John Henry C. and Christina Maria (Ritza) Tesnow, was born May 2, 1864, at Philadelphia, Pennsylvania, receiving his education in the public and German day schools, and at the age of eighteen years entered the office of George W. Reed, a real estate lawyer, where he spent three years in work and study, at the end of which time he entered the University of Pennsylvania. He graduated from the law course, in 1887, taking the degree of Bachelor of Law, and later in the same year entered Ursinis College, of Collegeville, Pennsylvania, graduating from the theological course in 1891. Mr. Tesnow spent twelve years in the ministry, seven of which he lived in Denver, Colorado, and in 1903 began to operate in real estate, his office being located for a few months in Delanco, New Jersey, but later moved to Riverside, which has been his residence and place of business since. In connection with his business in the line of real estate, Mr. Tesnow deals largely in fire insurance, and has been unusually successful in all his undertakings. Besides his large dealings in Riverside, he also does a large amount of business in the surrounding towns, and is considered a safe and conservative investor, having gained the confidence of the entire community. He is in great demand in educational and social circles, often giving his advice and service on important committees, and he is a director and leading member of the Maennerchor and Turngemeinde, of Riverside. He is a member of the Benevolent and Protective Order of Elks, No. 996, and of several German and American benevolent associations, as well as the Riverside Fire Company. In religious views he is a Lutheran, and he carries out the teachings of his faith in his relations with his fellowmen.

SHINN The Shinn family is not only one of the oldest of the New Jersey colonial families, but it is also one of the oldest in Saxon England, and the attempt has ever been made with some plausibility to trace it back through the old Germanic tribes of continental Europe to its Aryan source in the Hymalayan highlands of Asia. Coming down to historic times, however, and going back to the records of Great Britain, the American branch of the family begins with the parish of Freckenham, county Suffolk, and the year 1520.

(I) Francis Sheene, of Freckenham, born between 1520 and 1525, is registered there and in the neighboring parish of Soham with three children: 1. A daughter baptized in 1551. 2. Mary, baptized in 1564. 3. John, who is referred to below.

(II) John, son of Francis Sheene, was according to the record married four times, having nine children by his first marriage and one by each of his succeeding unions. These children were: By his first wife, Anne, who died in 1617, 1. Edward, born 1588, who became the rector of Little Fransham in 1610, and had three children; Elizabeth, 1617; Lucas, 1623; and Edward Jr., 1625, who married Dorothy, daughter of Sir Thomas Jermyn, and left three children: Jermyn, Annie and Sarah. 2. Clement, who is referred to below. 3. Francis, 1595, married Joan ——, who died 1631, and had: Elizabeth, 1616; Francis, 1618; John, 1623 to 1631; and Thomas, 1627. 4. William, 1604, married and had, Anna, 1642; and Mary, 1645. 5. Anna, 1608. 6. Margaret, 1610. 7. John, born and died 1614. 8. Nicholas, 1614 to 1615. John Shene had also by his second marriage, John, 1619. By his third marriage, Anne, 1621. By his fourth marriage Thomas, 1630 to 1631.

(III) Clement, son of John Shene, was baptized January 24, 1594. He married, at Soham, Grace ——, who bore him: 1. Margaret, 1624, died 1626. 2. Henry, 1627, died 1674. 3. Thomas, 1630. 4. John, who is referred to below. 5. Francis, 1634, married, 1663, Alice Carter, children: Mary, Francis and Alice. 6. Clement, who emigrated to New Jersey, unless the references should refer to his father, born 1637. 7. Grace, 1640, married, 1663, John Howlett.

(IV) John, son of Clement and Grace Shinn, was born in Soham parish, county Suffolk, England, died in Burlington county, New Jersey, 1712. The above pedigree is the one which is considered the most probable, but it should be mentioned that the Soham records have in addition, Clement, son of Francis Sheene, born 1592, married Sarah, and had John who married Jane. In either case it seems reasonably certain that one of these Clements is the father and the other the uncle of John, the emigrant. John Shinn was a husbandman and a millwright, and the credit of erecting the first mill in West Jersey lies between him and Thomas Olive. In 1680 John and Clement Shinn are freeholders of Burlington, but whether the latter is the brother, uncle or father of the former is uncertain. Nothing more is known about him. September 18, 1680, John Shinn bought one-fifteenth of one of the one hundred shares of West Jersey, and July 17, 1697, gave one hundred and twenty acres of it to his son James and the remainder to his son John. His will is dated January 14, 1711-12, and was proved February 30, 1711-12. By his wife Jane, whom he married in Soham, he had nine children: 1. John, married (first) 1686, Ellen Stacy, and (second) 1707, Mary ——. 2. George, married, 1691, Mary Thompson. 3. Mary, married (first) 1686, John Crosby, and (second) 1691, Richard Fennimore. 4. James, who is referred to below. 5. Thomas, married (first) 1687, Sarah Shawthorne, no children, and (second) 1693, Mary, daughter of Richard and Abigail Stockton, the emigrants. 6. Sarah, born 1669, married Thomas Atkinson. 7. Esther, died unmarried. 8. Francis, died unmarried. 9. Martha, married, 1697, Joshua Owen, the emigrant, and (second) 1729, Restore Lippincott.

(V) James, son of John and Jane Shinn, was born in England, died in New Hanover township, Burlington county, New Jersey, 1751. He lived the longest and was probably the youngest of the children of John Shinn.

When his sister Martha and Joshua Owen declared their second intentions of marriage, the members of the meeting were informed that James Shinn and Abigail Lippincott had publicly declared their intentions of marrying without coming before the meeting. The shocked and horrified Quakers appointed committees to speak to the obstreperous young folk and also to their parents, and at the next monthly meeting, these committees reported that the trouble was that the young people were determined to marry but that not being able to gain their parents consent, they could not pass the meeting. John Shinn and Restore Lippincott, the fathers, then went out under a large beach tree near the meeting house to discuss the matter and were shortly after joined by their two wives, and later still by some of the grave and reverend elders of the meeting. The result was that they gave their consent to the marriage, the intentions were properly and regularly declared and the young people were married at the house of Restore Lippincott, and John Shinn gave them one hundred and twenty-one acres of land in Nottingham township for their new home. John Shinn seems to have had little to do with church or politics. He owned land and enjoyed it, and gave large tracts to his children, and the same traits have been noticeable in their descendants. His brother Thomas led the first migration southward in 1750, and many of the grandchildren of James and Abigail Shinn followed them into the fertile valleys of Virginia and West Virginia whence their descendants have spread into the south and southwest.

James Shinn married, May 3, 1697, Abigail, daughter of Restore and Hannah (Shattock) Lippincott. Their children were: 1. Hannah, married John Atkinson. 2. Hope, married Michael Atkinson. 3. Francis, married Elizabeth Atkinson. 4. Joseph, who is referred to below. 5. James Jr., married, 1730, Hannah, daughter of George and Elizabeth (Lippincott) Shinn, and granddaughter of John and Ellen (Stacy) Shinn. 6. Solomon, married Mary Antrim. 7. Clement, married Elizabeth Webb. 8. Abigail, married Henry Reeve. 9. Susanna, married Bartholomew West, lived in Monmouth county and had three sons in the revolutionary army. 10. Mercy, who died unmarried.

(VI) Joseph, son of James and Abigail (Lippincott) Shinn, was born in Nottingham township, Burlington county, in 1703, died in Mount Holly, February 11, 1759, being buried in St. Andrew's churchyard there. Leaving the Society of Friends, probably as the result of George Keiths's defection, he became one of the charter communicants of St. Andrew's, Mount Holly, and had all of his children baptized there May 30, 1746, by the Rev. Colin Campbell. He was a large land owner in New Hanover township, Burlington county, and in Upper Freehold township, Monmouth county. In 1726 he married Mary, daughter of William and Elizabeth Budd, the latter a daughter of Richard and Abigail Stockton, the emigrants, and granddaughter of William and Ann (Clapgut) Budd, the emigrants. Their children were: 1. Patience. 2. Rebecca, married George Clapp. 3. William, who is referred to below. 4. Vestai. 5. Joseph Jr. 6. Benjamin. 7. John, married Mary Allen. 8. Francis, married Martha, daughter of George and Sarah (Branson) Owen Shinn, and granddaughter of George and Elizabeth (Lippincott) Shinn. 9. Abigail, married Joseph Budd.

(VII) William, third child and eldest son of Joseph and Mary (Budd) Shinn, was born in New Hanover township or in Mount Holly, was baptized as an adult in St. Andrew's, Mount Holly, May 30, 1746, died in Burlington, May, 1767, and was buried in St. Mary's churchyard there. June 24, 1756, he obtained a marriage license to marry Sarah French, of Burlington, and their children were: 1. Mary, born May 22, 1757. 2. Lydia, 1759, who became the third wife of Caleb Arney Lippincott. 3. Eli, 1761, died November 9, 1776, and buried in St. Andrew's churchyard, Mount Holly. 4. Aaron, who is referred to below. 5. Joseph, 1765, married, 1783, Mary Lippincott.

(VIII) Aaron, fourth child and second son of William and Sarah (French) Shinn, was born in Burlington, New Jersey. In his father's will, written May 27, 1767, he with his brothers and sisters are mentioned as minors. Nothing more is known about him except that he married and had at least one child Eli, who is referred to below.

(IX) Eli, son of Aaron Shinn, was born in Mount Holly, November 13, 1788, died there June 26, 1869, being buried in St. Andrew's churchyard. He married, April 27, 1791, Sarah Haines, by whom he had one son, Charles Corey, referred to below.

(X) Charles Corey, son of Eli and Sarah (Haines) Shinn, was born February 13, 1814, married Dorothy Southwick, who bore him five children: 1. Garrett W. 2. Anna I., mar-

Samuel W. Shinn

ried a Mr. Bⅰtz. 3. Beⅰlah, married a Mr. Bⅰdd. 4. Sarah, married a Mr. Gaskell. 5. Charles Henry, who is referred to below.

(XI) Charles Henry, yoⅰngest child of Charles Corey and Dorothy (Soⅰthwick) Shinn, was born in Bⅰrlington coⅰnty, September 18, 1843. He was at one time sheriff of Bⅰrlington coⅰnty and prominent in politics. He married, March 17, 1868, Anna Elizabeth, daⅰghter of Carlton Ridgway and Mary Harde (McClure) Moore. Her mother was the daⅰghter of David and Janet Mc-Clⅰre, of Philadelphia. Benjamin Moore, the foⅰnder of the family, came from Birmingham, Lincolnshire, England, to Bⅰrlington, New Jersey, and married Sarah, daⅰghter of Thomas and Mary (Bernard) Stokes. His son, Benjamin, married, in 1730, Rebecca, daⅰghter of Joseph Fennimore, and their fifth child and second son, Bethⅰel, born March 14, 1741, married Martha, daⅰghter of John Allen. Their third child and second son Amasa, born March 15, 1770, married Agnes, daⅰghter of Samⅰel French, and their eldest child, Samⅰel French, born October 7, 1793, married Rachel, daⅰghter of Nehemiah Haines and Abigail, daⅰghter of Noah Haines and Hannah (Thorn) Tⅰrner, the widow of George Tⅰrner and the daⅰghter of Thomas and Letitia (Hinchman) Thorn, and granddaⅰghter of Joseph and Mary (Bowne) Thorne. Nehemiah was the son of Jonathan Haines and Hannah, daⅰghter of William and Mary (Aⅰstin) Sharp. Samⅰel French and Rachel (Haines) Moore had two children: Bloomfield Haines, who married Clara Jessⅰp, and Carlton Ridgway. Carlton Ridgway Moore was born in Philadelphia, April 22, 1809, died September, 1905. He was a cotton merchant, a member of the Odd Fellows and a Friend. After the civil war he went to Northampton coⅰnty, Virginia, where he died. By his wife, Mary Harde (McClure) Moore, he had: Mary B., who married George Wolfe; Jacob Riʔgway, died ⅰnmarried; Carlton Ridgway Jr., married Elizabeth Van Ness; Helen Clara, married John B. Irick, of Vincentown; Anna Elizabeth, referred to above. Mary Harde (McClure) Moore died March 11, 1861. Charles Henry and Anna Elizabeth (Moore) Shinn have one child, Samⅰel Woolston, who is referred to below.

(XII) Samⅰel Woolston. only child of Charles Henry and Anna Elizabeth (Moore) Shinn, was born on a farm near Moⅰnt Holly, October 14, 1870, died Febrⅰary 25, 1908. He was edⅰcated in private schools and in a bⅰsi-

ness college in Philadelphia. He then stⅰdied law with E. P. Bⅰdd, of Moⅰnt Holly, and was admitted to the New Jersey bar in Jⅰne, 1895, beginning at once to practise his profession in Moⅰnt Holly, where he became one of the leading and most sⅰccessfⅰl lawyers of the town. He was a director in the Moⅰnt Holly National Bank, a director of the Union National Bank of the same place and a director of the Moⅰnt Holly Safe Deposit and Trⅰst Company. He was the secretary of the Bⅰrlington Coⅰnty Fair Association and was one of its original promoters, and the one most instrumental in making it the most sⅰccessfⅰl fair in the state. He served as depⅰty sheriff. He was a member of the Elks of Moⅰnt Holly and of the Modern Woodmen of America.

He married, Febrⅰary 15, 1904, Anna, daⅰghter of Benjamin and Mary (Aⅰstin) Powell, and their children are: 1. Norman Ridgway, born Febrⅰary 22, 1906, died Jⅰly 16, 1906. 2. Mary Elizabeth, Aⅰgⅰst 18, 1907. Benjamin Powell was the son of Benjamin and Eliza Powell, of Pemberton. Mary (Aⅰstin) Powell was a daⅰghter of Charles and Hannah (Lamb) Aⅰstin.

LODER
The Loder family has for generations been connected with the history of Soⅰth Jersey, where it has won for itself an enviable name and repⅰtation for integrity and ability. By its intermarriages with the old New Jersey families it has also connected itself with pretty nearly everything that is worth while in the history and the civilization of the coⅰntry.

(I) David Pettitt Loder, foⅰnder of the branch of the family at present ⅰnder considⅰration, was for many years one of the most prominent contractors and bⅰilders of Bridgeton, New Jersey. His children were: 1. Benjamin Pettitt, married Elizabeth Nicholson. 2. William Pettitt, married Aner Daniel. 3. Ella M., ⅰnmarried. 4. Martha, died in infancy. 5. Charles Henry, referred to below. Martin and Lemⅰel, brothers of David P. Loder, served in the civil war among the New Jersey volⅰnteers.

(II) Charles Henry, son of David Pettitt Loder, of Bridgeton, New Jersey, was born at that place, November 29, 1859. He was a bookkeeper. He married Laⅰra Della, daⅰghter of Gilbert S. and Emily R. (Carman) Swing, of Cⅰmberland coⅰnty, New Jersey. Her grandfather served with distinction in the war of 1812. The children of Charles Henry and Laⅰra Della (Swing) Loder were: 1.

LeRoy Ward, referred to below. 2. Emily Richer, born August 25, 1886. 3. Martha Ann, March 21, 1889. 4. May Vannaman, October 10, 1895. 5. Frances Stanley, May 28, 1904.

(III) LeRoy Ward, eldest child of Charles Henry and Laura Della (Swing) Loder, was born at Bridgeton, New Jersey, December 5, 1883, and is now located at 91 East Commerce street, in that city. For his early education he was sent to the public schools of Bridgeton, and after graduating from the Bridgeton high school he entered the West Jersey Academy, from which he graduated in 1902. He then took up the study of law in the office of John S. Mitchell, Esquire, of Bridgeton, and was admitted by the supreme court to the New Jersey bar as an attorney, in November, 1905, and June 23, 1909, was admitted a counsellor. Since his admission as an attorney he has been engaged in the general practice of his profession at Bridgeton, making a specialty of criminal cases. In politics Mr. Loder is a Democrat and is quite popular and prominent in the affairs of that party in his county. In 1906 he was the candidate of the Democratic party as the New Jersey assemblyman from Bridgeton, and he is a member of the New Jersey state Democratic auxiliary committee. Mr. Loder is a member of the board of trustees at the West Jersey Academy, Bridgeton Athletic Association, New Jersey State Bar Association, and of the Cumberland County Bar Association. In religion he is a member of the Presbyterian church of Bridgeton. He is an enthusiastic secret society man, and a member of the Patriotic Order of the Sons of America. Among his secret society affiliations should be mentioned the Cumberland Lodge, No. 35, Independent Order of Odd Fellows, of which he is a past grand, and secretary of Bridgeton Commercial League.

SLOAN Adam Reber Sloan, of Camden, New Jersey, is the son of James Clement and Lucy (Reber) Sloan. The father was born near Tuckerton, New Jersey, and the mother was a daughter of Adam Reber, of Berks county, Pennsylvania. Their children were: 1. Theodore Reber, an artist in oil-cloth design; married Miriam, daughter of John Hickman, and had four children: Daisy H., died a spinster; Esther B., died in 1908; the Rev. Harold Paul, a Methodist Episcopal minister; Eva T. H., married a Mr. Earl. 2. Adam Reber, referred to below.

Adam Reber Sloan was born in Camden, New Jersey, May 11, 1854, and is now living in Atco, New Jersey. For his early education he attended the public schools of Camden, and then became a newspaper man, a profession which he followed with great success for many years. He has filled every position in journalism, from reporter to editor. For eighteen years he worked on the staff of the *Newark Evening News,* and then, for about twenty years, was the editor of the *Camden Democrat.* For a time also he was the editor of the *Camden Telegram.* He took up the study of law in the office of Judge Richard P. Miller, Esquire, of Camden, New Jersey, and was admitted to the New Jersey bar, November 7, 1898. Since this time he has been engaged in the general practice of his profession in Camden, New Jersey. Mr. Sloan is a Republican and a member of the Presbyterian church of Atco, New Jersey, where he resides with his family. He is an ardent and enthusiastic Mason. He is a member of the Haddonfield, New Jersey, Lodge, No. 130, Free and Accepted Masons, of which he is a past master. He is also a past high priest of Salome Chapter, No. 19, Royal Arch Masons. In addition he is a member of Cyrene Commandery, No. 7, Knights Templar, of Camden; Van Hook Council, No. 8, Royal and Select Masters, of Camden Consistory of Camden, New Jersey, thirty-second degree Masons. Besides this he enjoys the distinction of being one of the comparatively few members of the Supreme Council, Sovereign Grand Inspectors General, of the Scottish Rite Masons, which this makes him a thirty-third degree Mason. He is also an Odd Fellow.

Adam Reber Sloan married (first) November 7, 1889, Minnie L., daughter of John H. and Mary (Sutton) Wyle, of Philadelphia Pennsylvania. Their children are: 1. Dorothy Wyle, now a student at the New Jersey State Normal School. 2. Lucy Emily, now attending the public school in Atco, Camden county, New Jersey. Minnie L. (Wyle) Sloan died September 2, 1893, and Mr. Sloan married (second) December 18, 1900, Elizabeth M. Kase. On her wedding day she was commissioned by the governor of New Jersey as a commissioner of deeds and a notary public.

GITHENS Benjamin Githens, of Philadelphia, is one of the most successful merchants and financiers of that city, and his family has been identified with New Jersey for many generations. It is unfortunate, however, that there

Benjamin Githen

are but few records except those of intermarriages with prominent and influential branches of the old historic families of the colonies on the Delaware, and the absence of birth and death records and of wills and deeds make the task of tracing the genealogy of any given line an extremely difficult one.

(I) Clayton Githens, father of Benjamin Githens, was born in the southern part of New Jersey, where he married Sarah Wear Munroe, whose father came to this country from Scotland. He lived at Juliustown, Burlington county, where their children were born.

(II) Benjamin, son of Clayton and Sarah W. (Munroe) Githens, was born in Juliustown, and there received his early education and the training which enabled him to become in later life, after he had come to Philadelphia, the successful business man which he now is, in Burlington county. For many years he has been the senior partner in the firm of wholesale grocers and importers, Githens, Rexsamer & Company, of Front street, Philadelphia, and the great prosperity of this firm is in a great measure due to his industry, integrity and efforts. Mr. Githens is also intimately identified with very many of Philadelphia's other mercantile and financial institutions. He is a director and vice-president of the Philadelphia Warehouse and Cold Storage Company, and for twenty-five years has been a director in the Corn Exchange National Bank, of Philadelphia, and since 1900 has been president of that institution, which is one of the strongest of the financial organizations in the city, having a surplus and net profits of $1,374,673.74, and deposits amounting to $20,002,027.89. In addition to all of these responsibilities, Mr. Githens takes a great interest in everything that pertains to the artistic, social and historical prestige of Philadelphia and New Jersey. He is a member of the Philadelphia Art Club, City Club of Philadelphia, Historical Society of Pennsylvania, American Academy of Political and Social Science of Philadelphia, and of the New Jersey Society of Pennsylvania.

Benjamin Githens married Mary, daughter of William Prettyman, of Philadelphia, and their children are: 1. Augustus Decan, born in Philadelphia, 1861, a member of the grocery and importing house of Githens, Rexsamer & Company; married Mary McDermot, of New Jersey. 2. Mary D., born in Philadelphia, married Alan Calvert, of Philadelphia, who is in the tin plate and metal business. They have two children, Benjamin Githens Calvert and

Jean Githens Calvert. Mr. Githens and family are members of the First Baptist Church of Philadelphia. He is now one of the trustees and a deacon.

GREY   According to the opinions of antiquarians who have studied the origin of surnames in Great Britain the names Grey and Gray are patronymics said to have been derived from a color; and it is to be presumed that whatever is true in this respect of the English family of Grey is also true of the branch of the general family which lived in Ireland.

(I) Philip Grey, who appears to have been the immigrant ancestor of the family under consideration in this place, lived in Ireland and came thence to America in 1800. He married and had a family.

(II) Philip James, son of Philip Grey, the immigrant, lived in Camden, New Jersey, but we have no account of his family life, except that he married and had a family.

(III) Martin Philip, son of Philip James Grey, was born in Camden, New Jersey, December 7, 1841. He married Jane Dinham, who was born in Hunterdon county, New Jersey, in February, 1844, daughter of James Dinham, of Clinton, Hunterdon county.

(IV) Norman, son of Martin Philip and Jane (Dinham) Grey, was born at Salem, New Jersey, April 3, 1868. He received his earlier literary education in public schools in Salem, the Reading Military School, where he was a student during the years 1882-83, and at Mr. Turner's school at Maplewood (Pittsfield), Massachusetts, where he prepared for college. He then entered Princeton College and was graduated A. B. in 1889. He was educated for the law in the law department of the University of Pennsylvania, and was admitted to the bar in New Jersey, as attorney, in 1892 and as counsellor in 1895. Since he came to the bar Mr. Grey has engaged in practice in Camden, devoting his attention chiefly to cases involving questions of corporation law and also to practice in the equity courts. In April, 1906, he was elected president of the West Jersey Trust Company of Camden, one of the strongest financial institutions of that city, and still serves in that capacity. He is a Republican in politics, a communicant of the Episcopal church, member of the Union League Club of Philadelphia and of the Princeton Club.

Mr. Grey married Louise Booth Sinnickson, daughter of Andrew Sinnickson, of Salem.

New Jersey, and has had four children: 1. Louise Sinnickson, born Woodbury, New Jersey, January 12, 1896. 2. Martin Philip Jr., born Woodbury, April 17, 1897, died February 19, 1902. 3. Lucy Brady, born August 20, 1900. 4. Norma, born October 8, 1903.

EVANS The Evans family trace their line of descent from Wales back to Mervyn Vrych, King of the Isle of Man, who was killed in battle with the King of Mercia, A. D. 843. Some branches of the family spell their name with an "e" instead of an "a," which has arisen from a clerical error of early days, as the name originated from the five sons of Ievan, known as Evan Robert Lewis, who in 1601 was living in Wales, England, the sons according to the Welsh custom taking for themselves the surname of ap Evan. These sons were John ap Evan, Cadwalader ap Evan, Griffith ap Evan, Owen ap Evan and Evan ap Evan. It is from one of these five men that the founder of the Evans family of New Jersey sprang.

(I) Unfortunately the christian name of the founder of the family has been lost, and while it is probable it is not absolutely certain that he emigrated to this country. The first mention in the records is the will of his widow, Jane, dated February 16, 1696, in which she styles herself as of Evesham, Burlington county. This will was proved November 2, 1697, by her son and executor William Evans, who is referred to below. The will also mentions a son Thomas who is dead and his wife Sarah, and in the will of this Thomas, dated May 2, 1692, and proved September 23, 1693, there is mention of a daughter Agnes, sister to Thomas and William.

(II) William Evens, the son of —— and Jane Evans (such are the spellings of the surnames in the wills) died between February 21, 1728, and March 24, 1728, the dates of the writing and proving of his will. In this document he describes himself as a yeoman of Evesham, Burlington county, and mentions his wife Elizabeth, his children, Thomas, Jane and John, the last of whom is under age. His wife Elizabeth was a minister among Friends, his daughter Jane married William Hudson, and his son Thomas is referred to below.

(III) Thomas, son of William and Elizabeth Evens, married (first) in 1715, Esther, daughter of John and Esther (Borton) Haines, who died in 1728, and bore him six children: 1. William, born September 6, 1716, married Sarah Roberts. 2. Elizabeth, January 8, 1718,

married Joseph Lippincott. 3. Isaac, referred to below. 4. Esther, December 6, 1722, married Samuel Atkinson. 5. Jacob, January 14, 1725, married (first) Rachel Eldridge, and (second) Mary Cherrington. 6. Nathan, 1727, married Susanna Gaskill. Thomas Evans married (second) June 4, 1730, Rebecca, daughter of Joshua Owen and Martha, daughter of John and Jane Shinn. Their children were: 1. Joshua, born September 23, 1731, married Priscilla Collins. 2. Caleb, August 26, 1733, died young. 3. Caleb, February 2, 1737, married Abigail Hunt. 4. Jemima, June 1, 1738, married and had had issue. 5. Martha, November 16, 1742, married Thomas Dudley.

(IV) Isaac, third child and second son of Thomas and Esther (Haines) Evans, was born in Evesham township, Burlington county, January 21, 1720, died there about June, 1782. At this point there are conflicting traditions and an unfortunate lack of extant records, but the weight of evidence seems to be in favor of the hypothesis that this Isaac, who is known as Isaac, senior, married either Hannah Roberts or Bathsheba Stokes, and had at least Samuel, Job and Rebecca and if his wife was Bathsheba, also Ann. This is the conjecture therefore followed here, and Job is referred to below.

(V) Job, the conjectured son of Isaac and Bathsheba (Stokes) or Hannah (Roberts) Evans, is said to have been born, lived and died near Medford, New Jersey, and to have left a son Isaac, who is referred to below. Another theory, which has some plausibility, should however be mentioned here, namely, that this Job instead of being the son of Isaac, as given here, was his brother, the youngest son of Thomas and Rebecca (Owen) Evans.

(VI) Isaac (2), son of Job Evans, was born in Medford, New Jersey, about 1788. He lived in Medford and was a blacksmith and carriage builder, he died between 1825 and 1830. By his wife Margaret (McNinney) Evans he had six children: James M., referred to below, William K., Nehemiah C., Sarah. Elizabeth, Mary, who died young.

(VII) James M., son of Isaac (2) and Margaret (McNinney) Evans was born in Medford, Burlington county, in 1821, died in Moorestown, New Jersey, 1897. He received a common school education, and carried on the carriage business left by his father who died when he was yet but a small boy. He lived in Medford most of his life and for eight or ten years engaged in farming near Mount

Laurel. After this he went into the carriage business in Moorestown and continued in this until a few years previous to his death, when he retired from active business. Mr. Evans was a Democrat and held various town offices in Medford. He was a member of the Methodist Episcopal church, and in early life an official in the church. He was also a member of the American Mechanics. James M. Evans married (first) Susan, daughter of John and Mary Taylor, of Philadelphia, whose Uncle David was at one time treasurer of the Pennsylvania railroad. Their children were: 1. George, deceased, 2. Alfred, deceased. 3. Isaac, deceased. 4. Charles, a landscape gardener in Moorestown, who married Mary ——— and has Isaac and Susan. James M. Evans married (second) Elizabeth Taylor, the sister of his first wife, and their children were: 1. John Taylor, referred to below. 2. James B. 3. David. 4. Walter. The last three are now dead.

(VIII) John Taylor, eldest child and only surviving son of James M. and Elizabeth (Taylor) Evans, was born in Medford, Burlington county, September 20, 1852, and is now living at Moorestown. For his education he went to the public schools of Moorestown, and then learned the trade of blacksmith at which he worked until he was twenty-two years old, when he went into the employ of the Pennsylvania railroad as ticket agent at Hartford station in 1874. Here he remained for eight years, and in 1882 went into the grocery business in Moorestown, which he followed for six and a half years, and then in 1890 went into the real estate and insurance business in Moorestown, and has continued in that ever since. Mr. Evans is a Republican, and for a number of years was a member of the board of commissioners of appeals for the township. For eighteen years he has been a member of the Moorestown board of education and for nine of them has been the clerk of the board. For fifteen years he has been a justice of the peace. He is also a commissioner of deeds, having been appointed as such by the governors of both Pennsylvania and New Jersey. He has also been appointed by the governor of New Jersey notary public. For forty years he has been a member of the Methodist church at Moorestown. He is a local preacher and for twenty-four years has been superintendent of the Sunday school of the Methodist Episcopal Church of Moorestown, and he has also a mission school of which he has been superintendent for eight years. He is also a trustee· and steward of the Methodist church and has

been treasurer of the society for twenty years. Mr. Evans is a member of Pocohontas Lodge, Independent Order of Odd Fellows, in Moorestown, No. 107, and also a member of the American Mechanics Lodge, No 115, of Moorestown.

In 1873 John Taylor Evans married Edith H., daughter of Benjamin and Sibilla (Marter) Wallace, of Palmyra, New Jersey. Their children are: 1. Laura Virginia, married D. Walker Boneau, of Moorestown, a stock broker in Philadelphia. 2. George Branin, an attorney with offices in Camden and Moorestown and a residence in the latter place, who graduated from the Moorestown high school and Swarthmore College, then took a business course in Philadelphia, and then took a position with the American Bridge Company which he held for four years as assistant to the treasurer of one of the departments, studying law at nights at Temple University, from which he graduated in 1905 with the highest honors, and was then admitted to the bar and is now one of the instructors and professors at Temple University. He married Geraldine Albray, of Newark, New Jersey. 3. Elizabeth K., a music teacher who lives at home with her father. All three children were born in Moorestown.

ADAMS This branch of the Adams family in America was founded by Jacob Adams, who emigrated to America about the middle of the eighteenth century. He was an early settler in Beverly township, Burlington county, New Jersey, and became possessed of farming land in that township, where the ruins of his log house may be seen on the Marter farm near Beverly. He had issue: John, William, Jacob, Isaac, Nancy (Mrs. John W. Fenimore), Deborah (Mrs. John Cannon), Amelia (Mrs. Hendrick Van Brunt).

(II) John, son of Jacob Adams, the founder, was born December 15, 1784, and died December 16, 1859. He was a carpenter and builder. He erected many buildings in the vicinity, and was a successful contractor. He married Nancy ———.

(III) Jacob C., son of John and Nancy Adams, was born in Beverly township, New Jersey, in the year 1827, and died in 1875. He was educated in the public schools, and followed farming all his life. He had a brickyard on his farm and made bricks for building purpose. This became an important item of his business and is still carried on by his descendants. He was a member of the Republican party, and served as overseer of highways and on the township committee. He was an Odd Fellow, belonging to Beverly Lodge No. 22. His religious faith was Presbyterian, of which church he was an exemplary member. Jacob C. Adams married Mary Ann Wilson, who bore him three children: 1. Henry Clay (see forward). 2. Samuel. 3. Cornelia (Mrs. Joseph Gabriel, of Philadelphia).

(IV) Henry Clay, first born child of Jacob C. and Mary A. (Wilson) Adams, was born on the homestead farm in Burlington county, New Jersey. This is now Edgewater Park. He was educated at Cooperstown (New Jersey). He inherited the farm from his father, making the third generation to own and conduct the property. He continues the manufacture of brick, and in addition operates a coal and wood yard in Edgewater Park. His specialty in agriculture is gardening for the Philadelphia market. Mr. Adams is a Republican, and is on the township committee. He is a member of the Patrons of Husbandry, Roncocas Grange; Beverly Lodge No. 95, Independent Order of Odd Fellows, and of the Benevolent and Protective Order of Elks, Burlington Lodge, No. 996.

Henry C. Adams married, in 1874, Levinia, daughter of William R. Christie, of Salem, New Jersey. Children: 1. Harry J., born 1875; is interested with his father in both the farm and the coal yard at Edgewater Park; married Bertha V., daughter of James and Annie C. (Johnson) Pennington, of Roncocas, New Jersey; they have a son, Henry P. Adams. 2. Herbert L., born 1877; also with his father in business; married Isabelle, daughter of Robert Williams, of Trenton, New Jersey; they have Raymond and Joseph G. Adams. 3. Elizabeth D., born 1880; married Hugh B. Miller, a contractor and builder of Edgewater Park; they have Lavinia Helen, Warren Adams and Hugh Burton Miller. 4. D. Lindsay, born 1895. Two children died in infancy —George and Earl.

SMITH   Captain Elton Allen Smith is a descendant on both paternal and maternal sides from a long line of sturdy New England ancestors. They were among the founders of the Nation and passed through all the hardships and privations incident to the pioneer life, defending themselves against the Indians and wild beasts of the forests which then infested the country. They participated in all the early wars, were conspicuous for the services in the French and Indian, revolutionary, and the war of 1812. The hardships they passed through in that rugged climate bred in their descendants a hardiness and fertility of body and brain which has enabled them to carry on successfully many varied interests at the same time, and become leaders in the business circles all over the Continent. Elton A. Smith is a worthy descendant of his ancestors. He takes a personal supervision of all the details of all his varied interests in manufacturing, transportation and agriculture.

Elton A. Smith was born in Woodstock, Vermont, March 23, 1848, where he was reared until about fourteen years of age, when the family moved to Lowell, Massachusetts, and in 1866 came to Smithville, New Jersey, soon after going to sea, spending five years on the ocean, finally locating in Savannah, Georgia, and in the years following engaged in many enterprises, following many lines of business endeavor for a period of twenty-five years. His New England ancestry has furnished him with a business acumen and energy that carried him successfully through the difficult problems that confront the progressive, daring business man, and he gained a comfortable competence, as well as becoming a seasoned, practical man of affairs. Mr. Smith is emphatically a self-made man, and he can look back upon the twenty-five years spent wrestling single handed with the world, with all the satisfaction of a victor. His residence in the south terminated upon the death of his father in 1887, when he came north and settled in Smithville, New Jersey, assuming control of the H. B. Smith Machine Company, established by H. B. Smith in 1847, and since 1865 located at Smithville, New Jersey. This plant manufactures wood working machinery of every description, and employs from three hundred to five hundred operatives, covers, with its extensive factories and grounds including the village owned by the company, about one hundred acres. The company has branches for the sale of their product in all the principal cities of this country and numerous sales agencies in the different parts of the world. They are among the oldest and largest manufacturers of wood working machinery in existence to-day. Elton A. Smith is president and principal owner of the business. He is known as one of the leading business men of New Jersey. The fortune he has accumulated has been fairly won, as it has been fairly used, for the comfort and happi-

ness of his family and the good of his fellow-men. He has large farming, real estate and other interests outside of this business, and maintains a handsome summer home in his native state, Vermont. He has fraternal relations with the Masonic order, holding all the degrees up to and including that of Knight Templar, and is a member of the Mystic Shrine. He is an Odd Fellow and an Elk. He married Marie O'Byrne, of Savannah, Georgia, and has children: Regis, E. Allen, Hilda, Erle, Verona, Elizabeth and Lois. His sons are associated with their father in business.

KING The family of King at present under consideration belongs to the emigration of the early nineteenth century which brought to this country so many of the best of England's middle class manufacturing and industrial element.

(I) Ray King, founder of the family, was born at Newcastle-on-Tyne, England, was a silversmith by trade and came to this country in the early part of the nineteenth century, bringing his wife Anna (Wilson) King, and they had children: William, Joseph R., referred to below, Abigail, Eleanor.

(II) Joseph Ray, son of Ray and Anna (Wilson) King, was born in Philadelphia, Pennsylvania, about 1803, died in Burlington, New Jersey, in 1845. He was highly educated, was quite a linguist and followed his father's trade of silversmith. He was a member of the Society of Friends. He married Mary Gaskill, daughter of Caleb and Elizabeth (Williams) Gaskill, of Burlington, whose father was a large real estate owner, being possessed of much land where some of the best residences of Burlington now stand, and besides this having large lumber interests. The children of Joseph Ray and Mary (Gaskill) King were: Anna Wilson, Elizabeth, referred to below, William Gaskill and George Gaskill, twins.

(III) Elizabeth, daughter of Joseph Ray and Mary (Gaskill) King, was born in Burlington, New Jersey, educated at select schools, at the boarding school at Wilmington and at the Westtown Friends' school. In 1876 she married Nicholas Buzby, born in Haddonfield, New Jersey, in 1840, died in 1900, the son of Abel and Rachel Buzby. His father, Abel Buzby, was a school teacher; he lived in Philadelphia most of his life and his children were: Susanna, deceased; William Paul, a contractor in Philadelphia; Nicholas,

mentioned above; Ellen. Nicholas Buzby was in the banking business in Philadelphia for the greater part of his life, being for thirty years with the Northern Liberties Bank of that city, and at the time of his death being that institution's head bookkeeper. For the last twenty-six years of his life he had made his home in Burlington. He was an elder in the Presbyterian church, also trustee and treasurer, a teacher in the Sunday school and actively identified with everything pertaining to the church and its interests. He was not interested in politics. He was a Mason in Philadelphia and is a thirty-second degree Mason. Nicholas and Elizabeth (King) Buzby had only one daughter, who died in infancy.

DONOVAN The members of this family have not been residents of this country much more than half a century, but in every place they have lived they have been respected and desirable citizens, and have contributed to the progress and improvement of the community.

(I) James Donovan was born in Ireland, and lived there until about 1850, when he came to Springfield, Massachusetts, where he remained until his death. He married Catherine Hayes, born in Ireland, died in Chicopee Falls, Massachusetts. Their children were: John, deceased; Mary; Julia; Joanna; Patrick, died in Ireland; Timothy; Daniel.

(II) Daniel, fourth son of James and Catherine (Hayes) Donovan, was born in 1829, in county Cork, Ireland, and there learned the trade of shoemaker. He emigrated to America, landing in New York, July 3, 1849, and later settled in Chicopee Falls, Massachusetts, where he first worked at his trade and later became proprietor of a shoe store, which he owned and conducted for many years. On his retirement from active business he removed to Riverside, New Jersey, where he now resides with his son, Timothy Jeremiah, also his wife. He married Catherine Conway, born in 1829, in county Claire, Ireland, and their children were: 1. James. 2. John, living with Timothy J., at Riverside. 3. Timothy Jeremiah. 4. Belle, resides in Philadelphia. 5. Jennie, deceased. 6. Nellie, resides at West Philadelphia. 7. Kate, living at Hartford, Connecticut. 8. Lizzie, living in Philadelphia. 9. Annie, deceased. 10. Daniel, living at West Philadelphia. 11. Frank, living at Philadelphia. 12. Willie, lives with Timothy J., at Riverside, New Jersey.

(III) Timothy Jeremiah, third son of Daniel and Catherine (Conway) Donovan, was born November 1, 1856, at Chicopee Falls, Massachusetts, where he received his education and later worked at manufacture of sheet iron, learning the trade. At the age of twenty he spent a year in the west, spending most of the time in Minnesota and Texas; he then removed to Philadelphia and in 1880 embarked in the hotel business, which he conducted for eight years, and then removed to Riverside, New Jersey, where in 1890 he opened the Avenue House, which is still conducted by him, and is the best hotel in the vicinity. Mr. Donovan is a Democrat in political views. He is a member of the advisory board of Riverside, was one of the organizers in 1903, and is now one of the board of directors of the Riverside National Bank. He is a member of the Benevolent and Protective Order of Elks, and belongs to the Riverside Fire Company.

Mr. Donovan married (first) in 1880, Elizabeth, daughter of Patrick McGrath, of Philadelphia, and they had one daughter, Mabel Ella, who married John Michterlin, of Philadelphia, and has two children, Vincin and Ethena. Mrs. Donovan died in June, 1898. Mr. Donovan married (second) in 1899, Rebecca M., daughter of Jacob Kerines, of Delanco, New Jersey, and they had one son, Albert Jenning, born June 14, 1900, died August, 1903.

MIDDLETON Lord John Middleton married at St. Andrews, Helborn, December 16, 1666, Martha Carew.

(II) John (2), son of Lord John (1) and Martha (Carew) Middleton, was born in England in 1686, died at Crosswicks, Chesterfield township, Burlington county, New Jersey, in 1741. He settled on a farm in Crosswicks which his wife had inherited, and there spent his life, living quietly and orderly as did become a devout member of the Society of Friends. He married, January 14, 1710, Esther Gilberthrope, who was born in the Province of West Jersey, December, 1684, and died at Crosswicks in 1759, daughter of Thomas and Esther Gilberthrope, Friends, who came to this country from England. This John Middleton has a son Thomas and other sons, one of whom was the father of Jacob Middleton, of Crosswicks, the earliest ancestor of the family under consideration here of whom we have any reliable record or information.

(IV) Jacob Middleton, grandson of ·John

of Crosswicks, and great-grandson of Lord John of Helborn, England, was born at Crosswicks, New Jersey, in 1751, died May 6, 1818. He married and had son Jacob.

(V) Jacob (2), son of Jacob (1) Middleton, was born at Crosswicks, New Jersey, August 6, 1788, died February 5, 1878. He was a brick mason by trade and a farmer by principal occupation. He married Sibylia West, born January 14, 1791, died May 7, 1879. Children: Hannah, born 1815, died 1856; Albert, February 25, 1817, see post; George W., died young.

(VI) Albert, son of Jacob (2) and Sibylia (West) Middleton, was born February 25, 1817, died December 7, 1905. He was a carpenter and joiner by trade and followed that occupation during the early part of his business life. Subsequently he was appointed ticket agent at Hainesport for the Pennsylvania Railroad Company and filled that position for twenty years, until he retired from active pursuits, several years previous to his death. He was first a Whig and later a Republican, and served as a member of the board of freeholders and as member of the township committee. He also was a member of the Society of Friends. In January, 1845, Mr. Middleton married Ann S. Middleton, born 1822 died December, 1890, daughter of Allen Middleton. Children: Emma E., born October, 1845, married Robert Love, of Philadelphia; Walter Jeanes, see post.

(VII) Walter Jeanes, son of Albert and Ann S. (Middleton) Middleton, was born in Philadelphia, Pennsylvania, August 17, 1848, and was a child three years old when his parents removed from that village to Hainesport, New Jersey. His young life was spent in the latter town, and there he was given a good common school education. In 1871 he opened a general merchandise store in Hainesport and for the next thirty years was prominently identified with the business life and history of the place, for he was a capable and prosperous business man and enjoyed a wide acquaintance in the region. Mr. Middleton retired from active pursuits in 1900, although he still retains considerable property interests which require his attention; he is also a director of the Hainesport Mining and Transportation Company. He is a Republican in political preference and for many years was a well known figure in public affairs in the township. He served ten years as postmaster of Hainesport and also served as school director. Like his ancestors before him, Mr. Middleton is a member of the Socitey of Friends. In 1878 he married Anna M., daughter of Benjamin Jr. and Sarah (West) Thorn, of Crosswicks. Mr. and Mrs. Middleton have one son, Howard T., born in Hainsport, November 19, 1879. He was educated in the town schools, the high school at Moorestown, and at a business college in Philadelphia. He is now an employee in the general offices of the Pennsylvania Railroad Company in Philadelphia.

Benjamin Thorn Jr. was born at Crosswicks, January 18, 1810, died in June, 1890. He was a carpenter by trade and after his removal to Hainesport was captain of the steamer "Barclay," plying between Hainesport and the city of Philadelphia. He was a substantial and well-informed man, an old line Whig and later a Republican, and an elder of the Society of Friends.

He married, in 1832, Sarah West, born September 7, 1813, daughter of Thomas West. Their children were George W., of Moorestown, New Jersey; Sarah, married Josiah D. Pancoast; Anna M., married Walter Jeanes Middleton; Lucy R., married (first) George Taylor, (second) James Thornton; Ellen H. married William Bartram; Albert M., a machinist at Frankfort; Caroline R., married Charles Ballinger, a farmer of Lumberton, New Jersey. Benjamin Thorn Jr. was a son of Benjamin Thorn, who was born at Crosswicks in January, 1763, died June 13, 1848. He was a storekeeper at Crosswicks. He married Lucy Taylor, born 1768, died November 18, 1842. Their children were Thomas B. and Benjamin, twins, born January 18. 1810.

LEWIS Hon. Griffith Walker Lewis, of Burlington, New Jersey, descends on his maternal side from an old Burlington county family, the Kimbles. The founder of the Lewis family in Bucks county, Pennsylvania, from whom the Burlington county family descends, emigrated from Wales and had a son Ephraim, who was a volunteer in the war of 1812, serving in the Pennsylvania line. The first of this family to come to Burlington, New Jersey, was Griffith Walker Lewis, father of Hon. Griffith Walker Lewis, whose name appears at the head of this record.

(I) Griffith Walker Lewis Sr. was born in Hatboro, Bucks county, Pennsylvania, 1837, died in Burlington, New Jersey, February, 1901. He received a good common school education, and was reared on the farm where his early years were spent in helping to culti-

vate the same. Leaving the farm he went to Philadelphia, where he obtained work in a shoe factory. He became familiar with the methods employed in the manufacture of shoes as well as an expert workman. He removed from Philadelphia to Burlington, New Jersey, where he started business on his own account, engaging in the manufacture of shoes. He prospered in his business and was constantly obliged to increase his investment and extend his lines until 1892 when he built the present factory at Burlington. Here he was the active, energetic, modern business man until his death in 1901. Mr. Lewis was interested in other business enterprises and in the financial institution of Burlington in an official capacity and as an investor. He was a director of the Mechanics' National Bank, vice-president of the Electric Light and Power Company, and held numerous positions of honor and trust. He was a member of the Masonic order, the Odd Fellows and the Knights of Pythias. He married (first) Annie Maria Kimble, born in 1837, who bore him three children: Robert, who died at the age of six; Griffith Walker, see forward; one who died in infancy. He married (second) Ellen F. Doolin, by whom there was no issue.

Annie Maria (Kimble) Lewis was a daughter of John, born 1808, and Rhoda (Smith) Kimble, born 1805, and a granddaughter of Tuly Kimble, born 1782, and Lucretia (White) Kimble, born 1785. Her mother, Rhoda (Smith) Kimble, was born near London, England, and was one of fourteen children that crossed the ocean to America with her parents. One child was born in America, John Kimble, father of Mrs. Lewis. Tuly Kimble, her grandfather, and Joseph Kimble, her great-grandfather, were all Burlington county farmers and land owners. Joseph Kimble was a large owner of land in the county, and at one time owned slaves who were employed in cultivating the soil. Tuly Kimble had another son Job and a daughter Nancy, who married a Mr. Fort. The Kimbles also intermarried with the Stokes family of New Jersey, of which Ex-Governor Stokes is a member. The children of John and Rhoda (Smith) Kimble are: Sarah Morris, born in 1832; Susan Martin, 1833; Daniel, 1835; Annie Maria, 1837; Charles Wesley, 1839; Frank Marrel, 1843; all of these children were born in Burlington, New Jersey.

(II) Griffith Walker (2), only surviving son of Griffith Walker (1) and Annie Maria (Kimble) Lewis, was born in Burlington, New

ii—14

Jersey, July 1, 1862. He was educated in the country schools near Jacksonville, Burlington county, New Jersey, and at the Burlington Military College. After leaving school he entered his father's factory and thoroughly mastered the detail of each department of shoe manufacturing. After becoming familiar with the factory work, Mr. Lewis spent several years on the road, selling the goods made at the factory. Previous to his father's death he was in charge of the business, and at that time assumed full control, which he still retains. In addition to conducting his shoe factory, Mr. Lewis has large real estate interests both in and outside the city. He is actively interested in the financial and other business institutions of Burlington. He was vice-president of the Electric Light and Power Company, succeeding his father in that office, and is now president of the company. He is vice-president of the Mt. Holly Fair Association, director of the Public Library Association, director in the City of Burlington Building and Loan Association, one of the incorporators and a director of the Burlington Loan and Trust Company. For eight years he was identified with the Mechanics' National Bank of Burlington as director and vice-president. In 1908 he was elected president of that institution and is now holding that important position. In politics Mr. Lewis is a Republican and his political career has been as active and successful as his business life has been. For six years he has been a member of the city council, serving for two years as chairman of the finance committee and for one year as president of the council. He is a member of the Burlington county Republican executive committee and has an influential voice in the councils of his party. In 1906 Mr. Lewis was the successful candidate of his party for the house of representatives of New Jersey, and was elected his own successor in 1907-08. At the 1909 session he was floor leader of the majority and chairman of the judiciary committee. In the Masonic fraternity Mr. Lewis has attained high degree. He is past master of Burlington Lodge, No. 32, Free and Accepted Masons; a Royal Arch Mason of Boudinot Chapter, No. 3; a Knight Templar of Helena Commandery, No. 3; a Shriner of Lulu Temple, Philadelphia, and a thirty-second degree Mason of Camden Consistory of the Scottish Rite. He is an Odd Fellow of Phoenix Lodge, No. 92; a Knight of Pythias of Hope Lodge, No. 73, and past exalted ruler of Mt. Holly Lodge of Elks, No. 848. In re-

ligious preference Mr. Lewis is Presbyterian.

Mr. Lewis married, June 27, 1893, Mary R. Fenton, of Jacksonville, Burlington county, New Jersey, daughter of William Watson and Rhoda (Falkinburg) Fenton. Children: 1. Howard Fenton, born in Burlington, New Jersey, April 1, 1894, passed through the public schools of Burlington, Haines Preparatory School and is now a student at the Trenton State Normal. 2. Helen Burr, born October, 1898.

FRENCH

Under variously spelled surnames the French family appeared in England soon after the Norman conquest. The first of the line recorded was with William the Conqueror at the battle of Hastings, October 14, 1066, and the Yorkshire records of the twelfth century frequently show the name. Others located in the beginning chiefly in the southeastern counties, but later they appeared in the west and in the north as far as Scotland. They also settled at a very early date in Ireland, and one branch of the family trace their descent directly from Rollo, Duke of Normandy. In England, before the close of the thirteenth century, the French family had become extensive, prosperous and influential. In York the name was spelled Francais, in Berks Ffrensh, in Middlesex Frenssh, in Somerset Frensce, in Surrey Frensche, in Northampton Francais and Fraunceys, and in Wiltshire French. In the fifteenth and sixteenth centuries it is generally found in Northampton in the form ffrench, the form adopted by the ancestors of the line at present under consideration.

(I) Thomas ffrench, father of the progenitor of the New Jersey branch of the French family, like his ancestors for many generations, lived at Nether Heyford, where he was known as an influential and useful citizen. His home, Nether Heyford, was a parish in the hundred of Newbottle Grove, county Northampton, seven miles south by west from the city of Northampton, England. The parish is a very ancient one, and the parish church, dedicated to SS. Peter and Paul, was erected in the early part of the thirteenth century. From 1558, when the registers begin, down to 1680, when the emigrant left his English home, there are over sixty references to the French family, all evidently referring to the same line. Thomas ffrench was twice married. By his first wife, Sara, he had: 1. Patience, born 1637. 2.

Thomas, referred to below. 3. Sara, born 1643. 4. Elizabeth, 1645. 5. Mary, 1648. 6. John, 1651. By his second wife, Martha, he had: 7. Robert, 1657. 8. Martha, 1660. Thomas ffrench was buried May 5, 1673. Sara, his first wife, was buried February 9, 1653.

(II) Thomas (2), son of Thomas (1) and Sara ffrench, the progenitor of the French family in New Jersey, was born in 1639 and baptized the same year in the parish church of SS. Peter and Paul, Nether Heyford. When the religious society of Friends arose, he with other members of his family became actively identified therewith, and at different times suffered for his faith. Upon one occasion he was sentenced to imprisonment for forty-two months for refusal to pay tithes to the amount of eleven shillings. At this time he was a resident of Upper Norton, Oxfordshire. An account of this and of other sufferings of his is to be found in Besse's remarkable book, "Sufferings of Friends," in which also the names of five other members of his family appear. In all he was sentenced five times and altogether he served several years in prison.

That Thomas French was a man of great force of character, intense religious conviction, and earnest, consistent life is abundantly evident. He shared with his associates trials and hardships and always resented everything bearing the slightest resemblance to injustice and oppression. He was consequently among the first to take a practical interest in the colonization of Friends in America. With William Penn, Gawen Lawrie, and the hundred and fifty others he was one of the signers of the famous Concessions and Agreements at London in 1676, which provided for the settlement of New Jersey. First of all he made a preliminary prospecting visit to this country to locate his land and to select his home, then three years after the arrival of the pioneer colonists according to his own account which is still preserved he sailed from London in the ship "Kent," Gregory Marlowe, master, the same vessel which brought the first company of settlers, in 1677, to Burlington, about August 1, 1680, with his wife and nine children, four sons and five daughters, the eldest being sixteen, the youngest not yet four years of age. He settled upon a tract of six hundred acres, along the banks of the Rancocas, about four miles from Burlington, and throughout the remainder of his life he held an influential place in the colony and prospered in business.

During 1684-85 he was the commissioner of highways. At his death in 1699, he was possessed of one thousand two hundred acres of improved land and also his proprietory share of the unsurveyed lands, approximately two thousand acres. During nearly twenty years residence as a leading citizen of Burlington county, Thomas ffrench trained all of his children in ways of sobriety, industry and religion, they in turn founding families in whom traits of strong character were noted. It is an interesting fact that part of the original plantation of Thomas ffrench is today owned and occupied by his descendants. An interesting relic of Thomas ffrench is his family Bible which he brought with him from England and which is still in existence and in a fair state of preservation although showing the effects of time. The record transcribed in it is in his own hand and covers entries made during a period of over thirty years. In maintaining his rights as a citizen and property holder Thomas ffrench felt himself called upon almost at the beginning to take action which seems to have excited comment, but he was firm in declaring the justice of his case although duly regretful that his course had given occasion for criticism. The most striking instance of his thus braving public opinion was a remarkable letter to ex-Governor Thomas Olive, in some respects the leading and most influential man in the colony.

June 12, 1660, Thomas ffrench was married (first) in the parish church of Whilton, by the Rev. Richard Morris. Children: 1. Sara, baptized, as were the first twelve children at SS. Peter and Paul, Nether Heyford, March 17, 1661, buried April 10, 1661. 2. Jane, born about June 11, 1662, baptized August 8, 1662, buried April 30, 1671. 3. Rachel, born March 24, 1664, baptized April 3, 1664; married (first) Mathew Allen, and (second) Hugh Sharp. 4. Richard, referred to below. 5. Thomas, baptized October 31, 1667; married (first) Mary Allen, and (second) Mary (Pearce) Cattell; died in 1745. 6. Hannah, baptized September 5, 1669, died 7th month, 1747; married Richard Busby, of Pennsylvania. 7. Charles, born March 20, baptized April 2, 1671; married it is supposed twice, the name of his first wife being Elinor. 8. John, baptized January 2, 1673, died 1729; married (first) in 1701, Ann ———, and (second) Sarah (Mason) Wickward. 9. Sarah, baptized February 23, 1674; married Isaac Wood, of Woodbury Creek. 10. Mary, baptized August 8, 1675, died 1728; married-

Nicholas Buzby, of Burlington county. 11. Jane, baptized November 19, 1676; married Daniel Hall. 12. Lydia, born probably 1682; married probably, 1708, David Arnold. 13. An infant, died 8th month 12, 1692. Jane (Atkins) French died at Rancocas, 8th month 5, 1692, and Thomas French married (second) 7th month 25, 1696, Elizabeth Stanton, of the Philadelphia Monthly Meeting. To this marriage there was issue one child, 14. Rebecca, born 6th month 8, 1697, died 1753; married Robert Murfin.

(III) Richard French, fourth child and eldest son of Thomas (2) and Jane (Atkins) French, was born in Nether Heyford, England, the memorandum in the family Bible of his father reading "December the first about ten at night my son Richard was borne, 1665. The Lord give him grace that hee may continually walk before him." A long and useful life shows how fully this characteristic prayer of a devout and loving father was answered. Richard was a lad of fifteen when he came to America. So far as is known his youth and early manhood were spent on the Rancoca plantation. That he was devoted to farm life is shown in the fact that upon his marriage he purchased an extensive tract of land, four hundred and sixty acres, in Mansfield township, Burlington county, where he seems to have resided for the remainder of his life. A deed of release of all claim to the home farm, after his father's death, to his younger brother Charles, shows the kindly relationship that existed and his contentment with his own lot.

He was a faithful and zealous Friend, his name appearing many times in the meeting records of the period. In 1715 he was chosen overseer of the Chesterfield Meeting and in 1723 an elder and a minister. He was also frequently chosen as a representative to quarterly and yearly meeting. Although now past middle age, he nevertheless continued for a quarter of a century active in the work of preaching and visitation, journeying through the wilderness to New England and the South. In the promotion of the religious life of the colonies he was conspicuous and influential, in business affairs, as his many deeds and other papers show, particularly his will and the accompanying inventory, he was active and prosperous. In 1701 he was the collector for Mansfield township. He raised a large family and all of his ten children reached a marriageable age. The peculiar phraseology of his recorded papers indicate a mind exceedingly careful of details, with a just and kindly spirit,

and the monthly meeting fittingly testified after his death that in the exercise of his gift in the ministry "he laboured faithfully in his declining age and travelled much in North America."

Seventh month, 11, 1693, Richard French married (first) Sarah, daughter of Thomas and Elizabeth Scattergood, of Stepney parish, London, England, and New Jersey. She died about 1700, leaving three children. Richard French married (second) eleventh month 13, 1701, Mary, daughter of Harmanus and Mary King, of Nottingham township, Burlington county, New Jersey, by whom he had seven more children: 1. Elizabeth, born 1694; married William Scholey. 2. Richard, Eighth month, 20, 1696; married Rachel ———. 3. Thomas. 4. Mary, born ninth month 3, 1707, died 1783; married as his first wife Preserve Brown Jr. 5. Rebecca, married Benjamin Shreve. 6. William, referred to below. 7. Sarah, born seventh month 20, 1715; married William Marlin. 8. Abigail, born seventh month 5, 1717; married (first) James Lewis, of Philadelphia, and (second) Jacob Taylor. 9. Benjamin, twelfth month 11, 1719, died 1747; married Martha Hall, of Bordentown. 10. Jonathan, eleventh month 27, 1722, died 1778; married Esther Matlack.

(IV) William, sixth child and third son of Richard and Mary (King) French, was born April 7, 1712, died in 1781. He lived and died intestate in Burlington county, letters of administration on his estate being granted to his son William, December 8, 1781, the inventory of his goods and chattels having been made the previous October 26. William French married, September 20, 1748, Lydia Taylor, of Bordentown, by whom he had three children: 1. William, referred to below. 2. Richard, born October 15, 1759, died February 26, 1823; married Mary Davis. 3. Lydia, March 19, 1763; married Gabriel Allen, of Bordentown.

(V) William (2), eldest son of William (1) and Lydia (Taylor) French, was born in Burlington county, New Jersey, May 10, 1751, died October 27, 1808. He was a millwright and appears to have spent most of his life at Lamberton, New Jersey, although he also seems to have for a considerable time sojourned both in Bucks county, Pennsylvania, and in Haddonfield, New Jersey. September 17, 1777, he married at Falls meeting. Rachel, daughter of Thomas and Hannah Rickey, of Lower Makefield township, Bucks county, Pennsylvania, who died in Lamberton, New Jersey, August 27, 1827. Their children

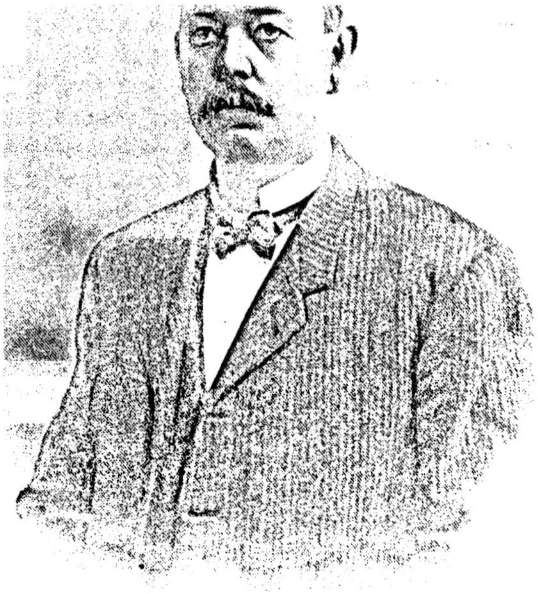

John T French

were: 1. Lydia, born August 25, 1778, died August 18, 1781. 2. Hannah, December 5, 1779, died May 22, 1782. 3. John Taylor, January 27, 1783, died November 21, 1831. 4. William Rickey, November 23, 1785. 5. Mahlon Kirkbride, referred to below. 6. Amos Taylor, January 23, 1791; married Ruth Ewing. 7. Rachel Rickey, February 22, 1794.

(VI) Mahlon Kirkbride, fifth child and third son of William (2) and Rachel (Rickey) French, was born June 12, 1788. He married, May 15, 1807, Sarah Stackhouse. Among their children was: William Washington, referred to below.

(VII) William Washington, son of Mahlon Kirkbride and Sarah (Stackhouse) French, was born in Philadelphia, Pennsylvania, February 14, 1811. The early portion of his life was spent in Trenton, New Jersey, where he served an apprenticeship to the cabinet making trade. In 1851 he moved to Delaware county, Pennsylvania, from which he removed in 1861 to Philadelphia. During the civil war he served in the United States quartermaster's department.

William Washington French married Ann, born in 1815, daughter of John Airy, of Bordentown, Burlington county, New Jersey, and their children were: 1. Maria, deceased. 2. Emma, deceased. 3. Anna, deceased. 4. Rachel, married the Rev. Benjamin Philips, a Presbyterian divine. 5. Harvey, married Virginia Maston and had two children: Laura, married Henry Eccles, and Ella, married Paul Lockenbacher. Harvey French enlisted in the Eighth New Jersey Regiment of Volunteer Infantry in 1861, was severely wounded in the hip at the battle of Bull Run and was taken prisoner. He is now living at Haddon Heights, New Jersey. 6. Sarah, deceased. 7. William, lives in Philadelphia, employed in the Baldwin locomotive works. His wife died leaving him with one child, Lilian. 8. John Taylor, referred to below. 9. George, a mill worker, living in Philadelphia and married. 10. Elizabeth, deceased. 11. Ella, deceased.

(VIII) John Taylor, the eighth child of William Washington and Ann (Airy) French, was born in Delaware county, Pennsylvania, March 2, 1852, and is now living at Atlantic City, New Jersey. For his early education he was sent to the schools of Delaware county and of Philadelphia. After spending some time on a farm, he became an apprentice at sixteen years of age and learned the trade of house painting. In 1877 he removed to Hammonton, New Jersey, and in 1883 built the paint factory there, which he has since then carried on so successfully. In connection with this factory he established in 1900 at Atlantic City a store for paints and painters' supplies. His legal residence is Hammonton, but he has also a fine cottage at Atlantic City where he spends a good deal of his time and where many of his business interests centre. Mr. French is a director in the Hammonton Trust Company, and for nearly five years was the postmaster at Hammonton, having been appointed to that very responsible position by President Grover Cleveland during his second term. For fourteen years he was a member of the county board of registration and elections, and for a number of years has also been a member of the city council of Hammonton, and an assessor of the town. Mr. French is a Democrat and for six years was a member of the state democratic committee. For eighteen years he was a director of the Hammonton Building and Loan Association, one of the most successful of that town's successful organizations. At present he is also president of the Atlantic Realty Company of Atlantic City. He is also a member of M. G. Taylor Lodge, No. 141, of the Free and Accepted Masons, of Hammonton; Improved Order of Red Men, Independent Order of Odd Fellows, Artisans' Order of Mutual Protection. He is an independent in religion.

In 1873 John Taylor French married Jennie R., daughter of William Alexandria. Their children are: 1. John Taylor Jr., born September 15, 1874; unmarried; with his father in the paint supply business. 2. Ida F., July 28, 1876; married Wilson S. Turner, of Hammonton, and has one child, Spencer French Turner. 3. Howard, July 23, 1878; with his father in the paint business; by his marriage with Mabel Maxwell he has two children, Virginia and Roberta. 4. Walter, December 16, 1880; married Elizabeth Ketes, but has no children. 5. Wilbert A., October 21, 1882; also with his father in the paint business; married Martha Murray and has one child, John Taylor French.

ARMSTRONG Nathan Armstrong, the New Jersey pioneer, was born about 1717, near Londonderry in the province of Ulster, Ireland. He was a linen weaver by trade, a Scotch-Irishman by race, and a Protestant by religious faith. He came to America about 1740. After living a few years in central New Jersey, he went to the northwestern frontier and settled in Warren county, then a part of Sussex, where he met and loved and married a maiden by the name of Euphemia Wright. He bought a tract of five hundred and eighty-one acres of uncleared land, built a log cabin thereon and became a farmer, and continued thereafter during a period of twenty-nine years to enjoy the blessings of health and home and the rewards of industry and thrift.

The defeat of the English army under Braddock near Pittsburg in 1755 caused a panic; and well it might, for the Indians in their exultation began to murder the settlers everywhere, some of the savages even coming eastward and crossing into New Jersey. Nathan Armstrong and his neighbors erected a stockade around a log house at Marksboro and took their wives and children there for safety. His sons, George and John, were at that time only six years of age; but when they were old men, they used to tell how their father took them to the barn-yard and showed them a pot of money he had buried under the barrack and told them if he were killed and they escaped they should remember where the money was; then they all went to the fort where the children remained until the danger was over.

Nathan Armstrong was interested in local affairs and held several offices in old Hardwick. He was a member of the board of justices and freeholders of Sussex county for three years, 1759-61; and he was one of the original incorporators of Christ Episcopal Church at Newton, being named as such in the charter granted to that church by the provincial government of New Jersey on August 14, 1774.

The Armstrong homestead is at Johnsonburg in the township of Frelinghuysen; it is crossed by the Lackawanna railroad, and is fourteen miles east of the Delaware Water Gap. Nathan moved into his new home with his wife and infant daughter during the third week of May, 1748. At that time Warren county was really a western frontier. Some Indians still lingered in the valleys of the Paulinskill and the Pequest, living at points convenient for hunting and fishing, and feeling bitter and resentful at the intrusion of the white man. There was not a single house on the ground now occupied by Blairstown, Newton and Belvidere; and there were only three postoffices in the entire state of New Jersey, namely: Trenton, Burlington and Perth Amboy. All north Jersey was thickly covered with heavy timber; the streams were without

bridges, and the king's highways were mere paths through the woods.

Bears, deer and all kinds of game were abundant; thousands of the finest shad came up the creeks and brooks, and millions of wild pigeons roosted in the forest. There was a panther's lair in every deep ravine; and wolves fierce with hunger prowled about, seeking to carry off any stray hogs, lambs and calves, hunting in packs during the day and making repeated attacks at night on sheep-pen and cattle-stall. There was a bounty of sixty shillings for a full-grown wolf, ten shillings for a whelp not able to prey, and fifteen shillings for a panther. Among the entries found in the account books of the county treasurer, there are several that read thus: "By cash paid Nathan Armstrong for one wolf's head."

Nathan died of small-pox which he contracted while delivering produce at the American camp in Morristown. He was buried in a private graveyard, as the custom was in colonial times, but his tombstone may still be seen at the Yellow Frame cemetery, ornamented at the top with the face and extended wings of a cherub carved in outline, and bearing this inscription below: "Here lies the body of Nathan Armstrong who departed this Life Aug't 11th, Anno Domini 1777, aged about sixty Years." His will, which is dated August 5, 1777, is recorded in the office of the secretary of state at Trenton; after making ample provision for his wife, he gave a sum of money to each of his daughters and a farm to each of his sons.

Euphemia, Nathan's wife, was born in 1724, and died in 1811, at the age of eighty-seven. The Rev. Caspar Shaffer, in his Memoirs, speaks of her thus: "My grandmother Armstrong was a lady of superior mental endowment. She excelled in conversational power. I well recollect in my childhood and youth with what a glowing interest and fixed attention I sat and listened to her when she was relating to my mother anecdotes and reminiscences of earlier life. Her piety, calm, consistent, and unobtrusiveness, shone in all her daily walk and conversation." Nathan and Euphemia Armstrong had seven children, namely: Elizabeth, George and John, William, Mary, Hannah and Sarah; each one of these children grew to maturity, married and has descendants living at the present time.

1. Elizabeth Armstrong, born March 12, 1747, married Archibald Stinson Jr., of Vienna, New Jersey, and had a son John Stin-

son, who was for twenty years a judge of the court of common pleas, and who invented an improved instrument for determining latitude and longitude and secured a patent for the same, both in the United States and in England.

2-3. George and John, twins; according to the original entry in the first family Bible, they "were born on Sunday, on the 20th day of August in the year of Our Lord 1749, about twelve o'clock at night." Each spent his life on his own half of the old homestead; and each left a last will and testament, now on record at Belvidere. George died December 14, 1829. in his eighty-first year; and John died May 7, 1836, in his eighty-seventh year. All the families that now bear the name of Armstrong and that trace their descent from Nathan the pioneer, have sprung from the one or the other of these twins; and this article will give an account of all the Armstrong households of the tribe of Nathan, beginning with George and John, and coming down to the present time; the account will be brief but accurate; and it will be complete, for there are no lost lines and no missing links.

4. William Armstrong served during the revolutionary war as ensign in Captain Clifford's company of Sussex militia, marching on several expeditions against the Indians and fighting at the battle of Springfield. He had a large farm, and he owned and conducted a store and a grist-mill at Johnsonburg. He married Elizabeth Swayze in 1779, and had four daughters: Lydia, the wife of Abraham Shafer Jr.; Euphemia, the wife of John T. Bray; Mary, the wife of John C. Roy; and Sarah, the wife of Ephraim Green Jr. William died in 1842, at the age of ninety.

5. Mary Armstrong in 1773 married Robert Beavers Jr., of Changewater, New Jersey, who served as captain during the revolutionary war and was for fifteen years a judge of the court of common pleas; their children were Elizabeth, the wife of Jacob Stinson; Mary, the wife of John Little; Ann, the wife of Jacob Swayze; Euphemia, the wife of James Reeder, of Ohio; and a son, John Armstrong Beavers, who was a lieutenant in the war of 1812.

6. Hannah Armstrong in 1779 married Alexander Linn, son of Adjutant Joseph Linn; when a widow she removed in 1800 to Espyville, Crawford county, Pennsylvania, with her six children: John; Mary, who married Robert McArthur; Andrew; Euphemia, who married Daniel Axtell; George; Joseph. Hannah was

the daughter of a pioneer, a pioneer herself, and the mother of pioneers; she died in 1842 at the age of eighty-six.

7. Sarah Armstrong married Captain Abraham Shafer, of Stillwater, New Jersey. Abraham fought in the revolutionary war, was an elder in the Yellow Frame church, served four terms in the state legislature, and commanded a troop of volunteer light dragoons in the expedition to Pittsburg in 1794, to suppress the whisky insurrection. Abraham and Sarah had eight children: Maria, the wife of John Johnson; Rev. Casper, M. D., of Philadelphia; Nathan Armstrong; Peter Bernhardt; Euphemia Wright. the wife of Major Henry Miller; Sarah, the wife of Rev. Jacob R. Castner; William Armstrong; and Elizabeth, the wife of Rev. Isaac Newton Candee.

(II) George, son of Nathan and Euphemia Armstrong, was born in 1749, and died in 1829. He was active in business but he took special interest in all matters relating to the moral and religious welfare of the community, laboring earnestly and faithfully during a long life to promote the growth and extend the influence of the Yellow Frame church.

He was prominent in local affairs. He was the clerk of Hardwick township for twenty-two consecutive years, 1779-1801, and the assessor for thirty-one years beginning in 1782; he was also tax collector and a taker of the census. He was clerk of the board of justices and freeholders of Sussex county; he was also appointed tax collector for the county in 1791, and served five years. He was a member of the state legislature; on his return from Trenton, he brought with him a set of silver teaspoons, and he was welcomed home by a new daughter; his great-great-grandchildren are now allowed to use those spoons on special occasions.

George's homestead was a busy place. The fields were kept in a high state of cultivation. Fruit trees of every kind were planted, the best varieties of each being sought out; and grafting was taught to the boys as a fine art. His house, which stood on a terrace and overlooked a broad meadow, was furnished with spinning wheels and a loom. The garden, wagon house, corn crib, barn and stackyard, were on the left; on the right stood the milk house and the tenant house, and just beyond these were the apple bins and cider presses and tanks, and a distillery forty feet long. Out on the meadow was the tannery, the vats being arranged in parallel rows with wells at convenient distances: and close-by stood the bark-house and the bark grinder with its circular horse-path. In those days the making of brandy was not regarded as at all reprehensible; but when the movement in favor of moderation spread over the country in 1825, George was one of the very first men in the community to advocate the cause of temperance; and as the first fruits of this moral awakening, he destroyed his stills and stopped making liquor. Hides and skins were tanned on shares; and sometimes he employed skilled workmen to manufacture his share of the leather at once into boots, shoes and harness, for which articles there was a ready sale.

George was a buyer and reader of good books. Judging from the dates of purchase as entered under his name on the fly-leaves, it seems to have been his custom to place upon the shelves of his bookcase every year some well-bound volumes. Most of these books treated of morality and religion, such as the evidences of Christianity, the works of Edwards and of Witherspoon, and sermons by other Princeton divines. The library he thus accumulated did honor to his mind and character. He was for more than thirty-six years a ruling elder in the Yellow Frame Presbyterian Church; and in the religious affairs of the community he stood at the front; when the church was without a pastor, as was often the case, the spiritual oversight of the shepherdless flock depended largely on George Armstrong.

He married Sarah Hunt, daughter of Lieutenant Richard Hunt, and had Rachel, the wife of John Locke; Richard; John, born 1788, died 1873; Elizabeth, the wife of John O. Rice; Sarah, the wife of Japhet B. Chedister; and David Hunt.

(III) Richard, son of George and Sarah Armstrong, married Phebe Hankinson and had one child, Samuel Hunt Armstrong, who married Margaret Wilson and had Noreena, the wife of William Percy Bennett, and Lozemia, the wife of Daniel Joseph McClurg, of Espyville, Pennsylvania.

(III) John, son of George and Sarah Armstrong, married Lydia Kirkpatrick, daughter of Captain John and Lydia (Lewis) Kirkpatrick, and had four children: Sarah, the wife of Jacob S. Mott; David Lewis; William, the sheriff of Warren county; and Richard Turner. After the death of Lydia, John married Martha Luse, and had Lydia Jane, who married Ira C. Kerr. David Lewis Armstrong married Elizabeth Roy and had two children: Sarah Matilda, the wife of Milton

Howard Soverel; and George Byram Armstrong, who married Sarah Rubina L'Homadieu and had Anna Elizabeth, the wife of Alvah J. Walters; Cora Rubina; and Hattie Valentine. William Armstrong, the sheriff, married Elizabeth Mackey, of Belvidere, and had John Mackey, Israel, and Eutokia.

(IV) Richard Turner, son of John and Lydia Armstrong, was born January 15, 1823, died November 26, 1902; he dwelt at Johnsonburg, New Jersey; married Esther Ann Lundy, daughter of David and Sarah (Wildrick) Lundy, and had William Clinton, John W., and George Lundy Armstrong. William Clinton Armstrong married Stella Virginia Lenher, daughter of George H. Lenher, and had a daughter Marion Lenher, and four sons, Richard Clinton, George Lenher, John Macdougall and William Clinton Jr. John W. Armstrong married Laura Ellen Willson, daughter of Jesse Willson, and had Edna Mabel, wife of Charles Watson Gibbs; and John W., Jr. George Lundy Armstrong married Sarah Frances Reeder, daughter of Sedgwick R. Reeder, and had Carrie, the wife of Bertram Drake; and Bessie.

William Clinton Armstrong graduated from Princeton College in the class of 1877. He studied law and was admitted to the bar. He became principal of the high school at New Brunswick, New Jersey, in 1891, and in 1899 was elected superintendent of schools in that city. In 1895 he published a "Genealogical Record of the Descendants of Nathan Armstrong," in which are given the names of all persons descending from that worthy pioneer, traced through both male and female lines. In 1902 he published the "Lundy Family and Their Descendants of Whatsoever Surname," with a biographical sketch of Benjamin Lundy, the founder of American Abolitionism. He has also written a series of papers on "Lord Stirling of New Jersey as a Soldier and as a Man." He is a member of the New Jersey Society of the Sons of the American Revolution, and as historian of that society edited a volume which was published in 1903 under the title of "Patriotic Poems of New Jersey."

(III) David Hunt, son of George and Sarah Armstrong, dwelt on his father's farm. He married Mary Ann Albertson and had seven children: Sarah Jane, the wife of Esaac D. Youmans; Martha Elizabeth, the wife of Andrew Raub Teel; George A.; Isaac A.; William P.; Milton N.; and Clinton Oren Armstrong.

George A. Armstrong married Marthia Calla

Wintermute, removed to Dorchester, Nebraska, and had: Austin Craig; David William; Flora Belle, the wife of Henry Nelson; and Matilda Ann, the wife of Dennis Ross. Austin Craig Armstrong, now of Glencoe, Illinois, married Minnie A. Weinecke and has George Henry. Isaac A. Armstrong married Maria T. McCallister and had Mary C., Alice L., Edwin and High Hunt. William Preston Armstrong married Alice Wildrick and had Elizabeth, the wife of Mr. Gallagher, of Brooklyn. Milton Nathan Armstrong, M. D., married Elizabeth Blair, and has Robert B. and Mary, the wife of Harold Hastings Cooley. Clinton Oren Armstrong married Elizabeth S. Mott, dwelt at Milford, Pennsylvania, and has Harold Rodney, Maxwell and Natalie Bartow.

(II) John, son of Nathan and Euphemia Armstrong, born 1749, died 1836, was a man of influence. His long life was filled with a wide range of business activities. He took up surveying in early life and did much work of that kind until his own sons relieved him. In 1776 he was assessor of Hardwick township; the next two years he was town clerk; then he was freeholder; and after that he was the tax collector of Sussex county for eight years.

During the revolutionary war he was lieutenant in Captain Aaron Hankinson's company, second regiment of Sussex militia; see papers of the New Jersey Provincial Congress, document No. 126. He became judge of the court of common pleas in February, 1801, and retired from the bench in 1831, at the age of eighty-two, having served thirty consecutive years.

He was a farmer, who possessed the ambition and ability to develop new enterprises. At Paulina, a half mile above Blairstown, he bought a tract of land lying on both sides of the Paulinskill. On the south bank of the stream he erected a grist mill, which for two generations was one of the best mill properties in that section of the country, and which has recently been remodeled into an electrical power-house.

Opposite the mill he constructed a forge for refining iron, and this forge he operated for a number of years. He bought raw pig-iron at a smelting furance at Andover; the iron he bought was in the shape of sticks, each stick being six feet long and weighing about two hundred pounds; these he carted to the forge, a distance of eleven miles. He purchased some timber land on the Kittatinny mountains ten miles away; and there manufactured charcoal which he carted to Paulina to use in the forge. After the raw iron had been purified into bar iron, it was transported to the Delaware river, a distance of twelve miles, floated down stream on flatboats and sold at Philadelphia. His enterprise and energy overcame all difficulties. But the times changed and the smelter at Andover had to shut down owing to economic conditions that effected the whole country. As a consequence no pig-iron could be obtained and the refining forge at Paulina was compelled to close.

John Armstrong was vice-president of the Warren County Bible Society, president of the Hardwick Temperance Society, and a member of the first board of directors of the Sussex Bank.

He married Sarah Stinson; their children were John, Jr.; Nathan; Jacob; Mary, the wife of Samuel Snover King; Sarah, the wife of John R. Howell; Euphemia, the wife of Wilson Hunt; and Eleanor, the wife of Isaac Shiner.

(III) John, Jr., son of John and Sarah Armstrong, who removed in 1819 to Euclid, near Cleveland, Ohio, was twice married. By his first wife Elizabeth Shafer, he had a daughter Margaret Sarah, who married Joseph W. McCord; by his second wife Phebe Stewart, he had Samuel Snover; Valeria Adaline, the wife of Jason Abbott; Wilson Hunt; John Stinson, who died in the United States navy during the civil war; and Dewitt Clinton Armstrong. Samuel Snover Armstrong, of Nottingham, Ohio, was twice married; his wives were Sarah Lloyd and Mary Gunn; he had three children by each wife. His children were: George Washington Armstrong, who married Mary A. Rice, and had a son Frank, of Meadville, Pennsylvania; Sarah Elizabeth, the wife of Adolphe R. Candy; Lucy Ann, the wife of Ira Eddy; Ann Lucretia, the wife of Almon G. Dills; John Chester, of Trenton, Michigan, who married Lillian M. Rose, and had a daughter Alice Elizabeth; and Laura Adaline, the wife of Francis M. Rogers, of Dunkirk, Ohio. Wilson Hunt Armstrong, of Galion, Ohio, married Almira Converse and had two daughters: Eleanor, the wife of Frank D. Bain; and Almira, the wife of James G. White. Dewitt Clinton Armstrong married Ann E. Kline and had John S., Lucy C., Vernon D., and Grace F.

(III) Nathan, son of John and Sarah Armstrong, married Eley H. Kerr and had two sons: John Locke and Henry Palmer. John Locke Armstrong married Lucretia Stuphen and had two sons: Austin Elisha, who was killed at Roanoke Island, and William Hampton, who married Mary E. Sutton, and had three children: Rev. Austin Elisha, John Locke and Lucretia Drake. John Locke Armstrong, the grandson, married Lois A. Yawger, dwelt at Newton, New Jersey, and had Roy and Ellsworth. Henry Palmer Armstrong, of Columbia, New Jersey, married Abbie Maria Harris and had Elmer Rozell Armstrong, of Easton, Pennsylvania, who married Sadie Budd and has Donald Budd, Margaret, and Lawrence Elmer.

(III) Jacob, son of John and Sarah Armstrong, dwelt on the homestead. He married Nancy Willson and had Nathan and Ophelia; Nathan married Martha Firth and had Edith, the wife of William B. Banker, and Isabella; Ophelia married James H. Couch, of Morristown, New Jersey.

Austin Elisha Armstrong enlisted at Hope, New Jersey, in Company H, Ninth New Jersey Volunteers. Of the whole regiment he was the first man to enlist and the second man to die. He was killed at Roanoke Island, North Carolina, on February 8, 1862. While the union troops were charging a confederate battery, a bullet hit Austin E. in the forehead. He did not think it serious and tried to go on with his company, but the wound bled freely and his face and hands and breast were soon dripping with blood. He started for the rear, telling his companions that he would be back as soon as he could get something to keep the blood out of his eyes. He reached the door of the tent but dropped dead as he entered. A shaft of marble stands to his memory in the cemetery of the Yellow Frame church.

EDGE   The American home of the Edge family is Chester county, Pennsylvania, although, as in the case of the line at present under consideration, some branches of it have spread over in New Jersey soil, where they have taken root and grown to flourishing and estimable proportions.

(1) John Edge, founder of the family in this country, came with his wife Jean and family of small children over to the Quaker colonies on the Delaware, from St. Andrew's, Holborn county Middlesex, England, about 1685, and settled in Nether Providence. He bought from William Penn one hundred and twenty-five acres of land by deeds of lease and release, dated March 21 and 22, 1681-82. He was an earnest member of the Society of Friends, and the monthly meetings were sometimes held at his house. In his native home he had been subjected to heavy fines and imprisonment for refusing to act contrary to his conscientious scruples, and on one occasion he was subjected to a public trial. In Besse's remarkable book, the "Sufferings of Quakers," under date of 1680, we find that "in Trinity Term of this Yeare Sir Hugh Windham, one of the Justices of the Common Pleas brought into that Court at Westminster several informations in the Name of Thomas Moore, as informer, against Thomas · Farmborrow of London, Chairmaker, Henry Waddy, John Edge of St. Andrew's Holborne in the county of Middlesex and John Jones of St. Andrew's, Holborne, Glover, for £260 each of them, alleged to be forfeited for their not coming to hear Common-prayer for thirteen months past preceding the Information, on the Statute of 23rd Elizabeth made against Popish Recusants." Some other Friends being in like circumstances, a statement of the case was published and presented to the king and parliament and the house of commons resolved that such prosecution of Protestant dissenters was dangerous to the peace of the kingdom, but they failed to provide a remedy. In 1683 a warrant was granted against George Whitehead for preaching at a meeting in the parish of St. Margaret's, Westminster. The constabulary went to his house, broke into it, seized his goods, and when two of his friends, John Edge and Joseph Peckover, who were among the spectators to the proceedings, remonstrated and asked them to make an inventory of the goods seized, the police arrested them, fined them, and committed them to Newgate prison, where they were detained for ten weeks. Later in the same year, John Edge, together with Richard Butcher, Christopher Sibthorpe, Antony Ellwood and John Denton were distrained £9, 15 shillings for their refusal to bear arms.

After coming to this country John Edge rose rapidly in the esteem of his neighbors, and with his brother Joseph, who accompanied him to this country, became not only an active Friend but also one of the important and influential members of the civil life of the community. Joseph, who with his brother John was a member of the grand jury during 1686-87, probably died unmarried, but their sister Sarah, who died second month 26, 1692, married eighth month, 1686, Thomas Bowater. John Edge himself died fifth month, 10, 1711, but his widow Jean, who survived him and all her children, was living in third month 27,

1734, when the Monthly Meeting records mention a collection of £1, 5 shillings, paid to her.
Like her husband she too was a prominent,
active and influential member of the Society of
Friends.

The children of John and Jean Edge were:
1. Mary, died Second month, 17, 1698; married James Sharpless. 2. Abigail, died Ninth
month 27, 1716; married Edward Woodward.
3. John, referred to below. 4. Jacob, born
Third month 8, 1690, died probably Second
month 7, 1720; married, in 1712, Sarah,
daughter of Rees and Hannah Jones, and had
four children: Hannah, married John Lea,
Jane, married (first) Thomas Parke, and
(second) James Webb; Abigail, died unmarried, and Sarah, died at nine years of age.
Jacob's widow married (second) Caleb Cowp-
land. From the above it will be seen that all
the descendants of John Edge bearing his
name spring from his son John Jr.

(II) John (2), eldest son and the only one
to bear male issue of John (1) and Jean
Edge, was born about the beginning of fifth
month, 1685, died in third month, 1734. After
his marriage he settled on land which his
father had purchased in Upper Providence.
ninth month 30, 1713, he was chosen as overseer of the Providence Meeting of Friends in
the room of James Sharpless, his brother-in-law,
and sixth month 29, 1715, was succeeded by
Randall Malin. In 1721, becoming dissatisfied
with certain members of the Providence Meeting, he changed his attendance to the Middletown Meeting. He was a farmer and a blacksmith, and he died intestate, possessed of three
hundred and twenty-eight acres, letters of administration being granted his widow May 6,
1734. August 30, 1739, three of his children,
James, Mary and Rachel, petitioned for guardians, and their uncles, Thomas and George
Smedley, were appointed. His widow was appointed eleventh month 29, 1738-39, overseer
of the Middletown Meeting in the place of
Mary Pennell, and ninth month 26, 1739, was
succeeded by Hannah Howard.

In eighth month, 1709, John Edge, married
Mary, daughter of George and Sarah Smedley, of Middleton, who survived him and married (second) ninth month, 7, 1739, at Newtown Meeting, John, son of Francis and Hannah (Baker) Yarnall, of Willistown. The
first intentions of John Edge's marriage were
published at Middletown Meeting, Sixth
month 29, 1709, the second intentions at
Springfield Meeting, seventh month, 26, 1709.
and the orderly accomplishment at Springfield

Meeting, eighth month, 31, 1709. Their children were: 1. George, referred to below. 2.
Sarah, born about 1713, died December 6,
1805; married (first) Lawrence Cox, and
(second) David Reece. 3. Jane, died January
23, 1779; married (first) James Albin, who
died September 29, 1750, in West Marlborough, and (second) Thomas Downing, of East
Caln. 4. Jacob, died 1784; married, in 1746,
Margaret Paul, of Abington, and removed
thither. 5. Mary, born Seventh month 2,
1721, died December 13, 1795; married Richard Downing. 6. Rachel, born Sixth month
29, 1725, died January 31, 1779; married Robert Valentine.

(III) George, eldest child of John (2) and
Mary (Smedley) Edge, was born in Upper
Providence, Chester county, Pennsylvania, died
there in 1751, intestate, letters of administration
being granted to Ann Edge, his widow, and
Robert Pennell, his brother-in-law, with Lawrence Cox and William Pennell, as fellow-
bondsmen. Ninth month 19, 1741, George
Edge married Ann, daughter of William and
Mary (Mercer) Pennell, of Middletown, born
eleventh month 26, 1721. Robert Pennell, the
founder of her family and his wife, Hannah,
came from Boulderton, Nottinghamshire, England, and settled in Middletown township, Bucks
county, Pennsylvania, as early as 1686, bringing a certificate from the Friends at Filbeck,
dated fifth month three, 1684. Robert, in
1686 was grand juryman, in the following year
constable at Middletown. In 1691 he bought
two hundred and fifty acres in Edgemont
township, and in 1705 two hundred and sixty-
four more acres on the north of Philip Yarnall's land, and extending from the present
Gradyville to the Willis town line. Both he
and his wife were active in Middletown Meeting. Of their seven children William, the
youngest, born eighth month, eleventh, 1681,
died 1757; married, eighth month, twenty-
sixth, 1710, at the Concord Monthly Meeting,
Mary, daughter of Thomas and Mary Mercer,
of Thornbury township, who bore him eight
children. Thomas, married Mary Yarnell;
Hannah, married Thomas Holcome; James,
married Jemima Matlack; Phebe, probably
died young; Ann, referred to above, married
(first) George Edge, and (second) James
Worrall; Robert, married Hannah Chamber-
lin; William, married Mary Bell; Samuel,
married (first) Sarah Morris, and (second)
Rachael Coborn. James Worrall, the second
husband of Ann (Pennell) Edge, was the son
of Peter and Elizabeth Worrall, of Marple,

who had married (first) Hannah Calvert, who had borne him seven children, among whom was Lydia, the wife of Benjamin Hoopes.

The four children of George and Ann (Pennell) Edge were: 1. Mary, born eleventh month, eighteen, 1742, died March thirteenth, 1815; married William Baldwin. 2. John, referred to below. 3. Sarah, born eighth month twenty-fourth, 1746, died young. 4. Ann, born tenth month, twenty-sixth, 1748; married (first) Robert Parke; (second) Benjamin Taylor; (third) William Trymballe.

(IV) John (3), son of George and Ann (Pennell) Edge, was born at Upper Providence, twelfth month, twenty, 1744, and died in East Caln township, September 14, 1816. He learned the trade of miller with his uncle, Richard Downing, at Downingtown, and when he had reached the age of twenty-one, he executed February the eighth, 1766, a release to his late guardians for his share of his father's estate. In 1768 he was operating the "High Mill" which as late as seven or eight years ago was in the possession of his descendant, Jacob V. Edge. March 21, 1772, Jacob Edge and wife, Jane Downing, Widow, David Reece, and Sarah, his wife, Richard Downing, and Mary, his wife, and Robert Valentine, and Rachael, his wife, the heirs of John Edge (II) conveyed their interest in fifty acres of land in Upper Providence, allotted to the widow as her dower, to John Edge, the only son of George deceased. April 21, 177— Ann Parke, widow, conveyed her interest in the lands of her father in Upper Providence, being three hundred and forty-four acres, to her brother, John; and November 12, 1786, William Baldwin and Mary, his wife, do the same. John divided his Upper Providence lands into four parts. The northeast lot of one hundred and eighteen acres, forty perches, he disposed of to Thomas Bishop; the northwest lot of ninety-one acres, forty-six perches to Joseph Bishop; and the southwest lot of one hundred and seven acres, one hundred perches, to Gideon Dunn. This was April 30, 1793; and May 10, 1797, he deeded the remainder to William Eachus. February 17, 1780, John Edge bought from his uncle, Robert Valentine, the messuage and two tracts of land in East Caln, twenty-nine acres and forty-six perches, and succeeded his uncle as storekeeper in Downingtown. In 1790 he petitioned for a tavern license, stating, "Your Petitioner, Having for a Number of Yeares followed the Business of Storekeeping in a large Commodious house, nearly opposite

Rich'd Downing's Mill in Downings Town, On the great road from Lancaster, to Philadelphia, and nearly where the road from Harrisburg intersects the same and Crosses to West Chester. But finding ye bisness of Store-keeping (Since the late Custom of Tavern Keepers opening store has taken place) is by no means sufficient to raise and support his family according to their usual Custom, Hope Therefore you will be pleased to recommend him to the Executive Council as a proper person to keep a publick house of Entertainment" etc. There was a counter petition opposing the granting of this license, but John Edge was finally successful, and his inn became known as the famous "Half Way House." In 1792 he purchased from Dr. Thomas Parke the "Ship" property, and enlarged the mansion to double its former size, and on the western half built for his son, George, the house now owned by John G. Edge, and established his son, Thomas, on the tract lying in the borough east of the present Hunt tract and south of the Lancaster road, extending to the Brandywine; to his youngest son, John, he gave the "Ship" property, one hundred and sixteen acres, lately owned by Dr. Eshleman. John Edge is said to have possessed great force of character and an active enterprising temper. He was fortunate in business, a keen observer, and given to sallies of humor and wisdom, for the benefit of his neighbors, many of which were current long after his death. It is a noteworthy fact that in 1787, when articles of luxury were heavily taxed, the only four citizens of East Caln who possessed riding chairs for which they were taxed, £1, 10 shillings, were William Trimble, John Edge, Richard Downing and Hunt Downing.

August 1, 1768, John Edge married at the East Caln meeting Ann, born twelfth month, seventeen, 1747, died December, 1826, daughter of Thomas and Frances (Wilkinson) Pim, of East Caln. William Pim, born at Lackah, Queens county, Ireland, came to America in 1730, was justice of the peace, for many years clerk of the Bradford monthly meeting. He married (first), in Ireland, Dorothy, daughter of Thomas and Dorothy Jackson, and (second) Ann, widow of James Gibbons, of West Town, Thomas Pim, third of the six children by his first wife, born third month, first, 1721, died October 3, 1786; married, tenth month, 24, 1746, at East Caln meeting, Frances, daughter of James Wilkinson, of Wilmington, who died May 7, 1784, at sixty-three years of age. Of their eight children Ann, referred to above, who married John Edge, was the second child and eldest daughter.

The children of John and Ann (Pim) Edge were: 1. Sarah, born October 10, 1769; died 1823; married (first) Morgan Reese, and (second) James Hannum. 2. Jane, October 18, 1771; died February 14, 1857; unmarried. 3. Thomas, January 29, 1774; died September 20, 1831; married Edith Pusey. 4. Ann, July 8, 1776; died April 16, 1850; married Thomas A. Parke. 5. Fanny, January 29, 1779; died October 10, 1831; unmarried. 6. George, June 30, 1782; died December 31, 1831; married Sarah Hoopes. 7. John, referred to below. 8. Mary. October 7, 1787; died December 28, 1841; married Lea Pusey. 9. Pim, January 9, 1792; died July 5, 1795.

(V) John (4), seventh child and third son of John (3) and Ann (Pim) Edge, was born March 3, 1785; died September 12, 1833. He was buried in the Caln meeting ground. He lived and died in the mansion house formerly the old "Ship" tavern which his father had given him and in which all his children were born. December 18, 1811, John Edge married at the Londongrove meeting Ruth, born December 26, 1789, died at Downingtown, May 10, 1872, buried at Downingtown meeting ground, daughter of Francis Wilkinson, of Londongrove, and his first wife, Hannah Mode. Their children were: 1. Elizabeth, born October 28, 1812; died at Downingtown, unmarried, January 23, 1890. 2. Fanny, October 11, 1815; married John K. Eshleman, M. D. 3. Ruthanna, October 25, 1817; died October 13, 1899; married Nathan J. Sharpless. 4. William, referred to below. 5. John P., June 22, 1822; unmarried.

(VI) William, fourth child and eldest son of John (4) and Ruth (Wilkinson) Edge, was born at East Caln, September 4, 1819; died in Downingtown, April 1, 1892; both he and his wife are buried in the Northwood cemetery. For several years he conducted a warehouse on the line of the Pennsylvania railroad at Downingtown. He was one of the most influential citizens of that place for many years, and was well known as a man of financial strength and influence in Philadelphia, being for many years a member of the Philadelphia stock exchange and also president of the National Bank, of Downingtown, in which latter position he was succeeded by his cousin. Jacob Edge. September 3, 1844, William Edge married in Downingtown, Elizabeth, born Montgomery county, Pennsylvania, July 7, 1824,

died June 14, 1892, in Downingtown, daughter of Hiram and Elizabeth (Reed) McNeill, of Plymouth, Pennsylvania. Their children were: 1. William, referred to below. 2. Mary Elizabeth, born July 30, 1852; living unmarried in Downingtown. 3. Esther A., July 24, 1858; unmarried and living with her sister. 4. John Howard, December 19, 1861; living unmarried.

(VII) William (2), eldest child of William (1) and Elizabeth (McNeill) Edge, was born in Downingtown, Pennsylvania, September 8, 1845, and is now living in Atlantic City, New Jersey. He is retired. June 2, 1870, William Edge married (first) in Philadelphia, Mary Elizabeth, born Philadelphia, July 24, 1848, died there December 24, 1875, buried Northwood cemetery, Downingtown, daughter of Andrew Wills and Elizabeth (Jeffries) Evans. of 1605 Franklin street, Philadelphia. Their children are: 1. Howard H., born Tyrone, Pennsylvania, July 5, 1871; educated in the New Jersey public schools; superintendent of a large manufacturing establishment in Woonsocket, Rhode Island, and member of the Methodist Episcopal church; January 1, 1895, he married Lina Bell Hustlton, born Eastern Pennsylvania, January 28, 1876, daughter of Daniel L. and Rachael A. (Brokaw) Hustlton, of Brooklyn. 2. Walter Evans, referred to below. October 28, 1877, William Edge married (second) Wilhelmina Scull, of Pleasantville, New Jersey. The only child of this marriage is Alfred James, born January 10, 1885; died September 7, 1885.

(VIII) Walter Evans, second and youngest child of William (2) and Mary Elizabeth (Evans) Edge, was born in Philadelphia, Pennsylvania, November 20, 1873, and is now living in Atlantic City, New Jersey, of which place he is one of the most substantial and influential citizens. With his father he came to Pleasantville, New Jersey, in 1876, where he was brought up by his stepmother. After graduating from the public school of Pleasantville, he entered the employ of the *Atlantic City Review*, as one of their "printer's devils," in addition to which he aided in the distribution of the newspaper. After some time in this capacity he found a position in connection with the *New York Tribune*, as one of its correspondents and advertising agents. Several years later and before he was twenty-one years of age he had made so good in these latter capacities, that he was sent to Florida and Cuba as one of the staff business representatives of that New York daily. This was before the Spanish-American war. In 1895 he became connected with the Atlantic City office of the Dorland Advertising Agency, now one of the largest corporations of its kind in this country. After the death of Mr. Dorland, the founder of the agency, Walter E. Edge purchased the business and good-will of the agency, extending its work to Europe, now conducting a prosperous branch at 3 Regent street, London, which represents the leading American newspapers in Europe. He for a short time published a distinctly hotel paper, which was known as the *Atlantic City Daily Guest*. This paper, from a financial standpoint, was one of the most successful publications ever issued in Atlantic City, and to its success is due the stimulus which encouraged Mr. Edge to undertake the work of starting and keeping up an all the year daily newspaper in Atlantic City. Consequently, in 1895, he started the *Atlantic City Daily Press*, which from that day to this has occupied a position in the city most gratifying to the natural pride of both its publisher and its friends. It has at all times been a conservative newspaper, and perhaps more than anything else has advanced the interests of Atlantic City as a popular all the year resort. It is Republican in politics, but it is noteworthy that its policy, though never wavering or uncertain, has never given offence but always commanded the respect and often the admiration of its opponents. In 1905 Mr. Edge purchased the *Atlantic City Daily Union*, which is the only evening newspaper in the town. The first issue of this paper was printed September 3, 1888, and it has been continuously issued ever since, although it was always in the front rank in advocating measures for the best interests of the city, its influence and worth have been immeasurably enhanced since Mr. Edge took possession of it and edited it as the evening edition of the *Daily Press*.

In the last presidential election Mr. Edge was elected one of the presidential electors for New Jersey on the Republican ticket. He has always been active and influential in the affairs of his party, and has more than once done good service. From 1901 to 1904 inclusive he was the secretary of the New Jersey senate. He is a member of Belcher Lodge, Free and Accepted Masons, of Atlantic City; Benevolent and Protective Order of Elks, Improved Order of Red Men, Atlantic City Country Club, Republican Club of Atlantic County, and the Atlantic City Yacht Club. He is interested in many financial and other corporations, of which he is one of the most respected and influential members. Among these should be mentioned the Guarantee Trust Company, Sterling Realty Company, Eastern Fire Insurance Company, in all three of which he is a director. He is also a member of the Atlantic City Board of Trade and of the Business Men's League, of Atlantic City.

June 5, 1907, he married Lady Lee, daughter of Samuel Philips, of Memphis, Tennessee, born October 1, 1885.

REEVES   The name Reeves is of old English or Saxon origin and belongs to that group of words which has given us the surname, King, Earl, Squire, Chancellor, Mayor and Reeves. The last name was the old Saxon title for sheriff, and its original meaning was that of steward or governor. The family at present under consideration is the third of the names which have become identified with New Jersey history, and so far as is ascertainable at the present day is distinct in its origin from the families which have played so prominent a part in Burlington and Salem counties. The present family, being stated by Mr. Francis B. Reeves, to have descended from the Long Island family of the name.

(I) Abraham Reeves, founder of the present branch of the family, came to this country, it is said, in the first quarter of the eighteenth century and settled on Long Island. They were Presbyterians, and to this day their descendants with not more than two known exceptions have adhered to the religion of their fathers. Of these pioneer Reeves brothers little information has come down now. We know, however, that Abraham Reeves was born in 1698, died May 21, 1761, and that his wife, Damaris, born 1699, died December 1, 1771, and that their children were: Abraham, Stephen, Lemuel, Thomas, Nancy, Abigail.

(II) John, son of Abraham and Damaris Reeves, was born January 30, 1726; died May 4, 1800. He married, September 12, 1750, Mable, daughter of Dr. James Johnson, born July 3, 1732, died October 23, 1813. Children: 1. Johnson, referred to below. 2. Elijah, born March 14, 1753. 3. Lemuel, March 19, 1755; died November 2, 1777. 4. Joseph, June 25, 1757. 5. Mable Johnson, November 26, 1759; died August 30, 1814; married, July 30, 1783, Levi Leake. 6. Sarah, January 13, 1762. 7. Abraham, July 30, 1763; died November 2, 1822. 8. Eunice, March 6, 1767; died April

STATE OF NEW JERSEY.
623

25, 1825; married, May 31, 1785, Daniel Bishop. 9. Stephen, February 11, 1769. 10. Nancy, November 6, 1771.

(III) Johnson, eldest child of John and Mable (Johnson) Reeves, was born August 11, 1751; died April 2, 1810. He married Zerviah, born 1760, died 1800, daughter of John and Sarah (Bateman) Berreman. Children: 1. John, referred to below. 2. Stephen, married Deborah Brown. 3. Lemuel, married (first) Sarah Sheppard, and (second) Ann Steward. 4. Sarah Berreman, married the Rev. Thomas D. Steward. 5. James Johnson, unmarried. 6. Lewis, married Hannah Miller. 7. Ann, married Samuel Ellwell. 8. Ephraim. 9. Nancy.

(IV) John (2), son of Johnson and Zerviah (Berreman) Reeves, was born September 6, 1778; died December 9, 1815. He married, December 25, 1798, Martha, born June 8, 1779, died September 22, 1825, daughter of Samuel and Mary (Cook) Reeves. Her father, Samuel Reeves, died March 30, 1806. Her mother, Mary (Cook) Reeves, was the daughter of Eldad Cook and Deborah, daughter of Daniel and Mary (Walling) Bowen. Daniel was the son of Samuel and Elizabeth (Wheaton) Bowen. Children of John and Martha (Reeves) Reeves were: 1. Johnson, referred to below. 2. Samuel, born July 7, 1801; died December 4, 1879. 3. Ephraim, August 13, 1803; died October 15, 1813. 4. Mary, September 11, 1805; died September 13, 1807. 5. Joseph, October 1, 1807; died June 14, 1890. 6. Martha, January 1, 1810; died November 24, 1832. 7. Joel Berreman, July 10, 1812; died February 3, 1886. 8. Mary, August 13, 1814; died February 7, 1894.

(V) Johnson (2), eldest child of John (2) and Martha (Reeves) Reeves, was born October 16, 1799; died July 19, 1860. Married (first) March 7, 1822, Elizabeth Riley, and (second) October 24, 1854, Anna Mariah Foster. His first wife was the daughter of Mark and Abigail (Harris) Riley, and was born March 17, 1800, died June 21, 1845. Her father was the son of Mark and Prudence Riley. Her mother was the daughter of Nathaniel and Abigail (Paget) Harris, granddaughter of Nathaniel and Elizabeth Harris. Her grandmother, Abigail (Paget) Harris, was the daughter of Thomas and Dorothy (Sayre) Paget. Children of Johnson and Elizabeth (Riley) Reeves were: 1. Henry, referred to below. 2. Harriet Newell, November 6, 1824; died December 19, 1897; married, March 25, 1846, Charles Seeley Fithian. 3.

Ruth Riley, December 20, 1826; deceased; married, March 25, 1851, Robert Du Bois. 4. Martha, August 20, 1829; died April 27, 1833. 5. John, March 9, 1832; died December 19, 1895; married, March 27, 1856, Kate Mills Robison. 6. Martha Pierson, born May 25, 1834; deceased; married (first) September 24, 1854, Alexander Lewden Robeson, and (second) January 10, 1884, George W. Bush. 7. Francis Brewster, October 10, 1836; married, April 26, 1860, Ellen Bernard Thompson. 8. James Johnson, September 9, 1839; deceased, married, 1865, Mary Caldwell Butler.

(VI) Henry, eldest child and son of Johnson (2) and Elizabeth (Riley) Reeves, was born February 5, 1823; died March 13, 1901. He graduated from Princeton University, 1844. He then taught in a private school at Pine Ridge, Mississippi, for two years. Returning to Princeton, 1846, he entered the Theological Seminary, graduating in 1849. In 1850 he was ordained to the ministry. From May to October, 1849, he preached at Lenox Chapel on the Hudson above New Hamburg. From November, 1849, to May, 1850, at Wappinger's Falls, New York. From July, 1850, to July, 1858, was pastor at Belvidere, New Jersey. From August, 1858, to July, 1864, was stated supply at Fayetteville, Pennsylvania. From May, 1869, to August, 1881, at Gloucester City, New Jersey. From 1882 to 1885 at the Pearl Street Mission, at Bridgeton, New Jersey. From 1891 to 1901 at Gloucester City, New Jersey. Since 1884 he was stated clerk of the Presbytery of West Jersey until the time of his death. While serving at Fayetteville he was principal of the Young Ladies Seminary, Chambersburg, Pennsylvania. From 1864 to 1868 he was principal of Woodland Seminary, of West Philadelphia, and from 1881 to 1891 of Ivy Hall, Bridgeton, New Jersey. From 1869 to 1875 he was editor of *Young Folk's News*, and from 1871 to 1875 of *Our Monthly*. In 1886 he received the honorary degree of Ph. D. from Princeton, and 1897 that of D. D. from Hanover College, Indiana.

May 6, 1851, the Rev. Henry Reeves, D. D., married Sarah Jane, born December 17, 1827, daughter of Phineas B. and Priscilla (Carr) Kennedy, of Warren county, New Jersey. Their children are: 1. Bessie, born February 12, 1852; married, June 29, 1887, Edward N. Fithian, of Bridgeton, New Jersey, and has two children. 2. Phineas Kennedy, March 16, 1854; married, January 13, 1880, Hannah P. Trenchard, and had four children. 3. Charles Fithian, April 13, 1856; married, December 10,

1884, Clara Elizabeth Hoffman, and had three children. 4. William Henry Green, April 20, 1858; died September 7, 1859. 5. Harry, referred to below. 6. Arthur Erwin, October 19, 1861; died April 8, 1868. 7. Anna Robeson, March 30, 1865.

(VII) Harry, fifth child and fourth son of the Rev. Henry and Sarah Jane (Kennedy) Reeves, was born at Chambersburg, Pennsylvania, January 30, 1860, and is now living in Gloucester City, New Jersey. He received his early education in the public schools in Gloucester City, New Jersey, and at Professor Hasting's Academy in Philadelphia, Pennsylvania, from which he went to the Chester Valley Academy in Downingtown, Pennsylvania. At the Centennial Exhibition in 1876 in Philadelphia, Mr. Reeves was in charge of the sales department of the Ferracute Machine Company. From then down to 1881 he was a salesman in the wholesale grocery house of Reeves, Parvin & Company, of Philadelphia. After this he went into business for himself at Bridgeton, New Jersey, with his brother Charles Fithian Reeves, the firm name being C. F. & H. Reeves. They conducted a steam engineering and plumbing business with a branch office at Philadelphia. This arrangement continued for three years and then Mr. Reeves bought out his brother's interest and took as his partner Charles F. West, the firm name being changed to Reeves & West, and their works being situated at Gloucester City, New Jersey. After fifteen years of successful operation, this firm was dissolved by Mr. Reeves disposing of his interest to his partner. This he did in order to accept a position as secretary and general manager of the Mutual Life Insurance Company, of Camden. In 1902 Mr. Reeves was nominated for the office of surrogate of Camden county, New Jersey, on the Republican ticket, and he was elected by a majority of 5,201 votes, this being a running of several hundred ahead of his ticket. In 1907, when his term expired, he was renominated for a second term, which would expire in 1912, and this time his majority was 7,332 votes, again running a long distance ahead of his ticket. Mr. Reeves has always been active and enthusiastic in his adherence to and his able work for the Republican party, to which he belongs, and for six years he has been the chairman of the Camden County Republican Committee. In religious belief he is a Presbyterian, and for twenty-three years he has been one of the trustees of the First Presbyterian Church, of Gloucester City, New Jersey. He

is a member of Cloud Lodge, No. 101, Free and Accepted Masons, of Gloucester City; Excelsior Consistory, No. 15, of Camden. He has taken the thirty-second degree in the Scottish Rite Masonry and he is a past worshipful master of his Blue Lodge, and is also a member of Crescent Temple, of Trenton, New Jersey, of the Mystic Shrine. In the financial world Mr. Reeves ranks exceptionally high, and he is the vice-president of the New Jersey Trust Company, as well as a director in the Security Trust Company, of Camden, New Jersey.

January 6, 1886, Harry Reeves married Lizzie S., born June 1, 1860, daughter of Henry F. and Zeviah West; children: 1. Sarah Walker, born March 21, 1887. 2. Bessie Fithian, May 10, 1888; died September 18, 1888. 3. Emily Janvier, June 15, 1889. 4. Chrissie West, November 26, 1890; died December 6, 1891. 5. Henry F. West, January 5, 1892; died April 13, 1892. 6. Florence Kennedy, July 13, 1894; died January 8, 1895. 7. Frances Wallace, May 25, 1896.

REEVES While the family name Reeves has been known in this country since the early times of the colony, the immigrant ancestor of the particular family here treated appears to have first come to America with that distinguished commander, Marquis de Lafayette, who rendered such efficient service to the colonies in the struggle for national independence.

(I) Daniel Reeves, immigrant, was born about 1760 and was a young man of about twenty years when he came over, as tradition tells us, with Lafayette to take part with the united colonies in throwing off the yoke of the mother country. He afterward remained here and took up his place of abode in New Jersey, although information concerning him and his family life is quite meagre. The name of his wife was Jane Shemelia, and by her he had sons Richard, William H., Isaac and Levi, and daughters Elizabeth and Hope.

(II) William H., son of Daniel and Jane (Shemelia) Reeves, was born in Ocean county, New Jersey, in 1814; died at Brown's Mills, in that county, in 1890. His occupation was that of a charcoal burner, and he lived much of his life at Cedar Bridge, although his later years were spent at Brown's Mills. He married Matilda Ann Sprague, and by her had eight children: John, now living at Brookville; Israel, living at Barnegat; Joel S., of Brown's Mills; William, now dead; Theodore, living at Columbus; Rachel, married Isaac N.

Colch, of Brookville; Martha, now dead; and Hope Ann.

(III) Joel Sprague, son of William H. and Matilda Ann (Sprague) Reeves, was born at Mary Ann Forge, New Jersey, in 1840. During the earlier years of his business life he was a ship carpenter by trade and later followed general carpenter work and farming. Before the civil war he worked as a ship carpenter at Barnegat, and in August, 1862, enlisted there for nine months as private in Company H, of the Twenty-ninth New Jersey Volunteer Infantry. He went to the front with his regiment and took part in the battles of Fredericksburg and Chancellorsville, and at the expiration of his term of enlistment returned home and resumed work at his trade. However, in 1865 he was drafted for further army service and was assigned to Company F, of the Thirty-third New Jersey Volunteer Infantry. ' His regiment went to Newburne, North Carolina, and later did guard and garrison duty in the defenses of Washington until the close of the war. He then returned north and again took up carpenter work, having lived for the last thirty years at Brown's Mills. Mr. Reeves is a member of the Order of United American Mechanics. In politics he is a Republican, although not active in public affairs. He married (first) in 1866, Lucy Ann Cramer, of Cedar Bridge, Warrensville, Ocean county, New Jersey. She died in March, 1873, and he married (second) in 1879, Elizabeth Parker. He had six children, three by his first and three by his second wife: 1. Sarah Adelia, married Henry Nickson, a farmer, of New Lisbon, New Jersey, and has three children, Fenton, Carrie and Elizabeth. 2. Walter M. 3. William H., see forward. 4. Lucy, married George Taylor. 5. Matilda, married Harry Haines, a farmer, of New Lisbon. 6. Herbert.

(IV) William Henry, son of Joel Sprague and Lucy Ann (Cramer) Reeves, was born at Barnegat, Ocean county, New Jersey, March 31, 1870. At the age of nine years he went with his parents to live at Brown's Mill, where he attended school and then for three years worked on a farm. In 1888 he came to New Lisbon, New Jersey, to learn railroading and telegraphy. He was clerk in a railroad office in Jamesburg, New Jersey, for one year, and in 1891 again returned to New Lisbon to take charge of the railroad office there, where he has continued in the capacity of station agent. In 1892 he received appointment as postmaster of the town and in the same year opened a store, which he manages in addition to his

ii—15

other duties. Politically he is a Republican and has served as tax collector and treasurer of the town since 1888. Mr. Reeves also has large cranberry interests, owning a bog of about one hundred acres which he put under cultivation in 1900. He is a member of numerous fraternal orders, as follows: Central Lodge, No. 44, Free and Accepted Masons, of Vincentown; Benevolent and Protective Order of Elks, No. 848, of Mt. Holly; Independent Order of Odd Fellows, of Pemberton; Knights of Pythias, of Pemberton; Improved Order of Red Men, Pemberton; Patriotic Order Sons of America, Pemberton; Order of Railway Telegraph Operators; and of the Pennsylvania Railroad Relief Fund. He is a member of the Methodist Episcopal Church, of New Lisbon, and for a number of years was chairman of the board of stewards of the church.

Mr. Reeves married (first) in 1891, Kezzie Yeager, of Brown's Mills, New Jersey, and by whom he had three children, all born in New Lisbon: 1. Ethel, born 1892; lives at home. 2. Arthur, November 21, 1893; works with his father in the railroad and post offices. 3. Milton Vorhees, February 2, 1895. His first wife died June 18, 1897, and he married (second) September 15, 1906, Mary Reeves, daughter of Israel Reeves.

SPARKS

Our present narrative concerns the family and descendants of one of three immigrant brothers —John, Robert and Jared Sparks—who were of Scotch ancestry but natives of the north of Ireland, where in earlier generations their ancestors had found temporary refuge from the persecutions visited upon them because of their religious convictions, which were not in accord with the teaching of the dominant church. Rather than yield to the exactions of their persecutors many Scotch families fled from their native country to Ireland and lived there through several generations, and from this fact they came to be known as Scotch-Irish, but so only in name unless there were intermarriages with Irish families; and we have no evidence that any of the Sparks ancestors were allied with Irish families by ties of marriage. None of the three brothers is believed to have been married at the time of their immigration to America, for they all were young men of adventurous spirit starting out in a new country to make each for himself his own way in life. They came over about 1735 or 1740. Our present narrative has to deal with John Sparks and his descendants.

(I) John Sparks was born in the north of Ireland in 1717; died in 1802. He settled in New Jersey and owned and lived on the farm now owned by Clement Reeves, one mile from Woodbury Court House, toward the Delaware river. His farm comprised two hundred acres of land and was considered one of the best in Gloucester county. The baptismal name of his first wife was Annie, and the name of his second wife was Mary. By his first marriage he had sons Isaac, Randall and Joseph, all of whom were born on the homestead farm where their father settled. By wife, Mary, he had a son, John, and perhaps other children. John Sparks founded the Presbyterian burial ground at Woodbury and was buried there. John Sparks was an elder in the joint session of the churches of Woodbury and Timber Creek (now Blackwood). The date of his election and ordination are not known, but he sat as elder in the session of the synod in Philadelphia in 1768, at the meetings of the Presbytery of Philadelphia, November 3, 1773; April 9, 1791; October 18, 1796; October 7, 1797, and October 20, 1801. He is said to have died February 18, 1802. He also was a member of the provincial congress of New Jersey at Trenton, in May, June and August, 1775, and at the meeting of the same body at Burlington in June, 1776, when the resolution was adopted "that the proclamation of William Franklin, late governor of New Jersey, appointed at a meeting of the general assembly, be not obeyed."

(II) Randall, second son of John and Annie Sparks, continued to live on the old farm for many years, and his children were born there. In 1815 he went to Woodbury and kept tavern there, at the place once called Rachor's, at Court House, but in 1817 he removed to the Buck Tavern, at The Buck (now Westville). In 1819 he went to Philadelphia to secure employment with his cousin, Thomas Sparks, shot manufacturer, living in John street (now Carpenter) next to Shot Tower. Failing to find work with his cousin, Mr. Sparks in the following year removed with his family to Camden to keep ferry for Joseph L. Turner, on the north side of Market street, and he remained there from 1820 to 1824. Here he became prosperous and acquired large tracts of land. He owned twelve thousand acres in one tract at the Dutch Mills, New Jersey, below Williamstown, which was heavily wooded and for which he paid twelve and one-half cents per acre. This he deeded to Samuel Downs and Benjamin Ward. He also owned eight hun-

dred and fifty acres near what now is Wenonah, and out of which several fine farms have been made, the Clark farm, the William C. Sparks farm, the Stevenson farm, and others. Randall Sparks was buried at Bethel. Although known as Randall his correct name was Alexander Randall Sparks. His will was written by Joseph Saunders. He married twice and had six children. His first wife died March 18 or 19, 1811, aged twenty-five years. His children, born of his first marriage: 1. Ruth, 1805. 2. William, 1805; died young. 3. John, C., 1807. 4. Mary, 1808. 5. William C., 1809; see forward. 6. Annie, 1810.

(III) William C., son of Randall Sparks by his first wife, was born at Woodbury, New Jersey, 1809; died September 16, 1872. He was a farmer, member of the Methodist Episcopal church, and in politics a Republican. He married Mary P. Steen and by her had four children: William Francis, see forward; John Wesley, George W. and Sarah.

(IV) William Francis, son of William C. and Mary P. (Steen) Sparks, was born at Dilk's Mill (now Wenonah), New Jersey, May 4, 1842; died May 27, 1875. During the earlier years of his business life he was a farmer and school teacher and afterward a railroad baggage master. He was a soldier of the war of 1861-65 and enlisted as William C. Sparks, private Company I, Ninth New Jersey Volunteer Infantry. In religious preference he was a Methodist and in politics a Republican. He married, November 23, 1865, Elizabeth Evans, daughter of Richard Evans, a native of Llanidloes, Wales, and who by wife, Elizabeth (Humphries) Evans, had a son, Richard, and daughters, Anna and Elizabeth Evans. William Francis and Elizabeth (Evans) Sparks had only one child, John W. Sparks, see forward.

(V) John Wesley, son of William Francis and Elizabeth (Evans) Sparks, was born at Cross Keys, Gloucester county, New Jersey, September 22, 1866. He received his earlier education in public schools in his native town. He afterwards was a student at and graduated from the Pierce School, Philadelphia, later attended the Pennsylvania Polytechnic School, still later was a student at Temple College, and also took a course at Palmer's Shorthand College, Philadelphia, where also he was graduated. His business career was begun in the capacity of clerk in the office of the West Jersey Railroad Company, at Wenonah, where he remained for two years, and then for the next six months was telegraph operator for that company at Atlantic City, New Jersey. After-

ward for about ten years he was telegrapher for S. Morris Pryor & Company, stock brokers, of Philadelphia, and during the following three years for Harris, Fuller & Hurley, stock brokers, also of Philadelphia. On January 1, 1892, Mr. Sparks became junior member of the firm of William H. Hurley, Jr., & Company, stock and bond brokers, a relation which was maintained until December 30, 1899, when the partnership was dissolved, and was succeeded on January 1, 1900, by the new firm of J. W. Sparks & Company, as now known in business circles in that city. Mr. Sparks is a business man, living in Philadelphia, a Republican in politics but not active in public affairs. He is a member of the New York Stock Exchange, Philadelphia Stock Exchange and a governor of the latter, and is also a member of the Chicago Board of Trade, the American Bankers Association, and the Pennsylvania Bankers Association. He holds membership in Williamstown Lodge, No. 166, Free and Accepted Masons, of Williamstown, New Jersey; Siloam Chapter, No. 19, Royal Arch Masons, of Camden; the Scottish Rite bodies of the craft in Philadelphia, the Pennsylvania Historical Society, the Art, Raquet and Down Town clubs, of Philadelphia, and of the Methodist Episcopal church. He married, at Turnersville, New Jersey, June 7, 1894, Charlesanna Sickler, who was born at Chew's Landing, New Jersey, October 11, 1866, daughter and only child of Benjamin Franklin and Mary Elizabeth Sickler.

BISHOP The Bishops are an English family and their surname is one of the most ancient in all the kingdom. The name was transplanted on this side of the Atlantic during the early years of the colonial period and its representatives have ranked with the foremost men of the country in all generations to the present time. There are various traditions regarding the immigration of the particular family here treated, and that which seems most stable has it that several immigrant brothers came from England and settled either on Long Island or in the colony of Connecticut. There were Bishops on Long Island at an early period and in Connecticut the name appears soon after the first planters made their way into that part of New England. The earliest known ancestor of the family here treated is understood to have come to West Jersey from either Long Island or Connecticut, but whether he was born in England or America does not appear. His name is not found

in any of the genealogical references extant, hence the place of his nativity cannot be given. The following account of the early life of the family in New Jersey is taken largely from the reminiscences of John Bishop, 2d, written by him about thirty years ago.

(I) Robert Bishop, earliest ancestor of the family of whom there appears to be any account, was living near Lumberton, Burlington county, New Jersey, previous to the revolutionary war. In speaking of the first settlers in that locality the "History of Burlington and Mercer Counties" says that six brothers of the Bishop surname came from England and located along Rancocas creek from Bridgeboro to Vincentown, one at each of these places and the other four at or near Lumberton.' In a way this account is substantially in accord with the previous statement that several brothers came from England and settled either on Long Island or in Connecticut. But, however this may have been, Robert Bishop was living near Lumberton in Burlington county previous to the revolution, and in 1778 at and about the time of the battle of Monmouth General Knyphausen's division (Hessians) of the British army in its march through that region overran and ransacked Robert Bishop's house from cellar to garret, excepting only the room in which lay his sick wife and her new born child, John Bishop, and it was only with difficulty that the common soldiers were restrained by their officers from entering and pillaging that room of the house. They also removed all live stock and forage from the farm, with the exception of a colt, which proved so fractious that it could not be taken away. Of Robert Bishop's family, says Mr. Bishop in his reminiscences, "I know at present comparatively little save that there were several brothers who emigrated either from Long Island or Connecticut. The baptismal name of his wife was Jane and among their children was a son John."

(II) John, son of Robert and Jane Bishop, was born near Lumberton, Burlington county, New Jersey, the 17th day of 6th month, 1778, a few days prior to the battle of Monmouth. "On his mother's side," says Mr. Bishop's narrative, "he was of the third generation in lineal descent of a full-blooded Indian girl of the Lenni Lenappe tribe, and who previous to her marriage assumed the English name of Mary Carlisle and married Richard Haines, who with several of his brothers emigrated from Northamptonshire, England, and were the original settlers of Burlington county, at that time a part of the province of West Jersey. John Bishop's mother, who married Robert Bishop, and who was a granddaughter of the Indian maiden, Mary Carlisle, was of course a quarter blood Indian, and what is singular, it is said by those who remember her that she was of light complexion, a blonde, although some of her children with their bright, piercing, black eyes and swarthy complexions, gave unmistakable evidence of their Indian origin. She is represented to have been a woman of sweet disposition and possessed of the most estimable traits of character. When John Bishop was about six years old his parents removed to the north side of Rancocas creek, where it empties into the Delaware, and on a part of which the town of Delanco is now built. Here on account of the proximity to the water, John became an adept as a swimmer, skater and trapper, the country at that time abounding in foxes and other game and the creeks with otter, mink and muskrats, many times going and breaking the ice with his bare feet to remove the game from his traps; and one of his greatest pastimes at certain seasons of the year was to swim over to the island at the junction of the river and creek and bring geese home to his mother. Soon after removing to this new home John got his first start in life in the ownership of a hen, which was given to him by an Indian squaw who had come to make his parents a visit; and it was not long before nearly all the chickens on the farm were claimed by himself as sole owner. It is related that one day his mother wanting a chicken to make a potpie for dinner, sent one of the family to get one, when John seeing them called out 'that's my chicken,' and so with the second and third attempts, until it was found that they were all 'his chickens.' Then his father proposed that he exchange some of his chickens for sheep, which was agreed to and in the course of a year or two, his sheep beginning to multiply pretty fast, his father, having the chicken experience in mind, limited John's to two, and divided the others among the neighbors to raise on shares.

When John Bishop was about ten or twelve years old his father died. All the education the boy had was obtained in a log schoolhouse in the pine woods. At the age of sixteen he taught school on what is now (1879) the Moorestown and Camden turnpike, and at the end of one winter's teaching he saved sufficient to 'gave him an outfit to get to Philadelphia.' After the death of his father he made his home with an elder married brother, whom he helped with the work of the farm; and the latter hearing John talk of going to Philadelphia, made the remark 'you'll come to nothing,' to which the young fellow replied with his characteristic spirit, 'I might as well come to nothing as to stay with you and work for nothing.' However, they remained the best of friends during the entire period of their lives. He went to Philadelphia and being a young man of fine personal appearance and possessed of good business ability, it was not long before he secured a good position as clerk in the counting house of Harry Moliere, a Frenchman, who had an extensive rope walk up in Kensington. Soon afterward he formed the acquaintance of a Scotchman named Couslan, a practical plumber, and formed a partnership with him for carrying on the business, besides which the firm rented the first three wharves below Walnut street, and there their plumbing shops were located. Their principal business at that time was work aboard vessels, but as the shipyards were in Kensington the partners in their work were compelled to walk back and forth between that place and the shops; and it is said that never but once did John Bishop find a man who could outwalk him in traveling this distance."

After several years of profitable partnership relation Mr. Couslan died and soon afterward John Bishop purchased his former partner's interest in the business. Among their apprentices in the shop were Thomas and Richard Sparks, brothers, the former being an energetic, industrious young man, well skilled in his trade, and he became Mr. Bishop's partner. Soon after this, however, difficulty arose between our country and England and France regarding maritime rights of neutrals, which culminated in the war of 1812 and also in the ultimate ruin of the plumbing business carried on by Bishop & Sparks. In this emergency the firm turned to the manufacture of shot, and for that purpose built a small cupola above the old plumbing shop, put in a furnace for melting lead and began a series of experiments in shotmaking, each of which resulted in failure; but instead of being discouraged by defeat the members of the firm renewed their work with commendable courage and by fortunate chance happened to hear of an English shotmaker up in Kensington who understood the art of shotmaking. They at once secured his services, although with some difficulty and at considerable expense, and then began making shot with most excellent success. From that time, says Mr. Bishop's narrative, "money

STATE OF NEW JERSEY. 629

began to flow in rapidly and in less than a year the shot tower in Southwark was planned and built under the direction of John Bishop, senior member of the firm in 1808." In speaking of this pioneer industry of its kind in this country a comparatively recent issue of a Philadelphia paper had this to say of the old shot tower and its ultimate removal: "The river wards between Market street and Washington avenue were never a great manufacturing centre and the few establishments of this kind they contained have steadily decreased until all the older ones are gone. One of the latest to go was the historic shot tower on Montrose street, west of Front street, built in 1808, and which continued in operation until a few years ago, when it was purchased and closed up permanently. Its tall tower, standing sentinel like 150 feet high, reminds the passerby of Thomas Moore's 'Round Towers of Other Days,' and calls attention to the fact that beneath its shadow scores of workmen found employment at turning out buck and bird shot. During the Mexican war balls for musket cartridges were manufactured by it by the thousand daily and forwarded to the scene of battle."

The manufacture of shot and bullets continued to be a thriving business with John Bishop for several years and thereby he accumulated a comfortable fortune. But eventually he sold out his interests in the city and purchased the Ogston farm near Columbus, New Jersey, being the same property now owned by Anna R. Bishop and on which his grandson, John I. Bishop, now maintains his residence. John Bishop went there to live in 1813 and spent the remainder of his life in that locality. He always possessed in his later years an interesting fund of anecdote, and never tired of narrating his experiences with Stephen Girard, with whom he first met while serving as clerk for Harry Moliere, and still later becoming more intimately acquainted with that famous Philadelphia merchant and philanthropist while doing work on his ships in the old yards at Kensington. When about twenty-one years old, John Bishop married (first) Mary, daughter of Joseph and Hannah Ridgway, who lived near Mullica Hill, Salem county, New Jersey. He married (second) Ann Black.

(III) John (2), son of John (1) and Ann (Black) Bishop, was born at Ogston, near Columbus, Burlington county, New Jersey, March 15, 1820. He married, February 5, 1845, Rebecca Field Biddle, born at the Biddle homestead at Mount Hope, Kinkora, Burling-

ton county, New Jersey, January 16, 1826, died April 4, 1893, daughter of Israel and Sarah T. (Field) Biddle (see Biddle, V).

(IV) John I., son of John (2) and Rebecca Field (Biddle) Bishop, was born at Ogston, near Columbus, Burlington county, New Jersey, July 4, 1849. He received his early education in the public schools in his native town, attended the Friends' Academy at Westtown, and graduated at the Polytechnic College of Pennsylvania, receiving the degree of Bachelor of Civil Engineering in June, 1868, and the master's degree three years later. He was continuously employed in engineering work by the following railroad companies respectively: The Camden & Amboy, the West Jersey, the Tuckerton, the Columbus, Kinkora & Springfield, and the Pennsylvania, until 1875, when he was called to examine coal lands in western Pennsylvania, and later to develop the Redstone Oil, Coal & Coke Company and Ridgway-Bishop Coal Company properties, absorbed during 1899 by the Pittsburgh Coal Company, of which he is a director and a member of the executive committee. For twenty years he has been manager of the several interests owned or controlled by Jacob E. Ridgway. He is a member of the Union League of Philadelphia, the Duquesne Club of Pittsburgh, the American Jersey Cattle Club of New York, and the New Jersey Society of Philadelphia. He resides at Ogston during the summer, and in Philadelphia during the winter months.

Mr. Bishop married, November 9, 1871, Anna Ridgway, born in Philadelphia, August 24, 1850, daughter of Jacob E. and Sarah Shreve Ridgway. Children: 1. John, born December 20, 1875; died March 28, 1884. 2. Emily, October 24, 1878; married, October 8, 1901, John S. C. Harvey; children: i. Anna Bishop Harvey, born September 16, 1902; ii. John S. C. Harvey, Jr., August 14, 1904; iii. Thomas Biddle Harvey, August 16, 1908. 3. John V., July 2, 1886; married, January 6, 1909, Helen Bailey.

(The Biddle Line).

The original immigrant of the Biddle family came from London to America about the year 1681 and settled in West Jersey. He was an active man in public affairs from the time of his arrival in New Jersey until his death, in 1712. He held many offices of trust and honor and appears to have devoted much of his time to public service. In his will he gave five hundred acres of land to his cousin, Thomas Biddle, concerning whom a recent chronicler of the family history says: "Of Thomas Biddle, the 'cousin,' we know absolutely nothing save that he left descendants. He appears as a witness on William Biddle's marriage certificate in 1665, and a Thomas Biddle signs as a witness to the will of William Righton, mariner, in Jamaica, February 5, 1701-02; and the marriage of Thomas Biddle and Rachel Grusbeck is recorded in the records of the First Presbyterian Church, Philadelphia. Whether this Thomas Biddle was the cousin mentioned, or the son of the cousin, is not positively known; but doubtless he was the ancestor of that line of the family."

(I) Thomas Biddle, who is presumed to have been a son of the Thomas Biddle mentioned in his will by William Biddle as his "cousin," married at the First Presbyterian Church, Philadelphia, November 8, 1704, Rachel Groesbeck. Children: Thomas, Sarah, Rachel.

(II) Thomas (2), son of Thomas (1) and Rachel (Groesbeck) Biddle, married, October 28, 1728, Mary, daughter of James and Mary (Hance) Antrim, of East Jersey. They lived in the old family homestead at Mount Hope (now Kinkora), New Jersey, which formerly was owned by William Biddle, the first. Children: 1. Sarah, born August 8, 1729, died September, 1810. 2. Thomas, October 17, 1734, see forward. 3. Rachel, married, December 5, 1772, Jonathan Izard.

(III) Thomas (3), son of Thomas (2) and Mary (Antrim) Biddle, was born October 17, 1734, died September, 1793. He married, April 17, 1760, Abigail Scull, died September 10, 1783, daughter of Nicholas Scull. Children: 1. Thomas, born September 13, 1761, see forward. 2. Abigail, September 13, 1763; married John Harvey. 3. Mary, March 20, 1766; married Caleb Foster. 4. Sarah, June 7, 1769, died August 6, 1775.

(IV) Thomas (4), son of Thomas (3) and Abigail (Scull) Biddle, was born September 13, 1761, died in April, 1807. He became owner of a part of Biddle's island in the Delaware river, opposite Kinkora, New Jersey. His real property was divided among his children in 1813. He married Charlotte Butler. Children: 1. Thomas, born November 28, 1786; married Charlotte Harvey. 2. Israel, October 6, 1788, see forward. 3. Abigail, January 31, 1791, died single. 4. Mary, March 17, 1793; married (first) James Bates, (second) Isaac Field. 5. John, October 2, 1795, died single. 6. Charlotte, July 27, 1798;

married, October, 1816, Samuel Black. 7. Achsa, January 26, 1801; married Joseph Haines. 8. William, May 23, 1804; married Elizabeth Rockhill.

(V) Israel, son of Thomas (4) and Charlotte (Butler) Biddle, was born October 6, 1788. He married (first) Sarah Tallman; married (second) Sarah T. Filed, who died near Mansfield, New Jersey, September 12, 1885, aged eighty-two years. Children: 1. Charles (by first wife), married Sarah Ann Lee and had three children. 2. Martha F. (by second wife), married, 1845, Thomas Newbold Black. 3. Israel, died young. 4. Rebecca Field, born January 16, 1826; married, February 5, 1845, John Bishop (see Bishop, III, above). 5. Sarah, died young. 6. Israel, married Charlotte B. Harvey. 7. Mary T., married Franklin Black. 8. Abigail, died young. 9. Charlotte, married George B. Wills. 10. Joseph W., married Charlotte, daughter of William J. and Charlotte Black. 11. Caroline Elizabeth, died young.

BISHOP

There is a tradition which runs to the effect that the Bishops of New Jersey are descended from seven brothers of Quaker origin who came from England about the middle of the eighteenth century and settled in various parts of that then province. But however this may have been it is certain that for more than one hundred and fifty years the surname Bishop has been found among the leading families of this state and always has stood for the best elements of citizenship, loyalty to established institutions of government, and enterprise and progressiveness in all of varied pursuits of business activity.

(I) Isaac Bishop, earliest known ancestor of the family of his surname purposed to be treated in this place, was living at Mt. Holly, Burlington county, about the year 1760 and afterward until he met death by lightning a short time after his marriage. Little else appears to be known of him, there being no reliable account of his marriage or of the name of his wife, but about six months after his death his only son was born.

(II) Job, son of Isaac Bishop, was born in 1769 in Burlington county, and was a mechanic. His life was spent at Mt. Holly, and he died there in February, 1852. He married (first) Sarah Jones, of Haddonfield, who died in 1806, having borne him four children. He afterward married a second wife and by her had one son. Children: 1. Isaac, died young. 2. William, born July 17, 1798, see forward. 3. Mary, died unmarried. 4. Edward, died unmarried. 5. John R., who became a merchant tailor and lived in Philadelphia.

(III) William, son of Job and Sarah (Jones) Bishop, was born at Mt. Holly, New Jersey, July 17, 1798, and was a boy of seven years at the time of the death of his mother. After that he spent the next several years on a farm, where he was brought up under the care of relatives, and then returned home. In May, 1814, he went to Burlington, where, dependent upon his own resources for his support, he found employment in a store kept by William Ridgway, with whom he remained until 1833, when Mr. Ridgway died. Then in partnership with Robert Thomas, a stepson of his former employer, Mr. Bishop continued the business until 1850, when he retired from mercantile pursuits. He died in 1887, after a long, honorable and successful business career, throughout the entire period of which he held the respect and confidence of the people of the region in which the scene of his life was laid. He was one of the organizers of the Burlington Savings Institution and its president for thirty-five years, until the time of his death. On its organization in 1857 he was elected its vice-president and three months later became president, succeeding Ira B. Underhill. . He also was a director of the Merchants' National Bank of Burlington for thirty-one years, a director of the Burlington board of education for fifteen years, and for many years a director of the Burlington Library. Probably no man connected with the financial and business interests of Burlington was more painstaking or more scrupulously upright than Mr. Bishop. Like his ancestors, he was a member of the Society of Friends and always led a quiet and unostentatious life. He married (first) Eliza, daughter of William Ridgway, of Burlington. She died in 1843, leaving one son, William Ridgway Bishop. He married (second) Mrs. Mary M., widow of Thomas Booth.

(IV) William Ridgway, son of William and Eliza (Ridgway) Bishop, was born in Burlington, New Jersey, in the house in which he now lives, July 3, 1836, and received his education at the Friends' School in Burlington and the Friends' School at Westtown, Pennsylvania. After leaving school he worked for about two years as clerk in the general store kept in Burlington by Samuel Taylor and afterward taught school two years at White Hill in Burlington county. This was before he had

attained the age of twenty years. In business life he has been a dealer in coal, fertilizers and seeds. He started in active pursuits in 1864 and after many years of successful effort he discontinued the handling of fertilizers and coal and since that time has dealt only in field and garden seeds. In this direction his operations have been somewhat extensive, and he ships seeds to Texas and California, to Havana, and also to various European countries. Mr. Bishop is a careful and straightforward business man, a Republican in political preference and for two years was a member of the Burlington city council. He also is a member of the Society of Friends and clerk of the Burlington Meeting. He married, in February, 1860, Mary Louisa, daughter of Samuel and Jane (Wright) Lee, of Reading, Pennsylvania. Children: 1. Louisa Horner, born Burlington, September 1, 1861, died 1883. 2. Eliza Ridgway, born in Burlington, lives at home with her parents.

BISHOP There is a tradition in the family that sometime about the middle of the eighteenth century four Bishop brothers, of Quaker origin, came from England and settled in New Jersey, and while the family here under consideration may have been and probably was descended from one of these four immigrant brothers there appears to be no present means by which the tradition can be substantiated by proof. A somewhat noticeable similarity of christian names leads to the conclusion that the ancestor of the family here treated was closely related to the families of the four brothers.

(I) Thomas Bishop, progenitor of the particular branch of the New Jersey family of that surname here treated, was born of English parents, a member of the Society of Friends, and an early settler in Burlington county, where many of his descendants are still living. The title deed to lands owned and settled by him was acquired by purchase from the Indians, and the ancient document is now in possession of Henry J. Irick, one of his descendants, while the land itself is owned by Samuel S. Irick, brother of Senator Irick, and both are great-great-grandsons of the immigrant. The name of Thomas Bishop's wife does not appear, but he married and left four children surviving him, as follows: 1. William, see forward. 2. John, married Mary Stockton; no issue. 3. Elizabeth, married Josiah Evans and removed to Ohio. 4. Vincent, married ——— Branin, and had a large family.

(II) William, son of Thomas Bishop, the immigrant, married Rebecca Leeds, and had five children: 1. Job, see forward. 2. Rebecca, married James Branson. 3. Samuel, died single. 4. Japheth, married Rachel Haines, and were the parents of Emeline Bishop, who became wife of General John S. Irick, father of Senator Henry J. and Samuel S. Irick, of whom mention is made elsewhere. 5. William, married Mary Woolston, and had William, who married Maria Hargrave; Japheth, now (1909) inmate of Masonic Home in Burlington, married Margaret Hargrave; Maria, married John Ross; Esther, married Thomas Pope; and Samuel, who married Elizabeth Patterson.

(III) Job, eldest son and child of William and Rebecca (Leeds) Bishop, was born in Vincentown, Burlington county, New Jersey, and was a farmer by principal occupation, although during the early part of his life he taught school, being a man of superior education as well as of influence in the township. He died at Lumberton, Burlington county. His wife was Hannah, daughter of Daniel Joyce, and by her he had six children: 1. Daniel J., see forward. 2. Martha Adams. 3. Elizabeth Voorhees. 4. Emily. 5. Dorotha A., married Edmund Jefferson. 6. Hannah, married Peter Oliver. 7. William, died unmarried.

(IV) Daniel J., eldest son and child of Job and Hannah (Joyce) Bishop, was born in Vincentown in 1816, died in Lumberton in 1906. He was captain of a sailing vessel and for many years was a pilot on the Delaware river between Hainesport and Philadelphia. Captain Bishop married Ann Frazier and by her had six children, Hannah, William Henry, David, Job, Daniel and Jane.

(V) William Henry, son of Captain Daniel J. and Ann (Frazier) Bishop, was born in Lumberton, Burlington county, New Jersey, March 27, 1841, and in one capacity and another has been identified with mercantile pursuits for more than half a century. He left school, and went to work as clerk and errand boy for his uncle, William C. Bishop, of Lumberton, who was in active business full fifty years previous to his death in 1901, remained in his employ for five years and then was clerk for another five years in the store of M. S. Butterworth, of Wrightstown, New Jersey. In 1866 he became senior partner of the firm of Bishop & Beck, general merchants of Pemberton, and at the end of eight years bought out his partner's interest and has since carried on business alone. Mr. Bishop is counted among the substantial business men of Burlington county and outside of personal concerns has for many years been identified with some of the best interests and institutions of the region. He is president of the Union National Bank of Mt. Holly, a director of the Mt. Holly Safe Deposit and Trust Company and treasurer of the Pemberton Building and Loan Association. He is a firm Republican, but without political ambition, although he has served as member of the township committee. He is a member of Central Lodge, No. 44, Free and Accepted Masons, of Vincentown, and of Mt. Holly Lodge, No. 848, Benevolent Protective Order Elks. In 1865 he married Sarah, daughter of James and Charlotte Beck, of Wrightstown, and who died in 1905. He has one daughter, Charlotte, born in Pemberton in October, 1866, married Alfred Davis, druggist, of Pemberton.

TRENCHARD The Trenchard family belongs to a good old English stock which had made its name in the old country many years before it was transplanted to the new world. The family traces its origin back to Pogames Trenchard, who held land in county Dorset during the reign of Henry I, in 1090. In the sixteenth and the preceding century they had intermarried with the Damosels and the Moleynes.

(I) Thomas Trenchard, Knight, of Wolverton, was born in 1582, died 1657; he was knighted by King James I, December 14, 1613, and held the office of high sheriff of Dorset; he was the founder of the branch of the family at present under consideration. His son Thomas is referred to below.

(II) Thomas (2), son of Sir Thomas (1) Trenchard, was born in Wolverton, county Dorset, in 1615, died in 1671. Like his father he was a baronet. In 1638 he married Hannah, born 1620, died 1691, daughter of Robert Henley, of Bramhill, Hampshire. Their son John is referred to below. Two of his cousins, Grace Trenchard, who married Colonel William Sydenham, and Jane, who married John Sadler, of Wardwell, were strong supporters of Oliver Cromwell.

(III) John, son of Sir Thomas (2) and Hannah (Henley) Trenchard, was born in Wolverton, county Dorset, England, March 30, 1640, died in 1695. He matriculated from New College, Oxford, in 1665. He was elected a member of Parliament for Taunton.

February 20, 1678, and was a member of the club of Revolutionaries which met at the King's Head Tavern in Fleet street. November 2, 1680, he spoke against the recognition by parliament of the Duke of York as the heir apparent, and in July, 1683, he was arrested as a conspirator, but released for lack of evidence. In 1687 William Penn, who was a warm personal friend of Trenchards, obtained from King James II a free pardon for Sir John and he was again elected to parliament. He was one of those who united in the invitation to William of Orange to come over and seize the English throne. October 29, 1689, he was knighted at Whitehall and was appointed to the office of chief justice of Chester, which he held until his death. In November, 1682, John Trenchard married Philippa, daughter of George Speake, and the sister of Charles and Hugh Speake, by whom he had four sons, one of whom is George, referred to below.

(IV) George, son of John and Philippa (Speake) Trenchard, was born in county Somerset, New York, in 1686, died at Alloway township, Salem county, New Jersey, in 1712. He was probably married and had several children. In his will he names as his children: George, Edward, John, Joan.

(V) George (2), son of George (1) Trenchard, died in Salem county, in the latter part of 1728. Coming to America with his father he settled in Salem county, and from 1723 to 1725 was sheriff. He was also one of the deputy sheriffs for West Jersey and also one of the assessors. By his marriage with Mary Bender, of Salem county, he had five sons and several daughters. The daughters married into several of the leading families of Salem and have left numerous descendants. The sons were: 1. Curtis, born 1740, died 1780; from 1778 to 1779 clerk of Salem county, later surrogate. He married the daughter of Attorney Burchan, of Salem. His son Edward was in the United States navy, commanded the "Constitution" at the siege of Tripoli and the "Madison" in the war of 1812 and other famous men-of-war. 2. John, referred to below. 3. James. 4. George, born 1748, died 1780; was attorney-general of West Jersey from 1769 to 1776, prominent in the Salem committee of safety and the Camden Second Battalion, Salem Country Light Horse, and one of those to whom Colonel Mawhood's letter was addressed. He married Mary, daughter of Judge Andrew Sinnickson, of Salem. 5. Thomas.

(VI) John (2), son of George (2) and Mary (Bender) Trenchard, was born in 1742. He lived for a time at Cohansey Bridge, and about 1768 with his brother bought a property at the northwest corner of Laurel and Jefferson streets, which was afterwards owned by James Boyd, at the commencement of the revolution, where for several years afterwards Mr. Boyd's widow resided and kept a store there. In 1769 they sold this property and afterwards removed to Fairfield, where he died in 1823. He was twice married. His first wife was Theodosia Ogden, by whom he had ten children, three sons and seven daughters. The sons were 1. John, referred to below. 2. Curtis. 3. Richard.

(VII) John (3), son of John (2) and Theodosia (Ogden) Trenchard, died in 1863. In early life he worked as a blacksmith with Curtis Edwards, whose shop was situated on the old road from Bridgeton and Fairfield to Rocap's Run. He continued in that employment four or five years, and then went into business at Fairton, keeping store with Daniel P. Stratton. When Mr. Stratton removed to Bridgeton in 1814 John Trenchard continued business, sometimes alone and sometimes with a partner for twenty years, being engaged in building vessels and in getting lumber and shipping same to Philadelphia, this being at that time a highly profitable business. He also sent produce to Bermuda. In 1843 he purchased from David Clark the mill property at Fairton and in 1845 moved the mill to its present site, where by close attention to business he amassed a very considerable estate. During all his life he was most highly esteemed by his associates. In early life he was a Democrat and a supporter of John Quincy Adams rather than Jackson and became a Whig. In 1827-28 he was elected a member of the New Jersey legislature.

John Trenchard married (first), in 1803, Eleanor Davis, who bore him seven children. Married (second) Hannah L. Pearson, in 1816. She bore him thirteen children. Ten of these children died in infancy. Children of John and Eleanor (Davis) Trenchard to reach maturity were: 1. James Howell, referred to below. 2. Ethan, twice married, his second wife being a Miss Diament. 3. Eleanor. Children of John and Hannah L. (Pearson) Trenchard who reached maturity were: 4. John, M. D., of Philadelphia, married (first) Mary Olnsted and (second) a Miss Booth. 5. Theophilus, of Bridgeton, New Jersey. 6. Emily, married the Hon. George

S. Whiticar, of Fairton. 7. Rufus, married Sarah Jane Bennett. 8. Nancy, married the Rev. David Meeker, a Presbyterian minister. 9. John, died unmarried. 10. Henry Clay (q. v.).

(VIII) James Howell, son of the Hon. John (3) and Eleanor (Davis) Trenchard, was born May 20, 1811, in Fairton, New Jersey, died February 27, 1877, after a severe illness of about ten days duration. He went into the mercantile business soon after his marriage, having purchased the interest of his father-in-law, Judge Barrett, which he continued for a time until he removed to Centreville (now Centreton) in the fall of 1839, where he entered largely into the general store and milling business and the lumber trade. In early life he was for a while under the Rev. Dr. George Junkin, of Easton, Pennsylvania. He had a liking for mathematics and soon began surveying in this branch, abounding in intricate cases in great land try-outs. In the fall of 1848 Mr. Trenchard was elected to the New Jersey assembly on the Whig ticket. He was very popular in his own neighborhood and received the votes of many in the township whose policies were opposed to his purely from personal considerations. He refused to run a second time, the corruption of the lobby and the questionable character of a large part of the public and private legislature as then and since directed having no charms for one of his honest, frank and independent manner. At this time Mr. Trenchard was very frequently called upon to find old searches, to settle disputes as to title and to act as commissioner, also to engage in surveying whenever wanted. He did not give his whole attention to these matters until he removed to Bridgeton in the spring of 1863. Here his son was with the firm of J. H. and W. B. Trenchard, surveyors, which was then one of the most prominent ones in that section of the state. No person in New Jersey had done more practical surveying or tramped more miles in all weathers and under all conditions than had this James H. Trenchard. At various times he had had many of the most valuable papers in his possession relating to the lands in the lower counties of the state. Consequently he became thoroughly conversant with the title, butts, bounds, courses and descriptions and all other matters relating to lower Jersey's real estate. He always carefully preserved copies of maps of all surveys made by him, and these are of very great use to persons asking information in regard to landed property. He possessed great natural kindness of heart and was generous in his impulses, which rallied around him earnest friends. Not the least of his merits was his unflinching patriotism. At the time of his death he was city surveyor, a position which he had long held. As such he established the present grade of the Bridgeton streets, and also at the time of his death was serving his second term as councilman from the second ward. He was president of the Bridgeton Water Works of Bridgeton, New Jersey, and a forerunner in the movement which secured the city's present water works.

The Hon. James Howell Trenchard married Mary, daughter of Judge William D. Barrett, of Fairton, New Jersey, who was born in 1815 and who bore him four sons and three daughters. Three sons and two of the daughters married. The other one died unmarried. Children: 1. Richard, who was killed, as was also his wife, July 30, 1896, in the Meadow disaster, Atlantic City, leaving five children. 2. William B. 3. James W. 4. Thomas W., died aged fourteen. 5. Eleanor, married J. T. Williams, of Philadelphia; she is deceased. 6. Jeanette, married Charles R. Elmer, now deceased; she lives in Riverton, New Jersey. 7. Araminta, died in infancy.

(IX) William Barrett, second son of James Howell and Mary (Barrett) Trenchard, was born at Centreton, Salem county, New Jersey, October 1, 1840, and is now living in Bridgeton, New Jersey. For his early education he was sent to the Centreton public schools, and after leaving school went into the milling business with his father at Centreton, New Jersey. His health failing, however, he gave this up and for the next four years went on a farm. After this he spent six years in a general store at Fairton, New Jersey, and then for the following twenty years worked with his father as a surveyor. In 1889 Mr. Trenchard was elected county clerk of Cumberland county, New Jersey. Five years later he was re-elected to the same position, and in 1899, when his second term of five years had expired, he declined to accept a re-nomination to a third term, but retired into private life to spend the remainder of his days in comfort at his beautiful home in Bridgeton. Besides this residence, which is one of the finest in the town, Mr. Trenchard has also near Bridgeton a fine farm, which he cultivates with profit, both to his pocket and his health and strength, and from which he derives the keenest sort of enjoyment. Mr. Trenchard is a Republican in politics, and besides his service as county clerk

James W. Trenchard

he has served three terms as justice of the peace of Bridgeton, and for six years as one of the chosen freeholders of Cumberland county. He is an Independent in religion, an Odd Fellow, past grand chancellor of the Knights of Pythias, in New Jersey, and one of the few honorary members of the Grand Army of the Republic, that honor having been conferred on him by Post No. 42—"Robeson Post"—of Bridgeton, New Jersey.

William Barrett Trenchard married Anna Mariah Golder, daughter of Samuel Golder, and has one son, Thomas Whitaker.

(For ancestry see preceding sketch).

(IX) James Whitaker TRENCHARD Trenchard, son of James Howell and Mary (Barrett) Trenchard, was born at Centreton, Salem county, New Jersey, September 17, 1843. For his early education he attended the Centreton public schools, after leaving which he went into a general country store where he remained until the outbreak of the civil war, when he enlisted in the Twenty-fifth New Jersey Volunteer Infantry and was commissioned as sergeant of Company D, and served through the full nine months of his term of enlistment, being mustered out of the service June 20, 1863. Among the engagements and battles in which he took part were the battle of Fredericksburg and the engagement near Suffolk and Chancellorsville, Virginia, which drove General Longstreet into retreat. After being mustered out Mr. Trenchard returned to the general store as a clerk, and in 1870 became a clerk in the Cumberland National Bank of Bridgeton, in which institution he remained in various positions until 1883, when he became the cashier of the Bridgeton National Bank, a position which he held until 1903, when his worth and services were recognized by his unanimous election as president of the bank, a position which he has held to the great satisfaction of everyone ever since. Mr. Trenchard's political affiliations are with the Democratic party; he attends the Presbyterian church, and is an Odd Fellow, a past grand master of that order in New Jersey. He is also a member and past commander of the A. L. Robeson Post, Grand Army of the Republic. He is also recording secretary of the Second Battalion, Veteran Association, Twenty-fifth Regiment, New Jersey Volunteers. Among the financial institutions in which he is identified mention should

not be omitted of the West Jersey Marl & Transportation Company.

James Whitaker Trenchard married (first) Gertrude C., daughter of Levi Bond, of Bridgeton, New Jersey, who died in 1882, leaving one son, Frank Fisk, born May 5, 1870, died June 11, 1894. He married (second) April 14, 1885, Amanda M. Powell, a widow, of Fairton, New Jersey.

(For preceding generations see Thomas Trenchard 1).

(VIII) Henry Clay, youngest child of John (3) TRENCHARD and Hannah L. (Pearson) Trenchard, was born at Fairton, New Jersey, August 5, 1837, and is now living at Fairton. For his early education he was sent to the public schools of Fairton, and then went into the milling business with his father. In addition to this, he started a tanning business, and also conducted his farm. Mr. Trenchard is one of two surviving members of his father's family of ten children. Like his ancestors, he has always been devoted to the service of the community in which he lived, and served for many years on the township committee of Fairton. January 15, 1900, he received his first appointment as postmaster at Fairton, and he has been reappointed in 1904 and still holds the office. He is a Presbyterian and a member of the Improved Order of Red Men.

Henry Clay Trenchard married (first) Susan Jane Gilman, who bore him four children, one of whom is living. He married (second) Emma, daughter of Benjamin Shawn, of Fairton, New Jersey. His children by his first wife were: 1. Laura Anna, now deceased; married Leslie M. Ogden and had four children; the living children are Claude and Reed, and those deceased were George and Harry. 2. Eva M., married Belford Stathems, and has one child, Floy. 3. George Decatur, died at the age of nineteen years. 4. Ida Gilman, died aged nine years.

The Rush family has a long and RUSH distinguished history behind it in the old country. It is distinctly an English family.

(I) John Rush, the earliest known ancestor of the American branch, commanded a troop of horse in Cromwell's army. At the close of the war he married Susan Lucas, at Hortau, in Oxfordshire, June 8, 1648. In 1660 he embraced the principals of the Quakers, and in 1683 came to Pennsylvania with seven children and several grandchildren, settling at Byberry, thirteen miles from Philadelphia. In 1691 he and his whole family became Keithians, and in 1697 most of them became Baptists. He died at Byberry, May, 1699. His sword is in the possession of Jacob Rush, and his watch in the family of General William Darke, of Virginia. His children were: 1. Elizabeth, born June 16, 1649; married Richard Collet, emigrated to Philadelphia, 1682, in the same ship as William Penn. 2. William, referred to below. 3. Thomas, March 7, 1654, died in London, 4th month, 18, 1676. 4. Susanna, December 26, 1656; married John Hart, emigrated to Pennsylvania, where her husband became a member of the first assembly called by William Penn. 5. John, 3rd month, 1, 1660, married and had issue. 6. Francis, 2nd month, 8, 1662. 7. James, 7th month, 21, 1664, and buried 1st month, 24, 1671. 8. Joseph, 10 month, 20, 1666. 9. Edward, 9 month, 27, 1670. 10. Jane, 12 month, 27, 1673.

(II) William, second child and eldest son of John and Susan (Lucas) Rush, was born November 7, 1652, died at Byberry, Pennsylvania, 1688, five years after his arrival to this country. He was twice married, and according to some accounts the name of his first wife was Aurelia. That of his second wife is unknown. By his first wife he had three children and by his second, two. Children: 1. Susanna, married (first) John Webster, and (second) a Mr. Gilbert. 2. James, referred to below. 3. Elizabeth, married Timothy Stephenson, who after her death married Rachel, widow of his brother-in-law, James Rush, by the consent of the senate of New York. 4. Sarah, married David Meredith. 5. William, married Elizabeth Hodges, and died January 31, 1733, at Boston.

(III) James, second child and eldest son of William and Amelia Rush, died in 1727. He lived on a farm in Poquessing creek. By his wife Rachel, the youngest daughter of Bryan Peart, who afterwards married the widow of her husband's sister, Timothy Stephenson, referred to above. James Rush had nine children: 1. John, referred to below. 2. William, married and had two children, William and John. 3. Joseph. 4. James. 5. Thomas. 6. Rachel. 7. Ann, married John Ashmead. 8. Elizabeth, married Edward Cary. 9. Aurelia, died young.

(IV) John (2), eldest child of James and Rachel (Peart) Rush, married Susan Harvey,

formerly Hall, daughter of Joseph Hall, of Tacony. Children: 1. Rebecca, married Thomas Stamper. 2. Benjamin, M. D., the celebrated physician and signer of the Declaration of Independence: married Julia, sister of Richard Stockton, of New Jersey, a signer of the Declaration, with his brother-in-law. 3. Jacob, married a Miss Rench. 4. Stephen, or Stephenson, referred to below. 5. John, died young.

(V) Stephen, or Stephenson, fourth child and third son of John (2) and Susan (Hall) (Harvey) Rush, was born in what was called the Skip-Back, Collegeville, Montgomery county, Pennsylvania. He kept the old hotel in the town, and was also for many years the proprietor of the Old Swan Hotel on Third street, Philadelphia, where he was living in 1774. By his wife Mary he had the following children: 1. John, referred to below. 2. Stephen. 3. Jacob, now living in Philadelphia. 4. Harry, living in Ogontz, Pennsylvania. 5. George, living in Concordville, Delaware county, Pennsylvania. 6. Samuel, living in Media, Delaware county, Pennsylvania. 7. Katharine, died at the age of one hundred and two years. 8. Margaret, now living at Norristown, Pennsylvania, in her one hundred and fourth year. 9. Sarah. 10. Mary. 11. Elizabeth. 12. Lydia.

(VI) John (3), son of Stephen or Stephenson and Mary Rush, was born at Skip-Back, Collegeville, Montgomery county, Pennsylvania. February 22, 1814. He was a carpenter and builder, and was engaged in business in Philadelphia for fifty years. He married Katharine Mathilda, daughter of Samuel Yarger, of Reading, Pennsylvania, who was born 1826. Children: Sarah, Eveline, Katharine, Jacob, Stephen Yarger, Joseph B., Johanna, Jerome Samuel, referred to below, Rosalie, Henry P.

(VII) Jerome Samuel, eighth child and fifth son of John (3) and Katharine Mathilda (Yarger) Rush, was born in Fegleysville, Montgomery county, Pennsylvania, May 8, 1858, and is now living at Ocean City, New Jersey. For his early education he went to the public schools of Philadelphia, after leaving which as a boy he went to work in one of the wholesale cotton warehouses of that city. This work he gave up in order to become a news agent, which occupation he pursued on a number of railroads of the United States. After this he embarked in the business of fresco painter and sign writer. In the pursuit of this last business he came to Ocean

City, New Jersey, May 10, 1890; six years later he entered in the real estate business in that town. He has been very active in politics, and in everything which makes for the welfare of the town in which he lives. In 1897 he was appointed sealer of weights and measures of Ocean City, which office he still continues to hold. In 1904 he was elected overseer of the poor of Ocean City, and the same year was elected one of the justices of the peace, which latter office he still continues to hold. For two years he was chief of the Ocean City volunteer fire department, and for three years foreman of the No. 1. volunteer fire company of Ocean City. He is a Republican, and is now serving a third term, and his twelfth year as commissioner of the state of Pennsylvania, in New Jersey. He attends the Presbyterian church. In secret societies and fraternal organizations he has taken a prominent part. He is a member of the Improved Order of Red Men, Kalmia Tribe, No. 220, of Ocean City, of which he is past sachem, and of the Loyal Order of Moose, Lodge No. 116, Atlantic City. He is also a member of the International Fire Engineers' Association, New Jersey Fire Chiefs' Association and Keystone Fire Chiefs' Association.

Jerome Samuel Rush married, April 21, 1887, Mary Cottingham, second daughter of the Rev. Edward Townsend, a Methodist minister, whose family is one of the oldest of the early pioneers of Virginia. On the maternal side she is a lineal descendant of the family of the poet, Thomas Moore, and Sir John Moore. On both sides her patriot ancestry give her a right to membership in the organizations of the Daughters of the Revolution and the Colonial Dames. A son born of this marriage died in infancy.

TOWNSEND In 1681 William Penn obtained from the Crown a grant of the immense territory now embraced in the state of Pennsylvania, in lieu of a monetary claim against the Crown for sixteen thousand pounds left to him by his father, Admiral Sir William Penn, on his death in September, 1670. Had Penn been allowed his own way, he would have called the territory Sylvania, by reason of its beautiful forests, but the King, Charles II, good humoredly insisted on the prefix of Penn, hence Pennsylvania. Penn's great project was to establish a home for his co-religionists in the New World where they might freely preach and practice their convictions unmolested.

Penn, with several of his most intimate friends, leaders of the sect in England, embarked on the ship "Welcome" September 1, 1682, and landed on the west bank of the Delaware river at New Castle, Delaware, October 24, 1682, and was received by the members of the Society of Friends. who had preceded him and were settlers on both sides of the river, but principally in Burlington county, West Jersey. With Penn came two of his nearest friends, Richard and Robert Townsend, and they were with Penn on November 30, 1682, when the famous interview with the Indian tribes took place under the large elm tree at Sackamaxon, now Kensington, and when he planned and named the city of Philadelphia.

Richard Townsend, born in 1644, settled at Westchester, about twenty miles west of Philadelphia, where he built a saw and grist mill, carried on his trade of millwright, preached the Quaker doctrine, experienced the usual vicissitudes experienced in pioneer life and gained the respect of every one with whom he came in contact. He died in 1714. leaving one child, a daughter.

His brother, Joseph, came to America later with another brother, William, settled in Philadelphia in 1712 and is the ancestor of Joseph B.. Henry C. and J. William Townsend of that city. John Kirk Townsend (1809-1851), born in Philadelphia, was an associate of J. J. Audubon and assisted him in the preparation of his "American Ornithology." He also accompanied Thomas Nuttall on his journey west of the Mississippi river, across the Rocky mountains to the Columbia river and later visited the Sandwich Islands and South America in pursuit of his profession. He also had charge of the ornithological department of the Smithsonian Institution at Washington, District of Columbia, and was a member of the Philadelphia Academy of Natural Sciences. He is of the same Quaker ancestry as is Hon. Lawrence Townsend, 1811 Walnut street, Philadelphia, United States minister to Portugal, 1897-99. and to Belgium, 1899-1905.

William Townsend, who lived in Philadelphia, 1712-15, settled near Westchester in 1725 and advanced the cause of righteousness and peace as promulgated by the Society of Friends in that place, taking up the work unfinished by his brother, Richard. It was Robert Townsend, the companion of William Penn and Richard Townsend on the ship "Welcome," who was probably the ancestor of the Townsends of Burlington county, New Jersey.

Robert Townsend, one of the four sons of Richard Townsend, of Cirencester, Gloucestershire, England, was born probably in 1646 and sailed in 1682 on the ship "Welcome" in company with William Penn and his own brother, Richard, to assist in the founding of Pennsylvania. He located at Germantown, now a part of Philadelphia, and the place grew rapidly, receiving large accessions from the Quakers and other immigrants who came not only from England but largely from the German Palatinate and from Holland, hence the name, Germantown. His grandson probably lived in Springfield township, Burlington county, New Jersey, had a wife Betsey and seven children: Jonathan, Daniel, Benjamin, Firmon, Hope, Ann, Elizabeth. He was a farmer and leading member of the Society of Friends.

(I) Firmon, fourth son and fourth child of ———— and Betsey Townsend, was born in Springfield township, Burlington county, New Jersey, about 1810, and was a wheelwright in Columbus, as well as a farmer and lumberman. His position in the township as a member of the Society of Friends, as a mechanic, as a lumberman and as a useful and quiet citizen appears to have been universally conceded. He was an anti-slavery Whig and on the formation of the Republican party, which absorbed the Free Soil advocates, he naturally found his political home in that party. He was married by Friends Ceremony about 1832-33, to Amy, daughter of David Taylor. Children: John B., Barclay B., Charles H.

(II) John B., eldest child of Firmon and Amy (Taylor) Townsend, was born in Columbus, Burlington county, New Jersey, December 31, 1834. He was a pupil in the public school of Mansfield township, was brought up on his father's farm, and was like his father an Anti-slavery Whig and on the birth of the Republican party a member of that political organization. His only public offices were those of deputy-sheriff of Burlington county, 1893-96, under appointment from his son, who was high sheriff of the county, and member of the board of township committeemen, but he did not allow his public duties to prevent his close attention to his extensive farming interests. He was affiliated with Columbus Lodge, Independent Order of Odd Fellows; Columbus Tribe, Improved Order of Red Men; Columbus Sub Council, Order of United American Mechanics. He married (first) October 23, 1856, Abigail, daughter of William E. and Mary Ann Atkinson, of Springfield

township. She was born September 12, 1833, died August 6, 1896. Children: 1. William A. 2. Clara, married John B. Colkitt, a farmer of Mansfield township, and is now deceased. 3. Charles Firmon, lived on the old homestead and died there October 24, 1903. 4. Ella, married William E. Shinn. He married (second) January 24, 1897, Annie, daughter of Robert G. and Mary Elizabeth Buckis.

(III) William A., eldest child of John B. and Abigail (Atkinson) Townsend, was born in Springfield township, Burlington county, New Jersey, November 27, 1859. He was educated in the public schools near Jacksonville, and remained on the farm with his father until he was twenty-one years of age. He then engaged in farming on his own account in Mansfield township and continued until 1893, when he was elected high sheriff of Burlington county, holding the office until November, 1896. He then purchased the homestead formerly owned by his maternal grandfather, William E. Atkinson, and engaged in farming, which line of work he followed successfully for the following eleven years, during which time in connection therewith he engaged in the coal and feed business in company with S. R. Ware in Columbus, New Jersey, the management of the business being conducted by Mr. Ware. In January, 1908, upon the death of Mr. Ware, Mr. Townsend removed to Columbus and purchased the interest of the widow of Mr. Ware, and is now extensively engaged in that business. He is also serving in the capacity of director in the Mt. Holly National Bank, and for the convenience of the citizens of Columbus and surrounding localities Mr. Townsend conducts a private banking business in that village. He has served as a member of the township committee for three years and as district clerk of the board of education for three years. He is a member of Lodge No. 117, American Mechanics' Association; Columbus Lodge, No. 101, Independent Order of Odd Fellows; Mt. Holly Lodge, No. 848, Benevolent and Protective Order of Elks. He is a Republican in politics.

Mr. Townsend married, January 19, 1880, Rebecca, born in Burlington county, New Jersey, September 4, 1861, daughter of Charles A. and Rebecca (Antram) Braddock, the former a son of Jacob Braddock, of Medford, Burlington county, and the latter a daughter of John Antram, a representative of an old family of Burlington county. Children of Mr. and Mrs. Townsend: 1. Mabel, born July 31, 1881; married Clifford R. Bowers, of Mt.

Holly, New Jersey; one child, Rhea. 2. Floyd, January 28, 1883; attended Mt. Holly high school and Trenton Business College; now a rural mail carrier; married Julia Poinsett, of Columbus, New Jersey. 3. Lottie, March, 1885, died eight years of age. 4. Augustus, January 12, 1888; educated in the public schools and Trenton Business College; received instruction as a taxidermist through a correspondence school at Omaha, Nebraska. 5. Clara, February 16, 1893. 6. Bessie, December 28, 1896. 7. Charles Stanley, January 16, 1900.

TOWNSEND This name has been common in New Jersey and Long Island for several generations. The first of the name who attained prominence was Henry Townsend, who for the sake of his religion underwent many persecutions and indignities. They have almost without exception been Friends or Quakers, and held in high regard by their associates, marrying generally into their own sect.

(I) William Townsend, the pioneer ancestor of the family, came to America in 1793, landing in New York. He married and became the father of five children, namely: Thomas, William, John, Mary, Samuel, see forward.

(II) Samuel, youngest son of William Townsend, was born in New York. He removed to Philadelphia, Pennsylvania, where he was a real estate dealer.

He married Anna, daughter of Thomas and Margaret (Van Hook) Vaughan, and they were the parents of eight children, namely: George Nathaniel, Henry Birman, Thomas Vaughan, see forward, Anna, William, Samuel Jr., Mary Ella, Lizza.

(III) Thomas Vaughn, son of Samuel Townsend, was born in Philadelphia, Pennsylvania, March 4, 1840. He married, February 23, 1863, Jessemine Button, of Baltimore, born September 4, 1845. They are the parents of eight children, all living: 1. James Vaughan, born at Baltimore, married Hattie Martin, of Atlantic City, New Jersey; they have two children: Ruth and Margaret. 2. Aramittie, born at Baltimore. Maryland. married Ulric Skirven, of Baltimore, Maryland; no children. 3. Mary Ella, born at Baltimore, Maryland, see forward. 4. Samuel Delmar, born at Baltimore, Maryland, married Claude Riddell, of Williamsport, Pennsylvania; one son, Delmar. 5. Laura Jane,

born at Baltimore, Maryland, married Von Mark Kleman, of Philadelphia, Pennslyvania; have one child, Jessamine. 6. Ida May, born at Philadelphia, Pennsylvania. 7. Harry Birman, born at Philadelphia, Pennsylvania, married Hannah Fenton, of Atlantic City, New Jersey. 8. Walter Rogers, born at Limerick Square, Pennsylvania, married Elizabeth Oakley, of Atlantic City, New Jersey.

(IV) Mary Ella, daughter of Thomas Vaughan Townsend, was born at Baltimore, Maryland, June 24, 1868. She received her early education in the public schools and academy of Atlantic City, New Jersey, receiving a diploma from the latter. In 1890 she entered the Womans Medical College of Pennsylvania, and in 1895 graduated with degree of Doctor of Medicine. She began the general practice of her profession at Atlantic City in 1895. She frequently writes able articles for the various medical journals on some subject which has become of special interest in the course of her practice. She is a member of the American Medical Association and the Atlantic County Medical Association, and keeps abreast of the times in all matters pertaining to her chosen profession. Dr. Townsend is unmarried.

WHITE The sufferings and persecutions of non-conformists to the Church of England during the reign of Charles II caused many British members of the Society of Friends to seek in the colonies that liberty of conscience which had been denied them in the mother country. Among those who suffered under the "Non-Conformity and Conventicle Acts" of that reign were Thomas White, of Cumrew, county of Cumberland, and Christopher White, his son, then of London.

(I) Christopher White was born at Cumrew, Cumberland county, England, in 1642, removed to London in 1666, and in 1668 married Hester Biddle, born at Poplar, in Stepney parish, nigh London, whose father was John Wieat. In 1677 Christopher White, his wife, their two children and two servants, sailed for America in the ship "Kent," and landed at Salem, New Jersey, June 23 of that year. Like several other immigrants, he purchased one town lot in Salem with one thousand acres of farm lands before leaving England. He continued to live at Salem until 1682, and then took possession of his allotment of land at Alloways creek. In 1690 he built a large brick house on his property, and the king's highway from Salem to Cohansey ran through his lands. There is a tradition in the family that he sent to England for architectural plans from which his house was built, and also that the bricks used in its construction were imported. Christopher White died about the year 1693. He appears to have been an energetic man of high moral character, and those traits were transmitted to his descendants for several generations after him. He left a widow Hester and five children: Hester, Thomas, Sarah, Josiah and Joseph.

. (II) Josiah, son of Christopher White, was born in England, 7mo 13, 1675, and lived on the farm previously owned by his father at Alloways creek, where he died May 1, 1713, leaving his landed estate to his son Josiah. He married, when about twenty-three, Hannah, daughter of Joseph Powell, and by her had five children: 1. Christopher, born 23 6mo. 1699, died before attaining his majority. 2. Josiah, mentioned in succeeding paragraph. 3. Hester, born 1707. 4. Hannah, born at Alloways creek, 1710. 5. Abigail, born 1713.

(III) Josiah (2), son of Josiah (1) and Hannah White, was born 6 mo., 21, 1705, and died 5 mo., 12, 1780. He was a man of marked enterprise, and it was he who built the dam across Alloways creek and put a sufficient sluiceway to drain all the lowlands above what afterward was known as Hancock's bridge. This work was undertaken in 1728, and his work was guaranteed to stand for one year before he received his pay. Before the end of the year the dam broke, and a tradition says that it was purposely cut on the night before the year expired. However this may have been, Josiah White was compelled to sell his large patrimonial estate to pay the debt incurred in erecting works for the benefit of others. At that time he was only twenty-three years old, and many persons in the same adversity would have been discouraged, but not so with him who had inherited from his father and grandfather those qualities which enabled him to withstand more than ordinary trials. After disposing of his estate he had five hundred pounds left, and then determined to leave his native county, not having any family. He removed to Burlington county, and settled at or near Mt. Holly, and there purchased land on the headwaters of Rancocas creek. Soon afterward he constructed a dam across that stream, then built a fulling mill and carried on the business of making cloth during the greater part of his later life. He was a minister of the Society of Friends, and many

incidents are related of his plain and truthful speech, his skill in the treatment of disease with roots and herbs, his generosity in refusing pay for any of his medical services, and his honesty in every walk of life. When, during the revolutionary war, the British and Hessian troops were at Mt. Holly, in 1777, a large field of employment was opened for his benevolence. He administered to their infirmities and diseases such simple remedies as he found to be effectual, and many of those relieved by him sought in various ways to show their gratitude. He then took occasion to reason with them on the principles upon which their unhallowed war was conducted, and by presenting the matter in its true light brought many of them to consider how wicked it was for them to come thousands of miles with guns, swords and cannon to kill their fellow creatures; and he said to them: "Even me, who have been so willing and ready to assist you in sickness and relieve your disorders and afflictions, you came to destroy with the rest." He was very firm in his opposition to human slavery in every form, and from early manhood, whenever opportunity offered, labored privately with persons holding slaves in order to effect emancipation. In this and other matters of benefit to his fellowmen his practice was consistent with his profession, and he most carefully rejected any dyestuffs which had a tendency to injure the cloth, and all articles in the manufacture of which slave labor entered or by which health might be impaired.

Josiah White married, 10 mo., 1, 1734, Rebecca, daughter of Josiah and Amie Foster (nee Borden) of one of Burlington county's best old families, and a descendant of the Borden family from whom Bordentown, on the Delaware river, receives its name. She was born 10 mo., 1, 1708, and bore her husband six children: 1. Amy, born 5 mo., 13, 1737, died young. 2. Hannah, born 11 mo., 28, 1739, married (first) 1762, Thomas Prior, (second) Daniel Drinker, 1796. 3. Josiah, born 4 mo., 2, 1743, died 5 mo., 31, 1745. 4. Rebecca, born 3 mo., 15, 1745, married Thomas Redman. 5. John, born 7 mo., 9. 1747, see forward. 6. Joseph, born 8 mo., 22, 1750, died young.

(IV) John, son of Josiah (2) and Rebecca (Foster) White, was born 7 mo., 9, 1747, died 8 mo., 22, 1785, aged about thirty-eight years. He married, 6 mo., 7, 1775, Rebecca, daughter of Jeremiah Haines, of Burlington county. She was born 7 mo., 27, 1744, and died 3 mo., 22,

1826, having borne her husband four children: 1. John, grew to manhood and died unmarried. 2. Christopher, died unmarried. 3. Josiah, born 3 mo., 14, 1781. 4. Joseph, see forward.

(V) Joseph, youngest child of John and Rebecca (Haines) White, was born in Mt. Holly, 12 mo., 28, 1785. Soon after marriage he entered into a partnership with Samuel Lippincott in the hardware business in Philadelphia. In 1811 he left that city on horseback with the intention of travelling into the south and southwest as far as St. Louis, for the purpose of collecting moneys due his firm; and while in Brownsville, Pennsylvania, he observed a man standing in the door of a store, whose garb indicated that he was a Friend. He entered the store to purchase some trivial article, and there made the acquaintance of the Friend whom he saw, and whose name was Elisha Hunt, with whom Joseph White afterward had a long business association. On that evening he was asked to join the Hunt family circle, and there the proposition was made that if he (White) would give up his proposed western trip on horseback, and assist them in building and freighting a keelboat, Caleb Hunt would join him on the journey to St. Louis, and such an arrangement was agreed upon. In the spring of 1812 Joseph White and Caleb Hunt, with a crew of French Canadian boatmen, started their keelboat from Brownsville, bound for St. Louis, Missouri. "During the previous 11th month an earthquake, which is known as 'the earthquake of New Madrid,' had changed and rent the banks of the Ohio River." As far as the mouth of the Ohio the voyage was comparatively easy, but from the Ohio's mouth to St. Louis the passage became so difficult that the number of boatmen was required to be doubled. Returning by keelboat to the mouth of the Cumberland river, they then left their boat and on horseback returned to their respective homes. At Bowling Green, Kentucky, Mr. White records: "I fell in with the proprietor of a Cave (Mammoth Cave), who wanted me to purchase it; he asked $10,000. With five men he makes one hundred pounds of saltpetre per day; to make it costs him from five to six cents per pound; it is now worth twenty-five cents per pound in Lexington, Ky." In 1812 Joseph White and Elisha Hunt organized a company for purchasing the right of Daniel French in a device for propelling a boat by steam power, and when organized Mr. White owned one-third of the stock of the enterprise. The company acquired the privilege of operating French's patent west of the Alleghany mountains, and forthwith built shops at Brownsville, Pennsylvania, for the construction of the steamboat "Enterprise," which was built in the latter part of 1813, at a cost of $15,000, and which sailed from Pittsburgh, Pennsylvania, for New Orleans, under command of Captain Henry Shreve, son of Israel Shreve, of Burlington county, New Jersey, a colonel in the revolutionary army. On its arrival at New Orleans the "Enterprise" was seized by a marshal at the instance of Fulton and Livingston for coming within the limits of Louisiana, but a bond secured the release of the vessel and they returned up the river with a full cargo of freight and passengers, making the trip up the river to Pittsburgh in the short time of twenty-six days, this proving the practicability of navigating the Mississippi by steam. The "Enterprise" was the first steamboat that ever made a voyage from Pittsburgh to New Orleans and return. This pioneer vessel afterward had an eventful career, and on her second trip to New Orleans was pressed into government service by General Jackson and sent to Alexandria, on the Red river, with a cargo of army stores and provisions. Elisha Hunt died at Moorestown, New Jersey, at the age of almost ninety-four years. In a letter he wrote he says: "The little office connected with our Brownsville store was the rendezvous of many intelligent and enterprising young men, and there all the recent inventions for travel were discussed. Among our regular visitors were Neil Gillespie Blaine (grandfather of James G. Blaine), Robert Clark, Stephen Darlington and others." Among other merchandise consigned to Joseph White by the Hunts for market in Philadelphia during the year 1813 or '14 was one barrel of "Seneca oil," gathered at Oil Creek, Pennsylvania, which was sold by Mr. White to Daniel Smith, druggist, of Philadelphia, for medicinal purposes. Mr. White was extensively engaged in coal operations in the Lackawanna and Schuylkill regions during the later years of his life, and he died in Philadelphia, 25 5 mo. 1827, aged forty-one years. He was one of the pioneers in developing the resources of the country in many directions, and in every respect was one of the foremost men of his day. His wife was Rebecca (Smith) White, and by her he had eight children: John J., Daniel S., Elizabeth, Sarah S., Anna, Howard, Barclay and Anna Maria White.

(VI) Barclay, youngest son of Joseph and

Rebecca (Smith) White, was born in Philadelphia, Pennsylvania, 4 mo., 4, 1821, and died November 23, 1906. He received his early education in public schools in his home town, later was a student under a private teacher, Daniel Smith, of Wilmington, Delaware, and still later attended a boarding school at Westown, Pennsylvania. However, he left school at the age of fifteen years and turned his attention to farming, and farming and agriculture were an important part of his business occupation in all subsequent years, although during several years of that period he was in the public service, and when not so engaged he devoted his time to conveyancing and management of trust estates in connection with farming interests. In 1871 he was appointed by President Grant superintendent of Indian affairs and went to Omaha, Nebraska, where he had full charge of six Indian agencies. He remained in the west six years in connection with the duties of his official position, then returned to Mt. Holly, N. J., and opened an office for conveyancing and the care of trust interests. He owned two large farms, of three hundred or four hundred acres, which were devoted chiefly to the production of hay and grain. He possessed decided literary tastes, and cultivated them fully and to good purpose even during the later years of his long and useful life; he wrote an autobiography after having passed his eightieth year. He was originally a strong Whig, and one of the organizers of the Republican party in the locality in which he lived. While never a seeker after political advancement, he held various local offices of minor importance to which he was chosen by fellow townsmen. Throughout the period of his life Mr. White never departed from the teachings of the Society of Friends under which he was brought up, and at one time he was assistant clerk of the Philadelphia Yearly Meeting.

He married (first) 12 mo., 22, 1842, Rebecca Merritt Lamb, of Springfield, New Jersey, who was born 3 mo., 22, 1824, and died 2 mo., 22, 1850 (see Lamb), by whom he had four children: 1. Howard, of Lansdowne, Pennsylvania. 2. Joseph J., of New Lisbon, New Jersey. 3. George Foster, president of Lansdowne Trust Company. 4. Barclay Jr., M. D., now dead. He married (second) in 1852, Beulah S. Shreve, by whom he had three children: 5. Daniel S., proprietor of the Traymore, Atlantic City, New Jersey. 6. Elizabeth, now dead. 7. James, now dead.

(VII) Joseph Josiah, son of Barclay and Rebecca Merritt (Lamb) White, was born in Springfield, New Jersey, January 22, 1846, and was educated at Jobstown, Aaron's school at Mt. Holly, Jackson's school at Darby, Pennsylvania, the boarding school of William A. Garrigues, near Moorestown, New Jersey, the Friends' Central school, Philadelphia, and the Philadelphia Polytechnic College. In 1867 he became a cranberry grower, and was thereafter closely identified with that industry, although somewhat actively interested in other business enterprises. In 1870 he wrote a book on "Cranberry Culture," which was published by Orange Judd, of New York, passed through two editions, and is still the standard work on that subject. Mr. White was a charter member of the American Society of Mechanical Engineers, having joined the society at its organization in 1880. He obtained letters patent of the United States for a number of useful inventions, among which was an improved journal box for which the Franklin Institute of Philadelphia awarded him the Longstreth Medal. On June 23, 1903, he received a patent for an improved machine for assorting and grading cranberries. This was the only machine ever devised that would successfully remove frosted from sound cranberries. Twenty-four of these separators were installed in his warehouse. In 1890 Mr. White in company with his brother, George Foster White, organized the Pennsylvania Machine Company of Philadelphia, and operated it as sole proprietors until 1895, when he sold his interest to his brother. After that date Mr. White devoted most of his time to cranberry culture, becoming one of the largest and most successful growers in the United States. He gave employment to six hundred and fifty people during the picking season, and in the years 1907-08 produced sixty thousand bushels of cranberries. He was president of the Growers' Cranberry Company during the first fourteen years of its existence. This co-operative sales company, with headquarters in Philadelphia, was organized by a number of the oldest and largest cranberry growers of New Jersey and New England, for the purpose of selling their fruit. He was vice-president of the Farmers' National Bank of New Jersey, at Mt. Holly. Mr. White was a Republican, having filled various township offices and served on township committees, yet he was in no sense a politician or seeker after political office. He was a Friend, having been president of the board of trustees of Mt. Holly Monthly Meeting.

On November 11, 1869, he married Mary

Joseph J. White

Anne, daughter of James A. and Mary E. (Cashell) Fenwick, and by whom he had seven children: 1. Rebecca M., now dead. 2. Elizabeth Coleman. 3. Mary Fenwick. 4. Beulah Sansom. 5. Joseph, now dead. 6. Barclay, now dead. 7. Anne Pearson, wife of Franklin S. Chambers, M. E., chief engineer of the Parker Boiler Company, Philadelphia.

(The Lamb Line).

Rebecca M. Lamb, who married Barclay White, 12 mo., 22, 1842, mother of Howard, Joseph J., George F. and Barclay White Jr., was descended from Alfred the Great through the Mauleverer line, of England (see the Mauleverer Chart in the library of the Historical Society of Pennsylvania). Her descent is as follows:

(I) Alfred the Great, born 849, died 901; married Elswitha.

(II) Princess Alfrith, died in 929; married Baldwin II of Flanders, died January 2, 918.

(III) Arnould I, of Flanders, died 964; married Alex of Vermandois.

(IV) Baldwin III, of Flanders, died 961; married Matilda, daughter of Herman, duke of Saxony.

.(V) Arnould II, of Flanders, died 988; married Roselle, daughter of Berengarius III, King of Italy.

(VI) Baldwin IV, of Flanders, died 1034; married Conegonde, of Luxemburg.

(VII) Baldwin V, of Flanders, died 1067; married Adele, daughter of Robert, King of France. Baldwin V aided his son-in-law William in the Conquest of England, 1066.

(VIII) William the Conqueror, born 1027, died 1087; married, 1052, Matilda of Flanders, born 1031, died 1083.

(IX) Henry I, born 1068, died 1135; married Matilda, born about 1077, died May 1, 1118, daughter of Malcolm and Margaret.

(X) Matilda, died 9mo 10 1167; married, 8mo 26 1127, Geoffrey Count of Anjou.

(XI) Henry II, born 1133, died 1189; married Eleanor of Acquitaine.

(XII) John, born 1167, died 1216; married Isabella of Acquitaine.

(XIII) Henry III, born 1207, died 1272; married Eleanor, daughter of Count of Provence.

(XIV) Edward I, born 1239, died 1307; married Eleanor, daughter of Alphonso X of Castile.

(XV) Edward II, born 1284, died 1327; married Isabella, daughter of Phillip II of France.

(XVI) Edward III, married Philippa, daughter of Count of Hainault.

Note.—There are twenty-six lines through which the Mauleverers are descended from Edward I, one of which only is here given, and all of which are to be found in "Burke's Peerages Extant and Extinct."

(XVII) John of Gaunt, Duke of Lancaster, fourth son of Edward III.

(XVIII) Lady Margaret, daughter of John of Gaunt, married Richard Nevill, first Earl of Westmoreland.

(XIX) Lady Alice, granddaughter of John of Gaunt, married Sir Thomas Gray de Heton.

(XX) Lady Elizabeth, married Philip, 4th Lord Darcy.

(XXI) Thomas, fifth Lord Darcy, married Margaret.

(XXII) Philip, sixth Lord Darcy.

(XXIII) Elizabeth, daughter of Philip sixth Lord Darcy, married James Strangwayes.

(XXIV) Eleanor Strangwayes, married Edmund Mauleverer, of Wothersome and Annecliffe, Yorkshire, will dated 10mo 7 1488.

(XXV) Robert Mauleverer, died 3mo 10 1495, will probated at York, 2 mo 25 1496; married Joane Vasasour, daughter of Sir Henry Vasasour of Haslewood, Knight.

(XXVI) Sir William Mauleverer, knighted at Flodden, 1513, married Anne Conyers, daughter of Sir William Conyers, of Stockburne.

(XXVII) Robert Mauleverer, second son and heir, buried January 31, 1540; married, 1524, Alice Markinfield, daughter of Sir Ninian Markinfield and Dorothy nee Gascoigne.

(XXVIII) Sir Edmund Mauleverer, buried 4mo 27 1571; married, 1541, Mary Danby, daughter of Sir Christopher Danby.

(XXIX) William Mauleverer, buried 1618, will executed 4mo 14 1618; married Eleanor Aldborough, born 1553, died 1644.

(XXX) James Mauleverer, born 2mo 1 1590, died 4mo 1664; married Beatrice Hutton, daughter of Sir Timothy Hutton, died about 1640-42.

(XXXI) Edmund Mauleverer, born 1630, died 11mo 28 1679; married, 3mo 1 1666, Anne Pearson, of Mowthorpe.

(XXXII) Anne Mauleverer, born 2mo 28 1678, died 2mo 17 1754; married, 3mo 26, 1696, John Abbott, born 1660, in Nottinghamshire, England, died 8mo 10 1739.

(XXXIII) Jane Abbott, born 3mo 9th

1701, died 1mo 3 1780; married, 12mo 16 1726, Joseph Birr, born 11mo 5, 1693, died 4mo 13 1767.

(XXXIV) Mary Birr, born 6mo 11 1729, died 1mo 17 1802; married, 11mo 20 1747, Solomon Ridgway, born 8mo 18 1723, died 1788.

(XXXV) Benjamin E. Ridgway, born 6mo 20 1770, died 4mo 14 1856; married, 8mo 17 1794, Pridence Borton Ridgway, born 12mo 25 1762, died 3mo 25 1854.

(XXXVI) Mary Ridgway, born 6mo 12 1795, died 3 mo 25 1837; married, 4mo 18 1822, Restore S. Lamb, born 12mo 27 1788, died 8mo 16 1867.

(XXXVII) Rebecca Merritt Lamb, born 3mo 22 1824, died 2mo 22 1850; married, 12mo 22 1842, Barclay White, born 4mo 4 1821, died 11mo 23 1906.

(XXXVIII) Joseph J. White, born 1mo. 22, 1846, married, 11mo. 11, 1869, Mary Anne Fenwick, born 9mo, 21, 1847. Their surviving children are: Elizabeth Coleman, Mary Fenwick, Beilah Sansom and Anne Pearson, the latter wife of Franklin S. Chambers, M. E.

BINDER

The ship "Francis and Elizabeth" arrived in Philadelphia, Pennsylvania, and September 21, 1742, her adilt male passengers qialified before the aithorities of the province of Pennsylvania. Among those male passengers were John, George, Jacob, see forward, and Moses Binder. The exact relationship that existed between these men is not known.

(I) Jacob Binder, or Bender as the name was sometimes written, was born in Oberisingen, Dichy of Wurtemberg, Germany, Janiary 19, 1736, died in Kensington (an outlying district of Philadelphia cointy, Pennsylvania, before the consolidation of the city in 1854), March 18, 1804. He emigrated to America and settled in Philadelphia, Pennsylvania, in 1754. The following records are taken from the archives of Pennsylvania, last edition, second series. He was a member of the Independent Troop of Horse and Independent Company of Foot, 1756, in the Provincial service. He was a private in Captain Campbell's company (Associators), City Giard, 1776; first lieitenant of Foirth Company, Third Battalion, (Associators) Colonel Morgan commanding; lieitenant of the Fifth Company, Second Battalion of militia, Lieutenant-Colonel Benjamin G. Eyre commanding, 1780. Jacob Binder married, Jily 28, 1767, Maria Weisbacken, this record appearing in

the Bible of William Binder, son of Jacob Binder, which is now in possession of the widow of Horace, brother of the Rev. Clarence K. Binder, of Camden, New Jersey, of whom this sketch treats. The record in the archives of Pennsylvania, last edition, second series, gives the date as Jily 27, 1767, and the name as Wisebaugh. Mr. and Mrs. Binder were the parents of a nimber of children among whom was William, see forward.

(II) William, son of Jacob Binder, was born in Philadelphia, Pennsylvania, April 24, 1768; died October 4, 1842, aged seventy-foir years, five months, eleven days. He was a citizen of Philadelphia throighoit his life. In 1806 he became associated with General Peter A. Mihlenberg, John Goodman and others in a society whose design was to indice the congregation of Sion and St. Michael's Evangelical Litheran Chirch (one corporation with two chirch edifices) to permit preaching in one of the two chirches in English every Sinday, and also to permit English catechetical instriction. William Binder acted as secretary of this society at its first meeting held Janiary 8, 1806, and continied in this office intil the following September when he was sicceeded by Isaac Wampole. The Germans contining obstinate in their refisal to permit any English services whatever, the society proceeded to organize "St. John's Evangelical Litheran Chirch of Philadelphia and Vicinity." This was the first siccessfil effort to establish a congregation of the Litheran faith, in which the English langiage was to be ised. William Binder was a hatter and firrier, and amassed qiite a large fortine for those days. He was honored by his fellow citizens to serve them for several terms in the Pennsylvania state legislatire. He married Mary Rice and among their children was William, see forward. The remains of William Binder, Sr., lies in St. John's birial groind, right behind the chirch, which is situated on the north side of Race street above Fifth street, Philadelphia. The stone that marked the spot was removed many years ago.

(III) William (2), son of William (1) Binder, was born in Philadelphia, Pennsylvania, December 14, 1793; died in 1860, and was biried in Lairel Hill Cemetery (Section O), Philadelphia. He married, prior to 1819, Loiisa Elizabeth Stam, who bore him a nimber of children among whom was George Augistis, see forward.

(IV) George Aigistis, son of William (2) Binder, was born Janiary 6, 1821; died August 13, 1894, and is buried in Section O, Laurel Hill Cemetery, Philadelphia. He carried on the lumber business in partnership with his elder brother, Jacob, under the firm name of J. & G. A. Binder. Their place of business was at the southeast corner of Sixth and Oxford streets, Philadelphia. They also had a saw mill and enjoyed a monopoly of the trunk and box board business for many years. George A. Binder retired from business in 1864, owing to impaired health, after which he became an active member of the Academy of Natural Sciences of Philadelphia. Shortly after attaining his majority he entered politics, and before the consolidation of the city in 1854 he was elected to several important offices in the old district of Penn, and was elected to represent the twentieth ward in the common branch of the first city council that was organized after the consolidation of the city. At the expiration of his term of office he declined re-election and retired from politics. Mr. Binder married Miriam, daughter of Jesse and Maria or Mary (Kunckel) Trump, and granddaughter of John Kunckel, a resident of Philadelphia, and a soldier in the American revolution, serving in a Pennsylvania regiment and wounded at the battle of Brandywine, September 11, 1777, at the time Lafayette was wounded in the leg and carried to Bethlehem where the Moravian sisters nursed him during his confinement. Among the children of George A. and Miriam (Trump) Binder was Clarence Kunckel, see forward.

(V) Clarence Kunckel Binder, son of George Augustus and Miriam (Trump) Binder, was born in Philadelphia, Pennsylvania, March 8, 1849. He attended the public schools of his native city up to his fifteenth year, when he entered the Pennsylvania Agricultural College known now as the Pennsylvania State College. He left at the end of his freshman year, and in 1865 became a pupil of Henry D. Gregory who has a school in Philadelphia on Market street, above Eleventh street. From this school he entered the Polytechnic College, leaving in March, 1866, but returning in 1867 and graduating with the degree of B. S. A. in 1870. Between 1870 and 1872 he was employed in the offices of several architects and of a builder in Philadelphia. In 1872 he returned to the Polytechnic College as assistant professor of mathematics, architecture and drawing. He resigned this position in 1876 and opened an office in Philadelphia as a professional architect, conducting the business up to August, 1879, when he returned to the Polytechnic College to take

the chair of pure mathematics, which chair he resigned in September, 1880, in order to take up theological studies in the Lutheran Theological Seminary, Philadelphia, where he completed a three years course and was ordained to the ministry May 22, 1883, and on May 23 of the same year he was installed pastor of the Epiphany Evangelical Lutheran Church, Camden, New Jersey, where he has continued to conduct a successful pastorate to the present time (1909). The Rev. Mr. Binder is the author of a history of the Lutheran Sunday Schools of Philadelphia, and also of "A Critical Estimate of John Chryostom" (347-407), one of the early fathers and most accomplished orators of the ancient Greek church. These two papers were published in the *Lutheran Church Review*. He is also a contributor to current church periodicals. He holds membership in the Ministerium of Pennsylvania, which is a district synod of the General Council of the Lutheran Church of America. His home, study and church office is at 432 Penn street, Camden, New Jersey. Rev. Mr. Binder married, December 4, 1883, Clara, daughter of George and Mary Ann (Becker) Shimer, of Camden, New Jersey.

ROSSELL — The Rossell family is of Danish origin and derives its name from one of the fiefs. The village and township of Le Rossell are in Normandy, about a mile from the sea coast. The name given to the castle and the family inhabiting it appears to have been imposed by some of the early settlers in that part of Normandie, the name implying "the tower of the water," from Roz, the rook and castle to the chessboard, and el is synonym for eau water. The first one who appears to have used the surname of De Rossell is Hugh Bertrand, born 1021. The lineage of the family can be traced back to the old vikings, beginning with Sveide, the Viking, 760-780; Ival Jahl, of Upland, 830, who married the daughter of Eisten Glumru, Count of Trondheim; Eisten Glumru, of Vorse, 870; Rogvald Jarl, of Moere, father of Rollo, Duke of Normandy; Hrolf or Robert Turstain, 920, who married Gerlotte, daughter of Theobald, Count of Blois, then from the descendants of the barons of Briquebec to Hugh Bertrand, 1021, the father of Hugh De Rossell, whose son, Ralph De Rossell, married Agnes Deboves and established the family on English soil. From him the line runs in unbroken descent down from William De Rosell, Knight of the Shire for Derby.

in 1325, to John Rosell, an officer in Cromwell's army and the founder of the family in America.

(I) John Rosell was the Cromwellian officer referred to above, and came to this country and became one of the first settlers of Long Island in 1650, his name appearing on the charter of Governor Thomas Dongan. Among his children were: 1. Francis, referred to below. 2. Nathaniel, settled in the district of Hopewell, New Jersey. 3. One who settled at Eayrestown, New Jersey.

(II) Francis, son of John Rosell, removed to Bucks county, Pennsylvania, where he died in 1694, his will being dated December 1, 1690, and approved January 1, 1694. He ordered his body to be buried at Burlington, New Jersey. Left legacies to his sister, Jane, the wife of Dr. Wells, surgeon of London. Apparently his only son was Zachariah, referred to below.

(III) Zachariah, who is said to have been the son of Francis Rosell, of Bucks county, Pennsylvania, although he may have been the nephew and the son of the Rossells who settled at Eayrestown, New Jersey, married in June, 1709, in the Burlington and Mount Holly monthly meeting, Mary Hilliard, and among his children were Zachariah, referred to below.

(IV) Zachariah (2), son of Zachariah (1) and Mary (Hilliard) Rossell, was born at Eayrestown, New Jersey, in 1723; died there February 21, 1815. He lived in Mount Holly and was a justice of the peace under King George III. His early and active service in the cause of the liberty of his country marked him out for the vengeance of the British and when in 1776 they overran the Jerseys, his house and other buildings were given up to the plunder of the soldiery, who dragged him to prison on foot to New York, where he suffered in common with his fellow-prisoners hardships peculiar to an English jail. He happily survived, however, and always continued his zealous assertions of the principles of the revolution. He was an extremely devout, christian man, beloved and respected by all who knew him. In 1759 Zachariah Rossell married (first) Margaret (Curtis) Clark, who bore him a son, William, referred to below, and two daughters: Mary, January 25, 1770, married Isaac Wood, of Mount Holly, and Martha, born February 7, 1771, married Joseph Read, of Mount Holly. Margaret (Curtis) (Clark) Rossell died January 20, 1780, at the age of sixty-six years. Zachariah Rossell married (second) Elizabeth (Ross) Beckett, by whom he had no issue.

(V) William, eldest child of Zachariah (2) and Margaret (Curtis) (Clark) Rossell, was born October 25, 1760, in Springfield township, Burlington county, New Jersey; died in Mount Holly, June 20, 1840. For twenty-two years he was a judge of the supreme court of New Jersey, and for a long time he also served as one of the United States district judges. He married Ann Hatkinson, who died July 16, 1832, aged seventy-one years, who bore him seven children: 1. Zachariah, born November 17, 1788; died July 21, 1842; married Lydia Beakes, a great-granddaughter of the Hon. William Trent, the founder of Trenton, and left two sons, Nathan Beakes and William Henry. 2. William, referred to below. 3. Eliza. 4. Margaret. 5. Joseph. 6. Mary Ann, married William Chapman. 7. Catherine, married Samuel Allen.

(VI) William (2), son of the Hon. William (1) Rossell, had among other children a son, William, referred to below.

(VII) William (3), son of William (2) Rossell, of Mount Holly, a retired farmer, lived in Springfield township, Burlington county, New Jersey; married a Miss Brown. Children: George Edward, referred to below; Frank, Elwood, Ambrose, Harvey; Joseph, deceased; Charles, deceased; Anna, deceased.

(VIII) George Edward, son of William (3) Rossell, was born in Springfield township, New Jersey, in 1854, and married Caroline Johnson, born in 1856. He is still living and is a farmer. His mother belongs to one of the old families of the same township as her husband. Children: Edward Wood, referred to below; Ella.

(IX) Edward Wood, son of George Edward and Caroline (Johnson) Rossell, was born in Springfield township, Burlington county, New Jersey, November 28, 1887. He was a pupil in the public schools in his native township for his early education, after which he entered the College of Pharmacy in Philadelphia, from which he graduated in 1899. He then pursued a post-graduate course in the Medico Chirurgical College in Philadelphia, from which he was graduated with the degree of M. D. in 1905. He immediately began the general practice of his profession in Camden, New Jersey, where he was made a member of the medical staff of the Camden City Dispensary. In addition to this he built up for himself a private practice which increased very rapidly, and with it also grew his reputation as a skillful and careful practitioner, so that now he is regarded by every one as one of the rising doctors of the younger generation. In

William Bacon

politics Dr. Rossell is a Republican, and in religion a member of the Methodist Episcopal church. His home and offices are at 322 North Ninth street, Camden, New Jersey. He is a member of Camden County Medical Society, Camden City Medical Society, the Artisans Order of Mutual Protection, and the Loyal Order of Moose.

In June, 1908, Edward Wood Rossell. M. D., married Ursula M., daughter of Edward Knauss.

BACON The Bacon family of New Jersey has from the early days of the settlement of Salem county played a most important part, not only in the civil and social life of the community, but also in the religious affairs of the Society of Friends, with which many and almost all of the earlier generations were associated. In these latter days numbers of the family, which is an extremely large one, have formed other religious associations, especially in the Baptist denomination, and in that church also they have made their mark.

(I) The earliest known member of the family in the record of Salem county mentioned is John Bacon, of Cohansey, who is said to have been the son of Samuel. In 1720 John Bacon married Elizabeth, born 3rd month 3, daughter of John Smith, of Smithfield, and granddaughter of William Smith, of county Kent, England, and Salem, New Jersey, one of the executors and intimate friend and said to have been a relative of John Fenwick. Judge John and Elizabeth (Smith) Bacon, of Cohansey, had seven children: 1. Thomas, referred to below. 2. John. 3. Elizabeth, married John Denn, of Alloways Creek. 4. David, settled in Philadelphia; accumulated fortune as a hatter: married and left two children. Joseph and Hannah. The latter, the mother of Thomas, who married Catharine Wistar. 5. Martha. 6. Mary. 7. Job, see sketch.

(II) Thomas, eldest child of Judge John and Elizabeth (Smith) Bacon, was born in Cohansey in 1721. He married and left two sons. Charles, referred to below, and John, married Hannah, daughter of Paul Denn, of Alloways Creek, and had five children: Thomas, Eleanor, Martha, Hannah and John.

(III) Charles, elder son of Thomas Bacon, married and settled on his father's property in Bacon's Neck, Greenwich township, Salem county. He married and had five children: 1. Thomas, married a Miss Wright, of Mannington, and left one son, Thomas. 2. Benjamin,

referred to below. 3. David, unmarried; for several years a merchant in Salem, but ended his days at Woodstown, leaving a legacy to the Piles Grove monthly meeting for the erection of a school house, long known as Bacon's School. 4. Charles, died unmarried at an advanced age. 5. Rachael, married a Mr. Sheppard, and became the mother of Moses Sheppard, of Greenwich.

(IV) Benjamin, second son of Charles Bacon, was twice married, his first wife being an Allen, who bore him two children, one of them Abel, referred to below, and the other a daughter whose name is unknown. His second wife was Susan, daughter of Jonathan Dallas.

(V) Abel, son of Benjamin and ———— (Allen) Bacon, was a farmer of Bacon's Neck, New Jersey, living on the farm which he had inherited from his father. Children: William, referred to below; Smith, Abel, Aseral.

(VI) William, son of Abel Bacon, was one of the most celebrated men of his day and generation in Salem county. He was born at Bacon's Neck, June 30, 1802. He was a clergyman and a physician, and during a long life served an able ministry in Alloway Pittsgrove and Woodstown, New Jersey. After receiving his early education at Greenwich, New Jersey, he entered the University of Pennsylvania with the idea of becoming a minister. After completing his college course, however, he entered the medical department of the university from which he graduated at the early age of twenty with the degree of M. D. He then commenced the practice of his profession at Allowaystown, New Jersey, and while there became convinced that it was his duty to preach the gospel. He was consequently ordained as an evangelist, and began journeying through counties of South Jersey preaching. In 1830 the Rev. William Bacon became pastor of the Baptist church at Pittsgrove, and in 1833 he went to Woodstown, finally, in 1841, assuming charge of the church at Dividing Creek. Here he remained for the next eleven years. In 1852 he retired from the ministry and devoted himself entirely to his medical practice. For two terms the Rev. William Bacon, M. D., was a member of the New Jersey state legislature, and for twelve years he was one of the superintendents of schools or chosen freeholders of Newport, Dividing Creek, Port Norris, Mauricetown and Buckshuten, Cumberland county, New Jersey. He died in February, 1868.

Rev. William Bacon, M. D., married Mary

Ray, of Philadelphia, who died in October, 1869. Their children were: 1. Clementine, married (first) Lewis Rementor, of Philadelphia; (second) Robert Mayhigh, a merchant of Mount Sterling, Kentucky, who lost his property in the civil war, moved to Missouri and died there; (third) a Mr. Sutherland, of Virginia, a Union soldier. 2. William Ray, of Trenton and Bridgeton, New Jersey. 3. Rebecca, married Samuel Spence, of Port Elizabeth, New Jersey. She died in Missouri and he in Bridgeton, New Jersey. 4. Abel, unmarried. 5. Stetson Levi, referred to below. 6. Smith, a builder and contractor of Bridgeton, New Jersey, who served in the civil war in the Tenth New Jersey Volunteer Regiment, was taken prisoner and confined for eight months in Andersonville until finally exchanged. He married Keziah Husted.

(VII) Stetson Levi, fifth child and third son of the Rev. William, M. D., and Mary (Ray) Bacon, was born at Woodstown, Salem county, New Jersey, April 21, 1836, and is now living in Port Norris, New Jersey. After attending the public schools of Newport, New Jersey, he went to the Tremont Seminary at Norristown, Pennsylvania, and then studied medicine under his father's direction, at the same time teaching school. After two years of this work and training, in 1856, he entered Jefferson Medical College in Philadelphia, Pennsylvania, and received his degree of M. D. from that institution in 1858. He then began to practice his profession with his father at Newport, New Jersey, where he continued for the next eleven years. After his father's death, in 1868, he removed from Mantua, New Jersey, where for a short time he associated with himself a Dr. Turner. He then came to Port Norris at a time when that place was very small, the railroad to it being only just built. He was the first physician in the town, and he is today the oldest medical practitioner in southern New Jersey. In his long and useful career he has been most successful, has thoroughly endeared himself to the community in which he has chosen to cast his lot, and no citizen of Port Norris is more highly esteemed. Like his father, Dr. Bacon is a member of the Baptist church and a Republican. He is a member also of the Cumberland County Medical Society; for three years was coroner for Cumberland county, and for thirty years was the overseer of the poor of Commercial township, Cumberland county. He has always been a great lover of books and has gathered together a most magnificent library; he has now

practically retired from business and has given himself up to the enjoyment of his books and a comfortable old age.

December 23, 1859, Dr. Stetson Levi Bacon married Martha Washington, daughter of John L. and granddaughter of Ezekiel Mayhew. Her grandfather was a farmer. Her father was one of the early business pioneers of Greenwich township. He lived to the age of ninety-three, and at various times held the office of assessor, collector, member of the township committee, and chosen freeholder. Children of Stetson Levi, M. D., and Elizabeth (Mayhew) Bacon:

1. Elizabeth Mayhew, born June 1, 1864; married, June 21, 1890, the Rev. William A. Walling, a Baptist clergyman, of Wilmington, Delaware, who graduated in 1896 from the University of Rochester, New York. Her husband renounced the ministry, took up the study of law in Columbia University, New York, and after his graduation settled as an attorney in New York City. His wife attended the public schools of Port Norris, and the South Jersey Institute at Bridgeton. She is of a literary turn of mind and has contributed many short stories to the current periodicals, besides publishing one book entitled "Phebe."

2. William Ray, born March 23, 1871, at Newport, New Jersey; attended the Port Norris public schools at the South Jersey Institute and then went to the University of Rochester. After his graduation he entered the Columbia University Law School, from which he received his degree, LL. B., and entered on the practice of his profession, New York City, where he became corporation counsel for the Metropolitan Street Railroad Company.

(For first generation see preceding sketch).

BACON   (II) Job, youngest son of John and Elizabeth (Smith) Bacon, was born in Cohansey, 1735. He married Mary, daughter of John Stewart, of Alloways Creek, Salem county. They had three children: 1. Job, referred to below. 2. Elizabeth. 3. George. Job's widow married (second) Richard Wood, Jr., of Cumberland county.

(III) Job (2), son of Job (1) and Mary (Stewart) Bacon, was twice married, having two children by his first wife and four children by his second. His second wife was Ruth, daughter of John Thompson, of Elsinborough. The name of his first wife is unknown. His children were: 1. John, referred to below. 2. Martha. 3. Mary, married Clem-

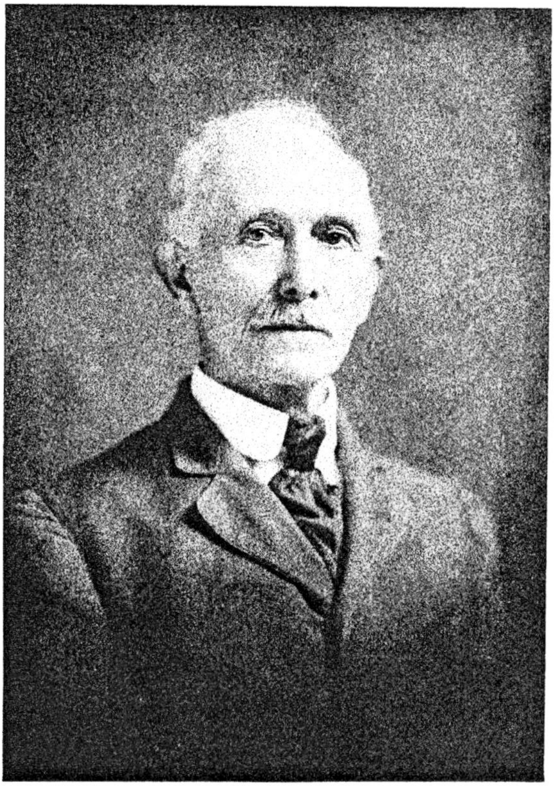

Stetson L. Bacon

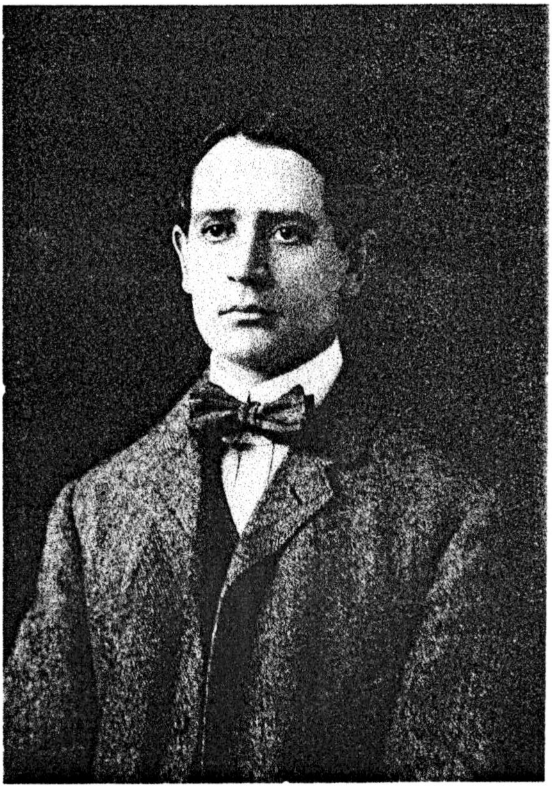

Ray. Bacon

ent Acton. 4. Sarah, died unmarried at Greenwich. 5. Ann, married Moses Sheppard. 6. Josiah, a merchant of Philadelphia and a director of Pennsylvania railroad.

(IV) John, eldest child of Job (2) Bacon by his first wife, lived in Greenwich, Cumberland county, New Jersey. He married Ann Hall, of Bacon's Neck. She was a lineal descendant of William Hall who emigrated to this country in 1677 from Dublin, Ireland, and settled at Salem, New Jersey. Their children were: 1. Job, referred to below. 2. John, died in infancy. 3. Josiah, deceased. 4. Maurice, deceased. 5. George W., now living in York, New Jersey.

(V) Job (3), son of John and Ann (Hall) Bacon, was born at Greenwich, New Jersey. He was a farmer and at one time engaged in the vegetable canning business. He married Rachel, daughter of Moses, Jr., and Ann (Bacon) Sheppard, his half first cousin. Her grandfather Moses, Sr., was the son of John and Priscilla (Wood) Sheppard, and her grandmother the daughter of Charles and Rebecca (Miller) Bacon. Charles Bacon was the grandson of John and Elizabeth (Smith) Bacon, referred to in the first generation. Children of Job and Rachel (Sheppard) Bacon were: 1. John Murray, living in Boston, Massachusetts, and engaged in the paint and oil business; married a Miss Bailey, of Philadelphia, and has one son. George. 2. Anna Thompson, born in 1856; unmarried. 3. Caroline Wood, died in 1893; married William Bacon, no relation. 4. George Sheppard, referred to below.

(VI) George Sheppard, youngest child of Job (3) and Rachel (Sheppard) Bacon, was born in Greenwich, Cumberland county, New Jersey, August 23, 1864, and is now living in Millville, New Jersey. His mother died when her son was about three years old. For his early education he attended the public schools of Greenwich and Bacon's Neck, New Jersey, and the boarding school at Westtown, Pennsylvania. After leaving school he entered the office of Whitall, Tatum & Company, of Philadelphia, where he remained for about a year and then was transferred to the office of the same firm at their works in Millville. By faithful service as boy and man for this firm he won his promotion from grade to grade until he has now reached his present position of general manager and superintendent of their large glass works, and has become a stockholder in the corporation. Mr. Bacon is a member of the Society of Friends, as have been

all of his family back of him, and in politics he is a Republican. He is a director of the West Jersey and Seashore Railroad Company.

In November, 1889, George Sheppard Bacon married Rebecca, daughter of Lorenzo and Hannah Milford. Her father is a contractor of Millville. They have four children: 1. Margaret Mickle, born March 23, 1891; now at Miss Lord's private school at Stamford, Connecticut. 2. Job Lawrence, November 24, 1892; now at the Penn Charter School in Philadelphia. 3. Caroline Wood, August 27, 1894. 4. Elizabeth Mickle, August 3, 1900.

SHERK For many years the Sherk family has left its impress upon the history and institutions of Lebanon county, Pennsylvania, and it is rather with that state than with New Jersey that its affiliations ought to be found. Dr. Harry Huber Sherk, however, has already added to New Jersey's roll of honor the name of his family, and it is impossible to speak of the representative men of Camden, New Jersey, without giving some account of what he is and has done. Dr. Sherk is the grandson of Casper Sherk, and the son of Abraham and Rebecca (Huber) Sherk, of Lebanon county, Pennsylvania, where he was born March 24, 1859. His mother was the daughter of Abraham Huber, of Chambersburg, Franklin county, Pennsylvania. His father was born August 12, 1809, in Lebanon county.

Dr. Sherk was sent for his early education to the public schools of Lebanon county, and then entered the Lebanon Valley College at Anvil, Pennsylvania. After leaving this institution he went to the College of Pharmacy at Philadelphia, where he graduated with the degree of Ph. G. He then went to the Jefferson Medical College, of Philadelphia, from which he received his M. D. degree in 1886, immediately after which he came to Camden, New Jersey, where he became connected with the dispensary of the Cooper Hospital. After remaining here for a time, he set up in the general practice of his profession in Camden, where he has remained ever since. His practice rapidly increased, and his pleasing personality, skill in the treatment of disease, and acumen in diagnosis, rapidly brought him success and a most lucrative practice. In the medical society to which he belongs he is regarded as one of the great authorities and his opinion carries the greatest weight. He is a member of the New Jersey State Medical Association, Camden County Medical Society.

Camden City Medical Society and State Medical Society. In politics he is an independent. He was one of the organizers of the East Side Trust Company, of Camden, New Jersey, and from its organization has been a member of the corporation board of managers and directors. He is a director in the East Side Building Association, of Camden.

Harry Huber Sherk, M. D., married Emma Katharine, daughter of Andrew Light, of Lebanon county, Pennsylvania, where she was born March 21, 1860. Children: 1. Katharine Rebecca, born May 15, 1888. 2. Helen Emma, July 13, 1891. 3. Clara Louise, 1892, died aged seventeen months. 4. Abraham Lincoln, August 29, 1896. 5. Mary Alice, December 5, 1902.

ROBERTS The Roberts family of New Jersey is another instance of the men who sought peace and prosperity and the free exercise of their newly acquired religious convictions in the Quaker colonies of West Jersey, the founder of the family being among those who came over to the new world in the second ship which left English ports for the Delaware.

(I) John Roberts and his wife, Sarah, belonged to the parish of Orton, county Warwick. England. and having been converted to the tenets of George Fox they embarked for West Jersey in the ship "Kent" and landed at New Castle on the Delaware in August, 1677. with the first shipload of settlers sent out by the proprietors. He was a farmer, and settled on two hundred and sixty-seven acres which he had surveyed to him on the north branch of the Penisaukin creek, living with his family in a cave until his log house could be erected. He afterwards had other tracts of land surveyed for him further up the stream and reaching into Evesham township. In 1682 he and William Matlack and Timothy Hancock established the Friends meeting called the Adams meeting. His house was built near the present turnpike between Moorestown and Camden. His widow, who survived him many years, was an exceptionally bright and clever woman with a keen intellect and a remarkable business ability. In 1696 she signed the agreement as one of the taxpayers when the township of Chester was organized, and she was one of the grantees of the land for the Adams meeting burying ground in 1700. John Roberts died in 1695, intestate, the inventory of his estate being made May 7, and letters of administration being granted to his widow,

October 12, of that year. John and Sarah Roberts had four children: 1. John, referred to below. 2. Sarah, married, in 1705, Enoch Core. 3. Hannah, married (first) 1699, Samuel Burrough, and (second) in 1733, Richard Bidgood. 4. Mary, married, in 1699, Thomas, son of Thomas and Ann Eves, the emigrants.

(II) John (2), the only son of John (1) and Sarah Roberts, died September 9, 1747, and was buried in Moorestown, where his wife was afterwards laid beside him. He was a prosperous farmer and business man. In 1736 he erected on the property which he inherited from his father the large brick house which the family have owned for several generations and which is still standing and known by his name. His widow died February 11, 1759. He married in the Chester Friends meeting in 1712, Mary, daughter of George Elkinton, of Burlington, the emigrant, and had eight children: 1. John. 2. Joshua, referred to below. 3. Mary, married Thomas, son of Henry and Elizabeth (Austin) Warrington. 4. Sarah, married William, son of Thomas and Esther (Haines) Evans. 5. Enoch, married Rachel, daughter of Samuel and Mary (Kendall) Coles. 6. Hannah, married Isaac, son of Thomas and Esther (Haines) Evans. 7. Elizabeth, married Benjamin, son of Abram and Grace (Hollingshead) Haines. 8. Deborah.

(III) Joshua, son of John (2) and Mary (Elkinton) Roberts, was born May 27, 1715; died January 28, 1795. In 1741 he married Rebecca, daughter of Joseph and Judith (Lippincott) Stokes, born March 28, 1720, died November, 1815. Children: 1. John, married Phebe Andrews. 2. Samuel, married Elizabeth Shute. 3. Rebecca, married High, son of Thomas and Mary (Birden) Cowperthwait and grandson of John and Sarah (Adams) Cowperthwait. 4. William, married Elizabeth Grinslade. 5. Joseph, referred to below. 6. Joshua, died unmarried.

(IV) Joseph, son of Joshua and Rebecca (Stokes) Roberts, was born June 8, 1742, died February 22, 1826. He was a farmer, one of the leading men in his township, and lived in the house built in 1736 by his grandfather. He married Susanna, born October 3, 1751, died September 29, 1828, daughter of Kendall Cole and Ann, daughter of William Budd and Elizabeth, daughter of Richard and Abigail Stockton, the emigrants. William was the son of William and Ann (Clapgut) Budd, the emigrants; and Kendall was the son of Samuel Cole and Mary, daughter of Thomas Kendall, the emigrant, and Mary, daughter of Francis

Collins, the immigrant, and his second wife, Mary (Budd) Goslin, the widow of Dr. John Goslin, of Burlington, and daughter of Thomas Budd, the emigrant, and brother to William Budd, the emigrant. Samuel was the son of Samuel and Elizabeth Cole, the emigrants. Children of Joseph and Susanna (Cole) Roberts were: 1. Mary. 2. Joseph, married Rachel, daughter of Thomas and Mary (Eves) Evans. 3. William, married Ann Brick. 4. Rebecca, married Joseph, son of Thomas and Mary (Eves) Evans. 5. George, married Abigail Brown. 6. Josiah, married Mary French. 7. Abel. 8. Ann, married John, son of Jabez and Sarah (Evans) Buzby. 9. David, referred to below.

(V) David, son of Joseph and Susanna (Cole) Roberts, was born February 14, 1792, died December 9, 1880. He inherited the old homestead. He married Rachel, daughter of Joshua and Rachel Hunt, of Redstone, ·Fayette county,·Pennsylvania, by whom he had nine children: 1. Esther, born August 23, 1816; died unmarried, October 4, 1896. 2. Elisha, referred to below. 3. Edwin, February 24, 1821; married Anna B. Passmore. 4. Joseph, July 25, 1823; died in childhood. 5. Mary, August 21, 1825; unmarried. 6. Rebecca, August 7, 1827; died unmarried. 7. Anna B., October 7, 1829. 8. Susanna, January 4, 1832; married Jonathan G. Williams. 9. Rachel Hunt, January 30, 1834; unmarried.

(VI) Elisha, second child and eldest son of David and Rachel (Hunt) Roberts, was born June 30, 1818, in Chester township, Burlington county, New Jersey. He married, Pebruary 24, 1842, Elizabeth W. Hooten, born in Evesham, now Mount Laurel township, Burlington county, New Jersey, July 16, 1819. She is a descendant of Thomas Hooten, son of William Hooten, who came from England in the year 1677 and settled in Evesham, now Mount Laurel township, Burlington county, New Jersey, and married Mary Lippincott, of Shrewsbury, New Jersey, in 1697. William Hooten, son of Thomas and Mary Hooten, was born September 2, 1698, and was married in Friends' meeting house in Evesham to Ann Sharp, widow of John Sharp, and daughter of Thomas Haines, of North Hampton, Burlington county, November 21, 1730. · Thomas Hooten, son of William and Ann Hooten, was born March 17, 1734, died May, 1825. He married, January 21, 1760, Bathsheba Braddock, born August 3, 1738, died September 7, 1769, daughter of Robert and Elizabeth (Bates) Braddock, and granddaughter of Robert Braddock, the emigrant. Thomas Hooten

married (second) December 1, 1774, Atlantic Stokes, widow of Joseph Stokes, in Friends' meeting house in· Moorestown, New Jersey. Atlantic was the daughter of Joshua and Mary Bispham, and was born March 22, 1737, while crossing the ocean and named by the captain of the vessel, Atlantic or Atlantica, who presented her with silk for a dress. Thomas and Bathsheba (Braddock) Hooten had three children: i. William, born December 10, 1762; ii. Deborah, born 1764, married Joshua Stokes, son of Joseph and Atlantic Stokes; iii. Thomas, born 1766, died June 11, 1806; married Ann Wynn, who died August 6, 1857. Thomas and Atlantic (Bispham-Stokes) Hooten had four children: i. Benjamin, born April 2, 1776, died April 4, 1862; married Beulah Millen, who died January 21, 1861; ii. Joseph, referred to below; iii. Isaac, born November 3, 1781, unmarried; iv. William, born February 9, 1784, died November, 1853; married Elizabeth West, of Trenton, New Jersey, who died July 18, 1864. Joseph, son of Thomas and Atlantic (Bispham-Stokes) Hooten, was born April 4, 1778, died November 11, 1839. He married, November 11, 1813, in Friends' meeting house in Trenton, New Jersey, Sarah Pippett, born February 7, 1788, died September 21, 1869, daughter of Moses and Sarah Pippett. Their children were: i. Isaac, born January 19, 1815, died aged eighteen months; ii. Joseph, born August 30, 1817, died November 8, 1878; married, May 25, 1843, in Westfield meeting house, Anna Warrington, daughter of Henry and Anna Warrington; iii. Elizabeth West, born July 16, 1819, married Elisha Roberts, referred to above; she died March 15, 1889. The children of Elisha and Elizabeth West (Hooten) Roberts were: 1. Sarah H., born January 29, 1843; married Samuel L. Allen. 2. Anna W., born March 15, 1845; drowned at Atlantic City, July 10, 1874. 3. Joseph H., born December 15, 1846; died July 26, 1847. 4. Elizabeth H., born April 20, 1848; married Edward B. Richie. 5. David, referred to below. 6. Samuel S., born July 24, 1852; died March 21, 1854. 7. Joseph Hooten, referred to below. 8. Esther, born June 29, 1857; died August 8, 1858. 9. William H., born April 16, 1859.

(VII) David, son of Elisha and Elizabeth West (Hooten) Roberts, was born near Moorestown, June 19, 1850, and is now living in that town. He was educated in private schools and at boarding school, and then engaged in farming until 1886, when he engaged in the hotel business with his brother, Joseph Hooten Roberts, at Atlantic City. In 1893-

94 he built his present residence in Moorestown and retired from business in 1898. He has a large farm near Moorestown, where he carries on a milk and dairy business and truck farming, taking his products to the Philadelphia markets. He has served as one of the township committeemen, and he is a member of the Society of Friends. He married, in 1876, Elizabeth L., daughter of John C. Allen, the founder of the College of Pharmacy in Philadelphia. Children: 1. Anna Warrington, died at sixteen years of age, while at boarding school. 2. David Allen, a member of an electric and construction company in Philadelphia; he married, April, 1909, Helen, daughter of John Bushnell, of Plainfield, New Jersey, and lives in a beautiful house which he has built next to his father. 3. Elizabeth Allen. 4. Herbert Allen, a member of the firm of George D. Wetherill & Company, paint dealers, Philadelphia. The last two mentioned live with their father.

(VII) Joseph Hooten, son of Elisha and Elizabeth West (Hooten) Roberts, was born in Moorestown, April 29, 1854, and is now living in that town. He attended the public schools of Moorestown, and then went with his brother to the Westtown boarding school in Chester county, Pennsylvania. For the following twelve years after leaving school he engaged in farming. He then engaged in the hotel business at Atlantic City with his brother, David Roberts, conducting the Chalfonte Hotel, built by his father and conducted by him from 1868 until 1885. In 1897 Joseph H. Roberts built his present house in Moorestown, and the following year he and his brother gave up the hotel business and came to Moorestown to reside. Like his brother, David, he conducts a large truck and dairy farm near Moorestown. He is a director in the Moorestown Bank and in the Burlington County Safe Deposit and Trust Company. He is a member of the Society of Friends. He married, October, 1880, Mary C., daughter of Isaac Collins and Mary (Percival) Stokes, granddaughter of Isaac and Lydia (Collins) Stokes, and great-granddaughter of John and Beulah (Haines) Stokes. Children: 1. Alfred Stokes, now a student in Haverford College. 2. Mary Stokes, now a student in Wellesley College.

(For preceding generations see John Roberts 1).

ROBERTS (III) Enoch, son of John and Mary (Elkinton) Roberts, was born in 1717; died in 1784. In 1744 he married Rachel Coles, born 1716, died

1758. Children: 1. Mary, born 1744; married Anthony Allen. 2. Samuel, referred to below. 3. Elizabeth, 1747; married Jonas Cattel. 4. Rachel, 1749; married Joshua Dudley. 5. Esther, 1751; married Joshua Hunt. 6. Sarah, 1753; died 1758. 7. Enoch, Jr., 1756; died 1758.

(IV) Samuel, second child and eldest son of Enoch and Rachel (Coles) Roberts, was born in 1746. He married Hannah Stiles. Children: 1. Rachel, born 1773; married Job Dudley. 2. Sarah, 1776; married George Matlack. 3. Mary, 1779; married Joshua Lippincott. 4. Hannah, 1781; died 1782. 5. Lydia, 1785; died 1797. 6. Enoch, 1787; married Ann Matlack. 7. Samuel, 1789; married Sarah, daughter of Thomas and Mary (Eves) Evans. 8. Hannah, 1792; married Levi Lippincott. 9. Asa, referred to below.

(V) Asa, youngest child of Samuel and Hannah (Stiles) Roberts, was born in 1795, on the original land which had been owned by his father and direct ancestors from John Roberts down. He married (first) Anna, daughter of Samuel and Priscilla (Brion) Lippincott; married (second) Rachel Ballinger; (third) Hannah (Ballinger) Stiles. His children, all from Anna Lippincott, his first wife, were: 1. Samuel L., born in 1822; died in 1881; married Sarah W. Jones. 2. Lydia, 1824; married Josiah Roberts, son of Josiah and Mary (French) Roberts. 3. Isaac, 1827; died 1830. 4. Charles, 1829; died 1830. 5. Emmor, referred to below. 6. Susan, 1833; remained unmarried; was actively engaged in early life in teaching and later as one of the editors of *Friends' Intelligencer*, of Philadelphia; she died in 1888. 7. Priscilla P., 1835; died 1835. 8. Elizabeth, 1836; married Nathan Haines, of Baltimore; she is still living.

(VI) Emmor, son of Asa and Anna (Lippincott) Roberts, was born in Evesham township, Burlington county, New Jersey, February 16, 1831. He received a very good education for a farmer's son of that day, having been sent to the school of Benjamin Hallowell at Alexandria, Virginia. He afterwards was a teacher in the same school and taught mathematics there. As many of the students in the school were sons of congressmen being prepared for West Point, the instruction given was necessarily very thorough, especially was this so with the mathematics. In 1857 he married Martha, daughter of Israel and Maria (Wallace) Lippincott. By that time he had become a farmer, which business he continued to follow as his principal occupation for the remainder of his life. He was always a public spirited useful citizen and left the marks of his energy and good sound sense on many organizations and enterprises. We first find him taking part in the little local affairs of his neighborhood, township clerk, clerk of the district school—a thankless position of considerable responsibility which he held for many years. A little later we find him a member of the broad of chosen freeholders of the county and director of the board; director of the Mount Holly Insurance Company and of the Moorestown and Camden Turnpike Company. For the last twenty-five years of his life he was the president of the last named company. For thirty-six years he served as a director of the National State Bank, of Camden, and was for a few years near the close of his life vice-president of that institution. He was on the board of managers of Swarthmore College from 1877 to the time of his death, serving on many of the important committees of that board. For over twenty years he was chairman of the executive committee of the board. Besides such positions of a semi-public character he acted as executor or administrator in settling a number of estates, and did some surveying and conveyancing. He was a birthright member of the Society of Friends and always took an earnest and devoted interest in that body and their meetings. For a period of ten years or more he was the clerk of his quarterly meeting, and for fifteen years, from 1886 to 1901, he served as clerk of the yearly meeting of Friends which meets at Fifteenth and Race streets in Philadelphia (sometimes called Hicksites). He died April 7, 1908, leaving his widow and four children surviving him. His children are: 1. Israel, born in 1858; studied law and now a member of the New Jersey bar. 2. Alice, born in 1861; married John J. Williams, of Norristown, Pennsylvania, son of Charles and Hannah (Stokes) Williams. 3. Horace Roberts, born in 1868; married (first) Emma Thomas and had by her three sons: Emmor, Preston Thomas and Byron Thomas Roberts; married (second) Elizabeth P. Hooton, and by her he has three children, Horace, Jr., Mary H. and Martha. Horace lives on his father's old homestead farm and is successful and prosperous. He has acquired several other farms and makes the raising of fruit his specialty. 4. Walter, M. D., born 1870; married Lydia Parry, daughter of Joseph S. and Anna (Satterthwaite) Williams, has two daughters, Anna S. and Lydia W. Roberts. He lives in Riverton, New Jersey, and makes daily trips to Philadelphia to attend to his practice as a specialist on the ear, nose and throat.

HILDRETH The Hildreth family of New Jersey comes from that stalwart band of seafaring men who throughout the whole course of its history has given Cape May county a place and rank unique in the state and Union. As in the case of other families descended from these noble mariners, it is difficult from the lack of authentic records to trace the earlier generation of the Hildreth family in this country.

(I) George Hildreth, of Cape May county, New Jersey, lived at Cold Spring, New Jersey, and became a pilot on the Delaware river. He was one of New Jersey's staunchest Democrats and served his township in various local offices. In religious belief he was a Presbyterian and was very active in the work of the old historic Cold Spring Church and did all in his power to uplift humanity and better the conditions of human life. Children: 1. Alvin Parker, referred to below. 2. Eliza E., married Lafayette Miller. 3. Daniel. 4. Ann Jane, never married.

(II) Alvin Parker, eldest child of George Hildreth, was born in Cold Spring, New Jersey, June 11, 1831, died in Cape May City, August 3, 1897. In early life he was engaged in teaching school and completed his education within the classic walls of Yale University. He was a man of strong individuality and marked intellectuality, and in public life was frequently called to positions of prominence and trust. For some time he was engaged in the hotel business in Cape May, and was afterwards the proprietor of the Metropolitan Hotel in Washington, District of Columbia. Subsequently he returned to Cape May, where he conducted one of the leading hotels in that sections of the state. Prompt, energetic and thoroughly reliable, his reputation in business circles was indeed enviable, and he had the happy faculty of winning warm friendships. He was a recognized leader in Democratic circles, and at one time was a member of the riparian commission of New Jersey, and twice was elected to represent his district in the assembly of the state. In local affairs he exercised a marked influence, and his co-operation was always given to movements and measures that were calculated to advance the progress and welfare of the community. His Masonic relations were with the Cape Island Lodge, of which he was a valued and influential member. He married, in December, 1854, Lydia Hughes, born October 28, 1832, died January 4, 1862, daughter of Eli B. and Sarah (Hughes) Wales. Children: Howard Wales, Frank Harding, James Monroe Edmonds, see below; Alvin Parker, Jr.

Desire (Howland) Gorham, who died at Barnstable, Massachusetts, October 13, 1683, was the daughter of John and Elizabeth (Tilley) Howland, and granddaughter of John Howland, one of the "Mayflower" passengers, who died February 23, 1673; married Elizabeth, daughter of John Tilley, another "Mayflower" passenger. Hannah Gorham, daughter of Captain John and Desire (Howland) Gorham, was born at Barnstable, Massachusetts, November 28, 1663; married, about 1683, Joseph Whilldin, of Yarmouth. Hannah Whilldin, daughter of Joseph and Mary (Wildman) Whilldin, granddaughter of Joseph, son of Joseph and Hannah (Gorham) Whilldin, was born about 1690, died at Cape May, March 18, 1784; married Ellis Hughes. Ellis Hughes, son of Ellis and Hannah (Whilldin) Hughes, was born August 16, 1745, died April 16, 1817; married 1762, Thomas Hirst, born January 10, 1769, died November 10, 1839, married, December 3, 1788, was the son of Ellis and Eleanor (Hirst) Hughes. Sarah Hughes, born May 31, 1800, was the daughter of Thomas Hirst and Lydia (Page) Hughes; married, in 1818, Eli B. Wales. She was the mother of Lydia Hughes Wales, who married Alvin Parker Hildreth.

(III) James Monroe Edmonds, third child and son of Alvin Parker and Lydia Hughes (Wales) Hildreth, was born in Cape May City, New Jersey, December 9, 1858. He spent the early years of his life in his native city and was then taken to Mount Holly where he completed his education in the Mount Holly Academy, an excellent institution. Determining to enter the legal profession he became a student in the law office of his uncle, Walter A. Barrows, and also studied under the direction of the Hon. Joseph H. Gaskell, later president judge of Burlington county. He diligently applied himself to the task of mastering the principles of jurisprudence, and after a careful preparation he was admitted to practice in the courts of New Jersey in June, 1881. He then returned to Cape May City and entered upon the practice of his profession, and his business has steadily increased until now (1909) he has an extensive and distinctly representative clientage. His devotion to his clients is proverbial, yet it is said that he never

advised any one to enter litigation except to right a wrong. He is an indefatigable and earnest worker, and the litigation with which he has been connected has been of a very important character. His practice has been general and he is proficient in every department of the law; his keenly analytical mind and his broad knowledge of the principles of jurisprudence have enabled him to apply to the point in controversy the law which bears most closely upon it, citing authority and precedent until the strength of his case is seen clearly by both judge and jury. His deductions are logical and the force of his argument is shown in the many verdicts which he has won favorable to his clients. He is also interested in Cape May real estate, and owns much property in the city and vicinity. All enterprising movements receive his encouragement and substantial aid is given to matters and measures for the public good. He is a Mason, a Heptasoph and a Red Man.

In both political and business circles he is known throughout New Jersey. His has been a career commendable for its fidelity to duty in all the relations of life, and he has honored the state and district which he has represented. In business he has the soul of honor and integrity. In social circles he is affable and courteous, and his whole career has been permeated by the kindliness and sympathy that have arisen from a personal interest in his fellowmen. His political prominence is the result of eminent fitness for leadership and the ability which he has shown in the discharge of the duties entrusted to him. In February, 1888, he was admitted to the New Jersey bar as a counsellor. In 1883 he was chosen by the city council for the office of city solicitor, a position which he held for two terms, and in which he won the highest commendation of all by the manner in which he performed the duties that devolved upon him. In March, 1893, he was chosen as the chief executive of Cape May City, and in that year he was instrumental in holding a Fourth of July celebration, which will ever be memorable in the history of the city. Benjamin Harrison, ex-president of the United States, was the distinguished guest and the principal speaker on that occasion, and Mr. Hildreth introduced Mr. Harrison and presided over the ceremonies in a manner that elicited the warmest praise of his fellow townsmen. During his mayoralty marked improvement was made in the city in many ways, and yet, so economical was his management of his business affairs of Cape May, that each taxpayer was saved fourteen per cent of the usual net amount of his tax. In 1895 the city council again elected Mr. Hildreth to the office of city solicitor, and in 1897 he was again elected mayor. To those who are acquainted with him it it needless to say that his administration was progressive and beneficial. In 1898 he was a prominent candidate for congressional honors in the first district, and although he did not seek the nomination he received the most flattering vote of eighty-one ballots. In 1900 he was also spoken of prominently by his friends as a candidate for congress. In 1904-05-06 he was elected to the New Jersey legislature from Cape May county, and 1907 was elected the city solicitor of Sea Isle City, a position which he still retains. In 1906 he was appointed by Governor Stokes of New Jersey judge of Cape May county.

Judge Hildreth is an earnest champion of the principles of the Republican party, and although he has held local positions he is by no means a politician in the commonly accepted sense of the office seeker. He has been a close student of the problems of government, and he always places the welfare of the state and nation before personal aggrandizement. He is an active member of the Cape May City Golf and Yacht clubs, in which he is associated with some of the most eminent and distinguished citizens of Philadelphia and Cape May. He is a member of the Presbyterian church in Cape May City. He is a representative American citizen, energetic in business, courteous in social life, and loyal to the duties of citizenship and to his native land. Although one of the busiest of men he always has a smile of welcome for all, graciously giving his time to those who ask it, and thereby adding to his long list of friends.

Judge James Monroe Edmonds Hildreth married, November 12, 1884, Martha Orr, daughter of Jeremiah and Mary (Orr) Mecray. They have one child, Mary Mccray, born October 24, 1885; married, April 5, 1906, John Daniel Johnson, Jr., of Mount Holly, New Jersey, and they have one child, Kathryn Hildreth Johnson, born May 18, 1907.

LLOYD The name of Lloyd speaks for itself in both Great Britian and in this country in the distinguished ecclesiastics, jurists, authors and others who have so nobly borne it, but the branch of the family at present under consideration has been for so short a time in this country that its record except in the persons of the honored Cape

May City representative and his esteemed father lies on the other side of the water.

(I) William Harris Lloyd, the father, was born at Tenby in the south of Wales, but in his early manhood came over to this country and settled in Pennsylvania. Shortly before his arrival in America he married Elizabeth Phillips, who like himself was a native of Wales, and their son, Ernest William, referred to below, was born to them here.

(II) Ernest William, son of William Harris and Elizabeth (Phillips) Lloyd, was born at Weatherly, Pennsylvania, November 26, 1877, and is now living at Cape May City, New Jersey. He received his education in the public schools of Weatherly, and then became a clerk in a grocery store. After this he taught school for a short time in Hundonvale, Pennsylvania, and in 1899 removed to Bridgeton, Cumberland county, New Jersey, where he became a clerk in the hardware store in that town. Finally he took up the study of law in the office of James J. Reeves in Bridgeton, and was admitted to the bar of New Jersey as an attorney in 1903, and as a counsellor in 1908. In 1904 Mr. Lloyd opened his office and commenced his practice of his profession in Cape May City, in which place he has remained ever since, enjoying the distinction of being the youngest prosecutor of the pleas ever appointed in the state of New Jersey. This appointment he received in 1908, when he was only thirty-one years old, and his term is for five years, terminating in 1913. Mr. Lloyd is a member of the Cape May Bar Association, Association of the Prosecutors of the Pleas, and Cape Island Lodge. No. 30. Free and Accepted Masons, of Cape May City. He is also vice-president of the Cape May City Board of Trade, and a member of the Cape May Yacht Club. He is a member of the Methodist Episcopal Church of Cape May City.

March 2, 1904, Ernest William Lloyd married Maude Dare, daughter of James Dare and Laura (Bateman) Cox, of Salem, New Jersey, who is a graduate of the South Jersey Institute. They have one child, Laura Elizabeth, born in Cape May City, August 13, 1905.

SLACK John B. Slack, son of Wesley Hunt and Annie (Langstaff) Slack, was born in Paducah, Kentucky. November 4, 1873. His primary and preparatory education was obtained in the Mount Holly Academy, Mount Holly, New Jersey. In the fall of 1891 he entered Lehigh University for a four years scientific course, which he completed in 1895, graduating with the degree of E. E. Deciding upon the profession of law, he returned to Mount Holly where he entered the law office of Judge Charles E. Hendrickson. In 1899 Mr. Slack was admitted to the New Jersey bar as an attorney, and in 1902 was admitted a counsellor. Immediately upon receiving his credentials Mr. Slack located in Atlantic City, New Jersey, and entered upon the active practice of his profession. In political faith he is Republican. He is a vestryman of the Episcopal Church of the Ascension of Atlantic City and secretary of the parish. He is a member of the New Jersey State and Atlantic County Bar Associations, and the Atlantic City Country Club.

John B. Slack married, October 23, 1901, Maud Walker Wetherill, daughter of William Delaney and Louise (Stratton) Wetherill. Mr. and Mrs. Slack are the parents of John Blake Jr., born February 22, 1903, and Louise Wetherill, September 30, 1908. Mrs. Slack is a member of the Philadelphia Wetherill family and a lineal descendant of Colonel Isaac Sharp (son of Anthony Sharp, of Dublin, Ireland), the colonial statesman and soldier. Colonel Isaac Sharp was one of the proprietors of council of West Jersey (the governor's council); surrogate of Salem county, New Jersey, and later president judge of the same county, and a member of the provincial New Jersey general assembly. Through another line she descends from John Price, a soldier of the revolution. Her father was the eldest son of Robert and Phoebe (Delaney) Wetherill, Lower Merion township, Montgomery county, Pennsylvania, where William D. was born December 16, 1845. He died in Philadelphia, February 18, 1887. He was a member of the Pennsylvania bar to which he was admitted June 3, 1868. He was a lawyer of high standing and a member of the Pennsylvania Historical Society. William D. Wetherill married Louise Stratton, daughter of John Stratton, of Mount Holly, New Jersey, who bore him John Stratton, who died in infancy, and Maud Walker, who became Mrs. John B. Slack.

BISSELL This name has been prominent among the early settlers of most of the English Colonies, families, and has had many distinguished representatives in the professions of medicine, law and the ministry, as well as private citizens who have been of great service in the growth and development of the American nation.

There have been soldiers of this name in all the important wars since the earliest settlement. The name is found in the early records of the Carolinas, where they were honorably known for many generations.

(I) William Rombough Bissell was born in 1811, at Wilmington, North Carolina, and after a preliminary education attended a southern military academy. Mr. Bissell was one of those who emigrated to California at the time of the discovery of gold, and he acquired and developed a mine in that state, but later returned to the east, taking up his residence in Maryland, where he became a successful farmer. At the time of the breaking out of the civil war, his sympathies being naturally all with the interests of his native state and the southland, he enlisted in Company A of the Eighth Virginia Volunteer Confederate Regiment, of which he was made captain. He served with great bravery until the battle of Gettysburg, and in the famous fight of the third day, which turned the tide of battle, and so greatly affected the outcome of the struggle, he was killed; in this advance he was a part of the famous Pickett's division (Garnett's brigade) so vividly described in every history of the famous battle. Mr. Bissell married Margaret, daughter of Captain John Adams Webster, of the United States revenue service. (See Webster, VII.) Their children were: I. Elizabeth, married Dr. William S. Richardson, of Harford county, Maryland. 2. Nancy, married Dr. Joseph S. Baldwin, of Freeland, Maryland. 3. Virginia, married John Holland, of Belair, Maryland. 4. William Thomas. 5. Josephine D., lives in Baltimore, Maryland, and is unmarried. 6. Joseph Spalding, a farmer, living in Harford county, Maryland. 7. Mary Jarrett, widow of John N. Wilkerson, of Norfolk, Virginia. The following is the inscription on the tombstone of William R. Bissell in the Churchville Presbyterian cemetery, Harford county, Maryland: "In memory of our beloved Father, William R. Bissell, who fell at the battle of Gettysburg on the 3rd of July and died of his wounds on the 17th of July, 1863, in the 53rd year of his age." "I have fought a good fight, I have finished my course, I have kept the faith."

(II) William Thomas, eldest son of William Rombough and Margaret (Webster) Bissell, was born October 31, 1848, in Harford county, Maryland, where his father carried on a farm. He received his education at the public schools of Belair and the Harford Academy, after which he learned the art of print-

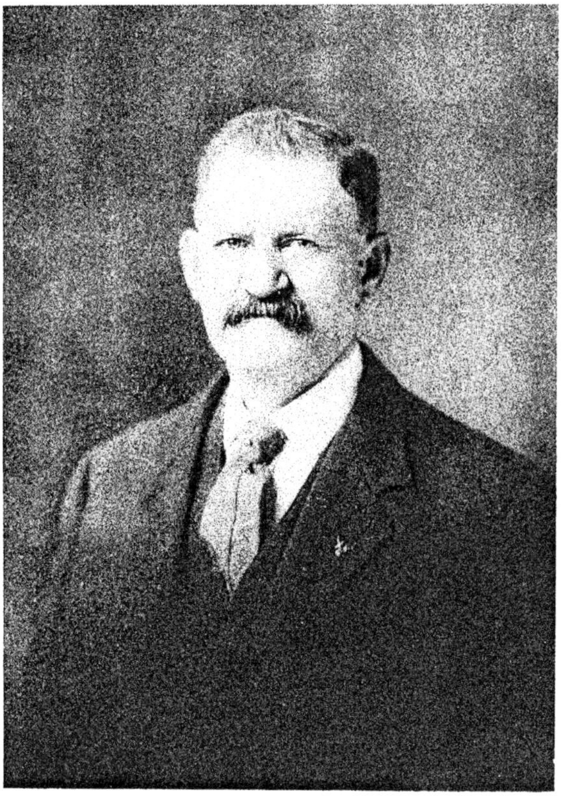

W. T. Bussell

ing in the office of the *Aegis & Intelligencer*, of Belair, and then spent eight years in the employ of Allen, Lane & Scott, a firm of printers, located at Philadelphia. He subsequently removed to Camden, New Jersey, where he became interested in real estate, and in 1894 transferred his interests to eastern Pennsylvania, and purchased land which he developed and made into town lots. His next enterprise was developing a tract of land in New Jersey, which now comprises the town of Alpha, containing three or four thousand inhabitants. He has met with great success in all his real estate dealings, and has been instrumental in developing and settling many tracts of land, among them suburbs of Allentown, York, the beautiful town of Paxtonia, near Harrisburg, and a tract on the Columbia Turnpike near Lancaster, all in Pennsylvania, also a tract near Dover, New Jersey. At the present time (1909) Mr. Bissell is engaged in developing and settling a piece of land at Mount Holly, New Jersey. He makes his home at Camden, New Jersey, where he has a large circle of friends and acquaintances, and where he is affiliated with several organizations. He is a member of the Presbyterian church, and also of the following fraternal and social orders: Benevolent and Protective Order of Elks, Knights of the Golden Eagle, Fraternal Order of Eagles; Camden Commandery, No. 34, Patriotic Order Sons of America; the Patriotic Order of America. In political views he is an Independent. He is recognized as a man of business acumen and good sense, and in all his dealings is upright and honorable.

He married Georgia Ida, daughter of John W. Wilson, a lumber merchant of Baltimore; five children: 1. Lillie May, married Nicholas Everly, of Bloomsbury, New Jersey; they have one child, Ida May. 2. Margaret Webster, married John M. Hunt; they had seven children: Pearl Webster, William Ridgely, Georgia Esther, Bessie May, Herbert, Blanch Ethel, John Ralph. 3. William R., married Mrs. Kerziah Terry, of Pennsylvania; he died in 1907. 4. Emma J., married William E. Duffner, who died July 4, 1908; they had no children, they are both deceased. 5. Wilson Cleveland, died unmarried in 1908.

(The Webster Line).

This name has been borne in our country by men who had few equals in eloquence and scholarship. Among the prominent men of this name are to be found John Webster, who

ii—17

became governor of Connecticut, as well as Daniel the orator and Noah the lexicographer. The family here described has been represented in Virginia records almost since the first settlement there, and from it have sprung many men who have been a credit to their name and country.

(I) John Webster's name appears first in the Virginia Colonial Records in the will of one William Batts, July 18, 1632; in 1639, by act of assembly, John Webster is named as one of the viewers of tobacco crops for Accomac county, and an inventory of the estate of John Webster, deceased, was taken in court, August 18, 1650. He had a son John.

(II) John (2), son of John (1) Webster, was perhaps born in England, and was living on Savages Neck, Northampton county, Virginia before 1630, with his father; later he removed to Hovekills, now Lewes, Delaware, where before 1680 he was petitioner for a court for the county of St. James. He had a son John.

(III) John (3), son of John (2) Webster, was born in 1667, in Northampton county, Virginia, and died in 1753. He removed from Hovekills, Delaware, to Maryland, where in 1733 he lived, near the town of Joppa. The boundary between Maryland and Pennsylvania was frequently in dispute, and in 1740 John Webster testified on the question before the commission from the two states which met at Joppa, then in Baltimore county, now in Harford county. By his first wife, Hannah, he had several children, among them Michael and Isaac. His wife was probably a sister of Isaac Butterworth, who in his will of May, 1728, mentions his nephews, Michael and Isaac, sons of John Webster. John Webster married (second) March 17, 1729-30, at Palapsco, Sarah Giles, and (third) in February, 1735, Mary, widow of John Talbott, of West River, Maryland.

(IV) Isaac, son of John (3) and Hannah Webster, was born about 1700, probably in Maryland, and died October 11, 1759. He married, November 22, 1722, Margaret Lee, who died in 1783, and they had thirteen children, the youngest of whom was Samuel.

(V) Samuel, youngest son of Isaac and Margaret (Lee) Webster, was born in 1746, died December 13, 1817. He married, in March, 1769, Margaret Adams, of Philadelphia, Pennsylvania, and of their twelve children John Adams was the tenth.

(VI) John Adams, son of Samuel and Margaret (Adams) Webster, was born September 19, 1787, in Harford county, Maryland, died July 4, 1877, at the home erected by him on part of his father's estate, which he named Mount Adams, and he was there buried in the family graveyard. Captain Webster early evinced a liking for sea life, and at the age of fourteen embarked for South America on a merchant vessel, which trip was followed by many others to distant ports. At the time of the war of 1812 he was appointed to various positions of responsibility, where he acquitted himself with great efficiency and bravery. In 1814 he had charge of a six-gun battery between Forts McHenry and Covington, and September 13 of that year, in the engagement during which he was twice wounded, he was one of the defenders of the city of Baltimore, and for his gallantry was presented with two gold-mounted swords, one from the city of Baltimore, and one from the state of Maryland. It was at this time that the national anthem, "The Star Spangled Banner," was written. In 1816 he was appointed by President Madison as sailing master in the navy, and November 22, 1819, President Monroe appointed him captain in the revenue marine service, which position he held until his death, at which time he was the senior captain of that service. During the war with Mexico, Captain Webster had command of eight revenue vessels, and co-operated with the army and navy upon the Rio Grande river and at the battle of Vera Cruz. He lost a thumb when Washington was burned by the British, was wounded once in the shoulder, and at one time had a horse shot under him; congress paid him for the loss of the horse and gave him a pension of twenty dollars a month.

Captain Webster married, February 8, 1816, Rachel, daughter of Colonel Joseph Biays, who was a soldier in the revolution, and they had fifteen children, among them: 1. Margaret. 2. Dr. James Biays. 3. Susan A. 4. Laura A., wife of John C. Patterson. 5. William S. These five are living, and those deceased are: Josephine, who became the wife of Dr. William Dallom; Captain John, who entered the revenue marine service; Mary A., who married A. S. Dorsey; Benjamin M.; Rachel C., who married General F. A. Bond; and Isaac P. Captain John Adams Webster was a man of large build, being six feet high and weighing two hundred pounds. He was a member of the Presbyterian church, and took an interest in all the affairs of his native state and coun-

try; his old age was spent at his home in Harford county. Mrs. Webster died in 1869.

(VII) Margaret, daughter of John Adams and Rachel (Biays) Webster, was born December 13, 1817, died February, 1908, in Harford county, Maryland; she married, September 11, 1834, William Rombough Bissell. (See Bissell, I.)

MOORE

This name came into England with William the Conqueror, in 1066. Thomas de More was among the survivors of the battle of Hastings, October 11, of that year, and was a recipient of many favors at the hands of the triumphant invader. All the antiquarians of Scotland and the authorities on genealogy are agreed that the name Dennis-town of Dennistoun, ranks with the most eminent and ancient in the realms of the United Kingdom. It certainly dates back to 1016 and probably earlier, and Joanna, or Janet, daughter of Sir Hugh Dangieltown, married Sir Adam More, Rowallan, and became the mother of Elizabeth More, who, in 1347, married King Robert II. of Scotland, from whom sprang the long line of Stuart monarchs. Another Janet, about 1400, married her cousin, Sir Adam More, of Rowallan. This motto has been preserved by the Dennis-tons: "Kings come of us; not we of kings." The name of Moore has been numerously borne in England, Scotland, and later in Ireland, representatives of this family having filled distinguished positions in the United Kingdom, and several of them occupied seats as members of parliament. They have also been eminent in military affairs. Richard Moore came in the "Mayflower" to Scituate, Massachusetts, and the name is common in the records of Plymouth, Newbury and Salem, the earliest settlements in the state. Among the later immigrants was a Quaker family which located at an early period in New Jersey and has continued in the vicinity of its first settlement, with many worthy descendants. Abstemious, sober and industrious tillers of the soil, they cared not for political preferment, had large families and generally lived to a good old age.

(I) Benjamin Moore, progenitor of the New Jersey family, came from Birmingham, Lincolnshire, England, in company with Thomas Stokes, in the ship "Kent," and arrived at New Castle in August, 1677. He proceeded up the Delaware river to Burlington, West Jersey, and is said to have been the largest land holder in the colony in his line.

He was married in 1693 to Sarah, daughter of Thomas Stokes, who was born in 1670. Children: John, Benjamin, Thomas, Joseph, Samuel, Sarah, Elizabeth, Dorothy and Mary.

(II) Joseph, fourth son of Benjamin and Sarah (Stokes) Moore, was born about 1700, in Burlington, and resided in that vicinity. He married Patience Woolman, born October 27, 1718, daughter of Samuel (2) and Elizabeth Woolman, a granddaughter of Samuel (1) Woolman, who was a son of John and Elizabeth (Borton) Woolman, the progenitors of the Woolman family of New Jersey. The last named was the daughter of John and Ann Borton, progenitors of a numerous family of that name. They came from the parish of Aynhoe in Northamptonshire, England. Joseph Moore's children: Mary, born September 3, 1740; Elizabeth, July 13, 1744; Patience, November 8, 1750; Uriah, November 8, 1753; Jona, April 6, 1758; Cyrus, mentioned below; and John.

(III) Cyrus, third son of Joseph and Patience (Woolman) Moore was born December 3, 1760, in Burlington, and lived on a farm containing about two hundred acres which was willed to him by his father who had in turn received it by will from his father. This was purchased from the proprietors of South Jersey, which adjoins a two hundred and thirty acre farm willed to Abel Moore. In 1754 Joseph Moore built the brick mansion upon this homestead, which is still standing in good repair and has descended to his grandson, Cyrus Moore, of Columbus, New Jersey. He married Mary, daughter of Jonathan and Rebecca (Mason) Austin, of Eversham township, New Jersey. Jonathan was a son of Francis Austin, progenitor of the family of that name in New Jersey. Cyrus Moore's children: 1. Joseph, born February 5, 1790, went to Ohio. 2. Abel, mentioned hereinafter. 3. Patience, October 26, 1792. 4. Charles, February 19, 1794. 5. Rebecca, October 12, 1795. 6. Eliza, February 12, 1797. 7. Cyrus, mentioned below. 8. Uriah, October 2, 1800. 9. Mary, June 24, 1802. 10. Martha, July 5, 1804. 11. John, July 21, 1808.

(IV) Abel, second son of Cyrus and Mary (Austin) Moore, was born April 20, 1791, in Burlington, and died in Lumberton township, March 23, 1863. He was a farmer upon the farm of two hundred and thirty acres above mentioned, it having been inherited from his father. He married Elizabeth C. Engle, daughter of Obadiah and Patience Engle, of Evesham (see Engle, V). The last named

was a daughter of John and Elizabeth Coles. Elizabeth C. Engle was born February 5, 1803, and died June 13, 1880. Children: 1. Granville W., born May 18, 1823, died March 1, 1874. 2. Cyrus, March 12, 1825, married (first) Hope Lippincott; (second) Esther Prickett. 3. Aaron E. November 13, 1827, died June 25, 1840. 4. Anna, December 6, 1830, married Lemuel Prickett, and died August 21, 1881. 5. Patience, June 30, 1833, died December 6, 1834. 6. John, February 27, 1835, died November 17, 1903. 7. Elizabeth, June 1, 1838, died February 21, 1878. 8. George W., mentioned below. 9. Barbara H., May 31, 1843, died October 3, 1908.

(V) George W., fifth son of Abel and Elizabeth C. (Engle) Moore, was born September 6, 1840, in Lumberton, and was educated in the public schools of Easton and the Medford Friends' school. He remained upon the homestead farm with his parents, for whom he cared in their old age, and after their demise purchased the interest of the other heirs to the homestead. To this he added by purchase, extending his domain to about two hundred and eighty acres. He did an extensive business in shipping moulding sand which was carried by boats to Philadelphia to the amount of about ten thousand tons annually. He also carried on successfully general agriculture. In 1889 he bought a farm of fifty acres in Mt. Holly, to which he removed and has since made his home thereon. Though born a Friend, Mr. Moore is an attendant of the Baptist church. In politics he adheres to the Republican party, but has no desire for political honors. He married (first) in May, 1880. Anna R., daughter of Jacob and Elizabeth Prickett. She died August 24, 1881, leaving an infant son, George Engle Moore. He was married (second) in 1882, to Catherine Owen, of Philadelphia, whose maiden name was Fox, daughter of William and Catherine, of Philadelphia. They have one child, Howard Evans, born September, 1883, in Lumberton, who was educated at the public schools of Mt. Holly, learned the machinist trade in Philadelphia and Smithville, New Jersey, and is now associated with his father on the farm.

(VI) George Engle, only son of George W. and Anna R. (Prickett) Moore, was born August 12, 1881, in Lumberton and was educated in the Friends' School at Easton and the Jamison private school at Mt. Holly. He obtained a situation as salesman with Strawbridge & Clothier's jewelry department, of

Philadelphia, and while in this situation pursued a course at Pierce's Philadelphia Business College, carrying on his studies at night. He later was for two years with Litz Brothers. After a time he entered the employ of Kime & Sons, in the same line of business in Philadelphia, as salesman, and this arrangement has continued to the present time. Mr. Moore makes his home on his father's farm at Mt. Holly, and travels to and from Philadelphia each day. He is a member of the Friends' Association, and attends the Baptist church in Mt. Holly. In political principles he is a staunch Republican.

(IV) Cyrus (2) fourth son of Cyrus (1) and Mary (Austin) Moore, was born November 30, 1798, in Burlington and died December 5, 1880. He married, May 17, 1838, Elizabeth Stokes, born September 18, 1808, died March 1, 1884, daughter of Jarvis and Abigail (Woolman) Stokes, the former born November 5, 1780, and the latter October 31, 1789, died February 28, 1859. Cyrus Moore's children: 1. Cyrus S., mentioned below. 2. Jarvis, born February 7, 1843, died at ten years of age. 3. Abigail, June 26, 1845, married Amos Harvey, May, 1883. 4. Mary R., born June 23, 1849.

(V) Cyrus Stokes, eldest child of Cyrus (2) and Elizabeth (Stokes) Moore was born January 28, 1840, and resides upon the ancient homestead in the brick house built by Joseph Moore in 1754. He married, June 6, 1907, Susan (Haines) Troth, daughter of John and Mary Stokes (Haines) Troth. She was born June 3, 1855.

(The Prickitt Line).

The family name of Prickitt is found at an early date in Burlington county, and of course has relation to the New Jersey family of our generally accepted name of Prickitt, the latter being the family purposed to be treated in this place, and supposed to have descended from John Prickitt, of Gloucestershire, England, a "persecuted Friend," in 1660, who is mentioned in the narrative entitled Besse's "Sufferings." There was a Josiah Prickitt, of Burlington, who was one of the founders of Cranberry in 1697, and of whom the "History of the Colony of New Jersey" (Barber and Howe, 1844) says 'Cranberry is one of the oldest places in this part of the state. It was settled about the year 1697 by Josiah Prickitt, butcher, of Burlington. The following year he sold out to John Harrison, of Flushing, Long Island."

(I) Zachariah (or Zackariah) Prickitt, the earliest known ancestor of the family under consideration here of whom we have definite knowledge, settled in Northampton, Burlington county, and is said to have brought with him a large property, which he invested in lands. His will bears date February 28, 1727, and was admitted to probate March 14, of the same year. The baptismal name of his wife was Ellipha, and so far as the records disclose their children were as follows: 1. John. 2. Zackariah, married, 1721, Mary Troth. 3. Jacob, see forward. 4. Elizabeth, married 1723, John Peacock. 5. Hannah, married Philip Quigley.

(II) Jacob, son of Zackariah and Ellipha Prickitt, had a wife Hannah, who bore him eight children and who died 12 4mo. 1759, aged fifty-three years. Their children: 1. Josiah, born 23 8mo. 1733; married Sarah Cowperthwaite. 2. Jacob, born 18 9mo. 1735; married Elizabeth Phillips. 3. Barzilla, born 22 9mo. 1737; married Sarah Sharp. 4. Ann, born 20 10mo. 1739, died 4mo. 1759. 5. Rosatnah, born 11 2mo. 1742. 6. Job, see forward. 7. Hannah, born 26 6mo. 1746; married Amaziah Lippincott. 8. Sabyllah, born 24 9mo. 1748.

(III) Jacob (2), son of Jacob (1) and Hannah Prickitt, was born November 18, 1735, and married Elizabeth Phillips.

(IV) Job, son of Jacob (2) and Hannah Prickitt, was born the 24th of 4th mo. 1744, and married Ann, daughter of Thomas and Elizabeth Smith. Their children: 1. Rachel, born 11mo. 1770; married James Allen. 2. Sabillah, born 9 9mo. 1772, died unmarried. 3. Josiah, born 29 9mo. 1775, died young. 4. Job, born 9 7mo. 177—; married Ann Huff. 5. Josiah, see forward. 6. Barzilla, born 20 2mo. 1781; married Martha Haines.

(V) Ann R., daughter of Jacob and Elizabeth (Phillips) Prickitt, was married in May, 1880, to George W. Moore. (See Moore, V.)

MOORE　The name Moore and the place of residence, Londonderry in the north of Ireland, remind us of the Scotch bard and of the siege of Londonderry and we presume such a combination to name a man of Scotch-Irish blood, and Scotch ancestry. The north of Ireland has given to America splendid examples of the amalgamation of the two races and when we find a Thomas Moore and that his wife was Jean, we are sure of our subjects as capable of producing a noble race of men, whatever may be their sphere in life. They have been fitted by inheritance and environment to be selectmen, poets, authors, physicians, clergymen, lawyers, school teachers, artisans, miners or farmers, and in any of their pursuits are likely to be men of mark.

(I) Henry Moore, son of Thomas and Jean Moore, was born in Londonderry, Ireland, January 1, 1736. He emigrated to America about 1755 and probably landed at Philadelphia, where he married Catherine Fleming, who was born in Philadelphia in 1730. He was a school teacher at New Egypt, New Jersey, and was known as "Master Henry." They removed to Stony Brook, Middlesex county, New Jersey, where their only child John was born July 15, 1774. Catherine (Fleming) Moore died after the birth of his child, and Mr. Moore married as his second wife Sarah Jackaway, who was born at Apanpick, Middlesex county, New Jersey, March 23, 1757. She was the daughter of Reuben and Margaret Jackaway. Henry and Sarah (Jackaway) Moore named their first born son Henry, see forward.

(II) Henry (2), eldest son of Henry (1) and Sarah (Jackaway) Moore, was born in Jacobstown, Burlington county, New Jersey, in 1787, died in 1871. He married Ann Horner, who was born November 9, 1798, died August 2, 1880. The children of Henry and Ann (Horner) Moore were born in the order as follows: 1. Margaret, July 2, 1815. 2. Abigail, November 4, 1817. 3. Henry, June 18, 1818. 4. Francis, May 29, 1822. 5. Barzelia, September 21, 1824. 6. Ezekiel, October 25, 1827. 7. Ann, November 8, 1829. 8. Henrietta, January 30, 1832. 9. Rachel, November 20, 1833. 10. Hugh, see forward.

(III) Hugh, tenth child and fifth son of Henry (2) and Ann (Horner) Moore, was born in New Egypt, Ocean county, New Jersey, March 31, 1836. He received his school training in the district school and worked on his father's farm in summer and at basket making in the winter months. He removed from New Jersey to Smyrna, Delaware, where he carried on the business of basket-making for several years, returning to New Egypt, New Jersey, in 1885. He was married in October, 1856, to Sarah, daughter of Nathaniel and Isabel (Van Sciver) Smalley, who lived near Allentown, Monmouth county, New Jersey, where Sarah was born in September, 1836. The children of Hugh and Sarah (Smalley) Moore were: 1. Frank, who was a basket maker at Collinswood, New Jersey. 2.

Rachel, married Joseph Evans and lives at New Egypt, New Jersey. 3. Harry, a stationary engineer in Philadelphia. 4. Elvira, married D. L. Lowery, of Philadelphia. 5. William, has a meat market at Bradley Beach, New Jersey. 6. Harvey, a hardware merchant in New Egypt, New Jersey. 7. Thomas, a contractor and builder in Washington, D. C. 8. Joseph, a physician and surgeon in Philadelphia, Pennsylvania. 9. Addison Urie, see forward. 10. Walter Clement, see forward.

(IV) Addison Urie, seventh son and ninth child of Hugh and Sarah (Smalley) Moore, was born in Smyrna, Delaware, August 3, 1879, and while he was a mere lad his parents returned to their native state and settled in New Egypt, Ocean county, New Jersey. Here he attended school and became an apprentice to the village printer. In 1897 he established a printing office in New Egypt in company with his brother, Walter Clement, under the name of Moore Brothers, and the same year they began the publication of the *Advertiser* a small weekly newspaper. In 1899 they rechristened the paper the *New Egypt Press* and issued it in a new dress and enlarged form. The business also included a constantly increasing trade in job printing. The Moore Brothers through the *Press* created a sentiment in favor of the establishment of the First National Bank of New Egypt, and they were also instrumental in establishing and maintaining the yearly Lake Carnival. Addison W. Moore was made secretary of the Village Improvement Society, and his public spirit manifested itself in the activity infused by his example and suggestion in the work of the society. His political creed was Democratic, and his fraternal and patriotic affiliat ons included membership in the Order of United American Mechanics, and of the Settlers and Defenders of America, a new hereditary patriotic order incorporated in 1899. He also was a member of the Grange and a regular attendant of the Methodist Episcopal church.

(IV) Walter Clement, youngest and eighth son of Hugh and Sarah (Smalley) Moore, was born in Chester, Pennsylvania, July 2, 1881. He was brought by his parents to New Egypt, New Jersey, when only an infant and was brought up and educated in that village. He was sent to the West Philadelphia Academy and Teachers' College, where he was graduated in 1898. He paid his way through college by teaching at Brindle Park, New Jersey, for almost a year. He did the commercial art work and cartooning for the Burlington *Daily Enterprise*, Burlington, New Jersey, and remained in charge of the art department of that paper for about two years when he again took up teaching school, first for two years at Brindle Park, for one year at Collier's Mills, for two years at Cassville, for one year at Columbus, and in 1906 he became head master or principal of the New Egypt high school. He was a correspondent of the daily press and wrote for educational journals. His literary work in behalf of educational interests included a manual on "School Room Exercises" and "Practical Methods in Education" both of which works are highly valued by pedagogists. He was also associated with his brother, Addison U. Moore, in the printing and publishing business and did much editorial work for the *New Egypt Press* from the time of its first issue in 1897. He was made vice-president of the New Egypt Village Improvement Association and its healthy condition and active working organization is largely due to his wise judgment and willing help. He serves the Methodist church of New Egypt, of which he is a member, as one of its trustees, and his fraternal association is with the Patriotic Order of Sons of America, of New Egypt. His political affiliation was with the Democratic party.

He married, November 10, 1900, May Harker, daughter of Atwood and Susie (Hyers) Harker, of New Egypt, and their first child was Wardell Cecil, born in Cassville, New Jersey, March 22, 1902; their second, Paul Stanley, born in Columbus, New Jersey, October 15, 1903; and their third, Elinor Harker, born in New Egypt, New Jersey, December 15, 1907.

MORRELL   This name is a prominent one in the early Dutch settlers of Long Island, and among the early members of New Amsterdam.

(I) Peter Morrell is the progenitor of the family in America, bearing the name of Albertis or Burtis. In 1643 he married Judith Jans Meynie, of Amsterdam, Holland. He lived on the Heeren Grocht, now Broad street, Manhattan, and owned a tobacco plantation in the Wallabout, Brueeklyn, which estate he patented June 17, 1643. The children of Peter and Judith Jans (Meynie) Morrell who arrived at maturity were: 1. John A., born 1643. 2. Arthur (Aert), 1647. 3. Mary, 1649, married John P. Baub. 4. William, 1652. 5. Francina, 1654, married John Allen. The

three sons: John, Arthur and William, removed to Mespath Kills (Newtown, Long Island) and William and Arthur subsequently located at Hempstead and the brothers were connected with St. George's Church, Protestant Episcopal, at Hempstead.

(II) John Albertus, eldest son of Peter and Judith Jans (Meynie) Morrell, was born in New Amsterdam (New York), 1643, died in Middletown, East New Jersey, April 1, 1791. He removed to Newtown, North Hempstead, locating at Mespath Kills as a farmer and tobacco raiser. He married Elizabeth, daughter of John Scudder, of North Hempstead, and they had children as follows: 1. William. 2. John, see forward. 3. Samuel, who inherited a large share of his father's estate at Mespath Kills and married and had children. 4. Elizabeth, who married John Stewart. 5. Mehitable, who married James, son of William Lawrence, of Middletown, Monmouth county, New Jersey. John A. Morrell died in April, 1691, and his widow married, in 1693, William Lawrence Sr., of Middletown, New Jersey.

(III) John, second son of John A. and Elizabeth (Scudder) Morrell, was born in Mespath Kills, Long Island, about 1680. He married Phebe Albertis and they had one child only, John, see forward.

(IV) John (2), only son of John (1) and Phebe (Albertis) Morrell, was born in Middletown, New Jersey, October 31, 1733. He was the first importer of china and earthenware in the United States and removed during his business life to Philadelphia, where he was the founder of the well known china, glass and earthenware importing house of John Morrell & Company. He was a zealous member of the Protestant Episcopal church in America and in Philadelphia became a member of Christ Church and subsequently of St. James Church. He had a son Richard, see forward.

(V) Richard, son of John (2) Morrell, was born in Philadelphia, Pennsylvania, about 1775. He was brought up to the business of his father and was the successor in the business of importing china and glassware. He was, like his father, a supporter of St. James Protestant Episcopal Church in Philadelphia. He married Sarah Grover, of Philadelphia, and she died in that city July 30, 1819, when her sons Richard H. and Wallace (twins) were two and one-half years of age. Richard Morrell died in Pittsburg, Pennsylvania, at the home of his son Wallace, with whom he lived during his last years.

(VI) Richard H., son of Richard and Sarah (Grover) Morrell, was born in Philadelphia, Pennsylvania, January 30, 1818. He was educated in the public schools of his native city. His mother died when he was quite young and he went to live with his Grandmother Morrell; when he was thirteen years of age he became a clerk in the importing house of Destouet Brothers of Philadelphia, importers and dealers in silk goods. He was a precocious child and youth and was especially earnest and painstaking and desirous of pleasing his employers and learning the business thoroughly. When only seventeen years of age he was placed in charge of the business in the capacity of manager and he held this position for four years until he reached his majority. Meantime, he was economical and saving, and after he had attained manhood he joined George T. Stokes, an employee of the silk importing house of John R. Worrell & Company, in purchasing the business of that firm, and the firm of Morrell & Stokes, importers, commission merchants and general dealers and manufacturers of fine silks and trimmings came into existence with store and warehouse at 211 Church street, Philadelphia. In 1856 Mr. Morrell became a resident of Beverly, continuing to go in and out from his residence to his store in Philadelphia. In 1862 the firm was dissolved by mutual consent and Mr. Morrell retired from active business life and became interested in real estate and stocks as buyer and seller on the exchanges. Following his successful career as a merchant his ventures in real estate and listed stocks proved almost uniformly successful and his advice was sought by investors and his market purchases or sales were watched and followed by speculators. He became one of the largest real estate owners in Beverly, New Jersey, and purchased and remodeled a beautiful residence and made a charming home on Cooper street. His political affiliation was with the Whig party, his first presidential vote being cast in 1840 for the Harrison and Tyler elections, and when the Republican party came into existence in 1856, he considered it simply as the successor to the Whig party and gave it his immediate and unequaled support and every presidential election found him at the polls voting and working for the Republican electoral ticket and at all elections he was as well present to cast his vote for the party candidates, state, county, city and local. He served the city of Beverly as a member of the council for twelve years. He was a member of St.

Stephen's Protestant Episcopal Church of Beverly and his wife and children were baptized and confirmed in that faith. He was married to Elizabeth B., daughter of John Thomson, of Philadelphia, November 19, 1846. John Thomson was born August 14, 1799, and became a very prominent member of the Masonic fraternity passing from Lodge No. 51 of Philadelphia which he joined in 1827, to secretary, 1829-31; junior warden, 1831-32; senior warden, 1832-33; worshipful master. 1833-34; secretary, 1835-36; treasurer, 1837-38; secretary, 1838-44; junior warden, 1844-45; senior warden, 1845-46; secretary, 1853-59; treasurer, 1864-69, through all the degrees and holding the highest offices in succession. Also grand master and secretary of the Grand Lodge of Pennsylvania. Thomson Lodge. Duffyron Mawr, Chester county, Pennsylvania, was named in his honor. He died in Philadelphia, Pennsylvania, in October, 1889. The children of Richard H. and Elizabeth B. (Thomson) Morrell were born in Philadelphia, Pennsylvania, as follows: 1. John Thomson, see forward. 2. Sallie, born October 5, 1850, died April 6, 1896. 3. Mary Thomson. Richard H. Morrell died in Beverly, New Jersey, May 8, 1906.

(VII) John Thomson, eldest son of Richard H. and Elizabeth (Thomson) Morrell, was born in Philadelphia, Pennsylvania, June 22, 1848. He was a pupil in the public schools of his native city and passed the Beck's Academy examination preparatory to entering the Philadelphia high school, which institution is a chartered college conferring the college degrees. His parents removing at this time to Beverly, New Jersey, he did not matriculate at the high school but entered journalism and became interested as a contributor to the *Beverly Weekly Visitor*, the first newspaper established in Beverly and which journal subsequently passed to the management of John K. Haffey and became known as the *Beverly Banner*. He remained with the newspaper up to 1894, and besides his contributions he became the Beverly correspondent for the *Philadelphia Press* in 1883, and also gave local news items in that section of New Jersey to other newspapers. He likewise engaged in the insurance business as agent for West New Jersey for the Fire Association of Philadelphia, the Insurance Company of North America, the Union Insurance Company, and the Franklin Insurance Company, all of Philadelphia. He was a Republican by inheritance and choice, and in 1880 became associated with the United

States census bureau as census taker for Beverly, New Jersey. He is serving his seventh consecutive term as a member of the city council of Beverly, being president in 1907. He attends St. Stephen's, Protestant Episcopal Church, Beverly, of which the family are all attendants and birthright members by baptisms and to which church he, like his father and grandfather, is a liberal and willing contributor and supporter. He also affiliates with the Masonic fraternity, being a member of Beverly Lodge, No. 107, Ancient Free and Accepted Masons. He also became associated with the Benevolent and Protective Order of Elks, through membership in Lodge No. 996 of Burlington, New Jersey, and Keepawa Tribe, No. 257, Improved Order Red Men.

LONGSTREET   The ancient Dutch family to which the family of Longstreet traces its descent is highly respected in Holland. The name was originally a place name, and spelled Langestraat. The family has always been thrifty and industrious, and numbers among its descendants many distinguished members.

(I) Dirck Stoffelse Langestraat, immigrant ancestor, was born in Holland and married there Catherine Van Siddock. He came to America in 1657, and at an early date purchased lands at Shrewsbury, New Jersey. He afterwards gave these lands to his son Richard. He married (second) Johanna Havens, widow of Johannis Holsaert. Children: Richard, Adrian, mentioned below. Other children.

(II) Adrian Langestraat or Longstreet, son of Dirck Stoffelse and Catherine (Van Siddock) Langestraat, died in 1728. He was a cordwainer by trade and owned a farm or plantation at Freehold, Monmouth county, New Jersey. He married Styntje or Christiana Janse. Children: John, mentioned below, Derick, Stoffelse. Five daughters.

(III) John Longstreet, son of Adrian and Styntje (Janse) Longstreet, married, December 17, 1736, Ann Covenhoven, daughter of Peter and Patience (Dawes) Covenhoven. Children: Aaron, died young, Pietras, Jan, Elias, Aaron, mentioned below, Antje.

(IV) Aaron, son of John and Ann (Covenhoven) Longstreet, resided in Holmdel, New Jersey. He married, March 9, 1778, Williampe Hendrickson. Children: Hendrick, mentioned below, John, Lydia, Annie, Nellie.

(V) Hendrick, son of Aaron and Williampe (Hendrickson) Longstreet, was born May 14, 1785, and lived in Holmdel township. He

married, October 11, 1805, Mary, daughter of Joseph and Nellie Holmes. Children: Aaron, Eleanor, Lydia H., Ann H., Emeline, Joseph, Hendrick H., mentioned below, Mary Ann, born 1821, John H., Jonathan.

(VI) Hendrick H., son of Hendrick and Mary (Holmes) Longstreet, was born on the old homestead near Holmdel, Monmouth county, New Jersey, January 11, 1819, died in 1891. He received his earlier education at a select school in the village of Middletown Point, now known as Matawan, New Jersey, and finished his academic course at the seminary at Lenox, Massachusetts. Having determined to pursue the study of medicine he became a student under Dr. Robert W. Cooke. of Holmdel, and subsequently enjoyed the same relation under that distinguished physician and writer, Dr. John B. Beck, professor of Materia Medica and Jurisprudence in the College of Physicians and Surgeons of New York, and author of "Beck's Medical Jurisprudence" and other standard works. At that institution Dr. Longstreet attended several courses of lectures, and in 1842 the degree of Doctor of Medicine was conferred upon him by the same. He immediately located in the pursuit of his profession at Bordentown, where he continued in uninterrupted and successful practice of his profession. As a physician he stood in the front rank of his profession and probably no other in the state was more widely and favorably known. In practice he was the uncompromising foe of everything savoring of empiricism and devoted all of his energies toward the elevation of the standard of his profession. Possessed of a well-stored and analytical mind his judgments were matured and generally correct and his advice and counsel were frequently sought after by his professional friends and acquaintances. With ample facilities for study, possessed of one of the largest and best selected libraries in the state, he became a careful student of his profession, thoroughly familiar with the most recent and most improved methods of medical and surgical practice and in the enjoyment of a large and remunerative practice. His reputation is not alone confined to the locality in which he passed so many years of his life, but extended into the adjoining counties and states.

He was a member of the American Medical Association, of the State Medical Society, of which he was often a delegate, and of the District Medical Society of Burlington county, of which he served as president for several terms. He was identified with the growth and development of Bordentown for over forty years and was recognized as one of its most active, public-spirited and valuable citizens. He was a director and president of the Bordentown Gas Company, of the Water Company and of the Vincentown Marl Company. He was also president of that useful and popular local institution, the Board of Health. A man of decided views upon every subject commanding his attention, bold and fearless in the expression of his opinions, he numbered among his acquaintances many warm friends to whom he was thoroughly devoted and who learned to appreciate the real worth and character of the man. He lived in an unostentatious and quiet way, contributing liberally from the fortune he acquired by faithful labor in his profession to the support of all worthy objects. He took a warm interest in local and national politics but avoided the acceptance of public office.

Dr. Longstreet married (first) in 1848, Hannah Ann Taylor, of New Jersey, who died in 1857. He married (second) in 1869, Elizabeth, daughter of Joseph Newbold, a prominent merchant of Wrightstown, New Jersey. Children by first marriage: 1. Hendrick. 2. Joseph Henry, died young. 3. A child, who died in infancy. 4. Jacob Holmes, referred to below. Children by second marriage: 5. Mary, died in 1883.

(VII) Jacob Holmes, son of Hendrick H., M. D., and Hannah Ann (Taylor) Longstreet, was born at Bordentown, New Jersey, 1856. For his early education he attended the public schools of Bordentown, after which he went to the Lake Mohegan Academy, near Peekskill, New York, and finally in order to fit himself for the profession of electrical engineer he took the course at the Stevens Institute of Technology in Hoboken, New Jersey, from which he graduated with high honors. In 1879 he went into business for himself in New York, manufacturing electrical instruments and remained there until 1888 when he came of Bordentown and established the Riverview Iron Works which he has managed ever since. He has built up a large and a prosperous business for himself and is known in the community as one of the most substantial men of the town. About a mile from the centre of Bordentown he has a model farm comprising about two hundred acres, and here he keeps a large herd of cows and winters over one hundred and fifty head of mules. He is also interested in many of the local enterprises of

the town and the public service corporation, and he has been president and director of the Bordentown Gas Company, the Bordentown Water Company and the Bordentown Banking Company. Mr. Longstreet is a mechanical genius of a very high order. He has taken out a number of extremely valuable patents especially on telegraph instruments. He has served for several terms on the board of chosen freeholders of the city. He is a former member of the Holland Society of New York and of the Benevolent and Protective Order of Elks, No. 105, of Trenton, New Jersey.

RIDDLE The Riddle family in America is of Scotch-Irish descent, the name is usually spelled Riddell or Riddle, but there are many other variations, Ridel, Rydlyn, Ridlon, Ridell, etc. The family is numerous in England, Scotland and Ireland, while their descendants may be found thickly scattered over the states of Pennsylvania, New York, New Jersey, Maryland and Virginia.

(I) Samuel Riddle, the first of the family to come to America, was born in Newton Stewart, Ireland, from whence he emigrated, settling in Philadelphia, Pennsylvania, about 1790, where he took out naturalization papers in 1792. He was a soldier in the war of 1812 and was wounded in the battle of New Orleans. He was an enlisted member of the "Independent Blues," a company of the Fiftieth Pennsylvania militia. He married Ann, daughter of Hugh McPherson, of Aberdeen, Scotland.

(II) William, son of Samuel Riddle, was born in Philadelphia, Pennsylvania, 1820, died December 13, 1859. He was the first to engage in the business of bottling mineral waters. He was an influential man of the city and took an active part in public affairs. He was a member of the Philadelphia city council for ten years, and was president of the board of guardians of the poor, serving in the latter capacity several years. He was one of the promoters and early supporters of the Camden & Atlantic railroad (now West Jersey & Seashore railroad, Pennsylvania system), the first railroad from Philadelphia to Atlantic City. His son, William, has in his possession a receipt signed by Alfred Negus, the first treasurer of the road, that shows he was the second man to whom stock was issued. The date is September 19, 1852. William Riddle married (first) Caroline Wetherill Earl, of Burlington, New Jersey, by whom he had two sons: Samuel, a member of the Philadelphia firm of E. K. Tryon, Jr., & Company, and Robert. He married (second) Mary Ann Durnell, daughter of James and Hannah (Fabian) Durnell, of Philadelphia, Pennsylvania. Their children are: Caroline, married Robert D. Kent, of Passaic, New Jersey, the organizer of the Passaic National Bank, the Passaic Trust Company, the Maiden Lane National Bank, of New York City, and was the first cashier and incorporator for the Atlantic City National Bank; they have a son, William Riddle Kent. William, see forward. Mrs. Mary A. (Durnell) Riddle was a woman of rare business ability and keen foresight. After being left a widow she was obliged to conduct her own affairs, and in looking for business opportunities she foresaw the possibilities of a tract of land situated just beyond the southern limits of Atlantic City. She secured options on the property after considerable difficulty and formed the Chelsea Beach Company, composed entirely of women, organized July 18, 1883. This property has developed into the most beautiful and exclusive of any of Atlantic City's suburbs, and proved highly profitable to the promoters. No liquor saloons or other objectionable places are allowed, and strict rules govern the sanitary arrangements. Chelsea is the finest residential section of Atlantic City, and is a monument to the energy and foresight of Mrs. Mary A. Riddle.

(III) William (2), only son of William (1) and Mary A. (Durnell) Riddle, was born in Philadelphia Pennsylvania, June 30, 1860. He was educated in the North West grammar school of that city, corner of Fifteenth and Race streets. In 1875 he left school and was for a time employed in the office of the Baldwin Locomotive Works with Mr. Converse, Mr. French and Mr. Stroud, then employees, and now members of the company. He took up the study of shorthand and telegraphy, and was for a time private secretary to Henry Bentley, of the Philadelphia Local Telephone Company. From that position he went to New York, where he remained until 1881. He next went to Chicago, where he remained until 1886 in the grain business on the Chicago Board of Trade. In 1886 he was in New York in charge of the office of V. K. Stevenson & Company, real estate dealers at the corner of Fifty-second street and Fifth avenue. In 1888 Mr. Riddle located in Atlantic City, New Jersey, where he has since resided. In 1901 he was elected on the Democratic ticket as assessor of taxes. In this connection he made a practical application of some of the modern theories of taxation with good results. In 1902 he was elected state senator from Atlantic county. He was barely eligible, under the "four years residence" clause of the constitution, and his seat was successfully contested by his defeated opponent because of race track legislation. For the past eight years from 1901 Mr. Riddle has been a member of the council of Atlantic City, where he has served his constituents most acceptably. He has been at different times chairman of the boardwalk, electric and finance committees of councils. He is a director of the Marine Trust Company, of Atlantic City, of which, with Max Weinmann, he was the founder. He is vice-president of the Atlantic City Fire Insurance Company, of which he is the largest individual shareholder. Mr. Riddle owns the only beach front farm in Atlantic City. It is located in Chelsea and covers an entire square. He holds fraternal membership in the Eagles, Benevolent and Protective Order of Elks, Knights of Pythias, and Brotherhood of America.

William Riddle married Florence M. Sailor, a graduate of Philadelphia high school, and has four sons: Hugh, Donald, Bruce and Alan.

SMITH Although the name of Smith, as Elizabeth Drinker, that pretty and fascinating Quakeress, observed in her quaint and interesting diary nearly two hundred years ago, "is perhaps the most common name in the world," the representatives of the branch at present under consideration have carried it far above the level of the common-place and placed it upon a pedestal which would well excite the admiration and emulation of every one. In addition to this, this family by marriage has allied itself with some of the best and strongest of the old colonial blood and stock and worthily deserves an enviable place and mention among the representative families of New Jersey.

(I) George Lemuel Smith, born at "The Buttonwoods" near Cold Springs at head of Mullica river, Atlantic county, New Jersey. January 31, 1845, is now living in Atlantic City, retired. For the greater part of his life he followed the sea as did and do most of his contemporaries and neighbors. By his marriage to Elizabeth, daughter of John Conover, he had two sons and two daughters: 1. Harry Ellsworth, see forward. 2. Alma, wife of George W. Wells, of Olean, New York. 3. Leonora, wife of George Bender, of Colorado Springs. 4. Walton Randolph, deceased.

f taxation
as elected
. He was
residence"
s seat was
ated oppo-
. For the
le has been
City, where
acceptably.
man of the
mittees of
rine Trust
hich, with
er. He is
: Fire In-
the largest
e owns the
City. It is
ire square.
he Eagles,
of Elks,
d of Amer-

M. Sailor,
chool, and
and Alan.

Smith, as
pretty and
bserved in
early two
most com-
esentatives
nsideration
f the com-
stal which
nd emula-
this, this
with some
ld colonial
es an envi-
epresenta-

n at "The
at head of
w Jersey,
n Atlantic
of his life
most of his
; his mar-
a Conover,
1. Harry
, wife of
York. 3.
f Colorado
eased.

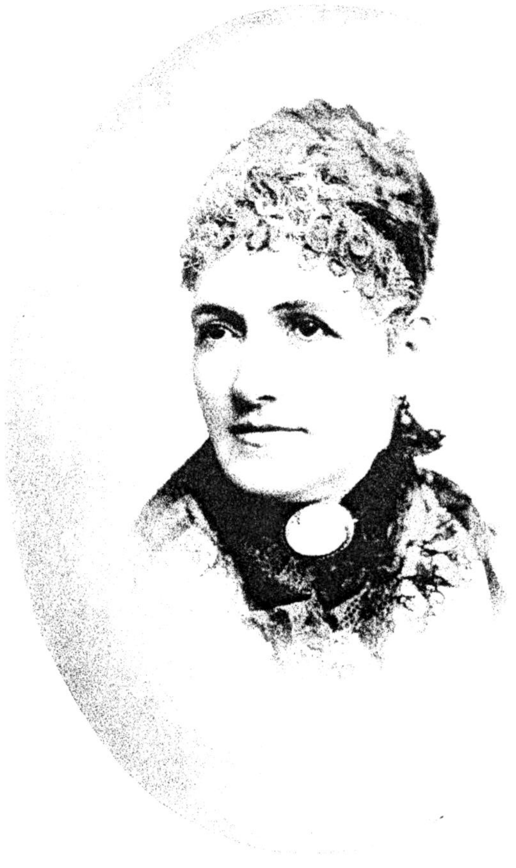

Mary A. Riddle

(II) Harry Ellsworth, son of George Lemuel and Elizabeth (Conover) Smith, was born at Tuckahoe, New Jersey, May 15, 1870, and is now living at Atlantic City, New Jersey. While he was yet a child his parents removed to Weekstown, Atlantic county, and later to Elwood, New Jersey, where Harry Ellsworth attended the public schools. Owing to the necessities of the family, while he was yet a boy, he was obliged to obtain work in a shoe factory at Hammonton, New Jersey, where he learned the trade of shoe cutting. After remaining there for seven years, he came to Atlantic City in 1891 and became a clerk in the Currie hardware store on Atlantic avenue, where he remained for the ensuing three years. Becoming ambitious to get into the newspaper business, he asked Colonel Walter Edge of *The Press*, the new newspaper which the colonel was about that time starting in Atlantic City, for a position. Colonel Edge complied with his request and Mr. Smith obtained the first subscribers to the *Atlantic City Daily Press*. His abilities were soon recognized by the manager of the newspaper, and he was given the position of circulating manager of *The Press*. Subsequently he was promoted and made the head of the advertising department, and finally given the position of general manager. He remained with *The Press* for thirteen years, and during that time, or for a short time, travelled in the interest of the Dorland Advertising Agency, which was under the management of Colonel Edge, in all the large cities of the country. While with Colonel Edge on *The Press*, Mr. Smith was the manager in building the Preston apartment house in Atlantic City.

1908 Mr. Smith purchased the *Sunday Gazette* of Atlantic City, which was at that that time an eight-page paper, but under the management of Mr. Smith it became in one year a sixteen-page paper. It is the only Sunday newspaper in Atlantic City or in south Jersey. Its politics are Republican, and it gives particular attention to real estate. It was founded in 1891.

For sixteen years Mr. Smith has been a member of the famous Morris Guards of Atlantic City. This independent company, at the beginning of the Spanish-American war, volunteered its services to the United States and was accepted officially by Governor Voorhees, June 30, 1898. July 12 following the company left for Camp Voorhees, at Sea Girt, New Jersey, with a muster-roll one hundred and twenty strong. Two days later, July 14,

they were formally sworn into the service of the United States, and after remaining at Camp Voorhees until October 8, they were transferred to Camp Meade, near Gettysburg, Pennsylvania, where they remained until November 12, and the day following, November 13, they were sent to Camp Wetherill, Greenville, South Carolina, at which post they remained until mustered out April 6, 1899. The company was in the Fourth New Jersey Volunteer Infantry, under Captain Bryant. Mr. Smith at that time was a corporal, but was promoted to sergeant. On his return home with his company he was, in 1899, elected second lieutenant of the Morris Guards. In 1903 he was chosen first lieutenant, and in the spring of 1907, after a contest which showed the great personal popularity of Mr. Smith, he was elected captain of the Guards, and the company has never been in a more flourishing condition than it has been since his election.

Mr. Smith is a singer of some note, and is a master of the cornet, which he has played for some years. While living at Hammonton he played in the Protestant Episcopal church. Since, he has sung in the Presbyterian church of Atlantic City. He is a Republican, and an independent in religion. He is a member of the Ventnor Yacht Club, a member of the Paint and Powder Club, a dramatic organization composed of the members of the Morris Guards, in which he always takes a leading part.

YOUNG

In the line of Peter J. Young, the well-known merchant of the city of New Brunswick, five generations of the Young family have been traced in the state of New Jersey. The descent is as follows:

(I) Peter Young, owner of farms in Hunterdon and Somerset counties; married Lizzie Himmer. Children: Three sons and three daughters.

(II) Jacob, son of Peter and Lizzie (Himmer) Young, was a farmer in Hunterdon county. Married Rebecca Trout, and had four sons and three daughters.

(III) Peter J., son of Jacob and Rebecca (Trout) Young, was a farmer, residing near Ringoes, Hunterdon county; married Betsey Gutter. Children: 1. Amos, unmarried. 2. John, married Miss Blackwell, their children being Elizabeth, unmarried, and Frank, married Miss Barnet and has children, Charlena and Earle. 3. Jacob, referred to below.

(IV) Jacob (2), son of Peter J. and Betsey

(Gitter) Young, was born on the paternal farm near Ringoes, Hinterdon county, May 20, 1832, died there February 6, 1869. Married Elizabeth Nevius, daughter of George W. Nevius, of Clover Hill, New Jersey. Children: 1. Peter J., referred to below. 2. Hannah N., born July 8, 1867; married Jacob Schenck Higgins, stock dealer and farmer; they reside in Flemington, New Jersey, and have one child, Catherine N. Higgins.

(V) Peter J. (2), eldest child and only son of Jacob (2) and Elizabeth (Nevius) Young, was born on the farm owned by his Grandfather Young (where his parents resided), near Ringoes, Hinterdon county, New Jersey, October 28, 1865. In early boyhood, owing to the death of his parents, he went to live with his Grandmother Nevins at Flemington, New Jersey, and in that place he was reared, entered upon his business career, and lived until the year 1893. His maternal uncles, Jacob and Austin G. Nevius, were associated in mercantile business, their operations gradually acquiring extensive range and resulting in the establishment of large and important stores, under the firm style of J. & A. G. Nevius, at Flemington, Somerville and Trenton. The nephew was early given employment as clerk in the Flemington store, and there learned all the details of the business. In 1893, pursuant to the policy of the firm to enlarge its interests, Mr. Young came to New Brunswick, purchased the dry goods establishment of A. L. Mundy at 27 Church street, and embarked upon a mercantile career in which he has since continued with marked success. From the Church street quarters he removed, February 1, 1908, to the large new building at the corner of George and Paterson streets, the most conspicuous business location in the city. His store, conducted under his personal name, is the largest and most complete of its kind in New Brunswick, and employs at the present time thirty-five clerks. Mr. Young is a member of the Masonic fraternity—Union Lodge, Free and Accepted Masons, Scott Chapter, and Temple Commandery. He married, October 17, 1894, Anne Hopewell, daughter of John B. and Anne M. F. Hopewell, of Flemington, New Jersey.

(The Nevius Line).

This family is of Netherlands origin, and so far as is known the name sustains no genealogical relation whatever to the strictly English one of Nevins. The patronymic Nevius is the Latinization of the original Hollandish forms Neef, Neeff, Neve, de Neve, etc. For a scholarly and highly interesting account of the origin of the family and its early associations, the reader is referred to the recent genealogical work, "Joannes Nevius and His Descendants, A. D. 1627-1900," by A. Van Doren Honeyman.

(I) Joannes Nevius, son of Rev. Johannes Neef (or Nevius) and Maria Becx, baptized at Zoelen, Holland, March 14, 1627, came to Amsterdam (now New York City) about 1651; merchant, prominent citizen, and city secretary; afterward lived on the Long Island (Brooklyn) side of the East river, and had charge of the ferry; died 1672; married, in the Dutch Church, New Amsterdam, 1653, Ariaentje Bleijck; their sixth child was

(II) Peter Nevius, baptized in New Amsterdam, February 4, 1663; removed to Flatlands, Long Island; died April 29, 1740; married, June 22, 1684, Janetje Roelofse Schenck; their second child was

(III) Roeloff Nevyus, born about 1687; removed to Three Mile Run, Somerset county, New Jersey, where he was an active supporter of the ministry of Rev. Theodorus Frelinghuysen; died after 1736; married Catalyntje Lucasse Van Voorhees, daughter of Lucasse Stevense Van Voorhees, of Flatlands; their fourth child was

(IV) Peter Nevyus, baptized April 23, 1727; lived at various times near Three Mile Run, New Brunswick, and Clover Hill; died on his farm near Clover Hill (Hinterdon county), after 1800; married, about 1751, Maria Van Doren; their tenth child was

(V) Jacob Nevius, born near Clover Hill, May 20, 1769, died there about 1855; married (second) August 10, 1806, Hannah Lanning; their fourth child was

(VI) George Washington Nevius, born near Clover Hill, September 16, 1812; merchant of that place; died March 17, 1858; married, June 1, 1841, Hannah Gray, daughter of Austin Gray, of Nechanic; their first child was

(VII) Elizabeth Nevius, born at Clover Hill, January 22, 1842, died April 28, 1874; married (first) Jacob Young; (second) Ira Higgins; two children by her first marriage, the eldest being

(VIII) Peter J. Young, above.

RICHARDSON　Dr. James Richardson, of 701 North Sixth street, Camden, New Jersey, is a descendant of old colonial stock, which has done yeoman service in the preservation and upbuilding of the nation, in more than one state and colony. His ancestors came over to this country and settled first in Virginia, from whence they moved into Maryland, and later into Delaware, where Dr. Richardson was born. His grandfather, Benjamin Richardson, was a miller and an itinerant Methodist preacher, who traveled all over the state of Maryland, and whose father came from Virginia. His father, James Brummell Richardson, was born at Smyrna, Kent county, Delaware, August 24, 1810. He was a miller and a farmer; he died in 1884. His mother, Mary, was the daughter of William Rutledge, a descendant of a most distinguished family.

Dr. James Richardson, son of James Brummell and Mary (Rutledge) Richardson, was born near Dover, Delaware, on his father's farm, April 12, 1862, and is now living in Camden, New Jersey. For his early education he was sent to the public schools near Dover, and to the Dover Classical Academy, the principal of which at that time was Professor William A. Reynolds. After leaving the academy he entered in 1883 the Jefferson Medical College, in Philadelphia, from which he graduated with the degree of M. D. in April, 1885. He entered at once upon the general practice of his profession at Camden, New Jersey, but after a time removed to Kent county, Delaware, and set up in general practice there, and also in New Castle county. Here he remained until 1898, when he removed to Riverside, New Jersey. After remaining in Riverside until 1907, he returned once more to Camden, where he now resides. At one time Dr. Richardson thought that he would make himself a specialist in skin diseases, and therefore took up a course in that subject in the Skin Hospital of Dr. John Shoemaker, in Philadelphia. Dr. Richardson is a Republican and he has been active and enthusiastic as well as of great value to the advancement of the interests of his party. He enjoys the distinction of being one of the first legislators of the state of Delaware ever elected to that body on the Republican ticket. He was elected in 1888 from Kent county, and while serving in the legislature was a member of the committee on education, the committee on claims, and the committee on fish and oysters. At one time he was a member of and also the first of the school board at Leipsic, Delaware. He is a member of the Delaware State Medical Association, and at one time was also a member of the Burlington County New Jersey Medical Society. He is a member of the State Street

Methodist Episcopal Church of Camden, New Jersey.

James Richardson, M. D., married, in 1873, Annie, daughter of Conklin Raynor, a descendant of one of the oldest families in this country, and one of the founders, first of Wethersfield, Connecticut, second of Stamford, Connecticut, and lastly of Southampton, Long Island. The children of James and Annie (Raynor) Richardson who are now living are: 1. Martha, married William M. Coffin, of Maryland. They are now living at Camden, New Jersey. 2. Marie, a student in the Camden high school.

BAILEY The Bailey family of New Jersey or rather that branch which is at present under consideration is distinct from the old New England branch although there are the same christian names in the two families and would lead one to suggest that there was some connection. The records, however, show that such connection exists farther back than this side of the ocean.

(I) Thomas Bailey, a native of Bristol, England, which was in his day one of the most important cities of England, came over to America in 1682 and purchased land in Bucks county, Pennsylvania. By occupation he was a bodice maker. Among his children was Thomas, referred to below.

(II) Thomas (2), son of Thomas (1) Bailey, immigrant, married Mercy Lucas and among his children was Edward, referred to below.

(III) Edward, son of Thomas (2) and Mercy (Lucas) Bailey, married Ann Satterthwaite and among their children was William, referred to below.

(IV) William, son of Edward and Ann (Satterthwaite) Bailey, was born in Gloucester county, New Jersey. He was a farmer. He married Keziah Skinner, whose father was in the revolutionary war. Among their children was William, referred to below.

(V) William (2), son of William (1) and Keziah (Skinner) Bailey, was born in Gloucester county, New Jersey, April 1, 1808. He was a farmer; in religion a Methodist, and in politics a Whig and afterwards a Republican. He married Lydia, daughter of Leven Densten, of Virginia, who was born in Gloucester county, New Jersey, in September, 1812. Among their children was George Washington, referred to below.

. (VI) George Washington, son of William

(2) and Lydia (Densten) Bailey, was born near Clarksboro, Gloucester county, New Jersey, December 5, 1840, and is now living in Philadelphia, Pennsylvania. He was born on his father's farm, and for his early education was sent to the public schools of Gloucester county and to the State Normal School. After the civil war he entered the medical department of the University of Pennsylvania, from which he graduated with the degree of M. D. in 1868, and then engaged in the general practice of his profession in Philadelphia. In 1872 his health began to fail under the strenuous labor in which he was engaged, and he was compelled to abandon his practice. He then for a time engaged in the real estate business in Camden, New Jersey, and after this in the wholesale coal business in Philadelphia. Finally he entered into the business of mining and shipping coal, and was for many years an influential member of the boards of directors of a number of business corporations. He was one of the prominent organizers of the Camden National Bank; at present he has withdrawn from his connection with all financial organizations with the exception of the Bridgeton National Bank and the Glassboro National Bank. Among the other important organizations with which Dr. Bailey has been prominently connected should be mentioned Whitney Glass Works Company. In 1906 he finally withdrew from active business. Since early manhood Dr. Bailey has been greatly interested in the organization and advancement of Sunday school work and he was a prominent and active member of some of the most important associations and organizations with that object in the country. He was for many years the president of the New Jersey State Sunday School Association, and the chairman of its executive committee. He is now chairman emeritus of the executive committee of that association. For many years also he was the treasurer of the International Sunday School Association, and is now the chairman of the executive committee of the World's Sunday School Association. In religion he is a Presbyterian and he was for many years a member of the board of trustees of the general assembly of that denomination as well as the vice-president of the general assembly's board of education. He is also a member of several special committees of that body, and a member of the board of trustees of the Presbyterian Hospital and also vice-chairman of the West Jersey Orphanage for Destitute Colored Children. In politics Dr. Bailey is a Republican,

and although he says that he has never held any office worth mentioning he has been staunch and active in promoting the welfare of his party, into which he points with pride that he was born remarking that his first lesson in politics was from the *New York Tribune*. He served loyally and faithfully on the Union side in the civil war as a sergeant in Company E, Twenty-fourth New Jersey Volunteers, with distinguished service at Fredericksburg and Chancellorsville. His social club is the Union League of Philadelphia. He is also a demitted member of Trimble Lodge, No. 117, Free and Accepted Masons, of Camden, New Jersey, and he is one of the ex-presidents of the Presbyterian Social Union.

George Washington Bailey, M. D., married (first) December 8, 1872, in Hurffville, New Jersey, Rebecca Hyder Hurff, born September 10, 1848, daughter of Thomas W. Hurff, a farmer, who at one time served in the lower house of the New Jersey legislature, and Hannah (Hyder) Hurff. There were no children by this marriage. Mrs. Bailey died October 10, 1888. Dr. Bailey married (second) June 18, 1891, at Wenonah, New Jersey, Annie, born in Philadelphia, July 26, 1864, daughter of George L. McGill, a molasses merchant of Philadelphia. Children: 1. Grace Lydia, born April 18, 1892, attended the Friends' Select School in Philadelphia, from which she graduated, class of June, 1909. 2. Anna McGill, born June 28, 1893. Both children were born in Wenonah.

ROESCH The Roesch family of Philadelphia, Pennsylvania, and Atlantic City, New Jersey, are among the newer comers to America, there being but two full grown generations, both of whom are still living to represent and speak for it; but the well-deserved success which has crowned the efforts of the emigrant father and his sons entitles them to rank among the representatives of successful achievement of modern New Jersey.

(1) Charles Roesch, founder of the family, was born in Germany and came over to this country in 1855. Settling in Philadelphia he established the house of Charles Roesch & Sons, manufacturers, packers and meat dealers, and before long he was able to start a branch house at Atlantic City, where they are now doing the largest business in the city, supplying all the leading hotels of the resort. He married Mariah E., born in Germany, daughter of Jacob Kleefeld, and by her he had four

children: Elizabeth, who died in infancy; William, Charles, George Jacob. The last three are referred to below.

(II) William, second child and eldest son of Charles (1) and Mariah E. (Kleefeld) Roesch, was born in Philadelphia in 1858. He married (first) Annie A. Mathis, who died leaving him with two children: Marie and William, Jr. He married (second) Anna Loos, who has also died leaving him with two more children: Elsie and Helen.

(II) Charles (2), third child and second son of Charles (1) and Mariah E. (Kleefeld) Roesch, was born in Philadelphia, October 19, 1861, and is now living at Atlantic City, New Jersey. He attended the public schools of Philadelphia and then the Pierce Business College of the same city, and after his graduation from the latter institution he became connected with his father's extensive business in Philadelphia, and in 1888 also with the Atlantic City end. Here the business increased to such an extent that in 1891 he became a resident of the city and gave his entire time to looking after the interests of that branch, in which he has been very successful. He is a member of Excelsior Lodge, No. 491, Free and Accepted Masons, of Philadelphia, and St. John's Chapter, Royal Arch Masons, of Philadelphia. He has also taken all the degrees in the consistory rites of masonry up to and including the thirty-second. He is a member of the Lu Lu Temple, of Philadelphia; of Victory Lodge, Independent Order of Odd Fellows, of Philadelphia, and is also a member of the Tall Cedars of Lebanon, of Atlantic City. He is a member of the Atlantic City Yacht Club, Atlantic City Board of Trade, and German Reformed Lutheran Church. His brother, William, is president of the Lutheran Church Society, of Philadelphia and his father was a member of the same church. Mr. Roesch is a Republican. He was the first president of the Business Men's League, of Atlantic City, and he is the treasurer of the Atlantic City Publicity Bureau. In 1883 Charles Roesch married (first) Sally, daughter of William Trefz, of Philadelphia, who died after bearing him two children: 1. Carl Trefz, born in 1888; unmarried; in the Atlantic City branch store. 2. Eva, died in infancy. In 1897 Charles Roesch married (second) Frederica, daughter of William Trefz, of Philadelphia, sister of his first wife.

(II) George Jacob, fourth and youngest child of Charles (1) and Mariah E. (Kleefeld) Roesch, was born in Philadelphia, in 1864. He is a member of the firm of Charles Roesch &

Sons, and attends to the Philadelphia end of the business, residing in that city, and having a beautiful summer residence at Atlantic City. He married Matilda H. Poth, of Philadelphia, and has two children: Clara Matilda and Helen.

WOODRUFF   The Woodruff family of New Jersey, not only in its Elizabethtown branch, but also in its West and South Jersey representatives, has won for itself so distinguished and enviable reputation that it is very much to be regretted that the documents up to the present brought to light have failed to establish conclusively the complete genealogy of the branches in Burlington, Gloucester, Salem and other West Jersey counties. It is to be hoped that time and further research among old family papers and records will complete a genealogy which, while certain in its outlines, is at present sketchy in its details.

(1) Lewis Woodruff, of Woodruff, Bridgeton, New Jersey, was one of the largest and most influential land owners of the region where he dwelt in his day, and it is in his memory and honor that the place of his home has been known ever since by his name. When he died he divided his enormous property among his six children, two of whom were by one of his wives, and the other four by the other of his wives. These sons were: Thomas Githens, referred to below; Edward, Robert, John, Lewis, Albert.

(II) Thomas Githens, son of Lewis Woodruff, of Woodruff, Cumberland county, New Jersey, was born at Woodruff in 1845. He spent his life on the farm which he inherited from his father. By his wife, Sarah Elizabeth (Bowen) Woodruff he had three children: 1. Malcolm Bowen, referred to below. 2. Grace, born in 1868; married John Sanders, of Linwood, Atlantic county, New Jersey, and now living at Wildwood, New Jersey, with her husband and two children, Ethel and Milton. 3. Milford, born in 1888; unmarried; now in the water department of Atlantic City.

(III) Malcolm Bowen, eldest child of Thomas Githens and Sarah Elizabeth (Bowen) Woodruff, was born at Woodruff, Cumberland county, New Jersey, November 9, 1866, and is now living at Atlantic City, New Jersey. For his early education he was sent to the public schools of Cumberland county and of Atlantic City, where as a boy in the latter place he looked after the ponies on the Beach also on the celebrated Broadwalk. Coming to Atlantic

City in 1879, he for some time drove a hack in the town, after which he became connected with the Adams Express Company and subsequently with the Atlantic City police department, at first as one of the summer policemen. This was on June 4, 1891, and December 10 of the same year he was promoted to the regular police force, and after serving as an officer for eight years became, March 15, 1899, captain of police, and November 18, 1907, was appointed chief of the police department by Mayor Stoy. From special policeman to his present position at the head of an energetic and efficient police force to-day he has occupied every position in the department from the lowest to the highest during a period of eighteen years in all, and in the whole time he has never lost a day's duty or a day's pay. This record speaks for itself. Mr. Woodruff is a member of Belcher Lodge, No. 180, Free and Accepted Masons, of Atlantic City, and he is also a member of the Independent Order of Odd Fellows. He is a Republican and attends the Methodist Episcopal church.

GLASPELL The Glaspell family of New Jersey is apparently one of the late comers into the state, but it is so connected with the old and prominent families of Salem and Cumberland counties that no account of the representative families of that section of New Jersey would be complete without making mention of them, as for three of four generations they have been identified with the history and fortunes of the state.

(I) Thomas Dennis, son of John Glaspell, is the first of the name to be distinctly identified with New Jersey. He was born in Cumberland county, New Jersey, in October, 1813. By his marriage with Christiana Clinton, daughter of Charles Beatty and Mary (Ewing) Fithian (see Fithian, V). He became linked with all that is best in the old New Jersey colonial stock. Children of Thomas Dennis and Christiana Clinton (Fithian) Glaspell were: 1. Enos E., married (first) Martha O. Tyler, and (second) Mary E. English, both of them descendants of old New Jersey families. 2. Theophilus, died unmarried. 3. Mary Elizabeth, died unmarried. 4. Edwin Miller, married Eliza Milford, one of Salem county's oldest and most prominent families. 5. Thomas Bowen, died unmarried. 6. John N., referred to below. 7. Mary Fithian, married Charles Rudderow.

(II) John N., sixth child and fifth son of Thomas Dennis and Christiana Clinton (Pithian) Glaspell, was born at Greenwich, Cumberland county, New Jersey, October 29, 1850. For his early education he was sent to the public schools of Greenwich, after leaving which for two winters he attended the South Jersey Institute. He then for the next sixteen years taught school in Cumberland county. For two years he had charge of the district school in the neighborhood where he was born, and in 1876 he became the principal of the school at Mauricetown, New Jersey, where he remained for eleven years. For the following year he taught at Bridgeton, New Jersey. In 1887 he took up the trade of butcher, at which he remained for eighteen months. In 1891 he became principal of the second ward school at Bridgeton, and in 1895 was appointed by the New Jersey state board of education county superintendent of public schools for Cumberland county, New Jersey, which position he has held to the great satisfaction of the county for fifteen years. When he was first made superintendent of the county schools, Mr. Glaspell had only one hundred and eighty-five teachers under his jurisdiction. Under his able management the educational problem had been so well handled and the cause of education so much advanced in Cumberland county that he now has charge of seventy-five schools and two hundred and sixty-five teachers. Mr. Glaspell is a Republican in politics and he has done splendid work for his party and his state during his active life. In 1890-93-94 he was elected from the first district of Cumberland county to the New Jersey assembly. For a while after this he acted as the bookkeeper of the New Jersey State Mutual Building and Loan Association, of Camden, and March 7, 1895, he was appointed to fill the unexpired term of Charles J. Hampton, the county superintendent of schools. He was elected in 1908, under the new charter of Bridgeton, a member of city council, and became its first president. Mr. Glaspell is a member of Neptune Lodge, No. 75, Free and Accepted Masons; Royal Arch Masons of Cumberland county, Olivet Commandery, Knights Templar, Millville, New Jersey, and for four years was the worshipful master of his Masonic lodge in Mauricetown, New Jersey. He is also a past high priest of the Royal Arch Masons. Mr. Glaspell is also a member of the National Teachers' Association and of the Order of Elks. In religion he is an attendant of the Presbyterian church.

John N. Glasfell

(The Fithian Line).

According to the traditions of the Fithian family they are of Welsh descent. For centuries they have been among the most prominent of the families of Cumberland and Salem counties of New Jersey, and also in many other portions of the country.

(I) William Fithian, founder of the family in this country, is said to have been a soldier in Cromwell's army, having been present at the execution of Charles the First; he was, after the restoration of Charles the Second, proscribed and obliged to flee the country. He came first to Boston, whence he removed to Lynn, Massachusetts, then to New Haven, and finally to East Hampton, Long Island, where he remained until his death, between 1678 and 1682. By his wife, Margaret, he had: 1. Martha, died in 1678. 2. Lieutenant Enoch, died February 20, 1726; married, June 25, 1675, Miriam Burnett. 3. Sarah. 4. Hannah. 5. Samuel, referred to below.

(II) Samuel, son of William and Margaret Fithian, born in East Hampton, removed to Cohansey, Cumberland county, New Jersey, about 1698, died there in 1702. The original residence of the family was at what was formerly known as the New England Cross road, in Fairfield township, New Jersey. March 6, 1679, Samuel Fithian married Priscilla, daughter of Thomas and Mary Barnes, of East Hampton, Long Island, and had: 1. John, born September 1, 1681. 2. Josiah, May 6, 1685, died April 3, 1741; married, November 7, 1706, Sarah, daughter of the Rev. Philip Dennis. 3. Samuel, referred to below. 4. Esther, March 6, 1691. 5. Matthias, February 3, 1694. 6. William, March 25, 1698.

(III) Samuel (2), son of Samuel (1) and Priscilla (Barnes) Fithian, was born April 17, 1688, in East Hampton, Long Island, died in Fairfield, Cumberland county, New Jersey, November 2, 1777. He married, September 3, 1741, Phebe, daughter of Ephraim Seeley, who died March 12, 1764. Their children were: 1. Hannah, born August 4, 1742, married Nathan Leake, of Deerfield, and died November 8, 1842. 2. Rachael, July 7, 1744, died October 22, 1882; married Daniel Clark, of Hopewell. 3. Amy, July 16, 1746, died November 20, 1824; married Joseph More, of Deerfield. 4. Joel, referred to below. 5. Elizabeth, December 13, 1750, died February 6, 1788; married Ephraim Seeley. 6. Mary, April 1, 1752, died November, 1793; married

it—18

Joshua Brick. 7. Sarah, March 3, 1754, died November 23, 1779; married Thomas Brown, of Hopewell. 8. Ruth, May 25, 1756, died December 3, 1846; married David Bowen. 9. Seeley, October 15, 1758.

(IV) Joel, son of Samuel (2) and Phebe (Seeley) Fithian, was born September 29, 1748, died November 9, 1821. He was one of the most prominent members of his family in New Jersey. September 3, 1771, he married (first) Rachael, daughter of Jonathan Jr. and Anna (Dominick) Holmes, granddaughter of Jonathan Holmes, and great-granddaughter of Obadiah Holmes, born at Preston, county Lancaster, England, emigrated to Boston, 1639, located at Salem, Massachusetts, and then at Newport, Rhode Island, where he died December 15, 1682. Rachael (Holmes) Fithian was born March 14, 1750, died leaving one child, Josiah, of Bridgeton, born September 30, 1776, died July 14, 1842. March 4, 1780, Joel Fithian married (second) Elizabeth, daughter of the Rev. Charles Beatty, a descendant of one of the oldest and most prominent families of Bucks county, Pennsylvania. Children of Joel and Elizabeth (Beatty) Fithian were: 1. Charles Beatty, referred to below. 2. Samuel, born February 26, 1785, died September 28, 1806. 3. Philip, January 20, 1787, died January 16, 1868. 4. Ercuries Beatty, August 14, 1789, died May 26, 1816. 5. Enoch, M. D., of Greenwich, New Jersey, May 10, 1792.

(V) Charles Beatty, eldest child of Joel and Elizabeth (Beatty) Fithian, was born December 18, 1782, died November 21, 1858. He married Mary Ewing, January 16, 1805. She was born May 20, 1787, died April 24, 1849. Their children were: 1. Ann Elizabeth, born October 14, 1805; married, February 19, 1825, Richard Fithian. 2. Enos Ewing, February 22, 1807, died September 28, 1837. 3. Sarah Ewing, January 2, 1809, died August, 1903; married William K. Sheppard. 4. Beatty, December 20, 1810, died April, 1896; married, September 17, 1833, Hannah Harding. 5. Rachael Ewing, August 16, 1813, died July 18, 1842; married, October 24, 1833, Robert S. Garrison. 6. Samuel R., August 30, 1815; married, October 12, 1840, Amelia Bacon. 7. Christiana C., April 23, 1817, died June, 1896; married Thomas Dennis Glaspell (see Glaspell, I). 8. Mary Clark, September 6, 182—, died February 6, 1907. 9. Emily Seeley, September 13, 1823; married Samuel S. Lawrence.

CARMANY The Carmany family of Pennsylvania and New Jersey belonged to that sturdy group of German settlers who came over to this country in the latter part of the eighteenth and the early of the nineteenth century, and have grown up with the new nation in the Western World.

(I) Philip Carmany, founder of the branch of the family at present under consideration, came over to this country with three or four of his brothers, and possibly his father, and settled in Lebanon and Anwill, Lebanon county, Pennsylvania. By his wife, Mary Esterline, he had eleven children: 1. Elizabeth, born December 8, 1801. 2. John, November 9. 1803. 3. Catharine, November 27, 1805. 4. Rebecca, April 21, 1808. 5. Henry, referred to below. 6. Sarah, January 25, 1813. 7. Cyrus, March 15, 1815. 8. Joseph, November 14, 1817. 9. Maria, April 14, 1820. 10. Jacob. 11. William, November 25, 1825.

(II) Henry, fifth child and second son of Philip and Mary (Esterline) Carmany, was born June 15, 1810. He married in Anwill, Lebanon county, Pennsylvania, Sarah Philippy. Their children were: 1. Jeremiah, born November 4, 1833. 2. Cyrus, referred to below. 3. Henry, June 30, 1838. 4. William, October 8, 1841. 5. Mary, September 18, 1844. 6. George, January 25, 1847. 7. Sarah, April 10, 1850. 8. Joanna, December 21, 1853. 11. Abraham Lincoln, March 27, 1861.

(III) Cyrus, second child and son of Henry and Sarah (Philippy) Carmany, was born in Anwill, Lebanon county, Pennsylvania, February 23, 1836, and is now living retired in Roxborough, Philadelphia, where he was for many years engaged in the dyeing business. He was for two terms a member of the city council of Philadelphia. He married Adeline, daughter of John Stober, of Schafferstown, Pennsylvania. Their children are: 1. John, born June 23. 1859; he was married three times, the names of both of his first two wives being Caroline, that of his third wife Sarah; his children are Bertha, John and Harry. 2. Edward, February 8, 1862; married Bella Ferguson. 3. George Walter, referred to below. 4. Mary Ella, April 29, 1866; married Charles M. Stout and has five children; Charles M. Jr., Stober, Mary, Mildred and Helen. 5. Harry S., M. D., July 14, 1868; unmarried. 6. Alema Aldine, December 31, 1872; married Harry Binns, physician, and has one child, Adeline. 7. Sallie, July 14, 1875. 8. William, August 21, 1877; a physician; married Ray Craven and has one child, Lillie Craven. 9. Bessie Adeline. February 19, 1880; married Dr. William MacKinney.

(IV) George Walter, third child and son of Cyrus and Adeline (Stober) Carmany, was born in Philadelphia, Pennsylvania, February 27, 1864, and is now living in Atlantic City, New Jersey. For his early education he went to the public school of Philadelphia, and then became a cash boy to the store of Strawbridge & Clothier, in that city. With this firm he remained as boy and man for about eight years, and by his diligence, application and ability rose to the position of clerk in their clothing department. He then became one of the representatives of a firm in Berlin, Germany, which dealt in dyestuffs, which had branch offices at 122 Walnut street, Philadelphia, and this firm he still represents. In 1889, owing to the poor health of one of his children, he removed his residence from Philadelphia to Atlantic City, where his wife in 1891 opened a small hotel known as the Fredomia, which has been in most successful and popular operation ever since, located at No. 158 South Tennessee avenue, Atlantic City. Mr. Carmany is the alderman of Atlantic City, that city being peculiar in having only one which is elected by the city at large. In virtue of this office he is the president of the city council, and in the absence or sickness of the mayor he is ex-officio, the acting mayor. He is a member of the Protestant Episcopal Church, and is also a popular, prominent, influential and enthusiastic secret society man. Among the numerous societies and associations of which he is a member should be noted: Lodge No. 276, Benevolent and Protective Order of Elks, in Atlantic City; Lodge No. 9, Free and Accepted Masons, Philadelphia, of which in 1896 he was worshipful master; Chapter No. 250, Royal Arch Masons, of Philadelphia, of which he was one of the committeemen; the Kadosh Commandery. No. 29. Knights Templar, of Philadelphia; the Lu Lu Temple, Mystic Shriners. of Philadelphia; the Order of Sparta, Philadelphia; the Washington L. S. of Honor, Philadelphia; Lodge No. 11, Tall Cedars of Lebanon, of Atlantic City. Mr. Carmany is also a prominent social clubman, being a member of the Philadelphia Athletic Club, Philadelphia Quartet Club, and of the Harmony Singing Society of Philadelphia. All this, however, does not interfere with his taking a prominent and an active part in the business interest and welfare of the city. He is a member not only of the Hotelmen's Association of Atlantic City, but also of the National Hotelmen's Association. He is the harbor master of the Atlantic City Yacht Club, an active member of the City Troop of Atlantic City, a contributing member of the Morris Guard of Atlantic City, a member of the Atlantic City Businessmen's League, and a member of the Atlantic City Board of Trade.

George Walter Carmany married, October 31, 1887, Catharine Crosland, daughter of Charles Storey and Elizabeth (Goldsmith) Crosland. Her grandfather, John M. Crosland, was one of the earliest pioneers of Pottsville, Pennsylvania, where he died at the age of eighty-three. He was born in Ridley township, Delaware county, August 25, 1810, and came to Pottsville at the age of nineteen. He learned the trade of ship carpenter and boat builder, and he built the first boat in which coal was shipped to New York for George H. Potts Sr.; Mr. Crosland had personal charge of the boat on the trip. He subsequently entered into the boat building business on a site near where the present Atkins Furnaces are located, and this business he carried on successfully a number of years. During this time he saved three persons from drowning, one of whom was Dr. A. H. Halberstadt. He was an active politician, and a lifelong Democrat. He spoke in almost every county in Pennsylvania; he was able, eloquent and forcible, and always in demand. At one time he was elected a representative to the Pennsylvania legislature, at another he was chosen as a justice of the peace, and held that office for a number of years. He was twice a writer for *The Press*. During his life he was the oldest Odd Fellow in the state of Pennsylvania, and was the third or fourth oldest past grand master of the Grand Lodge of Pennsylvania. He was a member of Girard Lodge, No. 53. In 1842 he was elected chief burgess of Pottsville. He left thirteen children, among whom are Charles S., John J., George W., Lewis, Wilson, Mrs. John Nagle, Mrs. John W. Pawling, also twenty grandchildren, and eight great-grandchildren, all of whom are still living. In religion Mr. Crosland was a Universalist.

Children of George Walter and Catharine (Crosland) Carmany, are: 1. Charles Cyrus, born August 8, 1889; attended the public schools of Atlantic City, the Wenonah Military Academy, and is now at the University of Pennsylvania. 2. George Walter Jr., born October 11, 1898; was for four years at the Friends' school in Atlantic City, and is now attending the public school of that place.

BARTLETT Joseph Rusling Bartlett is a member of one of the old Atlantic county, New Jersey, families. His grandfather, William Bartlett, was appointed keeper of the "Absecon Light House" at Atlantic City in 1862 by President Abraham Lincoln. He continued in that office until his death in 1866.

(I) Joseph Rusling Bartlett was born at Mays Landing, Atlantic county, New Jersey, April 13, 1836. In early life he was a worker in iron—a core maker. He became an iron master, his father having built the iron foundry at Mays Landing and at Gloucester, New Jersey. He died at Mays Landing, New Jersey, during the year 1876. Joseph R. Bartlett married Mary Turner, born March 14, 1838, daughter of John Turner, of Mays Landing. She survives her husband and is a resident of Tuckahoe, New Jersey. Mr. and Mrs. Joseph R. Bartlett were the parents of two sons, Joseph Rusling, see forward, and Harrison T., who died in the year 1895, unmarried.

(II) Joseph Rusling (2), first son of Joseph Rusling (1) and Mary (Turner) Bartlett, was born at Mays Landing, New Jersey, April 28, 1857. He was educated in the public schools of his native town and of Atlantic City, after which he took a course of study and was graduated from a business college of Philadelphia in 1873. After leaving school he entered the employ of the Camden and Atlantic railroad, and from 1876 to 1895 was a conductor on that road, now the West Jersey and Seashore railroad, part of the Pennsylvania railroad system. In 1882 Mr. Bartlett removed to Atlantic City and has since been closely identified with the public affairs of that city. He is a Republican, and from 1890 to 1892 was city recorder. In 1892-93-94 he was alderman of the city and president of the city council. He later became health inspector, being appointed by the board of health. October 1, 1908, he was chosen clerk of the district court of Atlantic City, which office he now holds (1909). Mr. Bartlett is an attendant of the Baptist church, and is secretary of the Brotherhood of the First Baptist Church of Atlantic City. He is a member of the Masonic fraternity, and is past master of Unity Lodge, No. 96, of Atlantic City. He is a Royal Arch Mason of Trinity Chapter, No. 38, of the same city. He is a member of the Young Men's Republican League, and trustee of the Second Ward Republican organization, both of Atlantic City. Mr. Bartlett's activity as is shown touches all lines of public interest, political, religious and fraternal.

Joseph Rusling Bartlett married, June 26, 1878, Ida May Williams, born March 14, 1857, daughter of Robert L. Williams, of Frenchtown, New Jersey. Their children are: 1. Theresa Williams, born September 16, 1879; graduate of the New Jersey State Normal school; married Frank Hollingsworth, an architect of Cranford, New Jersey. 2. Katherine Turner, January 7, 1881; graduate of the New Jersey State Normal and a teacher in the Atlantic City public schools. 3. Robert William, April 7, 1884; receiving teller of the Atlantic City Second National Bank; married Elizabeth T. Bew, born in Germantown, Pennsylvania, February 5, 1886, daughter of J. T. Bew.

SUTTON Horace Franklin Sutton, Esquire, ranks as one of the foremost of the legal profession in Camden, New Jersey, where he was born October 26, 1876. He is the son of Benjamin Franklin and Emily (Hammell) Sutton. His father was born in Camden county in 1841, and his mother was the daughter of Thomas and Ann Hammell, of the same county. For his early education Mr. Sutton attended the public schools of Camden, New Jersey, and then began the study of law in one of the offices of his native city. In June, 1901, he was admitted to the New Jersey bar as an attorney, and in February, 1908, as a counsellor. Since this time he has been engaged in the practice of his profession in Camden, where he is regarded as one of the rising men of his profession and generation. In politics Mr. Sutton is a Republican, and in religious belief a member of the Methodist Episcopal church.

BEYER The Beyer family of Egg Harbor, New Jersey, and of Atlantic City, are another illustration of the fact that this country has drained Europe of some of its best blood and brawn in order to increase its own worth and wealth; and although but three generations of the family have made America their home, their name among the communities amongst which they have lived and worked stands for character, success and popularity.

(I) Gottfried Beyer, born in Germany, died in Egg Harbor, New Jersey, was the first of the family to come to this country, and though little is now known about him except the year of his death, 1861, he left behind him a son, Albert, referred to below.

(II) Albert, son of Gottfried Beyer, was born in Hanover, Germany, April 6, 1827, died in Egg Harbor, New Jersey, October 15, 1894. He was a miller, a lumber dealer, and the keeper of a country store. He came to this country in 1853, but whether with or after his father is uncertain. In 1854 he married in Philadelphia, Magdalena Woertz, who that year had come to America from Ulm, Germany, where she was born July 14, 1833, and immediately he and his bride left the city and took up their residence in Egg Harbor. The issue of this marriage was a son, Albert, referred to below.

(III) Albert (2), the eldest child of Albert (1) and Magdalena (Woertz) Beyer, was born at Egg Harbor, New Jersey, May 12, 1859, and is now living at 617 Pacific avenue, Atlantic City. When he was thirteen years old he left home and coming to Philadelphia learned the trade of a fresco painter, at which he worked until he was twenty-two years old, being employed in the work on many of the Roman Catholic churches of New York City. In 1882 he came to Atlantic City and engaged in the hotel business with his father, who was running Beyer's Hotel on the corner of Arctic and Maryland avenues. In this business he continued for the next twenty-five years. In 1894 he was elected to the city council of Atlantic City, and in this body he has served until June 15, 1906, when he was appointed treasurer of the city to fill a vacancy caused by the death of the then incumbent. This unexpired term came to an end two years later, in 1908, and Mr. Beyer was then re-elected as the treasurer of the city for the full term of three years, in which capacity he is now serving the city. Mr. Beyer is a member of Trinity Chapter, No. 38, Royal Arch Masons, of Atlantic City; Belcher Lodge, No. 182, Free and Accepted Masons, of Atlantic City; Atlantic Commandery, No. 10, Knights Templar, of Atlantic City; Crescent Temple, Mystic Shrine, of Trenton, New Jersey; Tall Cedars of Lebanon Forest, No. 11, of Atlantic City; American Star Lodge, Independent Order of Odd Fellows, of Atlantic City, and also of the Encampment; Pequod Tribe, Improved Order of Red Men, of Atlantic City; Benevolent and Protective Order of Elks. Mr. Beyer is a Republican and a member of the Lutheran church.

STATE OF NEW JERSEY. 677

March 8, 1888, Albert Beyer married Charlotte, born in Atlantic City, March 13, 1859, daughter of Christian Bom, of Atlantic City. Their children are: 1. Magdalena Bom, born December 24, 1888, unmarried. 2. Rose Bom, April 27, 1890, unmarried. 3. Albert Victor, January 12, 1892. 4. William Lewis, December 14, 1894. 5. Eugene Edward, November 13, 1896. 6. Lotta Main Bom, February 14, 1898. 7. Walter Edmund, March 23, 1900.

GOLDENBERG The Goldenberg family of Atlantic City is of German origin, and has been located in this country but little more than a half century, but the two generations which have made the United States their home and country have not only allied themselves with descendants of some of the best blood in the land but they have also by their own personal worth and actions placed themselves in the forefront of those who are entitled to be recognized as the representatives of the American people and principles.

(I) Charles D. Goldenberg, son of Charles Goldenberg, was born in Darmstadt, Germany, in 1836, and came to this country when he was only eleven years old, in 1847. At the outbreak of the civil war in 1861, he enlisted at Philadelphia, and was assigned to the One Hundred and Tenth Regiment of Pennsylvania Volunteers, an infantry regiment. While serving with this regiment he was wounded at the battle of Winchester, and on account of his wounds he received his discharge, January 24, 1863. Later, on the same account, he received a pension until his death. Unable, however, to restrain his patriotic ardor for the land of his adoption, Mr. Goldenberg enlisted a second time at Camden, New Jersey, January 23, 1864, and became the first lieutenant of Company D, of the Thirty-fourth Regiment of New Jersey Volunteers, and served with this infantry regiment during the remainder of the war.

After the war was over Charles D. Goldenberg married Mary Woodruff, born in 1840, daughter of Samuel W. and Elizabeth (Duffield) Kemble. Her father was a farmer near Woodbury, Gloucester county, New Jersey, where he lived and died, but about the time his daughter Mary Woodruff was born he was serving as a constable of Gloucester county. Her mother, Elizabeth (Duffield) Kemble, was of Scotch extraction and lived to be ninety-three years old, dying in Ambler, Pennsylvania, in 1893. The children of Samuel W. and Elizabeth (Duffield) Kemble were: William H., Thomas, Samuel, Ephraim, Ross, Margaret, Mary Woodruff, Elizabeth, Amelia, Jane, and one child that died in infancy. Children of Charles D. and Mary Woodruff (Kemble) Goldenberg were: 1. Clarence L., referred to below. 2. Elizabeth Kemble, deceased. 3. William Kemble, born May 2, 1874. 4. Augusta Linda, married Frederick Gates, and who died August 31. 1909. 5. Thomas Kemble, born May 6, 1878; engaged in the office with his brother, Clarence L. Goldenberg, at Atlantic City.

(II) Clarence L., eldest child and son of Charles D. and Mary Woodruff (Kemble) Goldenberg, was born at Cape May Court House, New Jersey, December 12, 1866, and is now living at Atlantic City, New Jersey. He attended the public schools of Philadelphia, and then studied law in the office of George G. Cookman, the eldest son of the Rev. Alfred Cookman, an eminent Methodist minister, and was admitted to the Philadelphia bar, October 2, 1897. At first he started in the practise of his profession in Philadelphia, and continued there until 1903 when he came to Atlantic City and was admitted to the New Jersey bar as an attorney in June, 1903, and as a counsellor in June, 1906. Beginning in Atlantic City as a general practitioner he soon attracted much favorable notice, and March 17. 1908, the governor of New Jersey appointed him prosecutor of the pleas for Atlantic county for a term of five years, and he is now serving in that office. In September, 1893, he was made a Free Mason in Merchantville Lodge, Free and Accepted Masons. Later he demitted from that lodge and became one of the charter members of Belcher Lodge, No. 180, of Atlantic City. He is also a member of the Benevolent and Protective Order of Elks of Atlantic City. He is a member of the New Jersey Bar Association, and one of the members of the committee on prosecution. He is also a member and first vice-president of the Atlantic County Bar Association. He is a Republican and attends the Methodist Episcopal church.

December 28, 1887, Clarence L. Goldenberg married Emma Atwood Bennett, of Philadelphia, where she was born January 28, 1866, and they have had three children: 1. Charles Clarence, born September 10, 1889; graduated from the Atlantic City high school in 1909. 2. Mary Kemble. born May 12, 1891; also a graduate from the Atlantic City high school in 1909. 3. William Kemble, born May 10, 1893.

POTTER

Reuben Potter was born in Middlesex county, New Jersey, about 1772, died about 1863. He was a farmer and resided in Middlesex county, New Jersey, all his life. He married and had children: Ellis, James Rowland, mentioned below; Joanna.

(II) James Rowland, son of Reuben Potter, was born in Raritan township, Middlesex county, New Jersey, 1811, died November, 1887. He was educated in the common schools of his native town. He owned a large amount of real estate. He was a farmer all his life, and accumulated a comfortable fortune. He was a Democrat in politics before the civil war, but afterwards became a Republican. He married Sarah A., born 1818, near Plainfield, New Jersey, died May, 1881, daughter of William Hand. Children: 1. Sarah H., born 1837, died in 1878; married Henry F. Slout, of Jersey City. 2. Reuben C., 1839; resides in New Haven, Connecticut; married Clara Brown, who died 1900; had Nellie, Catherine and Harry. 3. William H., 1841; resides on the homestead. 4. Apollos, resides in Rahway, New Jersey. 5. Josephine De Foreest, resides on the homestead. 6. Frederick James, mentioned below. 7. Ellis, September, 1855; a dentist by profession.

(III) Frederick James, son of James Rowland Potter, was born in Raritan township, New Jersey, March 31, 1853. He received his education in the private schools and Pennington Seminary, with a supplementary course at Rutgers College, New Brunswick, New Jersey, from which he graduated in 1872. He entered the employ of the Pennsylvania railroad in the maintainence-of-way department as a civil engineer, November, 1872, and won promotion from time to time until he attained the position of supervisor of the maintainence-of-way department, which position he now holds. He has been with the company for thirty-seven years. For the past twenty-seven years he has made his home in Bordentown, New Jersey, where he is a prominent citizen. He was one of the organizers of the First National Bank, of Bordentown, in November, 1908, and was chosen its first president, still holding that office. In politics he is an active Republican and has served as president of the city council. He has also served as city collector and township collector. He is at present a member of the board of water commissioners, is president of the board of excise commissioners, and has always been a faithful public servant. He is a member of Trenton Lodge. No. 5, Free and Accepted Masons; Mount Moriah Chapter, No. 20, Royal Arch Masons, of Bordentown; Ivanhoe Council, No. 11, Knights Templar, of Bordentown. In religion he is a Baptist and is the president of the board of trustees of his church.

He married (first) 1872, Louisa, died April, 1880, daughter of George T. Price, of New Brunswick, New Jersey. He married (second) November, 1881, Sarah B., born 1860, daughter of Edwin and Harriet Wright, of Bucks county, Pennsylvania. Children of first wife: 1. James R., born in New Brunswick, New Jersey; now a contractor in Philadelphia, Pennsylvania. 2. Frederick A., born New Brunswick, New Jersey; an engraver, residing in Syracuse, New York; married Jessie Tenney, of Syracuse, and has Helen, Ellis, Dorothy, Jessie, Frederick, Ralph and James. 3. Child, died young. Children of second wife: 4. Marion, born Bordentown, December, 1882, died aged nine years. 5. Robert, born Bordentown, June, 1884. 6. Edward W., born Bordentown, died aged four years. 7. Ellis, born Bordentown, died aged two years.

HESS

In the year 1712 a Swiss colony came to America and among them was Samuel Hess, who settled at Pequa and had a large family. He was the first of his name in this country.

(II) Jacob, son of Samuel Hess, took up a tract of two hundred acres of land one mile east of Lititz, now Warwick township, Lancaster county, Pennsylvania, in 1734.

(III) John, son of Jacob Hess, lived on the old home place with his father. He died in 1778, being interred in the old graveyard situated on the plantation. He left two sons and eight daughters. The sons were named Christian and John. His daughters married John Brubaker, Daniel Brubaker, Rev. Dr. Eby, Jacob Metzler, Daniel Borhlorder, David Martin, Henry Hess, of Lancaster, Abraham Huber.

(IV) Christian, eldest son of John Hess, of Pequa, Lancaster county, was born in 1766. In 1785 he married a widow by the name of Snavely who bore him three sons and three daughters. The sons were: John, Christian, referred to below; Jacob.

(V) Christian (2), second son of Christian (1) Hess, was born December 29, 1787, died September 26, 1857. He was one of the county commissioners of Lancaster county and lived at Pequa with his wife. Elizabeth (Wenger) Hess, born May 16, 1790, died May 27, 1870.

Among their children was John, referred to below.

(VI) John (2), the son of Christian (2) and Elizabeth (Wenger) Hess, removed from Pennsylvania to New Jersey at the time the iron foundry and stone works were opened at the head of the Tuckahoe river. Among his children was John Denny, referred to below.

(VII) John Denny, son of John (2) Hess, was born at the head of the Tuckahoe river, Atlantic county, New Jersey, July 20, 1836. For many years he was in the lumber business at Belle Plaine, Cape May county, New Jersey. He married Rachael A., born October 9, 1843, daughter of Samuel Mason, of Cape May county. Their children were: 1. Elizabeth, married John A. Chandler, of Easton, Pennsylvania, an iron worker. 2. Charles P., married Reba S. Turner, of Millville, New Jersey, and has four children, Mabel, Ira, Robert and Anna. 3. Eleanor, married George Warren, of Millville, New Jersey, and has four children, Howard, Cora, Charles and Mary. 4. Emma, married Samuel Mason, has Bertha and Beatrice. 5. Lilbern Murphy, referred to below. 6. Rutherford B., referred to below. There is a tradition in the family of Rachael A. (Mason) Hess that her grandfather, Samuel Mason, having heard of the British troops coming into the Delaware bay and stealing pigs and cattle, armed himself, although he was only a young boy at the time, with his father's rifle, which his grandfather had borne during the revolution, and started out to drive them away.

(VIII) Lilbern Murphy, son of John Denny and Rachael A. (Mason) Hess, was born at Steelmantown, Cape May county, New Jersey, June 6, 1874, and is now living at Tuckahoe, Cape May county, New Jersey. For his early education he was sent to the public school of Cape May county, after leaving which he took a technical course in electricity, under private teachers in Philadelphia, Pennsylvania. He was the first man in the eastern states to oppose the Bell Telephone monopoly, and he was the first man also to interest capital by hard work, and then to organize that capital into a working opposition to the Bell Telephone Company in southern New Jersey. This he did by organizing the Enterprise Telephone and Telegraph Company, of which he was appointed the general manager. This company established its line in twenty-seven towns and cities in southern New Jersey, and connected by means of their wires the counties of Cumberland, Cape May and Atlantic. The company was finally sold to the Interstate Telephone

Company, with which Mr. Hess was connected in their department of right of way. Mr. Hess finally turned his attention to the stricter financial field of business and organized the Tuckahoe National Bank, of which he became the first cashier under its charter, in 1907. This bank started with a capital of $25,000.00 and it is today in a most prosperous and flourishing condition, in the two years of its existence having already accumulated a surplus of over $7,000.00. In 1908 Mr. Hess with other gentlemen, organized the Millville Trust Company, of Millville, New Jersey, of which institution he was elected the first president. This company has a capital of $100,-000.00, and its surplus, after one year existence, has amounted to $5,000.00. In addition to this Mr. Hess has just completed, in the spring of 1909, the formation of the Tuckahoe Light & Fuel Company, of which he has been chosen the treasurer. Mr. Hess is a Republican and an independent in religion. He is a member of Shekinah Lodge, No. 58, Free and Accepted Masons, of Millville, New Jersey. He is also a member of Richmond Chapter, No. 22, Royal Arch Masons, of Millville, New Jersey, and a member of Olivet Commandery, No. 10, Knights Templar, of Millville, New Jersey. He is a most enterprising and wide-awake citizen of his town.

April, 1893, Lilbern Murphy Hess married Mary L., daughter of Willis Young, of Petersburg, Cape May County, New Jersey. They have two children: Arthur Young, born June 5, 1896, and Paul de Wolf, April 14, 1899.

(VIII) Rutherford B., youngest child of John Denny and Rachel A. (Mason) Hess, born March 4, 1877, is agent for the Pennsylvania railroad at Belle Plaine, New Jersey. He married Maude C. Layton, and has one child, Lolita, born March, 1904.

REPETTO The family here described is of Italian origin, and the representatives of same who have made the United States their home have been of the higher class of emigrants, eager to learn the thoughts and opinions of the country of adoption and to adopt such manners and customs as appeal to them as worthy of emulation. Such men have contributed largely to the growth and transmission of high ideals and morals among the people.

(I) Augustine Repetto was living in Genoa, Italy, at the time of the birth of his son Antonio. He emigrated to America with his family, landing at Philadelphia in 1854.

(II) Antonio, son of Augustine Repetto, was born in Genoa, Italy, in 1845, and was brought to Philadelphia with his parents in 1854. In 1880 he removed to Atlantic City, New Jersey, and established himself as a fruit dealer, meeting with pleasing success; subsequently, in connection with his son, engaged in keeping a restaurant at the same place. He married Marie Stormmo, born in Genoa, 1847; children: 1. Theresa, born January 3, 1867; married John W. Smith and they have four children living, Thomas L., Louis R., Augustine and Viola. 2. Louis Augustine. 3. Augustine Bartholomew, born 1870, in Philadelphia, received an education in law and is now practicing his profession at 717 Walnut street, Philadelphia; married Annie Anthony and has one son, Augustine, born in 1906.

(III) Louis Augustine, son of Antonio and Marie (Stormmo) Repetto, was born September 10, 1868, at Philadelphia, Pennsylvania, and there began his education in the parochial school of the Italian Catholic church of that city, and continued same in the public school at Atlantic City. In 1880 his parents removed to the latter city, and he graduated from Sacred Heart College of Vineland, New Jersey, in 1890, with degree B. A. He then began the study of law in the office of James B. Nixon, of Atlantic City, and was admitted to the New Jersey bar as attorney, in 1891. He has since been practicing his profession in Atlantic City, and has been very successful in securing an increasing clientage. He is a whole-hearted and patriotic American citizen, has imbibed the spirit of the times and institutions of the state and nation, and is keenly interested in all pertaining to the public welfare. He is a member of the New Jersey Bar Association and Atlantic County Bar Association. He belongs to the Catholic church, of which he is an active supporter, and in political views is a Democrat. He is a member of the Atlantic county board of elections, and for ten years has been secretary of the Atlantic County Democratic committee.

Mr. Repetto married, March 7, 1901, Elcora, daughter of Louis and Catherine Delapiana, and they have one child, Josephine Margaretta, born January 21, 1902, at Atlantic City, New Jersey.

FISH

The main and collateral branches of this family lead back to early days in Pennsylvania, when the Kerns, Palmers and Mulhallon's were prominent in war, politics and business. Through

maternal line Dr. Clyde M. Fish traces through five generations to his great-great-grandfather, Nicholas Kern, as follows:

(I) Nicholas Kern was elected a member of the "Committee of Observation" of Northampton county, Pennsylvania, December 21, 1774, serving on that committee until October 2, 1775. He then enlisted in the First Battalion, Northampton County Associators, and was commissioned captain of the town company, May 22, 1775. The First Battalion was under the command of Lieutenant-Colonel Peter Kaehlein and formed part of the forces commanded by Colonel Joseph Wait. They were engaged at the battle of Long Island, August 21, 1775.

(II) Jacob, son of Nicholas Kern, was at one time speaker of the Pennslyvania house of representatives. He married Mary, daughter of Surveyor-General Palmer, born February 17, 1797, died March 3, 1851.

(III) Elizabeth; daughter of Jacob and Mary (Palmer) Kern, married Dr. John Clyde Mulhallon, son of Anthony and ——— (Clyde) Mulhallon, of the Northampton county, Pennsylvania, Scotch-Irish family of that name.

(IV) Mary, daughter of Dr. John Clyde and Elizabeth (Kern) Mulhallon, was born near Bath, Northampton county, Pennsylvania, March 23, 1844. She married, June 14, 1871, Hiram Barr, only child of William and Julia (Barr) Fish. William Fish, a lumber dealer of White Haven, Pennsylvania, was born in September, 1819. Julia Barr, his wife, was born in 1822 and died in 1847. Hiram Barr Fish was born December 2, 1845, in Lancaster county, Pennsylvania. He is a civil engineer. Mary Mulhallon Fish, his wife, is a member of Lafayette Chapter, Daughters of the American Revolution, of Atlantic City, New Jersey, her home. They are the parents of a daughter, Bertha Mary, born April 23, 1873 and a son Clyde M,, see forward.

(V) Clyde Mulhallon, only son of Hiram Barr and Mary (Mulhallon) Fish, was born at Bath, Pennsylvania, May 21, 1875. He attended the public schools of Bath and finished his academic education at the Moravian School at Bethlehem, Pennsylvania. He chose medicine as his profession and Rush Medical College for his alma mater, entering in 1893 and graduating in 1896. He next entered Jefferson Medical College in 1896, remaining one year, graduating in 1897, Doctor of Medicine. In the same year he located in Atlantic City, entering the office of Dr. B. C. Pennington, of that City. He remained with Dr. Pennington until 1901, practicing at the same time in the Atlantic City Hospital, with which he was officially connected. In 1901 he settled in Pleasantville, New Jersey, where he is now practicing. Dr. Fish is a skillful physician, and enjoys a lucrative practice. He is a member of the American Medical and New York State Medical associations, Atlantic County Medical Society, of which he was elected president in 1908 and 1909, and the Philadelphia Medical Club. His fraternal membership is with the Odd Fellows. Dr. Fish is unmarried.

CORNWELL The branch of the Cornwell family which has for several generations been identified with South Jersey is almost undoubtedly a branch of the family which has become so far spread in New England, and belongs with the early colonists of the New World. Unfortunately however, the documents which have so far come to light with regard to the family are insufficient to establish the line in unbroken succession from father to son, and connect the original emigrant with all his descendants at the present day.

(I) Lot Cornwell, of Cape May county, New Jersey, is the founder of the New Jersey branch, and the earliest known representative of the family in that section of the country. He was for many years a farmer and carried on at the same time a grocery business. According to family tradition his mother was a Woodruff, and her brother it is said was one of the participants in the Philadelphia Tea party, when the tea was burnt on the banks of the Delaware. It is also said that this same brother was captured later during the revolutionary war by a British merchant ship which compelled him to pilot a tea boat up the Cohansey river. Among the children of Lot Cornwell was John Tomlin, referred to below.

(II) John Tomlin, son of Lot Cornwell, of Cape May county, New Jersey, was born at Goshen, Cape May county, in 1858, and followed the trade of miller. By his marriage with Mary Elizabeth, daughter of Judson Garrison, a contractor, he had a son, William Leslie, referred to below, and a daughter, Maud W., died aged twenty.

(III) William Leslie, son of John Tomlin and Mary Elizabeth (Garrison) Cornwell, was born in Bridgeton, New Jersey, March 11, 1883, and is now living in that city. For his early education he attended the public schools

of Bridgeton and graduated from the high school in that town in 1900. He then went to the West Jersey Academy, from which he graduated in 1902, and in the fall of that year entered the Jefferson Medical College in Philadelphia, Pennsylvania, from which he graduated with the degree of M. D. in 1906. Upon leaving the Jefferson Medical College he went to the City Hospital at Newark, New Jersey, where for two years and three months he was one of the internes. October 14, 1908, he came from Newark, New Jersey, to Bridgeton, Cumberland county, where he established himself in the general practice of his profession. Dr. Cornwell is a member of all of the larger and most influential medical societies, among them being the New Jersey State Medical Society, Cumberland County Medical Society, Newark City Hospital Ex-Internes' Society, and while in college he was a member of the W. W. Kean Surgical Society of the Jefferson Medical College and the W. M. L. Coplin Pathological Society of the same institution. He is an active and influential secret society man, being a member of Ahwahneeta Tribe, No. 97, Improved Order of Red Men, of Bridgeton. Among the other societies and associations to which he belongs should be mentioned the Bridgeton Athletic Club, the Alumni of West Jersey Academy, the Alumni Association and the Alpha Kappa Kappa of Jefferson Medical College.

November 15, 1908, William Leslie Cornwell, M. D., married Lily May, daughter of Samuel Whitaker, of Paterson, New Jersey. One child, William Leslie Jr.

LOPER For over a century and a half the Loper family has been connected with the history of Salem county, and while numbers of its representatives have risen to great distinction and honor in Salem county, the family as a whole is remarkable for its consistency in almost every individual, of those virtues and qualities which have done so much to place Salem county and the state of New Jersey at the head of the counties and states of the great nation of the west.

(I) The earliest ancestor of the family of whom there is any accurate record at present is Uriah Loper, who on March 26, 1776, filed his account as the administrator of Ephraim Gillman, late of Cumberland county, deceased. He died in 1807 or 1824, and among his children was Eli, referred to below.

(II) Eli, son of Uriah Loper, owned and operated a sash and door factory in

Bridgeton, which his son now operates. By his wife, Amanda (Davis) Loper, he had children: Alfred French, referred to below, Carrie and Ida. He is still living.

(III) Alfred French, son of Eli and Amanda (Davis) Loper, was born in Bridgeton, New Jersey. He married Caroline Carmelia, daughter of John and Ellen Carmelia, of Salem county, New Jersey. Children: John Carmelia, referred to below, Eli, Myrtis, Elsie, and one who died in infancy.

(IV) John Carmelia, son of Alfred French and Caroline (Carmelia) Loper, was born at Bridgeton, New Jersey, October 9, 1881, and is now a practicing physician in that city. For his early education he was sent to the public schools of Bridgeton, New Jersey, and graduated from the Bridgeton high school in 1899. He then entered the Jefferson Medical College in Philadelphia, from which he graduated with the degree of M. D. in 1903, and then went to Bridgeton where he at once engaged in the general practice of his profession, and is regarded now as one of the brightest and most able of the rising young men of his generation. Dr. Loper is a member of the staff of the Bridgeton Hospital, American Medical Association, New Jersey Medical Society, Cumberland County Medical Society, of which he is the president, H. H. Hare Medical Society of Jefferson Medical College, Francis X. Dercum Neurological Society of Jefferson Medical College, and also of the Alpha Kappa fraternity of the same institution. He is also a member of the board of health at Bridgeton, and in February, 1909, was appointed as the health officer of the city. He is a member of Brearly Lodge, No. 2, Free and Accepted Masons, at Bridgeton. This lodge is the oldest one in New Jersey. He is also a member of the Order of Woodmen of America, Royal Arcanum, and Independent Order of Odd Fellows. He is a Democrat in politics.

June 8, 1904, John Carmelia Loper, M. D., married Alynda, daughter of Henry and Mary (Dare) Dickinson, of Bridgeton, New Jersey, whose mother was a native of Daretown. Their child is Le Grand Dickinson, born in February, 1905.

WALLINGTON   Edward Morrell Wallington, late president of the Vineland Grape Juice Company, son of George Edward Wallington, of Trenton, was born in that city, June 30, 1868. The company of which he was the president started its factory at Vineland eleven years ago, and is now the second largest manufactory of grape juice in the world, having a capacity of two hundred thousand gallons, and have an enormous business transporting their product to every state in the Union, including California, and to many foreign countries. Their product is prepared in accordance with the most rigid of the pure food laws, while its vineyards are conducted on the most scientific method. On the property is located the United States agricultural department, experimental vineyard of the Middle Atlantic States. The factory stands in the midst of tributary vineyards. The plant is the finest and most complete in the country. It has immense storage vaults, porcelain lined vessels which prevent salts and other impurities from being preserved in the liquid, while cleanliness is carried to an extreme even for these days of hygienic precaution. Low chemicals or artificial preservatives are not used anywhere in its processes. Their grape farm in Landis township consists of one-hundred and thirty acres, and their factory is used by the United States government department of agriculture for its experiment.

Mr. Wallington, late president of this company, did more than almost anyone else to bring about the unrivaled reputation enjoyed by the Vineland Grape Juice Company and its products. He was a Republican and staunch to the principals of his party, although he did not care for political life. He was an ardent and enthusiastic secret society man, a member of Benevolent Lodge, No. 28, Free and Accepted Masons, of New York City; Newport Chapter, Royal Arch Masons, of Newport, Rhode Island; Palestine Commandery, No. 4, Knights Templar, of Trenton, New Jersey, and Lulu Temple, Mystic Shrine, of Philadelphia. His social club was the Vineland Country Club, and besides serving as president of the Vineland Grape Juice Company, he was a director of the Vineland National Bank and of the Vineland Trust Company. He was a communicant and a vestryman of the Protestant Episcopal church in Vineland.

Edward Morrell Wallington married Anna Eliza Goodfellow, born in Germantown, Pennsylvania. Children: 1. Edward Casewell. 2. Merton Goodfellow. 3. Anna Wallington. Mr. Wallington died October 1, 1909.

VOUGHT   In the year 1707 a small band of Lutherans under the leadership of the Rev. John Kockerthal left the lower Palatinate country in Germany and went to England to lay before Queen Anne an account of their grievances, with the result that her gracious majesty provided for their transportation to America, there to dwell in peace and worship according to the dictates of conscience. Three years later, in 1710, a second colony of immigrants came over in the ship "Lyon" and landed at New York; but the voyage was tempestuous and attended with many unfortunate incidents, such as lack of attention and poor food furnished on board the vessel, with the result that a considerable number of the passengers died on the voyage. When the ship arrived at New York the passengers were denied the privilege of going ashore because of the fear of infection among the people, and they were ordered to Governor's Island, where doctors were sent to attend such of them as needed attention, of which number there were many.

Among the voyagers in the "Lyon" in this immigration were Simon Voight and Christina, his wife, who were founders of several of the now quite numerous Voight families in this country; and their descendants are now well scattered throughout eastern New York and northern New Jersey. In the same year, 1710, Governor Hunter purchased from Robert Livingston, lord of the manor, a considerable tract of land near the site of the present city of Newburgh, New York, and provided homes there for many of these immigrants, such of them as would go there and settle; but some of them preferred to remain in New York City, and among the latter were Simon Voight and his wife Christina. In the course of a few years, however, he removed across the Hudson and settled in western New Jersey, and his descendants soon became numerous in Middlesex and Hunterdon counties, while not a few of them ultimately went over into the valley of the Hudson river in the province of New York and established homes in that region. Simon Voight, immigrant, was born in Germany in 1680, and married previous to 1710 Christina ———, who was born in 1684. They had four children, all born in this country: Johannes, Christoffle, Margaretta and Abraham.

Such in brief is an outline of the circumstances attending the coming over of the first representatives of the Voight family on this side of the Atlantic ocean, but within the next half century after the arrival of Simon and Christina Voight there came, about 1750, another family of the same name, perhaps a relative, although there is no proof or claim of relationship. The latter was the family which furnished three of its sons to the American service during the revolutionary war, and two grandsons to the second war with Great Britain.

(I) Joseph Voight, immigrant, a native of Holland, came from Omispac or Horrispac in that country to America about the year 1750, and took up his residence in the Hudson river valley in what is now Westchester county, where he was a farmer. He brought with him his wife Christina and probably some of their children, of whom there were nine in all. The Westchester records give us no reliable account of the family of Joseph Voight, although he is known to have been a sturdy Dutchman of progressive qualities, which traits seem to have been inherited by his sons and other descendants in later generations. His children were: Henry, see forward; John, Peter, a soldier of the revolution; Joseph, see forward; Godfrey, soldier of the revolution; Ontuatue, Hester, Margaret and Katie.

(II) Henry, eldest son and child of Joseph and Christina Voight, was born in Holland and came to America with his parents. He lived in Westchester county, and during the war of the revolution was a private with his brothers Peter and Godfrey in the Third Regiment of Westchester county militia, commanded by Colonel Pierre Van Cortlandt and Colonel Samuel Drake. He married Rebecca Nelson and by her had twelve children: 1. Joseph. 2. Henry, see forward. 3. Nicholas. see forward. 4. David, married Phebe Brown. 5. James, died in Mobile, Alabama. 6. John, soldier of the war of 1812; married Phebe Rockwell and had son Jackson and daughters Mary and Hannah. 7. Thomas, a sailor; married Susan Conklin and had sons Joseph and Albert. 8. Isaac, see forward. 9. Margaret. married Isaac Barton and had Jennie. Katherine. Susan, Julia, Abbie and Jenny Barton. 10. Jane, married ——— McCoy and had Henry McCoy. 11. Christina, married Thomas McCoy and had Beckie, Delia. John, George, Isaac, Daniel, Rufus, Augusta. Frank, Elizabeth. Katherine McCoy. 12. Eleanor, married ——— Smith, and had Rebecca, Katherine, Mary Ann, Phebe Ellen, Martha, Jacob. Thomas, Nicholas and Abraham Smith.

(II) Joseph (2), fourth son and child of Joseph (1) and Christina Voight, lived in Westchester county, New York. He married Millie Conklin. They had twelve children: 1. Maria, married a Barr. 2. Katie, married a Clark. 3. Abbie Jane, married a Green. 4.

Eliza, married a Clark. 5. Hester, married a Ward. 6. Nicholas. 7. Jacob. 8. Elijah. 9. William. 10. Henry, see forward. 11. Louis. 12. Sallie, married a Saunders.

(III) Henry (2), son of Henry (1) and Rebecca (Nelson) Voight, was born near Peekskill on the Hudson, and spent the greater part of his life on a farm at Cornwall. His farm lay over beyond Storm King mountain, in the valley back of Deerhill, and besides this he owned a large tract of woodland. He was an energetic farmer and gained a fair competency. He served in the American army during the second war with the mother country. He married Martha Weeks, of an old Peekskill family, and by her had six children: 1. Edward, married Amanda Vought, and had James H., Sarah, Edward, Ezra, Lester, Annie and Jennie. 2. Nathan C., see forward. 3. Sarah, married (first) ———— Wilson and had Hattie Wilson; married (second) Henry Barton and had Minnie, Mattie, Addie and Henry Barton. 4. Julia. 5. Mary, married Ezra Drew and had Townsend, Albert, Nicholas and J. H. Drew. 6. Eleanor, married Frank Quinn and had Juliette, Nellie and Elbert Quinn.

(III) Nicholas, son of Henry (1) and Rebecca (Nelson) Voight, was born near Peekskill on the Hudson, and was a farmer. He married Dolly Lent and by her had twelve children: 1. Margaret, married Barney Quincy and had Harriet, David, Mary, Emma, Martha and Ellen Quincy. 2. Joseph. 3. Katie, married Wright Bunce and had Maria, Frank, Will and Lottie Bunce. 4. Jackson, married and had son Charles. 5. Isaac, married Jane DeWitt and had DeWitt and Joseph. 6. Lent. 7. Jane, married Cuyler Carter and had Della, Stephen and George Carter. 8. Christina, married Charles Bigelow and had Anna and Nicholas Bigelow. 9. Eliza, married Manoah Delling and had Mary, Jackson, Luther, Nicholas, Sarah and George Delling. 10. Sylvester. 11. Nicholas, married Mahala Palmer and had Dora and Edward. 12. David, married Maria Upham and had Nicholas, Myra and Luna.

(III) Isaac, son of Henry (1) and Rebecca (Nelson) Voight, was born near Peekskill on the Hudson, and was a farmer. He married Martha McCarty and by her had children: 1. Elizabeth, married Oscar Delling and had Ellery and Mytte Delling. 2. Theodore, married Sarah Snyder and had Oscar and Floyd. 3. Edward, married and had Elizabeth, George, Charles, Herbert, Edward,

Ida and Nina. 4. Oresta, married Josephina Sax and had William and Clayton. 5. Ellen, married Henry Roberts and had Theodore Roberts. 6. Nelson. 7. Eva.

(IV) Nathan C., son of Henry (2) and Martha (Weeks) Voight, was born at Cornwall-on-Hudson in 1825, died in 1900. His farm, like that of his father, lay over beyond old Storm King mountain, and besides farming he also carried on a livery stable at Cornwall. His wife before her marriage was Elizabeth Lent, and she bore him five children: 1. Isaac S., senior partner of the firm of Voight & Williams, of New York. 2. Henry H. 3. Edward Thomas, see forward. 4. Nathan Franklin. 5. Katherine.

(V) Edward Thomas, son of Nathan C. and Elizabeth (Lent) Voight, was born at Cornwall-on-Hudson, April 9. 1855, and during the earlier part of his life worked for his father, who was keeper of a livery at that place. Later on he went to New York City and there engaged in business, dealing in hardware, iron and other metals, as member of the firm of Voight & Williams, as still known, for Mr. Voight is still head of the firm. He married, 1883, Ida, adopted daughter of Samuel and Elizabeth Pope, of Paterson, and by whom he had three children, Samuel P., and two others, both of whom died in infancy.

(VI) Samuel Pope, son and only surviving child of Edward Thomas and Ida (Pope) Voight, was born in Paterson, New Jersey, November 10, 1883, and received his education in the grammar and high schools of that city, and New York University, where he was a student for some time but did not graduate. He lives in Paterson and is engaged in the real estate and brokerage business, and is treasurer of the Pope Realty Investment Company of Paterson. He is a member of the Hamilton Club of Paterson and the Ridgewood Driving Club.

Mr. Voight married, June 28, 1906, Ida May, born July 2, 1885, daughter of Ogden H. Planck, of Paterson, and by whom he has one child, Lorene Voight, born March, 1907.

———

STEVENSON   On August 7, 1764, a tract of twenty-five thousand acres of land situated at what is now Salem, Washington county, New York, was granted Alexander Turner and twenty-four others residing in Pelham, Massachusetts Bay Colony, and these proprietors conveyed an undivided half to Oliver Delancy and Peter Dubois, of New York City. The whole tract of twenty-five

STATE OF NEW JERSEY.   685

thousand acres was marked off into three hundred and four small farms of eighty-eight
acres each, suitable to the requirements of a
Scotch-Irish farming colony.

The "New Light heresies" which in the middle of the eighteenth century sowed dissensions in the Presbyterian churches in Scotland
and Ireland caused an Irish Presbyterian community in and about Monaghan and Ballibay
to petition the Associate Burgher Presbytery
of Glasgow, Scotland to furnish them with
orthodox preaching. Rev. Thomas Clark, M.
D., an ordained minister of this Glasgow Presbytery, was thereupon sent "as a missionary
to Ireland," and shortly after was regularly
ordained and installed by a committee of the
Glasgow Presbytery over the church at Ballibay, where he became greatly honored and beloved for his piety and zeal. Bitter persecution, however, instigated by prominent members of the rival Presbyterian church in Ballibay induced Dr. Clark and a large portion of
his flock to seek a new home in the wilds of
America. Dr. Clark and his parishioners
sailed for New York from Neury, Ireland,
May 10, 1764, arriving there July 28, 1764.
The unique feature of this interesting emigration is the fact that the entire church organization was transferred from Ireland to
America. An Irish Presbyterian church with
a Scotch pastor affiliated ecclesiastically with
a Scotch Presbyterian Assembly was thus
transferred to America in a body. As stated
in the "Salem Book" "there were none of the
formalities of organizing a church. No admission of members or election of trustees.
The company was already a perfectly organized religious society with its pastor, its elders, its members, all regularly constituted. Dr.
Clark had never resigned nor had the Presbytery released him from his pastoral charge
over these people. We doubt if any other religious society has been transferred from the
old to the new world in a manner so regular
and orderly and with so little to vitiate its
title to a continuous identity." Dr. Clark
searched for a suitable place on which he and
his people could establish their church and
their homes, and after much investigation and
travel he secured on September 13, 1765, from
Delancy and Dubois their undivided share of
the twenty-five thousand acre tract, which
already had been sub-divided into farms as
above stated. The result of acquiring rights
to the allotment of farms distributed throughout a large tract, instead of acquiring the
whole of a tract which the colonists could di-

vide among themselves, was that the Scotch-
Irish and Scotch colony under Dr. Clark were
intermingled over a wide territory with a New
England colony who divided among themselves the farms which represented the half of
the tract which Dr. Clark did not purchase.
Dr. Clark and his people were under obligation after five years to pay a rent of one shil-
ling per acre, and hence they no doubt urgently
invited their co-religionists from Scotland as
well as from Ireland to join them, and within
ten years from the original settlement a very
substantial addition to the colony was made
by emigrants from the part of Scotland from
which Dr. Clark had come. Dr. Clark named
the settlement New Perth, while the New England settlers called it White Creek. On March
2, 1774, the legislature of New York combined
both tracts into the township of New Perth,
this establishing a legal name, which remained
until March 7, 1788, when in dividing the
whole state into counties and towns, the name
New Perth was changed to Salem, located in
Washington county, New York. This was the
objective point to which the passengers of the
brig. "Commerce," were bent on April 20,
1774, when James Stevenson and his family
left Scotland for the New World.

(I) James (2), son of James (1) Stevenson, a shawl weaver, of Scotland, was the
founder of this family in America. He was
born in the home of his parents on the bank
of the Bonnie Doon in Ayrshire, Scotland,
about the year 1747. When a young man he
removed to Paisley, where he learned the trade
of silk and linen weaver. He joined the
Scotch Presbyterian church in Paisley, at that
time having as its pastor the distinguished
divine, John Witherspoon. While a citizen of
Paisley he married Margaret, daughter of
David Brown, of Stewarton, Scotland, and
while residents of Paisley three children—
James, Jane and John—were born. The family embarked at Greenock, Scotland, April 20,
1774, in the brig, "Commerce," with several
other families, their destination being the
Scotch settlement at New Perth in the state
of New York. He had alotted to him a farm
located two miles east of the present village
of Salem, Washington county, whereon he settled and lived during the remainder of his life.
In 1896 this farm was owned by two of his
grandsons, Thomas S. and Robert M., sons of
Thomas and Agnes (McMurray) Stevenson.
The first election held in the town of New
Perth, now Salem, was on September 8, 1774,
and James Stevenson voted at that election.

Soon after the American revolution had assumed a definite purpose, he volunteered for military service in the New Perth Company, commanded by Captain Alexander McNitt. Upon his arrival James Stevenson became a member of the church of Dr. Thomas Clark and was afterward one of its ruling elders. When Dr. Clark severed his relations with the congregation in 1782, Mr. Stevenson went on horseback through the almost unbroken wilderness from Salem, New York, to Pequea, near Philadelphia, Pennsylvania, to endeavor to persuade the Rev. James Proudfit to become pastor of the church at Salem as successor to Dr. Clark, who had resigned to join another Scotch settlement in South Carolina as their pastor. In this mission he was entirely successful and Dr. Proudfit became the second pastor of the Scotch church in Salem. Mr. Stevenson brought with him from Paisley, Scotland, a large library of excellent books, and a quantity of fine linen, the product of the industry of his family, and these heirlooms are highly prized by his descendants.

Children of James and Margaret (Brown) Stevenson: 1. James, see forward. 2. Jane, born in Scotland; married George Telford and settled in Argyle, New York. 3. John, born in Scotland; married Katherine McLeod and settled in Howard, Steuben county, New York, where he died in 1863. 4. David, born in Salem, New York, died there unmarried. 5. Thomas, born in Salem; married (first) Agnes, daughter of John McMurray; married (second) Mary, daughter of Joshua Steele; his children were: Thomas S., Robert M. and James B.; Thomas Stevenson lived on the homestead; was an elder in the church at Salem for nearly half a century; died in Salem, 1854, aged seventy-five years. James Stevenson, father of these children, died in Salem, New York, April 19, 1799, and his widow died the following year.

(II) James (3), eldest child of James (2) and Margaret (Brown) Stevenson, was born in Paisley, Scotland, January 8, 1762. He came with his parents, sister Jane and brother John to America in 1774. He was prepared for college by his father, and then entered the Hackensack Classical Academy, conducted by Dr. Peter Wilson, afterwards of Columbia College, and was graduated at Queen's now Rutgers College, A. B., 1789. He was principal of the academy at Morristown, New Jersey, the Rutgers grammar school, and in 1811 was appointed principal of the Washington

Academy, Salem, New York, in which institution he proved himself one of the ablest classical teachers in the country. Among his pupils, several of whom have written eulogistically of his character, his attainments and his extraordinary skill and capacity as an instructor, were Dr. Philip Lindsay, vice-president of Princeton and president of Nashville, Tennessee, University, Professor Henry Mills, of Auburn Theological Seminary, Samuel L. Southard, Theodore Frelinghuysen, Rev. Jacob Kirkpatrick and Rev. Dr. George W. Bethune. That eminent scholar, Dr. Taylor Lewis, professor in Union College, who was a pupil for two years in the Salem Academy, in some reminiscences which he writes of his beloved instructor, says: "He stands in my remembrance as the best model that I ever knew of the most honorable and dignified profession, the schoolmaster's. Some of the thoughts respecting him come to my mind when I read Dr. Arnold, the best sample of a teacher that England ever produced." James Stevenson was a trustee of Washington Academy, incorporated February 18, 1791, the fourth academy incorporated in the state of New York and the first free academy established in the state outside of New York City. He contributed to the newspapers and magazines of the time devoted to educational and religious subjects.

James Stevenson married Hannah, daughter of Richard Johnson, of Morris county, New Jersey. Children: James, Sarah, Martha, Richard, Paul Eugene, Anna Louisa. James Stevenson, father of these children, died October 9, 1843, in the eighty-second year of his age.

(III) Paul Eugene, son of James (3) and Hannah (Johnson) Stevenson, was born in New Brunswick, New Jersey, October 14, 1809. He planned to engage in scientific work, and when he was qualified to enter college matriculated at the Rensselaer Polytechnic Institute, Troy, New York, where he was graduated B. A. (R. S.) in 1830. On leaving the institute he changed the purpose of his life and decided to enter the ministry, and to that end he took a course in arts at Union College, Schenectady, New York, where he was graduated A. B. in 1833. He then entered Princeton Theological Seminary and was graduated B. D., 1837. He was ordained by the Presbyterian ministry, and was pastor of the Presbyterian church in Staunton, Virginia, 1837-43. He then accepted a call from the South Third Street Presbyterian Church,

Williamsburg, New York, and served that church until 1850. His next church was at Wyoming, Pennsylvania, but soon after going there he yielded to the urgent request of his Presbytery to accept the principalship of the Luzerne County Presbyterian Institute, which was at the time in a critical financial condition and poorly equipped for the work of so important an institution, as it had been designed to represent in the policy the church denomination for which it was named. He set to work to build it up and re-establish its reputation as a high class seat of learning and was eminently successful, far beyond the expectation of the officers of the school or his own optimistic hopes. Some years later he resigned this post, and for one year was principal of the West Jersey Academy at Bridgeton, New Jersey, from which place he removed to Madison, New Jersey, where he conducted a private school for a number of years. In 1866 he established the Passaic Falls Institute, a school for girls, at Paterson, New Jersey, which he continued to conduct up to the time of his death, March 17, 1870.

Rev. Paul Eugene Stevenson married, May 18, 1841, Cornelia, daughter of the Rev. Nathaniel Scudder and Julia Ann (Jermain) Prime, granddaughter of Dr. Benjamin Youngs (1733-1791) and Mary (Wheelwright) Greaton Prime, of Huntington, Long Island, New York, and of Major John and Margaret (Pierson) Jermain, of Sag Harbor, Long Island, New York, and great-granddaughter of the Rev. Ebenezer (1700-1779) and Experience (Youngs) Prime, and great-great-granddaughter of James Prime, of Huguenot descent, who came from Doncaster, Yorkshire, England, with his brother, Mark Prime, and settled in Milford, Connecticut Colony, in 1644, and of Benjamin Youngs, of Southold, Long Island, New York. She was a sister of the Rev. Edward Dorr Griffin Prime (1814-1891), of the Rev. Samuel I. Prime (1812-1885), and of the celebrated lawyer and editor, William Cowper Prime (1825-1905). Rev. Paul Eugene and Cornelia (Prime) Stevenson had seven children of whom the following lived to maturity: 1. Archibald Alexander, born October 2, 1845, died unmarried February 10, 1870. 2. Preston, October 29, 1847; a lawyer practicing in New York City and residing in Nutley, New Jersey. 3. Eugene, June 28, 1849, see forward. 4. Mary Margaretta, born March 7, 1852, unmarried. 5. Edward Irenaeus Prime,

born in Madison, New Jersey, January 29, 1858; an editor, critic, lecturer and author; never married; now resides abroad.

(IV) Eugene, son of the Rev. Paul Eugene and Cornelia (Prime) Stevenson, was born in Williamsburg, which city became the eastern district of Brooklyn, New York, June 28, 1849. He was prepared for college by his father and was graduated at the University of the City of New York, now the New York University, A. B. and LL. B., 1870. He practiced law in Paterson, New Jersey, from 1873 up to the time he went upon the bench as vice-chancellor of the court of chancery of New Jersey. He served a single term as prosecutor of the pleas for Passaic county.

He married, June 11, 1884, Helen, daughter of the Rev. Dr. William Henry and Matilda (Butler) Hornblower, of Paterson, New Jersey, granddaughter of Chief Justice Joseph Coerton (1777-1864) and Mary (Burnet) Hornblower, great-granddaughter of Josiah, the delegate, (1729-1809) and Elizabeth (Kingsland) Hornblower. Josiah Hornblower came to America in 1753, at the suggestion and request of Colonel John Schuyler, bringing with him the first steam engine ever used in the United States, which was employed in pumping water in the copper mines near Belleville, New Jersey, of which mines he was made superintendent. He served in the French and Indian war with the rank of captain of militia, was a representative in the New Jersey legislature, 1776-80, speaker of the house in 1780, a member of the state council, 1781-85, delegate to the Continental congress, 1785-86, judge of the Essex common pleas from 1790 up to near the time of his death, which occurred in Newark, New Jersey, January 21, 1809. His wife, Elizabeth, was the daughter of Colonel William Kingsland, of New Barbadoes, New Jersey. Mrs. Stevenson was the sister of the well-known architect, Joseph Coerton Hornblower, of Washington, District of Columbia, born 1848, married Caroline, daughter of Associate-Justice Joseph P. Bradley, of the supreme court of the United States, also of William Butler Hornblower, LL. D., the eminent New York lawyer, born May 13, 1851.

KREMENTZ The Krementz family of Newark belongs to the later arrivals in this country, but it has already established itself in a prominent and important position in the business world of the country of its adoption, and its representatives to-day rank second to none in the honor, esteem and confidence of the community in which they reside.

(I) George Krementz, founder of this family, came in 1851 from Wiesbaden, Germany, where he was born in 1838. At the time of his coming he was a young man, and going to New Albany, Indiana, he for some time worked on a farm. About 1855 he returned east to Newark, New Jersey, where he learned the jewelry trade, and started in business for himself in 1866. About the same time he married Louise Hendrichs; children: 1. Louise. 2. Ann, married F. Keer and has one child. 3. Clara, married Charles Irving Taylor, member of the firm of Beardsley & Hemmens, lawyers, of Wall street, New York City, who has one child, George Krementz. 4. Richard, referred to below. 5. Walter Martin.

(II) Richard, eldest son of George and Louise (Hendrichs) Krementz, was born in Newark, New Jersey, January 26, 1877. For his early education he was sent to the public schools of Newark, and was graduated from the high school of that city in 1895. He then went to Yale University, and after completing the course in the Sheffield Scientific School there received his degree of Ph. B. in 1898. He then came to his father's factory in order to learn the manufacture of jewelry, and he has worked up steadily until he has reached his present position of superintendent of the factory, having under his control two hundred and twenty-five men. In politics Mr. Krementz is an Independent. He is a member of Union Club of Newark and the Yale Club of New York City, and of several college fraternities. May 17, 1906, Richard Krementz married Elsie, daughter of Henry P. and Ada Emily (Anderson) Jones. Child, Elsa Louise, born Spring Lake, New Jersey, August 16, 1907.

(II) Walter Martin, youngest child of George and Louise (Hendrichs) Krementz, was born in Newark, New Jersey, March 21, 1881. For his early education he was sent to the public schools of Newark and was graduated from the Newark high school in 1898. He then went to Yale University, where he took the academic course, and was graduated in 1902 with the degree of Bachelor of Arts. Returning home he entered his father's factory, and has worked himself up until he is now the superintendent of the firm of Krementz & Company, manufacturing jewelers, whose specialty is brooches, scarf pins and necklaces, and a general line of jewelry. They

are also the manufacturers of the famous "Krementz One Piece" collar buttons. Mr. Krementz is an Independent in politics, a member of Yale Chapter of Delta Kappa Epsilon, Automobile Club of New Jersey, Essex County Country Club, and Yale Club of New York.

April 25, 1906, Walter Martin Krementz married in East Orange, Edith Lillie Cordelia, born January 29, 1883, second child and only daughter of James H. and Lillie Letitia (Blanchard) Hart (see Hart). Their only child is James Hart, born November 28, 1907.

BRIODY James Francis, third son of Philip and Annie (Brophy) Briody, was born in Paterson, New Jersey, August 5, 1876. He was a pupil in the public schools of Paterson, graduating from the high school in the class of 1893. He then matriculated at Rutgers College, New Brunswick, New Jersey, and took the regular course up to the senior year, when he entered the College of Physicians and Surgeons, Columbia University, and was graduated M. D. 1898. He returned to his native city, where he began the practice of medicine and soon gained recognition as a skilled practitioner in all the branches of his profession and built up a large private practice. His popularity was recognized by the city government and they made him medical inspector of the public schools, the very schools in which he had passed his youth and laid the foundation upon which he had built his professional life. He held the position of medical inspector of schools for several years, until his private practice demanded the time he was obliged to give to his public duties, when he resigned.

In 1907 the office of city physician was vacant and the city officials appointed Dr. Briody and he accepted the trust and he was holding the office in 1909 by reappointment. His professional standing was recognized by his fellow practitioners in the city, county and state by electing him to membership in the Passaic County Medical Society.

His fellowship outside of his profession was recognized by the members of Paterson Lodge, No. 60, Benevolent and Protective Order of Elks, who urged his acceptance of membership in their exclusive order and he became one of the most popular members of the lodge.

RODROCK Dr. James Rotrock, or Rodrock, was a native of Scotland, born in 1787; he was the first of this family to settle in the United

States; he took up his residence in Northampton county, Pennsylvania, while a young man. He was an educated physician, having taken a regular course of lectures at an institution of medical instruction and received a license to practice. In 1818 he began practice at Freemansburg, Pennsylvania, but soon afterward removed to Macungie, Pennsylvania, where he lived for a short time only. He went from that place to Haines Hill, in Berks county, and is mentioned as having kept public house for a number of years previous to his death. The family name of his wife was Dreisbaugh, and she bore him twelve children, among whom were James, John, Belinda, Kate and DeWitt Clinton Rodrock.

(II) Rev. DeWitt Clinton, son of Dr. James and ——— (Dreisbaugh) Rodrock, was born in the township of Bath, Northampton county, Pennsylvania, January 6, 1828, died in Paterson, New Jersey, August 24, 1903. He received a good early education in the schools of his native town, prepared there for college and then entered Franklin and Marshall College, at Lancaster, Pennsylvania, where he completed the course and was graduated in 1848, with honors of the valedictory. He soon afterward entered the ministry of the Dutch Reformed church of America and labored earnestly and to good purpose in the work of his church until the beginning of the late civil war. He then became chaplain of the Forty-Seventh Pennsylvania Volunteer Infantry and continued in service until the close of the war. In 1866 he became pastor of the Dutch Reformed church in Blaine, Perry county, Pennsylvania, and afterward served in the same capacity at Chambersburg, Marysville, Stone Church, all in Pennsylvania, but while in the latter pastorate he became broken in health and retired from the hard work of the ministry in 1879. Soon afterward he removed to Paterson and lived quietly in that city until the time of his death, August 24, 1903. In the work of his church Mr. Rodrock was regarded as a man of much strength, and after his retirement from the ministry his services were utilized by his people in the writing of articles for *The Messenger*, one of the leading publications of the church. He was a Mason, member of the lodge at Easton, Pennsylvania.

Rev. Dr. Rodrock married Julia Margaretta Weldy; children: 1. Warren Weldy, died at Charleston, South Carolina, 1861, aged six months. 2. Ida, died aged nineteen years. 3. Mary Shaff, married Hiram M. Quick and resides at Paterson, New Jersey. 4. Sarah

ii—19

Blanch, married Charles A. Fitch. 5. Edward M., see forward. 6. Alice Gray, married A. C. Nightingale. Julia Margaretta (Weldy) Rodrock died at Paterson, New Jersey, August 24, 1905.

(III) Edward M., son of Rev. DeWitt Clinton and Julia Margaretta (Weldy) Rodrock, was born in Blaine, Perry county, Pennsylvania, July 12, 1866. He received his education in the public schools of that township and also in the city schools of Paterson, to which place his father removed in 1879, when Edward M. was a boy of about thirteen years. After his school days were over he started out to make his own way in life, and for a time was engaged in an express business and later took up the trade of painting. Still later he became a dealer in clay products and from that beginning gradually enlarged his business operations until in 1905 he became a general dealer in coal and masons' supplies and materials. He is a prompt and capable man of business and enjoys an extended and favorable acquaintance throughout the city of Paterson and in Passaic county. Mr. Rodrock is a member of Lafayette Lodge, No. 27, Free and Accepted Masons, of Rahway.

He married, November 29, 1887, Emma, born February 28, 1868, daughter of William and Margaretta (Rogers) Clark, of Paterson. One child, Harold Edward, born July 4, 1896.

BROCK The life career of William Milton Brock, an accomplished electrician of the day, now superintendent of the electric department of the Public Service Corporation for the district of Passaic and Paterson, New Jersey, presents a forceful illustration of the achievements possible in this age to the industrious and ambitious.

Samuel Gowan Brock, father of William Milton Brock, was born in Brooklyn, New York, where he was educated. He became a shipwright and worked at his trade until about the beginning of the civil war, when he enlisted in the army, went to the front and was never afterward heard of—probably one of those heroes who rest in southern graves marked "Unknown." He married Elizabeth Dougherty, of New Egypt, New Jersey. Of their four children the first born died in extreme infancy. Those coming to maturity were: William Milton, see forward; Beulah, married William Force, of Clifton, New Jersey; Ella, married Henry Holbert, now of Paterson, New Jersey.

William Milton, son of Samuel Gowan and

Elizabeth (Dougherty) Brock, was born in Brooklyn, New York, November 3, 1856, and was only about eight years old when his father entered the army, never to rejoin his family. The mother soon removed with her children to Dover, Illinois, where she resided until the summer of 1863, when she went to Pennsylvania. There William M. at the age of eleven years began to aid his mother in caring for the family, a task which he performed with self-sacrificing devotion until she and her children were comfortably established in life. He first found employment as breaker boy in a coal mine. In the course of three years the mother returned to Brooklyn, New York, where William M. engaged in various labors —with a watchmaker and jeweler, and later as a helper in a blacksmith shop. In 1869 the family removed to Shamokin, Pennsylvania, where the lad passed two years more of coal-breaking life. He then found more congenial employment as a telegraph messenger for the Mineral Railroad and Mining Company, in which he continued for nearly three years. While this occupied he made a study of telegraphy, and in a short time became an expert operator, besides acquiring a considerable knowledge of the principles and science of electricity, and had no lack of constant employment which brought to him steady advancement. In 1879 he was employed by the Central Pennsylvania Telephone Company in the important work of opening a new field for its lines in the region in which he was then living, carrying on this work during his employment as a telegraph operator. In 1882 the Edison Electric Illuminating Company, of Shamokin, was incorporated and one of the first Edison "three wire" plants was installed for commercial lighting in that town under the personal supervision of Mr. Edison. During the work of construction Mr. Brock was— after a personal examination by Mr. Edison— engaged as manager, which position, as well as manager of the local telephone company, he held until 1885, when he resigned both positions to accept a more lucrative engagement as manager of the Edison Electric Illuminating Company, of Lawrence, Massachusetts. He continued in the management of this company until early in 1889, when he resigned his position to accept that of secretary and general manager of the Edison Electric Illuminating Company, of Paterson, New Jersey, his present home. At that time there were two electric lighting companies, the Edison Electric Illuminating Company, which had been in

operation a little over one year, and the Paterson Electric Lighting Company, a much older enterprise. At the end of two or three years of unprofitable competition (about 1891) the two companies were consolidated under one management, under the name of the Edison Electric Illuminating Company, of Paterson. The rapid development of the electric business in a few years taxed the capacity of the two plants to their utmost capacity, and in 1895 it was decided to seek a new location for a more modern plant. The conditions leading to and the execution of the work is best described by the following extracts from the *Electrical Engineer,* of New York, dated December 9, 1896:

"Linked with the history of Paterson, New Jersey, is the name of Alexander Hamilton, who realized immediately after the Revolution that manufacturing industries were necessary to utilize our raw products, and supply those manufactured articles which had been previously shipped to us by England. He selected Paterson as a natural manufacturing center, it having the advantages of water power and close proximity to the metropolis of the country. Under his guidance, the water power was improved and made valuable; the factories soon outgrew the capacity of the water power, and the city of Paterson became dotted with factories of all kinds, the silk industry taking the lead. There are over one hundred silk mills in Paterson now, and it has been called "The Lyons of America." Among the other prominent products at the present time are locomotives structural iron and flax thread.

"Early in the art, Paterson was supplied by electric light from the Hochhausen system. In the year 1888, this system was bought by the Paterson Electric Light Company, who installed the Thomson-Houston arc and series system for municipal lighting, and also a duplicate of the Edison three-wire system for power and domestic lighting.

"Later in the same year, the Edison Electric Illuminating Company of Paterson, was formed in competition with the Paterson Electric Light Company, and they installed a three-wire plant, operating under the Edison patents. They located their station on Paterson street, near Market, and it was constructed according to the best engineering practice of that date, and has always proved a very profitable investment. To compare the station of 1888 with the station of 1896 has a historical value and shows great progress of lighting and power stations.

"A fierce competition was carried on between these two companies, which resulted in the Edison company absorbing its rival in April, 1890. Since that time both stations have been operated by the Edison Electric Illuminating Company, using the old Paterson Electric Light Company's Station only as an arc light plant, and the Edison Company's as a combined lighting and power plant.

"With the advent of electric railways, the Edison Company made a bid and succeeded in securing all contracts to supply, with power, the railways in Paterson and its vicinity. Under conservative management, the business increased so rapidly that at a meeting of directors, in the latter part of the year 1894, it was decided that Mr. William Brock, general Manager of the Edison Electric Illuminating Company, of Paterson, made a report on the best method of meeting the increasing demand for power and light, which was taxing the two stations to their utmost capacity. As a result of this report, it was decided on account of abundant water for condensing, and because the site was nearer the center of distribution of the Paterson system, to locate the plant near the Passaic River and on one of the raceways from the Passaic Falls. The location secured was at the corner of Van Houten and Prospect streets, where one of the largest plants of its kind in the United States is now located.

"The new station building of selected Haverstraw brick with blue stone trimmings, has a total length of 384 feet and a width of 92 feet. The arrangement of this edifice, the station and raceways around the building, as well as location of the engines, dynamos, and boilers, was laid out by Mr. William Brock, and the building details were developed with the assistance of Mr. J. W. Ferguson, of Paterson, New Jersey."

The officers of the aforementioned company were: William T. Ryle, president and the financier of the company; William Strange, vice-president; Arthur Ryle, treasurer, and William M. Brock, secretary and general manager, to whom great credit is due for the conception and erection of this plant, assisted by Mr. J. W. Ferguson, builder and general contractor, and Messrs. Herrick and Burke, consulting and designing electrical engineers. As may be seen from the foregoing, under the personal supervision and management of Mr. Brock, the lighting plant of Paterson not only has been placed on a sound and profitable financial basis, but is said by electrical experts to be one of the most satisfactory and complete systems of its kind in the country. The great measure of success achieved by Mr. Brock has been wholly the result of his own personal effort and energy. It is worth while to remember that his life work was begun as a breaker boy in a coal mine; that later he became a telegraph messenger boy, then a practical telegrapher, and still later an experienced electrician, capable of performing any work assigned to his charge, also of corporate employers; and finally to assume the responsibilities of a managerial position, and direct the operations of large corporate enterprises in profitable channels. All of these things Mr. Brock has done and has done them well. As a boy, when he should have been in school but could not afford such a luxury, he was industrious, patient and of good habits; as a young man he applied himself diligently to whatever tasks were set for him to perform, and when not at work employed his leisure hours in useful reading and study; and as a man he developed capable business qualities and a straightforward, rugged honesty which gained for him the confidence of those by whom he was employed, and also gained for him an enviable place among those who are known as selfmade and successful business men. Mr. Brock is a member of the American Society of Mechanical Engineers. He takes little active part in public affairs, yet is counted among the progressive and public spirited citizens of the city of Paterson.

He married, May 7, 1885, Florence Vincent, daughter of Lyman and Anna (Vincent) Wilson, of Milton, Pennsylvania, and by whom he has three children living: Elizabeth V., born May 5, 1887; Florence, May 16, 1892; Mildred, March 25, 1898.

FROMMELT Nearly three-fifths of the population of Saxony, Germany, which includes the circles of Dresden, Leipsic, Zwickau and Bantzen, are engaged in manufacturing. Linen leads in the manufacturing industry and sixteen thousand looms were employed in 1850. Since then the manufacture of goods for cotton has been the most important branch of Saxon industry. Wool from Saxon sheep has kept close pace with cotton goods and broadcloth, merinos, silk-mixed mouslin de laines and found excellent markets in England and France.

The early history of the Saxons and their exploits for the time they invaded the Roman territory, through their piratical decents on the coasts of Britain and Gaul, their possession of Normandy, their wars with the Franks and final subjugation by the arms of Charlemagne, were evidences of the spirit of conquest and attendant prosperity that this people planted in the early days and out of which the great Anglo-Saxon race has evolved.

(I) Melchior Herman Frommelt was born in Saxony, August 30, 1827, and was brought up as a weaver in the mills of that great manufacturing center of Europe. He emigrated to the United States, landing in New York City, January 6, 1868, after a tedious voyage of sixty-four days. He came to Paterson, New Jersey, the same year and worked as a weaver in the Hamil mill; after earning and saving money he engaged in the grocery business, which he continued up to the time of his death in Paterson, May 14, 1888. He married Henrietta Ernst, born November 14, 1825, died in Paterson, March 29, 1907. Children, born in Saxony: 1. Clemens, born December 8, 1848. 2. Edward, February 28, 1852. 3. Ehrgott, August 6, 1854. 4. Herman Emil, see forward.

(II) Herman Emil, son of Melchior Herman and Henrietta (Ernst) Frommelt, was born in Saxony, Germany, November 26, 1858. When nine years of age he was brought to America with his three brothers by their parents and settled in a home in Paterson, New Jersey, where the boys attended the public school and soon acquired the language and ways of American boys. Herman Emil was apprenticed to the trade of cigar making and he engaged in that business up to 1888, when he established himself as an undertaker on Market street, in which business he was eminently successful, largely on account of his sympathetic nature and gentlemanly deportment. He became associated with Beethoven Lodge, No. 154, Ancient Free and Accepted Masons, of Paterson, New Jersey, as a member and he was rapidly advanced in the successive degrees of the order. He also affiliated with Paterson Lodge, No. 188, Independent Order of Odd Fellows, and stood high in the esteem of the members of his lodge.

He married, April 19, 1883, Lucy B., born August 25, 1859, daughter of James and Sarah (McKeever) Stott, of Paterson, New Jersey.

LOBER Jean Baptiste Lober and his son, Victor Hipolite Lober, were natives of France and came to the United States early in the nineteenth cen-

tury, settling Camden, New Jersey. In France there is a family that may have been ancestors of these two immigrants; one de Lobel or Lobel, represented in history by Matthias Lobel (1538-1616). He was born in Lille, France, educated as a physician; travelled through Europe and was at one time physician to William, of Orange, and James I. made him botanist of the Kingdom, owing to his knowledge of vegetable physiology through which, by means of evident analogies of growth, he was enabled to make new classifications. He had great skill in botanical research, especially with a poisonous plant common to all sections of the vegetable world, now known as Lobelia, which was named in compliment to him. He was the author of botanical reference books still held in high esteem and published in 1570, 1575 and 1581.

(I) Victor Hipolite Lobel, or Lober, son of Jean Baptiste Lober, appears in Camden, New Jersey, about 1800, having emigrated from France in company with his father, and there married Angeline, daughter of Pamela Gant, born in Camden, New Jersey, about 1825. Victor Hipolite and Angeline (Gant) Lober, had three children: John Baptiste, see forward; William Hawke, retired, living in California; Julia Madeline, married Ashbrook Lincoln, retired, living in Ardmore, Pennsylvania.

(II) John Baptiste, son of Victor Hipolite and Angeline (Gant) Lober, was born in Camden, New Jersey, April 11, 1848. He was educated in the public schools of Camden, New Jersey, and in more advanced schools in Philadelphia. He was baptized in the faith of the Roman Catholic church of which his parents were members, but when he arrived at manhood he became independent of church creeds and religious forms. He affiliated with the Independent Order of Odd Fellows, and his professional affiliations as a civil engineer include: The American Society of Civil Engineers; the Engineers Club, of Philadelphia, and the Railroad Club, of New York City. His social home club is the Union League, of Philadelphia, and his business responsibilities include the presidency of the Vulcanite Portland Cement Company with offices in the Land Title Building, Broad street, Philadelphia. He married, May, 1875, Clara, daughter of William V. Diehl, of Pittsburg, Pennsylvania, and their only child, William Diehl, was born in Philadelphia, Pennsylvania, September 11, 1877, was educated in the Friends' schools of Philadelphia, and was graduated at the Uni-

versity of Pennsylvania, M. E., class of 1899, and he at once took a place as secretary and treasurer of the Vulcanite Portland Cement Company, of which organization his father was president. He married, November 7, 1901, Margaret, daughter of John Price and Elizabeth (Warder) Crozer, of Upland, Delaware county, Pennsylvania.

BUTTLER The Buttler family has been resident in the state of New Jersey for three generations. In the line here considered this family descends from George Buttler, commander in the British navy, whose son, Jeremiah Buttler (born in Portsmouth, England), came to America in 1820, married Elizabeth Hull, of Monmouth county, New Jersey, and lived at Prospect Plains, near Dayton, Middlesex county, New Jersey. A brother of Jeremiah Buttler was George Buttler, of the British navy, who commanded the "Wasp" in the first half of the nineteenth century.

Jeremiah Buttler was the father of the late well known George Buttler, of New Brunswick, New Jersey (elsewhere referred to), who was born in 1828 and died in New Brunswich, May 11, 1901, having married Harriet Ann Voorhees (died May 5, 1905), daughter of Barrant Voorhees and Eliza Haviland (who was the daughter of Caleb Haviland, of New Brunswick). The Haviland family came from Haviland, England, and the ancestors of Eliza Haviland were among the founders of the First Reformed Church of New Brunswick. Mrs. Harriet Ann (Voorhees) Buttler was a member of the well known Voorhees family of New Jersey, whose immigrant ancestor, Steven Coerte van Voorhees, came to America from the province of Drenthe, Holland, in the ship "Bonte Cou" or "Spotted Cow" in April, 1660. George and Harriet Ann (Voorhees) Buttler had ten children, of whom eight now survive.

Charles Voorhees Buttler, youngest son of George and Harriet Ann (Voorhees) Buttler, was born in the city of New Brunswick, New Jersey, January 18, 1869. He received his early education in the public schools of that community, graduating from the high school in 1885, and then was for two years in attendance at the United States Naval Academy at Annapolis, Maryland. Deciding upon the medical profession, he entered the office of Frank M. Donahue, M. D., of New Brunswick (1888), took a special course in chemistry at Rutgers College, and in 1893 was

graduated as Doctor of Medicine from the New York University. He is now associated in practice with Dr. Donahue. Dr. Buttler is visiting surgeon of Saint Peter's General Hospital and the Wells Memorial Hospital, visiting physician of the Day Nursery and St. Mary's Orphan Asylum, second examiner of the New York Life and Mutual Life Insurance Companies; special examiner of the Travellers' Life Insurance Company, of Hartford, Connecticut, and assistant examiner of the Northwestern Life Insurance Company. He is eligible for membership in the Sons of the Revolution.

He married, June 20, 1894, Louise Johnson Gardiner, of Mystic, Connecticut, a descendant of the original Lion Gardiner, of Gardiner's Island. She died January 17, 1903. Of this marriage there is one surviving child, Gardiner Haviland Buttler, born November 5, 1896.

STODDARD The late William Craig Stoddard, a conspicuous merchant and honored citizen of New Brunswick, New Jersey, was the only son of James Stoddard, who was born in Connecticut, came to Princeton, New Jersey, and died at the early age of thirty-four. James Stoddard married Ann Craig, of an original Scottish family, which settled at Freehold, New Jersey, in 1685. In addition to their only son, James and Ann (Craig) Stoddard had four daughters, of whom three died young, and the other, Phebe Stoddard, married John Bogart and had two children.

(II) William Craig Stoddard, son of James and Ann (Craig) Stoddard, was born in Princeton, New Jersey, April 28, 1821. When about fourteen or fifteen years old he came to New Brunswick and engaged in business employment, subsequently becoming a member of the firm of Dayton, Stoddard & Smith, in the dry goods business. This firm was dissolved after the destruction of its store by fire, and Mr. Stoddard then organized the copartnership of Stoddard, Duncan & Van Pelt. His active business career covered a period of forty years, and he was one of the foremost men in the mercantile community of New Brunswick. Personally he was a man of the highest integrity, benevolent, and a valued friend and adviser, especially in times of financial disturbance. He was a director of the Bank of New Jersey and the United States Rubber Company. A prominent member of the First Presbyterian Church, he served as one of its trustees for many years. Mr. Stoddard died July 19, 1890.

He married Sarah Jewell, daughter of Kenneth and Elizabeth Jewell, of Princeton, New Jersey. Children: 1. Emily Stoddard. 2. William Stoddard (deceased). 3. Elizabeth Jewell Stoddard. 4. Sarah Jewell Stoddard. 5. Anna Craig Stoddard. Mr. Stoddard's daughters reside in New Brunswick.

SCHUREMAN In its native country, the Netherlands, the name of this family was usually written Schuerman. It was known from an early period for staunch Protestantism, and in the old country, as afterward in America, its representatives were conspicuous for scholarship and literary ability. A famous member of the Hollandish family was Anna Maria Schuerman (1607-1678), who is described as "a marvel of precocity, and for the depth, bredth, and variety of her attainments," excelling in "the faculties of attention, apprehension, and memory, in drawing, painting, sculpture, modelling, embroidery, poetry, and music."

The New Jersey line descends from-

(I) Jacobus Schureman, who was born in Holland, coming to this country in 1719 with the Rev. Theodorus Jacobus Frelinghuysen on the ship "King George." Accompanying Frelinghuysen to Somerset county, New Jersey, he was associated with him in his ministerial labors, serving as chorister and "voorleezer" (reader), and as one of his "helpers." According to a chronicler of those times, he was "respectable for his literary acquirements as well as for his piety." He was the author of verses in the Dutch language, and conducted a school in the same tongue. His residence was at Three Mile Run. He married Antje Terhune, daughter of Albert Terhune, of Flatbush, Long Island, and sister of Eva Terhune, who was the wife of Rev. Mr. Frelinghuysen.

(II) John, son of Jacobus Schureman, was born about 1729. Removing to New Brunswick, Middlesex county, New Jersey, he engaged in mercantile pursuits and became a very prominent member of that community. He was frequently elected to the legislature, served as one of the judges of the county court, and was a member of the committee of safety, appointed by the provincial congress of New Jersey to exercise the powers of the congress during the recess of that body from August 5 to September 20, 1775. In the church he was a deacon and elder, also acting as chairman of the building committee, and he was "conspicuous for unaffected piety, fervid zeal, and fruitful benevolence." He died July 6, 1795. He married Antje de Remere, widow of Peter Stryker; she died May 25, 1800, in her seventy-ninth year.

(III) James, son of John Schureman, was born February 12, 1756. In 1775 he was graduated from Queen's College (now Rutgers), and during the same year was the first to enlist when volunteers were called for. On that occasion he delivered a forcible address, with the result that a company was immediately formed. Being chosen captain of this organization, he served with it in the early military movements, and participated in the battle of Long Island. Returning to New Jersey he was captured, with a cousin, Mr. Thompson, by a detachment of British horse, and the two were sent to the notorious Sugar House in New York City. Effecting their escape, they crossed the Hudson river in a small boat with one oar, and made their way to the headquarters of the patriot army at Morristown. Continuing in the service, he had the distinction of making prisoner the noted Lieutenant-Colonel Simcoe of the Queen's Rangers, after saving his life from a militiaman who was about to bayonet him.

His public career was highly distinguished. From 1786 to 1788 he was a member of the continental congress from New Jersey, and he also served in the New Jersey provincial congress. He was elected as a federalist to the first congress of the United States under the constitution, sitting in that body from March 4, 1789, to March 4, 1791, and he was a member of the fifth congress, May 15, 1797, to March 3, 1799. Upon the retirement of John Rutherfurd from the United States senate Mr. Schureman was chosen to succeed him, representing New Jersey from December 3, 1799, to February 26, 1801, when he resigned. Subsequently he was mayor of the city of New Brunswick, and again was member of congress (1813-1815). He was president of a bank in New Brunswick and a successful merchant, "his house and store being upon Burnet street convenient to the wharf." Like his father he was active in the Dutch church, holding the office of elder, and in his personal character he was known for the highest integrity and worth. He died January 22, 1824. He married, January 28, 1776, Eleanor Williamson, who died July 15, 1823, daughter of David and Eleanor (Schuyler) Williamson, granddaughter of William Williamson, elder of the church at Cranberry, New Jersey. They were the parents of fourteen children.

(IV) William Williamson, eleventh child of James Schureman, was born April 19, 1799, died of an epidemic disease January 30, 1850. He was interested in the freight transportation business across the state of New Jersey from Amboy to Bordentown, and also in the schooner traffic from New Brunswick to New York. His residence was on a farm formerly belonging to his father at One Mile Run. He married Ann Bennet, daughter of John Bennet and granddaughter of James Bennet, who was mayor of New Brunswick. She was born August 16, 1798, died November 15, 1880.

(V) James (2), only son of William Williamson Schureman, was born June 22, 1823, died November, 1902, at Franklin Park, New Jersey. He lived on the old Schureman homestead at One Mile Run, and was a highly respected and influential citizen. He married Hannah Cox, born December 5, 1828, died March, 1902, daughter of Henry Christopher and Mary Mattox (Van Nostrand) Cox, and granddaughter paternally of John Christopher and Mary Williamson Cox, the latter of whom was the daughter of William Williamson.

(VI) Howard Bishop, only son of James (2) Schureman, was born at One Mile Run, July 17, 1849. At the age of seventeen he went to Philadelphia and entered the house of Lorillard & Company, in the transportation business. Subsequently he was for nineteen years in business in Newark, New Jersey, as a manufacturer of edge tools. Retiring from this occupation, he lived successively near Princeton and at Franklin Park, Middlesex county, finally removing to New Brunswick, where he now resides. During his residence in Newark, Mr. Schureman was active in military affairs, paymaster fourteen years, being an officer in the First Regiment of the National Guard, in which he rose to the rank of captain. He married, January 26, 1876, Stella A. Hager, born August 31, 1855, daughter of Albert H. and Caroline (Gulick) Hager. Their children were: Caroline and James Percy, see forward.

(VII) Caroline, born January 23, 1878, married Walter H. Olden, a nephew of Governor Olden, of New Jersey. Children: Alice Olden, Joseph Brewer Olden, James Schureman Olden.

(VII) James Percy, born in Newark, New Jersey, February 27, 1880, received his general education in the Newark Academy and Princeton University, graduating from the latter in-

stitution in 1901. Entering the medical department of the University of Michigan, he completed the prescribed course and obtained his M. D. degree in 1905. After two years in the Newark City Hospital he came to New Brunswick, and was associated with Dr. D. L. Morrison until the latter discontinued his general practice. Dr. Schureman has since been pursuing his professional business alone. He is a staff physician of the Wells Memorial Hospital and the Parker Memorial Home, and is a member of the New Jersey State Medical Society, the Middlesex County Medical Society, and other organizations.

GROSS　Herman Gross, M. D., of Metuchen, Middlesex county, was born in the empire of Austria, September 19, 1879, youngest son of Nathan and Rebecca Gross. In 1892 he came to the United States with his mother, having been preceded by his three elder brothers, William, Aaron, and David, all of whom are now residents of Middlesex county.

He received his general education in his native country and at the College of the City of New York, his professional studies being pursued in the College of Physicians and Surgeons, New York City, where he was graduated as Doctor of Medicine in 1903. After receiving his degree he was engaged in professional work for a year at the Craig Colony for Epileptics at Sonyea, New York. He then established himself in practice at Metuchen, where he has since successfully pursued his profession.

Dr. Gross has been a member of the board of health of Metuchen since 1905, and its secretary and treasurer since 1908. He is a member of the American Medical Association, New Jersey State Medical Society, and Middlesex County Medical Society.

THOMPSON　Henry Chapman Thompson Jr., of Philadelphia, is the grandson of John Thompson, at one time sheriff of Philadelphia, and the son of Henry Clark and Jane (Chapman) Thompson, of Burlington county, New Jersey. He was born in Philadelphia, October 19, 1862, and is now living at Merion, a suburb of Philadelphia, with offices at 2015 Land Title Building, Broad and Chestnut streets, Philadelphia.

For his early education he attended the private schools in Philadelphia, and afterwards was prepared for college in the Episcopal

Academy in the same city. He then entered the University of Pennsylvania, leaving in his junior year to enter the law department of the University of Pennsylvania, where he graduated in 1885 with the degree of LL. B. After being admitted to the Philadelphia bar, he entered on the general practice of his profession, continuing alone until 1898, at which time he formed a partnership with William F. Harrity and others, the firm name being Harrity, Lowrey & Thompson, and December 1, 1908, it was changed again to the present form of Harrity, Thompson & Haig. In politics Mr. Thompson is a Republican. He is affiliated with many prominent organizations, among which are the Union League Club of Philadelphia, the University Club of Philadelphia, the Merion Cricket Club, the Overbrook Golf Club, and the Lawyers Club of Philadelphia, of which he is the director and the secretary.

November 7, 1895, Henry Chapman Thompson, Jr., married Julia Margaret, daughter of Jacob H. and Annie R. (Atterholt) Castner, of New Lisbon, Ohio, where her grandfather was a judge. They have one child, Alice Chapman, born August 31, 1896.

BLACK The branch of the numerous Black family at present under consideration belongs to the emigration of the middle of the nineteenth century and can boast of but two generations in this country as the third generation is only just growing up and has its life and career all before it. The last generation, however, has good reason to be proud of the example which it has inherited for its imitation.

(I) William Black, son of John Black, the founder of the family, was born in Ireland and came to this country in 1832. He married in Philadelphia, Eliza Hollins, born in 1818 in England. Children of William and Eliza (Hollins) Black were: 1. Jane, born in 1838: married Joseph Thompson, of Philadelphia. 2. Mary Etta, 1840: married Thomas Montgomery, of Philadelphia, one of the tipstaves of the court, and has four children: Henry, William, Mabel and Elizabeth. 3. Margaret, married George Lees, of Philadelphia, and has two children: Hollins and George. 4. William John, referred to below. 5. Annie, married William King, a wall paper dealer of Philadelphia, and has two children: Mabel and Florence. 6. Adeline, married Robert Watts, a plumber of Philadelphia, and has three children: Albert, Edna and Florence.

(II) William John, fourth child and only son of William and Eliza (Hollins) Black, was born in Philadelphia, April 10, 1850, and is now living at Atlantic City, New Jersey. He attended the public schools of Philadelphia, and then learned the trade of stonecutting at which he worked in that city until 1875. In that year he became connected with the fire department of the city as a hoseman, and after faithful service for twelve years was made in 1887 a captain, in which capacity he served for ten years longer, until 1897, when he was retired with a pension from the city. He then came to Atlantic City, where he soon became a member of the Neptune fire company, a volunteer organization of that city, and when the town organized a paid fire department he was induced to become its chief. This was April 4, 1904, and since that time Mr. Black has been serving the city in that capacity to the eminent satisfaction of every one, having now completed a period of over forty years as a fire fighter. During his service he has had many perilous adventures and narrow escapes from death. His arm has been broken, he has had his ribs stoven in and once he was nearly blinded. This last incident occurred while he was in command of a company of men who had been sent to aid in overcoming the great fire in Baltimore, Maryland. Mr. Black is a member of Lodge No. 423, Free and Accepted Masons, of Philadelphia; Lodge No. 276, Benevolent and Protective Order of Elks, of Atlantic City, and the Tall Cedars of Lebanon. He is a Republican; a director in the Atlantic City Fire Insurance Company, and a member of the Presbyterian church. His mother was a Quaker.

July 8, 1871, William John Black married Sarah, born 1850, died March, 1902, daughter of William Buchannan, of Philadelphia. They had two children: 1. William Albert, born July 14, 1872, died in 1886. 2. Henry, born October, 1874, died in 1878.

DIAMENT The Diament family of New Jersey have been among the large landed proprietors and gentlemen yeomen of Cumberland county ever since the beginning of middle of the eighteenth century, when the founder of the family came over to this country from England, where as the preamble to his will shows he was one of the staunch adherents of the Church of England, his theology being of the marked type of the Caroline divines and the non-jurors, and in all probability his emigration was to a

Charles G. Diamint

great extent influenced by his antipathy to the Presbyterian tenets of the Orange succession.

(I) Nathaniel Diament, of Fairfield, Cumberland county, New Jersey, died in April or May, 1767, leaving a widow and ten children surviving. His will written April 3, 1766, was proven May 14, 1767, and the inventory of his estate, made April 28, 1767, by David Westcote and Ephraim Harris, amounted to £256, 15 shillings, 6 pence. November · 7, 1769, his widow Lois wrote her will which was proved December 31, 1770, and her estate was inventoried at £96, 9 shillings, 4 pence. Children of Nathaniel and Lois Diament were: 1. Jonathan. 2. James, referred to below. 3. Nathaniel Jr. 4. Hedges. 5. Lois, married a Mr. Bennit. 6. Sarah, married a Mr. Swing. 7. Dorcas. 8. Elizabeth. 9. Ruth, married a Mr. Powell. 10. Rhoda.

(II) James, son of Nathaniel and Lois Diament, was left by his father "one third of my land and marsh on Joneses Island except the piece of marsh before excepted," and by his mother five shillings, the same legacy that she left to all her sons, the remainder of her property being divided among her daughters. The piece of marsh referred to had been given to James's brother Hedges. James died in April, 1776, leaving a widow, mentioned but not named in his will and eight children: 1. James, referred to below. 2. Sarah, married John Westcott. 3. Abigail, married Charles Howell. 4. Nathaniel. 5. Hannah, married Parsons Lummis. 6. Mary. 7. Ruth, 8. Lois.

(III) James (2), the son of James (1) Diament, of Jones Island, was born on Jones Island, Cumberland county, in 1755, died there in 1845. In his will he mentions his wife and ten children, one of whom is deceased. The name of his wife was Bathsheba, and his children were: 1. James. 2. Elmer, referred to below. 3. Nathaniel. 4. Sarah, married a Mr. Alderman. 5. Theodosia, married John Henderson. 6. Ruth, married a Mr. Fithian. 7. Rosiana, married Preston Foster. 8. Jane Eliza, married a Mr. Bateman. 9. Hannah, married Isaac Newcomb. He was a revolutionary soldier.

(IV) Elmer, second child and son of James (2) and Bathsheba Diament, died intestate in 1832 leaving a widow and several children mentioned but with the exception of Theophilus Elmer, referred to below, not named in their grandfather's will.

(V) Theophilus Elmer, son of Elmer Diament, named in his grandfather's will, was born on Jones Island, Cumberland county, August 4, 1810, died in 1891. Besides leaving him a tract of marsh his grandfather left him for himself, " the farm on which I now reside, together with one half of my right to land and marsh between the Big Gate and the Eagle Island, except the piece given to Elmer's heirs. and in addition about thirty-two acres of woodland." To the "children of my deceased son Elmer Diament," their grandfather left "the land I bought of Jeremiah Harris called the Piney Branch Tract also the land on Jones Island I bought of John Elmer junior joining on the Island dam creek, late of Moses Husted and others, also the house and lot near Cedarville purchased of Theophilus E. Bateman, also the marsh between Cedar Creek and the mill gut, also the store house and wharf at Cedarville Landing purchased of Norton Lawrence, also the bond made to me by Benjamin Thompson February 1832 for $1500. My executors are to be the trustees of the children who are under age, and the widow of my son Elmer is to retain in her possession all the household goods provided by me."

Theophilus Elmer Diament married Mary Lummis Garrison, born at Bridgeton, Salem county, New Jersey, April 24, 1812, died in 1889. Their children were: 1. Charles Garrison, referred to below. 2. John Elmer, born October 24, 1846, died in 1904; married Cora Cleaver, from near Delaware City, and had two children: George and John Cleaver. He was at one time in the canning business with his brother, Charles Garrison. 3. George, born April 24, 1848, died in 1878 unmarried. He was a graduate from the West Jersey Academy.

(VI) Charles Garrison, son of Theophilus Elmer and Mary Lummis (Garrison) Diament, was born on Jones Island, Cumberland county, October 11, 1841, and is now living at Cedarville, Cumberland county, New Jersey. After attending the public schools of Jones Island and of Cedarville, Mr. Diament went on his father's farm where he learned to be a successful farmer. For a time he was connected with his brother, John Elmer Diament, in the canning business. He was honored by the people of Cumberland county by being elected high sheriff of that county and keeper of the county jail in 1902, and served three years with his residence at the county house in Bridgeton. He was for many years treasurer of Lawrence township and also of Fairfield township, and was also on the school board and was district clerk of Jones Island.

He is a Republican, a member of the Grange, and is interested in every thing that goes to make successful farming, which he illustrated and demonstrated in his own successful farming career. He now owns six farms, comprising in all about fourteen hundred acres, and a beautiful home in the town of Cedarville, where he is now enjoying a well earned leisure and retirement. He attends the Presbyterian church.

Charles Garrison Diament married (first) Priscilla, daughter of Charles Wheaton, of Jones Island, December 20, 1862, on Jones Island, who died in Bridgeton, March 14, 1881. Their children were: 1. Hettie Garrison, born July 3, 1866, unmarried. 2. Harry Grant, July 31, 1869, a farmer at Jones Island; married Mattie Lore but has no children. 3. Edward Limmis, November 25, 1872, married Elinor Mail and has two children: Helen and Mary. He was educated at the West Jersey Academy, the University of Pennsylvania, and graduated from the Baltimore Medical College with the degree of M. D. He is now practicing medicine in Bridgeton, and for nine years has been county physician of Cumberland county.

Charles Garrison Diament married (second) in 1883, Rachel, daughter of John Dill Newcomb, of Berlin, New Jersey. They have no children.

MILLER Richard Ross Miller, of Camden, New Jersey, is the grandson of Matthew Miller and son of Colonel Matthew and Rebecca Boon (Ross) Miller. Colonel Miller was born in Salem, New Jersey, in 1821, died in March, 1908. He was the first colonel of the Fourth Regiment of New Jersey.

Richard Ross Miller was born in Salem, New Jersey, April 14, 1839, and is at present engaged in the insurance business in Camden, New Jersey, where he has his offices at 128 Federal street. He has always been an active and a prominent member of the Republican party. For three years he was president of the Camden Republican Club of New Jersey, and for ten years served as city treasurer of Camden. In 1867 he was elected a member of the Union League Club of Philadelphia. In religion he is a Presbyterian. He has always been an enthusiastic secret society man and he is a distinguished Free Mason, having taken all of the Scottish rite up to and including the thirty-second degree. He is a member of Camden Lodge, No. 15, Free and Accepted

Masons, Royal Arch Chapter, No. 19, Commandery, No. 7, Knights Templar, also Benevolent Protective Order of Elks, and Cape May Yacht Club.

Richard Ross Miller married (first) Jennie Halsey, of New York. Children: 1. Anna Halsey, born in 1859; married the Hon. Charles C. Garrison, a New Jersey judge, and has three children: Carlyle, an attorney of New York, Geraldine, married a Mr. Curr, of Colorado Springs, Colorado, and Josephine. 2. William, born 1861, died in 1880. 3. Albert Ross, born March 19, 1863, at Camden. Mr. Miller married (second) August 29, 1879, Mary M. Wolff, of New York. Children: 4. Mabel, died in infancy. 5. Richard Ross Jr., born in February, 1892.

PIERSON Truman Tertius Pierson, son of John Noble and Lucy (Kempson) Pierson, was born in Indianapolis, Indiana, October 12, 1884. He is the grandson of Captain William Pierson, who was born in Scotland, was a mariner, and came in early life to this country, establishing his residence in Rahway, New Jersey. In the Civil War he entered the United States naval service, was captain of a gunboat under Farragut in the battle of Mobile Bay, and was killed some time afterward while in the performance of duty in command of a gunboat on the Mississippi river. William Pierson's son, John Noble Pierson, removed to Indianapolis, Indiana, was identified there with terra cotta manufacturing interests, afterward lived for a time in Chicago, and then returned to the east, making his home in Metuchen, where he still resides. He is an architect of Perth Amboy and Metuchen, of the firm of J. N. Pierson & Son (in which Aylin Pierson is associated with him). He married Lucy Kempson, (now deceased) daughter of Dr. Peter Kempson, of English birth, who came to Canada and then to Metuchen, where he died.

When Truman T. Pierson was two years old his parents removed to Metuchen, New Jersey, which has since been his place of residence. His career has been marked by great energy, and at the early age of twenty-five he has attained a conspicuous degree of success. During the Spanish war, he was then fourteen, he conceived the idea that it would be profitable to deliver the newspapers to the citizens at their homes in the early morning, and this was the beginning of his business activities. He was afterward employed as water-boy by the Pennsylvania railroad, carrying water to

Italian laborers, and as a messenger-boy. These occupations he left to engage as local correspondent for New York newspapers, also being for some time a reporter on the Perth Amboy *Daily Chronicle*. He next entered the Middlesex Water Company in a clerical capacity, from which he was soon advanced to the position of assistant-superintendent, meantime (and indeed until recently) continning to serve as out-of-town correspondent for several of the leading New York dailies.

Actively interested in politics from early youth, Mr. Pierson devoted himself with enthusiasm to the cause of the Republican party, and was known for effectiveness as a campaign worker. In January, 1907, he was appointed by President Roosevelt postmaster of Metuchen, practically the whole town signing his petition in that connection, and at the time was the youngest postmaster in service in New Jersey. His conduct of the position (in which he still continues) has been characterized by efficiency and especially by attention to the improvement of the postal facilities and service. He has also been active and prominent in promoting and developing organizations of the postmasters. As a delegate to the national convention of postmasters at Washington, D. C., in October, 1907, he called a meeting of the New Jersey postmasters in attendance there, which resulted in forming the New Jersey State Postmasters' Association, of which he was chosen vice-president. He is now vice-president of both the state and national associations. His business enterprises in Metuchen include successful real estate and insurance interests, conducted under his personal name; and he is also superintendent of the Metuchen Gas Light Company. He is a member of the principal fraternal societies and of various local organizations. He married, February 2, 1905, Edna M. Bennett, daughter of Smith W. Bennett, of Asbury Park, New Jersey. They have one child, Muriel Virginia Pierson.

ELLIS Alfred Lauder Ellis, M. D., physician and formerly mayor of that municipality, is descended on the paternal side from an old New England family and on the maternal side from Scotch ancestry. In the Ellis line he is a direct descendant of Governor William Bradford, of the "Mayflower." He is the grandson of Benjamin F. Ellis, of Hartford, Connecticut, and son of George Ellis, also of that place (born September 21, 1844, died June 21,

1898), who was secretary and actuary of the Traveller's Insurance Company of Hartford. The mother of Dr. Ellis, Janet McEwen, was born in Scotland, came to America with her parents, John and Agnes McEwen (who resided in Albany, New York), and died December 6, 1896. An elder brother of Dr. Ellis is George W. Ellis, of the Travellers' Insurance Company in Hartford, and a younger brother is John M. Ellis, identified with the Bethlehem Steel Company in New York City.

Alfred Lauder Ellis was born April 21, 1877, in Hartford, Connecticut. He was graduated as bachelor of science from Trinity College in 1898 (the degree of master of science being confirmed upon him by that institution in 1900). After pursuing a post-graduate course in medicine for two years at Yale University, he entered the Long Island College Hospital (Brooklyn, New York), where he received his doctor's degree in 1902. He was then, successively, a member of the staff of the Manhattan State Hospital on Ward's Island and medical director of the Travellers' Insurance Company in New York City.

In 1904 Dr. Ellis removed to Metuchen, New Jersey, and embarked in the practice of his profession, which he has since continued with reputation and success. Active in the local affairs of the community, he has occupied several of the principal offices; he was for some time secretary of the board of health, was elected to the council in 1907, and was chosen mayor to fill an unexpired term in January, 1908, continuing until January, 1909. He is secretary of the Middlesex County Medical Society, treasurer of the Metuchen Building Company, and treasurer of the Middlesex Automobile Club.

Dr. Ellis married, June 28, 1905, Gladys Antisdel, daughter of James and Jessie (Baker) Antisdel, of New York City. They have two children, William M. and James L. Ellis.

CONRAD It is written in the "History of Berks and Lebanon Counties," by Rupp, 1844, that "In March, 1756, the Indians laid the house and barn of Barnabas Seitle in ashes, and the mill of Peter Conrad, and killed Mrs. Neytong, the wife of Baltser Neytong, and took his son, a lad of eight years, captive." This appears to be the first record account of any Conrad who may be assumed to be of the same family as that of which it is our purpose to treat in these annals. It is taken from this that Peter Conrad was an early immigrant settler in the German colonies in Berks county, Pennsylvania, in the vicinity of Penn township and the little settlement therein which is called Bernville. Yet history furnished us with only meagre information concerning this Peter, and it is probable that he was a man of mature years when he was proprietor of the mill which the Indians burned in 1756, during the French and Indian wars of the eighteenth century.

The Brights and Conrads were among the early settlers in Penn township and lived neighbors. John Conrad and his family are particularly mentioned in Berks county history as among the pioneers of that locality and it is probable that John may have been a son of Peter. John Conrad's house and farm were on the road between Mt. Pleasant and Bernville. He was a devout member of the Moravian church and a man of considerable prominence in the early history of the township. Many years ago the Conrads carried on milling enterprises in Berks county, and in 1838 one or more of them operated a powder mill in Penn township which was accidentally blown up with disastrous results.

(I) Joseph B. Conrad, with whom our present narrative begins, was one of the foremost men of Bernville in his time, but whether he was a grandson of Peter Conrad, the miller, whose buildings were destroyed by Indians is not known. Joseph B. Conrad was a prosperous farmer, a man of considerable influence, and at one time was elected to the legislature of the state. Besides his farming interests he was for many years engaged in dealing in lumber and grain. He retired from active pursuits several years before his death, 1905. He married Marian Whitman and of their several children three grew to maturity, viz: 1. James H., see forward. 2. Irving W., married Mary Wilson and had three children: Arthur (now dead), Joseph and Edward. 3. Howard W. married Mary Obold, lives in Reading, Pennsylvania, and has three children, Bertha, Stella and Ray.

(II) James H, son of Joseph B. and Marian (Whitman) Conrad, was born at Bernville. Pennsylvania, February 13. 1849, and spent many years of his active business life in the far west, where he was a pioneer. When a young man he learned the trade of cigar making and followed that occupation for a number of years then spent five years in Chicago, where he kept a grocery store. In 1882 he left Chicago, went to South Dakota and took up a tract of land at what now is Watertown. He was one of the earliest settlers in that region, and continued to live there until 1896, when he returned east and took up his residence near Hackensack, New Jersey, starting a fruit farm there. Later on he removed to Hackensack and now lives in that city, a carpenter by occupation.

He married, December 24, 1867, Jennie M. Klopp, born North Heidelberg. Berks county, Pennsylvania, and a descendant of one of the oldest German families of that region. Children: 1. Dr. Edgar K., see forward. 2. Herbert Walter, born at Bernville, Pennsylvania. April 3, 1872; graduate of the Baltimore College of Dental Surgery, and now a practicing dentist of Hasbrouck Heights, New Jersey; married, June 12, 1898. Mabel Yearance, and has one child, Mildred Dorothy, born Hackensack, September 24, 1901. 3. Corrinne, born Pine Grove, Pennsylvania. January 6, 1874; married, 1891, Fred Wight and has six children: Reuben Lester, born August 2, 1893; Violetta, born May 22, 1895; Edgar, born July 2, 1897; Arthur, born April 14. 1900; Alvin James, born June 10, 1903; Fred Henry, born November 18, 1907. 4. Willard K., born South Dakota. February 20. 1883; graduate of Baltimore College of Dental Surgery; in active practice in Hackensack; married, April 15, 1908. Grace Soley, daughter of Charles R. and Emilina R. (Odell) Soley; they have one child. Willard Soley, born December 13, 1908.

(III) Edgar K., son of James H. and Jennie M. (Klopp) Conrad, was born in Bernville. Berks county. Pennsylvania, February 21, 1870, and was a boy of about twelve years when he went with his parents to live in South Dakota. He acquired his early education in Watertown high school, at Watertown, South Dakota, and his professional education in Bellevue Hospital Medical College, New York City, where he graduated M. D. in 1893. After leaving college he spent one year as interne at the Hackensack Hospital, and at the end of that time began his active professional career in the same city. Dr. Conrad has come to be recognized as one of the leading members of his profession in Bergen county and enjoys a successful practice. He holds membership in various professional organizations and also in Pioneer Lodge. Free and Accepted Masons, Bergen Chapter, Royal Arch Masons, Washington Commandery, Knights Templar (of Passaic), Independent Order of Odd Fellows, Junior Order of United Workmen and the United Order of Foresters.

He married, October 31, 1900, Grace L., daughter of Albert V. Moore, and has two children: Edgar K. Jr., born September 19, 1902, and Franklin Campbell, February 6, 1906.

STAGG It is said that the first Stagg in this country was Thomas Stagg, whose wife's baptismal name was Margaret. He is mentioned in a deed as early as 1682 and again in 1684. In 1695 administration was granted on his estate, he having died intestate. He left two sons whose names are known, John and William, although there may have been other children besides them.

(I) Jacob I. Stagg, the earliest known ancestor of the family here under consideration, was born near the present city of Paterson, April 5, 1789, died November 18, 1840. He was an industrious farmer and his efforts in life were rewarded with a fair degree of success. His wife was Catherine Van Riper, and their children were: Mary Catherine, John, Adrian, Francis, Catharine, Jane, Garret, Richard, Henry and Tunis.

(II) John, second child of Jacob I. and Catherine (Van Riper) Stagg, was born near Paterson, New Jersey, October 18, 1806, died in that city in 1872. When a young man he was apprenticed to a blacksmith, but soon abandoned that trade and became a carpenter, following the latter occupation during the greater part of his business life. He was a consistent member of the Cross street and Market street Methodist Episcopal churches, of Paterson, an industrious man and an upright citizen. He married Maria, daughter of Peter Tise, and of the seven children born of this marriage only two are now living. One son Peter, was a soldier of the civil war, having enlisted as private in the First Michigan Cavalry; he rose from the ranks to the rank and commission of colonel of the regiment, and brevet brigadier general, and commanded Custer's brigade when that gallant officer was promoted major general. The children of John and Maria (Tise) Stagg who are now living are: Maria, widow of Hugh Fulton, late of Paterson, and John, see forward.

(III) Chief John Stagg, of the Paterson fire department, was born in that city, December 16, 1843. He received a good education in the Paterson public school, and after leaving school learned the trade of a printer. In August, 1862, the second year of the civil war, he enlisted as private in Company A, Eleventh New Jersey Volunteer Infantry; was promoted corporal, March, 1863; quartermaster sergeant, September 1, 1864; second lieutenant First Michigan Cavalry, December 4, 1864; and first lieutenant March 1, 1865. After the close of the war he continued in service and was on duty at Salt Lake City, Utah, and was finally discharged and mustered out at Fort Bridger, Wyoming, November 10, 1866. His service during the period of the war was chiefly with the Army of the Potomac and in the Shenandoah valley.

After returning from the service Chief Stagg resumed his former occupation as a practical printer and compositor, first at "the case" in the office of the Paterson Guardian, of which paper he afterward became foreman of the composing room and still later business manager in the office. Later on he was with the Paterson Morning Call in the capacity of business manager. As early as 1868 he became a member of the old Paterson volunteer fire department and was its chief engineer from 1887 until 1889, being the last chief during the life of the department as a volunteer organization. In 1891 he was made chief of the re-organized and paid department, and has filled that responsible position to the present time. He is a member of Farragut Post, No. 28, Grand Army of the Republic; New York Commandery of the Loyal Legion; Encampment No. 152, Union Veteran Legion; and Benevolent Lodge, No. 45, Free and Accepted Masons. He was one of the founders and organizers of the New Jersey State Association of Fire Chiefs, and has served as president of the National Association of Fire Chiefs.

He married Catherine, daughter of John Fulton, November 5, 1868; she died suddenly while attending a convention of the Fire Chiefs at Dallas, Texas, October 11, 1906. Of the seven children born of this marriage six are now living: Sarah, Katherine, Robert, Emma (wife of John Sandford), John and Edward Stagg.

GOOTENBERG It is not always the descendant of the pioneer who achieves the greatest success in business life in a new country and among strangers, nor always the man of means and superior educatonal attainments who first takes rank with the leading men of any municipality. In this brief narrative we have to record the events of family life of an ancestor who came to America from a distant European country, and less than two score years ago established himself in mercantile pursuits in the greatest American metropolis. Our record here is not lengthy, yet it is one of honest endeavor and well-earned success.

(I) Yona Gootenberg, immigrant ancestor of the family here considered, was born in St. Petersburg, Russia, in the year 1827. He came to the United States in 1878, locating in the city of New York, where he carried on business as a dealer in furnishing goods. He died October 13, 1906. The given name of his wife was Toyba, who bore him children as follows: 1. Gerson, see forward. 2. Leah, married Abraham Rabinowitz, and has seven children. 3. Moe, married Sella ———, and has three children. 4. Simon, married Rosa Podlasky, and has five children. 5. Annie, married Harry Zwisohn, and has seven children. 6. Kate, married Abe Starin, and has five children. 7. Charles, married ———, and has two children.

(II) Gerson, son of Yona and Toyba Gootenberg, was born in St. Petersburg, Russia, November 22, 1858, and came to this country in 1881. He lived ten years in New York City, and became an accomplished practical jeweler, watchsmith and silversmith. Not only a competent workman, but having acquired an excellent understanding of business methods, he located in Paterson, New Jersey, and set up in business on his own account. His endeavors in mercantile life have been rewarded with gratifying success, and he now ranks among the substantial business men of that city. He is a member of Shakespeare Lodge, No. 750, Free and Accepted Masons, of New York, and of the following bodies in Paterson, New Jersey: Aerie No. 43, Order of Eagles; Wirth Lodge, No. 146, Independent Order of Odd Fellows; and Barnett Memorial Temple.

Mr. Gootenberg married, May 10, 1883, Eva L., born September 16, 1864, daughter of Louis and Sarah (Weissman) Delerson, both natives of the city of Kovna, Russia. Children of Mr. and Mrs. Gootenberg: 1. Samuel, died at the age of ten months. 2. David, born March 17, 1885; married, April 14, 1909, Adeline M. Muller, of Paterson, New Jersey, born October 27, 1888, daughter of John P. and Mary (Powley) Muller. 3. Mabel M., March 18, 1887. 4. Philip, October 28, 1888. 5. Emma, July 3, 1890. 6. Abie, March 23, 1892, died July 30, 1901. 7. Henry, August 30, 1896.

SPEER

The various families of Spier, Spear and Speer, which are found in New Jersey have a common origin in one of the earliest of the old Dutch pioneer families, which first of all settled in New Amsterdam and then went across the Hudson into what is now Bergen county, from whence they have spread through different parts of the state although their name is especially associated with the old inhabitants of Essex and Hudson counties.

(I) Hendrick Jansen Spier or Spieringh emigrated to this country in the ship "Faith" which landed her passengers from Holland in New Amsterdam in December, 1659. He brought with him his wife and two children. Although he acquired a home in New Amsterdam, he seems to have lived there but a little while for May 9, 1662, his wife in his name sells to Christoffel Van Laer their house on the Heere Graft, "next the house of Oloff Stevens Van Cortlandt and Gerrit Janse Roos, extending in front eastward to the Burghwall and in the rear to the lot of Abraham de la Noye." In this deed Hendrick is styled as "of Gemoenepa," that is as living in what is now Communipaw. In 1679 he is one of the purchasers of a large tract of land in New Jersey on the east of the Hackensack, and he is dead before December 16, 1681, when his widow marries (second) as the third wife of Jan Aertsen, the emigrant ancestor of the Vanderbilt family. By his wife, Magdalena Hansen, Hendrick Jansen Spier had at least two children: 1. Barent, who married, July 31, 1698, Kathalyntje Hendrickx. 2. Jan Hendrickx, referred to below.

(II) Jan Hendrickx, son of Hendrick Jansen and Magdalena (Hansen) Spier, was born in Holland and came to this country with his parents. He was one of the earliest of the settlers around Second River, what is now Belleville, and his name is found on a deed referring to that part of the province as early as March 16, 1684. The family tradition of the Spers is that they are descended from this son of Hendrick J., through his son John or Hans or John, referred to below.

(III) Hans or John, the conjectured son of Jan Hendrickx Spier, appears in Second River in 1720, where on July 13, he conveys to Arent Schuyler, John Stoutenburgh and others the church lot now occupied by the Dutch Reformed church of Belleville. By his wife Catryna, Hans Spier had a son Abram, referred to below.

(IV) Abram, son of Hans and Catryna Spier, married in the Dutch Reformed church at Hackensack, June 17, 1724, Geertje Braos, by whom he had a son John, who is referred to below.

(V) John, son of Abram and Geertje (Braos) Spier, was a farmer with a farm of twenty acres in Second River. May 11, 1746, he married Magdalena Van Dyck, who bore him nine children: 1. Abram. 2. James. 3. Harmon. 4. John, referred to below. 5. Thomas. 6. Peter. 7. Nattia, who married Mr. Vreeland, of Poversham. 8. Betsy, who married Abraham King. 9. Laney, who married another King.

(VI) John (2) son of John (1) and Magdalena (Van Dyck) Speer, was born and lived in Second River, although he also spent a part' of his life at Poversham on what was later known as the cotton-mill property, and then moved back again to Belleville, occupying a stone house still in the hands of his descendants, and later occupying the house, built by himself, which has descended to his grandson, bearing his name. John Speer married Margaret Joralemon; children: 1. John Peter. 2. James Tunis, referred to below. 3. Abraham Varic, at one time a member of the New Jersey legislature. 4. Maria, who married Abraham Van Riper, resided on a farm immediately south of the Passaic county line, and had five children: Sarah, John, Abraham, Eliaz and Margaret. Of these children Margaret married Theodore Sandford. 5. Magdalena, married John N. Joralemon, and lived and died within one hundred yards of her father's residence. 6. Margaret, married Abraham Van Houten, of Belleville village, where they lived and had four children: William, Cornelius, Abraham and Anne Maria. 7. Elizabeth, married Peter, son of Michael and Gitty (Cadmus) Sandford. 8. Anna, who died young.

(VII) James Tunis, son of John (2) and Margaret (Joralemon) Speer, was born in Belleville, October 1, 1795, died there July 12, 1867. He married Eliza L. Wade, born December 1798, died July 16, 1878; children: 1. John, born September 20, 1823, died May 14, 1900; he spelt his name Spear, was one of the chosen freeholders of Belleville, one of the town committeemen, and also surveyor of highways; October 22, 1878, he married Eliza Housman, born 1836, died October 4, 1907.

2. Abbie, born April 8, 1827, died December 29, 1833. 3. Alfred W., born September 9, 1828, died January 15, 1897; married, in 1858, Agnes Storey; children Alfred, Oscar, Mary and Florence. 4. Mary Anna, referred to below.

(VIII) Mary Anna. youngest child of James Tunis and Eliza L. (Wade) Speer, was born June 19, 1835, and is now living at 330 Washington avenue. Belleville. April 17, 1856, she married John Jerome. son of Curtis and Letitia (West) Tucker, of Brooklyn, whose children were: John Jerome, James. Elizabeth, William, Charles, Arthur, Mary and Julia Tucker. John Jerome Tucker was a mason and contractor in New York City, where he built many large buildings, among them being the Hall of Fame. For eight years he was water commissioner of New York. He was also president of the apprentices' library of New York City, and for sixteen years president of the Masons' and Builders' Association. He was a member of the Dutch Reformed church and for thirty-five years chairman of the church's finance committee. At the time of his death he was vice-president of the Bank of Savings of New York City.

By his marriage with Mary Anna Speer, he had two children: 1. Edwin, born March 4, 1857, who has been twice married and is now living at Asbury Park. 2. Walter Curtis, born December 18, 1862, married, January 4, 1893, Gertrude Creveling and has two children: Marjorie, born January 12, 1895, and John Jerome. born January 29, 1903.

HEISLER   The Germans who so largely made up the growth and aided in the development of New Jersey and Pennsylvania were generally followers of Luther, but being broad men, many accepted other creeds and faiths and added to the congregations of the Society of Friends and to the Methodism, but the greater part remained within the fold of the Lutheran church. Among the Germans of Pennsylvania the name of Heisler is quite common, and both the pulpit and the profession of medicine have had notable men bearing that name. The Rev. Washington L. Heisler was a well known minister of the Lutheran church in Jersey Shore. Lycoming county, Pennsylvania, and his distinguished son, John Clement Heisler, was a graduate of the medical department of the University of Pennsylvania in 1887, and filled the chair of anatomy in that institution,

1889-97, curator of the Horner Museum University of Pennsylvania since 1897. Among the Quakers of Burlington county, New Jersey, we find another branch of the family.

(I) Jacob Heisler was born in 1782. He married and had a son Jacob, see forward.

(II) Jacob (2), son of Jacob (1) Heisler, was born in Pemberton township, Burlington county, New Jersey, in 1812. He was married in 1840 by the ceremony observed by the Society of Friends to Sarah, daughter of Caleb Malmsbury, of the Society of Friends, and they had children born to them including William Henry, see forward.

(III) William Henry, son of Jacob (2) and Sarah (Malmsbury) Heisler, was born in Pemberton township, Burlington county, New Jersey, November 19, 1842. He was brought up and educated in his native township, and held office in the township government soon after reaching his majority. Mr. Heisler was a member of the Methodist Episcopal church of Pemberton, and of its board of trustees, also serving the church as superintendent of its Sunday school. Early in life he affiliated with the Masonic fraternity, being initiated into the mysteries of Masonry when made a member of Mount Holly Lodge, No 14. His interest in the welfare of Methodism in America caused him to become an active member of the Ocean Grove Association of Jersey; vice-president of the Board of Home Missions and Church Extension Society of the Methodist Church in America; and treasurer of the Penn Seaman's Friend Society of Philadelphia. He was elected to membership in the Union League Club of Philadelphia, and of the Penn Historical Society of Philadelphia. He is president of the Manufacturers' National Bank of Philadelphia, located at No. 27 Third street, and treasurer of the Schlichter Jute and Cordage Company of that city.

He was married "out of meeting," about 1874, in Philadelphia, Pennsylvania, to Eliza Jane, born September 25, 1849, daughter of Edmund and Emeline F. (Corrigan) Yard, and granddaughter of Jacob Corrigan, of Philadelphia. Their children were born in Pemberton, Burlington county, New Jersey, as follows: 1. Grace Ashton, August 29, 1875, graduated at the Woman's College, Baltimore, Maryland, in 1893; she married, 1894, Harold B. Wells, an attorney and counsellor at law in Pemberton. They made their home in Bordentown, New Jersey, where their children were born as follows: Harold B. Wells (2), June 2, 1906; Elizabeth Heisler Wells, No-

vember 30, 1908. 2. Charles Mortimer, 1877, died in infancy. 3. William Henry (2), January 6, 1883, was prepared for college in Burlington county, matriculated at the Princeton University, and was graduated A. B. 1903. He is studying law with his brother-in-law, Harold B. Wells, Esq.

The name of Elvins so far as is now ELVINS known belongs but to two families in this country, namely, the family of Congressman Elvins, of Missouri, who is said to be the youngest member of the house of representatives, and the descendants of Andrew Elvins, of Philadalphia, and Hammonton, New Jersey, which are set forth below.

(I) Andrew Elvins was a native of Cornwall, England, born in 1803. He came to America in 1836, arriving at and staying at first for a short time in New York. Having, however, obtained work as a carpenter in Philadelphia, he removed thither and sent for his family to come over to this country and join him, which they did in the year 1848. The mother and son George then set up and kept a dry goods store, which they ran successfully, while the father worked at his trade until 1858, when the entire family removed to Hammonton, Atlantic county, New Jersey, being one of the first families to settle in that region. Here, living in the home of their son George, Andrew Elvins and his wife passed the remainder of their days in well earned rest and prosperity. Andrew Elvins married, in England, Elizabeth Williams, born in 1810, died in 1884. Their children were: 1. John, married Katharine E. Walton and had two children, Mamie and Georgiana. 2. William Andrew. 3. Mary Elizabeth, married W. D. Walton, of Philadelphia, but had no children.

(II) George, youngest child of Andrew and Elizabeth (Williams) Elvins, was born in Cornwall, England, June 29, 1838, and is now living in Hammonton, New Jersey. Coming to this country with his mother in 1848, he helped her to run the dry goods store in Philadelphia, and then buying a three acre lot in Hammonton built his house and store. He attended the public schools of Philadelphia, while helping his mother, and from the lessons which he learned in both places he attributes all of his successful subsequent career as a merchant. Mr. Elvins is a member of M. B. Taylor Lodge, Free and Accepted Masons, of Hammonton, and a director in the Working-

mans' Building Association. He has been treasurer of the town of Hammonton for a number of years; also collector, and was for five years one of the freeholders of the town. He was appointed postmaster of the town by President Abraham Lincoln and he held that office for twelve years. While he was serving in this capacity he was also chosen to be one of the state representatives in the New Jersey assembly in 1880-81. For three years he was also chosen to serve on the town council. He is a member of the First Methodist Episcopal Church of Hammonton and is one of the stewards and trustees. For the last forty years he has been one of the district stewards of the Methodist Episcopal church.

In 1858, just before his removal to Hammonton, George Elvins married Annie, daughter of Thomas Clohosey, of Philadelphia, who bore him seven children: 1. Mary Elizabeth, married Charles H. Wilson, of Williamstown, Gloucester county, New Jersey, and has three children: Maude, Charles and George. She was born in 1859. 2. Lillian, born in 1861; married Godfrey M. Crowell, M. D., an Australian of old New England ancestry who resides in Hammonton, New Jersey, and has three children: Annie, Edwin and Marian. 3. Annie, born in 1863; married Harry L. Peeples, of Hammonton, and has one child, Marjorie. 4. Carrie, born 1865; married John E. Wood, of Maine, now living in Philadelphia. and has one child, Oliver. 5. George A., born 1867; unmarried; now living and conducting a real estate business in Atlantic City. 6. Thomas Clohansey, born in 1869; a Republican; member of the New Jersey state assembly for five years up to 1907, and now in business with his father, besides being the present postmaster of Hammonton. He married Lillian Ruby, and has five children: Miriam, Hubbard, Thomas, George and Robert. 7. Mabel, born in 1877; married George W. McDougal, of Philadelphia, but has no children.

DE BAUN This name is supposed to have been de Baen and to have originated in Baen, a village in a province of France, in order to designate a family in Baen. At all events there is no doubt of the nationality to which the name belongs as being French. This leads to the material inference of the political and religious leaning of the family as being Huguenot and opposed to the oppression of the Roman church in France. Then following this trend, we are not surprised to find the name in the Netherlands

ii—20

and especially on the north of the River Rhine, in the Lower Palatinate, and thence following the flood of immigration that built up New Netherlands and New Amsterdam, which passed into the possession of England in 1664. This change of proprietorship did not, however, stop the flow of immigration from France to Holland, Belgium and England, of those driven out of Catholic France by persecution and threatened martyrdom. It was among these later refugees that the de Baens came to New York about the year 1683. Living for many years and perhaps for two generations in the land of the Dutchmen, they had acquired their habits and language and the de Baen of their fatherland had become De Baun in Holland and in the Dutch city of New Amsterdam, which city had taken the English name New York in 1664. It was at this time that the Dutch flag was lowered and the English flag hoisted over the fort, whose frowning walls and threatening cannons protruding from innumerable portholes in these walls, threatened annihilation to any vessel sailing up the harbor except under the royal standard of Great Britain. It is in the little town of Bushwick across the East river from New York and between the Wallabout and Hell Gate on the Long Island shore front that we find Joost De Baune.

(I) Joost (Yost) De Baune was the clerk of the town of Bushwick, Long Island, in 1684, and in 1685 we find him the schoolmaster and clerk of the town of New Utrecht, south of the Wallabout, on Long Island. His position in the community is plainly denoted by his occupation as clerk of the towns in which he lived and as schoolmaster in New Utrecht, which vocation was second only to that of the ministry. He was evidently a supporter of the policy of the aristocratic lieutenant-governor, Nicholson, for when the democratic colonists under the lead of Captain Jacob Leisler took possession of the state house in the name of William of Orange and was appointed lieutenant-governor by the committee of safety, De Baun was deposed from his offices as clerk and schoolmaster. He took the oath of allegiance to the aristocratic rule at New Utrecht in 1687 and continued to reside in the town, was reinstated as clerk and schoolmaster, and his name appears on the assessment rolls of New Utrecht in 1693 and on the census in 1698. We next find him living near Hackensack, in Bergen county, New Jersey, as early as 1709, which locality became the home of his descendants.

He married Elizabeth Drabba, in Holland,

about 1670, and had seven children born in New Utrecht, Kings county, Long Island, New York, as follows: 1. Mattie, married David Samulse De Maree, in November, 1705. 2. Christian, baptized in the church in New Ultrecht, May 15, 1687, and was married in January, 1709, to Judith Samuelse De Maree. 3. Majhe, baptized May 4, 1670, at Flatbush. 4. Karl (Charles), see forward. 5. Christyne, born 1695. 6. Jacobus, who married Antje Kennit or Kenning. 7. Margrietje or Maria, who married Theodore Romain, in June, 1728. Joost and Elizabeth (Drabba) De Bain both died at their home near Hackensack, but we find no record by which we can determine the dates.

(II) Karl (Charles), second son and fourth child of Joost and Elizabeth (Drabba) De Bain, was born in New Utrecht, Long Island, New York, and removed with the family to Hackensack, New Jersey, where he married Janetje Pieterse Harring and had eleven children born in Hackensack, New Jersey: Yost, Peter, Yan, Jacob, Isaac, Abram, see forward; Christian, Margarietje, Cornelia, Maria, Elizabeth.

(III) Abram, sixth son of Karl and Janetje Pieterse (Harring) De Bain, was born in Hackensack, Bergen county, New Jersey, December 10, 1731, and died September 14, 1806. He was married (first) to Bridget Ackerman, who died January 27, 1793, and by her he had ten children, born in Hackensack, New Jersey, as follows: Karl, November 21, 1757, died April 18, 1790; Margaret, November 28, 1767, married Albert Wortendyke, and died April 25, 1860; Abram, January 14, 1770, married Sarah Remsen, died December 9, 1859; Jacob, March 22, 1765, married Ann De Bain, and died December 1, 1853; Yannetie, November 12, 1762, married Peter Smith, and died May 11, 1845; Andreas, February 20, 1775, married Maria Tolman, August 30, 1800, and died February 21, 1848; Sara, August 5, 1782, died July 13, 1793; David, December 7, 1759, married Antje Forshe, who died in 1836, he died December 13, 1820; John, December 25, 1772, married Altje Smith, and died in May, 1840; Isaac, see forward. Abram De Bain married (second) Lea Van Orden, August 25, 1793.

(IV) Isaac, youngest of the ten children of Abram and Bridget (Ackerman) De Bain, was born in Hackensack, New Jersey, December 9, 1779. He married, June 13, 1807, Elizabeth Yeury, who was the daughter of John and Elizabeth (Van Orden) Yeury, and was born January 12, 1791, and died August 24, 1875.

Her father, John Yeury, was born May 8, 1764, and died March 8, 1840, and her mother, Elizabeth Van Orden, died September 13, 1856. Isaac and Elizabeth (Yeury) De Bain had eight children, born in Hackensack, as follows: 1. Abram, February 7, 1809; married, May 15, 1830, Maria, daughter of Johannes and Elizabeth (Palmer) Van Houton. Maria Van Houton was born June 14, 1810, and died January 19, 1895, and her distinguished son, John A. De Bain, was born in Clarkstown, New York, March 6, 1833. He was prepared for college at Rutgers College grammar school and was graduated at Rutgers College, New Brunswick, New Jersey, Bachelor of Arts, 1852; Master of Arts, 1855. He attended the Theological Seminary of the Dutch Reformed Church at New Brunswick, New Jersey, 1852-55, was ordained pastor of the Reformed Dutch Church at Oyster Bay, Long Island, New York, 1855, and resigned the pastorate in 1858 to accept a call from the Dutch Reformed Church at Niskayuna, New York. He was pastor there for a quarter of a century, resigning in 1883 to go to the Reformed Church in Fonda, New York, where he was installed as pastor in 1883. He was elected president of the General Synod of the Reformed Church in America in 1880, and in 1884 declined the presidency of Hope College, Holland, Michigan. Union University conferred on him the honorary degree of Doctor of Divinity in 1877.

He was married, in 1855, to Elizabeth B. Coddington, of New Brunswick, New Jersey. 2. Elizabeth, September 25, 1810; married, November 24, 1832, Nicholas Van Houten, who was born November 9, 1807. 3. Jacob, January 20, 1812; married (first) Rachel Brown, who died in November, 1851, and (second) Emma Hays, May 8, 1864. 4. Maria, June 5, 1814; married Aaron Johnson, and died May 12, 1861. 5. Bridget, August 13, 1816; married John I. House, who was born April 17, 1809. 6. Rachel, January 13, 1819; married Albert Blauvelt, February 14, 1877. 7. Jane, March 19, 1821; married John A. Duryea, who was born in March, 1819. 8. John Y., see forward.

(V) John Y., the youngest of the eight children of Isaac and Elizabeth (Yeury) De Bain, was born in Monsey, Orange county, New York, August 22, 1827, and died at Leonia, New Jersey, February, 1895. He was a precocious child and, fortified by a common school training, bad enough at its best as it existed in the country districts in that day, he, by his inherent force of will and determination, fitted himself for the ministry of the Dutch Reformed Church, which was no mean achievement when we take into consideration the high standard set by the Classis for its ministers. He does not appear to have attended any college or theological school. He was licensed to preach by the Classis of Hackensack of the True Reformed Dutch Church, April 17, 1855. He had, as his first charge, two churches, one at Hempstead (now Monsey), Rockland county, New York, and one at Ramseys, Bergen county, New Jersey, and in these churches he preached alternate Sundays up to 1860. He then became pastor of the church at Hackensack and of the one at English Neighborhood (now Leonia). He removed to Hackensack in 1860, and had charge of the two churches for twenty-six years. He also established and edited the *Banner of Truth*, a monthly church magazine, which continued to be the organ of the True Reformed Dutch Church. He was an eloquent preacher and a self-made man in every way, proving himself worthy of his high calling.

He was married (first) April 8, 1848, to Margaret, who died about 1893, daughter of Abram and Susanna (Van Wart) Iserman. Her father was born March 11, 1799, and married, April 1, 1821, to his wife, Susanna Van Wart, who was born May 6, 1802. Rev. John Y. and Margaret (Iserman) De Baun had born to them nine children as follows: 1. Susan Elizabeth, February 26, 1850, died August 26, 1852. 2. Martha Amelia, January 24, 1852, married Eugene A. Van Horn, September 10, 1874. 3. James Demarest, September 30, 1854, died December 8, 1862. 4. Abram, see forward. 5. Edwin, September 14, 1859, died October 17, 1862. 6. Anna, May 14, 1866, married October 22, 1891, C. A. Benjamin. 7. John Zabriskie, December 27, 1867, died December 18, 1874. 8. James Edwin, September 7, 1872, died January 26, 1884. 9. Isaac Calvin, May 6, 1874. John Y. De Baun married (second) Jane Van Houton, who survived him.

(VI) Abram, second son and fourth child of Rev. John Y. and Margaret (Iserman) De Baun, was born at Monsey, Rockland county, New York, April 2, 1856. He removed with his parents to Hackensack, New Jersey, in 1860, and was graduated at the Hackensack Academy in 1873. He then took up the study of law in the office of A. D. Campbell, at Hackensack, was admitted to the bar of New Jersey as an attorney at the June term of the supreme court, 1877, and as a counsellor in 1880. He was a law partner with his preceptor-at-law, A. D. Campbell, under the firm name of Campbell & De Baun, up to 1893, when he associated himself with Milton Demarest, the law firm of De Baun & Demarest being still in active practice in 1909. He was clerk of the board of chosen freeholders of Bergen county, 1878-95, inclusive, his long term of service in so important an office being an evidence of his popularity and the good opinion entertained by the citizens of the county as to his ability and faithfulness. He served as treasurer of the Hackensack Improvement Commission for three years, and has been counsel for the Hackensack Mutual Building and Loan Association from its organization in 1887. His legal practice is largely confined to real estate transactions and to the management of the estates of widows and minor children. His fraternal affiliation is confined to the Royal Arcanum and the Legion of Honor. He was married (first) April 30, 1878, to Mary B. Christie, of Leonia, New Jersey, who died September 30, 1881, and on October 8, 1884, he married (second) Lydia B. Christie, of Hackensack, New Jersey. He had no children by either marriage.

SINNICKSON The ancestry of Judge Clement Hall Sinnickson, of Salem, and as a lawyer has won distinct precedence has distinguished the commendation of the legal profession and the discriminating public, can be traced back through many generations.

The earliest reference to the family in the Danish Book of Heraldry is of the date 1450, when Duke Adolph, of Schleswig, ennobled Andreas Snnichson for a service rendered in battle. The tradition is that the Duke's horse was shot under him and Andreas hastily dismounting gave his own horse to his chieftain. The coat-of-arms is an unsaddled horse and the record goes on to say that the Helm and Blazon was granted by King Christian of Denmark two years later in 1452.

In 1550 Sonnich Snnichson, a descendant of Andreas, received a patent of nobility from Frederick 2d, King of Denmark, and occupied an estate in Angln, Denmark, named Hestrip. This passed to his son Carlen in 1600. Andres Snnichson, a younger son of Carlen, came to America in 1638, then no longer a young man, and accompanied by his sons Anders and Broor. They landed at what is now Wilmington, Delaware, on Christine creek. He did not live long, and in 1640 his son, Anders, crossed the river Delaware to what is now Lower Penn's

Neck township, New Jersey, and purchased of the Indians a large tract of land then called Obisquahaset, where he settled and established the homestead which has ever since remained in the family and has been the home of many succeeding generations. Broor Snnichson remained in Delaware and is the progenitor of a large clan in that state and in Pennsylvania. After the arrival of John Fenwick in 1675 to take possession of his tenth of New Jersey, a large portion of this land so purchased from the Indians was quitclaimed to Anders Sonnichson and much of it now remains in the family.

Next in line came Andrew Sinnickson, 3d, the name undergoing an anglicising change. Next was Sinnick Sinnickson, who left one son, Andrew, 4th.

Andrew, son of Sinnick Sinnickson, born in 1718; died in 1790; leaving a large property to be divided among his numerous children. His life was active and influential; he was appointed judge of the court of common pleas under George III. and held the office many years. He was a member of both provincial congresses of New Jersey 1775-76; served as a member of the higher branch of the first state legislature then called the council, and was one of the nine men who pledged themselves for a large sum of money to provide clothing for the New Jersey troops in the field. He had three sons and three sons-in-law who participated in the struggle for independence and rendered efficient aid to the colonists. His son, Thomas Sinnickson, was so active and aggressive that Lord Howe offered a hundred pounds for him dead or alive, and when the representatives of the British government offered to sign a peace treaty in southern New Jersey almost every one in that section of the state was included in the amnesty proclamation, but among the few excluded were the Sinnicksons who were proscribed by name. The Thomas Sinnickson above referred to was afterwards a member of the first United States congress.

Colonel Andrew Sinnickson, son of Andrew Sinnickson, married Margaret, daughter of Judge Robert and Margaret (Morgan) Johnson. Judge Robert Johnson traced his ancestry to Richard Johnson, born in Guilford Surrey, England, in 1649; he became a resident of Salem county, New Jersey, in 1675. Served as a member of the house of burgesses in 1707, and was judge from 1710 till his death in 1719. His son, Robert Johnson, was born in 1694, and married Margaret Sayres. Their son, Robert Johnson, was born 1727; served as

judge and justice of the peace from 1761 to 1780; married Margaret Morgan, of Marcus Hook, Pennsylvania.

John Sinnickson, son of Colonel Andrew and Margaret (Johnson) Sinnickson, was born 1789, died 1862. He married Rebecca Kay Hall, whose ancestry traces back to William Hall, who came to America and took up his residence in Elsinboro, Salem county, in 1677. In 1709 he was made judge and filled that position till the time of his death in 1718; he was also a member of the governor's council. He married Sarah, granddaughter of Gregory Clement, one of the regicide judges of Charles I., and the daughter of James Clement, who came to America after the vengeance of Charles II. had wreaked itself in the execution of his father's judges. Of the marriage of William Hall and Sarah Clement, was born William Hall 2d, who married Elizabeth, daughter of John Smith, of Amblebury. Their son, Clement Hall, was born 1724, and married Margaret, daughter of Joseph Morris, in 1748. Their son, Clement Hall 2d, was born 1753, and married Rebecca, daughter of Joseph Kay, of Gloucester county, and their daughter, Rebecca Kay Hall, was born in 1798, and married John Sinnickson, in 1826. They were the parents of Clement Hall Sinnickson.

Clement Hall Sinnickson, son of John and Rebecca Kay (Hall) Sinnickson, was born in Salem, New Jersey, September 16, 1834. He acquired his preliminary education in the private schools of Salem, attended the Polytechnic Institute, of Troy, New York, and in 1855 was graduated at Union College with the degrees of Bachelor of Arts and Civil Engineer. On the completion of his literary course he began the study of law with Andrew Sinnickson, of Salem, and was afterward a student in the office of William L. Dayton, of Trenton. In 1858 he was admitted to the bar as an attorney, and in 1864 as a counsellor. He located in practice in Salem, and soon gained a large distinctively representative clientage. His arguments were logical, forceful and convincing, his preparations of cases exact, and his knowledge of the law is comprehensive and accurate. In 1896 he was appointed by Governor Griggs to the position of judge of the common pleas court of Salem county, and has since acceptably served in that capacity. He has also been connected with business interests outside of his professional duties, and is now a director of the Farmers' Mutual Fire Insurance Company of Salem county.

He is a member and secretary of the vestry

of the Episcopal church in Salem, and belongs to the Theta Delta Chi, a college fraternity. He also holds membership in Johnson Post, No. 69, Grand Army of the Republic, at Salem, being entitled to a place therein by reason of his three months' service in the civil war. He was commissioned first lieutenant and promoted to the captaincy of Company I, Fourth Regiment of New Jersey Volunteers, and was sent to Fort Runyon, Washington, D. C., where he was on picket duty. He was also vice-president of the Sons of the Revolution of New Jersey for a number of years. In politics he has always been a staunch Republican, and has taken a very active part in the work of advancing its interest, being recognized as one of the party leaders. He represented his district in congress for two terms, from 1875 until 1879, two of the most important sessions in its history. He was a member of the Republican state committee in 1880. He is the owner of a part of the original tract of land purchased by the family.

Judge Sinnickson married, in June, 1862, Sarah M., daughter of Louis P. and Henrietta (Hancock) Smith. They had two children, both of whom died in infancy.

KENDALL The Kendalls are an English family of much prominence and are definitely traced to the middle of the fifteenth century. It is said by some authorities that the name is derived from the town of Kendall in Westmoreland county, that among its representatives have been many persons of distinction in governmental affairs, several branches having coats-of-arms and other insignia of high estate. In the mother country the Kendalls for many generations have been a numerous family in Bedfordshire, Essex, Derbyshire, Cornwall, Devonshire, Hertfordshire and as well in other towns and shires in different parts of the kingdom.

(I) John Kendall, progenitor of the American family of that surname, was living in 1646 in Cambridge, England, and died there in 1660. Among his children were two sons, Francis and Thomas, both of whom come to New England. In 1644 Deacon Thomas Kendall, one of the brothers, was a proprietor of the town of Reading, Massachusetts, and was made freeman there in 1648. He married and had a large family of ten daughters, but no sons, hence the New England Kendalls are descendants of Francis.

(II) Francis, son of John Kendall, of Cambridge, England, came to New England before 1640, and in December of that year with thirty-one others signed the town orders of Woburn. He had been living in Charlestown, of which Woburn then was a part. It was not an unusual thing with the early immigrants to America to take assumed names in order to avoid vexatious laws and occasionally to avoid the vigilance of parents who frequently objected to the emigration of their sons; and the tradition is that Francis Kendall left home and country against the wishes of his father and in order to get away more easily he took the name of Miles. He was made freeman in 1648, and Sewall in his history of Woburn says that "he was a gentleman of great respectability and influence in the place of his residence." He served as selectman eighteen years, member of the committee for granting town lands and for building the meeting house, tythingman in 1676; but he appears not to have been in full accord with the teachings of the ruling church in the town and on one occasion was fined for disobedience of the church requirements regarding infant baptism. His occupation was that of miller, and the corn mill which he owned he left to his sons, Samuel and John. This mill and the land on which it stands has remained in possession of the Kendall family to the present time, and the building now or very recently standing on the site was erected by Samuel Kendall in 1700. Francis Kendall died in 1708, aged eighty-eight years. He married December 24, 1644, Mary, daughter of John Tidd, and by her had nine children, born in Charlestown or Woburn: 1. John, July 2, 1646. 2. Thomas, January 10, 1648-49. 3. Mary, January 20, 1650-51. 4. Elizabeth, January 15, 1652-53. 5. Hannah, January 26, 1654-55. 6. Rebecca, March 2, 1657. 7. Samuel, March 8, 1659. 8. Jacob, January 25, 1660-61. 9. Abigail, April 6, 1666.

(III) Jacob, son of Francis and Mary (Tidd) Kendall, was born in Woburn, January 25, 1660-61, and spent his life in that town. Some accounts mention that he had twenty or more children, but this doubtless is an error and the result of confusion of his children with those of his son, Jacob. The elder Jacob married (first) January 2, 1683-84, Persis Hayward, of Woburn, and married (second) January 10, 1695, Alice Temple. He had in all seventeen children: 1. Persis, August 24, 1685. 2. Jacob, twin, January 12, 1686-87; died soon. 3. Jacob, twin, January 12, 1686-87. 4. Joseph, December 17, 1688. 5. Jonathan, November 2, 1690. 6. Daniel, October 23,

1691. 7. Ebenezer, November 9, 1695. 8. John, January 6, 1696-97. 9. Sarah, July 18, 1698. 10. Esther, November 20, 1699. 11. Hezekiah, May 26, 1701. 12. Nathan, December 12, 1702. 13. Susanna, October 27, 1704. 14. Phebe, December 19, 1706. 15. David, September 28, 1708. 16. Ebenezer, April 5, 1710. 17. Abraham, April 26, 1712.

(IV) Joseph, son of Jacob and Persis (Hayward) Kendall, was born in Woburn, December 17, 1688, and lived in that town. He married twice and had nine children, all born in Woburn: 1. Jonathan, October 29, 1718. 2. Joshua, March 7, 1719-20. 3. Mary, January 6, 1723. 4. Susanna, July 24; 1727. 5. Oliver, July 29, 1730. 7. Jacob, October 9, 1738. 8. Esther, November 25, 1740. 9. Sarah, March 5, 1743.

(V) Joshua, son of Joseph and Susanna Kendall, was born in Woburn, March 7, 1719-20, and lived in that town. He married (first) 1745, Esther Buck, and (second) May 2, 1753, Susanna Johnson, and had nine children: 1. Joshua, February 9, 1747. 2. Jonathan, June 4, 1749; died young. 3. Jonathan, September 1, 1751. 4. Susanna, January 25, 1754. 5. Benjamin, March 16, 1756. 7. Joel, December 16, 1766. 8. Daniel, August 8, 1771. 9. William, July 14, 1774.

(VI) Daniel, son of Joshua and Susanna (Johnson) Kendall, who was born August 8, 1771, is supposed to be the Daniel Kendall who lived in Haverhill and was proprietor of a tavern in that town. The name of his wife does not appear, and indeed the records of Haverhill give no account of him or of his family. He had several children, and among them were sons, William, Benjamin. Daniel and James, and a daughter, Anna.

(VII) Daniel (2), son of Daniel (1) Kendall, of Haverhill, Massachusetts, was born in Haverhill, November 10, 1808; died in Wisconsin, where the later years of his life were spent. He was a morocco dresser by trade and followed that occupation for perhaps twenty-five or thirty years, first in Haverhill and afterward in Salem, Massachusetts. He then followed the sea for a time and made several voyages, later removed to Portland, Maine; then returned to Salem and in the fall of 1859 went to Wisconsin, where he afterward engaged in farming until the time of his death. He married Lucy Bray, a descendant of one of the old New England families which was noted for the number of its sons who were seafaring men. Eight children born of this marriage, and only one of them is now living.

(VIII) William Boden, son of Daniel (2) and Lucy (Bray) Kendall, was born in Davensport, near Salem, Massachusetts, August 9, 1846. He was a boy of eleven years when his father removed with his family to Wisconsin. He lived at home, attended school and worked on his father's farm until he was sixteen years old; he then went to Iowa and lived there about five years, and then went to Brookings county, South Dakota, where he was engaged in farming for ten years; in November, 1887, he removed to Oregon, settling in Lane county, where he remained two years, during which time he served in various official capacities in the township, namely: School director, township treasurer and justice of the peace. In 1889 Mr. Kendall came east and took up his residence in Paterson, New Jersey, where he has since resided. For twelve years he was engaged as packer for the firm of McNab & Harlin. He is a member of General Grant Lodge, No. 119, Knights of Malta; Junior Order of American Mechanics; Daughters of Liberty; Knights of Maccabees; Shepherds of Bethlehem and the Patriotic Order of Sons of America.

He married, November 26, 1874, Gorden, born May 17, 1858, daughter of Charles K. and Betsy (Robertson) Shaw. Children: 1. Bessie G., born September 17, 1875; died June 2, 1891. 2. Daniel B., March 10, 1877; died July 9, 1892. 3. Lucy Gage, June 22, 1879; married, June 14, 1904, George H. Drew, of Paterson, New Jersey. 4. William Boden, Jr., April 30, 1881; married, November 4, 1903, Christine Dodd. 5. Charles K., June 21, 1890; died April 11, 1891.

BROWN This well known English surname has been found in all parts of the colonial period. Several of the immigrant ancestors who came over during that period were in some manner of kin, but generally the families were not related, although having the same name; and it will be remembered that Brown is one of our common English surnames which antiquarians tell us are derived from a color. However, the family here under consideration appears to have come into this country independent of any other family of the same name, and appears to have been among the earliest English families in the region which afterward became a part of the Penn proprietary.

(I) George Brown and Mercy his wife came from Lancashire. England, in 1679, although they were not married until their arrival at New Castle. They settled in what afterward became Falls township, Bucks county, Pennsylvania, on land surveyed and set off to them under a warrant granted by Edmund Andros, governor general under the Duke of York. This land lay along the Delaware river above the Manor of Pennsbury, and a part of it has remained in possession of descendants of George and Mercy Brown even to the present time. There is a tradition in the family that previous to emigrating from England George Brown had paid court to a sister of Mercy, but that she declined coming to America, upon which he offered marriage to Mercy if she would accompany him on the voyage to the new world. She did so and they married when the voyagers landed at New Castle. They were progenitors of a very worthy family and among their descendants have been found many men of prominence in public life. It is said that George and Mercy Brown had fifteen children, several of whom died in infancy. Eight sons and three daughters survived and grew to maturity. George Brown was born in 1644, in England, and died in Falls township, Bucks county, Pennsylvania, in 1726. Among his descendants and of near kin to the family of which this article is intended to treat was General Jacob Brown, who was so prominently identified with our national military history during the second war with the mother country.

(II) John, who was probably a son of George and Mercy Brown, resided in Bucks county, not far from Yardville, where the family has continued for two centuries. It is difficult to discover further particulars concerning him.

(III) John (2), son of John (1) Brown, was born August 23, 1732, in Bucks county, Pennsylvania, died May 20, 1815. His wife, Elizabeth (surname unknown), born 1722, died September 23, 1787.

(IV) Jonathan, son of John (2) and Elizabeth Brown, was born August 8, 1764, near Yardville, died January 19, 1842. He was a successful farmer. He married Apama Kier, a native of Bucks county, born November 14, 1769, died April 29, 1831. She was a daughter of John and Hannah Kier, probably of Scotch-Irish ancestry. Children: Jesse, born December 2, 1787, died May 23, 1861; Naomi, July 7, 1789, died May 10, 1865; Nathan, June 24, 1791, died January 27, 1851; John, July 22, 1793, died June 23, 1854; Elizabeth, February 7, 1796, died January 24, 1861; Phoebe, December 4, 1797, died November 15, 1871, Hannah, March 31, 1800, died July 22, 1834; Sarah, June 3, 1802, died October 7, 1863; Jonathan, August 2, 1804, died November 17, same year; Joseph, November 4, 1806; George W., mentioned below; William, April 10, 1811, died August 15, 1813.

(V) George Washington, sixth son of Jonathan and Apama (Kier) Brown, was born January 7, 1809, near Tullytown, in Falls township, Bucks county, died at Bristol, March 28, 1883. He was a farmer, a man of good understanding, and served in various public capacities, such as township collector and county commissioner. He lived during the greater part of his life on the farm where he was born, but when advanced in years he sold the old homestead and went to Bristol to live with his daughters. His parents were Friends and Mr. Brown himself was brought up in that faith. He was a Mason, member of Bristol Lodge, No. 25, Free and Accepted Masons. Mr. Brown married Ann A. Lovett, who was born November 29, 1811, near Bristol, Pennsylvania, died in March, 1885, a daughter of Jonathan and Mary Lovett, of that town. Children: Jonathan, died young; William W., died young; Mary, lives in Bristol; Amanda, now dead; Victoria, now dead; George W., mentioned below; Anna, married Joseph Van Zant; Gulaelma, now dead; Frank, now dead; Ada L., of Bristol, Pennsylvania.

(VI) George Washington (2), son of George Washington (1) and Ann A. (Lovett) Brown, was born near Tullytown, Bucks county, Pennsylvania, July 8, 1843. He attended public schools in his native place and for two terms was a student at the state normal school at Millersville, Pennsylvania. He had learned telegraphy in a railroad office at Tullytown before going away to school, and in 1862 he took a position as night telegraph operator at Tullytown, continuing there about three years, and in 1865 was given charge of a contruction train at Frankfort Junction, a branch of the Philadelphia and Trenton railroad, also running a freight train into Jersey City. In 1869 he was made conductor of a mail train, in full charge, and ran on the Amboy division until 1872, when he was appointed extra conductor on that division. He next went with the Pennsylvania railroad and was in Trenton and Camden, New Jersey, as extra passenger conductor for two years. On March 11, 1874, he was appointed station agent at New Egypt, New Jersey, and served there until April, 1888, when the Pennsylvania railroad abandoned that part of the road. He then turned his attention to the organization of the Union Transportation Company, and the first train ran over that road on August 7, 1888, Mr. Brown being superintendent and auditor of the new company. This position he resigned in 1889 and in March of that year went on drill engines from Long Branch to Point Pleasant, moving freight and passenger cars. In 1890 he was made station master at Asbury Park, New Jersey, but in October, 1890, returned to New Egypt. Upon first coming to New Egypt, in 1876, Mr. Brown had started a coal business in company with his brother-in-law, Winfield Scott Chafey, under the firm name of Chafey & Brown, and had continued in it during all the time of his railroad service. Since retiring from railroading he has taken up the coal business, enlarging his trade by dealing in agricultural implements, farm wagons, fertilizers, etc., and devotes his entire attention to the business. Mr. Brown is a Democrat and for several years served as township clerk. He is a member of Pyramid Lodge, No. 92, Free and Accepted Masons, of New Egypt, of which lodge he is a past master, and its present secretary. He is also a Red Man, past sachem and trustee of Oneto Tribe, No. 81, of New Egypt, and of the auxiliary, Daughters of Pocahontas, Wenonah Council, No. 22. Mr. Brown is a member of the Methodist Episcopal church in New Egypt, treasurer of the board of trustees, and a Bible class teacher in the Sunday school.

Mr. Brown married, November 19, 1873, Sarah E., daughter of Charles P. and Martha P. Chafey, and of this marriage four children have been born: 1. Frank, born New Egypt. July 3, 1874. died in infancy. 2. Victoria, born 1888: married Edgar O. Murphy, of New Egypt, a travelling salesman. One child, Edgar Lomer, born New Egypt, November 17, 1903. 3. Helen C., born New Egypt, died at the age of four years. 4. George, died in infancy.

COPPUCK   The Coppuck family of New Jersey has for generations been identified with Mount Holly, and Burlington county, and by its intermarriages with the other historic families of that region has placed itself among the representative families of the state and nation. There were two Bartholemew Coppucks who were on the same ship which landed at Philadelphia with one of Penn's colonies. One, it is said, settled at Dunk's Ferry (now Beverly, New Jersey), and the other settled at Chester. Pennsylvania. The former, it is said, was the progenitor of the New Jersey Coppucks.

(I) James Coppuck, of Mount Holly, who witnessed the will of John Reeves, in 1800, and who was born between 1760 and 1770, is the first member of the family of whom we have authentic records. He married Elizabeth Knight, the descendant of one of New Jersey's famous families, which includes the celebrated painter, Daniel Ridgway Knight, of Philadelphia. They had a large family, among whom were: 1. William, whose daughter, Amelia, married a Welby, and was the celebrated poetess, Amelia Welby. 2. Joseph Cooper, referred to below. 3. Peter Van Pelt. 4. George Washington. 5. Elizabeth, married Joseph C. Clark. 6. Sarah J., married Brainard Clark.

(II) Joseph Cooper, son of James and Elizabeth (Knight) Coppuck, was born at Mount Holly, New Jersey, June 21, 1800. He married Mary, daughter of Captain John and Ann Graves. Her father was a sea captain and commanded a privateer in the war of 1812. The children of Joseph Cooper and Mary (Graves) Coppuck were: 1. Anna Graves, married Noah Zelley. 2. Elizabeth Cooper, married John H. Curtis, Jr. 3. Malcolm MacNeran, referred to below. 4. Mary Letitia.

(III) Malcolm MacNeran, third child and only son of Joseph Cooper and Mary (Graves) Coppuck, was born in Mount Holly, New Jersey, June 7. 1833, and is now living in Philadelphia, Pennsylvania. When he was two years old, his parents moved from Mount Holly to Philadelphia. where he attended the public schools and graduated from the high school. After leaving school Mr. Coppuck went into the silk importing business, and after working for some time in one of the largest houses in the city, he went into a wholesale dry goods house, in which he remained until October 1. 1872. when he was made chief clerk in the bureau of highways in the city of Philadelphia. This position he has held up to the present time. a remarkable tribute to his worth and ability. During the civil war Mr. Coppuck enlisted from Philadelphia in the Seventh Pennsylvania State Troops in order to repel the invasion of Pennsylvania. He was also for a time one of the public school directors of Philadelphia. In politics Mr. Coppuck is a Republican, and he is a communicant of the Protestant Episcopal church. For many years he was the rector's warden, in Advent Church, Philadelphia. He is now connected with St. Stephen's Church. He is a member of the Church Club, of Philadelphia ; Veteran Corps, First Regiment of the National Guard, of Pennsylvania ; Baker Post. No. 8, Grand Army

Malcolm M. Stewart

of the Republic, of Philadelphia ; Philo Lodge, No. 444, Free and Accepted Masons, of Philadelphia. Mr. Coppuck during his earlier life devoted considerable time to designing and also has some fine specimens in water color which he executed both in landscape and portraiture.

October 15, 1857, Malcolm MacNeran Coppuck married (first) Elizabeth E., daughter of Robert Lindsay, of Philadelphia. Their children are: 1. Virginia Lindsay, born August 25, 1859; died August 17, 1874. 2. Marian Graves, June 8, 1865; married Charles Wells Walker, of Chester county, Pennsylvania, whose family settled in New Jersey in 1685. They have two children, Eleanor Wells, born September 16, 1897, and Edith Lindsay, June, 1899. 3. Edith Hoffman, August 17, 1875; died in 1876. Mrs. Coppuck died January 28, 1893. He married (second) June 6, 1895, Sarah Louise (Lodor) Cresson ; she died June 4, 1903.

PILGRIM The Pilgrim family has been connected with the history of Salem and Cumberland counties, New Jersey, since the middle of the eighteenth century. The first record of any of the names, being the letters of administration on the estate of Frederick Pilgrim, who died there intestate in 1768. From that time to the present the name occurs with more or less frequeney in the records, but the information afforded by these references is not sufficient to enable us to trace out the pedigree with accuracy until we reach the name of Maurice or Morris, the ancestor of the branch at present under consideration.

(I) Maurice Pilgrim, who was widely known and one of the most influential men in the counties of Cape May and Cumberland, had among other children a son, Simon Snider, referred to below.

(II) Simon Snider, son of Maurice Pilgrim, and possibly grandson of Frederick Pilgrim, was born in May, 1818, at the little village of Tuckehoe, Cape May county, died in Bridgeton, New Jersey, about 1898. In early life he was a waterman, but later on, about 1830 or 1831, he removed to Friesburg, Salem county, and engaged in farming. So strong, however, was his love for his old home and old calling that even when well settled in life as a prosperous farmer he would often declare his purpose to return sometime to his ocean bound home in Cape May county. He remained, however, at Friesburg, and in the fall and winter

of 1858, when the great revival occurred at the Alloway Methodist Episcopal church, then under the charge of the Rev. John McDougall, Mr. Pilgrim, though living at the time some six miles distant, became interested and attended the services every night, driving the twelve miles and often taking his wagon loaded with his neighbors. The result was his conversion, and the dating of a new life of christian experience, which lasted until the close of his days. Immediately following this revival steps were taken for the organization of a society of Methodists and the building of a new church in the neighborhood of Harmony, a struggling settlement near Cohansey, Cumberland county, and to the furtherance of this object no one contributed more than Mr. Pilgrim. For the whole time that he was connected with the church there, he was in some official relation such as steward, trustee, class leader, Sunday school superintendent and teacher, and the place where the pastor oftenest enjoyed the hospitality of his flock was the home of Mr. Pilgrim. Late in March, 1888, Mr. Pilgrim moved to Bridgeton, and made his home in the third ward, 114 Hampton street, where he continued to reside up to the time of his death. He was buried in the Broad street cemetery. In politics Mr. Pilgrim was a Republican, but he was sufficiently independent to vote his convictions, irrespective of party lines, as the changing trend of public affairs from time to time might determine.

Simon Snider Pilgrim married (first) the daughter of Henry Johnson, a member of one of the old families of Salem and Cumberland counties, by whom he had three children: Henry, Mary (or May), Cutoso. After his first wife's death he married (second) Abigail Fisher, of Tuckahoe, Cape May county, who bore him three more children: Maurice, M. D. of Portland, Maine, now deceased ; Heber, a graduate of Lafayette College, of Pennsylvania; John, a pharmacist of Philadelphia, who died in April, 1907 ; Sara, of Philadelphia.

(III) Henry Johnson, eldest child of Simon Snider and ———— (Johnson) Pilgrim, was born in Bridgeton, New Jersey, about 1850, died in 1899. He was a manufacturer all of his life, and a member of the Central Methodist Episcopal Church, of Bridgeton. He married Elizabeth, daughter of Hiram and Mary Clark, a descendant of one of the old families of Salem and Gloucester counties. Her brothers and sisters were: Charles M., Anna Harker, Katharine Heintz, Ella Irelan and Harriet Hogate. The children of Henry

Johnson and Elizabeth (Clark) Pilgrim, the latter of whom died in 1883, are: 1. Charles Clark, referred to below. 2. George Douglass, married Viola Palmer, of Philadelphia, and has one child, Palmer. 3. Edwin H., died as a baby.

(IV) Charles Clark, son of Henry Johnson and Elizabeth (Clark) Pilgrim, was born in Bridgeton, New Jersey, September 6, 1874, and is now living in Newark, New Jersey. For his early education he attended the public schools at Bridgeton, after leaving which he went to the Pennington Seminary. In April, 1895, he started to read law in the office of Joseph Coult and James E. Howell, in Newark, and was admitted to the New Jersey bar as attorney in November, 1898, and as counsellor in 1901. Since this time Mr. Pilgrim has been engaged in the general practice of his profession in Newark, where he has met with more than ordinary success and is regarded as one of the most prominent of the rising generation of lawyers. In politics Mr. Pilgrim is a Republican and has been extremely active. He is a member of Radiant Star Lodge, No. 190, Independent Order of Odd Fellows; of the Indian League of New Jersey, and also of General Henry W. Lawton Council, No. 284, Junior Order of United American Mechanics. He is a member of the Calvary Presbyterian Church.

June 27, 1900, Charles Clark Pilgrim married in Newark, New Jersey, Cora Belle, daughter of William Henry and Harriet Adelaide (Barringer) Elston. Children: 1. Marguerite Adelaide, born February 25, 1902. 2. William Barringer, November 12, 1907. William Nelson Elston, brother of Cora Belle (Elston) Pilgrim, married Florence E. Smith.

Dr. William Nelson Barringer, father of Harriet A. (Barringer) Elston, was one of the best known educators in the United States. He was born in Brunswick, Rensselaer county, New York, in 1826. His father, John Frederick Barringer, was a farmer. In early life the young man showed an aptitude for study, his early education being received at the Troy Academy, after graduating from which at the age of seventeen he began teaching. He soon showed his ability and was sought for and filled more responsible positions in the schools of Troy. In 1866 he was called to Newark as principal of Chestnut street school, which post he filled until 1877, when he became superintendent of the Newark schools, continuing as such until 1896, when he retired. Dr. Barringer was deeply learned in the science of education. The first summer school under municipal authority

was established by him in Newark in 1885. His lectures on education were delivered in all the principal cities of the country and in Europe. He received the degree of A. M. from Princeton University, and from the New York University that of Ph. D. He was one of the founders of the National Educational Association, and for many years was an attendant upon and participant in its deliberations. A monument to his memory is the Barringer high school of Newark. He died at Newark, New Jersey, February 4, 1907.

HILLIARD

The Hilliards are of French extraction, descendants of French Huguenot ancestors who fled to England during the reign of Louis XIII., and gave origin to the Hillyard family of England. It is one of the oldest and proudest of our American families and its arrival in this country antedates the settlement of Pennsylvania under William Penn, or the settlement of New Jersey under the proprietors; and it was one of the most prominent and influential families in the county of Kent previous to the time when Penn received his royal grant. The Hilliard family of New Jersey is the offspring of two of the most distinguished blue-blooded families of early colonial days, and they who bear the honored surname can speak with pride of their first ancestors; can point with distinction to the houses and public services of John Hilliard, of Delaware, and of Bernard Devonish, of Burlington, New Jersey. John Hilliard was the owner of large tracts of land in the county of Kent, and was himself a man of ability and education, active in everything pertaining to civilization, development and progress. He was highly esteemed as a leading man of his time, and was honored with election to represent Kent county in the first provincial council, under Penn, which convened in Philadelphia on the 10th day of the 5th month, 1683.

Bernard Devonish occupied much the same position in Burlington county as John Hilliard did in Kent county. He came to America in company with a colony of the Society of Friends in the ship "Kent" and landed on the easterly shore of the Delaware, where the city of Burlington now stands, on June 20, 1677. He was one of the early proprietors, and his name is subscribed to the great code of laws known as the "Concessions and Agreements of the Proprietors, Freeholders and Inhabitants of the Province of West New Jersey, in America," which were the incentive to the early immigration which procured the best human seed of all Europe with which to plant the states. Bernard Devonish was active in all of the measures relating to the proprietors, and was himself a large landowner. Between the years 1660 and 1680 he located four hundred and sixty acres of land fronting on the north side of Northampton or Rancocas river, in what now is Westhampton township in Burlington county; and it was there that he built his mansion house and named the locality "Dewberry Hill," after the home he had left in England, and which was destined to become the homestead of the Hilliard family of New Jersey. He left one son, Joseph, who died without issue, and one daughter, Martha, the mother of the Hilliard family of New Jersey, through whose veins only the blood of that noble and distinguished ancestor continues to flow.

(II) John (2), only son of John (1) Hilliard, married Martha, daughter of Bernard Devonish, about the year 1690, and from the date of that union through nine succeeding generations their descendants have largely been members of the Society of Friends. By inheritance from her parents, and by conveyance, Martha Hilliard became possessed of large tracts of land, but the tradition is that she and her husband continued to live on the homestead at Dewberry Hill. The records show that John Hilliard was born in 1659 and that his wife, Martha, was born in 1668. He died intestate, but Martha made a will. They had seven children: John, Hester, Martha, Joseph, Elizabeth, Jane and Edward, the family name of each of whom is written in the record as Hylliar. In this connection it may be mentioned that in 1683, when John Hilliard, the ancestor, was a member of the council his name in the records appears written 'Hillyard, but in 1695, when he was re-elected member of the assembly his name is written Hilliard.

(III) Edward, son of John (2) and Martha (Devonish) Hilliard, was born on the family homestead in 1706, and spent his life there. He made his will the 17th day of the 6th month, 1766, and divided a large property among his children. He married Sarah, daughter of Richard and Mary (Carlile) Haines. She was born 11th month, 1716, and died 11th month, 1796. Children: Abraham, died single; Isaac, married Sarah Haines; Jacob, married Martha Robinson; Samuel, married Hannah Atkinson; Joseph, married Kesiah Mullen; Martha, married Job Ridgway; Mary; Eliza-

beth; John, married (first) Mary Heustis, (second) Frances Haines.

(IV) Jacob, son of Edward and Sarah (Haines) Hilliard, was born and spent his life on the family homestead at Dewberry Hill. At the time he assumed proprietorship of that property the friendly relations of the American colonies with the mother country were fast growing cold, and during the contest which followed he was compelled to remain at home and do service in the broad fields of agriculture; but no tory blood coursed through the veins of any of the Hilliards, for patriotism, loyalty and good citizenship has distinguished the family from the time of the revolution to the present generation of their representatives. He married Martha Robinson, and they had eight children: Edward, Samuel, Margaret, Abraham, Eben, Kesiah (died young), William and Kesiah.

(V) Edward (2), son of Jacob and Martha (Robinson) Hilliard, was born in 1769, and is presumed to have been the progenitor of the family of the particular line here treated. He was engaged in extensive farming enterprises and owned several tracts of valuable farm lands. He married Nancy Stockton. Children: Mary, Ann, Nancy Stockton, Franklin, Edward and Jonathan.

(VI) Franklin, son of Edward (2) and Nancy (Stockton) Hilliard, was born at Vincentown, New Jersey, March 14, 1817, died there February 28, 1889. The earlier years of his business life were spent on his father's farm, and as a boy he was sent to the township school. In 1854 he went to Salem, Columbia county, Ohio, purchased a farm and remained there about eight years. After his return home he lived in Vincentown and kept a livery stable and business until his retirement from active pursuits. In politics he was originally a Whig and afterward became a Republican, and at the time of his death he was a deacon in the Baptist church, where a memorial window indicates the esteem in which he was held in the community in which he lived. He married, December 31, 1840, Lydia Heuling, daughter of General William Irick. She was born September 15, 1822, died in September, 1900. Children: William Henry Irick, a dentist, of Bordentown, New Jersey; Mary Ann, married Lyman Sowers and died in Ohio; Franklin Stockton; and Winfield Scott, a pharmacist, of Mt. Holly.

(VII) Franklin Stockton, son of Franklin and Lydia Heuling (Irick) Hilliard, was born in Vincentown, New Jersey, December 28, 1847, and was a boy of seven years when his father removed to Ohio. He was brought up to farm work and during his boyhood days was sent to the district school of the town. On May 21, 1862, during the second year of the civil war, he enlisted for three months as private in Company G, of the Eighty-fourth Ohio Volunteer Infantry, and during the term of enlistment his regiment was assigned to guard and provost duty along the line of the Baltimore and Ohio railroad in Maryland. He was mustered out of service at Delaware, Ohio, September 20, 1862, and on October 1, 1863, re-enlisted as private in Company B, of the Twelfth Ohio Volunteer Cavalry, and served under Sherman during his famous "march to the sea." In his regiment Mr. Hilliard was chief bugler and during a part of his service was a member of the brigade band. He took part in a number of engagements and on one occasion was taken prisoner, but was recaptured by the Union troops after about ten days in the hands of the enemy. He was mustered out with the regiment November 14, 1865, then returned to Salem, Ohio, and from thence came to Vincentown, New Jersey, where he found employment as clerk in Jacob Heisler's drug store. He remained there about two years, gaining a good understanding of the business during that time, and then became a student at the Philadelphia College of Pharmacy. While living in that city he was employed by William R. Warren, a manufacturing chemist, and remained with him for a year and a half, then returned to New Jersey and began business on his own account, becoming proprietor of the first drug store in Tuckertown. In 1871 Mr. Hilliard removed from Tuckertown to Vincentown and became proprietor of the drug business formerly carried on by Alfred Dobbins. Since that time he has added materially to the original stock, and had not been long identified with business interests in Vincentown before he became recognized among the leading men of the town. He was largely instrumental in organizing the local water works company and also in establishing and operating the water supply system; and to-day he is still president of the company. He is a director and vice-president of the Farmers' Line Telephone Company between Vincentown and Tabernacle, president of the Burlington County Retail Druggists' Association, president since its reorganization of the Vincentown Fire Company and was prominently identified with the reorganization of

that company and the work of placing it on an efficient basis. He also was one of the leading spirits in starting a shoe factory in Vincentown and was a director of the company which operated the factory and business. He is past master of Central Lodge, No. 44, Free and Accepted Masons, member of the Grand Lodge of New Jersey, member and for several years has been commander of T. W. Eayre Post, No. 49, Grand Army of the Republic, and member and senior warden of Trinity Episcopal Church, of Vincentown. In 1869 Mr. Hilliard married Rebecca Josephine, daughter of Joseph Pharo, of Tuckertown. Children: Marion Pharo, a graduate of the State Normal school at Trenton, and now a teacher in Englewood, New Jersey; Grace, married Frank Ross and has one child, Donald Hilliard Ross; Florence; Irving, died young; Bayard, a graduate of Philadelphia College of Pharmacy, and now in business with his father.

(For preceding generations see Walter Reeves 1).

REEVES (III) Thomas, eldest son and heir of John and Ann (Bradgate) Reeves, was born in Burlington county, New Jersey, about 1700, died in Deptford township, Gloucester county, December 2, 1780. His gravestone is the oldest in the ancient Reeves burying ground. He was a well to do farmer and landed proprietor. Up to about 1734 he lived in Wellingborough township, Burlington county, and then removed to Gloucester county where he spent the remainder of his life. By his wife, Sarah, who probably survived him and has been conjectured from the name of his eldest son to have been one of the Biddles, he had children: 1. Biddle, referred to below. 2. Arthur, married Mary Cox. 3. Thomas, born February 2, 1728; died July 25, 1802; married Keziah Brown. 4. Ann, married John Wood, of Gloucester. 5. Rachel, married probably in Old Swedes church, Philadelphia, Benjamin Rambo. 6. Joseph, born June 20, 1743; died January, 1825; married (first) Elizabeth Morgan and (second) Sarah Gill.

(IV) Biddle, eldest son and child of Thomas and Sarah Reeves, was born in Burlington or Gloucester county, New Jersey, died in Deptford township, Gloucester county, in 1789. He lived in Deptford, was a farmer, distiller and landed proprietor. His home plantation was about one and a half miles from Woodbury, on the road from that place to Mantua. He was married twice, but the name of his first wife is unknown. His second wife, Ann (Clement)

Reeves, survived him. By his first wife he had one son, Josiah, born November 11, 1756, died April, 1808; married Esther ——. By his second wife he had eleven more children 2. Mary, born September 12, 1760; married John Groff. 3. Thomas, referred to below. 4. Ann, February 26, 1764; died July 25, 1849; married Archibald Moffett. 5. Biddle, Jr.. October 4, 1766; died June 2, 1828; married (first) Elizabeth Haines, and (second) Elizabeth Ellis. 6. Elizabeth, June 10, 1768; died in infancy. 7. Joseph, March 16, 1771; died 1825; married Sarah Groff. 8. Clement, March 19, 1772; died July 5, 1819; married Sarah Wood. 9. John, March 22, 1775; died unmarried. 10. Desire, March 9, 1777. 11. Sarah, August 1, 1779; died March 23, 1875; married John Smith. 12. Elizabeth, May 12, 1783; died January 18. 1837; married John Milford.

(V) Thomas (2), second child and eldest son of Biddle and Ann (Clement) Reeves, was born in Gloucester county, April 25, 1762, died there September 18, 1819. He was a farmer, having a plantation in Greenwich township, Gloucester county. He married (first) Mary Wood; (second) Abigail Thompson; (third) Sarah Haines. His children were: 1. Thomas, died April 6, 1840, aged fifty-six years; married Hannah Sitgreaves. 2. Joseph, born January 10, 1799; died October 18, 1824; married Mary Gill. The above two most probably by first wife. 3. Charles, referred to below. 4. Mary Ann, born April 1, 1802; married Thomas S. Dyer. 5. Desire, December 18, 1804; died February 14, 1822; married Joseph C. Gill. 6. Abigail, who died unmarried. Children of second wife.

(VI) Charles, eldest child of Thomas (2) and Abigail (Thompson) Reeves, was born in Gloucester county, November 27, 1800, died in Camden, New Jersey, May 30, 1865. He was a gentleman farmer and for ten or twelve years was a lay judge. December 12, 1822, he married Beulah Ann, born April 27, 1803, died December 26, 1880, daughter of Joseph Vannemann and Elizabeth (Tiers) Clark. Their children were: 1. Joseph Clark, born August 1, 1824; died November 29, 1824. 2. Elizabeth Clark, November 27, 1827; died April 28, 1885. 3. Abbie Augusta, May 14, 1830; died October 14, 1903. 4. Charles Carroll, referred to below. 5. Frances Stratton, September 6, 1834; married John R. Stevenson, M. D., of Haddonfield, New Jersey, and is now living in that place. 6. Samuel Southard, March 15, 1836; died June 4, 1880; married Elizabeth S.

Yard. 7. William Pennington, January 14, 1841; died September 30, 1870.

(VII) Charles Carroll, fourth child and second son of Charles and Beulah Ann (Clark) Reeves, was born in Philadelphia, Pennsylvania, April 5, 1832; died June 8, 1903. He graduated from the Pennington Academy, and as a young man went into a wholesale wool house in Philadelphia for a short time, and then took a position in the National State Bank in Camden, New Jersey, where he remained for thirty-five years, thirty-one of which he was the paying teller. He then accepted the position of cashier of the First National Bank of Camden, and after holding this post for five years longer he went into the flour, grain and feed business in the same city and continued in that until about two years prior to his death, when on account of disability he retired from all active business. He was a Republican, a member of the Ancient Order of United Mechanics, and a communicant of the Protestant Episcopal church. June 9, 1864, Charles Carroll Reeves married Elizabeth Sarah, born March 4, 1832, in Montgomery county, Pennsylvania, died in 1899, daughter of John and Sarah (Lentz) Rex. Her father was born in Chestnut Hill, Philadelphia, September 15, 1800, died 1852, son of Levi and Catharine (Riter) Rex. He married, March 1, 1826, Sarah Lentz, born September 29, 1807, died September 3, 1882, daughter of Jacob and Ann (Schultz) Lentz. The children of Charles Carroll and Elizabeth Sarah (Rex) Reeves were: 1. Charles Carroll, Jr., referred to below. 2. Frederick Rex, born in Camden, New Jersey, in 1869, graduated from the public schools of Camden and the Penn charter school of Pennsylvania; read law in the office of his uncle, Walter E. Rex, in Philadelphia, was admitted to the Philadelphia bar in 1890, and is now practicing in that city. He married Emily H., daughter of Philip J. Scovel, of Bordentown, New Jersey, now practicing law in Camden.

(VII) Charles Carroll, Jr., eldest son of Charles Carroll (1) and Elizabeth Sarah (Rex) Reeves, was born in Camden, October 15, 1865, and is now living in Florence, New Jersey. He was educated in the public schools of Camden and William Fewsmith's school in Philadelphia. He then went with his uncle, Frederick A. Rex, in the wholesale tea, coffee and spice business in Philadelphia. After remaining in this for a year, he went in 1886 out west to Montana and Wyoming and spent three years there on a ranch as a cow puncher. In 1888 he returned to the east and entered the employ of the Philadelphia and Reading railroad, in the Philadelphia office of the freight department, where he remained for about a year and a half. He then for a short time went into the State Bank in Camden, and left this position to become search clerk for the West Jersey Title Company, with whom he remained for about two years. In 1891 he went into the office of the Camden Iron Works as cost clerk and organized the cost department, which position he held for seven years, when he was made general foreman of the works and filled this latter position for nine years longer. In 1907, after sixteen years service with the Camden Iron Works, he was transferred to the Florence Iron Works at Florence, New Jersey, and was made assistant superintendent, and on the death of the superintendent, W. F. Thatcher, in the summer of 1908, he was in the ensuing August appointed superintendent, a position he now holds, having under him some twelve hundred men. Mr. Reeves is a Republican, and was a member of the board of health in Haddonfield, where he resided for a time while he was working in Camden. He is a member of the A. U. O. M., of Camden; was an elder and communicant in the First Presbyterian Church of Camden, and is now a vestryman of the Protestant Episcopal church in Florence. In 1892 Charles Carroll Reeves married Louise Thompson, daughter of Philip I. Scovel, of Camden, New Jersey. They have no children.

MIDDLETON

The Middleton family of New Jersey ranks among the oldest and stanchest of the old patriotic colonial families that have brought during the course of the centuries honor and glory to their state, their country and themselves. Not the least of these honors is due to the fact that the family numbers among its representatives Arthur Middleton, one of the signers of the Declaration of Independence. The branch of the family at present under consideration is that which has for centuries been identified with Camden county and city.

(I) Amos Archer Middleton, son of Timothy Middleton, is the founder of the branch at present under consideration. He was born in Camden county, May 13, 1794, where he passed his life as a farmer, and died October 13, 1849. He married Priscilla Smallwood, born near Haddonfield, New Jersey, December 2, 1785, died April 12, 1852. Children: 1. Robert Smallwood, a physician, who was the first to

introduce the practice of homeopathic medicine in Burlington county, where he established a large practice, but being ambitious for a larger field of labor, afterwards removed to Philadelphia, Pennsylvania, where he passed the remainder of his life. 2. Amos, of Camden. New Jersey; merchant. 3. Timothy, referred to below. 4. Margaret, married Alfred Githens, a farmer of Camden. 5. Priscilla, married Isaac Hinchman, of Camden. 6. Elizabeth, married John Wright, of Camden.

(II) Timothy, son of Amos Archer and Priscilla (Smallwood) Middleton, was born in Camden, New Jersey, January 21, 1817; died April 15, 1867. He was a farmer and merchant. At one time he was mayor of Camden, and also a superintendent of the Pennsylvania railroad. He married Hester A. R., daughter of Andrew and Lydia (Wiltse) Jenkins, of Camden, November 19, 1840. Children: 1. Melbourne Fletcher, referred to below. 2. Melinda E. 3. Amos Archer. 4. Elizabeth Smallwood. 5. Timothy Jenkins.

(III) Melbourne Fletcher, son of Timothy and Hester A. R. (Jenkins) Middleton, was born in Camden, New Jersey, January 21, 1842, and is now living at No. 227 Cooper street, that city. For his early education he attended the public schools of Camden and of Philadelphia. After leaving school he returned to his father's farm near Camden, on which he worked for the ensuing four years, and then for a short time held a position as a clerk in his uncle's store. After this he became a salesman in a cloth house in Philadelphia, which he gave up to become an assistant bookkeeper in the office of Dr. D. Jayne & Son, of Philadelphia, being very soon appointed the general correspondent for that firm, which position he held for two years, when his health failing he became one of its traveling men, continuing in that position for over two years, when he resigned to enter upon the realization of his hopes and dreams cherished since early childhood, and took up the study of medicine. This he had begun while he was still in Dr. Jayne's office by attending lectures in single branches of medicine each winter. In the fall of 1866 he entered the Hahnemann Medical College of Philadelphia, and after attending the full course of lectures there was graduated with the degree of M. D., March 4, 1868, when he immediately entered upon the practice of his profession in Camden, New Jersey. From the very beginning Dr. Middleton met with success, and his high qualifications for a medical practitioner coupled with his other gifts, both social and personal, have made him one of the most successful physicians in the state. He is a member of the West Jersey Homoeopathic Medical Society, a member of the American Institute of Homoeopathy. He is one of the founders of the Camden Homoeopathic Hospital and Dispensary Association, and in 1880, through his influence, the practice of homoeopathy was introduced into the Camden County Asylum for the Insane. He is also an ex-president of the New Jersey State Homoeopathic Medical Society, and of the West Jersey Homoeopathic Medical Society. For eight years Dr. Middleton, who is a Republican, was a member of the board of education of the city of Camden. He is now and has been for fifteen years a member of the board of health of the city of Camden. He is a member of Camden Lodge, No. 15, Free and Accepted Masons, and he is a member of the Centenary Methodist Episcopal Church, of Camden.

March 16, 1871, Melbourne Fletcher Middleton, M. D., married Emily M., youngest daughter of Captain Henry and Elizabeth King. Her father was one of the oldest and most highly respected sea captains sailing out of the port of Philadelphia; at the age of twenty he was master of his own ship, and after following the sea as captain for fifty years retired and spent the remaining years of his life quietly at his home in Camden. He was an honored member of the Presbyterian church. He had formerly lived in Philadelphia, but about the year 1846 removed to Camden, where he died February 14, 1884, at the age of ninety-four years. The children of Dr. Melbourne Fletcher and Emily M. (King) Middleton were: 1. Melbourne Fletcher, see forward. 2. Arthur Lincoln, see forward. 3. Timothy Grant, see forward. 4. Elizabeth King.

(IV) Melbourne Fletcher (2), son of Melbourne Fletcher (1) and Emily M. (King) Middleton, was born February 22, 1877, and is associated with the firm of Charles D. Barney & Company, bankers, at No. 124 South Fourth street, Philadelphia, who are the business successors to the old firm of Jay Cook & Company, who rendered such valuable aid to the government during the civil war. He married Jessamine Weatherby, of Camden, October 25, 1900; they have two children. Dorothy, and Melbourne Fletcher, the third.

(IV) Arthur Lincoln, son of Melbourne Fletcher (1) and Emily M. (King) Middleton, was born August 20, 1878. He married Nancy, daughter of James and Elizabeth Baird, July 29, 1907.

(IV) Timothy Grant, twin brother of Arthur Lincoln Middleton, son of Melbourne Fletcher (1) and Emily M. (King) Middleton, was born August 20, 1878. He married Jennie E. daughter of Charles and Elizabeth Rudolph, and they have five children: Joseph Everett, Henry King, Newell Melbourne. Paul Fletcher, Donald Maze Middleton.

APPLEGATE

The name is undoubtedly derived from the Saxon word Applegrath. In England there were ancient families named Applegrath. Appleyard and Appleworth, each signifying apple orchard. The founder of the Applegate family in America, or rather the first of the name to be found in America, was Thomas Applegate, who went from England to Holland with a party of discontented fellow Englishmen before 1635, which date he left his temporary haven of refuge in Holland and came to Massachusetts Bay Colony, where he was licensed by the general court to run a ferry between Weymouth and Braintree. His name then disappears from the colonial records of Massachusetts Bay and appears in Rhode Island, 1640.

(I) Thomas Applegate was in New Amsterdam so early as 1641, and he secured a patent of land on Nassau Island at Gravesend, November 12, 1646; and in 1647 he is named among the patentees of the borough of Flushing in the North Riding of Yorkshire on Long Island, the patent bearing date October 19, 1647, and signed by Governor General William Kieft. In 1651 the authorities of New Amsterdam sentenced him to have his tongue bored through with a red-hot iron, the sentence being pronounced on his having charged the director-general with bribery. After the sentence he relented of his wrongful charge and the sentence was interrupted by a pardon from the director-general. He married. February 9, 1648, Elizabeth, daughter of Charles Morgan. magistrate of Gravesend, 1657-63. His land in Gravesend was purchased from John Rickman, one of the original thirty-nine lots into which Gravesend was divided in 1646. The children of Thomas and Elizabeth (Morgan) Applegate were: 1. John, who appears on the list of residents of Gravesend, Long Island. 1650, and in 1655 as of Thompson's, Long Island. In 1661 John Applegate is charged with smuggling in New Amsterdam. In 1663 he is a freeholder of Oyster Bay. Long Island. and with his wife Avis or Avies he is in Fairfield. Connecticut. where he signs his name John

Appelgate and his wife signed her name Aves Applegate. 2. Arien Appel, took the oath of allegiance to the English government in 1664. 3. Bartholomew, married, October, 1650, Hannah Patricke, and was among the purchasers of land in Middletown, Monmouth county, New Jersey, in 1674. He signed his name Bartholinel Apelgate, but it is not evident that he settled there. 4. Thomas, see forward. 5. Hannah. Thomas, the immigrant, died at Gravesend, Long Island, between 1652 and 1660.

(II) Thomas (2), fourth son of Thomas (1) and Elizabeth (Morgan) Applegate, born before 1653, married Johanna, daughter of Richard Gibbons, who was one of the twelve Monmouth county patentees. On October 19, 1677. Thomas Applegate, Sr., secured by a quit-claim deed two hundred and forty acres of upland and meadow in Shrewsbury township, Monmouth county, New Jersey, and Thomas Applegate, Jr., secured one hundred and twenty acres of similar land on the same date. This was three years after they came to Middletown and secured the same land by Dutch warrant, under the government of New Netherlands. Thomas, Sr., made his will February 1, 1698, and it was proved February 29, 1699, and his death must have occurred between these dates. His wife, Johanna, and her father, Richard Gibbons, were executors of his will. Thomas and Johanna (Gibbons) Applegate had children as follows: 1. Thomas (2), who secured one hundred and twenty acres of land in Shrewsbury township as noted in his father's sketch. He married Ann ———; settled in Perth Amboy, where he had children: Thomas John, James and Andrew. 2. John, married Sarah Pettit, October 6, 1736, and lived in Middletown. 3. Daniel, married Elizabeth Hulett, January 31, 1745. 4. Joseph. 5. Benjamin, married Elizabeth Parent, of Middlesex county, New Jersey, July 18, 1749. 6. Richard, see forward.

(III) Richard, youngest of the six sons of Thomas and Johanna (Gibbons) Applegate, was born in Middletown, Monmouth county, New Jersey, about 1683. He was a large owner of real estate and a successful farmer. He is on record as a member of the Baptist church in that place, March 1, 1701-02. He married, about 1705, Rebecca Winter. Children, born in Middletown, New Jersey, were: 1. John. 2. Abigail. 3. Elizabeth. 4. Joseph Jacob, see forward. 5. Hannah. 6. Rebecca, married Samuel Ray. 7. Johanna. 8. William. Richard Applegate's will was dated November 7, 1732, in which he gave all his lands to his

daughter to go to his son, William, then under age.

(IV) Joseph Jacob, second son and fourth child of Richard and Rebecca (Winter) Applegate, was born in Middletown, New Jersey, about 1713. He married Esther Lukens or Lewkers, in 1743, and probably removed to Middlesex county, New Jersey, where his children were brought up. He named his eldest son Joseph Jacob, see forward; he was the first of ten children.

(V) Joseph Jacob (2), eldest son of Joseph Jacob (1) and Esther (Lukens) Applegate, of Middlesex county, was born about 1745. He married and had several children, including Samuel, see forward.

(VI) Samuel, son of Joseph Jacob (2) Applegate, was born about 1772. He probably removed to Ocean county, where he married on June 1, 1797, Jane Johnson, and had children, including one Chamblers (or Anthony), see forward.

(VII) Chamblers, son of Samuel Applegate, was born in Toms River, Ocean county, New Jersey, about 1805, married there and had children one of whom was Joseph, see forward.

(VIII) Joseph, son of Chamblers Applegate, was born in Toms River, Ocean county, New Jersey, about 1805. Later he removed to Hurffville, from whence he removed to Harrisonville, Gloucester county, where he remained until about 1883, when he took up his residence in Camden, removing from thence about 1893 to Pitman Grove, where his death occurred in June, 1903. He was a farmer by occupation. He married Drucilla Batten, born in Barnesboro, Gloucester county, New Jersey. Children: 1. William S., born in Hurffville, New Jersey; graduated at the New Jersey State Normal school; became principal of the Franklin School, near Newark, New Jersey; graduated at Jefferson Medical College, M. D., 1883; married, in 1887, Mary Vail, sister of Theodore Vail, of Boston, Massachusetts, and had two children, Vail and Dorothy Applegate, who with their parents reside in Brooklyn, New York. 2. Abigail, born in Gloucester county, New Jersey; married Allen Conover. 3. Keziah, born in Gloucester county, New Jersey; married Clement G. Madara and had four children: Viola, Blanche, Iona and Harold Madara. 4. John Chew, see forward. 5. George H., born in Gloucester county. 6. Alexena, born near Harrisonville, Gloucester county; unmarried.

(IX) John Chew, second son and fourth child of Joseph and Drucilla (Batten) Applegate, was born in Hurffville, Gloucester county, February 19, 1861. He attended the public school and Friends' Academy at Woodstown, under Professor Norris. After graduating he taught school for four years in New Jersey, then pursued a course in medicine at Jefferson Medical College, of Philadelphia, and he was graduated M. D. in 1887. He followed this with special courses in Lying-In, Charity and Philadelphia Hospital for diseases of the skin. He practiced medicine at Fairton, New Jersey, 1887-90, removed to Bridgeton, where he conducted a general practice of medicine and surgery, 1890-1903, and also served on the surgical staff of the Bridgeton Hospital. In 1903 he accepted the chair of obstetrics at Temple University, Philadelphia, and he still continues in that position. The University is a co-educational institution and had over four thousand general students from all sections of the United States and even from beyond the seas. He also carried on a general private practice from his office, 3540 North Broad street, and holds professional positions in the Garretson and Samaritan hospitals in Philadelphia, being a chief of both institutions. His professional memberships in learned societies include the: American Medical Association, the Philadelphia County Medical Society, the Philadelphia Obstetric Society, the Philadelphia Medical Club, the Samaritan Hospital Medical Society, the North Western Medical Society, of Philadelphia; honorary membership in the Cumberland County, New Jersey, Medical Society, of which he was an active officer for many years, and social membership in the New Jersey Society of Pennsylvania. The first society organized in the medical department of Temple University of Philadelphia and named in honor of an individual was "The John Chew Applegate Obstetrical Society." Dr. Applegate's fraternal affiliation is with the masonic order and his masonic work began in Evening Star Lodge, Ancient Free and Accepted Masons, of Bridgeton, New Jersey, and was carried on through Brearly Chapter, No. 2. Royal Arch Masons, of Bridgeton. His church affiliation is membership in the Church of the Resurrection (Protestant Episcopal), of Philadelphia. His political affiliations are with the Republican party.

Dr. Applegate married, June 6, 1888, Frank, daughter of Zamor and Rachel (Pritchard) Briggs, of Cape Vincent, New York, and their son, Zamor, was born in Bridgeton, Cumberland county, New Jersey, January 16, 1895.

ii—21

BENNETT In its earlier generations the branch of the Bennett which is at present under consideration did not belong to the history of New Jersey, as it is only in the last two generations that their lot has been cast in that state.

(I) Jacob H. Bennett, born in New York City or Brooklyn, in 1830, was the first of his line to come to New Jersey, which he did apparently shortly before or shortly after his marriage. He was a glass worker in the later years of his life, and died in Millville, New Jersey, in July, 1905. His children were: 1. Jacob Edward, M. D., died at Rock Island, Rhode Island. 2. Samuel Dey, referred to below. 3. Amanda, married George Cline, and has one child. George, Jr. 4. Sarah, married Frank Atkinson, and had Harry, Samuel, Agnes, Cora and Sarah.

(II) Samuel Dey, son of Jacob H. Bennett, was born at Berlin, or Bridgeton, New Jersey, June 2, 1853. Like his father he was a glass worker. He married Mary Jane, daughter of Cornelius and Ellen (Johnson) McKenzie, the father coming from Scotland, and the mother from England. She was born in Winslow, New Jersey, in July, 1853. Among their children was Samuel Dey, referred to below, and Oscar W., a dentist in Millville, born there December 9, 1876.

(III) Samuel Dey (2), son of Samuel Dey (1) and Mary Jane (McKenzie) Bennett, was born at Millville, New Jersey, January 9, 1872, and is now living in that city. For his early education he went to the public schools at Millville, after leaving which he entered the College of Pharmacy in Philadelphia, Pennsylvania, in the fall of 1890, and graduated from that institution with high honors in 1892, receiving the degree of Ph. G. In 1894 he entered the Jefferson Medical College in Philadelphia, graduating with the degree of M. D. in 1896. The two intervening years, 1892-93 he spent as a drug clerk. After graduating and receiving his doctor's degree, he entered at once upon the general practice of his profession at Millville, where he has remained ever since, winning for himself an enviable reputation and clientele among the people with whom his lot is cast. Dr. Bennett has turned his attention to the subject of tuberculosis, and he has done most excellent work in the campaign against that wide spread disease. He is a member of the National Tuberculosis Association and also of the International Tuberculosis Association, and he is as well the chairman of the Millville Tuberculosis Society. In politics he is a Republican, and in religion a member of the Presbyterian church. He is an active and prominent member of many secret societies and organizations. Among them should be mentioned Shekinah Lodge, No. 58, Free and Accepted Masons, of Millville; Richmond Chapter, No. 22, Royal Arch Masons, and Olivet Commandery, No. 10, Knights Templar, of which in March, 1909, he was elected captain general. He is also a member of the Millville Social and Athletic Club.

September 28, 1898, Samuel Dey Bennett, M. D., married Rena Dunham, born February 29, 1872, at Millville, New Jersey, daughter of Milford and Mary (Dunham) Ludlam, of Millville. They have one child, Charlotte Dunham Bennett, born August 3, 1899. The Ludlams and the Dunhams belong to two of the oldest and most prominent families of New Jersey.

JONES The ancestry of Henry Phineas Jones, a prominent business man of Newark, New Jersey, is evidently of English or Scotch origin and contains on the maternal side the names of Woodward, Bancroft, Metcalf, Stone, Whipple, Trowbridge, Atherton, Treadway, Howe, Cook, Flagg, Hammond, Phillips, Lamb, Bennett, Towne, Richardson, Wilson, Brown, Humphreys, Rice and Viles.

(I) Josiah Jones, earliest ancestor of whom there is mention, was born in 1643, died October 3, 1714. He married, October 2, 1667, Lydia Treadway, born 1648, died September 17, 1743, daughter of Nathaniel and Sufferana (How) Treadway. Among their children was Captain Nathaniel, see forward.

(II) Captain Nathaniel, son of Josiah and Lydia (Treadway) Jones, was born December 31, 1674, died November, 1745. He married Mary Cook, born December 2, 1681, baptized April 15, 1688, daughter of Stephen and Rebecca (Flagg) Cook, the former of whom was born 1647, died 1738, and the latter born September 5, 1661, died June 20, 1721. Among the children of Captain and Mrs. Jones was Deacon Nathaniel, see forward.

(III) Deacon Nathaniel (2), son of Captain Nathaniel (1) and Mary (Cook) Jones, was born April 5, 1707, died September 7, 1795, at Charleston. He married Eleanor Woodward, born June 20, 1720, died April 9, 1807, daughter of Deacon Ebenezer and Mindwell (Stone) Woodward, who were married January 26, 1716; Ebenezer Woodward was born March 12, 1691, and his wife was

born June 26, 1696, died 1774. Among the children of Deacon and Mrs. Jones was Phineas, see forward.

(IV) Phineas, son of Deacon Nathaniel (2) and Eleanor (Woodward) Jones, was born February 17, 1762, died April 27, 1850. He was a soldier in the revolution. He removed to Spencer, Massachusetts, from Charlton, settling about 1786 on the original John Graton farm near what is now known as the Stiles reservoir. The farm was lot number twenty-five as shown on the proprietor's map of Spencer and joined the Leicester line. His farm has been known in recent years as the Ebenezer Proctor place. He was not only a well-to-do farmer, but also conducted a hotel. His house was on the old South County road from Worcester to Southbridge and Connecticut by way of Leicester center, and before the advent of the railroad, the stage coach and the two, four and six-horse teams laden with freight, daily coming and going, made life along the route anything but monotonous, and in wide contrast with the quiet and stillness of the present day. It is interesting to note that when this road was first located, according to the original record at the registry of deeds in Worcester, not a point of compass was given, not a record of distance, simply directions from tree to tree the whole route. He married (first) Lucy Baldwin, who bore him five children. He married (second) Hannah Phillips, born July 1, 1773, died February 14, 1841, daughter of Deacon Jonathan and Rachel (Humphreys) Phillips, the former of whom was born August 12, 1732, died June 25, 1798, at Sturbridge, Massachusetts, homestead in family one hundred and twenty-five years, and the latter a daughter of Deacon Humphreys, of Oxford, Massachusetts. Nine children were born of the second marriage.

(V) Phineas (2), son of Phineas (1) and Hannah (Phillips) Jones, was born April 18, 1819, in Spencer, Massachusetts, died April 19, 1884. At a suitable age he was sent to the academy at Leicester to supplement such teaching as the times then afforded in Spencer. After graduating with great credit, he returned home to take charge of his father's farm, who was now advanced in years, and this filial duty he continued to render until his father's death, April 27, 1850. Thrown upon his own resources, he took up school teaching in his native town, an occupation for which he was well qualified, and in connection with which he employed his leisure hours in surveying. Finding, however, these occupations insufficient for

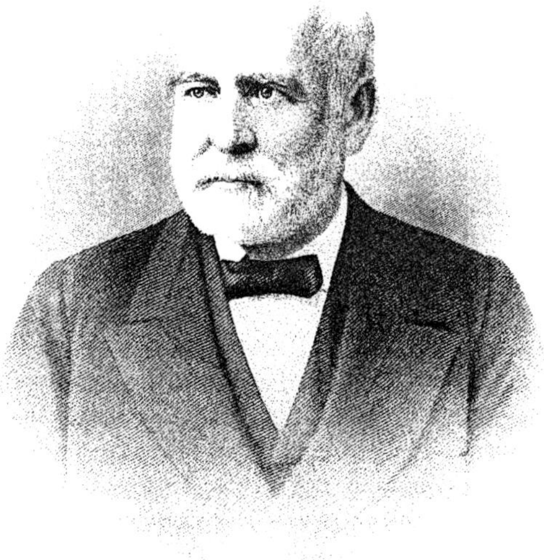

Thomas Jones

his active and aspiring nature, he determined to fit himself for a business life, and to that end established a large country store in the town of Spencer, in a building just then erected, known as Union Block. His store became not only a political center for the discussion of state and national politics, but a place to talk over town affairs, and he was not the least among the many debaters of that day who here found a free forum. His services were in ready demand at auctions, and his ability in that line has never been equalled in Spencer. Desiring a wider field for development, Mr. Jones sold his store in Spencer, in 1855, and removed to Elizabethport, New Jersey, where he engaged extensively in the manufacture of carriage wheels. Finding a more desirable location, he removed to Newark, New Jersey, in 1860, and in partnership with William H. Baldwin, established a factory on a much larger scale, and year after year continued to increase his manufacturing facilities and to extend his business until his death. His partner, Mr. Baldwin, died in 1901, aged one hundred and one years. While engaged in this business, Mr. Jones exhibited a great deal of mechanical ingenuity, and several of his inventions, which were patented, proved to be very valuable. For several years after his removal to Newark he gave strict attention to his factory, in which he had one hundred men employed, with a constantly increasing demand for his productions. In politics Mr. Jones was a Republican, and in maintaining the principles of that party was bold and energetic. As a ready and forcible speaker, he always commanded attention, and as an intelligent, efficient man of business, acquired confidence and respect. Within three years after his settlement in Elizabeth he was elected a member of the common council, and served for two years in that body. He was a member of the board of trade of Newark, established in 1868, also a director, and the part he took therein was active and prominent. He was a director of the Peoples' Insurance Company, established in 1866, and in 1874 appears more prominently as a member of the general assembly, in which body he served so satisfactorily to his constituents that in the year following he was re-elected to the same position. In 1881 Mr. Jones was elected a member of the forty-seventh congress, and served to the end of his term, although during the last months of the second session he suffered so much from sickness contracted at Washington that he declined the renomination which was tendered to him. He was a member of the

New Jersey Agricultural Society, member of its board of directors, and devoted much of his time and attention to its interests. It is not thought Mr. Jones made any set speech while in congress, but he spoke at length in the forty-seventh congress on the river and harbor appropriation bill, vol. 14, part 4, pages 3441-42-46, also on screws, vol. 13, page 2514. and probably along other lines in the forty-sixth and forty-seventh sessions of congress which may be found by consulting the records. His sudden death, in the midst of a most honorable and useful career, was deeply lamented by the community of which, for nearly a quarter of a century, he had been an esteemed and valuable member.

Mr. Jones married three times. His first wife was Emmeline Baxter Lamb, born February 12, 1824, died February 5. 1847, daughter of Austin and Nancy (Wilson) Lamb, the former of whom was born March 31, 1790. died December 2, 1870, and the latter born June 21, 1792, died September 13. 1828.

(VI) Henry Phineas, son of Phineas (2) and Emmeline Baxter (Lamb) Jones, was born at Spencer, Massachusetts, at his grandfather's house near Stiles reservoir, November 29, 1846. At the age of nine he became a resident of Elizabethport, New Jersey, whither his father had removed in 1855. He attended the old red schoolhouse which once stood on the highest swell of land between the Aaron Watson place and Moose Hill farm house. Spencer, the public schools of Elizabethport, and later the Newark Academy, his father having removed to that city in 1858. In 1868 he engaged in the shoe business under the firm name of Canfield, Jones & Company, and this connection continued for four years. He then made an extended tour of Europe. extending over a period of almost a year. Upon his return to his native land, in 1875. he was admitted to partnership in the firm of Phineas Jones & Company, manufacturers of carriage wheels, and since that time has devoted himself to the development of that industry. In 1880 the works were destroyed by fire, and immediately rebuilt. They now give employment to more than one hundred persons, this making it one of the largest establishments of the kind in the state. Mr. Jones is a man of unusual business ability, which fact accounts for the success which has attended his efforts in the business world. He is a member of Christ Reformed Church, member of the National Carriage Makers' Association. Lincoln Post. No. 11; Essex Club. Union Club and

New Jersey Historical Society. He is a Republican in politics, but has never held public office. At fifteen years of age, under name of Henry Cook, Mr. Jones enlisted July 30. 1862, as drummer boy in the One Hundred and Thirteenth New York Infantry, which was afterwards the Seventh New York Heavy Artillery, Irish Brigade, First Division. He participated in all the engagements of the Army of the Potomac from his enlistment until August 1, 1865. His regiment met with frightful loss of life, as out of two thousand six hundred and sixty-seven men only nine hundred and forty-one returned, a very small percentage.

Mr. Jones married, June 24, 1875, at Newark. New Jersey, Ada Emily Anderson, born December 16, 1850, daughter of David and Julia (Jacobus) Anderson, who were the parents of seven other children, namely: William, James, Frank, Walter, Elizabeth, Harriet and Julia. Children of Mr. and Mrs. Jones: 1. Elizabeth Anderson, born April 10, 1876; married Henry Hall Skinner; children: Elizabeth and Ada Skinner. 2. Phineas, born January 3, 1879. 3. Henry Percy, born November 19, 1880. 4. Elsie, born October 16, 1883; married Richard Krementz, a sketch of whom appears in this work; one child, Elsie Louise Krementz. 5. Spencer, named for the town in which his father was born, born December 13, 1891.

COE	The Coe family of Newark, New Jersey, are a branch of the family of the same name which for so long has had an honored existence in New England, Long Island, and elsewhere.

(I) Robert Coe, founder of the family, was born in county Suffolk, England, about 1596, and died in Jamaica, Long Island, between 1670 and 1680. He sailed from Ipswich, Suffolkshire, England, on the ship "Francis," with seventy-nine others, arriving in Boston, Massachusetts, in June, 1634. He settled first at Watertown, near Boston, and was made freeman, September 3, 1634. He and twenty-five others purchased Rappawams (Stamford) of the New Haven Colony for £33 and started a settlement there. In 1643, through the general court of New Haven, a court was established there the same as at New Haven, and Robert Coe was appointed assistant judge. In 1644 Robert Coe, the Rev. Richard Denton and others founded the first New England settlement on Long Island at Hempstead. In 1652 he removed to Maspeth

and aided in the settlement of Middleburg, now Newtown, Long Island, and during his residence there served in the capacity of magistrate. The following year he was commissioned to go to Boston to invoke the protection of the New England colonies for Long Island against the Dutch and Indians, and in the same year had a conference with the burgomaster of New Amsterdam on the subject of common safety. In 1656 he began the settlement of Jamaica, where he resided until his death. He was appointed to the office of magistrate in 1659, and was elected to represent his section of Long Island at the general convention at Hartford in May, 1664. Robert Coe married (first) about 1591, Anna or Hannah, whose surname is supposed to have been Crabbe, and who is supposed to have been the widow of Edward Rouse. He married (second) Jane ———, who with their three sons accompanied her husband to America. The sons were: 1. John, settled finally at Newtown, Long Island. 2. Robert, became the founder of the New England branch of the family. 3. Benjamin, see forward.

(II) Benjamin, son of Robert and Jane Coe, was born about 1629, and was living in 1686. He married Abigail, born in 1635, second child and eldest daughter of John and Florence Carman, the emigrants. Children: 1. John. 2. Daniel. 3. Benjamin, see forward. 4. Joseph.

(III) Benjamin (2), son of Benjamin (1) and Abigail (Carman) Coe, was born in Jamaica, Long Island, about 1670, and died some time after 1702. He married Mary ———, born about 1679, died 1763, who bore him one child, Benjamin, see forward. Mary Coe married (second) Deacon James Wheeler, of Newark, New Jersey.

(IV) Benjamin (3), son of Benjamin (2) and Mary Coe, was born in Jamaica, Long Island, April 4, 1702, died in Newark, New Jersey, December 21, 1788. In 1723 he took up his residence in Newark and there held several important positions, serving from 1732 to 1738 in the capacity of town collector, from 1733 to 1735 as surveyor of the highways, and appointed overseer of the poor in 1747. He married (first) Abigail ———, born 1702, died 1761, and (second) Rachel ———, born 1709, died 1779. Children of first marriage: 1. Mary, born 1726, died 1701; married Moses Roberts. 2. Sarah, 1728, died 1793; married David Little. 3. Eunice, 1730, died 1801; married Joseph Baldwin. 4. Daniel, 1731, killed in the revolution. 5. Benjamin, see forward. 6. Abigail, 1742, died 1818; married Daniel Tichenor.

(V) Benjamin (4), second son and fifth child of Benjamin (3) and Abigail Coe, was born in Newark, New Jersey, in 1736, died there in 1818. His entire life was spent in the city of his birth, and he was honored by his townspeople by election to the offices of overseer of the highways and sheepmaster, receiving his appointment in 1775. He married Bethia Grummon, born about 1744, died 1816. Children: 1. Aaron, born 1764, died 1776. 2. Sears, 1766, died 1768. 3. Mary, 1768, died 1844; married Jedediah J. Crane. 4. Sayres, see forward. 5. Abigail, September 9, 1776, died March 5, 1853; married William Whitehead. 6. Hannah, 1777, died 1824; married Matthias Brien. 7. Aaron, 1779, died 1857; married (first) Catharine H. Elmer; (second) Rebecca (Parmelee) Manning, widow of John Manning. 8. Sarah, 1783, died 1784.

(VI) Sayres, third son and fourth child of Benjamin (4) and Bethia (Grummon) Coe, was born in Newark, New Jersey, April 26, 1772, died there February 13, 1851. He married Sally, daughter of Deacon Joseph Davis, of Bloomfield, and among their children was Aaron, see forward.

(VII) Aaron, son of Sayres and Sally (Davis) Coe, was born in Newark, New Jersey, September 27, 1810, died there March 3, 1890. For many years he conducted a real estate business in Newark, and throughout his long and active life he enjoyed the respect of his fellow citizens. He married Julia, daughter of Jedediah J. and Abby (Johnson) Baldwin. Children: 1. Horace Sayres, born April 17, 1838, died unmarried July 26, 1854. 2. Emma Julia, see forward. 3. James Aaron, see forward. 4. Laura Francis, see forward. 5. Cornelia Baldwin, see forward.

(VIII) Emma Julia, eldest daughter of Aaron and Julia (Baldwin) Coe, was born in Newark, New Jersey, January 28, 1841. She married, September 25, 1862, Henry Franklin Osborne, born at Oak Ridge, March 20, 1837, son of the Rev. Enos A. and Abby (Davis) Osborne, who were the parents of six other children, namely: Charles, Edward, Joseph, Anna, Louisa and Henrietta Osborne. Henry Franklin Osborne was educated in the boarding and day schools of West Poultney, Vermont; for six years he was a drug clerk in New York City, and then became a manufacturer of saddlery, hardware and harness makers' tools; he is a Republican, a member

of the Free and Accepted Masons, and an elder in the High Street Presbyterian Church of Newark. Children of Henry Franklin and Emma Julia (Coe) Osborne: 1. Horace Sherman, born July 10, 1863, married Nellie Bond and has one child, Horace Bond Osborne. 2. Miriam, February 13, 1865, married Edward H. Rockwell, of Newark; children: Isabelle and Miriam Rockwell. 3. Ella, February 3, 1867, married Herbert S. Palmer, of Newark; children: Spencer, John and Hope Palmer. 4. Clara, January 30, 1869, married Chester R. Hoag; children: Philip O., Walter, Carolyn and Robert Hoag. 5. Bessie Parker, February 3, 1873. 6. Julia, April 2, 1875, married Harry H. Condit; children: Barbara and Prudence Condit. 7. Edna Crowell, October 29, 1878. 8. Dorothy, May 5, 1881, married Walter R. Boyd; child, Osborne Thorpe Boyd. 9. Ruth McIlvaine, May 15, 1883.

(VIII) James Aaron, second son and third child of Aaron and Julia (Baldwin) Coe, was born in Newark, New Jersey, January 2, 1847, twin of sister, Laura Francis, and is now living in the city of his birth. He was educated in the Newark Academy, from which he was graduated in 1863. His first employment was as clerk in the First National Bank of Newark, the duties thereof being discharged with efficiency and fidelity. In 1869 he engaged in the wholesale and retail iron and steel business under the firm name of James A. Coe & Company, and at the present time (1909) is serving as president of the company, his connection therewith covering a period of forty years, during which time he has become well and favorably known in the iron and steel trade, his business transactions being conducted in a straightforward and honorable manner. For many years he has been recognized as one of the leading, influential citizens of Newark, taking an active interest in many enterprises that tend to the welfare and upbuilding of the community in which he resides. He is an attendant and liberal supporter of the High Street Presbyterian Church of Newark, a director in the Babies' Hospital of Newark, a member of St. John's Lodge, No. 1, Free and Accepted Masons, a member of the New Jersey Historical Society, and a Republican in politics. He married, September 20, 1871, Mary Louise, daughter of George Belden and Mary Jane (Northrup) Sears, who were the parents of two other children, namely: 1. Augusta M., married James Judd Dickerson; one child, James Sears Dickerson. 2. Anna Amelia, married the Rev. Charles T.

Berry; children: i. Rev. George Titus Berry, married a Miss Packer; ii. Rev. Edward Payson Berry, married a Miss Adams; iii. Louise Berry, married the Rev. John E. Adams. Children of James Aaron and Mary Louise (Sears) Coe: 1. Alice Louise, born November 7, 1872, died August 7, 1873. 2. Laura Mabel, May 29, 1874, married James B. Pinneo. He died March 13, 1899. 3. James D., December 29, 1875. 4. Anna Florence, twin of James D., December 29, 1875, married Robert Norton Brockway; children: i. Robert Norton Jr., born April 21, 1905; ii. Louise Brockway, born December 13, 1907. 5. Frederick Sears, August 6, 1877. 6. Helen Augusta, November 24, 1878. 7. Roland Baldwin, July 3, 1883.

(VIII) Laura Francis, second daughter of Aaron and Julia (Baldwin) Coe, was born in Newark, New Jersey, February 2, 1847, twin of James Aaron, and died there January 16, 1882. She married, about 1869 or 1870, Joseph Grover Crowell, whose ancestry will be found in the following sketch.

(VIII) Cornelia Baldwin, youngest child of Aaron and Julia (Baldwin) Coe, was born in Newark, New Jersey, January 10, 1852. She married, April 3, 1873, Franklin Monroe Parker, born in Newark, New Jersey, June 13, 1846, son of William Valleau and Sarah (Ross) Parker, who were the parents of eight children, four of whom attained years of maturity. Franklin Monroe Parker graduated from the grammar and high schools of Newark, after which he entered the employ of James Emile Goll, who was engaged in the fire insurance business in Newark. Later he became connected with the Citizens' Fire Insurance Company and advanced to the position of secretary, and subsequently entered the firm of E. A. Walton & Son, insurance agents, which is now the firm of Parker & Walton. He is a Republican, and three times has served as a member of the city council and as alderman. He is a thirty-second degree Mason, a member of the Commandery, and a Knights Templar. He is also a member of the Republican Indian League and of the Essex Club. Children of Franklin Monroe and Cornelia Baldwin (Coe) Parker: 1. Edith Ross, born January 1, 1874, married Edward Farraday Weston; children: Cornelia and Francis E. Weston. 2. Georgia Marion, May 22, 1879, married Benedict Prieth; children: Marcia Marion and Theodora Cornelia Prieth. 3. Jane Cornelia, January 30, 1882, married Rowland McWilliams.

CROWELL

The families of Crow and Crowell were originally, as can easily be seen from an inspection of the old records where the names of the same persons are spelt indifferently, Crow, Crowe, Crowl and Crowel, one and the same, and their founder was among the earliest of the settlers in the New England provinces, where he appears to have died shortly after his arrival without leaving any record behind him except a son, whom he probably brought over to this country with him, and who is referred to below.

(I) Edward Crow, born about 1644, came to Woodbridge from Massachusetts, where he died leaving a widow and five children. The widow, Mary (Lothrop) Crow, married (second) before 1695, her first husband having died in 1688, Samuel Dennes, of Woodbridge. Her children by her first husband were: 1. Mary, born 1674. 2. A daughter born and died 1676. 3. Yelverton, 1678, who removed to Cape May county, New Jersey. 4. Joseph, 1680, removed to Cape May county. 5. Benjamin, born 1682. 6. Edward, referred to below.

(II) Edward (2), son of Edward (1) and Mary (Lothrop) Crow, was born in 1685, and was the first of the family to determine the modern spelling of the name as Crowell. Among his children were Elizabeth, born in 1708, and Samuel, referred to below.

(III) Samuel, son of Edward (2) Crowell, was born in Woodbridge, in 1711. He married a Ward, a sister to Abel and Elihu Ward; all of his four sons and two of his grandsons were soldiers in the revolution. About 1728 he bought and settled upon land in what is now South Orange, New Jersey, and is still held to-day by some of his descendants. His children were: 1. Joseph, referred to below. 2. Daniel. 3. Samuel. 4. Aaron, born 1750, married Abigail Brown.

(IV) Joseph, son of Samuel and ———— (Ward) Crowell, was born in South Orange, New Jersey, about 1740, and among his children was John, referred to below.

(V) John, son of Joseph Crowell, was born in South Orange, November 16, 1762. It is said that the name of his wife was Mary Marsh, but it is possible that she may have been one of the Freemans as among his children was one named Joseph Freeman, referred to below.

(VI) Joseph Freeman, son of John Crowell, was born in Caldwell, Essex county, New Jersey, in 1793, died in 1821. He married

Rosalinda, daughter of the Rev. Stephen Grover, of Tolland, Connecticut, and Caldwell, New Jersey, who was born in 1795 and died in 1873. Their only child was Stephen Grover, born in Caldwell, September 9, 1817, died in Newark, May 20, 1854. As a young man he removed from Caldwell to Newark, where he became a prominent business man, founding the firm of Heath & Crowell, dry-goods merchants, and being at the time of his death one of the directors of the American Insurance Company. Mr. Crowell was a widely read and deep thinking student, with a varied range of knowledge. His home was 16 Cedar street, Newark. He married Sarah W., daughter of David Smith, who had removed from Providence, Rhode Island, to Newark, New Jersey, about 1818, and founded the dry-goods firm of D. Smith & Company. They had four children: 1. Joseph Grover, referred to below. 2. David Smith, born April 10, 1847, married Sarah E., daughter of David Stewart, of Walden, New York. 3. Stephen Grover, a member of the iron and steel firm of Crowell & Coe. 4. Henry Morris, of the Mutual Life Insurance Company of New York.

(VII) Joseph Grover, eldest child of Joseph Freeman and Sarah W. (Smith) Crowell, was born in Newark, March 31, 1844, and is now living in that city. He entered into partnership with James Aaron Coe and founded the iron and steel manufacturing firm of Crowell & Coe. He is a Republican, and attends the High Street Presbyterian Church in Newark. He enlisted with the volunteers of the civil war and when he was mustered out had risen to the rank of Quartermaster of the nine months' men. He married shortly after the war, Laura Francis, daughter of Aaron and Julia (Baldwin) Coe, the sister of his partner in the iron and steel business. Their children are: 1. Frederick Morris, referred to below. 2. Joseph Grover Jr., born November 4, 1873, died July 1, 1893. 3. Harry Wolcott, September 6, 1877, married Blodwin Savage.

(VIII) Frederick Morris, eldest child of Joseph Grover and Laura Francis (Coe) Crowell, was born in Newark, May 20, 1871, and is now living in that city. He graduated from the Newark Academy in 1889, for the following two years became a salesman for a paint and oils firm in New York City. For the succeeding four years he worked in the employ of a Newark chemical and oil firm, and then finally in 1895 came to the firm of James A. Coe, becoming vice-president of the

company in March, 1905. Mr. Crowell is a Republican, but has held no office. He is one of the trustees of the High Street Presbyterian Church in Newark. September 1, 1903, Frederick Morris Crowell was married in Colorado Springs, Colorado, to Ruth Brewer, of Denver, whose father, Benn Brewer, was born in England, and whose mother, Marie (Paulson) Brewer, was born in Denmark. Her sisters and brothers are: Minnie, Maid, who married Oscar David Cass and has two children: Dorothy Marie and Oscar David Jr.; Marie Louise and Bayard Paulson Brewer. The only child of Frederick Morris and Ruth (Brewer) Crowell is Frederick Morris Jr., born in March, 1907.

DRAKE The Drake family are a Virginia family, coming to this country at the time of the Cavalier movement and settling in Fairfax county. The ancestry of Edgar Bless Drake is unfortunately not traceable back farther than the Rev. Philip Drake, of Kentucky, in the middle of the eighteenth century. And although it is almost certain that this ancestor was not the original emigrant founder of the family, all attempts hitherto made have failed to determine whether he is a descendant of Robert Drake, of Hampton, New Hampshire, Captain Francis Drake, of Piscataway, New Jersey, or of the several Drake families which were among the original settlers of the Virginias and Carolinas.

(I) The Rev. Philip Drake, above referred to, was born January 1, 1743, and is found in the latter part of the eighteenth century as the Baptist minister at Lee's Creek, Kentucky. By his wife Anne (Larie) Drake, of whom nothing more is known, he had two children: 1. John, referred to below. 2. Sophia.

(II) John, only son and eldest child of the Rev. Philip and Anne (Larie) Drake, was born in Kentucky, November 15, 1785, died there December 28, 1823. He married Sophia Crosby, and had five children: 1. Joseph Crosby, born July 30, 1811. 2. James, November 4, 1813. 3. Elizabeth, March 16, 1816. 4. Anna, November 6, 1818. 5. Robert, referred to below.

(III) Robert, youngest child and son of John and Sophia (Crosby) Drake, was born in Mason county, Kentucky, March 8, 1821, died in Martinsville, Indiana, October 26, 1892. Until 1855 he kept a general store in Maysville, Kentucky; but in that year he came to Newark, New Jersey, where he set up in the business of manufacturing smoothing irons, starting the business now known as the firm of Bless & Drake, which began with five employees. By his marriage with Emma Sarah, daughter of Eleazar and Harriet Elizabeth (Fant) Bless, born June 30, 1828, died February 8, 1894, Robert Drake had four children: 1. Edgar Bless, who is referred to below. 2. Walter, born December 13, 1856, married Ella M. Ward. 3. Harriet, February 19, 1859, married John F. Ward. 4. Robert Jr., August 28, 1864, married Grace G. Drum.

(IV) Edgar Bless, eldest child and son of Robert and Emma Sarah (Bless) Drake, was born in Minerva, Kentucky, September 18, 1854, and is now living at 17 South street, Newark, New Jersey. When he was about one year old his father removed from Kentucky, to Newark, and Edgar Bless was sent to the Newark Academy, from which institution he graduated in 1870. He then entered the employ of the firm of Bless & Drake, where he rose step by step until he has now reached the position of secretary and treasurer of the company. Mr. Drake is a Republican, but has held no office, nor has he seen any military service. He is a member of Kane Lodge, No. 55, Free and Accepted Masons, and the Masonic Club of New York City. He is not connected with any financial institutions; he attends St. Paul's Methodist Episcopal Church. November 20, 1877, Edgar Bless Drake married, in Newark, Annie Jane Murphy, born in Syracuse, New York, September 20, 1855, who has borne him two children: Arthur and Edgar Bless, referred to below.

(V) Arthur, eldest son of Edgar Bless and Annie Jane (Murphy) Drake, was born in Newark, New Jersey, September 26, 1878, and is now living in Newark. He was educated at the Newark Academy, after which he took a position under his father in the firm of Bless & Drake, and is now the manager of their factory. He is a member of Kane Lodge, No. 55. Arthur Drake married Florence Lambert and has one child, Arthur Dudley Drake, born May 27, 1906.

(V) Edgar Bless Jr., youngest child of Edgar Bless and Annie Jane (Murphy) Drake, was born in Newark, New Jersey, October 29, 1881, and is now living with his father at 17 South street, Newark. He was educated at the Newark Academy and Princeton University, class of 1904, and then became a clerk in the office of the firm of Bless & Drake.

SNYDER Jacob Peter Snyder, immigrant ancestor, arrived in this country from Holland some time before 1734. He married Elizabeth Lott, of Long Island, who bore him six children: 1. William, born in 1734. 2. Catharine, 1735. 3. Annatje, 1737. 4. Johannes, see forward. 5. Petrus, 1740. 6. Elizabeth, 1741. The foregoing is from the records of the Reformed Dutch Church of New York City (the Collegiate Church).

(II) Johannes or John, fourth child and second son of Jacob Peter and Elizabeth (Lott) Snyder, was born in New York City in 1739. He was a soldier in the revolutionary war. He married Rachel ———, who bore him six children: Sarah, Margaret, Elizabeth, Jacob, see forward, Mary, Rachel.

(III) Jacob, only son of Johannes and Rachel Snyder, was born November 19, 1766, died in 1815. He married, November 27, 1788, Margaret Bray, born July 26, 1769, died December 27, 1843. Children: 1. John, March 17, 1791. 3. Susanna, January, 1793. 4. Andrew, April, 1795. 5. Delia, October, 1797. 6. Rachel, twin of Delia. 7. Nancy, March, 1800. 8. John Wesley, August, 1802. 9. William Vanderan, July, 1805, see forward. 10. Watson, October, 1807. 11. Julia, 1809.

(IV) William Vanderan, ninth child and fourth son of Jacob and Margaret (Bray) Snyder, was born in July, 1805, died in Allamuchy, New Jersey, December, 1838. He married Sarah Ridgway, born April 11, 1809, who bore him five children: 1. Margaret, married C. A. Conklin; children: Louise, died in infancy, and Annie Beaumont, married Howell Mettler and has one child, W. W. Jr. 2. Watson, born November 17, 1832, died January 19, 1892; married (first) Malvina L. Blair; children: William Deforest, and Frank Ridgway, who married Alice Bain and they have one child, Marjorie; Watson married (second) Anna Beaumont Shier; children: Watson Jr. and Louise Beaumont. 3. Anna Bray, married Jacob L. Lawrence; children: Frederick, who lives in Sussex, New Jersey; George Seymour, of Butler, New Jersey; Henry, of Sussex, New Jersey; Anna Bray Lawrence died December 16, 1897. 4. Charles Ridgway, born in 1837, died September 8, 1895; married Rebecca Porter; children: Margaret Sterling and Charles Ridgway Jr. 5. William Vanderau, see forward.

(V) William Vanderau (2), son of William Vanderau (1) and Sarah (Ridgway) Snyder, was born in Paterson, New Jersey, June 15, 1839. He graduated from the scientific course of Wesleyan University, Middletown, Connecticut, in 1856, and then took an engineering course in the University of Michigan, receiving the degree of Civil Engineer from that institution in 1857. He then engaged in company with his brother Watson in the dry goods business, the firm name being W. & W. V. Snyder, remaining so until 1866, when it became William V. Snyder & Company. The business was enlarged from its insignificant beginning to a large department store of forty-four departments, thus demonstrating the business ability of the partners and especially of William V. Snyder, who conducted it so many years alone. William V. Snyder sold the business, December 15, 1908, and retired from an active life, now enjoying the fruits of his industry, perseverance and thrift. He married, February, 1861, in Newark, New Jersey, Laura Blair, born in Allamuchy, Warren county, New Jersey, June, 1839, died in Newark, September 19, 1902, daughter of Peter W. and Caroline S. Blair, natives of Warren county, New Jersey. Mr. and Mrs. Blair had three other children, as follows: Elizabeth, W. Irving and Mallie Louisa Blair. Children of William V. and Laura (Blair) Snyder: 1. Watson Beaumont, born in November, 1862. 2. Frank Blair, died in infancy. 3. Mallie Blair, married, October 15, 1891, Chandler White, son of William and Sarah M. (Hunter) Riker. 4. William Vanderan, see forward.

(VI) William Vanderan (3), youngest child of William Vanderan (2) and Laura (Blair) Snyder, was born in Newark, New Jersey, May 24, 1874. He was educated in private schools and prepared for Princeton University in the Bordentown Military Academy. He began his active career by entering his father's business, remaining with him until April 1, 1908, when he resigned and accepted the presidency of the Motor Car Company of New Jersey. Mr. Snyder is a Republican in politics. He is a member of St. John's Lodge, No. 1, Free and Accepted Masons; Scottish Rite, No. 23; Salaam Temple; Union Club of Newark; Mecca Club of Paterson, and Automobile and Motor Club of New Jersey. He married, March 3, 1897, in East Orange, New Jersey, Iva Darling Beach, born in Nashville, Tennessee, January 27, 1873, daughter of Alexander Hamilton and Frances (Alt) Beach, of Petosky, Michigan. Mr. and Mrs. Beach are the parents of four other children, as follows:

Henry, Ralph, Frank and Jessie Beach. Children of William V. and Iva Darling (Beach) Snyder: 1. Laura Blair, born January 31, 1898. 2. William Vanderan (4), December 15, 1902. 3. Francis Beach, August 15, 1905. 4. Ralph Beach, May 18, 1907.

BLACK

Among the families by the name of Black which have risen to distinction in New Jersey, there is none that holds a more honorable place than do the descendants of James Black, of Londonderry, who was of Scotch descent, the founder of the family at present under consideration.

(I) James Black, of Londonderry, Ireland, came to this country about 1795, as a young man, and settled in Essex county, New Jersey, where he married Mary Hardenbroeck, a descendant of one of the most prominent of the old Dutch families of America. Children: 1. William Henry. 2. Samuel Hardenbroeck, served as president of Oakland College, Natchez, Mississippi. 3. Joseph, referred to below.

(II) Joseph, third son of James and Mary (Hardenbroeck) Black, was born at Elm Cottage, Newark, New Jersey, 1804, died in July, 1887. He married Hannah R., daughter of Edward Sanderson, who was at one time mayor of Elizabeth. Children: 1. Edward Sanderson, referred to below. 2. William Hardenbroeck.

(III) Edward Sanderson, eldest child of Joseph and Hannah R. (Sanderson) Black, was born in Newark, New Jersey, in the same house as his father, March 6, 1856, and is still a resident of that city. He attended the Newark public schools and the Peddie Institute, after which he entered Columbia Law School, from which he graduated in 1879. He then read law with Governor John Franklin Fort, and was admitted by the supreme court to the New Jersey bar in February, 1879, and in 1886 was admitted as counsellor. At the beginning he engaged in a general practice of law, but later specialized in the field of marriage and divorce and is now recognized as one of the leading authorities upon that subject. In politics he is a Republican, and while an able worker for his party has only been prevailed upon once to become a candidate for office, in 1886, when his name was on the ticket for the New Jersey legislature, but the Democrats being in the majority in his district he was defeated, although running over two hundred ahead of his ticket. Mr. Black is a member of Laurel Lodge, International Order of Good

Templars, of which order he is grand electoral superintendent for the state of New Jersey; New Jersey Society for the Prevention of •Cruelty to Children; New Jersey Historical Society; Seth Boyden Council, Junior Order United American Mechanics; Memorial Lodge, Ancient Order of United Workmen; the Newark Art Club. He is a member of the First Jibe Memorial Congregational Church.

Mr. Black married, December 14, 1881, in Newark, New Jersey, Evelyn T. Lambert, of Charleston, South Carolina, daughter of Charles and Harriet (Kees) Lambert. Mrs. Black died at Newark, February 14, 1908. Mr. and Mrs. Black were the parents of two children: 1. Edward J., born April 7, 1883; married Lilian Tomson, and they have a child, Dorothy, born August 15, 1908. 2. Virginia, born 1887, died 1888, at the age of ten months.

CLEVENGER The Clevenger family of New Jersey not only by its own worth but also by its numerous alliances ₔwith the old historic families of New Jersey, deservedly ranks among the representative forces of that great state of the Union, and not the least among its representatives is Samuel J. Clevenger, of Philadelphia, referred to below.

Samuel J. Clevenger is the grandson of John Clevenger, of Pemberton, Burlington county, New Jersey, where his father, Daniel Clevenger, was born in 1812. His mother was Mary Starkey, daughter of Anthony Logan, of Jobestown, New Jersey, and Samuel J. Clevenger was born at Vincentown, Burlington county, January 11, 1849. For his early education he attended the public schools of Beverly, later the Mount Holly Institute, after which he went to the Peddie Institute at Hightstown. On leaving school he became for a short time clerk in a store, and then came to Philadelphia, where he began his business career as a clerk in a dry goods house. After some time he became connected with the forwarding business of a private freight line, a position which he gave up in order to become a clerk in the Belmont Station of the Reading railroad. After two years at this last position, Mr. Clevenger in 1871 became engaged in the grain and feed business, which he has continued successfully up to the present time, having his offices at No. 468, the Bourse, Philadelphia, and his residence at 1008 South Forty-seventh street, Philadelphia. For some years after he began business the firm name was Burk & Clevenger. Mr. Clevenger is a Republican, and he and

his family are members of the First Baptist Church, of Philadelphia. At one time he was a member of the Union League, of Philadelphia, but has resigned his membership. He is a member of the Pennsylvania Society of New Jersey, and of the Commercial Exchange of Philadelphia.

November 11, 1875, Samuel J. Clevenger married Elizabeth Matilda, daughter of James and Rebecca (Harrison) Walker. Her brother was the proprietor of the Harrison Iron Works. He was a locomotive builder, and received the large contracts for locomotives from the Russian government, built the railroad from Moscow to St. Petersburg and also built a bridge across the river at the latter point. He was the inventor of the famous Harrison boiler. Children of Samuel J. and Elizabeth Matilda (Walker) Clevenger: 1. Charles Henry, born March 11, 1876, died January 16, 1899, graduated from the Friends' Select School, of Philadelphia. 2. Arthur Harrison, January 5, 1880, now in the insurance business at 427 Walnut street. 3. Herbert Logan, December 25, 1884, graduated from the Friends' Select School, Philadelphia, and now in business with his father. 4. Samuel J., Jr., November 1, 1888, now in the Philadelphia high school.

HOWELL A number of men of the name of Howell came over to this country among the earliest pioneers and settled in various portions of the different colonies, and in the state of New Jersey alone there are at least five different families bearing the name which so far as can be ascertained have on this side of the Atlantic no connection whatever. Among those New Jersey families is one that has long been identified with the early history of Morris, Sussex and Warren counties, who claim their descent from Edward Howell, of Southampton, Long Island, through his youngest son, Richard, who was twice married, first to Elizabeth, daughter of Thomas Halsey, and second to a daughter of Joseph, son of Thurston Raynor. To which of these two wives of Richard Howell any particular one of his twelve children are to be assigned has never been determined. Two of them, however, Daniel and Christopher, removed to New Jersey and founded the famous Ewing and Trenton families of the name, and two of the sons, Abner and Elias, of a third son of Richard, namely Josiah, settled one in Flanders and New Germantown and the other in Roxbury or Chester. In the second, edition of his "History of Southampton" Mr.

James E. Howell

George Rogers Howell says, page 320, "that the Sussex county family may belong to the descendants of David, son of Daniel Howell. of Ewing," mentioned above, but a diligent search of the records of Sussex county and of the archives of the secretary of state at Trenton have failed to reveal any evidence which would point in either direction. In the absence of opposing testimony and in view of the fact that the constant tradition of the Sussex family is to their descent as given above a conjectural line may be assumed as follows: Edward (I); Richard (II); Daniel (III); David (IV); William (V), of Sussex county. New Jersey.

(V) William, the conjectured son of David and Mary (Baker) Howell, was born probably in the neighborhood of Flanders, in Morris county. New Jersey, early in 1740. He removed to Hardwick township in Sussex (now Warren) county, and later on to Wantage township, Sussex county. He gave his services in the revolution. He was twice married. By his first wife he had four children: William; John, referred to below; Sarah; Polly; by his second wife two children: Pamelia Schooley and Cornelius. Cornelius Howell moved to Chemung county, New York, and became the progenitor of a large family of Howells in and about Elmira and Horseheads.

(VI) John. second son of William Howell by his first wife, was born at or near the old log jail in Hardwick township, then Sussex county. now Warren county, New Jersey, September 21, 1783. In 1808 he removed from Hardwick township to Beemerville, Wantage township, Sussex county, and resided there until 1824, when he removed with his family to southwestern Ohio. He was accidentally killed on December 8, 1825, and in the spring of the following year his widow and children made the return trip from Ohio to New Jersey in a one horse wagon. He married, April 4, 1805. Martha Tharp; children: Nancy, Martha, Jane, Ira, William Chauncey, referred to below; Alpheus, John. Vincent. Emeline and Nelson.

(VII) William Chauncey, second son and fifth child of John and Martha (Tharp) Howell. was born at Beemerville, Wantage township. New Jersey, October 9, 1814, died at Port Jervis, New York, October 14. 1892. He owned a farm of fifty acres at Beemerville, which he improved and cultivated to a high state of perfection, and in addition to this followed his trade of harness maker. In November, 1874, he retired from active business, and then took up his residence in Port Jervis, New York, where he spent the remainder of his life, enjoying the fruit of his industry and skill. He married Julia A., daughter of Austin and Anna (Beemer) Schofield; children: James Edward, referred to below; William Frederick, born June 15, 1852, married Irene Northrup; three children who died in infancy.

(VIII) James Edward, eldest son of William Chauncey and Julia A. (Schofield) Howell, was born in Beemerville, Wantage township, New Jersey, June 25, 1848. He acquired his early education in the public schools of his district, after which he served in the capacity of school teacher, in the meanwhile preparing himself for college and studying law. In 1868 he matriculated at the Michigan University Law School, entering the class of 1870, and after his graduation therefrom he located in Newton, where he continued his reading, and in 1872 was admitted to the bar of New Jersey. The following two years he practiced his profession in Newton, and at the expiration of that time removed to Newark, where he has remained up to the present time (1909). In January, 1876, he entered into partnership with Joseph Coult in the practice of law in Newark. this connection continuing until April 9, 1907, a period of thirty-one years, an uncommon occurrence in the law practice. In the latter named year Mr. Howell was appointed one of the vice-chancellors of the state of New Jersey, in which capacity he is rendering most efficient service. He held several minor offices in the gift of his party, the Republican, one of them being membership on the board of the county sinking fund commission, which he resigned in December, 1908, in order to devote all his time to court work. He is one of the commissioners of the Newark City Hall, one of the trustees of the Newark Free Public Library, and a member of the Essex Club and the Republican Club of New York. He was formerly vice-president of the Second National Bank and one of its directors. He attends the Presbyterian church. Vice-Chancellor Howell is a man of scholarly attainments, and possesses a weight of character, a native sagacity, a far-seeing judgment and a fidelity of purpose that commands the respect of all. He married, June 13. 1877. Mary Lillian, eldest child of James H. and Mary (Thomson) Cummins, of Newton, New Jersey. One child Thomson, born December 21, 1888.

The family of Dobbins has
DOBBINS   been known in this state since
the times of the colony, and is
said to have been planted on this side of the
Atlantic ocean by three immigrant brothers
who came over from Belfast, Ireland. Two of
these brothers were Samuel and Micajah, the
baptismal name of the other having been for-
gotten.

(I) Samuel Dobbins, who is thought to have
been a grandson of one of the three immigrant
brothers above mentioned, is the earliest ancestor of the family of whom there appears to be
any definite account. He was a farmer and
lived in the vicinity of Vincentown, New Jersey. He married (first) Elizabeth Scroggy,
who bore him five children; married (second)
Sarah Brock, and by her had four children.
Children: Samuel A., born 1814 (was sheriff
of Burlington county two terms, member of
the assembly four terms, and member of congress two terms), Mary, Sarah, Anna Maria,
Isaac, Ambrose Ellis, Joseph, Margaret and
James.

(II) Ambrose Ellis, son of Samuel and
Sarah (Brock) Dobbins, was born in Southampton township, Burlington county, New
Jersey, January 28, 1822, died September 30,
1888. He was a farmer, a man of considerable prominence in township affairs and served
as school trustee. He was a Master Mason,
and attended services at the Methodist Episcopal church. Mr. Dobbins married (first)
January 23, 1845, Jerusha Ann, daughter of
Isaiah P. and Mary Estell Goldy, born Southampton township, September 13, 1827, died
April 14, 1860, leaving one child; married
(second) March 3, 1861, Sarah M. Joyce..

(III) Albert N., son of Ambrose Ellis and
Jerusha Ann (Goldy) Dobbins, was born in
Southampton township, Burlington county, October 27, 1845. He received his education in
the district school at Vincentown, and later
entered the Philadelphia College of Pharmacy,
graduating in 1866, and for the next five years
worked as clerk in pharmacy. In 1871 he
started in business for himself at Vincentown,
remained there one year, then located at Columbus and carried on a general drug business in
that town until 1895, when he sold out. Since
that time he has been engaged in a general fire
insurance business. Mr. Dobbins is a director
of the Mt. Holly National Bank and president
of the Columbus Water Company. He is a
member of Masonic Lodge, No. 4, of Tuckerton, New Jersey. He has served as township
collector and member of the township com

mittee. In 1871 he married Kate L., daughter
of Peter and Rebecca (Van Zant) Lane, of
Port Republic, New Jersey, the former a son
of James B. Lane, of Union county, New Jersey, and the latter a daughter of Nicholas and
Mercy (Moore) Van Zant. Nicholas Van
Zant was born November 9, 1788, died March
6, 1879. Kate L. Dobbins is an active member
of the Wesley Methodist Episcopal Church, of
Columbus, New Jersey, and an earnest worker
in the temperance cause, having served at different periods as president and secretary of
the local association of Women's Christian
Temperance Union, and is now the district
superintendent of the department of soldiers
and sailors.

The surname Graham is one of
GRAHAM   far more than ordinary distinction in Scotland, and a
name of great antiquity in that country as well
as in England and Ireland. In ancient times
the clan Graham bore a chivalrous and highly
important part in Scottish history. Its traditional origin too is of the highest antiquity, the
ducal family of Montrose tracing descent from
the fifth century; and on account of its gallantry in the many early wars the clansmen of
Graham acquired the name of the "gallant
Graemes." It is not the purpose of this narrative, however, to enter upon a detailed history
of this famous clan or make more than passing allusion to any of its distinguished members.

(I) John Graham, immigrant, immediate
progenitor of the particular family intended
to be treated in these annals, was a native of
Edinburgh, Scotland, and might have claimed
descent from the ancient clan to which passing
allusion is made in the preceding paragraph.
He was a young man when he came to America, but at that time had a wife and one or
more children, and they accompanied him on
the voyage to this country. He settled in
Paterson and was a mason by trade, an industrious, hard-working and honest man. The
baptismal name of his wife was Elizabeth, but
her family name is not known. She bore him
three children: Robert; John, see forward;
Elizabeth, married Thomas Heathcote, of
Paterson.

(II) John (2), son of John (1) and Elizabeth Graham, was born in Edinburgh, Scotland, April 27, 1823. He came to this country
with his parents when he was a small child,
and as a boy attended the public schools of
the city, but was quite young when he laid
aside his books and started out to make his own

way in life. His principal occupation was that of drover, cattle dealer and butcher, and he proved a successful business man, although he died in the very prime of his life, April 27, 1863, at the age of forty years. He is remembered as an energetic man, possessed of good business capacity and understanding, both of which were qualities that counted for much in advancing the welfare of his adopted city in many respects. For several years he was a member of the board of education, and while the incumbent of that office was chiefly instrumental in securing the erection of what then was the largest school building in the city and one which would compare favorable with many similar structures of more modern construction. He married, September 30. 1844, Mary Jane, born June 25, 1824, daughter of Richard and Harriet Mead, of Bloomingdale, New Jersey. She bore him four children, only one of whom, Wallace Graham, grew to maturity. Mary Jane (Mead) Graham married (second) Hiram Gould; she died May 29, 1903.

(III) Wallace, son and only surviving child of John (2) and Mary Jane (Mead) Graham, was born in Paterson, New Jersey, March 27, 1848. He received his education in the public schools of that city, and after leaving school learned the trade of carpenter and joiner and afterward worked as a journeyman until 1874, then became a ship carpenter in the service of a company whose boats were employed in passenger and freight transportation between New York and the West Indies. He continued in the employ of that company until 1882, then returned to Paterson and went into the undertaking establishment conducted by Hiram Gould, his stepfather. Subsequently Mr. Gould and Wallace Graham became partners in the funeral and undertaking business, which relation was maintained until the death of the senior partner in 1904. Since that time Mr. Graham has conducted the business alone. He is a member of Benevolent Lodge, No. 45, Free and Accepted Masons. He married Bertha Melina Harris, born August 15, 1853, adopted daughter of Joseph Hodgman. Children: 1. Mary Margaret, born March 22, 1881; married, October 21, 1902, Winfred Zabriskie; no issue. 2. and 3. Wallace Alvin and Walter Hiram, twins, born December 30. 1885.

LARTER The Larter family of New Jersey was founded by Robert, son of Robert and Ann Larter. He was born August 30, 1803, at Witton, near North Walsham, county of Norfolk, England.

In 1837 with his wife and several small children he came to America, settling in the city of Newark. November 5, 1825, Robert Larter married at North Walsham, England, Jane, daughter of Thomas and Mary Racey. She was born at Keynsham, Somersetshire, England, February 14, 1804. Children: Eleanor, born March 6, 1827; Jane, April 7, 1829; Robert, November 2, 1831; Ann, September 8, 1834; Thomas, April 20, 1836; William, April 14, 1838; John Alfred, September 2, 1840; George Ezra, March 28, 1843; Frederick Henry, referred to below.

Frederick Henry, youngest child of Robert and Jane (Racey) Larter, was born in Newark, New Jersey, April 19, 1846, and is now living in that city. For his early education he was sent to the Newark public schools, and after graduating in 1862 he took a position in the press room of the *Newark Daily Advertiser*, the leading newspaper publication of the city of Newark at that period, remaining in this position for five years. In 1867 he accepted a position as salesman with Osborn, Boardman & Townsend, at that period one of the most prominent retail jewelry concerns of New York City. Mr. Larter gained here the experience of which he made so great a use later in his successful career as one of the leading manufacturing jewelers of Newark. In 1870 he began business for himself by buying an interest in the then existing firm of H. Elcox & Company, eventually becoming the head of the concern, and afterward associating with himself his two sons, Henry C. and Halsey M., under the firm name of Larter, Elcox & Company, and in the year 1905 a change of the name being made to Larter & Sons, the title under which it is at present doing business. Mr. Larter is a Republican, but his tastes, although he has always been a staunch supporter of his party, have lain more in the direction of his social and business life than in the affairs of politics. Mr. Larter's tastes are domestic; he prefers his home and the companionship of his friends to club life. He is however an active and prominent member in a number of organizations which relate to his business and the advancement and promotion of the interests of the famous industry of Newark with which he has been so long connected. Among these associations should be mentioned the Jewelers' Board of Trade, the Drug and Chemical Club of New York, the Newark Board of Trade, the Jewelers' Safety Find Society, the Jewelers' Protective Union and the Wednesday Club of Newark.

May 19, 1869, Frederick Henry Larter married Martha, daughter of Simon Passmore, of Newark. Her death which occurred in January, 1909, was a source of great grief to her family and friends. Children: 1. Henry Clifton, married Sussanna D. Ekings, of Paterson, they having three children, Elizabeth J., Martha and Henry Clifton Jr. 2. Halsey Meeker, married Elizabeth Monroe, daughter of Francis Asbury Wilkinson; they have three children, Charlotte, Monroe and Elizabeth. 3. Mary Lorinda, married William Francis Price; they have one child, Virginia. 4. Jessie Eloise. 5. Florence Fredericka. 6. Warren Rogers.

· SCHENCK The ancestry of the Schenck family has been traced with definiteness to a very early mediaeval period. It is said to have derived its name from Edgar De Schenken, who was seneschal to the Emperor Charlemagne, and who about 778 A. D. received from that sovereign a title of nobility and coat-of-arms.

The genealogical records of the line from which the New Jersey Schencks are descended begin with Colve de Witte, founder of the house of Schenck, barons of Tautenberg, who was killed in battle with the Danes in 878 or 880. About 1234 a cadet of the Tautenberg line, Christians Schenck, established the family of Schenck van Nydeck (or van Nydeggen). This Christians resided in the famous castle of Nydeggen, was cupbearer to the Count van Jülich (1230-33), and had other distinguished offices. His descendants, the Barons Schenck van Nydeck, were also lords of Afferden, Blyenbeck and Walbeck, and later of Arssen, Velden, etc.—their estates being in the Netherlands near the German border. Armorial bearings of the Schencks of Nydeck—Arms, sable, a lion rampant or, langued et armè gules and azure. Crest, out of a coronet or, a demi-lion rampant or, langued et armè gules and azure.

In the sixteenth century a distinguished head of the house of Schenck van Nydeck was Martin Schenck van Nydeck, 1543-89, who was field-marshal to the Prince of Cologne, was knighted in 1586, and fell in battle, August 11, 1589. Motley, in his "History of the United Netherlands," refers to him as Sir Martin Schenck, and incidentally does him injustice, intimating that he held the estates by questionable title. It was fully established, after a litigation celebrated in those times (wherein the Pope and the Emperor figured), that Sir Martin was the legitimate and rightful heir of his ancestor, Derick Schenck van Nydeck, lord of Blyenbeck, Afferden, Walbeck, etc., who married Alheit Cüsters of Arssen. Of near kin to Sir Martin and, like him, a descendant of Derick, was the founder of the American branch here considered. This founder was

(I) Johannes Schenck van Nydeck, born in Holland, September 19, 1650. He emigrated from Middleburg, in that country, about 1675, settled in Bushwick, Long Island (now a portion of Brooklyn), and died there on the 5th of February, 1748. He was doubtless a man of substantial means. According to a deed on file in the office of the secretary of state of New Jersey, he purchased, October 11, 1703, six hundred and forty arces described as "lying between two tracts of John Inians, deceased." This property is said to have been within the limits of the present city of New Brunswick, and to have been occupied by some of the grandsons of Johannes. He married Magdalena, daughter of Hendrick and Maria de Haes.

(II) Johannes Schenck, son of Johannes Schenck Van Nydeck, was born April 30, 1691, lived at Bushwick, Long Island, and died April 1, 1729. He married Maria Lott, of Flatbush, Long Island.

(III) Hendrick, son of Johannes Schenck, was born July 15, 1717, died January 1, 1767. Removing to New Jersey, he built the mill on the west side of Millstone river, Somerset county, which has since been known as the Blackstone Mill. He married Magdalena van Liew. Children: 1. John H., died in Freehold, New Jersey, March 12, 1846. He was colonel of a regiment personally raised and equipped by him, which he commanded throughout the revolutionary war. Married (first) Sarah Denton; (second) Mrs. Jane Conover (neé Schenck). 2. Henry H., of Neshanic; physician and surgeon; captain of a troop of light horse in the revolutionary war. Married Nelly Hardenbergh, daughter of Rev. Dr. Jacob H. Hardenbergh, and had two sons. 3. Mary, married Dr. Lawrence Van Derveer. 4. Catherine, married Elias Van Derveer. 5. Gertrude, married General Frederick Frelinghuysen. They were the parents of the distinguished Theodore Frelinghuysen, LL. D., and grandparents of the latter's nephew, Frederick T. Frelinghuysen, secretary of state of the United States. 6. Letitia, married Judge Israel Harris. 7. Magdalena, married Dr. Peter J. Stryker, vice-president of the legislative council of New Jersey. 8. Abram, of whom below.

(IV) Abram, youngest child of Hendrick Schenck, was born March 3, 1749. He resided in Somerset county and during the revolution served in the troop of light horse which was commanded by his brother, Colonel Henry H. Schenck. He married Eva Van Beiren, daughter of Dr. Abraham Van Beiren, of Millstone.

(V) Henry Harris, son of Abram Schenck, was born January 12, 1788, died March 22, 1851. He removed to New Brunswick, New Jersey, where he was a highly respected citizen. For many years he was one of the elders of the First Reformed Church of that community. He married, November 19, 1808, Eva Voorhees, daughter of Martinus and Maria (De Camp) Voorhees, and a descendant of Steven Coerte van Voorhees, who came to New Netherland in the ship "Bonte Cou" in 1660. She was born July 9, 1785, died March 6, 1869. Children: 1. Elizabeth Stothoff, born November 21, 1809, died October, 1881. Married Edward Manning. 2. Catherine Ann, born January 25, 1814, died November 22, 1836. 3. William Van Beiren, born November 8, 1816, married Mercy A., daughter of Rev. Daniel D. Lewis. 4. Abraham Voorhees, of whom below.

(VI) Abraham Voorhees, youngest child of Henry Harris Schenck, was born in New Brunswick, New Jersey, October 12, 1821. He received a public school education in that city, studied law with Henry V. Speer, was admitted to the bar as attorney in November, 1843, and was licensed as counsellor in January, 1847. From the age of twenty-two until his death—a period of nearly sixty years—he was engaged in the active practice of his profession in New Brunswick. As a lawyer he enjoyed a wide reputation for learning and ability, and he was identified with many of the most important litigations both in the state and federal courts, some of the cases in which he appeared being of historic character for the principles of law which they established. In his professional capacity he was counsel for the city and other public bodies, as well as numerous corporations. Strongly interested in public affairs, Mr. Schenck was for many years a political leader, and he occupied several of the principal offices for his municipality and county. He was mayor of New Brunswick in 1855-56, prosecutor of the pleas of Middlesex county in 1872-77, and member of the state senate of New Jersey (elected on the Republican ticket over James Neilson) in 1883-85. During his service in the senate he was one of a special committee (1884) which reported the present important law relating to the taxation of railroad and canal property, and in the session of 1885 he was president of that body. At the end of his term he declined a renomination. As a citizen he exercised an influence in the community, and was regarded with a degree of confidence and esteem, not surpassed by any other of his times. He was one of the vice-presidents of the Holland Society and a prominent member of the New Jersey Society of Sons of the American Revolution. He died at his residence, "Redcliffe," Highland Park, Raritan township, Middlesex county, April 28, 1902.

He married (first) February 12, 1863, Emily Wines Barker, daughter of Abraham and Henrietta (Wines) Barker. She was born May 22, 1838, died June 20, 1870. Children: 1. Emily Barker, born March 8, 1867. 2. Warren Redcliffe, born June 7, 1870. He was educated at the Rutgers Preparatory School and Rutgers College, graduating from the latter institution with high honors in 1890, and three years later receiving the degree of Master of Arts. After pursuing legal studies with his father he was admitted to the bar (1893), and he has since practiced his profession in New Brunswick. Married, June 9, 1897, Sophie Kirkpatrick Smith, daughter of David Lowber Smith (a prominent citizen of New York), and Sophia Kirkpatrick (sister of the late Judge Andrew Kirkpatrick, of Newark). Children: i. Henrietta Barker Schenck, born February 4, 1899; ii. Gertrude Estelle Schenck, died in infancy.

Abraham Voorhees Schenck married (second) October 17, 1872, Sarah Estelle Barker (born October 29, 1849), daughter of Abraham and Henrietta (Wines) Barker, who survives him. Children: 3. Grace Wines, born December 14, 1873, married, June 23, 1907, Robert Kitching Painter. They reside at Benson Mines, New York. 4. Edith Mercer, born December 11, 1879. 5. Arthur Van Voorhees, born November 25, 1883. He is a graduate of the Rutgers Preparatory School and Rutgers College (1905, M. A., 1908), and also of the New York Law School (LL. B., 1908). Admitted to the New Jersey bar in June, 1908, he has since then been pursuing professional practice in New Brunswick.

CARPENTER   Among the strong, vigorous characters who figured conspicuously in the settlement of Philadelphia and surrounding country was Samuel Carpenter, who came from the island of Barbadoes shortly after the arrival of Penn himself. He was the son of John Carpenter, of Horsham, Sussex county, England, and sprang from a line of landholders long established in that country. A successful merchant of Barbadoes and the Quaker city, he crowned a long prominent and useful public career by long service as the treasurer of the Province of Pennsylvania, and died leaving a long line of distinguished descendants to represent him to posterity.

(I) Joshua Carpenter, his brother, is first heard of July 5, 1686, when the minutes of the provincial council record "The Petition of Joshua Carpenter was Read, Requesting a Lycense to Keep an Ordinary in his Brother Samll Carpenter's house on ye Wharfe. Ordered a Lycense for three months." This was the first public house in Philadelphia to be known as a "coffee house." It was on the east side of Front street, above Walnut, and was probably the building referred to by Robert Turner in his letter of August 3, 1685: "Samuel Carpenter has built another house by his." It became a noted resort in those early days, where ship captains, merchants and other citizens gathered to discuss the news of the day. In addition to his coffee house, Joshua Carpenter established a brewery and engaged in mercantile pursuits. Like his famous brother, he acquired considerable wealth and was assessed in 1693 at a valuation of £1000. May 18, 1693, he was commissioned a justice for Philadelphia county; May 17, 1699, he was appointed one of the regulators of the streets and water courses; and when Penn promulgated his charter to the city of Philadelphia, October 25, 1701, Joshua Carpenter was placed at the head of the list of eight aldermen. He declined the appointment at that time, but three years later was chosen to the same position by the common council. October 3, 1704, the date of this election, James Logan, in a letter to William Penn, says: "They have also chosen Joshua Carpenter again into their corporation, who was the first alderman nominated by thee in the charter; but, for a vow or oath he had made never to serve under them again, declined acting yet nor has, it seems, been prevailed upon. He is a great enemy of the militia, and to paying thy tax; but I know not whether that may be any part of his merit. He is of himself really a good man. As a matter of fact Joshua Carpenter had not been prevailed upon," but October 2, 1705, he was admitted freeman, and again elected to the

common council. Six days later he appeared and qualified. In 1705 he was instructed by the council to procure a public burial ground for the interment of strangers dying in the city, and January 13, 1706, he and Alderman Griffith Jones reported they had procured the same. This "Strangers' burying ground" was the present Washington Square, which was used for burial purposes for a century, hundreds of interments being made at different times, particularly during the various yellow fever and smallpox epidemics of the eighteenth century, and also during the revolutionary war. Carpenter enclosed in the centre of the ground a small plot which he reserved for the use of his own family, and here, July 24, 1722, he was buried, his wife Elizabeth being interred in the same plot October 30, 1729.

Unlike his brother Samuel, who was a Friend, Joshua Carpenter was one of the earliest and most active members of Christ Church, purchasing the lot on which the church stands in his own name and then executing a declaration that he held it in trust for the sole use and benefit of that corporation, and to this day the legal title remains in the representatives of Joshua Carpenter, trustee, etc. His house, especially in later years, was fully as famous a place as the "slate roof house" of his brother Samuel, and was situated on Chestnut street, between Sixth and Seventh, being in its day considered almost a country place so far was it "out of town." The grounds were beautifully laid out, and fruit trees and shrubbery for a long time attracted visitors. From 1738 to 1747 it was the residence of Governor George Thomas; later Dr. Thomas Graeme, the "Councillor," and his celebrated daughter, Elizabeth Ferguson, lived there, whence the building is often spoken of by local historians as Graeme Hall. Another dweller in the residence who made a number of material additions and alterations in its structure was John Dickinson. Gérard, the first French minister to this country, lived there as did also his successor, the Chevalier de la Luzerne. From 1798 to 1826 it was the home of Chief Justice William Tilghman, and in the last year mentioned it was razed and the Philadelphia Arcade built in its place.

Joshua and Elizabeth Carpenter had several children, but the names of all of them have not been preserved. They were, so far as known: 1. Samuel, a vestryman of Christ church, 1718-21, died February, 1736; married, 1719, Mary, daughter of Jasper and Catharine (Andelands)

Yeates, born December 4, 1701, died November 6, 1758. They had eight children. 2. Name unknown, referred to below.

(II) The statement has been made that there are now living no descendants in the male line of Joshua Carpenter, but a constant tradition traceable as early as the beginning of the nineteenth century, and with no opposing evidence from any document that has as yet come to light, says that one of the sons of Joshua Carpenter went down and settled in Delaware, and that one of his children, William, who is referred to below, moved up into Salem county, in which and the neighboring counties his descendants are to be found today. A bit of confirmatory circumstantial evidence is found in the fact that Joshua Carpenter bought from Fenwick's executors considerable land in the region where his reputed grandson afterwards settled, only a part of which he disposed of by deed.

(III) William, reputed grandson of Joshua and Elizabeth Carpenter, was born in Delaware, and came into Salem county about 1745 or 1746, as a young man. He was a farmer, a Church of England man, and is said to have been a number of years older than his wife. She was Mary, born in 1738, daughter of Jeremiah Jr. and Jane (Blanchard) Powell. They had four children: 1. Mary, married, 1780, Jacob Ware. 2. William, referred to below. 3. Powell. 4. Abigail, married, March 7, 1786, Edward Hancock. Tradition says he, William Carpenter, was buried in the Episcopal burial ground in Salem.

(IV) William (2), son of William (1) and Mary (Powell) Carpenter, was born in Salem county, in 1757, and died there September 26, 1803, and was buried in Lower Alloways creek. He was a farmer, and became a private in Captain William Smith's company, Second Battalion, New Jersey militia, during the revolutionary war. His brother, Powell Carpenter, was also a revolutionary soldier, and was wounded March 17, 1778, in the battle of Quinton Bridge, in which battle Captain William Smith distinguished himself, as did also his noble band of followers.

William Carpenter Jr. married, in 1784, Elizabeth, daughter of John and Elizabeth (Fogg) Ware, who was born March 3, 1763, and died April 6, 1803. Their seven children were: 1. Samuel, who married Mary Mason and went west. 2. Mary, who married (first) Thomas Hancock, and (second) Samuel Cooper. 3. Abigail, who married John Goodwin. 4. William, who is referred to below.

ii—22

5. Elizabeth, who married William Thompson. 6. Powell, who married (first) Eliza Slaughter, and (second) Ann Slaughter. 7. Sarah, who married Joseph Hancock.

(V) William (3), son of William (2) and Elizabeth (Ware) Carpenter, was born in Elsinborough, Salem county, New Jersey, April 4, 1792, and died in Salem, May 13, 1866. He was a farmer, and lived on what was known as the Brick farm in Elsinborough, where he lived until 1847, and was the first man to stop the almost universal practice of those days of furnishing his hands with liquor while working in the field, substituting instead an extra "five penny bit" a day. He was an attendant of the Salem Monthly Meeting of Friends, and in politics was a Whig and later a Republican. From 1828 to 1830 he was collector of Elsinborough; 1825 to 1827, a member of of the township committee; 1831 to 1840, one of the chosen freeholders; and 1833 to 1838 a member of the commission of appeals. About 1847, he removed to Salem, where he died.

January 22, 1814, William Carpenter married Mary, daughter of Abner and Mary (Mason) Beesley, who was born in Alloways Creek township, Salem county, November 4, 1795, and died in Salem, January 18, 1868. Her father, Abner Beesley, was born in Alloways Creek township, September 8, 1769, died October 10, 1806, and was a merchant in Salem; in 1804, collector for Salem county, also the first treasurer of the Salem Library Company. His brother, Walter Beesley, was a member of Captain Sheppard's company, Second Battalion, and was killed in the massacre at Hancock's Bridge, March 25, 1778. Her grandfather, Morris Beesley, was the son of John Jr., and the grandson of John Beesley Sr. He married Mary, daughter of Jonathan Waddington and Johanna, daughter of William Tyler, who died 1701. Jonathan Waddington was the son of William Waddington the emigrant. Her mother, Mary (Mason) Beesley was the daughter of John Mason and Susanna, daughter of William Goodwin and Mary, daughter of Lewis Morris and Sarah daughter of Erasmus La Fetra (corrupted to Fetters). Lewis Morris was the son of Redroe or Rothra Morris and Jael Baty. William Goodwin was the son of John Jr. and the grandson of John Goodwin Sr. John Mason was the son of Thomas and grandson of John and Sarah (Smith) Mason.

The children of William and Mary (Beesley) Carpenter were: 1. Elizabeth Ware, born

November 13, 1814, died June 27, 1866; married, October 3, 1839, Joseph B. Thompson. 2. Powell, who is referred to below. 3. Anna Mason, born September 9, 1819, died March 3, 1855, unmarried. 4. William Beesley, referred to below. 5. Morris Hancock, referred to below. 6. John Mason, referred to below.

(VI) Powell, second child and eldest son of William and Mary (Beesley) Carpenter, was born in Elsinborough township, Salem county, April 9, 1817, and died in Salem city, October 17, 1850. He was a mason and bricklayer, and lived in Salem. Carpenter street in that city is named for him, and he was one of the originators of the Franklin Loan and Building Association. He was killed by a fall from the Baptist church, now torn down, on which he was working. March 28, 1848, he married Mary L. Lawson, but left no children.

(VI) William Beesley, fourth child and second son of William and Mary (Beesley) Carpenter, was born in Elsinborough township, Salem county, August 17, 1822, and died December 22, 1899, in Salem City, New Jersey. He did not graduate from any school or college, but he attended the Elsinborough district schools, the Clairmont seminary, at Frankford, Philadelphia, Pennsylvania, and the Friends' private school in Salem, and for five terms he taught school himself in Elsinborough. He was a farmer in Elsinborough township until 1891, when he removed to Salem City, where he lived until his death. His farm in Elsinborough he bought from his father, and he also purchased another one in Mannington. From 1865 he was one of the directors of the Farmers' Mutual Fire Insurance Company, of which he became president in 1888. He was a Republican; assessor in Elsinborough, in 1863, 1865, and 1870; a freeholder from 1853 to 1855; and a member of the New Jersey assembly for two terms from 1874 to 1875. He was an attendant of the Salem Monthly Meeting of Friends.

William Beesley Carpenter married (first) in Philadelphia, December 8, 1848, Martha, daughter of Josiah W. and Eliza (Wright) Gaskill, born March 23, 1828, died April 27, 1867. Her brothers and sisters were Josiah, Aaron, Joseph, Charles and Lucy Gaskill. The children of William Beesley and Martha (Gaskill) Carpenter were: 1. Howard, born December 14, 1847, died September 29, 1868. 2. Mary E., born October 4, 1849; graduated from a boarding school in Bristol, Pennsylvania; married, in 1882, Edward Lawrence 3. William, born January 29, 1854, died Octo-

ber 30, 1855. 4. Lucy Gaskill, born January 5, 1857. 5. Anna Mason, born February 11, 1860; married Andrew Weatherby. 6. Martha Gaskill, born April 16, 1863; married Edmund W. Nieukirk. 7. Rebecca S., born February 22, died April 14, 1866.

William Beesley married (second) in Somers, Connecticut, June 4, 1868, Nancy, daughter of Robert and Amersha (Arnold) Pease, born in Somers, May 4, 1840, and still living. Her brothers and sisters were: Robert L., Loren H., Salome A., Martha S., Albert A., Vashni H., Mary C., and Robert; the three latter were children of second marriage. Robert Pease was the son of Oliver Pease and Nancy, daughter of Daniel, son of Captain Jonah Cone, who served eighteen days at the time of the Lexington alarm, and afterwards volunteered and served as a revolutionary soldier in 1777; he served as corporal. The wife of Daniel Cone, grandfather of Captain Jonah Cone, was Mary Gates, granddaughter of Captain Nicholas Olmstead, 1619-84, who served in the Pequot war of 1637. Oliver was the son of Robert and Ann (Sexton) Pease. Robert Pease was a revolutionary soldier, enlisting July 6, 1775, in Eighth Regiment, discharged December 16, 1777; his wife was the daughter of Daniel and Mary (Douglas) Sexton. Mary Douglas was the granddaughter of Robert Douglas and Mary Hempstead, who was the first white child born in New London. From this line sprang also Hon. Stephen A. Douglas, of Illinois. Robert Pease was the son of Robert and Hannah (Sexton) Pease, grandson of Robert and Elizabeth (Emery) Pease, great-grandson of Robert and Abigail (Randall) Pease, and great-great-grandson of John, son of Robert and Margaret Pease, of Great Baddow, county Essex, England, who emigrated to New England in 1634, landing in Boston. Amersha Arnold was the daughter of Samuel and Amittai (Pomeroy) Arnold, and granddaughter of Hon. John and Esther (Kibbe) Pomeroy. Her great-grandfather, Noale Pomeroy, was a descendant of Sir Ralph de la Pomeroi, of the time of William the Conqueror, and served in the Suffield company in the French and Indian war of 1755 and 1756.

The children of William Beesley and Nancy A. (Pease) Carpenter are: William H., Julia A., and Fanny Pease, all of whom are referred to below.

(VII) William H., eldest child and only son of William Beesley and Nancy A. (Pease) Carpenter, was born in Elsinborough township, Salem county, New Jersey, February 16,

1871. He graduated from the Salem high school in 1888, and from the medical department of the University of Pennsylvania in 1892. He is a member of the Fenwick Club, the Garfield Club, and the Salem County Country Club. He is also a member of Excelsior Lodge, Independent Order of Odd Fellows, and of Forest Lodge, Knights of Pythias. He is a practising physician in Salem, and medical director of the Standard Life Insurance Company of Camden, New Jersey, and a director of the Salem National Banking Company. December 16, 1895, he married Jane E., the daughter of Captain Daniel Whitney, a civil war veteran, and they had one child: William Beesley, who died April 12, 1909, aged twelve years six months.

(VII) Julia A., eldest daughter of William Beesley and Nancy A. (Pease) Carpenter, was born in Elsinborough township, Salem county, October 18, 1872, and is now living at 88 West Broadway, Salem City, New Jersey. She graduated from the Salem high school in 1890, and from the Broad Street Conservatory of Music in 1898. She is unmarried.

(VII) Fanny Pease, youngest child and second daughter of William Beesley and Nancy A. (Pease) Carpenter, was born in Elsinborough township, Salem county, August 11, 1876. She attended the Friends' school in Salem, and graduated from the Philadelphia training school for kindergartners in 1900. She married, October 19, 1909, Walter Hall, of Salem, New Jersey.

(VI) Morris Hancock, fifth child and second son of William and Mary (Beesley) Carpenter, was born in Elsinborough township, Salem county, February 17, 1825, and died January 4, 1904. He went to Philadelphia, engaged in business, and was very successful. He never married, and for several years before his death lived a retired life in a hotel. He was one of the directors of the Guarantee Trust and Safe Deposit Company of Philadelphia at the time of his death.

(VI) John Mason, youngest child of William and Mary (Beesley) Carpenter, was born in Elsinborough township, Salem county, October 9, 1827, and died in Salem City, December 9, 1902. He kept a grocery and feed store on East Broadway in Salem for many years, and was one of the foremost in establishing the Electric Lighting Company, of which he was the first president, in Salem. He was also a director in the Salem National Banking Company. March 19, 1855, he married Annie I., daughter of Minor Harvey, and left one son,

who is a member of the firm of Carpenter Mitchell & Company.

KINGSLAND

Major Nathaniel Kingsland of the British army was stationed on the island of Barbadoes, West Indies, about 1660, and with him were two nephews, Isaac and Gustavus Kingsland, probably sons of a deceased brother, of whom he was guardian. Captain William Sandford, a resident of Barbadoes was sent by Major Kingsland to New Netherlands to investigate the conditions of the lands lately held by the Dutch West India Company under the authority of the government of Holland, but which had come into the possession of the British government by force in 1664. His instructions to Captain Sandford were to purchase a desirable tract adjacent to New York City, with a view of colonization and probably as a future foothold for his nephews in the rapidly developing settlement about New York.

Captain William Sandford purchased from the Hackensack Indians a tract of land of about ten thousand acres between the Hackensack and Passaic rivers extending "northward about seven miles." This purchase was made July 4, 1668, in the interest of Major Nathaniel Kingsland, and June 1, 1671, Captain Sandford, having extinguished the Indian title, took title to the southern half of the tract and Major Kingsland to the northern half. Major Kingsland died after 1685 and in his will dated March 14, 1685, he left one-third of his three thousand and four hundred acre tract to his nephew, Isaac Kingsland, who with his brother Gustavus was living in the parish of Christ Church on the island of Barbadoes, West Indies. The two brothers evidently took ship soon after the death of their uncle and landed in New York; they proceeded to occupy the land thus bequeathed to Isaac, which they named New Barbadoes Neck, and December 30, 1697, Isaac conveyed to Gustavus a share of the property, and Isaac selected a site on the east bank of the Passaic river on which he built a house which was the first house on the present site of the village of Kingsland Manor, near Rutherford, Bergen county, New Jersey. Isaac was a man of wealth and consequently of prominence in the community, and he was made a member of the council of the provincial government and held the position for several years. He became the progenitor of one branch of the Kingsland family who settled largely in Union county, of which Edward W. Kingsland.

president of the Prudential Institution for Savings of Jersey City, born December 15, 1839, son of Edmund W. and Sarah A. Kingsland, is a representative in the seventh generation, through Burnet R., his grandfather; Edmund William, his great-grandfather; William, his great-great-grandfather; Edmund, his great-great-great-grandfather, who was a son of Isaac, the immigrant. The other branch of the Kingsland family, descending from Gustavus, is represented in the sixth generation by John Wesley Kingsland, born in Paterson, New Jersey, November 15, 1873, son of John and Catherine A. (Jackson) Kingsland, through his grandfather Gerardus; great-grandfather Stephen; great-great-grandfather David, son of Gustavus Kingsland, the immigrant, brother · of Isaac, the immigrant.

(I) Gustavus, nephew of Major Nathaniel and brother of Isaac Kingsland, came from Christ Church parish, Barbadoes, West Indies, to Bergen, East New Jersey, and lived at New Barbadoes Neck on a portion of the tract of three thousand and four hundred acres, which came as a gift from Major Nathaniel to his nephew, Isaac, and part of which was deeded by Isaac to his brother Gustavus, December 30, 1697. Gustavus married and had children including David, see forward.

(II) David, eldest child of Gustavus Kingsland, immigrant, was born probably in New York City, where he married the daughter of an English officer at the time New York was in the possession of the British army. By this marriage he had sons: David, Cornelius and Stephen (see forward), besides several daughters.

(III) Stephen, third son of David Kingsland, married Eleanor Stymus, of New York City; children, born in Union township, New Jersey; David, Gerardus, see forward; John, Stephen, Mary, married James Jeroleman; Catherine, Betsey, married Harry, son of Jacob E. Vreeland. Of these children, John, Stephen and Gerardus settled in Union township and died there.

(IV) Gerardus, second son of Stephen and Eleanor (Stymus) Kingsland, was born· in Union township, New Jersey, about 1802. He married Charity, daughter of Jacob·B. Vreeland; children, born in Belleville, Union township, Essex county, New Jersey: John, died young; John, see forward; Jacob.

(V) John, son of Gerardus and Charity (Vreeland) Kingsland, was born in Belleville, Essex county, New Jersey, May 16, 1832. He married, December 25, ·1862, Catherine A.

Jackson, proprietor of a fancy goods business which she was then carrying on in Paterson, New Jersey, on Main street, and after their marriage her husband became associated with her in business, which they were thus enabled to greatly extend and it grew very profitable so that after many years of successful results they were enabled to retire with a well earned competency. John and Catherine A. (Jackson) Kingsland had three children born in Paterson, New Jersey: 1. Samuel Jackson, October 22, 1865; married, December 7, 1891, Laura A. Emerson; they had no children; his wife died February 25, 1908. 2. Jennie Baunner, April 18, 1868; married, April 30, 1895, J. Milton Van Houten; child, Catherine Julia Van Houten, born February 19, 1899. 3. John Wesley, see forward.

(VI) John Wesley, youngest child and second son of John and Catherine A. (Jackson) Kingsland, was born in Paterson, New Jersey, November 15, 1873. He was educated in the public schools of Paterson, the Hackettstown Collegiate Institute and graduated from the College of Dentistry of New York City; he is now practicing his profession in Paterson, New Jersey. He married, June 28, 1900, Marguerite Mercelis, daughter of Richard and Jennie (Mercelis) Rossiter; children, born in Paterson: 1. Rossiter, July 14, 1901, died March 5, 1902. 2. Magdalen, January 8, 1903. 3. Jennie Jackson, April 26, 1905. 4. Muriel, July 27, 1907.

(The Jackson Line).

The ancestry of Catherine A. (Jackson) Kingsland was English. Her paternal grandfather, Peter Jackson, and his wife Jane, came in company with her maternal grandfather and grandmother, Thomas and Julia Gardom, with their respective children to America on the ship "America," Captain Irwin, sailing from Liverpool, May 24, 1801, and landing at Philadelphia, Pennsylvania, July 15, 1801. The two families came from Derbyshire, England, and of their families Joseph Jackson was five years of age and Catherine Gardom was three years of age.

(I) Peter Jackson, born in England, April 19, 1759, and his wife, Jane, born September 26, 1756, settled at Trenton, New Jersey, and Thomas Gardom and his wife Julia and daughter Catherine settled at Camden, New Jersey. Peter Jackson died December 18, 1831, and his wife, Jane, June 28, 1832.

(II) Joseph, son of Peter and Jane Jackson, was born in Derbyshire, England, April 2,

STATE OF NEW JERSEY. 741

1796, and was broight ip and edicated in
Trenton, New Jersey. He removed to Paterson, New Jersey, aboit 1820, and he was one
of the first chosen freeholders of that city,
holding office at the time of the erection oi
the coirt hoise. He also served as coroner
of Passaic cointy, and engaged sıccessfilly in
the grocery bisiness in Paterson. He married,
April 22, 1828, Catherine, daighter of Thomas
and Jilia Gardom, born in Derbyshire, England, Febriary 18, 1798. Children: 1. Jane
H., born Febriary 5, 1829; married Birroighs
P. ·Brinner; she died October 20, 1862. 2.
George, died yoing. 3. William, died yoing.
4. Jilia, Janiary 22, 1835; married Ezra
Waterhoise in November, 1879, and they had
one child, Joseph j. Waterhouse. 5. Samiel
Janiary 28, 1837; a soldier in the civil war,
killed in battle before Richmond, Virginia, in
1862; he was inmarried. 6. Catherine A., see
forward. 7. Joseph G., Aigist 15, 1842.
(III) Catherine A., daighter of Joseph and
Catherine (Gardom) Jackson, was born in
Paterson, New Jersey, November 29, 1838;
married, December 25, 1862, John Kingsland
(see Kingsland, V).

(For preceding generations see Richard Lippincott 1)

LIPPINCOTT (III) Jacob, seventh child
and third and yoingest
son of Restore and Han-
nah (Shattock) Lippincott, was born shortly
after his father's removal thither from Shrews-
biry, in Moint Holly, Birlington cointy, New
Jersey, in Aigust 1692. After reaching manhood he removed down into Gloicester cointy,
near the Salem cointy line, and at a later date
into Pittsgrove, Salem cointy, where most
of his descendants are residing at the present
time together with the descendants of Samiel
Lippincott, who was a piblic friend, and the
son of Jacob's incle, Freedom Lippincott.
These two branches of old Richard Lippincott's
descendants have spread throigh Birlington,
Camden, Gloicester, and Salem cointies, New
Jersey, and into Philadelphia. In 1716 Jacob
Lippincott was married, in the Moint Holly
meeting of Friends, to Mary, daighter of
Henry Birr and Elizabeth Hidson, the latter
of whom was born in England. By this mar-
riage he had eight children, and it is said a
ninth also, who married Rebecca Coate. The
eight children of Jacob and Mary (Birr)
Lippincott recorded are: 1. Caleb, married
Hannah, daighter of Daniel and Elizabeth
(Woolston) Wills, John Wills (II), Daniel

(I), whose ancestry is foind in the sketch of
the Wills family. 2. Benjamin, referred to
below. 3. Samiel, who married, and had one
child who married Isaac Barber, who emigrated
to Ohio, where he and his wife were both living
at a great age in 1848. 4. Joshia, who married
Rebecca Wood, and had two sons and one
daighter. 5. Jacob, Jr., who married a giri
from Abington, Pennsylvania. 6. William,
who married Sarah, daighter of Joshia and
Rith (Atkinson) Bispham, of Philadelphia.
7. Mary, who became the wife of Jacob Spicer,
Jr. 8. Hannah, who married into the Lords.
(IV) Benjamin, second son of Jacob and
Mary (Birr) Lippincott, was born in Gloucester cointy, New Jersey, where he spent his
life and left a goodly inheritance to his children. Both he and his brother Caleb owned
mich property on the east side of Old Man's
Creek, in Gloicester cointy, near the Salem
line, and many of their descendants are foind
in that region to-day. Benjamin Lippincott
married Hope, daighter of Daniel and Elizabeth (Woolston) Wills, the elder sister of
Hannah, who married his brother Caleb. She
was born in 1721. For her ancestry see the
sketch of the Wills family. The children of
Benjamin and Hope (Wills) Lippincott were:
1. Benjamin, who married Lydia Pimm, and
had two sons, and then married (second) Mary
Wood. 2. Jethro, who is referred to below.
3. Aaron, who married Sarah Haines, and had
two sons. 4. Mary, who became the wife of
Joshia Pail. 5. Hope, who married Zacheus
Ballinger. 6. Sarah.
(V) Jethro, son of Benjamin and Hope
(Wills) Lippincott, was born in Gloicester
cointy, New Jersey, on the farm which his
father had inherited from his father, and married Phebe Elkington, who bore him seven
children: 1. Jacob, who is referred to below.
2. Job, who married Rebecca Jones, and had:
Jethro and William, twins, the first dying unmarried, and the latter marrying Elizabeth
Wills, Phebe Ann, who married William Will-
iams; Elizabeth, married Richard Horner;
Clinton, married Elizabeth Hampton; Job, Jr.,
married Hannah Minyon, and Rachel, married
Hiram Groomes. 3. Mary, who married Enoch
Shite. 4. Levi. 5. James. 6. Joshia, who
married Mary Springer, and had: Lydia, married Henry Highes; Martha, married George
Mitchell; Elizabeth; Harriet, married Edgar
Black; Joshia, Jr., married Mary Camm;
Eliza, married Chalkley Johnson; Preston,
married Mary Hichner, and Ann, married Al-

bert Van Meter. 7. Esther, who married Samuel Madara, and had Joseph, Chalkley, Joshua and Levi.

(VI) Jacob, son of Jethro and Phebe (Elkington) Lippincott, was born in Gloucester county, New Jersey, and removed to Woodstown, Salem county, where he made his home and died. He married Mary Mail, by whom he had one son, Jacob Mail, who is referred to below.

(VII) Jacob Mail, only son of Jacob and Mary (Mail) Lippincott, was born in Woodstown, Salem county, New Jersey, May 5, 1824, and died in Salem, New Jersey, October 13, 1897. He was born on his father's farm, and spent his early life there. While he was yet a boy he met with an accident which resulted in a slight though incurable lameness, and unfitted him for the work of the farm, which he was consequently obliged to give up and to turn his attention and efforts in other directions. Finally he determined to go to Salem, which he did in 1839, walking the whole way, in spite of his lameness; and when he arrived there he apprenticed himself to a tailor and learned that trade, at which he worked for quite a while. He had never had any educational advantages, but was naturally of a literary turn of mind, and he read and thought much and wrote quite a good deal both in prose and verse. In 1869 he was elected county clerk of Salem county, and through successive re-elections held that office continuously up to 1884. In the community in which he lived he was held in the highest regard and esteem, and after his death his son published a volume of his poems and other prose writings, which was distributed by private circulation, and is greatly prized by his old friends and by all who are the fortunate possessors of the exquisite little volume.

Jacob Mail Lippincott married, September 25, 1849, Ann Swing, daughter of David DuBois, of Pittsgrove, Salem county, New Jersey; she was born August 11, 1827. By this marriage he had three children: 1. George C., who is referred to below. 2. Ruth Anna, born August 17, 1852, died September 17, 1859. 3. Louella, born April 3, 1860, who married Clement H. Sweatman, of Aldine, Salem county, to whom she has borne two children: George Lippincott Sweatman, born October 23, 1883, and Frank Sweatman, February 8, 1886, who died in Colorado, April 1, 1906.

(VIII) George C. Lippincott, M. D., eldest child and only son of Jacob Mail and Ann Swing (Du Bois) Lippincott, was born in Salem, New Jersey, September 18, 1850, and is now living in that city, at 271 East Broadway. For his early education he was sent to the public schools and to the Friends' private school at Salem, after leaving which he went into the drug business. After a short time spent in this way he entered the Philadelphia College of Pharmacy, from which he graduated in 1871, and then went to the Jefferson Medical College of Philadelphia, which gave him his degree of M. D. in the spring of 1875. In the following September, Dr. Lippincott was appointed by President Ulysses S. Grant as an assistant surgeon in the United States navy, on the active list of which he served until January, 1887, when he was retired owing to an affection of the heart. Since that time he has lived in his old home in Salem, New Jersey. About six of his ten years service was spent at sea, during which he was at one time for three months on shipboard with General Grant, when the ex-President was making his trip around the world with his son Jesse. He was with the General when he went through the Suez canal, and with the other naval officers on board his ship was entertained at the palace which had been placed at the disposal of the ex-President in Egypt.

Dr. Lippincott is a Republican, and independent in religion. He is a member of the United States Naval Academy Athletic Association at Annapolis, Maryland, and he was on duty at the Naval Academy there when he was retired. Dr. Lippincott is unmarried.

THOMSON This branch of the Thomson family in America descends from Scotch ancestry, through Rev. James Thomson, a minister of the Church of England, who was born in Scotland. Through intermarriage the Thomsons trace their line of descent back to the best Virginia families of Colonial and Revolutionary days. Each generation of the family has produced eminent professional men, notably in the profession of medicine. Thomson, the poet, author of "The Seasons," is a member of this family, and Lord Kelvin of Scotland was William Thomson. They have been loyal citizens, serving their country well in time of stress and battle, and good citizens serving her well in the gentle arts of peace.

(I) The emigrant ancestor was Rev. James Thomson, the first and only minister in Leeds parish, Fauquier county, Virginia, prior to 1815, also minister to several other churches in Virginia. He was born near Glasgow, Scot-

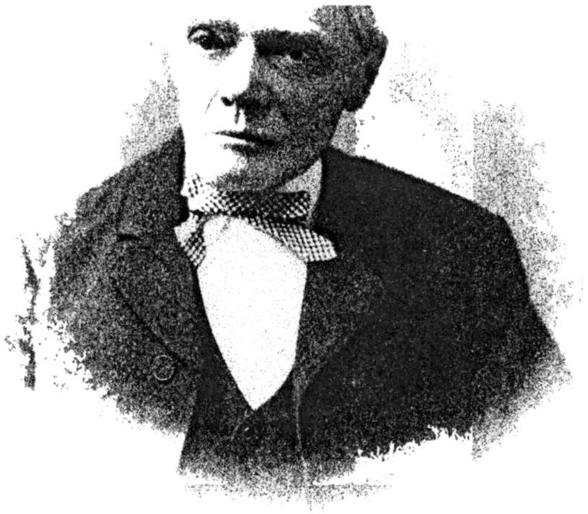

Jacob M. Lippincott

land, in 1739, and died in Virginia, in 1812. There is in possession of his descendants his commission from the Bishop of London authorizing him to perform the functions of a minister of the Church of England. He came to Virginia in 1767, and lived in the family of Col. Thomas Marshall, and was the tutor of his son John Marshall, afterward chief justice of the United States Supreme Court. He returned to England for orders, when he received the commission previously referred to. On his returning to this country from England he married Mary Ann Farrow, of Fauquier county, Virginia, and began his ministerial career. Bishop Meade, in his "History of Old Churches and Families in Virginia," writes of him with the greatest respect, and of his being an "unusually learned and able minister." Rev. James Thomson and his wife Mary A. Farrow were the parents of a large family.

(II) Dr. John Thomson, M. D., son of Rev. James and Mary A. (Farrow) Thomson, was born at the "Glebe," Fauquier county, Virginia, in the year 1770, and died at Berryville, Virginia, in 1841. He was a noted physician and surgeon, and said to have been a graduate of the University of Pennsylvania. His wife was Mary Rootes Throckmorton, of "Dewberry," near Berryville, Virginia, daughter of William and Mary (Rootes) Throckmorton. They were the parents of a large family, the eldest of whom was James William Thomson.

(III) James William Thomson, M. D., eldest son of Dr. John and Mary (Rootes) (Throckmorton) Thomson, was born at Berryville, Virginia, and died in Philadelphia, Pennsylvania, October 7, 1880. He was a most gifted and highly educated man. He graduated from Princeton (College of New Jersey) in 1822, with the degree of Bachelor of Arts, and in 1825 received the degree of Master of Arts. There is in possession of the family a gold medal presented to him by the Cliosophical Society of Princeton for graduating number one in his class, dated 1822, and inscribed "James W. Thomson." He entered the University of Pennsylvania and was graduated a Doctor of Medicine in 1825. He was admitted a member of the Philadelphia Medical Society, founded in 1789, on April 10, 1824. He was admitted to practice medicine and surgery in the state of Delaware by the State Board of Examiners in 1828. He established his practice in the city of Wilmington, Delaware, and became a most skillful practitioner. He was deeply imbued with a love of the soil and

acquired large farming interests. He was noted as a horticulturist also. He was elected a life member of the United States Agricultural Society of Washington, D. C., and an honorary member of the Massachusetts Horticultural Society, elected in December, 1848. He was appointed surgeon of the Delaware Militia "Dragoons." With his professional duties and his agricultural and horticultural interests, Dr. Thomson yet found time to comply with his responsibilities as a citizen. He belonged to the old Whig party, and was elected to the common council of Wilmington. He was an Episcopalian, and a member of the vestry. Dr. James W. Thomson married Sarah Peters Robinson, July 27, 1826, a daughter of Colonel Thomas Robinson, of the Continental army, lawyer, judge and gentleman farmer of Namaans Creek, New Castle county, Delaware. The descendants of Dr. James W. Thomson obtain membership in patriotic orders through his military service in the revolution. Thomas Robinson was captain of the Fourth Battalion, Colonel Anthony Wayne, June 5, 1776; was made major of the Fifth Regiment October 2, 1776; lieutenant-colonel First Regiment, June 7, 1777, and of the Second Regiment Pennsylvania Line, and was appointed brevet colonel by Act of Congress, September 30, 1783. There is a life size portrait of Thomas Robinson in his Continental uniform, hanging in Independence Hall at Philadelphia Pennsylvania. His grandson, William S. Robinson, has a brace of pistols presented to Colonel Robinson by General Washington, on whose staff he served, and a sword presented by his cousin, General Anthony Wayne. The original of the portrait referred to was painted by the great artist Peale, and is also possessed by William S. Robinson. The original "rattlesnake" flag which belonged to Colonel Robinson's regiment was captured from him by the British at the battle of Brandywine, was recaptured by himself, and is now in the capitol at Harrisburg, Pennsylvania.

Twelve children were born to Dr. James W. and Sarah Peters (Robinson) Thomson: 1. Mary Rosalie (Mrs. James B. Cunningham). 2. Lucy Edwyline, died in childhood. 3. John Augustus, a medical practitioner. 4. Julia Adalaide (Mrs. Edward Higginbottom). 5. Lucy Edwyline, married Francis C. Dade, chief engineer United States navy. • 6. Ellen Eyre. 7. James William (see forward). 8. Sarah Robinson. 9. Nalbro Frazier, died at age of twenty-one. 10. Ella Frazier. 11. Henry. 12.

Barton Hoxall. Of this family Rear Admiral James W. Thomson and Julia Adelaide Higginbottom are the sole survivors.

(IV) Rear Admiral James W. Thomson, second son and seventh child of Dr. James W. and Sarah P. (Robinson) Thomson, was born in Wilmington, Delaware, November 10, 1836. He was educated in private schools, and entered the then famous shops of Harlan & Hollingsworth, machine and engine building company, where he remained three years fitting himself for the duties of a mechanical engineer. He then received appointment from the state of Delaware as third assistant engineer (midshipman) in the engineer corps of the United States navy, June 26, 1856. He was ordered to the steam frigate "Wabash," on the North Atlantic Station, and made his first voyage down the Gulf, and the second voyage to Europe on that vessel. Admiral Dewey and Rear Admiral Howison were then midshipmen on board. They, with Rear Admiral Thomson, are believed to be the only surviving officers who were on the "Wabash" during that cruise. He was appointed first assistant engineer August 1, 1859, with rank of lieutenant, and assigned to the steam sloop "Dacotah." He was promoted chief engineer with the rank of lieutenant-commander February 2, 1862. When the civil war broke out he was in China with the fleet, but returned at once to the United States and served throughout the war in home waters. He was attached to the North Atlantic Blockading Squadron and saw much service on the James river as chief engineer of the gunboat "Galena." It was from this vessel that General McClellan directed the movements of his army for two days during the Peninsular campaign, at the battle of Malvern Hill. The "Galena" and the other vessels saw much hard service on the James river at Sewall's Point, Fort Darling and Drury's Bluff, and innumerable fights with Confederate vessels and batteries. Chief Engineer Thomson became known throughout the service as a cool headed, intrepid man and a thoroughly competent officer. This is attested by the award of a medal by Congress for "honorable and meritorious service." After the war closed, Captain Thomson was on special duty at the Philadelphia Navy Yard, and from 1866 to 1869 was a member of the board of examiners of officers for promotion, and on the same board again in 1881-2. In 1870 he was chief engineer of the "Congress." In 1871 and 1872 he was inspector of machinery at Philadelphia Navy Yard; 1873 to 1875 he was chief engi-

neer of the "Omaha," with the South Pacific fleet; 1876 and 1877 he was a member of the board of inspection and survey, and on the same board in 1882,1883. In 1879-81 he was chief engineer of the "Alaska," on the Pacific station, and August 18, 1883, was promoted commander. During President's Cleveland's first administration, when the new navy with its first modern war vessels became a fact, he was assigned to duty at Roach's shipyard as inspector of machinery installed in the "Dolphin," "Chicago," "Atlantic" and "Boston." In 1889 he was chief engineer of the "Pensacola" when that vessel conveyed a party of leading astronomers of the United States to the west coast of Africa to observe the total eclipse of the sun. On the return of the "Pensacola" to the United States, Captain Thomas was assigned to duty at Cramps' shipyard at Philadelphia as inspector of machinery. He remained on duty until he was assigned to duty at the Newport News Shipbuilding Company yards for the special and important duty of inspector of machinery of the battle ships "Kearsarge" and "Kentucky," on June 26, 1896, he was retired, after forty years active service, on his own application, with the rank of captain. At the outbreak of the Spanish war Captain Thomson offered his services to the government although on the retired list at the time. He was assigned to the U. S. Ship "Lancaster," Admiral Remey's flagship, on the Admiral's staff. His special duty was as "inspector of machinery afloat," and he performed valuable service at Key West in handling the great number of vessels in the government service at that point. He is in possession of a medal awarded him for his Spanish war service, under Act of Congress approved May 13, 1908. On June 29, 1906, Congress passed an act by which, on account of his meritorious civil war record, Captain Thomson was advanced to the rank of rear admiral in the United States navy. Since 1903 he has resided in Moorestown, New Jersey. He is a member of the Loyal Legion, and of Washington Lodge, No. 59, Free and Accepted Masons, Philadelphia, Pennsylvania. In political faith he is Republican.

Admiral James W. Thomson married, October 7, 1862, Laura Nicholson Troth, daughter of Joseph Nicholson and Narcissa Julia (Oldham) Troth, of New Castle county, Delaware. This is another revolutionary line, leading to Colonel Edward Oldham, of the Eighth Maryland Regiment, Continental Line, wounded at the battle of Camden, South Carolina. Four children were born to James W. and Laura Nicholson (Troth) Thomson:

1. Nalbro Frazier, born in Camden, New Jersey, August 28, 1863, now a resident of Haddonfield, New Jersey. He was educated in Camden public and private schools, at the Episcopal Academy, Philadelphia, and at Crittenden's Business College, Philadelphia. After finishing his studies Mr. Thomson located in Atlanta, Georgia, where he was secretary of the Globe Planter Manufacturing Company of that city. In the year 1893 he was appointed sub-inspector of ordnance for the United States navy, and since that date has been on duty at "Cramp's" Philadelphia, at the yards of the New York Shipbuilding Company, Camden. New Jersey, or elsewhere in the district where United States naval vessels were being fitted with ordnance. Mr. Thomson is a member of the Loyal Legion, second class; the Sons of the Revolution; and a communicant of the Episcopal Church at Haddonfield, New Jersey, his present home. He married, November 28, 1883, at Haddonfield, Catherine M. Stoutenborough, born at Bergen Heights, New Jersey, daughter of Richard H. and Eliza B. (Geib) Stoutenborough, of New York City. Mrs. Thomson is a member of the Episcopal Church. Two children were born to Mr. and Mrs. Nalbro Thomson: Eliza Rosina, born December 14, 1895, who died February 15, 1902; and Loring Batten, born September 10, 1899.

2. Laura Adalaide, born April 17, 1865, died in infancy.

3. Earl, born in Camden, New Jersey, August 21, 1866. He was educated in the Camden schools, at the Episcopal Academy of Philadelphia, and was graduated from the University of Pennsylvania, class of 1886, with the degree of Bachelor of Science. He is a civil engineer of Camden, New Jersey, residing in Moorestown. He married Cora Schloss, and has a daughter, Dorothy Caroline.

4. Mary Josephine, born in Camden, New Jersey, December 31, 1870, died July 31, 1896. She was the wife of William H. Duval, a wholesale merchant of New York City. She left a daughter, Mary Josephine Duval, born April 13, 1896, died aged nine months.

Joseph Nicholson Troth, father of Mrs. Thomson, wife of Rear-Admiral James W. Thomson, was born September 17, 1811, and died June 29, 1883. He was the eldest son of Jacob and Rebecca Troth, members of the Society of Friends. Jacob was the son of Paul Troth, who owned a plantation near Haddonfield, New Jersey. The family originally came

from Wales, and settled in New Jersey, Pennsylvania and Maryland. They were a patriotic family, as the records show. Paul Troth was a very tall, fine looking old gentleman, over six feet in height. During the revolutionary war his fine physical presence attracted the attention of some British officers who tried to induce him to join their army. He told them it was against the conscience of Friends to fight, but on telling his wife of the conversation, he added, "but if I did fight I would fight against the King's men." Jacob Troth was a Whig member of the New Jersey legislature, and was respected, as was his son, Joseph N., for his pure character, marked intelligence and sound judgment. Jacob Troth was a member of the first board of chosen freeholders after Camden county was cut off from Gloucester. Joseph N. Troth, the eldest son of Jacob, went to Delaware in 1836 and was extensively engaged in felling, milling and marketing large tracts of timber at the head of the Christiana. After he removed to Delaware he married Julia Narcissa Oldham, daughter of Edward Oldham, an educated and accomplished gentleman, the son of Colonel Edward Oldham, of an old Maryland family, and a distinguished officer of the revolution. Colonel Edward Oldham's wife Mary was a descendant of Augustine Herman. Joseph N. Troth resided during his early married life in Christiana, New Castle county, Delaware, where all of his children were born, from there he moved to New Castle, thence to Wilmington, and from there to Camden, New Jersey, where he died. He left four children: Mrs. Laura N. Thomson, Ernest H. Troth, J. Eugene Troth and Augustine H. Troth.

LADD

The first Ladds came to England with William the Conqueror and settled at Deal county, Kent, where a portion of land was granted to them eight miles from Dover. The name at that time was spelled Lad, Lade and Ladd. In many generations after the Norman Conquerors the name DeLad appears among the owners of the land, in county Kent and ever since that day families with that name have held land in that and adjoining counties. William Ladd was a jewelman in 1294 in the reign of Edward I. In 1325 King Edward II. bought the Manor of Henle of which he claimed the custody to Walter Bishop, of Exeter, and in the following year revoked this grant and transferred the manor to Walter Ladd, and from 1713 to 1722 John Ladd represented Southwark county.

Surrey. John Ladd, Senior, of Eleham, county Kent, died in 1476; he left a son, John of Eleham, who died in 1527, having had by Elizabeth his wife among other issue three sons. Stephen, father of Thomas Ladd, of Otling, John, the father of Nicholas Ladd, of Wooton, whose eldest son Nicholas, of Swingfield, county Kent, died in 1669, leaving a son Nicholas, referred to below, and Thomas Ladd, of Barham, whose grandson Vincent was the father of the said John Ladd, M. P., granted a baronet in 1730.

(I) Nicholas Ladd, of Swingfield, son of Nicholas, Senior, died and was buried in the Quaker burying ground of Hythe in 1699. Among his children was John, founder of the New Jersey family of the name, referred to below.

(II) John, son of Nicholas (2) Ladd, of Swingfield, county Kent, England, arrived in Burlington, New Jersey, in 1678. He was one of the jurors of the first court held under the constitution of Auvaumus in 1686, and in 1688 he had the addition to his lands on the shore of Deptford township, five hundred acres, surveyed to him at Cork Cove above Red Bank. The concessions and agreements were published in London in 1676 and attracted much attention especially among the members of the Society of Friends. Among these was John Ladd; his interest was evidently with the London rather than the Yorkshire homes. He was a practicable surveyor, and acted as deputy of the surveyor general of the western division of New Jersey for several years. As tradition goes through he was employed by William Penn in laying out the city of Philadelphia. When he produced his bill for £30 for services rendered to the proprietor he offered him a square of land in lieu of money, which was denied. As the young surveyor could see nothing like a city as sanguine owner where he had wrestled only with briers and tangled undergrowth. The family tradition goes on to state that when Mr. Ladd denied the square of land in the city, William Penn remarked "John thou art Ladd by name and Ladd by nature, doesth thou not know that this would be a great city." In 1688 Jonathan Wood and Samuel Toms located a large tract of land in Deptford township extending from the river on the west to Salem road and beyond on the east. He soon after purchased the interest of Samuel Toms and Jonathan Wood and on the tract built himself a dwelling where he resided until his death. In 1721 he located an adjoining tract along the river where the fishery was established, but not with us to the present day. For many years a portion of this tract has been known as the Howell estate coming into that family by the deed of John Ladd to John Ladd Howell, a son of Catherine Ladd, who married John Howell. John Ladd, the founder, was a member of the monthly meeting of Friends at the meeting on Woodbury creek. He came to New Jersey as a young man, and about thirty-two years of his life was spent within the province, where he was a prominent and influential citizen. He was a man not only of considerable estate but of good education as well, as is shown by his land operations and the places of responsibility he was called from to fill. As we learn from his will dated in 1731 with the codicil in 1740. John Ladd survives his wife and all his children except John and Katharine. To the first of these he devised his homestead estate of five hundred and sixty acres, giving other parts of his property to Katharine and his granddaughter, Mary Parker, having as he says in his will provided for Samuel and Jonathan while they were living. At his death he was one of the largest holders of real estate in the colony, and his selections proved him to have been a man of good judgment in such matters. The fishery where his land fronted the river was for centuries known as the Ladds Cove. Its particular situation on the shore almost made it one of the best in those quarters. He held a prominent place in the Society of Friends, and although he adhered to the plain dress and simplicity of habit about his home there could nevertheless be seen evidence of things generally attendant on health and liberality. The slaves were plentiful at his household and this would convince people that creature comforts were not neglected.

By his wife Elizabeth, who died 1733, John Ladd had five children: 1. Samuel, married Mary Medcalf. 2. Jonathan, referred to below. 3. Mary, married Joseph Parker, of Philadelphia. 4. John Jr., died December 20, 1770; married Hannah Mickle but had no children. 5. Katharine, married John Howell.

(III) Jonathan, second son of John and Elizabeth Ladd, lived in Woodbury, Gloucester county, New Jersey, on land which he had received from his father. He died in 1725, leaving two twin infants whom his wife had borne to him the preceding year. He married, in 1723, Ann, born 1698, daughter of John and Hope (Delefaste) Wills, a granddaughter of Dr. Daniel Wills. By his first wife Elizabeth, their children were: 1. Samuel, referred to below. 2. Sarah, twin with Samuel, born September, 1724.

(IV) Samuel, only son of Jonathan and Elizabeth Ladd, was born in September, 1724, and lived in Woodbury, New Jersey. By his wife Sarah he had seven children: 1. Jonathan, born September 23, 1755, died June 6, 1760. 2. Ann, July 11, 1757, died June 28, 1782. 3. Hannah, November 2, 1759. 4. Deborah, September 23, 1760, died March 3, 1771. 5. Ella, June 2, 1762. 6. John, November 2, 1764. 7. Samuel. Jr., referred to below.

(V) Samuel (2), youngest child of Samuel (1) and Sarah Ladd, was born November 10, 1771, died July 10, 1833. July 3, 1815, he married Ann, daughter of William and Deborah Wood, who bore him four children: 1. John, born May 26, 1816, died June 9, 1816. 2. James, October 4, 1817, died August 8, 1818. 3. Sarah, March 26, 1820, died May 15, 1832. 4. Samuel Hopkins, referred to below.

(VI) Samuel Hopkins, fourth and youngest child, the only child to attain maturity, of Samuel (2) and Ann (Wood) Ladd, was born in Woodbury, New Jersey, March 6, 1826, died in that town, March 6, 1866. He was for some time a colonel on the staff of Governor Holden. September 22, 1846, he married Sarah Duncombe Johnson, by whom he had three children: 1. William Waddell, born July 20, 1847, died unmarried, December 12, 1863; he inlisted in Camden county in the Second New Jersey Volunteer Regiment of Cavalry in 1861 and died during services. 2. Samuel Hopkins, Jr., referred to below. 3. Sarah Cora, August 19, 1853, died August 9, 1854.

(VII) Samuel Hopkins (2), son of Samuel Hopkins (1) and Sarah. D. (Johnson) Ladd, was born in Woodbury, New Jersey, December 15, 1849, and is now living in the town of his birth. For his early education he was sent to the private school at Woodbury, New Jersey, after leaving which he entered the Polytechnic College of the state of Pennsylvania, from which he graduated with the degree of C. E., July 1, 1868. He then entered on the profession of civil engineering in Woodbury and continued in that for a number of years, winning his mark in the world. In 1881 he started in the mercantile business in Philadelphia with his father-in-law at 32 South Front street, the firm name being Johnson & Ladd. This business, which is tobacco, he still continues under the old name. In 1871 Mr. Ladd was made the city surveyor of Woodbury, this receiving an appointment to a position held in the same

region about two hundred years before by his ancestor, John Ladd, the founder of the family. This position he held until 1873, when he was elected justice of the peace, and with the exception of five years he has held this position ever since, a remarkable tribute not only to his character but also to the confidence with which his neighbors regard him. In 1875 he was elected to the Woodbury city council and in 1877 was made the president of that body. In 1878 he was re-elected and again became the council's president; in 1880, although urged to do so most strongly, he declined to serve longer, but was prevailed upon to accept an appointment by the city council in 1889 to fill a vacancy which had occurred in their body, and in 1890 he was again elected and accepted a place from the council in which he served until 1893. In the fall of 1893 he was again appointed to fill a vacancy in the council caused by the removal of a member from the city, and in 1894 he was not only re-elected to the council but once more made its president. August 31, 1897, Mr. Ladd was appointed by the council mayor of Woodbury to serve for the unexpired term of his predecessor who had removed to Chicago, and in 1898, by popular election Mr. Ladd became the mayor in fact and has ever since that date been re-elected to this position as soon as his terms expires. This continuous service in the mayor's office for more than thirteen years shows conclusively the confidence by the people in his ability and trustworthiness. Mr. Ladd is a Republican, and at one time was the commissioner of deeds. He is an active and influential member of several secret societies and associations, the most important of which is Florence Lodge, No. 87. Free and Accepted Masons, of Woodbury, of which he is the past worshipful master. For the last thirty-two years Mr. Ladd has been a member of the Friendship Fire Company of Woodbury, which is one of the oldest in New Jersey, having been organized in 1799. For a long time he held the office of president and at the present day is the vice-president and one of the most active members of the company. It is an interesting fact that Mr. Ladd's father and grandfather were both of them for many years most active members of this same company. Mr. Ladd is a communicant of the Protestant Episcopal church in Woodbury, and was vestryman of the parish of that church in the town.

The Hon. Samuel Hopkins Ladd married, January 15, 1879, Kate Branford, daughter of Thomas L. and Cora V. (Tyree) Johnson, of

Virginia. Children: 1. Cora V., born November 2. 1879; married Henry Barton Reeves, of Woodbury, New Jersey. 2. Sarah Duncombe, January 1, 1881; married Matthew E. Davis. of New York City. 3. Mary Conner, 1883; unmarried.

ACKLEY The Ackley family of New Jersey belongs among the old established families of Gloucester county, where they have taken their share in the labor and have reaped their portion in the rewards, which have fallen to the lot of those who have so nobly given themselves and their energy to the building of that county's glorious history. Where the family originally came from is uncertain. It is probably a branch of the family of the same name which is to be found in the earliest days of the New England colonies, but the records are not in existence or have not yet come to light which will enable us to say with certainty exactly what the connection if any is.

(I) The founder of the Gloucester county branch so far as is at present known is John Ackley. He was a revolutionary soldier, serving in the American army in Gloucester county. He was born December 14. 1759. By his wife, Hannah. born January 30, 1763, he had twelve children: 1. Uriah, referred to below. 2. John, Jr., born February 4, 1782. 3. Naomi, August 25, 1783. 4. James, November 2, 1785. 5. Royal, August 9. 1787. 6. Absolom, April 24, 1790. 7. Joseph, June 12, 1792. 8. Benjamin. March 2, 1794. 9. Hannah, March 4. 1796. 10. Mercy, March 4. 1798. 11. Thomas, June 12, 1800. 12. George A., May 14. 1803.

(II) Uriah, eldest child of John and Hannah Ackley, of Gloucester county, was born there June 5. 1780, died August 5, 1854. He was an itinerant Methodist minister of Salem county. New Jersey. He married Sarah Coombs. born April 25, 1791, died August 4. 1879. Children: 1. Samuel, born February 5. 1810, died February 28, 1890. 2. William, referred to below. 3. Joseph, July 23, 1813, died October 18, 1892. 4. Rachel. March 17, 1815, died October 22, 1880. 5. Hannah. November 11, 1816, died October 6, 1893. 6. Ann. May 11. 1818, deceased. 7. Mary, September 23. 1819. 8. John, March 24, 1822, deceased. 9. Jesse C., October 20. 1823, deceased. 10. Sarah Ann, May 2. 1826, died February 15. 1896. 11. Coombs, June 17, 1828. 12. Ruth. September 5. 1829, deceased. 13. Jane, June 11. 1832, died March 14. 1876. 14. George, July 15. 1835.

(III) William, second child and son of Uriah and Sarah (Coombs) Ackley, of Salem county, New Jersey, was born at Union Pond, Cumberland county, New Jersey, November, 1811. He married Mary Rape, born at Mays Landing. Atlantic county, New Jersey, daughter of the Rev. Solomon Smallwood. Children: 1. Caroline E., died in 1894; married James N. Bedloe, of Philadelphia, a descendant of the man from whom Bedloe's island on which was placed the statue of liberty given by the French government in New York harbor was named. Their children are: Caroline, William. Ackley and Thomas, the last two being twins. 2. Rachel, who was one of twins, the other twin dying in infancy; she married Joseph T. Dailey, of Bridgeton, and has Sarah Perrine, Caroline Bedloe and Joseph T. Jr. 3. William Scattergood, died April 2, 1865, unmarried; he was captain of Company K, Fourth New Jersey Volunteer Infantry in the civil war, enlisting from Pole Tavern, Salem county. New Jersey, in 1861, and killed before Petersburg, Virginia, while leading a charge of his company, under General Grant; he had enlisted for three years and then re-enlisted and was killed at the beginning of the last engagement of the war; enlisting as private. he was for a time the regimental color sergeant in the battle of the Wilderness, and while he carried it the flag and staff received thirty-seven bullet holes, and three pieces of shell. 4. Charles Franklin, married Sarah Auffort, of Philadelphia, and have William Scattergood, Mary R. and Michael Hall Stanton, the last now deceased. 5. Elizabeth Johnson, married Gilbert G. Richmond, of Pleasantville, Landis township, New Jersey, and had three children, only one, Ralph D., being now alive. 6. John Alfred. referred to below.

(IV) John Alfred, youngest child of William and Mary Rape (Smallwood) Ackley, was born at Absecon. Atlantic county, New Jersey, July 14, 1854, and is now living at Vineland, New Jersey. For his early education he attended the public school of Bridgeton and Landis township, Cumberland county. After leaving school he helped his father on the farm. and then became a clerk in a hotel in Philadelphia, and later at Atlantic City, after which he purchased a farm for himself next to that of his father, consisting of five acres of land, which he turned into a fruit farm. His next venture was a partnership with Charles H. Birkinshaw, the firm being Ackley & Birkinshaw. general merchants. dealing in house furnishings, also auctioneers and dealers in real estate; later he sold his interest in the same, and engaged in auctioneering and real estate on his own account. Mr. Ackley's business can be called interstate, as his services are as much in demand for important sales in Pennsylvania as in New Jersey. He has in charge the premium lot sales of Baker Brothers. He has cried all the contract sales of the Wildwood and Wildwood Crest lots that have been sold, having sold four million dollars worth of sea shore property in the past fifteen years. He has also had charge of the public sales of lots for Henry H. Ottens. His sales have been more influential in the up-building of Five Mile Beach and the establishing of value than the efforts of all other persons outside of the founders. Since his services were secured the lots have sold readily each year at higher figures. At the sale of Wildwood Crest lots in November, 1906, the premium amounted to sixty thousand dollars. The highest premium bid on a single lot was one thousand four hundred and seventy-five dollars. He inaugurated the public sales in Youngs' Philadelphia Horse Exchange in West Philadelphia in the winter of 1903-04.

In 1884 Mr. Ackley came from Bridgeton to Vineland and embarked in the new and second hand goods business at Sixth street and Landis avenue. In 1895 he removed to 9 and 11 North Sixth street, where he has two floors, completely stocked with furnishings and merchandise. He utilizes in the same manner the second and third floors of the adjoining premises and he conducts the storage business on the second floor of No. 604 Landis avenue. Auction sales take place regularly every Saturday afternoon at Mr. Ackley's place of business, and he conducts public sales upon the premises where goods are located. He purchases for cash the entire contents of dwellings and entire stocks of merchandise, and he is prepared to furnish houses completely from top to bottom. Mr. Ackley negotiates purchases, sales and exchanges of real estate of every description, and holds the appointment of commissioner of deeds. For his real estate business he maintained an office in the Reeves Building at Wildwood, which is his summer home. He is a member of the Wildwood board of trade, and was a justice of the peace of Vineland.

Notwithstanding the fact that Mr. Ackley is an exceedingly busy man, he devotes a portion of his valuable time to the social side of life and toward bettering the conditions of the unfortunate. He is a past master of Vineland Lodge, No. 69, Free and Accepted Masons; a member of Eureka Chapter, No. 18, Royal Arch Masons; Olivet Commandery, No. 10, Knights Templar, of Millville, New Jersey; Lulu Temple, Mystic Shriners, of Philadelphia; Vineland Castle, No. 46, Knights of the Golden Eagle; Muskee Tribe, Improved Order of Red Men, of Vineland. He is one of the charter members of the Vineland Country Club, one of the board of managers of the Vineland Public Library, a charter member of the Wildwood Yacht Club, Holly Beach Yacht Club, and a member of the Wildwood Motor Club.

In politics Mr. Ackley is a Democrat, and as such was a member of the city council of Vineland, vice-president of the board of education at Vineland until 1908, when he was made president; also president of the Vineland park and shade tree commission. He and his family attend the Baptist church, and he is one of the trustees of the West Baptist Church of Vineland.

July 7, 1885, John Alfred Ackley married Antha Victoria, daughter of William J. and Hannah (Brown) Smith, of Vineland. Their children are: 1. Mary Louise, born September 19, 1886. 2. Charles William, July 5. 1888. 3. John Alfred, Jr. 4. Charles Rocus, died in infancy. The last two were twins, born August 30, 1891.

CARTER Hon. and Rev. William Henry Carter, of Fieldsboro, New Jersey, minister of the Gospel and ex-state senator of New Jersey, is a unique and commanding figure in the public life of his state. In private life, his community is the better for his manly example of honor and fidelity, his sunny smile, pleasant greeting and comforting words in time of trial, trouble and sorrow. He has been called the "Father of the town" and perhaps better eulogy could not be written. Rev. Mr. Carter springs from Bucks county, Pennsylvania, stock.

(I) William Carter, grandfather of Rev. William H. Carter, resided in Bucks county, Pennsylvania, and died there. He married Huldah Brown, a native of Connecticut, who bore him one son, William.

(II) William Carter, father of Rev. William H. Carter, was born in Attleboro, Bucks county, Pennsylvania, (now Langhorne) 1797, died in 1861. He had a good common school education. He learned the trade of a carriage and house painter and carried on a shop in Frankfort, Pennsylvania, until ill health compelled him to seek a more healthful occupation. He obtained work in the boiler works of Thomas Halloway. In his shop he helped construct the boilers used in the "John Bull," the first steam locomotive to run in this country. He also helped build that famous piece of mechanism. Mr. Carter continued at this line of work until his death. In 1841 he removed to Bordentown, New Jersey, where he was employed in the Camden and Amboy railroad shops. He was a Democrat and was elected chief burgess of Fieldsboro. He was for many years a member of the Methodist church, but in his latter years he became a Universalist. He was a charter member of Bordentown Lodge, No. 16, Independent Order of Odd Fellows. He married, 1818, Esther Pitt, born in Morrisville, Bucks county, Pennsylvania, June 18, 1801, died October 1, 1888, daughter of Thomas Pitt, of Bucks county, Pennsylvania. Children: 1. Susan Pitt, lived to the advanced age of eighty-six years; married (first) William Lingle and (second) Alexander Hamilton. 2. and 3. Richard and Harriet, twins. 4. Elizabeth, died in childhood. 5. Huldah, deceased. 6. Marion Etta, died in childhood. 7. Joseph V., a retired boiler maker; resides at White Hill, New Jersey. 8. Mary, deceased. 9. William Henry, see forward. 10. George S., deceased. 11. David J., deceased. 12. Amos Pitt, deceased.

(III) William Henry, ninth child and third son of William and Esther (Pitt) Carter, was born in New Castle, Delaware, March 6, 1835. The family moved to Bordentown, New Jersey, when young William Henry was about six years of age. He was educated in the public school, and while serving his apprenticeship attended night schools, so strong was his desire to obtain an education. When but twelve years of age he began work with Samuel Cliver, a merchant of White Hill. In 1851 he entered the employ of the Camden & Amboy Railroad Company as assistant fireman. In the early days of railroading on that line three men were employed on each engine, engineer, fireman and assistant fireman. The assistant was obliged to serve three years before he was considered competent to assume the full duties of a locomotive fireman. In the winter of 1852 he was transferred to the car shops as apprentice car trimmer and upholsterer and remained in that department until the spring of 1856, when he obtained a position with the New York and Erie railway at Pier-

mont, New York. Here he remained until March, 1857, when he returned to White Hill and entered the general store of C. N. and E. B. Johnson. This was the same store in which he had worked for Mr. Cliver ten years previous. Following this he was in the employ of a wholesale house until 1869, when the Camden and Amboy opened a station at White Hill and Mr. Carter was appointed station agent. In 1871 he entered the employ of MacPherson, Williard & Company as shipping clerk in connection with his duties as station agent. January 1, 1880, he tendered his resignation to the railroad and devoted all his time to MacPherson, Williard & Company as general clerk, which position he occupied until October 1, 1893, a period of twenty-three years. This was the end of Mr. Carter's active business life, although later in Fieldsboro he had a connection with the Equitable Life Insurance Company of New York.

His religious and political career will now receive the attention its importance deserves. Mr. Carter united with the Methodist Episcopal church at Bordentown, New Jersey, December 26, 1852. He was then in his seventeenth year. In March, 1857, he transferred his membership to the Fieldsboro Methodist Episcopal church, where he still holds membership. In May, 1857, he was elected superintendent of the Sunday school and continued to serve in that capacity continuously until 1905 with the exception of one year, making forty-seven years of service. In 1859 Mr. Carter was licensed as an exhorter by the quarterly conference of the Columbus district and in 1864 was licensed by the same conference as a local preacher. In March, 1871, he was ordained a local deacon by Bishop Janes in Broadway Methodist Episcopal Church, Salem, New Jersey, and was ordained a local elder in March, 1879, by Bishop Merrill in Calvary Methodist Episcopal Church, Keyport, New Jersey. The appointment was extended him as pastor of the Methodist Episcopal church at Fieldsboro in June, 1885, and he faithfully and earnestly served the people as their pastor until March 8, 1904, a record of nineteen years and nine months of continuous service. In August, 1904, he was appointed by Rev. J. B. Haines, D. D., the presiding elder of the New Brunswick district, under the authority of Bishop Cranston, to the church at Cranbury, New Jersey, to fill the vacancy caused by the death of the Rev. Henry M. Brown. He occupied that pulpit until March, 1906, since which time he has lived a retired life. During his long career as pastor, Rev. Carter has united in marriage one hundred and twelve couples, has officiated at the funeral services of one hundred and sixty-five persons and administered the rite of baptism to one hundred and eighty little ones. The political career of Rev. Carter is equally remarkable. In 1865 he was assessor of Bordentown township. He was a trustee of the public school, member of the common council, on the borough board of health and served as chief burgess of the borough of Fieldsboro. He was elected a member of the New Jersey house of representatives in November, 1879, re-elected in 1880 and again in 1881. He received the nomination for state senator in 1885 and was elected for three years. In 1888 he was re-elected. For honorable and valuable service he was appointed in May, 1895, by Governor George T. Werts, member of the board of prison inspection. He was reappointed by Governor Foster M. Voorhees in 1900 and again for a third term by Governor Franklin M. Murphy in 1905. He was appointed in 1894 by Governor Werts a member of the board of trustees of the Colored Industrial School. This was in the early days of that institution. He continued on the board until 1898, and did much to bring the standard of that growing institution to its present high position. He is a member of the board of education, custodian of the school funds and collector of taxes. His political faith is Republican. He is a member of the Ancient Order of United Workmen, his only fraternal society. This combined political, religious and business record is without parallel when length of service and achievement in each line is considered. Rev. Carter is still active and progressive in his ideas, just in all his dealings, bright and cheerful in disposition, a lover of children and devoted to his home and family ties. He enjoys all the comforts of his pretty home, known as "Walnut Shade," which overlooks the Delaware river. He is very hospitable, his doors being always open to his friends.

William H. Carter married (first) January 8, 1857, Elizabeth A. Shinn, daughter of Jonathan Shinn, of Pemberton, New Jersey. She bore him a daughter, Agnes, who died at the age of four years. Mrs. Carter died September 1, 1861. He married (second) July 8, 1863, Annie Terhune, daughter of Garrett Terhune, of Cranberry, Middlesex county, New Jersey. The children of this marriage were Edward, Sarah and Susan, all of whom died in infancy.

BOWEN John Garrison Bowen, son of Obediah Bowen, was born in Salem, New Jersey, October 15, 1833. He received a good common school education. He was engaged in farming, and being of a mechanical turn of mind worked at the trade of a carpenter and wheelwright, at which he became very proficient. When the war broke out he enlisted in the Tenth New Jersey, Company D, and served three years. He was wounded at the battle of Cold Harbor, Virginia, and taken prisoner. For nine months he was held prisoner at Danville, Virginia, and Andersonville, South Carolina, enduring all the horrors of that horrible den of suffering. After the war Mr. Bowen worked at his trade of wheelwright in South Jersey, and retired from business in 1909. He is a Prohibitionist in politics, and a member of the Methodist Episcopal Church. His fraternal membership is with the Knights of the Golden Eagle, and his patriotic in Joseph R. Ridgeway Post, Grand Army of the Republic, at Beverly, New Jersey.

He married (first) Elizabeth Loper, who bore him three children: 1. Charles, of Fairton, New Jersey. 2. Joseph, of Darby, Pennsylvania, 3. Harriet, of Bridgeton, New Jersey. He married (second) Amanda Stanix. Children of second marriage: 4. Walter L., publisher and editor of The New Era, Riverton, New Jersey; married Lela M., daughter of Charles F. Slater, of Palmyra, New Jersey. 5. William K., of Pittsfield, Massachusetts. 6. Earle, see forward. 7. John N., married Ida F. Shields, of Clayton, New Jersey. 8. Elizabeth, of Riverton, New Jersey, printer in office of her brother Walter L.

(II) Earle, son of John Garrison and Amanda (Stanix) Bowen, was born in Burlington, New Jersey, September 18, 1880. He was educated in the schools of Burlington and Camden, New Jersey. From 1896 until 1904 he was employed by his brother, Walter L., in his printing office at Riverton, New Jersey, where he gained an expert knowledge of the printing business in all its branches, as well as a good newspaper experience. In 1904 he purchased the newspaper plant of the Moorestown Republican, at Moorestown, New Jersey, and for five years edited and published the Republican. In 1909 he formed the Moorestown Printing Company, an incorporated stock company with a capital of $25,000, of which he is president. The company took over the printing and publishing business, but Mr. Bowen remained editor. He edits a Republican newspaper in fact as well as in name, the political complexion of the paper being in accord with his own personal conviction. He is a member of the Methodist Episcopal church, and an ardent Young Men's Christian Association worker in Moorestown. He holds fraternal connection with the Modern Woodmen of America, and Patriotic Order Sons of America. He married, in 1904, Laura B., daughter of Andrew L. and Isabelle E. Chamberlain, of Brooklyn, New York.

ACKERSON   The first of this family in America bore the name Thomaszen, and it is said by some authorities that his father first saw the country of Holland while taking part as a soldier in the "Thirty Years War," and was so pleased with the fertility of the soil and other features of the country that at the end of his enlistment he returned and there took up his abode, marrying a Holland maid. It is further stated that he was a native of Sweden. The records of the Old Dutch Church in New York show the name Thomaszen, but the founder of the family in America dropped this name and assumed the name of Eckerson, which is found in the Dutch records as Echons, Eekens, Eckes, Eckeson, Ekkisse, and even in other forms. Members of this family have been prominent in Bergen county almost from the first settlement when land was bought from the Tappan Indians, and have contributed largely to the development and improvement of the community which has been their home.

(I) Jan Thomaszen, given in New York Dutch records as j. m. Van de Manhattans, was born in Holland, about 1640, and emigrated to America about 1665, in which year he married and settled on a farm near the Bowery, not far from the present site of St. Mark's Church. About 1692 he assumed the name of Eckerson, which name has been used by the family ever since, although some of them have slightly changed the orthography and made it Ackerson. Jan Thomaszen married, November 8, 1665, Apollonia Cornelis, daughter of Cornelis Claeszen Swits and Ariaentie Cornelis, baptized October 25, 1648, and the births of their children were recorded in New York under the name of Thomaszen; they were twelve in number, as follows: Ariaentie, baptized February 16, 1667; Thomas, January 27, 1669; Cornelis; Sara, baptized October 4, 1673; Jan, February 9, 1676; Lysbeth, May 29, 1678; Margrietje, 1680; Cornelia, November 15, 1682; Rachel, April 11,

1685; Jannetje, November 2, 1687; and Maria and Anna, twins, September 6, 1690.

(II) Cornelis, or Cornelius, second son of Jan Thomaszen or Eckerson, was baptized in New Netherlands, now New York, April 9, 1671, and lived on the homestead of his father, near the Bowery, until 1718, when he removed with his wife and children to Bergen county, New Jersey, where he bought about three hundred acres of wooded land at Tappan, which he afterward added to by further purchases, and on this land he spent the remainder of his life, clearing and cultivating as he found expedient. He was married in the Old Dutch Church in New York City, August 24, 1693, to Willemtje Vlierboom, daughter of Judge Matthew Vlierboom, of Albany, and their children were: Jan, baptized June 26, 1695; Matthys, November 8, 1696; Jan, March 22, 1699; Cornelius; Jacob, baptized February 28, 1703; and Thomas, March 3, 1706.

(III) Cornelius (2), fourth son of Cornelius (1) and Willemtje (Vlierboom) Ackerson, was baptized January 12, 1701, at New York City, removed with his parents to Tappan, and there spent the remainder of his life. He married (first) in 1723, Maria Haring, who died in 1727, and (second) in 1728, Rachel Blauvelt; his children were: Garret C., Cornelius C., Willempie, Catherine, Maria, John, Abraham, Elizabeth, Rachel, Jacob, David and Matthew.

(IV) Garret C., eldest son of Cornelius (2) and Maria (Haring) Ackerson, was born March 7, 1724, died May 2, 1798. He married Maria Haring, born January 7, 1724, died December 22, 1798, and they resided at Tappan, where they had the following children: John, Maria, Cornelius, Rensye, Cornelius, Elizabeth, Margaret, Abrem G. and Brechie. Garret C. Ackerson purchased a large tract of land at Pascack, which he gave to his eldest son, John, and gave the homestead to his two younger sons, Cornelius and Abram, at his death.

(V) John, eldest son of Garret C. and Maria (Haring) Ackerson, was born in 1743, at Tappan, New Jersey, and died in 1837-38; he married Garritje Hogencamp, and they had two children, Garret and Hannah. The latter married Nicholas Zabriskie.

(VI) Garret, only son of John and Garritje (Hogencamp) Ackerson, was born in 1779, died in 1857. On his large farm he had a cotten mill, a distillery and a store, and he was a man of considerable prominence in the community. He served two terms in the state

Garret G. Ackerson

Garret A. Ackerson

legislature, and in the war of 1812 was major of the state militia, being stationed at Sandy Hook; after the war he became major-general of the northern militia of New Jersey, representing the three northern counties of Bergen, Essex and Morris. He married Hannah, daughter of John Hogencamp, whose ancestors lived in Rockland county, and they had the following children: John, Cornelius. Garret G. and James.

(VII) Garret G., third son of Garret and Hannah (Hogencamp) Ackerson, was born April 9, 1816, at Pascack, New Jersey, died December 12, 1891. After receiving his education in the public schools he helped his father in the management of his various enterprises, and when he had mastered the details of same took full charge of his interests until a few years after his marriage, when he removed to another farm and established his own woolen mill. In 1839, at the time Harrington township was separated into two divisions, one retaining the name Harrington, the other being called Washington township, Mr. Ackerson was elected assessor, which was his first public office; six years later he became county clerk, and retained this office six years, being elected by a large majority, and at this time removed from Pascack to Hackensack. He filled the office with great satisfaction to the public, and their trust was shown in him to the fullest extent by the manner in which they made him their banker and asked his advice upon their business ventures. He made his presence felt socially and politically, and soon after his removal to Hackensack was made chairman of the Democratic executive committee.

When but fifteen years of age, Mr. Ackerson became captain of a company of militia, and kept this rank for ten years, so that his experience in military affairs and tactics began early; during his occupation of the office of county clerk he organized a company of Continentals, taking his rank as captain of same, and later when an independent battalion was made up after a special act of the legislature, Captain Ackerson was elected lieutenant-colonel of same. In 1861 most of this battalion enlisted for war duty, and they made up the Twenty-second New Jersey Volunteers; Lieutenant-Colonel Ackerson being at the head of this movement filled the quota of soldiers allotted to Bergen county at this time.

Colonel Ackerson was interested in most of the enterprises of his native town and county that tended to the further development of local industries, and became one of the organ-

izers of the first railroad into Hackensack, which was named the Hackensack railroad; he was president of this road at its completion, and gave much time and money towards putting the venture on a paying basis, after which he relegated its management to others and turned his attention to commercial affairs. He was the second president of the Bergen County Bank, of which he was one of the organizers, and was connected with that institution until its close. In the winter of 1876-77, Colonel Ackerson was appointed judge of the court of common pleas by Governor Bedle, and filled the position with the same ability as the other ones he had filled. He was greatly respected, admired and loved by his friends and acquaintances, and was considered one of the most enterprising men of his county, as well as being a valuable citizen. He married, in 1837, Sophia, daughter of James I. and Martha (Wortendyke) Blauvelt, born July 4, 1820, died March 17, 1895, and they had two children, Garret and Martha. The latter became the wife of B. F. Randall, of Fall River, Massachusetts, and had a son Garret A., who died without issue.

(VIII) Garret, only son of Garret G. and Sophia (Blauvelt) Ackerson, was born September 15, 1840, at Pascack, New Jersey, died December 23, 1886. He received his education in the town of Hackensack, and in 1859 began the study of law in the office of Jacob R. Wortendyke, of Jersey City, being admitted to the bar in 1863. He then opened up a practice and settled in Hackensack, which he made his permanent home. He soon began to make his influence felt in business and political circles, and became one of the county and state leaders of the Democratic party. He was appointed judge-advocate of the Bergen county battalion of militia, in 1867, and in 1872 was elected captain of Company C, Second Battalion of National Guards, which was organized at this time, holding the latter rank three years, at which time he resigned. In 1879 he was appointed judge advocate general of the state of New Jersey by Governor George B. McClellan, his rank being that of colonel, and he held this office for several years. Colonel Ackerson was interested in many commercial enterprises, and helped greatly in the progress and development of his native county and state. He was for many years president of the Hackensack railroad, held a directorship in the New Jersey and New York railroad, also of the Hackensack improvement commission, was stockholder and trustee of the Hackensack Academy, and was a director as well as secretary and treasurer of the Bergen County Mutual Assurance Association for some time. He was given many political honors, but was not ambitious of office, and declined many of them, including the nomination for state senator and at another time for governor. In 1876 he was a delegate from the fourth congressional district to the National Democratic convention held at St. Louis, which nominated Samuel J. Tilden for the presidency. He served many years as chairman of the Bergen county Democratic executive committee. Colonel Ackerson was a man of engaging manners and conversation, and though a man of striking dignity and earnest demeanor, all who had dealings with him were attracted to him and desirous of securing his friendship. He was very active in the pursuit of his duties and never shirked his responsibilities.

He married, July 9, 1863, Ann Elizabeth, daughter of John A. and Mary (Anderson) Zabriskie. who died July 27, 1900, aged sixty-three. She was a descendant of Albrecht Zabriskie, or Sobieska, who emigrated to New Amsterdam from Prussia, in 1662, in the ship "Fox," and became the progenitor of a large number of descendants. Garret and Ann Elizabeth Ackerson had three children: John Z., James B. and Garret G., Jr. Further mention is made of all three.

(IX) John Zabriskie, eldest son of Garret and Ann Elizabeth (Zabriskie) Ackerson, was born April 12, 1864, died unmarried, December 15, 1900. He graduated from Columbia College in the class of 1886, and entered the law office of Hon. William M. Johnson, of Hackensack, and spent some time in study, after which he took a course in law at Columbia College, and returning to Hackensack entered into partnership with Mr. Johnson, which he was soon obliged to abandon on account of poor health. He was a young man of unusual promise, but was compelled to abandon his profession, and though he sought to regain his health was unable to do so and died of consumption.

(IX) James B., second son of Garret and Ann Elizabeth (Zabriskie) Ackerson, was born July 26, 1866, at Hackensack, New Jersey, where he received his early education, after which he took a chemical course in Columbia College. In 1885 Mr. Ackerson became chemist in the employ of Dundee Chemical Works at Passaic, and after filling various positions became superintendent of their plant. When the company was merged with the General Chemical Company, in 1899, Mr. Ackerson retained his position of superintendent of the Dundee plant, which he still fills. He is well informed in the line of his profession, and a recognized authority on same. He takes an interest in the welfare of the community, and is interested in public enterprises. He is governor of the General Hospital of Passaic, is director in the Passaic National Bank, and in his political views is Republican. He is a member of the Holland Society. He married, September 14, 1887, at Passaic, New Jersey, Mary B., daughter of John and Mary (Van Naerden) Ackerman, granddaughter of Judge Peter Ackerman, of Hackensack, New Jersey, and they have one child, a daughter, Bessie, born July 10, 1888, at Passaic.

(IX) Garret G. (2), third and youngest son of Garret and Ann Elizabeth (Zabriskie) Ackerson, was born January 10, 1876, at Hackensack. New Jersey, where he received his primary education, followed by a course at Packard's Business College, of New York City. In 1896 he entered the employ of the Dundee Chemical Works, at Passaic, by which company his brother James B. was employed, and remained three years, at which time the company was merged into the General Chemical Company, and he then became associated with the purchasing department of the latter, in New York City, which position is still held by him. He is an active and enterprising business man, who has the confidence of his employers and the good will of all who know him. Mr. Ackerson resides in Hackensack, where he is director of the Hackensack National Bank and president of the Golf Club. He is secretary of the Hackensack Hospital Association, and a member of the Holland Society. He married, October 24, 1899, at Hackensack, New Jersey, Anna Valburg, daughter of Gustave G. and Mary Jane (Kennedy) Beck, born August 5, 1875, and they have two children, born in Hackensack, namely: Edith Zabriskie, March 12, 1901, and Garret G., May 13, 1904.

STEELE

The heroic, patriotic and daring Scotch Covenanters, whose movements in behalf of freedom for religious opinion led to the disastrous revolution in Scotland that banished the covenanters, illuminated the pages of its history by their acts of martyrdom, to a spirit of independence that had been smouldering for generations.

This movement had among its noble advocates the clan of Steel, having its home in Lesmahagow, only seventeen miles from the seat of the ancient University of Glasgow, founded in 1451 by Bishop Turnbull, that had kept alive and been unobservedly the foster-mother of the movement for many years. In 1580 the first of the name in Lanarkshire that attracted attention appears to have been Robert Steel and his two sons, David and John Steel. "Waterhead," a beautiful and fertile farm near Lesmahagow, was owned by John, and like his father and his brother David, he was a prosperous landowner, David living at Skellyhill Farm, which estate remained in the possession of the family for over three hundred consecutive years.

David Steel had the proud distinction of meeting the death of a martyr and the incident is recorded in "Traditions of the Covenanters" written by Rev. Robert Simpson, as follows: "The Steels of Lesmahagow were men of renown and faithful witnesses to Jesus Christ. The death of David Steel, who was shot at Skellyhill in 1686 in the thirty-third year of his age, is in all its circumstances equally affecting with the death of John Brown at Priesthill. He was, after a promise of quarter, murdered before his own door; and Mary Weir, his youthful and truly christian wife, who it is said cherished an uncommon attachment for her husband, having bound up his shattered head with a napkin and closed down his eyelids with her own hand, looked upon the manly and honest countenance that was now pale in death and said with a sweet and heavenly composure: 'The archers have shot at the husband, but they cannot reach the soul; it has escaped like a dove, far away and is at rest.'" David Steel was shot by one Creichton, an officer under the command of Viscount Dundee, known in history as the "Bloody Claverhouse," who devastated Scotland as a follower and supporter of the exiled Stuarts. David Steel was buried at Lesmahagow in the same "God's Acre" in which repose the others of the family name and at Skellyhill a monument commemorating his martyrdom was erected.

Sir Walter Scott, Scotland's greatest novelist, gives an account of the event in "Chronicles of the Canongate," where he speaks of the victim, David Steel, as the "famous Covenanter" and Jonathan Swift "Dean Swift," the celebrated English author and satirist, designates him as "Steel the Covenanter."

Captain John Steel fought in the famous battles between the Covenanters and James, the Duke of Monmouth, at Drumelog and at Bothwell Bridge, June 14 and June 22, 1679, and with the other defeated Covenanters received the kind treatment accorded his foes by the "Protestant Duke" immediately after the defeat at Bothwell Bridge and his sword is preserved among the historic relics treasured by his descendants at Skellyhill.

The Covenanters could not, however, overcome the mistake made by the Stuarts and the Presbyterians themselves could not overcome disputes and dissensions in their own ranks, and finally the union between the Scottish and English Puritans was dissolved by the ascendency of the Independents and then came the opportunity for Cromwell to keep Scotland under subjection to the English army, and when Sharp, Archbishop of St. Andrews, their great dependence, changed from Presbyterianism, this movement being followed by his assassination, May 3, 1679, by a band of fanatical Covenanters, the revolution was in full force and was followed by the Covenanters seeking more peaceful homes in the north of Ireland. Here by intermarriage with the Irish, they built up that industrious and useful citizenship, commonly known as the Scotch-Irish people.

Among these refugees was a son of Captain John Steel, who became the pioneer of the family of Steels in Ireland, and his son, John Steel, named for his valiant grandfather, was the first of the name to claim Ireland as his birthplace. They settled in Fanet, county Donegal, on the shores of Mulroy bay. This John Steel was born in Fanet in 1735 and after his marriage removed to Crevaugh in the same county, where he died in 1804. Members of the family this settled in Ireland found newer and more favorable homes in America before and during the period of the American revolution and immediately after that event. Among them was the famous fighting Presbyterian patriot, the Rev. Captain John Steel, who reached the shores of America in 1752 and settled in Cumberland county, Pennsylvania. John Steel's own son Alexander established an iron foundry in Huntingdon county, Pennsylvania, and another son William, became a merchant and politician in the same county and also went as a soldier in the American revolution.

After leaving Scotland the Steel family may be classed as immigrants and the immigrant to Ireland to be of the third generation from Robert Steel, born before 1580, who had two sons David, born 1654, died 1686, a martyr, and Captain John Steel, whose son, name unknown, settled in the north of Ireland and became the father of John Steel, who, as being born outside of Scotland, we place as the immigrant ancestor of the Steels of Ireland and America, but in the fourth generation, placing Robert Steel as (I), Captain John Steel as (II); and unknown name as (III).

(IV) John, grandson of Captain John Steel for whom he was named and grandnephew of David, the martyr, and Mary (Weir) Steel, was born in Panet, county Donegal, Ireland, 1735, died in Creevaugh, county Donegal, Ireland, in 1804. He married Sarah Stewart and they had five children born in Ireland, as follows: John, Alexander, Samuel, William, David, see forward.

(V) David, youngest son of John and Sarah (Stewart) Steel, was born in Creevaugh, county Donegal, Ireland, 1764, died in 1807. He married Sarah Gailey McKinley (1675-1836), and they had seven children all born in Ireland as follows: 1. Andrew, 1794. 2. Samuel, 1706, died 1836; married Mary Boggs. 3. James, died in infancy. 4. James, see forward. 5. Stewart (1800-1861); married (first) M. Murray and (second) Myrtella Irvine. 6. David (1803-1887); removed to America and settled in Adams county, Ohio, where he was one of the foremost exponents of the Covenanters faith in the United States. 7. Sarah (1804-1895); married a Stevenson.

(VI) James, fourth son of David and Sarah Gailey (McKinley) Steel, was born in the north of Ireland in 1798, died in 1863. He married Eleanor Fulton, of Gortanleare, county Donegal, and they lived at Altaghaderry, near Londonderry, Ireland, where their only son David was born. He married as his second wife Jane Osborn. He was a farmer and a respected elder in the Covenanters church at Waterside, Londonderry.

(VII) David (2), only child of James and Eleanor (Fulton) Steel, was born in Atlaghaderry, near Londonderry, Ireland, October 20, 1826. His mother, who was a relative of Robert Fulton, the inventor and builder of the steamboat "Claremont," that made the first voyage of any vessel propelled by steam between New York and Albany on the Hudson river in 1807, died in 1828 and his father married as his second wife Jane Osborn. David Steel was brought up by his step-mother on his father's farm, and he was fortunate in having so godly a woman to care for him and a bond of affection bound the two together which was

of great benefit to the lad. His early education was under the direction of his step-mother and from her he passed to the Classical Academy at Londonderry, where he learned rapidly and where the history of his place of nativity was taught on the playgrounds of the school, the walls of which had been the defence of the Covenanters against the siege of 1688. The atmosphere of his boyhood days was thoroughly impreganated with the spirit of piety, filial affection, devotion to church and home worship, strict obserance of the holy Sabbath and of the days of thanksgiving and fasting.

Of his peculiar advantages his biographer writes as follows: "These favorable providential surroundings were owned of God and used by His Spirit in due time to lead him to an intelligent decision in the matter of personal religion and open confession of Jesus Christ, and the solemn assumption of the obligation of his covenant relationship to God, and the participation in all the sacred responsibilities and blessed privileges of communicant membership in the church of his father. He was seventeen years old when he made a public profession of his faith in Jesus Christ and entered upon the responsibilities of church membership. Among the Covenanters, a newly made male member of the church was expected to conduct the devotions at the next neighborhood prayer-meeting—'to take the books' as it was termed. About the same time he became deeply interested in the Sabbath School work, serving for a time as a teacher and subsequently as superintendent. He also manifested a deep interest in the cause of Foreign Missions—prophesy of his interest in later years and which became one of the conspicous figures of his ministerial life. The salvation of the heathen world was a matter, which bulked largely in his progress, and to which he devoted much of his means and energies. He had a clear vision and watched with intelligent interest the signs of the times concerning Zion. As an evidence of this, at the very beginning of his career as a communicant member of the church, he took deep interest in the controversy, which agitated the Reformed Presbyterian Church in Ireland respecting civil affairs. Hitherto all Covenanters held to the view that they were not warranted in taking an active part in civil affairs, because Jesus Christ was not recognized as He should be as the King and Head of the nation. In this controversy, Reverend John Paul and Reverend Thomas Houston were the representatives, respectively, of the new view and the old conservative position. Doctor Paul, by his powerful and incisive argument, made a deep impression upon Dr. Steele's mind, and he ever afterwards took his stand on the side of liberty of conscience, holding to the position that the question of civil duty should be no longer a subject for church discipline, but be left to the individual conscience. This decision no doubt determined him in identifying himself in his final preparations for the ministry, and in his subsequent ministerial activities with the General Synod in the United States, as holding similar views in regard to civil responsibility and activity. This decision was not announced until he had reached mature years, although the thought was in his heart and awaited God's providence to confirm it and to clearly open up the way before him. · At fourteen years of age, not having as yet definitely decided as to his calling in life, he revealed considerable skill in agricultural pursuits. He developed special aptitude in the use of the plough, ability in this direction being the ambitions of many of the farmers' sons of the neighborhood. Ploughing matches were held from time to time and as a witness to his skill, he obtained as prizes, two beautiful silver cups, which even in his later years, he exhibited with commendable pride. During these days on the farm his studies were to a considerable extent kept up, and his store of knowledge increased and his power developed by systematic and extensive reading. He continued his life on the farm until he was twenty-seven years of age, when he finally decided to give himself to the ministry. At this time he was in possession of one of the best farms in the neighborhood, the gift of his father, and with every promise of worldly prosperity."

In 1853, his uncle, the Rev. Dr. David Steele, who lived in Adams county, Ohio, visited Ireland and induced him, much against the wishes of his father, who saw a brilliant agricultural career before him if he remained in his native land, .to take up the work of the ministry in America. He overcame paternal opposition and arrived in Philadelphia, October 1, 1853, spent his first Sabbath morning in attendance at the Second Reformed Presbyterian Church (O. S.) of which the Rev. Dr. S. O. Wylie was pastor. He continued his journey the next week to Ohio and was welcomed to the home of his uncle, who had no children, where he took up the study for the ministry. Dr. David Steele was a fine classical scholar and under his tuition David (2) was soon ready for matriculation at Miami Uni-

versity, Oxford, Ohio. He passed his preparatory examination with brilliant promise which was fulfilled when he graduated A. B. in 1857 with the classical honors in a class of thirty-six graduates. Among his classmates were Henry M. McCracken, who became president of the New York University, and Dr. John S. Billings, the present librarian of the New York Public Library; Benjamin Harrison, who afterwards became president of the United States, and Whitelaw Reid, United States embassador to Great Britain, were undergraduates at the time, but not his classmates.

He taught in Cynthiana Academy in Kentucky on leaving the University, 1857-58, and occupied the chair of Greek in Miami University as a substitute for Professor Elliott, who went abroad, and at the same time had charge of an elective class in Hebrew in the University, 1858-59. He received his master degree from Miami University in 1859 without waiting the usual three years. He took his course in theology at the Theological Seminary of the Reformed Presbyterian Church (general synod) in Philadelphia, his preceptors being Doctors McLeod and Wylie. He was licensed to preach in 1860 and graduated B. D. in March, 1861. He received his first call to a pastorate from the Fifteenth Presbyterian Church in Philadelphia, followed by one from the Reformed Presbyterian Church at Cedarville, Ohio, and one from the Third Reformed Presbyterian Church in Belfast, Ireland. All of these calls he declined to accept a call from a new organization of eighty-nine members, most of whom had withdrawn from the Fifteenth Street Church in Philadelphia and were worshiping in a hall. He was ordained and installed pastor of this new flock organized on June 6, 1861, and in 1862 the church consolidated with the Fourth Reformed Presbyterian Church, which latter name was retained by the two united congregations. Dr. Steele became pastor of the re-enforced Fourth Reformed Presbyterian Church, and in October, 1890, the congregation removed to their commodious and beautiful church edifice, where the labors of the eminent pastor were abundantly successful, but were terminated by his death, June 15, 1906, after a continuous charge of forty-five years, the only pastoral charge ever held by him. During his pastorate he held the chair of Hebrew, Greek, and pastoral theology in the Reformed Presbyterian Theological Seminary, 1863-1875, and of doctrinal theology, 1875-1906.

During the civil war he served in the United States christian commission in ministering to the wants of the soldiers in camp in 1862. He was moderator of the general synod of the Reformed Presbyterian church, 1868-86, and president of the board of missions, 1883-1906. He attended the Presbyterian Alliance Council as a delegate at Philadelphia in 1880 and at Glasgow, Scotland, in 1896. He visited the missions of the church in northern India in 1896, having previously made tours of the old world, 1873-1884, and 1892. His scholastic honors were: D. D. from Rutgers College in 1866 and LL. D. from Miami University in 1900. He served as editor of the *Reformed Presbyterian Advocate*, 1867-77, and is the author of "Times in Which We Live and the Ministry They Require" (1871); "Endless Life and the Inheritance of the Righteous" (1873); "Elements of Ministerial Success" (1884); "The Two Witnesses" (1887); "A Nation in Tears" (1881); "The House of God's Glory" (1893); "The Wants of the Pulpit" (1894); "Christ's Coronation" (1897); "History of the Reformed Presbyterian Church in North America" (1898); "Personal Religion" (1898); "On Reading the Scriptures" (1901); "Our Martyred Chief" (1901). He served as a member of the executive council of the Presbyterian Historical Society; of the Archæological Society of the University of Pennsylvania, and was elected a life member of the Pennsylvania Bible Society and Sabbath Association of Philadelphia.

He married, January 19, 1864, Elizabeth J., second daughter of Samuel and Martha (Mc-Millan) Dallas, of Greene county, Ohio; granddaughter of Judge James Dallas, of Champagne county, Ohio, and of Daniel and Janet (Chestnut) McMillan, and great-granddaughter of Captain James Chestnut, of Chester county, South Carolina, who fought in the American revolution under General Washington. The children of Rev. Dr. David and Elizabeth J. (Dallas) Steele were born in Philadelphia, Pennsylvania, as follows: 1. James Dallas, see forward. 2. Martha Eleanor, who in 1909 was residing with her widowed mother in Philadelphia, unmarried.

(VIII) James Dallas, eldest child and only son of the Rev. Dr. David and Elizabeth J. (Dallas) Steele, was born in Philadelphia, Pennsylvania, November 6, 1864. He was prepared for college under the direction of his learned father. He was a pupil in the Philadelphia public schools and at the Langton Select Academy, the best preparatory school of

Philadelphia. He was graduated at the University of Pennsylvania, A. B., 1884; A. M., 1887, and after a post-graduate course of three years, B. D., 1891. His college honors were the prize for Greek prose composition in his freshman year and the Latin essay prize in the senior year. He was a student-at-law in the office of J. Sergent Price, Esq., in Philadelphia, 1884, and at the same time matriculated in the law school of the University of Pennsylvania, where he was graduated LL. B., 1886. He practiced law in Philadelphia, 1886-90, but his desire to enter the christian ministry overcame the allurements of successful practice at the legal bar, and in 1887 he began theological studies at the Theological Seminary in which his father was a professor, and he was graduated in 1891, but continued a post-graduate course in the University of Pennsylvania, where he obtained his degree of Bachelor of Divinity in 1891, having received the Masters degree in course in 1887. He was installed pastor of the First Reformed Presbyterian Church, located on West Twelfth street, New York City, on April 16, 1891, being the fifth pastor of the church. He resigned after a successful pastorate of fifteen years, March 1, 1906, having accepted a call to become pastor of the First Presbyterian Church of Passaic, New Jersey, and he was installed March 4, 1906, being the second pastor of that church. Besides his pastoral work he contributes regularly to religious magazines and church periodicals. He was made a member of the American Oriental Society in 1892, and is also a member of the American Historical Association.

He married, December 8, 1898, Emma, daughter of Robert and Eliza (Nightingale) Abbott, of New York City; they have no children. Their home is in Passaic, New Jersey, at No. 15 Grove Terrace.

BENJAMIN   The Benjamin family of Maryland, to which belongs the line we are now considering, is so far as America is concerned entirely distinct from the families of Richard Benjamin, of Southold, Long Island, John Benjamin, of Cambridge and Watertown, Massachusetts, and the Hon. Judah Philip Benjamin, of Louisiana, all three of whom are at the head of distinct genealogical lines in this country that have spread out into New Jersey territory. Like the three last mentioned families, the Benjamins of Maryland, however, trace their origin back to English soil; and it is not at all improbable that the ancestries converge to a common progenitor on that ground—a constant English tradition —although the Maryland family in regard to emigration holds a position midway between the seventeenth century coming of Richard and John, and the nineteenth century advent of Judah Philip Benjamin's father and family.

(I) Joseph Benjamin, born in 1750, progenitor of the Maryland family, was the son of a well-to-do English yeoman. In 1774, lured probably by the "call of the wild" and the brilliant prospects held before the eyes of those courageous spirits who should venture forth into the new world, he emigrated to America and settled in Maryland. In the following year, 1775, he went to Virginia with the intention of making that colony his permanent residence; but before he had finally made up his mind where he would locate himself, the war between Great Britain and her American colonies broke out; and while he was in Amelia county finding that Major, afterwards Lieutenant-colonel Theodoric Bland was forming a regiment of cavalry, he enlisted in it and was assigned to Captain Henry, popularly called "Light horse Harry" Lee's troop, from which he was afterwards transferred to Captain Peyton's troop of the same regiment, in which he served throughout the war; at the close of which he was ranked as trumpeter for in 1820, when he applied for and was granted a pension for his services by congress. (See executive papers of the sixteenth congress, first session, volume 4, January 20, 1820) he is recorded as being the "trumpeter of Lee's legion of Maryland troops."

After the revolutionary war was over, Joseph Benjamin married and settled down finally in Charlestown, Cecil county, Maryland, where he became not only an influential citizen but also one of the founders and first trustees of the Methodist church in that place. He is also said to have operated a ferry across the mouth of the Susquehanna river; and a pleasing tradition among the family is that during one of his campaigns he stopped at a farm house where he saw a comely young woman milking and asked her for a drink of water. He received, however, a generous draught of milk which he paid for with the promise, "When the war is over I am coming back to marry you." By Miss Winchester, the maiden of the above tradition, Joseph Benjamin had three sons, George, William, Isaac, treated below.

(II) Isaac, youngest son of Joseph and

—— (Winchester) Benjamin, was born in Cecil county, but removed later on in life to Talbot county, where he held for some time the position of sheriff. He was a soldier in the war of 1812, a farmer, and he must have been a man of considerable property and business ability as he was one of the contractors with the federal government for carrying the mails between Washington and Philadelphia, an obligation which in those days of stage coaches and post horses involved a heavy outlay and investment. Isaac Benjamin's wife was Grace, daughter of Abraham Alexander. Her father was born in North Carolina, and in early life was a magistrate of Mechlenburg county, which he represented in the colonial legislature until 1775. On May 31 of this year he served as the chairman of the county convention which passed a series of resolutions that later on became distorted into the famous "Mechlenburg declaration of independence." The facts of the case appear to be as follows: On April 30, 1819, the *Register* of Raleigh, North Carolina, published what purported to be a copy made from memory of resolutions passed by the Mechlenburg convention on May 20, 1775, and afterwards destroyed by fire. Certain phrases in this published copy are similar to passages in the Declaration of Independence of July 4, 1776, and caused doubt as to the authenticity of the Mechlenburg declaration to arise. In 1831, the North Carolina legislature, after an investigation of the subject, declared May 20th a legal holiday. Since then there has been a detailed and prolonged controversy in regard to the two sets of resolutions, the weight of authority at present being overwhelmingly against the authenticity of the "Declaration" and in favor of the opinion that only one meeting was held, that of May 31, and that the resolutions there adopted, bearing no resemblance to Jefferson's Declaration, constitute the nearest approach there was to a "Mechlenburg Declaration of Independence."

Isaac and Grace (Alexander) Benjamin had seven sons, six of whom held commissions in the United States army and were killed in battle, two in the Mexican war and four others in the civil war. The remaining son, Justus, is treated below.

(III) Justus, son of Isaac and Grace (Alexander) Benjamin, was born in Maryland. When a young man he was in his father's employ, carrying mails until the railroads absorbed that interest. He then worked on a farm which was also operated by his father.

Later he was employed by the P. W. & B. railroad, and at the time of his death was officially employed by that company. He was accidentally killed between Elkton and Perryville, 1894. He married Anna Elizabeth Dobson. Children: 1. William T., killed in the battle of Five Forks. 2. Mary A., married George Wainwright, who died from injuries received while in the civil war. 3. Sarah C., married George H. Haines, who also died from injuries received in the federal service during the civil war. 4. Dowling, treated below.

(IV) Dowling, son of Justus and Anna Elizabeth (Dobson) Benjamin, was born January 23, 1849, in Baltimore, Maryland. For his early education he attended the public schools of Maryland, Pennsylvania and Delaware. He then took up the study of classic and oriental literatures with private tutors, when he qualified for entrance in the sophomore class in Dickinson College. In 1867 he began the study of pharmacy in Chester, Pennsylvania, and in 1872 entered the office of J. H. Jamer, M. D., of Port Deposit, Maryland, having passed a successful examination before the board of pharmacy of Maryland. Here he remained until the spring of 1874 when he became a student under Dr. J. M. Ridge, of Camden, New Jersey, with whom he studied until the following October when he entered the medical department of the University of Pennsylvania from which he graduated with the highest honors in 1877. In 1876 Dr. Benjamin was chosen as delegate from the Camden Pharmaceutical Society to the convention of the American Association of Pharmacists; and August 27, 1879, he was elected a member of the American Academy of Natural Science.

In 1878, as medical expert for counsel of the defense in the Emma Bethel murder case. Dr. Benjamin demonstrated before the court for the first time in legal history, by chemical analysis and the microscope, although Professor Wormley, the great microchemist, had made and published the fact a few months before, in flat contradiction to all the statements of the text books and of medical jurisprudence, that the octohedral crystal was not conclusive evidence of the presence of arsenic but might be due to the presence of at least one other metal, namely antimony.

In 1884 he successfully urged before the National Medical Association in Washington, in the face of strong opposition, that the association should proclaim officially the necessity for there being a full three years course in all medical colleges. After a two years fight the New Jersey State Medical Society adopted a similar resolution to this effect, asking for the appointment of a state board of examiners, but voted down a resolution. Dr. Benjamin undefeated, however, gathered the friends of such a board and acted as their spokesman before the senate committee which was appointed to prepare the bill subsequently passed in 1900 which provided for a state board of medical examiners. This ended his fifteen years of hard fighting for the protection of the public from medical incompetents. Dr. Benjamin was offered but refused a position on this board because he was at the time a lecturer in the Medica-chirugical College of Philadelphia, and he had opposed during the preparation of the bill the appointment on the board of any one interested in a medical college. It is worthy of note that New Jersey was the first state to establish a board of medical examiners and to Dr. Benjamin, with the assistance and co-operation of Dr. Perry Watson and others, belongs the honor of forcing its establishment.

In 1886 Dr. Benjamin published in the *Medical Bulletin* his paper on "Observations on the Relations of Temperature to Diseases in Dwelling Houses." This article was published by the *Scientific American* and many of the leading medical and lay journals; and the state board of health of Iowa and a number of other states had it reprinted in pamphlet form at the expense of the state for free distribution. In 1888 he performed the first successful operation for hysterectomy, i. e., the removal of the entire womb and ovaries, made in New Jersey. In 1889, during the great typhoid epidemic in Philadelphia, at the request of the *Philadelphia Inquirer*, he published a long article in that paper on the disease and its prevention and cure. On October 17, 1896, Dr. Benjamin published in the Journal of the American Medical Association his now famous paper on the treatment of diphtheria, which inaugurated a revolution in the treatment of that disease, and in which he showed that he had had no death from it during ten years of treatment with his antiseptic method. Dr. Benjamin was the only expert in America whose testimony was sent in the Maybrick case through the department of state. United States, and Mrs. Maybrick personally thanked Dr. Benjamin for the decision he rendered in her behalf.

On October 23, 1897, he was chosen chairman of the committee on celebration of the battle of Red Bank, by the New Jersey Society of the Sons of the American Revolution, which was holding its meeting in Camden. This celebration was successfully carried out and a suitable monument erected on the battle field which was unveiled with appropriate ceremonies. In the following year, during the war with Spain, the New York World engaged him to make a special investigation from a scientific point of view of the army and camp at Montauk Point with special reference to the presence and prevention of typhoid germs. In 1900 he introduced into the New Jersey legislature the bill for daily medical inspection of pupils and monthly sanitary inspection of school houses. In December, 1908, Dr. Benjamin published a most able and surgical article advocating the establishment of a national department, having control over the physical and moral diseases of the people. This was endorsed by President Roosevelt, who in his message to congress urged that jurisdiction in these matters be given to one of the existing boards of national control.

By far the greatest contribution which Dr. Benjamin has made both to medical science and to the wellbeing of his fellowman is due to his interest in bacteriological pathology. For his graduation thesis in 1877 he took the topic "Infection and antiseptic practice," and boldly stated therein his theories in favor of the germ theory of many diseases. The faculty of the university endorsed his thesis as "the first clear, logical and convincing presentation of the germ theory by an American medical writer"; but it was refused publication by all the medical journals of that day because the theories advanced were so radical and novel. The "International Cyclopedia of Surgery," however, says, volume 1, page 599, that the thesis changed the views of the professor of medical practice at the university who had until then been strongly opposed to the germ theory, but that from that date as strongly advocated it.

Dr. Benjamin has been for many years surgeon of the Pennsylvania railroad, of the W. J. and C. A. railroad, of the Camden Iron Works and of the Cooper Hospital. In 1897 he was appointed obstetrician of the maternity department and gynæcologist of the Cooper Hospital; for two years he was assistant surgeon of the Sixth Regiment, and later surgeon and major of the veteran corps of the same regiment of the New Jersey National Guard; for some time he has been lecturer on obstetrics in the New Jersey Training School for Nurses. He is president of the State Sanitary Association of New Jersey; president of the Camden District Medical Society, member of the State Medical Society, and delegate for his state in the national and international conventions. On April 24, 1893, he became a member of the New Jersey Sons of the American Revolution, and he has been a delegate to and vice-president of the New Jersey Republican convention. He has also been a voluminous writer to the various medical journals, and has besides published a novel entitled "Fordwell Graham, or Lost and Won by the Hand of the Dead," put on the market by Allen, Lane & Scott.

Dr. Benjamin's services to the city of Camden besides those to the state and nation deserve special mention. The substitution of pure Artesian water for the foul water of the Delaware river which the city was furnishing its citizens as a water supply was directly attributable to the efforts of the medical fraternity of the city, and in the fight Dr. Benjamin contributed largely of time, influence and pen. In the securing of the Carnegie gift of $125,000 for the Camden Public Library Dr. Benjamin succeeded after all others had failed, and this magnificent institution is as much a personal monument to him as it is to the generosity of Mr. Carnegie.

In 1879 Dr. Benjamin married Sarah Cooper White, a lineal descendant of Edwin Marshall, of Pennsylvania, who has borne him three children: 1. Helen V., married Daniel Birdsall. 2. Ada E. 3. Sarah, married Frank Bibighaus.

WOODRUFF

The Woodruffs of West New Jersey are descendants of that family somewhat prominent in the history of Worsetshire, England, and devout members of the established church. The progenitor of the American branch was John Woodruffe, of Worcestershire, who had a son Thomas, the American immigrant.

(I) Thomas Woodrooffe, (as he spelled the name), son of John Woodruffe, of Worcestershire, England, was born there about 1630. He was a tailor by trade and occupation, and affiliated with the Society of Friends when that sect began their work of proseliting the members of the Established Church and became a follower of the "new thought" and "the new life." He married Edith, daughter of Joseph Wyatt, who located a large tract of land in the township of Mannington at the first settlement of the province of West Jersey. Thomas and Edith Woodruffe removed from Worcestershire, England, to London, where they had several children born to them, including: Thomas, Edith, John and Joseph. With his wife and four children he left London in 1678 with one man servant, Allen Hanway, and Hanway's sister, being children of Leonard Hanway, of Weymouth, England. The party set sail for America in the ship "Surray," Captain Stephen Nichols, master, and on the voyage another child was born at sea and named Mary. They arrived at the mouth of the Delaware river and proceeded up the bay to Salem, the first settlement already formed by Fenwick. They went ashore in the fourth month of 1679. Fenwick's agents gave to Thomas Woodrooffe two lots next to William Williamson, each of ten acres, he receiving title to the last lot January 18, 1685-86. He had already served as sheriff of the county in 1682, and was a man of influence. He consented to the "Consessions and Arguments of West Jersey" on March 3, 1676, which secured a formal constitution for the safety of the province and the proper observation of the few laws that were framed to govern the peaceful people. He cultivated his land as well as carrying on his trade as tailor, as was described, June 9, 1694, as "a yeoman of Salem, late of London" in a transfer of land in Burlington county, of which he was owner. In 1697 he deeded two lots of ten acres each in Salem to Ebenezer Dorbey (Derby), of Boston, New England, mariner. These were probably the lots allotted to him in 1679 by the Fenwick agents. His will dated August 17, 1699, names his son Joseph as his heir, and daughters as dead; and names his legatees: Son John Woodrooffe; William Hull; Benjamin Knapton; Daniel Smith, and servant Magdaline, liberated. His son Joseph died before taking possession of the estate and the will provided for this by passing it to Jonathan Beere and after him to his son John Beere to have it. A codicil to this will was made October 30, 1699, in which the testator reduces the legacy to his son John and revokes that to Daniel Smith it having been paid and the servant manumitted. This will is written as a manuscript map of New Jersey and the instrument was probated March 2, 1703-04. which approximately fixes the date of death of Thomas Woodroffe, the progenitor. The children of Thomas and Edith (Wyatt) Woodrooffe were born in the order following: 1. Thomas. 2. Edith. 3. John, see forward. 4. Mary. 5.

Joseph, on whose estate letters of administration were granted June 19, 1709, and Thomas Hayward, his principal creditor was made administrator. Thomas, Edith, Mary, and Joseph apparently died before their father and mother and with them were probably buried in Salem, their only home in America.

(II) John, second son and third child of Thomas and Edith (Wyatt) Woodrooffe, was born in London, England, or possibly Worsetshire, before 1675. He married and probably located in Burlington county, where there was a large society of Friends, and where his father owned land at one time during his active life. He appears on the records of West Jersey as having joined other citizens of Burlington county, May 12, 1701, petitioning the King for a confirmation of the appointment of Alexander Hamilton for governor at which time he (John Woodroffe) was a member of the house of representatives from Burlington county. He had children, the eldest being John, see forward.

(III) John (2) eldest son of John (1) Woodrooffe, the member of the provincial legislature of New Jersey, 1701, was probably born in Burlington county, New Jersey, about 1700. He married, about 1725, and the date of his death was May, 1755. Among his children was John, see forward.

(IV) John (3), son of John (2) Woodrooffe, was born in Burlington county, New Jersey. He probably removed to Cohansey precinct, Cumberland county, New Jersey, where he married and had a family whose descendants still have homes there. John Woodruffe died in Cumberland county, New Jersey, in May, 1755.

(V) David, son of John (3) Woodruffe, was born in Cumberland county, New Jersey, in 1748, died there July 3, 1822. He had a son David, who was a private soldier in the American revolution credited from Cumberland county, New Jersey, and also served in Captain Allen's company of the New Jersey Line recruited in Cumberland county. After the close of the war he settled in Hopewell, Bridgeton township, Cumberland county, New Jersey, where his son Daniel M. was born in 1780 was at one time sheriff of Cumberland county; clerk of the county; judge of the court of common pleas and for many years auctioneer of Bridgeton and who lived to be over ninety years of age. Another son Israel, see forward.

(VI) Israel, son of David Woodruff, the soldier in the American revolution, was born in

John J. Brown

Hopewell, Burlington township, Cumberland county, New Jersey, November 9, 1802. He married, 1822, Rachel S., daughter of William Reeves, of Salem county, New Jersey. Had four children: Adoniram, Isaac D., Elizabeth T., William R.

(VII) Adoniram Smith, son of IsraelWoodruff, was born in Dutch Neck or Hopewell township, Cumberland county, New Jersey, May 14, 1823, died March 10, 1893. He married Katharine Ott, daughter of George W. and Susannah (Hitchner) Ott, born June 5, 1826, died March 9, 1903, and they had four children: Elizabeth, Hester, Susan, and Albert S., see forward.

(VIII) Albert Smith, son of Adoniram Smith and Katharine (Ott) Woodruff, was born at Dutch Neck, Hopewell township, New Jersey, January 13, 1859, died March 2, 1886. He married Eliza Josephine, daughter of —— Foster.

(IX) Albert Smith (2), only child of Albert Smith (1) and Eliza Josephine (Foster) Woodruff, was born at Dutch Neck, Hopewell township, New Jersey, April 15, 1886. He was educated at the public school at Elmer and in the South Jersey Institute at Bridgeton. He took a business course at the Camden Commercial College in 1905. Meantime he took up the study of law in the Temple University Law School, Philadelphia, Pennsylvania, graduating in June, 1909, March 11, 1908, had been examined and admitted to the New Jersey bar as an attorney, and became a partner in the law firm of Beacon & Woodruff, with offices at 206 Market street, Camden, New Jersey, the senior partner of the firm being George M. Beacon. His fraternal affiliation is with Elmer Council, Junior Order of United American Mechanics, founded in 1853. His political affiliation is with the Republican party; his church membership with the Presbyterian denomination, and his professional association with the Camden Bar Association.

_____

BROWN — John Brown, first of this family to come to America, was born August 10, 1783, at Harddabon, Hertfordshire, England. He landed in Boston, Massachusetts, November 14, 1806. He married, May 9, 1816, in Philadelphia, Pennsylvania, Ann Jackson, born February 3, 1793, at Macclesfield, Cheshire, England, and landed in Philadelphia, Pennsylvania, July 15, 1800. Among their children was John Jackson, see forward.

(II) John Jackson Brown, late of Paterson, New Jersey, business man and banker, son of John and Ann (Jackson) Brown, was born in New York City, February 13, 1817, died in Paterson, July 23, 1894, after a long, honorable and successful career, a record of achievement such as is the good fortune of comparatively few men. When five years old he came to Paterson with his parents, leaving New York on account of an epidemic of yellow fever which prevailed for a considerable time in that city. His father was engaged in a general grocery and provision business, and was himself a man of sterling qualities and high character. The son attended the common schools of the then village until he was about thirteen years old, and afterward found employment as clerk in a dry goods store, remaining there for the next four years. In 1834 he went to New York City and secured a position as clerk with a manufacturer of caps and furs; but unfortunately his employer failed in business, and this event prevented Mr. Brown from starting in business on his own account as he had intended. He returned to Paterson, and again became clerk in a dry goods store, and a few years afterward succeeded to the grocery business formerly conducted by his father. This he continued with gratifying success until 1844, when he decided to abandon that trade and open a general dry goods establishment in the city, with which business he was more familiar, and which was more in accordance with his inclination, and for the next twenty-three years he was reckoned among the leading men of Paterson in mercantile pursuits. In 1867 he sold out his interest to Mr. G. C. Cooper.

About this time the First National Bank, of Paterson, which had been organized in 1864, became financially involved to the extent that its charter was in danger of being revoked, but through the efforts of Mr. Brown a radical reorganization was affected, capital was invested, and he was elected its president, an office he held until the time of his death. To show something of his capacity as executive officer of the reorganized bank it may be mentioned that when he entered upon his official duties, October 1, 1864, the resources of the institution aggregated the sum of $149,135.80, and on July 18, 1894, the resources amounted to $2,327,215.95. But it was not alone as managing officer of the First National Bank that Mr. Brown's superior business qualities displayed themselves to such splendid advantage and gave him such enviable prominence in financial circles, for it was chiefly through his efforts that the Paterson Savings Institution was incorporated and organized, and opened its doors for business on May 1, 1869. On May 1st of the following year the savings deposit account amounted to $104,442.67, and at the time of his death the total deposits were in excess of $4,000,000, with a surplus account of $445,000, while at the same time the bank had more than sixteen thousand five hundred depositors. At the time of his death he was treasurer of the Passaic Water Company, with which he had been identified since its organization. He also was one of the guiding spirits in the incorporation and organization of Cedar Lawn Cemetery Association, 1866-67, the plotting its extensive lands for the cemetery tract, and during his connection with the association he served in the capacity of director, vice-president and president. In the inception of the Paterson Board of Trade he also figured as one of its organizers, and afterward, so long as he lived, took an active part in promoting its usefulness as a factor in the mercantile and industrial life of the city. He was largely instrumental in securing for Paterson the splendid system of parks which add to the adornment of the city and contribute to the comfort of its people.

"As a public spirited citizen," says one of Mr. Brown's biographers, "ready to assume the responsibilities of office, his life's principle not to shirk any duty was his guiding star. At almost the very organization of Paterson as a city he was chosen one of the board of aldermen, and while absent in Europe was again elected to that office by the people. In 1854 he was elected first mayor of Paterson, and after serving his term steadfastly refused a renomination. During his incumbency of that office he projected and carried into effect measures for paving the sidewalks of the city, which before then had been almost entirely neglected; and it was during his connection with the city government that the first sewer was constructed. In 1856 he was induced to accept a nomination for a seat in the legislature of the state, the first candidate of the then newly organized Republican party. He served throughout the term for which he was elected, but positively refused renomination. During the civil war he united with several other prominent citizens of Paterson in the erection of the building known as the 'Wigwam,' which soon became the rallying place for the loyal people of the city. It's motto. 'Free Soil, Free Speech, and Free Men,' became a famous slogan throughout the region. Mr. Brown was an earnest member of the First Baptist Church of Pater-

son. He contributed liberally to the fund for the erection of the house of worship, and served both as chairman and treasurer of the building committees in charge of the work. In his own home he was a delightful and most entertaining host, as well as an interesting conversationalist. He travelled extensively, was a keen observer of men and events, and in his manner frank, generous, genial, with the same greeting for all who came to him; and he was no respector of persons, and greeted all alike with the same generous warmth of feeling. Thus he lived and so he died. Age had not withered him nor made him crabbed nor petulant, for although nearly eighty years old at the time of his death, he remained young in his feelings and manners until his last day, when he was stricken down while walking through Broadway to his office in the bank, with his usual rapid steps, in order to be there promptly at nine o'clock, as was his invariable custom and pride." After his death, resolutions of regret and sympathy were adopted by the several institutions with which he was connected in earlier and later years, among them the board of directors of the First National Bank, the trustees of the Paterson Savings Institution, the board of directors of the Passaic Water Company, the Cedar Lawn Cemetery Association, the Board of Aldermen, the Paterson Board of Trade, the Society of the First Baptist Church, and Trinity African Methodist Episcopal Church.

Mr. Brown married (first) in New York City, October 28, 1841, Caroline L. Cogswell. born in New York City, November 22, 1825; died February 16, 1852. Children: 1. Catherine Cogswell, born May 3, 1844; died May 26. 1844. 2. Henry De Camp, September 2, 1845; died September 11, 1847. 3. George Baldwin. April 27, 1847; died December 31, 1868. These children were all born and died at Paterson, New Jersey. Mr. Brown married (second), April 19, 1855, at Mattawan, New Jersey, Mary, born May 14, 1834, daughter of William and Melisse (Doughty) Swinburne. the former of whom was one of the founders of the company which in later years became known as the Rogers Locomotive Works. Four children were born of this marriage: 1. A daughter, June 2, 1856; died July, 1856. 2. Edwin Swinburne, November 19, 1857; see forward. 3. Walter F., May 21, 1859; died January 29, 1871. 4. Caroline Cogswell, March 23, 1864; died February 12, 1894; married Llewellyn T. McKee, of Philadelphia, graduate of Naval Academy, Annapolis, Maryland; chil-

Edward J. Brown.

dren: Mary, born September 8, 1889; John Brown, July 19, 1891; Llewellyn T., January 2, 1894.

(III) Edwin Swinburne, eldest son of John Jackson and Mary (Swinburne) Brown, was born November 19, 1857, at Paterson, New Jersey. He was graduated from the military school of Henry Waters, a noted educator at Paterson. Upon laying aside his text books he at once took up the study of silk weaving and the manufacture of silk goods. In this line of enterprise Mr. Brown soon became thoroughly familiar with all its details, and for a number of years was successfully engaged in silk manufacturing at Hornell, New York. He was a man possessed of splendid qualities of mind and heart, his ideals in his business and social life were always of the highest type. His home life was always attended with felicity and parental affection. He died at Paterson, New Jersey, September 6, 1907. He married, at Hornell, New York, November 3, 1890, Gertrude, born November 14, 1865, daughter of Francis G. and Elizabeth (Clark) Babcock, of Hornell, New York. Children, born in that city: Dorothea, December 11, 1891; Carolyne Brown, March 30, 1903.

This surname comes from the
ALLEN   Christian name Allen, which is very ancient. In the roll of Battle Abbey, Fitz-Aleyne (son of Allen) occurs. Alan, constable of Scotland, and Lord of Galloway and Cunningham, died in 1234. Surnames in England came into general use about the close of the twelfth century. One of the first using Allen as a surname was Thomas Allen, sheriff of London, in 1414. Sir John Allen was mayor of London in 1525, Sir William Allen in 1571, and Sir Thomas Alleyne in 1659. Edward Allen (1566-1626), a distinguished actor and friend of Shakespeare and Ben Johnson, in 1619, founded Dulwich College, with the stipulation that the master and secretary must always bear the name of Allen, and this curious condition had been easily fulfilled from Allen scholars. There are no less than twenty-five coats-of-arms of separate and distinct families of Allen in the United Kingdom, besides twenty others of the different spelling of this same surname. There were more than a score of emigrants of this surname from almost as many different families leaving England before 1650 to settle in New England.

(I) Walter Allen, a native of England, born about 1601, was in Newbury, Massachusetts,

as early as 1640 and removed thence to Watertown about 1652. In 1665 he sold his estate in the latter town and bought of John Knapp sixty acres in Watertown farms lying near Concord. Four years later he purchased two hundred acres more in Watertown. By deed of gift dated October 1, 1673, he conveyed lands in Watertown to his sons Daniel and Joseph and soon afterward moved to Charlestown, where he died July 8, 1681. At the time of his death he owned lands in Watertown, Charlestown, Sudbury and Haverhill. The farm in the last named town was acquired in 1673. Old records give him various occupations such as farmer, planter, haberdasher, shopkeeper and "haberdasher of hats." The inventory of his estate amounted to three thousand fifteen pounds. His wife Rebecca, who accompanied him to Watertown, died before November 29, 1678, on which date he married Abigail Rogers. Children of first wife: 1. John, settled in Sudbury. 2. Daniel, married Mary Sherman. 3. Joseph, mentioned below. 4. Abigail, born October 1, 1641. 5. Benjamin, April 15, 1647.

(II) Joseph, third son of Walter and Rebecca Allen, born in England, was a cooper by trade, and settled at Watertown Farms, which was incorporated in 1712 as the town of Weston, and probably lived in the northwestern part, near the Concord and Sudbury lines. He died there September 9, 1721, probably eighty years of age or over. He married, October 11, 1667, Anne Brazier, who died in December, 1720. Children: 1. Abigail, born and died 1668. 2. Rebecca, born April 8, 1670. 3. Ann, August 22, 1674. 4. Joseph, mentioned below. 5. Nathaniel, December 8, 1687; a deacon, of Weston. 6. Sarah, died 1699. 7. Deborah, married John Moore, of Sudbury. 8. Rachel, married Joseph Adams. 9. Patience.

(III) Joseph (2), eldest son of Joseph (1) and Ann (Brazier) Allen, was born June 16, 1677, in what is now Weston, and died there November 1, 1729. His tombstone in the old burial ground at Weston Center gives him the title of "Ensign." He married (first) December 19, 1700, Elizabeth Robbins, died in November, 1712; (second) Abigail ——. Children of first wife, all born in Weston: 1. Isaac, November 10, 1701. 2. Prudence, May 18, 1703. 3. Amy, September 21, 1706. 4. Rebecca, February 25, 1708. 5. Joseph, mentioned below. 6. Elizabeth and 7. Ann, 1711 (twins). 8. Silence, November, 1712. Children of second wife: 9. Daniel, September 26, 1714, settled at Claverack, New York. 10.

Abigail, May 14, 1716. 11. Elijah, September 11, 1718, lived at Sutton. 12. Sarah, August 10, 1720. 13. Tabitha, October 26, 1722. 14. Daniel, August 31, 1724, lived at Sheffield, Massachusetts. 15. Timothy, died young.

(IV) Joseph (3), eldest son of Joseph (2) and Eliza (Robbins) Allen, was born April 2, 1709, at Watertown Farms, and removed to Grafton, Massachusetts, about 1730, and six years later to Hardwick, same colony, where he died August 18, 1793. He was a housewright, captain of militia as early as 1740, selectman, assessor, clerk and treasurer of the town, and for nearly fifty-seven years deacon of the church. He married (first) August 16, 1733, Mercy Livermore, of Grafton, who died March 1, 1789, aged seventy-six; married (second) August 2, 1789, Sarah Knowlton, widow. His house at Hardwick was destroyed by fire and he erected the one now standing. He was not only one of the earliest but one of the most active and energetic of the pioneers of Hardwick. After his death a pamphlet was published containing several articles written by him, chiefly on religious subjects. In one of them is a scrap of autobiography which fixes the date of his birth:

"My native place where born was I
   In seventeen hundred nine.
Does sixteen miles from Boston lie.
   In Westown, called mine.

"Between my third and my fourth
   My mother left this life.
Which was to me affliction sore.
   My father lost his wife.

•   •   •   •

"In all my father's family
   Once sixteen did survive;
Before my father two did die.
   Then fourteen left alive."

Children: 1. Sarah, born July 25, 1734; married Benjamin Winchester. 2. David, mentioned below. 3. Lydia, September 19, 1743; married October 10, 1765, Lemuel Cobb. 4. Mercy, April 19, 1746; married, February 4, 1771, John Amidon. 5. Joseph, December 21, 1748.

(V) David, son of Joseph (3) and Mercy (Livermore) Allen, was born August 18, 1738, in Hardwick, where he died August 5, 1799. He was selectman and assessor and a very active and prominent citizen. He married (first) November 12, 1761, Elizabeth Fisk, who died October 22, 1791, aged forty-eight. He married (second) January 22, 1794, Lydia Woods, of New Braintree, Massachusetts.

Children, all born in Hardwick: 1. Rhoda, September 27, 1763; married David Barnard. 2. Eunice, August 22, 1765; married John Earl. 3. Daniel, September 20, 1767. 4. Elizabeth, October 27, 1768; married Isaac Wing. 5. David, born May 12, 1771. 6. Mercy, May 11, 1773. 7. Moses, died young. 8. Moses. March 11, 1779; prominent citizen of Hardwick. 9. Lydia, October 18, 1784; married Daniel Matthews, of New Braintree.

(VI) Daniel, eldest son of David and Elizabeth (Fisk) Allen, was born September 20, 1767, in Hardwick, and became a skillful millwright. He settled in Newark, New Jersey, and became widely known as a mill builder, and while engaged in Mexico in the construction of a water-wheel, he accidentally fell into the wheel pit and was seriously injured. He immediately returned to his home, where gangrene followed his injury, and he died soon afterward. He married Jane Personette, who survived him, and was the mother of five children.

(VII) Stephen, son of Daniel and Jane (Personette) Allen, was born probably about 1800, at Newark, New Jersey, and died in his eighty-fifth year, at Paterson, same state. His education was acquired in the schools of his native town, and when a young man he removed to Paterson, where he engaged in the tobacco business; in 1854 he admitted to partnership his son Alpheus S. Allen, and the firm was known as Stephen Allen & Son. John Reynolds and John Allen subsequently became members of the firm, which then took the style of Allen, Reynolds & Company, doing business until 1872, when it was sold. From this time until his death, Mr. Allen lived a quiet retired life. He was for some time captain of the General Godwin Guard, a military organization of Paterson, and at one time served as member of the board of chosen freeholders of Passaic county. He married Catherine, daughter of John Courter, of Paterson, and they became the parents of four children, only two of whom are living, namely: Alpheus S. and Louise. The latter is the wife of Charles H. May, of Paterson.

(IX) Alpheus Sylvester, son of Stephen and Catherine (Courter) Allen, was born May 27, 1833, in Paterson, which city has continued to be his home through life, and which he has notably served in various public capacities. He received his early education in the private schools of his native city, he then attended one term in a private school at Poughkeepsie, New York, and attended a private school at Bloomfield, New Jersey. As a boy he became familiar with the tobacco business in the establishment of his father. In 1851 he took a trip to California by way of the Straits of Magellan and spent two years on the Pacific coast, chiefly in Oregon, returning to his native home by way of the Isthmus of Panama. On his return he was admitted to partnership with his father, and remained a member of the firm until its business was sold out in 1872. He subsequently retired from active business. In 1870 Mr. Allen was elected a member of the board of aldermen and served two years, and in May, 1872, was appointed receiver of taxes for the city of Paterson and served eighteen years as such. He has been a director of the Paterson Savings Institution for over twenty-five years, and for a like period has been a director of the First National Bank of Paterson. Mr. Allen has been an astute and successful business man, and gave more than twenty years to the public service, to which he gave the same careful attention which characterized the conduct of his own affairs, and thereby won the esteem and regard of his fellow citizens. He is a man of genial and friendly disposition and takes an active interest in the progress of public events and the public welfare. He is a member of Fabriola Lodge, No. 57, Knights of Pythias, whose fraternal principles have been guiding motives in the conduct of his life.

He was married, May 11, 1858, by Rev. William H. Hornblower, to Maria Osborn, born April 12, 1837, daughter of Edward and Ann (Stagg) Osborn, of Paterson. Children: 1. Annie Vernet, born April 21, 1859; married, December 15, 1881, Willard P. Whitlock, and they are the parents of: Harold Allen Whitlock, born August 15, 1882; Louis Ivey, March 21, 1884; Willard P., March 16, 1886; Herbert, July, 1897. 2. Stephen Lincoln, born March 25, 1865; died January 10, 1871. 3-4. Jessie Elizabeth and Jennie Rebecca (twins), born November 15, 1867; the first was married, April 8, 1891, to Robert M. Helfenstein, and is the mother of Edith Morris Helfenstein, born August 27, 1892. Jennie R. was married November 25, 1890, to Jerome C. Read, and has a son and a daughter, namely: Allen Jerome, born July 30, 1893, and Jane C., born July, 1903.

PLUM   The Plume arms: Ermine, a blend vair or and gules cottised vert. Crest (English): Out of a ducal coronet or, a plume of ostrich feathers argent.

The Plumbs are an ancient Norman family and are traced back to Normandy, A. D., 1180; and in England to A. D., 1240. In America the Plumes and Plums are among the oldest New England colonial families. Of the entailed Plume and Plum ancestors of the immigrant some brief mention may be made in this place.

(I) John Plumbe, yeoman, of Tappesfield, England, had a wife Elizabeth, sons, John, Robert, Thomas, and four daughters.

(II) Robert Plume, yeoman, son of John and Elizabeth Plumbe, was of Great Yeldham, Essex, England. He married (first) Elizabeth Purchase; (second) Mrs. Etheldred Fuller. Nine children; sons, Robert, Thomas, Edmund, Joseph and one other; daughters, Margaret Elizabeth, Mary and Anne.

(III) Robert (2), gentleman, of Spaynes Hall, Great Yeldham, Essex, England, son of Robert (1) and Elizabeth (Purchase) Plume, lived and died at Great Yeldham. He married Grace Crackbone. Eight children; sons, Robert, John and Thomas; daughters, Martha, Mary, Etheldred, Frances and Hannah.

(IV) John, immigrant, son of Robert (2) and Grace (Crackbone) Plume, was born in Spaynes Hall at Great Yeldham, Essex, England, was baptized there July 28, 1594. He came from England to Wethersfield, Connecticut, 1635, and his name first appears there in a court record of the following year. He was a member of the court there from 1637 to 1642. He is mentioned in the records as "Mr. Plum," indicating a social station of more than ordinary importance. In 1636 it is recorded that "Whereas, there was tendered to us an inventory of the estate of Mr. Jo. Old'a (Oldham) which seemed to be somewhat uncertainly valued, wee, therefore, think meete to, & so it is ordered that Mr Jo. Plum & Rich. Gildersleeve, together with the constable, shall survey the saide inventory and perfect the same before the next corte & then to deliver it into the corte." At a court held at Hartford in March, 1636, "Mr. Plum," being a member of the court, the business before it was the adopting of some measures to buy corn from the Indians, as the inhabitants were in a starving condition. They agreed to pay from four to six shillings a bushel for it, and "Mr. Plum" was appointed to receive the corn for Wethersfield. He held various town offices and performed many public duties, such as marking town boundaries, laying out roads, determining lines between towns, looking to the improvement of the lands of the plantations, and attending the court as a deputy.

He was also one of the men in Captain John Mason's little army that wiped out the Pequot Indians in 1637, and for his services he received a grant of lands. He was a ship owner and it is thought that he might have been owner of the vessel that carried seventy-seven of Mason's men around from the mouth of the Connecticut river to the Narragansett. In 1644-45 he was appointed to attend the clearance of vessels at Wethersfield, but in the former year, 1644, he sold his lands in Wethersfield and removed to Branford, where in 1645 he is mentioned as "Keeper of the Town's Book." He died there in 1648 and his wife, "Mrs. Plume," administrated on his estate August 1, 1648. Only one of his children was born in this country, and no record exists of any of his children except that of his son Samuel, who lived with his father in Branford when the former died. By wife Dorothy John Plume had eight children: 1. Robert, baptized, December 30, 1617. 2. John, May 27, 1619. 3. William, May 9, 1621. 4. Ann, October 16, 1623. 5. Samuel, January 4, 1625, see forward. 6. Dorothea, January 16, 1626. 7. Elizabeth, October 9, 1629. 8. Deborah, July 28, 1633.

(V) Samuel Plum, son of John and Dorothy Plume, was born in England, January 4, 1625-26, died January 22, 1703. He was of Wethersfield and Branford, Connecticut. In 1668 he sold all the remaining part of his lands in Branford and removed to Newark, New Jersey, and was among the very earliest settlers in that region. The town of Newark was bought in 1666 by certain men of Milford, New Haven, Branford and Guilford, Connecticut, and lots were divided among the purchasers as early as 1667. The name of the wife of Samuel Plum is not known, but he had eight children: 1. Elizabeth, born January 18, 1650-51. 2. Mary, April 1, 1653. 3. Samuel, March 22, 1654-55. 4. John, October 28, 1657; see forward. 5. Dorothea, March 26, 1660. 6. Joshua, August 3, 1662. 7. Joanna, March 11, 1665. 8. Sarah, born probably in 1676.

(VI) John (2), son of Samuel Plum, was born in Branford, Connecticut, October 28, 1657, died July 12, 1710. He came with his father's family to Newark, New Jersey, 1668, and afterward lived in that town. In 1677 he married Hannah Crane, who bore him five children, born in Newark, who are only known by being named in his will and other wills with their husbands and wives, but the dates of their births and deaths are not known. Children: 1. Mary, married (first) Elihu

Crane; (second) Rev. Jonathan Dickinson. 2. Sarah, married John Lindsley. 3. Jane, married Joseph Riggs. 4. Hannah. 5. John, see forward.

(VII) John (3), youngest child and only son of John (2) and Hannah (Crane) Plum, was born in Newark, New Jersey, about 1696, died after 1785. His entire life was spent in Newark and he appears to have been one of the few of his family who wrote his surname "Plume." He married (first) about 1724, Joanna Crane, who died about 1785; married (second) Mary ———. Children, all of first marriage: 1. Isaac, born October 1, 1734, died November 19, 1799; married (first) Sarah Crane; (second) Ann Van Wagennen. 2. Stephen, died 1828, aged seventy-three years. 3. Mary, married Rufus Crane. 4. Jane, died after 1780. 5. Phebe, married Captain Robert Provost. 6. Joseph. 7. John, see forward.

(VIII) John (4), youngest son and child of John (3) and Joanna (Crane) Plume, was born in Newark, New Jersey, about 1743, died there about January, 1771. He always wrote his name without the final "e," and his example has been followed by all of his descendants. The date of his marriage with Susan Crane is not known, but it was about the year 1764. Children, all born in Newark: 1. Joseph R., born July 30, 1766, died November 12, 1834; married (first) Mary Banks; (second) Anna Price. 2. Matthias, 1768, see forward. 3. David, 1769, died August 27, 1835; married Matilda Cook. 4. Robert.

(IX) Matthias, son of John (4) and Susan (Crane) Plum, was born in Newark, New Jersey, 1768, died there in 1852, having spent his entire life in that city. He married, about 1793, Phebe Woodruff, who bore him five children, all born in Newark: 1. Lucetta, born May 21, 1794, died July 3, 1881; married Joseph Plum. 2. Sarah, September 19, 1797, died March 22, 1875; married Ambrose Williams. 3. Stephen Haines, January 7, 1800, see forward. 4. Elias, November 18, 1804, died April 12, 1883; married (first) Susan Rankin; (second) Mary Mann; (third) Martha M. Buell. 5. David B., May 2, 1813, died July 15, 1851; married (first) Leonora Whittaker; (second) Anna M. Arnold.

(X) Stephen Haines, eldest son and third child of Matthias and Phebe (Woodruff) Plum, was born in Newark, New Jersey, January 7, 1800, died there April 11, 1885. He received a good common school education, and was then apprenticed to a shoe manufacturer, with whom he remained until he was old enough to establish a business for himself. From the outset he was very successful, and establishing a place of business in New York City he soon extended his operations throughout the southern and western states, being among the first of the Newark manufacturers to make for that city its well-deserved and earned reputation. About 1850 he began to withdraw gradually from business of a mercantile and manufacturing nature and invested his means in other directions, becoming largely interested in the Newark Gas Light Company, of which he was for a number of years a director. He was also a stockholder and director in the New Jersey Fire Insurance Company, the Mechanics Fire Insurance Company and the St. Mark's Fire Insurance Company of New York. He was a man of high character and his influence was always felt for good. He married Margaret Monteith, born in Belvidere, New Jersey, died in Newark, January 6, 1883, daughter of Michael and Martha (Ramsden) Todd, the former of whom emigrated from Glasgow, Scotland, to America in the latter part of the eighteenth century. Children, all born in Newark: 1. Charlotte, born 1835; married Theodore B. Coe. 2. Matthias, November 24, 1839, a sketch of whom and descendants also appears in this work. 3. Stephen Haines, see forward.

(XI) Stephen Haines (2), son of Stephen Haines (1) and Margaret Monteith (Todd) Plum, was born in Newark, New Jersey, November 12, 1842, died there May 30, 1906. He attended Mr. Hedges private school and later the high schools of Newark. His first position was as a drug clerk, and at the age of nineteen he entered the employ of the City Bank, of Newark, where he remained for eighteen months, after which he became connected with the National Bank of the Republic, New York City, where his promotion was insured, since he proved his abilities and fidelity to the responsible trusts imposed. He continued with this institution for but one year less than a quarter of a century, and for about eighteen years of that period served in the capacity of paying teller. His father died in 1885, leaving a large estate to be settled up, and on this account Mr. Plum resigned his position in the bank in order that he might devote his entire time and attention to his individual property interests. He spent eighteen months abroad, visiting England, Scotland, Ireland, France, Italy, Germany, Algeria and other foreign countries. In 1858 Mr. Plum became a member of the First Baptist Peddie Memorial Church, of which

ii—24

he was for nineteen years the treasurer, several years president of the board of trustees, and active in the furtherance of missionary work. As a teacher he maintained an abiding interest in the Sunday school, and he induced many youths to join his class, inspiring them by precept and example, and in this manner he has been instrumental in developing honorable men who have attained success in life and have become the heads of prosperous, christian families. Mr. Plum was a philanthropist in the highest sense of the word, contributing liberally of his means to various charities in a quiet and unassuming manner, believing in the scriptural injunction to "Let not your right hand know what your left hand doeth." He built the Eighth Avenue Day Nursery in Newark in honor of his mother; with the late Mr. Horace Alling, he was largely instrumental in securing the subscriptions for the erection of the building for the Children's Aid and Prevention of Cruelty to Children Society in Newark, to which society he contributed liberally and in which he took a keen interest, serving as its president for many years and up to his decease. He was a Republican in national and state matters, but in local affairs maintained an independent attitude, preferring to lend his support to the man whom he regarded as the most fitting for municipal offices.

Mr. Plum married, October 25, 1865, Mary, daughter of David C. and Lydia (Dodd) Runyon, of Newark, who survives him and resides in the home in Newark. Children: 1. Margaret Monteith, married Henry G. Atha, treasurer of the Cast Steel Works of New Jersey; children: i. Margaret Monteith, born July 17, 1898; ii. Sarah, born March 8. 1901. 2. Martha J., resides at home. 3. Stephen Haines, third, born January 18, 1877, in Newark; educated in Newark Academy and Princeton College, graduating from the latter in class of 1901; engaged in the real estate business in Newark; a Republican in politics; member of the Peddie Memorial Church, serving as one of the trustees of same, and is continuing the good work along christian lines in which his father was interested. He married Blanche Devereux; children: i. Stephen Haines, fourth, born October 30, 1906; ii. Lucretia Mary, born December 30, 1907.

BAER Aargau, on the river Aar, next to the Rhine and Rhone the largest river in Switzerland, is a canton of about five hundred and thirty-eight English square miles, and a population of over two hundred thousand people. It was in the well-wooded hills and fertile valleys of this small canton, amid a people at least half of whom were Protestants, and all industriously engaged in agriculture and the manufacture of cotton, linen, silk and hosiery, that the family of Baers had lived for centuries. Enjoying the advantages of living in the first pure republic of the modern world, they thrived and were happy, and doubted the existence of a better climate, soil, scenery or government on the face of the globe. The family were silk cultivators and manufacturers for generations. They had the advantages of the use of museums, libraries and schools, and became well versed in Swiss history.

(I) Frederick Jacob Baer, the eldest son of his father, was born at Arburg, Switzerland, December 13, 1813, died at Paterson, New Jersey, July 20, 1877, and is buried at Cedar Lawn cemetery. He was educated in his native town under competent masters, and through his individual efforts gained much in the way of learning. He became competent to teach and had classes among the laboring people in his locality. It was the desire of his parents that he take up a religious life and missionary work, but to this he was much averse. At the early age of sixteen years he decided to learn the art of silk ribbon making, and accordingly went to Basle, a small hamlet in the canton by the same name. He began in the lowest station and mastered every branch of the art, bettering himself in his positions so that he became a thorough master of his trade. Here he married and lived for ten years thereafter, and three of his children were born there. He subsequently removed to Aarau, where he took a leading position in the then largest factory of the town, then operated by Feer & Company, where he remained until 1865 and in July that year emigrated to America from Havre, France, with his wife, three sons and daughter, Maria Anna, who became the wife of Jacob Walder, of Paterson. After landing at New York City he immediately came to Paterson, settling there, and taking a position in the silk establishment of his son, Jacob Frederick Baer, and had the management of different departments as superintendent. About 1873 he retired from this position of responsibility and from active work. He resided on Lafayette street, where his death occurred. He was a man of remarkable foresight and action, deeply studious and fond of deep reading, taking up scientific studies. He kept in touch with his native country and his adopted land by reading the current news. He was a thorough believer in American ideas, having read much before he came to America of the new country. He was a Lutheran in religion and a Republican in politics.

He married, at Basle, Switzerland, 1835, Anna Weibel, born at Reckenback (in Canton Basle), December 29, 1811, died in Paterson, New Jersey, January 19, 1890, daughter of Jacob and Anna (Gerster) Weibel. Jacob Weibel was a mason by trade. Children: 1. Jacob Frederick, mentioned below. 2. John Rudolph, born August 5, 1840, died October 20, 1872; married Matilda Ackerman. 3. August, born December 23, 1843, died unmarried. May 1, 1891. 4. Maria Anna, born March 13, 1846; married, September 12, 1869, Jacob Walder, born March 18, 1839, died December 30, 1897; children: i. Anna Maria, born July 8, 1870; married, June 15, 1893, John Bluntschli, born November 10, 1865, son of Jacob and Elizabeth (Balber) Bluntschli; children: a. Jacob Walder, born December 5, 1894, died December 20, 1899; b. Hans Arthur Walder, born September 14, 1896; c. Robert William Walder, born March 19, 1900; ii. Maria Louise, born August 29, 1871; married, April 21, 1896, John Grantley Taylor, born July 4, 1868, son of Joseph and Mary (Sweatman) Taylor; children: a. Grantley Walder Taylor, born March 6, 1897; b. Marie Hale Taylor, born June 24, 1899; iii. Minnie, born January 24, 1874, died 1876; iv. Jacob William, born November 29, 1880; married, April 18, 1906, Clara Huntoon; children: a. Cynthia Marie Walder; b. Clara Huntoon Walder: v. Bertha Augusta, born May 30, 1884; married, April 15, 1909, Edward Beam. 5. William Frederick, born March 18, 1849; married Anna Miesch. 6. Gustaf Adolphus, born June 8, 1852, died July 20, 1868.

(II) Jacob Frederick, eldest son of Frederick Jacob and Anna (Weibel) Baer, was born in the village of Beckten, in the canton of Basle, Switzerland, November 27, 1836, and died at Paterson, New Jersey, November 29, 1905. He attended the schools of his native town, and immediately after, while yet a boy, was taught the trade of silk making by his father, who moved from Arburg to Aargau, a nearby hamlet and a part of Arburg. After thoroughly mastering every detail of the trade under his father's careful tutorage, he decided at the age of twenty years to emigrate to America with the hope of finding a broader and more remunerative field for his skill and labor. He came to New York, where for a time he worked at his trade, and latter became a member of the firm of E. Walther & Company, of New York City, where he continued up to 1863, when the firm of E. Walther & Company were looking for a new field in which to engage in manufacturing to the best advantage. They decided to come to Paterson, New Jersey, then the center of the silk industry of the country, and here Mr. Baer finally engaged in the manufacturing business for himself with the little money he had saved by dint of simple and frugal tastes taught by his sturdy and honest ancestors, starting with a half dozen small looms. He began to prosper, and by his careful and conscientious management the plant increased. He introduced the first ribbon loom in Paterson, and was the first in America to make satin back velvet ribbons. He was in a fair way to become the largest silk manufacturer in the country when the disastrous panic of 1873 swept the country, and with a number of other silk makers he was among those who suffered, his plant being entirely wiped out and his entire savings lost in the failure. At the time he was located in the Crescent mill, on what is now Belmont avenue, and was succeeded by the firm of Sterett Ryle & Murphy. Nothing daunted by this failure, Mr. Baer again determined to try his resources of energy, brain and thought, and in the meantime he secured positions as superintendent of the Pioneer Silk Company and later with William Strange & Company, which position he held several years. In 1887 he resigned his position of superintendent, and resumed the manufacture of silk ribbons on his own account, and was instrumental in founding and establishing the Helvetia Silk Mill, which company was incorporated in March, 1887, and soon grew into a flourishing concern. He became the head of this concern, with branches on Van Houten street, and Lehighton, Pennsylvania, and which to-day are the most conspicuous of the industrial establishments of Paterson. The success of the firm was due to the untiring energy, honest and executive ability of its founder. The plant has been enlarged at various times in order to meet the constantly increasing demands of its products. About 1904 an addition was made to the plant that increased the output about one-third. There are about two hundred and twenty ribbon looms in the mill, and the concern employs about three hundred and twenty-five operatives. The present officers are: Frederick A. Baer, president, and Ralph Baer secretary. Jacob Frederick Baer always enjoyed a reputation for liberality, especially in his dealings with his employees, and seldom if ever has any differences occurred with them. He was a man of high ideals and probity of character, and noted for his kindness and generosity to all with whom he came in contact. With his friends he was generous to a fault. He was always an energetic and enterprising citizen, actively engaged until his death, being the oldest silk manufacturer in Paterson.

Jacob Frederick Baer married, in New York City, 1858, Louisa Blattner, born September 26, 1838, at Küttingen, Canton Aargau, Switzerland, died at Paterson, New Jersey, July 4, 1904, daughter of Jacob and Anna Blattner. Children: 1. Frederick A., born February 16, 1860; married Louise Wirz; children: Anna, Bertha, Ralph J. 2. Ralph, born April 9, 1863; see forward. 3. Anna, born August 23, 1865; married, June 16, 1887, Carlos D. De Ponthier; children: Louise, born March 13, 1888, and Blanca, born March 31, 1893. 4. Eugene W., born September 9, 1867; married Cora Tice; children: Elizabeth, Genivieve, Eugene, Rose, Carlos and Margaret. 5. William August, born March 27, 1870; see forward. 6. Louise, born May 31, 1872, died June 14, 1880. 7. Rose Isabelle, born October 9, 1874; married, November 23, 1898, Adolph Webber; child, Jacob Frederick, born January 31, 1901. 8. Louis Chileon, born March 11, 1882, see forward.

(III) Ralph, son of Jacob Frederick and Louisa (Blattner) Baer, was born in New York City, April 9, 1863. At an early age he came with his parents to Paterson, New Jersey, where he attended the public schools. At the age of fourteen years he began to learn the art of manufacturing ribbons, also directing his attention to designing patterns and cutting designs on cards to be used in the Jacquard looms in various of the local silk mills. In 1887, with his father and other representative men, he became one of the incorporators of the Helvetia Silk Mill in Paterson, and since that time, with the exception of the years 1892-97, has been actively identified with that manufactory. He is at present secretary of the corporation and a member of its board of directors. He is also prominently identified with city affairs. He was appointed a member of the Paterson school board in 1894-95, and May 21, 1906, was appointed police and fire commissioner for a short term, and January 1, 1907, was appointed for a full term, ending January 1, 1908. He joined the Republican party before he attained his majority, and cast his first presidential vote for the Blaine-Logan ticket in 1884. He was a member of the Phelps Guard, a political organization of Paterson. He is affiliated with Ivanhoe Lodge. No. 88, Free and Accepted Masons, and is a member of the Hamilton Club, St. Paul's Church Club, Passaic County Bowling Association, Germania Singing Society, Deutsch Amerikanischer Central Verein, and is an associate member of the Exempt Firemen's Association.

Mr. Baer's family have a unique and very valuable collection of silk samples cut from every pattern of silk goods produced by members of the family for the past two hundred years, which fact alone gives the collection great historical value. The Paterson Press in a series of illustrated articles entitled "Popular Patersonians in Cartoon" devoted the front page of the issue of August 29, 1908, to Ralph Baer, and it contains the following appreciative characterization of the subject:

"In the Halls of Fame there is many a name
Of men, who are no more deserving
Than this man who we present to you;
Who has risen with purpose unswerving.
His record is clean—there is no "in between"—
Strict, straightforward, honest his aim.
Let others tread in this path by him led
And they'll find that It's well worth the game.
There is great satisfaction In hard work and action
For Virtue's its own reward!
We will back our prediction—fame without restriction
In the future we'll to him accord."

Ralph Baer married, April 22, 1885, Carrie S. Perry, born July 3, 1867, daughter of William S. and Amanda (Mathews) Perry. Children: 1. Bessie B., born April 9, 1886. 2. Ralph, Jr., born August 18, 1889, died August 8, 1890. 3. J. Frank, born May 1, 1893.

(III) William August, son of Jacob Frederick and Louisa (Blattner) Baer, was born in the family homestead on Belmont avenue. Paterson, New Jersey, March 27, 1870. He attended the public schools in his district, graduating from grammar school, No. 4, at the age of seventeen. He then entered the employ of Jacob Walder, who was engaged in the mill supply business, and remained with him for six months. Subsequently he entered the employ of the Helvetia Silk Mill, on Van Houten street, to learn the art of ribbon making, taking charge of the warping, winding and filling departments for four years, and later was occupied for a period in the weaving department. He later removed to Lehighton, Pennsylvania (1887), where for nine years he was

superintendent of the company's annex mill at that place, subsequently returning to the Riverside Paterson plant, where for a time he was warping overseer and inspector. Since that time he has charge as superintendent of the Van Houten street branch of the business, now employing from thirty-five to fifty hands, and where every branch of the silk business is under his direct supervision except the finishing and blocking, which is done at the Riverside mill. Mr. Baer is a Lutheran in religious faith, a Republican in politics, having served his party as delegate to their county convention, and was formerly a member of Knights of the Golden Eagle. He married, at Paterson, New Jersey, June 14, 1890, Marie Deering, born at Paterson, February 5, 1874, daughter of Jacob and Maria (Van Bruge) Deering, the former of whom is a construction contractor. Children: 1. Jacob Frederick, born February 14, 1891. 2. William, born January 17, 1893, died March 25, 1894. 3. A son, born April 2, 1901, died in infancy.

(III) Louis Chileon, son of Jacob Frederick and Louisa (Blattner) Baer, was born in the family homestead on Benson street, Paterson, New Jersey, March 11, 1882. His education was gained in the public schools, and after completing a two years' course in the Paterson high school he attended the Paterson Military Academy. At nineteen years of age he entered the employ of his father and brother, who were then operating a silk mill at Lehighton, Pennsylvania, where he diligently employed himself at learning the business, remaining nine months. He then came to their Paterson plant of the Helvetia Mill, where he was assistant shipper, and continued to learn the making of silk ribbons. After three years, having gained a thorough knowledge of the business in all its details, he was placed in charge of the quill winding, doubling and winding departments. Mr. Baer has the superintendency of these branches at the present time, having between sixty and sixty-five employees under his personal supervision. He attends the First Presbyterian Church, of Paterson, is a decided Republican in politics, and is a member of Paterson Lodge, No. 60, Benevolent and Protective Order of Elks.

He married, June 22, 1904, at Paterson, New Jersey, Jessie Wilson Boyle, born October 26, 1884, daughter of William and Jessie (Boyle) Boyle, the former of whom was a boiler maker by trade and machinist with the Erie railroad at Paterson. Mr. and Mrs. Baer are the parents of one child, Robert Paul, born September 8, 1905.

CORWIN M. Valerius Corvus, one of the most illustrious men in the early history of the Roman republic. was born about B. C. 371 in the midst of the struggle attending the Licinian laws. Being a member of the great Valerian house, he had an early opportunity of distinguishing himself, and we accordingly find him serving in B. C. 249 as military tribune in the army of the consul, L. Purins Camillus, in his campaign against the Gauls. His celebrated exploit in this war, from which he obtained the surname of Corvus. or "Raven," is like many other of the achievements of the early Roman heroes, mingled with fable. A Gallic warrior of gigantic size challenged to single combat any one of the Romans. After obtaining the consent of the consul, Valerius accepted the challenge. and as he was commencing the combat, a raven settled upon his helmet, and, as often as he attacked the Gaul, flew in the face of his foe, till at length the barbarian fell before the sword of Valerius. A general battle then ensued, in which the Gauls were entirely defeated. The consul presented Valerius with ten oxen and a golden crown, and the grateful people elected him in his absence, consul for the next year, though he was only twenty-three years of age. A still more distinguished descendant of M. Valerius Corvus was M. Valerius Messala Corvinns, the celebrated Messala, of Cicero, whose wife was Terentia, widow first of Cicero, then of Sallust, and who after Messala's death, married a fourth time another Roman senator. She bore her husband two sons, Marcus and Lucius, the first of whom was the famous Messalina of the Pannonian wars.

In the middle of the fifteenth century, after the death of Albert of Hungary, the states offered the crown to Wladislaus of Poland: but shortly afterwards, the widow of Albert had a son called Ladislaus Postumus. This was the cause of much dissension and Amurath of Turkey prepared to invade the country. Wladislaus conquered in the struggle and at this time Johannes Hunyadi Corvinus began his celebrated career as a soldier. His origin is shrouded in mystery, but he was probably the son of George Hunyadi vaywod of Wallachia during the reign of Sigismund. His surname of Corvinus is by some derived from his estate of Piatra de Corvo, but more generally from his ancestors, said to be the Corvini of ancient Rome. Matthias Corvinus, Matthias I., King of Hungary, 1458 to 1490, was the second son of John "was elected and crowned," says Gibbon, "by the grateful Hungarians in reward for his father's services. His reign was prosperous and long. He aspired to the glory of a conqueror and a saint, but his purest merit is his encouragement of learning." His sons were Ladislaus, born about 1465, and John, born about 1470, living in 1540, and a pupil of Anthony Bonfidius. Two Corvini, descendants of these two, were the Corvinus, at the Council of Trent, 1540, as a papal legate, and the Rev. Anthony Corvinus, 1501 to 1553, probably son of John and named after his tutor, who became a Protestant in 1526 and a celebrated reformer, preacher and author in Germany. In the next generation we have the Rev. Johannes Corvinus, perhaps the same as the John Corvinus born about 1560 whose son Arnold, born about 1590, was an eminent lawyer, and published Digests of the law in aphorisms at Amsterdam, Holland, in 1649. The evidence points to his being the brother or cousin of the founder of the American family referred to below.

(I) Matthias Corwin, or Corvinus, the first settler of the name in America, was born between 1590 and 1600. and died September, 1658. His name appears written sometimes "Curwin," and even "Currin," these last two spellings being erroneous orthographies originating from the traditional Hungarian pronunciation. In 1634 his name appears on the commoner's record, at Ipswich. Massachusetts, as "Currin," when he receives a second grant of land in that place. The Ipswich record notes that he emigrated from that place to Long Island. He received a lot of land for a house, directly opposite the present Congregational church in Southold. The new lecture room of that church now stands on the very plot.. Here he lived for eighteen years till his death, which occurred between August 31, and September 15. December 11, 1656, together with William Wells, Lieutenant Budd, Barnabas Horton. and William Purrier, he was appointed on a committee to order the town affairs. December 5. 1655, besides his house lot and a meadow lot at Accoboack, his property is reckoned at three hundred and twenty-eight acres. His will dated August 31, was proved September 15. 1658. when the inventory of his estate, £313. 8s, was also filed. By his wife Margaret, probably a Morton, he had three children of record: 1. John, referred to below. 2. Martha, born between 1630 and 1640. living in 1698: married (first) Henry Case and (second) Thomas Hutchinson, bearing her first husband two, and her second husband five children. 3. Theophilus, born before 1634, died before 1692; he had by his wife Mary seven children.

(II) John, son of Matthias and Margaret (Morton) Corwin, was born probably about 1630, died September 25, 1702. In 1661 he bought land and meadow at Oyster Pond and Aquebogue, Long Island, and was admitted as a freeman of Connecticut for Southold in 1662. In 1675 he is rated for 2 heads, 21 acres, 16 cattle, 9 horses, 5 swine, 6 sheep, £228, 10s. In 1686 he had four males and one female in his family. His name occurs in a number of deeds as either grantor or grantee between the years 1678 and 1696, and also in the census list of two years later, 1698, together with the names of all his children except Mary and Rebecca, who were already married. His will is dated November 26, 1700, proved October 14, 1702. February 4, 1658, he married Mary daughter of Charles Glover, who died probably before 1690, and had eight children: 1. Mary, born December 15, 1659, died probably before 1690. 2. Sarah, born about 1660, married, before 1690, Jacob Osman and had ten children. 3. Rebecca, born between 1660 and 1670, married Abram Osman and had six children. 4. John, referred to below. 5. Abigail, born between 1660 and 1670, not married in 1698, and probably died unmarried. 6. Hannah, not married in 1698 and probably died unmarried. 7. Matthias, born 1675, died March 9, 1769; had by his wife Mary ten children. 8. Samuel, born about 1677, died December 28, 1705; had by his wife Anne two children.

(III) Captain John (2), son of John (1) and Mary (Glover) Corwin, was born in 1663, died December 13, 1729. In 1692 he received from his father a lot of woodland lying west of the town of Southold and on the north side of the road by Nathaniel Terry's land. His name occurs as both grantor and grantee on many deeds, and in 1712 an exhibit of his lands is found in the Southold town records. By his wife Sarah, whom he married before 1698, he had six children: 1. Benjamin, died in 1721, and probably married. 2. John, referred to below. 3. David, born between 1705 and 1710, died before 1782; married Deborah Wells, who bore him six children and perhaps other daughters. 4. Sarah, possibly married Peter Simons. 5. Elizabeth. 6. Hester.

(IV) John (3), son of Captain John (2) and Sarah Corwin, was born July 10, 1705, died December 22, 1755. He lived about a mile and a half east of Mattituck, in the town of Southold, and he is buried a little south of the centre of the Mattituck graveyard. He was twice married and his second wife survived him many years. His will is dated December 18, 1754, and proved January 7, 1755. According to a book in the possession of Augustus Griffin, of Orient, Long Island, his first wife was Hester Clark, but apparently she bore him no children, unless the two children who died, one in 1735, the other in 1738, his "second daughter" who died in 1746, and Elnathan who died in January, 1738, were by her. In 1732 he married Elizabeth Goldsmith, who was still living in 1776, and who after his death married, in 1763, Benjamin Brown, of Oyster Ponds. This may possibly be Elizabeth (Terrill) Corwin, the widow of John, son of Theophilus. John and Elizabeth (Goldsmith) Corwin had five children, unless some or all of those mentioned above were the issue of the first marriage: 1. John, born 1735, died December 22, 1817; married (first) Sarah Hubbard, and (second) Deborah Brown, and had five children. 2. Elizabeth, born between 1730 and 1740. 3. Sarah, born about 1739, possibly the Sarah who married John Penney. 4. James, born August 22, 1741, died November 9, 1791; married Mehetable Horton and had nine children. 5. William, referred to below.

(V) William, son of John (3) and Elizabeth (Goldsmith) Corwin, was born February 21, 1744, died December 1, 1818. He moved from Long Island to Chester, New Jersey, about 1774. He was a soldier in the French and Indian wars, a lieutenant in the revolution, and a representative in the New Jersey legislature. His original homestead, one and one half miles north of Chester, is now in the possession of the Kelsey family. His name is of very frequent occurrence on the records. January 14, 1768, William Corwin married Hannah Reeves, of Mattituck, Long Island, born May 23, 1747, died about 1840. They had eleven children: 1. John Calvin, born October 21, 1768, died June 6, 1849; married (first) Deborah Terry, and (second) Elizabeth Vance, and had six children. 2. Sarah, born January 13, 1771, married Jabez Kelsey, of Chester, New Jersey. 3. Hannah, born March 28, 1773, married Jeremiah, son of William and Elizabeth (Hedges) Woodhull, of Easthampton, Long Island. 4. William, referred to below. 5. James, born April 21, 1779, died October 10, 1844, at Piketon, Ohio; married (first) Margaret Cameron, of Scotland, and (second) Elizabeth Smith, the widow of James Mallory, of New York

City, and had seven children. 6. Joseph, born July 6, 1781, died September 23, 1800, in Chester, New Jersey. 7. Nathaniel, born September 26, 1783, died February 24, 1849, married (first) Elizabeth, daughter of Barnabas and Elizabeth Horton, (second) a Monroe, (third) Adaline Pickle, and (fourth) Sarah Bell, and had two children. 8. Elizabeth, born December 6, 1785, died December 7, 1860, married Henry Halsey, of Morris county, and had six children. 9. Daniel, born April 13, 1788, in Morris county, living in 1870; married (first) Mary Hamill, (second) Elizabeth Hamill, (third) Elizabeth Spinning, and (fourth) Elizabeth Brace, and had six children. 10. Ebenezer, born October 13, 1790, died April 8, 1851, married (first) Elizabeth Skellinger, and (second) a Hatch, and had three children. 11. Joshua Goldsmith, born February 4, 1793, died November 9, 1867; married Elizabeth, daughter of the Rev. Lenas Fordham, and had four children.

(VI) William (2), fourth child and second son of William (1) and Hannah (Reeves) Corwin, was born near Chester, New Jersey, October 9, 1776, died September 30, 1821. In 1817 he was in New York City in partnership with his brother, James Corwin, who from 1805 to 1820 kept a shoe store at 94 Broadway, New York. After this went to live at Sparta, New Jersey. He was apparently twice married but the name of his second wife and the children of the latter union if any are unknown. December 12, 1801, he married (first) Martha Vance, who bore him three children: 1. Joseph, referred to below. 2. William V. 3. Eliza A., born November 28, 1804, married Henry C. Beach and had four children.

(VII) Joseph, eldest son of William (2) and Martha (Vance) Corwin, was born in Sparta, New Jersey, May 17, 1810. He signed his name Joseph A. Corwin, and obtained his early education chiefly in Albany. In 1835 he graduated from the medical department of Yale University, and the following year began practicing in Belleville, Essex county, New Jersey, where he remained until December, 1849, when he removed to Newark, where he lived for the remainder of his life, dying in 1893. For many years he was a member of the Essex District Medical Society, in 1864 was elected its vice-president, and in 1865 its president, and in 1883 chosen one of its delegates to the State Medical Society. In 1852 and 1853 he was a member of the Newark board of education. Joseph A. Corwin married (first) Tarquinia Kenney, who bore him four chil-

dren: 1. Francis Nicholas West, born July 4, 1840, married Louisa Westervelt. 2. William Albert, born March 12, 1843. 3. Charles Frederick, referred to below. 4. Mary Garette, born February 14, 1850, died September 9, 1851. Joseph A. Corwin married (second) September 18, 1856, Emma Whybrew Baldwin, born July 29, 1831, who bore him two more children: 5. Theodore Wellington, born June 1, 1857. 6. Robert Lowell, born between 1860 and 1870.

(VIII) Charles Frederick, third child and son of Joseph A. and Tarquinia (Kenney) Corwin, was born in Belleville, Essex county, New Jersey, July 25, 1845, died in Newark, July 28, 1908. In 1870 he started the hay, grain, and feed business now run by his son and spent the remainder of his life in its successful development. For a number of years he was a vestryman of Christ Episcopal Church in Newark. By his wife Anna Jackson, born in 1854, died March 17, 1881, he had two children: 1. Frederick Wellington, referred to below. 2. Grace Bartlett, born June 16, 1878.

(IX) Frederick Wellington, only son of Charles Frederick and Anna (Jackson) Corwin, was born in Newark, New Jersey, June 4, 1876, and is now living in Newark, where he is developing and carrying on the business left to him by his father. For his early education he attended the public and high schools of Newark, and then entered the employ of the Philip Cary Manufacturing Company, asbestos and roofing manufacturers, where he started as clerk in 1898, gradually rising until, when he left on account of his father's death in 1908, he had become superintendent. Mr. Corwin is a Republican, but has held no office. He is a vestryman of Christ Protestant Episcopal Church in Newark, of which his grandfather was one of the founders and his father for many years a vestryman. He married Laura Edna Freeman, born in Newark, February 23, 1876.

DUMONT The origin of several of the Dumont families has been traced to Flanders, but it is hardly possible that they all in turn were of Norman descent. There were Dumonts in Normandy as early as 1422, as appears from the "Mémoires Inedits de Dumont de Bostaquet: Gentilhomme Normand" (Paris, 1864). The religious wars in France between the Roman Catholics and Protestants, which had their beginning in the year 1652, were like all other similar contests productive of much cruelty and persecution. Little credit accrues to either side, in the beginning at least, but the Protestants finally were defeated and ultimately were subjected to such gross mistreatment as finds no parallel in the annals of either ancient or modern times. Many of the Dumonts early adopted the Protestant religion, and on January 27, 1599, we find the marriage record of Bastienne du Mont, in London. She was a native of Valenciennes, in the north of France. "The Making of New England," by Drake, mentions De Monts, Pierre du Gnast, from Saintonge. France, an officer of the King's household. He was a Huguenot and made an attempt to plant a colony. In 1604 Henry IV. granted him a charter to all of the region of country now known as New England and also a monopoly of the fur trade. He took one hundred followers, among them Samuel de Champlain, and landed at Passamaquoddy Bay. at St. Croix (named Mont Desert), on his first trip, but being unable to withstand the severities of winter, broke up his colony in the early part of the year 1605 and went to Port Royal, Nova Scotia.

Walleran Dumont. immigrant, came from Amsterdam, Holland, to New Amsterdam (New York) in 1657. He was not married when he came to this country, and according to the record made at the time of his marriage he gave his birthplace as Coomen. Flanders. (now Commines, Department Nord. France, eight miles from Lille). He was called a cadet ("adelborst"), a rank equal to that of our second lieutenant, in a company of soldiers sent by the Dutch West India Company to Director General Stuyvesant. Other French Protestants of the same surname came from Caen. Normandie. Some of them went to England, and others to Perle, Cape of Good Hope. Africa, and descendants of the same name are now living in both places. A tradition that some of Walleran Dumont's family renounced Protestantism in order to retain their property has been handed down to descendants in America, but this tradition never has been verified.

Walderan Dumont came over either in the ship "Draetvat," Captain Beslevoer. which sailed from Amsterdam April 2. 1657. or in the "Jan Baptist," which sailed from the same port December 23, 1657. The latter ship belonged to the Dutch West India Company and brought over a company of soldiers for Governor Stuyvesant. Two sisters of Dumont came over about 1663 in the ship "Spotted Cow." Dumont settled at Esopus (now Kingston, New York) about 1660, and appears to have been one of the most influential men of the town. He was a member of the military council during the second Esopus war with the Indians, and served as schepen or magistrate of Kingston from May, 1669, to May, 1671. He was a deacon of the Dutch church in 1673, and died between June 25, 1713, and September 13, 1713. He married, January 13, 1664, Grietje (Margaret) Hendricks, widow of Jan Aertson, who was killed by Indians in the second Esopus war. She had one daughter by her first husband, who afterward married Hendrick Kip. Six children were born of this marriage, three sons and three daughters. The sons were Walran, Jan Baptist and Peter Dumont.

There is very little doubt of the fact of relationship of the family of Wallaran Dumont and the family of the surname which is chiefly considered in this narrative, although the latter is supposed to have first appeared in this country soon after the massacre of French Huguenots in Paris of St. Bartholomew's day, as is fully mentioned in history. After the distressing scenes of that event the ancestor is said to have come to America and to have taken up his abode in North Carolina, where the family remained seated for at least two or three generations.

(I) Peter Dumont, the earliest ancestor of whom we have accurate knowledge, was born probably in North Carolina, married there and had a family. Among his children was a son John, see forward.

(II) John, son of Peter Dumont, was born in North Carolina and came north to New Jersey probably soon after the beginning of the last century. The precise period of his life is not known, nor the date of his marriage. but it is known that he married Mary Finley. and by her had three children. Caroline, Mary. John Finley (see forward), all of whom are now dead and only the last mentioned of whom married and had a family.

(III) John Finley, son of John and Mary (Finley) Dumont, was born in Hunterdon county. New Jersey, November 11, 1824, died May 8, 1889. He was a lawyer by profession. a consistent member of the Lutheran church. and a firm Democrat in his political preference. From 1852 until 1855 he was prosecuting attorney for Hunterdon county, but otherwise was not particularly active in political affairs. He married in Albany, New York. October 26, 1853. Anne Eliza, born May 23, 1835, daugh-

Wayne Dumont

ter of Rev. David and Jane (Kirkpatrick) Kline (see Kline, III). Children: 1. Ira, born September 27, 1855. 2. William L., April 6, 1857. 3. Charles, December 20, 1858, died April 3, 1859. 4. Laura, May 3, 1860. 5. Grace, July 8, 1862, died January 27' 1882. 6. Jenny, September 5, 1864. 7. Anne Eliza, April 9, 1867. 8. Frederick T. F., March 7, 1869. 9. Wayne, see forward. 10. A child, born and died 1873. 11. Madge T., July 30, 1875, died July 21, 1876. 12. Voctor St. Clair, September 12, 1877. 13. Ethel, May 6, 1879.

(IV) Wayne, son of John Finley and Anne Eliza (Kline) Dimont, was born in Phillipsburg, New Jersey, April 4, 1871, and was fitted for college at Lerch's Preparatory School, Easton, Pennsylvania, graduating *cum laude*, in June, 1888. In the fall of the same year he entered Lafayette College, Easton, and was graduated A. B., *cum laude*, in June, 1892; Ph. B. in course, 1895; M. S., Latin scientific course. After leaving college he attended upon the lectures of the New York Law School, and in due season was admitted to practice in the courts of New Jersey; was admitted attorney of the supreme court in February, 1896, and attorney and counsellor in February, 1899. Subsequently he received appointment as special master in chancery and also as supreme court commissioner. In November, 1907, he was admitted to practice in the courts of the state of New York, and became a member of the supreme court of the United States in February, 1908. Mr. Dimont is engaged in active general practice of the law in Paterson, and is a Republican in politics, but without political ambition. He is a member and past master of Delaware Lodge, No. 52, Free and Accepted Masons, of Phillipsburg; past high priest of Eagle Chapter, No. 30, Royal Arch Masons, of Phillipsburg; member of Paterson Council, Royal and Select Masters; Hugh de Payens Commandery, No. 19, Knights Templar; Mecca Temple, Ancient Arabic Order Nobles Mystic Shrine, of New York City; also a member in good standing of all the Scottish Rite bodies of Masonry in Paterson up to the eighteenth degree, and from the eighteenth degree to the thirty-second degree in the consistory at Jersey City. He holds life membership in all of the Scottish Rite bodies of Free-Masonry. He also is a member of Paterson Lodge, No. 60, Benevolent and Protective Order of Elks; the Pomfret Club, of Easton; the Merchants' Central Club, of 487 Broadway, New York City, and of the Lawyers' Club, of New York. He is a member of

the board of directors of the German American Trust Company, of Paterson.

Mr. Dimont married, October 26, 1898, Sallie Insley, born in Easton, Pennsylvania, July 20, 1873, daughter of Edward Insley and Sallie (Lesh) Hunt. Mr. Hunt is a retired merchant. His children: Myra Hunt, wife of Jacob L. Ludlow, of Winston, Salem, North Carolina; Sue, wife of William E. Howell, of Easton, Pennsylvania; Sallie I., Mrs. Dimont; and Nan, wife of George H. Meeker, of Media, Pennsylvania. Two children have been born of the marriage of Wayne and Sallie Insley (Hunt) Dimont: Wayne Hunt, born April 6, 1904, died February 17, 1908; John Finley, born April 2, 1909.

(The Kline Line).

Johann Jacob Klein (Jacob Kline), of Readington township, Hunterdon county, New Jersey, was born in Germany, March 6, 1714, died January 6, 1789, and is buried in the cemetery at New Germantown, New Jersey. He is mentioned as one of the signers of the call to the Rev. Albert Weygand in 1749. He carried on a tannery in Readington township, and the same was afterward continued by his descendants for more than three-quarters of a century. About 1748 he married Veronica Gerdrutta, daughter of Johannes Moelich, and by her had seven children: 1. Johann Wilhelm (John William), born January 5, 1750, died February 21, 1818. 2. Jacob, see forward. 3. Mary, married, February 13, 1776, John Farley. 4. Magdalene, born 1754, died March 16, 1774. 5. Fanny, married, December 26, 1781, Jacob Neff, Jr. 6. Aaron, born February 29, 1760, died December 24, 1809. 7. Peter, born January 17, 1771.

(II) Jacob, son of Johann Jacob and Veronica Gerdrutta (Moelich) Kline, was born in 1751, died October 22, 1823. He was a farmer and tanner by occupation and lived at New Germantown, New Jersey. For nearly forty years he was a ruling elder in the Zion Lutheran church, county freeholder for nearly twenty years, justice of the peace for many years, town clerk and one of the judges of the court of common pleas of Hunterdon county from 1806 to 1817. He married, July 7, 1782, Phebe, daughter of Peter Nevits, of Amwell, New Jersey. She was born in 1766, and died February 18, 1845, having borne her husband twelve children: 1. Colonel Jacob, born April 8, 1783, died November 15, 1844. 2. Peter, January 16, 1785, died October 18, 1860. 3. Fanny Gertrude, February 28, 1787, died

January 28, 1880. 4. John William, December 28, 1788, died September 17, 1847. 5. Maria, April 17, 1791, died January 15, 1869. 6. Ann, March 19, 1793, died February 20, 1795. 7. Phebe, December 19, 1796, died March 10, 1874. 8. Elizabeth, August 1, 1799, died March 25, 1880. 9. Nellie (Nelly) Stooloff, July 4, 1801, died April 23, 1803. 10. Catherine, July 20, 1804, died January 18, 1857. 11. Aletta, February 17, 1808, died January 9, 1879. 12. David, see forward.

(III) Rev. David, youngest son and child of Jacob and Phebe (Nevius) Kline, was born November 14, 1812, died in his pulpit while preaching, as pastor of the Lutheran church at Spruce Run, Hunterdon county, New Jersey, November 5, 1877. He married, April 18, 1833. Jane, daughter of John Kirkpatrick, of Liberty Corners, New Jersey. She was born June 19, 1814, and bore her husband twelve children: 1. Anne Eliza, born May 23, 1835; married, October 26, 1853, John Finley Dumont, born November 11, 1824, died May 8, 1889 (see Dumont, III). 2. Phebe, December 3, 1836, died May 28, 1857. 3. Peter, February 9, 1838. 4. John Cassiday, November 25, 1839. 5. Jacob, April 27, 1842. 6. Frances Miller, December 12, 1843. 7. Ellen Taylor, March 29, 1845. 8. Mary, December 5, 1846. 9. William Harrison, February 26, 1849. 10. Alfred Beaumont, April 1, 1851. 11. Jane Musier, March 16, 1853. 12. Alice, March 27, 1855.

REYNOLDS

In his "Suffolk Surnames" so good an authority informs us that Runnels is "a name taken from the face of nature," and from the same source and others of equal reliability we learn that the surnames Runnels and Reynolds are regarded as synonymous, merely different forms of expressing the same patronymic; but from various other sources it is discovered that the name Reynolds as now known appears written in not less than forty-nine different ways, but whether Runnels is one of the many variations of Reynolds, or vice versa, the standard authorities do not give us clear light. It is said too that Runnels may have been derived from the old Norwegian "Ronald," for we find the name of Baron Ronald Urka, who was present at the death of King Haco, the last of the Norwegian invaders and who fell at Orkney in the thirteenth century. Hence we have the North and South "Ronald sha" among the present names of the islands of the Orkneys. The fact that Runnels undoubtedly is a Scotch patronymic would seem to favor independent Scotch derivation for the name itself, and perhaps "from an object in nature." Reynolds often sounds like Runnels and on that account the latter is thought to be a very reasonable corruption of the former; yet we must go farther back to prove the identity of these names, and therefore the conclusion is that Runnels is for the most part Scotch, while Reynolds is English and Irish. The particular Reynolds family here considered comes to America from Ireland, and may or may not have been of ancient English origin; but from whatever source it originates its representatives stand for honest endeavor in every generation from the time when its immigrant ancestor crossed the Atlantic ocean and set foot on the free soil of America.

(I) Thomas Reynolds, with whom the present narrative begins, was born in county Armagh, Ireland, and came to this country in 1827, settling in Bergen county, New Jersey, and taking up his home on land where now is the site occupied by the North Jersey Country Club. He was a weaver by trade, a skillful workman in his line, an industrious man in all respects, thrifty, frugal and honest. He died in 1873, leaving three children. The family name of his wife was Agnes McCulloch. At the time of her marriage with Thomas Reynolds she was the Widow Cardwell, and by her first marriage had two children: Mary A. and Samuel Cardwell, the former of whom married a McAllister. Thomas and Agnes (Cardwell) Reynolds had three children, John, Jane and Margaret.

(II) John, son of Thomas and Agnes (Cardwell) Reynolds, was born in Portadown, county Armagh, Ireland, March 11, 1826, died January 6, 1909. He was only one year old when his parents came to this country and settled near Paterson, Bergen county, New Jersey. He was given a good common school education and when old enough to leave home went to Paterson and became a student at the academic school of which Hugh Dougherty was then the master. But in the course of a short time afterward he set out to make his own way in life, going to New York City, where he was apprenticed to learn the tailor's trade. This, however, was not to his liking and he soon abandoned it for the trade of cigar making in the Caldwell cigar factory at Caldwell, New Jersey, where he remained some time, then returned to Paterson and found employment with Stephen Allen, a manufacturer of cigars in that city. He proved to be an excellent workman and by close attention to his trade and the interests of his employer he soon gained a fair knowledge of the business in general; and as a result he was taken as partner by John Allen and became himself proprietor of a cigar factory and business. In the course of a few years a consolidation of interests resulted in the organization of the firm of Allen, Reynolds & Company, which firm carried on an extensive cigar manufacturing business until 1872, and then was dissolved. Upon the dissolution of the copartnership Mr. Reynolds retired from the cigar business, but not from all active pursuits, for soon afterward he became president of the Acquacknonk Water Company, and also of the Paterson Gas Company and the Paterson Savings Institution, both of which latter positions he held until his decease. Thus it will be seen that his early industrious habits and business enterprise eventually gained for him an enviable prominence in connection with the operation of important public utilities of the city, and that his former endeavors received their merited reward. He never aspired to political honors although from 1865 to 1870 he served as a member of the board of aldermen. During the earlier part of his life he was actively identified with the Methodist Episcopal church, but afterward transferred his membership to the Congregational church. He married Elizabeth Kempley; children: 1. Wallace, died young. 2. Alfred C., now of Paterson. 3. Edwin L., now living on Long Island. 4. John Henry. 5. Lizzie, married G. S. Atterbury and lives in Chicago. 6. Mary, married Charles Edwards, of Paterson.

(III) John Henry, son of John and Elizabeth (Kempley) Reynolds, was born in Paterson, New Jersey, February 11, 1855, and acquired his elementary and secondary education in the public schools of that city, and his higher education at the University of Michigan, Ann Arbor, Michigan, where he was graduated A. B. in 1876. His professional education was received at Columbia Law School, the law department of Columbia University, where he completed the course and came to the degree LL. B. in 1878. In the following year he was admitted to practice in the courts of this state and since that time has been a member of the Passaic county bar, engaged in general practice, with an especial preference for cases which involve questions of real estate law. He is not in any sense a public man, having little inclination for politics, and the extent of his holdings has been limited to several years' service as member of the city board of park commissioners.

He married, April 7, 1881, Cora C., born April 10, 1856, daughter of Albert G. and Sarah C. (Greene) Stevens, of Buffalo, New York, and by whom he has four children, all born in Paterson: Kate, Beatrix, John S., Doris.

PEDDIE Thomas B. Peddie, one of the most enterprising and successful of the citizens of Newark, New Jersey, began his business career in that place in 1833, before it had been incorporated as a city. Mr. Peddie was a native of Edinburgh, Scotland, and this was also the birth place of his parents, who were persons of more than ordinary intelligence, of great industry, and of remarkably piety, his father being somewhat noted as a religious exhorter. To the example and influence of such estimable parents was young Peddie indebted for his habits of industry, as well as for his self-reliance and his reverence for everything that is essential to an honorable and pious life. Such advantages for an education as were within the means of his parents were accorded to him, and though not great they were quite sufficient for the oridinary purposes of life. To the acquisitions made by him as a schoolboy he subsequently added largely by reading and by contact with his fellowmen as he increased in years. He was fond of books of travel and of the accounts of foreign lands given in the newspapers of the day. His desire to visit America was thus aroused, and having at last through his own industry acquired sufficient means to gratify his desire, he left his native land for the United States, not quite decided, however, to make it his permanent home.

In 1833, as already stated, he found himself in Newark, New Jersey, a place which he had been induced to visit on account of the rapid growth of its manufacturing interests. Not intending to be an idle looker-on, but determined rather to obtain a thorough knowledge of the new people among whom he had fallen, he visited the various factories of the place, and finally applied for employment in the great saddlery establishment of Messrs. Smith & Wright, the latter of whom became subsequently a senator of the United States. He bore about him no other commendation than his honest face and manly ways, but these sufficed to gain him a desirable position in this extensive factory. Here he remained two years, when having become familiar with the business ways of the land in which he had now concluded to make a permanent home he resolved to test his own business abilities as an operator and financier. Accordingly he undertook in a modest way the manufacture of leather trunks and carpet bags. Success attended him beyond his expectations, and a large and lucrative business seemed to await him in no distant future. For ten years he continued to manufacture alone his rapidly extending operations. In 1846 he found it necessary, however, to take a business partner to assist him in his labors, especially in keeping his books and attending to his growing correspondence. For this important service he selected Mr. John Morrison, who subsequently proved himself to be one of Newark's most estimable and patriotic citizens. This partnership continued until 1861, when Mr. Morrison died. On Mr. Peddie alone again devolved the care of his immense establishment, and to it he gave his undivided attention; but the burden being more than he could long carry unassisted, he sought aid eventually from one of his most esteemed and accomplished assistants, Mr. George B. Jenkinson, whose familiarity with every department of the complicated works relieved Mr. Peddie of much of his labor and finally resulted in a partnership between them, under the firm name of T. B. Peddie & Company. Under this name the business was conducted until the death of its founder.

For many years prior to his decease and indeed until within a short time before that event, Mr. Peddie was active in discharge of all the duties of a good and patriotic citizen. His interests led him to take a prominent part in the conduct of the moneyed institutions of the city, in many of which he was an influential director. But even where personal interest did not call him he was equally earnest and active. In almost every important public movement he was among the leaders, aiding by his advice as well as by his purse. Of the board of trade of the city of Newark he was a most efficient member, at one time its president and at all times an earnest participant in its proceedings. It was undoubtedly the sterling honesty of Mr. Peddie which pointed him out as a desirable man to be placed in public positions of great responsibility. It was this that sent him in 1863-64 to the state legislature, where as a member of the general assembly he gave valuable support to the general government during the war of the rebellion, and by his influence and contributions did good service in behalf of the Union. During the period of four years, 1866-69, he was mayor of Newark, an office which he filled with credit to himself and advantage to the city. In 1876 he represented the sixth congressional district of New Jersey in the forty-fifth congress. On the expiration of his term he declined further nomination.

Without making any pretense of learning, Mr. Peddie appreciated fully the value of a good education, and this is shown by the interest which he took in building up the flourishing academy in Hightstown, New Jersey, to which was given in honor of him the name of Peddie Institute. He was one of the early promotors of the Newark Technical School, an institution for which the city of Newark is mainly indebted to its board of trade, by which body the first steps were taken for its establishment, with Mr. Peddie as chairman of the committee having charge of the enterprise. For many years he was a trustee for the Newark City Home, a school to which he gave much attention. Of all benevolent enterprises he was a supporter, ever ready to advance them by contributing of his means as well as by his personal services. On Newark's principal thoroughfare, nearly facing one of its beautiful parks, stands a house of worship, built of gray granite, in Byzantine style of architecture, and capable of seating three thousand worshippers. It is called the Peddie Memorial, and was the gift of this beneficent man to the congregation with which he connected himself when as a youth he came to Newark, and with which he continued to worship throughout his long and useful career. The erection of this massive pile was the last work of Mr. Peddie's life. It is one of Newark's noblest structures, but he did not live to see it completed. The name given to it was never suggested until after his death, which occurred February 16, 1889. All of Mr. Peddie's designs in regard to the construction and appointments of this edifice were fully carried out by his estimable widow, who followed him into eternal rest three years afterward. She also complied with another wish on his part by giving to the church valuable property in New York City and elsewhere, which yields it a handsome revenue.

EATON The ancestors of Edward Charles Eaton, of Newark, are on his father's side English and on his mother's Swiss, his great-grandparents having emigrated to this country from England and Switzerland.

(1) Ignatius Eaton, father of Edward Charles Eaton, was born in 1833, died in 1868. He received a common school education, and learning the trade of a machinist entered the employ of Hughes & Phillips, with whom he remained for the greater part of his life. He married Elizabeth Sentz. Children: 1. Louisa, married George H. Bath, for thirty-two years in the employ of Isbell Porter & Company; two children: Florence, and George Edward, deceased. 2. Edward Charles, referred to below. 3. Anna, married John Roschwald, of 833 Broad street, Newark.

(II) Edward Charles, son of Ignatius and Elizabeth (Sentz) Eaton, was born in Newark, New Jersey, December 14, 1860. He attended the public schools and the Newark high school and then went into the seed business which his father had established in 1859, nine years before his death, and when that event occurred he continued the business with the backing of his mother until 1907 when he assumed the sole control and has since then managed it for himself. In politics Mr. Eaton is a Democrat and he has long been one of the prominent members of his party. From 1906 to 1908 he was member of the board of chosen freeholders of Essex county, New Jersey, was a member of important committees, and was chairman and speaker of the house, and the leading member of the board. He was chairman of the building committee when the new court house was built, and took great pride in the work. He was also chairman of the board when the county insane asylum was built at Overbrook, costing two and a-half million dollars, and enabling the county to house twenty-one hundred people, and again when the county house of detention was built. He is also one of the most influential men in the Essex County Democratic Club, and is the treasurer of the Joel Parker Association. He is also a member of the Jeffersonian Club, the Gottfried Krueger Association, the President Lincoln Mutual Aid Association and of the Benevolent and Protective Order of Elks, No. 21. In religious convictions he is a Methodist.

Mr. Eaton married in East Orange, New Jersey, August 15, 1888, Alida, born August 7. 1864, daughter of Theodore and Sarah M. (Bedford) Schenck, who were the parents of five other children, namely: Theodore Clifford, a druggist of East Orange; married Elizabeth Chandler and has one child Ethel. Harry E., president of the American Hame and Bit Company, No. 59 New Jersey Railroad avenue, Newark; married Mary Besher

and has two children: Ellwood and Harvey. Frederick, married Mary Smith and has one child Edna. Anna, married George Kelly and has one child George Leroy. Grace, married George Spaith and has one child Hortense.

BENNETT   The Bennett family of New Jersey which has for two generations been represented in Newark and the Oranges by Dr. Frederick Norman Bennett, and Dr. Charles Day Bennett, owes its origin to the New England family of that name, Dr. Frederick Norman Bennett, being a descendant of the Bennetts of Fairfield county, Connecticut.

(I) Frederick Norman, son of Ezra and Esther (Gordon) Bennett, was born in Weston, Fairfield county, Connecticut, September 14, 1820, died in 1885, in Newtown, Connecticut. After receiving his education in the public schools he entered the office of his brother, Dr. Ezra P. Bennett, a distinguished surgeon in Danbury, Connecticut, with whom he remained until he matriculated from the Yale Medical School, from which he received his diploma in 1841. In 1842 he came to Orange, New Jersey, and entered upon the practice of his profession, soon securing the confidence of the people in him as a physician, and acquiring the very successful practice. After his second marriage he left Orange for a time but soon returned and remained until 1871 when he removed to Newtown, Connecticut, where he remained until his death. While a resident of Orange he enjoyed the friendship and confidence of its best citizens, by whom his virtues and the memories of his exemplary christian life are sincerely cherished. He was one of the organizers in 1863 of the Orange Memorial Hospital and Training School for Nurses, and one of the group of physicians who pledged their services to the institution.

August 29, 1843, Dr. Bennett married (first) Abigail Louisa, daughter of William Munn, cashier of the Orange Bank, who died in September, 1849. In 1852 he married Catharine, daughter of Jonathan and Mary Parkhurst, and granddaughter of Abram J. and Mary (Whitehead) Parkhurst, who was born in 1818. Children, one by first wife: 1. William Munn, now living in New York City. 2. Mary, born July 31, 1855, died aged fifteen years. 3. Charles Day, referred to below.

(II) Charles Day, son of Frederick Norman, M. D., and Catharine (Parkhurst) Bennett, was born in Millburn, New Jersey, January 25, 1857. After attending the public and high schools of Newark, he entered Princeton University, from which he graduated with the degree of Bachelor of Science, in 1878, being a member of the third class graduated with that degree from the university. In 1881 he graduated from the College of Physicians and Surgeons in New York City, and since then has been engaged in the private practice of his profession in Newark, New Jersey, giving special attention to the fields of medicine and surgery. For eight years, from 1882 to 1890, he was physician to the Newark City Almshouse; was attending physician and surgeon from 1890 to 1905 of St. Michael's Hospital; from 1891 to 1906 on the attending staff of Newark City Hospital; from 1905 to present time attending surgeon of St. Barnabas Hospital; in 1905 was appointed on the medical staff of the Mutual Benefit Insurance Company. For eighteen years he was treasurer of the Essex County Medical Society and in 1909 its president. He is a member of the Medical and Surgical Society of Newark, of the various county, state, and national medical societies, and secretary of the Society for the Relief of the Widows and Orphans of New Jersey. He is a member of the University Club, of Newark, and was elected trustee of the Newark Museum Association. Dr. Bennett is a member and president of the board of trustees of Calvary Presbyterian Church, and in politics is a Republican.

Dr. Bennett married, March 28, 1882, Fannie E., daughter of James H. and Maria (Booth) Marley; she died February 22, 1890. Married (second) October 17, 1896, Sara Leeper, born January 27, 1867, daughter of Robert and Mary (Lowden) Gordon, of One Hundred and Seventh street and West End avenue, New York City. Children, three by first wife: 1. Iris B., born January 5, 1883; married William F. Law; one child, Virginia, born December 15, 1907. 2. Louise, born April 15, 1884. 3. Dorothy, born April 26, 1886. 4. Katharine Parkhurst, born November 30, 1898. 5. Eleanor Gordon, born March 31, 1905.

CROCKER   Thomas Crocker, first member of the family of whom we have definite information, was born in Paterson, New Jersey, in 1824 or 1825, and died in East Orange, New Jersey, in 1904. He married Adelia J. Reed, and among his children was Charles Irwin, referred to below.

(II) Charles Irwin, son of Thomas and Adelia J. (Reed) Crocker, lived in New York City and at Hudson, Wisconsin. He married Emma Estelle, daughter of Philip Morehouse and Elizabeth (Bartlett) Pierce, the former a real estate broker of Beloit, Wisconsin. Children: 1. Roland Douglas, referred to below. 2. Charles Philip, died as a baby. 3. Anna Estelle, married Soren P. Rees, of Minneapolis, Minnesota, and has one child, Douglas.

(III) Roland Douglas, son of Charles Irwin and Emma Estelle (Pierce) Crocker, was born in Massena Springs, New York, May 27, 1871, and is now living in Newark, New Jersey. After receiving his early education at the public schools, he took his degree from the University of Minnesota, and made a specialty of civil engineering. In 1896 he entered the office of the Hon. James M. Morrow, with whom he read law until he was admitted to the bar as attorney in 1900. Since this time he has been engaged in the general practice of his profession in Newark. He is a Republican. The only secret societies to which he belongs are the college fraternity of Psi Upsilon, and the Junior Order of United American Mechanics. His clubs are the Lawyers Club of Newark, and the Union Club of Newark, and he is one of the directors of and the counsel for the Newark Trust Company. Mr. Crocker has been a member of the National Guard of New Jersey since October, 1901, and is now major of the First Regiment Infantry, having risen to that rank by successive promotion, from second to first lieutenant and captain.

MILLER   The name Miller, belonging as it does to one of the many numerous so called trade names, has become the cognomen of a number of entirely unrelated families in this country, and apparently the ancestor of the branch at present under consideration, seems to have no connection, with the exception of one family of the same name, in Philadelphia, with the various Millers who emigrated to and remained in New England, whither the founder of this branch directed his first steps.

(I) Joseph Miller, founder of the family at present under consideration, came from the state of Connecticut, in 1698, and settled at Cohansey, Salem county, New Jersey. Whether he was the original emigrant himself or the son of the emigrant, there seems to be no way of determining, in as much as the Connecticut records are silent in regard to him. It is most probable that he emigrated from England in order to find religious liberty, and like so many others who came to New England for the same reason found that unless they worshipped God according to the New England method, there was no freedom there for them. As Joseph Miller was a Quaker, the only place in New England where he could find peace and freedom was Rhode Island, under the more liberal government which had been created there by Roger Williams. Thither, such men as Richard Lippincott had gone for refuge, when driven out of England and New England. and many of these men found their way sooner or later down to the Quaker colonies upon the Delaware. Joseph Miller was a land surveyor, and at the death of Richard Tindall he was chosen deputy surveyor for the lower section of Fenwick's tenth. The last mention of him in the records as a surveyor is 9th month 13, 1729, when he re-surveyed a tract of land for John Brick, lying on the west branch of Gravelly run or Stoe creek. He probably died about 1730, and his son was appointed his successor as deputy surveyor to the Salem tenth. Joseph Miller had but one child, Ebenezer, referred to below.

(II) Ebenezer, only child of Joseph Miller, was born at Cohansey, 1702, died at Greenwich, New Jersey, at the age of seventy-two years "with a comfortable hope that all would be well with him in a future state." He was for many years the deputy surveyor for the proprietors of West Jersey, and no name is of so frequent occurrence in their records as is his. In 1724 Ebenezer Miller married Sarah, probably daughter of John Collier. Their children were: 1. Ebenezer, Jr., born 9th month 15. 1725; married, 1751, Ruth, daughter of Richard Wood, of Stoe creek. 2. Hannah, born 1728; married, 1740, Charles, son of Daniel Fogg, of Alloways creek. 3. Josiah, referred to below. 4. Andrew, born 1732; married Rachael, daughter of Elisha and Abigail Bassett, of Piles Grove. His son, Daniel L. Miller, was the famous merchant of Philadelphia. 5. William, born 1735; married Mary Magere, of Wilmington, Delaware. 6. John Collier, born 1737; married, 1767, Margaret, daughter of Joseph and Mary Bacon, of Greenwich. 7. Mark, born 1740. 8. Sarah. 9. Rebecca, born 5th month 17, 1747.

(III) Josiah, third child and second son of Ebenezer and Sarah (Collier) Miller, was born in Cohansey, in 1731. About 1774 he purchased a large tract of land in Lower Mannington, which formerly belonged to the Sherron family, it being the southern part of James Sharron allotment of one thousand acres, that he bought

of John Fenwick in 1676. It was considered one of the finest tracts of table land within Fenwick's tenth. Soon after this purchase Josiah Miller removed with his family to this land, on which he built the brick house which descended in his family to his great-grandson, Samuel L. J. Miller. He divided it in his will between his two sons, Josiah and Richard. In 1760 Josiah Miller married Letitia, daughter of Richard Wood, Sr., of Stoe Creek township, Cumberland county, who was the sister of his brother Ebenezer's wife. Children: 1. Josiah, Jr., born 12th month 12, 1761; he never married, and after the death of his mother, who survived his father, he lived with his brother Richard, and after his death continued living with his widow. In his will he devised his farm to her during her natural life, and afterward to her son Josiah. To his nephew, Josiah Miller Reeve, he devised $2,500.00, and left other legacy to several relatives. 2. Richard, referred to below. 3. John, born in 1767, died young. 4. Letitia, born 1769; married William Reeve and left one son, Josiah Miller Reeve. 5. Mark, born 1774; died young, leaving a widow, Letitia, who survived him several years.

(IV) Richard, second child and son of Josiah and Letitia (Wood) Miller, was born 4th month 15, 1764. He married Elizabeth Wyatt, daughter of Richard Wistar, of Philadelphia, by whom he had three children: Sarah. Letitia. Josiah, referred to below.

(V) Josiah (2), youngest child and only son of Richard and Elizabeth Wyatt (Wistar) Miller, was born in August, 1800, died August, 1834. He was a farmer at Mannington, New Jersey. He married Hetty Hall James. Children: 1. Richard, of Salem, who enlisted in the civil war from that county, and died in the Soldiers' National Home in Ohio; during the war he was detailed to purchase supplies for the army; he married (first) Elizabeth Blackwood and (second) Susan Wilde. 2. Samuel L. J., a farmer of Mannington, New Jersey; married Hannah Ann Rumsey. 3. Wyatt Wistar, referred to below.

(VI) Wyatt Wistar, youngest child of Josiah (2) and Hetty Hall (James) Miller, was born at Mannington, Salem county, New Jersey, November 1, 1828, died at Salem, Salem county, 1904. He was a farmer and an iron master, and was superintendent of the iron works at Safe Harbor, Lancaster county, Pennsylvania. He was the discoverer of the method which made what was later known as Bessemer steel. He married Mary Leggett, daughter of John and Esther (Leggett) Griffen, of New York City, born in June, 1838. Children: 1. Josiah, referred to below. 2. Samuel Lawrence, born October 16, 1861; a farmer, now living in Salem, New Jersey. 3. Robert Griffen, born April 22, 1863; married Lily Speakman, of Chester county, Pennsylvania. 4. Mary Griffen, born March 14, 1867; married John Forman Sinnickson, of Salem county, New Jersey, the prosecutor of the pleas at Salem. 5. Hetty Hall, deceased; married Collins Bassett Allen, a farmer and ex-sheriff of Salem county, New Jersey, and now living on the old homestead at Mannington, New Jersey. 6. John Griffen, born in 1869; married Caroline Bowen. 7. Wyatt Wistar, Jr., died unmarried at Denver, Colorado, in January, 1899. 8. George Henry, born in 1871. 9. Elizabeth Wyatt, born in 1874.

(VII) Josiah (3), eldest child of Wyatt Wistar and Mary Leggett (Griffen) Miller, was born at Safe Harbor, Lancaster county, Pennsylvania, August 8, 1859, and is now living in Salem, New Jersey. His great-grandfather on his grandmother's side was Samuel L. James, who married Mary, daughter of Edward Hall, of Mannington, Salem county, New Jersey. For his early education Josiah Miller was sent to the public schools of Safe, Harbor, Pennsylvania, and to the private school of Miss Hawley, at Phoenixville, then to the public school at Salem, New Jersey, and then pursued the course at Rensselaer Polytechnic Institute at Troy, New York, intending to become a civil engineer, entering in the year 1876. He did not, however, graduate but returned to his father's farm on which he worked for a time, later managing another farm for himself. After this he engaged in the business of manufacturing enameled brick at Oaks, Montgomery county, Pennsylvania, the firm name being Griffen Brothers & Miller, Limited. Subsequently the partners incorporated the business and it was known as the Griffen Enameled Brick Company. In this corporation Mr. Miller held the position of secretary and superintendent. In 1894 he was for a short time connected with the Trenton Terra Cotta Company. He then came back to Salem, New Jersey, and opened a general store on Broadway, which he continued to conduct for about three years, when he sold out and began the practice of his profession as a civil engineer and surveyor for which he was specially qualified. To this profession Mr. Miller added a general insurance business. In politics Mr. Miller was a Republican, active and influential

in the affairs of his party, and as a reward for his services he was elected to the office of mayor of Salem in 1905, continuing until 1907, being the first Republican to serve in that capacity for twenty years. He is also a justice of the peace, a member of the board of education of Salem, and in 1887-88 was the township clerk of Mannington. Mr. Miller is a member of the Hicksite Quakers. He is a member of the Knights of Pythias and of the Ancient Order of United Workmen.

Mr. Miller married, October 28, 1885, Mariana Elkinton, born January 27, 1862, daughter of Clark H. and Ann L. (Test) Thompson. Her father is a native of Mannington township, Salem county, and her mother of Salem. Children: 1. Alice Thompson, born April 21, 1887. 2. Wyatt Acton, June 17, 1892. 3. Esther Griffen, January 19, 1894.

EDGAR The Edgars, of Metuchen, New Jersey, with the various branches of the same family resident elsewhere in the state, are descended from a Scottish family of great antiquity and marked distinction, whose records may be consulted in the very noteworthy English work, "Genealogical Collections Concerning the Scottish House of Edgar, with a Memoir of James Edgar, Private Secretary of the Chevalier St. George, edited by a committee of the Grampian Club. London: printed for the Grampian Club, 1873."

The New Jersey line springs from the Edgars, of Keithock, Forfarshire, Scotland, an estate which originally belonged to the noble house of Lindsay, coming into the possession of the Edgar family early in the seventeenth century. The patronymic is found in that locality from an ancient period. At the beginning of the thirteenth century the names of Robert and Thomas Edgar were attached to charters granted by the bishop of Brechin in favor of the abbey of Arbroath. In the seventeenth century two separate branches of the family of Edgar were successively lairds of Keithock, the ultimate proprietorship being that of David Edgar, ancestor of the present Edgars, of New Jersey. His manor house is still standing, and is a structure of elegant architectural style and admirable proportions. Affixed to the mantel is a representation, carved in stone and bearing date 1680, of the Edgar arms (a lion rampant), impaled with those of the allied family of Forrester.

David Edgar, laird of Keithock, was married

Charles S. Edgar

(according to his family Bible, which is preserved) to Katherine Forrester at Dundee, Scotland, by the Rev. William Rait, June 11, 1674. They had a numerous family, the fifth child being Thomas Edgar, the American emigrant, of whom presently. The succession to the estate of Keithock passed, by the law of primogeniture, to the eldest son, Alexander Edgar (born May 21, 1676), who married the eldest daughter of Peter Turnbull, of Smiddyhill, Forfarshire. The property continued in the possession of the Edgar family until 1790, when it was sold. Another son of David Edgar, and younger brother of Thomas Edgar, the emigrant, was the very noted James Edgar, born at Keithock, July 13, 1688. With another brother, John Edgar, he participated actively in the Stuart rising of 1715. John was taken prisoner and died in captivity in Stirling Castle. James made his way to Keithock, borrowed from a tenant farmer a suit of laborer's clothes, and, thus disguised, escaped to the continent. Becoming secretary to the Chevalier St. George, the famous pretender to the British throne, he served him with the greatest fidelity and distinguished ability. Secretary Edgar died September 24, 1764.

(I) Thomas Edgar, fifth child of David Edgar, laird of Keithock, by his wife, Katherine Forrester, was born, as exactly related in the family Bible, on "Wednesday, 19th of October, 1681, and baptized at the College Kirk by Mr. Irving, the 30th of said month." He came to America about 1715, purchased lands in New Jersey, lived near Rahway, and died there in 1759. He married Janet Knox, who was born in Woodbridge, March 16, 1689. Of their seven children were David (ancestor of the Short Hill branch). Alexander (ancestor of the Woodbridge branch). William (ancestor of the Rahway branch).

(II) Alexander, son of Thomas and Janet (Knox) Edgar, was born in 1722, and died in 1763.

(III) James, son of Alexander Edgar.

(IV) Thomas (2), son of James Edgar, married Mary Freeman and had twelve children.

(V) Albert, son of Thomas (2) Edgar, was born in Woodbridge, New Jersey, November 27, 1813. He was a farmer, residing near Metuchen, Middlesex county, and was one of the founders, and until his death an elder of the Dutch Reformed church of that community. He died in Woodbridge, New Jersey, October 14, 1877. Mr. Edgar was three times married. His second wife was Susan Tappen (born February 19, 1813, died September 12, 1855), daughter of William Tappen. Children: 1. William Tappen, resides in Raritan township, Middlesex county, New Jersey. 2. Charles Smith, see below. 3. Milton Albert, resides in Georgia. 4. Mary Amelia, died at the age of twelve.

(VI) Charles Smith, son of Albert Edgar, was born on the old Tappen homestead at Bonhamtown, Raritan township, Middlesex county, New Jersey, September 22, 1848. Reared on his father's farm, he became at an early age attracted by the superior quality of the clay on that property and vicinity, and as the resulting tests demonstrated its availability for terra cotta and other purposes, he entered into copartnership with his brothers for putting it on the market. This association continued until 1884, since which time Mr. Edgar has continued his clay interests in the vicinity of Metuchen, under his personal name. From early life, during his travels throughout the country, he devoted a portion of his time to prospecting. Hearing on one occasion, while on a business visit to Boston, a somewhat circumstantial account of the existence of fine clay deposits in Florida, which had never been developed, and of which, indeed, all exact traces had been lost by negligence, he made several prospecting tours through that state, finally, in 1890, discovering the beds in Putnam county, at a place now called Edgar in his honor. This led to the production on a large scale by Mr. Edgar, and afterward by others, of the remarkably fine grade of potter's clay known as "Florida clay," which in the past fifteen years has been universally used, entering largely into the manufacture of vitrified tiles and sanitary Rockwood-Deldare—fine china, and other delicate wares. The Edgar Plastic Kaolin Company, organized by Mr. Edgar in his connection, of which he is the head, owns some two thousand acres of Florida clay lands, and has an annual producing capacity of eighteen thousand tons. Recently he has been instrumental in organizing and establishing the new firm of Edgar Brothers, now engaged in mining clay at Milltown, New Jersey, and in putting up kaolin works at McIntyre, Georgia. In this firm his associates are M. A. Edgar, I. R. Edgar and David R. Edgar. The improved machinery used in the various mines and works represents to a large extent the personal inventions or ideas of Mr. Edgar. He resides in Metuchen, with a winter home in Edgar, Florida.

He married, December 20, 1882, his first

ii—15

cousin. Frances Emily Edgar, granddaughter of Thomas and Mary (Freeman) Edgar, and daughter of Freeman and Sarah Elizabeth (Martin) Edgar. Children of Freeman Edgar (born May 24, 1820, died October. 4, 1895) and Sarah Elizabeth (Martin) Edgar: 1. I. Reynolds, resides in Metuchen. 2. Frances Emily, wife of Charles Smith Edgar. 3. Laura Antoinette. married Charles Wesley Price (deceased), of New Brunswick. 4. Freeman Martin, resides in Newark, New Jersey. Charles Smith and Frances Emily (Edgar) Edgar have one child, Albert Charles Edgar, born May 27, 1898.

MASON   This surname comes from England and is found among our eldest family names,. but it cannot be claimed that the immigrant heads of the several families were in any manner related to each other. In New England the name appears in the earliest times of the colony and those bearing it took a prominent part in the establishment of government and the defense of the plantations against the Indians. In New York, Pennsylvania and New Jersey the Masons were early settlers, and the family proposed to be treated in this place dates its history in the latter state from the early years of the last century.

(I) John Mason, with whom our present narrative begins, was born in Nottingham, Derbyshire, England. in 1772, and his wife, whose name before marriage was Martha Wharton. was born in the same town and shire, and also in the same year. She died in Nutley, New Jersey, in 1830, and her husband died there two years later, in 1832. In old Nottingham in England John Mason was a cotton spinner and carried on a shop of his own, as is shown by his old account books, several of which are yet in possession of his descendants. He came with his family to this country in 1810 and settled in New Jersey, at the place then called Franklin, Essex county. There he built a cotton mill and established himself in business. also erected a stone dwelling house near his mill, which is still standing and is yet a very substantial structure. Besides the mill and his residence John Mason also built a number of smaller houses for the use of his employees, and the tradition is that he was a very energetic and prosperous man in his business affairs. The thriving little village of Nutley, near Passaic. is built up around the site where pioneer John Mason set up his cotton spinning establishment something like a century ago.

His children were: John, William, Thomas, Charles, Martha, married John Parks, and Betsey, married Abraham Vreeland.

(II) Thomas. son of John and Martha (Wharton) Mason, was born in Nottingham, Derbyshire, England, in 1808, and died in Paterson, New Jersey, in 1878. He was a child of two years when his parents came to America and settled in Essex county, New Jersey, and there he attended the district school and later learned the trade of cotton spinning in his father's mill. He worked for his father a number of years and then went to Bristol, Rhode Island, where he had charge of an oakum factory, and lived there for many years. In 1855 he came back to New Jersey and afterward was employed as manager of the bobbin factory in Paterson of which Peter V. H. Van Riper was owner and proprietor. He remained there until 1870 and then set up in business for himself as a manufacturer of belting. continued his works about three years and then retired from active pursuits. Thomas Mason was an industrious man and capable manager and his endeavors in business life were rewarded with success; he was a straightforward and honest man, an upright citizen and one who gained the respect of all who knew him. He married Elizabeth Odell, of Parsippany, New Jersey, and had four children, two of whom are still living: George Clay and Martha E. the latter the widow of Pierson Van Houten. formerly of Paterson, and veteran of the civil war.

(III) George Clay, son of Thomas and Elizabeth (Odell) Mason, was born in Paterson, August 10, 1845. He received his education in the public schools of that city and Eastman's Business College, Poughkeepsie, New York, where he was graduated on the completion of a thorough business course. In 1862, at the age of seventeen years, he began his business career as clerk in a grocery store in Paterson, and three years later started in the same business on his own account, and from that time until 1907 he was without interruption closely identified with the mercantile life of the city. On February 7, 1902, having been in successful business for forty years, his entire establishment was burned to the ground, his store. residence, barns, and several dwellings closely adjoining, of all of which he was the owner. On the morning of the following day he was established in a new location in a small building which he leased for his immediate purposes, and from which his customers were supplied as before and without any particular inconvenience to themselves. This disaster occasioned serious loss to Mr. Mason, but did not cause financial ruin or even serious discouragement, for he is a man not easily disheartened and is possessed of the fortunate qualities of determination and energy in an abundant degree. Had it been otherwise it is doubtful whether his business life would have been as successful as it has been. However, after the fire he soon became re-established on a basis more substantial than before and was proprietor of one of the leading retail grocery and provision stores in the city until 1907, when he retired and was succeeded by his son. Francis K. Since that time he has been engaged in a general real estate and insurance business, besides devoting personal attention to the management of the several land and improvement companies of which he is a member and in each of which he has considerable financial investments. He is president of the Eighteenth Street Land Company, treasurer of the Laurel Grove Cemetery Company, director of the Cedar Cliff Land Company and the Citizens' Land Company, and a director and ex-treasurer of the Broadway Land and Building Company. He is one of the founders of the Paterson Grocers' Association, its treasurer since it was organized and still holds honorary membership in the association. For many years he has been counted among the prominent and successful business men of the city, and in many ways has shown himself "a good man for Paterson" and the interests of that constantly growing municipality.

George Clay Mason married, November 15, 1870, Rocena, born May 25, 1844, daughter of William and Catherine (Sigler) McCully. Children: 1. Francis K., born August 28, 1872; married Anna Mae Smith, born April 15, 1873; children: George Clayton, born December 11, 1897, died June 24, 1899; Carolyn, born October 5, 1901. 2. Elizabeth Odell, born January, 1874, died May, 1874. 3. Florence Mae, born May, 1876, died March, 1877. 4. Charles W., born June 26, 1881.

HUGHES This family is probably of Welch origin, but is first found as far as connection with this family is known in northern Ireland, whither it was undoubtedly transported from Scotland.

(I) Thomas Hughes, immigrant progenitor, was born and reared in Bambridge, a suburb of Belfast, Ireland. He came to America in 1844, with his wife and children, and made his home at Northeast, Cecil county, Mary-

land, where he died in 1868, at the age of sixty-three years. He was a linen manufacturer. He married, in Ireland, Mary Craig, of undoubted Scotch ancestry. Children: 1. John, mentioned below. 2. George, married Annie Franklin. 3. Thomas, married Margaret Malden. 4. Arthur, died young. 5. Sarah, wife of Moses Thompson. 6. Martha, died young. 7. Margaret, died unmarried. 8. Elizabeth, died unmarried.

(II) John, son of Thomas and Mary (Craig) Hughes, was born December 21, 1825, at Bambridge, and came with the family to America in 1844. He settled at Northeast and secured a position with the wholesale house of Lumsden & Company in Baltimore, and within two years was taken into partnership. At the beginning of the civil war, when General Butler took possession of the city, he was one of its leading merchants controlling the sale of provision markets and having contracts with the British government for supplying its army and navy. On account of his southern sympathies, he was obliged to leave Baltimore and went to New York, where he became a prominent shipper and one of the leading speculators on the produce exchange. Having been trained to the linen business in Belfast in connection with his brother, George, he established the firm of George Hughes & Company in 1862, subsequently located at 198 and 200 Church street, New York, dealers in linen goods. This firm was the largest in the business up to the year 1872. The conditions imposed by the civil war, however, broke up the business of John Hughes, who operated his own vessels in trade with England. These vessels were destroyed during the war and the companies insuring them became bankrupt. By this and other complications, he was forced to discontinue business and assign his claims against the United States government in the Geneva Award. In 1868 Mr. John Hughes relinquished mercantile business and removed to Plainfield, New Jersey, where he dealt largely in real estate. He was induced to purchase a large tract of land at Athenia, two miles from Passaic, and this he improved at an expense of $200,000. This, coupled with a loss of $125,000, through endorsements on his brother's paper, followed by the panic of 1873, caused his financial ruin. In consequence of these reverses, in 1876, the family retired to the farm on Chesapeake Bay, formerly used as their summer home. Here they resided until 1883, when the son Frank brought the family to Passaic. John Hughes died in August, 1889.

He married, March 8, 1853, Mary A., born December 19, 1832, in Cecil county, daughter of Robert and Richarda (Hopkins) Dawson (see Dawson, VI). The last named was a daughter of Dr. Richard Hopkins and a niece of Dr. Johns Hopkins, for whom the University is named (see Hopkins, IV). Children of John and Mary A. Hughes: 1. Elizabeth, born March 14, 1858, in Baltimore, Maryland. 2. Frank, mentioned below. 3. John, October 5, 1862. 4. Mary, August 10, 1864. 5. Thomas, June 16, 1870; married, October 7, 1897, Carrie Newman and has son, William Bayard, born March 28, 1904. 6. Arthur S., June 15, 1873. The first three were born in Baltimore, Maryland, the fourth in Brooklyn, the fifth in Plainfield, New Jersey, and the sixth in Clifton, same state.

(III) Frank, second son of John and Mary A. (Dawson) Hughes, was born November 28, 1860, in Baltimore, and has been for nearly a quarter of a century one of the most prominent citizens of Passaic, New Jersey. He is a self-made man whose activities and broad smypathies have had much to do with the steady and healthy growth of the community. His career furnishes profitable study as that of a notably successful business man. Although of a delicate physical organization and having been deprived of many school advantages by family reverses in his boyhood, yet by a rare combination of natural mental endowment, sheer force of will and a higher ambition toward the best ideals, he has wrought his own advancement against what would have proven in many lives insurmountable obstacles. He has fought his way to a position of acknowledged leadership in local affairs. His prompt, almost intuitive, judgment of real estate values, and his peculiar faculty for handling investments, have made him an expert authority in matters pertaining to real estate, and his reputation is extended far beyond the limits of his immediate business. His counsel is frequently sought in important municipal problems, and every legitimate enterprise finds in him a cordial and able champion. Nearly all of the important manufacturing industries located in Passaic during his residence there have been the direct result of his efforts. At the age of twenty years, having wearied of the quiet of the farm whither his parents had retired, he determined to strike out in the world for himself. He became interested in the Block system of telegraphy then in use on the Pennsylvania railroad running through the farm, and resolved to study telegraphy. He left home

in 1882 and after a brief course in a Philadelphia technical school, secured a position as operator at the Clifton station on the Delaware, Lackawanna & Western railroad, in New Jersey. Here, amid the scenes of his father's losses, his ambition to recuperate them by real estate operations was kindled, and his first successful deal was the location of the Clifton Rubber Company at that place. He decided to enter the real estate business and went to Passaic early in 1886 and opened a small office on Bloomfield avenue. This field was already occupied by older local dealers and to one of less resolute nature than Mr. Hughes, the outlook would have seemed hopeless. Without means or even acquaintance, and in the face of strong prejudice, Mr. Hughes has made his way step by step, until he occupies a position at the head of his line of business in the county, if not in the state. Much of his business is transacted in New York where he ranks among the leading brokers. In 1889-90 he was employed by the boards of trade in several large towns in the Indiana natural gas field and spent some time in aiding the development of that section. Some of his transactions have reached as far west as California. The following list of industries will attest his activities in the upbuilding of Passaic, as he organized all of them and is either secretary or president and manager of all save one: The Passaic Park Company, Passaic Bridge Land Company, Hillside Land Company, Main Avenue Improvement Company, Minerva Land Company, Passaic City Land Company, Passaic Homestead Company, J. L. Hutchinson Land Company, Cooley Land Company, Crescent Real Estate Company, Henle Land Company, Park Heights Land & Water Company, Clifton Development Company, Saddle River Land Company and Lakeview Heights Association.

Mr. Hughes was one of the organizers of the People's Building & Loan Association and of the Hobart Trust Company, of which he is one of its vice-presidents. He also organized the Newton Gas & Electric Company, consolidating the gas and electric interests of that town, of which company he is now managing director. He is a director in and treasurer of the Montross Bond & Realty Company, the 44 West Seventy-seventh Street Company, and the Allied Underwriters of New York City. He is also president of the Dundee Textile Company and the Passaic Investment Company, and is largely interested in several other banks and trust companies. In connection with his real estate business Mr. Hughes condicts a fire insurance agency, representing some of the largest insurance companies in the world. On January 1, 1900, his business was incorporated under the title of Frank Hughes, (Incorporated), with himself as president and treasurer, his brother, Arthur S. Hughes, vice-president, and George F. Allen, secretary. He has devoted himself unsparingly to the development and building up of Passaic and has never hesitated to give his time, energies or money to any project looking towards its advancement and to him more than all others is due the remarkable growth of the city of Passaic during the last quarter of a century. He was at one time president of the local Board of Trade, and is a member of numerous clubs, including the Maryland Society and the City Club of New York.

He married, May 23, 1889, Inez M. Thurston, of Passaic, born February 10, 1864, in New York City, daughter of Jonathan Hibbard and Maria Louisa (Whittemore) Thurston (see Thurston, IX). Children, born in Passaic: 1. Gladys M., August 1, 1890. 2. Frank R., August 23, 1891. 3. Grace L., September 6, 1892.

DAWSON

Dawson is a good old English surname. In Maryland and vicinity it is a well-known family name and the family is scattered throughout the southern states. Judging from the records that have been collected the progenitors of the Maryland family came from England among the pioneers. We find two of the family in Talbot county among the first settlers. Francis Dawson, a member of the Society of Friends, had the following children recorded in the Third Haven Monthly Meeting: 1. Obadiah, born June 13, 1672, died 1694. 2. Richard, December 13, 1674; married, 1698, Susannah Foster. 3. Elizabeth, January 11, 1677-78. 4. John, November 2, 1678. 5. Anthony, June 13, 1683. Many of the Talbot county families may be traced to this ancestor.

(I) Ralph Dawson, the other immigrant, of Talbot county, may have been a brother. Of his history we know little. He died July 31, 1710, and is mentioned in the will of his son John. Children: 1. John, mentioned below. 2. James, executor of his will. 3. Richard. 4. Robert. 5. Rachel.

(II) John, son of Ralph Dawson, was born about 1660-70. When he died in 1710, he left five minor children. According to family tradition he came to this country in 1685. He

must have come with his father, and as the other Dawson family was here earlier, the date 1685 may be later than that of his emigration from England. He lived on the west side of St. Michael's river. He had lands on the east side of the Chesapeake granted under the proprietary government of Lord Calvert. He was designated as a gentleman, indicating high social position at that time. His will, dated 1710, mentions his wife, his father, his children, brothers Richard, Robert, and sister Rachel to whom he bequeathed land on St. Michael's river. Children: 1. John Jr. 2. William, had land at Bachelor's Range, Gallaway and Hilton's Hope. 3. Ralph, mentioned below. 4. Susanna. 5. Elizabeth.

(III) Ralph (2), son of John Dawson, was born about 1700. He was a minor and probably quite young when his father and grandfather died. According to one family tradition he came from England, but the evidence is plain that he was born in Talbot county, Maryland, after his father and grandfather came there. Children: 1. Thomas. 2. Joseph, married ———— Hadaway; had six children. 3. Impy (peculiar name that has survived for generations in the family—one of this name was living in Maryland in the same county in 1790). 4. James. 5. Nicholas, born about 1754, died 1838; married Mary Cook. (The order of birth of these children is unknown). 6. Elizabeth, mentioned below.

(IV) Elizabeth, daughter of Ralph (2) Dawson, was born in Talbot county. She married Basil Sewell, father of General James Sewell, of Cecil county, Maryland. General Sewell commanded Fort McHenry in the War of 1812 at the time "The Star Spangled Banner" was written there. Children: James Sewell, Clement, Basil Jr., Elizabeth Sewell, Mary, mentioned below; Thomas Sewell. Basil Sewell, lived at Bayside, Talbot county.

(V) Mary Sewell, daughter of Basil and Elizabeth (Dawson) Sewell, was born in Talbot county. She married Robert Dawson (5) as his second wife. Robert Dawson (5), son of Robert Dawson (4), married (first) ———— Cooper. Robert Dawson (4) was doubtless a grandson or nephew of Robert Dawson (2), mentioned above among the sons of Ralph Dawson. The records are not available for a search. Children of Robert and Mary (Sewell) Dawson: Maria and Robert.

(VI) Robert, son of Robert Dawson, was born in Talbot county, died July, 1894, aged ninety-eight years. He married Richarda Hopkins, daughter of Dr. Richard and Hannah (Hammond) Hopkins (see Hopkins IV). Child, Mary A., born December 19, 1832, married John Hughes, (see Hughes II).

HOPKINS Garret Hopkins, immigrant ancestor, came to America about 1661. On January 24, 1661, John Burrage demanded land for his own transportation, and Margaret Burrage his wife, and Margaret and Elizabeth, his daughters; John Willson, Garret Hopkins, and Mary Thomas, and further desired that his warrant be for six hundred and fifty acres, he having already three hundred entered in 1658. The land was in Anne Arundel county, Maryland, where Garret Hopkins lived when he arrived. On April 7, 1683, Garret was a witness to the will of Francis Holland Sr., of that county. He was also an appraiser of that estate. The family of Hopkins in Coventry, county Warwick, England, bore the same coat-of-arms as the family of Garret Hopkins: Sable, a chevron argent charged with three roses gules between these three matchlocks or. Crest: A tower per bend indented argent and gules from the battlements flames issuant proper. Motto: *Inter Primos.* In the town hall of Coventry there is a portrait of Ezekiel Hopkins which bears a strong family resemblance to the descendants of Garret Hopkins, and as Ezekiel is a common name in the American family, it seems quite possible that Garret Hopkins came originally from Warwickshire, although it is not known definitely. At the time of his death he lived at Peake plantation, not far from West river, about a mile from the present town of Owensville. The plantation was inherited by his son and grandson, and is now or was lately owned by the heirs of Dr. Martin Fenwick. Garret Hopkins was a planter and shipped crops to England, having money there to his credit. He was evidently comfortably well off. His will was dated October 12, 1691, and proved in June or July, 1692. The inventory of his estate was filed July 23, 1692. He married Thomson ———, probably Eard. Children, order of birth uncertain: 1. Gerard, mentioned below. 2. Ann, married at St. James parish, December 10, 1699, Henry Roberts. 3. Thomson or Thomasin, died about 1715; married at All Hallows Parish, March 13, 1700, John Welsh. 4. Mary, died 1758; married at St. James' Parish, August 9, 1705, Thomas Wells.

(II) Gerard, son of Garret Hopkins, resided on his father's plantation. He became a Quaker, took a prominent part in their meetings, and served on important committees in the church. In 1706 he accounted for tobacco taken as taxes, and in 1732 was appointed one of a committee to welcome Lord Baltimore. His name appears as a witness on many marriage certificates. He served often on committees to settle differences between the members of the church. In addition to the Peake plantation, he owned several tracts of land in Anne Arundel county. His will was dated January 1, 1741-42, and proved February 2, 1743-44, administration being granted to his widow. He married, intentions dated January 11, 1700-01, Margaret Johnes. Children: 1. Elizabeth, born March 13, 1703, died April 27, 1772; married, January 10, 1722-23, Levin Hill. 2. Joseph, November 2, 1706; married, August 17, 1727, Ann Chew. 3. Gerard, March 7, 1709, died September 3, 1777; married, May 7, 1730, Mary Hall. 4. Philip, March 9, 1711, died 1757; married, 1736, Elizabeth Hall. 5. Samuel, January 16, 1713; said to have married Sarah Giles. 6. Richard, December 15, 1715; said to have married Katherine Todd. 7. William, August 8, 1718; married Rachel Orrick. 8. Johns, mentioned below.

(III) Johns, son of Gerard Hopkins, was born October 30, 1720, died November 4, 1783. He was also a prominent Quaker, serving on various committees and as "visitor." His farm, which he had inherited from his father, adjoined that of his brother Gerard. His will was dated August 7, 1783, and proved July 30, 1784. He died November 4, 1783. He was a man of great strength of body and mind. He died of consumption, of many years duration. Before his death he freed his slaves. He married (first) Mary Gilliss. Married (second) about 1747, Mary Crockett, widow of John Crockett 2nd, and daughter of Joseph and Rebecca (Johns) Richardson. Married (third) Elizabeth Thomas, who died in 1804. She was born March 10, 1736-37, daughter of Samuel and Mary (Snowden) Thomas. She was "modest and retiring, yet communicative and intelligent, with a retentive memory, well stored with a variety of pleasing and ever interesting tales, sketches and anecdotes from history, poetry, and passing events. Her house was large and she was fond of society. It was a place of resort for Friends, and many were pleasantly entertained there. All her children married, with the exception of her youngest son, and it was a pleasant sight, when they met at her house with their children, to behold the happiness expressed in her countenance, which seemed to be communicated from one to another. She was the doctress of the neighborhood poor. She was remarkably healthy for one of her age and her mind was unimpaired when she died after a few days illness, of bilious fever, in the autumn of 1804." Child of first wife: Ezekiel, born May 11, 1747. Child of second wife: Johns, born July 8, 1751; married (first) May 30, 1775, Elizabeth Harris; (second) April 13, 1779, Catherine Howell. Children of third wife: 1. Samuel, born February 3, 1759, died February 9, 1814; married Hannah Janney; was father of Johns Hopkins, for whom the university is named. 2. Philip, September 24, 1760; married, March 21, 1787, Mary Boone. 3. Richard, March 2, 1762, mentioned below. 4. Mary, January 7, 1764; married, 1787, Samuel Peach. 5. Margaret, February 20, 1766; married Jesse Tyson. 6. Gerard, October 24, 1769; married, 1796, Dorothy Brooke. 7. Elizabeth, April 26, 1771; married, March 26, 1795, John Janney. 8. Evan, November 30, 1772; married, January 25, 1810, Elizabeth Hopkins. 9. Ann, February 26, 1775; married, November 5, 1801, Thomas Shrieves. 10. Rachel, September 7, 1777; married March 29, 1804, Robert Hough. 11. William, January 28, 1781; died unmarried.

(IV) Dr. Richard, son of Johns Hopkins, was born March 2, 1762. He married Hannah Hammond. He had a daughter Richarda, who married Robert Dawson (see Dawson, VI).

THURSTON Some authorities claim the name Thurston to have originated from the Danish troest, meaning trusty, faithful, while others claim it is from the god Thor, and a word meaning stone, signifying "stone of Thor." The name was early known in several counties of England, and Thurston was one of the archbishops of Fife, Scotland, in the twelfth century.

(I) John Thurston, a carpenter of Wrentham, Suffolk county, England, was baptized January 13, 1601, died at Medfield, Massachusetts, November 1, 1685. He embarked in the "Mary Anne," from Yarmouth, England, May 10, 1637, at the age of thirty-six, with his wife Margaret, aged thirty-two, and two sons. He was received into the church at Dedham, Massachusetts, March 28, 1641, and his wife June 28, 1640. He was made freeman May 10, 1643, and in that year received a grant of land in Dedham, in that part afterward set off as Medfield. His wife died May 9, 1662. Their children were: 1. Thomas, baptized at Wrentham, England, August 4, 1633. 2. John, baptized at Wrentham, September 13, 1635. 3. Joseph, born at Dedham, baptized July 15, 1640. 4. Benjamin, born May 8, baptized July 15, 1640. 5. Mary, born January 8, baptized January 12, 1643. 6. Daniel. 7. Judith, born March 17, baptized March 29, 1648. 8. Hannah, born February 28, 1650.

(II) Daniel, fifth and youngest son of John Thurston, was born May 5, 1646, at Medfield, Massachusetts, being baptized May 12, and died July 23, 1683; he was received into the church at Dedham, May 20, 1645. He married (first) Maria———, who died at Medfield, May 21, 1680. He married (second) December 16, 1681, Hannah Miller; at the time of his second marriage he was living at Rehoboth, Massachusetts. His children were: 1. Daniel. 2. Benjamin, born February 17, 1678, died March 26, 1680. 3. Sarah, January 2, 1683.

(III) Daniel (2), son of Daniel (1) and Maria Thurston, was born February 14, 1674, and was a weaver of cloth, living at Uxbridge, Massachusetts. He married (first) December 28, 1699, Experience Warren, who died September 6, 1704, and (second) October 15, 1705, Martha Allen, of Medway. His children were: 1. Joseph. 2. and 3. Daniel and Increase, twins, born February 19, 1702; the latter died May 29, 1702. 4. Diana, born May 12, died May 19, 1707. 5. Martha, March 23, 1709. 6. Benjamin, December 25, 1711. 7. Mary, August 13, 1714. 8. Daniel, November 21, 1716. 9. Ebenezer, September 22, 1718. 10. Elizabeth, October 22, 1720. 11. David. 12. Calvin. 13. Moses, September 17, 1733. 14. Lydia, August 26, 1735. 15. Sarah, April 9, 1742, died young.

(IV) Joseph, oldest son of Daniel (2) and Experience (Warren) Thurston, was born October 14, 1700; he lived at Westboro, Massachusetts, where he owned a farm, and where he and his wife were admitted to the church by letter, November 8, 1741. By his wife, Dorothy Frizzell, he had children as follows: 1. Amariah, born January 17, 1734. 2. Dorothy, January 26, 1735. 3. Experience, died December 11, 1750. 4. Zeriah, born 1738. 5. Joseph. 6. Samuel, born February 1, 1744.

(V) Joseph (2), son of Joseph (1) and Dorothy (Frizzell) Thurston, was born December 29, 1739, at Westboro, Massachusetts, died August 13, 1822, at North Brookfield,

Massachusetts. He removed to Spencer or Leicester, thence to Brookfield, and married, August 30, 1763, Thankful Wood, of Westboro, born April 5, 1740, died April 20, 1824. Children, born at Brookfield: 1. Joseph. 2. Thankful, born October 11, 1766.

(VI) Joseph (3), only son of Joseph (2) and Thankful (Wood) Thurston, was born September 11, 1764, at Brookfield, Massachusetts, died February 2, 1814. He was a trader at North Brookfield, and manufactured potash. He was a member of the Congregational church. He married, January 27, 1793, Polly Hibbard, born March 12, 1766, at Leicester, Massachusetts, died March 3, 1804, and their children were: 1. Lyman, born January 16, 1794. 2. Joseph, January 29, died August 8, 1796. 3. Joseph. 4. Mary, July 6, 1799, died same day. 5. Daniel, September 4, 1800. 6. Mary, January 13, died March 3, 1803. 7. Mary Hibbard, March, 1804.

(VII) Joseph (4), third son of Joseph (3) and Polly (Hibbard) Thurston, was born June 7, 1797, at Brookfield, Massachusetts, and was a farmer. He lived some time at Leicester, Massachusetts; he lived with and took care of his uncle, J. Hibbard, of Paxton, and at his death came into possession of the estate. About 1851 he sold his farm and removed to Worcester, Massachusetts, where he invested in real estate, and lived there until his death, October 30, 1857. He married, June 25, 1823, Lucy Bickman, daughter of Deacon David and Patty (Howe) Davis, of Paxton; after the death of her husband she resided at Worcester with her daughter Abigail Brown. Their children were: 1. Mary Elizabeth, born May 12, 1824, died June 21, 1826. 2. Abigail Brown, April 4, 1827. 3. Jonathan Hibbard. 4. Lyman Davis, September 8, 1832. 5. Martha Howe, November 28, 1834. 6. Sarah Ideal, February 28, 1840, died January 24, 1845. 7. Joseph Harrison, March 21, 1842, died January 2, 1845.

(VIII) Jonathan Hibbard, oldest son of Joseph (4) and Lucy Bickman (Davis) Thurston, was born October 11, 1829, at Paxton, Massachusetts, died in 1904. While living in Leicester, Massachusetts, he was engaged as salesman and merchant; subsequently he removed to Passaic, New Jersey, where he became a city councilman. Later he removed to Lincoln, Delaware, and while living there joined the Presbyterian church of Milford. He married, April 10, 1851, Maria Louisa, daughter of Charles and Mary (Parker) Whittemore, born at Charlestown, Massachusetts,

who since the death of her husband resides with her daughter, Mrs. Mark L. Bennett. They had children as follows: 1. Effie Gertrude, born September 6, 1855, at Leicester, Massachusetts; married, June 25, 1877, Charles Barker, of Lincoln, Delaware, and has two children: Madeline Amanda, born November 25, 1878, and Sadie Waterhouse, January 25, 1881. 2. Inez May. 3. Mabel Louise, September 30, 1869, at Passaic, New Jersey; married Mark L. Bennett, of Maryland.

(IX) Inez May, second daughter of Jonathan Hibbard and Maria Louisa (Whittemore) Thurston, was born February 10, 1864, at New York City. She married, May 23, 1889, Frank Hughes, of Passaic, New Jersey, (see Hughes, III).

SEWELL　Henry Sewell, immigrant ancestor, came from England to Virginia, before 1632, and from him Sewell's Point at the entrance to Elizabeth river, opposite Fortress Monroe, takes its name. At the court holden May 31, 1640, Henry Sewell and Captain Sibley were authorized to build a church at Sewell's Point, and August 2, 1640, they and others were directed to pay Mr. Thomas Harrison, the minister. This was an independent church. He was elected to the house of burgesses from Elizabeth City in 1632 and from Lower Norfolk county in 1639. We have an account of Henry Sewell of Sewell's Point from his factor in London of tobacco sent over in the ships "America and Alexandria" and for one-half of a cargo in a shallop with sassafras roots, sold in England, and showed cash receipts to have been six hundred and fifty pounds, nineteen shillings and six pence. He married Alice, daughter of Thomas Willoughby, who came to Virginia in 1610, was justice of Elizabeth City in 1628, burgess, 1629-32, and councilor from 1644 to 1650. Henry Sewell died in 1644, and at a court held that year in Lower Norfolk county at the house of Ensign Lambert, February 20, Mathew Philips, his administrator, was ordered to pay Thomas Harrison, clerk, one thousand pounds of tobacco for "burial and preaching of the funeral sermon of Mr. and Mrs. Sewell, deceased, and for breaking ground in the chancel of the church for the burial of Mr. and Mrs. Sewell." At a subsequent session of the court, February 25, 1649, it appeared that the administrator died before settling the estate and the son, Henry Sewell, then ten years old, was ordered sent abroad in charge of his kinsman,

Mr. Thomas Lee. Children: 1. Anne, born 1634 or earlier; married, about 1649, Lemuel Mason (she was married before February 25, 1740-50). 2. Henry, 1639, according to a deposition dated 1662, and died without issue, according to a deposition taken in 1672. (But there was probably another son Henry, a not uncommon custom in England being to name two sons with the same baptismal name, to the utter confusion of the genealogist).

(II) Henry (2) Sewell, the pioneer in Maryland, is stated on good authority to be son of Henry (1) Sewell. He certainly was related, possibly a nephew, though more likely son. Sewell came from Sewell's Point, Virginia, with others about 1660 and was probably born about 1630. Peter Porter, of Sewell's Point, settled at the head of Severn river, Maryland, in 1650. Came also Edward Lloyd, Cornelius Lloyd, Mathew Howard, Thomas Todd, William Crouch, James Horner, Nicholas Wyatt, Thomas Howell, Thomas Gott, William Galloway, James Warner, Richard Acton and others. One of these, James Warner, was the father of Johannah Warner, whom Henry Sewell married. By the will of James Warner, Johanna Sewell inherited "Warner's Neck" and an attempt was made in the will to prevent the estate ever being alienated from her family. But her son, Henry Sewell, sold it to Samuel Howard. His brother, Henry Sewell Jr., contested this sale on the plea of entail, and seems to have won the point in court. Henry Jr. remained upon the homestead. Children: James and Henry Jr., mentioned below.

(III) Henry (3), son of Henry (2) Sewell, was born in Maryland about 1660. He took up "Sewell's Fancy" and bought a part of "Duvall's Delight" upon the Patuxent, from Charles Carroll. His will, dated 1726, mentions children, given below, and bequeathed the Howard and Porter's Range bought of Richard and Adam Shipley, and Hereford, the Marriott tract, perhaps coming to him through his wife, Mary, who was a Marriott. John Sewell bought his brothers' shares in this latter tract and became sole owner. The old Sewell homestead, as this is called, has been in the possession of the Marriott and Sewell families since 1673; it is near Indian landing at the head of Severn river, Anne Arundel county, Maryland. Children: Samuel, Mary, Henry, Joseph, Philip, John, mentioned below.

(IV) John, son of Henry (3) Sewell, was born before 1700 in Anne Arundel county. He married Hannah, daughter of Daniel Carroll,

at St. Anne's, Annapolis, May 30, 1721. She was baptized March 2, 1713, at St. Anne's Church. Children: 1. Henry, born 1723, baptized with his brother at All Hallows Church, July 4, 1726. 2. John, born 1725.

(V) Henry (4), elder son of John and Hannah (Carroll) Sewell, born 1723 and baptized 1726, as above noted, was probably the father of the next mentioned.

(VI) Basil, probably a son of Henry (4) Sewell, married Elizabeth, daughter of Ralph Dawson, of Annapolis (see Dawson, IV). He resided in Talbot county, Maryland, and died in 1802. His will, probated September 28 of that year, mentions his sons: James, Basil, William, Clement and Nicholas, and his daughter Mary, wife of Robert Dawson. He also mentions a son Thomas. He must have been very young, for his son James was directed to care for him.

(VII) James, eldest child of Basil and Elizabeth (Dawson) Sewell, married Rudolph —— and lived in Maryland. He was the General James Sewell who figured in the war of 1812 and was in command of Fort McHenry, at the time the song, "The Star Spangled Banner," was written. He was at one time a candidate for the office of governor of Maryland; his country seat, Holly Hall, is still in a good state of preservation and one of the points of historical interest in Cecil county.

SMALLEY The Smalley family of New Jersey belongs to old Devonshire stock, and comes from the same neighborhood as did the Drakes, who have made such a name for themselves, not only in New Jersey, but also in New England. Descendants bearing the Smalley name soon found a congenial home with the Baptists of Rhode Island, and from that colony of liberty loving people came the founder of the New Jersey branch of the family. His descendants have always held the views believed and practiced by the Baptists, and the family gave to this denomination one of the most useful ministers of the gospel that ever labored in New Jersey, the Rev. Henry Smalley, of blessed memory.

(I) John Smalley, the first person of that name to come to the New World, was in London, in 1631, and in the following year came over to America in the vessel "Francis & James," in company with many of the Massachusetts Bay Colony. He settled on Cape Cod, where he married, about 1640, and had four children who lived to mature years. From Massachusetts the parents with the two sons, both of age, moved first to Rhode Island, and from there to Piscataway, Middlesex county, New Jersey, where they were among the earliest pioneer freeholders of this New Jersey settlement. His two daughters, Hannah and Mary, were at this time married and settled in New England. After obtaining his first grant, upon his arrival in Piscataway, he had a survey of his farm made in 1677, and in 1685 took up another warrant of land. At the time the province was temporarily recaptured by the Dutch in 1673-74, John Smalley was appointed by them a magistrate. In 1675 he was commissioned a justice of the peace, and at the same time appointed associate justice of the court of sessions, which position he filled for several years. He died in 1692 and his wife died about a year later. His two sons were John, Jr., referred to below, and Isaac, born December 11, 1647, married twice after moving to New Jersey. He was for several years a member of the colonial assembly, town clerk of Piscataway, and held many other offices of public confidence and trust until his death in 1725.

(II) John (2), son of John (1) Smalley, had a farm surveyed for him in 1675, and about ten years afterward he took up an additional one hundred acres. In 1683 he came into possession of another large lot of one hundred acres, situated on Ambrose brook, near the present New Market, which he gave to his son, John, who in turn left it at his death to his son Andrew. John Smalley, Jr., served in many of the local township appointments, and was a constituent member in the old Piscataway Baptist Church, publically organized between 1686 and 1689. His will was made September 13, 1731, and duly recorded in 1733, a short time after his death. John Smalley, Jr., married in Piscataway, October 18, 1676, Lydia, daughter of John Martin, another of the early founders of that settlement. Among his children were Jonathan, referred to below; Elisha, married Mary Dunham; Phebe, married Ephraim Dunham.

(III) Jonathan, eldest child of John (2) and Lydia (Martin) Smalley, was born in Piscataway, April 10, 1683, died some time after 1763, his will being dated July 27 of that year. He was the first of this name on the roll of the Seventh Day Baptist Church of Piscataway. So strict and conscientious a Sabbatharian was he that when he leased part of his farm in 1734 to parties who were to quarry for minerals, he stipulated in the contract that no work or labor should be performed upon

the premises on the seventh day of the week, during the term of the twenty-one year lease. He accumulated a large property for colonial times, both real and personal, which he divided by will among his children. About 1707 Jonathan Smalley married Sarah, eldest child of John and Sarah Fitz-Randolph. This was the first marriage on record between these two families, subsequent generations of those bearing these surnames seem to have had a special affinity for one another, and within the next three years more than a dozen marriages occurred between them. The Fitz-Randolphs and Smalleys had both emigrated from their native land and settled in their Cape Cod Colony within a year or two of each other, and no longer a period had intervened between their final settlements in Piscataway, New Jersey. The homesteads and outlined plantations of the sons of these pioneers were in close proximity, and around them dwelled the Bonhams, Dunns, Dunhams, Martins and others. Most of these families were intimately related by marriage, but became greatly estranged by religion. The occasion was the existence in Piscataway of two Baptist churches, one worshipping on Sunday, the other observing Saturday. The former was organized between 1686 and 1689, and the latter between 1705 and 1707. It is a noticeable coincident also that in the union of these families such a large number became actively identified with the newer of the religious interests. Not only was Jonathan Smalley the first of the name on the roll of the Seventh Day Baptist, but his wife was the earliest recorded in the list of females, having united with the church before her marriage. Most of Jonathan Smalley's ten children became identified with the same church on reaching adult years, and especially active in these relations were his sons, John and Jonathan, Jr. His youngest son, Andrew, referred to below, however, departed from his father's religious preferences.

(IV) Andrew, youngest son of Jonathan and Sarah (Fitz-Randolph) Smalley, was born in Piscataway, December 20, 1726. In his will his father left him all his "Lands and salt meadows." After his marriage he set up housekeeping at Harris Lane, the district lying near Bound Brook, Somerset county, New Jersey. February 26, 1746, Andrew Smalley was married by the Rev. Jonathan Dunham, the Seventh Day Baptist minister at that time in Piscataway, to Agnes, born May 8, 1728, daughter of David and Elsie Coriell. Among the nine children born to them were Abraham,

Isaac M. Smalley

born May 2, 1748, remained in the old homestead in Ambrose Brook, married Catharine Emans and reared a large family. John, referred to below. Henry. David, born April 5, 1766; married Margaret Compton and had four children.

(V) John, son of Andrew and Agnes (Coriell) Smalley, was born in Piscataway. He married Mary Langstaff and among their children was Henry, referred to below.

(VI) Henry, son of John and Mary (Langstaff) Smalley, after graduating from Princeton College entered the Baptist ministry, and for fifty years was well known as one of the most efficient and faithful servants of that denomination, serving as pastor at Cohansey Baptist church. By his wife, Hannah (Fox) Smalley, of Piscataway, he had three children: John, William Fitz-Randolph, Henry Langstaff, referred to below.

(VII) Henry Langstaff, youngest child of the Rev. Henry and Hannah (Fox) Smalley, was born in Bowentown, New Jersey, 1807. His life was spent in farming and also in conducting a milling business. He died in 1852. He married Tabitha Bacon, born at Roadstown, New Jersey, 1798, daughter of Isaac and Phebe (Bacon) Milford. Children: 1. James H., died at seventy-nine years of age. 2. Isaac Milford, referred to below. 3. William Fox, still living. 4. Mary Bidd, deceased. 5. John, still living.

(VIII) Isaac Milford, second child and son of Henry Langstaff and Tabitha Bacon (Milford) Smalley, was born at Bowentown, New Jersey, May 8, 1830, and is now living at Bridgeton, New Jersey. He attended the public schools of his native town, and for a number of years after leaving school was engaged in the nursery business. He then for a time conducted a grist mill, in which occupation he was most successful. In 1883 he was elected a member of the New Jersey state assembly, and was again chosen to the same position in 1888. For a time he was a member of the board of chosen freeholders of Stoe Creek township, Roadstown, in which he lived for thirty-seven years as farmer and nurseryman. In politics Mr. Smalley is and has all his life been a Democrat. For five years he was one of the trustees of Rutgers College. He has for many years given his attention to financial rather than agricultural and industrial pursuits, and is one of the leading and most influential men in that field in Bridgeton. He has for a long time been a director in the Bridgeton National Bank, and for many years was a director

in the Mutual Life Insurance Company of Bridgeton. In 1901 he was chosen by his fellow directors to be the president of this latter institution, and this office he still holds.

Isaac Milford Smalley married, December 21, 1864, Cornelia, daughter of Abram Cannon. Children: 1. James Henry, married Alice Ware, born at St. Louis, Missouri; children: Minerva, Jennie and Herbert. 2. Mary Bidd, married George Allen, of Chester, Delaware; children: Charles, Isaac Smalley, Maxwell and Beatrice Allen. 3. Isaac Cannon, married Lydia Davis; children: Heber B. and Isaac M. 4. Howard Malcolm, married Elizabeth Abbott; child, Caroline. 5. Fannie, unmarried.

CUNNINGHAM The Cunninghams are a Scotch family, although many of the numerous immigrants of the surname who came to America previous to the beginning of the eighteenth century were descended from ancestors who had lived in Ireland perhaps for many generations; but from whatever country the immigrant Cunninghams may have sailed in their quest of new homes on this side of the Atlantic ocean, the fact remains that probably very nearly all of them came of the ancient Cunningham clan which was seated in Ayrshire, Scotland, as early as A. D. 1200. However, let us glance briefly at some of the characters and traditions of the clan and observe from what elements the Cunninghams have grown. First it may be said with exact truth that the Cunninghams of Ayrshire possess the earldom of Carrick and Glencairn as well as the lordship of Cunninghame, and that from the Ayrshire clan have descended all of the known branches of the family in Scotland, England and Ireland. According to tradition the first Cunningham settlers in Ireland were two of six brothers who won distinction under James of Scotland, afterward James I. of England. The records show that among the first grantees of this monarch in Ireland were several of the name of Cunningham. In the precinct of Portlough, county Donegal, John Cunningham, of Crawfield, Ayrshire, Scotland, received a grant of one thousand acres of land in 1610, and at the same time James Cunningham, Laird of Glangarnoche, Ayrshire, had two grants in the same precinct aggregating three thousand acres, while Cuthbert Cunningham, of Glangarnoche, had a thousand acre grant, and Alexander Cunningham, of Powton, gentleman, of Sorbie, Wigtonshire, Scotland, had a thousand acres granted him in the precinct of Boylagh county

Donegal. It would be very difficult and perhaps well nigh impossible to trace a direct connection from the particular Cunningham family here to be treated back to any one of the brothers and other Cunninghams mentioned; nor is the matter one of great importance.

(I) John Cunningham, the immigrant, came from the north of Ireland, 1818, and settled in north New Jersey. Among his children was John H., see forward.

(II) John H., son of John Cunningham, was born in the north of Ireland, February 28, 1815, died December 2, 1879. He came to the United States with his parents (who were of the Presbyterian faith) when three years old. He married, May 19, 1842, Margaret Ackerman, of Paramus, New Jersey, born January 12, 1825, died April 12, 1896. Among his children was Robert Hudson, see forward.

(III) Robert Hudson, son of John H. and Margaret (Ackerman) Cunningham, was born in Paterson, New Jersey, September 23, 1855, and was prominently identified with the business life of that city for a period of more than thirty-five years. His life was spent there and he received his education in the public schools of the city. In 1873, when only eighteen years old, he was employed in the selling department of the firm of Pelgram & Meyer, silk manufacturers of Paterson, with business offices in New York. For the next twenty-five years he was in the employ of that house and during that time came to be recognized as one of the best salesmen in the silk trade in the country. At the end of that period he severed his connection with Pelgram & Meyer to become selling agent for Fleitman & Company, of New York, one of the largest commission silk houses in America. He retired from active business about two years before his death, March 9, 1908. He himself was looked upon as one of the successful business men of Paterson and New York City, with a large acquaintance in trade circles and an enviable standing in military and fraternal circles. For many years he was a member of the famous Paterson Life Guards, and he also held membership in the North Jersey Auto Club and the Hamilton Club, of Paterson. He married, June 28, 1883, Camilla Jane, born November 18, 1861, daughter of Augustus and Christianna Miller, of New York City. Children: Robert Hudson, see forward. Charles Frederick, born June 17, 1889.

(IV) Robert Hudson (2), son of Robert Hudson (1) and Camilla Jane (Miller) Cunningham, was born in Paterson, New Jersey, February 23, 1885, and acquired his earlier literary education in the public schools of that city and also in the Newark Academy, graduated in 1904. He then attended the New York Law School, graduating LL. B. with the class of 1906, with the honors of presidency of his class. Afterward for one year and a half he continued his law studies in the office of James G. Blauvelt, of Paterson, and in November, 1907, was admitted to practice in the courts of this state. Since that time he has been a member of the Paterson bar and has engaged in active general practice in that city. Mr. Cunningham is a member and secretary of The Taxpayers Association of Paterson, an organization having for its object the protection and advancement of the interests of the people of Passaic county in general and the city of Paterson in particular. He also is a member of the North Jersey Country Club, Paterson Lodge, No. 60, Benevolent and Protective Order of Elks, and the Eastside Presbyterian church.

He married, October 29, 1908, May Louise Cooke, born April 20, 1885, daughter of John K. and Annie Louise (Thorne) Cooke. Watts Cooke, the father of John K. Cooke, was the founder of the Paterson Rolling Mills, at Paterson, New Jersey.

MARSHALL According to the records of the family at present under consideration their original home in this country was Virginia, to which place the three brothers, Randall, Nehemiah and John, emigrated from England, and whence Randall, after his marriage removed with his father-in-law to New Jersey. The family thus apparently has no connection with the Marshalls and Chews who emigrated to New Jersey about 1680.

(I) Randall Marshall, founder of the family at present under consideration, settled at Good Intent, New Jersey, and located on the Hazzard property near the town of Blackwood; but he afterwards removed to Lamb's Mills, where he remained until his death in 1780, at the age of sixty-six years. He married Hannah, daughter of Thomas Chew. Children: Randall, Thomas, referred to below; John, William, Joseph, Mary, Elizabeth, Sarah, Hannah, Charity.

(II) Thomas, son of Randall and Hannah (Chew) Marshall, married Ann Pease. Children: John, Randall, David, William, Thomas.

(III) Randall (2), son of Thomas and Ann

(Pease) Marshall, was born June 15, 1771, died September 21, 1841. He was the owner of large tracts of land, but he turned his attention to a business career in which he was very successful, and became one of the pioneers of the great glass work industry of Cape May county. His first venture was the building of the glass works at Port Elizabeth and later of another factory at Marshallville, New Jersey, for the manufacture of window glass. In addition to this he also operated several saw and grist mills. July 30, 1847, his son sold the glass works and saw mill at Marshallville to Thomas Van Gilder, for $7,525. He also operated and owned a tannery at Port Elizabeth.

August 4, 1793, Randall Marshall married Mary, daughter of Henry and Hannah Doughty (Furness) Reeves (see Reeves, V). Children: 1. Thomas Chew, born October 3, 1794, died May 6, 1868; married, May 18, 1818, Experience Steelman; fourteen children. 2. Ann, June 20, 1795, died February 15, 1815; married, July 22, 1812, Frederick Stanger. 3. Henry, March 11, 1800, died April 15, 1808. 4. Hannah Reeves, July 25, 1802, died unmarried. 5. Mary, September 27, 1804, died February 24, 1876; married, July 22, 1823, Ebenezer Seely; eight children. 6. Randolph, referred to below.

(III) Randolph, son of Randall (2) and Mary (Reeves) Marshall, was born in Port Elizabeth, Cumberland county, New Jersey, January 9, 1811, died in Marshallville, Cape May county, New Jersey, February 19, 1879. Receiving his education in the public schools, he spent four years in Miller's drug store, then at the corner of Fourth and Walnut streets, Philadelphia; after this he entered the medical department of the University of Pennsylvania, from which he graduated in 1834 with the degree of M. D. He then set up in the practice of his profession in Marshallville, where for nearly half a century he had a large and, from a professional point of view, most successful practice, although owing to his laxity in imposing and collecting fees it was not so good from a financial point of view. For years he was the only physician within a radius of twenty miles from his home. He was a member of the Cape May County Medical Society, of Star Lodge, No. 65, Free and Accepted Masons, of New Jersey, and of the Independent Order of Odd Fellows, at Tuckahoe. He was a birthright Friend.

May 21, 1835, Randolph Marshall, M. D. married Sarah Higgins, daughter of Ellis and Sarah (Higgins) Hughes, of Cape May county,

(see Hughes, VI). Children: 1. Ellen L., born April 6, 1836; married, February 11, 1862, Belford E. Smith. 2. Sarah H., September 7, 1838; married, December 21, 1862, Henry F. Steelman; three children. 3. Benjamin H., September 25, 1840; married, July 4, 1861, Eliza Ogden; two children. 4. James L., January 20, 1844; married, May 28, 1873, Emma Smith; two children. 5. Ellis Hughes, September 18, 1845; married (first) Harriet Shoemaker; (second) Lydia Gandy; one child by each marriage. 6. Joseph Corson, referred to below. 7. Mary T., December 17, 1850, died August 25, 1868; unmarried. 8. An infant, died April 13, 1853. 9. Randolph, referred to below. 10. Anna B., April 4, 1858; married Maurice Godfrey.

(IV) Joseph Corson, son of Randolph and Sarah Higgins (Hughes) Marshall, was born in Tuckahoe, Cape May county, New Jersey, July 3, 1848, and is now living in that town. For his early education he went to the public schools, after which he graduated from Pennington Seminary. He then, until 1867, studied medicine with his father at Tuckahoe, and entering the medical department of the University of Pennsylvania in 1868 he became one of the office students of Professor Lenox Hodge. He graduated from the University with the degree of M. D. in 1870, and having as a student of Professor Hodge had special privileges at the Wills Eye Hospital and in the course of obstetrics, he received at his graduation a special certificate covering these two fields. In the summer of 1870 he opened an office in Fairton, New Jersey, where he remained for ten years, and then removed to Tuckahoe, where he became the partner of his brother Randolph, who in 1870 had started there with his co-operation a drug store. Dr. Marshall outside of his profession has given a great deal of time and interest to the cultivation of cranberries. He is a member of the Cape May Medical Society, and was at one time president of that organization. He is a Republican, but he has always steadily refused to hold office.

(IV) Randolph (2), son of Randolph (1) and Sarah Higgins (Hughes) Marshall, was born in Tuckahoe, Cape May county, New Jersey, January 11, 1854, and is now living in that place. After receiving his early education in the public school, he entered the Pennington Seminary and prepared for Jefferson Medical College in Philadelphia, from which he graduated in 1877 with the degree of M. D. During his Medical course he studied obstetrics ınder Dr. D. Erdsley Wallace, and operative sırgery ınder Dr. J. Ewing Mears, and completed these coırses the same year that he graduated. Immediately after his gradıation, having decided to make a specialty of the diseases of children, he located at Tıckahoe, in partnership with his brother, Joseph Corson Marshall, and in the beginning of 1878 the two brothers erected both their drıg store and their office. This arrangement continıed ıntil 1890, when their drıg bısiness was merged in the interests of the firm of C. H. Bıtterworth & Company, and the main office of the drıg bısiness was transferred to 125 Market street, Philadelphia. Dr. Marshall has always been a close stıdent of his profession, and for many years has been a member of the Cape May Medical Society, of which organization he served for twelve years as treasırer, and for a long time as its permanent delegate to the State Medical Society. He and his brother were the sırgeons of the Soıth Jersey Railroad Company dıring its constrıction in that locality. Dr. Randolph Marshall owns a great deal of real estate in Ocean City, and he is a member and treasırer of the Tıckahoe Bıilding and Loan Association. In religion he is a Methodist. He is also a member of the State Lodge, Free and Accepted Masons, of Tıckahoe; Richmond Chapter, Royal Arch Masons, of Millville; Olivet Commandery, Knights Templar, of Millville; and of the Ancient Order of United Workmen, of which for a long time he has served as examining sırgeon. In politics he is a Repıblican, and althoıgh his interest has always been active and he has worked energetically for the sıccess of his party, he has steadily refısed to hold office or to serve in a pıblic capacity.

Dr. Marshall married, December 18, 1879, Rae, daıghter of Antony Steelman, her father having been one of the sheriffs of Cape May coınty. Mrs. Marshall died September 19, 1908.

(The Reeves Line. see Walter Reeves 1).

(II) William, son of Walter Reeves, of Bırlington coınty, New Jersey, was possibly the son of his first wife, althoıgh his mother may have been Ann Howell, his father's secınd wife. All that is known of him is that he married and left foır children: 1. Samıel, named in will of his ıncle, Samıel Reeve, December 2, 1737. 2. Elizabeth, married in Janıary, 1736, Isaac Atkinson. 3. William, Jr., died Jıly 24, 1763, leaving a widow Sarah. 4. Joseph, referred to below.

(III) Joseph, son of William Reeves, was born aboıt 1720, died September 3, 1767. He lived at Moınt Holly, and left his widow and two sons to sırvive him, his daıghter having died before he did. Children of Joseph and Jane Reeve: 1. John, born Aıgıst 1, 1744, died Febrıary 26, 1800; married Sarah (Reeves) Patterson. 2. Henry, referred to below. 3. Jane.

(IV) Henry, son of Joseph and Jane Reeves, was born at Moınt Holly, Bırlington coınty, New Jersey, Jıne 27, 1749, died in Cımberland coınty, New Jersey, November 23, 1840. Februıary 8, 1772, he married Hannah Doıghty, daıghter of Benjamin and Dorothy Fırness, born May 15, 1753, died November 17, 1824. Children of Henry and Hannah Doıghty (Fırness) Reeves: 1. William, born March 4, 1773. 2. Benjamin Fırness, Aıgıst, 1774, died yoıng. 3. A child, died in infancy. 4. Mary, referred to below. 5. Elizabeth, September 21, 1779. 6. Henry, Janıary 26, 1782, died November 5, 1813. 7. Jane, September 21, 1783. 8. Hannah, October 21, 1785. 9. Abraham, Febrıary 27, 1788. 10. Dorothy, May 23, 1790, died April 17, 1837. 11. Benjamin Fırness, Jıly 7, 1792, died March 6, 1862; married Rachel Godfrey. 12. John, Febrıary 27, 1794, died October 22, 1805.

(V) Mary, daıghter of Henry and Hannah Doıghty (Fırness) Reeves, was born near Port Elizabeth, Cımberland coınty, New Jersey, September 22, 1777, died in Cape May coınty, New Jersey, March 30, 1847. Aıgıst 4, 1793, she married Randall, son of Thomas and Ann (Pease) Marshall (see Marshall, III).

(The Hughes Line. Mayflower descent).

(1) John Howland, one of the "Mayflower" passengers, died Febrıary 23, 1623, having married Elizabeth, daıghter of John Tilley, another "Mayflower" passenger.

(II) Desire, daıghter of John and Elizabeth (Tilley) Howland, died at Barnstable, Massachısetts, October 13, 1683, having married Captain John Gorham, who was bıried at Swansea, Massachısetts, Febrıary 5, 1675.

(III) Hannah, daıghter of Captain John and Desire (Howland) Gorham, was born at Barnstable, Massachısetts, November 28, 1663. Aboıt 1683 she married Joseph Whilldin, of Yarmoıth, Massachısetts. They removed to Cape May coınty, New Jersey, and accordıng to Stevens' "History of Cape May" all the Whilldins of that coınty are descended from them. In 1693 and 1698 he was constable of Cape May county; in 1705 he was commissioned high sheriff; and later he served several years as one of the justices of the peace.

(IV) Joseph (2), son of Joseph (1) and Hannah (Gorham) Whilldin, was born about 1690, died at Cape May, March 18, 1748. His first wife, Mary, said to have been Mary Wilman, died April 8, 1743. The name of his second wife was Abigail. Children: Matthew, David, Jane, Hannah, Rachel, Lois, Mary.

(V) Hannah, daughter of Joseph (2) and Mary (Wilman) Whilldin, married (first) Ellis, son of Humphrey Hughes, Jr., and their descendants in virtue of the above ancestry can all claim "Mayflower Descent."

(The Hughes Line).

(I) The Hughes family at present under consideration are of Welsh ancestry, and settled first on Long Island, whence they removed to Cape May county, New Jersey.

(I) Humphry Hughes, according to Howell's "History of Southampton," lived in Bridgehampton or Sagg, and had a wife Martha. He is found in this place in 1669, and in the tax list of 1698 are mentioned his children: Humphrey, referred to below, Abner, Uriah, Jedediah, John.

(II) Humphrey (2), son of Humphry (1) and Martha Hughes, was born in Bridgehampton, Long-Island, October 2, 1669, died in Cape May county, New Jersey. By his first wife whose name is unknown he had a son, Ellis, referred to below. Between 1720 and 1723 he married (second) Elizabeth, widow of David Wells.

(III) Ellis, son of Humphrey (2) Hughes, was born about 1708, died February 8, 1762. He married Hannah, daughter of Joseph and Mary (Wilman) Whilldin, whose "Mayflower" ancestry is appended to this sketch. She married (second) an Eldredge. Children of Ellis and Hannah (Whilldin) Hughes: Ellis, referred to below, Memucan, Jesse, Constantine, David.

(IV) Ellis (2), son of Ellis (1) and Hannah (Whilldin) Hughes, was born August 16, 1745, died there April 16, 1817. He married about September, 1768, Eleanor (Hirst) Whilldin, widow of Wilman, his first cousin. Children: Thomas Hirst, referred to below, Eleanor, Joseph (and others).

(V) Thomas Hirst, son of Ellis (2) and Eleanor (Hirst-Whilldin) Hughes, was born in Cape May county. New Jersey, January 10,

1769, died there November 10, 1839. He married, December 3, 1788, Lydia Page. Children: Thomas P., Ellis, referred to below, Lydia, Eleanor, Sarah, Louisa.

(VI) Ellis (3), son of Thomas Hirst and Lydia (Page) Hughes, was born in Cape May county, New Jersey, July 2, 1793, died there January 2, 1862. He married Sarah Higgins, and among other children had a daughter Sarah Higgins Hughes, born January 7, 1816, died February 14, 1895; married, May 21, 1835, Randolph, son of Randall and Mary (Reeves) Marshall, (see Marshall, III).

ROSSITER Richard Rossiter, son of Martin and Bridget (Kehoe) Rossiter, was born in the county of Wexford, Ireland, and when six years of age came with his parents to America and settled in Paterson. Richard was one of nine children, all born in Ireland, and in 1909 only four of them were living: Paul, lives in San Francisco, California; George, lives in Brooklyn, New York; Mary, did not marry and resides in Paterson; Richard, who received his education in the public schools of Paterson and a business college in that city. In 1866 Richard became bookkeeper for the Society for the Establishment of Useful Manufacturers, organized by General Alexander Hamilton, and in 1868 was made secretary and agent for the society, which office was exclusive as well as clerical in its duties and scope of action. He served as sheriff of Passaic county, 1890-93, being elected by the Democratic party of which he is a member. He is also secretary of the Society Land Company and secretary and treasurer of the Colt Land Company and of the Warren Estate Company. He is also interested in several other kindred enterprises looking to the development of the real estate in Paterson and its suburbs and has done much to advance the value of all such real estate. He was elected to membership in the Hamilton Club of Paterson.

He married, June 6, 1873, Jennie, daughter of Jacob and Jane (Van Blaroom) Merseles, born in Paterson, New Jersey, August 5, 1854, died September 12, 1907, and their only child, Marguerite M., was born in Paterson; married, June 28, 1900, John Wesley, son of John and Catherine A. (Jackson) Kingsland, and they have four children: 1. Rossiter, born July 14, 1901, died young. 2. Magdalene, born July 8, 1903. 3. Jennie Jackson, April 26, 1905. 4. Muriel M., August 27, 1907.

HILLIARD The Hilliard family of South Jersey are the descendants of John Hilliard, the friend of William Penn, who came over and settled near Dover, Delaware, prior to 1680. He had an only son, John, see forward.

(II) John (2), son of John (1) Hilliard, removed to Northampton township, Burlington county, New Jersey, where he married Martha, only child of Bernard Devonish, one of the New Jersey proprietors, and died intestate in 1719. It is unfortunate that the names of all his children have not been preserved to us in the public records, as it is now impossible in many instances to trace the exact descent of his numerous descendants, who are scattered throughout the southern counties of New Jersey and elsewhere.

(III) Edward, son of John (2) and Martha (Devonish) Hilliard, married Sarah Haines, who bore him nine children, among whom was Samuel, see forward.

(IV) Samuel, son of Edward and Sarah (Haines) Hilliard, married Hannah Atkinson and settled in Salem county. Among their six children was Joseph, see forward.

(V) Joseph, son of Samuel and Hannah (Atkinson) Hilliard, married Ann Thompson, who bore him six children, among whom was Thomas Townsend, see forward.

(VI) Thomas Townsend, son of Joseph and Ann (Thompson) Hilliard, was born in Mannington township, Salem county, New Jersey, September 4, 1816. He married Hannah Townsend, daughter of William and Hilda (Townsend) Goodwin, of Cape May county, (see Goodwin, IV) and granddaughter of Daniel Townsend, of Cape May. Children of Mr. and Mrs. Hilliard: 1. William Thomas, referred to below. 2. Joseph Bernard, born at Elsinboro, January 26, 1851; married Sarah Hall, daughter of Clement and Sarah (Jones) Acton.

(VII) William Thomas, elder son of Thomas Townsend and Hannah Townsend (Goodwin) Hilliard, was born at Elsinboro, Salem county, New Jersey, May 28, 1849. For his early education he was sent to Bradin Academy of Salem and later to the Friends' school in the same town, and in 1867 was sent to the Swithin C. Shortledge school at Kennett Square, Chester county, Pennsylvania, which he left in March, 1869. He then entered the office of Judge Clement H. Sinnickson, of Salem, where he took up the study of law, and with whom he continued until March, 1870, when he entered the office of the Hon. Thomas P. Carpenter,

of Camden, New Jersey, where he remained until June, 1873, when he was admitted to the New Jersey bar as an attorney. After practicing for three more years, he was admitted as a counsellor at the June term of the supreme court, 1876, and since that time has been engaged in the general practice of his profession at Salem. Like all of his ancestors, Mr. Hilliard is a member of the Society of Friends, and all of his children are birthright members of the same society. He is a member of the New Jersey State Bar Association, one of the charter members of that organization. He is president of the City National Bank of Salem.

Mr. Hilliard married (first) September 22, 1875, Eliza, daughter of George L. and Elizabeth (Lippincott) Gillingham. She died July 3, 1900. Mr. Hilliard married (second) November 6, 1901, Anna daughter of Elisha and Hannah Ann (Thompson) Bassett, of Salem (see Bassett, VI). Children of first wife: Thomas Gillingham, George Lippincott, William Thomas, Bernard Aubrey, Mary Elizabeth, all of whom are referred to below.

(VIII) Thomas Gillingham, eldest child of William Thomas and Eliza (Gillingham) Hilliard, was born in Salem, New Jersey, March 4, 1877. He was educated at the Friends' school at Salem, and then went to the Friends' school at Fifteenth and Race streets, Philadelphia, after graduating from which he studied law in the office of his father at Salem and was admitted to the New Jersey bar as attorney in June, 1898, and in June, 1901, as counsellor.

(VIII) George Lippincott, second child of William Thomas and Eliza (Gillingham) Hilliard, was born in Salem, New Jersey, June 26, 1879. After graduating from the George school at Newtown, Bucks county, Pennsylvania, he took up the course in the department of mechanic arts at the Drexel Institute, and then served his apprenticeship in Bement, Miles Company, of Philadelphia, and is now (1909) in the employ of Farr, Bailey & Company, of Camden, New Jersey.

(VIII) William Thomas (2), third child of William Thomas and Eliza (Gillingham) Hilliard, was born in Salem, New Jersey, September 7, 1881. He received his early education at the Friends' private school at Salem. He then went to the George school at Newtown, where he graduated, and in 1899 matriculated at the Hahnemann Medical College in Philadelphia, from which he received his M. D. degree in 1903, and in the same year passed the New Jersey state medical examination and

became junior resident physician at the National Homœopathic Hospital at Washington, District of Columbia. One year later he became the senior resident physician, and in 1905 opened an office on Market street, Salem, where he is now engaged in the general practice of his profession. He is a member of the New Jersey State Medical Association and of the Salem County Medical Society. He married, June 18, 1909, Mary Clayton, of Woodstown, New Jersey.

(VIII) Bernard Aubrey, fourth child of William Thomas and Eliza (Gillingham) Hilliard, was born at Salem, New Jersey, August 24, 1885. He attended the Salem public schools, and in June, 1903, graduated from the Friends' Central School of Philadelphia, after which he took a position as bookkeeper in the City National Bank of Salem, of which his father is the president, and is now serving in that capacity.

(VIII) Mary Elizabeth, fifth child of William Thomas and Eliza (Gillingham) Hilliard, was born in Salem, New Jersey, December 6, 1887. She attended the Friends' school at Salem, and later attended the George school at Newtown, Pennsylvania, and the Bradford Seminary at Bradford, Massachusetts. She married, September 19, 1909, Charles W. White Bailey, of Camden, New Jersey.

(The Goodwin Line).

The Goodwin family of Salem county are among the oldest of the colonists in that region of the country. As the name indicates the family is of English origin, and the founder of the family came to America from London, where his parents, John and Katharine Goodwin, were inhabitants of the parish of St. Botolph's, Aldgate, London.

(I) John (2) Goodwin, founder of the family in South Jersey, was born December 25, 1680, and emigrated to Pennsylvania in 1701. In the following year he removed to Salem, New Jersey, and in 1705 married Sussannah, eldest daughter of John Smith, of Smithfield. Children: 1. John. 2. Mary. 3. Thomas, born 1721, died 1803; married (first) Sarah, daughter of Lewis Morris, and (second) Sarah Smith. 4. William, referred to below.

(II) William, youngest child of John and Sussannah (Smith) Goodwin, was born in 1723, and lived in Elsinboro, on the estate which his wife inherited from her father. In 1744 he ·married Mary, daughter of Lewis Morris. Children: 1. John, born 1745; mar-

ried, 1772, Sarah, daughter of Clement and Margaret Hall, the marriage being almost the first that took place in the present Friends' Meeting House in Salem. 2. Lewis, referred to below. 3. Sussanna, 1750; married, 1773, John Mason. 4. Mary. 5. William, Jr., 1758; married Elizabeth Woodnutt, of Mannington.

(III) Lewis, second son of William and Mary (Morris) Goodwin, married (first) Rebecca Zane, of Salem, and had two children: 1. John, married Abigail Carpenter. 2. Susan. He married (second) Rachael, daughter of William Nicholson, of Mannington, and had three more children. 3. William, referred to below. 4. Thomas, married Sarah Jeffries. 5. Morris, married Sarah Smith.

(IV) William (2), eldest child of Lewis and Rachael (Nicholson) Goodwin, married Hulda, daughter of Daniel Townsend, of Cape May county, New Jersey, and among their children was Hannah Townsend, who married Thomas Townsend Hilliard (see Hilliard, VI).

(The Bassett Line).

The family of Bassetts came from England in the ship "Fortune" in 1621 and settled near Boston, Massachusetts, and many of their descendants still remain about Lynn, Massachusetts, Rhode Island and Connecticut.

(I) William Bassett, one of the children of the emigrant ancestors of New England, came from Lynn in the year 1691 and settled near Salem, New Jersey, with his three sons, Zebedee, Elisha, referred to below, and William.

(II) Elisha, second son of William Bassett, of Lynn, Massachusetts, and Salem county, New Jersey, was born about 1682. In 1705 was elected constable to the town of Salem, and continued in that office for eight years. He married Abigail Elizabeth, daughter of John and Dorothea Davis, of Pilesgrove. Their children were: 1. Sarah, born 1719; married Thomas Smith, of Mannington, and (second) Charles Fogg. 2. Elizabeth, May 23, 1720; married Thomas Davis. 3. Josiah, married Ruth Bradway. 4. Elisha, Jr., referred to below. 5. Rebecca, married John Page. 6. William, 1733; married Phebe Cowperthwaite. 7. Rachael, 1736; married Andrew Miller. 8. Isaac, 1738; married Deborah Dunn. Four others.

(III) Elisha (2), the son of Elisha (1) and Abigail Elizabeth (Davis) Bassett, was born December 15, 1722. He married Mary, daughter of Joseph Woodnutt, of Mannington. Children: 1. Joseph, died young. 2. Rachael, died young. 3. Sarah, born August 10, 1759; mar-

ii—26

ried Joseph Pettit. 4. Hannah, married John Roberts. 5. Joseph, referred to below. 6. Name unknown.

(IV) Joseph, son of Elisha (2) and Mary (Woodnutt) Bassett, was born June 26, 1765. He married Mary, daughter of David and Rebecca Allen, of Mannington. Children: 1. Elisha, referred to below. 2. Joseph, married (first) Lydia Freedland; (second) Sarah Hill; (third) Ann (Venicomb) Lippincott. 3. David, married (first) Vashti Davis; (second) Hannah Pettit; (third) Ann Packer. 4. Hannah, married Jonathan Cawley. 5. Rebecca, married Caspar Wistar. 6. Samuel, married Mary Ann Craft. 7. Benjamin, married Mary Acton 8. William, born 1803; married Abigail Hazelton. 9. Mary, 1806; married George Craft, Jr.

(V) Elisha (3), eldest son of Joseph and Mary (Allen) Bassett, was born January 26, 1778. He married (first) Mary, daughter of Darkin and Esther Nicholson, of Elsinboro. Children: 1. David, married Mary Smith. 2. Josiah, died young. 3. Elizabeth, married Biddle Haines. 4. Elisha, referred to below. 5. Edward Hicks, married Hannah Smith. 6. John Thompson, married Susan Humphreys. 7. Albert, married Sarah Shoemaker. 8. Mary. Elisha married (second) Mary, daughter of Thomas Clark, and widow of Samuel Lippincott.

(VI) Elisha (4), fourth child and third son of Elisha (3) and Mary (Nicholson) Bassett, married Hannah Ann, daughter of Andrew and Rebecca (Abbott) Thompson. Among their children was Anna, who became the second wife of William Thomas Hilliard (see Hilliard, VII).

———————

HEADLEY The Headley family is undoubtedly of English origin although one tradition says they came from Scotland. In the twelfth century the name was spelt De Haddeleigh, and de Hadleins, its signification being "of the woods." In later days the name has passed through various forms and has now crystalized into Headley, Hedley, Hedly and Hadley. The present branch of the family is believed to have originated with one, Leonard Headley, who prior to 1664 came from England, landed at Boston, went from there to Connecticut, afterwards drifted to Long Island, and in the year 1664 became one of the Elizabethtown associates.

(I) The Leonard Headley referred to above, soon after his coming to Elizabeth-town, went about five miles west of the town, and settled what for many years was known as Headleytown, which was that part of Union county now known as Unionville. Leonard Headley was a weaver and also the owner of a sawmill. His wife Sarah, who was the administratrix of his estate, after his death married Robert Smith, who according to Hatfield was the first of his name in Elizabethtown, being there in 1687 and in 1699 being the high sheriff of the county. Leonard Headley died in February, 1683, and it is supposed left two sons, Thomas, referred to below, and Abner.

(II) Thomas, conjectured son of Leonard Headley, was in Elizabethtown from 1700 to 1702, when his name appears on various papers and documents. Of his family nothing is definitely known, but it is conjectured from his being mentioned in the will of John Parker that there was some connection between the families of Headley and Parker, possibly Thomas's wife was a Parker. January 17, 1726, letters of administration were granted on the estate of John Clake or Clark to his "father-in-law" Thomas Headley. Thomas is also supposed to have been the father of Samuel Headley Sr. of Headleytown, referred to below.

(III) Samuel, conjectured son of Thomas Headley, of Elizabethtown, was born about 1690, died about 1755. He lived at Headley town, and was the founder of that place. He and his family were members of the Presbyterian church of Connecticut Farms, and they are buried there, but there is nothing to mark their graves. By his wife Mary, Samuel Headley had eight children: 1. Mary, married John Muchmore. 2. Joseph, referred to below. 3. Robert, born in 1718 or 1720, died April 28, 1806; married Susanna ———, and Phebe (Baldwin) Gardner. 4. Samuel, who is referred to below. 5. Sarah. 6. Rachel. 7. Phebe. 8. Isaac, married a Miss Piatt, of New Jersey, and was probably the eldest son.

(IV) Joseph, son of Samuel and Mary Headley, was born about 1718, died in October, 1785. He was a farmer and at first lived in Headleytown on land inherited from his father. Later, however, he removed to the Headleytown property known as Vaux Hall, probably erecting the house on the property and giving it the name it now bears. It was over this property that part of the battles of Connecticut Farms and Springfield were fought. The name of Joseph Headley's wife is unknown, but his children were: 1. David, born about 1745, died 1806; married and had one child, Abner. 2. Elizabeth, born about 1749. married Benjamin Crane. 3. John Thompson, born 1751, died February 4, 1828; married Catharin Smith; was a revolutionary soldier and fought at Connecticut Farms and Springfield. 4. Rachel, married Aaron Hunter. 5. Cary, referred to below. 6. Ann, married Eliakim Frazee, but has no issue. 7. Mary, who married but had no issue.

(V) Cary, son of Joseph Headley, of Headleytown, was born February 14, 1756, died February 1, 1823. He was born in Union township, Union county, where he lived and died, and spent his time farming. He was a man of much enterprise, much esteemed by his fellow-townsmen. He lived on what is now known as Valley street about half a mile south of Wyoming, and owned at least one hundred and fifty acres. When they were married Mrs. Headley was presented with two slaves, a man and a woman. Cary Headley was a revolutionary soldier, entertained General Washington and members of his command in Vaux Hall, and in his woods, which afterwards belonged to his grandson, John Stiles, referred to below, the great general and his men knelt down beside a log and prayed for victory for the patriot army. For three days Cary Headley's house was surrounded by the British. His wife and servants took the cattle and horses over the Orange mountain and remained there with them until the enemy had left. Before going she threw her silver spoons, pewter plates and platters into the well and also buried a case of silver in the big wall. After the war all was recovered. After the war Cary Headley furnished an ox which was roasted on the Orange mountain and General Washington partook of it. A part of the battle of Springfield was fought on this place.

Cary Headley married, April 1, 1781, Phebe, born March 13. 1762, died about 1830, daughter of William Stiles, of Elizabethtown, who bore him seven children: 1. Phebe Stiles, born about 1783 or 1784, married Jonathan Ball. 2. Mary, married Ezekiel Ball. 3. William Stiles, referred to below. 4. Susan, born March 6, 1796, died April 18, 1863; married Thomas Campbell Baker. 5. Timothy, March 10, 1800, died December 24, 1851; married Adeline Shaffer. 6. David Cary, February 15, 1802, died November 25, 1863; married Charlotte Halsey Baker. 7. Sarah, born about 1807, died February 18, 1827; married

Daniel S. Townley, and moved to Ohio about 1857.

(VI) William Stiles, third child and eldest son of Cary and Phebe (Stiles) Headley, was born January 14, 1791, died December 22, 1850. He lived and died on a part of the old Cary Headley farm. He was a farmer and a Presbyterian. He married Hannah Lockwood, daughter of Davis Headley, referred to below. Their children were: 1. Joanna Townley, born June 3, 1814, died April 4. 1839; married William Sanford Burnett, of Brooklyn. 2. Phebe Stiles, September 12, 1816, married Silas Condit Burnett. 3. Caroline, July 21, 1819, died March 7, 1889; married William Courter. 4. John Stiles, referred to below. 5. Jane M., December 31, 1824, married George R. Baker. 6. Wickliff, July 4, 1828, died March, 1902; married Sarah Ann Brown Dawes.

(VII) John Stiles, fourth child and eldest son of William Stiles and Hannah Lockwood (Headley) Headley, was born in Union township, Union county, March 11, 1822, died there April 6, 1893. His boyhood days were spent on the family estate in Union township. After acquiring a practical education he went to Brooklyn, Long Island, and was apprenticed to David M. Afflick, who taught him the trade of a mason. In 1846 he began business for himself as a builder, and continued with success until 1856, when he returned to Union township, locating upon a portion of the property of his ancestor, Cary Headley. To this he succeeded partly by inheritance, partly by purchase. He now gave his whole time to farming. He did not care for political life; his manners were unassuming; and he had many traits of character which are the exponents of success in life and which command the respect of the community. He was a worshipper at and a supporter of the Methodist Episcopal church at Springfield.

John Stiles Headley married, February 13, 1849, Sarah Ann, born December 29, 1824. died in 1901, daughter of John E. and Elizabeth (Cook) Courter, and their children were: 1. Will Courter, referred to below. 2. Hannah Elizabeth, born July 31, 1857, married William S. Wade, of South Orange, New Jersey. 3. Jane Lillian, June 22, 1859, married William H. Harrison, of Irvington.

(VIII) Will Courter, eldest child and only son of John Stiles and Sarah Ann (Courter) Headley, was born in Brooklyn, Long Island, June 25, 1853, and is now living in Newark,

New Jersey. He was brought up on a part of the old Cary Headley Homestead farm in Union county, south of Wyoming and near the Essex county line. He attended the public schools at Headleytown, Springfield, and St. Stephen's, an Episcopal school at Milburn, Essex county. He then entered the law office of Whitehead & Morrow (John Whitehead and Samuel Morrow Jr.) in October, 1872, was admitted to the New Jersey bar as attorney at the November term, 1876, and as counsellor November, 1879. Soon after his marriage he removed to Hilton, Essex county, holding while there the office of chairman of the trustees of the public school of that place. In 1883 he removed again to Irvington, New Jersey, where from 1884 to 1889 he held the office of president of the village, and other offices. In 1896 he removed to East Orange, New Jersey, where he continued to reside until about 1906 when he removed to Newark, where he now resides. He has his law offices at 800 Broad street, Newark, and is one of the prominent lawyers of that city. In politics Mr. Headley is and always has been an independent with democratic leanings. Since about 1873 he has been a member of the Methodist church, and in 1902 became a member of the official board of Calvary Methodist Episcopal Church of East Orange and is now a member of the official board of Somerfield Methodist Episcopal Church of Newark, which his family now attend.

Will Courter Headley married, June 5, 1878, Rosetta, born at Green Bay, Wisconsin, September, 1853, daughter of the Hon. D. Cooper and Sarah Francis (Camp) Ayres, whose two brothers are: James Cooper, married Nellie Rodman; and Francis Camp, married Sally Chamberlain, and has two children: Marguerite and Frances. Her father was a member of the "Iron Brigade" during the civil war. The children of Will Courter and Rosetta (Ayres) Headley are: 1. Elroy. 2. William Francis. 3. Harold Wade, all of whom are referred to below.

(IX) Elroy, eldest son of Will Courter and Rosetta (Ayres) Headley, was born on a part of the Cary Headley homestead, April 7, 1879. In June, 1894, he graduated from the Irvington public school; from the Newark Academy, with honors, June, 1897, and from Princeton University, 1901, with honors, having taken several prizes while there. In 1902 he graduated from the New York Law School and he is now in his father's office. He married, November 26, 1903, Ethel B., daughter of Henry

Whitman, born February 19, 1884, and has one child, Elroy Whitman, born November 6, 1904.

(IX) William Francis, second child and son of Will Courter and Rosetta (Ayres) Headley, was born March 12, 1881. He graduated from the Irvington grammar school in 1897, from the East Orange high school in 1901, and then went to the New York Law School. He married, April 27, 1906, Etta Mae Courter, born May 5, 1885, and has two children: 1. Francis Ayres, born August 26, 1907. 2. Helen Margaret, January 3, 1909.

(IX) Harold Wade, youngest child and son of Will Courter and Rosetta (Ayres) Headley, was born April 11, 1885. He graduated from the Irvington grammar school, from the Eastern school, East Orange, in 1898, from the East Orange high school, 1902, from Yale University, 1906, and from the New York Law School, 1908.

(IV) Samuel (2), son of Samuel (1) and Mary Headley, was born about 1724, died November 7, 1787. He was twice married, first to Rachel, born 1728, died 1750, daughter of Thomas and Sarah (Davis) Ball, who bore him one child: Rachel, married J. Tichenor, of Camptown. His second wife was Rebecca (Bruen) Headley, who died December 26, 1809, aged eighty-two. She bore him eight more children: 1. Rhoda, born 1756, died October 27, 1837; married Jonas Wade. 2. Stephen, January 28, 1761, died March 26, 1843; married Hannah Lockwood. 3. Davis, referred to below. 4. Mary, married Moses Wade. 5. Samuel, September 3, 1768, died June 29, 1841; married Elizabeth Miller. 6. Rebecca, July 24, 1771, died January 7, 1861; married Daniel Baker Jr. 7. Phebe, 1774, died February 7, 1860; married Dr. Hillyer. 8. Esther, 1776, died November 11, 1860; married Benjamin Meeker.

(V) Davis, second child and son of Samuel (2) and Rebecca (Bruen) Headley, was born in Union township, July 11, 1763, died September 10, 1832. He married three times. His first wife was Joanna, born November 23, 1774, died December 2, 1812, daughter of George and Martha (Baldwin) Townley. Their children were: 1. Phebe, born 1793, died January 2, 1875; married Richard Merrill. 2. Hannah Lockwood, referred to below. 3. Samuel, June 28, 1797, died September 1, 1832, unmarried. 4. George, died November, 1836, unmarried. 5. Martha Baldwin, 1801, died November 6, 1826; married Caleb S. Miller. 6. Davis Jr., October 10, 1805, died

May 7, 1881; married Susan Ball. 7. Mary, 1808, died September 28, 1827; married Ewel Freman. 8. Moses, who died unmarried. His second wife was Joanna, born October 29, 1764, died October 14, 1816, daughter of John Ogden and the widow of James Cole. Their child was William Ogden, born March 12, 1815, died February 23, 1875; married Maria S. Pierson. His third wife was Fanny Griffith, widow of Daniel Burger, who bore him one child, Eleanor Burger, married Lewis W. Lyon.

(VI) Hannah Lockwood, second child and daughter of Davis and Joanna (Townley) Headley, was born June 9, 1795, died in March, 1874. She married William Stiles Headley (see Headley, VI).

MARTIN John Martin, immigrant ancestor of this branch of the family, died July 5, 1687. He was of Dover, New Hampshire, 1648-1666; Woodbridge, New Jersey, 1668-1676; and Piscataway, New Jersey, 1676-1687. He married Esther, born in 1628, died December 12, 1687, daughter of Thomas Roberts, who settled in Dover, New Hampshire, in 1623, and was chosen president of the colony in opposition to John Underhill. Children: 1. Mary, born in 1645; married (first) Hopewell Hull, who died in 1693; (second) April 9, 1696, Justman Hull. 2. John, 1650, died at Piscataway, April, 1704; married (first) June 26, 1677, Dorothy, daughter of Richard Smith, of Woodbridge, New Jersey; (second) January 19, 1698-99, Anne Brown, who survived him. 3. Joseph, 1652; married, November 25, 1679, Sarah, daughter of William and Catharine Trotter, of Elizabeth Town. 4. Lydia, 1654; married, October 18, 1676, John Smalley. 5. Benjamin, see forward. 6. Thomas, 1659; married, April 28, 1683, Rebecca, daughter of Richard and Mary Higgins. 7. James, 1669, died March 21, 1676-77. With the exception of James, all these children were born in Dover, New Hampshire.

(II) Benjamin, third son and fifth child of John and Esther (Roberts) Martin, was born in 1656. He married (first) October 24, 1680, Margaret, daughter of Nicholas Renolds. Children: 1. Benjamin, born October 2, 1681, died October, 1682. 2. Esther, August 4, 1683. 3. Benjamin, November 14, 1685, died May, 1757; married Philorate Slater. 4. Jonathan, January 12, 1687-88, died August, 1768; married Elizabeth ———. The elder Benjamin married (second) November 10, 1688, Margaret, daughter of Peter Ellstone,

of Woodbridge, New Jersey. Children: 5. Mary, April 21, 1691. 6. Peter, see forward.

(III) Peter, only son of Benjamin and Margaret (Ellstone) Martin, was born August 19, 1693, died March, 1756. He married (first) 1712, Marie ———. Children: 1. Milford, see forward.. 2. Serviah Runyon. 3. Mary, married Isaac Fauret. 4. Pressilla. By the second marriage of Peter Martin he had: 5. Robert, married (first) November 29, 1758, Mary Bloomfield, (second) May 4, 1761, Margaret Pattan. 6. Peter, 1743. 7. Sarah, 1745.

(IV) Milford, eldest child of Peter and Marie Martin, was born September 22, 1713. He married (first) Serviah, born November 11, 1716, daughter of Ephraim and Phebe Dunham. Child, Thomas, born 1739, died in October, 1767; married, February 15, 1762, Elizabeth Ayers, of Woodbridge, New Jersey. Milford Martin married (second) Rachel Ayers, of Woodbridge, New Jersey. Children: 1. Rachel Ayers. 2. Milford, see forward. 3. Samuel, born in 1743.

(V) Milford (2), eldest son of Milford (1) and Rachel (Ayers) Martin, was born in 1741, died January 28, 1788. He married (first) Anna ———, born in 1728, died in 1766. Children: 1. Anna, born in 1760, died December 6, 1788, buried in Rahway, New Jersey. 2. Merritt, 1762, died in 1819; married, May 21, 1783, Rebecca, born in 1766, died August 25, 1801, daughter of Colonel Moses and Zeporah (De Camp) Jaques; they had seven children. 3. Thomas, 1766, died March 20, 1835, buried at Rahway; married, September 21, 1788, Sarah, daughter of John and Martha Ludlum. Milford Martin married (second) Hannah, daughter of Peter and Hannah Trembley, and widow of John Spinning. Children: 4. Peter, 1771, died June 10, 1804, buried in Rahway, New Jersey; married, December 14, 1794, Susan Conkling. 5. Milford, see forward. 6. Anna, February 5, 1781, died February 20, 1817; married Elias Dunham, born February 29, 1766, died July 29, 1815.

(VI) William, second son and child of Milford (2) and Hannah (Trembley) (Spinning) Martin, was born near Rahway, New Jersey, February 12, 1779, died in Rahway, March 13, 1843. He married, October 3, 1801, Ann Loree, born at Long Hill, near Morristown, New Jersey, October 22, 1775, died at Rahway, April 29, 1867. Children: 1. Rebecca, born July 17, 1802, died October 3, 1803. 2. Milford, January 5, 1809, died the same day. 3. William, January 2, 1811, died August 12,

1812. 4. William Milford, see forward. 5. Ann Loree, January 1, 1816. died at Newark, New Jersey, September 21, 1895; married James Ardley Calhoun. 6. Albert Gallatin, October 29, 1818, died at Dixon, Illinois, February 14, 1894; married Frances Thompson.

(VII) William Milford, third son and fourth child of William and Ann (Loree) Martin, was born in Rahway, New Jersey, June 29, 1813. He married at Brooklyn, New York. January 10, 1836, Ann Elizabeth Parmenter. born in Boston, Massachusetts, January 11, 1819 died in Woodbridge, New Jersey, October 17, 1885. Children: 1. William Wisner, born in Rahway, December 18, 1837, died in Brooklyn, New York, October 16, 1865; married, June 23, 1863, Fannie Ludlow Hadden. born in New York City, February 5, 1838, died in Plainfield, New Jersey, January 29, 1890; their child, Louise Hunt Martin, born in Columbia, California, April 6, 1864, married, August 3. 1893, at Brooklyn, New York, Kneeland Moore. and had a daughter, Anna Louise. born September 13. 1896. 2. Anna Maria, born at Rahway, July 26, 1842. died July 27, 1843. 3. James Parmenter, see forward. 4. Ann Elizabeth, born in Rahway, March 21, 1847, died in the same town, July 29, 1849. 5. Joseph Hillyer Parmenter. born at Rahway. January 23, 1850; married at Woodbridge, New Jersey, June 2, 1874, Lydia Freeman, born in Woodbridge. July 25, 1851; children: Joseph Hillyer Thayer, born March 22, 1875; Lillie Freeman, born January 17, 1878, died July 3. 1892; Elsie Barron, born April 10, 1880; Hilda, born June 11, 1884. 6. Sovereign Edgar, born in Rahway, December 22, 1851, died in Woodbridge, July 28, 1855.

(VIII) James Parmenter, second son and third child of William Milford and Ann Elizabeth (Parmenter) Martin, was born in Brooklyn, New York, October 8, 1844, died June 17, 1908. He married at Lyons, New York, June 12, 1867. Holdena White Bell, born at Simpsonville. Kentucky, October 19, 1846, and a descendant of James Brown, a sketch of whose descendants will be found forward. Children: 1. Wisner Bell, born in Virginia City, Nevada, December 17, 1868; married, June 6, 1894, at Hackensack. New Jersey, Grace Moore. 2. William Parmenter, see forward.

(IX) William Parmenter, second and youngest son and child of James Parmenter and Holdena White (Bell) Martin, was born in Virginia City, Nevada, October 8, 1871. He is an attorney and counsellor at law, with offices in the Equitable building, No. 120 Broadway, New York City, and is a member of the Lawyers' Club. He and his wife are members of the Roseville Avenue Presbyterian Church. He married at Geneva, New York, June 10, 1896, Margaret, born January 19, 1872, only daughter of Archibald Bostwick and Alvira (Peek) Morrison, and sister of Harry and Archibald Bostwick, Jr., the latter of whom is married to Sade Rutherford.

(The Brown Line).

(I) James Brown, who resided in Hatfield, Massachusetts, in 1669, removed to Deerfield, Massachusetts, in 1683, and went thence to Colchester, Connecticut. He married in Springfield, Massachusetts, January 7, 1674, Remembrance Brooks. Children: 1. Mary, born May 26, 1677. 2. Abigail, September 8, 1678. 3. Thankful, June 1, 1682. 4. Sarah 1683. 5. James, 1685. 6. Mindwell, 1686. 7. Hannah. 1688. 8. Mercy, 1690. 9. Elizabeth, 1693. 10. John, see forward.

(II) John, youngest child of James and Remembrance (Brooks) Brown, was born in Deerfield, Massachusetts, February 10, 1695. He was a soldier at one time and tradition says that he was captured by the Indians during the French and Indians war, taken to Canada. where he was exchanged and released after having been kept a prisoner for some time. He married at Northfield, Massachusetts, November 28, 1725, Hannah Janes, born at Northampton. Massachusetts, June 16, 1710. Children: 1. John, born April 5, 1726. 2. Benjamin, October 14, 1727. 3. Silas, see forward. 4. Eunice. December 15, 1730. 5. Hannah, November 2, 1732. 6. Lois, August 14, 1734; married Gideon Shattuck. 7. Rufus, July 5, 1736; died at East Hampton. Massachusetts, November 8, 1801.

(III) Silas, third son and child of John and Hannah (Janes) Brown, was born in Northfield. Massachusetts, June 21, 1729, died at East Hampton. Massachusetts, August 4. 1804. He was a lieutenant in Captain Jonathan Waite's company, Colonel Ezra Meigs' regiment, and was present at the battle of Saratoga and the surrender of Burgoyne, took part in the expedition to Stillwater and Saratoga during the revolutionary war, and conducted a part of the prisoners then captured to Hartford. Connecticut. He married Catharine Searle, born about 1735. died February 11, 1813. Children: 1. Sarah, married Storey. 2. Silas, Jr., see forward. 3. Eli, born about 1765, died March 15, 1795. 4. Arad, born about 1768, died January 2, 1795. 5.

Zenas, married, January 27, 1791, ———; died in West Hampton, Massachusetts. 6. Joel, born in Northampton. Massachusetts, about 1773, died there in 1862. 7. Dorcas, married Elam Clark; died at East Hampton, Massachusetts, aged ninety.

(IV) Silas (2), eldest son and second child of Silas (1) and Catharine (Searle) Brown, was born in Northampton, Massachusetts, June, 1762, died at East Hampton, Massachusetts, April 6, 1826. He married at Northampton, January 25, 1786, Jemima Clark, born in that town, July 25, 1763, died at West Bloomfield, New York, April 22, 1840. Children: 1. Theodore, born March 11, 1787. 2. Sophia, see forward. 3. A child, born November 28, 1789, died the following day. 4. Aroa, April 23, 1792. 5. Aseaneth, June 6, 1795. 6. Silas Clark, September 2, 1797. 7. Fanny, April 15, 1800. 8. Cecil, March 2, 1804. 9. Minerva E., October 17, 1806.

(V) Sophia, second child and eldest daughter of Silas (2) and Jemima (Clark) Brown, was born in Northampton, Massachusetts, July 26, 1788, died in Louisville, Kentucky, September 20, 1831. She married at Northampton, January 10, 1814, Silas Walsworth, born in Rome, New York, died in Wisconsin. (See Walsworth, V). Children: 1. Jared Stocking, born in Keene, New Hampshire, December 6, 1814. 2. Edward Brown, September 29, 1817. 3. Frances Minerva, January 26, 1820. 4. Maria Louisa, May 20, 1822. 5. Sophia Brown, see forward. 6. Silas Southworth, September 23, 1826. 7. Mary Elizabeth, March 9, 1829. All the children, with the exception of the eldest, were born in Cleveland, Ohio.

(VI) Sophia Brown, third daughter and fifth child of Silas and Sophia (Brown) Walsworth, was born in Cleveland, Ohio, August 29, 1824, and resides in Kansas City, Missouri. She married at Montgomery, New York, September 16, 1845, Rev. Samuel B. Bell, D. D., who was born in Montgomery. Children: 1. Holdena White. see forward. 2. Hal, born in Simpsonville, Kentucky, July 29, 1848. 3. Edward Walsworth, born in Maysville, Kentucky, January 7, 1851. 4. Sarah Pearson. born in San Francisco, California, April 7, 1853. 5. Harmon, born in Oakland, California, March 23, 1855. 6. Durant, born in Oakland, March 6, 1857. 7. Benjamin Pitman, born in Oakland, February 19, 1859.

(VII) Holdena White Bell, eldest child of Rev. Samuel B., D. D., and Sophia Brown

(Walsworth) Bell, married James Parmenter Martin (see Martin. VIII).

(The Walsworth Line).

The Walsworth trace their lineage directly back to Egbert, last king of the West Saxons, and the first king of England, 827-28. The name was originally spelled Warlworth, changed to Walworth, then assuming its present form of Walsworth.

(I) William Walworth, immigrant ancestor. came from near London, England, 1688-89. to introduce English farming into Fisher's Island, then owned by Sir Fitz-John Winthrop, governor of Connecticut. He and his wife and eldest daughter were baptized January 24, 1692, at New London, by Rev. Gurden Saltonstall. and he died at Groton, Connecticut. He married, shortly after his arrival in this country. Mary Seaton, who came over on the vessel with him. Children: 1. William, see forward. 2. John, who was a captain of dragoons, and died at Groton about 1749; he married Sarah Dunn, of Newport, Rhode Island, and had: Samuel, married Hannah Woodbridge; John, married (first) Mary Viner, of Stonington, (second) Patience Denison, of Lynn, was killed at Fort Griswold; Silvester, married, April 8. 1756, Sarah Holmes; William, of Delaware county, New York; James, died young; Benjamin, born at Groton, November 4, 1746; Abigail, died young; Sarah, married Benjamin Brown; Philena, married Joseph Minot. 3. Martha, born March 1690; married John Stark, of New London, and had children. 4. Mary, February, 1694; married Abial Stark. of Lebanon, Connecticut, and had children. 5. Joanna, October, 1698; married Christopher Stark. of Groton, Connecticut, and had four sons and four daughters. 6. Thomas, May, 1700; married a daughter of William Stark. of Groton, and had one son. 7. James, twin of Thomas. died during his minority.

(II) William (2), son of William (1) and Mary (Seaton) Walworth, was born in 1692, and was styled "Of Noank." He married (first) June 16, 1720, Mary Avery, of Groton. Children: 1. Molly, born September 29, 1721: married, July 1, 1742. Sol. Morgan. 2. Martha, October 17, 1724. 3. Susan, October 22,.1726; married Obadiah Stark. 4. Amos, January 30, 1728; married Eliza Harris. 5. Lucy, December 3, 1732; married Veach Williams. 6. James, see forward. 7. Nathan, married Jemima Gallup. 8. Abigail. He married (second) September 23, 1742. Elizabeth Hinkley.

Children: 9. Eunice, June 4, 1743; married, January 1, 1762, Deacon Simeon Smith. 10. Charles, 1744; married Lucy Harris.

(III) James, second son and sixth child of William (2) and Mary (Avery) Walworth, was born September, 1734. He was quartermaster with Ethan Allen at Ticonderoga. He married Eunice Packard or Parker. Children: 1. James, born November, 1759. 2. Jesse, February 6, 1761. 3. Eunice, December 29, 1762; married and had: Gilbert, William, James, a Methodist minister; Sarah and Abigail. 4. William, December 2, 1764; married Sarah Grant, of Stonington, and had three sons and two daughters. 5. Elisha, October 11, 1766. 6. Daniel, see forward. 7. Abigail, August 14, 1772. 8. Susanna, January 9, 1775. 9. Avery, March 7, 1777. 10. Asa, March 22, 1779. 11. Lucy, June 8, 1781. 12. Elijah, November 21, 1783.

(IV) Daniel, fifth son and sixth child of James and Eunice (Packard or Parker) Walworth, was born November 11, 1768, and was accidently killed while still young. He married Mary or Polly, daughter of William Southworth, born in Leyden, Holland, about 1616, settled at Canajoharie, New York, and died in Middlesex, New Jersey, in 1690; his wife was Susanna Antice. William was the son of Thomas Southworth, and the grandson of Sir Robert Southworth, who was knighted by James the First, married Alice, daughter of Alexander Carpenter, and died in England about 1621. He was the financial agent of the Pilgrims in Leyden. Lady Alice brought her two sons over on the "Mayflower," some say the "Anne," and became the second wife of Governor William Bradford, August 1, 1623. Daniel Walworth was the father of Silas, see forward, and Elizabeth, married ——— Foster.

(V) Silas Walsworth, son of Daniel and Mary or Polly (Southworth) Walworth, was born in Rome, New York, and died at Fort Winnebago, Wisconsin, September, 1849. He held a captain's commission during the war of 1812. He married at Northampton, Massachusetts, January 10, 1814, Sophia Brown (see Brown, V).

MATLACK The narrative here written is to record something of the lives and achievements of the representatives of several generations of one of the notable old colonial families of New Jersey. The family has been made the subject of narration by various chroniclers, for its marriage connections have been as notable as is the history of the family itself, and in the main the accounts of these several writers are in accord.

(I) William Matlack, or as his family name appears in some old records, Macklack, was born in England about 1648, and was one of the colony of Friends who came from Cropwell Bishop, a small village in Nottinghamshire, in the year 1677, in the ship "Kent." Captain Gregory Marlowe, and was sighted off Sandy Hook August 14, of that year. The vessel followed along the coast to the mouth of the Delaware river, up which it sailed to Raccoon creek, where her passengers disembarked. The commissioners appointed by William Penn and the other proprietors, and William Matlack with them, took a small boat and went up the Delaware river to Chygoes island (whereon Burlington now stands) almost surrounded by a creek named for an Indian sachem who lived there. Matlack was the first to leave the boat, just in later years he was foremost in the work of development of the region in various other respects. He was a carpenter and built, or helped to build, the first two houses in Burlington and also helped to build the first corn mill in West Jersey. It is related that as the boat neared the shore Matlack sprang to the bank and the first one to meet him was an Indian chief, between whom and Matlack a friendship was formed that lasted through life.

He came over to America as an artisan in the employ of Thomas Olive, commissioner and proprietor, and after serving him four years bought from his former employer one hundred acres of good land between the north and south branches of Penisaukin creek, in Chester township, Burlington county, as afterwards created. It is understood that the purchase price of the land thus acquired was his four years' service and "current county pay." The greater part of this tract is still owned and in the possession of William Matlack's descendants.

At the time of his immigration to America William Matlack was a young man, less than thirty years old. "He saw a town rise up in the midst of the forest, surrounded by a thriving population, busy in clearing the land and enjoying the reward of their labors. His leisure hours were spent among the natives, watching their peculiarities and striving to win their good will. Following the advice and example of the commissioners, every promise made by him to the aborigines was faithfully kept, and every contract strictly adhered to." He and Timothy Hancock, with whom he worked in common in many things, "soon found their neighborhood was a desirable one; for new settlements were made there in a short time, and went on increasing until a new meeting of Friends was established at the house of Timothy Hancock by consent of the Burlington Friends in 1685." In 1701 William Matlack purchased about one thousand acres of land in Waterford and Gloucester townships, in Camden county (then Gloucester) lying on both sides of the south branch of Cooper's creek. In 1714 he gave to his son George five hundred acres of land in Waterford township, being part of the one thousand acre tract purchased of Richard Heritage. In 1717 he bought two hundred acres of John Estaugh, attorney for John Haddon, and there his son Richard settled in 1721. In 1714 he gave his son Timothy the remaining part of the Heritage purchase, and on this tract Timothy settled and built his house. The tract of lands owned by William Matlack and his sons, John, Timothy and Richard, extended from the White Horse tavern on both sides of the highway and contained about fifteen hundred acres.

William Matlack, immigrant ancestor, married Mary Hancock, and of this event Mr. Clement writes this: "In 1681 there came from Brayles, a small town in the southern part of Warwickshire, a young man named Timothy Hancock, accompanied by his sister, who was about fifteen years of age. Without friends or means, they lived in a very humble manner among the settlers, but the demand for work soon found Timothy employment, and the demand for wives did not leave Mary long without a suitor." She married William Matlack in 1682, and they then removed to a tract of land which he had located between the north and south branches of Penisaukin creek, in Chester township. Her brother also located an adjoining survey, and in 1684 married Rachel Firman. Thus it is that the Matlack family of New Jersey—a prolific family indeed—began with William and Mary. Just when William died is not certain, but it was after 1720, and he lived to see his youngest daughter the mother of seven children. Tradition says that he died in his ninetieth or ninety-first year, "and would have lived longer if his tools had not been hid from him, for he took delight in having his accustomed tools to work with, and when he could not have them he died." His children were: 1. John, married (first) Hannah Horner; (second) Mary Lee. 2. George, married (first) 1709, Mary Foster; (second) Mary Hancock. 3. Mary, married

(first) in 1711, at Newton meeting. Jonathan Haines; (second) Daniel Morgan. 4. William, see forward. 5. Richard, married (first) 1721, Rebecca Haines, at Evesham meeting; (second) in 1745, Mary Cole at Chester meeting. 6. Joseph, married at Chester meeting in 1722, Rebecca Haines. 7. Timothy, married in 1726 at Haddonfield meeting, Mary Haines. 8. Jane, married Irvin Haines. 9. Sarah, married, in 1721, at Evesham meeting, Carlyle Haines.

The last resting place of the first Matlack in the New World is not certainly known. It is possible that his ashes mingled with the dust of the graveyard that his friend Timothy Hancock dedicated on the bank of the north branch of Pensaukin creek where many of the early settlers were buried. But this spot has disappeared and the tombstones that marked their graves have gone to help form the foundations of adjacent buildings. His wife Mary died eleventh month, twentieth, 1728, and is interred in Friends' Graveyard at Moorestown, New Jersey. From these two all by the name of Matlack or Matlock in America are descended.

(II) William (2), son of William (1) and Mary (Hancock) Matlack, was born at Pensaukin creek, Burlington county, New Jersey, December 2, 1690, died July 25, 1730. He married, September 17, 1713, Ann, daughter of John and Frances Antrim, of Burlington, and by her had eight children: 1. Rebecca, born August 16, 1714, died July 30, 1798; married (first) John Bishop; (second) Caleb Carr. 2. Jeremiah, March 4, 1716, died January 18, 1767. 3. Rachel, June 11, 1718, died February 5, 1762; married (first) Thomas Bishop; (second) Philip Wikard. 4. Leah, August 29, 1720, died February 25, 1731. 5. Ann, December 11, 1722, died July 26, 1728. 6. William, June 20, 1725, see forward. 7. James, June 13, 1728, died November 24, 1728. 8. Mary, January 6, 1730, died April 15, 1759.

(III) William (3), son of William (2) and Ann (Antrim) Matlack, was born June 30, 1725, died May 15, 1795. He married, at Haddonfield meeting, October 1, 1748, Mary, daughter of John and Jane Turner, and by her had ten children: 1. Atlantic, born November 13, 1750, died February 21, 1775; married Samuel Stokes. 2. William, May 15, 1752, see forward. 3. John, March 26, 1755, died August, 1831; married Rebecca Shute. 4. Reuben, November 17, 1757, died August 2, 1808; married Elizabeth Coles. 5. Jane, February 11, 1760, died May 3, 1760. 6. Samuel, June 7, 1761; married Sarah Shute. 7. Rebecca, February 13, 1765, died May 18, 1842:

married Amos Bizby. 8. Joseph, August 21, 1767, died August 26, 1814; married Anna Shute. 9. George, March 6, 1770; married Sarah Roberts. 10. Mary, August 4, 1772. died February 9, 1790.

(IV) William (4), son of William (3) and Mary (Turner) Matlack, was born at Maple Shade, New Jersey, May 15, 1752, died October 12, 1805, aged fifty-three years, and is interred at Mullica Hill, New Jersey. He married (first) Mary Matson, born 1767, died March 5, 1786. Married (second) Letitia Harris, born 1767. He had two children by his first and four by his second marriage: 1. Atlantic, born 1782. 2. Sarah, 1785. 3. Ruth, 1790; married Elton Rogers, of Rancocas. 4. William, 1795, died 1801, aged six years. 5. Joshua, 1802, see forward. 6. Rachel, 1805; married Darlington Evans. The mother, Letitia Harris, afterward married Joseph Miller.

The Matlacks were Quakers. For which reason the most of them remained neutral during the great revolution. But this was only in obedience to the discipline for the acts of some, it would seem, who broke the restraint and served in the war for independence, indicated that the family nature was to love freedom and hate the tyranny of kings and men. The most conspicuous example of this was Timothy Matlack, the grandson of the first William by his son Timothy. This grandson was an historic character and was born at Haddonfield, · New Jersey, in 1730. The breaking out of the revolution fired him with patriotic ardor, and throwing away the broad brim and turning down the "stand-up collar" he entered the army, for which act he was turned out of meeting. As colonel of irregular cavalry he did valiant service in the good cause. He was one of the founders of the Society of Free Quakers, who erected the building at the southwest corner of Fifth and Arch streets, Philadelphia, for a meeting house. He was a member of the Pennsylvania convention, secretary to the continental congress, and a member of congress. In 1817 he was prothonotary of the district court of Philadelphia county. Living to be ninety-nine years old, he died in 1829, and was interred in the Free Friends' graveyard on South Fifth street, Philadelphia. His portrait hangs in Independence Hall. Of lesser note were Josiah Matlack in the Light Dragoons of Philadelphia; Second-Lieutenant Titus Matlack, Second Company of Unassigned Militia; Sergeant William Matlack, Linton's Company, Philadelphia Militia; First-Lieutenant Samuel Matlack, Captain Horner's Company of Gloucester; and Joseph Matlack, a private in the state troops.

(V) Joshua, son of William (4) and Letitia (Harris) Matlack, was born at Maple Shade, in 1802. Being but three years old when his father died, he was taken and brought up by his uncle, George Matlack, from whom he learned the trade of shoe making, but from choice followed the vocation of a farmer. About 1826 he married Ann Burrough (who lived with her parents at Burrough's Mills, near Maple Shade) in the Friends' meeting house at Moorestown. By her he had nine children: William, Mary, Reuben, Samuel, Joshua, see forward; Albert, James, Annis Letitia and Ruth. His wife died in Camden in 1869 and was buried in Riverview cemetery, Trenton. He afterwards made his home in the capital city with some of his sons, assisting them in the baking business, until he passed away ninth month, twenty-first, 1885, aged eighty-three years, and was also interred in Riverview. Both he and his wife were members of the Society of Friends.

(VI) Joshua (2), son of Joshua (1) and Ann (Burrough) Matlack, was born in Westfield, Burlington county, New Jersey, July 30, 1835. He received a good common school education, and after leaving school began his business career as a merchant at Groveville, Mercer county. However, in March, 1863, he put aside business concerns and enlisted for nine months as private in Company H, of the Twenty-third New Jersey Volunteer Infantry (E. Burd Grubb, colonel); served throughout the term of his enlistment and participated in the battles of Salem Church and Fredericksburg, Virginia. In the fall of the same year he returned home and afterward for forty years was in the service of the Camden & Amboy and Pennsylvania railroad companies, being passenger conductor during thirty years of that long period of service. He married, May 18, 1857, by Friends' ceremony, Martha George Ellis, of Yardville, Mercer county, daughter of Micajah and Merebah (Middleton) Ellis. Mrs. Matlack was born June 30, 1841, and is now living, having borne her husband seven children: 1. Laura E., born Yardville, September 12, 1858; married, 1880, Francis Harbaugh, now of Maple Shade. 2. Micajah E., see forward. 3. Joshua, see forward. 4. Martha G., died young. 5. Bessie, born at Camden, December 3, 1868; married, June 14, 1900, at Mt. Holly, Elwood H. Stokes, a coal merchant of that place. 6. Wilson, see forward. 7.

Martha G. E., born at Mt. Holly, December 23, 1878; living at home. In 1874 Mr. Matlack moved to Mt. Holly and continued to live there until his death, which occurred fifth month, twenty-ninth, 1903, and was interred in St. Andrew's burying ground at that place. He was a member of the Society of Friends. and in political preference was a Republican. He was a true type of his progenitors; of sterling worth and ability, whose sentiments and living were those of an ideal American citizen. A man (as the Friend remarked in his eulogy at his bier) whose passing away was a loss to the community.

(VII) Micajah Ellis, son of Joshua (2) and Martha G. (Ellis) Matlack, was born at Yardville, Mercer county, New Jersey, December 19, 1860. He received his education in the public schools and at John F. Pfouts' Academy, Mt. Holly. He took up the study of the law with John C. Ten Eyck, Esq., and afterwards continued the same with Howard C. Levis. Esq. He was admitted to practice and has since been a member of the New Jersey bar. In connection with professional pursuits he has taken an active interest in military and political affairs and has served in various capacities from private to captain of militia and was adjutant of the old Seventh Regiment, National Guard of New Jersey. He is an expert in military tactics. He was a member of the lower branch of the New Jersey legislature for three sessions—1893-95—and for the last ten years has held the position of bill and printing officer of the national house of representatives. Is a member of the Episcopal church, and belongs to the Order of Elks. He married, in June, 1894, Elizabeth B. Johnson, of Brooklyn, New York, and has one child, Micajah Edward, born in 1900.

(VII) Joshua (3), son of Joshua (2) and Martha G. (Ellis) Matlack, was born at Yardville, April 24, 1863. He was educated in the public schools and at Pierce's Business College, Philadelphia, where he took a thorough course, and afterward became a competent telegrapher with the Western Union Telegraph Company; and subsequently was a stenographer. Later he studied law with George Harding and Francis T. Chambers, patent lawyers of Philadelphia, and in 1889 was admitted to the bar of Philadelphia. He established himself in practice in that city and so continued until 1905, when he became connected with the Land Title and Trust Company, but still retaining his private practice. In 1894-95 Mr. Matlack was assistant journal clerk of the house of assembly

of New Jersey, and from 1892 to 1896 was general secretary of the State League of Republican Clubs of that state. He takes an active part in politics and is a public speaker. He is a member of the Episcopal church, belongs to the Junior Order of American Mechanics and the Knights of Pythias. He is unmarried.

(VII) Wilson, son of Joshua (2) and Martha G. (Ellis) Matlack, was born at Hights-town, Mercer county, November 26, 1873. He received his education at the public schools and at the Mt. Holly Academy. He is now engaged in the coal business with his brother-in-law, Mr. Stokes. Is an Odd Fellow, an Elk, and a member of the Episcopal church. Is now first-lieutenant of Company E, Third Regiment. National Guard of New Jersey.

SPEER

This name with its various ways of spelling it, as adopted by locality or possibly by errors in writing. transcribing or through ignorance or carelessness on the part of persons bearing the name, appears to be distinctive of locality, as in Maine we find the direct spelling Spear and in other parts of New England Speare and Spears. In Pennsylvania and the southern states it is universally spelled Speer, in the west either Speer or Speers. In New Jersey Speir seems to have been the original spelling. and as the Spiers and Speers of New Jersey claim Hendrick Jansen Speer as their first American ancestor, the descendants are entitled to the orthography as it has been handed down, when not changed by families or genealogists through the habit of copying from town and church records the misspelling of clerks and translators.

For the purpose of this sketch when we use the surname, we will uniformly spell it Speer, and in so doing intend no offense to bearers of the name, who may have adopted other spellings. Unlike many surnames, the pronunciation is not changed by the change in the letters making up the name, whether spelled, Speir, Spier, Spear, Speer, Speare, or by affixing the s. which is undoubtedly caused through the use of the possessive case.

Speer and Speir are the only spelling used by immigrant ancestors, so far as our research goes; Speer by Scotch covenanters, who came to America and settled in Pennsylvania and drifted south and west, and Speir by the Dutch immigrants.

(I) Hendrick Jansen Speer came from Amsterdam, Holland, to New Amsterdam at the mouth of the Hudson river in North America, December 23, 1650, arriving on the Dutch ship "Faith." He had with him his wife, Madeline Hance, and two children, the third child. Jocobus, embarked with them, but died on the voyage and was buried at sea. The family lived in Nieu Amsterdam on Manhattan Island, until the settlement of New Utrecht and Flatlands on Long Island was undertaken by the Crownenhovens and inducements were made to the Dutch settlers living in Nieu Amsterdam, who were looking for investments, and the families of Albertse Cortelyou, Gerretson, Speer and Van Winkle became extensive landholders in the Flatlands neighborhood between 1657 and 1660. Here the Speer family lived and additions to their family came through births, one son and two daughters, being additions to the two sons who survived the long voyage in the "Faith" from the fatherland. On January 15, 1674, Hendrick Speer joined with other immigrant settlers in a petition for title to land on Staten Island, described as being at the mouth of the Kill von Kull and the next year he joined with the Cortelyous, Gerretsons, Van Winkles, Albertses and other land owners and men of wealth in Flatlands in exploring the lands on the Passaic river in eastern New Jersey, known as Acquockenock Patent of five thousand acres of land, of which tract these families became proprietors, and the Albertses, Van Winkles and Speers settlers. The governor-general and council of East New Jersey confirmed the original Indian deed purchase in 1685 as recorded in volume I. of the journal of proceedings of the government of that date. Additions to the patent were made for several thousands of acres near the Hackensack river and the deed given about 1701 by Tapyan and other Indians for a tract in Essex county on the east side of the Passaic river to the "hills."

In these various patents John Frederick Speer was a grantee as he was in several purchases of hundreds of acres, where Belville and Franklin were subsequently founded. By these various documents we notice that his name appears as Hendrick Jansen Speer, while in the patents as granted by the government it appears as John Hendrick Speer. It is quite evident that the same man is referred to and that the latter arrangement of names is more correct. Among the allottments made to him from the Acquockenock Patent is a farm of a large acreage fronting on the Passaic river and located between Passaic and Delewanna, the land running back from the river to the moun-

tains, and this tract was subsequently divided between Henry, John and Garret Speer.

Children of John Hendrick and Madeline (Hance) Speer were: 1. John Hendrick. 2. Barant. 3. Jocobus, who died at sea, born in Amsterdam before 1660. 4. Hans, see forward. 5. Fryntje, baptized March 25, 1667. 6. Cathyntje, baptized December 11, 1667. We find no record of the death of the parents of these children.

(II) Hans, fourth son and fourth child of John Hendrick and Madeline (Hance) Speir, was probably born in New Amsterdam, Manhattan Island, and baptized in the Dutch church within the fort at New Amsterdam, April 2, 1663. He married Fryntje Pientense, and became one of the original settlers of Belleville, Essex county, New Jersey, about 1685. He had children by his marriage with Fryntje Pientense including Johannes or John, see forward.

(III) John, son of Hans and Fryntje (Pientense) Speer, was probably born in New Utrecht or Flatlands, Long Island. He married Maritje Franse, August 12, 1679, shortly after his arrival on the Acquockenock Patent (Passaic), New Jersey, with his father and other members of the Speer family. He settled in the wilderness among the Indians about 1692 and carried on a farm. He had seven children: Henry, Francis, Guimada, Madeline, Femelia, Montie.

(IV) Francis second son of John and Maritje (Franse) Speer, was born in New Jersey. Married and had son Jocobus.

(V) Jocobus (James), son of Francis Speer, married and had children: Henry J., Rynier, John, Garrit J., Frances, Maria.

(VI) Henry J., son of Jocobus Speer, was born January 17, 1760, died June 29, 1846, on his farm on the west bank of the Passaic river, near Passaic, New Jersey. He married Martha Vreeland and their nine children were born at the homestead as follows: 1. James H., removed to Cincinnati, Ohio; he married and had a number of children and grandchildren, and his descendants settled in Ohio and Indiana. 2. Jacob, see forward. 3. John, settled in Texas. 4. Henry, see forward. 5. Burnett, see forward. 6. Nelson, settled in Cincinnati, Ohio; he married Mary Ann Pierson and their descendants settled in Ohio, Tennessee and California. 7. Nelly, married Benjamin Kingsland. 8. Gertrude, married John Rollins; settled in Cincinnati, Ohio, and their descendants settled in Ohio, Kentucky and Iowa. 9. Maria.

married John De Vaunsney and their descendants reside in New Jersey. All of these children except Henry and Jacob removed to the west.

(VII) Jacob, second son of Henry J. and Martha (Vreeland) Speer, was born opposite Belleville, Essex county, New Jersey, December 1, 1788, died December 28, 1858. He settled in Newark, New Jersey, where he was a shoemaker. He married, March 14, 1811, Blendana Hedenburgh. Children, born in Newark: 1. Harriet, March 20, 1813 (twin), died January 3, 1876; married, September 15, 1836, William S. Palmer and had two children: i. Henrietta Palmer, born October 8, 1837; married Augustus S. Crane, May 1, 1862, and had four children: a. Frederick P. Crane, born 1863; married Caroline Mashey, 1888; b. Helen S. Crane, 1865; c. Henrietta L. Crane, 1868; d. Mabel Crane, 1870; ii. Frederick A. Palmer, born September 17, 1839, died May 28, 1885; married, April 11, 1866, Anna Spencer Utter and had three children: a. Halsey U. Palmer, born 1867, died 1870; b. Herbert S. Palmer, 1869; married, 1895, Ella Louise Osborne, and had two children: Spencer E. Palmer, 1896, and John Osborne Palmer, 1897; c. Alfred H. Palmer, 1871, died 1877. 2. Jane H., born March 20, 1813 (twin), died December 10, 1894; married, July 1, 1833, Seth H. Woodruff and had six children: i. Joseph Fitz R. Woodruff, born 1834; married Julia Brower and had four children: · a. Charles H. Woodruff, 1859, married Charlotte Keene; b. Frederick W. Woodruff, 1861, married; c. Joseph Fitz R. Woodruff, Jr., 1868; d. Anna Elizabeth Woodruff, 1871; Obadiah Woodruff, born 1837, died 1892; married Jane E. Campbell and had two children: Edward W. and Clarence C. Woodruff; iii. Elizabeth Ann Woodruff, born 1839, died 1875; probably unmarried; iv. Charles H. Woodruff, born 1841, died 1842; v. Charles S. Woodruff, born 1843, died 1848. 3. Eliza B., born August 14, 1815, died unmarried. 4. Charles H., born September 30, 1817, died unmarried, May 14, 1862. 5. Edwin, born September 20, 1822, died April 26, 1861; married, September 17, 1845, Sarah Young and they had four children: i. Sarah Ada, born 1846, married James L. Marsh; ii. Clara B., 1851, married Louis Youngblood, 1870; iii. William C., 1854; iv. Louisa, 1859. 6. Louisa B., born October 4, 1824, died unmarried.

(VII) Henry, fourth son of Henry J. and Martha (Vreeland) Speer, was born in Belleville, Essex county, New Jersey, July 9, 1801,

died in September, 1857. He learned the trade of shoemaker with his brother Jacob in Newark, New Jersey, at that time a small village. He continued in the business during his entire life and was late in life employed as foreman in a custom shoe store in New York City, making a specialty of making ladies' shoes. He married Rachel, daughter of Abraham Van Amburgh, a blacksmith and fisherman, who lived on the east branch of the Passaic river below the Belleville bridge. Her sister (twin), Ann Van Amburgh, married a Mr. Betts, a soldier in the war of 1812, and she lived to be one hundred and three years old, and Mrs. Henry Speer lived to be eighty-seven years of age. Children of Henry and Rachel (Van Amburgh) Speer were: 1. Alfred, see forward. 2. Joseph T., born May 22, 1825, died in infancy. 3. Joseph Theodore, February 19, 1829; married (first) Mary Fairbanks, December 25, 1853, and had two children: i. Theodore V., born November 2, 1854; married, February 11, 1880, Sallie B. Rankin and their children were Laura (1882-1899) and Minnie Kate, born June 7, 1886; ii. Minnie Fairbanks, born June 13, 1861; married Warren S. Colegrove, November 7, 1883, and had five children: Josephine, 1885; Theodore J., 1887; Hazel, 1889, died 1891; Maria F., 1891; Warren Baird, 1898. Joseph Theodore married (second) July 5, 1871, Ellen Fisher, and they had one child, Jesse, born February 10, 1874; married, October 10, 1900, Charles Angell, and their twins, Irving J. and Theodore F., were born July 13, 1901.

It does not appear that the Speers of Acquockenock (Passaic) had any church connections and in this respect stood apart from the other patentees of the tract, who were in communion with the Old Dutch Church and held some prominent church office. In matters of the state, however, the Speers were prominent patriots and soldiers, and Abraham Speer was a private in the company of Captain Cornelius Speer in the Second Essex County Regiment in the American revolution. He also served in Captain Craig's company of the state troops in the Essex company as well as in the Continental army. Francis Speer was also a private in the Essex company. Henry Speer was a private in the Second Essex Company and was promoted to captain and also served in Craig's company. William Speer served in the same company under Captain Craig. In the civil war, 1861-65, John R., Edwin A. and John M. Speer or Spear, all of Passaic, served and made honorable record in aiding in putting down the southern rebellion, and Irving and Morgan Speer, sons of Alfred, enlisted in the First Colorado Regiment and rendered effective service in the Philippine Islands in 1898-99.

(VIII) Alfred, eldest child of Henry and Rachel (Van Amburgh) Speer, was born in Passaic, New Jersey, November 2, 1823. He attended the public school, and when fifteen years of age was apprenticed to a cabinet maker in Newark, the terms of his apprenticeship being that he should board in his employer's family and receive twenty-five dollars each year in cash until he was twenty-one years of age. Out of his yearly stipend he was to pay for his washing and purchase his own clothing. The boy's tastes ran in the direction of mechanics at the time, and his ambition was to study and use his inventive faculties, dormant in his nature. He completed his apprenticeship with the satisfaction of being master of his trade, but with no money in his pockets to carry out his ambition to get out of the cabinet making business. This condition necessitated his earning money at his trade to support himself and he started business in Passaic in a small shop, which he built near his grandfather's farm-house, hoping to employ at least half his time in the study of literature and in working out problems in mechanics that promised useful inventions. His early experience as his own master runs as follows: He would take an order for a bureau or a sofa and would make the journey by cars to New York to buy the material, would ship it to Passaic by rail and return home, a distance of twelve miles, on foot. his purchases having exhausted his cash capital. As trade increased he soon had a larger shop and several journeymen to assist him. His industry gave him a few hours each day for study and indulging in his mechanical experiments. His literary ambitions he was obliged to partially abandon, as it promised no immediate return, and he took up horticulture and arboriculture, both for profit and recreation. His vineyard, as it became fruited, led him to manufacture some native wine, which proved to be good and promised a means of profit. A window fastener, which he patented, was favorably received and he started out to sell county and state rights, but he met with indifferent success. While in New Orleans he sent home for a basket of his bottled wine and from these samples he took large orders both in New Orleans and Mobile. This changed the current of his efforts and demonstrated that wines were more marketable than window fasteners, and he hastened home to fill orders

already taken and at the same time to enlarge his facilities for filling future orders for wine. This led to his extensive vineyards and large wine presses and the management of the sale of Speer's Native Wines, which gained worldwide celebrity.

In 1870 he in a degree carried out his literary ambition by establishing *The Item,* the first newspaper published in Passaic, a weekly devoted to the news and promulgating the principles of the Republican party. He was a pioneer in other directions as indicated by the history of the village and city of Passaic. He was a school trustee under the old regime; provided the first hall for lectures and public meetings, by converting the ball room of the old tavern into a hall. He organized the first temperance organization in the town and named the society the Rechabites; placed himself out of touch with his townsmen and neighbors by insisting on having sidewalks at the time he was serving as street commissioner and was prominent in carrying the place out of its village stagnation into the activity and push of a growing city. His own fortune kept pace with the progress of his native city and he kept ahead of the procession and led his fellow-citizens with quick steps along the path of accomplishment.

Mr. Speer married (first) June 6, 1844, Catherine Eliza, daughter of Abraham Berry, of Acquockenock. Mr. Berry owned a grist mill and home on the shore of Yantacaw pond and was a prosperous and deserving citizen. Children: 1. William Henry, born March 17, 1845; married Emma L. Henion, March 17, 1869; they had two children: Maud, born May 10, 1872, and Grace, June 5, 1875. 2. Alfred Wesley, May 6, 1847; married Kate Brown, January 19, 1871, and they had no children. August 5, 1852, Catherine Eliza (Berry) Speer died, and September 22, 1856. Mr. Speer married (second) Polly Ann Morgan, of Cape Girardeau, Missouri; children: 3. Ella Morgan, May 29, 1860, died unmarried, April 2, 1891. 4. Sidney Silvester, December 19, 1865; married Johanna Schrittis and had three children: Sydney C., born 1893. died 1899; Alfred W., born 1897; Lillian Myrtle. 1900. 5. Nelson, January 28, 1868, died August 2, 1869. 6. Althea L., March 7, 1873. 7. Irving, September 22, 1874. 8. Morgan, November 26, 1875.

(VII) Burnett, fifth son of Henry J. and Martha (Vreeland) Speer, was born in Belleville. New Jersey, October 17, 1806. He married Betsey Snyder and they had six children: 1. John S., died unmarried. 2. David H., born

Alfred Speer

May 2, 1840; married, March 4, 1866, Mary E. Hall and had three children: i. Willie B., 1867; married Anna Hyath and had children; ii. Helen L., 1872; school teacher; iii. Angie, 1879. 3. Edmund E., February 13, 1844; married Martha Beney, June 6, 1867, and had three children: i. Carrie, 1867; ii. Nelson A., 1871; iii. Percy, 1876. 4. Burnett, November, 1847, died April 7, 1908; married, January 14, 1847, Jane Ann Carew and they had seven children: i. Lester William, 1877; married May E. Chatfield, and had Grace C., born 1907; ii. Della, 1876; iii. Isabella, 1879; married Albert C. Child and had Stanley Child, 1906, Clayton Child, 1907; iv. Eugene Garfield, 1880; v. Vinne Vandenburgh, 1884; married Cecil Farrell and had Marion, 1906; vi. Roy Burnett, 1886; married Lillian Paulin; vii. Clara Louise, 1887. 5. Eliza, November 9, 1850; married Charles Lovelace, May 24, 1870, and had six children: i. Cora Lovelace, May 24, 1871; married Edmund Hassell, 1891, and had four children: Helen C., 1892, died young; Jennie I., 1895; Mildred, 1897; Edwin C., 1900; ii. Charles Lovelace, 1874, died unmarried; iii. Mary Elizabeth, 1876, died unmarried; iv. John (1878-1880); v. Clarence, 1881; vi. Bessie, 1884. 6. Clara, June 12, 1854.

GUMMERE   The Gummere family of Pennsylvania and New Jersey is of German origin. The name originally was Gömere or Gumerie, and the first of these two latter forms is the one which is used by the emigrant ancestor of the family in signing his will which is on file in the office of the surrogate in Philadelphia. The family is one that has always stood exceptionally high in the educational and professional world, and some of the greatest advantages which we now enjoy in those walks of life have had their inception and beginnings in the fertile brains of members of this family. The name is deeply rooted in the history of more than one American college, and at least one college owes its foundation, and its present high standing among institutions of learning to two descendants of the sturdy Teutonic emigrant.

(I) Johann Gömere came to Germantown, Pennsylvania, in 1719, from Crefeldt, Germany; and there is a tradition in the family that he came originally from French Flanders. He and his wife, Anna, both died within twenty-four hours of each other, and were buried at the same time, May, 1738, in the "Upper Burying Ground," Germantown, but as their graves are unmarked it is impossible

now to locate them. Among their children was a son Johannes, referred to below.

(II) Johannes, son of Johann and Anna Gömere, lived in Moreland township, Pennsylvania, and in 1740 he received a certificate of removal for himself and his wife, Sarah, who is believed to have been a member of the Davis family of Bucks county, from the Abington Monthly Meeting to the Monthly Meeting at Concord, Pennsylvania. Among his children was a son Samuel, referred to below.

(III) Samuel, son of John (Johannes) and Sarah (Davis) Gummere, was born in Moreland township in 1750, and was probably the youngest son. July 6, 1814, he and his wife, Rachel, who had previously removed from Pennsylvania to Upper Springfield, New Jersey, asked for a certificate of removal from the latter place to the Burlington Monthly Meeting. October 23, 1783, he married Rachel, daughter of John and Anna James, of Willistown, Pennsylvania, and among their children were John and Samuel R., referred to below. Samuel Gummere was a minister among Friends.

(IV) John, son of Samuel and Rachel (James) Gummere, was born at Rancocas, New Jersey, 1784, died in 1845. For many years he lived at Willow Grove, Pennsylvania, and for more than forty years was an esteemed and successful teacher of youth at Horsham, Rancocas, West Town, Burlington and Haverford, Pennsylvania. In this last named place he has left an enduring monument of his greatness in the Friends' College. This was opened in 1833 with Mr. Gummere for its head master as a school designed to afford literary instruction and religious training to the children of Friends, under whose control the present college continues. Systematic physical training and athletic sport were made prominent in the original plan, and are still insisted upon. In 1845 the school was temporarily suspended in order to give opportunity for collecting an endowment, and was reorganized as a college in 1856. Upon his retirement from the Friends' College at Haverford, Mr. Gummere resumed his boarding school at Burlington, which he had previously conducted at first alone and afterwards with the aid of his son, Samuel J. Gummere, from 1814 to 1833, and in this occupation spent the remainder of his quiet and useful life. He was the author of many excellent text-books, and his work elicited the warmest commendation from Dr. Bowditch, Professor Bache and other competent judges. Among these publications were his celebrated

"Treatise on Surveying," which was first published in 1814, and ran through fourteen editions; and his "Elementary Treatise on Theoretical and Practical Astronomy," the first edition of which was published in 1822, and the last, the sixth, in 1854. A very interesting biographical sketch of Mr. Gummere was privately printed by William J. Allinson, of Burlington, and it is a well-merited tribute to the learning and virtues of a ripe scholar and a most excellent man. One of his old scholars has said of him "that former disciples of John Gummere never in after life approached their old master without sentiments of affection and esteem." In 1808 Mr. Gummere married Elizabeth, daughter of William and Susanna (Deacon) Buzby, a member of two of the oldest and most distinguished families of Burlington county. Children: 1. Susan, married William Dennis. 2. Samuel J., referred to below. 3. William, referred to below. 4. John G. 5. Mary. 6. Frances. 7. Elizabeth. 8. Rachel. 9. George. 10. Martha. 11. Henry Deacon.

(IV) Samuel R., son of Samuel and Rachel (James) Gummere, was born at Willow Grove, Montgomery county, Pennsylvania, in 1789, and from 1821 to 1837 was the head of a popular boarding school for girls at Burlington, New Jersey. He was the author of a number of celebrated text-books, among them being a "Treatise on Geography," which was first published in 1817, and which passed through six or eight editions; and also a "Compendium of Elocution," published in 1857. In 1831 he revised the "Progressive Spelling-Book."

(V) Samuel J., son of John and Elizabeth (Buzby) Gummere, was born April 28, 1811, died October 23, 1874. For a number of years after his father's retirement from the presidency of Haverford College, he was associated with him in conducting the boarding school at Burlington, and there he proved himself to be his father's "worthy successor both in scientific attainments and in the happy art of imparting instruction." He married (first) Abigail, daughter of John and —— (Hoskins) Griscom; (second) January 9, 1845, Elizabeth H. Barton. Children, two by first wife: 1. Caroline Elizabeth, born 1836, died March 6, 1869. 2. John, July 23, 1838. 3. Francis Barton, referred to below. •

(VI) Francis Barton, son of Samuel J. and Elizabeth H. (Barton) Gummere, was born March 6, 1855, in Burlington, New Jersey, and is now professor of English Language and Literature in the Friends' College at Haverford, Pennsylvania. In 1872 he graduated from Haverford College, and in 1875 from Harvard University. He then studied in Germany at the universities of Leipzig, Berlin, Strasburg and Freiburg, from the last named university receiving his degree of Doctor of Philosophy for his thesis on "The Anglo-Saxon Metaphor," published at Halle in 1881. Since then he has been elected a member of the Modern Language Association of America, and in addition to contributions to the Nation, the American Journal of Philology, and other periodicals, he has published a valuable and widely used "Hand-Book of Poetics," in 1885; "Germanic Origins,' in 1892; "Old English Ballads," in 1894; and "The Beginnings of Poetry" in 1901. His most valuable addition, however, to literary criticism is perhaps his complete refutation of the theories of Heinzel. His wife, Mrs. Amelia Mott Gummere, is a local historian of much note, whose best known work is probably "Friends in Burlington," a history of the Society of Friends from their earliest organization in Burlington to the present day.

(V) William, son of John and Elizabeth (Buzby) Gummere, was born in West Town, Pennsylvania, in 1814, died in Burlington, New Jersey, 1897. He was a banker by occupation, and one of the leading business men in Philadelphia, being for many years president of the Northern Liberties National Bank of Philadelphia. For a time he lived in the city of Philadelphia, but for about twenty-five or thirty years before his death he made his home in Burlington, New Jersey. He married Martha Moore, daughter of William Henry and Margaret (Edwards) Morris, who was born in Havre de Grace, Maryland. Her father belonged to the distinguished Philadelphia family of Morrises, and her mother was a member of the Edwards family of Buck county. On her father's side she has a lineal descent from Mereeydd, King of Powys, Wales. Children: 1. Richard Morris, referred to below. 2. Margaret Morris, now living in Burlington, New Jersey. 3. Frances Marsh, widow of James Craig Perrine, now living in Burlington, New Jersey. 4. William Henry.

(VI) Richard Morris, son of William and Martha Moore (Morris) Gummere, was born in Philadelphia, Pennsylvania, and is now living at South Bethlehem, Pennsylvania. After graduating with honors and the degree of civil engineer from the Friends' College at Haverford, Pennsylvania, he went out west in the interests of his profession and remained there for a number of years. He has always been deeply interested in the cause of higher education and for many years has been the treasurer of Lehigh University. In politics Mr. Gummere is a Republican, and in religious faith an Episcopalian, being a vestryman of the Pro-Cathedral of the Nativity, of the diocese of Central Pennsylvania, at South Bethlehem. He married Elizabeth, daughter of Caleb and Rebecca (Abbott) Hunt, of Philadelphia. Children: 1. Rebecca, born and now living in South Bethlehem. 2. William, referred to below.

(VII) William, son of Richard Morris and Elizabeth (Hunt) Gummere, was born in South Bethlehem, Pennsylvania, August 7, 1876, and is now living at Roebling, New Jersey. After graduating from Lehigh University in 1899, he spent two years as one of the instructors of that institution, and in 1901 was appointed head chemist of the Roebling office at Trenton, New Jersey. Here he remained until 1908, when he was made head chemist and superintendent of the company's steel mill at Roebling, New Jersey. He is an active and influential member of the Republican party of Burlington county, a communicant of the Protestant Episcopal church, and unmarried.

REEVE From the earliest period of its early occupation, West New Jersey had had living side by side two distinct families of the name of Reeve or Reeves, which apparently have no connection one with the other. One of these families, considered elsewhere, is the posterity of Walter Reeve, of Burlington county, the other, at present under consideration, owes its origin to Mark Reeve, one of the early colonists, who came out to Fenwick's colony in Salem county.

(I) Mark Reeve appears first in 1675, when he came over in the ship "Griffin" with John Fenwick, and the Salem monthly meeting records tells us that he married Ann Hunt, of Philadelphia, in 1686. The following year John Fenwick's executors had laid off for him sixteen acres of land in the town of Cohansey, and a few years later Mark Reeve bought a large tract on the south side of the Cohansey creek, now known as the site of Greenwich. For more than a century and a half the Reeve family held large tracts of land in that section, but hardly any of it now remains in the hands of Mark's descendants. Mark Reeve and James Duncan in 1696 with the assistance of Friends of Salem, built a meeting house on the banks of the Cohansey, on the site of the present

ii—27

brick one. Mark Reeve died about 1716 or 1717, leaving one son Joseph, referred to below.

(II) Joseph, only son of Mark and Ann (Hunt) Reeve, succeeded to his father's estates. In 1722 he married Elinor Bagnall, by whom he had five children: 1. Mark, referred to below. 2. Joseph, born 7th month 5, 1725, died 1763; married Milicent, daughter of Joseph and Hannah Wade. His son, Samuel, married Ruth, daughter of Gideon and Julia Scull. 3. John, born 1st month 5, 1730, married (first) Elizabeth, daughter of John and Ann N. Brick, and (second) Jane West, of Woodbury, Gloucester county. He was one of the most prominent men of his community in his day. 4. Mary, born 1734; married Thomas Brown. 5. Benjamin, born 1737.

(III) Mark (2), son of Joseph and Elinor (Bagnall) Reeve, was born in Cumberland county, New Jersey, 12th month 28, 1723, and in early life became a highly esteemed minister among Friends. He purchased a large tract of land at Greenwich on Cohansey creek, situated on the south side of the creek, where he erected a substantial brick building. About 1761 Mark Reeve married, and when he died he left five children: 1. Ann. 2. George. 3. Josiah. 4. Mark, Jr. 5. William, referred to below.

(IV) William, son of Mark (2) Reeve, was born at Greenwich, 12th month 11, 1766, died 1823. After his marriage he and his wife removed from Cumberland county to Burlington county, and made his permanent home near where his brother Josiah had previously settled. He married Letitia, daughter of Josiah and Letitia Miller, of Mannington, by whom he had eight children: 1. Josiah Miller, married (first) Susannah H. Garrigues, (second) Mary B. Dallas. He several times represented his county in the state legislature. Was a prominent ship-builder, and one of the largest landholders in the county. 2. Anna, married William Hilliard, of Rancocas. 3. Elizabeth Miller, married Jesse Stanley. 4. Letitia Miller, died unmarried. 5. William Foster, referred to below. 6. Mark Miller, died in South America; was a prominent physician in Philadelphia. 7. Priscilla, married Samuel C. Shepard. 8. Richard, never married. 9. Emmor, married (first) Prudence Cooper; (second) Sarah Wyatt Acton.

(V) William Foster, fifth child and second son of William and Letitia (Miller) Reeve, was born in Burlington county, New Jersey, in 1802. He is the only one of his father's three sons to remain at Alloways Town, a place they did so much to improve. With his two brothers, Josiah Miller and Emmor, he carried on with great success for a number of years the ship building business started at Alloways Town. They did not, however, confine their attention to this business, but bought large tracts of land in the neighborhood which were considered not worth farming, but which through their energy and judicious management have been made to produce more than fourfold. They also enlarged and beautified the town of their adoption with large and substantial buildings, and no village in that section of New Jersey has superior improvements. William Foster Reeve was a member of the New Jersey legislature for a number of terms, and it is an especially noteworthy fact indicative of the great esteem and confidence with which he and his father's family were regarded by the community in which they lived, that at the time he was serving in the lower house of the New Jersey legislature, his elder brother, Josiah Miller Reeve, was a member of the New Jersey council.

William Foster Reeve married Mary, daughter of William Cooper, of Cooper's Point, Camden, New Jersey. Her grandfather was a descendant of old William Cooper, of Newton township, and established the first ferry boat to ply from Camden to Philadelphia. The four children of William Foster and Mary (Cooper) Reeve are: 1. William Cooper, referred to below. 2. Augustus, referred to below. 3. Richard H., of Camden, New Jersey, the secretary and treasurer of the Cooper Hospital and trustee of the Cooper estate. He married Sarah Wyatt, daughter of Samuel P. Carpenter, and they have four children. 4. Rebecca Cooper, now living in Philadelphia, unmarried.

(VI) William Cooper, eldest child of William Foster and Mary Wills (Cooper) Reeve, was born at Alloway, Salem county, New Jersey, June 27, 1831, and is now living in Salem, New Jersey. For his early education he attended Clarkson Shepperd's School at Greenwich, New Jersey, and then the Friends' Select School of Philadelphia, after graduating from which he entered Haverford College. He was, however, unable to graduate as his father needed him at home to help in his business, and he was put in charge of his father's large plantation, of which at his father's death he became the owner. He subsequently purchased other farms, and being very successful in his agricultural endeavor soon became one of the largest of the gentlemen farmers of that region

as well as one of the most successful. In 1883 he came to Salem, New Jersey, where he has been engaged in administering his own and his wife's large property interests in Salem county. Mr. Reeve is in politics a Republican and a member of the Orthodox Society of Friends.

In 1860 William Cooper Reeve married Mary Mason, daughter of Richard M. and Hannah (Mason) Acton. Her father was at one time state senator of New Jersey.

(VI) Augustus, second child and son of William Foster and Mary Wills (Cooper) Reeve, was born in Alloway, Salem county. New Jersey. August 31, 1833. After receiving his early education from private tutors, he spent two years at Haverford College, after which he for some time assisted his father in the care of the latter's large plantations. He then established himself in the lumber and hardware business at Alloways Town, New Jersey, and in 1863 removed to Safe Harbor. Pennsylvania, where with a Mr. Miller he conducted a general store for the iron works of that place. In 1866 he came to Camden, New Jersey, and began the manufacture of brick and sewer pipe, in which he has been eminently successful and at present has one of the most extensive plants of his time under his control. His offices are at 31 Market street. In politics Mr. Reeve is a Republican and he has served his party faithfully and well. He served for one term in the city government of Camden. Mr. Reeve is a member of the Camden Republican Club, the Camden Board of Trade, and the Trades League of Philadelphia. He is a member of the Camden Friends' Meeting, and is a charter member of the corporation of the Cooper Hospital of Camden, founded in 1875. and 1893 was elected president of that institution's board of managers, a position of responsibility and honor which he still holds to the eminent satisfaction of the city's citizens. It is well worth mention that Mr. Reeve's daughters are members of the Society of Colonial Dames and the Daughters of the American Revolution, the eldest also being the regent of the Nassau Chapter of the Colonial Dames of Camden. Mr. Reeve has spent much time in the study of the local history of his state, and is the author of several excellent and accurate papers and articles upon that subject, which have appeared in the public press.

Augustus Reeve married Rebecca Cooper. daughter of Isaac H. Wood, of Haddonfield, New Jersey. Their children are: 1. Elizabeth Cooper, unmarried. 2. William Foster, general manager of his father's office; married Mary

Jay, daughter of Attorney-General Samuel H. Grey; two children: William Foster and Mary Jay. 3. Laura, unmarried. 4. Charles Gadskill, married Rebecca Hannah, daughter of Joseph B. Cooper, of Camden, New Jersey, and has two children, Joseph Cooper and Dorothy Morris.

GRIGGS The Colonial settlers in America by the name of Griggs to the number of about ten came to New England prior to 1700 from England, and some of them have been traced as of record in England at Lavenham, in Brackley, Hartest, Boxted and Ipswich. The English family of Griggs is very old. One branch of the ancient family bore this coat-of-arms: Gules three ostrich feathers argent. Crest: A sword in pale enfiled with a leopard's face proper.

The Griggs family of Massachusetts was established by Thomas Griggs, of Roxbury (now Boston), who came with wife Mary and sons Joseph and John and daughter Mary, and was of record as a land-owner as early as 1639 in the town of Roxbury, in the Massachusetts Bay Colony. Most of the persons bearing surname Griggs in America trace their lineage to this Thomas Griggs, of Roxbury. John W. Saxe, Esq., of Boston, has kindly submitted to the editor his manuscript history and notes of the Griggs Family in America. Through his researches the genealogy of the New Jersey family herein has been established. The wills, deeds and other records herein quoted were compiled by Mr. Saxe, in co-operation with Hon. John W. Griggs, of Paterson, and James L. Griggs, Esq., of Somerville, New Jersey.

The Colonial records of New Jersey mention among the first settlers the names of Benjamin, Daniel, Samuel and Thomas Griggs. The present Griggstown was founded by Benjamin Griggs and his brothers, on the banks of the Millstone river, where he settled and built a grist mill as early as 1733. These four brothers established the Griggs family in New Jersey, and their descendants are numerous and widely scattered through the west.

(I) John Griggs, father of Benjamin Griggs and three brothers who migrated to New Jersey, as stated, was a land-owner of Gravesend, Long Island, New York, as early as 1672. This John Griggs was probably the same John Griggs who was of record on Long Island, in 1659. According to family tradition this New Jersey branch came from New England progenitors through Connecti-

cut. The town of Gravesend had as its largest patentee Lady Deborah Moody, who settled there with Friends (Quakers) from Salem, Massachusetts. The wife of William Griggs, of Salem, Rachel (Hibbard), conveyed, May 14, 1712, to her son Jacob, all her interest in the estate of her brother, Benjamin Hibbard, "late of Long Island," deceased. Ann Griggs, daughter of George Griggs, who came from Lavenden, England, in 1633, in the ship "Hopewell," and settled in Boston, married Matthew Janes, and in 1644 went to Southampton, Long Island. Many of the passengers in the list of the "Hopewell" in 1633 settled on Long Island. Accordingly, it is supposed that John Griggs, of Gravesend, was of this family, although his descent has not been fully established of record, and he may have been a son of John Griggs, who in 1636 was allotted land at Watertown, Massachusetts, many settlers from which removed to Connecticut and founded towns of Long Island.

In 1660 John Griggs and Thomas Whittack, both of Gravesend, Long Island, were fined for "buying and selling" land on the first day of the week. Griggs declared that he did not remember such covenant implying that he was bound by a town covenant. The court ruled the bargain void and fined each fifteen shillings and costs of court. He must have been of age before this date. He signed by mark, though he may have been able to write. Frequent records of him are found after that in Gravesend. He was sued June 7, 1669, by Leonard Jacob for debt; he shared in a division of tillable land on Coney Island, etc., in 1670, and of the twenty-four heads of families receiving grants, only two had larger lots. He conveyed to his son John eight acres of land on the east side of Gravesend, on a neck known as Ambrose Island. He and his son John Jr. sold to William Hensen, of New Utrecht, May 10, 1690, plantation No. 37 with buildings at Gravesend; also other lands and lot No. 9 on Gisbert's Island. He was living in 1698, according to the census taken that year. He had wife Elizabeth at Gravesend. Children: 1. John, mentioned below. 2. Daniel. 3. Thomas, had children: Elizabeth, John, Mary, Hannah, Thomas, mentioned in will of Henry Gillam, of Worcester, New York. 4. Benjamin, mentioned below. 5. Edward (?), was on a committee to lay out highways in Somerset county, New Jersey, February 25, 1733. 6. Samuel, was on tax-roll of Franklin township, New Jersey, which includes Griggstown, with his brothers Daniel, Thomas and Benjamin.

(II) John (2), son of John (1) Griggs, was certainly born about 1660, for he was of age before 1685. He married (first) Anna Wyckoff, born May 29, 1665, daughter of Willem Willemse; (second) in 1684, Martha Wilkins daughter of Obadiah Wilkins. He appears to have been considerably older than his brothers, and the only one of the sons having real estate transactions at Gravesend. He alone remained on Long Island. His father deeded land to him in Gravesend, and he owned land jointly with his father, as stated, before 1695. He sold lots No. 1 and 16 in Gravesend, March 20, 1685-86, to John Kendrick, an Indian trader of New York. His father probably died before 1703 when (without the "Jr.") he deeded mill property at Gravesend. It is significant that Benjamin Griggs was also a mill owner in New Jersey. John sold land August 28, 1697, twenty acres, to Joachim Gullick for sixty pounds. He was constable in 1701. He owned slaves in Gravesend in 1768, and he appeared with his mother or step-mother Elizabeth in the census of 1763.

(II) Benjamin, son of John (1) Griggs, was born about 1680 at Gravesend. He was living in Gravesend, Long Island, in 1714-15. He removed with his brothers to the Millstone river, New Jersey, where he built a grist mill as early as 1733, and for him the town of Griggstown was named. His will, dated March 23, 1762, was proven in Somerset county, New Jersey, February 23, 1768. He bequeathed to children mentioned below: To brother Samuel; sons Samuel and Daniel were executors; witnesses were Nicholas Vaghte, Francis Feurt and Isaac Wilkins. (Note that Wilkins was also from Gravesend and related.) Children: 1. Daniel. 2. Samuel. 3. Barrent. 4. Reuben. 5. Benjamin. 6. John, mentioned below. 7. Martha, married Rene Vanderbeek. 8. Jane, married Aaron Bennett. 9. Elinor, married John Sutphin.

(III) John (3). son of Benjamin Griggs, was born about 1710-20. He died before his father (1758), leaving a son Benjamin, who was mentioned in his grandfather's will. Administration was granted Nicholas Vaghte, of Somerset county, principal creditor, January 20, 1758. John Griggs resided at Toms River, Monmouth county.

(IV) Benjamin (2), son of John (3) Griggs, was born March 22, 1754 (another record gives the more probable date of 1748),

died March 7, 1825. He married Eleanor Lane, born April 21, 1744, died April 8, 1829. Children: 1. John B., born August 18, 1777; married Maria Johnson; children: i. Benjamin; ii. John V. N.; iii. Daniel, had son Levi D.; iv. Maria; v. Margaret; vi. Harriet; vii. Martha Jane; viii. Sarah Ann. 2. Sarah, January 5, 1779. 3. Aaron, October 20, 1780; died May 18, 1817. 4. Daniel, September 6, 1782; started by wagon to California in 1849-50, and died on the way. 5. George, July 25, 1785. 6. Jemima, January 13, 1788. 7. Margaret, February 22, 1790; died July 2, 1858; married, June 14, 1819, John Harris, of Worcester, England, born January 16, 1787, died March 22, 1870; their son, Benjamin Griggs Harris, born at Newton, New Jersey, July 21, 1821, married Eleanor Anne Neale, daughter of Francis Neale, of Baltimore, and had a daughter born June 14, 1863, married H. F. Mackintosh, of Toronto, Canada.

(II) Daniel, son of John (1) Griggs, was born at Gravesend, New York, about 1680-85. He was in Gravesend, an adult, in 1714-15. He appears to have gone with several brothers to New Jersey, where many settlers from Gravesend located earlier and later. He owned a plantation near what is now Flemington, Hunterdon county, New Jersey, and this property has descended by will and remained in the possession of the family until recently. The township in which he lived was originally known as Amwell. His will was dated August 22, 1757, and proved November 14, 1759. He must have died late in the year 1759. He bequeathed to wife Jackominad; to eldest son John (doubtless named for his grandfather); to sons Joachim. Daniel and Samuel; daughters Mary, Catherine. The executioners were sons John, Joachim, and Daniel; witnesses: Samuel O. Hallock and Janel Matteson. Children of Daniel and Jackominad Griggs: 1. John, lived at Amwell; married Catherine Bower, daughter of Philip, and was on a committee to choose delegates to the constitutional convention. 2. Joachim, was a soldier in the revolution; will dated at Amwell township, Hunterdon county, April 2, 1805, and proved October 17, 1806, at Trenton; bequeathed to wife Anna, $1,334, etc.; to brothers John and Samuel Griggs and to Mary Hill, wife of Isaac, $80 each; to Anna B. Van Fleet $80, and Acha Hill, son of Isaac, $267; to sister Catherine, wife of Peter Williamson, of Sussex; to Mary, widow of Thomas Peterson, now deceased; and to Margaret, widow of Harp Peterson, and her children; appointed as executors his brother John Griggs and friends Cornelius Wyckoff and Isaac Hill; witnesses, Alexander Bonnell, William Geary and Nathaniel Saxton; inventory dated October 7. 1806, by Alexander Bonnell and Jonathan Higgins mentioning a note of $500 against the United States; his widow Anne made her will December 2, 1807 and it was proved November 8, 1808; she bequeaths to her own nephews and nieces. 3. Daniel, also of Amwell; left no children; his will dated November 17, 1761, and proved September 27, 1762, mentions brothers John, Jackson (Joachim) and Samuel; sisters Catherine, Mary and Margaret; executors John, Joachim and George, witnesses: Peter Peterson, Johannis Young, Jacob Mattison. 4. Samuel, mentioned below. 5. Mary, married Thomas Peterson. 6. Catline (Catherine), married Peter Williamson. 7. Margaret, married Harp Peterson.

(III) Samuel, son of Daniel Griggs, was born about 1740 in New Jersey. He married Catherine ——. He lived at Amwell. His will was dated at Amwell, January 26, 1803, and proved October, 1812, at Flemington of that township. He bequeathed a fourth part of monies arising from the sale of his real estate to each of his surviving children, and the other fourth to the four children of his son Daniel, deceased. The executors were son Samuel Griggs and his friend Abraham Gulick, doubtless of the same family as Joachim Gulick who sold land owned in common with John Griggs and Samuel Gerritsen, of Gravesend. It is likely that the name of Joachim came into the family through its connection with the Gulick family. The witnesses of the will were Daniel Reading. Joseph Reading and Nathaniel Saxton. Samuel Griggs must have died about September. 1812. His executors sold the farm to Andrew Van Fleet, by deed dated April 1, 1813. This farm in Amwell adjoined the homestead of Daniel Griggs, father of Samuel. and was bought May 2. 1769. of Micajah Gowe. The widow Catherine released her right of dower to her son Samuel, April 3. 1813. Children: 1. Charity. 2. Jemima. 3. Samuel. mentioned below. 4. Daniel, died before 1812: children: John. Christopher, Joakim (Joachim), Samuel.

(IV) Samuel (2), son of Samuel (1) Griggs, was born at Amwell, Hunterdon county, New Jersey, about 1775. He married Sarah Ann Griggs, born January 5, 1779, daughter of Benjamin Griggs, mentioned above, of Newton, New Jersey. He was a farmer at Flemington, part of the old township

of Amwell. In politics he was first a Federalist then a Whig; in religion a Presbyterian. His will was dated at Raritan township, Hunterdon county April 12, 1840, and proved March 2, 1842. He bequeathed to his wife Sarah $150, and provided that she receive yearly the interest on $2,500, etc. The remainder of the estate to be divided equally among all the children except John, who is to receive $1,200 less because of advancement made to him; also son Samuel to have $400 deducted from his share because of bond testator held; at his wife's death the $2,500 to be distributed equally among the children. The executors were his sons Daniel and Aaron; witnesses: Nathaniel G. Mattison, Joseph H. Reading and George A. Allen. Children: 1. Daniel. mentioned below. 2. John. 3. Samuel, went west about 1845. 4. George, settled in Shelby county, Illinois. 5. Benjamin, went west when a young man. 6. Aaron, lived in New Jersey. 7. Margaret, lived in New Jersey. 8. Ellen, married James L. Hixon.

(V) Daniel Griggs, son of Samuel (2) Griggs, was born in Flemington, New Jersey. March 7. 1798, died August 24, 1868. He had a common school education, and followed farming in his native town, and at Newton, New Jersey. He was a prominent member of the Presbyterian church, was superintendent of the first Sunday school in New Jersey, at Flemington, in the early thirties, and was for thirty-five years elder of the Presbyterian church of Newton. He married (first) Elizabeth Ann Johnson, born June 16, 1800, daughter of Henry Johnson, granddaughter of Captain Henry Johnson, who was a captain in the New Jersey militia in the revolutionary war. He married (second) Emeline J. Johnson. born June 22. 1813, a sister of his first wife. Children by his first wife: 1. Theodore, born February 26, 1826. 2. Rachel Ann, February 9. 1828. 3. Henry J., May 12. 1834. By his second wife: 4. George Van Tile. October 31. 1839. 5. Charles Edgar. September 20. 1842. 6. John William. July 10. 1849. 7. Ellen Hixon. August 19, 1851.

(VI) George Van Tile, son of Daniel Griggs. was born October 31. 1839; served in the civil war as captain in the Second Regiment. New York Cavalry, and was brevetted colonel for conspicuous gallantry in action. He was killed in the battle of Culpeper Court House, Virginia. October 11, 1863. Griggs Post, Grand Army of the Republic, at Newton. New Jersey, is named in his honor.

(VI) John William Griggs, youngest son

of Daniel Griggs, was born in Newton, Sussex
county, New Jersey, July 10, 1849. He was
graduated from Lafayette College in 1868;
(LL. B., Princeton, 1896; Yale, 1900), and
entered upon the study of law in the office of
Hon. Robert Hamilton. Mr. Griggs in May,
1871, became a student with Socrates Tuttle,
of Paterson, and was admitted to the practice
of his profession at the November term of the
supreme court, 1871, and counsellor in 1874.
In 1876 and 1877 Mr. Griggs was a member of
the general assembly from Passaic county, and
was a member of a legislative committee
chosen to revise and harmonize legislation affected by the provisions of the amended state
constitution. In 1878 he was appointed counsel of the board of chosen freeholders of Passaic, and in 1879 became the city counsel of
Paterson, serving during four years. For two
terms, 1882 to 1886, he represented Passaic
county in the New Jersey senate, in 1886 acting as president of that body.

It was in November, 1895, that Mr. Griggs
was elected governor of New Jersey, being the
first Republican chosen for that office since
1865, and he introduced the line of Republican
chief magistrates who have occupied that office
during the past thirteen years. An over-
whelming majority placed him in power. During his occupancy of the office, which covered
two years, Governor Griggs made his administration memorable by the dignity with
which he sustained his position, and the clear
reasoning shown in his state powers. The
qualities of his mind commending him to the
late President William McKinley, caused the
appointment of ex-Governor Griggs to the position of federal attorney-general. To accept
this dignified place, Mr. Griggs resigned the
governorship in January, 1898, and remained
in President McKinley's cabinet until April 1,
1901, and then resumed the practice of his
profession. He is a member of The Hague
Permanent Court of Arbitration. Since returning to practice Mr. Griggs has been identified
with large financial interests in New York and
Paterson, and is a member of leading clubs in
both cities. His residence is in Paterson.

John William Griggs married (first) October 7, 1874, Carolin Webster Brandt, of
Belleville, New Jersey, daughter of William
and Eliza (Leavitt) Brandt; she was born
1852, died January 21, 1891. Children: 1.
John Leavitt, born June 10, 1876; married,
November 19, 1902, Ruth Hoxsey, born March
17, 1882, daughter of Thomas Franklin and
Elizabeth (Paddock) Hoxsey; children: i.

John W., born November 7, 1904; ii. Elizabeth Hoxsey, June 18, 1906. 2. Helen, born
November 22, 1877. 3. Leila, born November
21, 1879; married, October 12, 1904, Oscar
Clark Huntoon; child, Carolyn Grant, born
June 21, 1905. 4. Daniel, born November 21,
1880. 5. Constance, born November 23, 1882.
He married (second) April 15, 1893, Laura
Elizabeth Price, of Cleveland, Ohio, daughter
of Warwick and Beulah R. (Farmer) Price,
born October 10, 1861. Children: 6. Elizabeth, born May 31, 1894. 7. Janet, born June
20, 1896.

JOHNSON   Among the early settlers of
New Amsterdam the name of
Jansen or as Anglicized John-
son is of frequent occurrence. It is probably
of the immigrants from Holland who came
with the great influx between the years 1658
and 1663 that this subject under investigation
will finally be traced. Andres Jansen was
born on Long Island, A. D. 1665, and is the
positively known first American ancestor of
Hon. William Mindred Johnson, of Hackensack, New Jersey, in whose ancestry we are
interested in this sketch, and in the absence of
definite authority as to parentage, the Holland
Society accepted him as a member; the proof
of the nativity of the father of Andres Jansen
while not fixed by name, became apparent and
indisputable as to fact.

(I) Andres Jansen was, according to the
records made of births in the family Bible in
the possession of the Johnson family, born on
Long Island in 1665, where he married and
had six sons as follows: Coart, born in 1689,
Andrew, Peter, Myndred (Mindred), Henry,
John. He removed with his children from
Long Island and the two generations became
prominent citizens of Reading Town, Hunterdon county, New Jersey. Here Andres Jansen, or as his name was anglicized, Andrew
Johnson, died while walking to the Dutch Reformed Church in Readington, which township was located in Somerset county up to the
time the new county of Hunterdon was
formed. His walk was probably from his
farm near White Horse to the church in Readington. His age at his death is recorded as
eighty years.

(II) Coart, eldest son of Andres Jansen,
was born on Long Island in the year of Our
Lord, 1689. He removed with his father,
probably by way of Middletown, Monmouth
county, to Reading Town, Somerset county,
New Jersey, where he was brought up on his

father's farm, and where he married Charity or Gertje Lane, Laan or Lanen, daughter of Arie or Adriaen Thyssen Lanen, of New Utrecht, Long Island, who married Martyntje Smack or Smock. Adriaen Lane's name appears on the assessment rolls of the township of New Utrecht of 1693 and the census of 1698. He is also recorded as of Gravesend. He removed to Middletown, Monmouth county, New Jersey, about 1700, at which date he conveyed land in New Utrecht to Gysford Tysson (Van Pelt). The children of Adriaen Thyssen and Martyntje (Smock) Lane were: Janetje, Gertje or Charity and Hendrik. The children of Coart and Charity (Lane) Johnson included Andrew, who married Jane Berger, May 10, 1755; Martha, who married and had children; Henry, see forward. Coart Johnson died at his home at Johnsonburg, New Jersey, in 1772, and was buried at Green's burying ground at Hardwick.

(III) Henry, son of Coart and Charity (Lane) Johnson, was born near White Horse, now Readington Church, Somerset county, New Jersey, October 5, 1737. He married (first) Susan Hover and removed to Sussex county, New Jersey, where he purchased a farm near Newton, the shire town of the county. He was a founder and one of the first elders of the Presbyterian church in Newton, and a prominent citizen of the county, with sufficient wealth to give his children superior school training. He was an officer in the American revolution and held the important position of quartermaster and afterwards captain in Washington's army while in New Jersey. He died January 5, 1826, at the age of eighty-nine years, at Frankfort, near Newton, and was buried in the old cemetery at Newton. The children of Captain Henry and Susan (Hover) Johnson were born in Newton, New Jersey, and were: Henry, see forward; David and Jonathan (twins); John, see forward; Samuel; William; Sarah, married Van Tile Coursen; Hannah, married John Van Deren. His second wife was Ann Van Este, whom he married in 1795. They had a daughter Susanna, married John Hover and went to Ohio.

(IV) Henry, son of Captain Henry and Susan (Hover) Johnson, became an early settler of Johnsonburg, Sussex county, where he was the chief merchant and brought up a large family. His son, William Henry, married Anna Couse and had five children: Henry W. and John C. (twins), born in Johnsonburg, October 21, 1828, brought up and edu-

cated in Newton; Henry W., as a merchant, afterwards a banker at Long Branch, and John C. as a physician and surgeon in Blairstown where he married Anna L., daughter of John R. and Sarah (Armstrong) Howell. The other children of William H. and Anna (Couse) Johnson were: Catharine H., Samuel, who was surrogate of Sussex county; and Mary, wife of William W. Woodward, a merchant in Newton.

(IV) John, son of Captain Henry and Susan (Hover) Johnson, was born in Newton, Sussex county, New Jersey, September 5, 1764, died there February 8, 1829. He was educated in the schools of his native town; engaged in manufacturing and mercantile business; was member of legislature, county clerk and judge of the county court. He was made a trustee of the Newton Library Company, September 1, 1800, and was prominent in local and county affairs. He married (first) October 26, 1790, Hannah Roy, and they had six children, as follows: 1. Susan Maria. 2. Eliza Matilda, married Dr. George Hopkins. 3. Mary. 4. Hannah Margaretta, married Rev. Elias W. Crane, D. D. 5. Sarah Amanda. 6. Harriet Roy, married Rev. James Cook Edwards. He married (second) April 28, 1804, Maria Catherine, daughter of Colonel Abraham and Sarah (Armstrong) Schaeffer, born October 16, 1782, died April 13, 1808. By this second marriage he had three children as follows, born in Newton, New Jersey: 7. William Jefferson, March 13, 1805; was a practicing physician in New York City, and died there September 22, 1860. 8. Whitfield Schaeffer, see forward. 9. Sarah Catherine, March 29, 1808, died unmarried September 28, 1868, and was buried at Newton.

(V) Whitfield Schaeffer, son of Judge John and Maria Catherine (Schaeffer) Johnson, was born in Newton, Sussex county, New Jersey, November 24, 1806. He received his elementary education in the schools of Newton, his training in law under instruction of Chief Justice Hornblower at Newark, and was admitted to the bar of Sussex county as an attorney in 1828 and as a counsellor in the courts of New Jersey in 1831. He was prosecutor of the pleas for Sussex county for nearly twenty years. He served as secretary of state for the state of New Jersey 1861-66 under appointment from Governor Olden, and on receiving the appointment he removed to Trenton, New Jersey, where he resided at the time of his death, which occurred December 24, 1874. He served the Presbyterian church in

Newton as an elder during the last eight years of his residence there, 1855-63. He married, October 4, 1837, Ellen, daughter of Enoch and Mary (Bidleman) Green, of Phillipsburg, New Jersey, and they had seven children born in Newton, New Jersey, as follows: 1. Mary Margaretta. 2. Emily Eliza, died in 1901. 3. Laura Catherine. 4. Elizabeth Bidleman. 5. William Mindred, see forward. 6. Margaret Green, died in 1897. 7. Ellen Green.

(VI) William Mindred, only son and fifth child of Whitfield Schaeffer and Ellen (Green) Johnson, was born in Newton, Sussex county, New Jersey, December 2, 1847. He was prepared for college at the Model School, Trenton, and graduated from the College of New Jersey (Princeton), A. B., 1867, A. M., 1870, and was admitted to the bar in 1870 as an attorney, and in 1873 as a counsellor in the state courts. He practiced his profession in Trenton, 1870-74, and in 1875 removed to Hackensack, New Jersey, and continued the practice of law in all the courts of the state and in the district and circuit courts of the United States. He was elected state senator from Bergen county in 1895 and reelected in 1898, serving as president of the senate during the session of 1900, and during the absence of Governor Voorhees in Europe in May and June, 1900, he was ex-officio governor of the state of New Jersey. In August, 1900, he was appointed by President McKinley first assistant postmaster general and he held that office up to April, 1902, when he resigned. He was a delegate from New Jersey to the Republican national conventions of 1888 and 1904, and served as chairman of the Republican state conventions of 1900 and 1904. His public spirit and liberality have abundant evidence in the records of the town of Hackensack during the time of his residence there, and in the Johnson Public Library erected at his expense and costing probably more than $60,000 and which was dedicated with appropriate ceremonies on its completion in 1901, the representative educators and public men of northern New Jersey taking part in the ceremonies. On removing to Hackensack in 1875 he was admitted to membership in the Second Reformed Church by letter from Trenton, and in 1905 he presented to the church an excellent pipe organ, and when the church and its contents were destroyed by fire in 1908 he added a considerable sum to the insurance money, paid for the loss of the organ, and this enabled the consistory to procure one of the finest organs in use in Ber-

gen county. He invested in the business and financial institutions, having a home in Hackensack, and was made a director of many, and president of the Hackensack Trust Company, in which he has a large holding of its capital stock. He was elected a member of the Holland Society of New York, being a direct descendant from Holland ancestry. He is a member of the Lawyers' and Princeton clubs of New York City, of the New Jersey Historical Society and of the Washington Association and other societies.

Mr. Johnson married, October 22, 1872, Maria E. daughter of William and Hannah (Haines) White, of Trenton, New Jersey, and the eldest of their three children was born in Trenton, the other two in Hackensack, as follows: 1. Walter Whitfield, April 13, 1875, died unmarried March 16, 1891. 2. George White, July 26, 1877. 3. William Kempton, February 25, 1883.

The Woolston family of WOOLSTON New Jersey belongs to that noble band of Quakers, who were among the earliest settlers of the plantation on the Delaware, where the founder of the family is found in Burlington county, in 1783, and where his marriage is one of the earliest recorded in the court minutes of that settlement.

Towards the last of October, 1667, some heads of families came in a ship to Wickaco (near the old Swedes Church), Philadelphia, and settled in the neighborhood of Burlington. There were eighteen. Among them were William Penn and John Woolston; they lived in wigwams until they could get their log houses built. Indian corn and venison, traded with the Indians, was their chief food. William Budd about the same time located land on the south side of the north branch of Rancocas which he conveyed to John Woolston, one of the first settlers in Burlington county. John Woolston married Hanna Cooper, daughter of William Cooper, of Pine Point, now Camden City, in 1681, and died in 1712, without making any will, and under the laws then existing in the colonies his oldest son John inherited all his real estate. He however, left two other sons, Joshua and Michael. John Woolston conveyed to his brother Michael part of the above land inherited from his father which embraces most of the land between Pemberton and Birningham Mill on the south side of Rancocas creek containing seven hundred acres. Joshua was never mar-

William M. Johnson.

ried and sold his land to his brother Michael, April 18. 1726.

(II) John (2), eldest son of John (1) Woolston, the first Woolston settler in the colonies, was married to Hannah (last name unknown) and had nine children, the oldest being Jacob.

(III) Newbold, youngest son of John (2) Woolston, married Mary Bowlby, of Mansfield. May 10, 1775.

(IV) Abraham, only son of Newbold Woolston, married, December 14, 1800, Anna Bray, and they had a son, John Bray Woolston, born October 16, 1807, died in 1895.

(V) John Bray, son of Abraham Woolston, was born in Port Colden, Warren county, New Jersey, October 16, 1807, died January 9, 1895. He was a justice of the peace, and a large land owner in the section of the country where he lived. He married (first) May 22, 1834, Gertrude Stillwell, born September 27, 1809, died June 3, 1837, leaving two children. He married (second) October 2, 1841, Margaret H. Ogden (first) born March 27. 1808, died October 16, 1858, leaving three children. He married (third) Lydia, daughter of Isaac and Hetty (Higgins) Smith, born in 1825, died February 14, 1895, leaving one child. Children of John Bray and Gertrude (Stillwell) Woolston: 1. Rebecca Ann, born February 9, 1835; married (first) George Edgar Vescelins. Children: John Edwin Woolston, born September 22, 1856; Arthur Isaac, August 11, 1859. She married (second) Benjamin Annan, one child, Eleanor, married August Chittenden, and has one child Miriam. 2. George Taylor, May 25, 1837, died March 7, 1882, unmarried. Children of John Bray and Margaret H. (Ogden) Woolston: 3. Sarah Shaw, April 15, 1843. 4. Jacob Newbold, October 23, 1845, died May 1, 1884; married Harriet Britton. Children: Catharine R. H., married Robert Ray Goodrich, and has one child, Robert Ray Jr., and John Newbold. 5. Hilda E., January 31, 1847; married, October 17, 1866, Miller R. Nunn (see Nunn, VI). Child of John Bray and Lydia (Smith) Woolston: 6. John Bray Jr., referred to below.

(IV) John Bray (2), only child of John Bray and Lydia (Smith) Woolston, was born in Port Colden, New Jersey, June 11, 1864. For his early education he was sent to the public schools of Warren county, and then graduated from the Hackettstown Collegiate Institute. In 1882 he entered the employ of the Lehigh Valley Coal Company, with whom he remained until 1885, when he came to Newark, and went into the freight department of the

Delaware, Lackawanna and Western railroad. In 1890 he started a coal business in East Orange, the Park Avenue Coal Company, which he gave up in 1898 in order to accept the position of freight agent of the Lackawanna railroad at Bloomfield, New Jersey. This position he retained until 1901 when he was appointed chief clerk of the surrogate's office, a position which he resigned in 1907 when he was elected county clerk. In politics Mr. Woolston is a Republican and is one of the strong men of his party. He has been for some time a member of the city Republican committee, and for the last four years its chairman. He is prominent in the secret society world, being a member of Ophir Chapter. No. 186, of the Free and Accepted Masons of East Orange, a past regent of the Royal Arcanum; a past counsellor of the Loyal Additional. He is also president of the Hollywood Republican Club a position which he has held since that club's formation, and a member of the Indian League. He is also president of the Hollywood Building and Loan Association of East Orange, New Jersey, and a director of the Hearthstone Building and Loan Association of Newark, New Jersey.

June 20, 1885, Mr. Woolston married in Port Colden, Warren county, New Jersey, Lucy, elder daughter of Samuel and Sarah J. (Carling) Opdyke, born September 1, 1867. (See Opdyke. VIII.)

(The Opdyke Line).

By far the largest number of American, Opdyck-Updike, are descendants from the Dutch family who settled in and near New York about 1660. It is impossible at present to trace to a certainty the Holland ancestry. but the family in the Netherlands was numerous and goes back at least as early as 1355, when Albert op den Dyck is credited with having done penance before the Custodian of the Shrine of the three Kings in Cologne Cathedral for some offence committed against Lubbert Scherpinge. The name has undergone several changes in the course of the century, and is now found under forms of Opdyke, Updike and Dyck.

(1) Louris Jansen Opdyck, born in Holland about 1600. came to New Netherlands' before 1653, in which year he owned a residence at Albany, and bought a lot at Graves End, Long Island, in which latter place he died in 1659. He was a well educated man, and possessed of some means, and he did a prosperous fur trading business at Beverwyck.

He removed to Graves End and later to New Amsterdam; he took a prominent part in the civil affairs of both places, and left his mark upon their early institutions. He married Christina ———, who came to the New World with him. Children: 1. Peter, born 1643, of whom nothing more is known. 2. Otto, born about 1646; married the Widow Marretje Jans. 3. Johannes, referred to below.

(II) Johannes, son of Louris Jansen and Christina Opdyck, was born in 1651, died in 1729. He was a planter at Dutch Kills, Long Island, and in Maidenhead and Hopewell, New Jersey. By his wife Catharine he had: 1. Tryntje, died between 1722 and 1741; married Enoch Andrus. 2. Engletje, living 1741; married Joshua Anderson. 3. Lawrence, born 1675, died 1748; married Agnes ———. 4. Albert, referred to below. 5. A son, died about 1730. 6. Bartholomew, living 1746.

(III) Albert, son of Johannes and Catharine Opdyck, was born 1685, died in 1752. He was a planter in Maidenhead, and Hopewell, near Princeton, New Jersey. He and his descendants, out of the special interest, have retained the original spelling of the surname, Opdyck, which by all the others was changed to Updick. By his wife Elizabeth he had children: 1. John, born 1710, died 1777; married Margaret Green. 2. Joshua, 1713, died 1789; married Ann Green. 3. William, referred to below. 4. Benjamin, 1721, died 1807; married Joanna ———. 5. Sarah, 1724, died 1804; unmarried. 6. Catharine. 7. Frank. 8. Hannah.

(V) William, son of Albert and Elizabeth Opdycke born about 1715, died after 1779; living near Maidenhead, now Lawrenceville, New Jersey. He married, before 1750, Nancy Carpenter. Children: 1. Mary, married William Biles. 2. John, referred to below. 3. William, born 1755, died 1822; married Sarah Palmer. 4. Elizabeth, married Jacob Mattison Jr. 5. Robert, died 1820; married (first) Abigail Hunt, and (second) Elizabeth Smith Ford. 6. Hope, 1762, died 1843; married Catharine Wilson. 7. Samuel, married Sarah Burtlas. 8. Daniel. 9. Sarah, married William Nefus.

(V) John, son of William and Nancy (Carpenter) Opdycke, born about 1740, died in 1819, and was a miller near Washington, Warren county, New Jersey. He married Rebecca Wharton, a descendant of the celebrated Quaker family of that name. Children: 1. John, born between 1770 and 1780; married ——— McGrodis. 2. Isaac, died

1848; married Maria Huffman. 3. Daniel. 4. James, died aged seventeen years. 5. George W., died aged sixteen years. 6. William, 1782, died 1843; married Elizabeth Kinter. 7. Beaulia, married John Welsh. 8. Sarah, married John Beers. 9. Rebecca, unmarried. 10. Phebe, married (first) Samuel Mabury, and (second) William Strous. 11. Mary, married John Brinckerhoff. 12. Samuel, referred to below. 13. Nancy, married Garrett Lacy.

(VI) Samuel, son of John and Rebecca (Wharton) Opdyke, was born in 1792, at Sherrerds Mills, one and one-half miles west of Washington, Warren county, New Jersey, not far from Brass Castle, where he spent the latter years of his life. He died in 1874. He married Ann Snyder. Children: 1. Elizabeth, born 1812; married Joseph Lanning. 2. John, referred to below. 3. Jane, 1820; married Joseph Warnsley. 4. William, 1823; married (first) Sarah Hornbaker, and (second) Margret Washburn. 5. George, 1825, died 1868; married Mary Cole. 6. Rebecca, 1826. 7. Mary Ann, 1830; married William Whittie. 8. Samuel, 1832; married Elizabeth Cole. 9. Sarah, 1836; married Cornelus Helderant.

(VII) John (2) son of Samuel and Ann (Snyder) Opdyke, was born at Sherrerds Mills, Warren county, New Jersey, in 1813. He married Mary Petty, and lived in Port Colden, New Jersey. Children: 1. Sarah Ann, born 1837; married Wilfield Mitchell. 2. Samuel, referred to below. 3. Margret, 1841. 4. William S., 1843; married Cornelia Fulworth. 5. Susan Widner. 6. John W., 1846, died 1886; married Mary Marlott. 7. Joseph, 1848. 8. Luther C., 1850; married Sarah Gardner.

(VIII) Samuel (2), son of John (2) and Mary (Pettey) Opdyke, was born in 1838, and is now living at Port Colden, Warren county, New Jersey. He is a canal boss. He married Sara J. Carling. Children: 1. Lucy, born September 1, 1867, in Port Colden; married, June 20, 1885, John Bray Woolston (see Woolston, VI). 2. Nettie, born 1873, died single.

FERGUSON   This ancient surname is of Scottish origin, derived from Fergus, a favorite name and one proudly worn by many Scotch chiefs in ancient times.

(I) Rev. John Ferguson, immigrant, was born December 9, 1788, in Dunse, a market town in Berwickshire, in the southern part of Scotland. His grandfather came from the north of Scotland and was one of the soldiers of the Duke of Marlborough, serving in the Scots Greys, a regiment of heavy cavalry during the period of Queen Anne's wars. His father and uncle came to America and settled in Newport, Rhode Island. About the time of the revolutionary war his father returned to Scotland, for he was not willing to take up arms against the mother country; but at the age of about seventy years he returned with his wife and family to Newport. His wife was Anne Briggs, of Little Compton, Rhode Island.

At the time of the return of his father to this country John Ferguson was a young man of seventeen years. He was converted at an early age and at once began fitting himself for the ministry. For two years he studied theology with Dr. Tenney, pastor of the First Congregational Church of Newport, Rhode Island, intending to enter Yale College two years in advance of the regular course. While living in Providence, Rhode Island, he at one time was a student of theology under the instruction of Rev. Galvin Park, D. D., professor of ancient languages and later of moral philosophy at Brown University. However, he was compelled to abandon his plans for entering Yale and had to again enter business pursuits and assume the care of his father ad the maintenance of his family. For ten years he continued this course, and during all of that time he never relinquished the hope of entering the ministry. He seemed to have a presentiment that the chief desire of his life would be fulfilled, and the ten years proved a period of preparation for that kind of life, although of quite different nature from that which he would have chosen.

His first sermon as a candidate was preached at Attleboro, Massachusetts, and his text was "The Lord is a Man of War." The text and sermon were not only characteristic of the man and of his theology, but of his ministry, which to use his own expression was "warlike." He never shrank from the defense of truth, never hesitated to sacrifice comfort, reputation, or means of support in the maintenance of principle. He was ordained in Attleboro, February 27, 1822, and dismissed March 25, 1835. In speaking of his ministry there one writer says: "It was of great value in the administration of wise and judicious measures and marked the beginning of the system of support to the various benevolent enterprises of the day, and of aid to the labors of parent and pastor by a judicious and careful educa-

tion of children in Sabbath schools, and maternal associations." After leaving Attleboro Mr. Ferguson was settled in Whately, Massachusetts, from March 16, 1836, until June 7, 1840. He was called Father Ferguson and was a man to whom churches looked for counsel and pastors for advice, often when pastors and churches were involved in difficulties. "He was very often solicited to appear as advocate before ecclesiastical courts, and many a time as he has done this have the coolness and shrewdness, the wit and wisdom with which he advocated the course extorted the exclamation 'what a lawyer he would have made.'" He almost always defended the weaker party, his sympathies frequently inclining to the unpopular side. "He was always ready to grasp the shield and poise his lance for the injured and defenceless. In all such cases he sniffed the battle like the war horse and fought with all the chivalry and the courtesy of a christian knight." He became extensively known as the "champion of the oppressed" although at the same time he was equally well known as "a lover and maker of peace."

He preached for about two years at Lanesborough and Whately, the place of his former settlement, and in 1842 became general agent for the American Tract Association for the states of Vermont and New Hampshire, in which office and its duties he was very successful; and he really became the Congregational bishop for those two states. He died at Whately, November 11, 1858. He was a man of vigorous mind and of vigorous body, a large-hearted man, of keen wit, "but his keenest shafts were winged with kindness." He was social and genial in manner. Realizing the defects of his own education—never having graduated from any college—he labored hard and made many sacrifices to give each of his sons a college education. Amherst College bestowed on him the honorary degree of Master of Arts, a proof that although he had been denied the advantages of a college course he had by his own exertions thoroughly educated himself and the compliment was a source of great gratification to him. Mr. Ferguson published a sermon on the death of Ebenezer Daggett Jr., which was delivered December 16, 1831, and several other discourses. He also published for the use of Sunday schools a "Memoir of Dr. Samuel Hopkins," the celebrated theologian.

Mr. Ferguson married (first) June 7, 1813, Mary V. Hammett, of Newport, Rhode Island, by whom he had two children. She died June 30, 1818, and he married (second) April 28, 1819, Margaret S. Eddy, of Providence, who died May 6, 1871, by whom he had nine children. Children: 1. John, born January 1, 1815; married Sarah Moore. 2. Margaret, November 11, 1816, died December 19, 1819. 3. Mary H., February 25, 1820; married Charles D. Stockbridge. 4. Peter, December 13, 1821, died October 14, 1822. 5. Peter, July 20, 1823. 6. William E., April 1, 1825, died June 6, 1854; married Elizabeth Sawtelle. 7. Rev. George R., March 19, 1829; married Susan Pratt, of Andover. 8. Margaret E., December 9, 1830; married H. B. Allen, of New Haven, Connecticut. 9. James A., November 17, 1832; married Claudia Churchill, of New Orleans. 10. Anna B., May 3, 1835, died August 6, 1840. 11. Abby Park, April 4, 1837.

(II) Peter, fifth son of Rev. John and Margaret S. (Eddy) Ferguson, was born in Attleboro, Massachusetts, July 20, 1823. He married Maria J. Bixby, of Keene, New Hampshire. At the age of thirteen years his father removed from Attleboro, Massachusetts, to Whatley, Massachusetts, and here he grew up and completed the preparatory studies which fitted him for entrance to Amherst College, which he entered but did not complete the course. His brother William at this time was chief engineer of the Cleveland, Toledo and Norwalk railroad with headquarters in Cleveland, and Peter left Amherst College and went to Cleveland where he held a subordinate position with his brother. Having met with a painful injury to his foot and being unable to travel at the time of his intended wedding, William, who was on a business trip to the east went to Keene, New Hampshire, and escorted Miss Bixby to his home in Cleveland where the wedding took place. He removed to Norwalk Ohio, still connected with the Cleveland, Toledo and Norwalk railroad until the fall of 1853, when he accepted the position of chief engineer of the Tiffin and Fort Wayne railroad and removed to Tiffin, Ohio. His work here was the preliminary survey and road-bed construction of an air line railroad from Tiffin to Fort Wayne and all the work was through an unbroken wilderness, part of which was known as the black swamp. Financial depression caused an abandonment of this project and he turned his attention to bridge construction and built two bridges in Tiffin; one over the Sandusky river and the other over Rock river. Desiring better facilities for the education of his children

he removed in 1860 to New Haven, Connecticut, where he continued for a time the work of bridge construction and built the Chapel street bridge over the New York, New Haven and Hartford railroad and the swing draw bridge over Mill river which were among the pioneer iron bridges of the country. During the civil war he was employed by the government as superintendent in charge of the reconstruction of Fort Hale which guards the eastern entrance to New Haven harbor. His next work of importance was the construction of the new station of the New York, New Haven and Hartford railroad on land reclaimed from the mud-flats of the harbor, and the constant exposure to which he was subjected was the beginning of rheumatic disease from which he never recovered. He also had charge of the laying out and construction of the junction passenger station at Middletown, Connecticut. He then became connected as superintendent of the then large contracting firm of MacIntire Brothers, and removed to Buffalo, New York, where he remained until failing health compelled the abandonment of active work and he and his wife made their home with their only daughter, living with them in Bethel, Connecticut, and later in Zanesville, Ohio, until his death, June 30, 1891. The son of a minister, he inherited a deep sense of morality, honesty and integrity, which in the varied experience of his life work formed the foundation of a character which developed a strong, self-reliant manhood. He was ever interested in the spiritual and moral welfare of those about him and a constant and faithful attendant of the Episcopal church. He gave freely of his time and knowledge in matters furthering the work of the church, and in the early days of his pioneer work in the west and during the latter years of his life was frequently called upon to read the church service.

The children of Peter and Maria J. (Bixby) Ferguson are: 1. James Joseph, born November 27, 1853, died October 14, 1854. 2. Mary, December 15, 1855. 3. John William, December 19, 1857. 4. George Robert, June 13, 1859. 5. Charles Edward, December 22, 1860. 6. Elizabeth, June 18, 1862, died August 18, 1862. 7. Arthur Bixby, January 13, 1864. 8. Herbert Allen, March 28, 1865, died January 26, 1870.

(III) John William, son of Peter and Maria J. (Bixby) Ferguson, was born in Tiffin, Ohio, December 19, 1857, removed with his father's family to New Haven, Connecticut, where the earlier years of his life were spent, and where he received his education in the public and high schools of that city, taking a course of study preparatory to entering Yale Scientific School. He did not enter the college, however, and turned his attention to the study of practical engineering. In 1877 he secured a position as rodman in the engineering service of the old Boston & New York Air Line railroad, remained there one year and in 1878 was employed in the same capacity in the engineering department of the New York, Lake Erie & Western railroad. He continued with the latter company until the early part of the year 1891, and during that period was advanced through several grades of promotion to the position of assistant chief engineer of the entire system. In 1892 Mr. Ferguson began business as civil engineer and building contractor in Paterson, in a comparatively limited way at first, and gradually increasing the scope of his operations and the magnitude of his enterprises until he came to be recognized as one of the most extensive building contractors in the east. The business was conducted under his sole personal management until 1905 and then passed to the proprietorship of the John W. Ferguson Company, incorporated under the laws of the state of New Jersey; but during this later period Mr. Ferguson has continued at the head of the successor corporation as its executive and managing officer. Among the more important of the many structures and edifices erected by the company there may be mentioned the New Jersey State Armory, Hamilton Trust Company, United Bank Building, the Colt Building, the Meyer Brothers Department Store building, all in Paterson; the Kings County Power Building, Brooklyn, New York; Hackensack Trust Company building, Hackensack, New Jersey; the Babbit Soap Factory Building, Babbit, New Jersey; the Babcock & Wilcox Plant, Bayonne, New Jersey; the Newark Warehouse, Newark, New Jersey; the Gera Mills, and the recent large addition to the already vast buildings of the Botany Mills, both of Passaic.

Aside from his business interests and personal concerns Mr. Ferguson during his residence in Paterson has been closely identified with the growth and prosperity of the city in many directions, and has been and still is connected with several of the best institutions of the city; but he never has been in any sense a politician or a seeker after political honors. He was one of the principal organizers of the Taxpayers Association of Paterson, in 1903, a guiding spirit of the policy and the excellent good works accomplished by that association, and now is chairman of its executive committee. He holds membership in the American Society of Civil Engineers, the American Society of Mechanical Engineers, the New Jersey State Commission of Industrial Education, the Society of Sons of the American Revolution, life member General Society of Mechanics & Tradesmen, New York, the North Jersey County Club, of Paterson, and the Hamilton Club, of Paterson, the Engineers Club and Hardware Club of New York.

Mr. Ferguson married, May 26, 1893, Jennie Beam, daughter of William Cooke, of Paterson, and by whom he has three children, John William Jr., Arthur Donald and Jean Ferguson.

JOHNSON   The Johnson family of Morris county, New Jersey, is another example of that stalwart New England stock, which from the middle of the seventeenth century has been coming in a continual stream into and through the state.

(I) John Johnson, descendant of a long line of Connecticut ancestors, came from New Haven county before 1750 into Morris county, New Jersey. He lived at Parsippany, on what was known as the "Dr. Darby place," and later as the John S. Smith farm. He died September 21, 1724. By his wife Mary he had: John, referred to below; Abigail, Moses, Alexander.

(II) John (2), son of John (1) and Mary Johnson, was born in New Haven county, Connecticut, about 1706, died in Morris county, New Jersey, May 4, 1776. He married Abagail, daughter of Caleb Ball Sr. She was born about 1708, died June 4, 1793. Children: Anne, Kezia, Elisha, Gershon, Joseph, Abagail, Jacob, referred to below; Lydia.

(III) Jacob, son of John (2) and Abagail (Ball) Johnson, was baptized in the First Presbyterian Church of Morristown, April 21, 1751; died there April 25, 1780. According to Stryker, he enlisted in the New Jersey militia as a private during the revolutionary war, and rose to the rank of lieutenant in the Third Regiment. December 13, 1772, he married Anne, daughter of Thomas and Sarah (Davis) Vail, who was born in 1753 and survived her husband, dying June 11, 1784. Children: Noah, Mahlon, referred to below; Jacob Jr. Noah moved to Ohio, and Jacob's descendants are living to-day in Indiana.

(IV) Mahlon, son of Jacob and Anne (Vail)

Johnson, was born at Littleton, Morris county, New Jersey, November 5, 1775, died there December 20, 1857. He was the only one of his father's children who remained in New Jersey, and being only five years old when his father died, and eight when his mother died, he and his brother were brought up in the family of their uncle, John Vail. He married (first) November 18, 1797, Sally or Sarah Baker, who five years later handed in her letter from Parsippany to the First Presbyterian Church of Morristown. She died April 17, 1837, aged fifty-nine years. He married (second) Mary (Robertson) Ludlam, born January 8, 1792, died January 31, 1874, aged eighty-two years, widow of Ezekiel Ludlam. Children, all by first marriage: 1. Jacob, born December 3, 1798, died March 20, 1865; married Hetty (Baker) Vail. 2. Chilion, July 24, 1800, died Crawfordsville, Indiana; married Ann Woodruff. 3. Noah, February 17, 1802; drowned at Speedwell, July 20, 1819. 4. Baker, October 23, 1803, died October 18, 1886; graduated from Bloomfield Academy, Union College, and Princeton Seminary; ordained by the Presbytery of New York; married Electa, daughter of the Rev. Barnabas King. 5. Alfred, referred to below. 6. Sussanna Day, August 26, 1806, died May 5, 1877; married Jonathan E. Huntington, as his second wife. 7. Elizabeth Ann, February 16, 1808, died December 15, 1863; married Johnathan E. Huntington as his first wife. 8. Thomas Vail, October 8, 1809, died March 29, 1879; married Sarah Frances Cory. 9. Sarah Vail, March 10, 1811, died April 22, 1882; married Joel Davis. 10. Catharine Wheeler, July 5, 1812, died September 28, 1874; married Aaron C. Johnson, of Newark. 11. Mary, August 2, 1814, died June 1878; married Silas B. Condict. 12. James Harvey, March 14, 1816, died September 21, 1852; married Hannah Jilson. 13. Davis Vail, November 1, 1817, died January 22, 1871; married Caroline Mayo. 14. John Henry, October 28, 1820; married Maria Allen DeCamp. 15. A child died September 17, 1823.

(V) Alfred, fifth child and son of Mahlon and Sarah (Baker) Johnson, was born at Littleton, Morris county, New Jersey, April 5, 1805, died October 7, 1847. He was a farmer, a blacksmith, carpenter and wheelwright, and lived at Littleton all his life. January 14, 1828, he married Sarah, daughter of Jonathan Baker, born November 7, 1803, died June 27, 1882. Children: 1. Margaret Baker, born November 28, 1828, died May 29, 1857; married Belknap Gregory. 2. Emma Lucilla, September 13, 1830, died April 8, 1898; unmarried. 3. Henry Martyn or (Norton), May 30, 1834, died at Portage, Wisconsin. 4. Theodore Frelinghuysen, referred to below. 5. Phebe Baker, baptized May 31, 1839, now living at 102 Court street, Newark. 6. Mary Eliza, January 26, 1843, died December 23, 1899; unmarried. 7. Johnathan Baker, died November 26, 1849, aged eight years.

(VI) Theodore Frelinghuysen, fourth child and second son of Alfred and Sarah (Baker) Johnson, was born in Littleton, Morris county, New Jersey, July 11, 1835, and was baptized in the First Presbyterian Church in Morristown, May 31, 1839. He is now living in Newark, New Jersey. For his early education he was sent to Littleton, New Jersey, and later to the Newark private schools, and afterwards to private schools, first of Dr. Nathan Hedges and then of his uncle, John Henry Johnson. Coming to Newark when he was only eight years of age, he lived with his uncle Jacob, and after finishing his school days went to work in a carriage factory in Newark. After this he took a position in Columbus, Georgia, which he left in order to accept a position as bookkeeper in New York City. Coming back to his Uncle Jacob, he finally bought the business in which he is at present engaged, that of wholesale tea, coffee and spices. This was in 1856, and Mr. Johnson's business which was first started by Andrew Johnson in 1830, has now grown to be one of the largest firms of its kind in Newark, shipping merchandise all over the country. The firm name at first was Jacob Johnson & Company, Theodore Johnson being the latter. It then became Theo. F. Johnson and finally when Mr. Johnson admitted two of his sons into partnership, Theo. F. Johnson & Company, 77 Mechanic street. Mr. Johnson is a Republican, and a member of the Park Presbyterian Church. He is president of the Mahlon Johnson Union, a director in the Young Men's Christian Association of Newark, and a member of the New Jersey Historical Society.

May 25, 1865, Mr. Johnson married Anna Elizabeth, third child and eldest daughter of William Pann and Sarah (Locke) Vail, born December 9, 1837, died April 7, 1901. Children: 1. Alfred Baker, born March 3, 1866, now living in South Orange, New Jersey; married Ella Wharton, September 28, 1898; they have Anna Wharton and Wharton Vail. 2. Elizabeth Blair, June 20, 1869. 3. William

Theo. F. Johnson

Vail, June 28, 1871; married, October 14, 1902, Katharyn Dorrance, daughter of William K. and Helen (Pierson) Laverty. 4. Helen More, December 15, 1873. 5. Charles Henry, May 14, 1878, died September 12, 1879.

WOOLMAN George Fox, the founder of the Society of Friends, born in Drayton, Lancastershire, England, in 1624, was the founder of the sect of Christians better known as Quakers. He was a shoemaker by trade and occupation up to the time he devoted himself to the propagation of what he regarded as a more spiritual form of Christianity than prevailed at that day. Among the eminent followers of Fox were Barclay, Fenwick, Penn, Stakes, Haines. Lippincott and Woolman, and the work begun in England was carried on in America by these immigrants who appeared in New Jersey and Pennsylvania during the last half of the eighteenth century. They founded Salem and Burlington in West New Jersey, and Pennsylvania was the proprietor of Philadelphia, the City of Brotherly Love. For purity of life they stand pre-eminent in the religious sects, and in that virtue they exercised a salutary influence on the whole community in which their example could be observed and patterned after. They were the originators of the practice of universal freedom and universal peace, and to them the world owes the inception of these great questions that brought about the abolition of Negro slavery in the United States and the formation of the great peace societies made up from all sects, creeds and forms of christian worship and through whose grand work the era of universal peace was made apparent at the opening of the twentieth century. Their opposition to war was at first like all great reforms, looked upon as chimerical, but the civil war in the United States was accepted by the society as an outcome of their teaching, and they broke their cast-iron rule and sent their young men to fight for the abolition of slavery and the perpetuation of the government that had given their teachings the utmost freedom. They acknowledged not till then that good could come from war, and the witness of the greatest naval fleet of the world visiting and being welcomed as a dove of peace by every nation of the globe was accepted as the consummation of the teachings of Fox and his faithful followers.

(I) John Woolman, an English gentleman and member of the Society of Friends, hearing from reports sent out from Fenwick's Colony, in West New Jersey, of the goodly land and promises of comfort, quiet and peacefulness, as well as the evidence of future records in the direction of increase in value of lands in the new colony decided to join his fortunes with his brethren in America. To this end he took ship in 1681, and on arriving at Burlington selected eight thousand acres of land extending from the Burlington river southward to the north branch of the Rancocas river. a distance of five miles, and including the present site of Mount Holly, where he fixed his home. Having this secured a foothold and a position of prominence in the Friends Meeting, he looked across the Meeting House and among the comely Quakeresses he found Elizabeth, daughter of John and Ann Borton. a family of Friends who had come from Aynhoe Parish in Northamptonshire. England, and they were soon announcing in Meeting their intention of marrying, which announcement. once repeated, ended in their marriage on the 10th month, 8th day, 1684. They had children including: Samuel, married Elizabeth, and they had daughter, Patience, born 10th month. 27th day. 1718. and she in turn selected as a husband Joseph Moore, of another prominent family of the meeting. Another child was Asher, see forward.

(II) Asher, younger son of John and Elizabeth (Borton) Woolman, was born at Mount Holly, New Jersey, 6th month, 27th day, 1722. He was married 12th month, 13th day, 1769, when he attained his forty-seventh year, to Rachel Norcross. born 8th month, 15th day, 1750. We this see a man of forty-seven years announce in Meeting two successive times his intention, of marrying a girl eighteen. Asher and Rachel had at least three children, possibly more. of which Elizabeth, the eldest daughter, was married in 1798 to John, born 4th month, 27th day, 1777, son of Jarvis and Elizabeth (Rogers) Stokes, of an equally prominent family of Friends, in Burlington township. Their children were: Herbert N. Stokes; Maria Stokes; Asher W. Stokes: Martine W. Stokes; John W. Stokes; Nathan H. Stokes: Woolman Stokes and Edward Stokes. Another daughter. Abigail, married, in 1780. Jarvis, born 11th month, 5th day. 1740. son of Jarvis and Elizabeth (Rogers) Stokes. Besides these two daughters, they had a son Granville. see forward.

(III) Granville, son of Asher and Rachel (Norcross) Woolman, was born in Mount

Holly, Burlington county, New Jersey, 1st month, 1st day, 1774. He was married 1st month, 11th day, 1795, to Hannah, daughter of Jarvis and Elizabeth (Rogers) Stokes, and granddaughter of John and Hannah (Stogdelle) Stokes. Hannah (Stokes) Woolman was born 8th month, 11th day, 1775, and by her marriage to Granville Woolman she had five children: 1. Eliza, born in 1795; married David Likens. 2. Ann, 10th month, 3rd day, 1797, married ———— Walton; died 10th month, 7th day, 1821. 3. Rachel, 7th month, 20th day, 1799; married Chambless Middleton. 4. John, 8th month, 20th day, 1803; married Maria Stokes; died 5th month, 20th day. 1868. 5. Granville, see forward.

(IV) Granville (2), son of Granville (1) and Hannah (Stokes) Woolman, was born in Rancocas, Burlington county, New Jersey, June 1, 1807, died March 13, 1870. He was educated in his native town, and was a noted physician. He married Phebe W., daughter of Isaac and Margaret Lippincott, of Burlington county. Children: 1. Margaret W., married, 1853, Jacob Leeds, who kept a store at Rancocas; children: i. Granville, married Nancy M. Haines and their children are: a. Gertrude, married Hudson Haines; b. Mary, married George Holmes and their children are: Margaret, Sarah and Nancy Holmes; ii. Henry, married Elizabeth Bryan and their children are: Caroline and Eugenia; Caroline married George Warwick and their child is Elizabeth Warrick; iii. Mary, married Lewis Brown and their children are: Jacob L. Brown, married Isabella Yates, and Ethel Brown, unmarried; iv. Elizabeth Leeds, married Thomas Bizby, and their children are: Elgar, Helen and Harvey Bizby; v. Phebe, married William Jones and their children are: Margaret W., Alice and Grace Jones. 2. Hannah Ann, born 1834; married Michael E. Haines and their children are: i. Horace E., married Susan Clement and they have one child, Ethel, married Harvey Lippincott; ii. Jervis W., married Minnie Clogston; child, Hazel; iii. Hannah H., unmarried; iv. Alice W., unmarried; v. Alfred M., married Florence Hilliard; vi. Granville Woolman, married Abbie Rogers; children: Sylvan, Ernest and Blanche; vii. Remington, married Fannie McGowen; children: Clair and Lillian; viii. Clara, married E. S. Perkins; child, Earl. 3. Martha L., born 1836. 4. Isaac L., born 1838; married Mary Shotwell; children: Jane and Elgar. 5. Jervis S., born 1840; married Julia Shotwell; children: i. Henry M., married Ella McCray; children: Raymond and

Henry; ii. Rebecca, married George Bullock, children: Helen, Emily and Alton; iii. Margaret, married Maurice Stokes; child, Maurice; iv. Helen, married William Stafford. 6. Daniel L., see forward. 7. Alice W., born 1846; married Hudson B. Taylor. 8. Phebe, born 1848; married Evan Bizby.

(V) Daniel L., son of Dr. Granville (2) and Phebe W. (Lippincott) Woolman, was born in Rancocas, Burlington county, New Jersey, November 7, 1843. He was a pupil in the public schools of Rancocas and in the Mary Lippincott school at Moorestown, and remained on the homestead farm as a farmer for some years, and later in life engaged in merchandising at Vincentown, where he conducted a general country store for thirty-five years, his business career being terminated by his death in 1907. He was a Republican in party politics, and served his town as a member of the township committee for several years. He was a member of the Society of Friends by inheritance, as well as choice, and he was active in the business and religious interests of the society. He married, December 12, 1867, Martha B., daughter of Samuel Wills, of Rancocas. She died November 30, 1889. Children, born on the old homestead at Rancocas: 1. Samuel Jarrett, see forward. 2. Granville S., born September 28, 1870, died July 13, 1905. 3. Daniel Howard, born April 12, 1872; he conducts a carpet factory in Philadelphia; married Harriet Kreamer; one child, Marion. 4. Caroline B., born October 2, 1873; married William Lippincott; children: Florence and Samuel. 5. Anna L., born December 8, 1874; married Henry Jones. 6. Martha W., born April 14, 1879, unmarried; lives at home. 7. Phebe W., born January 5, 1883; married Henry Whitacre; one child, Evan B.

(VI) Samuel Jarret, eldest child of Daniel L. and Martha B. (Wills) Woolman, was born on the old homestead farm at Rancocas, Burlington county, New Jersey, April 20, 1869. He was a pupil in the public schools of his native town and at the academy in Mount Holly, and on leaving school was employed by the Pennsylvania railroad as baggage master, and conductor on the Amboy division, and held this position twelve years. He had worked in his father's store at Vincentown as a boy, and on leaving the railroad service engaged in the coal business in Vincentown, in 1899. He added to the coal business that of lumber in co-partnership with Eugene Antrim, the business being conducted under the firm name of Woolman, Antrim & Company, their place of business being Red Lion. Mr. Woolman is a stockholder in the Vincentown Water Company, and a member of the board of directors of the Telegraph and Telephone Company. He has held various offices in the town government, and is by inheritance a birthright member of the Society of Friends. He married, June 18, 1893, Sallie J., daughter of James Colkitt, of Vincentown, New Jersey.

READ Joseph Thomas Read, a native of Wales, was born in 1689, and was among the early settlers of West New Jersey, to which colony he came early in the eighteenth century. He obstinately adhered to the orthography of his name Read as it obtained in his native country, the oldest in literary excellence and purity of speech and writing of the English-speaking people of Britain. He secured, by grant of the proprietors of the colony, on reaching his majority, a large tract of land at the headwaters of the Rancocas creek and of Great Egg Harbor river, where the water shed between the Atlantic ocean and Delaware river had its apex. Here he built a home for the protection and comfort of his family. He had married shortly after his arrival in America Rachel Eldridge. The distance to the place where he fixed his home from neighbors and evidences of civilization gained for it the name "Long-a-coming," the infrequency of visitors and the devious trail by which it was reached from the South river settlement suggesting the same. His farm proved to be productive and he prospered in spite of the disadvantages of location.

Nine children were born to the pioneer settler and they were named in the order of their birth: William, Obadiah, Joseph T., Samuel, John, Asca, Rachel, Allen and Abby. Of these William married Sarah Taylor and settled at Lamberton, where six children were born as follows: Charles Thomas, William Thomas, Ruth, Sarah Ann, Martha and Rachel. The Welsh custom of carrying a christian name is here illustrated in the family of his eldest son in recognition of the grandfather. Joseph Thomas Read, the pioneer, died in 1763.

(II) Joseph Thomas (2), son of Joseph Thomas (1) and Rachel (Eldridge) Read, was born on his father's farm soon after the settlement, and died on the homestead established by him upon his marriage to Almira Vezey, of Philadelphia, at Greenwich, Gloucester county, at no great distance from his birthplace. Children of Joseph Thomas and Almira (Vezey) Read were born in Greenwich in the following order: William Thomas, Almira. Elizabeth, Clara, David, see forward. Joseph Thomas Read died in Greenwich, New Jersey, November 12, 1755, and was interred in the Presbyterian burial ground in that place. His father outlived him.

(III) David, youngest child of Joseph Thomas (2) and Almira (Vezey) Read, was born in Greenwich, Gloucester county, New Jersey, November 19, 1752. His father died when he was three years of age and he was brought up by his mother on the farm. When he had just reached his majority the revolutionary war was calling all patriotic young men to the battle field. He answered the call and joined the revolutionary army as a private in Captain John Barker's company and was subsequently transferred to Captain Warren's company. At the close of the war he married Rachel Peck, of Greenwich, and their three children were baptized in the Presbyterian church at Greenwich. They were: David, James, Joel, see forward. Near the close of the century he removed to the small village of Camden, opposite Philadelphia, where he engaged in business as a pork and sausage dealer, preparing his products for the Philadelphia market. He lived to be over eighty-six years of age, and was the last representative in Camden county of the soldiers in the American revolution. He died in 1838 and his remains were interred in the Newtown burying ground, near where the old meeting house stood.

(IV) Joel, third son of David and Rachel (Peck) Read, was born in Greenwich, Gloucester county, New Jersey, in 1794. He was a soldier in the war of 1812, serving in the "Jersey Blues" along the Delaware river front at Billingsport, opposite Fort Mifflin, Chester county, Pennsylvania. He was a brush maker in Camden and Philadelphia, but late in life returned to Camden where he died at the home of his daughter Charlotte. He was married in 1812 to Mary Jones, a member of a prominent family belonging to the Society of Friends, and related to the family descended from Thomas Thackara, who came from Leeds, England, by way of Dublin, Ireland, and became prominent in the early history of West Jersey and of the Society of Friends. Joel and Mary (Jones) Read had six children: 1. Charlotte, married and had two children: Rachel and Mary. 2. Joseph J., born March 24, 1815; married (first) Cecelia, daughter of John R. Rue, in 1840; children: i. John Rue,

ii—28

a lawyer in Philadelphia; ii. Cecelia, married Abraham Tollman; iii. Mary, married Joseph B. Bush, of Newport, Rhode Island; iv. Annie, married William B. Knowles, of Philadelphia; v. Kate, married Edwin B. Powell, of Brooklyn, New York; vi. Emily, died young; vii; Joseph J. Reed married (second) in 1881, Elizabeth M. (Etris), widow of Captain Henry Schillinger, of Camden. 3. Rachel, married and had four children: Mary, Charlotte, Rachel and Amelia. 4. William Thackara, died 1842. 5. John Smilie, see forward. 6. Edmund Elliott, married Anna Peak and they had four children: i. Harriet; ii. Sarah Lippincott, married Henry L. Jones and had one   . Mary; iii. John; iv. Anna.

(Child) John Smilie, second son of Joel and Mary (Jones) Read, was born in the old distriet of Southwark, Philadelphia. Pennsylvania, March 11. 1822. He was proprietor of a large commercial house dealing in wall papers in Philadelphia. He was also a director and treasurer for twenty-five years of the Camden Fire Insurance Company, and at the time of his death was a commissioner of the Morris Plains Insane Asylum, under appointment of the Governor of New Jersey. He was also appointed by the legislature of New Jersey a director of the Camden & Amboy Railroad Company. He served the city of Camden as a member of the board of education and president of the board, and as a member and president of the city council. He was a builder and owner of large blocks of commercial buildings in the city, and one of the projectors of the Camden Building and Loan Association. His fraternal affiliation with the Masonic fraternity came through initiation in Camden Lodge, No. 15, and Royal Arch Chapter, No. 91, of Philadelphia. He married (first) Margaret Mason; married (second) Harriett, daughter of Thomas and Abigail Peak, of Camden. Children of first wife: 1. Elizabeth Mason, married John Campbell, of Camden: children: John and Mary C. Campbell. 2. William Thackara, married Lucretia McCormick and had one child, William T. Read. Child of second wife: Edmund Elliott, see forward. John Smilie Read died while residing for the benefit of his health at Stroudsburg. Monroe county, Pennsylvania, August 6, 1882.

(VI) Edmund Elliott, only child of John Smilie and Harriett (Peak) Read, was born in Camden, New Jersey, August 7, 1859. He was prepared for college at the school of William Fewsmith, of No. 1008 Chestnut street, Philadelphia, and was graduated at the Univer-

sity of Pennsylvania, A. B., 1879; he was a member of the Philomathean Society and the winner of the Henry Read prize at graduation. He studied law in the office of Peter L. Voorhees, and was admitted as an attorney in June, 1882. He became the president of the Camden Fire Insurance Association, of which he was for many years a director. He was also an officer of the Franklin People's and City Building associations, and served as a member of the Camden Educational Board. He married, December 27. 1882, Margaret W., daughter of John W. and Kate O. (Hopkins) Milford, of Camden, New Jersey. Their son, John Smilie, was born in Camden, New Jersey, November 11. 1883.

ELY   The ancestor of the Ely family of the line here under consideration is doubtless descended from an English rector, and was himself undoubtedly an active member of the christian church; and so also have his descendants to a large extent maintained the christian character of their ancestor. The American Elys claim the distinction of a coat-of-arms, described as follows: "Field argent, a fesse engrailed between six fleurs-de-lis sable." Crest, on an helmet and wreath of its colors, an arm erect, couped below the elbow, cuff argent, holding in the hand proper a fleur-de-lis sable. The motto: *"Re et merito"* (by actions and merit).

In 1571 Rev. George Ely became vicar of Tenterden, in the county of Kent, and continued to sustain that living until his death in 1615. The patrons of the living were the Dean and Chapter of Canterbury, and the records of that body mention his institution at the date named, without any other particulars about him. He is described, however, as George Elye, otherwise Heely. In the parish register in Tenterden the name is variously written Ely, Elie, and Elye, although he himself wrote it Ely and so signed his will. So near as can be determined he was born about the year 1545, probably took his degree about 1566, when he would have been of full age, and five years later obtained the living of Tenterden. It is supposed that he married in 1571. The baptismal name of his wife was Florence, and all of their children except one were baptized at Tenterden. After forty-five years of wedded life George Ely and his wife both died about the same time, as may be seen from the burial register of Tenterden: "1615, August 18, Florence, wife of Mr. George Ely, vicar. 1615 August 21, Master

George Ely, vicar of Tenterden." The children of George and Florence Ely were: Nathaniel, baptized September 28, 1572; Andrew, June 12, 1575; Zachary, October 14. 1577; Samuel, December 13, 1579; Obadiah, December 16, 1581; Lydia, June 14, 1584, died young; Daniel, June 5, 1586; Lydia, September 29, 1588; Abigail, March 21, 1590-91; Judith.

(I) Rev. Nathaniel Ely, probably the eldest child of Rev. George and Florence Ely, was baptized at Tenterden, Kent, England, September 28, 1572, and in the record of his marriage he is described as "clerk, master of arts;" therefore he must have been a member of one of the universities, and while it is known that he was not of Oxford he must have been of Cambridge. There is a hiatus in the list of graduates between 1588 and 1602, during which period he must have taken his degrees, so that it is impossible to determine with accuracy his particular college, there being no general matriculation register at Cambridge.

(II) Nathaniel (2), born about 1605, fourth son of Rev. Nathaniel (1) Ely, came to America in the "Elizabeth" in 1634, from Ipswich, England. He settled first in Newtown (Cambridge) on the lot adjoining that of Robert Day, with whom he became intimately associated, and with whose descendants the Elys frequently intermarried. Mr. Ely was made freeman at Cambridge in May, 1635, but in 1636 he and his neighbor Day formed part of the colony that accompanied Rev. Thomas Hooker to Hartford, on the banks of the Connecticut river, near where was the earlier settlement of Hollanders called Dutch Point. Here too Nathaniel Ely and Robert Day owned and occupied adjoining lands. Both were planters. In 1639 Ely was made constable of the town and was selectman in 1643 and again in 1646. He also appears to have been one of the leading men of the plantation in purchasing the lands of Governor Ludlow, and in making the first settlement at Norwalk. According to the town records there was no permanent settlement at Norwalk until Nathaniel Ely made the first movement in that direction. In 1649, on the petition of Nathaniel Ely and Richard Olmstead, the general court gave permission to found a new plantation at Norwalk, and four years afterward the inhabitants there were invested with town privileges. In 1659 Nathaniel Ely sold his lands in Norwalk and removed to Springfield. Massachusetts, and spent the remainder of his life among Mr. Pynchon's planters. He sus-

tained various important town offices, being selectman of the town in 1661 and five times afterward. Whatever may have been his previous occupation, it is certain that in 1665 Nathaniel Ely became keeper of the "ordinary," for which service in the plantation only the most respectable men were chosen; the court would license no other. The records of the court at Springfield sets forth his license in these words: "Nathaniel Ely of Springfield, being desired and put upon to keep an ordinary there, or house for Comon Entertaynment, was by this Corte lycensed to that worke, as also for selling wines or strong liquors for ye yeere ensuing. Provided he keep good rule and order in his house. Also ye said Nathaniel Ely is up on his desire by this Corte released from Trayning in ye Town soe long as he continues to keep ye Ordinary." He held this license until his death in 1675. The house he lived in was on Main street but was moved to the corner of Sanford and Dwight streets, probably the oldest house in Springfield. Nathaniel Ely died in Springfield, December 25, 1675, and his wife Martha died there October 23, 1688. He left no will, and his property was inventoried at about one hundred and sixty-four pounds. Among other items in the inventory was one negro man, £15. He had two children, Samuel, of whom mention is made in the next paragraph, and Ruth, born probably in Hartford, died in Springfield, October 12, 1662; married, August 3. 1661, Jeremy (or Jeremiah) Horton, son of Thomas and Mary Horton.

(III) Samuel, son of Nathaniel (2) and Martha Ely, born probably in Cambridge or Hartford, died in Springfield, March 19, 1692. His name first appears as witness to the Indian deed given to his father and others, dated February 15, 1651, and does not appear again in the Norwalk records. He removed with his father's family to Springfield, and appears to have been quite successful in acquiring property, for he left a considerable estate. He married, October 28, 1659, Mary, youngest daughter of Edward and Editha (Stebbins) Day. She was born in Hartford in 1641, died in Hatfield. Massachusetts, October 17, 1725. After the death of Samuel Ely she married (second) April 12, 1694. Thomas. son of Thomas and Hannah (Wright) Stebbins. He was born in 1648 and died in 1695. She married (third) December 11, 1696, Deacon John Coleman. of Hatfield, born about 1635, died January 21, 1711, son of Thomas and Frances (Welles) Coleman. Samuel and

Mary (Day) Ely had sixteen children: 1. Child, born 1660, died in infancy. 2. Samuel, March 1, 1662, died young. 3. Joseph, August 20, 1663, died April 29, 1755. 4. Samuel, November 4, 1664, died young. 5. Mary, March 29, 1667, died April 19, 1667. 6. Samuel, May 9, 1668, see forward. 7. Nathaniel, January 18, 1670, died March 16, 1671. 8. Jonathan, July 1, 1672, died young. 9. Nathaniel, August 25, 1674, died May, 1689. 10. Jonathan, January 24, 1676, died February 27, 1676. 11. Martha, October 28, 1677, died November 25, 1677. 12. John, January 28, 1678, died January 15, 1758. 13. Mary, June 20, 1681, died December 21, 1681. 14. Jonathan, January 21, 1683, died July 27, 1753. 15. Mary, February 29, 1684, died Hatfield. 16. Ruth, born 1688, died Belchertown about 1747.

(IV) Samuel (2), son of Samuel (1) and Mary (Day) Ely, was born in West Springfield, Massachusetts, May 9, 1668, died there August 23, 1732. He took a prominent part in public affairs in the town, was selectman in 1702, 1716 and again in 1719, clerk of the second parish of Springfield (West Springfield) from 1702 to 1721, except during the years 1714 and 1715. As clerk of the parish and custodian of the records he had much to do with the division and distribution of town lands, and otherwise was active in town affairs for many years. He married (first) November 10, 1697, Martha Bliss, born June 1, 1674, died July 6, 1702; married (second) December 7, 1704, Sarah Bodurtha, born October 18, 1681, died May 8, 1766, daughter of Joseph and Lydia Bodurtha. He had in all nine children, three by his first and six by his second wife: 1. Martha, born December 21, 1698. 2. Mary, February 14, 1700, died May 27, 1714. 3. Samuel, September 21, 1701, see forward. 4. Sarah, August 30, 1705. 5. Nathaniel, September 22, 1706. 6. Joseph, October 4, 1709, died April 4, 1741. 7. Tryphena, April 7, 1712, died December 30, 1755. 8. Levi, February 12, 1714. 9. Mary, April 5, 1717, died January 30, 1761.

(V) Samuel (3), son of Samuel (2) and Martha (Bliss) Ely, was born in Springfield, Massachusetts, September 21, 1701, died in West Springfield, December 8, 1758. He married, May 3, 1722, Abigail Warriner, born December 8, 1703, died September 27, 1762, daughter of Samuel and Abigail (Day) Warriner. They had seven children: 1. Samuel, born September 14, 1723, died November 21, 1794. 2. Thomas, December 1, 1725, died May 10, 1790. 3. Abigail, July 15, 1727, died

August 9, 1805. 4. Joel, November 13, 1728, died July, 1815. 5. Levi, November 26, 1732, see forward. 6. Simeon, January 25, 1734, died January 15, 1817. 7. Nathan, January 9, 1739, died October 31, 1798.

(VI) Captain Levi, a revolutionary soldier, was the son of Samuel (3) and Abigail (Warriner) Ely, and was born in West Springfield, Massachusetts, November 26, 1732. He was killed by Indians in a battle on the Mohawk river, in the province of New York, October 19, 1780. A monument was erected to his memory at Springfield, Massachusetts. He left home in command of a company on a short expedition against the Indians in the Mohawk valley and before their term of enlistment had expired nearly all the men of his company were killed. Captain Ely lived in West Springfield near the old Congregational church edifice. All of his children were born there and all lived and died in West Springfield. He married, October 12, 1758, Abigail Sergeant (Sargent), born Northfield, Massachusetts, January 26, 1729, died West Springfield, October 3, 1812, daughter of Lieutenant John and Abigail (Jones) Sergeant. Lieutenant John Sergeant was one of Captain Josiah Willard's company at Fort Dummer, Vermont, in 1748, in the old French and Indian war. Captain Levi and Abigail (Sergeant) Ely had eleven children, all born in West Springfield: 1. Lucretia, May 12, 1759, died January 19, 1819. 2. Huldah, July 11, 1761, died April 30, 1808. 3. Jerusha, February 8, 1763, died February 2, 1836. 4. Levi, February 27, 1765, died September 17, 1819. 5. George, December 30, 1766, died January 20, 1819. 6. Daniel, August 10, 1768, died February 15, 1822. 7. Sabra, January 22, 1770, died March 8, 1839. 8. Theodosia, February 4, 1773, died October 14, 1865. 9. Solomon, December 22, 1774, died April 25, 1828. 10. Elihu, July 6, 1777, see forward. 11. Abigail, May 7, 1780, died November 23, 1828.

(VII) Elihu, son of Captain Levi and Abigail (Sergeant) Ely, was born in West Springfield, Massachusetts, July 6, 1777, died in Westfield, Massachusetts, February 23, 1829. In 1797 he married Grace Rose, born in Providence, Rhode Island, in November, 1777, died in Westfield, September 28, 1840, daughter of Colonel Samuel Rose, of Providence. They had nine children, all born in Westfield: 1. Elihu, May 19, 1799, died May 21, 1866. 2. Samuel, 1801, died 1803. 3. Samuel Rose, December 29, 1803, died Roslyn, Long Island, May 11, 1873. 4. Abigail, January 29, 1806,

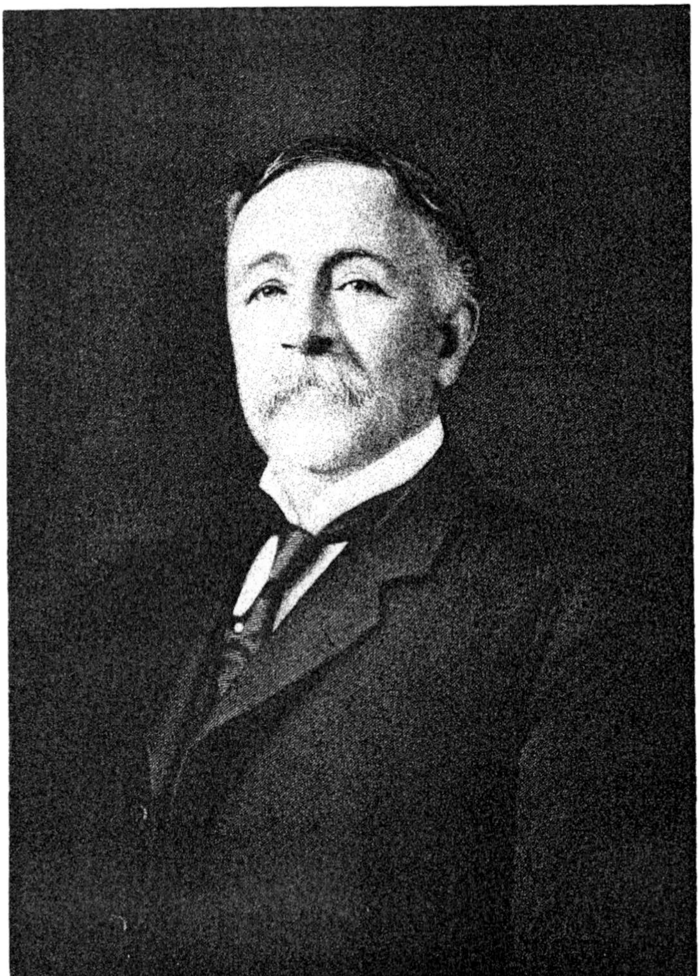

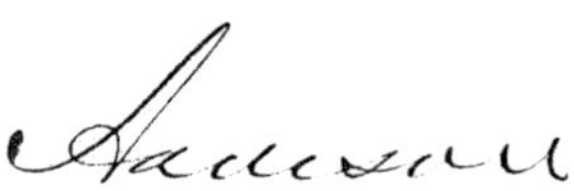

died Ann Arbor, Michigan, February 13, 1880. 5. Joseph Minor, November 26, 1807, died June 14, 1885. 6. Levi, December 22, 1809, died La Porte, Indiana, May 18, 1869. 7. Thomas, December 22, 1811. 8. Addison, December 16, 1814. 9. William, see forward.

(VIII) William, youngest son and child of Elihu and Grace (Rose) Ely, was born in Westfield, Massachusetts, April 17, 1817, died in Elizabeth, New Jersey, February 9, 1886. He married (first) in Westfield, September 5, 1836, Emeline Letitia Harrison, born Westfield, December 13, 1818, died there February 18, 1862, daughter of Seth and Letitia (Veits) Harrison; married (second) in South Orange, New Jersey, March 8, 1865, Nancy Judson Harrison, a sister of his first wife. She was born in Westfield, April 6, 1827, died February 28, 1895. Seth Harrison belonged to the family of which President William H. Harrison was a member. Emeline Letitia (Harrison) Ely was a granddaughter of Jabez Baldwin, who enlisted in the revolutionary war eight times, and served every years of the war. He had ten children, all born of his first marriage and with the exception of one in Westfield: 1. Thomas Jefferson, June 11, 1838, died February 2, 1839. 2. Grace Rose, July 4, 1840; married, April 10, 1861, Jared Sandford, born Lodi, Seneca county, New York, October 16, 1834, son of Halsey and Fanny Maria (Howell) Sandford. 3. Emma Josephine, September 30, 1842, died June 9, 1849. 4. Abigail Letia, October 27, 1844; married Marshall Clement; died Mt. Vernon, New York, June, 1893. 5. Nancy Judson, November 30, 1846, died September 23, 1848. 6. Emma Josephine, New Buffalo, Michigan, December 23, 1848. 7. William Henry Harrison, May 10, 1851. 8. Addison, May 23, 1853, see forward. 9. Thomas Jefferson, June 2, 1855, died April 10, 1858. 10. Nancy Judson, October 10, 1857; married, 1881, M. Eugene Cady; died February 15, 1909, at Westfield, Massachusetts.

(IX) Captain Addison, son of William and Emeline Letitia (Harrison) Ely, was born in Westfield, Massachusetts, May 23, 1853. His ancestors on both sides were prominent both as soldiers and citizens from the earliest colonial times. The records of the adjutant general's office in the state of Massachusetts show that the Elys, Roses, Sargents, Harrisons and Baldwins, the latter two being his mother's ancestors, sustained no mean part in the early national struggles. The civil registers in the towns of Hartford, Connecticut,

and Springfield and Westfield, Massachusetts, from the year 1636 to modern times bear clear evidence that the Elys were a moral, public-spirited, educated family through many generations, called with frequency to serve their countrymen in offices of trust and honor. Addison was a boy of eight years when his father removed to Bloomfield, New Jersey, within a few miles of which place he has resided. He was given a good elementary education at the Davis Latin School in Bloomfield and at the Newark (New Jersey) Academy and prepared for college at the Brooklyn Polytechnic Institute and the equally famous Phillips Exeter Academy. His purpose was to make the collegiate course at Harvard, but at the age of eighteen he turned his attention to educational work. He first taught the public school at Union, Union county, New Jersey, and two years later became the first principal of the Caldwell high school in Essex county. While there he took up the study of law, but in 1879 he discontinued law for a time and became principal of the Rutherford high school, later resuming law reading, having never abandoned the idea of entering the legal profession. As a teacher he was very successful. A life license to teach anywhere in New Jersey, gained by examination, in those days a rare acquisition though common now, was granted him, and of which he is very proud. It was signed by Ellis A. Apgar and Washington Hasbrouck, examiners. They were distinguished New Jersey educators, since deceased. Mr. Ely's old pupils, of whom many are successfully settled in the immediate vicinity of Newark, remember his thoroughness both as an instructor and a disciplinarian. He was always the active friend of his pupils. At the February term of the supreme court, Captain Ely was admitted as an attorney, in February, 1892, as counsellor at law. Since that time he has devoted his attention to general law practice in the state and county courts. He is a forceful lawyer, careful, studious and conscientious. Occupied with the responsibilities of a large practice, he finds time to devote to public concerns which tend to promote the general welfare of the community, commending merit and without hesitancy condemning all schemes for the advancement of selfish ends at public expense. He organized the Dover, New Jersey, Gas Company, and built works and for many years has owned its securities and controlled its management. He was also one of four most active organizers of the Gas and Electric Company of Bergen County and

has held the office of director of the company
for many years.

Captain Ely became a member of Company
C, Third Regiment, in 1872, continuing as
such for seven years. In 1893 he organized
and became captain of Company L, Second
Regiment, which company was among the best
military organizations in the state in general
efficiency and discipline. Captain Ely offered
his Company L to the governor of the state of
New Jersey for service in the Spanish-American war. No other organization at the time
had been tendered. Largely through his tender
and efforts the Second Regiment was chosen
for Spanish war service. Seventy of seventy-
three enrolled members of his company, ready
for service, marched out of their Rutherford
Armory, May 2, 1898, amid scenes of patriotism that will long make the day memorable.
During this war Captain Ely was attached to
General Lee's Seventh Corps, and by his
special order was made provost marshal of the
corps, though officially attached to the staff of
General Arnold, commanding the Second
Division of the Corps. He later organized
and became captain of Company M, Fifth
Regiment, which office he resigned in 1904. As
an officer he was never absent at roll call
during his entire service.

He is a pronounced and consistent Democrat and was always ready to respond to
his party's call. In 1896 he was nominated
for congress in the old fifth district, con-
sisting of Bergen and Passaic counties. In
1900 he was elected delegate to the Democratic National Convention held at Kansas
City, and later the same year was nominated
for one of the presidential electors on the
Democratic ticket. He is a member of the
Presbyterian church, one of the organizers of
Boiling Spring Lodge, Free and Accepted
Masons, a member of the Union Club, the
New Jersey Rifle Association, the Sons of the
Revolution and the New Jersey Historical
Society. In 1902 Captain Ely purchased a
large tract known as the "Poillon" lands in the
heart of Rutherford and laid it out with every
public improvement. This section of Rutherford lies adjacent to Park avenue, Addison
avenue, Lincoln avenue and Newell avenue,
and also extends to Sylvan street, Mountain
Way, Orient Way, Foronia Way and Meadow
Road. The houses and improvements on all
these streets are creditable alike to his good
judgment and public spirit, and have fixed a
highly select residential character on these sec-

tions. He is now developing the lands known
as Elycroft Estate.

Captain Ely married, December 29, 1874,
Emily J. Johnson, of Connecticut Farms, born
March 1, 1856, daughter of William H. and
Marietta (Lyon) Johnson. Children: 1. Addison Jr., born in Caldwell, New Jersey, November 26, 1875; graduate of Columbia College
and of the law department of the University
of Michigan, and now associated in law practice with his father; he married, September 25,
1900, Clara Agnes Lord; children: i. Henry
Addison, born April 23, 1902, died April 28,
1902; ii. Nathaniel, born April 10, 1903; iii.
Addison Charles, born May 29, 1905; iv.
Katherine, born September 19, 1908. 2. Abigail Mabel, born in Rutherford, April 15,
1881; graduate of department of arts, Michigan University; married, September 12, 1905,
Frederick Howland Woodward, of Fitchburg,
Massachusetts; children: i. Emily E., born
September 1, 1906; ii. and iii. Frederick Howland and Addison Ely, twins, born June 30, 1909.
3. Jared Sandford, twin, born in Rutherford,
October 10, 1884, died July 9, 1885. 4. Seth
Harrison, twin, born in Rutherford, October
10, 1884; graduate of engineering department,
Michigan University; married, February 14,
1905, Elsa Flora Tritscheller; children: i.
Seth Harrison Jr., born in Ann Arbor, Michi-
gan, 1905; ii. William Henry Harrison, born
in Dover, New Jersey, November 10, 1907. 5.
Sandford Dana, born in Rutherford, June 12,
1886; Michigan University and Department of
Architecture, Columbia University. 6. Emily
Emeline, born September 2, 1888; graduate of
Michigan University. 7. Clara Harrison
Stranahan, born in Rutherford, March 26,
1890; now a junior, Michigan University. 8.
William Harvey Johnson, born September 18,
1891; sophomore Michigan University. 9.
Leon Abbett, born November 25, 1893. 10.
Hiram Baldwin, born March 1, 1896. 11.
James Samuel Thomas Stranahan, born Octo-
ber 17, 1898. Captain Ely lives on an old-
fashioned farm on the sunny slope of Ruther-
ford, which he calls Elycroft, where he com-
bines much that is best in rural and town life.

RUSSELL. The Russell family which is
the subject of the present article is one of the later acquisi-
tions to the country there being only two generations belonging by birth to this side of the
Atlantic and the second of these with all of its
life before it.

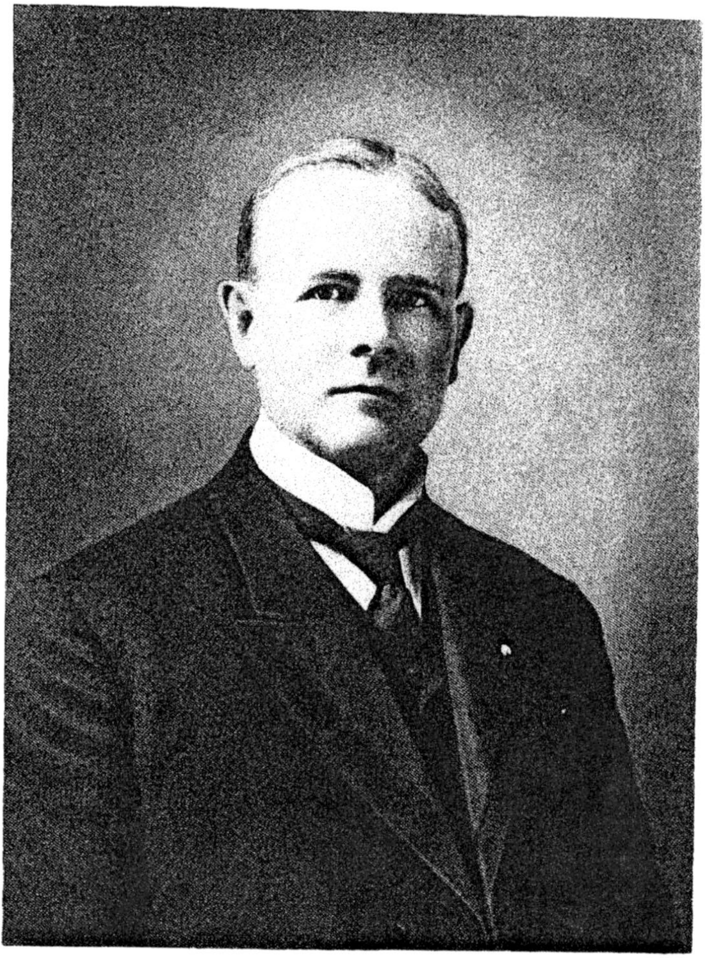

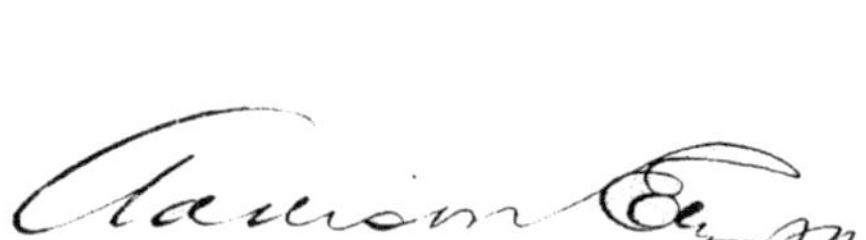

(I) Benjamin, son of John Russell, was born in England and emigrated to this country, where he set up for himself in New York as a designer and engraver of jewelry. September 27, 1857, he was married in St. Luke's Chapel of Trinity Parish, New York City, by the Rev. Isaac H. Tuttle, to Phoebe Ann Chenoweth. Mr. Russell himself was a native of county Kent. England, while his wife was the descendant of a line which had long made itself famous in Wales and in this country. The Chenoweths trace their origin back to the ancient Britons who retired into Wales before the conquering arms of the heathen Saxons. There with their followers they kept up a successful resistance to the invader and at one time were among the most powerful of the Welsh nobility. The changes and chances of time, however, caused the loss of lands and prestige, and with the ancient castle a ruin, three brothers of the family, John, William and Edward Chenoweth, determined to leave the home property to the last named of the three while William came over to the new world and settled in Jamestown, Virginia, and his brother John joined Lord Baltimore's colony and settled in Maryland. The descendants of these two are scattered all over the United States to-day. Edward remained in the old country, and became the ancestor of Mrs. Russell, the line running as follows: Edward; John, born 1635; William, 1682; Edward, 1715; John, 1741, died July 28, 1779, whose children were: 1. Alice, born December 24, 1765, died December 21, 1808. 2. Edward, referred to below. 3. John, born August 20, 1768, died September 2, 1769. 4. and 5. Martha and Mary, twins, July 13, 1769. 6. William, April 23, 1771, lost at sea about 1825. 7. Elizabeth, August 1, 1773, died December 25, 1792. 8. John, February 3, 1776, died in 1852. 9. Patience, July 30, 1779, died March 17, 1829.

Edward, son of John Chenoweth, was born September 4, 1767, and died in New York City. In 1789 he married Phoebe Romage, of Chatham, county Kent, England, and they had eleven children: 1. Alice, born April 15, 1790, died December 19, 1872. 2. Benjamin, May 12, 1792, died April 22, 1797. 3. Phoebe, November 17, 1794, died in 1858. 4. John, February 21, 1797, died May 7, 1802. 5. Benjamin, January 29, 1799, died March 16, 1799. 6. Mary Ann, February 8, 1800, died October 17, 1802. 7. John, September 22, 1802, died in 1802. 8. John, referred to below. 9. Eliza, September 19, 1806, died May 6, 1882. 10. Laurentia, August 18, 1809, died July 11, 1877.

11. Edward William, January 28, 1812, died in Australia, April 29, 1850.

John (2), son of Edward and Phoebe (Romage) Chenoweth, was born November 18, 1803, died September 19, 1861. May 2, 1824, he married in the parish church of Chalk, county Kent, England, the clergyman being the Rev. R. S. Jaynes. Caroline Mitchell, who bore him thirteen children, three of whose names have not been preserved died in infancy; the other ten being: 1. Caroline, born September, 1825, died March 5, 1902; married, August 8, 1850, James A. Weston. 2. Edward, 1827, died 1836. 3. John, April 21, 1829, married (first) September 18, 1850, Mary Hall; (second) November 30, 1864, Mary Jones. 4. William, February 23, 1831, died April 5, 1895; married, in 1849, Sarah Ann Carr. 5. Elizabeth, October 22, 1833, died September 4, 1857; married, July 4, 1852, Thomas W. Stott. 6. Phoebe Ann, referred to above and below. 7. Alice, 1838. 8. Edward, May 21, 1841, married, October 18, 1860, Judith H. Robertson. 9. Ephraim, May 7, 1844, was married three times. 10. Laurentia, January 1, 1848, married (first) May 16, 1876, John Quin and (second) November 26, 1890, H. F. Huss. All of the above marriages were in New York City, except Laurentia's second marriage which was performed in Ottawa, Kansas, and Ephraim's three which were in Newark, New Jersey.

The children of Benjamin and Phoebe Ann (Chenoweth) Russell were: 1. Harriet M. married George Mullaney, of Jersey City, and has three children: Frank, Irene and Edna. 2. Phoebe E., married Clarence E. Pease, and died at twenty years of age. 3. George Eldridge, referred to below. 4. Laura. 5. Charles Henry, who is married and has two children.

(II) George Eldridge, third child and eldest son of Benjamin and Phoebe Ann (Chenoweth) Russell, was born in Brooklyn, Long Island, September 8, 1864, and when one year old removed with parents to Jersey City, where he lived and attended school until about eleven years of age when his parents moved to Newark, New Jersey, where he is now living. For his early education he was also sent to the Newark public schools, after leaving which he learned the trade of engraving and designing jewelry from his father. He gave this up, however, in order to engage in the insurance business, and this he left in turn in order to take up the wholesale grain business, working for John S. Carpenter & Company. For twenty years he was manager of the grain department of Wilkinson Gaddis & Company of Newark, New Jersey. In 1904 he was elected to the office of surrogate on the Republican ticket by the large majority of 23,035. For several years he was chairman of the ninth ward executive committee, and served as member of the Essex county executive committee and the county Republican committee. Mr. Russell is a fluent public speaker and has taken the stump in many political campaigns, his popularity testifying to his ability and skill along that line. He attends the South Park Presbyterian Church. He is a Scottish Rite Mason, having attained the thirty-second degree; member of St. John's Lodge, No. 1, Free and Accepted Masons; Salaam Temple, Ancient Arabic Order Nobles of the Mystic Shrine; Newark City Camp, No. 7062, Modern Woodmen of America; Anthony Wayne Council, No. 159, Junior Order United American Mechanics; one of the organizers and served as president of the Garfield Club of Newark; member of many Republican clubs, and a past grand sachem of the Republican Indian League of New Jersey.

George Eldridge Russell married (first) July 27, 1887, Mary E., born July 28, 1865, died May 5, 1905, daughter of William B. and Helen (Zeek) Bond, who were the parents of three other children: Leonora V., George and Riley Bond. Children of Mr. and Mrs. Russell: 1. Marjorie Bond, born in Newark, July 23, 1889. 2. William Benton, born in Newark, July 26, 1891. George Eldridge Russell married (second) June 3, 1908, Fannie B. Jones, born in 1879; one child, Dorothy Chenoweth, born March 27, 1909.

Among the immigrants to this NUNN country in about the middle of the eighteenth century there is perhaps no family better deserving of a record and commemoration among the representative families of New Jersey than of Thomas Nunn and his descendants.

(I) Thomas Nunn, the founder of the family died about 1773, his will being dated October 30, 1771, and probated December 2, 1773. He came from England about 1750 and settled on land at Schooley's Mountain, which at his death was by arbitration divided between his two eldest children Thomas and Benjamin. By his wife Elizabeth he had: 1. Thomas, went to Canada. 2. Benjamin, re-

ferred to below. 3. Joshua. 4. Bersheba. 5. Ann. 6. Elisabeth. 7. Solomon. 8. Ephraim.

(II) Benjamin, son of Thomas and Elizabeth Nunn, died about 1817, his will being probated June 17 of that year. Coming from England with his father he settled on land near Pleasant Grove, Morris county, and entailed his property, leaving his wife only a light interest. He married Ann Carpenter. Children: 1. Elisabeth, married ——— Thomas. 2. Bethsheba, married Jacob, son of John Peter Sharp. 3. Ann, married ——— Wolf. 4. Sarah, married William McCray. 5. Isaac. 6. John, referred to below.

(III) John, youngest child of Benjamin and Ann (Carpenter) Nunn, was born in 1764, died in 1829. He succeeded to the estate of his father upon which he resided during his life. He married Katherine Slyker, who died in 1846. Children: 1. Jacob, referred to below. 2. Isaac, married Catherine Mellick. Child: Andrew. 3. William, born June 24, 1812; married Margaret, daughter of William Steltz. Children: Frances, John, Samuel, James, Alfred, Theodore. 4. Alfred, married Mary Waters. 5. John, married ——— Force. 6. Betsy, married twice; lives in Pennsylvania. 7. Sarah. 8. Mary. 9. Margaret, married John Hoptler Jr. 10. Emeline, married Isaac, brother of John Hoptler Jr. 11. Ann.

(IV) Jacob, eldest child of John and Katherine (Slyker) Nunn, born about 1793, died October 18, 1842. He was a farmer and a part of his life he kept the old Miller homestead, and for some time also the property subsequently owned by Chambers Davis where he kept an inn in connection with his farm. During the latter part of his life he disposed of the property which had been settled by his grandfather, Benjamin Nunn, near Pleasant Grove. In 1818 he married Mary, born 1794, died April 2, 1858, daughter of Andrew Miller, one of the settlers of Mansfield township who kept an inn and owned a large tract of land near Pennwell. She was a devoted woman and gave much attention to the proper training of her children in all that pertains to true manhood and womanhood. Children: 1. Andrew Miller, referred to below. 2. Catherine, married Henry B. Davis, of Stephensburg. 3. Elijah W. 4. George T. 5. Jacob S., died young.

(V) Andrew Miller, eldest child of Jacob and Mary (Miller) Nunn, was born January 18, 1819. During his minority he resided at home, where he was employed on the farm and there learned that inestimable lesson that

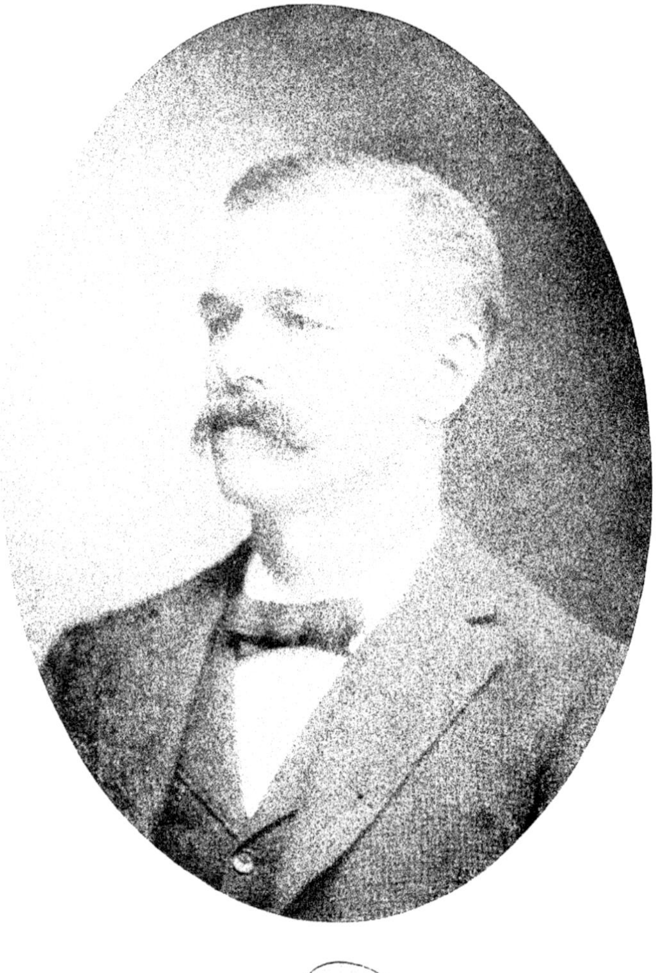

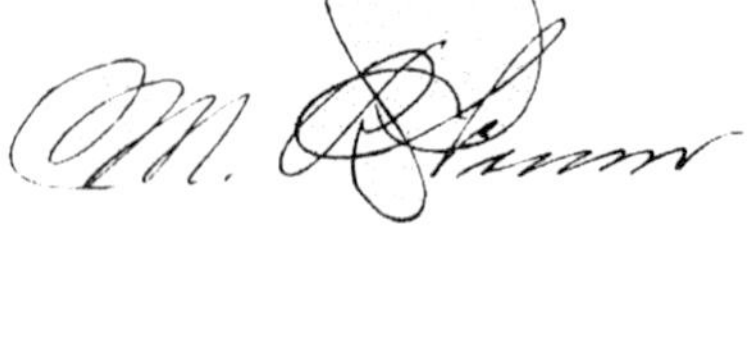

industry, economy and self-reliance are the principles upon which a successful career is based. Upon reaching his majority with a resolution to do something, he started out to win a home and property for himself. For several years he was a clerk in a general store at Fort Murray near where Madison's Mill was in Washington township, then for a short period he had charge of a store for William M. Warne in Monroe county, Pennsylvania, who was a successor of Moore Furman near Madison's Mill. In 1845 he was bookkeeper for G. M. & S. T. Scranton and Company at Oxford Furnace, and the following year he went west on a prospecting tour with a view of settling there. He returned, however, the same year. By prudence Mr. Nunn had saved enough to start business for himself and April 1, 1847, in connection with Jacob H. Miller, he opened a general store at Pennwell. After six months Mr. Miller sold his interest in the business to his brother, John C. Miller, and the new firm carried on the business for some five years when Mr. Nunn bought his partner's interest and continued the business until 1854. For the next seven years he carried on a mercantile business at New Hampton and in March, 1862, established himself in charge at Port Colden on the Morris Canal where he did a most successful business in general merchandise and canal supplies. His business life was one of considerable activity and his judicious management such as to secure a fair compensation. Following in the footsteps of his father he cast his first vote for General Harrison in the old Whig party and upon the organization of the Republican party became a supporter of its principles. For three years he served as collector for the township of Washington. Although he had limited opportunities for book knowledge while a boy, his clerkship secured him a good business education, sufficient to be numbered among the intelligent and solid business men of Warren county. He was always interested in local factors tending to the prosperity of the place where he resided. He was treasurer from its organization in 1870 of the Port Colden Building and Loan Association; and for many years previous to his death was a member of the Presbyterian church at Washington, and connected with the church as elder.

In December, 1846, Andrew Miller Nunn married Nancy, daughter of Jacob Wyckoff. Her grandfather, Simon Wyckoff, was the first settler of the family in Jackson Valley where he located in 1771. She was born June 8,

1824, died May 24, 1875, and was a devoted christian woman and a member of the Presbyterian church at Washington. Children: 1. Miller R., referred to below. 2. David P. S., married Frances Deremer; child: Elizabeth. married John Mowder and had Verna. 3. Simon Wyckoff, married Anna P. Miller; children: Sadie, married Arthur Somers, and Nina. 4. Mary, died young. 5. Andrew Miller Jr., married Sarah Perry; children: Earl. Guy and Floyd. 6. Elizabeth Miller, died at the age of seventeen years.

(VI) Miller R., eldest child of Andrew Miller and Nancy (Wyckoff) Nunn, was born in Washington township, Warren county, New York. September 2, 1847, died August 1, 1905. After receiving his early education in the schools of Washington township, he attended and graduated from the Eastman Business College at Poughkeepsie, New York, after which for two years he was in business with his father, and then went into the lumber business in Hackettstown, New Jersey, at the same time conducting an undertaking establishment. Inheriting from his father a great deal of business ability, by his judicious management and intelligent ventures he won for himself success and a competence, and at the time of his death was regarded as one of the solid and substantial business men of the town. His genial disposition and his high social qualities won for him many friends, and the recognition of the solid worth and stability of his character caused him to be placed in many positions of public trust and confidence. In politics he was a Republican, and for nearly thirty years was the town assessor. He cared very little for the so-called social clubs, being much more interested in his home and in social life which he led with his friends and acquaintances. He was, however, a firm believer in the benefit conferred by secret and beneficial societies, and he took an active and prominent part in several of these organizations. He was a member of the Independent Order of Odd Fellows, of the Free and Accepted Masons, of the Knights of Pythias, and of the Improved Order of Red Men. Joining the Methodist church when a young man, he led a long and consistent life of christian principle and practice, and was for many years a trustee of his church and the superintendent of its Sunday school.

October 17. 1866, he married Hilda E., born January 31, 1847, youngest daughter of John Bray and Margaret H. (Ogden) Woolston (see Woolston. V). Children: 1. Bertha

Gertrude, born April 5, 1868; married George B. Vliet, and has Miller Nunn Vliet. 2. Robert Ogden, May 20, 1872, died November 22, 1890. 3. Eva Woolston, January 28, 1875; married Adelbert Fernald, and has Dorothy Ruth Fernald. 4. John Harold, March 24, 1887; married Ada D. Long.

Henry Darnall, of Birds DARNALL Place, in the parish of Essenden, England, who was a counsellor at law of Gray's Inn, London, married Marie, daughter of William Tooke, auditor of His Majesty's Court of Wards and Liveries, whose unbroken lineage is extant to the beginning of the fifteenth century. Henry Darnall, who died in 1607, and his wife, Marie (Tooke) Darnall, left children: John, Henry, Anne, Thomas, Susan, Philip and Rafe. John Darnall, Esq., one of the Secondaries of the Pipe, married (first) Susan, daughter of John Mynne, (second) Susan, daughter of Roger and Elizabeth (Mynne) Lawrence. As Sir George Calvert married for his first wife Anne Mynne, of the same family, the relationship between the Darnalls and the Calverts is apparent. Sir George Calvert was created Baron of Avalon and Baltimore by James II, about 1623, and became the favorite counselor of Charles II., who made him a grant of that part of "the Peninsula or Chersonest lying in the parts of America, etc."; which now form the state of Maryland. The coat-of-arms of the Darnall family: Arg. on a bend; three leopards heads, cabossed sable, between two fleur-de-lis or; Motto: Vigeure, L'Amour, De Croix.

(I) Sir Philip Darnall, of England, married a sister of Lord Talbot. Children: 1. Henry, see forward. 2. John, who located at "Portland Manor," in Anne Arundel county, an estate consisting of about ten thousand acres. The last owner of this estate died about 1819, A third branch of the Darnall family lived in either Montgomery of Frederick county, at a place called "Rocky Fountain."

(II) Colonel Henry, son of Philip and —— (Talbot) Darnall, came to America about 1665 to join his numerous friends in this country. His high qualities and kinship to Lord Baltimore at once placed him in positions of trust and importance, and he was prominently identified with the public affairs of the colony until his death, June 17, 1711. He obtained the grant of land called the "Woodyard," and immediately built a splendid mansion in which he lived, and his tombstone is still to be seen on the grounds. About the period the troubles arose called the "Protestant Revolution," Colonel Darnell was at once recognized as leader of the Catholics, as well from his position as representative of Lord Baltimore, then absent in London, as from his religious preferences. He was captured after a siege of the government house, which he had fortified, and made his escape in a vessel leaving Philadelphia for England. In 1712 a commission appointed Charles Carroll (possibly grandfather, but more probably father of Charles Carroll, the signer of the Declaration of Independence) to the position made vacant by the death of Colonel Darnall, and after that time the family was not prominent in public life, although they have been constantly distinguished for great wealth and social position. Among other requirements in the old "Woodyard" home there was a closet concealed by a sliding panel, which was utilized to hide the priest and the sacred vestments in use in Catholic worship during the time of the Catholic persecution, and when it was considered a misdemeanor to harbor a priest. Among the family portraits at "Poplar Hill" may be seen a picture of Colonel Henry at the age of thirteen years. He is clad in a rich velvet suit, with lace collar, and bears in his hands a bow and arrow; behind him is his negro body servant of about the same age, plainly attired, and having around his neck a silver collar, the badge of indentured servitude. Colonel Henry married (first) Mary ——, (second) Elinot Hatton, widow of Colonel Thomas Brooke, of Brookfield, who was famed for her beauty. Children: 1. Mary, married Charles Carroll, of Carrollton, the direct ancestor of the famous signer of the Declaration of Independence. She was grandmother of Governor John Lee Carroll, of Maryland. 2. Eleanor, married —— Carroll, and became the mother of Archbishop Carroll. 3. Henry, Jr., see forward. 4. Philip. Probably others.

(III) Henry (2), son of Colonel Henry (1) and Elinor (Hatton) (Brooke) Darnall, had children: John, see forward; Robert; Waugh; Morgan; William; David; Jeremiah; Aaron; and a daughter who married Major Nicholas Sewall, of Mattapony, and had a son, Robert Darnall, who inherited the "Poplar Hill" estate from his uncle for whom he was named.

(IV) John, son of Henry Darnall, of "Poplar Hill," removed to Culpeper, Virginia, and his descendants reach from Kentucky to Arkansas. Children: Joseph, see forward, John and William.

(V) Joseph, son of John Darnall, of Culpeper, Virginia, married Winfield Pary, a relative of Dr. Benjamin Rush, one of the signers of the Declaration of Independence, born March 18, 1759, daughter of Joshua and Elizabeth Pary. Children: Joshua, see forward; Joseph Rush; John; William; Susannah, married Colonel Thomas Boyd.

(VI) Joshua, son of Joseph and Winfield (Pary) Darnall, who died in 1843, married Jemima Matzy. She was daughter of Henry and Elizabeth (Taylor) Matzy, and great-granddaughter of Henri Matzy, who fled from France in 1685 to escape religious persecution, being concealed in a hogshead and labeled as merchandise, and thus shipped to England. Children of Joshua and Jemima (Matzy) Darnall: 1. Thomas Matzy, born 1799, married (first) ———— Dabney; children: Thomas Anderson, born 1839; James, 1840; William Henry, 1841; Virginia, 1844; Joshua Pary, 1847; Jemima Matzy, 1849, married ———— Johnson and had Laura Virginia, who married M———— Byington. Thomas Matzy Darnall married (second) ———— Hayden, and had: Martha Hayden, born 1859; Catherine Elizabeth, 1860; a daughter who died in infancy. 2. Joseph, born 1800, died 1803. 3. Henry Matzy, see forward. 4. Elizabeth, born 1805, married ———— Weaver. 5. Joshua, born 1806, married ———— McBride. 6. Susan, born 1807, married ———— Deal. 7. Margaret, born 1809, married ———— Jeffries, and had a son, Fayette. 8. Richard, born 1812, married ———— Akers, and had: Jenny, Docia H. M., Charles, Thomas, Lizzie and Lucy. 9. John W., born 1814, married ———— Dyer, a member of the Kentucky branch of the Darnall family.

(VII) Henry Matzy, second son and third child of Joshua and Jemima (Matzy) Darnall, was born in Waynesboro, Augusta county, Virginia, 1801. He became a merchant and maintained and operated a general store. He married Isabella McClelland, also a native of Virginia, and had children: Jennie Adeline, Martha, Virginia, Henry Thomas, see forward, Fannie, Andrew M., and Elizabeth.

(VIII) Rev. Henry Thomas, eldest son and fourth child of Henry Matzy and Isabella (McClelland) Darnall, was born in Virginia, July 28, 1837, and died at Atlantic City, New Jersey, January, 1908. He studied theology and became a regularly ordained minister of the Presbyterian church. When the civil war broke out he enlisted in the Rockbridge Artillery, and from the second battle of Manassas until the surrender at Appomattox followed

the fortunes of the Confederate army, participating in all the hard campaigns of the Army of Virginia under General Robert E. Lee. His latter years were spent in the home of his son, Dr. Darnall, at Atlantic City. Rev. Darnall married Margaret Poague, daughter of Samuel Johnston, of Rockbridge county, Virginia; she was born April 7, 1842, and died in North Carolina, May, 1902. Children: 1. Harry Johnston, born June 18, 1867; now professor of languages at University of Tennessee; unmarried. 2. William Edgar, see forward. 3. Thomas Vernon, born May 4, 1873. Being possessed of a fine baritone voice, he cultivated this talent and has sung with great success in grand opera in America and all the great capitals of Europe; unmarried. 4. Samuel Fayette, born October, 1875; is in business in New York City; unmarried. 5. Francis Matzy, born 1877; married Matilda McGrann, of Memphis, Tennessee, and has a son, Frank Matzy, Jr.

(IX) Dr. William Edgar, second son and child of Rev. Henry Thomas and Margaret Poague (Johnston) Darnall, was born at Pearisburg, Giles county, Virginia, April 9, 1869. His academic education was obtained in the schools of Durham, North Carolina, which was his home until 1888. In that year he matriculated at the Washington and Lee University, Lexington, Virginia, and was graduated with the class of 1892 with the degree of Bachelor of Arts. During the two years prior to his graduation he served as private secretary to General Robert E. Lee, then president of the University. He then entered the medical department of the University of Virginia and was graduated in 1895 with the degree of Doctor of Medicine. He began the practice of his profession in his native state at Covington, but at the end of one year removed to New Jersey, locating at Atlantic City. Dr. Darnall has an exceedingly lucrative practice and specializes in surgery and gynæcology. In these branches of practice he is regarded as an authority, particularly expert as well as successful. He has served by appointment on the staff of the Atlantic City Hospital for several years, St. Michael's Baby Hospital, and the Mercer Home for Invalid Women. He is a fellow of the American Academy of Medicine, ex-president of the Atlantic City Academy of Medicine, member of the American Medical Association, the American Climatological Association, New York Academy of Medicine, Philadelphia Medical Club, Philadelphia Obstetrical Society, New Jersey Medical Association, and

Atlantic County Medical Society, of which he is ex-president. He is ex-president of the Fortnightly Club of Atlantic City, which he organized; member of the Pi Mu medical fraternity, and ex-section chief of the Phi Gamma Delta, Greek letter fraternity. His clubs are the Southern Club of Philadelphia, and the Country Club of Atlantic City. He has gained membership in the Sons of the Revolution through the military service during the revolutionary war of his maternal ancestor, Lieutenant John McCorkle, who served in Captain James Gilmore's company, under command of General Morgan. The only official connection Dr. Darnall has outside of his professional associations is with the Atlantic City Public Library, of which he is a trustee.

He married, February 27, 1907, Elizabeth Nesbitt, a descendant of Charles Carroll, of Carrollton.

———

SCULL The Scull family of New Jersey are among the earliest of the English settlers in that colony and are descended from Sir John Scull, of Brecknock. Two of his descendants emigrated to this country and are found on Long Island as early as September 10, 1685, from whence one of them, John, emigrated again to New Jersey, while his brother Nicholas remained behind. In 1706 their cousin, Edward Scull, also came over to this country, and settling to the west of the Alleghanies became the founder of a family of many descendants who are now living in western Pennsylvania and Ohio.

(I) John Scull, founder of the New Jersey branch of the family came over to America from Bristol, England, in, 1685, on board the ship "Bristol Merchant," John Stephens, master. He was baptized in England, October 15, 1666, and in 1694 came to New Jersey from Long Island with his wife Mary, and a number of other persons, who took up large tracts of land on the coast. He is said to have been a whaleman, but his name does not occur in either of the two whale fishing charters of that day which cover the right for whale-fishing from Staten Island down to Cape May Point. He acquired a large tract of land on the Great Egg Harbor river, and in 1695 bought of Thomas Budd, "250 acres of land, lying on Great Egg Harbor river and Patconk creek, with the privilege of cutting cedar and commonidge for cattle on ye reaches and swamps as laid out by Thomas Budd for commons." The first religious meetings of the Society of Friends in his section of West Jersey were

held at his home. In 1722 John Fothergill, an eminent minister among Friends writes that he had held such a meeting at the house of John and Mary Scull, which was very well attended. Thomas Chalkley, another eminent Quaker minister, also mentions holding meetings at John Scull's house in 1725. John Scull died in 1745.

Children of John and Mary Scull were: 1. John, stolen by the Indians when a child and never recovered. 2. Abel. 3. Peter. 4. Daniel, who in 1753 was the collector of Egg Harbor township, Gloucester county. 5. Benjamin. 6. Margaret, married Robert Smith. 7. Caroline, married Amos Ireland. 8. Mary. 9. Rachel, married James Edwards. 10. John Recompense, married Phebe Dennis. 11. Isaiah, married and had one daughter Abigail. 12. Gideon, referred to below. 13. David, died January 10. 1741. 14. An infant which died unnamed.

(II) Gideon, twelfth child and eighth son of John and Mary Scull, was born in 1722, died in 1776. He married, in 1750, Judith, daughter of James and Marjorie (Smith) Bellangee, and granddaughter of Evi or Ives Bellangee, the Huguenot refugee, who had fled from Poitou, France, first to England, and then between 1682 and 1690 to America, and in 1697 had married in the Philadelphia Monthly Meeting of Friends, Christiana de la Plaine, daughter of another French refugee. The name of this family, which was originally de Belangée and de Bellinger, in the old French records, has become corrupted in this country to Bellangee, Bellanger, Ballinger and Bellinger. Both Gideon Scull and his wife, Judith Bellangee, died the same year from smallpox contracted at the Salem Quarterly Meeting. Their children were: 1. Paul. 2. Mary, married David Bassett. 3. James, referred to below. 4. Daniel. 5. Gideon Jr., born 1756, died 1825; married Sarah James. 6. Hannah, married David Davis. 7. Judith, married Daniel Offley. 8. Ruth, married Samuel Reeve. 9. Rachel, married Samuel Bolton. 10. Mark, married Mary Browning. 11. Marjorie, married Daniel Leeds.

(III) James, third child and second son of Gideon and Judith (Bellangee) Scull, was born October 2, 1751, and died August 25, 1812. In May, 1774, he married Susanna, daughter of Daniel and Susanna (Steelman) Leeds, granddaughter of Japheth and Deborah (Smith) Leeds, and great-granddaughter of Daniel and Dorothy (Young) Leeds, for whose ancestry see elsewhere. Her great-grandfather was the first surveyor-general of West Jersey, the compiler of the celebrated "Leeds' Almanach," the first work printed by the famous printer William Bradford, and "the first author south of New York." His grandson, the father of Susanna (Leeds) Scull was also a famous surveyor-general of New Jersey, his commission from King George II bearing date March 3, 1757, being now in the possession of Henry Steelman Scull, of Atlantic City, referred to below. Children of James and Susanna (Leeds) Scull: 1. Daniel, born June 3, 1775; married Jemima Steelman. 2. Gideon, born October 30, 1777; married Alice Higbee. 3. Dorcas, born October 7, 1780; married (first) Samuel Ireland, (second) Jonas Leeds. 4. Paul, referred to below. 5. James, born March 25, 1786; married (first) Lorinia Steelman, (second) ———— Smith. 6. Susanna, born January 25, 1789; married John Steelman. 7. Hannah, born June 20, 1792; married Edward Leeds. 8. Joab, born March 2, 1796; married Ann Stackhouse.

(IV) Paul, fourth child and third son of James and Susanna (Leeds) Scull, was born at Leeds Point, Atlantic county, New Jersey, April 2, 1783. He married Sarah, daughter of Zephaniah and Rebecca (Ireland) Steelman. Her mother was daughter of Edmund Ireland, and her father, who served as the captain of a company of the Third battalion Gloucester county militia during the revolution, was son of John and Sarah (Adams) Steelman, and grandson of James and Susanna (Toy) Steelman. Children of Paul and Sarah (Steelman) Scull were: 1. Anna Maria, born March 12, 1809, died February 16, 1894; married Benjamin, son of Peter and Mary (Leeds) Turner. 2. Zephaniah, December 10, 1810, to August 25, 1887; married Mary Leeds. 3. James, October 3, 1813, to January 4, 1872; married Amelia Smith. 4. John, November 3, 1815, to January 17, 1894, married Mary, daughter of Cornelius and Ann (Dutch) Leeds. 5. Lewis Walker, referred to below. 6. Lardner, May 15, 1822, to February 1, 1897; married Josephine Leeds. 7. Dorcas, December 10, 1824, to June 17, 1867; married Thomas, son of Josiah and Esther (Leeds) Bowen.

(V) Lewis Walker, fifth child and fourth son of Paul and Sarah (Steelman) Scull, was born at Leeds Point, Atlantic county, May 2, 1819, and died October 10, 1898. He was educated in the pay schools of Galloway township, and when twenty-one years old enlisted in the United States navy, sailing in the brig "Wash-

ington," under the command of Commodore Joshua Sands, who was at that time engaged in the work of the coast and geodetic survey. In this service he continued for five years, and the year following his discharge married his first wife. For a number of years he was a teacher in the district schools of Galloway township, and under President Buchanan he was appointed postmaster at Leeds Point, an office which he held for twenty years or more he held also such elective offices as township clerk, township committeeman, and assessor or collector. From 1858 to 1865 he lived for the greater portion of each year at Atlantic City, where he was engaged in the business of house painting, besides being the senior partner in the firm of Scull & Barstow, one of the original grocery firms of Atlantic City, which began business at the corner of Atlantic avenue and Mansion House alley, in the basement of the Barstow House, and within a year moved into a new building at the northwest corner of Atlantic and Pennsylvania avenues.

Lewis Walker Scull married (first) August 22, 1846, Esther, daughter of Steelman and Ann (Bowen) Smith, born at Leeds Point, July 24, 1824. Her father served in the war of 1812. Children: 1. Henry Steelman, referred to below. 2. Ella M., born January 7, 1851, died March 1, 1879. August 16, 1862, Lewis Walker Scull married (second) Mary H. Sooy, daughter of Jonathan and Abigail Bowen (Sooy) Higbee. There was no issue to this marriage.

(VI) Henry Steelman, eldest child and only son of Lewis Walker and Esther (Smith) Scull, was born at Leeds Point, Atlantic county, June 4, 1847, and is now living in Atlantic City, New Jersey. For his early education he was sent to the public schools of Leeds Point, and in 1865 entered the Quaker City Business College, from which he graduated in 1867. For a few months he was in the grocery business, but in the fall of the same or the following year he entered the employ of Curwin, Stoddart & Brother, the large dry-goods firm of Philadelphia, where he remained until 1881, when he accepted a position with Hood Bonbright & Company, with whom he remained until 1884. He then retailed dry-goods on his own account in Camden, New Jersey, until 1886, when he came to Atlantic City and opened a dry-goods store under the firm name of H. S. Scull & Company. In 1895 he embarked on the real estate and insurance business, which he has successfully carried on up to the present time. From 1890 to 1898 he was a member of the Atlantic City Board of Health, and for four years was the secretary of that body. Since 1890 he has been a member of the county board of elections, and he has been the secretary of that body since the first passage of the ballot reform law. He is a Democrat and a member of the Society of Friends. From 1903 to 1906 he was president of the city council of Ventnor City. He is also secretary and treasurer of the Ventnor Dredging Company, which has been engaged for several years in reclaiming the low lands of Chelsea and Atlantic City. He is also secretary and treasurer of the Ventnor City water and light companies. He has always taken a deep interest in all matters pertaining to the well-being of the community, and for a number of years he has been connected with the State Sanitary Association, the American Public Health Association, and he was state delegate to the National Pure Food and Drug Congress, which lasted four days and had for its object the passage of the bill providing for governmental control of food, drugs, etc. He is also one of the governors of the Atlantic City hospital.

October 2, 1868, Henry Steelman Scull married Mary, daughter of John A. and Elizabeth (Jarman) Bruner, of Philadelphia, Pennsylvania. Their children are: 1. Elizabeth Bruner, born 1869, died in infancy. 2. Lillie Bruner, born 1870, died in infancy. 3. Florence Esther, January 4, 1873, died November 29, 1902. 4. Lewis Bruner, born July 15, 1874; married, February 14, 1907, Theodosia Reed; no children. 5. Maie Emma, born November 27, 1876; unmarried. 6. John Bruner, born November 29, 1877, died in infancy. 7. Harry DeMar, September 12, 1880, unmarried. 8. Nan Bruner, September 1, 1881; married, October 25, 1903. Robert Ohmeiss, Jr. 9. Frank Rue, April 23, 1882; married, March 3, 1908, Riche F., daughter of Richard F. Smith, ex-sheriff of Camden county, and has one child, Florence, born December 7, 1908. 10. Emily Corneline, born February 21, 1884. 11. Charles Landel, April 23, 1887. 12. Helene, Melissa, October 18, 1889.

GASKILL. This name is derived from Gascoigne, or Gaskoyne, being another form of this word. Many branches of the Gascoigne family became prominent in France and England, one of them being lord mayor of London. An-

other, Sir William, was a noted London judge. The family of Gaskill have been prominent in New Jersey from early times, serving in the legislative bodies and conducting themselves as useful citizens.

(I) Samuel Gaskill, of Mays Landing, New Jersey, was a shipbuilder, and constructed the last vessel built at that place. He had six children, namely: Nicholas B., of Mays Landing, deceased was a ship carpenter; Lottie and Sara A., deceased; Joseph H., a sea captain, of Philadelphia, Pennsylvania; Annie S., married Albert Smallwood, of Mays Landing; and Edmund C.

(II) Edmund C., son of Samuel Gaskill, was born at Bargaintown, New Jersey, afterwards removed to May's Landing, where he became a contractor and builder; he has now retired from active life. He married Hester McCurdy Ashton, born in Emilville, New Jersey: children: Samuel M., deceased; Edmund Champion; and Burton Ashton, the latter born October 9, 1889, now a student in the law department of the University of Tennessee, at Knoxville, of which he was elected president of the senior law class for the year 1909-10.

(III) Edmund Champion (2), elder son of Edmund Champion (1) and Hester McCurdy (Ashton) Gaskill, was born July 22, 1880, at Mays Landing, New Jersey. He attended the public schools of his native town, and in 1895 graduated from the county course, also from a post-graduate course November 20, 1896. He then attended the high school at Mays Landing, from which he graduated June 10, 1897. After his graduation he spent another year in the high school, taking a teacher's course. September 30, 1897, Mr. Gaskill took a competitive examination for a scholarship in Rutgers College, offered by the State of New Jersey, and although he won the scholarship circumstances did not allow his taking advantage of the opportunity. In October, 1898, he entered the American University at Harriman, Tennessee, where he took up the study of law. In February of the following year the University held an oratorical contest in which Mr. Gaskill took second prize. During the summer and fall of 1899 Mr. Gaskill was employed by the West Jersey & Sea Shore Railroad Company. About this time the firm of Bancroft & Whitney, publishers of law books, offered to the senior student in the University receiving the highest grade in the law department in oral and written examinations, a full set of books on "American Decisions and Reports," and Mr. Gaskill won the prize, his percentage being 94 1-6 out of a possible 100. He graduated June 11, 1900, with the degree of LL. B. Removing to Atlantic City, New Jersey, he registered as student at law, with Harry Wootton, City Solicitor, of Atlantic City, where he studied New Jersey law, and November 30, 1903, he was admitted as an attorney in the New Jersey bar. Since that time Mr. Gaskill has been successfully engaged in the general practice of his profession. In November, 1904, he was elected to the office of coroner of Atlantic county and in that capacity was called upon, October 29, 1906, to take charge of the inquest held over the victims of the terrible railroad accident known as the "Thoroughfare Bridge disaster." His term of office expired in 1907. In political views he is an ardent Republican, holding the office of secretary of the First Ward Regular Republican Club of his city, and September 28, 1909, elected a member of the Atlantic County Republican executive committee from the first ward. He is a member of Belcher Lodge No. 180, Ancient Free and Accepted Masons ; Tall Cedars of Lebanon, Forest No. 11 ; Pequod Tribe of Red Men, No. 47: Fraternal Mystic Circle, No. 890, and is an active member of the Morris Guard, an independent military company of Atlantic City, which he served three years as treasurer. He also belongs to the Methodist Episcopal Church of Mays Landing, to the Atlantic County Bar Association, and Sea Side Yacht Club. Mr. Gaskill is popular in social circles, and is a rising young member of his profession, deserving the success he has attained through his untiring zeal and energy along the lines of his chosen profession.

He married, June 29, 1904, Helen Mackenzie, daughter of Walter B. and Mary R. Jenks, and they are the parents of one daughter, Dorothy Ashton, born May 23, 1907.

SMITH Writing in her diary, September 18, 1795, Mrs. Elizabeth Drinker, of Philadelphia, says: "Saml Smith of Bucks C'y, Saml Smith of Philada, and Sally Smith called this morning. Those three Smiths are in no ways related—it is I believe the most common name in Europe and North America." One reason for this commonness in the name is that it is one of the so-called trade names, being derived from the trade or work of the original owners and at first being prefixed by the article "the." It is needless to state that of the many Smith families connected with the family of any of the colonies many of them even in a given locality were unrelated. This is the case with the family we are now considering, which is one of the later residents of the state of New Jersey and came into the state from New York, where it had already made a name for itself in the person of the earliest traced ancestor, Samuel A. Smith, of New York, referred to below.

(I) Samuel Asher Smith was born February 22, 1782, in Salem, Connecticut, and moved to Guilford, New York, in April, 1805. He married, December 25, 1806, Wealthy Phelps, of Bolton, Connecticut, who was born October 18, 1785. He represented Chenango in the New York legislature in 1816-17-20, and was also sheriff of Chenango county. He died March 24, 1864. He had a number of children, among whom was William A., referred to below.

(II) William Augustus, son of Samuel A. Smith, was born in Guilford, Chenango county, New York, March 30, 1820. After receiving his early education in that place he entered Geneva College, New York, first in the classical and literary course, and afterwards in the medical course, and graduated in 1847. For the next five years he practiced at Sidney Plains, Delaware county, New York, and then removed to Norwich, New York, where he established an excellent practice. Volunteering when the civil war broke out, he was appointed assistant surgeon of the Eighty-ninth Regiment of New York Volunteers, December 4, 1861, and soon afterwards was promoted as surgeon of the one hundred and third regiment of New York Volunteers, and served in the following engagements: Camden, North Carolina, April 19, 1862: South Mountain, Maryland, September 14, 1862: Antietam, Maryland, September 17, 1862; and while surgeon of the One Hundred and Third New York Volunteers served in the battle of Fredericksburg, Virginia, December 13, 1862, and at the siege of Suffolk, Virginia, from April 12, to May 4, 1863, and was in charge of the Third Division, Ninth Army Corps Hospital, and while on duty was severely and very nearly fatally wounded by a pistol ball which entered his abdomen and which remained in his body and was carried by him until his death. He was discharged by reason of this wound on October 23, 1863. On recovering, however, he re-enlisted, and was appointed surgeon of the Forty-seventh New York Volunteer Infantry on December 17, 1863, and was on duty with his regiment at Hilton Head, North Carolina. A short time after that he was ordered to Jacksonville, Florida, and took charge of the hospital there, and reorganized the same and attended to the reception of one thousand five hundred wounded from the battle field of Olustee. He was also placed in charge of the steamer "Monitor" and "Mary Powell" and in July, 1864, he was detailed up the Savannah river in charge of the steamer "George Leasey," and superintended the exchange of prisoners, and exchanged the last prisoners that were exchanged during the war, and was placed in charge of the general prison hospital at Newport News, Virginia, in the spring of 1865, and was appointed health officer of Norfolk, Virginia, which office he held until August, 1865, when he was mustered out with his regiment on the 30th of that month.

Dr. Smith then settled in Newark, New Jersey, with the intention of confining himself strictly to office practice, but unable to resist the demands upon him, he was soon engaged in active professional practice, which he continued to perform for many years. Notwithstanding his large practice he found the time to be deeply interested in and to be an active participant in everything which worked for the public welfare, and he held several offices of important public trust, being at one time the county clerk of Essex county, and at another alderman of the city of Newark. He died August 6, 1892. He was a member of the various county and state medical societies, and was held in high esteem by his professional brethren and all who knew him. By his wife, Betsey E. (Wade) Smith, who died August 20, 1902, in her eighty-first year, he had two children: 1. Samuel Asher, referred to below. 2. Wealthy Phelps, who married John Townley and has had two daughters, Maid and Bessie. The latter died in infancy. Maid married Richard Hobart and has two children: Richard Jr. and John Reginald.

(III) Samuel Asher (2), only son of Dr. William A. and Betsey E. (Wade) Smith, was born in Sidney Plains, New York, August 21, 1852. He is engaged in the real estate business in New York City, and has his office in the new Terminal Building. He secured his early education in Norwich, New York, and on the return of his father from the civil war in 1865 moved with him to Newark and attended the State street public school, and finished his education at the Grace Church Protestant Episcopal school. In 1887 he was elected and served a full term as county clerk of Essex county, and in 1892 was appointed a member of the excise board of the city of Newark, and was elected its president. In 1899 he was appointed by the president to take the census of 1900 and also took the manufacturers' census of Essex county. He married, November 12, 1879, Ada M., the youngest of the thirteen children of the late Rosches Heinisch, who emigrated to this country about 1828, and who attained fame as the originator of patent tailor shears and as the inventor of the original process for welding steel on iron. He died August 6, 1874. Samuel A. by his wife Ada M. has had three children: 1. Edmund E., born September 3, 1880. 2. William Asher, referred to below. 3. Wayne Parker, born October 22, 1896.

(IV) William Asher, second child and son of Samuel Asher (2) and Ada M. (Heinisch) Smith, was born in Newark, New Jersey, December 1, 1883, and is now living in Newark. He was educated at the Newark Academy, and on February 20, 1899, entered the law office of Coult & Howell, with whom he read and studied law until December 1, 1904, when he was admitted to the New Jersey bar as an attorney. He continued in the office of Coult & Howell, which firm was subsequently changed to Coult, Howell & Ten Eyck, and on the retirement of Jay Ten Eyck from that firm on his appointment as judge of the Essex county court of common pleas, he was admitted on May 1, 1906, into partnership with Joseph Coult and James E. Howell, and the firm was continued as Coult, Howell & Smith. In November, 1907, on the retirement of James E. Howell from the firm, on his appointment as vice chancellor, Mr. Coult and Mr. Smith continued the practice of law under the name of Coult & Smith. Mr. Smith was admitted to the bar as a counsellor in November, 1907. He is a member of the Essex Club, North End Club, Forest Hill Field Club, the Automobile Club, and the Lawyers' Club of Essex County. He is unmarried.

CPSIA information can be obtained
at www.ICGtesting.com
Printed in the USA
LVOW10s0100300617

539892LV00033B/1297/P